THE
CHURCHILL
DOCUMENTS

BOOKS BY MARTIN GILBERT

THE CHURCHILL BIOGRAPHY

Volume I: *Youth, 1874–1900* by Randolph S. Churchill
The Churchill Documents, Volume 1, *Youth, 1874–1896*
The Churchill Documents, Volume 2, *Young Soldier, 1896–1901*
Volume II: *Young Statesman, 1900–1914* by Randolph S. Churchill
The Churchill Documents, Volume 3, *Early Years in Politics, 1901–1907*
The Churchill Documents, Volume 4, *Minister of the Crown, 1907–1911*
The Churchill Documents, Volume 5, *At the Admiralty, 1911–1914*
Volume III: *The Challenge of War, 1914–1916* by Martin Gilbert
The Churchill Documents, Volume 6, *At the Admiralty, July 1914–April 1915*
The Churchill Documents, Volume 7, *"The Escaped Scapegoat", May 1915–December 1916*
Volume IV: *World in Torment, 1917–1922* by Martin Gilbert
The Churchill Documents, Volume 8, *War and Aftermath, December 1916–June 1919*
The Churchill Documents, Volume 9, *Disruption and Chaos, July 1919–March 1921*
The Churchill Documents, Volume 10, *Conciliation and Reconstruction, April 1921–November 1922*
Volume V: *The Prophet of Truth, 1922–1939* by Martin Gilbert
The Churchill Documents, Volume 11, *The Exchequer Years, 1922–1929*
The Churchill Documents, Volume 12, *The Wilderness Years, 1929–1935*
The Churchill Documents, Volume 13, *The Coming of War, 1936–1939*
Volume VI: *Finest Hour, 1939–1941* by Martin Gilbert
The Churchill Documents, Volume 14, *At the Admiralty, September 1939–May 1940*
The Churchill Documents, Volume 15, *Never Surrender, May 1940–December 1940*
The Churchill Documents, Volume 16, *The Ever-Widening War, 1941*
Volume VII: *Road to Victory, 1941–1945* by Martin Gilbert
The Churchill Documents, Volume 17, *Testing Times, 1942*
Volume VIII: *Never Despair, 1945–1965* by Martin Gilbert

OTHER BOOKS

The Appeasers (with Richard Gott)
The European Powers, 1900–1945
The Roots of Appeasement
Winston Churchill (Clarendon edition)
Sir Horace Rumbold: Portrait of a Diplomat
Churchill: A Photographic Portrait
Exile and Return: The Struggle for Jewish Statehood
Final Journey: The Fate of the Jews of Nazi Europe
Churchill: An Illustrated Biography
Auschwitz and the Allies
Churchill's Political Philosophy
Winston Churchill: The Wilderness Years
Jews of Hope: The Plight of Soviet Jewry Today
Jerusalem: Rebirth of a City
The Holocaust: The Jewish Tragedy
Shcharansky: Hero of Our Time
The Second World War
In Search of Churchill
The First World War
The Day the War Ended: VE Day 1945
Jerusalem in the Twentieth Century
The Boys: Triumph over Adversity
Holocaust Diary: Travelling in Search of the Past
Israel: A History

History of the Twentieth Century, Volume I
Empires in Conflict, 1900–1933
History of the Twentieth Century, Volume II
Descent into Barbarism, 1934–1951
History of the Twentieth Century, Volume III
Challenge to Civilization, 1952–1999
'Never Again': A History of the Holocaust
The Jewish Century: An Illustrated History
Letters to Auntie Fori: The 5,000 Year History
of the Jewish People and Their Faith
The Righteous: The Unsung Heroes of the Holocaust
Churchill at War in Photographs
Churchill's War Leadership:
Continue to Pester, Nag and Bite
D-Day
Churchill and America
Kristallnacht: Prelude to Destruction
The Will of the People: Churchill and
Parliamentary Democracy
Somme: Heroism and Horror in the First World War
Churchill and the Jews
The Story of Israel
In Ishmael's House: A History of Jews in Muslim Lands
Churchill: The Power of Words

HISTORICAL ATLASES

Atlas of American History
Atlas of the Arab–Israel Conflict
Atlas of British Charities
Atlas of British History
Atlas of the First World War

Atlas of the Holocaust
Historical Atlas of Jerusalem
Atlas of Jewish History
Atlas of Russian History
Atlas of the Second World War

Children's Illustrated Bible Atlas

EDITIONS OF DOCUMENTS

Britain and Germany Between the Wars
Plough My Own Furrow: The Life of Lord Allen of Hurtwood
Servant of India: Diaries of the Viceroy's Private Secretary, 1905–1910
Churchill: Great Lives Observed
Lloyd George: Great Lives Observed
Surviving the Holocaust: The Kovno Ghetto Diary of Avraham Tory
Winston Churchill and Emery Reves: Correspondence, 1937–1964

THE CHURCHILL DOCUMENTS

Martin Gilbert

VOLUME 17
TESTING TIMES
1942

Hillsdale College Press, Hillsdale, Michigan

Hillsdale College Press
33 East College Street
Hillsdale, Michigan 49242
www.hillsdale.edu

Printed in the United States of America

Printed and bound by Edwards Brothers, Ann Arbor, Michigan

Cover design by Hesseltine & DeMason, Ann Arbor, Michigan

THE CHURCHILL DOCUMENTS
Volume 17: *Testing Times, 1942*

Library of Congress Control Number: 2006934101

ISBN: 978-0-916308-46-9

First printing 2014

The Churchill War Papers are
dedicated to the memory of
Emery Reves
who helped to carry the books
of Winston Churchill
to the world

Testing Times is dedicated to the memory of

Ruth and Harold Geller

for whom Winston S. Churchill represented
all that was light
during the dark and bleak days covered by this volume

and to

Laurence Geller

for his passionate commitment
to Winston Churchill and
to Churchill's biographer

Contents

———

Note

W inston Churchill's personal papers are among the most comprehensive ever assembled relating to the life and times of one man. They are so extensive that it was only possible to include in the narrative volumes of his biography a part of the relevant documents.

The Companion Volumes, now titled *The Churchill Documents*, were planned to run parallel with the narrative volumes, and with them to form a whole. When an extract or quotation appears in a narrative volume, the complete document appears in an accompanying volume of *The Churchill Documents*. Where space prevented the inclusion of a contemporary letter in the narrative volume, it is included in the document volume.

Foreword

I write this introduction in the place of Sir Martin Gilbert, who in 2012 reached his fiftieth year of labour on the official biography of Winston Churchill. First engaged as a research assistant in 1962, for forty-four of the subsequent years he has been the official biographer. It is a fact of deep sadness that Sir Martin, incapacitated by complications from an arrhythmia of his heart, is unable to continue with the work at this time or in the immediate future.

At the time he fell ill, Sir Martin had completed the selection of the documents to be included in this volume and the work of annotation was well under way. We have completed the work according to the design that he laid out, and his name is upon the title page.

THE HISTORY OF MARTIN GILBERT'S INVOLVEMENT WITH THE CHURCHILL BIOGRAPHY

The story of this biography and of the remarkable man who has completed most of it should be stated here, within the pages of the work itself.

Winston Churchill's only son Randolph was the first author of the official biography. Randolph had first proposed to write the biography of his father in 1932, eight years before the elder man would take up the task of leading his nation through the Second World War, and thirty-three years before his death. Winston Churchill's own idea about the biography was plain from the terms in which he discouraged his son's 1932 plan, writing to Randolph of his hopes that 'someday you will make thousands instead of hundreds on my archives'.[1] Already he felt that his story would be important. Randolph began the work as official biographer nearly thirty years later, in 1961, and he did indeed make not hundreds but thousands.

---

[1] *The Churchill Documents*, Volume XII, *The Wilderness Years, 1929–1935* (Hillsdale, MI: Hillsdale College Press, 2009), page 406.

Within a year of Randolph's embarking on what he called 'The Great Work', Martin Gilbert was hired as one of five assistants. He began work on 25 October 1962, his twenty-fifth birthday.

The project began grandly. Setting out to write a record for the ages, Randolph Churchill insisted that the publishers produce document volumes to accompany the biographical narrative he was writing. This has proven to be, especially under Sir Martin, a task of immense scope in itself. It is one thing, and no easy thing, to cite a document in the course of explaining its meaning in a narrative history, especially when that narrative is constructed almost entirely from these original sources. It is another difficult thing to publish that document so that the reader may understand it independently of a surrounding narrative account. This requires extensive indexing and annotation of a different kind. People and events must be, so far as possible, identified and explained. Moreover, one must select the documents to be included, as the total corpus is much too numerous and lengthy to publish in a book or a series of books, even if the books are large and even if there are many of them. The selection must be made on the grounds of relevance, explanatory power, and importance. The provenance of everything must be explained. This activity is a service to history in itself and a major portion, probably by far the largest portion in actual volume of work, of the task.

Martin Gilbert worked as a researcher on the biography for almost five years until June 1967. At this point he withdrew, citing the pressure of work on the biography under the demanding Randolph in combination with his own historical work and his teaching at Merton College, Oxford. His wife was at that time expecting their first child, Natalie, now a successful schoolteacher in north-east London. He worried in a letter about his health,[1] which however would prove to hold up for decades longer. In a subsequent letter to Randolph he indicated that he would be prepared to return when work on Volume IV of the biography commenced.[2] In May 1968 Randolph telephoned Martin to say that 'a lamp is always burning for you here', and they agreed in that conversation

---

[1] For an account of Martin Gilbert's withdrawal from work on the biography and Randolph's response, see Winston S. Churchill, *His Father's Son: The Life of Randolph Churchill* (London: Orion House, 1997), pages 489–90.

[2] That volume, published in 1975, is entitled *The Stricken World* and covers the years 1916–22. Martin Gilbert would write that volume in its entirety, and he would also write Volume III, entitled *The Challenge of War*, covering the years 1914–16; published in 1971, it bears Martin's dedication to 'the memory of Randolph Churchill'.

that Martin would rejoin the staff shortly.[1] Three weeks later he received a telegram that Randolph had died.

Randolph had made it plain that he wanted his son, Winston, to succeed him as biographer. The British publisher, Heinemann, favoured this, but Lord Hartwell, owner of the *Daily Telegraph* newspaper and of certain rights to serialize the Churchill biography, favoured Lord Birkenhead, the son of Churchill's great friend F. E. Smith, the first Lord Birkenhead. Weeks passed while the pros and cons were discussed among the parties. Eventually the American publisher, Houghton Mifflin, suggested that the young Martin Gilbert – who had been present at some of the discussions through his friendship with the grandson Winston – finish the job. Martin met with Lord Hartwell and proposed a compromise. He writes:

> Then, in desperation I think at the thought of missing my train, I made the following suggestion: Lord Birkenhead, a noted one-volume biographer (of, among others, Lord Halifax and Lord Cherwell) would write a single-volume biography of Churchill based on the papers of which Lord Hartwell was the effective copyright holder. I would finish the multi-volume work on which Randolph had embarked. Lord Birkenhead's book would be short and stimulating. Mine would be long and academic.[2]

The compromise was accepted, and the young historian was given the job in October 1968.

During the forty-four years that have passed since Martin Gilbert took up this great task, the number of his published books has risen to eighty-eight. The Churchill biography has become a thing of magnificence in scale, scope, and accuracy. It is without doubt the longest biography ever written, as befits one of the largest lives ever lived. It is built upon an effort of research that has consumed the best efforts of this prolific author for most of his life. He has maintained throughout the rigorous commitment to careful chronology, to attention to accuracy in every detail, and to reliance upon original documents that is the hallmark of his scholarship.

I was privileged to work for Martin Gilbert for three years in the late 1970s; since then, I have endeavoured to be his friend continuously, and

[1] Sir Martin recounts his final conversation with Randolph in his 'Introduction to the New Edition' of *Winston S. Churchill*, Volume II, *Young Statesman, 1901–1914* (Hillsdale, MI: Hillsdale College Press, 2007), page xxxv.

[2] For Sir Martin's account of his meeting with Lord Hartwell, see his book *In Search of Churchill* (London: HarperCollins, 1994), pages 44–6.

have often been privileged to be his colleague. In those three years I witnessed and wondered at the care and energy he put into his work. Martin was not a wealthy man, then or now, but he would spare no expense to make sure that every document that could be found was found. Sensing that the expense of gathering and copying material was serious to him, I asked him once if I should be more careful what I copied at the Public Record Office and other archives. He replied with feeling: 'You must get everything. We must have it all here.'

His commitment to finding every relevant document was nothing less than fierce, although his manner was never so. Many times he would say: 'You have a good memory, and I have a good memory; we do not rely upon our memories.' One learned to look things up, again and again. One learned to write with the evidence directly before one. One learned that it is an infinite job to find all the evidence, but that this knowledge must spur one to further effort rather than despair. The best efforts would in fact yield results: he liked to say, 'In the writing of nineteenth- and twentieth-century history, there is no room for the word "perhaps".' If you used that term with him, his eyebrow would go up, and he would say: 'Perhaps not!'

Regarding Churchill, the abundance of the record is an obstacle as well as an opportunity. Martin wrote once that the first step is simply to read what Churchill wrote, and that itself requires months of application. Thinking he would live a short life as his father had, Churchill applied himself to his work with something approaching fury. By the time he was twenty-six, he had won distinction in three wars and had written best-selling books and widely read articles about all of them. Only then did he become a Member of Parliament, remaining in the House of Commons, with only brief interruption, for fifty-five years. Those were the most eventful years in history, at least to that time, and to all the offices he held over that period Churchill brought a restless interest and a massive ability to discharge business. He seemed to make his influence felt in whatever came up. I keep his published speeches in the edition by Robert Rhodes James, which is not quite comprehensive, on my bookshelf, not far from the complete writings of Abraham Lincoln. Churchill's speeches alone are many times more voluminous than all that Lincoln wrote of which we have record. In addition Churchill wrote about fifty books, countless articles, and memoranda and official minutes in the thousands. And this is only what he wrote himself; famously, Churchill inspired opinions about himself and the enterprises with which he was involved from friends and adversaries in their legions.

The official biography turned out to be bigger than Martin Gilbert foresaw, almost bigger than even he could do. But hardly anything is quite so big as that.

The method Martin established is partially responsible, along with his energy and ability, for the fact that this work could be carried on for so many decades with consistency. The method was simple yet ambitious. He looked everywhere possible for every original source. He covered secondary sources with care: more care when the authors were original witnesses to or participants in the events, more care still when their recollections were recorded at the time of the events. This vast treasure of material, once collected, was placed in strict chronological order. The documents were put in 'wodges', as he called them, and each wodge had a blank sheet of paper with the beginning date on it. The wodges were held together with 'black clips' or 'bulldog clips'. The biography deployed hundreds, then thousands of these. When a wodge got too big, it was split into several wodges. They were all kept on his desk, which was about thirty feet long, in their own chronological order. Secondary sources were photocopied and placed at the appropriate point in the chronology. One had to be careful not to put any wastebasket under the edge of a desk: something might fall into it. One did not carry the documents away anywhere. If he needed to use one, he made a photocopy.

Martin would sit at his long desk for long hours, beginning at the latest at 9.00 a.m. sharp, writing from these documents. Sometimes 'flags', long strips of paper held by a paper clip, would be placed alongside a document of particular importance. Sometimes these flags would carry a little summary at the top of what the document was or the theme it concerned. Until the last fifteen years or so, he wrote everything by hand in a clear script. He liked the Lami Safari fountain pen, and had many of them lying about the desk. He owned one or two of Churchill's own fountain pens, but did not use them. Once one went missing and a frantic search began, enlisting all hands, until it was uncovered. When it was found, to great relief, he went about the room checking to be doubly sure that no wastebaskets were positioned so that something could fall into them by accident.

A friend said to me once: I do not see how he produces so much; I could never do so. I replied: Probably none of us could do it, but we could try to follow his example in one respect. We could sit down every day not later than 9.00 a.m. and get on with the work. Martin was stricken once with Bell's palsy, as a result of which part of his face was paralysed. He worked anyway, the same hours, holding his pen in one hand and in the other a handkerchief which he held against his mouth to keep it fully closed.

I have thought since I first met Martin that he was made for this work and it was made for him. I have been privileged to know and to study with a few great scholars in my life, and now I work with some here at Hillsdale College. I have never seen any with such capacity to master detail and render it into order and sense. I have never seen any so diligent in making sure that what he wrote reflected the evidence that was before him.

His efforts remind me of one of the most brilliant passages that Churchill wrote. The passage concerns the art of painting, of which Churchill was a loving practitioner. Churchill stood in awe before the great painters, and of them he wrote:

> One begins to see, for instance, that painting a picture is like fighting a battle; and trying to paint a picture is, I suppose, like trying to fight a battle. It is, if anything, more exciting than fighting it successfully. But the principle is the same. It is the same kind of problem, as unfolding a long, sustained, interlocked argument. It is a proposition which, whether of few or numberless parts, is commanded by a single unity of conception. And we think – though I cannot tell – that painting a great picture must require an intellect on a grand scale. There must be that all-embracing view which presents the beginning and the end, the whole and each part, as one instantaneous impression retentively and untiringly held in the mind. When we look at the larger Turners – canvases yards wide and tall – and observe that they are all done in one piece and represent one single second of time, and that every innumerable detail, however small, however distant, however subordinate, is set forth naturally and in its true proportion and relation, without effort, without failure, we must feel in the presence of an intellectual manifestation the equal in quality and intensity of the finest achievements of warlike action, of forensic argument, or of scientific or philosophical adjudication.[1]

Let this be a description of Sir Martin's achievement in making this Great Work.

---

[1] From Churchill's essay 'Painting as a Pastime', first published in *Strand Magazine* in December 1921 and January 1922. For the full essay, see James Mueller, ed., *Thoughts and Adventures* (Wilmington, DE: ISI Books, 2009), pages 323–38.

FUTURE VOLUMES

Sir Martin had planned to produce six additional volumes of documents, one for each of the war years 1942–5 and two for Churchill's life after the wars. Our task is to complete them.

We will labour to gather and publish collections of documents as comprehensive, and as accurate, as he would have gathered and published. I do not expect that we will meet this standard, but at least we have learned from him what it is, and we have seen him work to exhaustion for decades to meet it. This will be on our minds as we go about the task. We are blessed to have the help of many skilled historians who know the Churchill story, and the students both graduate and undergraduate here at Hillsdale will lend much assistance. I have studied and taught Churchill without interruption since even before I met Martin.

I was privileged to sit beside Martin for many days to watch him make the selections for the document volumes over many years. We will in future, so far as we are able, follow the method that he followed. This task is not quite impossible, for the narrative volumes exist and can serve as a guide. Sir Martin's own archive, now available to us, contains the fruits of the work he did over many decades to make the writing of the narrative volumes possible. He selected the documents for publication from that archive, and we will follow his example. We will also look for new things and old that have been discovered that are not in his archive; this work is under way now in Britain and America and will continue urgently, or rather in the spirit of Sir Martin.

THE YEAR 1942

This volume covers the third year of the largest war in human history and enters on the third year of Churchill's premiership. Every month and every year of that war was a tale of tragedy and woe. For the Allies, much of it hitherto had been a tale of consistent defeat; in 1942 that began to change.

In June 1941 Hitler had invaded his ally the Soviet Union. In December 1941 Imperial Japan had attacked the United States at Pearl Harbor, and four days later Germany declared war on America. These two acts of aggression brought massive resources and manpower to the conflict that Britain had been fighting alone since the fall of France. In his *The Second World War*, Churchill would call this coalition 'The Grand Alliance', and he would refer to the year 1942 as the 'Hinge of Fate'. In it, he writes, 'we turn from almost uninterrupted disaster to almost unbroken success'.[1] This Grand Alliance would remain firm if not untroubled until the war ended in its triumph.

The year opened brightly. Churchill was in North America to address the Canadian Parliament in Ottawa, and to visit Franklin Roosevelt in Washington. He spent a few days in the sun in Florida and Bermuda. Now there were allies, and they were making big plans to win the war and to govern the world in peace after it.

Then bad news began to arrive; and it worsened until almost the end of the year. The defences of Singapore, long prepared against a sea attack, were weak to non-existent against a land attack from the north, precisely the direction from which the Japanese were approaching. During a Parliamentary vote later in the month Churchill warned that more bad news would come before good. He asked the House for a vote of confidence, and was given it overwhelmingly on January 29. By several accounts Churchill's performance in the confidence debate was masterful. Harold Nicolson records in his diary that his 'love and admiration of Winston surge round me like a tide!'[2]

On February 15 Singapore fell, and then Dutch and American positions in Asia were rolled up one by one.[3] In response to the devastating news about Singapore, Franklin Roosevelt wrote to Churchill:

> I realise how the fall of Singapore has affected you and the British people. It gives the well known back seat driver a field day but no matter how serious our setbacks have been and I do not for a moment underrate them, we must constantly look forward to the next moves that need to be made to hit the enemy.[4]

Churchill restructured his Government, giving up the leadership of the House of Commons to the Labour Member Sir Stafford Cripps while remaining Prime Minister, Minister of Defence, and a member of

---

[1] From the Preface to *The Second World War*, Volume IV, *The Hinge of Fate* (Boston: Houghton Mifflin, 1950), page vi.

[2] See page 177 below.

[3] At the news of the fall of Singapore, John Colville, Churchill's private secretary, records in his diary that Churchill seemed 'sorely pressed by his critics and opponents at home' (see page 259 below). Eighty-five thousand British soldiers, sailors, and airmen were captured. Like other captives in the Pacific theatre, these men were consigned to more than three years of privation, ill-treatment, and in many cases death. Among them was Lieutenant-Colonel Denis Houghton, a solicitor from Lancashire who in captivity fashioned a flute from a pipe and other materials he found about the camp in order to play in the camp orchestra. He also carved a set of chessmen in *Alice through the Looking Glass* figures. The flute, the chessmen, and the Colonel all survived the war. Later he produced three children, one of them my wife, Penny. The flute can be viewed in the Imperial War Museum.

[4] See page 285 below.

a War Cabinet reduced in size from nine to seven members. Of these changes, Churchill wrote to Roosevelt: 'I am most deeply grateful to you for your warm-hearted telegram No. 106. The pressure here has never been dangerous and I have used it to effect wholesome changes and accessions. You may take it everything is now solid.'[1]

The harmony between Churchill and Roosevelt was disturbed in April by a fundamental disagreement about the British Empire in India. Roosevelt's letter to Churchill on April 12 complains of the 'British Government's unwillingness to concede the right of self-government to the Indians'. This letter and Churchill's reflection on it in his *The Second World War* are printed on pages 512–15 of this volume.

At home, criticism mounted with bad news. British convoys over the northern route to Russia suffered heavy losses. Rommel took Tobruk in North Africa on June 20, while Churchill was visiting Roosevelt again at his home in Hyde Park and travelling with him by train to Washington. This was terrible news to receive while in the company of the new ally. Anthony Eden writes in his memoirs that Churchill 'felt the humiliation bitterly'.[2] Churchill returned home to face another confidence vote. Newspapers predicted the fall of the Government, but again Churchill survived. The opposition supporting the vote of no confidence found itself in disorder when one of its number, Admiral Sir Roger Keyes, Churchill's friend and colleague from the First World War Dardanelles campaign, insisted that Churchill must remain in power.

In North Africa Churchill changed generals twice. His first choice to replace Auchinleck, Lord Gott, was killed in a plane crash within hours of his selection; in his place Churchill appointed General Bernard Law Montgomery, later Viscount Montgomery of Alamein. On August 10–15 Churchill made a difficult and hazardous journey by plane to Moscow to explain to Stalin why there could be no second front in Europe in 1942 and why Allied convoys over Norway to Russia, which had taken losses of two-thirds, would have to be suspended. To a frowning Stalin, he promised instead a new front in North Africa, where the British had just been defeated. Stalin accused the British of being 'afraid of fighting'. Churchill bit his tongue.

On August 23 one of the decisive battles of the war began with the German attack on Stalingrad. This would be one of the largest and fiercest battles in history. Losses on both sides amounted to 1,900,000.

[1] See page 287 below.
[2] See page 818 below.

Fighting would continue street to street and building to building for almost six months, and for nearly half this time the Germans were slowly advancing. By the middle of August they had reached the Volga to the north of the city and came close to driving the Soviets back across the river. The Soviets held on by their fingernails until November, when they began the counter-attack that would destroy the German forces at Stalingrad and change the momentum of the war in the east.

The gloom that had hung over the Western Allies since May 1940 began finally to lift with signs of success in North Africa. In 1942 there were two battles around El Alamein, a city on the Egyptian coast. The first was fought in July and brought a halt to Rommel's advances into Egypt. The second began with a British counter-attack by Montgomery's 8th Army, launched on October 23. By November 6 the German army under Rommel was routed, with the capture of 20,000 prisoners, 350 tanks, and 400 guns. Two days later British and American troops landed in Algiers, Oran, and Casablanca, and the second front in North Africa was open. The war took on a new aspect, and henceforth the Allies would proceed from strength to strength. The first victory of Churchill's premiership was celebrated at home with the ringing of church bells throughout Britain on November 15.

The year closed as it had begun, with Churchill once again travelling to meet Roosevelt; and this time the two national leaders had good news to celebrate.

One will find in this document volume a rich account of these events, cataclysmic and glorious in alternation. One can see the statesmen grappling with enormous difficulties, guessing the future, taking enormous risks on inadequate knowledge. Sir Martin believed that the story is found nowhere if not in the writings of the time, and that its drama is fully apparent only in those sources. Here the records of Churchill's war effort in 1942 are published in unprecedented detail.

CONCLUSION

I will close with two points of a personal nature. The first is a word of condolence to the members of Sir Martin's immediate family. I have known most of them – Helen, Susie, Natalie, David, Josh, Margaret, and Esther – for decades, and their loss at Martin's incapacity is grievous. Martin's wife Esther has been brave, strong, and loving in caring for him during these hard months, and to her especially my heart goes out.

The second is a word about this man who was my teacher and employer. To such as he a student owes a debt that cannot be repaid. In my case the debt is compounded by the fact that I met my wife, now of thirty-three years, in his home. For much of the time while we worked for Martin, Penny Houghton, now Arnn, was the only other member of the staff, and this gave me the privilege I still treasure of coming to know her. Sir Martin's example, which we have observed and sought to follow now for more than three decades, is one of the greatest benefits we have reaped. We miss him deeply and pray for his recovery.

LARRY P. ARNN
Hillsdale College
Hillsdale, Michigan
May 2013

Hillsdale College Press
Acknowledgements

The following foundations and individuals gave generous support for the publication of *Testing Times*, volume 17 of *The Churchill Documents*, the first companion document volume to the seventh narrative volume, *Winston S. Churchill: Road to Victory, 1941–1945*: the Lynde and Harry Bradley Foundation, Milwaukee, Wisconsin; the Earhart Foundation, Ann Arbor, Michigan; the late George B. Ferguson, Peoria, Arizona; Mr. and Mrs. William L. Grewcock, Omaha, Nebraska; Mr. and Mrs. Thomas N. Jordan, Jr., Healdsburg, California; Mr. and Mrs. Tim M. Roudebush, Lenexa, Kansas; Mr. and Mrs. Emil A. Voelz, Jr., Akron, Ohio; and the Saul N. Silbert Charitable Trust, Sun City, Arizona.

Acknowledgements

This volume of Churchill documents came into being in three stages. The first stage took place during the twenty-year period between 1968 and 1988, when Sir Martin researched and wrote six of the eight narrative volumes that complete the Churchill biography; the second when, in 2008, he began the process of editing and preparing the specific documents that he had set aside for this 1942 volume; and the final stage in 2011, when the process of footnoting and the final preparation was undertaken. Throughout these stages, he was assisted by many in this important work.

While deep in the footnoting stage in spring 2012, Sir Martin was taken ill abruptly and has not been able to return to his desk. Work continued and it is due to the determination and diligence of President Larry Arnn and his able staff at Hillsdale College, and the Hillsdale College Press, that this book has come into being.

Sir Martin kept a list of those he wanted to acknowledge in this book, but the list is far from complete. I have had to rely on memory, and hope that those who are mentioned will understand how much their contribution has been appreciated, and those who have been omitted due to my negligence are no less appreciated. For this, and for my simple words that will not do justice to those who have helped, I apologize.

During the twenty years that Sir Martin was ensconced in the basement of the Bodleian Library and later at his own desk, turning over page after page of the estimated fifteen tonnes of documents that comprised the Churchill papers, he made note of the documents he wanted to use for these volumes, documents that 'flesh out' the narrative volumes. Throughout much of this period, Susie Gilbert was at his side, and encouraged and supported him in his mission to present Winston Churchill's life and work in the truest possible light.

In his 'Sources' to his first volume, Volume III of the biography, Sir Martin writes: 'I have tried wherever possible to find the original text of every document quoted in this volume, because in many instances I have discovered large discrepancies between the original document and later published versions.' In order to resolve discrepancies, he sent those who worked for him to the archives to photocopy the original documents. In this way William Sturge, Taffy Sassoon, Larry Arnn, and Abe Eisenstat each helped at different times during those early years to compile and sort the volume of materials that created the original day-to-day group of documents. Roger Nixon helped in later years with forays to the Public Record Office, Kew, now the National Archives.

In the years following the publication of the 1941 volume, Sir Martin worked to secure funding in order to finish the task he so wanted to complete, and that Hillsdale College Press wanted to publish. David Boler, with the help of Glynne Jenkins, suggested a sponsorship proposal, and David approached Laurence Geller who enthusiastically and generously stepped in to fund the work on the volume. Lord Rothschild of the Rothschild Foundation helped. It is due to their passion and dedication that this volume came into being.

In 2008 work was taken up to compile the 1942 volume. Sir Martin studied the day-to-day bundles of papers and chose the ones for this volume, augmenting them as needed. The following are the archivists who have helped with information and answering queries: Pearl Alderson, the Customer Host, Woodhorn Museum and Northumberland Archive; Pamela Clark, Archivist, Windsor, Royal Archives; Adrian Cooke, Network Support Analyst, Random House Group, UK; Sebastian Cox, Head of Air Historical Branch (RAF); Dr Christopher Joyce, Eastern Research Group, Foreign and Commonwealth Office; Jennifer Kelly, Librarian, North of England Institute of Mining and Mechanical Engineers; Rodney Melville, the Chequers Estate; Andrew Riley, Winston Churchill Archives, Churchill College, Cambridge; Oleg Rzheshevsky, President, the National Committee of Russian Historians, Association of the Second World War Historians; Merav Segal, Director, Weizmann Archives; Margaret Shannon, Washington Historical Research; Julia Sheppard, Archivist, Contemporary Medical Archives Centre, The Wellcome Institute for the History of Medicine; Vick Subbs, House Manager, Chartwell; Alycia J. Vivona, Archivist, Franklin D. Roosevelt Library; and Sebastian Wormell, Archivist, Harrods.

The permission of Her Majesty Queen Elizabeth II is gratefully acknowledged in allowing Sir Martin to make use of material from the Royal Archives, Windsor Castle.

In addition to the archivists who answered queries, these individuals were of enormous help: Max Arthur, Sir Tony Brenton, HM Ambassador to Russia, Moscow, and Anne Pringle; Sarah Brown; Lord Chadlington, and his Executive Assistant Tina Westfallen; Sally Falk, the Cabinet Office; and The Earl of Halifax. Richard Langworth, the editor of *Finest Hour*, Allen Packwood, Director, Churchill Archives, Churchill College, Cambridge, and Andrew Roberts were of assistance in the preparation of the book, and have been of great support to me in dealing with general Churchill queries with which I have been faced. The Lady Soames, LG, DBE, and her brother's grandson Randolph Churchill have been both a help to the book and of kind support to me.

The technical organization of the material was orchestrated by Kay Thomson. The massive task of typing the documents was undertaken by Brenda Harry, who had worked on the typescript for Volume VII of the biography that these documents cover, Avinoam Miller, who came especially from the United States to spend his holiday working with Sir Martin, and Stephani Francl at Hillsdale College.

Elzbieta Gottwald was at Sir Martin's right hand throughout the whole process and knew where to look to answer remaining queries when he took ill. At that precarious time, Gillian Somerscales took on the massive task of copyediting the manuscript and skilfully dealt with whatever queries came up. Estelle Botsman helped retrieve materials from the archives. Tim Aspden has prepared Sir Martin's maps.

When it looked as though Sir Martin would not be able to lend assistance to the final stages of publishing the book, Kevin Bishop, and later Kyle Murnen, organized the Hillsdale College team, which, working with Elzbieta Gottwald and Gillian Somerscales on the UK side, consisted of Aaron Kilgore, Linda Moore, and Hillsdale College students Brianna Landon, Tom Ohlgren, Andy Reuss, Kayla Cash, Ryne Bessmer, Andrew Koehlinger, and Giana Schena. Matthew Bell and Jonathan Walker helped with the maps, Ann Hart served as the final proofreader, and Christina Bych created the index. Soren Geiger has taken on overseeing the publication of the series.

In addition, Hillsdale College benefited from the expertise of Mary Burtzloff, Archivist, Dwight D. Eisenhower Library, Bonhams, BBC Heritage, Richard Langworth, Dr James W. Muller, Dr John Mather, and Winston Churchill's great-grandson Randolph Churchill.

Through this process, Dr Larry Arnn has been a great source of support to me in seeing this project through to completion. I am grateful to him and to the transatlantic cooperation between his office and Sir Martin's that achieved a victorious result – the goal that as yet still lay out of the Allies' reach in 1942.

In his notes, Sir Martin listed the cataclysmic events confronting Churchill in 1942: the conclusion of the Washington War Conference, the growing American commitment to Britain, the fall of Singapore ('my confidence . . . never stronger'), helping Russia, the Arctic convoys, intensification of the air war against Germany, dispute with Roosevelt over India, return to Washington, the atomic bomb agreement, talks in Cairo, Cairo endangered, first visit to Moscow, setback at Dieppe, victory at Alamein, Christmas at Chequers. Quite a year.

In his September 1939 to May 1940 volume of Churchill documents, Sir Martin writes: 'No historian can work on an island or in a vacuum. Without the help and encouragement of colleagues and friends the work could not have been completed. To all of them my thanks are due, and are given with gratitude.'

From my heart, I thank these generous individuals, too.

Esther Gilbert
London, England
August 2013

Sources and Bibliography

In the course of compiling this volume, I have used material from the following collections of public and private papers:

Lord Balfour of Inchrye papers; Lord Beaverbrook papers; Robert Barrington-Ward papers; Cecil papers; the Chartwell Trust; Sir John Colville papers; Earl of Derby papers; Sir George Harvie-Watt papers; General Sir Ian Jacob papers; Sir John Martin papers; Maxton papers; Phillimore papers; Sir Richard Pim papers; Lady Soames papers.

The principal archival collection used in this volume is the Churchill papers, now permanently housed at Churchill College, Cambridge. I have also been given access to material in the following collections: the Royal Archives; the BBC Written Archives Centre; Franklin D. Roosevelt papers; National Archives (Admiralty, Air Ministry, Cabinet, Foreign Office, Premier, Secret Intelligence Service, and War Office papers); Baroness Spencer-Churchill papers (Churchill College, Cambridge).

For those documents and recollections that were drawn from published works, I gratefully acknowledge the authors of the following books:

Alan Brooke, *War Diaries, 1939–1945, Field Marshal Lord Alanbrooke*, London, 1957.

Arthur Bryant, *The Turn of the Tide, 1939–1943: A Study Based on the Diaries and Autobiographical Notes of Field Marshal the Viscount Alanbrooke KG, OM*, London, 1957.

David Dilkes (editor), *The Diaries of Sir Alexander Cadogan OM, 1938–1945*, London, 1971.

Winston S. Churchill, *The End of the Beginning*, London, 1943.

Winston S. Churchill, *Secret Session Speeches*, New York, 1946.

Winston S. Churchill, *The Second World War*, volume one, *The Gathering Storm*, London, 1948.

Winston S. Churchill, *The Second World War*, volume two, *Their Finest Hour*, London, 1949.

Winston S. Churchill, *The Second World War*, volume three, *The Grand Alliance*, London, 1950.

Winston S. Churchill, *The Second World War*, volume four, *The Hinge of Fate*, London, 1951.

Winston S. Churchill, *The Second World War*, volume five, *Closing the Ring*, London, 1952.

Anthony Eden, *The Eden Memoirs, The Reckoning*, London, 1965.

Lord Birkenhead, *The Life of Lord Halifax*, London, 1965.

William Averell Harriman, *Special Envoy to Churchill and Stalin, 1941–1946*, London, 1976.

John Harvey (editor), *The War Diaries of Oliver Harvey 1941–1945*, London, 1978.

Lord Ismay, *The Memoirs of General the Lord Ismay*, London, 1960.

Robert Rhodes James (editor), *Chips, The Diaries of Sir Henry Channon*, London, 1967.

Robert Rhodes James (editor), *Winston S. Churchill, His Complete Speeches, 1897–1963*, volume six, London and New York, 1974.

Donald McLachlan, *In the Chair, Barrington-Ward of 'The Times', 1927–1948*, London, 1971.

Lord Moran, *Winston Churchill, The Struggle for Survival, 1940–1965*, London, 1966.

Nigel Nicolson (editor), *Harold Nicolson, Diaries and Letters, 1939–1945*, London, 1967.

Ben Pimlott (editor), *The Second World War Diary of Hugh Dalton, 1940–45*, London, 1985.

Robert E. Sherwood, *The White House Papers of Harry L. Hopkins, an Intimate History*, London, 1948.

Mary Soames, *Clementine Churchill*, London, 1979.

Charles Stuart (editor), *The Reith Diaries*, London, 1975.

A. J. P. Taylor, *Beaverbrook*, London, 1972.

January
1942

Winston S. Churchill: recollection
('The Grand Alliance', page 605)

1 January 1942   Washington DC

The President[1] was wheeled in to me on the morning of January 1. I got out of my bath, and agreed to the draft. The Declaration could not by itself win battles, but it set forth who we were and what we were fighting for. Later that day Roosevelt, I, Litvinov,[2] and Soong,[3] representing China, signed this majestic document in the President's study. It was left to the State Department to collect the signatures of the remaining twenty-two nations.

[1] Franklin Delano Roosevelt, 1882–1945. United States Assistant Secretary of the Navy, 1913–20. Governor of New York State, 1929–33. President of the United States, 1933–45. Churchill's pre-war support for Roosevelt had been frequently repeated in his articles in both Britain and America. 'I am,' he wrote in *Colliers* magazine in the first year of Roosevelt's presidency, 'though a foreigner, an ardent admirer of the main drift and impulse which President Roosevelt has given to the economic and financial policy of the United States' (*Colliers*, 4 November 1933).

[2] Maxim Litvinov, 1876–1952. Born Meier Wallakh in Bialystok (then Tsarist Russia) of Jewish parentage. A revolutionary, in exile in France and Britain from 1902 to 1917. Married an English-woman, Ivy Low. The first Bolshevik representative in London, November 1917 to September 1918 (when he was deported). In effective control of Soviet foreign policy, as Deputy Commissar for Foreign Affairs, 1926–30. Commissar for Foreign Affairs, 1930–9 (when Stalin dismissed him in favour of Molotov). Soviet Ambassador in Washington, 1941–3. Neither purged nor exiled, he lived his final years in quiet retirement. After his death, his widow returned to live in England.

[3] T. V. Soong, 1894–1971. Born in Shanghai. His brothers-in-law included Sun Yat-sen and Chiang Kai-shek. Minister of Finance, 1919–31, 1932–3. Minister of Foreign Affairs, 1942–5. Head of the Chinese delegation to the founding conference of the United Nations, San Francisco, 1945. Lived in New York from 1949 to his death.

Joint Declaration
('The Grand Alliance', pages 605–6)

1 January 1942   Washington DC

A Joint Declaration by the United States of America, the United Kingdom of Great Britain and Northern Ireland, the Union of Soviet Socialist Republics, China, Australia, Belgium, Canada, Costa Rica, Cuba, Czechoslovakia, the Dominican Republic, El Salvador, Greece, Guatemala, Haiti, Honduras, India, Luxemburg, The Netherlands, New Zealand, Nicaragua, Norway, Panama, Poland, South Africa, and Yugoslavia.[1]

The Governments signatory hereto,

Having subscribed to a common programme of purposes and principles embodied in the Joint Declaration of the President of the United States of America and the Prime Minister of the United Kingdom of Great Britain and Northern Ireland, dated August 14, 1941, known as the Atlantic Charter.[2]

Being convinced that complete victory over their enemies is essential to defend life, liberty, independence, and religious freedom, and to preserve human rights and justice in their own lands as well as in other lands, and that they are now engaged in a common struggle against savage and brutal forces seeking to subjugate the world, declare:

(1) Each Government pledges itself to employ its full resources, military or economic, against those members of the Tripartite Pact and its adherents with which such Government is at war.

(2) Each Government pledges itself to co-operate with the Governments signatory hereto, and not to make a separate armistice or peace with the enemies.

The foregoing declaration may be adhered to by other nations which are, or which may be, rendering material assistance and contributions in the struggle for victory over Hitlerism.

---

[1] Of these governments, eight had been conquered by Germany between September 1939 and April 1941: Belgium, Czechoslovakia, Greece, Luxemburg, The Netherlands, Norway, Poland, and Yugoslavia.

[2] For the full text of the Atlantic Charter, see Martin Gilbert, *The Churchill War Papers*, Volume III, *The Ever-Widening War, 1941*, Volume XVI of *The Churchill Documents* (New York and London, 2001), pages 1055–6.

Winston S. Churchill to Clement Attlee[1]
(Churchill papers, 20/88)

1 January 1942   Washington DC

I discussed all points raised by Cabinet fully with the President and Hull[2] this evening. Beaverbrook[3] and Halifax were also present. President showed himself most anxious to secure psychological effect of signature of Declaration on first day of New Year. If this were done it would obviously have been impossible to secure agreed amendments among parties concerned. Litvinov has expressly said that he had no powers to accept any change whatever without reference to Moscow.

2. Reference order of signatories in title, I could hardly press strongly for rearrangement, as Canada and Australia preferred President's order, which South Africa and New Zealand had also accepted.

3. Free French. – I pressed this strongly. President felt it impossible to include Free French among original signatories for reasons with which you are familiar. He undertook, however, to do utmost to get Soviet assent to insertion of words 'or authorities' in last paragraph after word 'Nations'. This would enable Free French to accede immediately. I anticipate no difficulty with Soviet, though Litvinov may have to refer it. If by chance Soviet Government is unwilling to accept verbal change, I suggested, and President agreed, that de Gaulle[4] might send a letter to

[1] Clement Richard Attlee, 1883–1967. Educated at Haileybury and University College, Oxford. Called to the Bar, 1906. Tutor and lecturer, London School of Economics, 1913–23. On active service, Gallipoli, Mesopotamia (wounded), and France, 1914–19; Major, 1917. First Labour Mayor of Stepney, 1919, 1920; Alderman, 1920–7. Labour MP for Limehouse, 1922–50; for West Walthamstow, 1950–5. Parliamentary Private Secretary to Ramsay MacDonald, 1922–4. Under-Secretary of State for War, 1924. Chancellor of the Duchy of Lancaster, 1930–1. Postmaster-General, 1931. Deputy Leader of the Labour Party in the House of Commons, 1931–45. Leader of the Opposition, 1935–40. Lord Privy Seal, 1940–2. Deputy Prime Minister, 1942–5. Lord President of the Council, 1943–5. Prime Minister, 1945–51 (Minister of Defence, 1945–6). Leader of the Opposition, 1951–5. Created Earl, 1955.

[2] Cordell Hull, 1871–1955. A member of the United States Congress for Tennessee, 1907–21, 1922–31. Senator, 1931–3. Secretary of State, 1933–44. Nobel Peace Prize, 1945. He published *The Memoirs of Cordell Hull* (two volumes) in 1948.

[3] William Maxwell Aitken, 1879–1964. Known as 'Max'. Canadian financier and newspaper proprietor. Conservative MP, 1910–16. Knighted, 1911. Canadian Expeditionary Force Eye-Witness in France, May–August 1915; Canadian Government Representative at the Front, September 1915–16. Bought the *Daily Express*, his largest-circulation newspaper, in December 1916. Created Baron Beaverbrook, 1917. Chancellor of the Duchy of Lancaster and Minister of Information, 1918. Minister for Aircraft Production, 1940–1. Minister of State, 1941. Minister of Supply, 1941–2. Lord Privy Seal, 1943–5.

[4] Charles de Gaulle, 1890–1970. On active service on the Western Front, 1914–16 (thrice wounded; despatches). Prisoner of war, 1916–18 (five attempts to escape). An advocate between the wars of armoured divisions as an essential part of warfare. Commanded 4th Armoured Brigade, 5th Army, September 1939; 4th Armoured Division, May 1940. Under-Secretary for War and National Defence,

all signatories saying that he acceded to the Declaration. He thought it unlikely that any of the signatories would object.

4. Your paragraph 3. We discussed this point fully. It seemed clear to us that a pledge of no separate peace could only fairly be held to cover those who were at war with particular parties. It would be possible, if thought necessary for those Powers at war with Japan to conclude a document between themselves that they should show the Soviet, making claim that, so long as Soviet was not at war with Japan, she could not claim voice in the fulfilment of the pledge *inter se* of those who were at war with Japan.

5. Hitlerism. – Your paragraph 4. President said that Hitlerism had assumed, both in United States and in Soviet, the general implication covering all aggression. Everybody would understand it, and it dotted the i's of what we all know, namely, that Japan has acted under German dictation. Moreover, from our point of view, I think the phrase has value as keeping the American mind and effort directed against the main target. I did not, therefore, press this, especially as the President was convinced that Stalin[1] could not accept it.

6. Your paragraph 5. President said he had been advised that the term 'high contracting parties' would make it impossible for him to sign as an executive act without concurrence of Senate. Canada also did not like 'high contracting parties'. I recognise difficulty about Indian States, but this difficulty must, I fear, be accepted.

7. Your paragraph 6. Here, again, Russian difficulty was felt, and I thought that, as Declaration speaks of human rights and justice, and as reference is made to Atlantic Charter, we could rightly claim, when Declaration is discussed, that social security was by clear implication covered.

8. I am sure Cabinet will appreciate the difficulty of securing a draft entirely agreeable to ourselves where so many others are involved, and, as United States Government have succeeded in securing agreement

6 June 1940. Chief of the Free French (later President of the French National Committee), London and Brazzaville, 1940–2. President of the French Committee of National Liberation, Algiers, 1943. President of the Provisional Government of the French Republic, and head of its armed forces, November 1943 to January 1946. Prime Minister, June 1958 to January 1959. President, December 1958 to June 1969.

[1] Josef Vissarionovich Djugashvili, 1879–1953. Born in Georgia. A Bolshevik revolutionary, he took the name Stalin (man of steel). In exile in the Siberian Arctic, 1913–16. Active in Petrograd during the October Revolution, 1917. Commissar for Nationalities, 1917–18. General Secretary of the Central Committee of the Communist Party, 1922. Effective ruler of Russia from 1923. Purged his opponents with show trials, 1936–8, murdering without compunction opponents, critics, and ordinary citizens who had committed no crime. Authorized the Nazi–Soviet Pact, August 1939. Succeeded Molotov as Head of Government, May 1941. Marshal of the Soviet Union, May 1943. Buried beside Lenin in the Lenin Mausoleum, 1953. 'Downgraded' to the Kremlin Wall, 1960. In 1989 Mikhail Gorbachev began the official process inside the Soviet Union of denouncing Stalin's crimes.

from almost everybody, we could only have adopted your amendments at the risk of reopening the whole discussion all round, leading to further complications. I have therefore signed *sub spe* and request all necessary formal authority. I am sure Cabinet will believe I did my best.[1]

Winston S. Churchill: recollection
('The Grand Alliance', page 606)

1 January 1942   Washington DC

At the outset a misunderstanding arose with Chiang Kai-shek,[2] which, though it did not affect the course of events, involved high politics. At Washington I had found the extraordinary significance of China in American minds, even at the top, strangely out of proportion. I was conscious of a standard of values which accorded China almost an equal fighting power with the British Empire, and rated the Chinese armies as a factor to be mentioned in the same breath as the armies of Russia.

I told the President how much I felt American opinion over-estimated the contribution which China could make to the general war. He differed strongly. There were five hundred million people in China. What would happen if this enormous population developed in the same way as Japan had done in the last century and got hold of modern weapons?

I replied that I was speaking of the present war, which was quite enough to go on with for the time being. I said I would of course always be helpful and polite to the Chinese, whom I admired and liked as a race and pitied for their endless misgovernment, but that he must not expect me to adopt what I felt was a wholly unreal standard of values.

---

[1] Churchill's minutes were generally initialled 'WSC', usually in red ink. This signature is not reproduced in this volume; signatures other than WSC are included wherever they exist on the archival version cited.

[2] Chiang Kai-shek, 1887–1975. Joined Sun Yat-sen's revolutionary party in 1907. Member of the revolutionary army in Shanghai on the outbreak of the Chinese Revolution, 1911. Served at Chinese General Headquarters, 1918–20. Visited the Soviet Union to study its military and social systems, 1923. Founder and Principal, Whampoa Military Academy, Canton, 1924. Member of the General Executive Committee of the Kuomintang, 1926. Commander-in-Chief, Northern Expeditionary Forces, 1926–8. Chairman of State, and Generalissimo of all fighting services, 1928–31. Resigned, 1931. Director-General of the Kuomintang Party, 1938. Chairman of the Supreme National Defence Council, 1939–47. President of the Republic of China, 1948. Retired, 1948. Formed a Government on behalf of the Chinese Nationalists in Formosa (Taiwan), 1949.

Lord Halifax:[1] diary
(*'The Life of Lord Halifax', page 596*)

[1 January 1942]   Washington DC

When I was fixing up with him last night what would be a good time to come and see him in the morning, I said what about 12 o'clock. He thought this was a bit late as that was about the time the President was apt to blow into his bedroom. He had, two or three days before, and found Winston with nothing on at all, and he had quickly to drape himself in a towel! 'He is the only head of State I have ever received in the nude.'

War Cabinet: minutes[2]
(*Cabinet papers, 65/25*)

1 January 1942   10 Downing Street
12 noon

CONFIDENTIAL RECORD

The Vice Chief of Naval Staff[3] said that no less than 130 wireless signals had been sent out from the vessel during the outward journey of the Prime Minister's party. The advice of the Admiralty was that an unwarrantable risk would be incurred if there were signalling on anything like this scale during the homeward passage. It was very desirable that wireless silence should be observed.

The War Cabinet:

Invited the Lord Privy Seal[4] and the First Lord of the Admiralty[5] to communicate with the Prime Minister to the above effect.

[1] Edward Frederick Lindley Wood, 1881–1959. Educated at Eton and Christ Church, Oxford. Conservative MP for Ripon, 1910–25. Parliamentary Under-Secretary of State for the Colonies, 1921–2. President of the Board of Education, 1922–4. Minister of Agriculture, 1924–5. Created Baron Irwin, 1925. Viceroy of India, 1926–31. President of the Board of Education, 1931–4. Succeeded his father as 3rd Viscount Halifax, 1934. Secretary of State for War, 1935. Lord Privy Seal, 1935–7. Lord President of the Council, 1937–8. Foreign Secretary, 1938–40. Ambassador in Washington, 1941–6. Order of Merit, 1946. One of his three sons was killed in action in Egypt in October 1942.

[2] In Churchill's absence in Washington, Clement Attlee, Lord Privy Seal, was in the chair.

[3] Henry Ruthven Moore, 1886–1978. Naval cadet, 1902. Served in the Grand Fleet, 1914–18 (DSO, 1916). Royal Naval Staff College, 1920–1. Imperial Defence College, 1927. Rear-Admiral Commanding 3rd Cruiser Squadron, 1939–40. Vice-Chief, Naval Staff, 1941–3. Knighted, 1942. Second-in-Command, Home Fleet, 1943–4. Commander-in-Chief, Home Fleet, 1944–5. Head of British Naval Mission, Washington, 1945–8.

[4] Clement Attlee.

[5] Albert Victor Alexander, 1885–1965. Educated at an elementary school, and technical classes, in Bristol. Labour (Co-operative) MP for Hillsborough, 1922–31, 1935–50. Parliamentary Secretary, Board of Trade, 1924. First Lord of the Admiralty in Ramsay MacDonald's second Labour Govern-

Winston S. Churchill to Admiral of the Fleet Sir Roger Keyes[1]
(Churchill papers, 20/57)

1 January 1942   Washington DC

Please accept my great sympathy in the loss of your gallant son.[2]

Winston

General Claude Auchinleck[3] to Winston S. Churchill
(Churchill papers, 20/68)

1 January 1942   Cairo

[...]

Your telegram 154 of Dec. 31st just received. Entirely agree as to desirability of clearing up Bardia, Halfaya, Sollum and so does General Ritchie.[4] As you see process has begun but all these positions are strongly held wired and mined and the enemy has plenty of artillery. Halfaya will

ment, 1929–31; in Churchill's wartime Coalition Government, 1940–5; and in Attlee's Labour Government, 1945–6. Member of the Cabinet Delegation to India, 1946. Minister of Defence, 1947–50. Created Viscount, 1950. Chancellor of the Duchy of Lancaster, 1950–1. Leader of the Labour Peers in the House of Lords, 1955–65. Created Earl, 1963; Knight of the Garter, 1964.

[1] Roger John Brownlow Keyes, 1872–1945. Entered the Royal Navy, 1885. Naval Attaché, Athens and Constantinople, 1905–7. Commodore in charge of submarines, North Sea and adjacent waters, August 1914 to February 1915. Chief of Staff, Eastern Mediterranean Squadron (Dardanelles), 1915. Director of Plans, Admiralty, 1917. Vice-Admiral in Command of the Dover Patrol (and Zeebrugge raid), 1918. Knighted, 1918. Created Baronet, 1919. Deputy Chief of the Naval Staff, 1921–5. Commander-in-Chief, Mediterranean, 1925–8; Portsmouth, 1929–31. Admiral of the Fleet, 1930. National Conservative MP for North Portsmouth, 1934–43. Director of Combined Operations, 1940–1. Created Baron, 1943. Churchill wrote the foreword to Keyes' memoirs, *Adventures Ashore and Afloat* (1939).

[2] Geoffrey Charles Tasker Keyes, 1917–41. Royal Armoured Corps; Royal Scots Greys (2nd Dragoons). Killed on 18 November 1941, while serving as a Lieutenant-Colonel in the Commandos, leading a raid on Rommel's headquarters in the Western Desert, 250 miles behind enemy lines. Buried in the Commonwealth War Graves Commission Cemetery in Benghazi. For his part in the raid, he was posthumously awarded the Victoria Cross.

[3] Claude John Eyre Auchinleck, 1884–1981. Known as 'The Auk'. Entered the Indian Army, 1903. On active service in Egypt and Aden, 1914–15; Mesopotamia, 1916–19 (DSO, 1917). On active service on the North-West Frontier of India, 1933, 1935. Deputy Chief of the General Staff, Army Headquarters, India, 1936. Member of the Expert Committee on the Defence of India, 1938. Commanded Anglo-French ground forces in Norway, May 1940. Knighted, 1940. Commander-in-Chief, Southern Command, 1940. Commander-in-Chief, India, 1941, when he sent troops to Iraq to crush the pro-German Rashid Ali revolt. Commander-in-Chief, Middle East, 1941–2. Commander-in-Chief, India, 1943–7. Field Marshal, 1946. Lived in retirement in Marrakech. After his death at the age of 96, he was buried in the Commonwealth War Graves Commission plot in the European cemetery in Casablanca.

[4] Neil Methuen Ritchie, 1897–1983. On active service in France, Mesopotamia, Palestine, 1914–18 (despatches, DSO, Military Cross). On active service in Palestine, 1938–9 (despatches). Brigadier, General Staff, 1939. Commander, 51st Highland Division, 1940. Deputy Chief of Staff, Middle East, 1941. Commander, 8th Army, Libya, 1941–2 (rank of Lieutenant-General). Commander, 52nd Lowland Division, 1942–3. General Officer Commanding-in-Chief, Scottish Command, and Governor of Edinburgh Castle, 1945–7. Knighted, 1945. Commander-in-Chief, Far East Land Forces, 1947–9. Commander, British Army Staff, Washington, 1950–1.

be tackled next and sacrifices accepted if necessary but I am desirous not repeat not to incur very heavy casualties especially as troops engaged will be South Africans whose manpower situation is as you know none too good. We will be as quick as we can.

We all wish you the best with luck in 1942 and hope we will be able to play our part to the fullest possible extent.[1]

Winston S. Churchill to General Claude Auchinleck
(Churchill papers, 20/88)

1 January 1942   Washington DC

I have a feeling that it would be well if you could arrange it to finish up Bardia, Sollum, Halfaya pockets as soon as possible, and that some sacrifice might well be made to this end. Have you no siege batteries available? Everyone here is delighted with progress made towards the West.

Winston S. Churchill to Brigadier Leslie Hollis[1]
(Churchill papers, 20/67)

2 January 1942   Washington DC

What has been done about the New Zealand telegram asking for a large quantity of weapons, &c.? They have behaved so well and deserve every help possible.

Winston S. Churchill to Brigadier Leslie Hollis
(Churchill papers, 20/67)

2 January 1942   Washington DC

Considering we have arranged that they are to be represented, through us, in London, is it not rather unnecessary for all these high Dutch authorities to come over here? How does the matter stand?[2]

---

[1] Leslie Chasemore Hollis, 1897–1963. Entered the Royal Marine Light Infantry, 1914. Served with the Grand Fleet and Harwich Force, 1915–18, including the Battle of Jutland. Assistant Secretary, Committee of Imperial Defence, 1936–9. Lieutenant-Colonel, 1937. Senior Assistant Secretary in the office of the War Cabinet, 1939–46. Brigadier, 1939. CBE, 1942. Major-General, 1943. Sole representative of the Defence Office with Churchill during the Prime Minister's illness at Carthage and recuperation at Marrakech, 1943–4. Knighted, 1946. Chief Staff Officer to the Minister of Defence, 1947–9. Commandant General, Royal Marines, 1949–52. Author of *One Marine's Tale* (1956) and *War at the Top* (1959).

[2] Sir Alexander Cadogan, Permanent Under-Secretary of State at the Foreign Office, wrote in his diary on 4 January 1942: 'Dutch are furious at decisions being taken in Washington without being given a chance of expressing their opinion. They are quite right! I got van Kleffens on telephone

Winston S. Churchill to Lord Halifax
(Churchill papers, 20/67)

2 January 1942   Washington DC

What do you think about this?[1] Should I break it to the President or to Hopkins,[2] or would it not be better for you to take it up with Hull?

General Claude Auchinleck to Winston S. Churchill
(Churchill papers, 20/68)

2 January 1942   Cairo

Have just had following from General Ritchie. Begins. Capture of Bardia completed reported 1,000 British prisoners of war released. Our casualties believed slight. Ends.

Will send details later.[3]

and gave him ridiculous message (very tactfully) from PM telling him to cancel his departure for Washington tomorrow. He – in a huff – had already decided not to go' (*The Diaries of Sir Alexander Cadogan,* page 428). Van Kleffens was the Netherlands Minister for Foreign Affairs.

[1] A telegram from the British Admiralty to the British Admiralty Delegation in Washington reporting that the Americans might try to placate the Argentines by asking them to take over the defence of the Falkland Islands, and suggesting that it should be made clear to the Americans that this would be undesirable.

[2] Harry Hopkins, 1890–1946. Director of the (New Deal) Works Progress Administration, 1935–8; Secretary of Commerce, 1938–40; Administrator of Lend-Lease, 1941–5. President Roosevelt's closest aide, he lived at the White House when he was not on wartime missions to London or Moscow, or in hospital (in 1937 he underwent surgery for cancer of the stomach). Travelled to Moscow on a mission for President Truman, May 1945.

[3] Ten hours later, at 9.55 p.m. on 2 January 1942, Auchinleck telegraphed to Churchill: 'Surrender of Bardia was un-conditional. Estimated number prisoners over 3,000 (repeat 3,000) including Major-General Schmidt Chief Administrative Staff Officer German Panzer-gruppe. Estimated over 1,000 (repeat 1,000) our own men previously captured by enemy will be released but no (repeat no) firm figures yet. General Ritchie success due to determination and skill of all troops under command General De-Villiers under direction of General Willoughby-Norrie and consisting of units of 1 and 2 South Africa Divisions 1 British (?Army) [query in transcript] Tank Bde., NZ Cavalry Regt., 3 British Medium Artillery Regts., and Polish Field Artillery Regt., supported magnificently by HM ships. Moonlight attack of Tank Regts., and South Africa Infantry all using bayonets proved too much for enemy. British, Australian and Free French Air Force squadrons all largely contributed to success of operation which was carried out in cold and most inclement weather. 4. Our casualties in moonlight attack last night very light believed less than 100' (*Churchill papers, 20/68*).

Winston S. Churchill to Clement Attlee
(Churchill papers, 20/88)

2 January 1942   Washington DC

Directive for General Wavell,[1] and arrangements for higher direction of war in ABDA[2] area have been approved by the President and myself. Text of former follows.

2. Much thought has been given to inclusion of Burma in ABDA area. Decision was reached that for operational purposes it should be so included, the overriding consideration being that we must give Chiang Kai-shek the feeling that the new command stretches out his left hand to him. It is of great importance that he should be supported in every way, and the General Officer Commanding, Burma, should be placed in direct touch with him and should be instructed without fail to establish good relations with him.

3. To include Australia and New Zealand in the area would be to overburden General Wavell. We are, however, pressing the Americans to extend the area of operations of their Pacific Fleet to include the whole region between 180° and the coast of Australia. They would thus cover Fiji, and strengthen the defence of New Zealand. Admiral King[3] is studying the possibility of this arrangement.

4. General Wavell's directive should be telegraphed to him as soon as possible. In the meanwhile he should be told that the President and I attach much importance to his taking over as soon as he can. He should be asked to specify the earliest date. The announcement cannot be delayed, but it will say that General Wavell will be taking over shortly.

---

[1] Archibald Percival Wavell, 1883–1950. On active service in South Africa, 1901, and on the Western Front, 1914–16 (wounded, Military Cross). Military Attaché with Russian Army in the Caucasus, 1916–17, and with the Egyptian Expeditionary Force, Palestine, 1917–18. CMG, 1919. Commanded British troops in Palestine and Transjordan, 1937–8. General Officer Commanding-in-Chief, Southern Command, 1938–9. Knighted, 1939. Commander-in-Chief, Middle East, 1940–1; India, 1941–2; ABDACOM (American–British–Dutch–Australian Command), 1942; India and Burma, 1942–3. Field Marshal, 1943. Created Earl, 1947. Biographer of Field Marshal Allenby, and author of an anthology of poetry, *Other Men's Flowers* (1944).

[2] ABDA: American British Dutch Australian [Command].

[3] Ernest Joseph King, 1878–1956. Highest-ranking cadet at the United States Naval Academy, 1901. While still at the Academy, served during the Spanish–American War of 1898. On active service at sea during the First World War. A submariner, 1923–5. Commander Aircraft Carriers, 1926–32. Commander-in-Chief, United States Fleet, from 30 December 1941, and Chief of Naval Operations from March 1942 to the end of the war. Fleet Admiral, 1944. Honorary knighthood, 1945.

5. I approve Pownall[1] as his Chief Staff Officer, and latter should be informed. He and all commanders concerned should receive copies of the Directive.

6. Netherlands Government should be informed.

7. Let me know who is proposed to command in India.

Winston S. Churchill to General Archibald Wavell
(Churchill papers, 20/88)

3 January 1942   Washington DC

The United States Government considers it politically important that you should set up your headquarters at first in Java, and they have told the Dutch Government that you will be doing so, basing themselves on the sentence in my original telegram, which read 'General Wavell, whose headquarters should in the first instance be established at Sourabaya.'

2. I do not wish your hands to be tied in any way, but if possible you should select a headquarters in Java. I believe both Sourabaya or Bandoeng have good communications.

Winston S. Churchill to Josef Stalin
(Churchill papers, 20/132)

3 January 1942   Washington DC

I am much concerned to read in American papers the article in *Pravda* of 31st December,[2] as it is assumed that such articles have the approval of the Russian Government. I feel you will allow me to point out to you the very great danger which might be caused here by a continuance of such criticism. From the very first day of the Nazi attack upon you I

---

[1] Henry Royds Pownall, 1887–1961. Entered the Army, 1906. On active service, 1914–18 (DSO, Military Cross). Director of Military Operations and Intelligence, War Office, 1938–9. Chief of the General Staff, British Expeditionary Force, 1939–40. Knighted, 1940. Inspector-General of the Home Guard, 1940. General Officer Commanding British Forces in Northern Ireland, 1940–1. Vice-Chief of the Imperial General Staff, 1941. Commander-in-Chief, Far East, 1941–2. General Officer Commanding Forces in Ceylon, 1942–3. General Officer Commanding-in-Chief, Persia, 1943. Chief of Staff to the Supreme Allied Commander, South-East Asia (Lord Mountbatten), 1943–4. Chief Commissioner, St John's Ambulance Brigade, 1947–9. Chancellor, Order of St John, 1951. Churchill's principal helper on the military aspects of his war memoirs, 1945–55.

[2] The article, a prominent editorial entitled 'Pétain methods in the Philippines' (actually published on December 30), contained bitter criticism of the United States' declaration of Manila as an 'open city' and likened American policy to that of a 'ladybird' (i.e. weak).

have laboured to get all possible support for Soviet Russia in the United States, and therefore I venture to send you this most private and entirely friendly comment.[1]

Winston S. Churchill to Alfred Duff Cooper[2]
(Churchill papers, 20/88)

3 January 1942   Washington DC

As you have no doubt seen in the Press reports, I took the opportunity of paying a tribute to Dutch assistance in my speech before the House of Commons at Ottawa.[3]

---

[1] Stalin replied to Churchill on January 9: 'Thank you for your message and your solicitude for the favourable development of Soviet–American relations. The article in *Pravda* referred to by you had no official character whatever and certainly was not directed to any other purpose but the common interests of our countries in the struggle against aggression. The Soviet Government for its part is doing and will do everything possible for the further strengthening of Soviet–American relations' (*Churchill papers, 20/132*).

[2] Alfred Duff Cooper, 1890–1954. Known as 'Duff'. Educated at Eton and New College, Oxford. Entered the Foreign Office as a clerk, 1913. On active service, Grenadier Guards, 1917–18 (DSO, despatches). Conservative MP for Oldham (Churchill's first constituency), 1924–9. Financial Secretary, War Office, 1928–9, 1931–4. MP for St George's, Westminster, 1931–45. Financial Secretary, Treasury, 1934–5. Privy Councillor, 1935. Secretary of State for War, 1935–7. First Lord of the Admiralty, 1937–8. Minister of Information, 1940–1. British Representative, Singapore, 1941. Chancellor of the Duchy of Lancaster, 1941–3. British Representative, French Committee of National Liberation, 1943–4. Ambassador to France, 1944–7. Knighted, 1948. Created Viscount Norwich, 1952.

[3] In the course of his speech to the Canadian House of Commons on 30 December 1941, Churchill made reference to the Dutch: 'What a contrast has been the behaviour of the valiant, stout-hearted Dutch, who still stand forth as a strong living partner in the struggle! Their venerated Queen and their Government are in England, their Princess and her children have found asylum and protection here in your midst. But the Dutch nation are defending their Empire with dogged courage and tenacity by land and sea and in the air. Their submarines are inflicting a heavy daily toll upon the Japanese robbers who have come across the seas to steal the wealth of the East Indies, and to ravage and exploit its fertility and its civilization. The British Empire and the United States are going to the aid of the Dutch. We are going to fight out this new war against Japan together. We have suffered together and we shall conquer together' (BBC Written Archives Centre).

Winston S. Churchill to Oliver Lyttelton[1]
(Churchill papers, 20/88)

3 January 1942   Washington DC

All points in your telegram No. 87 from Cairo to Washington of 31st December have for a long time been under detailed study.[2] Your general outlook agrees with ours. Should it be possible to make landings you mention on Atlantic shore, operation against Islands[3] would be superseded as continental bases would be available. Your paragraph 6 is particularly concurred in. Everything is dependent upon speed of Auchinleck's advance and available shipping, upon which there are many other calls. You may be sure 'Gymnast'[4] and its transatlantic development rank very highly in our thoughts. Meanwhile, utmost secrecy should be preserved.

2. I was much interested in your accounts of desert battle. Every good wish for New Year. I feel very thankful for great improvement in our fortune which 1941 has seen.

Winston S. Churchill to Clement Attlee
(Churchill papers, 20/88)

3 January 1942   Washington DC

You will have got my two telegrams about what we did yesterday. President has chosen the title 'United Nations' for all the Powers now

---

[1] Oliver Lyttelton 1893–1972. Son of Alfred Lyttelton, Colonial Secretary in Balfour's Government. Educated at Eton and Trinity College, Cambridge. 2nd Lieutenant, Grenadier Guards, December 1914; on active service on the Western Front, 1915–18 (Military Cross, DSO, despatches three times, wounded April 1918). Entered merchant banking, 1919. Joined the British Metal Corporation, 1920; later Managing Director. Appointed Controller of Non-Ferrous Metals, September 1939. President of the Board of Trade, and Privy Councillor, July 1940. Conservative MP for Aldershot, 1940–54. Minister of State, Middle East (based in Cairo), and Member of the War Cabinet, June 1941 to March 1942. Minister of Production, March 1942 to May 1945. Chairman of Associated Electrical Industries, 1945–51 and 1954–63. Secretary of State for Colonial Affairs, 1951–4. Created Viscount Chandos, 1954. Chairman of the National Theatre Board, 1962; Life President, 1971. Knight of the Garter, 1970. One of his three sons was killed on active service in Italy in 1944. The second of the Royal National Theatre's three auditoria bears his name.

[2] Lyttelton's memorandum 'On future military operations'.

[3] St Pierre and Miquelon.

[4] 'Gymnast': the British plan for an amphibious landing in French North Africa in the spring of 1942 to bring United States ground forces into action against Germany and Italy and end the Vichy Government's control of Morocco and Tunisia. It was later developed into 'Torch', the landings that took place from 8 to 16 November 1942.

working together. This is much better than 'Alliance' which places him in Constitutional difficulties, or 'Associated Powers', which is flat.

2. We could not get the words 'or Authorities' inserted in the last paragraph of the Declaration, as Litvinov is a mere automaton, evidently frightened out of his wits after what he has gone through. This can be covered by an exchange of letters making clear that the word 'Nations' covers authorities such as the Free French or insurgent organisations which may arise in Spain, in North Africa or in Germany itself. Settlement was imperative because with nearly thirty Powers already informed leakage was certain. President was also very keen on 1st January.

3. Speed was also essential in settling letter of instructions to Wavell. Here again it was necessary to defer to American views, observing we are no longer single, but married. I, personally, am in favour of Burma being included in Wavell's operational sphere; but, of course, the local Commander-in Chief, Burma, will be based on India, and will have a job of his own to do. He will have to get into friendly touch with Chiang Kai-shek, upon whom, it appears, Wavell and Brett[1] made a none-too-good impression.[2]

4. The heavy American troop and air force movements in Northern Ireland are to begin at once, and we are now beating about for the shipping necessary to mount 'Super-Gymnast',[3] if possible, during their currency.

5. We live here as a big family, in the greatest intimacy and informality, and I have formed the very highest regard and admiration for the President. His breadth of view, resolution and his loyalty to the common cause are beyond all praise. There is not the slightest sign here of excitement or worry about the opening misfortunes, which are taken as a matter of course and to be retrieved by the marshalling of overwhelming forces of every kind. There will, of course, be a row in public presently.

6. Please thank the War Cabinet for their very kind New Year's message. I am so glad you like what I said in Canada. My reception there was very moving.

---

[1] George H. Brett, 1886–1963. 2nd Lieutenant, United States Cavalry, 1911. United States Air Force, 1915; 1st Lieutenant, 1916. Brigadier-General, 1936; Major-General, 1940; Lieutenant-General, 1942. Among his many decorations and honours were the Distinguished Service Medal with Oak Leaves Cluster, the DFC, and an honorary knighthood (KCB).

[2] On 3 January 1942 President Roosevelt and Churchill jointly announced from Washington the setting up of the South-West Pacific area under General Wavell, with Major-General Brett (US) as his Deputy and General Pownall (UK) as his Chief of Staff; Admiral Hart (US) to be Commander in Chief naval forces in the same area; General Chiang Kai-shek to be Commander-in-Chief land and air forces in Chinese area (including Indo-China and Thailand).

[3] 'Super-Gymnast': the despatch, authorised on 13 January 1942, of 21,000 United States troops with aircraft and other equipment from the East Coast of the United States to Australia.

Winston S. Churchill to Clement Attlee
(Churchill papers, 20/88)

3 January 1942   Washington DC

There would inevitably be delay if Australian and New Zealand representatives sat in with representatives of British Chiefs of Staff at Washington, as they would be sure to wish to consult their Governments before giving an opinion. If Australia and New Zealand were in a position to make representations both in London and Washington there would be confusion.

There is no reason why Australian and New Zealand representatives should not be called into Conference by COS in London at the earliest stage, and that was our intention.

It would be most undesirable that any difference between us and the Dominions would be argued in front of the American COS.[1] The proposed procedure has been explained in detail to Mr Casey[2] who raised no objection.

Winston S. Churchill to John Curtin[3]
(Churchill papers, 20/88)

3 January 1942   Washington DC

General Wavell's command area is limited to the fighting zone where active operations are now proceeding. Henceforward it does not include Australia, New Zealand and communications between the United States and Australia, or, indeed, any other ocean communications. This does not, of course, mean that these vital regions and communications are to be left without protection so far as our resources admit. In our view, the American navy should assume the responsibility for the communica-

---

[1] The American Chiefs of Staff: Admiral William D. Leahy, United States Navy; General George C. Marshall, United States Army; General Henry Arnold, United States Army Air Forces.

[2] Richard Gardiner Casey, 1890–1976. Born in Australia. Educated in Australia and at Trinity College, Cambridge. On active service at Gallipoli and in France (DSO, Military Cross), 1915–18. Active in Australian politics between the wars. Australian Minister for Supply and Development, 1939–40. Australian Minister to the United States, 1940–2. British Minister of State Resident in the Middle East (based in Cairo), and Member of the British War Cabinet, 1942–3. Governor of Bengal, 1944–6. Minister of External Affairs, Australia, 1951–60. Created Baron, 1960. Governor-General of Australia, 1965–9.

[3] John Curtin, 1885–1945. Member of the Australian House of Representatives, 1928–31 and 1934–45. Leader of the Opposition, 1935–41. Prime Minister of Australia, 1941–5 (Minister of Defence, 1942–5). Chairman of the Advisory War Council, 1941–4.

tions to the eastwards, including the islands right up to the Australian or New Zealand coast. This is what we are pressing for. Admiral King has only just been given full powers over the whole of the American navy and he has not yet accepted our views. Obviously, if I cannot persuade the Americans to take over, we shall have to fill the gap as best we can, but I still hope our views will be accepted, in which case, of course, any vessels we or you have in that area will come under United States direction while operating there. There never has been any intention to make the main Allied concentration in the newly defined South-West Pacific theatre, and I do not know where you got this from.

2. I now send you the letter of instruction to General Wavell which has been agreed to by the President and the American chiefs. A statement upon the Wavell appointment will be made public shortly and I will see that you get it in good time for synchronization of release.

3. Your 166 of the 29th December. Staff appreciation to which you refer was prepared in London and all like documents of this character constitute a general survey of the situation rather than the final plans for action. It is, in any case, largely superseded by the appointment of Wavell as Supreme Commander. Nevertheless, I have laid it before the Chiefs of Staff who are with me here, and I have no doubt they will take to heart the various comments you have been good enough to make upon it.

4. Night and day I am labouring here to make the best arrangements possible in your interests and for your safety, having regard to the other theatres and the other dangers which have to be met from our limited resources. It is only a little while ago that you were most strongly urging the highest state of equipment for the Australian army in the Middle East. The battle there is still not finished, though the prospects are good. It would have been folly to spoil Auchinleck's battle by diverting aircraft, tanks, &c., to the Malay Peninsula at a time where there was no certainty that Japan would enter the war. The ease-up of the Caucasian danger through the Russian victories and the Auchinleck successes have made possible the considerable reinforcements, at the temporary expense of the Middle East, of which you have been advised and which are also justified because Malaya has now become a war theatre.

5. I have been in close consultation with Casey, who has been of great help in presenting your view and anxieties.

Winston S. Churchill to Anthony Eden[1]
(Churchill papers, 20/88)

3 January 1942   Washington DC

You should try and persuade Netherlands Foreign Minister[2] to defer his visit and that of his officers.[3]

British-American clamping machinery taking shape, and will work well if allowed to develop naturally.

Dutch collaboration must be centred in London under our general guidance.

Visit of Dutch authorities here at this moment would cause confusion and embarrassment.

Winston S. Churchill to Lord Halifax
(Churchill papers, 20/67)

3 January 1942   Washington DC

ST PIERRE AND MIQUELON ISLANDS

I have just seen Foreign Office telegram No. 7340.[4] I hope you have been able to make this point with the State Department. Vichy chatters as if they were a sovereign state; whereas they are helpless prisoners.

---

[1] Robert Anthony Eden, 1897–1977. Educated at Eton and Christ Church, Oxford. Served on the Western Front, 1915–18 (Military Cross). Conservative MP for Warwick and Leamington, 1923–57. Parliamentary Under-Secretary, Foreign Office, 1931–3. Lord Privy Seal, 1934–5. Minister for League of Nations Affairs, 1935. Foreign Secretary, 1935–8. Secretary of State for Dominion Affairs, September 1939 to May 1940. Foreign Secretary, May 1940 to July 1945, October 1951 to April 1955. Knight of the Garter, 1954. Prime Minister, 1955–7. Created Earl of Avon, 1961. One of his brothers was killed near Ypres in October 1914; another in 1916 at the Battle of Jutland. His elder son was killed in action in Burma on 23 June 1945, aged 20.

[2] Eelco Nicolaas van Kleffens, 1894–1983. Worked in the Secretariat of the League of Nations between the wars. Appointed Netherlands Minister of Foreign Affairs shortly before the outbreak of war in 1939. Served as Foreign Minister of the Dutch Government-in-Exile, 1940–5. Netherlands Representative on the United Nations Security Council, 1946, and Ambassador to the United States, 1947–50. President of the United Nations General Assembly, 1954.

[3] Eden had informed Churchill of the proposed visit of the Netherlands Foreign Minister and several senior Dutch officers to Washington.

[4] Opposing Vichy claims to be in charge of the French islands of St Pierre and Miquelon, off the Dominion of Newfoundland. The islands lie six miles from the nearest part of Newfoundland (Green Island). The fishing grounds off St Pierre and Miquelon had been a source of repeated conflict between Britain and France: taken by Britain from France in 1713 and regained by France in 1763, they were subsequently taken and retaken several times until France finally acquired them in 1815. In June 1940, the islands declared for Vichy. On 24 December 1941, without the knowledge of the Canadian or United States Governments, a Free French flotilla took over the islands. The Vichy authorities still claimed to be in charge. A referendum among the islanders then declared in favour of de Gaulle.

Winston S. Churchill to Anthony Eden
(Churchill papers, 20/88)

3 January 1942   Washington DC

ST PIERRE AND MIQUELON ISLANDS

I made some suggestions to Hull about Miquelon to clear up this squall, which is rather serious, as the State Department is being so heavily attacked, and we have agreed on the following draft. I explained to Hull that this draft was only provisional and dependent first on your agreement and secondly on that of the Canadian Government. I am sure the State Department will be grateful for being got out of a hole. However, let me know your full opinion. I will then communicate with Canada. If you agree, you will have to make it clear to de Gaulle that he must himself give the orders to Muselier[1] to withdraw. Otherwise very grave issues might arise for him. The President is very anxious to have this matter settled as at one moment it looked like Hull's resignation. You will, of course, take care of the press at your end:

> The United States, British, and Canadian Governments view this incident as on a very small scale compared to what is going on all over the world. The problems involved relate to the safeguarding of British, Canadian and American shipping in the North Atlantic and existing international commitments. None the less, it must be made clear that the Free French action was taken not only without their assent, but in the face of the declared wishes of the British Government.

> Accordingly, the three Governments have agreed that the principle that these islands are to be regarded in the present phase as demilitarized and out of the war shall be maintained. All armed forces will be withdrawn, it being understood that at the same time adequate steps shall be taken to assure that no radio station situated on the islands shall be used contrary to the interests of the United Nations. The local inhabitants will be left in full exercise of their rights of domestic self-government, arrangements being made both to continue the supplies from the United States and Canada on which they are dependent and also to provide for the seasonal supply of fish to the French inhabitants of Martinique.

---

[1] Emile Henry Muselier, 1882–1965. Entered the French Navy, 1902. Captain, 1918. Admiral Commanding the Navy and Defences of Marseille, 1938–40. Joined General de Gaulle, July 1940. Commander-in-Chief of the Free French Naval Forces, 1940–2, and of the Free French Air Forces, 1940–1. Chief of the French Naval Delegation, Military Mission for German Affairs, 1944–5. Honorary British knighthood, 1946.

Meanwhile, in the light of the relevant facts there should be no occasion for confusion or misunderstanding since there is no divergence of policy and there is complete co-operation and understanding between the United States, Great Britain and Canada in this as in other matters.

General Claude Auchinleck to Winston S. Churchill
(Churchill papers, 20/68)

3 January 1942   Cairo

Bardia. 5,000 prisoners counted. 1,150 our prisoners released including 650 New Zealanders. Only 2 officers recovered enemy having evacuated rest by sea. Our casualties for whole operation about 60 killed and 300 wounded. Water pumping station just saved from demolition. Roads and bridges all intact. Maximum damage has been done to town by enemy who has destroyed pier.

Winston S. Churchill to General Hastings Ismay,[1]
for the Chiefs of Staff Committee
(Churchill papers, 23/10)

4 January 1942   [Washington DC]
Most Secret

I have availed myself of a few days' quiet and seclusion to review the salients of war as they appear after my discussions here.

1. The United States has been attacked and become at war with the three Axis Powers, and desires to engage her trained troops as soon and as effectively as possible on fighting fronts. Owing to the shipping stringency this will not be possible on any very large scale during 1942. Meanwhile the United States Army is being raised from a strength of a little over thirty Divisions and five Armoured Divisions to a total strength of about sixty Divisions and ten Armoured Divisions. About 3 million

---

[1] Hastings Lionel Ismay, 1887–1965. Known as 'Pug'. Educated at Charterhouse and Sandhurst. 2nd Lieutenant, 1905; Captain, 1914. On active service in India, 1908, and Somaliland, 1914–20 (DSO). Staff College, Quetta, 1922. Assistant Secretary, Committee of Imperial Defence, 1925–30. Military Secretary to the Viceroy of India (Lord Willingdon), 1931–3. Colonel, 1932. Deputy Secretary, Committee of Imperial Defence, 1936–8; Secretary, 1938. Major-General, 1939. Chief of Staff to the Minister of Defence (Churchill), 1940–5. Knighted, 1940. Deputy Secretary (Military) to the War Cabinet, 1940–5. Lieutenant-General, 1942. General, 1944. Chief of Staff to the Viceroy of India (Lord Mountbatten), 1947. Created Baron, 1947. Secretary of State for Commonwealth Relations, 1951–2. Secretary-General of NATO, 1952–7. Created Knight of the Garter, 1957. He published his memoirs, *The Memoirs of General the Lord Ismay*, in 1960.

men are at present held or about to be called up for the Army and Air Force (over a million). Reserves of manpower are practically unlimited, but it would be a mis-direction of war effort to call larger numbers to the armed forces in the present phase.

2. It does not seem likely that more than between a quarter and a third of the above American forces can be transported to actual fighting fronts during the year 1942. In 1943, however, the great increases in shipping tonnage resulting from former and recent shipping programmes should enable much larger bodies to be moved across the oceans, and the Summer of 1943 may be marked by large offensive operations which should be carefully studied meanwhile.

3. The United States Air Force, already powerful and rapidly increasing, can be brought into heavy action during 1942. Already it is proposed that strong bomber forces, based on the British Isles, should attack Germany and the invasion ports. American Fighter Squadrons can participate in the defence of Great Britain and the domination of such parts of the French shore as are in Fighter reach. Additional United States Fighter and Bomber forces are much needed in Egypt and Libya, and it may be that the attack of the Roumanian oilfields from Persia by the heaviest American bombers is a project which should be entertained. Meanwhile, also, continuous streams of American bombers are proceeding both westward and eastward to the Pacific theatre of war, which will, of course, be the main scene of United States air action in 1942.

4. The Declaration by the President to Congress of the enormous increases in United States output of munitions and shipping to proceed during 1942, and reach full flow in 1943, makes it more than ever necessary for Hitler to bring the war to a decision in 1942 before the power of the United States can be fully brought to bear. Hitler's need to invade the British Isles has always been great. The difficulties of the operation are also very great. Our preparations to resist have continually improved during the past year, and will be still further augmented by the time the Spring invasion season is reached. Improvements in British preparations comprise:

(a) a far better trained and equipped Army;
(b) stronger and more elaborate beach defences, including substantially increased coast batteries;
(c) the marshalling by the Spring of between three and four thousand medium and heavy tanks in Great Britain, forming the equivalent of seven or eight Armoured Divisions;
(d) by the need imposed upon the invader, arising from the above, of bringing a very large invading Army across the sea, with con-

sequent aggravated difficulty of finding the shipping and of assembling it in the ports and river mouths, and of the greater target presented to British naval and air action;

(e) by the increase in the actual and relative power of the British Fighter Command which can now, instead of fighting at odds, bring superior numbers to bear upon the enemy Air Force over British soil, and can moreover dominate the French coastal regions nearest to the British Isles, viz., from Dunkirk to Dieppe, as well as Cherbourg, during the daytime, thus permitting daylight bombing under Fighter escort of the nearest and most dangerous regions of hostile embarkation.

5. Notwithstanding all the foregoing, we must continue to regard the invasion of the British Isles in 1942 as the only supreme means of escape and victory open to Hitler. He has had the time to prepare, perhaps in very great numbers, tank transporting vehicles capable of landing on any beach. He has no doubt developed air-borne attack by parachutes, and still more by gliders, to an extent which cannot be easily measured. The President, expressing views shared by the leading American strategists, has declared Great Britain an essential fortress of the United Nations. It is indeed the only place where the war can be lost in the critical campaign of 1942 about to open. It would be most imprudent to allow the successful defence of the British Isles to be hazarded. We have, of course, to continue to send about 40,000 men a month, with proportionate munitions and air forces, to the Armies of the Middle East. We have to send, as soon as shipping can be found, several additional Divisions to the Far East, or to replace Divisions withdrawn from the Middle East for the Far East. We also hold certain Divisions ready for particular overseas enterprises. The naval position in the Eastern Mediterranean also requires a very marked increase in British air power along the North African and Levantine shores. We must, therefore, face a continued outward flow of strength from the British Isles, and apart from equipment and armour there is no way in which our home defence army can be sensibly augmented by us. Indeed, the despatch of further Divisions abroad cannot be replaced by us.

6. The sending of four United States Divisions (one armoured) into Northern Ireland is therefore a most necessary war measure, which nothing should be allowed to prevent. The replacing of the British troops in Iceland liberates an additional British Division. It is suggested, however, that the United States authorities should be asked to consider:

(a) the training in Iceland of as many troops as possible to work in mountains and under snow conditions, as only the possession of such trained mountain and ski troops in considerable numbers can enable a liberating operation in Scandinavia to be prepared for the future; and

(b) that the American troops, once settled down in the North of Ireland, should pass in rotation, first by Brigades and then by Divisions, for tours of duty on the beaches of England and Scotland. This would be of interest to the American troops as well as adding to their experience and the defence of the island.

(c) It is further suggested that, in the absence of other more urgent calls, American Divisions beyond those already under orders may be sent into the United Kingdom, where they can, if need be, perfect their training.

7. The Operation 'Super-Gymnast' might become ripe, or might be forced upon us in the near future by unpredictable political or military events. It would be a misfortune if it were to interrupt the movement called 'Magnet.'[1] Provided the situation in North Africa, France or Spain undergoes no sudden deterioration, some months' delay might be accepted. Moreover, the military fact which would set French North Africa in a ferment and bring matters to a head would be the arrival of General Auchinleck's vanguards at the frontiers of Tunis. We cannot tell yet if and when this will be possible. Certainly the stubborn resistance of the enemy in Cyrenaica, the possibilities of General Von Rommel[2] withdrawing, or of being able to escape with a portion of his troops; the reinforcements which have probably reached Tripoli, and others which must be expected during the delay, and, above all, the difficulties of supply for our advancing troops – all will retard, or may even prevent, the full completion of 'Acrobat'.[3] We are therefore in a position to study 'Super-Gymnast' more thoroughly, and to proceed with 'Magnet' with the utmost speed.

8. For reasons which are known, the Italian Navy in the Mediterranean is greatly in excess of the British, and it is only the poor morale of the Italian Fleet that enables us to dispute the command of the sea, having

[1] 'Magnet': the movement of United States troops to Northern Ireland.

[2] Erwin Rommel, 1891–1944. Entered the German Army, 1910. On active service in the First World War in France, Italy, and Roumania; awarded Germany's highest decoration for bravery, *Pour le Mérite*, at the Battle of Caporetto, 1917. Colonel commanding Hitler's Headquarters Guard, 1939–40. In France, February–June 1940. Commanded the Afrika Korps, February 1941 to March 1943. Inspector of Coastal Defences, 1944, with responsibility for preparing France against an Allied assault; wounded by an Allied attack, 17 July 1944 (three days before the anti-Hitler bomb plot). Under suspicion of implication in the bomb plot, he accepted the option of suicide and was given a state funeral.

[3] 'Acrobat': the imminent advance from Cyrenaica into Tripolitania (planned for 11 January 1942).

regard especially to the very numerous well-posted air bases which the enemy has in Tripoli, in Sicily, in Italy, in Greece and in Crete. The concentration of German aircraft in large numbers at these air bases and the number of U-boats they maintain in the Mediterranean may conceivably portend an overseas expedition to the African shore, or alternatively or as a preliminary an attack upon Malta, that cruel thorn in their sides. It is, therefore, most important that the maximum air-power – bomber, fighter and torpedo-carrying types – we can gather and transport should be installed along that portion of the North African coast which is under our control. Substantial British air reinforcements are already on the way. The employment of American squadrons, based primarily on Egypt and extending westwards, would be invaluable. It would be for our advantage to develop air war in the Mediterranean on the largest scale on both sides, with constant bombing of enemy airfields and sea traffic. The German front-line Air Force is already less strong numerically than the British. A considerable portion of it must now be left opposite Russia. But the bulk of the British Air Force has to be tied up at home facing, at the present time, a much smaller concentration of German bombers and fighters, and yet not able to be moved because of the good interior communications possessed by the enemy and his power of rapid transference. In addition, there is the Italian Air Force to consider. What comparable value should be placed upon them is a matter of opinion.

11.[1] The object we should set before ourselves is the wearing down by continuous engagement of the German air power. This is being done on the Russian front. On the British front it can only be done to a limited extent, unless the enemy resumes his bombing or daylight offensive. But in the Mediterranean the enemy shows an inclination to develop a front, and we should meet him there with the superior strength which the arrival of the American Air Forces can alone give. It is of the utmost importance to make the German Air Force fight continuously on every possible occasion, and at every point of attack. We can afford the drain far better than they can. Indeed, like General Grant in his last campaign,[2] we can almost afford to lose two for one, having regard to the immense supplies now coming forward in the future. Every German

---

[1] The printed document does not include any item 9 or 10.

[2] Churchill is referring to General Ulysses S. Grant's military strategy at the end of the American Civil War. Grant had at his disposal far more soldiers than the Confederates could ever hope to muster, and so he adapted his strategy to his prize resource – men – by relentlessly overwhelming the enemy with numbers, despite the huge casualties incurred. Churchill is recognizing that, given their superior numbers of aircraft in Africa, the Allies could afford numerically to engage the Luftwaffe at every possible instance in order to wear down the enemy's air strength.

aircraft or pilot put out of action in 1942 is worth two of them in 1943. It is only by the strain of constant air-battle that we shall be able to force his consumption of air-power to levels which are beyond the capacity of his air-plants and air schools. In this way the initiative may be regained by us, as the enemy will be fully occupied, as we have been hitherto, in meeting day-to-day needs and keeping his head above water.

12. Coming further east we must acclaim the very great deliverance to us afforded by the successful Russian resistance along the Don and in the Crimea, carrying with it the continued Russian command of the Black Sea. Three months ago we were forced to expect a German advance through the Caucasus to the Caspian and the Baku oilfields. That danger is almost certainly staved off for perhaps four or five months till the winter is over and, of course, continued successful Russian resistance in the south gives complete protection to us. This fact alone has enabled us to divert the 18th Division, the 17th Indian Infantry Division and to plan the withdrawal of two out of the three Australian Divisions in Palestine, together with considerable air reinforcements and much material, from the Levant–Caspian front to the new emergencies in Malaya and the Far East. It must be emphasised that we could not possibly have provided for the Libyan operations, the maintenance of the Levant–Caspian front and the Malayan needs simultaneously. Even without the war with Japan we could only have maintained a very doubtful defence of Palestine, Iraq and Persia.

13. The danger may, however, recur in the late Spring. The oil stringency which is already serious in Germany and the German conquered countries makes the seizure of the Baku and Persian oilfields objects of vital consequence to Germany, second only to the need to successfully invade the British Isles. No one can forecast the future course of the Russo-German struggle. Evidently the Germans will suffer increasingly heavy losses during the winter. They may even sustain disasters so great that the Russian counter-strokes will reach the former frontier with consequences to the Nazi régime, both military and internal, which cannot be measured. On the other hand, the enormous power of the German Army may be able to reassert itself as soon as weather conditions improve. In this case they might well be content to adopt a defensive attitude along the northern and central sectors of the Russo-German front, and thrust an offensive spearhead south-east through the Caucasus to the oilfields which lie beyond.

14. They may also persuade or compel Turkey to grant them passage through Anatolia to attack successively Syria, Palestine and Egypt. It

would, however, seem unlikely, first, that Turkey would agree in view of the Russian strength in the north and of the British activities in Egypt and Libya, and also of the world situation, now that the United States is a full belligerent. Secondly, in the event of a Turkish refusal it seems unlikely that Germany would, after her Russian losses, wish to bring into the field against her the 50 Turkish Divisions by which the inhospitable and difficult mountainous regions of Anatolia would certainly be stubbornly defended. Moreover, if the south-eastward spear-thrust through the Caucasus were successful, the Anatolian line of advance would not be indispensable to the acquisition of the oilfields. The resistance of Turkey as a friendly neutral should be stimulated in every way, and especially by sending whatever supplies are possible in aircraft, anti-aircraft, tanks and anti-tank equipment. Great Britain has already made promises to aid the Turks with considerable air and land forces if they are attacked and resist. Our ability to fulfil these promises has been prejudiced by the diversions necessary for making head against Japan. On the whole, however, it would seem reasonable to assume that the main danger to be faced in the spring of 1942 in this theatre will be a breakdown in Russian defence of the Caucasus and Baku, and the German advance thence to the oilfield of Persia, and to Basra at the head of the Persian Gulf.

15. We thus see ourselves drawn away towards the West by 'Crusader,'[1] 'Acrobat' and perhaps 'Gymnast' and 'Super-Gymnast,' while at the same time we are drawn farther to the East by the increasing scale of the Japanese war. How are we to meet the danger outlined in the two preceding paragraphs? It will not be possible for Great Britain to replace the 18th British, 17th Indian, and two Australian Divisions moved or already assigned to the Far East, especially if 'Gymnast' or 'Super-Gymnast' should develop. The monthly drafts for North Africa, for the Levant–Caspian front and for the Malayan theatre, which have already averaged for many months 35,000 a month, will probably rise to 50,000 if existing units are to be maintained and if the necessary British contingents of the five new Divisions being raised in India are to be supplied. This will strain to the utmost both the escorts and the shipping necessary to move these monthly convoys in and out of the danger zones in the British Isles, and it is a three or four months' round voyage via the Cape of Good Hope to Suez, Basra or Malaya. It is doubtful whether more than one, or at the outside two, new Divisional formations can be transferred from Great Britain to the various eastern theatres in six or even eight months. It would not be wise to call upon India for further reinforcements for the

---

[1] 'Crusader': proposed operation in the Western Desert, planned for 24 January 1942.

Levant–Caspian theatre, as all her resources will be needed to nourish the war against Japan in the Malayan theatre, to defend Burma (and it may be India) and keep open the Burma Road to China. After the move to the Far East of the Divisions mentioned above has been completed we shall, therefore, have in the Levant–Caspian region only the 5th Indian Division in Cyprus, the 50th British Division at Baghdad, one Australian and one Armoured Division (as yet only partly formed) in Palestine, the 8th, 9th and 10th Indian Divisions in Persia and Iraq – total 7 Divisions. We shall have in Egypt and North Africa three British Armoured, the 70th British, the New Zealand Division, 2 South African Divisions, 4th Indian Division, and various British Brigade Groups and Polish and French contingents the equivalent of, say, three Divisions – total 11 Divisions. It seems likely that this force will be fully occupied in maintaining the North African shore, especially if the fighting front should extend westwards into Tunis.

16. It is a question to be profoundly considered whether the United States would not be wise to contemplate the development of an American army, based on the Persian Gulf ports, to operate to the northward with the British and Empire forces set out above. The monster liners sailing from United States' east coast ports could perhaps find their fullest employment in carrying American troops through the great ocean spaces via the Cape to the Persian Gulf. If an American army of six or eight Divisions could be developed north of the Persian Gulf, it would, added to the seven we have and proportionate air forces, with any reinforcements we can send, be a powerful factor in the war against Germany. Whether this army of, say, 15 Divisions, or any part of it, should stand purely on the defensive or should move forward to the Caucasus and even to the Russian southern front north of the Black Sea, would be dependent upon events on the Russo-German front, on where that front would be standing in the third quarter of 1942 and on the development of the communications by road and rail from the Persian Gulf to the Caspian Sea. It must be observed that any large force moved and maintained from the Persian Gulf in the Caspian basin will, of course, choke the southern warm-water supply lines by which it is proposed to carry munitions into Russia. If nothing can be done and the Russian southern front is beaten in (which may not happen), a frightful gap will be open which at present there is nothing in sight to fill, and the loss of the oilfields of the Caspian and Persia, and of all the regions between the present Russian Front and the frontiers of India cannot be excluded from our thoughts. It is suggested that the Joint

Staffs should study and report on the possibilities which are open, the precise object being the development of at least fifteen Divisions in the Levant–Caspian theatre.

FAR EAST

THE WAR AGAINST JAPAN

17. It is generally agreed that the defeat of Germany entailing a collapse will leave Japan exposed to overwhelming force, whereas the defeat of Japan would not by any means bring the world war to an end. Moreover, the vast distances in the Pacific and the advantageous forward key-points already seized or likely to be seized by the Japanese will make the serious invasion of the home-lands of Japan a very lengthy business. Not less lengthy will be the piece-meal recovery, by armies based mainly on Australia and India, of the islands, airfields and naval bases in the South-West Pacific area now confided to General Wavell. It seems, indeed, more probable that a decision can be reached sooner against Germany than against Japan. In any case, we cannot expect to develop adequate naval, air and military superiority in the aforesaid area for a considerable time having regard to other calls made upon us and the limitation of shipping.

18. While, therefore, it is right to assign primacy to the war against Germany, it would be wrong to speak of our 'standing on the defensive' against Japan; on the contrary, the only way in which we can live through the intervening period in the Far East before Germany is defeated is by regaining the initiative, albeit on a minor scale. Certain measures stand out clearly and are indeed imposed upon by events:

   (a) The Philippines must be held as long as possible, if only to detain Japanese forces there.
   (b) The supply lines to China via Burma must be kept open and fought for with the utmost energy.
   (c) The Singapore fortress and its immediate approaches must be defended to the utmost limit.
   (d) The Dutch Possessions in Java and Sumatra must be disputed on a constantly increasing scale.
   (e) The air routes from Australia to the South-West Pacific area, and the sea routes from the United States to Australia must be maintained.

19. None of the above defensive operations will be successfully accomplished apart from the development of a counter-stroke offensive on a minor but nonetheless considerable scale. In a theatre of a thousand islands, many capable of being converted into make-shift air and naval

bases, insoluble problems are set to purely passive defence. The Japanese having obtained temporary command of the sea, and air predominance over considerable areas, it is within their power to take almost any point they wish, apart, it is hoped, from the fortress of Singapore. They can go round with a circus force and clean up any local garrisons we or the Dutch have been able so far to hold. They will seek to secure their hold by a well-conceived network of air bases, and they no doubt hope to secure, in a certain number of months, the possession of the fortress of Singapore. Once in possession of this as well as Manila, with their air bases established at focal points, they will have built up a system of air and naval defence capable of prolonged resistance. They may succeed in doing this, in which case the end of 1943 or 1944 may well see them still ensconced in the possessions they have so easily won. On the other hand, the wider they are spread the greater the weight of the war upon them and the larger the target they expose. Their air power cannot be replenished or maintained at strength comparable to that of United States and Great Britain. The naval superiority of the United States, to which Great Britain will contribute to the best of her ability, ought to be regained by the summer of 1942.

20. It is not proposed here to discuss the steps by which the American–British naval superiority will be attained. Thereafter, or at least as soon as possible, raids should be organized upon islands or seaports which the Japanese have seized. The President has, I understand, ordered the formation of a force, on the West Coast of America, akin to the Commandos. Such a force, on account of its individual qualities, will be exceptionally valuable by gaining key-points and lodgments in amphibious operations. It would require to be supported by a number of small Brigade Groups whose mobility and equipment would be exactly fitted to the particular task foreseen, each task being a study in itself. It is not necessary, unless required on strategic grounds, to stay in the captured or recaptured islands. It will be sufficient to destroy or make prisoners of the garrison, demolish any useful installations, and depart. The exact composition of the forces for each undertaking and enterprise is a matter for separate study. According to our experiences, it would seem essential that there should be adequate cover by sea-borne aircraft and detachments of tanks and tank-landing craft. The enemy cannot possibly be prepared and must be highly vulnerable at many points. After even a few successful enterprises of this character, all of which are extremely valuable experiences to the troops and Commanders for instructional purposes, he will be terrorized out of holding places weakly, and will be forced to concentrate on a certain

number of strong points. It may then be possible for us to secure very easily suitable islands, provided we do not try to hold too many, in which air and refuelling bases of a temporary or permanent character can be improvised. The establishment of a reign of terror among the enemy's detached garrisons would seem to be an extremely valuable preliminary to the larger operations for reconquest and the building up of strong bases as stepping-stones from Australia northward.

Winston S. Churchill to Lord Linlithgow[1]
(Churchill papers, 20/68)

4 January 1942   Washington DC

I very much regret I cannot meet your wish to remove Auchinleck from his present command, which is of highest war importance. General Hartley[2] is strongly recommended as war appointment. Would he be agreeable to you? Alternatively, have you considered General Platt,[3] who took Keren largely with Indian troops and is certainly a man of mark.[4]

Winston S. Churchill to General Archibald Wavell
(Churchill papers, 20/68)

4 January 1942   Washington DC

Regret impossible to remove Auchinleck from great operations which he is controlling.

---

[1] Victor Alexander John Hope, 1887–1952. Known as 'Hopey'. Educated at Eton. Earl of Hopetoun until 1908, when he succeeded his father as 2nd Marquess of Linlithgow. On active service, 1914–18 (despatches). Civil Lord of Admiralty, 1922–4. Deputy Chairman of the Conservative Party Organisation, 1924–6. Chairman, Royal Commission on Indian Agriculture, 1926–8. Chairman, Joint Select Committee on Indian Constitutional Reform, 1933–4. Chairman, Medical Research Council, 1934–6. Privy Councillor, 1935. Viceroy of India, 1936–43. Knight of the Garter, 1943.

[2] Alan Fleming Hartley, 1882–1954. Entered the Army, 1901. On active service in South Africa, 1901–2; France, Belgium, the Balkans, and Iraq, 1914–18 (DSO). Major-General commanding the Waziristan District, 1937–8; the Rawalpindi District, 1939–40. Lieutenant-General, 1940. General Officer Commanding-in-Chief, Northern Command, India, 1940–1. Knighted, 1941. General, 1941. Commander-in-Chief, India, January–March 1942. Deputy Commander-in-Chief, India, 1942–4.

[3] William Platt, 1885–1975. On active service, North-West Frontier of India, 1908 (despatches, DSO); in France and Belgium, 1914–18. Major-General commanding the troops in Sudan, and Commandant of the Sudan Defence Force, 1938–40. General Officer Commanding-in-Chief, East African Command, 1941–5; a Free French detachment under his command captured Massawa on 8 April 1941. Knighted, 1941. Colonel of the Wiltshire Regiment, 1942–54.

[4] The post at issue is that of Commander-in-Chief, India. In the event General Hartley was appointed, and served in this capacity from January to March 1942, when he was succeeded by Auchinleck.

Winston S. Churchill to Clement Attlee
(Churchill papers, 20/88)

4 January 1942   Washington DC

Most Secret as to date. It is impossible to wind up the various important arrangements we have on hand in satisfactory manner without more time. The two staffs are working well together and establishing an excellent understanding. I should hope to be with you around 21st, but please let this be most secret.

Winston S. Churchill to Clement Attlee
(Churchill papers, 20/88)

4 January 1942   Washington DC

A series of meetings has been held on supply issues. These were presided over by the President himself and the Vice-President.[1] Negotiations were carried forward and discussions of details took place every day.

Then on Friday there was a meeting presided over by the President and myself. There are two meetings on Saturday. Final conclusions were:

It was decided to raise United States output and merchant shipping in 1942 to 8,000,000 tons deadweight and in 1943 to 10,000,000 tons deadweight. New 1942 programme is increase in production of one third.

War weapons programmes for 1942 and 1943 were determined as follows:

Weapons		1942	1943
Operational aircraft	. . . .	45,000	100,000
Tanks	. . . .	45,000	75,000
Anti-Aircraft guns	. . . .	20,000	35,000
Anti-tank guns	. . . .	14,90	not fixed
Ground and tank machine guns	. . . . .	500,000	not fixed

[1] Henry Agard Wallace, 1888–1965. United States Secretary of Agriculture, 1933–40 (his father had held the same post, 1921–4). Vice-President of the United States, January 1941 to January 1945 (when he was succeeded by Truman). Chairman of the Board of Economic Warfare and of the Supply Priorities and Allocations Board, 1941–4. Delivered his 'Century of the Common Man' speech in New York, 8 May 1942, with its positive vision of a post-war world beyond the defeat of the Nazis. Toured Latin America, 1943, helping to persuade 12 countries to declare war on Germany. Secretary of Commerce, 1945–6. Nominee of the Progressive Party in the 1948 Presidential election, advocating friendly relations with the Soviet Union and an end to the Cold War (and gaining 2.4% of the popular vote).

New 1942 programme represents increase on programme for 1942 which had been fixed after United States entry into the war as follows:

Operational aircraft	31,250
Tanks	29,550
Anti-Aircraft guns	8,900
Anti-tank guns	11,700
Ground and tank machine guns	238,000

Directives have been issued to all the departments concerned. Message to Congress this week will give abridged account of programme. Budget will contain necessary financial provisions.

Max[1] has been magnificent and Hopkins a godsend. Hope you will be pleased with immense resultant increase in programme.

Winston S. Churchill to Clement Attlee
(Churchill papers, 20/88)

5 January 1942   Washington DC

I am going south for a few days, hoping to remain in complete privacy, and President will go to Hyde Park.[2] Meanwhile the staffs are working hard, and on our return we shall deal with results. There are many difficulties to be overcome in making offensive plans, but we must persevere. The big movement of United States troops into Ireland is all arranged at this end. You must make sure that everything is getting prepared on our side. Please see that a fine job is done over this, and their special food, etc., studied.

2. I suppose you realise we are trying not only to meet the immediate needs, but to make a plan for the effective application of the American armies to the enemy's fronts wherever possible. Shipping is the limiting factor.

3. I shall be glad to have everything necessary sent forward, as I shall be in constant telegraphic touch. They are trying here to keep my whereabouts secret. It would be well to discourage speculation in our Press about my return or movements.

---

[1] Lord Beaverbrook.
[2] Hyde Park: Roosevelt's home on the Hudson River, New York State, near the town of Poughkeepsie.

Itinerary
(Franklin D. Roosevelt papers)

5 January 1942   The White House
                                                  Washington DC

Trip to Palm Beach and Pompano, Florida. The Prime Minister left Washington by Army plane early morning, Jan. 5. Landed Morrison Field, West Palm Beach, and motored to Pompano (Stettinius home).

John Martin:[1] diary
(Sir John Martin papers)

5 January 1942   Pompano Beach

Left Washington with PM, Sir Charles Wilson[2] and Tommy,[3] in Gen. Marshall's[4] plane. Arrived West Palm Beach airport. Staying in Stettinius's bungalow at Pompano.

Sir Charles Wilson: diary
('Winston Churchill, The Struggle for Survival', pages 20–1)

5 January 1942   Florida

The PM decided to come here because he did not want to tax the hospitality of the President, who likes to get away over the weekend to

[1] John Miller Martin, 1904–91. Entered the Dominions Office, 1927. Seconded to the Malayan Civil Service, 1931–4. Secretary, Palestine Royal Commission, 1936–7. Private Secretary to the Prime Minister (Churchill), 1940–1; Principal Private Secretary, 1941–5. Assistant Under-Secretary of State, Colonial Office, 1945–56; Deputy Under-Secretary, 1956–65. Knighted, 1952. High Commissioner, Malta, 1965–7. His memoir, *Downing Street: The War Years,* was published shortly after his death in 1991.

[2] Charles McMoran Wilson, 1882–1977. Physician. On active service as Medical Officer, 1914–18; Major, Royal Army Medical Corps (Military Cross, despatches twice). Dean of St Mary's Hospital Medical School, 1920–45. Knighted, 1938. Churchill's doctor from 1940 to 1955. President of the Royal College of Physicians, 1941–50. Created Baron Moran, 1943. In 1965, immediately after Churchill's death, he published *Winston Churchill: The Struggle for Survival.*

[3] Charles Ralfe Thompson, 1894–1966. Known as 'Tommy'. Midshipman, 1911. Served mainly in submarines, 1915–31. Flag Lieutenant and Flag Commander to the Board of Admiralty, 1936–40. OBE, 1938. Retired with rank of Commander, 1939. Personal Assistant to the Minister of Defence (Churchill), 1940–5. CMG, 1945.

[4] George Catlett Marshall, 1880–1959. 2nd Lieutenant, United States Infantry, 1901. On active service in France, 1917–18; Chief of Operations, 1st Army; Chief of Staff, 8th Army Corps. ADC to General Pershing, 1919–24. Chief of Staff of the United States Army, 1939–45. Chairman of the newly created Joint Chiefs of Staff Committee to advise the President on strategy, 1941–5. An advocate of the principle of 'Germany First' in Anglo-American military priorities. Representative of the President (Truman) to China with the rank of Ambassador, 1945–7. Secretary of State, 1947–9. Architect of the Marshall Plan to rebuild the shattered economies of Europe. Secretary of Defense, 1950–1. Nobel Peace Price, 1953.

Hyde Park. It was a thoughtful move to give the White House a respite, and we are seeing Winston in a new role.

General Marshall brought us in his own plane from Washington to Florida. The air here is balmy after the bitter cold of Ottawa – oranges and pineapples grow here. And the blue ocean is so warm that Winston basks half-submerged in the water like a hippopotamus in a swamp.

Winston S. Churchill: recollection
('The Grand Alliance', page 617)

5 January 1942   Florida

While at Palm Beach I was of course in constant touch by telephone with the President and the British Staffs in Washington, and also when necessary I could speak to London. An amusing, though at the moment disconcerting, incident occurred. Mr Wendell Willkie[1] had asked to see me. At this time there was tension between him and the President.

Roosevelt had not seemed at all keen about my meeting prominent members of the Opposition, and I had consequently so far not done so. Having regard however to Wendell Willkie's visit to England a year before, in January 1941, and to the cordial relations I had established with him, I felt that I ought not to leave American shores without seeing him. This was also our Ambassador's advice. I therefore put a call through to him on the evening of the 5th. After some delay I was told, 'Your call is through.' I said in effect, 'I am so glad to speak to you. I hope we may meet. I am travelling back by train tomorrow night. Can you not join the train at some point and travel with me for a few hours? Where will you be on Saturday next?'

A voice came back: 'Why, just where I am now, at my desk.' To this I replied, 'I do not understand.' 'Whom do you think you are speaking to?' I replied, 'To Mr Wendell Willkie, am I not?' 'No,' was the answer, 'you are speaking to the President.' I did not hear this very well, and asked, 'Who?' 'You are speaking to me,' came the answer, 'Franklin Roosevelt.' I said, 'I did not mean to trouble you at this moment. I was trying to speak to Wendell Willkie, but your telephone exchange seems to have made a mistake.'

[1] Wendell Lewis Willkie, 1892–1944. Born in Indiana. A lawyer and a Democrat. Became a Republican in opposition to Roosevelt's New Deal. Unlike many Republicans, he was not an isolationist. Won the Republican Party nomination for the Presidency, 1940. Lost to Roosevelt, but gained a larger Republican popular vote than any previous contender (a vote eventually exceeded by Eisenhower in 1952). Visited Britain, the Soviet Union, and China as Roosevelt's personal emissary, 1940–1.

'I hope you are getting on all right down there and enjoying yourself,' said the President. Some pleasant conversation followed about personal movements and plans, at the end of which I asked, 'I presume you do not mind my having wished to speak to Wendell Willkie?' To this Roosevelt said, 'No.' And this was the end of our talk.[1]

Winston S. Churchill: recollection
('The Grand Alliance', pages 612–13)

5 January 1942   Florida

My movements were kept strictly secret, and a notification was given from the White House to the Press that all movements by the President or by me were to be regarded as if they were the movements of American battleships. Consequently no word ever appeared. On the other hand, numbers of people greeted me in Florida, and many Pressmen and photographers, with whom I had pleasant interchanges, waited outside the entrance to our retreat; but not a trickle ever leaked into print.

Winston S. Churchill to Brigadier Leslie Hollis
(Churchill papers, 20/67)

5 January 1942   Washington DC[2]

These[3] seem quite all right, and the Dutch are a real fighting partner. Pray see how far their wishes can be met.

---

[1] Churchill noted in his memoirs: 'It must be remembered that this was in the early days of our friendship, and when I got back to Washington I thought it right to find out from Harry Hopkins whether any offence had been given. I therefore wrote to him: "I rely on you to let me know if this action of mine in wishing to speak to the person named is in any way considered inappropriate, because I certainly thought I was acting in accordance with my duty to be civil to a public personage of importance, and unless you advise me to the contrary I still propose to do so."' Hopkins said that no harm had been done (*The Grand Alliance*, pages 617–8).

[2] Although Churchill was actually in Florida at this time, his official communications continued to be sent as from Washington.

[3] The Dutch Government-in-Exile's amendments to Annex II of the directive to General Wavell as Supreme Commander, South-West Pacific.

Winston S. Churchill to Alfred Duff Cooper
(Churchill papers, 20/68)

5 January 1942   Washington DC

The very large arrangements which have developed from our discussions here, and Wavell's appointment as Supreme Commander-in-Chief of the South-West Pacific, necessarily bring your Mission to an end.[1] You should at your convenience, and by whatever is the safest and most suitable route, come home. If possible, without undue risk, you should confer with Wavell at his Headquarters in Java, and tell him what you think and know. Pray let me know your plans.

2. His Majesty's Government are entirely satisfied with the way in which you have discharged your difficult and, at times, dangerous task, and I look forward to our future work together, in a world situation which, with all its troubles, has changed decisively for the better.

Winston S. Churchill to Pieter Gerbrandy[2]
(Churchill papers, 20/88)

5 January 1942   Washington DC

I most deeply regret that you should have been embarrassed by the publication of the arrangements made here.[3] I am sure you will realise that in a crisis of this kind events proceed at a certain rate and it is not always possible to get everything in the right order. You may be sure that the President and I appreciate the enormous contribution you are making to the common cause in the new war against Japan. It is our fixed resolve to have your High Command thoroughly woven into the new organisation, and to profit in every way by the commanding knowledge which you possess of this area, as well as to work in the closest concert with the Netherlands Government in London. I have shown this to the President before despatching it, and it may well be he will send you a message himself.

---

[1] On 19 December 1941, Churchill appointed Duff Cooper Chancellor of the Duchy of Lancaster, with instructions to proceed to Singapore as the Resident British Cabinet Minister there. He was recalled on 22 January 1942.

[2] Pieter Sjoerds Gerbrandy, 1885–1961. Netherlands Minister of Justice, 1939. Joined the Government-in-Exile in London, 1940. Queen Wilhelmina, rejecting the defeatism of Prime Minister Dirk Jan de Geer, appointed Gerbrandy in his place. He served in this office from 3 September 1940 to 24 June 1945. While Prime Minister he was also in turn Minister of Justice, Minister for the Colonies and Minister of the Conduct of the War. Opposed the separatist movement in Indonesia, 1946–50.

[3] The Netherlands Prime Minister had protested against an announcement being made 'with the concurrence of the Netherlands Government'.

Winston S. Churchill to Lord Leathers[1]
(Churchill papers, 20/88)

5 January 1942   Washington DC

In our discussions here the shortage of personnel ships for military movements stands out as main obstacle. I am told United States method of fitting out these ships gives third more accommodation per ship, and is quite satisfactory. This is proved by experience of 18th Division.

Pray inform me what can be done to expedite provision of United States style accommodation in our ships, a matter which I regard as urgent. Please also see what can be done to arrange conversion of some of the fast cargo vessels now building in United States to troop carriers.

Winston S. Churchill to Admiral of the Fleet Sir Dudley Pound[2]
(Churchill papers, 20/67)

6 January 1942   Pompano

I see in the papers today rumours from London that Admiral Tovey[3] is to be the Joint Commander of the United States and British forces in the Atlantic. This would be quite unsuitable, and the publication of such a statement would be likely to lead to trouble. Any naval co-operation would have to be arranged through the Admiralty. Pray make this clear to the Admiralty, and, if necessary, let the report be contradicted.

---

[1] Frederick James Leathers, 1883–1965. Shipowner and company director. Served at the Ministry of Shipping, 1915–18. Chairman of William Cory and Son Ltd; Mann, George and Co. Ltd; R. and J. H. Rea Ltd; and the Steamship Owners' Coal Association Ltd. A director of several steamship companies. Adviser to the Ministry of Shipping on all matters relating to coal, 1940–1. Created Baron, 1941. Minister of War Transport, 1941–5. Companion of Honour, 1943. Secretary of State for the Co-ordination of Transport, Fuel and Power, 1951–3. Created Viscount, 1954.

[2] Alfred Dudley Pickman Rogers Pound, 1877–1943. Entered the Royal Navy, 1891. Torpedo Lieutenant, 1902. Captain, 1914. Second Naval Assistant to Lord Fisher, December 1914 to May 1915. Flag Captain, HMS *Colossus*, 1915–17. Took part in the Battle of Jutland. Served on the Admiralty Staff, 1917–19. Director of Plans Division, 1922. Commanded Battle Cruiser Squadron, 1929–32. Second Sea Lord, 1932–5. Knighted, 1933. Commander-in-Chief, Mediterranean, 1936–9. Admiral of the Fleet, 1939. First Sea Lord and Chief of the Naval Staff, 1939–43. Declined a peerage, 1943. Order of Merit, 1943, bestowed by the King's Private Secretary in hospital, October 6. Pound died on 21 October 1943; after his funeral at Westminster Abbey, his ashes were scattered at sea.

[3] John Cronyn Tovey, 1885–1971. On active service as a destroyer captain, 1914–18 (despatches, DSO). Appointed Commander after the Battle of Jutland, 1916, for 'the persistent and determined manner in which he attacked enemy ships'. Rear-Admiral, Destroyers, Mediterranean, 1938–40. Vice-Admiral, Second-in-Command, Mediterranean Fleet, 1940. Commander-in-Chief, Home Fleet, 1940–3 (including responsibility for Murmansk and Archangel convoys). Knighted, 1941. Admiral of the Fleet, 1943. Commander-in-Chief, the Nore, 1943–6. Created Baron, 1946.

Clementine Churchill[1] to Winston S. Churchill
(Baroness Spencer-Churchill papers)

6 January 1942   10 Downing Street

My Darling,

Randolph[2] has just walked in looking brown & well & very happy.

Consequently, as I have been talking to him I have time for only this one line to bring you my love.

I am happy that you are slipping away to the South for 3 days rest & sunshine.

I miss you dreadfully. Time seems to stand still.

I am pegging away at my Russian Fund.[3] It now stands at 1 million!

Tender love
Clemmie

Winston S. Churchill to King George VI[4]
(Churchill papers, 20/57)

6 January 1942   Florida

Sir,

Your Majesty has most graciously done me the honour of consenting to dine with me to meet the members of the War Cabinet on the night

---

[1] Clementine Hozier, 1885–1977. Married Winston Churchill in 1908. They had five children, Diana (born 1909), Randolph (born 1911), Sarah (born 1914), Marigold (born 1918), and Mary (born 1922). Active in the First World War, through the YWCA, in providing canteens for munitions workers. In the Second World War she presided over the Red Cross Aid to Russia Fund and the Fulmer Chase Maternity Home. From 1941 to 1947 she was also President of the YWCA War and National Fund, and from 1949 to 1951, Chairman of the YWCA National Hostels Committee. Created Baroness Spencer-Churchill, 1965; took her seat on the cross-benches, and voted in favour of the abolition of the death penalty on 20 July 1965. A Trustee of Lord Attlee's Memorial Foundation, 1966.

[2] Randolph Frederick Edward Spencer Churchill, 1911–68. Churchill's only son. Educated at Eton and Christ Church, Oxford. On leaving Oxford in 1932 without taking his degree, he worked briefly for Imperial Chemical Industries as Assistant Editor of their house magazine. Joined the staff of the *Sunday Graphic*, 1932; wrote subsequently for many newspapers, including the *Evening Standard* (1937–9). Reported during Hitler's election campaign of 1932, the Chaco War of 1935, and the Spanish Civil War; accompanied the Duke of Windsor on his tour of Germany, 1937. Unsuccessful Parliamentary candidate 1935 (twice), 1936, 1945, 1950, and 1951. Conservative MP for Preston, 1940–5. On active service, North Africa and Italy, 1941–3. Major, British mission to the Yugoslav Army of National Liberation, 1943–4 (MBE Military, 1944). Historian; editor of several volumes of his father's speeches, and author of the first two volumes of his biography, and the first two sets of document volumes.

[3] The Red Cross Aid to Russia Fund, which was raising money for hospitals throughout the Soviet Union.

[4] Albert Frederick Arthur George, 1895–1952. Second son of King George V. Educated at the Royal Naval Colleges, Osborne and Dartmouth. Lieutenant RN, 1918. Succeeded his brother as King, December 1936. Crowned (as George VI), May 1937.

of Tuesday, January 12. We are all greatly looking forward to this occasion. However, the weather in the Atlantic at this season is so uncertain and delays in flying have been so numerous and protracted that if the 11th or the 12th showed highly favourable conditions it would, I think, be my duty to take advantage of them rather than run the risk of failing to meet the President who travels through more tranquil latitudes.[1] I should be very grateful therefore if your Majesty would allow the date of the dinner to be changed until after my return, thus leaving me free to choose the best moment for my flight. Arrangements are also being made by the Admiralty to have a cruiser standing by from Sunday on in case the forecast of the weather in that week is very forbidding.

Only my wish to render Your Majesty the most effective service in my power would have induced me to proffer this suggestion which I do remaining with my humble duty.

Your Majesty's
Most faithful & devoted Servant
Winston S. Churchill

General Claude Auchinleck to Winston S. Churchill
(Churchill papers, 20/68)

6 January 1942   Cairo

No change Agedabia area. Our forward troops are in close touch with enemy and are keeping up pressure on him. Some further indications of possible enemy intention to withdraw. RAF bombed Halfaya heavily again yesterday. Bardia prisoners meantime about 8,000 including 1,800 Germans. Enemy aircraft approaching Benghazi yesterday were destroyed or driven off by our fighters.

John Martin: diary
(Sir John Martin papers)

7 January 1942   Pompano

More bathing mixed with some work. Walk with Sir C. Wilson. Mme. Balsan[2] to lunch. PM on medicine after dinner.

---

[1] In the event Churchill travelled to Washington to meet Roosevelt by train: see itinerary on page 51 below.

[2] Consuelo Vanderbilt, 1877–1964. Born in New York. Married Churchill's cousin, the 9th Duke of Marlborough, in 1895, at the age of 18, and obtained a divorce in 1921 (after which she married Lieutenant-Colonel Jacques Balsan, CMG). In the 1920s and 1930s Churchill was a frequent visitor at her chateau, St Georges Motel, near Dreux (some 50 miles to the west of Paris), and at her villa, Lou Seuil, at Eze in the South of France. In 1952 she published her memoirs, *The Glitter and the Gold.*

Winston S. Churchill to Peter Fraser[1]
(Churchill papers, 20/88)

7 January 1942   Florida

Reference your Telegram 263.

We have tried our best in consultation with United States Authorities to meet your most urgent requirements. List of what we and Americans can do is contained in my immediately following telegram. This includes some of the material about which your Liaison Office here has already telegraphed to New Zealand Government.

2. You will see that we have been able to make up a fairly good instalment and will try and do more as soon as we can.

3. It was not possible to consult you more fully about the South-West Pacific Supreme Command, as speed of execution was essential, but I hope results are satisfactory to you.

4. I am trying hard to get Americans to assume naval responsibility for area south of Equator and west of 180° up to east coast of Australia, and I think they will probably agree. Australian and New Zealand naval forces in the area would, of course, come under American operational command.

5. I am doing my utmost to build up and restore the Allied position in the Far East as soon as possible. We are all deeply grateful for the splendid courage and loyalty to the Mother Country shown by New Zealand under stress of danger.

Winston S. Churchill to Clement Attlee
(Churchill papers, 20/88)

7 January 1942   Florida

I am leaving Dill[2] behind here. He will represent me in my capacity as Minister of Defence. His directive is now being worked out. He will be at the President's disposal at any time Mr Roosevelt wishes to consult

---

[1] Peter Fraser, 1884–1950. Born in Scotland. Joined the Independent Labour Party in London, 1908. Emigrated to New Zealand in 1910 and became prominent in the labour movement there. Minister of Education, Health, Marine and Police, 1935–40; Prime Minister, 1940–9; Minister of External Affairs and Minister of Island Territories, 1943–9. Companion of Honour, 1945. Minister of Maori Affairs, 1946–9.

[2] John Greer Dill, 1881–1944. Born in Northern Ireland. Entered the Army, 1901. On active service, 1914–18 (DSO). Commanded British Forces in Palestine, 1936–7. Knighted, 1937. General Officer Commanding Aldershot Command, 1937–9. Commanded I Army Corps, France, 1939–40. Chief of the Imperial General Staff, 1940–1. Head of the British Joint Staff Mission, Washington, from 1941 until his death.

him. He will have direct link with United States Chiefs of Staff, guide and supervise work of our Joint Staff Mission and keep in touch with Heads of British Civil Missions.

2. Proposals for his pay and allowances will be telegraphed separately.

Winston S. Churchill to Clement Attlee
(Churchill papers, 20/88)

7 January 1942   Florida

Am resting in the South on Wilson's advice for a few days after rather a strenuous time. President is stopping all mention in the United States press. Please make sure no notice is issued in England, otherwise American press will be vexed, and I shall be overrun with them and tourists. Please tell Clemmie place is near Consuelo's. She will explain to you. We are in communication by telephone and air mail daily.

Winston S. Churchill to Clement Attlee
(Churchill papers, 20/88)

7 January 1942   Florida

INDIA

With reference to Cabinet Conclusion No. 4 of 19th December,[1] I hope my colleagues will realise the danger of raising constitutional issue, still more of making constitutional changes, in India at a moment when enemy is upon the frontier. The idea that we should 'get more out of India' by putting the Congress in charge at this juncture seems ill-founded. Yet that is what it would come to if any electoral or parliamentary foundation is chosen. Bringing hostile political element into the defence machine will paralyse action. Merely picking and choosing friendly Indians will do no serious harm, but will not in any way meet the political demands. The Indian liberals, though plausible, have never been able to deliver the goods. The Indian troops are fighting splendidly,

---

[1] 'The Minister of Labour and National Service [Ernest Bevin] said that he thought there was some anxiety in this country about the position in India, both from the point of view of defence and of the Constitutional issue. For example, was our policy calculated to get the fullest war effort from India? Ought we to be doing more to increase war production in India? He thought that the position might give rise to a demand for a discussion in Parliament at short notice, and that it might therefore be desirable that the War Cabinet should have a general discussion on the position at the first convenient opportunity. The War Cabinet took note of this suggestion' (*Cabinet Conclusions*, 19 December 1941, Conclusion 4).

but it must be remembered that their allegiance is to the King Emperor, and that the rule of the Congress and Hindoo Priesthood machine would never be tolerated by a fighting race.

2. I do not think you will have any trouble with American opinion. All press comments on India I have seen have been singularly restrained, especially since they entered the war. Thought here is concentrated on winning the war as soon as possible. The first duty of Congress nominees who have secured control of provincial government is to resume their responsible duties as ministers, and show that they can make success of the enormous jobs confided to them in this time of emergency. Pray communicate these views to the Cabinet. I trust we shall not depart from the position we have deliberately taken up.

Winston S. Churchill to General Hastings Ismay,
for the Chiefs of Staff Committee, and Sir Archibald Sinclair[1]
(Churchill papers, 20/88)

7 January 1942   Florida

In view of Naval position in Mediterranean, it is evidently urgent and important to send strong air reinforcements, especially torpedo planes, from Coastal or Bomber Command. Proportionate relaxation of bomber offensive against Germany, &c., and shipping must be accepted. General Arnold[2] tells me he is sending as soon as possible two bomber groups, i.e. 80 bombers, forthwith, as well as some fighter squadrons from Ulster. Pray tell me what you are doing and whether Admiral Cunningham[3] is comforted.

[1] Archibald Henry Macdonald Sinclair, 1890–1970. Entered the Army, 1910. Succeeded as 4th Baronet, 1912. Captain, 1915. Second-in-Command (under Churchill) of 6th Royal Scots Fusiliers, January–May 1916. Squadron Commander, 2nd Life Guards, 1916–18. Major, Guards Machine Gun Regiment, 1918. Private Secretary to Churchill, Ministry of Munitions, 1918–19. Churchill's Personal Military Secretary, War Office, 1919–21. Churchill's Private Secretary, Colonial Office, 1921–2. Liberal MP for Caithness and Sutherland, 1922–45. Secretary of State for Scotland, 1931–3. Leader of the Parliamentary Liberal Party, 1935–45. Secretary of State for Air in Churchill's Coalition Government, 1940–5. Created Viscount Thurso, 1952.

[2] Henry Harley Arnold, 1886–1950. Born in Pennsylvania. Pioneer airman: learned to fly with Orville Wright. Chief of the United States Army Air Corps, 1938. Member of the United States Joint Chiefs of Staff, 1941–5. Commanding General of United States Army Air Forces, 1942. An advocate of the decisive influence of air power on strategy.

[3] Andrew Browne Cunningham, 1883–1963. Entered the Royal Navy, 1898. On active service, 1914–18 (DSO and two bars). Vice-Admiral Commanding the Battle Cruiser Squadron, 1937–8. Deputy Chief of the Naval Staff, 1938–9. Knighted, 1939. Commander-in-Chief, Mediterranean, 1939–42. Head of the British Admiralty Delegation, Washington, 1942. Naval Commander-in-Chief, Expeditionary Force, North Africa, 1942. Commander-in-Chief, Mediterranean, 1943. Admiral of the Fleet, 1943. First Sea Lord and Chief of the Naval Staff, 1943–6. Created Baron, 1945; Viscount, 1946. Published his memoirs, *A Sailor's Odyssey*, in 1951.

Winston S. Churchill to Lord Cranborne[1]
(Churchill papers, 20/88)

7 January 1942   Florida

I hope there will be no question of giving any additional arms to
Southern Ireland or asking the United States to do so at this juncture.
It is much better to allow events to develop. The American-Irish pressure will grow. The arrival of American forces in strength in Northern
Ireland will create a powerful impression. We must give full play to the
powerful forces working on our behalf and not weaken their action by
minor concessions.[2]

Winston S. Churchill to Anthony Eden
(Churchill papers, 20/88)

7 January 1942   Florida

We are most anxious that Dutch views should be given fullest consideration at all states of ABDA discussions.

If decisions are to be obtained quickly, however, representation
on the High Executive Body in Washington, who will issue the final
instruction to General Wavell, must be cut down to the smallest possible
number. If Dutch have official status as members of the ABDA machine
in Washington, Dominions will also demand representation, resulting
in confusion and delay.

For the above reason it was considered right that machinery for consulting Dutch and Dominion governments should be centred in London,
and that British Government should be responsible for obtaining their
views and agreement and for forwarding them to Washington.

Naturally, if Washington required information about local conditions or technical advice from the Dutch, their representatives would

---

[1] Robert Arthur James Gascoyne-Cecil, Viscount Cranborne, 1893–1972. Known as 'Bobbety'.
Eldest son of 4th Marquess of Salisbury. Conservative MP for South Dorset, 1929–41. Parliamen-
tary Secretary of State for Foreign Affairs, 1935–8; resigned with Anthony Eden, February 1938.
Paymaster-General, 1940. Summoned to the House of Lords in his father's barony of Cecil of
Essendon, 1941. Secretary of State for Dominion Affairs, 1940–2, 1943–5; for the Colonies, 1942.
Leader of the House of Lords, 1942–5. Knight of the Garter, 1946. Succeeded his father as 5th
Marquess, 1947. Lord Privy Seal, 1951–2. Leader of the House of Lords, 1951–7. Secretary of State
for Commonwealth Relations, 1952. Lord President of the Council, 1952–7.

[2] Churchill hoped the build-up of American troops in Northern Ireland would lessen the pressure
on Southern Ireland to amass its own supply of arms from the United States. *WSC to Cranborne*, 7 January 1943.

be consulted, but they would not attend meetings as a regular practice unless invited to do so.

Following amendments to Annex 2 to General Wavell's Directive are, therefore, proposed:

Paragraph 1. – After 'Minister of Defence' Insert 'on behalf of ABDA Governments.'

Paragraph 2 (b). – After 'London' Insert 'having consulted Dutch Staff.'

Paragraph 3. – After 'agreement' Insert 'at every stage.'

Paragraph 4. – Delete 'both of them.' Substitute 'the ABDA Governments and respective Governments will be fully informed.'

President has approved the foregoing.

We feel sure that if given a trial Dutch Government will find this arrangement satisfactory.

Winston S. Churchill to General Hastings Ismay,
for the Chiefs of Staff Committee
(Churchill papers, 20/88)

7 January 1942   Florida
LOFOTEN ISLANDS RAID

If the fact that the enemy assembled a certain number of aircraft within striking distance of 'Anklet'[1] was to be held a good reason for an immediate retreat, this operation should never have been undertaken. It was always understood that we should be attacked from the air, whether we occupied Bodo or the 'Anklet' Islands. The proposal of the 'Anklet' Islands was based upon adequate A/A artillery being mounted afloat or ashore, and the configuration of the Fjord affords the necessary protection. Moreover, the object was the interruption over an indefinite period of the German north and south traffic in iron-ore and supplies against Russia. The 'Anklet' episode must therefore be judged a marked failure, as it was abandoned hastily and without any facts being apparent which were not foreseen at the time of its inception and preparation.

---

[1] 'Anklet': an allied naval and commando raid on the Lofoten Islands (26 December 1941), to intercept the flow of Swedish iron ore to Germany along the Norwegian coast. Twenty-two ships participated from three navies: the Royal Navy, the Royal Norwegian Navy, and the Polish Navy; 223 British and 77 Norwegian commandos went ashore.

George Harvie-Watt[1] to Winston S. Churchill
(Sir George Harvie-Watt papers)

8 January 1942   House of Commons
SECRET SESSION

Mr Attlee, then in open session, gave a review of the progress of the War. It was a dull speech which did not at all impress the House. He added little to what was already known.

It was really a 'marking time' debate. Members felt that there was little use in raising points unless you yourself were present, and until a full report of your American and Canadian visit had been made to the House. In consequence, very little interest was taken in the debate throughout the Sitting.

[...]

The Foreign Secretary wound up the debate in a speech which was by no means his best. The House adjourned for a further recess with many questions relating to withdrawals in the Far East not answered. There is a very strong desire for a full dress debate on the general war situation lasting two, possibly three days, when you get back.

The House is delighted with your visit to the United States and Canada. The universal opinion is that your mission and speeches have been an outstanding success, and that you have undoubtedly gained a great personal triumph.

I look forward to welcoming you home again soon.

Winston S. Churchill to John Curtin
(Churchill papers, 20/88)

8 January 1942   Florida

I fully sympathise your feelings and largely share your views. When Japan attacked United States and British Empire, immediate war danger confronted Australia. However, accession of United States to full warfare most favourably affected issue of final struggle. Indeed, it probably decides it. I therefore came here.

---

[1] George Steven Harvie-Watt, 1903–89. Called to the Bar, 1930. Conservative MP for Richmond, Surrey, 1937–59. Assistant Government Whip, 1938–40. Lieutenant-Colonel commanding 31st Battalion, Royal Engineers, Territorial Army, 1938–41; Brigadier, 6th Anti-Aircraft Brigade, 1941. Parliamentary Private Secretary to the Prime Minister (Churchill), July 1941 to July 1945. Created Baronet, 1945. He published his memoirs, *Most of My Life*, in 1980.

2. First step which President and I arranged was putting Supreme Commander with adequate representative staff over actual area of operation. This area is defined by General Wavell's command. Into this area we and United States are trying to press Naval, Air and Military Forces as far as possible. In our case regard must be paid to other commitments.

3. The second step is the organization of approaches. That has not yet been settled; but I have very little doubt United States will take over communications between themselves and Australia, taking command of any Australian Naval Forces which you may be willing to place at their disposal. The above covers case of New Zealand as well. The staffs are working hard, and I hope before I leave to reassure you upon this aspect.

4. There remains, of course, the defence of Australian soil. This rests primarily with you, and I thought you would prefer it to be in the hands of Australian Commander-in-Chief. United States would be quite willing, I believe, to reinforce your home defence troops with 40 or 50 thousand Americans. The limiting factor is not so much escort as actual shipping. Do you think you are in immediate danger of invasion in force? It is quite true you may have air attacks, but we have had good dose already in England without mortal harm resulting.

5. I contemplated these three commands:
(a) The South-Western Pacific under Wavell,
(b) The communications between United States and Australasia under an American commander, and
(c) Defence of mainland of Australia under your own Commander-in-Chief.

Surely that is a reasonable lay-out.

6. Now as to machinery of control. The President proposed General Wavell for the South-Western Pacific. The exact method by which orders should be transmitted to him was admittedly not solved by statement 'an appropriate body.' The British Chiefs of Staff in Washington are at work on this problem. Obviously there are two solutions. The first is to locate the whole control in Washington, in which case Australia, New Zealand, the Dutch and Great Britain will be represented on appropriate Joint Body set up in Washington.

7. The alternative is that orders to Supreme Commander, South-Western Pacific, will be transmitted formally and finally through Washington. They will embody the agreement between me and the President. I, or a Senior Minister, representing His Majesty's Government will be responsible for collecting in the Staff as well as the ministerial sphere the

views of Australia, New Zealand and Dutch, who will consult together in London. We shall transmit a combined representation to our officers in Joint Staff in Washington, which will certainly receive utmost consideration from President before any final decisions are reached.

8. Of these two processes, I have (?)[1] no doubt latter is better. Once a Supreme Commander has been appointed it is hoped he will be given free hand to use all forces given him and not be worried by endless reference to councils of 5 States and 3 Arms – total 15. Nothing would be easier than to set bunches of this kind at various Nodal points, and nothing would be more paralyzing to warfare direction.

9. The British, Dutch, Australian and New Zealand Governments standing outside this fighting field will not have to give continual orders to Supreme Commander, upon whose staff all will be represented. They will be concerned with finding and moving forward reinforcements of every kind. It is only occasionally that any tactical or even local strategical decision will be expressed at Washington, and then only after fullest consultation in London.

10. One thing is certain. We cannot have a control of United States, Great Britain, Australian, New Zealand and Dutch land, air and navy both in London and in Washington.

11. I advise, therefore, subject to your concurrence, the representation of Australia in London where Dutch Government is (?located) and where New Zealand is content to lie. You have sent Sir Earle Page[2] as an envoy of the Commonwealth Government. He has been invited to every Cabinet where Australian affairs have been concerned. He will certainly have all opportunities of presenting Australian views as you propose continuously. However, it is not possible to promise that nothing will ever be said or done which has not previously received full approval after consultation of all five Governments concerned. I may have to speak to the President on the telephone in matters of great urgency. These occasions should arise only rarely, since supreme commander will be doing fighting and there will probably be time to discuss (?larger) strategic and supply issues among ourselves before decisions.

[1] The items in parentheses were inserted by the transcriber of the telegram when it was received in London; they relate to words or phrases that were garbled in transmission.

[2] Earle Christmas Grafton Page, 1880–1961. Born and educated in Australia. On active service with Australian forces in France and Egypt, 1914–18. Acting Prime Minister of Australia, 1923–4, 1926–7. Minister of Commerce and Deputy Prime Minister, 1934–9. Minister of Health, 1937–8. Knighted, 1938. Prime Minister, 1939. Minister of Commerce, 1940–1. Special Australian Envoy to the British War Cabinet, 1941–2. Companion of Honour, 1942. Member of the Australian War Council, 1942–5. Minister of Health, Australia, 1949–56.

12. I must beg you to realise these matters of organization, where so many partners and factors are involved, take time to shape. I hope you will not judge structure before it is (?complete). Believe me, I am thinking of your interests at every moment. Within a week I hope to present you with entire draft which you will be able to criticize or, if you will, reject. I am sure no other method of making a good scheme for your approval could have been found than the one I have adopted. I hope, therefore, you will accord me the week for which I ask, remembering all operational measures are proceeding at highest speed and that much has been achieved already.

Winston S. Churchill to Anthony Eden
(Churchill papers, 20/88)

8 January 1942   Florida

We have never recognised the 1941 frontiers of Russia except <u>de facto</u>. They were acquired by acts of aggression in shameful collusion with Hitler. The transfer of the peoples of the Baltic States to Soviet Russia against their will would be contrary to all the principles for which we are fighting this war and would dishonour our cause. This also applies to Bessarabia and to Northern Bukovina and in a lesser degree to Finland, which I gather it is not intended wholly to subjugate and absorb.

2. Russia could, upon strategical grounds, make a case for the approaches to Leningrad, which the Finns have utilised to attack her. There are islands in the Baltic which may be essential to the safety of Russia. Strategical security may be invoked at certain points on the frontiers of Bukovina or Bessarabia. In these cases the population would have to be offered evacuation and compensation if they desired it. In all other cases transference of territory must be regulated after the war is over by freely and fairly conducted plebiscites, very differently from what is suggested in your paragraph 3, section (iv). In any case there can be no question of settling frontiers until the Peace Conference. I know President Roosevelt holds this view as strongly as I do, and he has several times expressed his pleasure to me at the firm line we took at Moscow. I could not be an advocate for a British Cabinet bent on such a course.

3. Your paragraph 2. You suggest that 'the acid test of our sincerity' depends upon our recognising the acquisition of these territories by the Soviet Union irrespective of the wishes of their peoples. I, on the

contrary, regard our sincerity involved in the maintenance of the principles of the Atlantic Charter, to which Stalin has subscribed. On this, also, we depend for our association with the United States.

4. I am not impressed with Mr Curtin's opinion, as he clearly, in his panic, cares little for the Australian connection with Great Britain. Happily he does not speak for Australia. I doubt very much whether New Zealand would adopt so cold-blooded a view. I am sure Smuts will not do so, and the Canadians would follow the United States.

5. About the effect on Russia of our refusal to prejudge the peace negotiations at this stage in the war, or to depart from the principles of the Atlantic Charter, it must be observed that they entered the war only when attacked by Germany, having previously shown themselves utterly indifferent to our fate, and indeed, they added to our burdens in our worst danger. Their armies have fought very bravely and have shown immense unsuspected strength in the defence of their native soil. They are fighting for self-preservation and have never had a thought for us. We, on the contrary, are helping them to the utmost of our ability because we admire their defence of their own country and because they are ranged against Hitler.

6. When you say in paragraph 2 that 'nothing we and the United States can do or say will affect the situation at the end of the war,' you are making a very large assumption about the conditions which will then prevail. No one can foresee how the balance of power will lie, or where the winning army will stand. It seems probable, however, that the United States and the British Empire, far from being exhausted, will be the most powerfully armed and economic *bloc* the world has ever seen, and that the Soviet Union will need our aid for reconstruction far more than we shall then need theirs.

7. You have promised that we will examine these claims of Russia in common with the United States and the Dominions. That promise we must keep. But there must be no mistake about the opinion of any British Government of which I am the head, namely, that it adheres to those principles of freedom and democracy set forth in the Atlantic Charter, and that these principles must become especially active whenever any question of transferring territory is raised. I conceive, therefore, that our answer should be that all questions of territorial frontiers must be left to the decision of the Peace Conference.

Oliver Harvey:[1] diary
(*'The War Diaries of Oliver Harvey'*, *page 86*)

8 January 1942

PM replied today to AE's telegram advocating a realistic acceptance of 1941 Soviet frontiers. A flat and shocked refusal! All the arguments about the Atlantic Charter, our promise to Roosevelt to make no promises before the Peace Conference, these poor little peoples brutally invaded, dressed up afresh. I'm afraid we're going to have great difficulty over this. AE will have a lone fight as no one else in the Cabinet will speak up to the PM – least of all Bevin[2] & Co.

AE thinks PM staying away too long and getting out of touch with opinion here which thinks much more of Russia than of America at present. Winston is *au fond* a diehard imperialist – bad about India (much trouble coming to us here over his refusal to countenance Dominion status) and bad about Russia. He not only hates the Bolsheviks but is jealous of them because of their bigger and more successful armies.

Henry Channon:[3] diary
(*'Chips'*, *page 316*)

8 January 1942

The Government had another bad day. Without Winston it would not last a week; and I wonder whether even he will be able to save it?

---

[1] Oliver Charles Harvey, 1893–1968. Educated at Malvern and Trinity College, Cambridge. On active service in France, Egypt, and Palestine (despatches), 1914–18. Entered the Foreign Office, 1919. First Secretary, Paris, 1931–6. Counsellor, and Principal Private Secretary to successive Secretaries of State for Foreign Affairs, 1936–9, 1941–3. Minister to Paris, 1940. Assistant Under-Secretary of State, 1943–6. Knighted, 1946. Deputy Under-Secretary of State (Political), 1946–7. Ambassador to France, 1948–54. Created Baron, 1954.

[2] Ernest Bevin, 1881–1951. National Organizer, Dockers' Union, 1910–21. General Secretary, Transport and General Workers' Union, 1921–40. Member of Trades Union Congress General Council, 1925–40. Labour MP for Central Wandsworth, 1940–50; for East Woolwich, 1950–1. Minister of Labour and National Service in Churchill's Coalition Government, 1940–5. Secretary of State for Foreign Affairs, 1945–51. Lord Privy Seal, 1951.

[3] Henry Channon, 1897–1958. Known as 'Chips'. American by birth. Educated privately, and at Christ Church, Oxford. In 1933, he married Lady Honor Guinness, elder daughter of the 2nd Earl of Iveagh. Conservative MP for Southend-on-Sea, 1935–50; for Southend-on-Sea (West), 1950–8. Parliamentary Private Secretary to the Under-Secretary of State for Foreign Affairs (R. A. Butler), 1938–41. Knighted, 1957.

Sir Charles Wilson: diary
(*'Winston Churchill, The Struggle for Survival'*, page 22)

9 January 1942   Florida

Lunch with Madame Balsan. When we left, Winston mused a little, and then said half to himself: 'Wealth, taste and leisure can do these things, but they do not bring happiness.'

Tomorrow we go back to Washington.

Winston S. Churchill to Lord Halifax
(*Churchill papers, 20/67*)

9 January 1942   Florida

[...] is not Denmark in a special position?[1] If my memory serves me, the President used the Danish Minister in Washington to cover the occupation by American troops of Iceland.

What is the harm in having Denmark in, any way? They certainly would have been on our side if they had not been grabbed by the Huns and overrun. They only submitted to brute force against which they had no means of resistance. I cannot see why the Norwegian Government should make a fuss.

Kindly let me know your views.

Winston S. Churchill to Admiral of the Fleet Sir Dudley Pound
(*Churchill papers, 20/67*)

9 January 1942   Florida

The incident at Alexandria,[2] which was so unpleasant, has raised in my mind the question of the security of Scapa Flow against this form of

[1] The Foreign Office was being pressed by the Norwegian Government-in-Exile to exclude Denmark – then under German occupation – from the Joint Declaration by the United Nations.

[2] The 'human torpedo', a small rideable submarine with a detachable warhead used as a limpet mine, was invented by two Italian naval architects in 1935. It was first used, by the Italians, in a raid on Alexandria in August 1940, when it was spotted and sunk by aircraft from a British aircraft carrier. An attack on Malta on 26 July 1941 was also foiled. But on the night of 18–19 December 1941, the Italians successfully penetrated Alexandria harbour using six human torpedoes, which inflicted considerable damage by affixing mines to the battleships *Queen Elizabeth* and *Valiant*, the oil ship *Saguna* and the destroyer *Jervis*. The limpet mine was placed on *Valiant* by Luigi Durand de la Penne, who after the September 1943 armistice was given the choice of remaining a prisoner of war or joining the Allies: he became an Allied frogman and participated in the Anglo-Italian attack on German-occupied La Spezia harbour on 22 June 1944.

attack. Are we, in fact, patrolling the entrances with depth charges every twenty minutes? No doubt the strong currents would give far greater protection than the calm water of Alexandria.

How does the matter stand?

Winston S. Churchill to General Archibald Wavell
(Churchill papers, 20/68)

9 January 1942   Florida

As you know from telegrams, I have been anxious that British forces in the Malayan Peninsula should be conserved as much as possible for the defence of the Singapore fortress and its Johore Hinterland. I therefore highly approve of the manner in which rear-guard operation is being conducted so as to inflict greatest loss and delay upon the enemy and to demolish all that might be of use to him. Nevertheless I do not understand why our position should be repeatedly turned by sea borne movements of the enemy brought down the west coast of the peninsula in unarmed steamers, junks or fishing vessels which come up various rivers and creeks and force us to retire.

Surely one or two submarines could operate to bar these likely river mouths by sinking with their 4-inch guns or torpedoes these unarmed troop carrying vessels. They could always dive when enemy aircraft arrived; thus, they would protect the western flank of our troops in the peninsula and enable every inch of ground to be sold as dear as possible without compromising our forces.

I should be very glad if you would let me know how this matter stands and whether anything can be done about it so that I may explain it to the President with whom I am constantly discussing all aspects of the war.

Itinerary
(Franklin D. Roosevelt papers)

10 January 1942   The White House
Washington DC

Left Pompano Jan. 10, drove to West Palm Beach. Boarded train at 2:25 p.m. and arrived Washington 11:00 a.m. Jan. 11. Movement in two Pullman 'room cars' attached to rear of regular train. Route via Florida East Coast rr., Atlantic Coast Line rr., and Richmond, Fredericksburg and Potomac rr.

Winston S. Churchill to Brigadier Leslie Hollis
(Churchill papers, 20/67)

10 January 1942

MALAYAN SITUATION

The 11th and which other Indian Divisions are engaged? How many Brigades in each? Is there a British battalion in each Brigade?

2. How many guns and AA guns? Are they British-manned?

3. What is the strength of the 2-Brigade Australian Division in Johore? Has it been weakened in any way?

4. What is the name, number and strength of the remaining Indian Division? Has it a British battalion in each Brigade?

5. What is the strength of the garrison at Singapore apart from field troops? How many gunners, engineers, infantry, civilian volunteers, &c. How many *bouches inutiles* have been flung out in accordance with my instructions? How many remain, i.e., what is the total non-combatant population? For how long have they full rations?

6. Give particulars of convoys, including dates.

7. How many armoured vehicles are there (a) inside the fortress; (b) with the mobile troops?

8. What is the air strength (a) today; (b) the 1st February?

Winston S. Churchill to Admiral of the Fleet Sir Dudley Pound
(Churchill papers, 20/67)

10 January 1942

LOFOTEN ISLANDS RAID

It may have been right to withdraw in the circumstances and at the time, but my complaint is that we ought not to have been led to believe an operation was to be carried out, in spite of air attack, which would result in the stopping of the traffic for a long time to come if at the first threat of air attack it was to be abandoned. You must remember how this operation was commended to us as one which would have a continuous effect upon the north and south traffic. It was never expected that the Germans would not react with their air force.

2. I do not know Admiral Hamilton,[1] but several things about Admiral Tovey have disquieted me. I have no doubt he would fight his ship or

---

[1] Louis Henry Keppel Hamilton, 1890–1957. Entered the Navy as a Midshipman, 1909. Son of an Admiral and grandson of an Admiral of the Fleet. On active service, Cameroons, 1914–15 (DSO). Narvik Operations, 1940 (bar to DSO). Rear-Admiral Commanding Home Fleet Destroyer

his squadron, but he strikes me as negative, un-enterprising and narrow-minded. He has protested against almost every positive proposal put to him. This, however, is entirely between ourselves.

Winston S. Churchill to Lord Halifax
(Churchill papers, 20/67)

10 January 1942

I must regard my conversation with the President as private and unofficial. Therefore, I do not feel at liberty to allow it to be quoted. It is, however, a very good guide to my action or inaction, and it squares entirely with my own feelings.

2. All this fussing about what is to happen after the war is premature at the present time, when we are probably a long way from any satisfactory conclusion. It is only the State Department which is pressing. Mr Morgenthau[1] assured me he was not troubling about it. The views and requests of the State Department were formed in a period separated from us by the gulf which marks the United States involvement in full war through being attacked by the three Axis Powers. Therefore, it is clear the views formed on the earlier basis have no relation to the present situation.

I told the President that Imperial Preference would raise great difficulties in England if raised as a separate issue now, but that, if raised at the end of the war as part of a large economic settlement, in which the United States would become a low tariff country, it would probably be easy to handle. He seemed to think this very sensible, and I am sure he felt, as I did, that we had better address our minds to the struggle on which the lives of our peoples depend. I should recommend you to stall any demand from the State Department with the usual diplomatic arts. I told the President that I personally was incapable of discussing the subject.

For your own information, if the matter became extremely pressing, I should have to send over the Chancellor of the Exchequer. But with

Flotillas, 1941–2; Commanding the First Cruiser Squadron, 1942–3. Flag Officer-in-Charge, Malta, 1943–5. Knighted, 1944.

[1] Henry Morgenthau, Junior, 1891–1967. A gentleman farmer in New York State before the First World War. Lieutenant, United States Navy, 1918. A neighbour and early supporter of Governor (later President) Roosevelt. New York State Conservation Commissioner, 1931. Chairman of the Federal Farm Board, 1933. Secretary of the Treasury, 1934–45. A strong supporter of active American defence preparations, and of Lend-Lease. His plan in 1944 to reduce post-war Germany to a pastoral condition, with almost no industry, was rejected by President Truman, who would not take him to the Potsdam Conference, whereupon he resigned.

every month that passes the fighting comradeship of the two countries as allies will grow, and the haggling about the lend-lease story will wane. After all, lend-lease is practically superseded now.

Winston S. Churchill to Clement Attlee
(Churchill papers, 20/88)

11 January 1942   Florida

The President is returning from Hyde Park to Washington, arriving on the morning of the 11th.[1] I meet him there. I shall require Sunday, Monday and Tuesday in order to settle finally what has been prepared in our absence by the staffs. Thereafter we return. Admiralty will explain that we cannot count on being in London before 22nd Thursday. I therefore cannot make any statement to Parliament before the 27th.

2. If, as I hope, we land in Scotland late the 21st or early the 22nd, you could announce in your business statement of the 22nd that I will make a statement to the House on Tuesday the 27th. I should be grateful if you would consider asking the House to allow gramophone record to be taken, thus avoiding the burden of my having to deliver the speech again on the 9 o'clock broadcast.

All that would seem to be necessary would be resolution *ad hoc* that the House approves taking the gramophone record of the statement to be delivered by the Prime Minister on the day in question. The innovation would, therefore, be in the nature of an experiment which need not be repeated if it is not successful. I hope that in view of the undoubted wish of the public to hear the statement, I may make this consideration. It could be arranged that in the event of any interruption which gave away national military secrets, the Speaker[2] might have the same power to amend the broadcast as he has when such indiscretions are committed in the ordinary course of debate. Alternatively, if you

---

[1] From time to time in these documents the date at the head of the document is at variance with dates referred to within the text. These discrepancies, which have not been corrected, may result from differences in time and/or calendar between the location of sending and that of receipt, or the passage of time between writing and despatch.

[2] Edward Algernon Fitzroy, 1869–1943. Son of 3rd Baron Southampton. Educated at Eton and Sandhurst. A page of honour to Queen Victoria. Conservative MP for Daventry, 1900–6, 1910–43. Captain, 1st Life Guards, 1914 (wounded at First Battle of Ypres). Commanded the mounted troops of the Guards Division, 1915–16. Deputy Chairman of Committees, House of Commons, 1922–8. Privy Councillor, 1924. Speaker of the House of Commons from 1928 until his death. His widow was created Viscountess Daventry in 1943. Their son Michael (born 1895) was killed in action on 15 April 1915.

think the House will object to this procedure, which I cannot believe, I could make a broadcast on Sunday night to the nation, and would give a résumé of it to the House on the Tuesday following. I think, however, they would prefer the course I suggest. Please put this matter to the Cabinet, including Sir A. Sinclair, saying that I attach importance to it, and let me know what can be done.

3. You will have seen by the telegrams which are passed that I have not been idle here. Indeed, the seclusion in which I have lived has enabled me to focus things more clearly than was possible in the stir of Washington. I am in the midst of preparing a considerable paper on Anglo-American co-operation, which I shall discuss with the Staffs and then with the President as soon as I get back.

4. I am so glad the debate on the 8th passed off peacefully, and that the House was willing to postpone the discussion on the main issue. Of course, the naggings and snarling has been fully reported over here, and one would think that they represented the opinion of the House. Several remarks have been reported which are not very helpful to American opinion, and I am pointing out to the President we can no more control the expression of freak opinion by individual members than he can those of Congress backwoodsmen. Try to let me have the gist of what you and Anthony said.[1]

5. It might be convenient if I made my statement on Tuesday as a statement, and that the adjournment was moved by somebody else immediately after. This would enable the usual criticisms to be made without my having exhausted my right of reply. Perhaps, however, you will not think this necessary. I cannot help feeling we have good tale to tell, even though we cannot tell the best part of it.

Winston S. Churchill to Clement Attlee
(Churchill papers, 20/88)

11 January 1942   Florida

BRITISH NAVAL POSITION IN THE MEDITERRANEAN

I greatly regret this vital secret[2] should be spread about the world in this fashion. We do not give our most secret information to the

---

[1] In the debate in the House of Commons on 8 January 1942, Attlee (who opened the debate) and Eden (who closed it) both defended the Government vigorously.

[2] Reports of the sinking of HMS *Barham* in the Mediterranean were beginning to appear in the American press. The attack on the British battleship had occurred on 24 November 1941, but the news was not made public in Britain until 29 January 1942 (see page 186 below).

Dominions or, indeed, even to the whole of our own Cabinet. It might be necessary to tell Washington if they became too insistent upon further naval support, but every day that this secret can be kept is a help to Australia as well as to everyone else. As it is, I think it will only alarm them needlessly. But what can they do about it? All this applies still more to telling Canada and South Africa. Every additional person who is told these matters is an added danger to the life of the State. I should not hesitate to use these arguments to Dominions should matters become known to the enemy and they ask why they had not been told before. The matter is all the more serious on account of what happened at Pearl Harbour, which is being kept strictly secret.[1] It is not a question of trusting people, but of not spreading the secrets over a needlessly large area when no action is required from parties informed.

John Martin: diary
(Sir John Martin papers)

11 January 1942   In the train
Florida to Washington DC

We are on our way back from a few days' break in Florida. The high up conversations were necessarily suspended while the Chiefs of Staff on both sides cleared up a mass of detailed business, and the PM took advantage of this to escape to the south and the sunshine. It was an opportunity for him to clear his mind on various things, but we by no means escaped from the daily conduct of the war, for we were of course connected with Washington by telephone and a courier once, and sometimes twice, a day brought down a pouch to us by aeroplane [...]

We were on the coast some way north of Miami – between that and Palm Beach – in a secluded bungalow on the beach, an ideal place for a seaside holiday. It wasn't always sunny or warm, though on our first morning I had to buy some exotic clothes because my ordinary ones were much too hot; but the sea was always hot and we had marvellous bathing, sometimes in surf against which it was hardly possible to stand upright.

We were closely guarded by Secret Service men and, though the Press soon scented our presence, we were not molested in any way. The story

---

[1] Oliver Harvey wrote in his diary on 11 January 1942: 'Long talk with Charles Peake today – just back from USA. He told me American Navy had had 6 out of 8 battleships knocked out in Pearl Harbour. No one believed air attack by Japan was possible. About 300 aeroplanes took part and the Americans shot down 2! America had been stunned by the disaster, tho' they didn't yet know the full truth' (*The War Diaries of Oliver Harvey*, page 86).

was put about that a Mr Lobb, an invalid requiring quiet, was staying in the house and, to explain my untransatlantic accents when answering the phone, I was his English butler.

We flew down, a wonderfully easy flight of over 800 miles. [...]

Winston S. Churchill to General Claude Auchinleck
(Churchill papers, 20/88)

11 January 1942   Washington DC

Your Taut No. 440, paragraph 3.[1] I fear this means that bulk of 72 enemy divisions have got away round the corner, and will now be retreating directly along their communications. I note also that 9 M/V[2] ships of 10,000 tons are reported to have reached Tripoli safely.

It was understood that you believed your advance down Trig-el-Abd would certainly cut off Rommel's Italian infantry, but now it appears they are out of the net. How does this all affect 'Acrobat'?

I am sure you and your armies did all in human power, but we must (?face) facts as they are, which greatly influence both 'Gymnast' and 'Super-Gymnast'.

Winston S. Churchill to Josef Stalin
(Churchill papers, 20/132)

11 January 1942

I am very glad to receive your kind telegram which reached me through M Litvinov on 9th January. The papers here are filled with tributes to the Russian armies, and may I also express my admiration of the great victories which have rewarded the leadership and devotion of the Russian forces.[3] I am emphasising in my talks here the extreme importance of making punctual deliveries to Russia of the promised quotas. I send you every good wish for the New Year.

---

[1] Auchinleck's telegram forecasting possible German action in Cyrenaica.

[2] M/V: merchant vessel.

[3] Starting on 7 January 1942, Soviet forces, many rushed to the Eastern Front from the Far East, began to push back the German armies that were within sight of Moscow and had almost surrounded the Soviet capital.

Winston S. Churchill to Anthony Eden
(Churchill papers, 20/88)

11 January 1942

Baghdad telegram No. 20 to Foreign Office.[1]

I am not aware of having made any such remarks to any Jew, Arab or Christian in the presence of Lord Halifax, but I am certainly not prepared to have anything said in public which would seem to dissociate myself from the Balfour declaration as interpreted by me in 1921.[2] The reply to Cornwallis[3] should be that we cannot undertake to contradict every assertion on the enemy broadcast. Now that he has the bulk of the 50th Division in Baghdad, surely he has no need to fret over matters of this kind.

Winston S. Churchill: recollection
('The Grand Alliance', page 624)

12 January 1942   Washington DC

When I got back to the White House I found that great progress had been made by the Combined Chiefs of Staff, and that it was mostly in harmony with my views. The President convened a meeting on January 12, when there was complete agreement upon the broad principles and targets of the war. The differences were confined to priorities and emphasis, and all was ruled by that harsh and despotic factor shipping.

'The President', says the British record, 'set great store on organising a "Super-Gymnast" – i.e., a combined United States–British expedition to North Africa. A tentative time-table had been worked out for putting 90,000 United States and 90,000 British troops, together with a considerable air force, into North Africa.' It was settled to send two divisions of American troops to Northern Ireland, with the objects which have been described.[4]

[1] Reporting allegations heard by the Ambassador that Churchill had made anti-Semitic remarks in Washington, in the presence of Lord Halifax.

[2] The Balfour Declaration of 1917, stating Britain's support for a Jewish National Home in Palestine; and Churchill's decision at the Cairo Conference in 1921, confirmed in his Palestine White Paper of 1922 (and endorsed in 1922 by the League of Nations), that Palestine would be open to Jewish 'close settlement' on the land 'of right and not on sufferance'.

[3] Kinahan Cornwallis, 1883–1959. Sudan Civil Service, 1906–14; Egyptian Civil Service, 1914–24. Director of the Arab Bureau, Cairo, 1916–20. On active service with the Arab Revolt, 1916–18 (despatches). Seconded to the Iraq Government, 1921. Adviser to the Minister of the Interior, Iraq, 1921–35. Knighted, 1929. Retired, 1935. Served in the Foreign Office, 1939–41. Ambassador in Baghdad, 1941–5. Chairman, Middle East Committee, Foreign Office, 1945–6. His younger son was killed in action in 1945.

[4] Operation 'Magnet'.

The President had told me privately that he would, if necessary as quickly as possible, send 50,000 United States troops to Australia and the islands covering its approach by the Japanese. Twenty-five thousand were to go as soon as possible to occupy New Caledonia, and other stepping-stones between America and Australasia. On 'Grand Strategy' the Staffs agreed that 'only the minimum of forces necessary for the safeguarding of vital interests in other theatres should be diverted from operations against Germany'. No one had more to do with obtaining this cardinal decision than General Marshall.

Winston S. Churchill: recollection
('The Grand Alliance', pages 624–5)

12 January 1942   Washington DC

One evening the General came to see me and put a hard question. He had agreed to send nearly thirty thousand American soldiers to Northern Ireland. We had of course placed the two 'Queens' – the only two 80,000-ton ships in the world – at his disposal for this purpose. General Marshall asked me how many men we ought to put on board, observing that boats, rafts, and other means of flotation could only be provided for about 8,000. If this were disregarded they could carry 16,000 men.

I gave the following answer: 'I can only tell you what *we* should do. You must judge for yourself the risks you will run. If it were a direct part of an actual operation, we should put all on board they could carry. If it were only a question of moving troops in a reasonable time, we should not go beyond the limits of lifeboats, rafts, etc. It is for you to decide.'

He received this in silence, and our conversation turned to other matters. In their first voyages these ships carried only the lesser numbers, but later on they were filled to the brim. As it happened, Fortune stood our friend.

Winston S. Churchill: recollection
('The Grand Alliance', page 625)

12 January 1942   Washington DC

The time had now come when I must leave the hospitable and exhilarating atmosphere of the White House and of the American nation, erect and infuriate against tyrants and aggressors. It was to no sunlit prospect that I must return. Eager though I was to be back in London, and sure of ultimate victory, I felt continually the approaching impact of a period of immense disasters which must last for many months. My hopes of a victory in the Western Desert, in which Rommel would be destroyed, had faded. Rommel had escaped. The results of Auchinleck's successes at Sidi Rezegh and at Gazala had not been decisive. The prestige which these had given us in the making of all our plans for the Anglo-American descent on French North Africa was definitely weakened, and this operation was obviously set back for months.

Lord Beaverbrook to Winston S. Churchill
(Churchill papers, 20/52)

12 January 1942   Mayflower Hotel
Washington DC

Dear Prime Minister,

My health is gone and I must now retire from my office.[1]

I propose to stay in my Island home in the Bahamas for a few days and then return to England by air. After a week or two I will go away again if there is no objection.

May I announce my resignation now and arrive in London a day after your return to hand over to my successor?

I leave everything better than I found it including <u>Rubber</u> and tin and after helping Russia.

You may rely on me to help your administration in every direction and by all the methods in my scope.

Yours ever,
B

Winston S. Churchill to Lord Beaverbrook
(Churchill papers, 20/53)

12 January 1942   The White House
PERSONAL   Washington DC

My dear Max,

I refuse to accept your resignation, which would be deeply detrimental to the Allied cause, and would undo much of the splendid work you have done over here.

---

[1] Lord Beaverbrook had been appointed Minister of Supply on 29 June 1941.

I am sorry if you were vexed at the line I took in our talk this evening. I really could not allow the Americans to go away with the impression that we could easily manage on an import of 28 million tons when all my instructions to Salter[1] and others have been to fight for 33 million tons of imports, and when 31 is absolutely necessary. As things are shaping, it will only be with a struggle that we shall get the shipping for that. Neither did I understand the reasons which prompted you to refuse the 100 thousand tons of rubber which the Americans were prepared to offer. Perhaps, however, I did not fully understand what you had in your mind.

Of course, if you want a few weeks' rest in the South I cannot deny it to you, but I had hoped you would share our homeward voyage and resume your duties at the Ministry of Supply, which were never more urgent and onerous than now.

Would you come and see me in the morning.

Yours ever,

W

War Cabinet: minutes
(Cabinet papers, 65/25)

12 January 1942   10 Downing Street
12 noon

The Lord Privy Seal[2] said that the Prime Minister would make a statement in Parliament at a fairly early date after his return. It was suggested that the Prime Minister should first make a statement, and that an adjournment motion should then be moved so that the Prime Minister would be in a position to reply.

General agreement was expressed with this proposal.

The Lord Privy Seal added that the Prime Minister wished to avoid the strain of making a statement in Parliament and a broadcast on the same day. This raised the question whether his statement on this occasion could be recorded and subsequently broadcast.

[1] James Arthur Salter, 1881–1975. Transport Department, Admiralty, 1904. Chairman, Allied Maritime Transport Executive, 1918. Knighted, 1922. Director, Economic and Finance Section, League of Nations, 1919–20, 1922–31. Professor of Political Theory and Institutions, Oxford University, 1934–44. Independent MP for Oxford University, 1937–50. Parliamentary Secretary, Ministry of Shipping, 1939–41; Ministry of War Transport, 1941. Head of the British Merchant Shipping Mission, Washington, 1941–3. Privy Councillor, 1941. Chancellor of the Duchy of Lancaster, 1945. Conservative MP for Ormskirk, 1951–3. Minister of State for Economic Affairs, 1951–2. Minister of Materials, 1952–3. Created Baron, 1953. Head of a special economic mission to Iraq, 1954.

[2] Clement Attlee.

Discussion showed that, while the War Cabinet was determined that the Prime Minister ought not to undergo the strain of making a statement in the House and also broadcasting on the same day, the wisdom of recording the Prime Minister's statement in the House was doubted. There was the difficulty of dealing with possible interjections. Again, once a statement in the House had been recorded and broadcast, it would be difficult to refuse the request that other speeches should be broadcast. The broadcasting of the proceedings of Parliament generally was strongly deprecated.

Further, statements in the House were usually longer and of a different character from broadcast speeches. It was also felt that there was no real reason why the Prime Minister's broadcast should not be delayed until some days after his return.

The War Cabinet

(1) Invited the Lord Privy Seal to reply in this sense to the Prime Minister.

(2) Invited the Parliamentary Secretary to the Treasury to inform certain leading members of the House that the question whether the Prime Minister's statement, on his return from the United States, should be recorded had been considered by the War Cabinet, who had decided against this course.

Winston S. Churchill to William Mackenzie King[1]
(Churchill papers, 20/68)

12 January 1942   The White House
                                         Washington DC

We cannot entirely exclude the possibility of a Japanese raid on the Falkland Isles with the object of interfering with the free flow of traffic around Cape Horn, or even with the idea of establishing for themselves submarine re-fuelling base. In the main, security of the islands must depend on naval dispositions made by United States fleet in whose area of strategical responsibility they are. I feel nevertheless that some strengthening of the garrison would be desirable, as it only consists at the present of some 300 local volunteers who also man the three 6″ coast-defence guns.

---

[1] William Mackenzie King, 1874–1950. Born in Ontario. First entered the Canadian Government as Minister of Labour, 1909. Leader of the Liberal Party of Canada, 1919. Leader of the Opposition, 1919–21, 1930–5. Prime Minister of Canada, 1921–30, 1935–48. Secretary of State for External Affairs, 1935–46. Order of Merit, 1947.

2. Before considering other possible ways of providing a small force for the island I felt it right to ask whether you would be prepared to undertake this task. One or two battalions with a battery of field guns would be all that need be sent. We positively do not want the Argentines who lay claim to the island shoving their nose in there. I do not want to propose to the President that the United States troops should take over. I should naturally much prefer that Canada should participate in the defence of a vital British outpost in the western hemisphere, and I hope you will see your way clear to agree to my suggestion. I shall personally be most grateful.

General Archibald Wavell to Winston S. Churchill
(Churchill papers, 20/68)

12 January 1942   Batavia

I send you for your private eye only my first impressions of personalities here and of my task.

2. Hart[1] is quiet attractive character and seems shrewd. But he is old and openly says so and gives me the impression of looking over his shoulder rather too much. His experiences at Manila seem to have given him exaggerated idea of Japanese efficiency. Palliser[2] will help to keep his eyes to the front. Hart should be easy to work with but may be over depressed if things go wrong.

3. Brett is pleasant and knows his job but is somewhat apt to lose his sense of proportion when unexpected happens. He soon recovers and was well described to me as man whose second thoughts are usually much better than his first. I will try to arrange that he always thinks twice.

[1] Thomas Charles Hart, 1877–1971. Admiral in the United States Navy who had first seen action in the Spanish–American War of 1898. Acting Chief of Staff to the Commander, Submarine Force, Atlantic Fleet, 1917–18 (DSM). Commander-in-Chief, Asiatic Fleet, 1939–42; on the day after Pearl Harbor, proclaimed unrestricted submarine warfare against Japan. Commander of the ABDA naval forces against Japan, 1942 (second DSM). Retired from the Navy, July 1942. From February to April 1944, conducted a one-member investigation, the Hart Inquiry, into the attack on Pearl Harbor; the purpose of the investigation was not to determine fault, but to ensure that the statute of limitations did not run out before courts-martial could be considered. Served as United States Senator for Connecticut (Republican), February 1945 to November 1946. Died in 1971, aged 94.

[2] Arthur Francis Eric Palliser, 1890–1956. Entered the Royal Navy, 1907. On active service, 1914–18 (DSC). Chief of Staff to the British Naval Commander-in-Chief, China, 1936–8. Commander HMS *Malaya*, 1940–1. Chief of Staff to the Commander-in-Chief, British Eastern Fleet, 1941; Deputy Commander, Naval Forces, ABDA Command, 1942. Fortress Commander, Trincomalee (Ceylon), 1942. Commander 1st Cruiser Squadron (Home Waters), 1943. Fourth Sea Lord and Chief of Supplies and Transport, Admiralty, 1944–8. Knighted, 1945.

4. Generally Americans strike me as rather shaken by the first reverses they have suffered within memory in fact since the Civil War. They have never had batterings we have endured in the last war and this and for the moment are surprised and hurt. From what Burnett[1] tells me Australian Government seems to have lost nerve temporarily.

5. Dutch appear at present both more solid and more enterprising. They are all for fighting as far forward as possible and quite prepared for sacrifices. Ter Poorten[2] is most co-operative but of moderate ability I should say. Admiral Helfrich[3] is shrewd and gives good impression. I think he is inclined to be jealous of Ter Poorten to whom he is senior and to feel rather out in the cold. Hart realises this and will do his best to keep him feeling important. He considers him competent to command Allied fleet in these waters and so I understand does Layton.[4]

6. It is going to be a race against time to secure our positions here and at present we are behind the clock. Things are not going too well in Malaya and Japanese are pushing south in Borneo and Celebes. It looks too as if our convoys will have increasingly dangerous passage. Our vital need is air and plenty of it. Aeroplanes as you realise are soon out of action without spare stores ground personnel and all these take time to collect. Hope that Dawson[5] from Middle East whom Brett has asked for can be sent to help with this problem.

7. Our picture may not look too bright at the moment but am sure enemy's is little brighter and his ultimate outlook completely black.

[1] Charles Stuart Burnett, 1882–1945. On active service, South Africa (1900–1), Northern Nigeria (1904–7), First World War (1914–18, DSO), and Iraq (1920). Director of Operations and Intelligence, Air Ministry, and Deputy Chief of the Air Staff, 1931–3. Air Officer Commanding, Iraq Command, 1933–5; UK Training Command, 1936–9. Knighted, 1936. Inspector-General, Royal Air Force, 1939–40. Chief of Air Staff, Royal Australian Air Force, 1940–2.

[2] Hein ter Poorten, 1887–1968. Born in Java. One of the founders of the Netherlands Army Air Force. Chief of Staff, Royal Netherlands Indies Army, 1939–41. Commanded the Royal Netherlands Indies Army, December 1941. Appointed Commander of ABDA forces, January 1942. Head of all Allied forces in Java, March 1941, when he unconditionally surrendered Java to the Japanese. Prisoner of war of the Japanese, 1942–5.

[3] Conrad Emile Lambert Helfrich, 1886–1962. Naval cadet, Royal Netherlands Navy, 1903. Commander-in-Chief, Netherlands Naval Forces in the Netherlands East Indies, 1939–42; Allied Naval Forces in the Netherlands East Indies, 1942. Honorary knighthood, 1942. Netherlands representative at the Japanese surrender, Tokyo Bay, September 1945. Commander-in-Chief, Royal Netherlands Navy, 1945–8.

[4] Geoffrey Layton, 1884–1964. Entered the Royal Navy, 1903. On active service, 1914–18 (Commander, 1916; DSO, 1918). Rear-Admiral, 1935. Vice-Admiral Commanding 1st Battle Squadron and Second-in-Command, Home Fleet, 1939–40. Knighted, 1940. Commander-in-Chief, China Station, 1940–2; Ceylon, 1942–5; Portsmouth, 1945–7.

[5] Grahame George Dawson, 1895–1944. Joined the Royal Engineers, 1914. Sub-Lieutenant, Royal Naval Air Service, 1915 (Dunkirk, Dardanelles). Captain, Royal Air Force, 1918. Advanced engineering specialist: in charge of the RAF School of Aeronautical Engineering, 1934–8. Engineer, Staff Duties, Headquarters Fighter Command, 1939–40. Director of Canadian and American Production,

Winston S. Churchill to Anthony Eden
(Churchill papers, 20/88)

12 January 1942   The White House
                                                   Washington DC

President raised the Miquelon issue with me tonight as an urgent matter. He pressed that we consider it in connection with 'Super-Gymnast.' United States relations with Vichy have strengthened since the German–American war. He does not wish to break sharply with Vichy. The State Department for their part are boring along on their old line quite oblivious of the fact that the further they go against de Gaulle the worse they will fare in American opinion. Nevertheless I am of the opinion that the following proposals should be embodied in the communiqué representing the policy of the United States, Canadian and British Governments. I understand that Mackenzie King says he will agree to whatever the President and I settle. It would have to be understood that Vichy will have to conform:

(i) The Islands are French and will remain French.

(ii) To avoid any potential threats to the shipping and interests of the Governments concerned, the use of the wireless stations on the Islands will be subject to the supervision and control by observers appointed by the American and Canadian Governments and attached to their respective consulates.

(iii) The Islands shall be neutralised and demilitarised and shall be considered out of the war.

(iv) The present Administrator shall be withdrawn for the period of the war; the appointment of an Administrator shall be withheld for the same period, and the administration of the Islands shall be left in the hands of a consultative Council.

(v) All armed forces will be withdrawn.

(vi) The Canadian and American governments agree and undertake to continue economic assistance to the inhabitants of the Islands and the respective Consuls of those countries will confer with the Local authorities as to the nature of the assistance to be given. Arrangements are being made both to continue the supplies from the United States and Canada on which the Islands are dependent and to provide a seasonal supply of fish to the French inhabitants of Martinique.

Ministry of Aircraft Production, 1940–1, commanding the Atlantic Ferry Organization (ATFERO). Headquarters Staff, Middle East Command, 1941–3 (CBE for distinguished service); Mediterranean Command, 1943–4; Mediterranean Allied Air Forces, 1944. Killed in an air accident (in which Air Vice-Marshal Trafford Leigh-Mallory also died) en route to Far East, 14 November 1944.

2. I think this is a reasonable compromise, and that in the circumstances it is only prudent to accept and enforce it. This means that you should tell de Gaulle that this is our settled policy and that he must bow to it. He has put himself fully in the wrong by his breach of faith. If he is to retain any measure of our recognition he must send orders to Muselier which the latter will obey. You should dwell on the many advantages gained by the Free French and that many of the points agreed will be a bitter pill to Vichy, but however you dish it up he has got to take it. I cannot believe he will refuse to give Muselier orders or that Muselier will disobey. If he were to, they are in a mood here to use force, i.e., the United States battleship *Arkansas,* which the President mentioned or starvation without stint. It is intolerable that the great movement of events should be obstructed, and I shall certainly not intervene to save de Gaulle or other Free French from the consequences.

3. I hope to hear from you tomorrow that it is all fixed. Personally, I think the terms are very reasonable considering the embarrassing position in which the United States has been placed by its agreement with Admiral Roberts,[1] and the breach of faith by de Gaulle. By all means consult the Cabinet if you will, but we shall soon be flitting and I must settle this before I go.

Winston S. Churchill to Clement Attlee
(Churchill papers, 20/88)

12 January 1942   The White House
                                                   Washington DC

As I shall soon be silent for a while, though I trust not for ever, pray cable tonight any outstanding points which require decision here before leaving.

---

[1] Georges Robert, 1875–1965. Commander-in-Chief, French Atlantic Forces, 1939–40. High Commissioner, French West Indies (including French Guiana and St Pierre and Miquelon), 1940–3. In December 1941, refused a Free French request to use his ships against the Germans. On 18 December 1941, agreed with the United States to discuss terms for neutralizing French Caribbean possessions (but later rejected the terms). Condemned to ten years' imprisonment by a French court in 1947, but freed on appeal.

General Claude Auchinleck to Winston S. Churchill
(Churchill papers, 20/68)

12 January 1942   Cairo

I do not think it can be said that bulk of enemy divisions have evaded us. It is true that he still speaks in terms of divisions but they are divisions only in name. For instance we know that strength of 90th German Light Division originally 9,000 is now 3,500, and has only 1 field gun left.

2. I estimate that not (repeat not) more than one third of original German Italian forces got away round corner totalling 17,000 German 18,000 Italian. These are much disorganised short of senior officers short of material and due to our continuous pressure are tired and certainly not as strong as their total strength 35,000 might be thought to indicate.

3. I have reason to believe 6 ships recently reached Palermo averaging 7,200 tons.

4. I am convinced that we should press forward with 'Acrobat' for many reasons not the least in order that Germany may continue to be attacked on two fronts Russia and Libya. I promise you I will not (repeat not) be led into any rash adventure nor (repeat nor) will General Ritchie but in view of heartening news from Russian front, I feel that we should do all we can to maintain the pressure in Libya. We have very full and interesting records of daily conversation between our prisoner Generals Ravenstein[1] and Schmidt.[2] Making all allowances for mental depression natural in prisoners of war there is no doubt that German morale is beginning to feel the strain not only in Libya but in Germany. They speak freely also of great losses in the recent fighting, mis-management and disorganisation and above all of dissatisfaction with Rommel's leadership. I am convinced the enemy is hard pressed more than we dared to think.

[1] Johann 'Hans' Theodor von Ravenstein, 1889–1962. Member of a Prussian military family: one of his ancestors fought, as Britain's ally, at Waterloo. Entered the German Army, 1909. On active service in the First World War, including at Verdun (1916), on the Somme (1916), and at the Chemin des Dames (1918). On active service in Poland (1939) and France (1940). Major-General commanding 21st Panzer Division, Afrika Korps, Western Desert, May–November 1941. Promoted Lieutenant-General, 1 October 1941. Captured by New Zealand troops, 28 November 1941: the first German general to be taken prisoner during the Second World War. Held initially in Cairo, where his conversations with his fellow prisoner of war, General Schmitt, were monitored.

[2] Artur Schmitt, 1888–1972. Entered the Royal Bavarian Army, 1907. On active service in the First World War, when he was taken prisoner by the British. Served with the Bavarian Police, 1920–35. Colonel, German Army, 1935. On active service in France (1940). Commanded Sector East, North Africa, November 1941 to January 1942. Taken prisoner by South African troops, Bardia, 2 January 1942. Joined General Ravenstein in captivity in Cairo. Taken to Canada later in 1942, and held there as a prisoner of war until transferred to a prisoner of war camp in Wales, 1946–7.

Winston S. Churchill to General Claude Auchinleck
(Churchill papers, 20/68)

13 January 1942   The White House
                                                    Washington DC

Very pleased with your number 1697 Susan.[1] Am showing it to the
President today. I am sure you are quite right to push on and bid highly
for decision in battle on Agheila–Marada front. Will support you whatever the result.

Winston S. Churchill to Frank J. Wilson[2]
(Churchill papers, 20/53)

13 January 1942   The White House
                                                    Washington DC

Dear Mr Wilson,
    I write to thank you most warmly for all the trouble which you and
the members of the United States Secret Service concerned have taken
during my visit to this country. I have been much struck by the versatility
of your officers and their thoroughness. There was no requirement, large
or small, whether strictly within their province or not, which they were
not ready to meet, if indeed it had not already been anticipated. The
work has, I am sure, been often arduous and exacting, and I am most
grateful for all that you and the members of your staff have done for my
comfort as well as my security in the course of my stay in Washington
and during my journeys to Canada and to Florida.

                                              Yours sincerely,
                                            Winston S. Churchill

---

[1] General Auchinleck's telegram of 12 January 1942, reproduced above.
[2] Frank J. Wilson, 1887–1970. Joined the United States Treasury Department's Intelligence Unit,
1920. An agent of the Treasury Department's Bureau of Inland Revenue (involved in the prosecution of Al Capone and in the Lindbergh kidnapping case). Chief of the United States Secret Service, 1936–47. Introduced innovations in Presidential security that subsequently became standard
practice.

Winston S. Churchill to John Curtin
(Churchill papers, 20/88)

13 January 1942   The White House
                                                   Washington DC

I do not see how any one could expect Malaya to be defended once the Japanese obtained command of sea and whilst we are fighting for our lives against Germany and Italy. The only vital point is Singapore Fortress and its essential hinterland. Personally, my anxiety has been lest in fighting rearguard action down the Peninsula to gain time we should dissipate the force required for the prolonged defence of Singapore. Out of the equivalent of 4 divisions available for that purpose, one has been lost and another mauled to gain a month or six weeks' time. Some may think it would have been better to have come back quicker with less loss.

2. It is clearly your duty to give all support to decisions of the Supreme Commander. We cannot judge from our distant post whether it is better to fight on the north-western side of the Peninsula at some risk to Mersing, or whether all troops should now withdraw into the Island Fortress (?leaving) naval base to be destroyed? Personally, I believe Wavell is right, and that view is supported by the Chiefs of Staff. I feel sure that you will agree to most of this.

3. I have great confidence that your troops will acquit themselves in the highest fashion in the impending battles. So far, the Japanese have only had two white battalions and a few gunners against them, the rest being Indian soldiers.[1] Everything is being done to reinforce Singapore and the hinterland. Two convoys bearing the 45th Indian Brigade group and its transports have got through, and a very critical convoy containing the leading brigade of the British 18th Division is timed to arrive on the 13th. I am naturally anxious about these 4,500 men going through the Straits of Sunda in a single ship. I hope, however, they will arrive in time to take their stand with their Australian brothers. I send you in immediately following telegram the full details of what we have on move towards this important battlefield, with the dates of arrival. There is justification in this for Wavell's hope that a counter-stroke will be possible in the latter part of February.

4. You are aware, no doubt, that I have proposed your withdrawal of two Australian Divisions from Palestine to the new theatre of (?so) much direct interest in Australia. The only limiting factor on their

---

[1] This sentence was omitted when Churchill published this telegram in his war memoirs.

movement will be the shipping. We shall have to do our best to replace them from home.

5. I do not accept any censure about Crete and Greece. We are doing our utmost in the Mother Country to meet living perils and onslaughts. We have sunk all party differences and have imposed universal compulsory service not only upon men but women. We have suffered the agonising loss of two of our finest ships, which we sent to sustain the Far Eastern War. We are organising, from reduced forces, the utmost further naval aid. In the battle of Libya, British and Empire losses to 7th January are reported at 1,200 officers and 16,000 men out of the comparatively small force it is possible to maintain forward in the desert. A heavy battle around Agheila seems to be impending. We have successfully disengaged Tobruk, after previously relieving all your men who so gallantly held it for so long. I hope, therefore, you will be considerate in the judgment which you pass upon those to whom Australian lives and fortunes are so dear.

6. I now send you the text of the draft (?arrangements) sub-joined which we have made with United States for the defence of the Anzac area. You will naturally comment, as I did when the staffs first told me, upon the fact that the United States, who will have the command, contribute only one heavy, or perhaps only one light, cruiser. The 1st Sea Lord is of the opinion, and I agree with him, that the advantage of persuading the United States to undertake the responsibilities for this area as a part of their main Pacific Command, outweighs such criticism. I have no doubt that this will also be your view. They have a stream of important convoys moving along the whole route, and will no doubt detach other naval forces from time to time. There are still other matters to be settled as between the ABDA and the Anzac areas, upon which we are still working. I spent all last night with Mr Casey, who explained to me very fully the views which your Government holds.

Winston S. Churchill to Lord Moyne[1]
(Churchill papers, 20/88)

13 January 1942

The White House
Washington DC

THE POSITION AT SINGAPORE

This is a shocking tale, and everybody seems to blame. Why did not Duff Cooper report the lack of preparation and provision of gas-masks, civilian hats, &c., for civil population? These elements of deficiency must have been known to him before war broke out.

2. His reports on Shenton Thomas[2] appear most damaging, and I do not see how he can continue unless you have reason to doubt them. The proposal Fraser[3] (?should) succeed the Colonial Secretary is one I cannot judge on merit, but case seems to be made out. Your suggestion about Bede Clifford[4] would certainly not meet case. He is very well where he is, and I should think would be the last man to become Governor, Singapore.

3. My suggestion is that, as this fortress is to stand a siege, the Commander-in-Chief, General Percival,[5] should be the Governor, and he

---

[1] Walter Edward Guinness, 1880–1944. 3rd son of the 1st Earl of Iveagh. Educated at Eton. On active service in South Africa, 1900–1 (wounded). Conservative MP for Bury St Edmunds, 1907–31. On active service, 1914–18 (despatches thrice). Under-Secretary of State for War, 1922–3. Financial Secretary, Treasury, 1923–4, 1924–5. Minister of Agriculture and Fisheries, 1925–9. Created Baron Moyne, 1932. A director of Arthur Guinness, Son, and Company, brewers. Elected to the Other Club (founded by Churchill and F. E. Smith), 1934. Secretary of State for the Colonies, 1941–2. Minister Resident, Cairo, 1944: murdered there by Jewish terrorists.

[2] (Thomas) Shenton (Whitelegge) Thomas, 1879–1962. Entered the Colonial Civil Service, 1909. Assistant Chief Secretary, Uganda, 1918. Principal Assistant Chief Secretary, Nigeria, 1921. Colonial Secretary, Gold Coast Colony, 1927. Governor of Nyasaland, 1929–32. Knighted, 1930. Governor of the Gold Coast, 1932–4. Governor of the Straits Settlements and High Commissioner for the Malay States, 1934–42. Prisoner of war of the Japanese in Changi Prison, Singapore, February 1942 to August 1945. On release from captivity, returned as High Commissioner until the Malayan Union took over the British administration, 1 April 1946.

[3] Hugh Fraser, 1890–1944. Appointed Acting Colonial Secretary, Singapore, January 1942. Captured by the Japanese. Died in Changi Prison on 25 July 1944.

[4] Bede Edmund Hugh Clifford, 1890–1969. Private and Military Secretary to the Governor-General of Australia, 1919–20; to the Governor-General of South Africa (Prince Arthur of Connaught), 1921–4. Governor and Commander-in-Chief, Bahamas, 1932–7; Mauritius, 1937–42; Trinidad and Tobago, 1942–6. Knighted, 1933. Among his books were *Irrigation and Hydro-Electric Resources of Mauritius* and an autobiography, *Proconsul.*

[5] Arthur Ernest Percival, 1887–1966. Clerk in a City office in London, 1907–14. On active service, 1914–18 (DSO, Military Cross, wounded). Served in North Russia, 1919 (bar to DSO), and in Ireland, 1920–2 (OBE, despatches twice). General Staff Officer, Malaya, 1936–8. Brigadier, General Staff, I Corps, British Expeditionary Force, France, September 1939 to February 1940. Assistant Chief of the Imperial General Staff, 1940. General Officer Commanding 44th (Home Counties) Division, 1940–1. CB, 1941. General Officer Commanding, Malaya, May 1941. Surrendered to the

should have the very best Colonial Secretary under him who can be found in the district. This follows arrangements of Gibraltar and Malta at present time. Alternatively, could not Admiral Layton become Governor, thus avoiding throwing too much strain upon Percival, who may actually have to conduct operations in Johore Tip personally? Let me know your views after consulting Lord Privy Seal and Defence Committee.

Winston S. Churchill to Anthony Eden
(Churchill papers, 20/88)

13 January 1942   The White House
Washington DC

I think Netherlands Foreign Minister is under a misapprehension.

2. The appointment of a Supreme Commander in the South-West Pacific was hailed by all as an essential measure if best use was to be made of ABDA forces in that area.

3. We have done our best to devise machinery which will strike a balance between:

(a) Preserving General Wavell's authority to execute the Supreme Command of the ABDA forces in his area with a reasonable degree of freedom; and

(b) Preserving the rights of the ABDA Governments to reach agreed decisions on such matters of major policy as may be referred to them by General Wavell or initiated by any one Government.

4. It would, of course, have been possible to set up high-level ABDA Combined Defence Committees in London, in Washington, and indeed at General Wavell's Headquarters. Clearly, such an arrangement, while ostensibly satisfying (b) above, would have destroyed at the outset any chance of successful execution of the unified Supreme Command in the South-West Pacific.

5. The procedure proposed seems to me to give all concerned a fair deal. Let me restate it.

6. When a decision of major policy is required, it is referred to Washington and London. It will first be sifted in London by the British and Dutch Governments and the representatives of Australia and New Zealand. It should be noted that America has not asked to be represented at this stage. The resultant views then go to Washington, and, if advice

Japanese, 15 February 1942. Released from captivity in Manchuria, August 1945. Present on board USS *Missouri* for the Japanese surrender.

of Dutch Representatives there is needed, it will be readily sought. Washington views, if divergent, would then be referred back to London, where, again, Dutch Government and Dominion Representatives would be given full and equal rights of comment. Finally, the agreed decision will be promulgated by Washington in the name of the ABDA Governments.

7. The very fact of the establishment of General Wavell's Headquarters in Netherlands East Indies territory affords him ample opportunity to seek and obtain the advice of Netherlands authorities there if he should so desire.

8. Surely this is the limit to which we can go. One of the main objects in establishing the Supreme Command in the South-West Pacific was to enable quick decisions to be taken. It is therefore most undesirable at the same time to set up machinery which will merely introduce delay at another and even more difficult level.

9. I expect to hear from General Wavell any day now that he is ready to assume the Supreme Command. It would be unfortunate in the extreme if we were unable to assure him that he had at his back the unanimous support of the ABDA Governments.

Winston S. Churchill to Peter Fraser
(Churchill papers, 20/88)

13 January 1942

The White House
Washington DC

NEW ZEALAND REQUEST FOR AIR REINFORCEMENTS

Air reinforcements for New Zealand have been examined by staff and their proposals, which are the best we can do at the moments, are as follows:

(i) Your paragraph 3 (a). United States have already agreed to send Squadron of 25 P.39 fighters with full service, including 2 RDF[1] sets and 700 personnel. Discussions are continuing and further American contribution is possible.

(ii) Your paragraph 3 (b). It is hoped to complete 1942 programme, except for Catalinas,[2] as follows:

---

[1] RDF: Radio Direction Finding, which became known as radar. A detection system using radio waves to calculate the range, altitude, direction, and speed of objects, developed in Britain by Robert Watson-Watt before the Second World War to detect aircraft and ships.

[2] Catalina: formal name Consolidated PBY Catalina; American flying boat used for anti-submarine attacks, convoy escorts, and search-and-rescue missions.

(i)　34 Hudsons,[1] 6 a month from December 1941 to April 1942.

(ii)　14 Ansons,[2] 7 a month in January and February 1942.

(iii)　14 Tanker Trailers and 7 RDF sets are already allocated for as soon as possible.

(iii) Catalinas situation is very difficult owing to set-back in American deliveries. Present expectation is limited to 36 Catalinas for the first half of 1942, which will fall far short even of meeting wastage. Improved deliveries of Catalinas should be available in second half of 1942 and when this happens everything possible will be done to help New Zealand.

(iv) Your paragraph 3(c). We are now entirely dependent upon American allocations for Hudson deliveries. The Hudson situation will be exceedingly tight in the first half of year, but we are pressing hard for improved allocations. If we are successful, you may be assured that we shall endeavour to meet your requirements. Further allotments of tanker trailers and RDF sets will be considered immediately [as] supplies become available and we hope to meet your requirements.

(v) Your paragraph 3 (d). We will try to send you some Hurricanes I's for anti-invasion work and some Ventura bombers may also be available towards the end of the year. Air Ministry is communicating direct with Goddard on question of OTU[3] training in New Zealand.

Winston S. Churchill to Clement Attlee
(Churchill papers, 20/88)

13 January 1942　　　　　　　　　　The White House
　　　　　　　　　　　　　　　　　　Washington DC

Would it not be well to form in London a Council of the Far East on the Ministerial plane? I would preside, with you or, when he returns, Duff Cooper, who is now well informed on the area and whose departure seems to be much regretted, as my Deputy. Members, Earle Page, a New Zealand representative who might be the High Commissioner to begin with, and a Dutch Cabinet Minister. This Council would be assisted by the kind of Staff group you outline in your Taut No. 503. The duties of this

---

[1] Hudson: formal name Lockheed Hudson; lightweight bomber built by United States for the Royal Air Force.

[2] Anson: British twin-engine, multi-purpose aircraft; originally built for light transport and coastal reconnaissance, but most effectively used during the Second World War as training aircraft.

[3] OTU: Operational Training Unit.

Council will be to focus and formulate views of the represented Powers to the President, whose views will also be brought before the Council. This would not interfere with Earle Page's attending the Cabinets as at present, when Australian affairs are affected, thus enabling them to be heard in the general sphere of the war.

Let me have your views back, 'clear the line.'[1]

Winston S. Churchill to Clement Attlee
(Churchill papers, 20/88)

13 January 1942   The White House
                                                  Washington DC

Much regret decision.[2] I certainly cannot undertake to make two speeches on the same situation within a few days.

Winston S. Churchill to Clement Attlee
(Churchill papers, 20/88)

13 January 1942   The White House
                                                  Washington DC

DETENTION OF U SAW[3]

Congratulate you on timely action.

---

[1] An instruction whereby this telegram would have immediate precedence over all other telegrams already marked for despatch.

[2] The decision of the Cabinet not to allow Churchill's speech on his return to be recorded in the House of Commons, and then broadcast.

[3] U Saw, 1900–48. Lawyer by training; defended the leader of the Burmese Peasant Rebellion (1930–2). Prime Minister of Burma, 1940–2. In November 1941, having come to London and failed to obtain a promise that Burma would be granted Dominion Status after the war, he made contact with the Japanese to secure his own future should Japan invade Burma. When papers relating to these contacts were discovered, the British arrested U Saw and detained him for four years in Uganda. In 1947 he was one of only two members of the Burmese delegation to London who refused to sign the Attlee–Aung San agreement for eventual Burmese independence. In 1948 he was tried, condemned, and sentenced to death by a Burmese court for his part in the assassination of Aung San and six of his Cabinet ministers. He was executed on 8 May 1948.

Winston S. Churchill: recollection
('The Grand Alliance', pages 625–6)

14 January 1942

On the 14th I took leave of the President. He seemed concerned about the dangers of the voyage. Our presence in Washington had been for many days public to the world, and the charts showed more than twenty U-boats on our homeward courses. We flew in beautiful weather from Norfolk to Bermuda, where the *Duke of York*, with escorting destroyers, awaited us inside the coral reefs. I travelled in an enormous Boeing flying-boat, which made a most favourable impression upon me. During the three hours' trip I made friends with the chief pilot, Captain Kelly Rogers,[1] who seemed a man of high quality and experience. I took the controls for a bit, to feel this ponderous machine of thirty or more tons in the air. I got more and more attached to the flying-boat. Presently I asked the captain, 'What about flying from Bermuda to England? Can she carry enough petrol?' Under his stolid exterior he became visibly excited. 'Of course we can do it. The present weather forecast would give a forty miles an hour wind behind us. We could do it in twenty hours.' I asked how far it was, and he said, 'About three thousand five hundred miles.' At this I became thoughtful.

However, when we landed I opened the matter to Portal[2] and Pound. Formidable events were happening in Malaya; we ought all to be back at the earliest moment. The Chief of the Air Staff said at once that he thought the risk wholly unjustifiable, and he could not take the responsibility for it. The First Sea Lord supported his colleague. There was the *Duke of York*, with her destroyers, all ready for us, offering comfort

---

[1] John Cecil Kelly-Rogers, 1905–81. Entered the Royal Air Force, 1927, piloting flying boats. Joined Imperial Airways, 1935. Flew the first Empire Flying Boat Service along the Nile to Lake Victoria, and from Lake Victoria to Durban. A regular captain on the Egypt–India–Australia flying boat route. Commanded the first Imperial Airways route across the Atlantic, 1939. Chief Pilot on Churchill's Boeing flying-boat flight from Virginia to Bermuda, 1942. OBE, 1945. Later first Chief Pilot of Aer Lingus.

[2] Charles Frederick Algernon Portal, 1893–1971. Known as 'Peter'. On active service, 1914–18 (despatches, DSO and bar; Military Cross). As a 2nd Lieutenant, Royal Engineers, he was in both the advance to and the retreat from Mons in 1914. Seconded to the Royal Flying Corps, 1915. Major, commanding 16 Squadron, 1917 (working for the Canadian Corps, then carrying out night bombing tasks). Air Ministry (Directorate of Operations and Intelligence), 1923. Commanded British Forces in Aden, 1934–5. Instructor, Imperial Defence College, 1936–7. Director of Organization, Air Ministry, 1937–8. Air Member for Personnel, Air Council, 1939–40. Air Officer Commanding-in-Chief, Bomber Command, April–October 1940. Knighted, July 1940. Chief of the Air Staff, October 1940 to November 1945. Created Baron, 1945; Viscount, 1946. Order of Merit, 1946. Knight of the Garter, 1946. Controller, Atomic Energy, Ministry of Supply, 1946–51. Chairman, British Aircraft Corporation, 1960–8.

and a certainty. I said, 'What about the U-boats you have been pointing out to me?' The Admiral made a disdainful gesture about them, which showed his real opinion of such a menace to a properly escorted and fast battleship. It occurred to me that both these officers thought my plan was to fly myself and leave them to come back in the *Duke of York*, so I said, 'Of course there would be room for all of us.' They both visibly changed countenance at this. After a considerable pause Portal said that the matter might be looked into, and that he would discuss it at length with the captain of the flying-boat and go into weather prospects with the meteorological authorities. I left it at that.

Two hours later they both returned, and Portal said that he thought it might be done. The aircraft could certainly accomplish the task under reasonable conditions; the weather outlook was exceptionally favourable on account of the strong following wind. No doubt it was very important to get home quickly. Pound said he had formed a very high opinion of the aircraft skipper, who certainly had unrivalled experience. Of course there was a risk, but on the other hand there were the U-boats to consider.

So we settled to go unless the weather deteriorated. The starting time was 2 p.m. the next day. It was thought necessary to reduce our baggage to a few boxes of vital papers. Dill was to remain behind in Washington as my personal military representative with the President. Our party would consist only of myself, the two Chiefs of Staff, and Max Beaverbrook, Charles Wilson, and Hollis. All the rest would go by the *Duke of York*.

War Cabinet
(Cabinet papers, 65/25)

14 January 1942   10 Downing Street

THE FUTURE OF ST PIERRE AND MIQUELON

The Secretary of State for Foreign Affairs then gave the War Cabinet the gist of a telephone conversation which he had had with the Prime Minister, to whom he had recounted the upshot of his discussions with General de Gaulle. (At this time he had not received the reply of the Council of Free France.)

[...]

The Prime Minister had said[1] that it was most important to reach a decision on the matter that day. He had arrived at a settlement of a

---

[1] In a telegram to the War Cabinet.

number of very important questions with the United States Government. The issues concerned in regard to these Islands were of relatively far less importance, and we ought to be prepared to make substantial concessions to meet the strong feelings of the United States Government in this matter. The Prime Minister had added that he strongly condemned General de Gaulle's attitude on the whole affair. He thought that the communiqué should be issued on behalf of all three governments (USA, UK, and Canada). If, however, it was necessary to take any action, to enforce the decision reached, that would be left to the United States. The Foreign Secretary said that he had then told the Prime Minister that he proposed to see General de Gaulle again later that evening, and to endeavour to persuade him to accept the communiqué, subject to the substitution for Clauses (iii) and (v) of a phrase which admitted General de Gaulle's intention in practice to withdraw his forces.

As regards Clause (ii), he had gathered from the Prime Minister that the United States Government were not now prepared to agree to the terms of a statement which explicitly recognized the sovereignty of the islands as residing either in the Council of Free France, or in the Vichy Government. If the amendments which General de Gaulle was prepared to agree to were unacceptable to the United States Government, the Prime Minister felt that, in view of the strong feelings which that Government had in regard to the matter, it would be necessary to agree to the issue of the communiqué in its present form.

The Foreign Secretary said that he would be grateful if the Cabinet would let him know what message he should give to the Prime Minister as representing the view of the War Cabinet, as to the action which he (the Prime Minister) should take, if the United States Government were not prepared to accept the amendments which he could persuade General de Gaulle to agree to in the draft communiqué. His own view was that it was very doubtful whether His Majesty's Government should be associated with the issue of the communiqué in its present form. In this event the communiqué, if issued, would be issued by the United States Government.

The Lord Privy Seal said that in effect the communiqué, as it stood, asserted the right of the United States Government to determine what happened in places in the American continent which did not belong to the United States. These two islands were in fact very close to our own territories, and a long way from the United States. Further, he did not think the Monroe Doctrine was applicable. No change in Sovereignty was involved since, in either event, the islands were French territory. It was only a question whether Sovereignty over the islands was exercised by the National Committee of the Free French or by the Vichy Government.

[...]

(3) The Foreign Secretary was authorized to inform the Prime Minister that it was the unanimous view of the War Cabinet that it would be impossible for us to support or associate ourselves either with the issue of a communiqué such as was proposed (unless, of course amendments which General de Gaulle would agree to were accepted) or with the kind of action proposed.

(4) The Foreign Secretary was asked to remind the Prime Minister of the importance of Mr McKenzie King[1] being consulted before any public announcement was made. This would be of special importance if we found it necessary to dissociate ourselves from the issue of the communiqué.

Sir Charles Wilson: diary
('Winston Churchill, The Struggle for Survival', page 22)

14 January 1942   The White House
                                                                   Washington DC

The Americans have got their way and the war will be run from Washington, but they will not be wise to push us so unceremoniously in the future. Our people are very unhappy about the decision,[2] and the most they will agree to is to try it out for a month. They were, however, brought back to good humour by the final figures of the production estimates. Harry[3] gave me some figures which meant something even to me: 100,000 aircraft in 1943 for 45,000 in 1942, and 75,000 tanks in 1943 for 45,000 in 1942. The PM gives Max most of the credit; Harry hands it to the President. I would bracket them together: to set a seemingly impossible target requires a particular cast of mind, and they have both got that kind of mind. I think Winston, more than anyone here, visualizes in detail what this programme means to the actual conduct of the war. He is drunk with the figures.

---

[1] William Mackenzie King, Prime Minister of Canada.
[2] The decision to establish an Anglo-American Combined Chiefs of Staff.
[3] Harry Hopkins.

Winston S. Churchill to Lord Halifax
(Churchill papers, 20/53)

14 January 1942   The White House
                                                   Washington DC

Before leaving Washington I must ask you to convey to all at the Embassy my most grateful thanks for the assistance they have rendered in connection with my Mission here. I feel sure that the conversations between the President and myself and between the British and American Chiefs of Staff will be found to have been of great value in promoting co-operation between our two countries in the conduct of the war, and I should like the members of your staff to know that they have made a substantial contribution to the success of our visit.

2. Sir Anthony Rumbold[1] has acted most successfully as Liaison Officer between the Embassy and the Mission and has cheerfully undertaken a great variety of tasks. In particular with other members of the Embassy he has relieved my staff of the burden of dealing with the mass of unofficial correspondence addressed to me from all parts of the United States and he has assisted in many other ways.

3. I would refer also to the excellent arrangements made under Mr Thorold,[2] Commander Dawn[3] and Commander Coleridge[4] for handling telegraphic correspondence. It has been evident that these were organised with the greatest throroughness and efficiency.

4. I wish at the same time to thank those responsible for ensuring so successfully that I was kept in touch with all important developments in foreign affairs during my stay.

5. I am glad to find that His Majesty's Representative in Washington is assisted by so able and efficient a staff. I send them all my good wishes in the important work in which they are engaged.

[1] (Horace) Anthony Claude Rumbold, 1911–83. Entered the Foreign Office, 1935. Second Secretary, Washington, 1940–2. Succeeded his father as 10th Baronet, 1941. British Minister, Paris, 1960–3. Knighted, 1962. Ambassador to Thailand, 1965–7; to Austria, 1967–70.

[2] Guy Frederick Thorold, 1898–1970. Educated at Winchester and New College, Oxford. Served in the Army, 1917–19. Ministry of Economic Warfare, 1939–45; First Secretary, British Embassy, Washington. Member of UK delegation to Organisation for European Economic Co-operation, Paris, 1948. Head of Treasury Delegation and Economic Minister, Washington, and UK Executive Director, IMF and IBRD, 1957–9. KCMG, 1959.

[3] Commander Dawn RN, Cypher Section, British Embassy, Washington.

[4] Richard Duke Coleridge, 1905–84. Entered the Royal Navy, 1919. Seconded to the Offices of the War Cabinet and Ministry of Defence, French General Headquarters, Vincennes, May–June 1940; War Cabinet Offices, London, July 1940 to May 1941. Joint Staff Mission, Washington, 1941. British Joint Staff and Combined Chiefs of Staff, 1942–5 (attended the conferences in Washington, 1942, and Quebec, 1943). OBE, 1944. British Joint Services Mission, Washington, 1948. CBE, 1951. Executive Secretary, North Atlantic Treaty Organisation, 1952–70. Succeeded his father as 4th Baron, 1955.

Winston S. Churchill to John Curtin
(Churchill papers, 20/68)

14 January 1942   The White House
                                                                 Washington DC

The vital convoy including the American transport *Mount Vernon*,[1] carrying 50 Hurricanes, one Anti-Tank Regiment, 50 guns; one Heavy AA Regiment, 50 guns; one Light AA Regiment, 50 guns and the 54th British Infantry Brigade Group, total about 9,000, reached Singapore safely and punctually yesterday.

Winston S. Churchill to General Archibald Wavell
(Churchill papers, 20/88)

14 January 1942   Washington DC

I hope you will tighten up the censorship at Singapore. President and I were both alarmed yesterday at a press statement coming from Singapore to the effect that air supremacy would be gained in three days. Another report said three weeks. Considering that this corresponded to the impending arrival of DS1,[2] it might easily have endangered a vital reinforcement. Whoever allowed such a report to go out from the Fortress is unfit for his task.

2. Please let me know your idea of what would happen in the event of your being forced to withdraw into the Island. How many troops would be needed to defend this area? What means are there of stopping landings as in Hong Kong? What are the defences and obstructions on the landward side? Are you sure you can dominate with Fortress cannon any attempt to plant siege batteries? Is everything being prepared, and what has been done about the useless mouths? It has always seemed to me that the vital need is to prolong the defence of the Island to the last possible minute, but, of course, I hope it will not come to this.

3. The Colonial Secretary informs me that he has telegraphed you my opinion about proclaiming a state of siege and appointing a military governor for the Fortress. I should be glad to know what you think.

---

[1] The USS *Mount Vernon* (24,289 tons) was a former luxury ocean liner, SS *Washington*, launched in 1933 and operating from New York to Plymouth and Hamburg. Acquired by the United States Navy on 6 June 1941, she was converted for naval use at the Philadelphia naval yard. On 4 June 1944 she began regular transatlantic voyages bringing United States troops from the United States to Britain for the northern European theatre of operations.

[2] The 'vital convoy' of the previous document.

4. Everyone here is very pleased with the telegrams you have sent, which give us all the feeling how buoyantly and spaciously you are grappling with your tremendous task. All the Americans seem to have the same confidence in you as have your British friends.

Winston S. Churchill to Anthony Eden
(Churchill papers, 20/88)

14 January 1942   The White House
                                                                 Washington DC

THE FUTURE OF ST PIERRE AND MIQUELON

I talked with the President about the Consultative Council at Miquelon, and asked him what assurances we had that the Council was friendly to the Free French. The President stated that the State Department had been advised by American Consul as follows:

That the Council consists of eleven members, four appointed and seven elected; that of the four appointed members, two of them had been appointed by Admiral Muselier since he took over; that Muselier left two of the others on his belief that they were friendly to the Free French; that Muselier has made no objection to the seven elected members, they having indicated to him their allegiance to the Free French. The President is of the opinion as a result of this that the Consultative Council is thoroughly sympathetic to the Free French. He stated that he did not know the date of the next regular election, but believed that it would be more desirable not to call an election until the normal date unless untoward circumstances should make another course desirable.

2. On my putting the points in Halifax's telegram reflecting on this Council as a 'rump', the President agreed that a fresh election shall be held within 90 days. Therefore, the last lines of paragraph 1, sub-section 4 would run 'this Consultative Council, for which new elections shall be freely held within 90 days.'

3. Your paragraph 3. The 'present Administrator,' means the Vichy Administrator with the German wife who is to be withdrawn.

4. It is, of course, understood that these terms will be enforced upon Vichy equally with de Gaulle. It seems quite likely that they will not accept, in which case they will have to lump it.

5. If de Gaulle will not settle on these terms, I shall authorise the issue of the amended communiqué, and it will be for the United States to enforce it – which they will certainly do. The President will probably

appoint a Trustee in the name of the United States and will not hesitate to use whatever force is necessary. You may tell de Gaulle this from me.

6. Reply, 'clear the line.' This business must be settled.

Winston S. Churchill to Clement Attlee
(Churchill papers, 20/88)

14 January 1942   The White House
                                                   Washington DC

It seems to me that the formation of a War Council of Far East should be publicly announced, as this concedes continuous representation which Dominion and Dutch demand. This announcement would not be possible if it is represented to be merely enlarged meetings of Defence Committee. The latter plan would simply amount to saying the representatives of the three other Governments will be invited to attend British Defence Committee meetings when Far Eastern matters are under consideration. This would not satisfy at all. What they have demanded is continuous representation with power of suggestion upon waging of war against Japan. I am responsible for determining these opinions and presenting them at first on Chiefs of Staff level to President, and ultimately for reaching agreement with him. I can only do this if this Japanese war, separated from the other by many thousands of miles, is the subject of special study. As Chiefs of Staff would be advisers in both cases, and as chairman and deputy chairman will be same, there should be no difficulty in reconciling British views on Defence, &c., and on council of Far East.

2. I do not think it would be a good thing to bring Australians, New Zealanders and Dutch into our general war policy by means of their attendance at regular Defence Committee meetings apart from Far Eastern matters. Australia's and New Zealand's associations with general war would be effected as at present, the former by frequent attendances at War Cabinet of Earle Page, and latter by one of High Commissioner. It would be my responsibility to invite Foreign Secretary or any or all of Service Ministers to attend Far Eastern Council, if necessary. I do not think your plan will give the other partners satisfaction, and I think it might be inconvenient from our point of view. I had only to put proposal to Australia and New Zealand and see what they had to say, but if we cannot agree on the matter it will have to stand over.

Harold Nicolson:[1] diary
('Harold Nicolson, Diaries and Letters', page 205)

14 January 1942   London

Meeting of the National Labour Executive. Kenneth Lindsay[2] says that we must concentrate on a long-term policy – the relations between the State and the individual and the State and industry. Frank Markham[3] says that, on the contrary, we must concentrate on winning the war. In order to do this, we must get rid of Churchill, who will never win the war.

Others say that Winston is not an organiser and is no judge of men. His faith in Beaverbrook is lamentable. The latter thinks only of the sensational and the dramatic: for instance, he did produce a lot of tanks, but only at the expense of their own spare-parts, and the result was that most of our tanks in Libya went out of action.

Kenneth Lindsay says that Shinwell[4] is the only man in the House prepared to make a stand against Winston, and Cripps[5] is the only possible alternative Prime Minister.

Stephen King-Hall[6] says that the mistake is for Winston to be both Prime Minister and Minister of Defence, and that he neglects produc-

[1] Harold George Nicolson, 1886–1968. Educated at Wellington and Balliol College, Oxford. Entered the Foreign Office, 1909; Counsellor, 1925. Served at the Paris Peace Conference, 1919; Teheran, 1925–7; Berlin, 1927–9. On editorial staff of *Evening Standard*, 1930. National Labour MP for West Leicester, 1935–45. Parliamentary Secretary, Ministry of Information, 1940–1. A Governor of the BBC, 1941–6. Joined the Labour Party, 1947. Author and biographer. Knighted, 1953.

[2] Kenneth Lindsay, 1897–1991. On active service, 1916–18. President of the Oxford Union, 1922. Secretary, Political and Economic Planning (PEP), 1931–5. Independent National MP for Kilmarnock Burghs, 1933–45. Civil Lord of the Admiralty, 1935–7. Parliamentary Secretary, Board of Education, 1937–40. Independent MP for the Combined English Universities, 1945–50.

[3] Frank Markham, 1897–1975. Labour MP for Chatham, 1929–31. Parliamentary Private Secretary to the Prime Minister (Ramsay MacDonald), 1931–2. National MP for South Nottingham, 1935–45. Between 1940 and 1945, saw active service in France and North Africa; also served with Eastern Command, Staff College, and the Hertfordshire Sub-Area, June 1940 to November 1942. Conservative MP for Buckingham, 1951–64. Knighted, 1953.

[4] Emanuel Shinwell, 1884–1986. Unsuccessful Labour candidate for Linlithgowshire, 1918; elected, 1922; re-elected, 1923; defeated, 1924; re-elected at a by-election in April 1928 and again at the general election of 1929; defeated, 1931. Parliamentary Secretary, Mines Department, 1924, 1931. Financial Secretary, War Office, 1929–30. Labour MP for Seaham, 1935–50; for Easington, 1950–70. Minister of Fuel and Power, 1945–7. Secretary of State for War, 1947–50. Minister of Defence, 1950–1. Chairman of the Parliamentary Labour Party, 1964–7. Created Baron (Life Peer), 1970.

[5] Richard Stafford Cripps, 1889–1952. Educated at Winchester. Barrister-at-law, 1913. Served with the Red Cross, France, 1914. Assistant Superintendent, Queen's Ferry Munitions Factory, 1915–18 (when his work much impressed Churchill, then Minister of Munitions). KC, 1927. Knighted, 1930. Labour MP for East Bristol, 1931–50; for South-East Bristol, 1950. Solicitor-General, 1930–1. Ambassador to Russia, 1940–2. Lord Privy Seal and Leader of the House of Commons, 1942. Minister of Aircraft Production, 1942–5. President of the Board of Trade, 1945. Minister of Economic Affairs, 1947. Chancellor of the Exchequer, 1947–50.

[6] William Stephen Richard King-Hall, 1893–1966. On active service in the Royal Navy, 1914–18. Admiralty Naval Staff, 1919–20. China Squadron, 1921–3. Intelligence Officer, Mediterranean

tion in one capacity and confuses strategy in the other. They all feel that he must be brought down, and yet they all agree (a) that there is no apparent successor, and (b) that his fall would [have] given an immense moral shock to the country.

I am disgusted by all this, since they are only thinking in political and departmental terms, and have no conception of the effort of will involved. Winston is the embodiment of the nation's will.

Itinerary
(Franklin D. Roosevelt papers)

14–15 January 1942   The White House
                                                          Washington DC

The Prime Minister and party left Washington by special train just before midnight, Jan. 14, and arrived Naval Operating Base, Norfolk, Va., early morning, Jan. 15, and <u>flew</u> back to England. This movement by R. F. and P. rr., Richmond-Petersburg and Virginian rr., into the Naval Operating Base. The PM used the Pullman private car Roald Amundsen.

Winston S. Churchill: speech
('The Gathering Storm', pages 627–8)

15 January 1942   Bermuda

It is a sudden descent which I have made upon you, and I must express my gratitude that so many members of the Assembly should have found it possible at such very short notice – excusable only by wartime conditions – to attend this meeting. Here I come, as leader of the House of Commons, to call upon you in the second oldest Parliament in the world. Here is a representative parliamentary institution with an unbroken continuity almost as long as that of the House of Commons, an institution which began even before the House of Commons attained its full authority. It is a long way back to 1620. Yet these ideas of parliamentary government, of the representation of the people upon franchises, which extend as time goes on, and which in our country have

Fleet, 1925–6; Atlantic Fleet, 1927–8. Admiralty War Staff, 1928–9. Founded the *King-Hall News Letter*, posted weekly to subscribers, 1936. Independent MP for the Ormskirk Division of Lancashire, 1939–44. Served in Ministry of Aircraft Production, 1940–2; Ministry of Fuel and Power, 1943–5. Founded the Hansard Society for Parliamentary Government, 1944. Radio and television commentator on public events. Knighted, 1954. Created Baron (Life Peer), 1966.

reached the complete limits of universal suffrage, these institutions and principles constitute at this moment one of the great causes which are being fought out in the world. With all our weakness and with all their strength, with all their faults, with all their virtues, with all the criticisms that may be made against them, with their many shortcomings, with lack of foresight, lack of continuity of purpose or pressure only of superficial purpose, they nevertheless assert the right of the common people – the broad masses of the people – to take a conscious and effective share in the government of their country.

That is one of the great causes which are at stake now. We are confronted with embattled powers not based upon the public will, allowing no freedom of discussion, of speech or even of thought, but seeking to subjugate great nations and, if they can succeed, the whole world, on the basis of a party caucus, on the basis of a military hierarchy, on the basis of tyranny, terror and brute force. We are confronted with totalitarian States which deny as a fundamental principle the right of free debate and the expression of popular opinion.

It is against these evil forces that we have been in arms since the third of September, 1939. At one time it seemed that we should be alone. We were for a long time alone. We have stood alone all through the summer and the autumn and the winter of 1940 and 1941. But we did not flinch, we did not weaken. We did not worry because we could not see our way through. We said we will do our duty, we will do our best. The rest we must leave to Providence. And what a reward has come! What a lesson it is never to give in – never to give in when you guard the cause of freedom. What a moral there is to be drawn from that, because now we see great Powers rising that have come to our aid, not wholly because of association with the British Empire but because of association with the cause of which, I will venture to say in no boastful spirit, the British Empire is the oldest custodian, namely, representative government based on the freedom and the rights of the individual.

We have had some great and blessed accessions of help. In the first place we all see now what a service has been rendered to the cause of freedom by the valiant resistance for four and a half years of the Chinese people, fighting the same kinds of tyranny in Asia as have sought to molest us in the Western World. Secondly, we have had the valiant resistance of the Russian armies and peoples to the cruel and unprovoked invasion of their country and the slaughterous attack which had been made upon them – men, women and children alike. And now we see the United States, which under its great President showed its sympathy with our cause at every stage, set upon by those same three villainous Powers, and assaulted with every circumstance of treachery and malice. And so now the situation is widely different from what it was when we for more than a year alone held high the flaming torch of freedom. It is greatly changed. We are now no longer alone. We are marching in a great concourse.

We signed the other day at Washington the agreement of twenty-six countries, including four of the largest masses of population, comprising altogether much more than three-quarters of the entire population of the globe. And we shall march forward together in comradeship until those who have sought to trample upon the rights of individual freedom, the strong principles inculcated in the birth of the English parliamentary system and by the American revolutionary war, by Hampden and by Washington, are beaten down, and until those principles are finally established.

In this vast world struggle, in this convulsion, you in Bermuda happen to be called upon to play a part of especial importance and distinction. Everybody has to do his duty to the cause – first to the British Empire, but above that to the world cause. You had your own life in these Islands. It has run for centuries in a more unbroken course than, perhaps, the life of any civilized community in the world. Suddenly great changes have to be made. I thought it right to ask you, with the full authority of Parliament and of His Majesty the King, to make such alterations in your long-established life as would facilitate the ever closer connection and unity of spirit, and the reciprocity of practical measures for common security, between the British Empire and the United States.

I have got in my pocket the message which I sent you, and on which you decided that you would co-operate heart and hand, that you would put up with many changes and alterations in the balance of your community here for the sake of the old country and the Empire, and of those larger ideas which unite men of all races and all nations and all the creeds.

I said to you: 'I have today signed a document' – this was on the 25th March, 1941 – 'implementing the agreement of September last for the leasing to the United States of bases in Bermuda and elsewhere – and I wish to express to you my strong conviction that these bases are important pillars of the bridge connecting the two great English-speaking democracies. You have cause to be proud that it has fallen to your lot to make this important contribution to a better world.'

You have done so. It is not a question whether it is more profitable; this is a question of duty, of world duty, and these Islands on which I

have had the honour to set foot this morning have unfailingly and un-
falteringly answered the call. Now let me say to you what a reward has
come, because we have seen, as events have unfolded, that the whole
English-speaking world stands together.

We have had other Allies, important and honoured, who are fighting
with great valour against the common foe. Still one has the feeling that
the English-speaking world have only to march forward together, have
only to pool the luck, to guide the forward march of mankind. And for
your contribution to these supreme and even, if I may say so, sublime
ends, I am very happy to have found myself here today to express on
behalf of the Motherland and of the British House of Commons our
profound gratitude.

Josef Stalin to Winston S. Churchill
(Churchill papers, 20/68)

16 January 1942

Received your message of January 15th.[1] My sincere thanks for your
good wishes for the New Year and in connection with the successes of
the Red Army. My best greetings to you and to the British Army on their
important successes in Northern Africa.

Winston S. Churchill: recollection
('The Grand Alliance', pages 627–8)

16 January 1942   Bermuda

I woke up unconscionably early with the conviction that I should certainly not go to sleep again. I must confess that I felt rather frightened.
I thought of the ocean spaces, and that we should never be within a
thousand miles of land until we approached the British Isles. I thought
perhaps I had done a rash thing, that there were too many eggs in one
basket. I had always regarded an Atlantic flight with awe. But the die
was cast. Still, I must admit that if at breakfast, or even before luncheon,
they had come to me to report that the weather had changed and we
must go by sea I should have easily reconciled myself to a voyage in the
splendid ship which had come all this way to fetch us.

---

[1] Dated 11 January 1942 in this volume. The Soviet Union did not adopt the Gregorian Calendar
until 1922.

Divine sunlight lapped the island, and the favourable weather prospects were confirmed. At noon we reached the flying-boat by launch. We were delayed for an hour on the quay because a picket-boat which had gone to the *Duke of York* for items of baggage had taken longer than expected.

[...]

It was, as the captain had predicted, quite a job to get off the water. Indeed, I thought that we should hardly clear the low hills which closed the harbour. There was really no danger; we were in sure hands. The flying-boat lifted ponderously a quarter of a mile from the reef, and we had several hundred feet of height to spare. There is no doubt about the comfort of these great flying-boats. I had a good broad bed in the bridal suite at the stern with large windows on either side. It was quite a long walk, thirty or forty feet, downhill through the various compartments to the saloon and dining-room, where nothing was lacking in food or drink. The motion was smooth, the vibration not unpleasant, and we passed an agreeable afternoon and had a merry dinner. These boats have two storeys, and one walks up a regular staircase to the control room. Darkness had fallen, and all the reports were good.

We were now flying through dense mist at about seven thousand feet. One could see the leading edge of the wings, with their great flaming exhausts pouring back over the wing surfaces. In these machines at this time a large rubber tube which expanded and contracted at intervals was used to prevent icing. The captain explained to me how it worked, and we saw from time to time the ice splintering off as it expanded. I went to bed and slept soundly for several hours.

Winston S. Churchill: recollection
('The Grand Alliance', pages 628–9)

17 January 1942   Above the Atlantic Ocean

I woke just before the dawn, and went forward to the controls. The daylight grew. Beneath us was an almost unbroken floor of clouds.

After sitting for an hour or so in the co-pilot's seat I sensed a feeling of anxiety around me. We were supposed to be approaching England from the south-west and we ought already to have passed the Scilly Islands, but they had not been seen through any of the gaps in the cloud floor. As we had flown for more than ten hours through mist and had had only one sight of a star in that time, we might well be slightly off our course. Wireless communication was of course limited by the normal war-time rules. It was evident from the discussions which were going on that we did not know where we were. Presently Portal, who had been studying the position, had a word with the captain, and then said to me, 'We are going to turn north at once.' This was done, and after another half-hour in and out of the clouds we sighted England, and soon arrived over Plymouth, where, avoiding the balloons, which were all shining, we landed comfortably.

As I left the aircraft the captain remarked, 'I never felt so much relieved in my life as when I landed you safely in the harbour.' I did not appreciate the significance of his remark at the moment. Later on I learnt that if we had held on our course for another five or six minutes before turning northwards we should have been over the German batteries in Brest. We had slanted too much to the southward during the night. Moreover, the decisive correction which had been made brought us in, not from the south-west, but from just east of south – that is to say, from the enemy's direction rather than from that from which we were expected. This had the result, as I was told some weeks later, that we were reported as a hostile bomber coming in from Brest, and six Hurricanes from Fighter Command were ordered out to shoot us down.

However, they failed in their mission.

The flying boat reached Mount Batten, Plymouth, at 9.45 a.m. on 17 January 1942. Churchill then travelled from Plymouth to London by train.

Sir Charles Wilson: diary
('Winston Churchill, The Struggle for Survival', page 23)

17 January 1942

As the train carried the Prime Minister towards London, he sat for a time with his white hands laid out on his thighs, his head poked forward, absorbed in thought. The five weeks that he had been out of the country had not been wasted, he felt; the close friendship he had established with President Roosevelt had smoothed out every difficulty.

'I have done a good job of work with the President,' he said yesterday. 'We got on together. I think we shall soon see dividends. I am sure, Charles, the House will be pleased with what I have to tell them.'

When, however, he picked up a pile of morning papers, he was pained to find that the country did not share his satisfaction. On the contrary, public opinion seemed to be baffled by the way things had gone wrong; the nation was frankly puzzled and worried. He put down the *Manchester Guardian* with an angry gesture.[1]

'There seems to be plenty of snarling,' he said in a tired voice.

Winston S. Churchill to President Franklin D. Roosevelt
(Churchill papers, 20/88)

17 January 1942   10 Downing Street

Your message of January 16 relating to Wavell's 00048[2] of January 14, I entirely agree. Action was most urgent.

We got here with a good hop from Bermuda with a thirty-mile wind. Will cable you again shortly.

General Claude Auchinleck to Winston S. Churchill
(Churchill papers, 20/68)

17 January 1942   Western Desert

Capture Bardia and Halfaya with 14,000 prisoners and much war material at cost of less than 500 casualties represent fine performance reflecting credit Generals Ritchie, Norrie[3] and De-Villiers.[4] Was proposing to feature this in today's communiqué but am withholding it in case

---

[1] The *Manchester Guardian* of 17 January 1942 contained several articles reflecting dismay and discontent arising primarily, but not solely, from news of the surge of the Japanese military into Malaya. One article (headlined 'Malayan Mistakes') criticized the apparent incompetence with which the Government had organized Malaya's defences and demanded that Churchill, upon his return from America, answer for these failures. Another, unrelated to the Malayan defeats, accused the Government of neglecting to remedy the shortcomings of the homeland war industry.

[2] In which General Wavell expressed his reluctance to take military command in the Philippines.

[3] (Charles) Willoughby (Moke) Norrie, 1893–1977. 2nd Lieutenant, 1913. On active service, 1914–18 (DSO, Military Cross and bar, wounded four times). Commanded 1st Cavalry Brigade (mechanised), 1938–40; 1st Armoured Brigade, 1940; 1st Armoured Division, 1941. Lieutenant-General commanding XXX Corps, Western Desert, 1941–2. Knighted, 1944. Head of British Military Mission to French Committee of National Liberation, 1944. Governor of South Australia, 1944–52. Governor of New Zealand, 1952–7. Created Baron, 1957.

[4] Isaac Pierre de Villiers, 1891–1967. Born in South Africa. Served in German South-West Africa and on the Western Front, 1914–18 (Military Cross). Commissioner of Police, South Africa, 1928–40. General Officer Commanding 2nd South African Infantry Division, 1940–2 (CB). Commanded Coastal Area Command, South Africa, 1942–5. Chairman of the Union of South Africa Immigration Selection Board, 1947–67.

you might like to stress it yourself. Will merely say Halfaya has fallen with so many prisoners etc.

Winston S. Churchill to General Claude Auchinleck
(Churchill papers, 20/68)

17 January 1942   10 Downing Street

Hearty congratulations on another brilliant and timely success.[1]

General Sir Alan Brooke:[2] diary
('War Diaries, Field Marshal Lord Alanbrooke', page 220)

17 January 1942

Usual COS meeting where we discovered that PM was flying through from Bermuda, and had landed Mount Batten at 9 a.m. After lunch went to Paddington to meet his special, due at 3 p.m. A queer crowd of Cabinet Ministers in black slouch sombreros and astrakhan collars to meet him! He arrived about 3.15 and was given a great welcome. Went back to WO[3] to find he was having a War Cabinet meeting which Chiefs of Staff were to attend at 6 p.m. This lasted till 7.30 p.m., and was very interesting as it contained a full account of the trip to America and his impressions.

War Cabinet: conclusions
(Cabinet papers, 65/25)

17 January 1942   10 Downing Street
6 p.m.

The Prime Minister gave the War Cabinet a general account of his visit to the United States. He, the Minister of Supply[4] and the Chiefs of

---

[1] Auchinleck replied on 18 January 1942: 'Thank you very much. Credit is due to Commanders and Troops on the spot and I will tell them' (*Churchill papers, 20/68*).

[2] Alan Francis Brooke, 1883–1963. Entered the Army, 1902. On active service, 1914–18 (DSO and bar, despatches six times). General Officer Commanding-in-Chief, Anti-Aircraft Command, 1939. Commanded II Army Corps, British Expeditionary Force, 1939–40. Knighted, 1940. General Officer Commanding-in-Chief, Home Forces, 1940–1. Chief of the Imperial General Staff, 1941–6. Field Marshal, 1944. Created Baron, 1945; Viscount Alanbrooke, 1946. Order of Merit, 1946. Master Gunner, St James's Park, 1946–56. His brother Victor, a fellow subaltern and close friend of Churchill in 1895–6, died from exhaustion on the retreat from Mons in 1914. Churchill was also a good friend of Brooke's brother Ronnie, whose Assistant Adjutant he was in South Africa for some months, and with whom he galloped into Ladysmith on the night of its liberation in 1900.

[3] War Office.

[4] Lord Beaverbrook.

Staff had been received throughout with the greatest kindness. He had lived on the closest personal terms with the President. The United States Administration were tackling war problems with the greatest vigour, and were clearly resolved not to be diverted from using all the resources of their country to the utmost to crush Hitler, our major enemy.

The Prime Minister gave an account of the general course of the discussions which had taken place. Among the most important results had been the decision to set up (1) a Combined Raw Materials Board, and (2) two Committees, one in London and one in Washington, to deal with munition assignments; (3) Anglo-American Shipping Adjustment Boards both in Washington and in London. The idea underlying all these bodies was that the resources of Great Britain and the United States were regarded as a common pool to be used for the prosecution of the war. A paper setting out particulars of these bodies would be circulated to the Cabinet for consideration at their meeting on Monday. It had been agreed that for the present no public announcement would be made in regard to these bodies, which would be subject to review in, say, a month's time, in the light of experience gained of their working.

There had been virtually no discussion in regard to the question of consideration under the Lease-Lend Agreement.

The Prime Minister said that he had taken the line that the question need not be settled as a matter of urgency, and that he had not been pressed on the point.

[...]

2. The Prime Minister suggested that at the meeting of the House on Tuesday, the 20th January, he should say that he would like further time to prepare his statement to the House, and that he hoped he would not be pressed to make a statement until Tuesday, the 27th January. There might then, he thought, be a debate of, say, two days' duration on the war situation.

The Joint Parliamentary Secretary to the Treasury[1] said that there might be some demand for a statement by the Prime Minister at an earlier date, but that this demand would probably be satisfied if a debate, extending for three days was offered. This suggestion was met with general approval.

[...]

[1] James Gray Stuart, 1897–1971. 3rd son of the 17th Earl of Moray. Educated at Eton. On active service, 1914–18 (Military Cross and bar). Conservative MP for Moray and Nairn, 1923–59. Entered the Whips' Office, 1935; Deputy Chief Whip, 1938–41; Government Chief Whip, 1941–5; Chief Opposition Whip 1945–8. Privy Councillor, 1939. Secretary of State for Scotland, 1951–7. Created Viscount, 1959.

4. The War Cabinet were informed that Halfaya had surrendered and 5,500 prisoners had been captured. Altogether, 14,000 prisoners had been taken in Bardia, Sollum and Halfaya at very slight loss to ourselves.

The Prime Minister asked that no comparative statement of the total casualties on both sides, since our offensive in the Western Desert had been started on the 18th November, should be published in advance of his statement on the 27th January.

OTHER POINTS TOUCHED ON IN THE DISCUSSION

The Prime Minister said that the President and Mrs Roosevelt[1] had throughout the visit shown him the greatest kindness and hospitality. He had lived on terms of the greatest intimacy with them. He had lunched everyday with the President, Mr Harry Hopkins being usually the only other person present.

Besides addressing Congress, he had attended a meeting of the United States Cabinet. On leaving, the President's last words to him had been 'Trust me to the bitter end'. An Olympian calm had obtained at the White House. It was perhaps rather isolated. The President had no adequate link between his will and executive action. There was no such organisation as the Secretariat of the Cabinet or of the Chiefs of Staff Committee. When the President saw the Ministerial heads of the Fighting Services, who were really little more than Private Secretaries and responsible to him only, meetings were quite informal. Although Mr Harry Hopkins lacked experience of military matters, his instincts were fundamentally sound, and he played a great part in helping the President to give effect to his policies.

[...]

The Prime Minister thought that there was little risk of the Americans abandoning the conventional principles of war. They were not above learning from us, provided that we did not set out to teach them.

The State Department was apt to be somewhat jumpy, and had been very much upset over the action taken by General de Gaulle at St Pierre and Miquelon.

The Americans were setting about the war with great vigour. Lord Beaverbrook had performed the most valuable service in getting them to extend greatly the production programmes which they had in mind.

---

[1] (Anna) Eleanor Roosevelt, 1884–1962. Married Franklin Roosevelt, 1905. United States Representative at the United Nations General Assembly, 1945–52. In 1950 she published *This I Remember* and in 1962 *The Autobiography of Eleanor Roosevelt.*

The fact that these programmes had now been published would provide a stimulus to their fulfilment.

The Prime Minister, in referring to the three instruments which had been prepared (dealing with munitions assignments, shipping and raw materials), said that the President had said that he did not much mind what appeared on papers, since he (the President), the Prime Minister, Mr Harry Hopkins and Lord Beaverbrook would be able to compose any difficulties which might arise.

The Prime Minister said that these Agreements were, in his view, wholly favourable to us. In practice, as we were already fully engaged in the war, our resources would not be drawn upon. In assessing the value of these instruments, regard should be had to the personalities behind them.

As regards the appointment of a Supreme Commander in the Far East, the Prime Minister said that at first he had been against the proposal, which had been strongly urged by General Marshall, who had made a great impression on him in a talk on the matter which had lasted for an hour. The suggestion that General Wavell should be appointed as Supreme Commander came from the Americans. The beneficial results of this appointment had already been seen. General Wavell's telegram since his arrival in Batavia had given the greatest confidence.

On the suggestion that an Australian Minister should have a seat in the War Cabinet, the Prime Minister said that he thought before this was considered, the Australians ought to lay aside their Party feud and set up a National Government.

Incidental reference was made to the request of Mr R. Stokes, MP,[1] to visit Turkey. In view of Mr Stokes' attitude, the view taken was that this request should be refused.

War Cabinet: Confidential Annex
(Cabinet papers, 65/29)

17 January 1942   10 Downing Street
6 p.m.

The Prime Minister said that the disaster at Pearl Harbour had had a great effect in the United States. They were resolved to settle matters finally with Japan. But they realised that the main pressure must be kept

---

[1] Richard Rapier Stokes, 1897–1957. On active service in the Royal Artillery, 1915–18 (Military Cross and bar). Unsuccessful Labour Parliamentary candidate, 1935. Labour MP for Ipswich from 1938 until his death. A persistent critic of the conduct of the war, 1940–5. Minister of Works, 1950–1; Minister of Materials, 1951.

on Germany. As a means to this end they were keen on the project of occupying the North and West Coast of Africa. He (the Prime Minister) had explained to them that our aim should be to marshal our forces, on a line Iceland – British Isles – North Africa, ready for an offensive in 1943. But it was clear that shipping was the limiting factor in any plans that were made.

The shortage of shipping would delay the move of US troops into Northern Ireland. Everything possible should be done for the comfort of the US troops; and, subject to such secrecy as to actual troop movements as was necessary for their safety, their arrival should be featured.

It would be useful to arrange for the US troops to take a turn at beach defence, a Brigade at a time.

As a result of events at Pearl Harbour, the United States had lost their naval supremacy. By the middle of February they would have 7 battleships in the Pacific. If the two new Japanese battleships were then serviceable, it was probable that two US 16″ capital ships,[1] now in the Atlantic, would be moved to the Pacific. If, however, they left these two ships in the Atlantic, it would be for consideration whether the two *Nelsons*,[2] when available, should be sent out to the Pacific.

As regards naval building programmes, the three new American battleships which had been scheduled for completion in 1943 had now been brought forward to 1942. A large number of auxiliary aircraft-carriers were to be improvised. Of the first 30 delivered, 15 were to be allotted to us.

Two columns of heavy bomber aircraft were now on their way to the Far East; the one, across Africa and India; the other, across the Pacific.

The Prime Minister said that he had been impressed by the American attitude towards China. They held General Chiang Kai-shek in considerable esteem, and they intended to assist him in raising and training a very large Chinese army. They were also keen on developing communications with China <u>via</u> the Burma Road. He (the Prime Minister) felt that we should look at the China problem from a wider angle than hitherto. At the back of the United States attitude was the fear that, unless we paid sufficient regard to China, there was the risk that she might make a separate peace. It would not be a long step from such a peace to a combined Asiatic movement.

The First Sea Lord said that the Chiefs of Staff had had many meetings with the two American Chiefs of Staff and with General Arnold,

---

[1] 16″: ships with 16-inch guns.

[2] Nelson class battleships. On 29 September 1943 the Italian instrument of surrender was signed on board HMS *Nelson* in Valetta Harbour, Malta, by Marshal Badoglio and General Eisenhower.

the head of the Army Air Staff. The secretarial arrangements for these meetings had been undertaken by our own staff. The Americans had as yet no central secretariat, but they were setting one up. It had been agreed that there should be meetings at least once a week of the Combined Chiefs of Staff, i.e., the US Chiefs of Staffs, and the representatives in Washington of the British Chiefs of Staff; and that the American and British Joint Planners should also work together. The Americans had realised the advantages of our system, and were prepared to work with it and through it.

As for the United States Navy, each of its Fleets had three Commanders-in-Chief, the President, Admiral King and the local Commander-in-Chief. The system had perhaps certain advantages, but was not one to which we were accustomed.

The Prime Minister had already mentioned the possibility of the two United States battleships now in the Atlantic being moved to the Pacific, but the Americans had agreed to two US 8″ cruisers being stationed in the Iceland area. We, on the other hand, had agreed to let them have 10 corvettes as they were very short of all small craft.

The War Cabinet took note of these statements.

Winston S. Churchill to Peter Fraser
(Churchill papers, 20/68)

17 January 1942   10 Downing Street
Most Secret and Personal

I am grateful to you for your telegram. I welcome as always the frank expression of your views with which, in the main, I am much in sympathy, and the well-balanced reasoning with which you have presented them to me.

2. I fully endorse the remarks in your opening paragraphs. The Government and people of New Zealand have always adopted a helpful and realist attitude to this war which, beginning in the narrow confines of Europe, has gradually spread over almost the entire world and is now at the doorstep of New Zealand.

3. If you have thought us unmindful of your necessities in the past, although indeed we have never been so, I can assure you that the vast distance in miles which separates London from Wellington will not cause us to be unmindful of you or leave you comfortless in your hour of peril.

4. You will I am sure forgive me if in the time at my disposal I do not take up each of your points in detail. From the telegram which you have now received since sending your telegram to me you will know of the army and air reinforcements which we and America are sending to you. The establishment of a new Anzac naval area will I hope also be agreeable to you.

Moreover, the United States contemplate the despatch at an early date of considerable land and air forces to the Far East area.

5. Nevertheless you would not expect me to make promises of support which cannot be fulfilled, or of the early redress of a situation in the Far East which must take time to rectify, as rectified it will be.

6. I sense your (corrupt group)[1] having been misled by a too complacent expression of military opinion in the past on probable dangers in the Pacific area in general and to New Zealand in particular. But who could have foretold the serious opening setback which the United States fleet suffered on the 7th of December, with all that this, and subsequent losses of our two fine ships, entail.

The events of this war have been consistently unpredictable, and not all to our advantage. I am not sure that the German general staff have always forecast events with unerring accuracy. For example, the Battle of Britain, the Battle of the Atlantic, and the Russian resistance must have shaken Hitler's faith in careful calculation of military appreciations.

7. Turning now to the strategic areas in the Pacific, you suggest that the establishment of the ABDA area under General Wavell is too narrow in conception, and should be extended to cover the whole Pacific and Indian Oceans.

Frankly, I find this idea more attractive in theory than, in my view, it could work out in practice, unless it were possible for the United States Navy Department and the British Admiralty, with the naval boards of Australia and New Zealand and of the Dutch Government, to be merged into one large United National Navy Department.

8. As at present arranged the United States Navy will have control in the Pacific, Anzac and, under General Wavell's general direction, the ABDA areas. This is no rigid line of responsibility and ensures that the predominant Allied Naval Power in the Pacific, i.e. the United States, exercises naval control in all three areas.

9. In establishing the ABDA areas, there was no intention to ignore or to starve the other Pacific areas, but to ensure a virile defence, and in due time offence, in the area which must bear the first shock of the

---

[1] 'Corrupt group': a phrase indicating words indecipherable in the telegram as received.

attack, and if held will secure vital lines of communication to Australia and New Zealand.

10. Our object, and in this I include all the ABDA powers, is to hold Singapore and to build up a fleet in the Pacific which will wrest naval control from the Japanese. All this is being worked out with the greatest despatch and in ceaseless consultation with our American allies.

11. I and my advisers have given much thought to the question of Dominion representation on our war councils, and in this connection I am not repetition not referring to the larger question of an Imperial War Cabinet. In considering this we have not been free agents. We have had to take into full account the views of the United States and Dutch Governments. It would be lamentable if, after appointing General Wavell to his great responsibilities, we were, at the same time, to impose controlling machine which, by its ponderous workings, would make rapid decisions virtually impossible. I am, however, entirely sympathetic to your feelings that New Zealand should have rightful place in framing of a major military policy in the Far East.

I have, therefore, suggested to my colleagues that a body should be formed in London with representatives on the ministerial plane of Australia, New Zealand and the Dutch governments to which major (?Pacific) problems, and in particular problems raised by General Wavell in accordance with his directive, would be referred. I would propose myself to preside over this body. Our view would of course have to be concerted with the President and the United States Staff in Washington. In the Staff sphere it has already been proposed that the service representatives of Australia and New Zealand and Dutch should be given expression in London.

12. I have had a preliminary report from General Wavell whom I expect to assume Supreme Command any day now. Whilst acknowledging the gravity of the present situation he takes a robust view of the final outcome and I am most anxious he should feel at the outset of his difficult task that he will receive our unstinted and united confidence.

Winston S. Churchill: recollection
('The Hinge of Fate', page 23)

17 January 1942   London

Immediately on my arrival, amid a surge of business, I was forced to prepare myself for a full-dress Parliamentary debate. The immense world events which had happened since I last addressed the House of Commons at length had now to be presented to the nation. From what I could see of the newspapers, to the reading of which I gave at least an hour a day, there was a rising swell of discontent and apprehension about our evident unreadiness to meet the Japanese onfall in the East and Far East. To the public the Desert battle seemed to be going well, and I was glad to lay the facts before the Parliament. I asked my colleagues to give me reasonable time.

General Sir Alan Brooke: diary
('War Diaries, Field Marshal Lord Alanbrooke', page 221)

18 January 1942

After a nice sleep and breakfast, a telephone call from PM saying he wanted me to dine with him tonight! So left home 5.30, motored back on snow covered roads to WO, where I got into picture as to latest wires and then went on to the Annexe at Storey's Gate.[1] Only Mrs Churchill and youngest daughter[2] for dinner. A very pleasant, quiet, homely dinner. He could not have been nicer. After dinner went to his study where I remained till after midnight discussing the possibilities of Singapore Island holding out. Also drew his attention to the danger of Rangoon.

Winston S. Churchill to General Hastings Ismay,
for the Chiefs of Staff Committee
(Churchill papers, 20/67)

18 January 1942   10 Downing Street

Please report what is being done to emulate the exploits of the Italians in Alexandria harbour and similar methods of this kind. At the begin-

---

[1] The Annexe: also known as 'No. 10 Annexe'; the above-ground quarters in the New Public Offices (now part of the Treasury) facing St James's Park, in which Churchill frequently worked, ate, and slept between October 1940 and May 1945, after 10 Downing Street had been damaged in a number of bombing raids on Whitehall in September and October 1940. The Annexe contained a map room, a dining room, a sitting room, a bathroom, a kitchen, Clementine Churchill's bedroom, Churchill's bedroom, Churchill's study, the Private Secretaries' room, a typists' room, and several offices, all above ground level, protected by metal shutters that could be closed during an air raid. Cabinet meetings were still held in Downing Street, except during bombing raids, when they were held underneath the Annexe, in the underground Central War Rooms (later known as the Cabinet War Rooms).

[2] Mary Churchill, 1922–. Churchill's youngest child. Served in the Second World War in the Red Cross and WVS, 1939–41; in the ATS, 1941–6. MBE (Military), 1945. Married Captain Christopher Soames, Coldstream Guards (later Baron Soames), 1947. Created DBE, 1980. Chairman, Royal National Theatre Board, 1989–95. Among her published books are *Clementine Churchill by her Daughter Mary Soames* (1979) and *A Daughter's Tale* (2011).

ning of the war Colonel Jefferis[1] had a number of bright ideas on this subject, which received very little encouragement. Is there any reason why we should be incapable of the same kind of scientific aggressive action that the Italians have shown? One would have thought we should have been in the lead.

Please state the exact position.[2]

Winston S. Churchill to Lord Moyne[3]
(Churchill papers, 20/67)

18 January 1942   10 Downing Street
Secret

It seems necessary to remove Sir Hubert Young[4] from Trinidad. The Americans have removed the offending General,[5] and we cannot have friction, which Young will, I am sure, cause.

I wonder, however, whether you could not find him employment at the Colonial Office. He is a Civil Servant of distinction, and would, I should think, be of great assistance to you in his proper setting.

[1] Millis Rowland Jefferis, 1899–1963. Joined the Royal Engineers, 1918. Major, 1939; that November he constructed a small floating mine to be used in rivers (for Churchill's 'Royal Marine' operation, mining the Rhine). Commanded 1st Field Squadron in Norway, April–May 1940, on sabotage duties (despatches). In charge of rocket and bomb experimentation, first under the War Office, then, from August 1940 until the end of the war, under Churchill's direct auspices. Responsible for, among other weapons, the scatter bomb, anti-tank mortars, the CLAM magnetic explosive device to attach to tanks and ships, and the PIAT hand-held anti-tank rocket. Promoted Lieutenant-Colonel, August 1940, at Churchill's specific request. Brigadier, 1942. CB, 1942. Knighted, 1945. Deputy Engineer-in-Chief, India, 1946. Engineer-in-Chief, Pakistan (with the rank of Major-General), 1947–50. Returned to England to become Chief Superintendent, Military Engineering experimental establishment, 1950–3.

[2] An Under Water Working Party (UWWP) was working at Gibraltar on a British 'human torpedo', the 'Chariot'. Trials were later held in Portsmouth, and then in Loch Cairnbawm, Scotland, for an attack on the *Tirpitz* in Trondheim Fjord. There were in all five 'Chariot' operations: against *Tirpitz* (1 November 1942), against Italian warships in Palermo harbour (2 January 1943, 18 January 1943 and May/June 1943) and against Italian liners at Phuket, near Penang, Malaya (27 October 1944).

[3] Secretary of State for the Colonies, 8 February 1941 to 22 February 1942.

[4] Hubert Winthrop Young, 1885–1950. 2nd Lieutenant, Royal Artillery, 1904. Transferred to Indian Army, 1908. Adjutant, 116th Mahrattas, 1913. Assistant Political Officer, Mesopotamia, 1915. Deputy Director, Local Resources Department, Mesopotamia, 1917. In March 1918, at the request of T. E. Lawrence, transferred to operations at Hedjaz, where he organized transport and supplies for the Arab forces. President of the Local Resources Board, Damascus, 1918. Major, 1919. Member of the Eastern Department of the Foreign Office, 1919–21. Assistant Secretary, Middle East Department, Colonial Office, 1921–6 (accompanying Churchill to the Cairo Conference). Colonial Secretary, Gibraltar, 1926–9. Counsellor for the High Commissioner, Iraq, 1929–32. Knighted, 1932. Minister to Baghdad, 1932. Governor and Commander-in-Chief, Nyasaland, 1932–4; Northern Rhodesia, 1934–8; Trinidad and Tobago, 1938–42. Unsuccessful Liberal Parliamentary candidate at the 1945 election.

[5] Brigadier-General Ralph Talbot Jr. Young was opposed to the hardships experienced by Trinidadians as a result of the agreement whereby Britain traded 99-year leases on bases in its colonies for American destroyers. The disagreements between Young and Talbot centred on where authority lay: with the British colonial governor or with the American general.

Winston S. Churchill to Sir Archibald Sinclair
(Churchill papers, 20/67)

18 January 1942   10 Downing Street

I hear you are in default of 45 aircraft for December for Russia, and that this will not be rectified until 25th January, and that the January quota will not be cleared until February.

It seems a very great pity to fall short in Russian deliveries by these comparatively small quantities which cannot affect your main problem here.

I must emphasise that exact and punctual deliveries to Russia are of the utmost importance, as this is all we can do to help them.

Winston S. Churchill to General Claude Auchinleck
(Churchill papers, 20/68)

18 January 1942   10 Downing Street
Personal

I think it quite likely that the remaining Australian division will move to the Far Eastern theatre as soon as transport is available. It would be natural to place the Australians together and in their home theatre. I myself suggested the beginning of this movement which was justified by the new war against Japan and the great improvement on the Southern Russian front. At the same time, in all my talks with the President and General Marshall, I have emphasised the importance of the Levant–Caspian front. The question of basing an American Army on the Persian Gulf ports is receiving favourable attention. Indeed it was from American sources that this proposal was first made to me. There is a genuine desire in high quarters at Washington to bring the largest number of United States troops into action against the Germans at the earliest moment. There is no lack of troops. The limiting factor in 1942 is of course shipping.

2. The President is placing four American divisions, including one armoured, in Northern Ireland as quickly as possible. The movement began on January 15 and should be completed in two months. These troops will also take part in defence of Great Britain. The name of this Operation[1] will be imparted to you in a separate telegram which should be read with this telegram. Additional American forces will take over

---

[1] 'Magnet'.

Iceland in considerable strength, and I have urged their training in ski work with a view to the future. The above moves would enable us, subject to the limitations of shipping, to send you British Divisions to replace some or all of those which have been or are to be diverted from your Command to the Far East.

3. The President is very much set on 'Gymnast', which with American participation will be called 'Super-Gymnast'. For this, owing to the need of large movements of American Air Force ground personnel to the Far East, it is now said that May will be the earliest date for strong combined operations. We are trying to reduce this date by more stringent use of United States shipping. The President is therefore deeply interested in 'Acrobat', and there is no need to delay it in any way. Indeed I feel it is going to be a harder job than we anticipated. Should the success of 'Acrobat' or any other cause precipitate a crisis in the 'Gymnast' area, an Operation is being prepared by the British and American Staffs which pre-supposes French co-operation instead of French opposition. The name of this Operation will be contained in a separate telegram, reference being made to this para. 3.[1]

4. The Americans are fully impressed with the idea that Germany is the main enemy, and there is no intention to sacrifice any profitable operation against Germany for the sake of a Far Eastern offensive. Nevertheless, should the battle for the approaches to Singapore turn in our favour, which is by no means certain, it will be advisable to drive the enemy from the Malay Peninsula, as his presence there will be just as costly in troops as a counterstroke. Very considerable American Air forces are being moved into the Far Eastern theatre. By May, superior naval strength should once again be gathered in the Pacific.

5. I do not intend to make a statement to the House before Tuesday, January 27. There is therefore no reason why your Cairo communiqué should not dilate upon solid and highly profitable character of your success in clearing up the Bardia Halfaya pockets entailing such heavy losses to the enemy. I should be glad however, if the general statement of profit and loss and casualties on both sides could be left to me. Let me have the latest figures up to say January 23 or 24, together with any other information about material or about the general course of the campaign which you think may be of interest. I have of course followed it with the closest attention day by day but I shall wish to do full justice to the splendid achievements of the Desert Army.

[1] The name chosen for the North African landings with French co-operation (which never took place) was 'Semi-Gymnast'.

Henry Channon: diary
('Chips', page 317)

18 January 1942   5 Belgrave Square

The newspapers splash the Prime Minister's return and his welcome, and all my agents report that he will defy, or at least forestall his critics, by playing for time; he will ask the indulgence of the House and plead pressure of work, etc., before making any important statement. A wise course. Probably he is unaware how great the prevailing anxiety in political circles is.

Winston S. Churchill to John Curtin
(Churchill papers, 20/68)

19 January 1942   10 Downing Street
Personal and Most Secret

I thank you for your frank expression of views. I have no responsibility for the neglect of our defenses and policy of appeasement which preceded the outbreak of the war. I had been for eleven years out of office, and had given ceaseless warnings for six years before the war began. On the other hand, I accept the fullest responsibility for the main priorities and general distribution of our resources since I became Prime Minister in May 1940. The eastward flow of reinforcements and aircraft from this Island has been maintained from that date forward to the utmost limit of our shipping capacity and other means of moving aircraft and tanks. I deemed the Middle East a more urgent theatre than the new-christened ABDA area. We had also to keep our promises to Russia of munitions deliveries. No one could tell what Japan would do, but I was sure that if she attacked us and you the United States would enter the war and that the safety of Australia and ultimate victory would be assured.

2. It must be remembered that only three months ago we faced in the Middle East, where the Australian Imperial Force lay, the threat of a double attack by Rommel from the west and the overrunning of the Caucasus, Persia, Syria, and Iraq from the north. In such a plight all the teachings of war show that everything should be concentrated on destroying one of the attacking forces. I thought it best to make a job of Rommel while forming with the rest of our resources the best Levant–Caspian front possible. This latter was largely beyond our resources. Since then two-thirds of Rommel's army has been destroyed, and Cyrenaica cleared,

but only by a very narrow margin. In fact it hung in the balance at the moment when Auchinleck rightly superseded Cunningham.

3. Although I cannot promise total destruction of Rommel, we have at least gained a very substantial success, which has already rid us of one serious danger and liberated important forces. At the same time the tremendous, unexpected resistance of Russia has given a considerable breathing-space, and it may be more, on the Levant–Caspian front. Thus we are able to move the 17th Indian Division and soon several other Indian infantry divisions previously assigned to the Levant–Caspian front, together with the 18th British and the 7th and 8th Australian Divisions, with substantial aircraft and some armoured forces, from the Middle East to the Far Eastern theatre. This we are doing with all speed. You may judge how melancholy our position would have been if we had been beaten by Rommel, and if the Caucasus, the Baku oil-wells, and Persia had been overrun by the enemy. I am sure it would have been wrong to send forces needed to beat Rommel to reinforce the Malay Peninsula while Japan was still at peace. To try to be safe everywhere is to be strong nowhere.

4. We have to be thankful, first, for the Russian victories, secondly, for our good success against Rommel, and thirdly, that the United States was attacked by Japan at the same time as ourselves. The blame for the frightful risks we have had to run and will have to run rests with all those who, in or out of office, failed to discern the Nazi menace and to crush it while it was weak.

5. No one could foresee the series of major naval disasters which befell us and the United States around the turn of the year 1941–42. In an hour the American naval superiority in the Pacific was for the time being swept away. In another hour the *Prince of Wales* and *Repulse* were sunk. Thus the Japanese gained the temporary command of Pacific waters and no doubt we have further grievous punishment to face in the Far East. In this new crisis affecting you, I should have approved the sending of the three fast Mediterranean battleships to form, with the four 'R's' and the *Warspite*, just repaired, a new fleet in the Indian Ocean, to move to your protection as might be most helpful.

6. I have already told you of the *Barham* being sunk. I must now inform you that the *Queen Elizabeth* and *Valiant* have both sustained underwater damage from a human torpedo which put them out of action, one for three and the other for six months.[1] As the enemy do

---

[1] On the 'human torpedo' attacks in Alexandria harbour, see note on page 50 above.

not yet know about these three last-mentioned ships, you will see that we have no need to enlighten them, and I must ask you to keep this last deadly secret to yourself alone.

7. However, these evil conditions will pass. By May the United States will have a superior fleet at Hawaii. We have encouraged them to take their two new battleships out of the Atlantic if they need them, thus taking more burden upon ourselves. We are sending two and possibly three out of our four modern aircraft-carriers to the Indian Ocean. *Warspite* will soon be there and thereafter *Valiant*. Thus the balance of sea-power in the Indian and Pacific Oceans will in the absence of further misfortunes turn decisively in our favour, and all Japanese overseas operations will be deprived of their present assurance. Meanwhile we are trying to make up by air-power in the Mediterranean for our lack of a battle-fleet and the impending arrival of *Anson* and complete working up of *Duke of York* enable us to face large reductions in American strength in the Atlantic for the sake of the Pacific.

8. We must not be dismayed or get into recrimination but remain united in true comradeship. Do not doubt my loyalty to Australia and New Zealand. I cannot offer any guarantees for the future and I am sure great ordeals lie before us, but I feel hopeful as never before that we shall emerge safely and also gloriously, from the dark valley.

Winston S. Churchill to General Hastings Ismay,
for the Chiefs of Staff Committee
(Churchill papers, 20/67)

19 January 1942   10 Downing Street

I must confess to being staggered by this[1] and other telegrams on the same subject. It never occurred to me for a moment nor to Sir John Dill, with whom I discussed the matter on the outward voyage, that the gorge of the fortress of Singapore with its splendid moat half-a-mile to a mile wide was not entirely fortified against an attack from the northward. What is the use of having an island for a fortress [if] it is not to be made into a citadel? To construct a line of detached works with searchlights and cross-fire combined with immense wiring and obstruction of the swamp areas and to provide the proper ammunition to enable the fortress guns

---

[1] Telegram 'Abdacom 00118' of 19 January 1942, reporting on the lack of defences on the north side of Singapore Island.

to dominate enemy batteries planted in Johore, was an elementary peace-time provision which it is incredible did not exist in a fortress which has been twenty years building. If this was so, how much more should the necessary field works have been constructed during the two and a half years of the present war? How is it that not one of you pointed this out to me at any time when these matters have been under discussion? More especially should this have been done because in my various minutes extending over the last two years I have repeatedly shown that I relied upon this defence of Singapore Island against a formal siege, and have never relied upon the Kra Isthmus plan. In England at the present time we have found it necessary to protect the gorges of all our forts against a landing raid from the rear, and the Portsdown Hill forts at Portsmouth show the principles which have long prevailed.

2. Another case where you all seem to have been misinformed by all the Joint Planners and Joint Intelligence Committees is on the state of the terrain between Singora and Johore. I was repeatedly informed at the time of the Japanese landing that owing to the season of the year the ground was so water-logged that there could be no question of an advance southward in force until the spring. Pray look this up and find out who and what was the foundation for this opinion, so violently falsi-fied by events. It is most disquieting to me that such frightful ignorance of the conditions should have prevailed.

3. Seaward batteries and a naval base do not constitute a fortress, which is a <u>completely encircled</u> strong place. Merely to have seaward batteries and no fort or fixed defences to protect their rear is not to be excused on any ground. By such neglect the whole security of the fortress has been at the mercy of 10,000 men breaking across the Straits in small boats. I warn you this will be one of the greatest scandals that could possibly be exposed.

4. Let a plan be made at once to do the best possible while the battle in Johore is going forward. This plan should comprise:

(a) An attempt to use the fortress guns on the northern front by firing reduced charges and by running in a certain quantity of HE if none exists.

(b) By mining and obstructing the landing-places where any consid-erable force could gather.

(c) By wiring and laying booby traps in mangrove swamps and other places.

(d) By constructing field works and strong points with field artillery and machine-gun crossfire.

(e) By collecting and taking under our control every conceivable small boat that is found in the Johore Straits or anywhere else within reach.

(f) By planting field batteries at each end of the Straits carefully masked and with searchlights, so as to destroy any enemy boat that may seek to enter the Straits.

(g) By forming the nuclei of three or four mobile counter-attack reserve columns upon which the troops when driven out of Johore can be formed.

(h) The entire male population should be employed upon constructing defence works. The most rigorous compulsion is to be used, up to the limit where picks and shovels are available.

(i) Not only must the defence of Singapore Island be maintained by every means, but the whole Island must be fought for until every single Unit and every single strong point has been separately destroyed.

(j) Finally, the city of Singapore must be converted into a citadel and defended to the death. No surrender can be contemplated, and the Commander, Staffs and principal Officers are expected to perish at their posts.

Lord Ismay: recollection
(*'The Memoirs of General The Lord Ismay'*, pages 246–7)

[19 January 1942]

From my earliest youth, 19 January had always been rather a special date in my calendar as the anniversary of my mother's birthday. In 1942 it was a very dark day. When I reported to the Prime Minister in the morning, I found him in a towering rage. Why had I not told him that there were no defences on the north side of Singapore island? Before I could protest that he must have been misinformed, he thrust into my hand a telegram from Wavell reporting that little or nothing had been done in the way of constructing defences to prevent the crossing of the Johore Straits. I could scarcely believe my eyes. The Prime Minister continued: 'You were with the Committee of Imperial Defence for several years before the war broke out. You must have known the position. Why did you not warn me?' I was tempted to explain that the Committee of Imperial Defence had concerned themselves solely with the installation of heavy guns at Singapore to meet sea-borne attack, and with the period for which the fortress must be prepared to hold out until relief came, and that it had been taken for granted that the commanders on the spot would see to the local defences against land attack from the north. But I remained silent. What did my own feelings matter when so ghastly and humiliating a disaster loomed ahead?

The next few weeks were a hideous nightmare.[1]

Winston S. Churchill to Anthony Eden and the Chiefs of Staff Committee
(Churchill papers, 20/67)

19 January 1942   10 Downing Street
Action this Day

About Timor. We should say to the Portuguese Government that we are guarding Timor until their reinforcements arrive. Nevertheless, when they do arrive, we should not go. We should leave our troops, the Dutch troops and their troops all on the spot. The Portuguese are obviously not capable of protecting their neutrality, and Timor is a key-point. General Wavell should be authorized to take all necessary steps for the military security of Timor, regardless of the effects produced on Portuguese pride. There is no need to raise the question yet with the Portuguese Government, as we have several weeks (how many?) before the Portuguese troops can arrive.[2]

Winston S. Churchill to General Archibald Wavell
(Churchill papers, 20/68)

19 January 1942   10 Downing Street
Personal

Your 00048 to which President has given approval caused some perturbation to American Chiefs of Staff, who thought that by not taking over Philippines you were cutting the loss and giving up all hope. You have no doubt seen their reaction which seems quite reasonable. I hope you will be able to assure President that you are taking over the whole show as desired, it being clearly understood that you can only do your best.

---

[1] Singapore surrendered on 15 February 1942, Java on March 8, Rangoon on March 10.

[2] Japanese forces invaded the part-Dutch, part-Portuguese island of Timor on 20 February 1942. After three days of fighting, most of the Australian and Royal Netherlands troops were forced to surrender, as were the small numbers of British, American, and Portuguese (the last being volunteers, as Portugal remained neutral). Several hundred Australian troops continued to fight a guerrilla war, supplied by air from Darwin, 400 miles to the south-east. The last Australian troops were evacuated on 10 February 1943.

Winston S. Churchill to Lord Camrose[1]
(Churchill papers, 20/68)

19 January 1942   10 Downing Street
Personal

Have read with so much pleasure your series of leading articles in the *Daily Telegraph*.[2] Stop. Hope to see you soon.

Winston

General Archibald Wavell to Winston S. Churchill
(Churchill papers, 20/68)

19 January 1942   Batavia[3]
Private and Most Secret

Officer whom I had sent to Singapore for plans of defence of island has now returned. Schemes are now being prepared for defence northern part of island. Number of troops required to hold island effectively probably are great or greater than number (4 groups missing) Johore. I have ordered Percival to fight out the battle in Johore but to work out plans to prolong resistance on island as long as possible should he lose Johore battle. I must warn you however that I doubt whether island can be held for long once Johore is lost. Fortress guns sited for use against ships and have mostly (?ammunition) for that purpose only, many can only fire sea-wards. Part of garrison has already been sent into Johore and many troops remaining are of doubtful value. I am sorry to give you depressing picture but I do not want you to have false picture of island fortress. Singapore defences were constructed entirely to meet seaward attack. I still hope Johore may be held till next convoy arrives.[4]

---

[1] William Ewart Berry, 1879–1954. Newspaper proprietor. Founder of *Advertising World*, 1901. Editor-in-Chief of the *Sunday Times*, 1915–36. Chairman, Financial Times Ltd, 1919–45; Allied Newspapers Ltd, 1924–36. Created Baron Camrose, 1929. Chief Proprietor and Editor-in-Chief of the *Daily Telegraph* and *Morning Post*, 1936–54. Principal Adviser, Ministry of Information, 1939. Created Viscount, 1941. One of Churchill's close friends (elected to the Other Club in 1926), and from 1945 a principal financial adviser; in 1946, he negotiated both the sale of Churchill's war memoirs and also the purchase of Chartwell by a group of Churchill's friends and its conveyance to the National Trust (Camrose himself contributing £15,000 and 16 other friends £5,000 each).

[2] A series of leading articles in the *Daily Telegraph* defending London's military policy in the face of the disastrous turn of events in the Far East.

[3] Wavell had taken up his headquarters at Batavia (now North Jakarta), then the capital of the Netherlands East Indies.

[4] Johore held out until 31 January 1942.

War Cabinet: Confidential Annex
(Cabinet papers, 65/29)

19 January 1942   10 Downing Street
6 p.m.

The Chief of the Imperial General Staff and the Chief of the Air Staff reported on the military and air reinforcements now arriving in Malaya and Burma, and due to arrive there during the remainder of January and February.

The First Sea Lord reported on the convoy arrangements for these reinforcements.

The Chief of the Imperial General Staff said that, following upon General Wavell's decisions, the front in Malaya was being re-organised. In Burma the situation appeared to be developing unfavourably. There were pockets of Japanese in the neighbourhood of Tavoy, Mergui and Moulmein. The situation of the American forces in Luzon appeared precarious. In Mindanao the situation was better, although there was a shortage of small arms ammunition. There had been Japanese landings on both the east and west coasts of Dutch Borneo, and on the northern promontory of the Celebes.

The Prime Minister emphasised the importance of maintaining the Burma Road in operation. It should also be made clear that it was the duty of the Singapore garrison to hold out to the last, should military resistance in Johore collapse.

The Prime Minister said that he was prepared to take upon himself the full responsibility for the political decisions which had governed the size of our forces in Malaya at the outbreak of hostilities with Japan. There were, however, certain matters connected with the defence of Malaya which called for inquiry. He instanced the following:

(1) On several occasions our forces had been out-flanked by Japanese landings on the west coast. Our Naval forces had failed to stop this, although it was believed that the enemy had moved his troops along the coast in small, unarmed vessels.

(2) He wished to be assured that the defence plans for the Naval Base at Singapore, and for Singapore Island, made adequate defence for the following:

      (a) Obtaining control of all small craft, which might other-wise fall into enemy hands, and their destruction when necessary.

      (b) The destruction of any small craft attempting to cross the straits between the mainland of Johore and Singapore Island.

Had batteries for this purpose been installed at each end of the straits?

(c) What steps were being taken to extend the ground defences to the landward side of the fortress?

(d) Had a complete scheme of demolitions, covering all the objects of military importance, been drawn up? How far had the preparations for carrying out this scheme, if need arose, advanced?

(e) Was the water supply secure?

(3) What progress had been made in evacuating <u>bouches inutiles</u> from Singapore? If a siege was likely, it was important to reduce the size of the population, both European and Asiatic, before the fortress was invested.

The Chiefs of Staff were invited to submit a Report on these matters.

Winston S. Churchill to General Archibald Wavell
(Churchill papers, 20/68)

20 January 1942   10 Downing Street
Immediate

Now that you have become Supreme Commander of the ABDA nations in the South Western Pacific I cannot of course send you any direct instructions. All your operative orders which I hope will be as few as possible will come through the combined COS Committee from the President at Washington. Nevertheless I propose to continue our correspondence whenever I have suggestions to make or questions to ask. This will be especially the case where the local defence of a fortress like Singapore is involved. It is in this light that you must view the telegram sent you today by the COS Committee about the landward defence of Singapore Island. I was greatly distressed by your No. 00079 of 16/1 and No. 00018 of 19/1 and I want to make it absolutely clear that I expect every inch of ground to be defended, every scrap of material or defences to be blown to pieces to prevent capture by the enemy and no question of surrender to be entertained until after protracted fighting among the ruins of Singapore City.

House of Commons: Oral Answers
(Hansard)

20 January 1942   House of Commons

HOUSE OF COMMONS SPEECHES
(ELECTRICAL RECORDING)

Captain Plugge[1] asked the Prime Minister whether he will consider making arrangements for the broadcasting of important speeches made in the House of Commons, in view of the fact that such arrangements were made in connection with the most recent speeches by the British Prime Minister to Congress in Washington and in the Canadian House of Commons?

The Prime Minister (Mr Churchill): I have considered this matter long and carefully and also with diffidence, as to some extent at the present time it affects myself. It certainly would be a very great convenience, and would, I believe, be welcomed by the public, if an electrical record of major statements about the war could be made. This record could be used for subsequent broadcasting, which might be deemed an advantage. In my own case I have been constantly asked to repeat the speech I have delivered in the House over the broadcast later. This imposes a very heavy strain, and is, moreover, unsatisfactory from the point of view of delivery.

It has been represented to me that in the Dominions and in the United States there are very large numbers of people who would like to listen to a record of the actual speech or parts of it rather than to a news summary, such as are usually compiled – very well compiled – by the British Broadcasting Corporation. Moreover, such a record could be used at the most convenient hours in the various countries concerned, which now encircle the entire globe. I should hope, therefore, that the House might be disposed from time to time to grant me or any successor I may have during the war this indulgence. As an innovation of this kind in our practice should be most carefully watched, I should

---

[1] Leonard Frank Plugge, 1889–1981. On active service, Lieutenant, Royal Naval Volunteer Reserve, 1917; Captain, Royal Air Force, 1918. Department of Scientific Research, Air Ministry, 1918. Inter-Allied Aeronautical Commission of Control, Berlin, 1919. Member of the General Committee, Radio Society of Great Britain, 1923–5. Created International Broadcasting Company, 1931, as a commercial rival to the BBC, buying air time from radio stations in France, Italy, and Spain (the first station on which he broadcast to Britain was Radio Normandy, transmitting from Fecamp). Conservative MP for Chatham, 1935–45. Chairman of the Parliamentary Science Committee, 1939–43. Scientist, writer, painter, and sculptor, and inventor; among his inventions was a two-way radio telephone for use in cars.

propose that an experiment should be made in the case of the statement I have been asked to make at an early opportunity upon the present war situation. There must necessarily be in this statement a good deal that is of some interest both in America and Australasia as well as in India and South Africa. A Motion will, therefore, be placed on the Paper for discussion allowing this procedure to be followed on this particular occasion only. As a separate Motion will be required in each individual case, the House would have full control of the practice; and if it were found to be objectionable or invidious or not in the public interest, it could be dropped. Evidently the practice would not be suitable to periods of Party Government.

The record would be the property of this House and its use, in the event of any controversy arising, would be a matter for decision by the House under Mr Speaker's guidance. As this is a matter which affects the customs of the House, I shall leave the decision to a free Vote.

Sir Hugh O'Neill:[1] I take it that my right hon. Friend did not mean that he would actually broadcast to the public while making his speech? (Hon. Member: 'No'.) In any case is it not a fact that the main function of this House is debate and criticism, and if the practice of broadcasting is to be adopted, or possibly even taking records of *ex-parte* statements by the Prime Minister or anybody else, ought not replies to these speeches to be similarly recorded?

Mr Hore-Belisha:[2] While I recognise, of course, the great importance of my right hon. Friend's statements and the keen and appreciative desire of the public to hear him, will he bear in mind that Parliament, of its nature, is not a platform but a representative Assembly intended to express the whole will of the nation? Will he, therefore, see that any account that is given of the proceedings of Parliament will be impartial and unbiased and will give expression to all points of view? Before the House is committed to this course and before the Motion is put down,

[1] Robert William Hugh O'Neill, 1883–1982. Ulster Unionist MP for Mid-Antrim, 1915–22; County Antrim, 1922–50; North Antrim, 1950–2. On active service, France and Palestine, 1915–18. Created Baronet, 1929. First Speaker of the House of Commons for Northern Ireland, 1921–9; MP for County Antrim in the Parliament of Northern Ireland, 1921–9. Parliamentary Under-Secretary of State for India and Burma, 1939–40. Created Baron Rathcavan, 1953. His son Con O'Neill, a diplomat, was one of those who interrogated Rudolf Hess in 1941.

[2] Leslie Hore-Belisha, 1893–1957. Known, on account of his Jewish origins, as 'Horeb Elisha'. His father, an Army officer, died when he was nine months old. Educated at Clifton and St John's College, Oxford. On active service in France, 1915–16, and at Salonika, 1916–18. President of the Oxford Union, 1919. Liberal MP for Plymouth Devonport, 1923–42; National Liberal from 1931; Independent 1942–5. Parliamentary Secretary, Board of Trade, 1931–2. Financial Secretary, Treasury, 1932–4. Minister of Transport, 1934–7 (with seat in Cabinet from October 1936). Privy Councillor, 1935. Secretary of State for War, 1937–40 (Member of War Cabinet, 1939–40). Minister of National Insurance, 1945. Created Baron, 1954.

would it not be possible to appoint a Committee under your aegis, Mr Speaker, to consider this proposal in all its implications?

Captain Plugge: While I thank my right hon. Friend for his reply, does he think it right that the British listening public should be granted, through the BBC, facilities for listening to an Allied Prime Minister in an Allied Parliament such as a President of the United States in Congress, yet be denied the same facilities for listening to their own Prime Minister in their own Parliament?

Sir William Davison:[1] Are we not right in thinking, from the statement of the Prime Minister, that this would be a purely exceptional war measure when all parties are united under his leadership and that it is not intended to be a precedent for the broadcasting of ordinary matters of party politics?

Mr Shinwell: Who said so?

Mr Thorne:[2] Will the Prime Minister consider the advisability of having the speech he made in Canada printed for circulation?

Commander Sir Archibald Southby:[3] Will my right hon. Friend bear in mind that the two speeches to which the Question refers were not made in the course of Debate, whereas any speech made by my right hon. Friend in this House must be made in the course of Debate and may be criticised by Members of this House, whose criticism may be divorced from his speech?

Mr Mander:[4] Is it the intention that the whole speech, with any interruption which might occur, would be recorded just as it is made, or would there be editing by Mr Speaker or anybody else?

[1] William Henry Davison, 1872–1953. Company director, connected with several educational foundations. Chairman of the Improved Industrial Dwellings Company and the East Surrey Water Company. President of the Kensington Chamber of Commerce. Mayor of Kensington, 1913–19. Raised and equipped two battalions for territorial service, 1914. Knighted, 1918. Conservative MP for Kensington South, 1918–45. Chairman of the Metropolitan Division of the National Union of Conservative Associations, 1928–30. Created Baron Broughshane, 1945.

[2] Will Thorne, 1857–1946. Began work at the age of six, in a barber's shop. Founder member of the National Union of General and Municipal Workers, 1889; General Secretary, 1889–1934. CBE, 1930. Member of West Ham Town Council from 1890 until his death. Labour MP for West Ham, 1906–45.

[3] Archibald Richard James Southby, 1886–1969. Entered the Royal Navy as a cadet, 1901; Lieutenant, 1908. Served in the Grand Fleet and on the North America and West Indian Station, 1913–18. Member of the Naval Armistice Commission, 1918–19; the Naval Inter-Allied Commission of Control, 1919–20. Commander, 1920. Conservative MP for Epsom, 1928–47. Assistant Government Whip, 1931–5. Junior Lord of the Treasury, 1935–7. Created Baronet, 1937. Member of Parliamentary Delegation to Buchenwald Concentration Camp, April 1945.

[4] Geoffrey Le Mesurier Mander, 1882–1962. Head of Mander Bros, paint and varnish manufacturers. Liberal MP, 1929–45. A leading Parliamentary critic of the Munich Agreement, 1938. Parliamentary Private Secretary to the Secretary of State for Air (Sir Archibald Sinclair), 1942–5. Knighted, 1945. Joined the Labour Party, 1948.

The Prime Minister: The idea is that a record should be made for subsequent use. This would be convenient because of the great difference in time between this country and the United States, Australasia, India, South Africa and so forth. I also have the feeling that in the circumstances of this war, when matters have to be spoken of which intimately affect many of our Dominions and Allies, there might be advantages in taking this course. But I am entirely in the hands of the House. If they do not feel they can give me this easement on this occasion as an experiment, I shall not take it amiss in any way, and I will do my best over the broadcast that evening to repeat what I have said.

Mr Hore-Belisha: Would my right hon. Friend consider the proposal I have made, which is not made in any way to hamper? Would he appoint some small representative committee of experienced Members of this House who might consider all the implications and various difficulties which might arise – for instance, the difficulties of interruptions?

The Prime Minister: No, Sir, I am leaving it to the House. I think the House is quite as competent as any particular group of individuals to consider this matter. I dealt myself very carefully with the question of the records. It would be a matter for decision by the House, under Mr Speaker's guidance, as to whether anything should be left out or should not be reproduced – for instance, if anything was said which revealed a military secret. This is now removed from the published records, and similar latitude would be provided for in this case. I do not propose to adopt the right hon. Gentleman's suggestion.

House of Commons: Oral Answers
(Hansard)

20 January 1942   House of Commons

INDIA CONSTITUTION

Dr Russell Thomas[1] asked the Prime Minister what reply he has given to the suggestions recently made to him by Sir Tej Bahadur Sapru,[2] and

---

[1] William Stanley Russell Thomas, 1896–1957. Surgeon Sub-Lieutenant, Royal Naval Volunteers, Northern Patrol, 1915–18. Member of the Council of the National Liberal Party, 1937–40. National Liberal MP for Southampton, 1940–5. Member of the Executive Committee of the British–American Parliamentary Committee, 1942–5.

[2] Tej Bahadur Sapru, 1875–1949. Member of the United Provinces Legislative Council, 1913–16. Member of the Imperial Legislative Council, 1916–20. Law Member of the Viceroy's Council, 1920–3. Knighted, 1923. President of the Indian Liberal Federation. Member of the All India Congress Committee, 1927–8. Represented the Government of India at the Imperial Conference,

other distinguished Indian leaders, in regard to the government of India?

Mr G Macdonald[1] asked the Prime Minister whether it has been possible for him to formulate his reply to the appeal made to him by a group of distinguished Indian leaders; and whether he is prepared to state the terms of his reply?

The Prime Minister: The communication referred to only reached me at the moment of my departure from the United States, and I could do no more than send an acknowledgement. I will, however, give careful attention to the suggestions which are made, and will thereafter send an answer in terms which can be made public.

Mr Macdonald: While appreciating that any good military strategy in the Far East at present may be nullified by political strategy which is not equally as good, does the right hon. Gentleman realise that this question of India is arousing great interest throughout this country and other countries, and will he see that there is no delay whatever in dealing with the problem of the maximum war effort from India?

The Prime Minister: That is always my desire, but I am not sure that the raising of far-reaching constitutional issues at this time, when the enemy is so near the gates of India, would be advantageous to the war effort.

Mr Macdonald: Does not the right hon. Gentleman realise that any delay over this question, in view of the present situation in India, may do more harm than good to the war effort?

House of Commons: Oral Answers
(Hansard)

20 January 1942   House of Commons

HONG KONG DEFENCE

Mr Thorne asked the Prime Minister what undertakings were given at the Washington Conference, 1921, by the British Government with regard to not making Hong Kong a first-class fortress; and why, in these

London, 1923. An Indian Delegate at the London Round Table Conferences of 1930, 1931, and 1932. Privy Councillor, 1934.

[1] Gordon Macdonald, 1888–1966. Began working underground in the coal mines at the age of 13. Labour MP for Ince, 1929–42. Chairman of Committees, House of Common, 1939–41. Resigned from Parliament, July 1942. Knighted, 1946. Governor of Newfoundland (then a Dominion), 1946–9 (when Newfoundland formed a confederation with Canada). Privy Councillor, 1951. National Governor, BBC for Wales, 1952–60.

circumstances, was an attempt made to defend Hong Kong under conditions which led to the eventual surrender of the garrison?[1]

The Prime Minister: Under Article 19 of the Washington Treaty of Limitation of Naval Armaments of 6th February, 1922, the United States of America, the British Empire, and Japan agreed to maintain the *status quo* with regard to fortifications and naval bases in the United States of America, the British Empire and Japanese insular territories and possessions in the Pacific Oceans. The Japanese Government denounced the Treaty on 29th December, 1934, and by virtue of that denunciation the Treaty lapsed on 31st December, 1936. Until the latter date, therefore, His Majesty's Government were precluded from erecting additional fortifications at Hong Kong. As regards the second part of the Question, it is the policy of His Majesty's Government that British territory should be defended to the utmost of our ability with such resources as are at our disposal.

Mr Noel-Baker:[2] Was sufficient effort made to fortify Hong Kong after the Japanese denounced the Treaty in 1934?

The Prime Minister: That is going back to the year 1936, and I cannot without notice say what steps were taken by the Government of those days, but I think it always has been obvious that the position of Hong Kong would become very precarious, lying as it does so near to the homeland of Japan, in the event of war with that country.

Henry Channon: diary
('Chips', page 317)

20 January 1942

At the House the Prime Minister arrived and was given a cheer, though hardly could his welcome be called enthusiastic – civil, perhaps. He looked fat and cross, and when he rose to answer his questions it was

---

[1] The Battle of Hong Kong (8–25 December 1941) began about eight hours after the attacks on Pearl Harbor. Allied (British, Canadian, and India) forces were outnumbered by Imperial Japanese about four to one; they had only five aircraft, and two out of three destroyers were ordered to Singapore. The Governor of Hong Kong formally surrendered on Christmas Day.

[2] Philip John Noel-Baker, 1889–1982. A Quaker; First Commandant, Friends Ambulance Unit, France, 1914–15 (subsequently on the Italian front). League of Nations Secretariat, 1919–22; active in publicising and supporting the work of the League of Nations. Labour MP for Coventry, 1929–31; for Derby, 1936–70. Parliamentary Secretary, Ministry of War Transport, 1942–5. Secretary of State for Air, 1946–7; for Commonwealth Relations, 1947–50. British delegate to the United Nations Preparatory Commission, 1945; member of the British Delegation to the UN General Assembly, 1946–7. Minister of Fuel and Power, 1950–1. Nobel Peace Prize, 1959. Created Baron, 1977.

obvious that he was disappointed with his reception, and that he had a cold, since his voice was husky. Such was the reappearance of the great hero, and I was almost sorry for him. ... He has announced that he will make a broadcast speech next Tuesday, and the House took his suggestion ungraciously; indeed, Members were querulous but I remembered Rab's[1] words last night at dinner when he warned us that Churchill is the greatest asset the Conservative Party has, and we had best exploit him. Rab said many wise things; how difficult it was for him to co-operate with Winston, etc.

Harold Nicolson: diary
('Harold Nicolson, Diaries and Letters', page 206)

20 January 1942

I arrive at the House a bit late and do not hear the reception given to Winston at his entry. Some say that it was most enthusiastic; others say that it had about it a note of reserve. I ask Randolph Churchill how it struck him. He said, 'Nothing like the reception Chamberlain got when he returned from Munich.'

Winston S. Churchill: speech
(Hansard)

20 January 1942   House of Commons

The Prime Minister (Mr Churchill): I beg to move,

'That an humble Address be presented to His Majesty to express the deep concern of this House at the loss which His Majesty has sustained by the death of His Royal Highness Prince Arthur William Patrick Albert, Duke of Connaught and Strathearn,[2] and to condole with His Majesty

---

[1] Richard Austen Butler, 1902–82. Known as 'Rab'. President of the Cambridge Union, 1924. Conservative MP for Saffron Walden, 1929–65. Under-Secretary of State, India Office, 1932–7. Parliamentary Secretary, Ministry of Labour, 1937–8. Under-Secretary of State for Foreign Affairs, 1938–41. Privy Councillor, 1939. Minister of Education, 1941–5. Minister of Labour, 1945. Chancellor of the Exchequer, 1951–5. Lord Privy Seal, 1955–61. Home Secretary, 1957–62. Deputy Prime Minister, 1962–3. Secretary of State for Foreign Affairs, 1963–4. Created Baron, 1965. Master of Trinity College, Cambridge, 1965–78.

[2] Arthur William Patrick Albert, 1850–1942. Seventh child and third son of Queen Victoria. Served in the British Army from 1866 to 1916. Created Duke of Connaught and Strathearn, and Earl of Sussex, 1874. Commanded the Aldershot District, 1893–6 (when Churchill was under his command). Commander-in-Chief, Ireland, 1900–4. Field Marshal, 1902. Inspector-General of the Forces, 1904–7. Governor-General of Canada, 1911–16. He died on 16 January 1942.

on this melancholy occasion; and to assure His Majesty that this House will ever participate with the most affectionate and dutiful attachment in whatever may concern the feelings and interests of His Majesty.' The late Duke of Connaught lived a life so long that it was not only a link with the tranquil days of the Victorian era, when a large number of people had persuaded themselves that most of the problems of society were solved, but also a link with the life of the Duke of Wellington. During the whole of his career, mainly in the British Army, he was a devoted, faithful officer and servant of the Crown. He filled a position of delicacy, not free from difficulty, beset on every side by the possibility of indiscretion when such a position is occupied by one who is a son of a Queen, afterwards a brother of a King, uncle of another Sovereign and the great uncle of a fourth Ruler. In that position, never did anything occur which did not make the public realise how true the Duke of Connaught was to all the constitutional implications of his position, and all who came into contact with him were impressed by his charm of manner, by his old-world courtesy, and knew that they were in the presence of a great and distinguished representative of the beloved Royal House.

I have had many opportunities of meeting his Royal Highness, who was a friend of my family, and I enjoyed his friendship. I served under his command, in 1895, as a young officer at Aldershot, and I know the respect and esteem in which he was held by all the troops and all the ranks in the Forces. For my part, I am very glad to feel that he lived long enough to see the dark, frightful crisis with which we were confronted 18 months ago broaden out into a somewhat clearer and more hopeful light.

Winston S. Churchill to General Hastings Ismay,
for the Chiefs of Staff Committee
(Churchill papers, 20/67)

20 January 1942   House of Commons

REINFORCING BURMA

This[1] is surely a matter for the Supreme Commander, but an opinion should be expressed by the COS Committee. Obviously nothing should distract us from the battle of Singapore, but should Singapore fall, quick transference of forces to Burma might be possible. As a strategic

---

[1] A telegram from the Governor of Burma, Sir Reginald Dorman-Smith, stressing the importance of reinforcing Burma.

object, I regard keeping the Burma Road open as more important than the retention of Singapore. What is the truth of the story about Wavell having refused Chiang Kai-shek's large offers of Chinese troops?[1]

Oliver Harvey: diary
('The War Diaries of Oliver Harvey', page 87)

20 January 1942

After his lunch today AE told me he had had a long talk to PM on best of terms. PM prepared to give Cripps a post in M. of Supply – but not prepared to get rid of Kingsley[2] 'who had been very helpful to him'. 'I'd rather have a Cabinet of obedient mugwumps[3] than of awkward freaks!' AE mentioned Crookshank[4] and Llewellyn[5] as having deserved promotion but PM said there were no places for them if Cabinet Ministers didn't die.

PM most anxious to have record made for broadcasting after of his speech in H of C next week. AE much opposed to it because it will mean practice couldn't be restricted to PM but would have to be extended to

[1] See Churchill's note to Wavell of January 23, and Wavell's reply of January 26, at pages 133 and 150 below.

[2] Kingsley Wood, 1881–1943. Member of London County Council, 1911–19. Chairman, London Insurance Committee, 1917–18. Conservative MP for Woolwich West, 1918–43. Knighted, 1918. Parliamentary Private Secretary to Minister of Health, 1919–22. Parliamentary Secretary, Ministry of Health, 1924–9 (when Neville Chamberlain was Minister). Board of Education, 1931. Privy Councillor, 1928. Chairman, Executive Committee of the National Conservative and Unionist Association, 1930–2. Postmaster-General, 1931–5. Minister of Health, 1935–8. Secretary of State for Air, 1938–40. Lord Privy Seal, April–May 1940. Chancellor of the Exchequer from May 1940 until his death in September 1943.

[3] Mugwump: a word derived from the Algonquian dialect of Native Americans in Massachusetts. In their language, it meant 'war leader'. The Puritan missionary John Eliot used it in his translation of the Bible into their language in 1663 to convey the English words 'duke', 'officer', and 'captain'. Brought into English in the early nineteenth century as a humorous term for a boss, bigwig, grand panjandrum, or other person in authority, although often one of a minor and inconsequential sort.

[4] Harry Frederick Comfort Crookshank, 1893–1961. On active service, 1914–18. Captain, 1919. Foreign Office, 1919–24 (Constantinople and Washington). Conservative MP, 1924–56. Secretary for Mines, 1936–9. Financial Secretary, Treasury, 1939–43. Postmaster-General, 1943–5. Minister of Health, 1951–2. Lord Privy Seal, 1952–5 (Churchill's second premiership). In 1954 and 1955 he was one of the Conservative Cabinet Ministers most determined that Churchill should retire. Created Viscount (under Eden), 1956.

[5] John Jestyn Llewellin, 1893–1957. On active service, Royal Artillery, 1914–18. Colonel Commanding Dorset Heavy Brigade, 1932–8. Called to the Bar, 1921. Conservative MP for Uxbridge, 1929–45. Civil Lord of the Admiralty, 1937–9. Parliamentary Secretary, Ministry of Supply, 1939–40. Parliamentary Secretary, Ministry of Aircraft Production, 1940–1. Parliamentary Secretary, Ministry of War Transport, 1941–2. President of the Board of Trade, 1942. Minister of Aircraft Production, 1942. Minister Resident in Washington for Supply, 1942–3. Minister of Food, 1943–5. Created Baron, 1945.

all, and it would end by speakers talking to microphone instead of to House. But PM mad to do it and it is to be tried as experiment.

Winston S. Churchill to General Archibald Wavell
(Churchill papers, 20/88)

20 January 1942   10 Downing Street

The eventuality of the battle of Johore going against you should be taken into account and all preparations should be made for the utmost possible defence of the Island. Following are some particular points:

1. Full preparations should be made to use fortress guns against landward attack and effective fire control should be organized. Report most urgent requirements high explosive when possibility of provision will be examined.

2. Land approaches from the Straits and landing places and exits therefrom in the Island should be obstructed with wire, mines, booby traps, or any other means possible.

3. A proportion of beach defence guns and machine guns should be diverted from the south sectors to the north and west of the Island.

4. All boats or small craft in the Straits or outside them within reach of the Island should be collected under our control or destroyed.

5. Defence must be based on system of localities for all ground defence sited to cover most dangerous avenues of approach. In view of the difficulty of siting beach defences in the swamps, a good system of mobile reserves ready to deliver rapid counter-attack should be built up. A system of switch lines should also be developed in the interior to prevent exploitation of successful landings. Full use should be made of all available civilian and military labour for this and generally for defence works of all kinds.

6. All possible measures should be taken to guard against attempted night landings succeeding by surprise. In this connection unlikely landing places should again be reconnoitred in the light of Japanese tactics and mobility.

7. Adequate measures should be made for the defence of aerodromes and other possible landing grounds in Johore and Singapore against Japanese airborne force reported under preparation in Indo-China. Full use must be made of RAF personnel.

8. Effective measures should be worked out to disperse and control the civil population and to suppress fifth column activity.

9. Personnel for fixed defences should be armed and assigned tasks in the local defence scheme.

10. The best possible signal communications should be developed throughout the Island and also to aerodromes in Sumatra on which close support aircraft may be based.

11. Realise that action will already have been taken on many of these points, in which case we shall be grateful for an early report. Action on the remainder should be initiated without delay and all possible steps taken to prepare for protracted defence.

House of Commons: Motion
(Hansard)

21 January 1942   10 Downing Street

RECORDING OF PRIME MINISTER'S STATEMENT

The following Motion stood upon the Order Paper in the name of The Prime Minister. 'That the statement on the War Situation to be made by the Prime Minister in this House on the First Sitting Day after 25th January be electrically recorded, with a view to being subsequently broadcast.'

The Prime Minister (Mr Churchill): As there appears to be so much difference of opinion about this Motion which stands on the Order Paper, I do not intend to press it.

Sir Hugh O'Neill (Antrim): In view of the statement which the Prime Minister has just made, can he say whether it is still his intention to broadcast to the country on the same day as he makes his speech in the House of Commons?

The Prime Minister: Yes, Sir. I shall do so.

Sir H. O'Neill: In view of the fact that it is obviously a great strain on the Prime Minister to make two speeches on the same day, one in the House of Commons and one on the wireless, would it not be better in future if he arranged to make his broadcast statements on days when he does not have to make an important speech in the House of Commons?

The Prime Minister: I will bear that in mind, but my reluctance to do the same thing twice over on the same day arises less from fatigue than from certain inartistic qualities naturally inseparable from a re-hash.

Captain Plugge (Chatham): While appreciating the reasons prompting my right hon. Friend to withdraw this Motion, may I ask him if he will not consider appointing a small Committee of the House of Commons to look more fully into the implications of this question as a result of my suggestion yesterday?

The Prime Minister: I think I have had enough of it.

Sir Percy Harris[1] (Bethnal Green, South-West): Does the Prime Minister realise how much the House of Commons appreciates his democratic instinct and his desire to defer to the general feeling of the House?

Mr Shinwell (Seaham): Has the Prime Minister ever considered whether there is another Member of the Government capable of undertaking these broadcasts?

Sir William Davison (Kensington, South): Does the Prime Minister realise that the objections which are felt to his original proposal arise from fears that it would set a precedent for ordinary matters of party politics, and would not democracy be well advised to show that it can adapt its procedure to deal with times of national emergency?

Mr Hore-Belisha (Devonport): Further to what the right hon. Baronet the Member for South-West Bethnal Green (Sir P Harris) has just said, may I say how much this action will be appreciated as being in marked, significant contrast to what would have happened in dictatorship countries? It is a most generous gesture.

Henry Channon: diary
('Chips', page 317)

21 January 1942   10 Downing Street

Winston bowed to the will of the Members by withdrawing his motion for his speech to be broadcast direct. The feeling of the House was strongly against it; and in deciding not to challenge it, he has acted wisely. It is better to placate Parliament on a small matter than to have a row on a minor issue. The boys – the naughty boys – have won a round.

[1] Percy Alfred Harris, 1876–1952. Barrister. Member of London County Council, 1907–34 and from 1946 until his death. Assistant Director, Volunteer Services, War Office, 1916. Liberal MP for Market Harborough, 1916–18, and for South-West Bethnal Green, 1922–45. Created Baronet, 1932. Chief Whip, Liberal Parliamentary Party, 1935–45; Deputy Leader, 1940–5. Privy Councillor, 1940. Author of *Forty Years In and Out of Parliament* (1946).

Winston S. Churchill to General Hastings Ismay,
for the Chiefs of Staff Committee
(Churchill papers, 20/67)

21 January 1942   10 Downing Street
Most Secret

In view of the very bad telegram from General Wavell,[1] we must reconsider the whole position at a Defence Committee meeting tonight.

We have already committed exactly the error which I feared when I sent my 'Beware' telegram from the ship on the way out. Forces which might have made a solid front in Johore, or at any rate along the Singapore waterfront, have been broken up piecemeal. No defensive line has been constructed on the land-ward side. No defence has been made by the Navy to the enemy's turning movements on the west coast of the Peninsula. General Wavell has expressed the opinion that 'it will take more troops to defend Singapore Island than to win the battle in Johore.' The battle in Johore is almost certainly lost.

Paragraph 3 gives little hope for prolonged defence. It is evident that such defence would be only at the cost of all the reinforcements now on the way. If General Wavell is doubtful whether more than a few weeks' delay can be obtained, the question arises whether we should not at once blow the docks and batteries and workshops to pieces and concentrate everything on the defence of Burma and keeping open the Burma Road.

2. It appears to me that this question should be squarely faced now and put bluntly to General Wavell. What is the value of Singapore above the many harbours in the south-west Pacific if all naval and military demolitions are thoroughly carried out? On the other hand, the loss of Burma would be very grievous. It would cut us off from the Chinese, whose troops have been the most successful of those yet engaged against the Japanese. We may, by muddling things and hesitating to take an ugly decision, lose both Singapore and the Burma Road. Obviously the decision depends upon how long the defence of Singapore Island can be maintained. If it is only for a few weeks, it is certainly not worth losing all our reinforcements and aircraft.

3. Moreover, one must consider that the fall of Singapore, accompanied as it will be by the fall of Corregidor, will be a tremendous shock to India, which only the arrival of powerful forces and successful action on the Burma front can sustain. Pray let all this be considered this morning.

[1] Telegram 00187 of 20 January 1942, about the deteriorating military situation in Malaya.

War Cabinet: Confidential Annex
(Cabinet papers, 65/29)

22 January 1942
6 p.m.

The Prime Minister said that, subject to the views of our own and the United States military authorities as to security, he thought that the arrival of the United States troops in Northern Ireland should be made the occasion of a demonstration of welcome.

The question had also been raised as to whether a submission should be made to the King with a view to His Majesty visiting Northern Ireland to inspect the United States troops soon after their arrival.

The War Cabinet thought that the occasion would justify such a visit, and that it would be appropriate that His Majesty should be accompanied by the Home Secretary and the United States Ambassador in London.

The Prime Minister undertook to approach the King on this subject.

Winston S. Churchill to the Air Ministry and War Office
(Churchill papers, 20/67)

22 January 1942
6 p.m.

DEFENCE OF AERODROMES

It is important that the arrangements should be simple and easy to understand. The first object is the local defence of the aerodrome, which requires unity of command both in the preparation and the event.

2. This immediate local defence falls to the RAF because they have the bulk of the people on the spot. It is also most important to release as many as possible of the young soldiers' battalions[1] and other military personnel from this static defence for the mobile field army.

3. In order to take over all existing aerodromes, the RAF will require an additional 13,000 men over and above the 66,000 RAF ground personnel already serving. This additional 13,000 will not, however, constitute an additional burden on the country's man power, since they will be deducted from the ceiling allotted to the Army for aerodrome defence.

---

[1] Eight 'young soldiers' battalions, comprising some 10,000 males too young for conscription (some of them as young as 15), were created for homeland airfield defence purposes and stationed as static guards at about 20 different airfields. The idea had first been put into practice in the First World War.

4. Nothing in the above conflicts with the general responsibility of the War Office for attacking any invader or intruder wherever found, and especially acting promptly in the defence and relief of airfields. The Commander-in-Chief, Home Forces,[1] will make all arrangements necessary for this purpose, and he will concert the operations of Home Forces so far as may be necessary with the airfield defence personnel. He will assist the Air Force stations by advising on their plan of local defence and will possess independent right of inspection to report to the War Office for transmission to the Air Ministry upon the standards of efficiency obtained.

Winston S. Churchill to Admiral of the Fleet Sir Dudley Pound
(Churchill papers, 20/67)

22 January 1942

BRITISH NAVAL ACTIVITIES ON THE COASTS OF MALAYA

This is really not good enough. Here we have been absolutely out-manoeuvred and apparently out-fought on the west coast of Malaya by an enemy who has no warship in the neighbourhood. Consequently our forces are made to retire from successive positions, precious time is gained by the enemy and a general state of insecurity engendered in our fighting troops. The shortcomings are only too evident. Why were the enemy allowed to obtain all these craft? We apparently have none or very few, although these were waters we, until recently, controlled. Secondly, when mention is made of heavy machine-gun fire from the banks, as in B, how is it the enemy hold these banks? They cannot be manning with machine-gun points commanding every part of the sea down which these barges must come.

You should surely call for much more precise reports. This command of the western shores of Malaya by the Japanese without the possession of a single ship of war must be reckoned as one of the most astonishing

[1] Bernard Charles Tolver Paget, 1887–1961. Son of Francis Paget, Bishop of Oxford. Entered the Army, 1907. On active service, 1914–18 (wounded twice, despatches four times, DSO, Military Cross). Major-General, 1937. As Commander, 18th Division, in Norway in 1940, he extracted two brigades from the Dombaas–Aandalsnes area during a seven-day action that won specific praise from Churchill in the House of Commons. CB, 1940. Chief of the General Staff, Home Forces, 1940–1. Commander-in-Chief, South-Eastern Command, 1941.Commander-in-Chief, Home Forces, 1941–3. Knighted, 1942. General, 1943. Commander-in-Chief, 21st Army Group, 1943. Commander-in-Chief, Middle East Force, 1944–5. His younger son died of wounds received in action in Germany in 1945 (posthumous DSO).

British lapses recorded in naval history. I am sorry to be disagreeable, but I look for a further report of a far more searching inquiry.

House of Commons: Business of the House
(Hansard)

22 January 1942   House of Commons

Mr Ness Edwards:[1] May I ask the Prime Minister whether, in accordance with the pledge given by the Minister of Labour on behalf of the Government, he would arrange to give time in the near future for a discussion of the Motion standing in my name and the names of some of my hon. Friends in regard to a Ministry of Production?

'That, in the view of this House it is imperative that a Minister of Production should be appointed with a seat in the War Cabinet, to centrally plan all production vital to the winning of the war, and to which the activities of the Ministry of Supply, the Ministry of Aircraft Production, and the Naval Supply Department should be subordinated.'

Would he regard it as more appropriate that that Question should fall within the scope of the Debate which is to take place during the next Sittings, or should it be taken separately?

The Prime Minister: The Debate at the next Sittings will range over the whole topic of the war, and, obviously, references to the sinews of war will be in Order. As to whether there should be a separate Debate on the proposals which have been several times advanced for the creation of a Ministry of Production, that is a matter which must be arranged at a later date, through the usual channels.

Mr Ness Edwards: May I put it to the right hon. Gentleman that it would be very inconvenient and undesirable to have a Motion of the sort I have mentioned moved as an Amendment to a Motion of Confidence should such a Motion be put down, because in that case it would not receive the unbiased consideration to which it is entitled? We would like an assurance that time will be given subsequently for the consideration of the Motion.

The Prime Minister: I really cannot undertake now, on the spur of the moment, to mortgage the time of the House in advance. The object of the Government is to facilitate the fullest Debate on the most burning

---

[1] Ness Edwards, 1897–1968. Worked in a coal mine from the age of 13. Labour MP for Caerphilly, 1939–68. Parliamentary Secretary, Ministry of Labour and National Service, 1945–50. Privy Councillor, 1947. Postmaster-General, 1950–1.

questions and to ascertain which are those burning questions, by the long established procedure of the House.

Winston S. Churchill to King George VI
(Royal Archives)

22 January 1942   10 Downing Street

The Prime Minister with his humble duty to your Majesty expresses his gratitude for the gracious letter of January 22. The present position is best epitomized in the telegram from Mr Curtin and the Prime Minister's reply of which the Cabinet cordially approved, which reappended. Your Majesty will see that in spite of all the arguments we have used, the Commonwealth Government, which has a majority of two, is determined to recur to the United States. They have the idea that they can get better service and more support from the United States than they can from us. It would be foolish and vain to obstruct their wishes. From what I know, I fear they will have a very awkward reception at Washington. Access to the supreme power is extremely difficult. It is only granted to few, and then in abundant measure. The lengthy telegrams they send will be addressed to subordinate officials and officers. It may be that, having knocked at this door, they will come back again to ours. If so, they will be very welcome.

2. Meanwhile we are welcoming Sir Earle Page at our discussions and are in fact putting him much more fully into the picture than Paragraph 3 of Mr Curtin's telegram requests. It will be wise, I am sure, to wait a day or two to let some realization of these problems sink into the Commonwealth Government before embarking upon further argument or pleading. It is always good to let people do what they like and then see whether they like what they do. I do not think they will succeed in displacing the effective centre of gravity from London. I am keeping New Zealand informed.

3. The Cabinet today took a very favourable view of the idea that Your Majesty, accompanied by the Home Secretary and the American Ambassador, should at a time convenient to yourself visit Northern Ireland and see the American troops, the vanguard of whom are arriving in two or three days' time. By the end of February I expect that 15,000 American troops will be in Northern Ireland. I should be most reluctant to press so arduous a task upon Your Majesty, although I think it would be most gratifying to the United States and impressive to all Europe if films

were made of Your Majesty taking the salute from the American Army. Perhaps I might venture to suggest to Your Majesty that your personal advisers should consider the matter, and that I might receive later on some indication of Your Majesty's pleasure.

I am, with my humble duty,
Your Majesty's faithful and obedient servant,
Winston S. Churchill

Winston S. Churchill to President Franklin D. Roosevelt
(Churchill papers, 20/69)

22 January 1942
Personal and Secret

Documents dealing with (1) Munition Assignments, (2) Anglo-American Shipping Adjustment Board, and (3) Combined Raw Materials Board, have been circulated to Ministers concerned.

2. These documents have met with warm approval from the War Cabinet and we see no objection to early announcement of all three; but would wish, before this is done, to inform the Dominions and let them know of the arrangements we propose for co-ordination of their needs and resources with ours. This however must not prevent an early publication of 2 and 3 or of all three at a time convenient to both of us.

3. Thus, as regards raw materials, we propose to form a clearing-house here for supplies from all the Empire and the needs of the whole Empire. This clearing-house will enable us to present the Empire position as a whole in Washington through Baillieu,[1] the representative of the Ministry of Supply. It may also be convenient to include within the scope of this clearing-house certain Allies whose demands we have hitherto sponsored or have made ourselves responsible for. On the other hand the position of Canada may require special consideration.

4. The question of Oil Products will be dealt with in a separate telegram which will be sent later.

---

[1] Clive Latham Baillieu, 1918–67. Educated at Melbourne University and Magdalen College, Oxford. On active service, 1915–18. An Australian Representative on the Imperial Economic Committee, 1930–47. Knighted, 1938. Director-General, British Purchasing Commission, Washington, 1941–2. Member of the British Supply Council in North America, 1941–3. Chairman, Fairey Aviation Company, 1943–5; of Central Mining, 1945–59; and of Dunlop, 1949–57. Chairman of the English Speaking Union, 1951–65. Created Baron, 1953. First President of the British Institute of Management, 1959.

5. As regards shipping, we shall continue and, as necessary, develop the existing arrangements whereby the shipping resources and needs of the Dominions are co-ordinated in London with our own.

We are also proposing to continue the same procedure as regards the shipping resources of the Allied Governments resident in London.

6. We anticipate some difficulty from the reference in paragraph 7 of the document setting up the Anglo-American Shipping Adjustment Board, which refers to USSR and China by name, but not to any other united nation. Several of the United Nations have important mercantile marines far in excess of that of China.

7. This difficulty could be got over if there was a common heading to all three documents, in the following terms:

'To further the co-ordination of the Allied War effort, the President and the Prime Minister have set up bodies to deal with Munition Assignments, Shipping Adjustment and Raw Materials. The functions of these bodies are outlined in the annexed documents.

These bodies will confer as necessary with representatives of the Union of Soviet Socialist Republics, China, and such others of the United Nations as may be necessary to the attainment of common purposes.'

8. The paragraph of each document which refers to conferring with USSR, China, and others of the United Nations, would then be omitted. The document setting up the Combined Raw Materials Board would be headed simply 'Combined Raw Materials Board.'

9. As I hope to refer to these matters in my speech in the House of Commons on Tuesday, I should be grateful for an early reply. We shall have to adjust the timing.

Henry Channon: diary
('Chips', page 318)

22 January 1942

I picked up all the gossip. No. 10, now known as 'The Dixième Bureau',[1] is in a flap. The 1922 Committee has sent an ultimatum, or at least a strongly-worded request, to the Prime Minister asking him not to insist upon a Vote of Confidence in the coming full-dress debate, as many Conservative Members would be obliged by their consciences to accept the challenge, and many more might abstain. At first the PM

---

[1] A pun on the French 'Deuxième Bureau', France's external military intelligence agency from 1871 to 1940 (*dixième* = 'tenth').

was adamant, but is now alarmed, though he still refuses to re-construct his Government. He may climb down, but he is in angry mood; the ineffectual Whips are in a frenzy and a first class crisis, no doubt chuckled over by the Germans, is upon us.

John Martin: diary
(Sir John Martin papers)

23 January 1942

To Chequers in afternoon. Much snow on roads. PM getting worked up for speech in House next Tuesday demanding vote of confidence. To bed 4 a.m.

Winston S. Churchill to General Hastings Ismay,
for the Chiefs of Staff Committee
(Churchill papers, 20/67)

23 January 1942

This[1] is very serious. If the figures are true they amount to a breach of faith. Pray let me have the explanation and the correct figures, together also with the amounts which have been sent. Any short fall on the part of the Service Departments will be in direct disobedience of the Cabinet instruction.

Winston S. Churchill to Anthony Eden and L. S. Amery
(Churchill papers, 20/67)

23 January 1942

THE DETENTION OF U SAW AND U TIN TUT[2]

The Cabinet thought this line[3] was precipitate. We must certainly not lose sight of the possibility of a trial, and nothing must be done to make a trial impossible. Prolonged, skilful questioning of both men separately may yield satisfactory evidence. They should both be kept in

---

[1] The complaint by the Soviet Ambassador in London to Anthony Eden, on 13 January 1942, about deficiencies in British supplies to the Soviet Union.

[2] U Saw's Oxford-trained secretary.

[3] The decision to detain U Saw without trial for the duration of the war.

strict seclusion. The Viceroy's recent telegram shows how important it is to bring traitors to justice.

Winston S. Churchill to Sir Archibald Sinclair
(Churchill papers, 20/67)

23 January 1942

The vanguard of the American troops, numbering over 4,000 men, arrives at Belfast on Sunday evening or Monday morning. I am inviting the American Ambassador[1] to meet them there, together with the Governor-General[2] and the Prime Minister of Northern Ireland.[3] I should also like one of the Service Ministers to meet these troops on their arrival, and I should be obliged if you would undertake this journey. Perhaps you will get in touch with the Home Secretary in order to concert arrangements.

Winston S. Churchill to General Archibald Wavell
(Churchill papers, 20/69)

23 January 1942
Personal

I am still puzzled about your reasons for refusing Chinese help in the defence of Burma and the Burma Road. You have I understand now accepted 49th and 93rd Chinese Divisions, but the Chinese Fifth Army and the rest of the Sixth Army are available just beyond the frontier. Burma seems in grave danger of being overrun. When we remember how long the Chinese have stood up alone and ill-armed against the Japanese, and when we see what a very rough time we are having at Japanese hands, I cannot understand why we do not welcome their aid.

[1] John Gilbert Winant, 1889–1947. Known as 'Gil'. On active service in France, 1917–18. Governor of New Hampshire, 1925–7, 1931–5. Chairman of the Social Security Board (an integral part of Roosevelt's New Deal), 1935–7. United States Ambassador in London, 1941–6. Order of Merit, 1946. Author of *A Letter from Grosvenor Square* (1947) and his wartime speeches, *Our Greatest Harvest* (published posthumously, 1950).

[2] James Albert Edward Hamilton, 1869–1953. Succeeded his father as 3rd Duke of Abercorn, 1913. Senator of Northern Ireland, 1921. Governor of Northern Ireland, 1922–45. Knight of the Garter, 1928.

[3] John Miller Andrews, 1871–1956. Unionist MP in the Parliament of Northern Ireland, 1921–53. Minister of Finance, Cabinet of Northern Island, 1937–40. Prime Minister of Northern Ireland, 1940–3. CH, 1943.

2. I must enlighten you upon the American view. China bulks as large in the minds of many of them as Great Britain. The President, who is a great admirer of yours, seemed a bit dunched[1] at Chiang-Kai-Shek's discouragement after your interview with him. The American Chiefs of Staff insisted upon Burma being in your command for the sole reason that they considered your giving your left hand to China and the opening of the Burma Road indispensable to world victory. And never forget that behind all looms the shadow of Asiatic solidarity, which the numerous disasters and defeats through which we have to plough our way may make more menacing.

3. If I can epitomize in one word the lesson I learned in the USA, it was 'China'.

Winston S. Churchill to President Franklin D. Roosevelt
(Churchill papers, 20/69)

23 January 1942
Personal and Secret

ST PIERRE AND MIQUELON ISLANDS

I saw General de Gaulle yesterday and after a severe conversation he agreed to the communiqué which I left with you being published by the United States, British and Canadian Governments without any acceptance by us of his proposed secret conditions. He feels it necessary to consult Admiral Muselier who is a member of the National Committee, but I understand I am to receive final assent of the Free French tomorrow, when I will immediately telegraph confirmation to you.

2. Assuming the above, what procedure do you want followed? Will Mr Hull put it to Vichy, or will you simply issue the communiqués straight away? I think the latter course would be the better, and these two tiny islands can then relapse into the obscurity from which they have more than once emerged since the Treaty of Utrecht.[2]

3. Meanwhile we are also informing Canada and asking them to communicate through the appropriate channels with you. It is important that no statement should be made in public till Canada's definite agreement has been received.

---

[1] Knocked over. Literally: pushed with a short, rapid blow.

[2] The Treaty of Utrecht, 1713, was concluded between France and Spain on the one hand and Britain, Savoy, Portugal, and the United Provinces on the other. Under the treaty, France ceded to Britain its claims to the Hudson's Bay Company's territories in Prince Rupert's Land, Newfoundland, and Acadia, but retained Prince Edward Island, Cape Breton Island, and St Pierre and Miquelon.

4. I do hope the solution for which I have worked hard will be satisfactory to Mr Hull and the State Department. I understood fully the difficulty in which they were placed. Public opinion here was of course delighted at the Vichy-ites being overthrown by an overwhelming popular vote, and coercion of de Gaulle would have been very unpopular.

General Claude Auchinleck to Winston S. Churchill
(Churchill papers, 20/69)

23 January 1942   Cairo
Personal and Most Secret

2. It seems clear that Rommel's eastwards move on Jan 21st was made in anticipation [of] expected attack by us. Finding only light forces confronting him he evidently decided to push on with the intention of disturbing our main L of C,[1] which he appears to believe rests on Benghazi. During withdrawal on 21st Jan in difficult sand dune country south west of Jedabya columns of support group first Armoured division reported to have lost 9 guns and 100 mechanical transport also a number of casualties details as yet unknown.

3. If Rommel persists in his advance, particularly on the Benghazi axis, he is likely to expose his eastwards flank to attack by our Armour which in that area now amounts to about 150 cruiser and American tanks. The small enemy column which penetrated almost into Antelat last night is presumed to be a commando.

4. I realize the public at home may be upset by enemy re-occupying Jedabya but it may well be that Rommel may be drawn on into a situation unfavourable to him. Rommel's move has held up reconnaissances and other preparations for our planned offensive against Agheila but as you know prime retarding factor was and still is need for building up adequate reserve in and forward of Benghazi. Meanwhile our forward troops are maintaining close touch with the enemy and our Air force have inflicted casualties on them.

5. 4 Indian Division is concentrating at Benghazi and is being reinforced with artillery.

6. Am confident that General Ritchie is watching for opportunity to force encounter battle in conditions which may be more favourable to us than those obtaining round Agheila with its swamps and bad going.

---

[1] L of C: line(s) of communication.

You may remember we were disappointed when enemy withdrew from Jedabya as this increased our maintenance difficulties.

Winston S. Churchill to Peter Fraser
(Churchill papers, 20/69)

23 January 1942　　　　　　　　　　　　　　　　　　　　Cairo
Most Secret and Personal

I have carefully studied your telegram No. 36 of the 20th January. Like you, I will deal in this telegram only with the proposal for a Far Eastern Defence Council in London. I cannot but think that there may have been some misunderstanding as to the precise scope of the arrangement which was discussed by the President and myself, and I think it will be best if I set out in fuller detail the whole scheme as we arranged it. The President proposed to me the appointment of a British General as Supreme Commander in the ABDA area. As part of this arrangement, the orders to that Supreme Commander on major strategy and policy will finally emanate from the President acting on behalf of the ABDA Governments. The President will be advised by combined Chiefs of Staff Committee in Washington. This Committee consists of three United States Chiefs of Staff sitting with the British Joint Staff Mission, at the head of which I propose to place Field-Marshal Dill. In London, there will be a Far Eastern Council, presided over by myself as Chairman, and comprising one ministerial representative each from Australia, New Zealand and the Netherlands, other ministers and advisors being summoned to attend as necessary.

2. The arrangements for inter-working between the Combined Chiefs of Staff Committee in Washington and the Far Eastern Council in London will be as follows. Any proposals emanating either from the Supreme Commander or from any of the ABDA Governments will be forwarded simultaneously to the Combined Chiefs of Staff Committee in Washington and to London for consideration by the Far Eastern Council. I shall be responsible, as Chairman of the Far Eastern Council for focusing and formulating the views of the Governments represented on the Council and for presenting them to the Combined Chiefs of Staff Committee in Washington. If there are differences, these will be reported. The members of the British Joint Staff Mission sitting in Washington, who are, of course, throughout in the closest touch with the British Chiefs

of Staff in London, will be responsible not merely for bringing the views of the Far Eastern Council before the Combined Chiefs of Staff Committee in Washington, but for making sure that those views are properly understood and for clearing up any difficulties.

3. In the event of disagreements between the United States Chiefs of Staff and the British Joint Staff Mission which would imply disagreement between the United States Chiefs of Staff and the Council of the Far East in London, the matter would be referred back to London for further consideration by the Council.

4. As an essential part of the arrangements for the Far Eastern Council in London, it is proposed that Planning Liaison Officers of Australia, New Zealand and the Netherlands should be brought into consultation in London with the Joint Planning Staff of the British Chiefs of Staff Committee, in order to ensure that the views of Australia, New Zealand and the Netherlands are given full weight in the preparation of any joint staff report or appreciation relevant to the ABDA area. For this purpose, it is suggested that the three Governments concerned should each provide a Service representative of equivalent rank to a colonel or lieutenant-colonel to act as Planning Liaison Officer. These officers would be given accommodation in the War Cabinet Offices and would be afforded all the facilities necessary for their work.

5. Such is the scheme in detail. It will be seen from it that the Far Eastern Council in London, so far from being an advisory body, will be the centre on which the views of the United Kingdom, Australia, New Zealand and the Netherlands Government are focused and formulated on the staff as well as on the ministerial plane and effective decisions reached, and further that no decision can be taken either in Washington or in London which does not take full account of the views of the Australian, New Zealand and the Netherlands Governments.

6. If the orders of ABDA powers to the Supreme Commander were to be framed by a body in Washington representing all those powers, the representatives of the Governments concerned, other than of the United States, would be less favourably placed for expressing the views of their Governments. Since, under the arrangement proposed, the Australian and New Zealand Governments will be represented in London not merely on the ministerial plane as full members of the Far Eastern Council, having an equal voice in its decisions, but also on the Joint Planning level, their representatives on the Council will be able to speak with the knowledge of the strategic and other considerations which have been taken into account in the formation of detailed plans.

7. Above is the plan to which the President was prepared to agree, and I feel that it is the one which offers the best opportunity to New Zealand to make her voice effectively heard in the Allied Councils. It is not possible for the United States both to give the command in the Pacific to a British General and to entrust their interests to a representative sitting in London as one of the members of a Far East Council here. On the other hand, we cannot have two Far Eastern Councils, one sitting in Washington and the other in London. The result would only lead to confusion and to machinery so cumbrous that it would fall to the ground of its own weight.

8. I hope, therefore, that, on studying this fuller explanation of the scheme, New Zealand will agree to take part in the Far Eastern Council in London in the manner suggested above. Pending your reply, we will proceed on the assumption that the Far Eastern Council here will come into being as proposed.

George Harvie-Watt to Winston S. Churchill
(Sir George Harvie-Watt papers)

23 January 1942
Personal and Most Secret

There is little to report from the House of Commons this week, apart from what you already know. The Debates have been, on the whole, dull. The only general point of interest in the House arose over the suggestion that our speech might be recorded and subsequently broadcast. As you know, opinion on all sides of the House was sharply divided on this subject. The Parliamentary Socialist Party had decided by a considerable majority that they would oppose the Motion. Your decision to withdraw was generally approved, and Members were delighted by the way you did it.

Now, however, the decision not to record your speech has been taken, there have been considerable qualms of conscience on the part of many Members who think the House might have been more generous.

At the 1922 Committee[1] on Wednesday, as you have seen from the Press, there was a certain amount of criticism of the suggestion to have

---

[1] The 1922 Committee (formally the Backbench 1922 Committee), made up of all backbench Conservative Members of Parliament. Founded in 1923, after the Conservative victory in the 1922 General Election, it meets every week when Parliament is in session, enabling Conservative backbenchers to have their views heard by frontbenchers. Frontbench MPs have a standing invitation to attend, but only backbenchers may vote.

next week's Debate made the subject of a vote of confidence. The subject was raised by Levy,[1] and supported by H. G. Williams.[2] They considered it unfortunate that you should have thrown out this challenge because it would look as if Members who voted against or refrained from voting, were opposed to your Premiership. This was not so. Irving Albery,[3] Arnold Gridley,[4] W. W. Wakefield,[5] W. Spens,[6] and Victor Cazalet[7] also supported this view.

It was stressed over and over again by speakers that

(i) it would be a catastrophe if anything happened to you as leader of the House and the Nation.

(ii) the Members who were taking this view were whole-heartedly loyal to you in every way and

(iii) while they had every confidence in you as Prime Minister, they had not the same confidence in your team as a whole.

This feeling of the 1922 Committee is also reflected in the attitude of many Liberals and Socialists. They likewise have stressed the fact that there is no challenge to your leadership.

[1] Thomas Levy, 1874–1953. Officer in command of transport during the transport strike, 1919. Conservative MP for the Elkland Division of Yorkshire, 1931–45. Chairman of the British Wool Central Advisory Committee, 1939–40.

[2] Herbert Geraint Williams, 1884–1954. Educated at University of Liverpool. Electrical and marine engineer. Secretary, Machine Tool Trades Association, 1911–28. Secretary, Machine Tool Department, Ministry of Munitions, 1917–18. Conservative MP for Reading, 1924–9; for South Croydon, 1932–45; for Croydon East, 1950–4. Parliamentary Secretary, Board of Trade, 1928–9. Knighted, 1939. Member of the House of Commons Select Committee on Expenditure, 1939–44. Chairman, London Conservative Union, 1939–48; National Union of Conservatives and Unionist Associations, 1948. Created Baronet, 1953.

[3] Irving James Albery, 1879–1967. Member of the Stock Exchange, 1902–64. On active service in South Africa, 1900, and on the Western Front, 1914–18 (Military Cross, despatches). Conservative MP for Gravesend, 1924–45. Knighted, 1936.

[4] Arnold Babb Gridley, 1878–1965. Consulting engineer. Controller of Electric Power Supply, Ministry of Munitions, 1916–19. KBE, 1920. Conservative MP for Stockport, 1935–50; for Stockport South, 1950–5. Created Baron, 1955.

[5] William Wavell Wakefield, 1898–1983. Royal Naval Air Service, 1916–18. English Rugby Union player, 1920–7; 13 times captain of England. Conservative MP for Swindon, 1935–45. Knighted, 1944. Conservative MP for St Marylebone, 1945–63. Created Baron, 1963.

[6] William Patrick Spens, 1885–1973. On active service in Mesopotamia, 1915–18 (despatches thrice, OBE). QC, 1925. Conservative MP for Ashford, 1933–43. Member of the Bacon Marketing Board, 1935. Director of Southern Railway, 1940–3. Knighted, 1943. Chief Justice of India, 1943–7. Conservative MP for South Kensington, 1956–9. Created Baron, 1959.

[7] Victor Alexander Cazalet, 1896–1943. Educated at Eton and Christ Church, Oxford. Oxford half blue for tennis, racquets, and squash, 1915. Served on the Western Front, 1915–18 (Military Cross). Member of General Knox's staff in Siberia, 1918–19. Conservative MP for Chippenham from 1924 until his death. Parliamentary Secretary, Board of Trade, 1924–6. Political Liaison Officer to General Sikorski, 1940–3. Killed in the air crash in which Sikorski died. His sister, Thelma Cazalet-Keir, was Conservative MP for Islington East, 1931–45.

There has been some talk of an amendment suggested by some Socialists – I haven't been able to find out who – expressing confidence in you but calling for a Ministerial reconstruction and for the inclusion in the Government of a Minister of Production. Whether this amendment will be put down or not, and what support it will get, I cannot yet say.

There is a general hope that you will not ask for a vote of confidence. If, however, there is a vote of confidence I doubt very much if more than a handful of Members on all sides will vote against the Government, though some, a larger number – may refrain. The abstentionists would include Winterton.[1]

The Debate on Aerodrome Defence fizzled out. The Secretary of State for Air[2] made a good speech as did his Under Secretary[3] in winding up the Debate. Certain misgivings were expressed, however, especially regarding division of responsibility between the Army and Air Force. It was felt that this responsibility was still not properly defined.

Despite the agitation for a secret session, the whole Debate took place in public.

[1] Edward Turnour, 1883–1962. Educated at Eton and New College, Oxford. Conservative MP for Horsham, 1904–51. Succeeded his father as 6th Earl Winterton, 1907. As an Irish peer, he continued to sit in the House of Commons. Served at Gallipoli, in Palestine and in Arabia, 1915–18. Under-Secretary of State for India, 1922–4, 1924–9. Chancellor of the Duchy of Lancaster, 1937–9. Paymaster-General, 1939. Chairman, Inter-Governmental Committee for Refugees, 1938–45.

[2] Sir Archibald Sinclair.

[3] Harold Balfour, 1897–1988. A great-grandson of Field Marshal Lord Napier of Magdala. Educated at Royal Naval College, Osborne. Joined 60th Rifles, 1914; Royal Flying Corps, 1915–17 (Military Cross and bar). Served in the Royal Air Force, 1918–23. Conservative MP for Isle of Thanet, 1929–45. Parliamentary Under-Secretary of State for Air, 1938–44. Privy Councillor, 1941. Minister Resident in West Africa, 1944–5. Created Baron, 1945. Member of the Board of British European Airways, 1955–66. He published *An Airman Marches* in 1935 and *Wings Over Westminster* in 1973. His elder brother, a Lieutenant Commander in the Royal Navy, was killed on active service in 1941.

John Martin: diary
(Sir John Martin papers)

24 January 1942   Chequers

Capt. Tennant[1] of *Repulse*[2] to lunch. PM working on speech. To bed 3.20 a.m.

Winston S. Churchill to Air Chief Marshal Sir Charles Portal
(Churchill papers, 20/67)

24 January 1942

AIRCRAFT LOSSES FOR WEEK ENDING 10 JANUARY 1942

This[3] is a frightful total, in a week while so little has been going on. I must request you to make me proposals for effecting a substantial reduction. I hope you will be able to reassure me that this is possible.

Meanwhile, please let me have the figures for operational losses at the hands of the enemy, and the rest separately.

Winston S. Churchill to John Moore-Brabazon[4]
(Churchill papers, 20/67)

24 January 1942

AIRCRAFT PRODUCTION FOR WEEK ENDING
17 JANUARY 1942

Pray let me have the reasons for this extremely bad week, which is not a holiday week. All your figures for January are most disappointing and far below target.

---

[1] William George Tennant, 1890–1963. Entered the Royal Navy, 1905. On active service at Gallipoli (1915) and Jutland (1916). Oversaw the evacuation of Dunkirk, 1940 (CB; nicknamed 'Dunkirk Joe'); Captain, HMS *Repulse*, 1940–2. Rear-Admiral, 1942. Normandy Landings, 1944 (CBE). Flag Officer, Levant and Mediterranean, 1944–6. Knighted 'for services in the War in Europe', 1945. Vice-Admiral, 1945. Commander-in-Chief, America and West Indies Station, 1946–9. Admiral, 1948.

[2] Launched in 1916, HMS *Repulse* was in action at the Second Battle of the Heligoland Bight, 1917; in the Norwegian campaign, 1940, and the search for the *Bismarck*, 1941; and in the Cape convoys, 1941. Sunk by a Japanese air attack off the coast of Malaya, 10 December 1941, with the loss of 508 officers and men.

[3] Aircraft loss and damage return for the week ending 10 January 1942.

[4] John Theodore Cuthbert Moore-Brabazon, 1884–1964. Educated at Harrow and Trinity College, Cambridge. Pioneer motorist and aviator; holder of Pilot's Certificate No. 1. Won the *Daily Mail* £1,000 prize for flying a circular mile, 1909. Lieutenant (later Lieutenant-Colonel) in charge of the Royal Flying Corps Photographic Section, 1914–18 (Military Cross, despatches thrice). Conservative MP for Chatham, 1918–29; for Wallasey, 1931–42. Chairman, Air Mails Committee, 1923. Parliamentary Private Secretary to the Lord Privy Seal, 1939–40. Minister of Transport, 1940–1.

Winston S. Churchill to General Claude Auchinleck
(Churchill papers, 20/69)

24 January 1942
Personal

Thank you for your explanation about Agedabia. I had read the situation exactly as you put it. I thought the Cairo bulletins printed in today's papers gave needlessly full revelation of your mind, but I suppose you were satisfied that the enemy understood our outlook already.[1]

2. Mind you let me have the figures of casualties and prisoners on both sides since November 18 to reach me Sunday.[2] We are having a fairly rough time about the Far East.

Oliver Harvey: diary
('The War Diaries of Oliver Harvey', page 87)

24 January 1942

Saw Cripps today.[3] He is to lunch with PM at Chequers on Sunday (?And be offered post of Minister of Supply). Government apart from PM is being attacked more and more and the big debate is this week. PM is disposed, tho' without enthusiasm, to make Cripps M. of Supply, while making the Beaver a sort of super Cabinet Minister overseeing the whole field of production.

Minister of Aircraft Production, 1941–2. Resigned after expressing the hope that Germany and the Soviet Union (then embattled at Stalingrad) would destroy each other. Created Baron, 1942. Published *The Brabazon Story* in 1956.

[1] Several newspapers – British, American, and Canadian – reported Rommel's advance into a triangle between Agedabia, Saunnu, and Antelat, and quoted British sources as saying that British strength in that area was 'perhaps lying in wait for just the opportunity that has come to it'.

[2] General Auchinleck replied that 262 officers and 2,646 other ranks had been killed; 565 officers and 6,774 other ranks had been wounded; and 446 officers and 3,011 other ranks were missing ('Personal', 24 January 1942, *Churchill papers, 20/69*).

[3] Sir Stafford Cripps had returned from Moscow, having been replaced as British Ambassador by Sir Archibald Clark Kerr.

Winston S. Churchill: recollection
(*'The Hinge of Fate'*, pages 56–7)

25 January 1942

Although I was kept well informed about the Left Wing ideas I acted wholly on the merits of the case. In the First World War, while I was Minister of Munitions, Cripps had been assistant superintendent of the largest explosives factory in the British Empire, and had filled the post with remarkable efficiency. This practical administrative experience was combined with his outstanding intellectual gifts. It seemed to me that his appointment to the Ministry of Supply would be in best accord with the public interest, and might form a part of the major design for creating a Ministry of Production. Sir Stafford and Lady Cripps[1] came to luncheon at Chequers on January 25, and he and I had a long and agreeable talk in the afternoon. When I made him a definite proposal and explained the position which the office in question would have in the general sphere of war production he said he would reflect upon it and let me know.

Winston S. Churchill to General Hastings Ismay,
for the Chiefs of Staff Committee
(*Churchill papers, 20/67*)

25 January 1942
Action this Day

The presence of *Tirpitz* at Trondheim has now been known for three days. The destruction or even the crippling of this ship is the greatest event at sea at the present time. No other target is comparable to it. She cannot have ack-ack[2] protection comparable to Brest or the German home ports. If she were even only crippled, it would be difficult to take her back to Germany. No doubt it is better to wait for moonlight for a night attack, but moonlight attacks are not comparable with day attacks. The entire naval situation throughout the world would be altered, and the naval command in the Pacific would be regained.

2. There must be no lack of co-operation between the Bomber Command and the Fleet Air Arm and aircraft carrier. A plan should be made

---

[1] Isobel Cripps, 1891–1979. 2nd daughter of Commander Harold Swithinbank RN. Married Cripps in 1911. They had one son and three daughters. DBE, 1946.

[2] Ack-ack: slang for 'anti-aircraft' (weaponry/defence).

to attack both with carrier-borne torpedo aircraft and with heavy bombers by daylight or at dawn. The whole strategy of the war turns at this period on this ship, which is holding four times the number of British capital ships paralysed, to say nothing of the two new American battleships retained in the Atlantic. I regard the matter as of the highest urgency and importance. I shall mention it in Cabinet tomorrow and it must be considered in detail at the Defence Committee on Tuesday night.[1]

Winston S. Churchill to Air Chief Marshal Sir Charles Portal
(Churchill papers, 20/67)

25 January 1942

I am of opinion that another four squadrons of Hurricanes will have to be found for the second trip of the *Indomitable* to the Malay Peninsula. These must come from the Middle East, and must be replaced as soon as possible by fighter aircraft flown to Malta.

2. The report attached[2] shows that there is difficulty in fuelling and servicing in the East the aircraft already on the spot. The report I received yesterday about the Takoradi route shows a substantial congestion of Hurricanes and Blenheims at Takoradi. There is at present no immediate hurry, because *Indomitable* has not yet flown off her first party, but a decision will have to be taken this week by the Defence Committee and a timetable should be worked out.

---

[1] The German battleship *Tirpitz* (52,600 tons loaded) had been commissioned on 25 February 1941. She was first attacked on 9 March 1942 by 12 RAF torpedo bombers, but evaded the torpedoes. In October 1942, while undergoing repairs in Fættenfjord outside Trondheim, she was attacked by British 'Chariot' human torpedoes. Rough seas caused the attack to fail. In a second Chariot attack, in Altafjord, on 22 September 1943, *Tirpitz* was badly damaged. Repairs were completed on 2 April 1944. The next attack, as a result of Enigma decrypts revealing *Tirpitz*'s departure for trials, was on 3 April 1944, by 40 RAF dive-bombers; *Tirpitz* was again badly damaged, and at least 132 men killed. Repairs were completed on 2 June 1944. On 22 August 1944, 38 RAF bombers attacked, causing only minor damage. On 29 August 1944, 34 bombers attacked, but heavy fog prevented any hits being scored. An attack on 15 September 1944 by 23 Lancasters caused serious damage, as did an attack on 29 October 1944, when she was moored off Hakoy Island (outside Tromsø). On 12 November 1944, 32 Lancaster bombers, carrying 12,000-pound 'Tallboy' bombs, attacked *Tirpitz*, which capsized; 950 men were drowned (some accounts say 1,204).

[2] A telegram from Air Marshal Tedder (see note on page 182 below), sent on 23 January 1942, about diversions of aircraft from the Middle East to the Far East.

Winston S. Churchill to General Claude Auchinleck
(Churchill papers, 20/69)

25 January 1942
Personal

I am much disturbed by No. 1005 B/24 from NLO 8th Army which speaks of evacuation of Benghazi and Derna. I had certainly never been led to suppose that such a situation could arise. All this movement of non-fighting personnel eastwards, and statement that demolition work at Benghazi has not (repeat not) been ordered yet, places the campaign on different level from any we had considered. Have you really had a heavy defeat in the Antelat area. Have your fresh armour been unable to compete with the resuscitated German tanks. It seems to me this is a serious crisis and one to me quite unexpected. Why should they all be off so quickly. Why should not the 4th Indian Division hold out at Benghazi like the Huns at Halfaya. The kind of retirement now evidently envisaged by subordinate officers implies the failure of 'Crusader' and the ruin of 'Acrobat'.[1]

Sir Alexander Hardinge[2] to Winston S. Churchill
(Royal Archives)

26 January 1942   Buckingham Palace

My dear Prime Minister,

The King wishes me to thank you sincerely for your letter of January 22nd. His Majesty fully realizes that the Commonwealth Government are in a very sensitive mood at the moment, and feels sure that you are quite right to let it simmer for a few days.

The King will, of course, be much interested to read the conclusions which you reach in your discussion at this evening's Cabinet.

As regards a visit to Northern Ireland to see the American troops, when a sufficient number have arrived, the idea certainly commends itself to His Majesty, who has instructed me to keep him informed of how the situation develops.

[1] Auchinleck's military operations in the Western Desert: 'Acrobat' (launched on 11 January 1942) and 'Crusader' (launched on 24 January 1942).

[2] Alexander Henry Louis Hardinge, 1894–1960. Educated at Harrow and Trinity College, Cambridge. On active service, 1914–18 (wounded, Military Cross). Adjutant, Grenadier Guards, 1919–20. Equerry and Assistant Private Secretary to King George V, 1920–36. Private Secretary to King Edward VIII, 1936; to King George VI, 1936–43. Privy Councillor, 1936. Knighted, 1937. Succeeded his father as Baron Hardinge of Penshurst, 1944 (his elder brother having died of wounds received in action on 18 December 1914). Extra Equerry to Queen Elizabeth II, 1952–60.

The King hopes that the debate which begins tomorrow will be satisfactory, and that the speeches which you have to make in it may not place too great a strain on you.

Yours very sincerely,
Alexander Hardinge

War Cabinet: conclusions
(Cabinet papers, 65/25)

26 January 1942   10 Downing Street
6 p.m.

The Prime Minister said that, in the course of his speech on the following day, he proposed to indicate that, under the organisation which had at first been proposed, it had been intended to set up a Far Eastern Council in London, but that the Australian and New Zealand Governments preferred representation on a Council in Washington.

In discussion, the view was expressed that there was still considerable misunderstanding both in Australia and New Zealand as to the practical working of the proposed Far Eastern Council in London. Those Governments might well be assuming that the main strategic planning of the war would now be conducted in Washington. It did not follow that this would happen, more especially since those working in London had behind them the whole machinery of the Chiefs of Staff organisation – an organisation to which there was no parallel in the United States.

Further, the view was very generally expressed that the needs of the Dominions would be better served by a Far Eastern Council in London than by the establishment of such a Council in Washington.

Sir Earle Page said that this was certainly his own view, and he was not without hope that the Australian Government would come round to it, provided that some time could be given for further consideration and that a fuller explanation could be sent to them not only as to the practical advantages of the proposed Far Eastern Council in London, but also of the arrangements which he understood were under consideration for improving the means of consultation in London with the Dominion Governments.

The Prime Minister said that he wished to avoid forcing upon the Dominion Governments a view which they were unwilling to adopt on a matter on which they felt strongly, more especially seeing that we might have to face a very serious situation in the Pacific. Nevertheless, while he was under an obligation to transmit the views of the Australian and New Zealand Governments to Washington without delay, he would consider whether he could avoid making any very specific reference to the matter in his speech on the following day, thus affording time for further explanations to be given.

The War Cabinet took note of this discussion.

The Prime Minister said that, in his speech in the House on the following day, he proposed to say that the Australian Government had stated that they desired that an accredited representative of the Commonwealth Government should have the right to be heard in the War Cabinet in the formulation and the direction of policy; and that they had been informed that we agreed to this request. New Zealand had asked for, and would be granted, the same privilege. Representatives of Canada and the Union of South Africa would also be welcomed here on the same terms.

War Cabinet: Confidential Annex
(Cabinet papers, 65/29)

26 January 1942   10 Downing Street
6 p.m.

The War Cabinet had before them a telegram from the Prime Minister of Australia to the Prime Minister, dated 24th January 1942.

The Prime Minister said that a very depressing report had been received from General Wavell, indicating that it looked as though Singapore might only be able to hold out for a few weeks. In this event we should have to consider whether we might not have to send to Burma some of the reinforcements destined for Malaya. It had, therefore, been necessary for the Defence Committee to consider what our action should be if we were unable to hold the fortress. But he thought that Sir Earle Page had unintentionally misled the Australian Government when he had reported to them that the Defence Committee had considered the evacuation of Singapore. The decision reached at the Meeting had been that the Battle of Johore and the defence of Singapore Island should be given the highest priority. Further, the orders issued to General Wavell had been that the battle should be fought out, if need be, in the ruins of Singapore.

The account given by Sir Earle Page to his Government was, therefore, incomplete. Clearly no decision could have been taken on such a grave matter without full consultation with the Dominions. Proceedings at the Defence Committee would be gravely hampered if an incomplete discussion, which formed no part of the Conclusions of the Meeting, was to be reported to the Dominion Governments.

The Prime Minister added that he did not propose to answer the telegram, but to refer it to the Chiefs of Staff.

Sir Earle Page said that his telegram to the Australian Prime Minister had been a factual statement of the position disclosed to the Defence Committee (Operations), together with his own observations. He conceived that he was within his rights in despatching such a telegram. In sending this telegram he had also had in mind that he could use this as an instance to reinforce the view which he had already laid before the Australian Government, that it was in their interest that the Far Eastern Council should be established in London, and not in Washington.

Turning to the passage in the part of the telegram which dealt with the reinforcement of the Pacific, Sir Earle Page said that it had undoubtedly been in Mr Curtin's mind, in drafting his telegram, that since the beginning of the war Australia had never been unwilling to send her Imperial Forces overseas. In doing so she had denuded herself to a dangerous extent.

The Prime Minister said that it went without saying that the Australian troops and air squadrons serving overseas must move homewards to the defence of their own country, now that danger threatened it. But effect could only be given to this process very gradually. All the available shipping was mortgaged for essential military movements.

In reply to a question, Sir Earle Page said that the Australian Government had accepted President Roosevelt's offer to send a large force of American troops to Australia.

Reference was also made to the movement of United States troops to New Caledonia.

The Minister of Supply[1] thought that it would be of advantage if the Australian Government could be informed that this movement of troops had been made possible by our having surrendered the use of ships which had been promised to us for other purposes.

Sir Earle Page referred to the need for sending fighter aircraft to Australia.

---

[1] Lord Beaverbrook.

The Prime Minister said that this country and the United States were sending a steady flow of aircraft to the Pacific theatre.

The Chief of the Air Staff[1] said that over 300 fighters and 300 aircraft of other types were being sent by the United States to Australia for onward despatch to the Pacific theatre. By far the quickest method of obtaining fighter aircraft for Australia would be if some part of these reinforcements could be retained in Australia.

The War Cabinet:

(1) Asked the Chiefs of Staff to report within two days on:

    (a) The reserves of men and materials available in Australia for the defence of that country:

    (b) The ways and means of despatching early reinforcements for Australia.

(2) Instructed the War Office and Air Ministry to prepare a Note setting out the steps which had already been taken to arrange for the despatch of British and US troops and air forces to the Far East.

(3) Took note that the Prime Minister and the Minister of Supply were in consultation regarding the possibility of making available to Australia reinforcements of armoured fighting vehicles.

Margot, Countess of Oxford and Asquith,[2] to Winston S. Churchill
(Churchill papers, 20/59)

26 January 1942   Savoy Hotel
London

Dearest Winston,

I feel <u>no</u>[3] anxiety for the outcome of tomorrow's debate. But there are <u>2</u> men of importance, and who would help you. One, you know – Stafford Cripps, the other <u>I</u> know – Oliver Lyttelton. Oliver is <u>wasted</u> in Cairo. When Gladstone[4] gave Henry the Home Office (out of the blue) you will remember that he was only known in 'Paper Buildings' and by a few good speeches in the House of Commons. You should promote Oliver Lyttelton. He is young, and very quick, and loyal. Above all he is

[1] Air Chief Marshal Sir Charles Portal.

[2] Emma Alice Margaret Tennant, 1864–1945. Known as 'Margot'. Married Herbert Henry Asquith (Home Secretary, 1892–5; Prime Minister, 1908–16) in 1894, as his second wife. Published four separate volumes of memoirs, including *The Autobiography of Margot Asquith* in 1921. Her husband died in 1928.

[3] Double underlining in original.

[4] William Ewart Gladstone, 1809–98. Four times Prime Minister, 1868–77, 1880–5, 1886, and 1892–4.

not <u>always</u> speaking to a dull public. Your Cabinet Ministers speak <u>far</u> too often.

Love,
Margot

General Thomas Blamey[1] to Winston S. Churchill
(Churchill papers, 20/69)

26 January 1942

It is at present difficult to know situation in Cyrenaica but last report indicates enemy thrust is not (repeat not) yet spent. There are indications that we have suffered a tactical reverse in Antelat area.

8th Army has not (repeat not) yet reported evacuation [of] Benghazi but shall not (repeat not) be surprised to hear it. Our withdrawal was planned before enemy counter thrust as normal precautionary measure in view weakness of our forces in forward area and Administrative difficulties over long L of C.

General Archibald Wavell to Winston S. Churchill
(Churchill papers, 20/69)

26 January 1942   Batavia
Personal

I did <u>not</u> (<u>underlined</u>) refuse Chinese help. You say I have 'now' accepted 49 and 93 Divisions. I accepted both these divisions when I was at Chungking on December 23rd and any delay in moving them down has been purely Chinese. These two divisions constitute 5th (?Chinese) Army I understand except for one other division of very doubtful quality. All I asked was that 6th Army should not be moved to Burmese frontier as it would be difficult to feed and communications inside Burma could not deal with it after Generalissimo demanded a line of communication purely Chinese and that Chinese troops should not be mixed with ours a condition impossible to fulfil at that time.

---

[1] Thomas Albert Blamey, 1884–1951. Born in New South Wales. On active service, 1914–18 (despatches seven times, DSO). Chief of Staff, Australian Corps, 1918; Australian Imperial Force, 1919. Chief Commissioner of Police, Victoria, 1925–37. Knighted, 1935. Chairman of the Australian Man Power Committee, 1939–40. General Officer Commanding 6th Australian Division, Australian Imperial Force, 1939–40; I Australian Corps, 1940–1; Australian Imperial Force, Middle East, 1941. Deputy Chief of Staff, Middle East, 1941. Commander-in-Chief, Allied Land Forces, South-West Pacific Area, 1942–5. Field Marshal, 1950.

2. I felt and still feel that to un-cover Yunnan by moving practically all Chinese troops in that province down to Burma would be unsound. Shortly Chinese had been proclaiming Yunnan and Burma Road seriously threatened by Japanese direct advance on Kunming from Siam.

3. British troops due for Burma from India and Africa should have been (?sufficient) if all went well and as many as communications could support. It was obviously better to defend Burma with Imperial troops than with Chinese and Governor particularly asked me not to accept more Chinese for Burma than was absolutely necessary.

4. Japanese advance in Tenasserin ought not to have had success it had as you will see by my telegram to CIGS.[1] GOC, Burma[2] has told me that even had whole of 5th and 6th Armies been available it would not have altered his dispositions in (?South).

5. I am of American sentiment about Chinese but democracies are apt to think with their hearts rather than with their heads and General's business is or should be to use his head for planning. I consider my judgment in accepting the Chinese help I did (2 divisions of 5th Army) and asking that 6th Army should be held in reserve in Kunming area was quite correct and I am sorry that my action seems to have been so misunderstood. I hope you will correct (?President)'s (?impression) if you get opportunity. I agree British prestige in China is low and can hardly be otherwise till we have had some success. It will not be increased by admission that we cannot hold Burma without Chinese help.

Winston S. Churchill: recollection
('The Hinge of Fate', pages 53–4)

27 January 1942

I was expected to make a full statement to Parliament about my mission to Washington and all that had happened in the five weeks I had been away. Two facts stood out in my mind. The first was that the Grand Alliance was bound to win the war in the long run. The second was that a vast, measureless array of disasters approached us in the onslaught of Japan. Everyone could see with intense relief that our life as a nation and Empire was no longer at stake. On the other hand, the fact that the sense of mortal danger was largely removed set every critic, friendly or malevolent, free to point out the many errors which had been made. Moreover,

[1] CIGS: the Chief of the Imperial General Staff, General Brooke.
[2] General Alexander.

many felt it their duty to improve our methods of conducting the war and thus shorten the fearful tale. I was myself profoundly disturbed by the defeats which had already fallen upon us, and no one knew better than I that these were but the beginnings of the deluge. The demeanour of the Australian Government, the well-informed and airily detached criticism of the newspapers, the shrewd and constant girding of twenty or thirty able Members of Parliament, the atmosphere of the lobbies, gave me the sense of an embarrassed, unhappy, baffled public opinion, albeit superficial, swelling and mounting about me on every side.

On the other hand, I was well aware of the strength of my position. I could count on the goodwill of the people for the share I had had in their survival in 1940. I did not underrate the broad, deep tide of national fidelity that bore me forward. The War Cabinet and the Chiefs of Staff showed me the highest loyalty. I was sure of myself. I made it clear, as occasion required, to those about me that I would not consent to the slightest curtailment of my personal authority and responsibility. The Press was full of suggestions that I should remain Prime Minister and make the speeches but cede the actual control of the war to someone else. I resolved to yield nothing to any quarter, to take the prime and direct responsibility upon myself, and to demand a Vote of Confidence from the House of Commons. I also remembered that wise French saying, '*On ne règne sur les âmes que par le calme.*'[1]

It was necessary above all to warn the House and the country of the misfortunes which impended upon us. There is no worse mistake in public leadership than to hold out false hopes soon to be swept away. The British people can face peril or misfortune with fortitude and buoyancy, but they bitterly resent being deceived or finding that those responsible for their affairs are themselves dwelling in a fool's paradise. I felt it vital, not only to my own position but to the whole conduct of the war, to discount future calamities by describing the immediate outlook in the darkest terms. It was also possible to do so at this juncture without prejudicing the military situation or disturbing that underlying confidence in ultimate victory which all were now entitled to feel. In spite of the shocks and stresses which each day brought, I did not grudge the twelve or fourteen hours of concentrated thought which ten thousand words of original composition on a vast, many-sided subject demanded, and while the flames of adverse war in the Desert licked my feet I succeeded in preparing my statement and appreciation of our case.

[1] One does not rule over peoples' souls except through calm.

Winston S. Churchill: speech
(Hansard)

27 January 1942

From time to time in the life of any Government there come occasions which must be clarified. No one who has read the newspapers of the last few weeks about our affairs at home and abroad can doubt that such an occasion is at hand.

Since my return to this country, I have come to the conclusion that I must ask to be sustained by a Vote of Confidence from the House of Commons. This is a thoroughly normal, constitutional, democratic procedure. A Debate on the war has been asked for. I have arranged it in the fullest and freest manner for three whole days. Any Member will be free to say anything he thinks fit about or against the Administration or against the composition or personalities of the Government, to his heart's content, subject only to the reservation which the House is always so careful to observe about military secrets. Could you have anything freer than that? Could you have any higher expression of democracy than that? Very few other countries have institutions strong enough to sustain such a thing while they are fighting for their lives.

I owe it to the House to explain to them what has led me to ask for their exceptional support at this time. It has been suggested that we should have a three days' Debate of this kind in which the Government would no doubt be lustily belaboured by some of those who have lighter burdens to carry, and that at the end we should separate without a Division. In this case sections of the Press which are hostile – and there are some whose hostility is pronounced – could declare that the Government's credit was broken, and it might even be hinted, after all that has passed and all the discussion there has been, that it had been privately intimated to me that I should be very reckless if I asked for a Vote of Confidence from Parliament.

And the matter does not stop there. It must be remembered that these reports can then be flashed all over the world, and that they are repeated in enemy broadcasts night after night in order to show that the Prime Minister has no right to speak for the nation and that the Government in Britain is about to collapse. Anyone who listens to the fulminations which come from across the water know that that is no exaggeration.

Of course, these statements from foreign sources would not be true, but neither would it be helpful to anyone that there should be any doubt about our position.

There is another aspect. We in this Island for a long time were alone, holding aloft the torch. We are no longer alone now. We are now at the centre and among those at the summit of 26 United Nations, comprising more than three-quarters of the population of the globe. Whoever speaks for Britain at this moment must be known to speak, not only in the name of the people – and of that I feel pretty sure I may – but in the name of Parliament and, above all, of the House of Commons. It is genuine public interest that requires that these facts should be made manifest afresh in a formal way.

We have had a great deal of bad news lately from the Far East, and I think it highly probable, for reasons which I shall presently explain, that we shall have a great deal more. Wrapped up in this bad news will be many tales of blunders and shortcomings, both in foresight and action. No one will pretend for a moment that disasters like these occur without there having been faults and shortcomings. I see all this rolling towards us like the waves in a storm, and that is another reason why I require a formal, solemn Vote of Confidence from the House of Commons, which hitherto in this struggle has never flinched. The House would fail in its duty if it did not insist upon two things, first, freedom of debate, and, secondly, a clear, honest, blunt Vote thereafter. Then we shall all know where we are, and all those with whom we have to deal, at home and abroad, friend or foe, will know where we are and where they are. It is because we are to have a free Debate, in which perhaps 20 to 30 Members can take part, that I demand an expression of opinion from the 300 or 400 Members who will have sat silent.

It is because things have gone badly and worse is to come that I demand a Vote of Confidence. This will be placed on the Paper today, to be moved at a later stage. I do not see why this should hamper anyone. If a Member has helpful criticisms to make, or even severe corrections to administer, that may be perfectly consistent with thinking that in respect of the Administration, such as it is, he might go farther and fare worse. But if an hon. Gentleman dislikes the Government very much and feels it in the public interest that it should be broken up, he ought to have the manhood to testify his convictions in the Lobby. There is no need to be mealy-mouthed in debate. There is no objection to anything being said, plain, or even plainer, and the Government will do their utmost to conform to any standard which may be set in the course of the Debate. But no one need be mealy-mouthed in debate, and no one should be chicken-hearted in voting. I have voted against Governments I have been elected to support, and, looking back, I have sometimes

felt very glad that I did so. Everyone in these rough times must do what
he thinks is his duty.

Mr Shinwell (Seaham): A free vote?

The Prime Minister: A vote under all the conditions which hitherto
have made the conduct of Parliamentary government possible. Surely
the hon. Gentleman is not the man to be frightened of a Whip? The
House of Commons, which is at present the most powerful representative Assembly in the world, must also – I am sure, will also – bear in
mind the effect produced abroad by all its proceedings. We have also to
remember how oddly foreigners view our country and its way of doing
things. When Rudolf Hess flew over here some months ago he firmly
believed that he had only to gain access to certain circles in this country
for what he described as 'the Churchill clique' –

Mr Thorne (Plaistow): Where is he now?

The Prime Minister: Where he ought to be – to be thrown out of power
and for a Government to be set up with which Hitler could negotiate a
magnanimous peace. The only importance attaching to the opinions
of Hess is the fact that he was fresh from the atmosphere of Hitler's
intimate table. But, Sir, I can assure you that since I have been back in
this country I have had anxious inquiries from a dozen countries, and
reports of enemy propaganda in a score of countries, all turning upon
the point whether His Majesty's present Government is to be dismissed
from power or not. This may seem silly to us, but in those mouths abroad
it is hurtful and mischievous to the common effort. I am not asking
for any special, personal favours in these circumstances, but I am sure
the House would wish to make its position clear; therefore I stand by
the ancient, constitutional, Parliamentary doctrine of free debate and
faithful voting.

Now I turn to the account of the war, which constitutes the claim
I make for the support and confidence of the House. Three or four
months ago we had to cope with the following situation. The German
invaders were advancing, blasting their way through Russia. The Russians were resisting with the utmost heroism. But no one could tell what
would happen, whether Leningrad, Moscow or Rostov would fall, or
where the German winter line would be established. No one can tell
now where it will be established, but now the boot is on the other leg.
We all agree that we must aid the valiant Russian Armies to the utmost
limit of our power. His Majesty's Government thought, and Parliament
upon reflection agreed with them, that the best aid we could give to
Russia was in supplies of many kinds of raw materials and of munitions,

particularly tanks and aircraft. Our Forces at home and abroad had for
long been waiting thirstily for these weapons. At last they were coming
to hand in large numbers. At home we have always the danger of invasion to consider and to prepare against. I will speak about the situation
in the Middle East presently. Nevertheless we sent Premier Stalin – for
that I gather is how he wishes to be addressed; at least, that is the form
in which he telegraphs to me – exactly what he asked for. The whole
quantity was promised and sent. There has been, I am sorry to say, a
small lag due to bad weather, but it will be made up by the early days of
February. This was a decision of major strategy and policy, and anyone
can see that it was right to put it first when they watch the wonderful
achievements, un-hoped for, undreamed of by us because we little
knew the Russian strength, but all the more glorious as they seem – the
wonderful achievements of the Russian Armies. Our munitions were
of course only a contribution to the Russian victory, but they were an
encouragement in Russia's darkest hour. Moreover, if we had not shown
a loyal effort to help our Ally, albeit at a heavy sacrifice to ourselves, I do
not think our relations with Premier Stalin and his great country would
be as good as they are now. There would have been a lack of comradeship, and the lack of comradeship might have spread reproaches on all
sides. Far from regretting what we did for Russia, I only wish it had been
in our power – but it was not – to have done more.

Three or four months ago, at a time when the German advance was
rolling onwards, we were particularly concerned with the possibility of
the Germans forcing the Don River, the capture of Rostov and the invasion of the Caucasus, and the reaching of the Baku oil wells before the
winter by the Panzer spearheads of the German Army. Everyone who has
been giving careful study and independent thought to this war, knows
how deep an anxiety that was in all our breasts three or four months
ago. Such an advance would not only have given the Germans the oil
which they are beginning seriously to need, but it would have involved
the destruction of the Russian Fleet and the loss of the command of the
Black Sea. It would have affected the safety of Turkey, and it would, in
due course, have exposed to the gravest dangers Persia, Iraq, Syria and
Palestine, and beyond those countries, all of which are now under our
control, it would have threatened the Suez Canal, Egypt and the Nile
Valley. At the same time as this menace defined itself with hideous and
increasing reality as it seemed, General von Rommel, with his army of
10 German and Italian divisions entrenched in his fortified positions at
and behind the Halfaya Pass, was preparing to make a decisive attack

on Tobruk as a preliminary to a renewed advance upon Egypt from the West. The Nile Valley was therefore menaced simultaneously by a direct attack from the West and by a more remote but in some ways more deadly attack from the North.

In such circumstances it is the classical rule of war, reinforced by endless examples – and some exceptions – that you prepare to fight a delaying action against one of the two attacks and concentrate, if possible, overwhelming strength against the other and nearer attack. We therefore approved General Auchinleck's plans for building up a delaying force in the vast region from Cyprus to the Caspian Sea, along what I may call the Levant–Caspian front, and preparing installations, airfields and communications upon which larger forces could be based, as time and transport allowed. On the other flank, the Western flank, we prepared to set upon Rommel and try to make a good job of him. For the sake of this battle in the Libyan Desert we concentrated everything we could lay our hands on, and we submitted to a very long delay, very painful to bear over here, so that all preparations could be perfected. We hoped to recapture Cyrenaica and the important airfields round Benghazi. But General Auchinleck's main objective was more simple. He set himself to destroy Rommel's army. Such was the mood in which we stood three or four months ago. Such was the broad strategical decision we took.

Now, when we see how events, which so often mock and falsify human effort and design, have shaped themselves, I am sure this was a right decision. General Auchinleck had demanded five months' preparation for his campaign, but on 18th November he fell upon the enemy. For more than two months in the desert the most fierce, continuous battle has raged between scattered bands of men, armed with the latest weapons, seeking each other dawn after dawn, fighting to the death throughout the day and then often long into the night. Here was a battle which turned out very differently from what was foreseen. All was dispersed and confused. Much depended on the individual soldier and the junior officer. Much, but not all; because this battle would have been lost on 24th November if General Auchinleck had not intervened himself, changed the command and ordered the ruthless pressure of the attack to be maintained without regard to risks or consequences. But for this robust decision we should now be back on the old line from which we had started, or perhaps further back. Tobruk would possibly have fallen, and Rommel might be marching towards the Nile. Since then the battle has declared itself. Cyrenaica has been regained. It has still to be held. We have not succeeded in destroying Rommel's army, but nearly two-thirds of it are wounded, prisoners or dead.

Perhaps I may give the figures to the House. In this strange, sombre battle of the desert, where our men have met the enemy for the first time – I do not say in every respect, because there are some things which are not all that we had hoped for – but, upon the whole, have met him with equal weapons, we have lost in killed, wounded and captured about 18,000 officers and men, of whom the greater part are British. We have in our possession 36,500 prisoners, including many wounded, of whom 10,500 are Germans. We have killed and wounded at least 11,500 Germans and 13,000 Italians – in all a total, accounted for exactly, of 61,000 men. There is also a mass of enemy wounded, some of whom have been evacuated to the rear or to the Westward – I cannot tell how many. Of the forces of which General Rommel disposed on 18th November, little more than one-third now remain, while 852 German and Italian aircraft have been destroyed and 336 German and Italian tanks. During this battle we have never had in action more than 45,000 men, against enemy forces – if they could be brought to bear – much more than double as strong. Therefore, it seems to me that this heroic, epic struggle in the desert, though there have been many local reverses and many ebbs and flows, has tested our manhood in a searching fashion and has proved not only that our men can die for King and country – everyone knew that – but that they can kill.

I cannot tell what the position at the present moment is on the Western front in Cyrenaica. We have a very daring and skilful opponent against us and, may I say across the havoc of war, a great General.[1] He has certainly received reinforcements. Another battle is even now in progress, and I make it a rule never to try and prophesy beforehand how battles will turn out. I always rejoice that I have made that rule. (An Hon. Member: 'What about the Skaggerak?') That was hardly a battle. Naturally, one does not say in a case like that that we have not a chance, because that is apt to be encouraging to the enemy and depressing to our own friends. In the general upshot, the fact remains that, whereas a year ago the Germans were telling all the neutrals that they would be in Suez by May, when some people talked of the possibility of a German descent upon Assiut, and many people were afraid that Tobruk would be stormed

---

[1] Churchill later wrote: 'My reference to Rommel passed off quite well at the moment. Later on I heard that some people had been offended. They could not feel that any virtue should be recognised in an enemy leader. This churlishness is a well-known streak in human nature, but contrary to the spirit in which a war is won, or a lasting peace established' (*The Hinge of Fate*, page 59).

and others feared for the Nile Valley, Cairo, Alexandria and the Canal, we have conducted an effective offensive against the enemy and hurled him backward, inflicting upon him incomparably more – well, I should not say incomparably, because I have just given the comparison – but far heavier losses and damage than we have suffered ourselves. Not only has he lost three times our losses on the battlefield, approximately, but the blue waters of the Mediterranean have, thanks to the enterprise of the Royal Navy, our submarines and Air Force, drowned a large number of the reinforcements which have been continually sent. This process has had further important successes during the last few days. Whether you call it a victory or not, it must be dubbed up to the present, although I will not make any promises, a highly profitable transaction, and certainly is an episode of war most glorious to the British, South African, New Zealand, Indian, Free French and Polish soldiers, sailors and airmen who have played their part in it. The prolonged, stubborn, steadfast and successful defence of Tobruk by Australian and British troops was an essential preliminary, over seven hard months, to any success which may have been achieved.

Let us see what has happened on the other flank, the Northern flank, of the Nile Valley. What has happened to Palestine, Syria, Iraq and Persia? There we must thank Russia. There the valour of the Russian Armies has warded off dangers which we saw and which we undoubtedly ran. The Caucasus and the precious oilfields of Baku, the great Anglo-Persian oilfields, are denied to the enemy. Winter has come. Evidently we have the time to strengthen still further our Forces and organizations in those regions. Therefore, Sir, I present to you, in laying the whole field open and bare and surveying it in all its parts, for all are related, a situation in the Nile Valley, both West and East, incomparably easier than anything we have ever seen since we were deserted by the French Bordeaux–Vichy Government and were set upon by Italy. The House will not fail to discern the agate points upon which this vast improvement has turned. It is only by the smallest margin that we have succeeded so far in beating Rommel in Cyrenaica and destroying two-thirds of his forces. Every tank, every aircraft squadron was needed. It is only by the victories on the Russian flank on the Black Sea coast that we have been spared the overrunning of all those vast lands from the Levant to the Caspian, which in turn give access to India, Persia, the Persian Gulf, the Nile Valley and the Suez Canal.

I have told the House the story of these few months, and hon. Members will see from it how narrowly our resources have been strained and by what a small margin and by what strokes of fortune – for which we claim no credit – we have survived – so far. Where should we have been, I wonder, if we had yielded to the clamour which was so loud three or four months ago that we should invade France or the Low Countries? We can still see on the walls the inscription, 'Second Front Now.' Who did not feel the appeal of that? But imagine what our position would have been if we had yielded to this vehement temptation. Every ton of our shipping, every flotilla, every aeroplane, the whole strength of our Army would be committed and would be fighting for life on the French shores or on the shores of the Low Countries. All these troubles of the Far East and the Middle East might have sunk to insignificance compared with the question of another and far worse Dunkirk.

Here, let me say, I should like to pay my tribute to one who has gone from us since I left this country, Mr Lees-Smith,[1] who, I remember, spoke with so much profound wisdom on this point at a moment when many opinions were in flux about it. His faithful, selfless and wise conduct of the important work which he discharged in this House was undoubtedly of great assistance to us all, not only to the Government but to us all, in the various stages of the war. His memory as a distinguished Parliamentarian will long find an honoured place in the recollection of those who had the fortune to be his colleagues.

Sometimes things can be done by saying 'Yes,' and sometimes things can be done by saying 'No.' Yet I suppose there are some of those who were vocal and voluble, and even clamant, for a second front to be opened in France, who are now going to come up bland and smiling and ask why it is that we have not ample forces in Malaya, Burma, Borneo and the Celebes. There are times when so many things happen, and happen so quickly, and time seems to pass in such a way that you can neither say it is long or short, that it is easy to forget what you have said three months before. You may fail to connect it with what you are advocating at the particular moment. Throughout a long and variegated Parliamentary life this consideration has led me to try and keep a watchful eye on that danger myself. You never can tell. There are also people who talk and bear themselves as if they had prepared for this war with great armaments and long, careful preparation. But that is not true. In two and a half years of fighting we have only just managed to keep our heads

<hr>

[1] Hastings Bertrand Lees-Smith, 1878–1941. Liberal MP for Northampton, 1910–18. Joined the Labour Party in 1919. Labour MP for Keighley, 1922–3, 1924–31, and from 1935 until his death. Postmaster-General, 1929–31. President of the Board of Education, 1931. Privy Councillor, 1931. Acting Chairman of the Parliamentary Labour Party, 1940–1.

above water. When I was called upon to be Prime Minister, now nearly two years ago, there were not many applicants for the job. Since then, perhaps, the market has improved. In spite of the shameful negligence, gross muddles, blatant incompetence, complacency, and lack of organising power which are daily attributed to us – and from which chidings we endeavour to profit – we are beginning to see our way through. It looks as if we were in for a very bad time, but provided we all stand together, and provided we throw in the last spasm of our strength, it also looks, more than it ever did before, as if we were going to win.

While facing Germany and Italy here and in the Nile Valley we have never had the power to provide effectively for the defence of the Far East. My whole argument so far has led up to that point. It may be that this or that might have been done which was not done, but we have never been able to provide effectively for the defence of the Far East against an attack by Japan. It has been the policy of the Cabinet at almost all costs to avoid embroilment with Japan until we were sure that the United States would also be engaged. We even had to stoop, as the House will remember, when we were at our very weakest point, to close the Burma Road for some months. I remember that some of our present critics were very angry about it, but we had to do it. There never has been a moment, there never could have been a moment, when Great Britain or the British Empire, single-handed, could fight Germany and Italy, could wage the Battle of Britain, the Battle of the Atlantic and the Battle of the Middle East and at the same time stand thoroughly prepared in Burma, the Malay Peninsula, and generally in the Far East against the impact of a vast military Empire like Japan, with more than 70 mobile divisions, the third navy in the world, a great air force and the thrust of 80 or 90 millions of hardy, warlike Asiatics. If we had started to scatter our forces over these immense areas in the Far East, we should have been ruined. If we had moved large armies of troops urgently needed on the war fronts to regions which were not at war and might never be at war we should have been altogether wrong. We should have cast away the chance, which has now become something more than a chance, of all of us emerging safely from the terrible plight in which we have been plunged.

We therefore have lain – I am putting it as bluntly as I can – for nearly two years under the threat of an attack by Japan with which we had no means of coping. But as time has passed the mighty United States, under the leadership of President Roosevelt, from reasons of its own interest and safety but also out of chivalrous regard for the cause of freedom and democracy, has drawn ever nearer to the confines of the struggle.

And now that the blow has fallen it does not fall on us alone. On the contrary, it falls upon united forces and United Nations, which are unquestionably capable of enduring the struggle, of retrieving the losses and of preventing another such stroke ever being delivered again.

There is an argument with which I will deal as I pass along to pursue my theme. It is said by some, 'If only you had organized the munitions production of this country properly and had had a Minister of Production (and that is not a question which should be dogmatised upon either way) it would have made everything all right. There would have been enough for all needs. We should have had enough supplies for Russia, enough well-equipped squadrons and divisions to defend the British Islands, to sustain the Middle East and to arm the Far East effectively.' But that is really not true. As a matter of fact, our munitions output is gigantic, has for some time been very large indeed, and it is bounding up in a most remarkable manner. In the last year, 1941, although we were at war in so many theatres and on so many fronts, we have produced more than double the munitions equipment of the United States, which was arming heavily, though of course a lap behind on the road. This condition will naturally be rapidly removed as the full power of American industry comes into full swing.

But, Sir, in the last six months, thanks to the energies of Lord Beaverbrook and the solid spadework done by his predecessors and the passage of time – he particularly asks me to say that – (An Hon. Member: 'Who did?') – Lord Beaverbrook; I should have said it anyway – our munitions output has risen in the following respects: We are producing more than twice as many far more complicated guns every month than we did in the peak of the 1917–18 war period, and the curve is rising. The guns are infinitely more complicated. Tank production has doubled in the last six months. Small arms production is more than twice what it was six months ago. Filled rounds of ammunition have doubled in the last six months. I could go on with the catalogue, but these are not doublings from early very small totals, they are doublings from the totals we boasted about, as far as we dared, six months ago. There has been an immense leap forward. In aircraft production there is a steady increase not only in the numbers but also in the size and quality of the aircraft, though I must say there has not been all the increase which I had hoped for.

But all this has nothing to do with the preparations it was open to us to make in Malaya and Burma and generally in the Far East. The limiting factor has not been troops or even equipment. The limiting factor has been transport, even assuming we had wished to take this measure and had had this great surplus. From the time that this present Government was formed, from the moment it was formed I may say, every scrap of shipping we could draw away from our vital supply routes, every U-boat escort we could divert from the Battle of the Atlantic, has been busy to the utmost capacity to carry troops, tanks and munitions from this Island to the East. There has been a ceaseless flow, and as for aircraft they have not only been moved by sea but by every route, some very dangerous and costly routes, to the Eastern battlefields. The decision was taken, as I have explained, to make our contribution to Russia, to try to beat Rommel and to form a stronger front from the Levant to the Caspian. It followed from that decision that it was in our power only to make a moderate and partial provision in the Far East against the hypothetical danger of a Japanese onslaught. Sixty thousand men, indeed, were concentrated at Singapore, but priority in modern aircraft, in tanks, and in anti-aircraft and anti-tank artillery was accorded to the Nile Valley.

For this decision in its broad strategic aspects, and also in its diplomatic policy in regard to Russia, I take the fullest personal responsibility. If we have handled our resources wrongly, no one is so much to blame as I am. If we have not got large modern air forces, and tanks in Burma and Malaya tonight no one is more accountable than I am. Why then should I be called upon to pick out scapegoats, to throw the blame on generals or airmen or sailors? Why, then, should I be called upon to drive away loyal and trusted colleagues and friends to appease the clamour of certain sections of the British and Australian Press, or in order to take the edge off our reverses in Malaya and the Far East, and the punishment which we have yet to take there? I would be ashamed to do such a thing at such a time, and if I were capable of doing it, believe me, I should be incapable of rendering this country or this House any further service.

I say that without in the slightest degree seeking to relieve myself from my duties and responsibility to endeavour to make continual improvements in Ministerial positions. It is the duty of every Prime Minister to the House, but we have to be quite sure that they are improvements in every case, and not only in every case but in the setting. I could not possibly descend to, as the German radio repeatedly credits me with, an attempt to get out of difficulties in which I really bear the main load by offering up scapegoats to public displeasure. Many people, many very well-meaning people, begin their criticisms and articles by saying, 'Of course, we are all in favour of the Prime Minister because he has the people behind him. But what about the muddles made by this or that Department; what about that General or this Minister?' But I am the man that Parliament and the nation have got to blame for the general way in which they are served, and I cannot serve them effectively unless, in spite of all that has gone wrong, and that is going to go wrong, I have their trust and faithful aid.

I must linger for a moment on our political affairs, because we are conducting the war on the basis of a full democracy and a free Press, and that is an attempt which has not been made before in such circumstances. A variety of attacks are made upon the composition of the Government. It is said that it is formed upon a party and political basis. But so is the House of Commons. It is silly to extol the Parliamentary system and then, in the next breath, to say, 'Away with party and away with politics.' From one quarter I am told that the leaders of the Labour party ought to be dismissed from the Cabinet. This would be a return to party Government pure and simple.

From opposite quarters it is said that no one who approved of Munich should be allowed to hold office. To do that would be to cast a reflection upon the great majority of the nation at that time, and also to deny the strongest party in the House any proportionate share in the National Government, which again, in turn, might cause inconvenience. Even my right hon. Friend the leader of the Liberal party – (An Hon. Member: 'Who is he?') – the Secretary of State for Air,[1] whose help today I value so much and with whom, as a lifelong friend, it is a pleasure to work, even he has not escaped unscathed. If I were to show the slightest weakness in dealing with these opposite forms of criticism, not only should I deprive myself of loyal and experienced colleagues, but I should destroy the National Government and rupture the war-time unity of Parliament itself.

Other attacks are directed against individual Ministers. I have been urged to make an example of the Chancellor of the Duchy of Lancaster,[2] who is now returning from his mission in the Far East. Thus, he would be made to bear the blame for our misfortunes. The position of the Chancellor of the Duchy of Lancaster at the head of the Council which he had been instructed to form at Singapore was rendered obsolete by the decision which I reached with the President of the United States to set up a Supreme Commander for the main fighting zone in the Far East. The whole conception of a Supreme Commander is that, under the direction of the Governments he serves, he is absolute master of all authorities in the region assigned to him. This would be destroyed if

[1] Sir Archibald Sinclair.
[2] Alfred Duff Cooper.

political functionaries representing the various nations – for it is not only this country which would be represented; others would have to be represented as well as ours – were clustered round him. The function of the Chancellor of the Duchy was therefore exhausted by the appointment of General Wavell to the Supreme Command. I may say that regret was expressed at his departure by the New Zealand and Australian Governments, and still more by the Council he formed at Singapore, which, in a localised and subordinate form, it has been found necessary to carry on. When I am invited, under threats of unpopularity to myself or the Government, to victimise the Chancellor of the Duchy, and throw him to the wolves, I say to those who make this amiable suggestion, I can only say to them, 'I much regret that I am unable to gratify your wishes,' – or words to that effect.

The outstanding question upon which the House should form its judgment for the purposes of the impending Division is whether His Majesty's Government were right in giving a marked priority in the distribution of the forces and equipment we could send overseas, to Russia, to Libya, and, to a lesser extent, to the Levant–Caspian danger front, and whether we were right in accepting, for the time being, a far lower standard of forces and equipment for the Far East than for these other theatres. The first obvious fact is that the Far Eastern theatre was at peace and that the other theatres were in violent or imminent war. It would evidently have been a very improvident use of our limited resources – as I pointed out earlier – if we had kept large masses of troops and equipment spread about the immense areas of the Pacific or in India, Burma and the Malay Peninsula, standing idle, month by month and perhaps year by year, without any war occurring. Thus, we should have failed in our engagements to Russia, which has meanwhile struck such staggering blows at the German Army, and we should have lost the battle in Cyrenaica, which we have not yet won, and we might now be fighting defensively well inside the Egyptian frontier. There is the question on which the House should make up its mind. We had not the resources to meet all the perils and pressures that came upon us.

But this question, serious and large as it is by itself, cannot be wholly decided without some attempt to answer the further question – what was the likelihood of the Far Eastern theatre being thrown into war by a Japanese attack? I have explained how very delicately we walked, and how painful it was at times, how very careful I was every time that we should not be exposed single-handed to this onslaught which we were utterly incapable of meeting. But it seemed irrational to suppose that in the last six months – which is what I am principally dealing with – the Japanese, having thrown away their opportunity of attacking us in the autumn of 1940, when we were so much weaker, so much less well-armed, and all alone, should at this period have plunged into a desperate struggle against the combined Forces of the British Empire and the United States. Nevertheless, nations, like individuals, commit irrational acts, and there were forces at work in Japan, violent, murderous, fanatical and explosive forces, which no one could measure.

On the other hand, the probability, since the Atlantic Conference, at which I discussed these matters with Mr Roosevelt, that the United States, even if not herself attacked, would come into a war in the Far East, and thus make final victory sure, seemed to allay some of these anxieties. That expectation has not been falsified by the events. It fortified our British decision to use our limited resources on the actual fighting fronts. As time went on, one had greater assurance that if Japan ran amok in the Pacific, we should not fight alone. It must also be remembered that over the whole of the Pacific scene brooded the great power of the United States Fleet, concentrated at Hawaii. It seemed very unlikely that Japan would attempt the distant invasion of the Malay Peninsula, the assault upon Singapore, and the attack upon the Dutch East Indies, while leaving behind them in their rear this great American Fleet. However, to strengthen the position as the situation seemed to intensify we sent the *Prince of Wales* and the *Repulse* to form the spear-point of the considerable battle forces which we felt ourselves at length able to form in the Indian Ocean. We reinforced Singapore to a considerable extent and Hong Kong to the extent which we were advised would be sufficient to hold the island for a long time. Besides this in minor ways we took what precautions were open to us. On 7th December the Japanese, by a sudden attack, delivered while their envoys were still negotiating at Washington, crippled for the time being the American Pacific Fleet, and a few days later inflicted very heavy naval losses on us by sinking the *Prince of Wales* and the *Repulse.*

For the time being, therefore, naval superiority in the Pacific and in the Malaysian Archipelago has passed from the hands of the two leading naval Powers into the hands of Japan. How long it will remain in Japanese hands is a Matter on which I do not intend to speculate. But at any rate it will be long enough for Japan to inflict very heavy and painful losses on all of the United Nations who have establishments and possessions in the Far East. The Japanese no doubt will try to peg out claims and lodgments over all this enormous area, and to organize, in the interval before they lose command of the seas, a local command of the air which will render their expulsion and destruction a matter of considerable time and exertion.

Here I must point out a very simple strategic truth. If there are 1,000 islands and 100 valuable military key points and you put 1,000 men on every one of them or whatever it may be, the Power that has the command of the sea and carries with it the local command of the air, can go around to every one of these places in turn, destroy or capture their garrisons, ravage and pillage them, ensconce themselves wherever they think fit, and then pass on with their circus to the next place. It would be vain to suppose that such an attack could be met by local defence. You might disperse 1,000,000 men over these immense areas and yet only provide more prey to the dominant Power. On the other hand, these conditions will be reversed when the balance of sea power and air power changes, as it will surely change.

Such is the phase of the Pacific war into which we have now entered. I cannot tell how long it will last. All I can tell the House it that it will be attended by very heavy punishment which we shall have to endure, and that presently, if we persevere, as I said just now about the Russian front, the boot will be on the other leg. That is why we should not allow ourselves to get rattled because this or that place has been captured, because, once the ultimate power of the United Nations has been brought to bear, the opposite process will be brought into play, and will move forward remorselessly to the final conclusion, provided that we persevere, provided that we fight with the utmost vigour and tenacity, and provided, above all, that we remain united.

Here I should like to express, in the name of the House, my admiration of the splendid courage and quality with which the small American Army, under General MacArthur,[1] has resisted brilliantly for so long, at desperate odds, the hordes of Japanese who have been hurled against it by superior air power and superior sea power. Amid our own troubles, we send out to General MacArthur and his soldiers, and also to the Filipinos, who are defending their native soil with vigour and courage, our salute across those wide spaces which we and the United States will presently

---

[1] Douglas MacArthur, 1880–1964. 2nd Lieutenant, Engineers, United States Army, 1903. On active service, 1917–18 (twice wounded). Temporary Brigadier-General, 1918. Chief of Staff, United States Army, 1930–5. Field Marshal of the Philippine Army, 1936. Retired, 1936. Returned to active duty, 1942. Commander-in-Chief, Allied Forces, South-West Pacific Area, 1943–51. Honorary knighthood, 1943. Commander-in-Chief, United States Forces, Far East Command, 1943–51. Supreme Commander, Allied Powers in Japan, 1945–51. Commander-in-Chief, United Nations Forces in Korea, 1950–1.

rule again together. Nor must I fail to pay a tribute, in the name of the House, to the Dutch, who, in the air and with their submarines, their surface craft, and their solid fighting troops, are playing one of the main parts in the struggle now going on in the Malaysian Archipelago.

We have to turn our eyes for a moment to the hard-fought battle which is raging upon the approaches to Singapore and in the Malay Peninsula. I am not going to make any forecast about that now, except that it will be fought to the last inch by the British, Australian and Indian troops, which are in the line together, and which have been very considerably reinforced. The hon. Member for the Eve Division of Suffolk (Mr Granville)[1] had a very sound military idea the other day, when he pointed out the importance of sending reinforcements of aircraft to assist our ground forces at Singapore and in Burma. I entirely agree with him. In fact, we anticipated his suggestion. Before I left for the United States, on 12th December, the moment, that is to say, when the situation in Singapore and Pearl Harbour had disclosed itself, it was possible to make a swift redistribution of our Forces. The moment was favourable. General Auchinleck was making headway in Cyrenaica; the Russian front not only stood unbroken but had begun the advance in a magnificent counter-attack, and we were able to order a large number of measures, which there is no need to elaborate, but which will be capable of being judged by their results as the next few weeks and the next few months unfold in the Far East.

When I reached the United States, accompanied by our principal officers and large technical staffs, further important steps were taken by the President, with my cordial assent, and with the best technical advice we could obtain, to move from many directions everything that ships could carry and all air power that could be flown, transported and serviced to suitable points. The House would be very ill-advised to suppose that the seven weeks which have passed since 7th December have been weeks of apathy and indecision for the English-speaking world. Odd as it may seem, quite a lot has been going on. But we must not nourish or indulge light and extravagant hopes or suppose that the advantages which the enemy have gained can soon or easily be taken from him. However, to sum up the bad and the good together, in spite of the many trag-

[1] Edgar Louis Granville, 1899–1998. Served with Australian Infantry Force, Gallipoli, Egypt, and France, 1915–18. Liberal MP, 1929–31; National Liberal, 1931–42; Liberal, 1942–51. Parliamentary Private Secretary to Herbert Samuel, 1931; to Sir John Simon, 1931–6. Captain, Royal Artillery, 1939–40. Created Baron, 1967. Sat in the Lords as an Independent.

edies past and future, and with all pity for those who have suffered and will suffer, I must profess my profound thankfulness for what has happened throughout the whole world in the last two months.

I now turn for a short space – I hope I am not unduly wearying the House, but I feel that the war has become so wide that there are many aspects that must be regarded – to the question of the organization, the international, inter-Allied or inter-United Nations organization, which must be developed to meet the fact that we are a vast confederacy. To hear some people talk, however, one would think that the way to win the war is to make sure that every Power contributing armed forces and every branch of these armed forces is represented on all the councils and organisations which have to be set up, and that everybody is fully consulted before anything is done. That is in fact the most sure way to lose a war. You have to be aware of the well-known danger of having 'more harness than horse,' to quote a homely expression. Action to be successful must rest in the fewest number of hands possible. Nevertheless, now that we are working in the closest partnership with the United States and have also to consider our Alliance with Russia and with China, as well as the bonds which unite us with the rest of the 26 United Nations and with our Dominions, it is evident that our system must become far more complex than heretofore.

I had many discussions with the President upon the Anglo-American war direction, especially as it affects this war against Japan, to which Russia is not yet a party. The physical and geographical difficulties of finding a common working centre for the leaders of nations and the great staffs of nations which cover the whole globe are insuperable. Whatever plan is made will be open to criticism and many valid objections. There is no solution that can be found where the war can be discussed from day to day fully by all the leading military and political authorities concerned. I have, however, arranged with President Roosevelt that there should be a body in Washington called the Combined Chiefs of the Staff Committee, consisting of the three United States Chiefs of the Staff, men of the highest distinction, and three high officers representing and acting under the general instructions of the British Chiefs of the Staff Committee in London. This body will advise the President, and in the event of divergence of view between the British and American Chiefs of the Staff or their representatives, the difference must be adjusted by personal agreement between him and me as representing our respective countries. We must also concert together the closest association with Premier Stalin and Generalissimo Chiang Kai-shek as well as with the rest of the Allied and Associated Powers. We shall, of course, also remain in the closest touch with one another on all important questions of policy.

In order to wage the war effectively against Japan, it was agreed that I should propose to those concerned the setting-up of a Pacific Council in London, on the Ministerial plane, comprising Great Britain, Australia, New Zealand and the Dutch Government. Assisted by the British Chiefs of the Staff and the great staffs organisations beneath them, I was to try to form and focus a united view. This would enable the British Commonwealth to act as a whole and form part of plans – plans which are at present far advanced – for collaboration at the appropriate levels in the spheres of defence, foreign affairs and supply. Thus the united view of the British Commonwealth and the Dutch would be transmitted, at first, on the Chiefs of the Staff level, to the combined Chiefs of the Staff Committee sitting in Washington. In the event of differences between the members of the Pacific Council in London, dissentient opinions would also be transmitted. In the event of differences between the London and Washington bodies, it would be necessary for the President and me to reach an agreement. I must point out that it is necessary for everybody to reach an agreement, for nobody can compel anybody else.

The Dutch Government, which is seated in London, might be willing to agree to this arrangement, but the Australian Government desired and the New Zealand Government preferred that this Council of the Pacific should be in Washington, where it would work alongside the Combined Chiefs of the Staff Committee. I have therefore transmitted the views of these two Dominions to the President, but I have not yet received, nor do I expect for a few says to receive, his reply. I am not, therefore, in a position today to announce, as I had hoped, the definite and final arrangements for the Pacific Council.

I should like to say, however, that underlying these structural arrangements are some very practical and simple facts upon which there is full agreement. The Supreme Commander has assumed control of the fighting areas in the South-West Pacific called the 'ABDA' area – ABDA – called after the countries which are involved, not the countries which are in the area but the countries which are involved in that area, namely, America, Britain, Dutch and Australasia. We do not propose to burden the Supreme Commander with frequent instructions. He has his general orders, and he has addressed himself with extraordinary buoyancy to his most difficult task, and President Roosevelt and I, representing, for my part, the British Government, are determined that he shall have a chance and a free hand to carry it out. The action in the Straits of Macassar undertaken by forces assigned to this area apparently has had very considerable success, of the full extent of which I am not yet advised. The manner in which General Wavell took up his task, the speed with which he has flown from place to place, the telegrams which he has sent describing the methods by which he was grappling with the situation and the forming of the central organism which was needed to deal with it – all this has made a most favourable impression upon the high officers, military and political, whom I met in the United States. This is all going on. Our duty, upon which we have been constantly engaged for some time, is to pass reinforcements of every kind, especially air, into the new war zone, from every quarter and by every means, with the utmost speed.

In order to extend the system of unified command which has been set up in the 'ABDA' area – that is to say, the South-West Pacific – where the actual fighting is going on, in order to extend that system to all areas in which the forces of more than one of the United Nations – because that is the term we have adopted – will be operating, the Eastward approaches to Australia and New Zealand have been styled the Anzac area, and are under United States command, the communications between the Anzac area and America are a United States responsibility, while the communications across the Indian Ocean and from India remain a British responsibility. All this is now working, while the larger constitutional, or semi-constitutional, discussions and structural arrangements are being elaborated by telegrams passing to and fro between so many Governments. All this is now working fully and actively from hour to hour, and it must not, therefore, be supposed that any necessary military action has been held up pending the larger structural arrangements which I have mentioned.

Now I come to the question of our own Empire or Commonwealth of Nations. The fact that Australia and New Zealand are in the immediate danger zone reinforces the demand that they should be represented in the War Cabinet of Great Britain and Northern Ireland. We have always been ready to form an Imperial War Cabinet containing the Prime Ministers of the four Dominions. Whenever any of them have come here they have taken their seats at our table as a matter of course. Unhappily, it has not been possible to get them all here together at once. General Smuts may not be able to come over from South Africa, and Mr Mackenzie King could unfortunately stay only for a short time. But Mr Fraser was with us, and it was a great pleasure to have him, and we had a three months' visit from Mr Menzies,[1] which was also a great success, and we were all very sorry when his most valuable knowledge of our affairs and the war position, and his exceptional abilities, were lost. For the last three months we have had Sir Earle Page representing the Commonwealth Government at Cabinets when war matters and Australian matters were under discussion and also, in similar circumstances, upon the Defence Committee. As a matter of fact this has always been interpreted in the most broad and elastic fashion. The Australian Government have now asked specifically 'that an accredited representative of the Commonwealth Government should have the right to be heard in the War Cabinet in the formulation and the direction of policy.' We have of course agreed to this. New Zealand feels bound to ask for similar representation, and the same facilities will of course be available to Canada and South Africa. The presence at the Cabinet table of Dominion representatives who have no power to take decisions and can only report to their Governments evidently raises some serious problems but none, I trust, which cannot be got over with good will. It must not, however, be supposed that in any circumstances the presence of Dominion representatives for certain purposes could in any way affect the collective responsibility of His Majesty's Servants in Great Britain to Crown and Parliament.

I am sure we all sympathise with our kith and kin in Australia now that the shield of British and American sea power has, for the time being, been withdrawn from them so unexpectedly and so tragically and now that hostile bombers may soon be within range of Australian shores. We shall not put any obstacle to the return of the splendid Australian troops who volunteered for Imperial service to defend their own homeland or whatever part of the Pacific theatre may be thought most expedient. We are taking many measures in conjunction with the United States to increase the security of Australia and New Zealand and to send them reinforcements, arms and equipment by the shortest and best routes. I always hesitate to express opinions about the future, because things turn out so very oddly, but I will go so far as to say that it may be that the Japanese, whose game is what I may call 'to make hell while the sun shines,' are more likely to occupy themselves in securing their rich prizes in the Philippines, the Dutch East Indies and the Malayan Archipelago and in seizing island bases for defensive

---

[1] Robert Gordon Menzies, 1894–1978. Prime Minister of Australia, 1939–41. Minister for Coordination of Defence, 1939–42. Minister for Information and Minister for Munitions, 1940. Leader of the Opposition, 1943–9. Prime Minister, 1949–66. Knight of the Garter, 1963.

purposes for the attack which is obviously coming towards them at no great distance of time – a tremendous onslaught which will characterise the future in 1942 and 1943. (An Hon. Member: '1944 and 1945?') No, I do not think we can stretch our views beyond those dates, but, again, we must see how we go. I think they are much more likely to be arranging themselves in those districts which they have taken or are likely to take than to undertake a serious mass invasion of Australia. That would seem to be a very ambitious overseas operation for Japan to undertake in the precarious and limited interval before the British and American navies regain – as they must certainly regain, through the new building that is advancing, and for other reasons – the unquestionable command of the Pacific Ocean. However, everything in human power that we can do to help Australia, or persuade America to do, we will do; and meanwhile I trust that reproaches and recriminations of all kinds will be avoided, and that if any are made, we in Britain will not take part in them.

Let me, in conclusion, return to the terrific changes which have occurred in our affairs during the last few months and particularly in the last few weeks. We have to consider the prospects of the war in 1942 and also in 1943, and, as I said just now, it is not useful to look further ahead than that. The moment that the United States was set upon and attacked by Japan, Germany and Italy – that is to say, within a few days of December 7, 1941 – I was sure it was my duty to cross the Atlantic and establish the closest possible relationship with the President and Government of the United States, and also to develop the closest contacts, personal and professional, between the British Chiefs of the Staff and their trans-Atlantic deputies, and with the American Chiefs of the Staff who were there to meet them.

Having crossed the Atlantic, it was plainly my duty to visit the great Dominion of Canada. The House will have read with admiration and deep interest the speech made by the Prime Minister of Canada yesterday on Canada's great and growing contribution to the common cause in men, in money, and in materials. A notable part of that contribution is the financial offer which the Canadian Government have made to this country. The sum involved is one billion Canadian dollars, about £225,000,000. I know the House will wish me to convey to the Government of Canada our lively appreciation of their timely and most generous offer. It is unequalled in its scale in the whole history of the British Empire, and it is a convincing proof of the determination of Canada to make her maximum contribution towards the successful prosecution of the war.

During those three weeks which I spent in Mr Roosevelt's home and family, I established with him relations not only of comradeship, but, I think I may say, of friendship. We can say anything to each other, however painful. When we parted he wrung my hand, saying, 'We will fight this through to the bitter end, whatever the cost may be.' Behind him rises the gigantic and hitherto unmobilised gigantic power of the people of the United States, carrying with them in their life and death struggle the entire, or almost the entire, Western hemisphere.

At Washington, we and our combined staffs surveyed the entire scene of the war, and we reached a number of important practical decisions. Some of them affect future operations and cannot, of course, be mentioned, but others have been made public by declaration or by events. The vanguard of an American Army has already arrived in the United Kingdom. Very considerable forces are following as opportunity may serve. These forces will take their station in the British Isles and face with us whatever is coming our way. They impart a freedom of movement to all forces in the British Isles greater than we could otherwise have possessed. Numerous United States fighter and bomber squadrons will also take part in the defence of Britain and in the ever-increasing bombing offensive against Germany. The United States Navy is linked in the most intimate union with the Admiralty, both in the Atlantic and the Pacific. We shall plan our Naval moves together as if we were literally one people.

In the next place, we formed this league of 26 United Nations in which the principal partners at the present time are Great Britain and the British Empire, the United States, the Union of Socialist Soviet Republics of Russia, and the Republic of China, together with the stout-hearted Dutch, and the representatives of the rest of the 26 Powers. This Union is based on the principles of the Atlantic Charter. It aims at the destruction of Hitlerism in all its forms and manifestations in every corner of the globe. We will march forward together until every vestige of this villainy has been extirpated from the life of the world.

Thirdly, as I have explained at some length, we addressed ourselves to the war against Japan and to the measures to be taken to defend Australia, New Zealand, the Netherlands East Indies, Malaya, Burma, and India against Japanese attack or invasion.

Fourthly, we have established a vast common pool of weapons and munitions, of raw materials and of shipping, the outline of which has been set forth in a series of memoranda which I have initialled with the President. I had a talk with him last night on the telephone, as a result of which an announcement has been made in the early hours of this morning in the United States, and I have a White Paper for the House which will be available, I think, in a very short time. Many people have been staggered by the figures of prospective American output of war weapons which the President announced to Congress, and the Germans have affected to regard them with incredulity. I can only say that Lord Beaverbrook and I were made acquainted beforehand with all the bases upon which these colossal programmes were founded, and that I myself heard President Roosevelt confide their specific tasks to the chiefs of American industry and I heard these men accept their prodigious tasks and declare that they would and could fulfil them. Most important of all is the multiplication of our joint tonnage at sea. The American programmes were already vast. They have been increased in the proportion of 100 to nearly 160. If they are completed, as completed I believe they will be, we shall be able to move across the ocean spaces in 1943 two, three or even four times as large armies as the considerable forces we are able to handle at sea at the present time.

I expect – and I have made no secret of it – that we shall both of us receive severe ill-usage at the hands of the Japanese in 1942, but I believe we shall presently regain the naval command of the Pacific and begin to establish an effective superiority in the air, and then later on, with the great basic areas in Australasia, in India and in the Dutch East Indies, we shall be able to set about our task in good style in 1943. It is no doubt true that the defeat of Japan will not necessarily entail the defeat of Hitler, whereas the defeat of Hitler would enable the whole forces of the United Nations to be concentrated upon the defeat of Japan. But there is no question of regarding the war in the Pacific as a secondary operation. The only limitation applied to its vigorous prosecution will be the shipping available at any given time.

It is most important that we should not overlook the enormous contribution of China to this struggle for world freedom and democracy. If there is any lesson I have brought back from the United States that I could express in one word, it would be 'China.' That is in all their minds. When we feel the sharp military qualities of the Japanese soldiery in contact with our own troops, although of course very few have as yet been engaged, we must remember that China, ill-armed or half-armed, has, for four and a half years, single handed, under its glorious leader Chiang Kai-shek, withstood the main fury of Japan. We shall pursue the struggle hand in hand with China, and do everything in our power to give them arms and supplies, which is all they need to vanquish the invaders of their native soil and play a magnificent part in the general forward movement of the United Nations.

Although I feel the broadening swell of victory and liberation bearing us and all the tortured peoples onwards safely to the final goal, I must confess to feeling the weight of the war upon me even more than in the tremendous summer days of 1940. There are so many fronts which are open, so many vulnerable points to defend, so many inevitable misfortunes, so many shrill voices raised to take advantage, now that we can breathe more freely, of all the turns and twists of war. Therefore, I feel entitled to come to the House of Commons, whose servant I am, and ask them not to press me to act against my conscience and better judgment and make scapegoats in order to improve my own position, not to press me to do the things which may be clamoured for at the moment but which will not help in our war effort, but, on the contrary, to give me their encouragement and to give me their aid. I have never ventured to predict the future. I stand by my original programme, blood, toil, tears and sweat, which is all I have ever offered, to which I added, five months later, 'many shortcomings, mistakes and disappointments.' But it is because I see the light gleaming behind the clouds and broadening on our path, that I make so bold now as to demand a declaration of confidence of the House of Commons as an additional weapon in the armoury of the United Nations.

Harold Nicolson: diary
('Harold Nicolson, Diaries and Letters', page 207)

27 January 1942   London

Down to the House. Winston speaks for an hour and a half and justifies his demand for a vote of confidence. One can actually feel the wind of opposition dropping sentence by sentence, and by the time he finishes it is clear that there is really no opposition at all only a certain uneasiness. He says that we shall have even worse news to face in the Far East and that the Libyan battle is going none too well. When he feels that he has the whole House with him, he finds it difficult to conceal his enjoyment of his speech, and that, in fact, is part of his amazing charm. He thrusts both his hands deep into his trouser pockets, and turns his tummy now to the right, now to the left, in evident enjoyment of his mastery of the position.

Herbert Williams and Henderson-Stewart[1] attack the Government. But
the House is not with them. Winston has won in the very first round, and
the future rounds will be dull and sad. My God, my love and admiration
of Winston surge round me like a tide!

Henry Channon: diary
('Chips', page 318)

27 January 1942

One of the great days in Parliamentary history is over, and it was a
splendid spectacle. I went early. As I arrived, I met the whole Churchill
family. Mrs Churchill, her hair grey now, was with Diana Sandys;[2] both
were hatless. Clarissa[3] was with her father, Jack Churchill;[4] Pam[5] was not
far behind, and she pressed my hand in her affectionate, conspiratorial
way: immediately behind them, followed by his secretaries, came the
Prime Minister. He had his angry bull manner and seemed to charge into
a rope barrier which he did not see; indeed, he very nearly toppled over
it; he was greeted with perfunctory cheers, but when he rose, he quickly
revealed that he was in high fettle, with his voice clear, and his manner
confident. I watched the House; there was not an empty place, and I had
to sit on the steps[6] between Anthony Eden and Brendan Bracken.[7]

[1] Sir James Henderson-Stewart, 1897–1961. Served in the Royal Artillery, 1914–18 (wounded).
Liberal MP for East Fife, 1933–61. Sessional Chairman of the Liberal National Parliamentary Party,
1945. Joint Parliamentary Under-Secretary of State for Scotland, 1952–7. Created Baronet, 1957.

[2] Diana Churchill, 1909–63. Churchill's eldest child. Married Sir John Milner Bailey, 1932
(divorced, 1935). Married Duncan Sandys, MP, 1935 (divorced, 1960). An officer in the Women's
Royal Naval Service, 1939–41. An Air Raid Warden, 1941–5; her parents were particularly anxious
about her during flying bomb attacks. Began working as a volunteer for the Samaritans, 1962.
Committed suicide, 1963.

[3] Clarissa Churchill, daughter of Winston Churchill's brother Jack. In 1952 she married Anthony
Eden (as his second wife).

[4] John Strange Spencer-Churchill, 1880–1947. Known as 'Jack'. Churchill's younger brother. Educated at Harrow. On active service in South Africa, 1900 (wounded). Major, Queen's Own Oxfordshire Hussars, 1914–18. Served at Dunkirk, 1914; on Sir John French's staff, Flanders, 1914–15; on
Sir Ian Hamilton's staff at the Dardanelles, 1915; on General Birdwood's staff, France, 1916–18. A
stockbroker, he served as a partner with the City firm of Vickers da Costa, 1918–40.

[5] Pamela Digby, 1920–97. Daughter of 11th Baron Digby. In 1939 married Randolph Churchill
(divorced, 1946); their son Winston was born at Chequers in 1940. Subsequently married Leyland
Hayward, and then Averell Harriman. Took US citizenship, 1971. United States Ambassador to
Paris from 1993 until her death.

[6] Of the Royal Throne; the Throne itself had been removed when the House of Commons took
over the Chamber of the House of Lords in 1941, after the severe bomb damage in the Chamber
of the House of Commons in May 1941.

[7] Brendan Bracken, 1901–58. Journalist and financier. Educated in Australia and at Sedbergh
School. Chairman of the *Financial News*, 1928. Conservative MP for North Paddington, 1929–45;
for Bournemouth, 1950–1. Elected to the Other Club, 1932. Parliamentary Private Secretary to the

The PM's carefully prepared speech rolled on like a vivid film, and it completely captivated the House for 90 minutes or more. I was won over, as were many others. Opposition was dead, or so it seemed. But perhaps he was just too long, for some Members left before he sat down, and when he did, the atmosphere had chilled. But another great Parliamentary moment had passed into history.... The House emptied. The lobbies buzzed; one's first impressions were entirely favourable, but I soon detected an undercurrent of hostility, and of criticism, for he had mollified nobody. Soon the debate began to lose reality.... Pethwick Lawrence was dull; Erskine-Hill[1] (of the 1922 Committee) recanted and tried to insinuate himself in the Government's good graces; Herbert Williams openly attacked Winston, who by that time was sitting in the smoking-room, with his full neck bulging over his collar, surrounded by Members....

It is always a bad sign when the PM comes to the smoking-room; he is either angling, or anxious.

I will not vote against the Government on Thursday, if vote there be. I do not think it would be in the interests of the country to do so. But why is the PM so unpopular in the House, he, a life-long House of Commons man? Perhaps his intolerance, his arrogance and his bad judgement are the reasons, and yet his many magnificent qualities are obvious to all.

Harold Balfour: recollections
(Lord Balfour of Inchrye papers)

27 January 1942

On January 27th Mr Churchill spoke in the House. Afterwards he took his usual place in the Members Dining Room, at the head of the Ministers' table. The Chancellor of the Exchequer and some other Ministers, including myself, had already commenced lunch. Mr Churchill turned to me saying that he had just returned in one of the 'Balfour Boeings' and that he withdrew entirely his censure on myself for having bought them. They were, he said 'fine ships'. 'You apologised to me' he added.

Prime Minister (Churchill), 1940–1. Privy Councillor, 1940. Managing Director of the *Economist*, 1940, 1941. Minister of Information, 1941–5. First Lord of the Admiralty, 1945. Chairman of the *Financial Times*, 1945. Created Viscount, 1952.

[1] Alexander Galloway Erskine-Hill, 1894–1947. On active service, 1916–18. Called to the English Bar, 1919; to the Scottish Bar, 1920. KC, 1935. Unionist MP for North Edinburgh, 1935–45. Created Baronet, 1945.

'It is rather I who should apologise to you'. Though I had 'not obeyed the rules' he was glad I had done the transaction. I was indeed grateful for this generous absolution.

One more incident completes my saga of the Boeings. After his return with the Prime Minister Lord Beaverbrook rang me up at my home on Sunday morning, January 18th to say he had just landed and that he had received 'hell' from the Prime Minister for having opposed the purchase once Mr Churchill had discovered the character of the giant boat he was travelling in. Lord Beaverbrook wished me to know that he admitted to me his mistake.

Winston S. Churchill to A. V. Alexander
(Churchill papers, 20/67)

27 January 1942

Is it really necessary to describe the *Tirpitz* as the *Admiral von Tirpitz* in every signal?

This must cause a considerable waste of time for signalmen, cipher staff and typists. Surely *Tirpitz* is good enough for the beast.

Winston S. Churchill to Air Chief Marshal Sir Charles Portal
(Churchill papers, 20/67)

27 January 1942
Action this Day

The latest telegrams from Singapore show only 1 Hurricane in action and 14 in twenty-four hours. We know 51 arrived on the 13th but had to be uncrated, &c. It is necessary for me to know how many of these are ready. Have they all been uncrated, or are they still only coming into action? I must have a clear account of each of the 51 Hurricanes landed; is it born, is it alive, is it wounded, or is it dead?

2. It is most important to get this before the 48 now being flown off *Indomitable* come into action. It is a fortnight ago since I asked for a daily return of Singapore Hurricanes and I have not had a single word since then. Pray see that I am properly informed. The whole battle turns on the arrival of these Hurricanes and of the rest of the 18th Division.

Winston S. Churchill to Chiang Kai-shek
(Churchill papers, 20/53)

27 January 1942

My dear Generalissimo,

The appointment of Sir Horace Seymour[1] as His Majesty's Ambassador at Chungking[2] gives me the opportunity to send this message to Your Excellency by his hand.

Sir Horace Seymour is leaving to take up his post at a critical hour for the United Nations in their war against Japan. But both you and I have known critical hours before and I firmly believe that the prospects for the future are bright.

Let us compare the situation with what it was a year ago. Then the brunt of the fighting was borne by China and the British Empire who were in the East and in the West the bulwarks against Axis aggression. Each was fighting at a great disadvantage against enemies more powerfully armed. Now the two wars have been linked together; now we have on our side the United States and Russia and the Twenty-six Nation Pact has been signed in Washington.

Japan's initial successes in her new venture are spectacular and she has enjoyed the advantages of a treacherous surprise. But her spectacular successes place her in a sensationally precarious position, and the advantages which she has gained will be exhausted as quickly as will some at least of her supplies of vital war materials. She will have to meet an ever increasing preponderant production of munitions and ships on the part of her opponents and the fate that is slowly but surely overtaking Germany will stare her too in the face. On that day the territories she has seized will turn into liabilities and she will either have to retreat or dissipate her forces in trying to retain them against the growing naval strength of the United Nations.

The gallant defence which China maintained alone for four years will be found to have played a vital part in the ultimate defeat of Japan and to have exercised a decisive effect on the course of the world war, and it remains to ensure this defeat of Japan by the close co-operation which is now developing between the forces of China and those of the

---

[1] Sir Horace James Seymour, 1885–1978. Entered the Diplomatic Service, 1908. British Minister, Teheran, 1936–9. Knighted, 1939. Assistant Under-Secretary of State, Foreign Office, 1939–42. Ambassador to China, 1942–6.

[2] Chungking: the provisional capital of China, 1937–45, following the Japanese occupation of Peking; frequently and heavily bombed by the Japanese Air Force. Many Chinese factories were moved to Chungking after 1937 from areas overrun by Japan.

British Empire, the United States and the Netherlands. I have no doubt about ultimate victory and it is in the confident hope and belief that China will then secure complete reparation and satisfaction from the vanquished enemy that I send you this message of greeting.

Sir Horace Seymour, who delivers it, is already conversant with the problems of the Far East from his experience in the Foreign Office where he was Under-Secretary charged with Far Eastern affairs. I hope Your Excellency will place in him the fullest confidence and thus help him to fulfil his task of maintaining and strengthening by every means the co-operation between our two countries which will result in victory.

Yours very sincerely,
Winston S. Churchill

John Curtin to Winston S. Churchill
(Churchill papers, 20/69)

27 January 1942
Most Secret

At the meeting of the Advisory Council yesterday, a review was made of our aircraft strength. The position is so serious that the Council feels it imperative that we should press again for the allotment of additional aircraft, which is the subject of my representations to you in cable of 23rd January.

So that you may be fully aware of our grave weakness, I am sending you the following information as to the strength of our operational aircraft to provide for the defence of the whole of Australia, New Guinea and Papua but excluding Darwin, which we had previously suggested should come within the ABDA area:

Fighter aircraft	Nil
Hudsons	29
Catalinas	14
Total	43

A large part of this force is located in the New Guinea area, where losses are being sustained daily and the numbers available to deal with raids against vital centres of Australia are extremely small.

In addition, there are in operational squadrons eighty Wirraways which can only be classed as advanced training aircraft. These have proved quite ineffective in operations against the Japanese. I cannot emphasise too strongly the urgency of our need and I would ask that immediate measures be taken to fulfil our requirements. In the air, we are left almost defenceless against our enemies.

Since the institution of the Empire Air Training Scheme 6,500 aircrew personnel and 2,300 ground staff have left Australia for the RAF. In addition, six squadrons of the RAAF are operating overseas.[1]

As you state that you have not been responsible for earlier neglect of the defence services under the control of the United Kingdom Government, so the present Australian Government feels that it has inherited a situation for which it was not responsible.

General Claude Auchinleck to Winston S. Churchill
(Churchill papers, 20/69)

27 January 1942   Advance Headquarters
Personal and Most Secret   Eighth Army

Summary. There is no doubt I fear that our armoured forces failed to compete with enemy satisfactorily and that they have had heavy losses without prospect able to inflict comparable damage on enemy. Cause of this not repeat not yet clear but probably that our troops being dispersed widely were unable to concentrate for concerted action against enemy compact mass. This is probably only one reason of several. 1st Armoured division or what remains of it is now concentrated and covered by armoured car screen and I hope it may be fit for offensive action at once but repeat but I await report from its commander. Other aspect of the operations demands enquiry which will be made. Meanwhile object is to regain initiative, close in on enemy, destroy him if we can, otherwise push him back. Am confident General Ritchie is fully determined to effect this object. Tedder[2] and I staying here for the present.

---

[1] More than 20,000 Australians from the Royal Australian Air Force served in RAF Bomber Command; 3,486 were killed in action.

[2] Arthur William Tedder, 1890–1967. Educated at Whitgift and Magdalene College, Cambridge. Colonial Service (Fiji), 1914. On active service, Royal Flying Corps, France, 1915–17, and Egypt, 1918–19 (despatches thrice). Commanded 207 Squadron, Constantinople, 1922–3; Royal Navy Staff College, 1923–4; No. 2 Flying Training School, 1924–6. Director, RAF Staff College, 1921–9. Director of Training, Air Ministry, 1934–6. Air Officer Commanding RAF Singapore, 1936–8. Director-General, Research and Development, Air Ministry, 1938–40. Deputy Air Officer Commander-in-Chief, RAF, Middle East, 1940–1; Air Officer Commander-in-Chief, RAF, Middle East, 1941–3. Knighted, 1942. Air Chief Marshal, 1942. Air Commander-in-Chief, Mediterranean Air Command, 1943. Deputy Supreme Commander (under General Eisenhower), 1943–5. Created Baron, 1946. Chief of the Air Staff, and First and Senior Air Member, Air Council, 1946–50. Chairman, British Joint Services Mission, Washington, 1950–1. Chancellor of the University of Cambridge from 1950 until his death.

General Sir Alan Brooke: diary
('*War Diaries, Field Marshal Lord Alanbrooke*', page 223)

27 January 1942

I was sent for on my way over to COS to see PM. Found him in bed with the red and golden dragon dressing gown on and a large cigar in his mouth. Busy working at his momentous speech. He wanted to discuss a sentence connected with move of Australian forces from Syria which I had asked him to withdraw, also one connected with continuance of supply of tanks to Russia.

Lord Alanbrooke: recollection
('*War Diaries, Field Marshal Lord Alanbrooke*', page 223)

[27 January 1942]

The interview was typical of many future ones of the kind. The scene in his bedroom was always the same and I only wish some artist could have committed it to canvas. The red and gold dressing gown in itself was worth going miles to see, and only Winston could have thought of wearing it! He looked rather like some Chinese Mandarin! The few hairs were usually ruffled on his bald head. A large cigar stuck sideways out of his face. The bed was littered with papers and despatches. Sometimes the tray with his finished breakfast was still on the bed table. The bell was continually being rung for secretaries, typists, stenographers, or his faithful valet Sawyers.[1]

---

[1] Frank Sawyers, 1903–72. Churchill's valet throughout the war years. On 14 August 1945 he was awarded the new Defence Medal in Churchill's Resignation Honours List. On leaving Churchill in 1947, he was valet to the Assistant Governor-General of Rhodesia, then to Lord Astor at Hever Castle in Kent, then to a Colonel in Chicago. When Churchill died, Sawyers was flown to the funeral in the same plane as General Eisenhower. In a letter of recommendation penned in 1946, Churchill wrote: 'Sawyers came everywhere with me in these six and a half tempestuous years, and showed many excellent qualities. He is absolutely honest, capable of attending to a great many personal details as a valet, and always rises to the occasion. In my illnesses he has been very attentive, and he stood up to the bombardment well. He was particularly good in the air journeys which at first had to be made in uncomfortable machines . . . He is leaving me at his own wish, and I am sorry to lose him' (*Churchill papers, 1/65*).

Winston S. Churchill to General Claude Auchinleck
(Churchill papers, 20/88)

28 January 1942

Your Susan 1712.[1] Many thanks. I have complete confidence in you, and am glad you are staying up.

2. You have no doubt seen the most secret stuff[2] about Rommel's presumed intentions, namely, clearing up the triangle Benghazi–Msus–Mechili, and then withdrawing to waiting line about Agheila. This seems to reinforce the importance of our holding on.

3. I am most anxious to hear further from you about defeat of our armour by inferior enemy numbers. This cuts very deep.

General Claude Auchinleck to Winston S. Churchill
(Churchill papers, 20/69)

28 January 1942   Advance Headquarters
Personal   Eighth Army

Situation deteriorated today and I fear we shall have to evacuate Benghazi temporarily at any rate.

[...]

5. Summary. Must be admitted that enemy has succeeded beyond his expectations and mine and that his tactics have been skilful and bold. Much will depend now on extent to which he may have to think out his panzer units round Msus to maintain large force used to attack Benghazi. Rommel has taken considerable risks and so have we. So far he is justified by results but Gen. Ritchie and I are seeking every possible means to turn the tables on him. Losses of 1 Armd. Div., in tanks and guns are heavy and (?future) fighting value of this key formation may be temporarily impaired though I hope not.

There is no disorganisation or confusion or any loss of morale so far as I can see.

---

[1] General Auchinleck's telegram of 27 January 1942, reproduced above.
[2] The 'most secret stuff' was information of German military, naval and air dispositions and plans, derived from Signals Intelligence (including Enigma decrypts).

Harold Nicolson: diary
(*'Harold Nicolson, Diaries and Letters', page 208*)

28 January 1942   London

Wardlaw-Milne[1] makes an impressive speech attacking the Government over Malaya. But the whole thing seems to me unreal since our misfortune is due entirely to the collapse of the American Navy. It is difficult for Winston to say this, and indeed he slid over the point neatly in his speech yesterday. But it is really absurd to expect our people at Singapore to have taken measures of defence on the assumption that the command of the sea would pass suddenly to the Japanese. And even if they had, we could not have provided sufficient to meet such a disaster.

Shinwell makes a vicious speech.[2] Randolph Churchill intervenes to defend his father. He attacks most cruelly those who had abused him, and says that Winterton 'clowned himself out of office within a few days'.[3] He is amusing and brave. Bob Boothby[4] says to me, 'I am enjoying this very much, but I hope it does not go on for long'. I have a dreadful feeling that Randolph may go too far. I see his little wife squirming in the Gallery, and Winston himself looks embarrassed and shy. But I am not so sure that it has done Randolph harm.[5]

[1] John Wardlaw-Milne, 1879–1967. Member of the Bombay Municipal Corporation, 1907–17. Lieutenant-Colonel Commanding 4th (Bombay) Artillery, Indian Defence Force, 1914–19. President, Government of India's War Shipping Advisory Committee, 1914–18. Conservative MP for Kidderminster, 1922–45. Knighted, 1932. Chairman, House of Commons Committee on National Expenditure, 1939–45. Chairman, Conservative Foreign Affairs Committee, India Committee, and Anglo-Egyptian Committee, 1939–45.

[2] Speaking of Churchill, Emanuel Shinwell declared: 'while grateful for his resource and courage, we are not enamoured of his challenge to the House [...] If he were as well equipped for war as he is for meeting a challenge from hon. Members, our forebodings regarding future events might be less melancholy [...] My right hon. Friend may receive the confidence of hon. Members, and emerge with a great Parliamentary triumph. But while we are debating and marching through the Division Lobbies the war position will be steadily deteriorating, no matter how triumphant he may be, and no matter how strong his majority, This will not bring us nearer to victory, nor will speeches, however inspiring.'

[3] According to Hansard, Randolph Churchill actually said that Lord Winterton 'clowned himself out of a job in one afternoon'.

[4] Robert John Graham Boothby, 1900–86. Educated at Eton and Magdalen College, Oxford. Conservative MP for East Aberdeenshire, 1924–58. Parliamentary Private Secretary to the Chancellor of the Exchequer (Churchill), 1926–9. Parliamentary Secretary, Ministry of Food, 1940–1. A British Delegate to the Consultative Assembly, Council of Europe, 1949–57. Knighted, on Churchill's recommendation, 1953. Created Baron, 1958. Chairman, Royal Philharmonic Orchestra, 1961–3. Published *The New Economy* (1943), *I Fight to Live* (1947), *My Yesterday, Your Tomorrow* (1962), and *Recollections of a Rebel* (1978).

[5] Randolph Churchill ended his speech with words of which he was afterwards rather proud: 'if we all realise that victory is now certain – though great dangers still remain to be gone through,

Harold Nicolson: diary
('*Harold Nicolson, Diaries and Letters*', *page 209*)

29 January 1942   London

As I pass the tape I find it ticking imperturbably. It tells us that the Germans claim to have entered Benghazi, and that the Japs claim to be only eighteen miles from Singapore. Grave disasters indeed. At the same time we have released the news of the sinking of the *Barham*.[1]

A black day for a vote of confidence.

Harold Nicolson: diary
('*Harold Nicolson, Diaries and Letters*', *page 209*)

29 January 1942   London

There was a scene earlier in the day between Winston and Southby. Yesterday, during Randolph's rather unfortunate speech, Southby had interrupted and hinted that Randolph was not a fighting soldier ('The Honourable and Gallant Member – I call him that because of the uniform he wears'). The Speaker shut him up, and in the corridor afterwards he went up to Winston and said that had he been allowed to finish, he would have congratulated Randolph on his rapid promotion. Winston shook his fist in his face. 'Do not speak to me', he shouted. 'You called my son a coward. You are my enemy. Do not speak to me.'

Winston S. Churchill: speech
(Hansard)

29 January 1942   House of Commons

Prime Minister (Mr Churchill): I must apologise to my Noble Friend[2] for not being in my place when he began a speech which, I think everyone will say, was in his best form and in the expansive Parliamentary style of former days. I shall do my best to answer his questions as they occur, and I assure him and other hon. Members who have likewise suffered an

and can only be surmounted by a continuation of national unity – I do not doubt that we shall pull through in the end.'

[1] The battleship *Barham* had been torpedoed in the Mediterranean on 25 November 1941 with the loss of 848 lives. News of the sinking of the *Queen Elizabeth* and *Valiant* in Alexandria harbour on 18 December 1941 had still not been released.

[2] Lord Winterton.

apparent discourtesy on my part that it is not because I have been idle during the previous hours of the Debate. No one can say that this has not been a full and free Debate. No one can say that criticism has been hampered or stilled. No one can say that it has not been a necessary Debate. Many will think it has been a valuable Debate. But I think there will be very few – the Noble Lord spoke of himself as being almost alone – who upon reflection will doubt that a Debate of this far-reaching character and memorable importance, in times of hard and anxious war, with the state of the world what it is, our relationships to other countries being what they are, and our own safety so deeply involved – very few people will doubt that it should close without a solemn and formal expression of the opinion of the House in relation both to the Government and to the prosecution of the war.

Sir, in no country in the world at the present time could a Government conducting a war be exposed to such a stress. No dictator country fighting for its life would dare allow such a discussion. They do not even allow the free transmission of news to their peoples, or even the reception of foreign broadcasts, to which we are all now so hardily inured. Even in the great democracy of the United States the Executive does not stand in the same direct, immediate, day-to-day relation to the Legislative body as we do. The President, in many vital respects independent of the Legislature, Commander-in-Chief of all the Forces of the Republic, has a fixed term of office, during which his authority can scarcely be impugned. But here in this country the House of Commons is master all the time of the life of the Administration. Against its decisions there is only one appeal, the appeal to the nation, an appeal it is very difficult to make under the conditions of a war like this, with a register like this, with air raids and invasion always hanging over us.

Therefore, I say that the House of Commons has a great responsibility. It owes it to itself and it owes it to the people and the whole Empire, and to the world cause, either to produce an effective, alternative Administration by which the King's Government can be carried on, or to sustain that Government in the enormous tasks and trials which it has to endure. I feel myself very much in need of that help at the present time, and I am sure I shall be accorded it in a manner to give encouragement and comfort, as well as guidance and suggestion. I am sorry, as I have said, that I have not been able to be here throughout the whole Debate, but I have read every word of the Debate, except what has been spoken and has not yet been printed, and I can assure the House that I shall be ready to profit to the full from many constructive and helpful lines of thought which have been advanced, even when they come from the most hostile quarter. I shall not be like that saint to whom I have before referred in this House, but whose name I have unhappily forgotten, who refused to do right because the devil prompted him. Neither shall I be deterred from doing what I am convinced is right by the fact that I have thought differently about it in some distant, or even in some recent past.

When events are moving at hurricane speed and when scenes change with baffling frequency, it would be disastrous to lose that flexibility of mind in dealing with new situations on which I have often been complimented, which is the essential counterpart of a consistent and unswerving purpose. Let me take an instance. During my visit to America, events occurred which alter in a decisive way the question of creating a Minister of Production. President Roosevelt has appointed Mr Donald Nelson[1] to supervise the whole field of American production. All the resources of our two countries are now pooled, in shipping, in munitions, and in raw materials, and some similar office, I will not say with exactly the same scope, but of similar scope, must be created here, if harmonious working between Great Britain and the United States is to be maintained upon this very high level. I have been for some weeks carefully considering this, and the strong opinions which have been expressed in the House, even though I do not share their reasoning in all respects, have reinforced the conclusions with which I returned from the United States. I will not of course anticipate any advice that it may be my duty to tender to the Crown.

I was forced to inflict upon the House two days ago a very lengthy statement, which cost me a great deal of time and trouble, in the intervals of busy days and nights, to prepare. I do not desire to add to it to any important extent. It would not be possible for me to answer all the criticisms and inquiries which have been made during this Debate. I have several times pointed out to the House the disadvantage I lie under, compared with the leaders of other countries who are charged with general war direction, in having to make so many public statements, and the danger that in explaining fully our position to our friends we may also be stating it rather too fully to our enemies. Moreover, the Lord Privy Seal,[2] in his

[1] Donald Marr Nelson, 1888–1959. Chemical engineer, Sears, Roebuck and Co., 1912–21; Manager, Men's and Boys' Clothing, 1921–6; Vice-President in charge of merchandising, 1930–9. Appointed by Roosevelt to be Coordinator of Purchases of the newly created Office of Production Management, 1941. Director of Priorities, Office of Production Management and Executive Director of Supplies, Priorities and Allocations Board, 1942–4. Chairman, War Production Board, 1942–4. Personal Representative of the President to Russia and China, 1944. In 1946, he published *Arsenal of Democracy*.

[2] Clement Attlee.

excellent speech yesterday, has already replied to a number of the controversial issues which were raised. There are therefore only a few points with which I wish to deal today, but they are important points.

The first is the advantage, not only to Britain but to the Empire, of the arrival of powerful American Army and Air Forces in the United Kingdom. First of all, it meets the wish of the American people and of the leaders of the Republic that the large mass of trained and equipped troops which they have under arms in the United States shall come into contact with the enemy as closely and as soon as possible. Secondly, the presence of these forces in these Islands imparts a greater freedom of movement overseas, to theatres where we are already engaged, of the mature and seasoned divisions of the British Home Army. It avoids the difficulty of reinforcing theatres where we are engaged with troops of another nation, with all the complications of armament and command which arise there from. Therefore we must consider this arrival of the American Army as giving us a latitude of manoeuvre which we have not hitherto possessed. Thirdly, the presence in our Islands of a Force of heavy but unknown strength, and the establishment of a broader bridgehead between us and the New World, constitutes an important additional deterrent to invasion at a time when the successful invasion of these Islands is Hitler's last remaining hope of total victory. Fourthly – and here I address myself to what my noble Friend has said about aiding and succouring Australia and New Zealand – the fact that well-equipped American divisions can be sent into these islands so easily and rapidly will enable substantial supplies of weapons and munitions, now being made in the United States for our account, to be sent direct on the other side of the world to Australia and New Zealand, to meet the new dangers of home defence which are cast upon them by the Japanese war. Lastly, this whole business cannot do Mr de Valera[1] any harm, and it may even do him some good. It certainly offers a measure of protection to Southern Ireland, and to Ireland as a whole, which she could not otherwise enjoy. I feel sure that the House will find these reasons, or most of them, solid and satisfactory.

[1] Eamon de Valera, 1882–1975. Born in New York. A leading figure in the Irish Easter Rebellion, 1916. Sentenced to death; sentence commuted to life penal servitude on account of his American birth. Released under the general amnesty, June 1917. President of Sinn Fein, 1917–26. Elected to Parliament as a Sinn Fein MP, 1918. Imprisoned with other Sinn Fein leaders, 1918; escaped from Lincoln gaol, February 1919. President of the Irish Republic, 1919–22. Rejected the Irish Treaty and fought with the Irregulars against the Free State Army, 1922–3. President of Fianna Fáil, 1926–59. Leader of the Opposition in the Free State Parliament, 1927–32. Prime Minister and Minister for External Affairs, 1932–48. Prime Minister for a second and a third time, 1951–4 and 1957–9. President of the Republic of Ireland, 1959–73.

The course of this Debate has mainly turned upon the admitted inadequacy of our preparations to meet the full onslaught of the new and mighty military opponent who has launched against us his whole force, his whole energies and fury in Malaya and in the Far East. There is not very much I wish to add, and that only by way of illustration, to the connected argument which I deployed to the House on Tuesday. The speeches of the hon. Members for Kidderminster (Sir J. Wardlaw-Milne) and Seaham (Mr Shinwell) dwelt from different angles upon this all-important issue. I do not, of course, pretend that there may not have been avoidable shortcomings or mistakes, or that some oversight might not have been shown in making use of our resources, limited though those resources were. While I take full responsibility for the broad strategic dispositions, that does not mean that scandals, or inefficiency or misbehaviour of functionaries at particular moments and particular places, occurring on the spot, will not be probed or will be covered by the general support I gave to our commanders in the field.

I am by no means claiming that faults have not been committed in the minor sphere, and faults for which the Government are blameworthy. But when all is said and done, the House must not be led into supposing that even if everything on the spot had gone perfectly – which the Noble Lord, who has experience, will agree is rare in war – they must not be led into supposing that this would have made any decisive difference to the heavy British and American forfeits which followed inexorably from the temporary loss of sea power in the Pacific, combined with the fact of our being so fully extended elsewhere. Even that is not exhaustive, because before the defeat of Pearl Harbour – I am speaking of eight or nine months ago – our ability to defend the Malay Peninsula was seriously prejudiced by the incursion of the Japanese into French Indo-China and the steady building-up of very powerful forces and bases there. Even at the time when I went to meet the President in Newfoundland the invasion of Siam seemed imminent, and probably it was due to the measures which the President took as the result of our conversations that this attack was staved off for so long, and might well have been staved off indefinitely. In ordinary circumstances, if we had not been engaged to the last ounce in Europe and the Nile Valley, we should ourselves, of course, have confronted the Japanese aggression into Indo-China with the strongest possible resistance from the moment when they began to build up a large military and air power. We were not in a position to do this.

If we had gone to war with Japan to stop the Japanese coming across the long ocean stretches from their own country, and establishing themselves within close striking distance of the Malay Peninsula and Singapore, we should have had to fight alone, perhaps for a long time, the whole of the Japanese attacks upon our loosely-knit establishments and possessions in this vast Oriental region. As I said on Tuesday, we have never had the power, and we never could have had the power, to fight Germany, Italy and Japan single-handed at the same time. We therefore had to watch the march of events with an anxiety which increased with the growth of the Japanese concentrations, but at the same time was offset by the continuous approach of the United States ever nearer to the confines of the war. It must not be supposed that endless, repeated consultations and discussions were not held by the Staffs, by the Defence Committee, by Ministers, and that Staff conferences were not held at Singapore. Contact was maintained with Australia and New Zealand, and with the United States to a lesser degree.

All this went on; but, when all was said and done, there was the danger, and the means of meeting it had yet to be found. Ought we not in that interval to have considered the question which the House must ask itself – I want to answer the case quite fairly – that, in view of that menace, apart from minor precautions, many of which were taken and some of which were not, ought we not to have reduced our aid in munitions to Russia? A part of what we sent to Russia would have made us, I will not say safe, because I do not think that that was possible in view of what happened at sea, but far better prepared in Burma and Malaya than we were. Figures were mentioned by the hon. Member for Seaham yesterday. He will not expect me to confirm or deny those figures, but, taking them as a basis, half of that would have made us far better off, and would have dazzled the eyes of Sir Robert Brooke-Popham,[1] who so repeatedly asked for more supplies of all those commodities of which we were most short. We did not make such a reduction, and I believe that the vast majority of opinion in all parts of the House, and in the country, endorses our decision now, even after the event. If they had to go back, they would take it again, even although they see now what serious consequences have arisen.

[1] Henry Robert Moore Brooke-Popham, 1878–1953. Entered the Army, 1898; Royal Flying Corps, 1912. On active service, 1914–18. Director of Research, Air Ministry, 1919–21. Commandant, Royal Air Force Staff College, 1921–6. Knighted, 1927. Air Officer Commanding Fighting Area Air Defences of Great Britain, 1926–8; Iraq Command, 1928–30. Air Officer Commanding-in-Chief, Air Defence of Great Britain, 1933–5. Inspector-General Royal Air Force, 1935–6. Retired list, 1937. Governor and Commander-in-Chief, Kenya, 1937–9. Recalled to the RAF, as Commander-in-Chief, Far East, 1941. Reverted to the retired list, 1944.

Let me say, in answer to the Noble Lord, as it is a question which he put, that I entirely agree with him about the vital importance of the Burma Road and of fighting with every means in our power to keep a strong hand grasp with the Chinese Armies and the closest contact with their splendid leader Chiang Kai-shek. He may rest assured that nothing has prevented the employment of Indian troops in that area, except the use of them in other theatres and the immense difficulties of transport in those regions. So much for the Russian policy, which, for good or for ill, has played a very great part in the thoughts and actions of the people of this country in this struggle, and I believe has played a very important part – not by any means a decisive part, but a very important part – in the crushing defeats which have been inflicted on the German army and the possible demoralisation of the wicked régime which uses that army.

But, apart from Russia, what about the campaign in Libya? What were the reasons which made that a necessary operation? First, we had to remove, and probably we have removed, the menace to the Nile Valley from the West for a considerable time, thus liberating important forces and still more important transport to meet what seemed to be an impending attack through the Caucasus from the North. Secondly, this was the only place where we could open a second front against the enemy. Everyone will remember, conveniently short as memories may be, the natural and passionate impatience which our prolonged inactivity aroused in all our hearts while Russia seemed to be being battered to pieces by the fearful machinery of the Germany army. There is no doubt whatever that, although our offensive in Libya was on a small scale compared with the mighty struggle on the Russian front, it nevertheless drew important German air forces from that front. They were moved at a most critical moment in that battle and transferred to the Mediterranean theatre. Thirdly, this second front in the Western Desert afforded us the opportunity of fighting a campaign against Germany and Italy on terms most costly to them. If there be any place where we can fight them with marked advantage, it is in the Western Desert and Libya, because not only, as I explained, have we managed to destroy two-thirds of their African army, a great amount of its equipment and air power, but also to take a formidable toll of all their reinforcements of men and materials and above all of their limited shipping across the Mediterranean by which they were forced to maintain themselves. The longer they go on fighting in this theatre the longer that process will go on, and there is no part of the world where you have a chance of getting better results for the blood and valour of your soldiers.

For these reasons, I am sure that it was a sound decision, and one with which all our professional advisers agreed, to take the offensive in the Western Desert and to do our utmost to make it a success. We have been over this ground in Cyrenaica already. The first time we took a quarter of a million Italian prisoners without serious loss to ourselves. The second time we have accounted for 60,000 men, including many Germans, for the loss of only one-third to ourselves. Even if we have to do part of it a third time, as seems possible, in view of the tactical successes of the enemy attacks upon our armoured brigade last week, there seems no reason why the campaign should not retain its profitable character in the war in North East Africa and become a dangerous drain, a festering sore, upon the German and Italian resources.

This is the question: Should we have been right to sacrifice all this, and stand idly on the defensive in the Western Desert and send all our available Forces to garrison Malaya and guard against a war against Japan which nevertheless might not have taken place, and which, I believe, did take place only through the civil Government being overwhelmed by a military coup d'état? That is a matter of opinion, and it is quite easy for those who clamoured eagerly for opening an offensive in Libya to dilate upon our want of foresight and preparedness in the Far East. That is a matter on which anyone can form an opinion, and those are lucky who do not have to form one before the course of events is known.

I come now to this battle which is raging in Johore. I cannot tell how it will go or how the attack upon the Island of Singapore will go, but a steady stream of reinforcements, both air and troops, have flowed into the island for several weeks past. The Forces which have been sent were, of course, set in motion within a few days, and some within a few hours, of the Japanese declaration of war. To sum up, I submit to the House that the main strategic and political decision to aid Russia, to deliver an offensive in Libya and to accept a consequential state of weakness in the then peaceful theatre of the Far East was sound and will be found to have played a useful part in the general course of the war and that this is in no wise invalidated by the unexpected naval misfortunes and the heavy forfeits which we have paid, and will have to pay, in the Far East. For this Vote of Confidence on that I rest.

There is, however, one episode of a tactical rather than a strategic character about which many questions have been asked, both here and in another place, to which it is not so easy to refer as my Noble Friend opposite seems to suggest. I mean, of course, the despatch from this country of the *Prince of Wales* during November last and, secondly, the operation which led to the sinking of the *Prince of Wales* and of the *Repulse*, which had started earlier. This sinking took place on 9th December. It was the policy of the War Cabinet and the Defence Committee, initiated by the Naval Staff, to build up in the Indian Ocean and base mainly on Singapore, a battle squadron to act, it was hoped, in co-operation with the United States fleet in general protective work in Far Eastern waters. I am not at liberty to state how these plans stand at the present time, but the House may be assured that nothing has been left undone, which was in our power, to repair the heavy losses which have been sustained. My right hon. Friend the Member for East Edinburgh (Mr Pethick-Lawrence)[1] has asked very properly – and the Noble Lord opposite made a specific point of it – why the *Prince of Wales* and *Repulse* were sent to Eastern waters if they could not be properly protected by aircraft. The answer to this question is that the decision to send those ships in advance to the Far East was taken in the hope, primarily, of deterring the Japanese from going to war at all, or, failing that, of deterring her from sending convoys into the Gulf of Siam, having regard to the then position of the strong American fleet at Hawaii.

After long and careful consideration it was decided, in view of the importance of having in Far Eastern waters at least one ship which could catch or kill any individual vessel of the enemy – the Americans then not having a new battleship available – to send the *Prince of Wales*. Moreover, she was the only ship available at the moment which could reach the spot in time for any deterrent effect to be produced. The intention was that these two fast ships, whose arrival at Cape Town was deliberately not concealed, would not only act as a deterrent upon Japan coming into the war but a deterrent upon the activities of individual heavy ships of the enemy, our ships being able to choose their moment to fight. The suggestion of the hon. and gallant Member for Epsom (Sir A. Southby) that the Naval Staff desired to send an aircraft-carrier and were overruled by me is as mischievous as it is untrue. It was always the intention that any fast ships proceeding to the Far East should be accompanied by an aircraft-carrier. Unfortunately, at the time, with the exception of an aircraft-carrier in home waters, not a single one of this

---

[1] Frederick William Pethick-Lawrence, 1871–1961. Educated at Eton and Trinity College, Cambridge. Opposed the South African War. Editor, *The Echo*, 1902–5. Editor, *Labour Record and Review*, 1906–7. Joint Editor, *Votes for Women*, 1907–14. Sentenced to nine months in prison for conspiracy in connection with a militant suffragette demonstration, 1912. Unsuccessful Peace Negotiation Parliamentary candidate for South Aberdeen, 1917. Labour MP for West Leicester, 1923–31; for East Edinburgh, 1935–45. Financial Secretary to the Treasury, 1929–31. Secretary of State for India and Burma, 1945–7. Created Baron, 1945. Member of the Political Honours Scrutiny Committee, 1949–61.

type was available. Through a succession of accidents, some of very slight consequence, all of them, except the one with the Home Fleet, were under repair. Accordingly, the *Prince of Wales* and the *Repulse* arrived at Singapore, and it was hoped they would shortly leave again for secret bases and the broad waters, which would enable them to put a continuous restraining preoccupation on all the movements of the enemy. That is the first phase of the story.

I now come to the further question of why, the presence of the two ships having failed to achieve the deterrent object, Pearl Harbour having occurred, and the Japanese having begun war, they were sent North from Singapore to oppose the Japanese landings from the Gulf of Siam on the Kra Peninsula. Admiral Tom Phillips,[1] as Vice-Chief of the Naval Staff, was fully acquainted with the whole policy I have described, and had sailed in the *Prince of Wales* to carry it out. On 8th December he decided, after conferring with his captain and staff officers, that in the circumstances, and in view of the movement of Japanese transports with a weak fighting escort towards the Kra Peninsula, drastic and urgent naval action was required. This action, if successful, would have presented the Army with a good prospect of defeating the landings and possibly of paralysing the invasion of Malaya at its birth. The stakes on both sides were very high. The prize was great if gained; if lost, our danger most grievous. Admiral Phillips was fully aware of the risk, and he took steps for air reconnaissance to see whether there was an enemy aircraft-carrier about and for fighter protection up to the limit of the short-range fighters available. Only after he left harbour was he informed that fighter protection could not be provided in the area in which he intended to operate, but in view of the low visibility he decided to stand on. Later, in accordance with his pre-determined plans, he turned back, because, as he had always made up his mind to do, the weather began to clear, and he knew he had been sighted. However, later still, during his retirement, a further landing more to the South of the peninsula was reported, presenting an even more serious threat to Malaya, and he decided to investigate this. It was on returning from this investigation, which proved to be negative, that his force was attacked, not, as has been supposed, by torpedo or bomber aircraft flown off a carrier, but by very

[1] Tom Spencer Vaughan Phillips, 1888–1941. Entered the Royal Navy, 1903. Director of Plans, Admiralty, 1935–8. Commodore Commanding the Home Fleet Destroyer Flotillas, 1938–9. Rear-Admiral, 1939. Vice-Chief of the Naval Staff, 1939–41. Knighted, 1941. Commander-in-Chief of the Eastern Fleet, 1941. Drowned when his flagship, the *Prince of Wales*, was sunk by Japanese torpedo bombers on 10 December 1941.

long-range shore-based heavy two-engined torpedo bombers from the main Japanese aerodromes 400 miles away.

In the opinion of the Board of Admiralty, which it is my duty to pronounce, the risks which Admiral Phillips took were fair and reasonable, in the light of the knowledge which he had of the enemy, when compared with the very urgent and vital issues at stake on which the whole safety of Malaya might have depended. I have given an account of this episode. No doubt the Admiralty will have its own inquiry for the purpose of informing itself and of studying the lessons, but I could not bring myself, even on the first day that this matter was mentioned, although the information I had was most scanty, to pronounce condemnation of the audacious, daring action of Admiral Tom Phillips in going forward, although he knew the risks he ran, when the prize might have been 20,000 of the enemy drowned in the sea, and a relief from the whole catalogue of misfortunes which have since come upon us, and have still to come.

I have finished, and it only remains for us to act. I have tried to lay the whole position before the House as far as public interest will allow, and very fully have we gone into matters. On behalf of His Majesty's Government, I make no complaint of the Debate, I offer no apologies, I offer no excuses, I make no promises. In no way have I mitigated the sense of danger and impending misfortunes of a minor character and of a severe character which still hang over us, but at the same time I avow my confidence, never stronger than at this moment, that we shall bring this conflict to an end in a manner agreeable to the interests of our country, and in a manner agreeable to the future of the world. I have finished. Let every man act now in accordance with what he thinks is his duty in harmony with his heart and conscience.

Admiral of the Fleet Sir Roger Keyes (Portsmouth, North): I hope that the Prime Minister will receive a unanimous vote, because we want to show to the whole world that this country is behind him in his determination to carry this war to a victorious issue. We are very grateful to the Prime Minister for the great inspiration which he gave us in our blackest hour. We are grateful to him for the wonderful and inspiring speeches he has made, which have expressed the opinion of this country in words which we should all like to emulate. At the same time I adhere to what I said in this House on 25th November, that until he overhauls the war machine and the War Cabinet, victory will be delayed and the issue will be prolonged, with all this means in cost of life and material. I do trust that he will consider what I have said.

Winston S. Churchill: recollection
(*'The Hinge of Fate'*, page 62)

29 January 1942

I had to wind up on the 29th. At this time I feared that there would be no division. I tried by taunts to urge our critics into the Lobby against us without at the same time offending the now thoroughly reconciled assembly. But nothing that I dared say could spur any of the disaffected figures in the Conservative, Labour, and Liberal Parties into voting. Luckily, when the division was called the Vote of Confidence was challenged by the Independent Labour Party, who numbered three. Two were required as tellers, and the result was four hundred and sixty-four to one. I was grateful to James Maxton, the leader of the minority, for bringing the matter to a head. Such a fuss had been made by the Press that telegrams of relief and congratulation flowed in from all over the Allied world.

[...]

The naggers in the Press were not however without resource. They spun round with the alacrity of squirrels. How unnecessary it had been to ask for a Vote of Confidence! Who had ever dreamed of challenging the National Government? These 'shrill voices', as I called them, were but the unknowing heralds of approaching catastrophe.

Henry Channon: diary
(*'Chips'*, page 319)

29 January 1942
Personal

I went to the House; the Lords' Chamber, which we continue to occupy, was packed. Half a hundred Members had to stand; the Prime Minister was already speaking and again he held the vast audience enthralled. He was conciliatory, tactful – and, finally, successful. He spoke for 42 minutes and after glancing at the clock, sat down. The Speaker, in his tired voice, put the question twice and called a division. The Aye Lobby, or more accurately, the 'content Lobby', since it is the Lords, was at once so crowded that many of the Members were forced to wait in the Chamber. The six-minute rule was suspended and it was a quarter of an hour at least before we filed through; one good bomb would have destroyed the whole democratic apparatus of this country – or does

Hitler think that the House of Commons is doing that on its own? When at last the figures were announced – 464 to 1 – there was a faint cheer. The victory is a triumph for Winston, though there was no alternative and he knows it. Nevertheless, he is the most inspiring leader we have, and the masses and the Americans both adore him.

Lord Halifax to Winston S. Churchill
(Churchill papers, 20/69)

29 January 1942   Washington DC
Personal

Warm congratulations on your House of Commons vote. I hope you were satisfied. Your speeches have been most helpful here.

Harold Nicolson: diary
('Harold Nicolson, Diaries and Letters', page 209)

29 January 1942

Third day of the Vote of Confidence debate. Winston winds up. He is very genial and self-confident. He does not gird at his critics. He compliments them on the excellence of their speeches. When he reaches his peroration he ceases to be genial and becomes emphatic. He crouches over the box and strikes it. 'It only remains for us to act. I offer no apologies. I offer no excuses. I make no promises. In no way have I mitigated the sense of danger and impending misfortunes that hang over us. But at the same time I avow my confidence, never stronger than at this moment, that we shall bring this conflict to an end in a manner agreeable to the interests of our country and the future of the world. I have finished.' (Then that downward sweep of the two arms, with the palms open to receive the stigmata.) 'Let every man act now in accordance with what he thinks is his duty in harmony with his heart and conscience.' Loud cheers, and we all file out into the thin and stifling lobby.

It takes a long time to count the votes, and finally they are recorded as 464 to 1. Huge cheers. Winston gets up and we rise and cheer him. He turns round and bows a little shyly. Then he joins Mrs Winston, and arm-in-arm and beaming, they push through the crowds in Central Lobby.

Winston S. Churchill to Captain Henry Margesson[1] and Brendan Bracken
(Churchill papers, 20/67)

30 January 1942
Action this Day

I am concerned about the fullness of the information given in the newspapers of the Singapore position. For instance, why is it necessary to state that a mile has been evacuated for defensive purposes on the north side of the island? In today's *Daily Express*[2] there is a perfectly clear, correct account of the whole position which, though written quite innocently, would certainly be a help to the enemy.

Considering that the siege is now entering on its vital phase, we cannot afford to have our point of view about it so candidly disclosed. Sir John Wardlaw-Milne's statement in the House of Commons should be examined by the Staffs. I asked General Wavell some time ago to have a stricter censorship on Singapore. What has been done about this? They seem to give everything away about themselves in the blandest manner. After all, they are defending a fortress and not conducting a Buchmanite revival.[3]

Winston S. Churchill to Lord Beaverbrook
(Churchill papers, 20/67)

30 January 1942
Most Secret

This is a complete collapse. The 15,000 United States troops are to fall down to 9,000; we are to lose one group of 25,000 capacity for 'Gymnast'; all amphibious operations by United States will be hamstrung; and, in addition, the power to reinforce the French, should they move, will be halved. What can have happened to bring this about? You should hold

---

[1] Henry David Reginald Margesson, 1890–1965. Educated at Harrow and Magdalene College, Cambridge. On active service, 1914–18 (Military Cross). Captain, 1918. Conservative MP for Upton, 1922–3; for Rugby, 1924–42. Assistant Government Whip, 1924. Junior Lord of the Treasury, 1926, 1926–9, 1931. Chief Government Whip, 1931–40. Privy Councillor, 1933. Secretary of State for War, 1940–2. Created Viscount, 1942.

[2] *Daily Express* of January 30, article on 'Singapore Situation'.

[3] Frank Buchman, 1878–1961. Protestant Christian evangelist. Born in Pennsylvania. Ordained a Lutheran minister, 1902. Founded the Oxford Movement (known as Moral Re-Armament from 1938 to 2001) in 1922. Attended Nuremberg rally, 1935. In 1936 he told the *New York World-Telegram*: 'I thank heaven for a man like Adolf Hitler, who built a front of defence against the anti-Christ of Communism.'

a meeting tomorrow with Lord Leathers and the Chiefs of the Staff and necessary officers, and see what can be made of it.

2. I am of opinion that 'Gymnast' may be considered off till the 1st April.

3. Lord Leathers should also furnish me with a statement of how the monster liners are to be employed.

Winston S. Churchill to President Franklin D. Roosevelt
(Churchill papers, 20/69)

30 January 1942

Many happy returns of the day, and may your next birthday see us a long lap forward on our road. Please give my kindest regards to Mrs Roosevelt.

Winston Churchill

Winston S. Churchill to President Franklin D. Roosevelt
(Churchill papers, 20/69)

30 January 1942
Most Immediate and Secret

I am informed that there is a danger that the fighter squadrons of the American Volunteer Group now helping so effectively in the defence of Rangoon may be withdrawn by Chiang Kai-shek to China after 31st January. Clearly the security of Rangoon is as important to Chiang as to us, and withdrawal of these squadrons before arrival of Hurricanes, due 15th to 20th February, might be disastrous. I understand that General Magruder[1] has instructions to represent this to the Generalissimo, but I think the matter is sufficiently serious for you to know about it personally.

---

[1] John Magruder, 1887–1958. Born in Virginia. Graduated from Virginia Military Institute, 1909. On active service in Europe, 1917–18. Chief of Intelligence, War Department, 1938–41. Chief, Military Advisory Group, China, 1941–3. Deputy Director (Intelligence), Office of Strategic Services, 1944–5. Director of Strategic Services Unit, War Department, 1945–6. His son, Lieutenant Munro Magruder, was killed in action in Korea in 1950. Father and son are buried in the same grave in Arlington Cemetery.

Winston S. Churchill to Sir Stafford Cripps
(Churchill papers, 20/53)

31 January 1942

My dear Stafford Cripps,

Many thanks for your letter of January 29.[1] I am sorry that you do not feel able to help us by taking over the vast business of the Ministry of Supply, except under conditions which it is not in my power to meet.

That the Minister of Supply should be a Member of the War Cabinet would vitiate the policy, upon which Parliament has lately shown itself so strongly set, of having a Minister of Production with general supervisory duties over the whole field of war supply. It would also still further depart from the principle of a small War Cabinet upon which so much stress was laid by public opinion at the time and after the formation of the present Government. We have already increased our numbers from five to eight, and if you count the Minister of State in Cairo, we should be nine. If the Minister of Supply were added, it would be impossible to exclude the Minister for Aircraft Production. If the Heads of these two Supply Departments were in the War Cabinet, it would be necessary to include the Ministerial Heads of the Fighting Departments whom they serve. Thus the two principles of a War Cabinet and of a Minister of Production would both be equally frustrated. I am sure neither the House of Commons nor the public would approve of this.

It will be a pleasure for me to see you from time to time as you suggest. I shall always be ready to receive your friendly advice, though what I had wanted was your active help. Perhaps I may be able to obtain this some day.

Yours sincerely,
Winston S. Churchill

Winston S. Churchill to Sir Archibald Sinclair
(Churchill papers, 20/53)

31 January 1942
Private & Confidential

My dear Archie,

I must draw your attention to the voting of the Liberal Party in the House on the Vote of Confidence. Out of a total of twenty, six abstained

---

[1] Explaining his conditions for becoming Minister of Supply.

or were absent, leaving fourteen to represent the Party. Of these four-teen, three were Ministers, viz: - yourself, Crinks[1] and Foot.[2] You also have an Under-Secretaryship in the Lords.[3] This is a lot of sail to carry on so small a hull and I fear that the Conservative Party, which in the three Divisions during the life of the present Government has voted 252, 281 and 309 respectively, will become critical of the lack of support given to the Government.

At the same time, the *News Chronicle* has become one of the most criti-cal and often hostile newspapers, and fallen sadly below the splendid but instructed independence of the *Manchester Guardian*.

I suggest to you that these matters require your very earnest attention. As you know, I have never measured the strength of the Liberal Party by its Parliamentary representation. Nevertheless when its numbers are so small it seems to me all the more necessary to have unity of action on occasions of Confidence in the Government, which the Party has formally and officially decided to join and support.

Yours sincerely,
Winston S. Churchill

Winston S. Churchill to Oliver Lyttelton
(Churchill papers, 20/69)

31 January 1942
Personal and Secret

I cannot conceal from you that I am very much disappointed by the poor servicing of our tanks during the present battle. Out of 987 British

[1] Harcourt Johnstone, 1895–1945. Known as 'Crinks'. Educated at Eton and Balliol College, Oxford. On active service, 1914–18. Liberal MP for Willesden East, 1923–4. Unsuccessful Liberal Parliamentary candidate for Eastbourne, 1925. Liberal MP for South Shields, 1931–5, and for West Middlesborough, 1940–5. Secretary, Department of Overseas Trade, 1940–5. A member of the Other Club from 1932, and its Joint Honorary Secretary (with Brendan Bracken) from 1937.

[2] Hugh Mackintosh Foot, 1907–90. Administrative Officer, Palestine Government, 1929–37. Assistant British Resident, Transjordan, 1939–42. British Military Administrator, Cyrenaica, 1943. Colonial Secretary, Cyprus, 1943–5; Jamaica, 1945–7. Chief Secretary, Nigeria, 1947–50. Knighted, 1951. Captain-General and Governor-in-Chief, Jamaica, 1951–7. Governor and Commander-in-Chief, Cyprus, 1957–60. Created Baron Caradon, 1964. Minister of State for Foreign Affairs and British Ambassador to the United Nations, 1964–70.

[3] Hugh Michael Seely, 1898–1970. Lieutenant in Grenadier Guards, 1917. Served until 1919. Held commission in South Notts Hussars, 1920–3. Liberal MP for East Norfolk, 1923–4; for Berwick-upon-Tweed, 1935–41. Joint Under-Secretary of State for Air, 1941–5. Created Baron Sherwood, 1941. In March 1942 he married Molly Patricia Chetwode, daughter of Viscount Camrose, who owned the *Daily Telegraph*.

and American Cruiser Tanks in the Command, only 422 are serviceable, and out of 308 Infantry Tanks only 101 are serviceable. I thought you were going to look after this aspect, and General Haining was put at your disposal for that purpose. I have followed your advice in recalling him, but I had expected that you yourself would have been able to give warning of the failure of the workshops to handle repairs. Actually you have in ME Command, as at 23.1.42, 1,295 Cruiser and Infantry Tanks, out of which only 523 are reported serviceable.

2. I had also hoped you would form a view of the waste of manpower, which is proved by the struggle to find a few fighting units from the Poles and the Free French while at the same time well over 600,000 soldiers are on our ration strength. I hoped you would give me a good clear check on all this and, as the head of the Council you have set up which the Commander-in-Chief attends, you might have drawn attention to these disparities. Surely you ought to try to grip this situation more closely.

Winston S. Churchill to General Hastings Ismay,
for the Chiefs of Staff Committee
(Churchill papers, 20/67)

31 January 1942
Most Secret

I am increasingly of opinion that the only way to marshall an adequate army south of the Caspian will be by using the monster liners to carry American forces to that theatre. You will by now have seen the Appreciation which I wrote while in the United States and which I left with the President.

I had reason to believe from Mr Hopkins that they by no means excluded the possibility of an American army based on Persian Gulf ports, or even upon Suez, or both. Do you wish me to take this up with the President, or will you put it to the Combined Staffs in the first instance, or are you against it? The matter turns largely on the use marked out in the next few months for the monster liners. What is their future programme? Pray let me have your views.

Winston S. Churchill to General Hastings Ismay,
for the Chiefs of Staff Committee
(Churchill papers, 20/67)

31 January 1942
Most Secret

DENIAL TO THE JAPANESE OF AMMUNITION IN THE
MAIN MAGAZINE ON SINGAPORE

The obvious course is to fire the ammunition at the enemy. Should evacuation become inevitable, which is by no means admitted, there will be two or three days to do this. Even in the week before the decision, ammunition should be brought to the gun sites and fired at the best enemy targets available. What are the number of rounds per gun for the different natures? Surely there is nothing that could not be fired away in 48 hours?

2. There is no objection to hiding shells in various holes and corners with delay action fuzes as booby-traps if there is any doubt about being able to fire it all away.

3. You do not mention firing away this ammunition at the enemy, which is the natural and long-prescribed course when the fall of a fortress is imminent.

4. The telegram requires to be redrafted around this central principle.

5. There ought to be plenty of time to make good arrangements. If the fortress is properly defended, we are more likely to have a shortage of ammunition towards the end than be left with large dumps.

6. Pray let this have your consideration, and perhaps you will furnish me with a further draft.

Winston S. Churchill to Air Chief Marshal Sir Charles Portal
(Churchill papers, 20/67)

31 January 1942

Please observe that, out of 1,550 serviceable aircraft, Fighter Command has managed to smash up 126, or one aircraft in 12, during a week in which there has been hardly any fighting. Let me know how many sorties there have been against the enemy. Let me have also a detailed analysis of the accidents during the week in question in Fighter Command, showing at least a dozen classes of cause.

Fancy all this wanton waste happening at a time when we have got so few in the kitty and ought to be fattening up for the spring fighting.

Winston S. Churchill to Lord Halifax
(Churchill papers, 20/67)

31 January 1942   Washington DC

Surely we need not worry too much about this.[1] The President's idea is that we keep the lead as patrons of the Free French while the United States tries to maintain contacts with Vichy. The Vichy contacts are extremely important at the present time in view of certain projects which are being considered. I certainly do not mind the United States strengthening their contacts with Vichy. On the contrary, it is on the influence of the United States with Vichy that I count for the decisive reactions in France.

Winston S. Churchill to Captain Henry Margesson,
General Sir Alan Brooke, and Brendan Bracken
(Churchill papers, 20/67)

31 January 1942
Secret

Ought all this[2] to be made public? Will the Americans like it being made public? I have not seen that they have made any announcement of their flying reinforcements. Of course, if there is no military objection, and no American objection, the information is quite helpful.

2. I am increasingly disturbed by the stream of information now pouring out from Singapore. Everything is discussed with great and accurate knowledge, and with the fullest publicity. I have already telegraphed once to General Wavell about the censorship at Singapore. Pray advise me of any further action you suggest.

---

[1] Assurances by the State Department in Washington to the Vichy French Embassy, also in Washington, that the crews of Vichy French ships taken over by the United States would be repatriated to Vichy France.

[2] A report in the *Daily Mirror* of 31 January 1942 headed 'Non-stop U.S. air raid to East'.

February
1942

Winston S. Churchill to President Franklin D. Roosevelt
(Churchill papers, 20/88)

1 February 1942

Thank you for your telegram just received. I send you herewith Wavell's message to me of 29th. Please remember it was not written for your eye, but we have got to a point where none of that matters.

2. I entirely agree about the balance being maintained, especially as I guessed who you are leaving the Supreme Command vacancy for. Nothing must stand in the way of the big layout, namely, Supreme Commander, Wavell; Deputy, unknown; Naval, the Dutchman[1]; Air, Brett, or whoever you choose. I have cabled Wavell on these lines, as it would be well to have his view before us before final decision.

3. I will reply to your paragraphs 3–7 inclusive after I have put them before the Cabinet on Monday. You may be sure there will be no disagreements between you and me.

4. Your paragraphs 8 and 9. Thank you so much for all your kindness. I cannot tell you how sorry I was to leave the White House. I enjoyed every minute of it, which is more than all of those whose portraits adorn the walls can say.

Winston S. Churchill to Peter Fraser
(Churchill papers, 20/88)

1 February 1942

The Staff has been giving consideration to the matter of including the Australians, the Dutch and the New Zealanders in the joint staff conferences. While they have not given me a final answer, I think I can say that their general feeling, with which I concur, is that all political and Govern-

[1] Admiral Helfrich.

ment matters concerning New Zealand, Australia and the Netherlands East Indies should continue to be handled in London and that military matters be resolved here. However, to have all of these countries represented each by three men on the joint staff considering ABDA problems would provide for an altogether unwieldy body. We are all strongly of the opinion that the present working organization is functioning very efficiently for the collaboration of British–United States affairs which will constitute the major portion of the matters to be handled. We think it would remain as at present but with this important supplementary arrangement to meet the special complications of the ABDA area: That in cases in which the Dutch, the Australians and the New Zealanders are concerned the combined staff will invite their participation in discussion of such matters as involve their national interest and collaboration. It is essential, however, that in those cases where immediate action is required the individual advice of the officers concerned be given without waiting for formal word from their respective Governments. We will undertake here to work out a close and intimate working relationship with the three Military Missions of Australia, New Zealand and the Netherlands East Indies and make sure that their advice is in no sense perfunctory but will be considered important and essential in determining the general policies of the war in the ABDA Area. This seems to be our joint staff opinion here.

Winston S. Churchill to General Hastings Ismay
(Churchill papers, 20/67)

2 February 1942
Action this Day
Most Secret

I should like to have a Staff meeting at 10 p.m. tonight with the Chiefs of the Staff, in order to discuss further reinforcements of Malaya and Burma and the defence of the Indian Ocean.

The following points occur to me:

1. Singapore. – How is it that we were only told last week that two out of the three aerodromes on the island were commanded by artillery from the mainland? Why were no others constructed? What progress has been made on the northern shore defences? What has been done about interior communications, radial roads, &c.? I presume the causeway which has been partly breached, is specially covered by artillery

and machine-gun fire. What plans are in hand for counter-attacks from the sea upon the Japanese communications to Malaya, observing that they seem to be able to do everything, and we nothing, in the matter of landings?

2. What plans are being made for the relief of Singapore by running in convoys of reinforcements, troops, aircraft and food? What arrangements have been made to give relief by attacking the Japanese aerodromes with heavy bombers from Sumatra and Java? Have any plans been made to establish new air bases on the subsidiary islands? What has been done about enforcing compulsory labour on the male population remaining in Singapore Island? A further effort must be made to reduce the useless mouths. Many of these matters are within General Wavell's province, but we must have full knowledge of the position and make sure that no point is overlooked.

3. Indian Ocean Bases. – What is being done to make sure of these? For instance, Trincomalee: what is its garrison? What are its guns? Has anything been done to protect its gorge? What aerodromes are available in the neighbourhood? The Navy is responsible for the defence of the Indian Ocean. What is the programme of reinforcements? When will the three aircraft carriers be at work? What are the proposed future movements of *Warspite*? How are the repairs of *Valiant* getting on? I observed that a U-boat sank a merchant ship by gunfire in the Bay of Bengal. Are merchant ships in those areas armed? Have they proper gunners on board? What measures are being taken to secure local command of the Bay of Bengal? At present we seem to have no naval forces, light or heavy, that can operate. What destroyers, corvettes and cruisers is it proposed to assign to Indian waters? Let me have the proposed time-table month by month, for the next four months, of reinforcements.

4. After the two Australian divisions have been moved into the Abda area, what other reinforcements are proposed? It would seem that at least four divisions should be sent from this country agreeably with the arrival of the Americans under 'Magnet' and the retardation of the date of probable invasion due to Russia and other causes. Whether these divisions should go to Egypt, to the Levant–Caspian front, to India or to the Abda area must be considered later. The great thing is to get them on the move. We must be prepared for substantial reductions in rations and in imports in order to carry out larger troop movements. The movements of troops by the smaller type of merchant ships must be considered. What about the West Indian Brigade from Freetown? We must have more men east of Suez. The whole field must be surveyed.

5. The reinforcement of India has become most urgent. I am deeply concerned with the reactions from Japanese victories throughout Asia. It will be necessary to have an additional number of British troops in India. These need not be fully formed divisions, as they are for internal security against revolt. In this connection, beach divisions should be considered and also separate battalions.

6. On other papers, I have already mentioned the possibility of the Americans coming into the Persian Gulf area and forming an army on the Levant–Caspian front.

Let me have proposals with time-tables for giving effect to the above, and pray add to these queries as you think best.

Winston S. Churchill to General Hastings Ismay,
for the Chiefs of Staff Committee
(Churchill papers, 20/67)

2 February 1942
Action this Day
Secret

SINGAPORE

What is indispensable is: first, the naval base should be completely wrecked so that the docks and workshops are rendered utterly useless for at least eighteen months; and secondly, that the fortress guns should all be destroyed and rendered unusable for a similar period. Thus Singapore will lose its value to the enemy as an effective naval base. The preparation for the above demolitions ought not to cause alarm because they are all in military areas from which the public is rigorously excluded, and also the actual work of putting in the explosive charges could be done by the engineers.

2. Plans should also be made for the destruction of other valuable property, but preparations for this should not be allowed to weaken the defence which, as the General rightly says, must be prolonged to the last possible hour. Every day gained is vital.

Winston S. Churchill to General Archibald Wavell
(Churchill papers, 20/69)

2 February 1942
Most Immediate
Personal

I observe that you have ordered the Hurricanes which had just reached Singapore to Palembang. Should be grateful for some explanation of this new decision which appears at first sight to indicate despair of defending Singapore.

Lord Beaverbrook to Harry Hopkins
(A. J. P. Taylor, 'Beaverbrook', pages 506–7)

2 February 1942

Churchill has had many experiences in a life full of colour but came up against a new situation on his return from Washington. Some ten or fifteen of his followers set themselves up as authorities on the Far East and on Singapore in particular. They had two or three good days of popularity and then they were required to present their case to public opinion. A most extraordinary reaction set in and by the weekend Churchill had been established in authority and power exceeding all that had gone before.

King George VI: diary
(Royal Archives)

3 February 1942   Buckingham Palace

The Prime Minister came to lunch. I could see he was very relieved that last week in the H of C was over & I told him so. He is glad of his new mandate, and he told me that he had had a census of the voting of the Conservative Party made on the 3 big votings since he became PM, & that on each occasion the Conservative vote was getting bigger. Most of his critics come from his own Party. Many Labour Members abstained from voting this time. Both Baldwin[1] and Chamberlain taught their supporters to be 'good boys' & the plums would fall on them. Winston in

---

[1] Stanley Baldwin, 1867–1947. Educated at Harrow and Trinity College, Cambridge. Conservative MP for Bewdley, 1908–37. Financial Secretary to the Treasury, 1917–21. President of the Board of Trade, 1921–2. Chancellor of the Exchequer, 1922–3. Prime Minister, 1923–4, 1924–9. Lord President of the Council, 1931–5. Prime Minister for the third time, 1935–7. Created Earl, and Knight of the Garter, 1937.

his own words says he has 'treated them rough' & given the plum jobs to others.

The only changes he wants to make in the Govt. are, Beaverbrook, Minister of Production, to look after Supply & MAP.[1] Andrew Duncan[2] to go back to Supply from the Bd. Of Trade, & Llewellin, A Conservative Under Secy to go to the Bd of Trade. The PM is worried & angry over events in the Far East. Singapore has not been fortified from the landward side even with tank traps & pill boxes hidden in the jungle. These could have been done by the troops themselves. 15″ gun emplacements pointing out to sea are no form of defence. He fears great loss of life by air bombardment. Only two aerodromes on the island. Can Hurricanes fly from Sumatra if the aerodromes are near enough? This is being found out. The Libyan campaign is going all wrong, & Rommel has done the same trick which made us retire last year. Our tanks & 2 pr guns are not as good as the German & their repair services are better. W is threatening to go out there.

Curtin (Australia) is still panicking for political representation on the Pacific Council in Washington & not in London, against Winston's judgement. FDR is being asked about it. Latter wants only Service representatives [at] his end.

Winston S. Churchill to Air Chief Marshal Sir Charles Portal
(Churchill papers, 20/67)

3 February 1942

I agree about the importance of Burma, but the rest of it seems rather confused.[3] How do you attack Japan from Burma, except by traversing China, which is a friendly Ally; and even when you get to China, it is quite a long way to attack Japan. What does he mean by 'in these islands'? Does he mean the British Islands or the islands of the Netherlands East Indies?

---

[1] Ministry of Aircraft Production.

[2] Andrew Rae Duncan, 1884–1952. Coal Controller, 1919–20. Chairman of the Advisory Committee of the Mines Department, 1920–9. Vice-President, Shipbuilding Employers Federation, 1920–7. Knighted, 1921. Chairman of the Central Electricity Board, 1927–35. A Director of the Bank of England, 1929–40. Chairman of the Executive Committee of the British Iron and Steel Federation, 1935–40 and 1945–52. National MP for the City of London, 1940–50. President of the Board of Trade, 1940 and 1941. Minister of Supply, 1940–1 and 1942–5. A Director of Imperial Chemical Industries, and of the Dunlop Rubber Company. One of his two sons was killed in action in the Second World War.

[3] A telegram of 1 February 1942 from Air Marshal Peirse to Sir Charles Portal.

He omits altogether from his survey a direct attack upon Japan, first by sea-borne air raids, and later on a larger scale.

2. Instead of writing all this it would have been better to explain why he sent all the Hurricanes away from Singapore, leaving its defence to Buffaloes[1] which are vulnerable and perfectly useless.

Winston S. Churchill to President Franklin D. Roosevelt
(Churchill papers, 20/69)

3 February 1942

[…]

5. About the Pacific Council. I have not heard from Australia or New Zealand, to whom I sent text of your proposals. We still think it will be necessary to have Far East Council in London and that Australians will eventually agree. The Dutch beg that it may be here because it is to be on the Ministerial level and it would be impossible for them to lose touch with Holland by transporting themselves to Washington. This is in accordance with your view. The Far East Council would of course make recommendations to you on military as well as political matters. The purely military would go from our Chiefs of Staff Committee in London to the Combined Chiefs of Staff Committee in Washington. The political aspects would be dealt with either through the Foreign Office and State Department, or, when necessary, between you and me.

6. There is no reason why the above arrangements should not fit in with what you have offered Australia, New Zealand and the Dutch. In fact I think it an admirable solution. The Combined Chiefs of Staff Committee in Washington would receive the military recommendations, on which the Far East Council would have been consulted beforehand, from our Chiefs of Staff Committee as arranged. But when the Combined Chiefs of Staff Committee in Washington were dealing with something affecting the ABDA or the ANZAC area, or even larger matters, it would be natural for them to invite representatives of Military Missions of Australia, New Zealand and Holland to attend the discussion. The representatives of these Missions would of course act under instructions from their Governments but they would be available to state their arguments in their own way and supply additional information to the Combined

---

[1] Buffalo: an American-designed monoplane fighter aircraft, 150 of which made up the bulk of the British fighter defence of Burma, Malaya, and Singapore. It proved no match for the Japanese Zero, and was known to its pilots as a 'flying coffin'. The Finnish Air Force found it effective, however, in shooting down Soviet aircraft.

Chiefs of Staff Committee in Washington. I have a feeling this will gratify all parties and not clog in any way the major American–British machinery which, as you say, is already working well.

7. But what about China? She has not hitherto been concerned with ABDA and ANZAC. Nevertheless two Chinese armies are coming down into Burma and on the Burma Road. I suggest China is primarily your concern and that you will weave her in with the Combined Chiefs of Staff Committee in Washington while keeping us constantly informed and will bring everything to final solution there.

8. Pending receipt of replies from Australia and New Zealand I should like to know how this strikes you. Again it looks to me a pretty good and practical layout.

General Archibald Wavell to Winston S. Churchill
(Churchill papers, 20/69)

3 February 1942
Most Immediate

Decision to withdraw majority fighters to Sumatra was taken during my visit to Singapore with Peirse[1] on January 29. Withdrawal of troops into Singapore exposes three out of four of island's aerodromes to artillery fire. Increased scale air attacks on aerodromes had already necessitated withdrawal bombers to more secure bases in Sumatra. Loss of Malaya emphasises vital importance of holding southern Sumatra and maintenance of aerodromes there for offensive operations to reduce scale of attacks on Singapore. Fighter defence of these aerodromes essential.

2. To leave fighters on exposed aerodromes in Singapore would be to invite their destruction in few days. Meanwhile every effort being made to maintain fighter defence by keeping equivalent of one squadron on Kallang aerodrome and by using other aerodromes as circumstances permit for refuelling fighters operating from Sumatra.

3. Consider these dispositions offer best prospects of air defence of Singapore which there is every intention and hope of holding.

[1] Richard Edmund Charles Peirse, 1892–1970. Pilot in the Royal Naval Air Service, 1913–14, and one of Churchill's flying instructors at that time. On active service, 1914–18 (DSO, AFC). Deputy Director of Operations and Intelligence, Air Ministry, 1930–3. Air Officer Commanding British Forces, Palestine, and Transjordan, 1933–6. Deputy Chief of the Air Staff, 1937–40. Knighted, 1940. Vice-Chief of the Air Staff, 1940. Air Officer Commanding-in-Chief, Bomber Command, 1940–2; India, 1942–3. Allied Air Commander-in-Chief, South-East Asia, 1943–4.

Winston S. Churchill to Chiang Kai-shek
(Churchill papers, 20/69)

3 February 1942
Personal and Secret
Most immediate

It gave us all the greatest pleasure to know that Your Excellency would visit India and consult with the Viceroy and the Commander-in-Chief upon all the measures we must take in common to safeguard Burma and the Burma Road and thus ensure the steady flow of munitions and supplies upon which the efficient action of the brave and successful Chinese armies depends. However I am sure you will understand that such a visit could only be made as the guest of the Viceroy, staying either at Government House or, if secrecy is specially desired, at one of his private houses on his own estates either at Delhi or Calcutta.

2. With regard to your seeing persons like Mr Gandhi[1] and Mr Nehru,[2] who are in a state at least of passive disobedience to the King Emperor, this you will readily see is a matter which requires very grave consideration. It might make a most grievous impression in Great Britain and throughout the British Empire if anything of this kind occurred otherwise than by arrangement with the Viceroy after you and he have talked over the whole position.

3. In any case, if you begin seeing the leaders of the Indian Congress Party it would be necessary that you should also see Mr Jinnah[3] representing 80,000,000 Moslems, and representatives of the 40,000,000 depressed classes and of the Indian Princes who rule over 80,000,000,

---

[1] Mohandas Karamchand Gandhi, 1869–1948. Born in India. Called to the Bar, London, 1889. Practised as a barrister in South Africa, 1889–1908; gave up his practice to devote himself to championing the rights of Indian settlers in South Africa, 1908; leader of the Passive Resistance Campaign, South Africa, 1908–14. Started the Non-Cooperation Movement, India, 1918; given sole authority to lead the national movement for independence by the Indian National Congress, 1921. Inaugurated the Civil Disobedience Campaign, 1930. Frequently imprisoned by the British. Opposed the partition of India into Hindu and Muslim states; severely critical of the Hindu caste system. Assassinated by an orthodox Hindu in 1948, within a year of the creation of India and Pakistan as independent States.

[2] Jawaharlal Nehru, 1889–1964. Educated (like Churchill) at Harrow. Barrister-at-law, Inner Temple, 1912. Member of the All-India Congress Committee, 1918–47. President, Indian National Congress, 1929. Imprisoned by the British several times, for his political activities and calls for non-cooperation. Vice-President, Interim Government of India, 1946. Prime Minister of India from 1947 until his death. Both his daughter, Indira Gandhi, and his grandson, Rajiv Gandhi, were subsequently Prime Ministers of India; both were assassinated.

[3] Mohammed Ali Jinnah, 1876–1948. Member of the Imperial Legislative Council from 1910. President of the all-India Muslim League 1916, 1920, and from 1934. 'Founder of Pakistan' and its first Governor-General, 1948.

to whom the Imperial Government is bound by solemn treaties. I must point out that the Congress Party, although successful some years ago in the provincial elections, in no way represents the martial races of India who are fighting so well, in their allegiance to the King-Emperor, to defend the very objects upon which the safety of India and the interests of China equally depend.

4. I must therefore beg that Your Excellency, with whom I hope to collaborate in the closest possible way in conjunction with President Roosevelt and Premier Stalin, not only in this war but in the world settlement which will follow it, will be so very kind as to consider these serious words of mine. Pray accept my best wishes for your safe and pleasant journey.

Winston S. Churchill to Lord Linlithgow
(Churchill papers, 20/69)

3 February 1942
Most immediate
Private and Personal
Secret

I have sent in immediately preceding telegram message for Generalissimo for delivery at best point of interception (either Burma or Calcutta to both of which it has been telegraphed) and I trust that you will be most careful to be guided by it. It represents view taken by Cabinet in assenting to the visit proposed. We cannot possibly agree to Head of Foreign State intervening as a kind of impartial arbiter between representative of King Emperor and Messrs Gandhi and Nehru. I hope indeed that when he has seen you and Members of your Council he will not wish to have discussions with parties mentioned and that you will guide him to that conclusion by showing how necessary it will be for him also to see representatives of other masses of the Indian public. In no circumstances must he be allowed to see Nehru as you apprehended by getting off at Allahabad or wherever Nehru may be. There could be no possibility of such meeting remaining secret and nothing would be more likely to spread pan-Asiatic malaise through all the bazaars of India.

Winston S. Churchill to Peter Fraser
(Churchill papers, 20/69)

3 February 1942
Most Secret

I have given fullest consideration to your requests for supplies of war material, and in particular to those set out in your message to me of 30th January No. 48, with the earnest wish to meet your needs to the maximum extent.

Our further proposals have been conveyed to you in the Secretary of State's telegram of today No. 87. I can assure you that they result from a careful review of the requirements of the various theatres of war in which the requirements of the United Kingdom have been placed last in order of priority and I hope that you will find that they meet your most pressing needs.

You recognise, as I know, that the task of allocation is one of extreme difficulty at the moment with a rapidly changing situation in several parts of the world. I should like to bring to your notice two considerations:

(a) there is a large flow of reinforcements of all kinds into the ABDA area. In addition to what we are sending to you an important consignment is being provided for the defence of Australia. This will contribute, directly or indirectly according as the situation develops, to the defence of New Zealand.

(b) we are already heading dangerously near the point where the spreading of our resources must lead to a general weakness. There is a point beyond which we cannot interfere with the flow to the Middle East whence so many Army and Air Units with their equipment have already been withdrawn for the Pacific.

As stated in the Secretary of State's telegram we shall be undertaking a further review at the end of March and I can indeed assure you that we are watching the situation in all its bearings from day to day.

Haile Selassie[1] to Winston S. Churchill
(Churchill papers, 20/69)

3 February 1942

On the occasion of the conclusion of agreement between the Government of the United Kingdom and myself I desire to thank Your Excel-

---

[1] Haile Selassie, 1892–1975. Ascended to the Imperial Throne of Abyssinia, 1930. Exiled after the Italian invasion, 1936. Returned to Abyssinia, 1941. Deposed, 1974. Died in custody, 1975.

lency once again for all you have done for myself and my people and to express my admiration for your inspiring leadership. It will be a cause of lasting and heartfelt gratitude to myself and my people that in the throes of their desperate and glorious struggle the great British people spared so generously their resources to give freedom to our country.[1] We pray God that victory will soon crown your efforts.

Oliver Lyttelton to Winston S. Churchill
(Churchill papers, 20/69)

3 February 1942   Cairo

[...]

6. Recovery of mobile workshops behind armoured formations depends on uncertain factors such as the course of battle, action by the enemy, good or bad weather. It is not yet possible to give full figures but, as an example, unit workshops of the seventh armoured division repaired and put back into the lines 280 tanks between November 18th and December 23rd. I think that in the early part of the battle their recoveries were good and do not compare unfavourably with the much-praised German system. After all, Rommel started with 253 German tanks and has now only about 40 German Runners. I cannot yet state definitely that in the later stages of the battle the same degree of efficiency has been achieved.

7. Everything possible is being done to dilute rearward services in order to free British forces for reinforcing fighting formations. Since his appointment Riddell Webster[2] has been working on dilution by non-British men and women and the results will begin to show shortly.

[1] Between 10 June 1940 and 1941, British and Commonwealth forces were in action in Abyssinia against the Italian forces that had conquered the country in 1936. On 3 August 1940, Italian troops invaded British Somaliland. In November 1940, the British Government's Code and Cypher School at Bletchley Park broke the high-grade cypher of the Italian Army in Italian East Africa. Later that month the replacement cypher for the Italian Royal Air Force was broken by the Combined Bureau, Middle East (based in Cairo). From that moment, the British commanders-in-chief knew of the Italian battle plans as soon as they were issued to the Italian commanders. On 18 January 1941, Haile Selassie re-entered Abyssinia. The final defeat of the Italian forces in Abyssinia and Italian East Africa came on 27 November 1941 (the Battle of Gondar). The troops participating in the defeat of the Italians were from Britain, Anglo-Egyptian Sudan, British Somaliland, Kenya Colony, British India, Northern and Southern Rhodesia, Nyasaland, South Africa, Belgium, the Belgian Congo, the Free French, and the Free Ethiopian forces.

[2] Thomas Sheriden Riddell-Webster, 1886–1974. Educated at Harrow and Sandhurst. Entered the Army, 1905. On active service, 1914–18 (despatches, DSO). Director of Movements and Quartering, War Office, 1938–9. Deputy Quartermaster General, 1939–40. General Officer Commanding-in-Chief, Southern India, 1941. Lieutenant-General in charge of Administration, Middle East (Cairo),

8. This, however, is mainly a long-term project. Having regard to the immense area of this command and the very large-scale administrative undertakings and improvements which we have in hand, it seems to me clear that the number of men employed in the rear areas will always compare very unfavourably with the proportions which it is possible to maintain in a European theatre of war or in any country where communications of all kinds are less primitive.

9. There has never been any shortage of man-power for the present battle. None of the three Dominion divisions have been used in the western part of the battle for some time. The limiting factor has been our ability to maintain troops at great distances from the railhead or port. The Free French were originally moved into Cyrenaica for political reasons. They arrived too late to take part in the Halfaya battle and they and the Poles were in the back areas and nearest to the scene of the new battlefield when the emergency arose.

10. I do not feel I have left anything undone on these subjects. I must say that I found your telegram profoundly discouraging and hardly just to me.

11. I shall not cease to try and improve recovery and manpower problems.

Oliver Lyttelton to Winston S. Churchill
(Churchill papers, 20/69)

4 February 1942   Cairo
Most Immediate

[...]

I want you to understand the background here.

(2) I have been having a very sticky time and the need for taking a firm line over Egyptian political crisis has not eased my task with the military. There was I felt loss of proper aggressive spirit in Cyrenaica and a tendency to take in sail. I will not (repeat not) have this, and the immediate task which Auchinleck and I have, is to restore the temporarily shaken confidence. I am happier tonight. Godwin Austin[1] is being relieved of his command and the general signs are better.

1941–2 (despatches). Knighted, 1942. Quartermaster General to the Forces, War Office (London), 1942–6. President of the British Legion (Scotland), 1949–65.
[1] Alfred Reade Godwin-Austen, 1889–1963. 2nd Lieutenant, 1909. On active service, Gallipoli and Mesopotamia, 1915–19 (Military Cross). Commanded 14th Infantry Brigade, Palestine (Arab revolt), 1938–9 (despatches). Major-General, 1939. Officer Commanding 8th Division, on active service in East Africa and Abyssinia (for which he was awarded the CB), 1940. Principal Adminis-

(3) I do not believe that we have been guilty of any major lapse in preparations made for the battle, but in any case the essential thing is now to put all our hearts and minds into ensuring a successful renewal of the offensive immediately [if] this is possible.

(4) I shall play my part to the full whatever happens, but I should like to feel that you have complete confidence and will support me as heretofore.

Winston S. Churchill to General Archibald Wavell
(Churchill papers, 20/69)

4 February 1942
Immediate
Personal

I am relieved to learn that you intend to maintain fighter defences of Singapore by re-fuelling Hurricanes operating from Sumatra.

2. Nevertheless, it is a grievous disadvantage that the bulk of your fighter force should be unable to intercept from their base and should have to waste so much flying time between Sumatra and Singapore.

3. Although I realise the risks to which aeroplanes based on Singapore would be exposed, I am not clear that the need for fighter defence at the Sumatra bases will be strongly felt so long as the Japanese are engaged with Singapore. Moreover, we hope to send you about 90 more Hurricanes by *Athène* and *Indomitable* before the end of February. I therefore hope that all proper risks will be taken in supporting Singapore with fighters.

4. It is difficult to see why half of the fighters left in the Island should be Buffaloes. If numbers must be limited, surely they should be of the highest quality available.

Winston S. Churchill to Lord Moyne
(Churchill papers, 20/67)

5 February 1942

JEWISH IMMIGRANTS HELD AT ATHLIT CAMP, PALESTINE

The situation has changed entirely since these illegal immigrants were rounded up and put in a concentration camp pending transmission to Mauritius. At that time it looked as if we should be subjected to a wave of illegal immigration, but now that the whole of South-Eastern Europe

trative Officer, India Command, New Delhi, 1945–6. Knighted, 1946. General, 1946. Chairman, South-Western Division, National Coal Board, 1946–8.

is in German hands, there is no further danger of this, and I suggest that you let them join their compatriots in Palestine.[1]

President Franklin D. Roosevelt to Winston S. Churchill
(*Churchill papers, 20/69*)

5 February 1942

I have asked the State Department through Halifax and Winant to express to the British Government my strong hope that it promptly agree to the present draft of Interim Lend Lease Agreement and I now ask your personal help in bringing this about.[2]

I understand your need of maintaining unity at home in the great task of winning the war. I know you also understand how essential it is that we maintain unity of purpose between our two governments and peoples to this end, equally important, in the unfinished tasks which will follow it.

I am convinced that further delay in concluding this agreement will be harmful to your interests and ours. I am likewise convinced that the present draft is not only fair and equitable but that it meets the apprehensions which some of your colleagues have felt and which Halifax has brought to our attention.[3]

No one knows better than I how busy you are. I should not add this matter to the long list of your worries if, after giving it much personal attention, I were not convinced that a failure to sign this agreement would do much mischief.

War Cabinet: Confidential Annex
(*Cabinet papers, 65/29*)

6 February 1942
12 noon

FUTURE FRONTIERS OF THE SOVIET UNION

The Minister of War Production[4] said that all that M Stalin was asking for was recognition of his frontiers as they had existed in June, 1941, when

---

[1] At the end of January 1942, 793 Jewish refugees from Europe, on board the *Darien*, had been intercepted by the Royal Navy off the coast of British Mandate Palestine, and were held in custody in Palestine awaiting deportation to the Indian Ocean island of Mauritius. On 4 February 1942, Randolph Churchill had written to his father to inform him of this, and to protest against the deportations.

[2] On 12 February 1942 Roosevelt wrote to Churchill: 'We have tried to approach the whole matter of lend-lease in a manner that will not lead us into the terrible pitfalls of the last war' (*Churchill papers, 20/70*).

[3] On Churchill's reservations about this draft of the agreement, see paragraph 9 of his cable to Roosevelt of 8 February 1942, reproduced at page 230 below.

[4] Lord Beaverbrook.

Germany had invaded Russia. At the same date we had made a Treaty with Russia which had wiped out everything which had passed between our two countries up to that date. M Stalin had, however, qualified his request for recognition of the 1941 boundaries on the West by making it clear that these boundaries would be subject to a special arrangement so far as Poland was concerned. Moreover, these frontiers were necessary for Russia's security and security was one of the factors dealt with in the Atlantic Charter. We should therefore (subject, of course, to the views of the United States on this subject) agree to M Stalin's request.

The Minister said that our relations with Russia were deteriorating; we could not afford to wait but should hold out a hand of friendship and seal the bond with them as quickly as possible. It was worth remembering that so far Russia had contributed far more to the war effort than the United States to whom we had made such frequent concessions. In a number of matters we had not acceded, or, not acceded at all promptly, to Russia's requests, e.g. her requests for military aid or her request that we should declare war on Finland.

The Foreign Secretary[1] said that he wished to ask the Cabinet to look at the matter from the point of view of Anglo-Russian relations in their wider sense. It was of the utmost importance that these relations should be put on a better basis. M Stalin wished to sign Treaties with us relating, not merely to our alliance in the war, but also to post-war co-operation. Unless we were in a position to sign Treaties with him, we should not get any real co-operation. He felt sure that no treaty could be signed except on the basis of Russia's June 1941 frontiers with Finland, the Baltic States and Roumania.

[...]

The Secretary of State for Air[2] said that provided we won the war, there was no doubt that M Stalin's forces would be in occupation of the Baltic States and Bessarabia at the end of the war, and it would not be in our power to get them to leave. By agreeing to accept these frontiers now, we should go a long way to remove the risk of bad feeling between this country and Russia.

The Prime Minister referred to the uncertainty as to what the position would be at the end of the war. In his view, the right plan was that all these matters should be settled at the Peace Conference. The immediate point at issue was how this matter should be presented to the United States. For his own part, he favoured a balanced presentation.

[1] Anthony Eden.
[2] Sir Archibald Sinclair.

Several Ministers thought that, if this was done, the result would be that the United States would immediately ask what our views were. They favoured giving the United States some indication of how our minds were moving.

The Minister of Labour and National Service[1] attached importance to it being clearly understood whether M Stalin's claim to his 1941 boundaries in Finland, the Baltic States and Bessarabia represented his ultimate aims in this direction.

The Foreign Secretary said that M Stalin's statement was quite specific on this point.

Winston S. Churchill to General Hastings Ismay
(Churchill papers, 20/67)

6 February 1942   Chequers[2]

Make sure I have all papers, files and minutes of any kind in the possession of any of the Military Departments which deal with the human torpedo, limpet bomb method or any cognate variations of attack on warships in harbour.

Winston S. Churchill to Admiral of the Fleet Sir Dudley Pound
(Churchill papers, 20/67)

6 February 1942   Chequers

Please give me the dates on which the following may be expected to join or rejoin the Fleet fit for duty: *Valiant, Nelson, Duke of York, Illustrious, Formidable* and *Queen Elizabeth.*

I am hoping that an intense day-to-day effort is made to get these ships fit for service.

---

[1] Ernest Bevin.

[2] Among Churchill's guests at Chequers on the weekend of 6–8 February 1942 were Lord Beaverbrook, Ernest Bevin, Randolph and Pamela Churchill, Averell Harriman and his daughter Kathleen, the United States Ambassador Gilbert Winant, the Secretary of State for India and Burma, L. S. Amery, and the pianist Bénno Moiseiwitsch.

Winston S. Churchill to Air Chief Marshal Sir Charles Portal
(Churchill papers, 20/67)

6 February 1942 Chequers

The New Zealand Government asked for 36 fighter airplanes, of which only 18 were given. Surely they should have their 36. How can this be managed? The 4 Fighter Squadrons for which they asked is more difficult. What is being done for them? As they are so much smaller they should have priority above Australia.

Winston S. Churchill to Lord Linlithgow
(Churchill papers, 20/69)

6 February 1942 Chequers
Personal and Secret

CHIANG KAI-SHEK'S PROPOSED VISIT TO INDIA

On what grounds would he regard himself as having been (quote) tricked (unquote). He proposed himself and will be an honoured guest, but he has no right to intervene between the Government of the King-Emperor and any of the King's subjects. It would be disastrous if you put yourself in a position where we had Gandhi and Nehru on the one side and the Viceroy of India on the other, with Chiang Kai-shek arbitrating between the two.

If you could bring about the desired result according to telegram 142[1] without showing him the actual text of the message there is no objection to your withholding it, but I rely on you to see that the result is achieved. Do not hesitate to use the message if there is any real necessity for it.

Winston S. Churchill to Haile Selassie
(Churchill papers, 20/69)

6 February 1942 Chequers

I am very glad to receive your Majesty's cordial message on the conclusion of the Agreement between our countries. His Britannic Majesty's Government have been proud to aid the Abyssinian people in driving out the invader and the aggressor, and we shall be ready without any thought of national gain to help Your Majesty in the task of reconstruc-

[1] Churchill's telegram to Chiang Kai-shek of 3 February 1942.

tion which is necessary to enable your Empire to play its full part in the better and broader world which we hope will emerge from the struggles and sufferings of the war.

Winston S. Churchill to Harry Hopkins
(Churchill papers, 20/69)

6 February 1942   Chequers
Personal and Secret

It would be well to make sure that the President's attention has been drawn to the very heavy sinkings by U-boats in the Western North Atlantic.[1] Since January 12 confirmed losses are 158,208 and probable losses 83,740 and possible losses 17,363, a total of 259,311 tons.

President Franklin D. Roosevelt to Winston S. Churchill
(Cabinet papers, 20/69)

7 February 1942
Triple Priority
Most Urgent

Admiral Hart[2] has asked to be relieved because of ill health. I believe the thing to do is to let the Dutchman go in as Acting C in C of all naval forces leaving all other Commands under Wavell as at present constituted including Peirse. This will handle the matter satisfactorily for the present and will permit us to make changes later if that seems desirable. This proposal is in the hands of Chiefs of Staff here but I wanted to send you my personal view. Can we not settle this with finality by Sunday.

Harry gave me your message about sinkings in Western Atlantic. This matter is being given urgent consideration by Stark,[3] King and me.

We had a good go at the Japs in Marshall Islands.

We are pushing on with Magnet.

---

[1] The German Navy had just adopted new Enigma settings, which were not to be broken by Bletchley Park until December 1942.

[2] Admiral Thomas Hart, Commander of the ABDA naval forces against Japan (see Wavell to Churchill, 12 January 1942).

[3] Harold Raynsford Stark, 1880–1972. Commissioned into the United States Navy, 1905. Served in European waters, 1917–18. Rear-Admiral, 1934. Officer Commanding the Cruisers, Battle Force, 1938–9. Chief of Naval Operations, 1939–42. Commander, United States Naval Forces in Europe, 1942–5. Honorary British knighthood, 1945.

Winston S. Churchill to General Archibald Wavell
(Churchill papers, 20/69)

7 February 1942   Chequers
Most Secret

I have now heard from President to whom I put the whole case. He says that Hart has asked to be relieved on grounds of health and that the best thing is quote to let the Dutchman go on acting C in C of all naval forces[1] leaving all other forces under Wavell as at present including Peirse unquote. I have closed with this as it clearly leaves the future open. It is certain that the Americans will require to fill one of the places, sea or air, and that this point will arise whenever The Unknown is free to become your Deputy. The Americans are very broadminded but if they think they are being squeezed out by what they call Britishers you will get the contrary reaction in a vehement form. There is no need for you to make Peirse acquainted with these uncertainties. All good wishes.

Peter Fraser to Winston S. Churchill
(Churchill papers, 20/69)

7 February 1942
Most Secret

We have just been advised by Major-General Freyberg[2] that the New Zealand Division has again been ordered to move for a full operational role in the Western Desert. We have of course told Freyberg that we must accept the position but that we are most disappointed that circumstances now require further operations by the New Zealand Division so soon after recent heavy losses and that we assume that nothing but the serious nature of the emergency has necessitated this step. We have asked him also to convey this communication to the Commander-in-Chief.

[1] It is perhaps worth noting the minor but interesting discrepancy here between Churchill's words, 'to let the Dutchman go on acting C in C of all naval forces', and Roosevelt's actual words in the telegram quoted, 'to let the Dutchman go in as Acting C in C of all naval forces' (see above).

[2] Bernard Freyberg, 1889–1963. Born in London. Educated in New Zealand. Sub-Lieutenant, Royal Naval Division, 1914. On active service at Antwerp, 1914, the Dardanelles, 1915, and in France, 1916–18 (despatches six times; wounded nine times; DSO and two bars); Victoria Cross, awarded for 'conspicuous bravery and brilliant leadership' at Beaumont Hamel during the Battle of the Somme, 1916). General Staff Officer, War Office, 1933–4. Posted to India, 1937, but invalided out of the Army after breakdown in health. Passed fit for general service, September 1939. General Officer Commanding Salisbury Plain Area, October 1939. General Officer Commanding New Zealand Forces from November 1939 until the end of the war. Commander-in-Chief, Allied Forces in Crete, 1941. Knighted, 1942. Awarded the third bar to his DSO, Italy, 1944. Governor-General of New Zealand 1946–52. Created Baron, 1951.

I think you should know that the recent ill-informed comments emanating from America and elsewhere as to the very large forces retained inactive in the United Kingdom as compared with the needs elsewhere, the despatch of American troops to Northern Ireland and the use of Dominion forces in the Middle East have been taken up with some force in this Dominion and were indeed reflected with some degree of embarrassment to us at the secret session of Parliament yesterday. I greatly fear that the renewed employment of New Zealand forces, who certainly have had their full share of heavy fighting and have, as you know, suffered very grievous losses, will add weight to this point of view, especially having regard to the fact that their renewed employment now will be misrepresented here as an indication that their last campaign was useless and that the job must be done again. Indeed it may well add point to a demand that New Zealand forces should be returned to the Pacific Area to meet the danger nearer home. Consensus of such sentiments may, as you know, have mischievous results. In order to counter any such propaganda and to allay any possible public feeling I should be most grateful if you would let me have, as far as possible for public use, a full statement of the number of troops at present held in the United Kingdom and of the reasons, which I do not for a moment suggest are not completely conclusive, for their retention.[1]

Winston S. Churchill to John Curtin
(Churchill papers, 20/69)

7 February 1942
Most Immediate
Most Secret and Personal

I am very glad to get your No. 102. I am sure we can give you better service in London than could be at present arranged in Washington. The fact that we cannot all be in one place is the fault of the various oceans. I read this morning that the President has said that the Pacific Councils on both sides of the Atlantic have been functioning for a month. We must not let him down by saying anything inconsistent with this.

2. I shall now call the first meeting of the Pacific Council in London on Tuesday. It does not deal only with the ABDA area but with the whole problems of the war against Japan, and the sooner we get functioning the better.

[1] For Churchill's reply, see 9 February 1942.

3. We are also asking the Americans to arrange for the organisation for the Anzac Area, not so large but on the same lines as Wavell's ABDA machine on which we are informing you. This will be set up in Australia under and around the American Naval Commander-in-Chief, and I hope soon to reach a settlement which will be satisfactory to you. One cannot make the whole new structure at once, and I think we have made immense progress considering the difficulties of time and communication.

4. The general layout is as follows:
1. The ABDA fighting area.
2. The Anzac approach area.
3. The Indian Ocean approach area.
4. The Australian home defence and war base area.
5. The Indian home defence and war base area.
6. The United States main Fleet area radiating from Hawaii.
It is the relation of all these that we have to concert.

5. I have remitted your paragraph 4 and its many sub-heads to the Chiefs of Staff Committee as it is largely technical. They will supply a memorandum which I will send you.

Winston S. Churchill to Peter Fraser
(Cabinet papers, 20/69)

7 February 1942

I am very glad to receive your assent to the proposed Far Eastern Council in London. I am sure you will get far better service here than in Washington, and that our joint views will weigh heavily with Washington, with whom we are in close touch.

There has been no overlooking of the Anzac area, but the distances are so great that it is necessary to establish a separate organisation from that of the ABDA area. We are proposing to Washington the setting up in Eastern Australia of a combined staff under the American Naval Commander-in-Chief, which will comprise representatives of New Zealand, Australia, the United States and Great Britain.

The whole of the affairs of the Anzac area will be dealt with from this combined command, and their relations with the ABDA area will, so far as they affect or overlap one another, be dealt with either directly between the two commands or, when necessary, by the London and Washington organisations. We have cabled to you, Australia and the United States on this matter, and do not anticipate any serious difficulties.

Winston S. Churchill to President Franklin D. Roosevelt
(Churchill papers, 20/69)

8 February 1942
Most Secret

Your latest received today, proposing: 'to let the Dutchman go in as Acting Commander-in-Chief of all Naval Forces, leaving all other Commands under Wavell as at present including Peirse' is absolutely agreed by me and will I am sure please Wavell. When certain other changes are ripe we can review the whole situation.

2. Both Australia and New Zealand have now agreed to our plan about the Pacific Council being on a Ministerial level in London constituted and functioning as proposed coupled with the arrangements you have made for the representation of the Dominions and Dutch on the Combined COS Committee in Washington on occasions when they are interested. This is a great step forward and I agree with you that the new machinery, ponderous and complicated though it was bound to be, is functioning smoothly and well. I even think we may plume ourselves a little on having brought it all into action so soon.

3. I presume you will take China under your wing at Washington, keeping us informed, while we maintain our normal contacts. I sent a strong telegram to Wavell about the importance you personally attach to China, and about bringing Chinese troops down into Burma. The Fifth and Sixth Chinese Armies have now come a long way south. There is plenty of rice in Burma, and this part of the field looks better. I am doing all I can to reinforce Burma from India with British troops and refilling India from home. As you know Chiang is visiting the Viceroy.

4. Although the French nation increasingly centres its hopes on the United States, the Vichy attitude described by you and manifesting itself in many ways is rotten. They have certainly been helping Rommel with supplies. I see that Vichy does not like the Miquelon St. Pierre communiqué and that Darlan[1] threatens to retaliate by pushing American observers out of Morocco. It seems to me vital that Donovan's[2] activities

---

[1] Jean Louis Xavier François Darlan, 1881–1942. Entered the French Navy, 1899. On active service, 1914–18 (three citations). Admiral, 1933. Commander-in-Chief of the French Navy, April 1939 to June 1940. Minister of Marine (under the Vichy Government) from June 1940 to April 1942. Distrusted by the Germans. He was in North Africa visiting his sick son when the Allies landed on 8 November 1942. Chief of State in French North Africa (with General Eisenhower's approval) from 11 November 1942 until his assassination on 24 December 1942.

[2] William Joseph Donovan, 1883–1959. On active service, France, 1917–18 (Congressional Medal of Honour). Assistant to the Attorney General of the United States, 1924–9. Chairman, Boulder Dam Canyon Project Commission, 1934–9. Unofficial observer in Britain for the Secretary of the

of which you told me should have full play and that American observers should in no circumstances be withdrawn. Otherwise what becomes of 'Gymnast' and its variants? You hold the master key in Martinique where there are reputed to be 20 French ships, 4,500 seamen many of whom would join Free France, 50 millions of gold from the *Emil Bertin*, and 100 American fighter planes which contrary to previous reports, are said to have been kept in good condition.

5. I hope nothing will be done to give guarantees for the non-occupation of Madagascar and Reunion. The Japanese might well turn up at the former one of these fine days, and Vichy will offer no more resistance to them there than in French Indo-China. A Japanese air, Submarine and/or Cruiser base at the Diego Suarez would paralyse our whole convoy route both to the Middle and to the Far East. We have therefore for some time had plans to establish ourselves at Diego Suarez by an expedition either from the Nile or from South Africa. At present action is indefinitely postponed as our hands are too full, but I do not want them tied. Of course we will let you know before any action is resolved.

6. I am delighted 'Magnet' is going forward. As it develops I hope to send four matured British divisions round the Cape for employment where most needed, but the shipping is the stranglehold.

7. Seventy per cent of our forces which fought in Malaya got back to the Island. Eleven convoys of stores and reinforcements including the whole 18th Division and other strong good AA and A/T[1] units are now deployed making the equivalent of four divisions, a force very well proportioned to the area they have to defend. I look forward to severe battles on this front, where the Japanese have to cross a broad moat before attacking a strong fortified and still mobile force. Unhappily the 100 Hurricanes which have arrived cannot work from the four bombarded airfields except in small detachments. Thus we are condemned to heavy Air inferiority. Tobruk was held for six months under these conditions, so I have good confidence. Every day that Singapore holds out gives Wavell time to get a strong grip on Sumatra and Java.

8. The Libyan setback has been both a shock and a disappointment, but I do not think Auchinleck has yet shot his bolt.

Navy, 1940. Sent by President Roosevelt on missions to south-east Europe and the Middle East to observe resistance movements, 1940–1. Co-ordinator of Information (Intelligence), 1941–2. Head of the OSS (Office of Strategic Services), 13 June 1942 to 1 October 1945, recruiting agents in Europe, North Africa and Burma. Brigadier-General, 1943. Major-General, 1944. Assistant to Judge Jackson at the Nuremberg Trials, 1945–6. Ambassador to Thailand, 1953–9.

[1] AA: Anti-aircraft; A/T: anti-tank.

9. Your telegram about Lease-Lend. I found Cabinet at its second meeting on this subject even more resolved against trading the principle of Imperial preference as consideration for Lease-Lend. I have always been opposed or lukewarm to Imperial preference, but the issue did not turn on the fiscal aspect. This might well form part of a Tariff or Economic discussion, the latter of which we are ready to begin at once. The great majority of the Cabinet felt that if we bartered the principle of Imperial preference for the sake of Lease-Lend we should have accepted an intervention in the domestic affairs of the British Empire, and that this would lead to dangerous debates in Parliament as well as to a further outbreak of the German propaganda of the kind you read to me on the second night of my visit about the United States breaking up the British Empire and reducing us to the level of territory of the Union. We should only play into the enemy's hands if we gave the slightest colour to all this nonsense. On the other hand we are all for sweeping away trade barriers and it is quite likely that we shall be willing to go further than Congress in this direction. Our whole aim is to work with you in constructing a free, fertile, economic policy for the post-war world. I hope most earnestly therefore that you will make allowances for all these difficulties and try to help forward the suggestions being made by us through the Foreign Office and State Department.

10. I trust Harry is improving. Please give him my regards. You would I am sure like an American film I saw last night *The Remarkable Andrew.*[1] It stirs one's dander.

11. Lastly, would you kindly number your telegrams to me for sake of reference. I suggest that you begin at 100 and I at '25',[2] which I am numbering this.

---

[1] Released in 1942, *The Remarkable Andrew* tells the story of Andrew Long (played by William Holden), a small-town accountant, who finds a $1,240 discrepancy in the city budget. His superiors try to explain it away. When he insists on pursuing the matter, he is in danger of being blamed himself. At that moment, the spirit of Andrew Jackson (the seventh President of the United States, 1829–37), whom Long idolises, visits him and summons great figures from American history – whom only Long can see. His problem is to get out of trouble before too many people think he is mad.

[2] Churchill numbered this telegram '25'.

Winston S. Churchill to Lord Quickswood[1]
(Cecil papers)

8 February 1942
Private

My dear Linky,

Your letter to Bobbety.[2] There are no movements which suggest so early an attack. On the contrary, all the authorities are feeling much easier for the present.

There is no danger of our sending too many troops out of Britain. We are doing all we can, but the shipping is too short.

[...]

Every good wish,
Yours ever,
W

Winston S. Churchill to Colonel Stewart Menzies[3]
(Churchill papers, 20/52)

8 February 1942
Most Secret

'C'

Does this draft,[4] which I have put in a personal form, give full effect to yours? I am sending it by the Ambassador in a sealed envelope. Do the Americans know anything about our machine?[5]

Let me know by tomorrow afternoon.[6]

---

[1] Hugh Richard Heathcote Gascoyne-Cecil, 1869–1956. Known as 'Linky'. Fifth son of the 3rd Marquess of Salisbury (and so uncle to Cranborne). Educated at Eton and University College, Oxford. Conservative MP for Greenwich, 1895–1906; for Oxford University, 1910–37. Provost of Eton, 1936–44. Created Baron Quickswood, 1941. In 1908 he was 'best man' at Churchill's wedding.

[2] Viscount Cranborne (see Churchill to Cranborne, 7 January 1942).

[3] Stewart Graham Menzies, 1890–1968. A nephew of Muriel Wilson, to whom Churchill had proposed marriage in the late 1890s. Educated at Eton. Served in the Grenadier Guards, 1909–10; the Life Guards, 1910–39. On active service, 1914–18; involved from 1915 in counter-espionage and security duties at General Headquarters, France (despatches, DSO, Military Cross). Lieutenant-Colonel, 1919. Chief of the War Office Secret Service, 1919 (under Churchill). Military Representative of the War Office, Secret Intelligence Service, 1919. Personal Assistant to the Head of the Secret Intelligence Service (Admiral Sir Hugh Sinclair) from 1923. Colonel, 1932. Head of the Secret Intelligence Service ('C'), November 1939 to May 1952. CB, 1942. Knighted, 1943.

[4] Of the letter that follows, addressed to President Roosevelt.

[5] A copy of the German Enigma machine, on which British cryptographers were able to read many tens of thousands of top secret German radio signals.

[6] Colonel Menzies replied on 9 February 1942: 'The draft puts matters clearly. The American Naval Authorities have been given several of our Cipher Machines. C' (*Churchill papers, 20/52*).

Winston S. Churchill to President Franklin D. Roosevelt
(Churchill papers, 20/52)

8 February 1942[1]

My dear Mr President,

One night when we talked late, you spoke of the importance of our cipher people getting into close contact with yours. I shall be very ready to put any expert you care to nominate in touch with my technicians. Ciphers for our two Navies have been and are continually a matter for frank discussion between our two Services. But diplomatic and military ciphers are of equal importance and we appear to know nothing officially of your versions of these. Some time ago, however, our experts claimed to have discovered the system and constructed some tables used by your Diplomatic Corps. From the moment when we became allies, I gave instructions that this work should cease. However, danger of our enemies having achieved a measure of success cannot, I am advised, be dismissed.

I shall be grateful if you will handle this matter entirely yourself, and if possible burn this letter when you have read it. The whole subject is secret in a degree which affects the safety of both our countries. The fewest possible people should know.

I take advantage of the Ambassador's homeward journey to send you this by his hand, to be delivered into yours personally.

Winston S. Churchill

Winston S. Churchill to Josef Stalin
(Churchill papers, 20/69)

8 February 1942

Words fail me to express the admiration which all of us feel at the continued brilliant successes of your Armies against the German invader, but I cannot resist sending you a further word of gratitude and congratulation on all that Russia is doing for the common cause.[2]

---

[1] This letter was eventually sent on 25 February 1942, with Ambassador Winant.

[2] On 28 January 1942, Marshal Timoshenko crossed the Upper Donetz River and advanced into Ukraine, recapturing Lozovo (30 miles from German-held Dnepropetrovsk). Further north, a Soviet advance at the junction between German Army Group North and Army Group Centre, between Lake Seliger and Rzhev, had created a gap between the two German army groups.

Winston S. Churchill to Ismet Inönü[1]
(Churchill papers, 20/70)

8 February 1942
Personal and Secret
NOT SENT

I have received the report of Your Excellency's conversation with the Military Attaché, and I take this occasion to assure you that I perfectly understand and approve of the Turkish policy in this particular period of the war of arming as strongly as possible and of allowing no one to pass through her territory or violate her neutrality. It is most important however to arm, and I hope that by the end of 1942 there will be good supplies of all modern weapons flowing from the American and British arsenals. No thoughtful man can doubt how this war is going to end, or that the Germans are going to have a worse defeat than last time. When it will end is a more difficult question. It should not however be supposed that Great Britain and the United States will be exhausted by a prolonged struggle. On the contrary in a year or two they will for the first time be thoroughly armed and militarised, whereas those nations which started fully armed cannot well get any stronger.

I send my most cordial greetings and good wishes to Your Excellency.

Winston S. Churchill to Peter Fraser
(Churchill papers, 20/70)

9 February 1942
Most Secret

The American troops brought to Britain are not their fully trained divisions, but they set free a larger number of mature British divisions for service in the Middle East and Far East. The mere sending of a few American divisions to Suez, Basra or the Dutch East Indies would hardly justify the opening of a new front with a new power, different weapons and independent rearward services. This may come, but not yet.

---

[1] Ismet Inönü, 1884–1974. Born in Smyrna. Served in the Ottoman Army, 1904–18. Active in the defence of Gallipoli, 1915. Chief of Staff to Mustapha Kemal, 1920; defeated the Greeks near the village of Inönü (1921), from which he took his surname. Prime Minister of Turkey, 1924–38; President, 1938–50. Leader of the Parliamentary opposition, 1950–61. Prime Minister, 1961–5. Leader of the Parliamentary opposition for a second time, 1965–72.

2. Meanwhile only one thing keeps British divisions in this island, namely shortage of troop-carrying tonnage. The use of shipping on the short haul from the United States to Britain is not comparable with the round-the-Cape voyage to the East. Are you aware that for more than a year past we have sent every month the equivalent of one New Zealand division from here to the Middle East? The great bulk of this is for upkeep. So hard pressed was I for tonnage to send some new divisional formations to the Middle East, that six months ago I begged from the President the use of some of his fast transports, which was granted. But for this the 18th Division would not be at Singapore today, and much may turn on that. Every effort is being made to find the additional shipping over and above the monthly upkeep to send divisions out of this country. The limiting factor is not and has not for many months been the safety of the United Kingdom but the difficulty of moving by sea at the necessary speeds for troop convoys and with the proper escorts the monthly quotas which have frequently exceeded 35,000 men. Do not therefore allow anyone to reproach the Mother Country with an undue regard for her own security.

3. I am grieved that it is necessary to use the New Zealand Division again so soon, and the fact proves the emergency. I am of course disappointed with what has happened on the Desert front, but I have confidence in Auchinleck. I believe he has not yet shot his bolt, and the position of the enemy seems highly delicate. We must abide with fortitude the issue of the event.

4. Now that the Japanese war has broken out upon us I am most anxious to work all New Zealand and Australian troops back into the Japanese theatre. But this again entirely depends upon shipping. Night and day we work to find more tonnage. All is continually filled.

January's losses in American waters and in the Far East have exceeded the three preceding months combined. The big tide of American shipbuilding has only just begun to flow. I keenly appreciate your consent to the renewed engagement of your Division. I wish there were time to exchange them with the 5th Indian Division in Cyprus, or with the remaining bulk of the British 50th Division in Syria and Iraq, but evidently the crunch is coming quicker than that. Hard times are the test, and New Zealand has never failed.

Every good wish.

Oliver Harvey: diary
('The War Diaries of Oliver Harvey', page 92)

9 February 1942

AE[1] told me today in the greatest secrecy that PM is considering going to India next week (by air) to meet Chiang Kai-shek and also to consult with Indian leaders as to formation of an Assembly to work out a constitution for after the war. On his return he would stop in Cairo and clear up the mess there (as to which he is very worried). The complication is that the doctors have told him that his heart is not too good and he needs rest.

AE asked him what he felt himself and he said he would go if the Cabinet wanted him to go. He confessed that he did feel his heart a bit – he had tried to dance a little the other night but found that he very quickly lost his breath!

AE asked my view. I said I thought no one else could do such a job successfully unless it were AE himself but he hadn't got the Cabinet status to reform India or deal with the military in Cairo. Halifax could deal with India if he were sent on special mission and this had occurred to me as a way of handling that particular impasse. He is held in high regard both in India and at home on India. But we agreed he would be useless with Chiang or with the generals. PM was the only person who could do it all. But for his heart there could be no question he was the right one to go. But the heart? AE and I finally thought that if he won't rest here (and he told AE he meant to go on 'till he dropped'), then perhaps the journey would be a sort of rest and it would be best that he should go. There should, however, be a secret War Cabinet of members only to decide.

What a decision to take, and how gallant of the old boy himself! But his age and more especially his way of life must begin to tell on him. He had beer, 3 ports and 3 brandies for lunch today, and has done it for years.

PM said he was very worried over Libya and thought Lyttelton had failed badly in not looking after the tanks and the Generals more. L was taking too much interest in local politics and foreign affairs, and not enough in what he was intended to do. Auchinleck had been bad over his choice of generals in spite of advice from home to use Wilson[2] and

[1] Anthony Eden, usually referred to as AE in Oliver Harvey's diary.
[2] Henry Maitland Wilson, 1881–1964. Known as 'Jumbo'. On active service in South Africa, 1899–1902; on the Western Front, 1914–17 (despatches, DSO). General Officer Commanding-in-Chief, Egypt, 1939; in Cyrenaica, 1940; in Greece, 1941; in Palestine and Transjordan, 1941. Knighted, 1940. Commander-in-Chief, Allied Forces in Syria, 1941; Persia–Iraq Command, 1942–3; Middle

Gott.[1] Now at last, after these defeats, he had appointed Gott to take charge of the battle – but why this delay and obstinacy?

Winston S. Churchill to General Archibald Wavell[2]
(Churchill papers, 20/70)

10 February 1942
Clear the Line

I think you ought to realise the way we view the situation in Singapore. It was reported to the Cabinet by the CIGS[3] that Percival has over 100,000 men of whom 33,000 are British and 17,000 Australian. It is doubtful whether the Japanese have as many in the whole Malay Peninsula, namely five divisions forward and a sixth coming up. In these circumstances defenders must greatly outnumber Japanese forces who have crossed the Straits and in a well-contested battle they should destroy them. There must at this stage be no thought of saving the troops or sparing the population. The battle must be fought to the bitter end at all costs. The 18th Division has a chance to make its name in history. Commanders and Senior Officers should die with their troops. The honour of the British Empire and of the British Army is at stake. I rely on you to show no mercy to weakness in any form. With the Russians fighting as they are and the Americans so stubborn at Luzon, the whole reputation of our country and our race is involved. It is expected that every unit will be brought into close contact with the enemy and fight it out. I feel sure these words express your own feeling and only send them to you in order to share your burdens.

East, 1943. Supreme Allied Commander, Mediterranean Theatre, 1944. Field Marshal, 1944. Head of the British Joint Staff Mission, Washington, 1945–7. Created Baron, 1946.

[1] William Henry Ewart Gott, 1897–1942. Educated at Harrow. On active service in the First World War (wounded, Military Cross). Brigadier, commanding the Support Group in the Western Desert during the Italian invasion of Egypt, 1940, conducting a planned withdrawal, and then Operation Compass (December 1940 to February 1941), which saw the destruction of the Italian 10th Army. When German troops pushed back the British Commonwealth forces to the Libyan border with Egypt, Gott was placed in command of planning and conducting Operation Brevity (mid-May 1941, which failed), and took part in Operation Battleaxe (June 1941, which failed). Thereafter he was promoted to command the 7th Armoured Division, which was defeated by the Africa Corps at Sidi Rezegh in November 1941. CBE and DSO, 1941. Lieutenant-General commanding XIII Corps, 1942 (battles of Gazala and First Alamein). CB, 1942. Chosen to succeed General Auchinleck as Commander-in-Chief Middle East and acting General Officer Commanding 8th Army, but killed on 7 August 1942, before he could take up his post, when an unarmed transport plane in which he was returning to Cairo from the front line was shot down.

[2] Wavell, Commander-in-Chief, ABDACOM, was then at Luzon, in the Philippines.

[3] Chief of the Imperial General Staff, General Brooke.

Winston S. Churchill to Anthony Eden
(Churchill papers, 20/67)

11 February 1942
Action this Day

Nothing was settled between me and the President on this question, but I have not the slightest doubt he would be willing to consult with us about new Members of the Club. If you wish I will speak tonight on the point to Hopkins. It would be a very good thing in my view to have both Persia and Ethiopia in.

Will you kindly meanwhile draw me up a list of the candidates for election and mark those you want blackballed. It is rather like Grillons,[1] the other way round.

Winston S. Churchill to the Most Reverend William Temple[2]
(Churchill papers, 20/53)

11 February 1942
Private & Confidential

My dear Archbishop,

I write to inform you that I propose to recommend to The King that you should be translated to the Archbishopric of Canterbury.

Few in the long succession since St Augustine can have received the summons to Canterbury at a time when the burden of the Primacy was heavier.

I trust that I may have your consent to this course which I commend with a deep sense of responsibility.

Yours sincerely,
Winston S. Churchill

---

[1] Grillons Club, a dining club to which both Eden and Churchill belonged. Founded in 1813 by members of both Houses of Parliament who wanted to meet on neutral ground, any discussion of politics being strictly excluded.

[2] William Temple, 1881–1944. Fellow and Lecturer in Philosophy, Queen's College, Oxford, 1904–10. President of the Oxford Union, 1904. President of the Workers Educational Association, 1908–24. Ordained priest, 1909. Chaplain to the Archbishop of Canterbury, 1910–21. Headmaster of Repton School, 1910–14. Canon of Westminster, 1919–21. Bishop of Manchester, 1921–9. Privy Councillor, 1929. Archbishop of York, 1929–42. Archbishop of Canterbury from 1942 until his death in 1944.

Winston S. Churchill to President Franklin D. Roosevelt
(Churchill papers, 20/70)

11 February 1942
No. 27

Now that Helfrich[1] has been made Acting Naval C in C ABDA area, Air Ministry would like to announce Peirse as C in C. It is of course understood that this appointment will be reviewed when the larger changes you have in mind come to pass and generally all will be done in accordance with the telegrams we have exchanged.

2. For your information I mention we need Harris, now one of our representatives on the Combined Staffs Committee, for the Bomber Command over here, and we are replacing him by Air Marshal Evill[2] who is admirably suited to represent us.

3. We have 106,000 men in Singapore Island, of which nearly 60,000 are British and Australian, 40,000 being British. I am very glad Wavell is there today. The battle must be fought to the bitter end, regardless of consequences to the city or its inhabitants. Every good wish.

General Archibald Wavell to Winston S. Churchill
(Churchill papers, 20/70)

11 February 1942
Most Secret
Personal

I returned today from 24 hours in Singapore. I received your telegram 69733 just before I left. I had seen all Divisional Commanders and the Governor and had already spoken to them on the lines of your telegram. I left with Percival written message to same effect.

2. Battle for Singapore is not going well. Japanese with usual infiltration tactics are getting on much more rapidly than they should in West of Island. I ordered Percival to stage counter attack with all troops possible on that front. Morale of some troops is not good and none is as high as I should like to see. Conditions of ground are difficult for defence where wide frontages have to be held in very enclosed country. The chief troubles are lack of sufficient training in some of reinforcing

---

[1] The Dutch Admiral (see Wavell to Churchill, 12 January 1942, page 64 above).

[2] Douglas Claude Strathern Evill, 1892–1971. Naval cadet, 1908. On active service, Royal Naval Air Service, 1914–18 (DSC, AFC). Air Vice Marshal, 1939. CB, 1940. Head of the Royal Air Force delegation in Washington, 1942. Vice-Chief of the Air Staff, 1943–6. Knighted, 1943. Air Chief Marshal, 1946.

troops and inferiority complex which bold and skilful Japanese tactics and their command of the air have caused.

3. Everything possible is being done to produce more offensive spirit and optimistic outlook, but I cannot pretend that these efforts have been entirely successful up to date. I have given the most categorical orders that there is to be no thought of surrender and that all troops are to continue fighting to the end.

4. I do not think that Percival has the number of troops at his disposal that you mention. I do not think that he has more than 60 to 70 thousand repetition 60 to 70 thousand at the most. He should however have quite enough to deal with enemy who have landed if the troops can be made to act with sufficient vigour and determination.

5. One of three northern aerodromes now in hands of enemy and other two under shell fire and out of use, remaining aerodrome in south of Island has been reduced by constant bombing to extremely limited use.

6. While returning from Singapore I fell from quay in dark and have broken two small bones in back. Damage not serious but I shall be in hospital for few days and somewhat crippled for two or three weeks probably.

President Franklin D. Roosevelt to Winston S. Churchill
(Churchill papers, 20/70)

11 February 1942
Secret and Personal
No. 102

I am giving careful attention to China and sent the Generalissimo another personal wire last night assuring him that an adequate air transport scheme would be set up between India and China in the immediate future. Incidentally, I have taken 25 good commercial transports away from the airlines to add them to our African ferry service at once and will take more if necessary.

2. Pressure on MacArthur is getting more acute.

3. The new Naval Command in the Abda Area is all set.

4. We had a bad break last night in the loss of the *Normandie* and will not know for a few days whether she is a total loss or not.[1]

---

[1] *Normandie*: built in France (St Nazaire), entering service in 1935 as the largest (83,673 tons) and fastest (31.14 knots) passenger liner afloat. Made the fastest transatlantic crossings on several of her 139 westbound and 138 eastbound crossings between Le Havre and New York. Seized by the United States in 1940, after the fall of France. While being converted to a troop ship (as USS

5. You can be sure there will be no guarantees given about non-occupation of Madagascar or Reunion.

6. Our stream of big bombers is getting blocked up at Bangalore because of the difficulties of landing fields in Sumatra and Java but we hope to break that jam soon.

7. I do hope Auchinleck can give Rommel a push soon.

8. Harry is much better but I am trying to confine him to barracks until he learns to take care of himself.

Oliver Harvey: diary
('The War Diaries of Oliver Harvey', page 94)

11 February 1942   London
CHURCHILL'S PROPOSED VISIT TO INDIA

PM is not going on his trip because of Singapore. He feels he must be here when it falls.

Winston S. Churchill to Chiang Kai-shek
(Churchill papers, 20/70)

12 February 1942
Personal and Secret

We think here in the Cabinet that your suggested visit to Mr Gandhi at Wardha[1] might impede the desire we have for rallying all India to the war effort against Japan. It might well have the unintended effect of emphasizing communal differences at a moment when unity is imperative, and I venture to hope that Your Excellency will be so very kind as not to press the matter contrary to the wishes of the Viceroy of the King Emperor. I look forward most hopefully to the increasing co-operation of the British, Indian, and other Imperial forces with the valiant Chinese armies who have so long withstood the brunt of barbarous Japanese aggression.

I take the occasion to convey my respectful compliments to Madame Chiang Kai-shek[2] and trust that her all too brief sojourn to India has been interesting and agreeable.

Lafayette), on 9 February 1942 caught fire, capsized, and sank in the mud at the New York Passenger Ship Terminal.

[1] Wardha: in the western Indian state of Maharashtra. Gandhi was then living in an ashram, at Sevagram, five miles to the east of Wardha.

[2] Soong May-ling, 1898–2003. Born in Shanghai, the daughter of a Methodist minister. Educated in the United States. Married Chiang Kai-shek, 1920. Member of the Chinese legislature, 1930–2.

Winston S. Churchill to Field Marshal Sir John Dill
(Churchill papers, 20/70)

12 February 1942
Secret and Personal

The Cabinet thought it would be a great mistake in this moment when heavy misfortunes must be expected to put out a cry of this kind for help from China.

Effect would probably be exact reverse of what was hoped for. We are taking great care of Chiang in India and have no reason to suppose he intends to fall out of the line. Anyhow, flattery of this kind is not likely to be effective unless accompanied by American and British military victories.

Peter Fraser to Winston S. Churchill
(Churchill papers, 20/70)

12 February 1942

[...]

3. Public opinion here is sound and is reacting healthily to bad news. Hard times as you say are the test and you may rely upon us. But we do need equipment badly and we look to you to do the best you properly can for us.

Winston S. Churchill to Peter Fraser
(Churchill papers, 20/70)

12 February 1942
Most Secret

Am most grateful to you for your very kind message. Am cabling you separately about equipment. The resolution of the New Zealand Parliament is a great encouragement in this dark hour.

On 18 February 1943, became the first Chinese national and only the second woman to address the United States Congress. Member of the Central Executive Committee of the Kuomintang, 1945. Lived in Taiwan, 1949–75, then in the United States, where she died in 2003 aged 105 (or 106).

Harold Nicolson: diary
('Harold Nicolson, Diaries and Letters', page 211)

12 February 194

What has saddened me is not merely the bad news from Singapore and Libya, but a conversation with Violet Bonham Carter.[1] She had been to see Winston yesterday, and for the first time in their long friendship she had found him depressed. He was querulous about criticism, unhappy at Cripps not consenting to take office,[2] worried by the absence of alternative Ministers whom he could invite to join the Government. But underneath it all was a dreadful fear, she felt, that our soldiers are not as good fighters as their fathers were. 'In 1915', said Winston, 'our men fought on even when they had only one shell left and were under a fierce barrage. Now they cannot resist dive-bombers. We have so many men in Singapore, so many men – they should have done better.' It is the same, of course, in Libya. Our men cannot stand up to punishment. And yet they are the same men as man the merchant ships and who won the Battle of Britain. There is something deeply wrong with the whole morale of our Army.

Clementine Churchill to Winston S. Churchill
(Baroness Spencer-Churchill papers)

12 February 1942

My Own Darling,

I am ashamed that by my violent attitude I should just now have added to your agonising anxieties – Please forgive me. I do beg of you to reflect, whether it would not be best to leave Lord B entirely out of your Reconstruction.

It is true that if you do he may (& will) work against you – at first covertly & then openly. But is not hostility without, better than intrigue & treachery & rattledom within? You should have peace <u>inside</u> your Government – for a few months at any rate – & you must have that with

---

[1] Helen Violet Asquith, 1887–1969. Elder daughter of H. H. Asquith. Educated in Dresden and Paris. Married, 1915, Sir Maurice Bonham-Carter (who died in 1960). President of the Women's Liberal Federation, 1923–5 and 1939–45; President of the Liberal Party Organization, 1945–7. A Governor of the BBC, 1941–6. Member of the Royal Commission on the Press, 1947–9. Unsuccessful Liberal Parliamentary candidate, 1945 and 1951. DBE, 1953. Created Baroness Asquith of Yarnbury, 1964. Published *Winston Churchill as I Knew Him*, 1965.

[2] Cripps had refused Churchill's offer to become Minister of Production because the post would not bring him a seat in the War Cabinet.

what you have to face and do for us all – Now that you have (as I understand) invited Sir Stafford, why not put your money on him.

The temper & behaviour you describe (in Lord B) is caused I think
by the prospect of a new personality equal perhaps in power to him &
certainly in intellect.

My darling – Try ridding yourself of this microbe which some people
fear is in your blood – Exorcise this bottle Imp & see if the air is not
clearer & purer – You will miss his drive & genius, but in Cripps you may
have new accessions of strength. And you don't mind 'that you don't
mean the same thing'. You both <u>do</u> in War & when Peace comes – we
can see. But it's a long way off.

Your devoted
Clemmie

George Harvie-Watt to Winston S. Churchill
(Sir George Harvie-Watt papers)

12 February 1942

The House this week has been somewhat perturbed at the news from
the Far East. Members cannot understand how our large army in the
island has failed to put up a better show, especially after all the assurances
that were given that Singapore could and must be held. The setbacks
have come as a surprise and somewhat of a shock. The immediate reaction in the House has been two-fold:

1. Granville and Henry Morris Jones[1] have resigned from the Liberal
National Party and Hore-Belisha has resigned in sympathy. These three
Members now presumably become independent.

2. The usual critics of the Government of all Parties have raised their
heads again and are now talking about a drastic re-organization of the
Government. I think it is likely that the House will expect a statement
from you early next week on the situation in Singapore.

[...]

There has been much talk regarding the constitution and scope of
the new Minister of Production. The Socialist Party at a Meeting on

---

[1] John Henry Morris-Jones, 1884–1972. On active service, 1914–18, serving as a doctor at Wimereux
(Military Cross). A medical practitioner for 20 years. MP for Denbigh, as Liberal, 1929–31, and
National Liberal, 1931–50. Assistant Government Whip, 1932–5. A Lord Commissioner of the Treas-
ury, 1935–7. Knighted, 1937. Chairman of the Welsh Parliamentary Party, 1941–2. Member of the
Parliamentary Delegation to Buchenwald Concentration Camp, April 1945. Author of *Doctor in the
Whips' Room*, 1955.

Wednesday decided to ask for a Debate, probably extending over two days. Many Members consider that Lord Beaverbrook is not the ideal man for the job, while others consider that the War Production Minister should have full executive power over the whole war effort. There is likely to be some criticism that the supply of Labour is left out of the Production Minister's province.

Winston S. Churchill to President Franklin D. Roosevelt
(Churchill papers, 20/70)

12 February 1942
Personal and Secret
No. 28

[...]

4. *Scharnhorst* and *Gneisenau*[1] are beating their way up Channel and have run the batteries at Dover. We are out after them with everything we have.

5. A fierce battle is raging at Singapore and orders have been given to fight it out.

Winston S. Churchill to General Claude Auchinleck
(Churchill papers, 20/70)

12 February 1942
Most Secret
Personal

Have been thinking much about you and your affairs with complete confidence you will come out on top. Every good wish.[2]

---

[1] In the early hours of 12 February 1942, two German battle cruisers, *Scharnhorst* and *Gneisenau*, and the cruiser *Prinz Eugen*, slipped out of Brest harbour and sailed up the English Channel in broad daylight, passing the Dover gun batteries and reaching the North Sea. All six British Swordfish aircraft and four of the Hampden bombers sent to attack the ships were shot down. On the morning of February 13 the three warships reached the safety of German ports.

[2] On 29 January 1942, Rommel recaptured Benghazi (the North African port for supplies from Italy) and advanced eastward to the British lines at Gazala. On February 4, Auchinleck evacuated Derna. Rommel halted his troops and prepared for a new offensive.

General Claude Auchinleck to Winston S. Churchill
(Churchill papers, 20/70)

13 February 1942
Personal

Most grateful for your No. 163 Feb 12th. Much appreciate your continued confidence and unfailing support which is greatest possible source of strength to me.

Winston S. Churchill to Anthony Eden
(Churchill papers, 20/67)

13 February 1942

I have seen no suggestion 'to restrain forcibly' Chiang Kai-shek. It would, I am sure, be a great mistake for him to travel many hundreds of miles across India to parley with Gandhi about whether the British Empire in India should come to an end or not. Guests have duties as well as hosts, and I have very little doubt he will defer to the wishes so courteously expressed. At 1 o'clock in the morning it was impossible to consult you. You do not need to labour the point with me about the importance of keeping China in the war. I am in the fullest agreement with your views. There is no doubt that great offence was given at Chungking when Wavell boggled over their help. You have perhaps seen my telegram[1] to him on this subject of about three weeks ago.[2]

[1] Churchill's telegram of 23 January 1942.

[2] On 13 February 1942, Chiang Kai-shek telegraphed to Churchill from India: 'Since my arrival at Delhi I have decided to modify my itinerary and given up the intention of visiting Wardha. Please be assured that my personal movement is a matter of small concern to me when interests of our joint war efforts are involved. Madame Chiang Kai-Shek joins me in expressing to you our heartfelt appreciation of the cordial hospitality that is extended to us during our stay in India and in sending you our warmest personal regards' (*Churchill papers, 20/70*).

General Hastings Ismay to Harold Laski[1]
(Churchill papers, 20/62)

13 February 1942
Personal and Confidential[2]

My dear Professor,

The Prime Minister has asked me to thank you for your letter of the 11th February, and to tell you, for your personal information, that it had already been appreciated that Major Wingate's talents might be of great value in the Far Eastern theatre of war.[3]

General Wavell, who is of course fully aware of Wingate's achievements in Ethiopia, was informed some time ago that Wingate could be sent out to him if he so wished; and he welcomed the offer. Arrangements are therefore being made to send Wingate out by the fastest route at the first opportunity.

[1] Harold Joseph Laski, 1893–1950. Political philosopher and historian. Son of Nathan Laski (an influential member of the Jewish community in North-West Manchester, Churchill's former constituency). Lecturer in History, McGill University, Montreal, 1914–16; Harvard University, 1916–20. Vice-Chairman of the British Institute of Adult Education, 1921–30. Member of the Fabian Society Executive, 1922. Lecturer in Political Science, Magdalene College, Cambridge, 1922–5. Professor of Political Science, London, 1926–50. Member of Executive Committee of Labour Party, 1936–49.

[2] On 13 February 1942, General Ismay wrote to John Martin, Churchill's PPS: 'I do not think that the Prime Minister ought to be troubled with this, and I propose to send the attached reply to the Professor whom I happen to know fairly well. If you agree, will you post it? (*Churchill papers, 20/62*).

[3] Orde Charles Wingate, 1903–44. Born in India. Entered the Royal Artillery, 1923. Served with Sudan Defence Force, 1928–33. Captain, 1936. Special Appointment, Palestine and Transjordan, 1936–9 (despatches, DSO). While serving in Palestine (under Wavell) during the Arab Revolt, he trained Jewish Special Night Squads to anticipate and prevent attacks from neighbouring villages. Major, 1940. On active service in Ethiopia, 1941 (where his force of 1,700 men took the surrender of 20,000 Italians); in Burma, 1942–4, as Commander of Special Forces, India Command (acting Major-General, despatches, two bars to DSO). Killed in an air crash in India while returning from a visit to one of his Indian 77th Infantry Brigade (Chindits) Long-Range Penetration squads behind Japanese lines, 24 March 1944. Buried in India; in 1950 his body was reburied in the United States National Cemetery in Arlington, Virginia, at the wishes of his family.

Winston S. Churchill to Lord Simon[1]
(Churchill papers, 20/53)

13 February 1942

THE CHANNEL DASH

My Dear Lord Chancellor,

I propose that an Enquiry should be instituted into the circumstances of the passage of the Straits by the German warships yesterday. For this purpose I am sure that Mr Justice Singleton[2] is undoubtedly the man to assist the Naval and Royal Air Force Officers who will take part in the Enquiry.

The Enquiry would last I think about a week and it would be most convenient if Mr Justice Singleton could be spared from his other duties so as to be able to start work on Monday, 16 February.

Yours very sincerely,
Winston S. Churchill

Henry Channon: diary
('Chips', page 321)

13 February 1942

[. . .] sleepily I stretched for the newspapers which were emblazoned with *Scharnhorst* and *Prinz Eugen* and *Gneisenau* – and the whole story. Everything seems to be going against us. Then Harold rushed into my bedroom, 'Read this!' he said. He referred to a violently anti-Churchill, anti-Government leader in the *Daily Mail*. It is the first that has ever appeared. Everyone is in a rage against the Prime Minister. Rage; frus-

---

[1] John Allsebrook Simon, 1873–1954. Educated at Fettes and Wadham College, Oxford. Fellow of All Souls. Liberal MP for Walthamstow, 1906–18; for Spen Valley, 1922–31. Solicitor-General, 1910–13. Knighted, 1910. Attorney-General, with a seat in the Cabinet, 1913–15. Home Secretary, 1915–16; resigned in opposition to conscription. Major, Royal Air Force, serving in France, 1917–18. National Liberal MP for Spen Valley, 1931–40. Secretary of State for Foreign Affairs, 1931–5. Home Secretary, 1935–7. Chancellor of the Exchequer, 1937–40. Created Viscount, 1940. Lord Chancellor, 1940–5.

[2] John Edward Singleton, 1885–1957. Called to the Bar, 1906. On active service, 1914–18; Captain, Royal Field Artillery. KC, 1922. Conservative MP for Lancaster, 1922–3. Recorder of Preston, 1928–34. Knighted, 1934. A Judge of the King's Bench Division, 1934–48. Among the wartime inquiries that Singleton headed were one on bombsights and another on German Air Force strength. Privy Councillor, 1949. A Lord Justice of Appeal from 1948 until his death. On 22 April 1942 Churchill wrote to Lord Selborne, the Minister of Economic Warfare, that Singleton had 'during this war conducted some of the most responsible inquiries which I have had made into technical and service Air Force and Army matters. He is, as you know, a man of exceptional and wide experience, with a first-rate war record in the last war. You could not have a better man in my opinion for the Inquiry.' This was in reply to Lord Selborne's letter of April 20 on the proposal to appoint Singleton to conduct an inquiry into the Special Operations Executive (*Churchill papers, 20/67*).

tration. This is not the post-Dunkirk feeling, but ANGER. The country is more upset about the escape of the German battleships than over Singapore.

[...]

The capital seethes with indignation and were Londoners Latins there would be rioting. I have never known so violent an outburst.

At the House I heard that there is a flap on at 10 Downing Street and that Winston, angered by the *Daily Mail* leader, is in a defiant, truculent mood. Attlee hinted to someone this afternoon that 'outside men' would be brought into the Government, that is non-parliamentary. And there is some talk about the formation of a so-called 'Centre Party' composed of Liberals, disgruntled Conservatives, etc., with Beaverbook at its head.

Winston S. Churchill to Sir Archibald Sinclair and
Air Chief Marshal Sir Charles Portal
(Premier papers, 3/11/3)

14 February 1942
Secret

The Brest question has settled itself by the escape of the enemy.

2. I am entirely in favour of the resumption of full bombing of Germany, subject always of course to our not incurring heavy losses owing to bad weather and enemy resistance combined. It is to be expected that better weather is at hand.[1]

Josef Stalin to Winston S. Churchill
(Churchill papers, 20/70)

14 February 1942   Kremlin
                                                                   Moscow

Thank you for your congratulations on the successes of the Red Army.[2] In spite of the difficulties on the Soviet–German front, as well as

---

[1] On 22 February 1942, Air Marshal Sir Arthur Harris was appointed Commander-in-Chief, Bomber Command. The first major raid under his command was on the Renault factory at Billancourt, just outside Paris, on March 3–4; 235 aircraft took part, the largest to any single target in the war thus far. Massive damage was done to the factory, but 367 French people were killed and more than 9,000 lost their homes. The next heavy bombing raids on Germany were on the nights of 8–9, 9–10, and 10–11 March (all on Essen), 12–13 March (Kiel), 13–14 March (Cologne), 25–6 and 26–7 March (Essen), and 28–9 March (Lübeck, where more than 300 people were killed and one-third of the city's buildings destroyed by fire, including the historic Marienkirche and a factory making oxygen equipment for U-boats).

[2] See Churchill's message to Stalin of 8 February 1942 (page 232).

on other fronts, I have not the slightest doubt that the Alliance created between the USSR, Great Britain and the USA will break the enemy and achieve complete victory.

Stalin

General Archibald Wavell to Winston S. Churchill
(Churchill papers, 20/70)

14 February 1942
Most Immediate
Private

SINGAPORE

You are of course sole judge of the moment when no further result can be gained at Singapore and should instruct Percival accordingly. CIGS concurs.

Winston S. Churchill to General Archibald Wavell
(Churchill papers, 20/70)

14 February 1942
Personal and Private

Have received telegram from Percival that enemy are close to town and that his troops are incapable of further counter attack. Have ordered him to continue inflict maximum damage to enemy by house to house fighting if necessary. Fear however that resistance not likely to be very prolonged.

General Archibald Wavell to Winston S. Churchill
(Churchill papers, 20/70)

14 February 1942
Most Secret
Private

Have had two telegrams from Percival in last 48 hours indicating that due to shortage of water in the town and other difficulties his powers of resistance are now much diminished. On both occasions have ordered him to fight on to the last. I have now sent him [the] following.

General Archibald Wavell to General Arthur Percival
(Churchill papers, 20/73)

14 February 1942
Most Secret

In all places where sufficiency of water exists for troops they must go on fighting.

General Arthur Percival to General Archibald Wavell
(Churchill papers, 20/73)

14 February 1942
Most Secret

We are fighting on but all troops except those on islands are now on Singapore perimeter and dependent with civil population upon one water supply. Both petrol and food supplies are also short owing to most of our dumps being outside the town area. Morale of Asiatic civil population is low under bombing and shelling from which they have no protection. Will continue to comply with your intention but feel must represent the situation as it exists today.

General Archibald Wavell to General Arthur Percival
(Churchill papers, 20/73)

15 February 1942
Most Secret

Your gallant stand is serving purpose and must be continued to limit of endurance.

General Archibald Wavell to General Arthur Percival
(Churchill papers, 20/70)

15 February 1942
Most Secret

Emergency operation. So long as you are in position to inflict losses and damage to enemy and your troops are physically capable of doing so you must fight on. Time gained and damage to enemy are of vital importance at this crisis. When you are fully satisfied that this is no longer possible I give you discretion to cease resistance. Before doing so all arms equipment and transport of value to enemy must of course be rendered useless. Also just before final cessation of fighting opportunity should be given to any determined bodies of men or individuals to try and effect escape by any means possible. They must be armed. Inform me of intentions. Whatever happens I thank you and all troops for your gallant efforts of last few days.

General Arthur Percival to General Archibald Wavell
(Churchill papers, 20/73)

15 February 1942

Owing to losses from enemy action, water, petrol, food and ammunition practically finished. Unable therefore [to] continue the fight any longer. All ranks have done their best and are grateful for your help.

On 15 February 1942, Singapore fell to the Japanese Army, after eight days of fierce fighting. It was the largest surrender of British-led troops – British, Australian, Indian, and Malayan – in British history: 85,000 in all. Of the 40,000 Indian soldiers who surrendered, as many as 30,000 joined the pro-Japanese Indian National Army, and fought against the British and Indian forces in Burma. Of the 55,000 other soldiers taken prisoner, 49,000 were killed while prisoners of war in slave labour camps throughout the Japanese-occupied territories.

Winston S. Churchill: broadcast
(BBC Written Archives Centre)

15 February 1942   Chequers

Nearly six months have passed since at the end of August I made a broadcast directly to my fellow countrymen; it is therefore worthwhile looking back over this half year of struggle for life, for that is what it has been, and what it is, to see what has happened to our fortunes and to our prospects.

At that time in August I had the pleasure of meeting the President of the United States and drawing up with him the declaration of British and American policy which has become known to the world as the Atlantic Charter. We also settled a number of other things about the war, some of which have had an important influence upon its course. In those days we met on the terms of a hard-pressed combatant seeking assistance from a great friend who was, however, only a benevolent neutral.

In those days the Germans seemed to be tearing the Russian armies to pieces and striding on with growing momentum to Leningrad, to Moscow, to Rostov, and even farther into the heart of Russia. It was thought a very daring assertion when the President declared that the Russian armies would hold out till the winter. You may say that the military men of all countries – friend, foe, and neutral alike – were very doubtful whether this would come true. As for us, our British resources were stretched to the utmost. We had already been for more than a whole year absolutely alone in the struggle with Hitler and Mussolini. We had to be ready to meet a German invasion of our own Island; we had to defend Egypt, the Nile Valley and the Suez Canal. Above all we had to bring in across the Atlantic in the teeth of the German and Italian U-boats and aircraft the food, raw materials and finished munitions without which we could not live, without which we could not wage war. We have to do all this still.

It seemed our duty in those August days to do everything in our power to help the Russian people to meet the prodigious onslaught which had been launched against them. It is little enough we have done for Russia, considering all she has done to beat Hitler and for the common cause. In these circumstances, we British had no means whatever of providing effectively against a new war with Japan. Such was the outlook when I talked with President Roosevelt in the middle of August on board the good ship *Prince of Wales*, now, alas, sunk beneath the waves. It is true that our position in August, 1941, seemed vastly better than it had been a year earlier in 1940, when France had just been beaten into the awful prostration in which she now lies, when we were almost entirely unarmed in our own Island, and when it looked as if Egypt and all the Middle East would be conquered by the Italians who still held Abyssinia and had newly driven us out of British Somaliland. Compared with those days of 1940, when all the world except ourselves thought we were down and out for ever, the situation the President and I surveyed in August, 1941, was an enormous improvement. Still, when you looked at it bluntly and squarely – with the United States neutral and fiercely divided, with the Russian armies falling back with grievous losses, with the German military power triumphant and unscathed, with the Japanese menace assuming an uglier shape each day – it certainly seemed a very bleak and anxious scene.

How do matters stand now? Taking it all in all, are our chances of survival better or are they worse than in August, 1941? How is it with the British Empire or Commonwealth of Nations? Are we up or down? What has happened to the principles of freedom and decent civilisation for which we are fighting? Are they making headway, or are they in greater peril? Let us take the rough with the smooth, let us put the good and bad side by side, and let us try to see exactly where we are. The first and greatest of events is that the United States is now unitedly and whole-heartedly in the war with us. The other day I crossed the Atlantic again to see President Roosevelt. This time we met not only as friends, but as comrades standing side by side and shoulder to shoulder in a battle for dear life and dearer honour in the common cause and against a common foe. When I survey and compute the power of the United States and its vast resources and feel that they are now in it with us, with the British Commonwealth of Nations all together, however long it lasts, till death or victory, I cannot believe there is any other fact in the whole world which can compare with that. That is what I have dreamed of, aimed at and worked for, and now it has come to pass.

But there is another fact, in some ways more immediately effective. The Russian armies have not been defeated, they have not been torn to pieces. The Russian people have not been conquered or destroyed. Leningrad and Moscow have not been taken. The Russian armies are in the field. They are not holding the line of the Urals or the line of the Volga. They are advancing victoriously, driving the foul invader from that native soil they have guarded so bravely and loved so well. More than that: for the first time they have broken the Hitler legend. Instead of the easy victories and abundant booty which he and his hordes had gathered in the West, he has found in Russia so far only disaster, failure, the shame of unspeakable crimes, the slaughter or loss of vast numbers of German soldiers, and the icy wind that blows across the Russian snow.

Here, then, are two tremendous fundamental facts which will in the end dominate the world situation and make victory possible in a form never possible before. But there is another heavy and terrible side to the account, and this must be set in the balance against these inestimable gains. Japan has plunged into the war, and is ravaging the beautiful, fertile, prosperous, and densely populated lands of the Far East. It would never have been in the power of Great Britain while fighting Germany and Italy – the nations long hardened and prepared for war – while fighting in the North Sea, in the Mediterranean and in the Atlantic – it would never have been in our power to defend the Pacific and the Far East single-handed against the onslaught of Japan.

We have only just been able to keep our heads above water at home; only by a narrow margin have we brought in the food and the supplies; only by so little have we held our own in the Nile Valley and the Middle East. The Mediterranean is closed, and all our transports have to go round the Cape of Good Hope, each ship making only three voyages in the year. Not a ship, not an aeroplane, not a tank, not an anti-tank gun or an anti-aircraft gun has stood idle. Everything we have has been deployed, either against the enemy or awaiting his attack. We are struggling hard in the Libyan Desert, where perhaps another serious battle will soon be fought. We have to provide for the safety and order of liberated Abyssinia, of conquered Eritrea, of Palestine, of liberated Syria and redeemed Iraq, and of our new ally, Persia. A ceaseless stream of ships, men, and materials has flowed from this country for a year and a half, in order to build up and sustain our armies in the Middle East, which guard those vast regions on either side of the Nile Valley. We had to do our best to give substantial aid to Russia. We gave it [to] her in her darkest hour, and we must not fail in our undertaking now. How then in this posture, gripped and held and battered as we were, could we have provided for the safety of the Far East against such an avalanche of fire and steel as has been hurled upon us by Japan? Always, my friends, this thought overhung our minds.

There was, however, one hope and one hope only – namely that if Japan entered the war with her allies, Germany and Italy, the United States would come in on our side, thus far more than repairing the balance. For this reason, I have been most careful, all these many months, not to give any provocation to Japan, and to put up with Japanese encroachments, dangerous though they were, so that if possible, whatever happened, we should not find ourselves forced to face this new enemy alone. I could not be sure that we should succeed in this policy, but it has come to pass. Japan has struck her felon blow, and a new, far greater champion has drawn the sword of implacable vengeance against her and on our side.

I shall frankly state to you that I did not believe it was in the interests of Japan to burst into war both upon the British Empire and the United States. I thought it would be a very irrational act. Indeed, when you remember that they did not attack us after Dunkirk when we were so much weaker, when our hopes of United States help were of the most slender character, and when we were all alone, I could hardly believe that they would commit what seemed to be a mad act. Tonight the Japanese are triumphant. They shout their exultation round the world. We suffer. We are taken aback. We are hard pressed. But I am sure even in this dark hour that 'criminal madness' will be the verdict which history will pronounce upon the authors of Japanese aggression, after the events of 1942 and 1943 have been inscribed upon its sombre pages.

The immediate deterrent which the United States exercised upon Japan – apart of course from the measureless resources of the American Union – was the dominant American battle fleet in the Pacific, which, with the naval forces we could spare, confronted Japanese aggression with the shield of superior sea-power. But, my friends, by an act of sudden violent surprise, long-calculated, balanced and prepared, and delivered under the crafty cloak of negotiation, the shield of sea-power which protected the fair lands and islands of the Pacific Ocean was for the time being, and only for the time being, dashed to the ground. Into the gap thus opened rushed the invading armies of Japan. We were exposed to the assault of a warrior race of nearly eighty millions, with a large outfit of modern weapons, whose war lords had been planning and scheming for this day, and looking forward to it perhaps for twenty years – while all the time our good people on both sides of the Atlantic were prating about perpetual peace, and cutting down each other's navies in order to set a good example. The overthrow, for a while, of British and United States sea power in the Pacific was like the breaking of some mighty dam; the long-gathered pent-up waters rushed down the peaceful valley, carrying ruin and devastation forward on their foam, and spreading their inundations far and wide.

No one must underrate any more the gravity and efficiency of the Japanese war machine. Whether in the air or upon the sea, or man to man on land, they have already proved themselves to be formidable, deadly, and, I am sorry to say, barbarous antagonists. This proves a hundred times over that there never was the slightest chance, even though we had been much better prepared in many ways than we were, of our standing up to them alone while we had Nazi Germany at our throat and Fascist Italy at our belly. It proves something else. And this should be a comfort and a reassurance. We can now measure the wonderful strength of the Chinese people who under Generalissimo Chiang Kai-shek have single-handed fought this hideous Japanese aggressor for four and a half years and left him baffled and dismayed. This they have done, although they were a people whose whole philosophy for many ages was opposed to war and warlike arts, and who in their agony were caught ill-armed, ill-supplied with munitions and hopelessly outmatched in the air. We must not underrate the power and malice of our latest foe, but neither must we undervalue the gigantic, overwhelming forces which now stand in the line with us in this world-struggle for freedom, and which, once they have developed their full natural inherent power, whatever has happened in the meanwhile, will be found fully capable of squaring all accounts and setting all things right for a good long time to come.

You know I have never prophesied to you or promised smooth and easy things, and now all I have to offer is hard adverse war for many months ahead. I must warn you, as I warned the House of Commons before they gave me their generous vote of confidence a fortnight ago, that many misfortunes, severe torturing losses, remorseless and gnawing anxieties lie before us. To our British folk these may seem even harder to bear when they are at a great distance than when the savage Hun was shattering our cities and we all felt in the midst of the battle ourselves. But the same qualities which brought us through the awful jeopardy of the summer of 1940 and its long autumn and winter bombardment from the air, will bring us through this other new ordeal, though it may be more costly and will certainly be longer. One fault, one crime, and one crime only, can rob the United Nations and the British people, upon whose constancy this grand alliance came into being, of the victory upon which their lives and honour depend. A weakening in our purpose and therefore in our unity – that is the mortal crime. Whoever is guilty of that crime, or of bringing it about in others, of him let it be said that it were better for him that a millstone were hanged about his neck and he were cast into the sea.[1]

Last autumn, when Russia was in her most dire peril, when vast numbers of her soldiers had been killed or taken prisoner, when one-third of her whole munitions capacity lay, as it still lies, in Nazi German hands, when Kiev fell, and the foreign Ambassadors were ordered out of Moscow, the Russian people did not fall to bickering among themselves. They just stood together and worked and fought all the harder. They did not lose trust in their leaders; they did not try to break up their Government. Hitler had hoped to find quislings and fifth columnists in the wide regions he overran, and among the unhappy masses who fell into his power. He looked for them. He searched for them. But he found none.

---

[1] Luke 17: 2.

The system upon which the Soviet Government is founded is very different from ours or from that of the United States. However that may be, the fact remains that Russia received blows which her friends feared and her foes believed were mortal, and through preserving national unity and persevering undaunted, Russia has had the marvellous come-back for which we thank God now. In the English-speaking world we rejoice in free institutions. We have free parliaments and a free press. This is the way of life we have been used to. This is the way of life we are fighting to defend. But it is the duty of all who take part in those free institutions to make sure, as the House of Commons and the House of Lords have done, and will I doubt not do, that the National Executive Government in time of war have a solid foundation on which to stand and on which to act; that the misfortunes and mistakes of war are not exploited against them; that while they are kept up to the mark by helpful and judicious criticism or advice, they are not deprived of the persisting power to run through a period of bad times and many cruel vexations and come out on the other side and get to the top of the hill.

Tonight I speak to you at home; I speak to you in Australia and New Zealand, for whose safety we will strain every nerve; to our loyal friends in India and Burma; to our gallant Allies, the Dutch and Chinese; and to our kith and kin in the United States. I speak to you all under the shadow of a heavy and far-reaching military defeat. It is a British and Imperial defeat. Singapore has fallen. All the Malay Peninsula has been overrun. Other dangers gather about us out there, and none of the dangers which we have hitherto successfully withstood at home and in the East are in any way diminished. This, therefore, is one of those moments when the British race and nation can show their quality and their genius. This is one of those moments when it can draw from the heart of misfortune the vital impulses of victory. Here is the moment to display that calm and poise combined with grim determination which not so long ago brought us out of the very jaws of death. Here is another occasion to show as so often in our long story – that we can meet reverses with dignity and with renewed accessions of strength. We must remember that we are no longer alone. We are in the midst of a great company. Three-quarters of the human race are now moving with us. The whole future of mankind may depend upon our action and upon our conduct. So far we have not failed. We shall not fail now. Let us move forward steadfastly together into the storm and through the storm.

Oliver Harvey: diary
('The War Diaries of Oliver Harvey', page 95)

15 February 1942   London

PM broadcast tonight. In his usual style he painted a magnificent backcloth for the fall of Singapore – but it didn't meet the point which is that nobody believes the Government machine is working efficiently. He never mentioned the Channel episode.[1]

Sir Alexander Cadogan:[2] diary
('The Diaries of Sir Alexander Cadogan', page 434)

15 February 1942

Winston broadcast at 9. Announced fall of Singapore. His broadcast not very good – rather apologetic and I <u>think</u> Parliament will take it as an attempt to appeal over their heads to the country – to avoid parliamentary criticism.

John Colville:[3] diary
(Sir John Colville papers)

15 February 1942   Pretoria[4]

Outside in Church Street I heard a familiar voice coming from the wireless in a small café. It was Winston announcing the fall of Singapore. The nature of his words and the unaccustomed speed and emotion with

---

[1] The escape of the *Scharnhorst* and *Gneisenau* from Brest on 12 February 1942.

[2] Alexander George Montagu Cadogan, 1884–1968. Seventh son of 5th Earl Cadogan. Educated at Eton and Balliol College, Oxford. Attaché, Diplomatic Service, 1908. British Minister to China, 1933–5; Ambassador, 1935–6. Knighted, 1934. Deputy Under-Secretary of State for Foreign Affairs, 1936–7; Permanent Under-Secretary, 1938–46. Permanent British Representative at the United Nations, 1946–50. Government Director, Suez Canal Company, 1951–7. Chairman of the BBC, 1952–7. His brother William George Sydney Cadogan, born in 1879, was killed in action in France on 14 November 1914.

[3] John Rupert Colville, 1915–87. A grandson of the Earl of Crewe. Page of Honour to King George V, 1927–31. Educated at Harrow and Trinity College, Cambridge. Entered the Diplomatic Service, 1937. Assistant Private Secretary to the Prime Minister: Neville Chamberlain, 1939–40; Churchill, 1940–1. Royal Air Force Volunteer Reserve, 1941–3. Assistant Private Secretary to the Prime Minister again: Churchill, 1943–5; Clement Attlee, 1945. Private Secretary to Princess Elizabeth, 1947–9. CVO, 1949. Joint Principal Private Secretary to the Prime Minister (Churchill), 1951–5. CB, 1955. Active in the development of Churchill College, Cambridge. Knighted, 1974. Author of a number of volumes of recollections and history, as well as *The Fringes of Power, Downing Street Diaries* (1985). Five years before publication, Sir John Colville gave me access to these diaries, from which I made the transcripts published in this volume.

[4] Colville was on a pilot training course in South Africa.

which he spoke convinced me that he was sorely pressed by critics and opponents at home. All the majesty of his oratory was there, but also a new note of appeal lacking the usual confidence of support. Probably the breakaway of the *Scharnhorst* and *Gneisenau* from Brest has contributed to the volume of criticism with which he is faced. Even greater than the loss of Singapore, with all its strategic significance, I felt the poignancy of the PM's position; and the fact that I was here in Pretoria, so closely associated with his early notoriety, made me feel it all the stronger.[1] Perhaps distance and the fact of being out of it makes me imagine things blacker than they are; but there was something about his voice and delivery which made me shiver and dissipated the pleasure of a happy evening.

Harold Nicolson: diary
(*'Harold Nicolson, Diaries and Letters'*, page 211)

15 February 1942

In the evening Winston Churchill speaks. He tells us that Singapore has fallen. He is grim and not gay. Unfortunately he appeals for national unity and not criticism, in a manner which recalls Neville Chamberlain. Moreover, although he is not rhetorical, he cannot speak in perfectly simple terms and cannot avoid the cadences of a phrase. I do not think his speech will have done good, and I feel deeply depressed and anxious.

Harold Nicolson: diary
(*'Harold Nicolson, Diaries and Letters'*, page 211)

16 February 1942

I find that people are more distressed about the escape of the *Scharnhorst* and *Gneisenau* than they are even by the loss of Singapore. They cannot bear the thought that the Germans sailed past our front door. Winston will have to face a bad situation in the House tomorrow. There will have to be a serious Government reconstruction. But what striking figures (other than Cripps) can Winston bring in? People are even suggesting that Wavell should be brought back to become Minister of Defence.

---

[1] During the Boer War (1899–1901) Churchill was confined in the States Model School, Pretoria, a prisoner-of-war camp, for 27 days, including his 25th birthday. Despite his protest that he was a journalist (as indeed he was) when captured, and not therefore a combatant, his request for release was rejected. He escaped on 12 December 1899, making his way in much danger to the Indian Ocean port of Lourenço Marques, in Portuguese East Africa, and thence by ship to Durban, where he found himself suddenly famous.

I fear a slump in public opinion which will deprive Winston of his legend. His broadcast last night was not liked. The country is too nervous and irritable to be fobbed off with fine phrases. Yet what else could he have said?

General Claude Auchinleck to Winston S. Churchill
(Churchill papers, 20/70)

16 February 1942   Cairo
Most Secret
Personal

We all realise situation consequent on fall of Singapore and you may rely on us to hang on and do our bit to help you through to victory.

Sir Alexander Cadogan: diary
('The Diaries of Sir Alexander Cadogan', page 434)

16 February 1942

Cabinet at 5 p.m. PM truculent and angry – and havering. I should have thought that he, with his 40 years' experience of the House, would know it's no use getting prickly about stupid criticism. All news as bad as it can be.

Winston S. Churchill to Lord Cherwell[1]
(Churchill papers, 20/67)

16 February 1942
Most Secret

The First Sea Lord told me yesterday that the captured German U-boat was built of a steel stronger and much more flexible than anything we have used for warships, and that explosions which crack and hole our armour merely dented the German craft.

[1] Frederick Alexander Lindemann, 1886–1957. Born at Baden Baden (where his mother was taking the cure); son of Alsatian father who had emigrated to Britain in the early 1870s and American mother. Educated at Blair Lodge, Scotland; Darmstadt, 1902–5; Berlin University, 1906–10. Doctor of Philosophy, Berlin, 1910. Studied physical chemistry in Paris, 1912–14. Worked at the Physical Laboratory, RAF, 1915–18, when he helped organize the kite balloon barrage. Learned to fly, 1916. Personally investigated the aerodynamic effects of aircraft spin. Professor of Experimental Philosophy (physics), Oxford, 1919–56. Member of the Expert Committee on Air Defence Research, Committee of Imperial Defence, 1935–9. Unsuccessful by-election candidate, Oxford University, 1937. Personal Assistant to the Prime Minister (Churchill), 1940–1. Created Baron Cherwell, 1941. Paymaster-General, 1942–5 and 1951–3. Privy Councillor, 1943. Created Viscount, 1956.

I should be glad if you could show this minute to the First Sea Lord, so that you can acquire the necessary information and tell me about it.

War Cabinet: conclusions
(Cabinet papers, 65/25)

16 February 1942
5 p.m.

JEWISH 'ILLEGAL' IMMIGRANTS
INTERNED IN PALESTINE

The Prime Minister raised the question whether these internees should not now be released. At the time when the War Cabinet considerred this matter in November 1940 it had looked as though we might be subjected to a wave of illegal immigration. But now that the whole of South-Eastern Europe was in German hands this risk must be greatly diminished.[1]

Winston S. Churchill: note[2]
(Churchill papers, 20/60)

16 February 1942

Although the honourable Member's[3] question[4] is couched in a form of personal discourtesy which seems to be characteristic of him, I am glad he has raised the matter, and will give him a full reply.

At the time when I was called upon by The King to form the present Government, now nearly two years ago, I sought His Majesty's permission to create & assume an office of Minister of Defence. My new position (of Prime Minister) in time of war is inseparable from the general supervision of its conduct and final responsibility for its results. As Prime Minister I am

---

[1] See Churchill's note to the Colonial Secretary, Lord Moyne, of 5 February (page 219 above). As a result of Churchill's intervention, and despite Moyne's opposition, the 793 internees were allowed to remain in Palestine.

[2] Drafted by Churchill as an answer to a Parliamentary Question about the Ministry of Defence, and drawn upon in his speech to the House of Commons on February 24 (see page 299 below). It was redrafted in the third person and sent to Brendan Bracken for him to use 'as he thought best' (F. D. W. Brown to B. C. Sendall, Ministry of Information, 16 February 1942, *Churchill papers, 20/60*).

[3] Richard Stokes.

[4] 'Mr Stokes asked the Prime Minister, whether, in view of the military situation in Libya and the Far East, and in order to ensure the best practical use of the resources at our disposal, he will now appoint a Minister of Defence to advise on war strategy?' and continued: 'May I ask whether the Prime Minister has read the speech made on this subject by Lord Chatfield in another place on 28 January, and whether he is aware of the growing volume of competent opinion that it is wrong for the Offices of Prime Minister and Minister of Defence to be held by the same person?' See House of Commons, Oral Answers, 17 February, reproduced below (page 268).

able to deal easily and smoothly with the three Service Departments and without prejudice to the constitutional responsibilities of the Secretary of State for War & Air and of the First Lord of the Admiralty.

I have therefore not found the need of defining formally or precisely the relationship between the Office of Minister of Defence, when held by the Prime Minister, and the Service Departments, as was found necessary, for instance, in the case of the office of Minister of Production wh was created the other day, or as would be necessary in the case of any Minister of Defence who was not also Prime Minister.

There is of course no Ministry of Defence and the three Services remain under separate autonomous Departments. For the purpose of maintaining general supervision over the conduct of the war, which I do under the authority of the War Cabinet and of the Defence Committee, I have at my disposal a Secretariat headed by Major-General Ismay and based upon the long-established staff and machinery of the pre-war Committee of Imperial Defence. While, as I have said, I take constitutional responsibility for everything that is done or not done, and am quite ready to take the blame when things go wrong, as they very often do, and as they are very likely to do in the future in many ways, I do not of course conduct the war myself. The war is conducted from day to day by the three Chiefs of the Staff, namely: the First Sea Lord, the Chief of the Imperial General Staff, and the Chief of the Air Staff. These Officers sit together every day and often twice a day. They give all the necessary directions and orders to the Commanders-in-Chief in the various theatres. They also advise me, the Defence Committee and the War Cabinet, on larger questions of strategy & war policy.

I am represented on this body by Major-General Ismay, who is also responsible for keeping the Defence Committee and the War Cabinet informed, upon all matters requiring higher decision. On account of the immense scope and complexity of our task when fighting is going on all over the world and where strategy and supply are so closely intermingled, the Chiefs of the Staff Committee are assisted by a Vice-Chiefs of the Staff Committee which relieves them of a great mass of important questions of secondary order. At the disposal of the Chiefs of the Staff Committee and the Vice-Chiefs' Committee are the Joint Planning Staffs and the three General Staffs of the Navy, Army and Air Force. Each of the three Chiefs of the Staff has, it must be remembered, the professional executive control of the Service he represents. When therefore they meet together, they are in a position to take immediate and responsible action in which each can carry out his share either singly or in combination.

I do not think there has ever been a situation in which the professional Heads of the Fighting Services have had a freer hand, have had more complete control of the course of events or have received more constant, harmonious support from the Prime Minister and Cabinet under whom they serve. It is my practice to leave the Chiefs of the Staff alone to do their work, subject to my general supervision and guidance. For instance, in 1941, out of 420 meetings, most of them lasting over two hours, I only convened 32 myself.[1] In addition, however, there are of course the meetings of the Defence Committee at which the Service Ministers are present as well as the other Ministerial Members of the Defence Committee, and there are the Cabinets at which the Chiefs of the Staff are always present except when domestic matters are concerned. In my absence from this country, or should I at any time be incapacitated, the Lord Privy Seal, representing the second largest Party in the Coalition, acts as my Deputy.[2]

Such is the machinery which, as Minister of Defence and Prime Minister, I have brought into existence. I am satisfied it is the best that can be devised to meet the extraordinary difficulties and dangers through which we are passing. There is absolutely no question of making any change in it of a serious or fundamental character as long as I retain the confidence of the House and of the country.

Winston S. Churchill to President Franklin D. Roosevelt
(Churchill papers, 20/70)

16 February 1942
Personal and Secret
No. 29

Wavell wires that he would like an American Admiral to be appointed as deputy to Helfrich but that he wants to keep Palliser[3] (British) as chief assistant. He is most anxious that Palliser should not be replaced at the present crisis.

2. You will have seen Wavell's telegrams about new situation created by fall of Singapore and Japanese strong landings in Sumatra. We are con-

---

[1] Of the 631 Chiefs of Staff meetings between May 1940 and December 1941, Churchill had presided over 56; when he was in the Chair they were known as Staff Conferences.

[2] Before finalising this note, Churchill altered this sentence to read: 'In my absence from this country or should I at any time be incapacitated the FM acts for me.' The Foreign Minister was Anthony Eden; the Lord Privy Seal was Clement Attlee.

[3] For Admirals Helfrich and Palliser, see Wavell to Churchill, 12 January 1942 (pages 63–4).

sidering new position tonight on the Defence Committee and tomorrow on the Pacific Council, and will send you our recommendations. Unless there is good prospect of effective resistance in Sumatra and Java, the issue arises whether all reinforce[ments] should not be diverted to Rangoon and Australia. The Australian Government seem inclined to press for the return of their two divisions to Australia. I could not resist them for long, and probably their third division, now in Palestine, will follow. It seems to me that the most vital point at the moment is Rangoon, alone assuring contact with China. As you see, Wavell has very rightly already diverted our Armoured Brigade, which should reach there on the 20th instant. The Chiefs of the Staff will send you the result of our discussions tomorrow through the military channel.

3. A battle is impending in Libya in which Rommel will probably take the offensive. We hope to give a good account of ourselves. Preliminary air fighting yesterday was very good.

4. The naval position in home waters and the Atlantic has been definitely eased by the retreat of the German naval forces from Brest. From there they threatened all our east-bound convoys, enforcing two battleships' escort. Their squadrons could also move either on to the Atlantic trade routes or into the Mediterranean. We would far rather have it where it is than where it was. Our bomber effort instead of being dispersed can now be concentrated on Germany. Lastly, as you may have learnt from most secret sources,[1] *Prinz Eugen* was damaged and both *Scharnhorst* and *Gneisenau* were mined, the former twice. This will keep them out of mischief for at least six months, during which both our Navies will receive important accessions of strength. Naturally we were very sorry we did not sink them, and an inquiry is being held as to why we did not know at daylight they were out.

Winston S. Churchill to Lord Linlithgow[2]
(Churchill papers, 20/70)

16 February 1942
Personal and Secret

PROPOSED NEW LEGISLATIVE COUNCIL FOR INDIA

I am greatly obliged to you for your telegram. You may be sure every aspect will be most carefully considered. My own idea was to ask the dif-

---

[1] Enigma. In Churchill's war memoirs, the words 'from most secret sources' were omitted (*The Hinge of Fate*, page 101).

[2] Viceroy of India.

ferent communities of India – Hindus, Moslems, Sikhs, Untouchables, etc. – to give us their best and leading men for such a body as has been outlined. However, the electoral basis proposed which was the best we could think of here might have the effect of throwing the whole Council into the hands of the Congress Caucus. This is far from my wish.

Winston S. Churchill to Sir Reginald Dorman-Smith[1]
(Churchill papers, 20/70)

16 February 1942

I have not hitherto troubled you with a message, but I want to tell you how much I and my colleagues have admired your firm, robust attitude under conditions of increasing difficulty and danger. Now that Singapore has fallen, more weight will assuredly be put into the attack upon you. The substantial reinforcements including the Armoured Brigade and two additional squadrons of Hurricanes should reach you soon. We are meeting tonight to discuss further possibilities. I regard Burma and contact with China as the most important feature in the whole theatre of war. All good wishes.

Oliver Harvey: diary
('The War Diaries of Oliver Harvey', pages 95–6)

16 February 1942

The press is strongly urging a separate Ministry of Defence. I thought the crisis might come in 2 stages if PM yielded now – a stage with Winston and a separate M of D, and then a latter stage when Winston faded out. Dick[2] said the country had lost all confidence in Government, and AE

---

[1] Reginald Dorman-Smith, 1899–1977. Educated at Harrow and Sandhurst. 2nd Lieutenant, Indian Army, 1918; served in 15th Sikhs. Major, Queen's Royal Regiment (Territorial Force), 1930; Honorary Colonel, 1937. A County Alderman, Surrey, 1931–5; Justice of the Peace, 1932. Conservative MP for Petersfield, 1935–41. President of the National Farmers Union, 1936–7. Knighted, 1937. Minister of Agriculture and Fisheries, January 1939 to May 1940. Privy Councillor, 1939. Governor of Burma, 1941–6. High Sheriff of Hampshire, 1952. A Justice of the Peace for Hampshire, 1960.

[2] Richard Kidston Law, 1901–80. Youngest son of Andrew Bonar Law (two of his brothers were killed in action on the Western Front). Editorial Staff, *Morning Post*, 1927; *New York Herald-Tribune*, 1928. Conservative MP for Hull South-West, 1931–45; for South Kensington, 1945–50; for Haltemprice, 1950–4. Member of the Medical Research Council, 1936–40. Financial Secretary, War Office, 1940–1; Parliamentary Under-Secretary of State, Foreign Office, 1941–3. Privy Councillor, 1943. Minister of State, 1943–5. Minister of Education, 1945. Created Baron Coleraine, 1954. Chairman, National Youth Employment Council, 1955–62.

should tell PM so and that if he didn't make change, then it would lose confidence in him (the PM) – Jim Thomas[1] who joined us, confirmed this – AE agreed and said he would say this and urge appointment of a separate M of D. What if Winston offered M of D to AE? AE was pretty sure he wouldn't. As regards Erskine Hill, AE was most anxious not to lend himself to any intrigue. He proposed to say we must all rally round PM and try to strengthen the Government.

AE said if it were his choice as PM he would favour putting a professional in as M of D, e.g. Dill. I suggested Trenchard[2] but AE said too old and too identified with separate air force controversy.

Bobbety[3] has written to AE from the country, advocating AE as M of Defence if PM permitted as best solution and urging that all Ministers should place resignations in PM's hand to facilitate reconstruction.[4]

Winston S. Churchill to General Archibald Wavell
(Churchill papers, 20/70)

17 February 1942
Personal and Most Secret

Keep the strictest censorship on all journalists, especially messages by telephone. I hear of very panic-stricken messages being sent. On the other hand, a good account from your staff of what happened would be welcomed.

---

[1] James Purdon Lewes Thomas, 1903–60. Educated at Rugby and Oriel College, Oxford. Conservative MP for Hereford, 1931–55. Assistant Private Secretary to Stanley Baldwin, 1931. Parliamentary Private Secretary to Anthony Eden, 1932–8 and 1940 (when Eden was Secretary of State for War). Lord Commissioner of the Treasury, 1940–3. Financial Secretary to the Admiralty, 1943–5. Vice-Chairman of the Conservative Party, 1945–51. Privy Councillor, 1951. First Lord of the Admiralty, 1951–6. Created Viscount Cilcennin, 1955.

[2] Hugh Montague Trenchard, 1873–1956. Entered the Army, 1893. On active service in South Africa, 1899–1902 (dangerously wounded). Major, 1902. Assistant Commandant, Central Flying School, 1913–14. General Officer Commanding the Royal Flying Corps in the Field, 1915–17. Major-General, 1916. Knighted, 1918. Chief of the Air Staff, 1918–29. Air Marshal, 1919. Created Baronet, 1919. Air Chief Marshal, 1922. Marshal of the Royal Air Force, 1927. Created Baron, 1930. Commissioner, Metropolitan Police, 1931–5. Created Viscount, 1936. His elder son, and both his stepsons, were killed in action in the Second World War.

[3] Viscount Cranborne, Secretary of State for the Dominions since 3 October 1940, who on 22 February 1942 was appointed Secretary of State for the Colonies.

[4] Oliver Harvey added: 'An unpleasant feature is that the American press is now demanding changes in the Government here.'

Lord Beaverbrook to Sir Samuel Hoare[1]
(Lord Beaverbrook papers)

17 February 1942
Personal

We are in the midst of a political crisis in Britain. The newspapers made it. But the Prime Minister keeps it alive.

Every day he adds a new touch of drama to the story. Indeed, if it were not for this, the crisis might die away altogether.

Already it has passed through several phases. There was the production phase, when it appeared that nothing would satisfy the people but the setting up of a full-fledged Production Ministry. The Ministry was set up. It had not many feathers, but the public have got used to the ugly duckling. They may think it will grow up to be a swan. The ugly duckling does not think this at all.

The next phase was the Cripps phase. Cripps must be given a place in the Government and indeed in the War Cabinet. Cripps was necessary to the effective conduct of the war.

I am a Crippsite. So is the Prime Minister. We are for Cripps. We want him to lead the House. Mr Attlee has imposed his veto. Having excommunicated Cripps in the peace, he is not going to make him assistant pope in the war.

So Cripps is still out of the Government. He is also, I believe, beginning to sink out of the public mind.

The latest cry is that there should be a Minister of Defence. The Prime Minister's critics are solicitous for his health. They think that he is carrying too many burdens. And they propose that he should appoint some other Minister to guide our strategy. The trouble about this suggestion is that either the new Minister of Defence will disagree with the Prime Minister on strategy and get the sack, or agree with the Prime Minister, in which case his appointment will be superfluous.

So it appears probable that this phase in the crisis will pass away. What the next one will be I know not. But I am bound to say that there is no sign of the agitation coming to an end.

---

[1] Samuel John Gurney Hoare, 1880–1959. Educated at Harrow and New College, Oxford. Conservative MP for Chelsea, 1910–44. Succeeded his father as 2nd Baronet, 1915. Lieutenant-Colonel, British Military Mission to Russia, 1916–17, and to Italy, 1917–18. Deputy High Commissioner, League of Nations, for care of Russian refugees, 1921. Secretary of State for Air, October 1922 to January 1924 and 1924–9. Secretary of State for India, 1931–5; for Foreign Affairs, 1935. First Lord of the Admiralty, 1936–7; Home Secretary, 1937–9; Lord Privy Seal, 1939–40; Secretary of State for Air, April–May 1940. Ambassador to Spain, 1940–4. Created Viscount Templewood, 1944.

No doubt, before this letter reaches you the denouement will be reached.[1]

House of Commons: Oral Answers
(Hansard)

17 February 1942

MINISTER OF DEFENCE

Mr Stokes asked the Prime Minister whether, in view of the military situation in Libya and the Far East, and in order to ensure the best practical use of the resources at our disposal, he will now appoint a Minister of Defence to advise on war strategy?

The Prime Minister (Mr Churchill): No, Sir.

Mr Stokes: May I ask whether the Prime Minister has read the speech made on this subject by Lord Chatfield[2] in another place on 28th January,[3] and whether he is aware of the growing volume of competent opinion that it is wrong for the Offices of Prime Minister and Minister of Defence to be held by the same person?

The Prime Minister: I would be quite ready to test the opinion of the House by putting down my salary for Debate.

BOARD OF ADMIRALTY

Mr Silverman:[4] Is the House to understand from the original answer that the Board of Admiralty does not meet regularly, and that, except

---

[1] Sir Samuel Hoare was in Madrid.

[2] Alfred Ernle Montacute Chatfield, 1873–1967. Entered the Royal Navy, 1886. Served at the battles of Heligoland (1914), Dogger Bank (1915), and Jutland (1916). Fourth Sea Lord, 1919–20. Knighted, 1919. Rear-Admiral, 1920. Assistant Chief of the Naval Staff, 1920–2. Third Sea Lord, 1925–8. Commander-in-Chief, Atlantic Fleet, 1929–31. Vice-Admiral, 1930. Commander-in-Chief, Mediterranean, 1931–2. First Sea Lord, January 1933 to September 1938. Admiral of the Fleet, 1935. Created Baron, 1937. Privy Councillor, 1939. Minister for Co-ordination of Defence, 1939–40 (with a seat in the War Cabinet). Chairman, Civil Defence Honours Committee, 1940–6. Author of *The Navy and Defence* (1942), and *It Might Happen Again* (1947).

[3] Speaking in the House of Lords on 28 January 1942, Lord Chatfield said, of 10 May 1940: 'The new Prime Minister became the Minister of Defence, he became Chairman of the Chief of Staffs Committee, and he removed from the War Cabinet the Service Ministers [. . .] How could you expect, with that powerful advocacy which that wonderful man has got, those in the Cabinet who are not equipped by strategical knowledge or Imperial experience to criticise what he advises? How could you expect in those circumstances, that you really could have a free and full discussion which would ensure the avoidance of vital mistakes? In my opinion, you cannot do so.'

[4] Sydney (Samuel) Silverman, 1895–1968. Born in Liverpool, son of a poor draper. Imprisoned three times (in Preston, Wormwood Scrubs, and Belfast prisons) as a conscientious objector, 1914–18. Lecturer in English, National University of Finland, 1921–5. Admitted Solicitor, 1927. Labour MP for Nelson and Colne from 1935 until his death. Member of the National Executive

for the exceptional circumstances in which it does meet in full session, the Board of Admiralty is really only a circumlocution office for the Minister of Defence?

The Prime Minister: The hon. Gentleman seems to have got the Minister of Defence very much in his head. There has been no change in the composition or character of the Board of Admiralty, or the way in which it does its work. It was established in the last war, and it is well known that the Chief of the Naval Staff, subject to the general supervision of the First Lord and of the Cabinet, is responsible for all the movements and dispositions of the Fleet.

Mr Silverman: Will the Prime Minister answer that part of the Question which I addressed to him, as to whether it can be taken as a general rule that the Board does not meet regularly and meets in full session only occasionally?

The Prime Minister: The Board meets, as it has always met, when questions of a certain class affecting the Naval Service or the general naval policy are to be discussed. The Board does not meet to decide on operations, and I hope that it will never be encouraged to do that.

House of Commons: Debate
(Hansard)

17 February 1942

WAR SITUATION

GERMAN WARSHIPS' ESCAPE: INQUIRY

The Prime Minister (Mr Churchill): I beg to move, 'That this House do now adjourn.'

I shall deal first with the naval episode which has attracted attention in the last few days. In March last the two German cruisers *Scharnhorst* and *Gneisenau* took refuge in Brest harbour, where they were joined in May by the *Prinz Eugen* after the destruction of the *Bismarck*. The position of these three ships became a serious preoccupation for the Admiralty. They lay on the flank of our main convoy route to the East, and they

Committee of the Labour Party from 1956 until his death. As a protest against bipartisan support for British nuclear weapons, he voted against the Royal Air Force, Royal Navy, and British Army estimates in the House of Commons, and was suspended from the Labour Party Whip, March 1961 to May 1963. A leading opponent of judicial hanging, in 1965 he successfully piloted the Murder (Abolition of Death Penalty) Bill through Parliament. The Act abolished capital punishment for murder in Britain and in the British Armed Forces for a period of five years, with provision for abolition to be made permanent by affirmative resolutions of both Houses of Parliament before the expiry of the period; these resolutions were passed in 1969.

could make a sortie at any time on to the Atlantic trade routes or into the Mediterranean. Accordingly, the Admiralty have pressed for their continued attack from the air in the hopes of disabling them and preventing them being repaired.

This process continued for more than 10 months, during which time the ships were undoubtedly hit several times and repair work was made very difficult. No less than 4,000 tons of bombs were dropped, and 3,299 bomber sorties were made upon them, with a loss of 247 Air Force personnel and 43 aircraft. As we were never in a position to know when some or all of these ships might put to sea, the situation entailed almost continuous naval precautions in the hope of being ready at all times to meet the various threats which these ships constituted. A further serious feature was the very grave subtraction from the bombing effort against Germany.

The bombing of these ships was, however, so severe that the Germans evidently came to the decision that they could not maintain them any longer at Brest and that they must return to Germany. We do not know whether this was for the purpose of effecting final repairs or to enable them to work up to full efficiency in the sheltered waters of the Baltic. However this may be, the Germans resolved to try to bring the ships back to Germany.

This was a very hazardous operation. It could be done either by sailing round the British Isles and returning via Norway, or by a dash up the Channel. The Germans rejected the plan of returning northabout and preferred to run the admittedly serious risks of the Channel passage. In the Atlantic Ocean they would have run a great risk of being picked up by our extensive air reconnaisances from the shore and from aircraft carriers, or of being slowed down by torpedo attacks and brought to action against overwhelming forces, as was the *Bismarck*. The Channel route, on the other hand, was a run of under 24 hours, part of which could be made in darkness, possibly by surprise, and they had the opportunity of choosing the weather which would be most favourable. The whole way through the Channel and along the Dutch coast they had the advantage of a powerful air umbrella. The dangers of running past the Dover batteries, under suitable weather conditions, were not great.

Our slow convoys repeatedly traverse the Straits of Dover, and are repeatedly bombarded by the German guns on the French shore, but this has not stopped our convoy traffic. One great danger was mines, but this they might hope to avoid by energetic sweeping. There remained, therefore, the action of surface ships and aircraft. Air reconnaissance would show the Germans that neither heavy ships nor even cruisers were in these narrow waters, and, therefore, attacks by flotillas of destroyers and of small torpedo boats were all that need be expected, apart from the air.

Some people seem to think that heavy forces should have been stationed so as to be able to intercept them in the Channel or the North Sea. Had we done so, our ships would have been open to the same scale of air attack as were the German ships at Brest. Further, any such disposition would have dangerously weakened the preventive measures which we have to take to safeguard our convoys and guard the Northern passage, and to deal with the other German heavy ships, the *Tirpitz*, *Lutzow* and *Scheer*. The Admiralty did not consider that the attempt to run through the Channel would be an impossible operation under the conditions which prevailed, and this was certainly much less to be apprehended than that the ships should break out on to the trade routes or into the Mediterranean.

No one can doubt the vigour and courage with which the enemy squadron was attacked as soon as its movement was perceived, and, of course, everyone is very sorry that these ships were not sunk. The only questions which are open are, first: Why was their movement not detected shortly after daylight, and secondly, Was the contact and liaison between the Coastal Command and the Admiralty, and also between the other RAF Commands and the Admiralty, as close as it should have been? At the suggestion of the Admiralty and of the Air Ministry, I have directed that an Inquiry shall be held into these points. The Inquiry will be secret. I doubt very much whether, when completed, its results will be suitable for publication. I am not prepared to give any information about the Inquiry or any undertakings that its results will be made public.

Although it may somewhat surprise the House and the public, I should like to state that, in the opinion of the Admiralty, with which I most cordially concur, this abandonment by the Germans of their position at Brest has been decidedly beneficial to our war situation. The threat to our convoy routes has been removed, and the enemy has been driven to leave his advantageous position. The diversion of our air bombing effort, which, though necessary, was so wasteful, is over. A heavier scale of attack on Germany is now possible, in which all the near misses will hit German and not French dwellings. Both the *Scharnhorst* and the *Gneisenau* have received damage in their passage which will keep them out of action for some time to come, after which they will have to be worked up in gunnery and other practices. Before they can again play any part in the war, the Royal Navy will be reinforced by various important units of the highest quality, and the same strengthening process is going forward in the Navy of the United States. Whatever smart of disappointment or annoyance may remain in our breasts that the final forfeit was not exacted, there is no doubt that the naval position in the Atlantic, so far from being worsened, is definitely eased.

FALL OF SINGAPORE

I have also been asked whether the Government have a statement to make about the fall of Singapore. This extremely grave event was not unexpected, and its possibility was comprised within the scope of the argument I submitted to the House on the occasion of the Vote of Confidence three weeks ago. The House has, of course, many opportunities of discussing this and other aspects of the war situation. I am sure it would be a great mistake to try to discuss it today in the short time available. I have no information to give to the House other than that contained in the public press, nor would it be prudent to speculate in detail upon the various evil consequences which will follow from the fall of Singapore. Moreover, it would ill become the dignity of the Government and the House, and would render poor service to the Alliance of which we are a part, if we were drawn into agitated or excited recriminations at a time when all our minds are oppressed with a sense of tragedy and with the sorrow of so lamentable a misfortune. Perhaps, at a later date, when we are more fully informed and when a carefully considered statement can be made, the House may seek for a further Debate upon the situation in the Far East and the prospect of its being retrieved by the combined action of the Allied Powers concerned. I could certainly not take part in any such discussion now.

However, as some hon. Members may be otherwise inclined, and as I did not wish to prevent them from expressing their opinions, I decided to move the Adjournment, as I have done. The Government will, of course, listen to the Debate, if it takes place, but I hope I may be permitted to remind the House of the extremely serious situation in which we stand, of the use that is made in hostile and even in Allied countries of any loose or intemperate language into which anyone may be drawn, and the importance of the House of Commons maintaining its reputation for firmness and courage in the face of adversity [. . .]

Mr A. Bevan[1] (Ebbw Vale): Would it not be to the convenience of the House if the Prime Minister could indicate what his intentions are,

---

[1] Aneurin Bevan, 1897–1960. A coal miner from the age of 13. Miners' Disputes Agent, 1926. Labour MP for Ebbw Vale from 1929 until his death. Forced in 1944 to give the Labour Party a written assurance of loyalty or be expelled (he gave the assurance). As Minister of Health, 1945–51, introduced the National Health Service. Minister of Labour and National Service, 1951; resigned in protest against defence spending and National Health Service charges (as did the President of the Board of

because we are neither having a Debate nor are we not having a Debate? It would be very much more to the point if the Prime Minister could tell the House when he proposes to give the House an opportunity of having a full-dress Debate on this matter; and may I implore him to be as resilient as he sometimes claims he is and to realise that it is our duty to express the anxieties of the country in this House?

The Prime Minister: I certainly had thought that sometime during the next series of Sitting Days would be appropriate for a Debate. It is not very long since we had a three-day Debate. [An Hon. Member: 'Something has happened since then.'] If hon. Gentlemen would be so kind as to read carefully what I said, they will see how very clearly – as clearly as I could without giving away military information – I indicated how grave the position was in the Far East, and how terrible are the forfeits that have been and will be exacted from us. I certainly feel that the House should have a Debate; there is not the slightest reason to object to a Debate; on the contrary, I will give every facility for a Debate and for a Division. The House is absolutely master. If its confidence is not extended to the Government, if it does not believe that the war is being well managed, if it thinks it can make arrangements which would lead to the war being better managed, it is the duty and the right of the House to express its opinion, as it can do in a proper and a constitutional manner.

Therefore, as I say, I certainly consider that a matter of this kind should be the subject of a Debate, but at the present time I have absolutely no news which has not been published in the Press – no news of any importance or interest. I do not quite know when the news will be received, but still I think that during the course of the next series of Sitting Days there should be a Debate on the subject, and I hope it will be a long Debate. I do not know whether it can all take place in public. I am absolutely certain that I could say things to this House which would arouse hon. Members to the seriousness of the situation and to the way in which the dangers may be aggravated by action we may take or fail to take, but I do not think I could say them in public at all. Let us say then that there will be a Debate; I was only deprecating that it should be held now, as it seems, in a mood of panic. [Hon. Members: 'No.'] I think that a very excited Debate taking place here today, while our minds are oppressed by what has happened, may easily have the effect of causing a bad and very unfavourable reaction all over the world. That is what I say. I stick

Trade, Harold Wilson, later Prime Minister). Treasurer of the Labour Party, and Deputy Leader of the Opposition, from 1956 until his death. His often acerbic manner (he was reported to have called the Conservatives 'lower than vermin') caused Churchill to dub him a 'merchant of discourtesy'.

to it. I think it would have been a bad thing to have had a Debate today. I certainly do not think I could undertake to prepare a full statement on this matter again by the third Sitting Day.

I must ask the House to realise the enormous burdens falling on me, not by my work as Minister of Defence, but by repeated and constant attendance on this House, which I never expected I should have to face, but which I will face. But I think I should be more prepared to make a statement next week. I hope that some information will come in which will enable me to make it. I beg that the Debate shall be absolutely frank, measured only by regard to the public interest. I beg that it shall be searching; I beg, I implore hon. Gentlemen – their manhood and honour require it – that they shall give effect to their opinions.

There is one point I have been asked about the Inquiry. It is quite true that I said I did not propose to give information about the Inquiry. I still think it would have been better that it should have been an Inquiry conducted for the purpose of giving information to the people responsible for carrying on the war, but as the question has been asked, I do not mind changing what I said on that subject, in deference to the wishes expressed by the House. This has already been decided; what I propose is that Mr Justice Bucknill[1] should preside and that Air Chief Marshal Sir Edgar Ludlow-Hewitt[2] and Vice-Admiral Sir Hugh Binney[3] should represent the two Services concerned.

Mr Hore-Belisha (Devonport): Are there any exact terms of reference?

[1] Alfred Townsend Bucknill, 1880–1963. Called to the Bar, 1903. Staff Officer, France, Egypt and Ireland, 1914–18. OBE, 1919. KC, 1931. Knighted, 1935. Judge of the High Court of Justice, 1935–45. Privy Councillor, 1945. Lord Justice of Appeal, 1945–51.

[2] Edgar Rainey Ludlow-Hewitt, 1886–1973. Royal Irish Rifles, 1905–14. Royal Flying Corps, 1914. On active service, 1914–18 (CMG, DSO, Military Cross, despatches six times). Commanded 10th Brigade, Royal Air Force, 1918. Chief Staff Officer, Headquarters, RAF in France, 1918–19. Air Officer Commanding, Iraq Command, 1930–2. Knighted, 1933. Director of Operations and Intelligence, Air Ministry, 1933–5. Air Officer Commanding, RAF India, 1935–7. Air Officer Commanding-in-Chief, Bomber Command, 1937–40. Inspector General of the RAF, 1940–5.

[3] Thomas Hugh Binney, 1883–1953. Gunnery Officer, *Queen Elizabeth*, 1914–18 (DSO, 1919). Deputy Director, Plans Division, Admiralty, 1925–7. Director, Tactical School, 1931–2. Commanded HMS *Hood*, 1932–3. Rear-Admiral, First Battle Squadron, 1936–8. Commandant, Imperial Defence College, 1939. Admiral Commanding Orkneys and Shetlands, 1939–43. Knighted, 1940. Governor of Tasmania, 1945–51. Despite Churchill's suggestion, Binney received no 'exceptional honour' for his work on Operation 'Rubble', when Norwegian merchant ships based in the Swedish port of Gothenburg ran the German naval blockade, escorted by the Royal Navy, in 1941.

The Prime Minister: Their scope is on those points which I indicated in my statement. I hope that the Inquiry will be quickly conducted. Of course, if anyone is found to have been guilty of a dereliction of duty, obviously disciplinary action will follow. Certainly, in that case, I am sure it will be possible to make some statement to the House, but I do not want this Inquiry, which deals with secret matters of defence around these Islands upon which our lives and safety depend, to be subject to a fought-out discussion and wrangling and intricate Debate in the same way as has been done in time of peace, when a submarine like *Thetis* was lost. I think it would be a great pity to do that. I hope the House will realise there is a very great desire to do as well as possible among all those who are serving them, whether in the House or in the Forces.

Mr Pethick-Lawrence: I am very much indebted to the Prime Minister for meeting the House in the way he has done in what he has just said. I am very glad he has consented to give us the particulars he has done. I think he owed it to the House. With regard to the Debate, I think, after consultation with my hon. Friends, that if we have a debate next week, that will also meet the case satisfactorily. Perhaps I might be allowed to say one thing. The Prime Minister said something which I think was misunderstood. I should like the Prime Minister to take the opportunity of explaining that he did not mean what I think was thought in parts of the House. When he used the word 'panic', I think the context of his remarks seemed to suggest that there was panic in this House or, at any rate, in the country. I am quite sure that the Prime Minister himself did not envisage that, because it is quite unnecessary for me to assure him that there is no panic whatever in this House and I do not think that there is any panic in the country. I feel convinced that what he had in his mind was that there might be panic in other parts of the world, and I hope that my interpretation of the Prime Minister's remarks is that which he would put upon them himself.

The Prime Minister: I gladly give the assurance that I was not imputing panic to any Members of this House, but I think, none the less, that a Debate held today in excitement, and pierced with charges and counter-charges interchanged across the House at this moment of great anxiety and distress would undoubtedly be contributing to what I might have called the 'rattling' process which is going on in some parts of the Press, not only in the Press of this country, but freely telegraphed both to Australia and the United States, which tends to give a feeling of insecurity, which I am quite sure the House would agree is detrimental.

Oliver Harvey: diary
('The War Diaries of Oliver Harvey', page 97)

17 February 1942

AE back from H of C where PM had made his statement on Singapore and ships, said he really thought he was riding for a fall, so <u>cassant</u>[1] and ill-tempered he seemed. H of C not unfavourably disposed, surprisingly so, but PM petulantly defiant.

Harold Nicolson: diary
('Harold Nicolson, Diaries and Letters', page 212)

17 February 1942

Winston made his statement this afternoon. It started all right, but when people asked questions, he became irritable and rather reckless. He spoke about 'anger and panic' which infuriated people and will, I fear, be broadcast throughout the world by our enemies. The pity of it is that he had a good case, and if only he had kept his head and produced his promises in the right order,[2] all would have gone well. He was not at his best.

Henry Channon: diary
('Chips', page 322)

17 February 1942

The House of Commons was restless, crowded and angry, yet it does not seem to know its own mind [...]

The PM came into the Chamber and I saw him scowl. No cheer greeted him as he arrived. Nor as he answered Questions. He seemed to have 'Lost the House'. Then at twelve o'clock he rose and in a curiously nonchalant, indeed uninterested, manner, read a prepared statement about the passing through the Channel Straits of the German ships. He convinced nobody, and particularly his attempt to turn an inglorious defeat into a victory displeased the House.

There was soon a barrage of questions. Several times the PM intervened and each time his reception was increasingly hostile; never have I known the House growl at a Prime Minister. Can he ever recover his

---

[1] Brusque.

[2] Nicolson noted in explanation: 'For instance, announcing the court of enquiry into the escape of the two German battle-cruisers.'

waning prestige? He is such a Schwärmer[1] that he basks only in approval; smiles and praise encourage him; criticism irritates and restricts him.

Today the august assembly nearly blew up; he was only saved by several dull speakers who so bored the House (Hugh O'Neill and Gallacher the Communist[2]) that Members began to file out in dozens. It was a disgraceful scene, which lasted an hour and there was no dignity or force; all sense of reality seemed to have left the elected representatives of the people.

We have the first dictator since Cromwell, and much as I distrust Winston (and I fear that he has the evil-eye, or ill-luck – certainly nothing that he has ever touched – Dardanelles, Abdication, India Bill, has come off well), I have even less faith in the Commons – a more moribund collection of old fogies and nit-wits I have never met.

Eventually the House resumed its ordinary business after having extracted a promise for a two days debate next week from the Prime Minister. But he was obviously disgruntled and shaken by his reception. I felt sorry for him.

Lord Beaverbrook to Winston S. Churchill
(Churchill papers, 20/52)

17 February 1942

Dear Prime Minister,

Here is the letter, which I mentioned on the telephone. The people have lost confidence in themselves and they turn to the Government, looking for a restoration of that confidence. It is the task of the Government to supply it.

What can be done, by means of changes in the structure of the administration, to give the people what they want?

(1) The addition of Sir Stafford Cripps to the Government? But the desire of the public for Cripps is a fleeting passion. Already it is on the wane.

(2) The appointment of a Minister of Defence or, perhaps, a deputy Minister of Defence? But no one can be found for this post who will at once give satisfaction to the public and to you, under whom he would serve.

---

[1] Used derogatorily, a gusher (when kindly meant, an enthusiast, a utopian, a visionary).

[2] William Gallacher, 1881–1965. Began work as a grocer's delivery boy at the age of 12. Chairman, Clyde Workers' Committee, 1914–18. Imprisoned four times for political activities, 1917, 1918, 1921, and 1925. Attended the 2nd Congress of the Communist International, Moscow, 1920 (where he met Lenin). Member of the Executive Committee of the Communist International, 1924, and again in 1935. Stood, unsuccessfully, against Churchill in Dundee, 1922. Communist MP for West Fife, 1935–50 (the only Communist MP 1935–45, then one of two). President of the Communist Party of Great Britain, 1953–63.

It might be possible to appoint some one who, like Cripps, would satisfy the public in its present mood. But Cripps would not be satisfactory to you.

(3) The setting up of a War Cabinet composed of a few Ministers, each of whom would preside over groups of departments and would be free from departmental duties. This plan should be adopted.

The War Cabinet should consist of Bevin, the strongest man in the present Cabinet; Eden, the most popular member of the Cabinet; and Attlee, the leader of the Socialist party.

The other members of the Cabinet should be wiped out. They are valiant men, more honourable than the thirty, but they attain not to the first three.

(4) Lastly, some members of the Government, especially Lord Moyne, are looked on by the public as unsatisfactory Ministers. Their names are well known to you.

One at any rate of the Defence Ministers is in trouble with the public. Maybe two of them.

This is, of course, a personal letter with no intention on my part to help or give countenance to any public agitation.

Yours ever,
Max

Brendan Bracken to Winston S. Churchill
(Churchill papers, 20/52)

17 February 1942

Lord Beaverbrook asked me to give you this letter.

I told him that I regarded his advice as unsound. And I beg you to make a thorough reconstruction of the government.

The Ministry of Information's agents in many parts of the world say that England's domestic political wranglings are doing infinite harm.

You are being looked upon as the faithful friend of Ministers who have outlived their usefulness.

BB

Lord Linlithgow to Winston S. Churchill
(Churchill papers, 20/70)

17 February 1942

Burma is under Wavell for operations and not under India, so I hope you will forgive me for speaking out of my (omission).[1] But I think you should know that after hearing many accounts from all kinds of people it is my opinion that our troops in Burma are not fighting with proper relish. I have not least doubt that this is in great part due to lack of drive and inspiration from the top. I watched Hutton[2] for two years as a Staff Officer. As Chief of the General Staff he was excellent. But he is uninspiring and entirely without those (6 corrupt groups) of leadership which draw best out of troops. Wavell appointed him when he himself was suddenly spirited away to cope with Japan and I had grave doubts then about appointment.

I do not waste time by stressing obvious importance of Rangoon and Burma. I have good reason to know that my personal opinion chimes with that of my senior officers in India. But it would be unfair to them to suggest that they share the least responsibility for this telegram. If you consult Auchinleck who was served by Hutton I have no doubt he will support my view. Wavell is having hell of a time and has much in hand. If you feel disposed to follow my judgement my advice to you is to act without delay, for there is no time to spare.[3]

2. I have not consulted or informed Dorman-Smith[4] about this telegram.

---

[1] Word not decipherable: probably 'turn'.

[2] Thomas Jacomb Hutton, 1890–1981. Royal Artillery, 1909. On active service, 1914–18 (wounded three times, despatches four times, Military Cross and bar). General Officer Commanding, Western Independent District, India, 1938–40. Deputy Chief of the General Staff, Army Headquarters, India, 1940–1. Chief of the General Staff, India, 1941; General Officer Commanding, Burma, 1942. War Resources and Reconstruction Committees, Council of India, 1942–4. Knighted, 1944. Regional Officer, Ministry of Health (UK), 1947–9. Director, British Productivity Council, 1953–7.

[3] General Hutton retained his Burma command.

[4] Sir Reginald Dorman-Smith, Governor of Burma.

Captain Richard Pim:[1] recollection
(Sir Richard Pim papers)

18 February 1942

On the 17th February the Prime Minister made a statement in the House about the escape of these ships and also reported the fall of Singapore. There was considerable adverse comment and some criticism. Next morning I found the Prime Minister very much depressed and from what he said it was obvious that he felt the irksomeness of having to put up with criticism as soon as events went badly – circumstances which he had prophesied when he spoke of tears and blood many months before. He said he was tired of it all and hinted that he was very seriously thinking of handing over his responsibilities to other shoulders.

My reply was, and I remember the words, 'But, my God, sir, you cannot do that'. He then said he wondered what were the views of the ordinary citizen, did they also accept the views of the Press or were they prepared to support him in bad days as well as fair. I gave it as my view that the loudest shouts, certainly in Parliament, came from those who saw the possibility of a re-shuffle and hoped to be in the running for some greater or smaller Government position and of course the Press would follow the dictates of the Party which they normally supported in the criticism which the Party was making.[2]

[1] Richard Pike Pim, 1900–87. Served in the Royal Naval Volunteer Reserve, 1914–18. Commander, RNVR Ulster Division, 1929. Joined Royal Irish Constabulary, 1921. Assistant Secretary, Ministry of Home Affairs, Northern Ireland, 1935. In charge of Churchill's War Room at the Admiralty, 1939–40; at Downing Street, No. 10 Annexe, and on Churchill's wartime travels (from Newfoundland 1941 to Potsdam 1945), 1940–5. Knighted, 1945. Inspector-General, Royal Ulster Constabulary, 1945–61. Member of Council of the Winston Churchill Memorial Trust, 1965–9.

[2] Pim added: 'The following week my wife and I had tea with Mrs Churchill who still obviously felt very sore at the way that some sections of the Press had been criticising the Prime Minister. It was a pleasant surprise for me when on the 5th March in the early hours of the morning he handed me a signed copy of his photograph.'

Lord Reith:[1] diary
('The Reith Diaries', pages 286–7)

18 February 1942

6.30 to 7.50 at No. 10. Churchill (who was looking awful) gave us bits of news about the war. Six divisions against the Jap twenty-four. 106,000 troops in Singapore; 60,000 captured. Where are the rest? And very bad work in letting the Japs in so quickly and easily. Duff Cooper there, just back. Churchill asked him to talk in the secret session obviously with a view to his saying there were plenty of troops in Singapore so that it shouldn't have been taken. He said it was obvious that his job must come to an end when a generalissimo was appointed.

Churchill said he was making considerable changes but did not say what they were. He said he was going to give up the leadership of the House of Commons and that it was better to yield to public pressure. Such sycophantic attitude on the part of Simon, Woolton,[2] Leathers and all. Leathers has the manners and attitude of a shop walker. I loathe these meetings. I expect Churchill will have his favourites around him still.

Winston S. Churchill: speech[3]
('The End of the Beginning', page 62)

18 February 1942   10 Downing Street

It is not without deep emotion that I attend this simple ceremony. Here we see the heart of Austria, although trampled down under the Nazi and Prussian yoke. We can never forget here in this island that Austria was

---

[1] John Charles Walsham Reith, 1889–1971. Educated at the Royal Technical College, Glasgow. Engineer's apprentice; then joined S. Pearson & Son Ltd, as an engineer, 1913. On active service, Royal Engineers, 1914–15 (seriously wounded in the head). Major, 1915. Mission to America, for munitions contracts, 1916–17. Admiralty, Engineer-in-Chief's Department, 1918. In charge of liquidation of munitions engineering contracts, 1919. First General Manager, BBC, 1922; Managing Director, 1923; Director-General, 1927–38. Knighted, 1927. Chairman, BOAC, 1939–40. Minister of Information, 1939–40. Minister of Transport, 1940. National MP for Southampton, 1940. Created Baron, 1940. Minister of Works, 1940–2. Director of Combined Operations, Materials Department, Admiralty, 1943–5. Member, Commonwealth Telecommunications Board, 1946–50.

[2] Frederick James Marquis, 1883–1964. A successful businessman, statistician, and economist. Chairman of Lewis's Investment Trust. Knighted, 1935. Director-General of Equipment and Stores, Ministry of Supply, 1939–40. Created Baron Woolton, 1939. Privy Councillor, 1940. Minister of Food, 1940–3. CH, 1942. Member of the War Cabinet, and Minister of Reconstruction, 1943–5. Chairman of the Conservative and Unionist Central Office, 1946–55. Chancellor of the Duchy of Lancaster, 1952–5. Created Viscount, 1953; Earl, 1956.

[3] Churchill made this speech outside 10 Downing Street when the Austrian Minister to Britain presented a trailer canteen to the Women's Voluntary Service (WVS) on behalf of Austrian refugees in Britain.

the first victim of Nazi aggression. We know that happy life which might have been led by scores of millions in central Europe. We remember the charm, beauty, and historic splendour of Vienna, the grace of life, the dignity of the individual; all the links of past generations which are associated in our minds with Austria and with Vienna.

Sir George Franckenstein,[1] you are here as a link with us between the dark past, the haggard present, and what I still believe will be the glorious future. We shall struggle on and fight on. The people of Britain will never desert the cause of the freeing of Austria from the Prussian yoke. We shall go forward. Many long miles have to be marched and many leagues at sea to be covered by ships; many millions of miles of aeroplane flights be accomplished; great heart and effort will be needed from large masses of human beings but we have three-quarters of the human race upon our side. Only our own follies can deprive us of victory; and in the victory of the Allies, Free Austria shall find her honoured place.

General Archibald Wavell to Winston S. Churchill
(Churchill papers, 20/70)

18 February 1942
Private and Most Secret

I am very disturbed altogether at lack of real fighting spirit in our troops shown in Malaya and so far in Burma. Neither British Australians or Indians have shown real toughness of mind or body though Australians fought well in Johore. Causes go deep, softness last 20 years, lack of vigour in peace training, effect of climate and atmosphere in east. Conditions of fighting admittedly difficult but should not have been insuperable.

2. Leaders real drive and inspiration are key. I looked for one for Malaya and Singapore and could not find him. Hutton has plenty of determination behind quiet manner and will never get rattled but lacks power personal inspiration. At time I selected him reorganisation of whole military machine in Burma was imperative I knew he would do this excellently and considered also he would be resolute and skilful commander. I have no reason to think otherwise but agree that Alexander's[2]

---

[1] Georg Freiherr von und zu Franckenstein, 1878–1953. Austro-Hungarian diplomat (serving in Washington, St Petersburg, Rome, Tokyo, India, London, Belgium, and the Caucasus). Austrian Envoy Extraordinary and Minister Plenipotentiary, London, 1920–38. Following the German annexation of Austria in 1938, he was knighted by King George VI. In 1939 he published *Facts and Features of My Life*.

[2] Harold Rupert Leofric George Alexander, 1891–1969. Educated at Harrow and Sandhurst (as was Churchill). On active service, 1914–18 (wounded three times, despatches five times, DSO, Military Cross). Lieutenant-General commanding I Corps, 1940 (despatches). General Officer Commanding

forceful personality might act as stimulus to troops. Dorman-Smith when I last visited Rangoon spoke well of Hutton and said he had impressed his ministers.

3. I am reluctant to make change but it would help me to decide if you would inform me (a) is it proposed to send whole or part of Australian Corps to Burma if so presume Australians may want to be consulted.

(b) what would become of Hutton, best solution might be if he could remain as CGS in Burma or return to India in that capacity.

(c) how quick could Alexander reach Burma after decision made, it should be within week if possible.

4. Your para. 3. Ordered myself out of hospital after 24 hours and somewhat to scandal of doctor am making rapid recovery.

On 19 February 1942 the new War Cabinet was announced:

Prime Minister and Minister of Defence	Winston Churchill
Deputy Prime Minister and Secretary of State for Dominion Affairs	Clement Attlee
Lord Privy Seal and Leader of the House of Commons	Sir Stafford Cripps
Lord President of the Council	Sir John Anderson[1]
Foreign Secretary	Anthony Eden
Minister of Production	Oliver Lyttelton
Minister of Labour	Ernest Bevin

Southern Command, 1940–2; Burma, 1942; the Middle East, 1942–3. Commander-in-Chief, 18th Army Group, North Africa, 1943; Allied Armies in Italy (15th Army Group), 1943–4. Knighted, 1942. Field Marshal, 1944. Supreme Allied Commander, Mediterranean Theatre, 1944–5. Created Viscount, 1946. Knight of the Garter, 1946. Governor-General of Canada, 1946–52. Created Earl Alexander of Tunis, 1952. Minister of Defence (in Churchill's second premiership), 1952–4. Order of Merit, 1959. In 1962 he published *The Alexander Memoirs.*

[1] John Anderson, 1882–1958. Educated at Edinburgh and Leipzig Universities. Entered the Colonial Office, 1905; Secretary, Northern Nigeria Lands Committee, 1909. Secretary to the Insurance Commissioners, London, 1913. Secretary, Ministry of Shipping, 1917–19. Knighted, 1919. Chairman of the Board of Inland Revenue, 1919–20. Joint Under-Secretary of State in the Government of Ireland, 1920. Permanent Under-Secretary of State, Home Office, 1922–32. Governor of Bengal, 1932–7. National Government MP for the Scottish Universities, 1938–50. Lord Privy Seal, 1938–9. Home Secretary and Minister of Home Security, 1939–40. Lord President of the Council, 1940–3. Chancellor of the Exchequer, 1943–5. Chairman of the Port of London Authority, 1946–58. Member of the BBC General Advisory Council 1947–57. Created Viscount Waverley, 1952. Order of Merit, 1957.

Winston S. Churchill to Sir Kingsley Wood
(Churchill papers, 20/53)

19 February 1942

My dear Kingsley,

I send you the enclosed composition of the new War Cabinet which I have found it necessary to form. You will see that I have not been able to include the Chancellor of the Exchequer in it, and have thus reverted to our original plan when the present Government was formed.

I am very sorry about this, but in all the circumstances there is no choice. Of course you will always have to come when your affairs are involved.

Yours very sincerely,
Winston S. Churchill

Winston S. Churchill to Lord Moyne
(Churchill papers, 20/53)

19 February 1942

My dear Walter,

It is with very deep regret on every ground, personal and public, that I find myself compelled to make a change in the Colonial Office. The considerable reconstruction of the Government which events and opinion alike require, makes it necessary for me to give Attlee the Dominions Office, which many have pressed should be held by a Member of the War Cabinet. That being so, I am anxious that Cranborne should take your place, and I feel sure that from all I know of you and from your previous conduct in this war, that you will be willing to fall in with my wishes and needs.

It has been a great pleasure for me to work with you during this stormy period, and I thank you most earnestly for all the help and friendship you have always shown me, as well as for the high competence with which you have discharged your functions, both as Colonial Secretary and Leader of the House of Lords.

Yours very sincerely,
Winston S. Churchill

Robert Menzies to Winston S. Churchill
(Churchill papers, 20/70)

19 February 1942

As one compelled by political circumstances to be very much of an onlooker in these days,[1] I have watched recent events with clear understanding of your problems, warmly sympathising and with the greatest admiration for your sustained and sustaining courage and leadership. Kind regards.

Robert Menzies

Winston S. Churchill to Robert Menzies[2]
(Churchill papers, 20/58)

19 February 1942

Am indebted to you for yr kind telegram and for all you are doing for our common cause.[3]

Winston S. Churchill

President Franklin D. Roosevelt to Winston S. Churchill
(Churchill papers, 20/70)

19 February 1942
Secret and Personal
No. 106

I realise how the fall of Singapore has affected you and the British people. It gives the well known back seat driver a field day but no matter how serious our setbacks have been and I do not for a moment underrate them, we must constantly look forward to the next moves that need to be made to hit the enemy.

---

[1] Robert Menzies, who had become Prime Minister of Australia on 26 April 1939, had stood down after John Curtin led the Labour Party to victory in the general election of October 1941. Menzies was Prime Minister a second time from December 1949 to January 1966.

[2] Churchill wrote out this reply in his own handwriting at the bottom of Menzies' telegram.

[3] Churchill wrote in his war memoirs of how the Australian Government under Menzies 'had raised the Australian Imperial Force and had sent no less than four divisions, composed of the flower of their military manhood, across the world to aid the Mother Country in the war, in the making of which and in the want of preparations for which they had no share. From the days of Bardia Australian troops and the New Zealand Division had played a foremost part in the Desert war for the defence of Egypt. They had shone in the van of its victories and shared in its many grievous reverses. The 9th Australian Division had yet to strike what history may well proclaim as the decisive blow in the Battle of Alamein, still eight months away' (*The Hinge of Fate*, page 137).

I hope you will be of good heart in these trying weeks because I am very sure that you have the great confidence of the masses of the British people. I want you to know that I think of you often and I know you will not hesitate to ask me if there is anything you think I can do.

When I speak on the radio next Monday evening I shall say a word about those people who treat the episode in the Channel as a defeat. I am more and more convinced that the location of all the German ships in Germany makes our joint North Atlantic naval problem more simple.

I have been giving a good deal of thought during the last few days to the Far East. It seems to me that we must at all costs maintain our two flanks – the right based on Australia and New Zealand and the left in Burma, India and China.

It seems to me that the United States is able because of our geographical position to reinforce the right flank much better than you can and I think that the United States should take the primary responsibility for that immediate reinforcement and maintenance, using Australia as the main base.

While the defence of Java looks difficult, I believe we both should fight hard for it but we must plan for the more southerly permanent base to strike back from. This will include some of the islands further north, such as New Caledonia and Fiji.

Britain is better prepared to reinforce Burma and India and I visualize that you would take responsibility for that theatre. We would supplement you in any way we could just as you would supplement our efforts on the right flank. The United States should continue to move our supplies principally aircraft through into China because I think that it is important that we have an effective offensive operation from there. Let me know what you think of this.

Because of the possibility of the loss of most of the ABDA area active operations will move fairly rapidly into the Burma area on the West and the Anzac area on the East. This would cause reconsideration of the ABDA commands and the shifting of personnel. I have not heard how Chiang Kai-shek is getting on but I am under the impression that his visit will be useful. Do let me hear from you.

Winston S. Churchill to President Franklin D. Roosevelt
(Churchill papers, 20/70)

20 February 1942
Personal and Secret
No. 30

I am most deeply grateful to you for your warm-hearted telegram No. 106. The pressure here has never been dangerous and I have used it to effect wholesome changes and accessions. You may take it everything is now solid.

2. I am grieved about Max, but he really does need two or three months in sunshine for his asthma and I know you will realize what friends we are and how helpful his driving power will be when he has recovered his health.

3. I do not like these days of personal stress and I have found it difficult to keep my eye on the ball. We are however in the fullest accord in all main things, and I will teleprint you more at large over the weekend. Democracy has to prove that it can provide a granite foundation for war against tyranny. I am looking forward to your rubbing it in about the easement in the Atlantic by the German flight from Brest, but of course we cannot dwell too much upon the damage they sustained.[1] Every good wish and very many thanks.

Winston S. Churchill to Anthony Eden
(Churchill papers, 20/67)

20 February 1942

WHAT TERM TO USE ABOUT THE UNITED STATES' WARTIME RELATIONSHIP WITH BRITAIN

The expression 'co-belligerent' is awful. To all intents and purposes the United States are Allies. To evade the Senate difficulty we use the term 'United Nations' rather than 'Allied Powers', but I see no reason why we should not refer to the United States as an Ally. In formal and official documents they will call themselves what they like. There would, however, be no harm in asking them first.

---

[1] Because the details about the damage had been derived from Enigma.

Winston S. Churchill to General Archibald Wavell
(Churchill papers, 20/70)

20 February 1942
Private and Secret

Obviously whole plan for defence ABDA Area for Commands, etc. is affected by rapid progress of enemy in all directions. It has been decided to fight to the utmost for Java with existing forces and some that were en route, and to divert main reinforcements to Burma and India. The President's mind is turning to United States looking after the Australian flank and we concentrating everything on defending or regaining Burma and Burma Road, of course after everything possible has been done to prolong the resistance in Java. He also realizes vital importance of Ceylon which is our only key of naval re-entry.

2. I surmise that it is not unlikely that General MacArthur, if extricated, will look after the Australian side. I have not heard from you where you would move your headquarters if forced to leave Java.

3. My own idea is that you should become again C-in-C in India, letting Hartley go back to his Northern Command. From this centre you would be able to animate the whole war against Japan from our side.

4. We are sending Alexander as fast as possible to command the considerable army now being assembled on the Burma front. If he arrives in time and there are favourable developments, he might well be given command of the local Air and Naval forces. I am much impressed with the advantages of not having three separate Commanders-in-Chief but letting the biggest one or the best one be the boss of all three Services.

5. Pray let us have your general views.

Winston S. Churchill to John Curtin
(Cabinet papers, 20/70)

20 February 1942
Most Secret

I suppose you realise that your leading division the head of which is sailing south of Colombo to Netherlands East Indies at this moment in our scanty British and American shipping (*Mount Vernon*)[1] is the only

---

[1] The ocean liner USS *Washington*, built in 1933, acquired by the United States Navy in June 1941, and converted to a troopship as USS *Mount Vernon* in December 1941. She had helped disembark British troops at Singapore.

force that can reach Rangoon in time to prevent its loss and the severance of communication with China. It can begin to disembark at Rangoon about 26th or 27th. There is nothing else in the world that can fill the gap.

2. We are all entirely in favour of all Australian troops returning home to defend their native soil, and we shall help their transportation in every way. But a vital war emergency cannot be ignored, and troops en route to other destinations must be ready to turn aside and take part in a battle. Every effort would be made to relieve this division at the earliest moment and send them on to Australia. I do not endorse the United States request that you should send your other two divisions to Burma. They will return home as fast as possible. But this one is needed now, and is the only one that can possibly save the situation.

3. Pray read again your message Johcu No. 21 in which you said that the evacuation of Singapore would be 'an inexcusable betrayal.' Agreeably with your point of view we therefore put the 18th Division and other important reinforcements into Singapore instead of diverting them to Burma and ordered them to fight it out to the end. They were lost at Singapore and did not save it, whereas they could almost certainly have saved Rangoon. I take full responsibility with my colleagues on the Defence Committee for this decision; but you also bear a heavy share on account of your telegram Johcu No. 21.

4. Your greatest support in this hour of peril must be drawn from the United States. They alone can bring into Australia the necessary troops and air forces, and they appear ready to do so. As you know, the President attaches supreme importance to keeping open the connection with China, without which his bombing offensive against Japan cannot be started, and also most grievous results may follow in Asia if China is cut off from all allied help.

5. I am quite sure that if you refuse to allow your troops to stop this gap which are actually passing, and if in consequence the above evils affecting the whole course of the war follow, a very grave effect will be produced upon the President and the Washington circle on whom you are so largely dependent. See especially the inclination of the United States to move major naval forces from Hawaii into the Anzac area.

6. We must have an answer immediately, as the leading ships of the convoy will soon be steaming in the opposite direction from Rangoon and every day is a day lost. I trust therefore that for the sake of all interests, and above all your own interests, you will give most careful consideration to the case I have set before you.

Winston S. Churchill to President Franklin D. Roosevelt
(Churchill papers, 20/70)

20 February 1942
Most Immediate
No. 31

The only troops who can reach Rangoon in time to stop the enemy and enable other reinforcements to arrive are the leading Australian division. These can begin to arrive there by 26th or 27th. We have asked Australian Government to allow this diversion for the needs of battle, and promised to relieve them at earliest. All other Australian troops going home at earliest. Australian Government have refused point blank. I have appealed to them again in the interests of the vital importance of keeping open Burma Road and maintaining contact with Chiang.

2. In view of your offer of American troops to help defend Australia and possible naval movements I feel you have a right to press for this movement of Allied forces. Please therefore send me a message which I can add to the very strong cable I have just sent off. Our Chiefs of Staff here are most insistent and I have no doubt our combined Chiefs of Staff Committee in Washington feel the same way. There is no reason why you should not also talk to Casey.[1]

George Harvie-Watt to Winston S. Churchill
(Sir George Harvie-Watt papers)

20 February 1942

The atmosphere in the House this week has been quite different from the atmosphere during recent sittings. The House welcomes the Government changes. There is an earnest desire, however, that the change in personnel will also result in a greater determination and an increase in the offensive spirit.

Your speech on Tuesday was well received in all quarters, and there is a general feeling of satisfaction that you dealt with the position of Minister of Defence and explained the structure and workings of the defence machine. This explanation has swept away many of the criticisms and misunderstandings which existed. Members are generally satisfied that you will not be relieved of many of your routine burdens, especially so far as the House of Commons is concerned.

[...]

---

[1] Richard Casey, Australian Ambassador in the United States, 1940–2.

The changes in the Government have undoubtedly had a marked effect on the House, which is now in a much less critical and a much more co-operative mood.

President Franklin D. Roosevelt to Winston S. Churchill
(Churchill papers, 20/70)

21 February 1942
No. 107

I hope you can persuade Australian Government to allow proposed temporary diversion of their leading Australian division to Burma. I think this is of utmost importance. Tell them I am speeding additional troops as well as planes to Australia and that my estimate of the situation there is highly optimistic and by no means dark. Harry[1] is seeing Casey at once.

Hugh Dalton:[2] recollection
('The Second World War Diary of Hugh Dalton', page 383)

21 February 1942

[...] it was snowing hard. In the afternoon we had a procession, headed by a Police Sergeant and myself marching side by side, immediately followed by the band of the Royal North Lancs, and then by detachments of Army, Air Force and various Civil Defence Services. Large crowds lined the route.

At the Hippodrome I made a short and urgent speech. I had just sat down when I received a telephone message:

'Don't interrupt your speech, but, as soon as you can, ring up White-hall 4464.' I rose and left the meeting, saying, with a wave of the hand, 'I have to telephone to London about the war.' I did so from an ARP[3] shelter

---

[1] Harry Hopkins.

[2] Edward Hugh John Neale Dalton, 1887–1962. Educated at Eton and King's College, Cambridge. Barrister, 1914. On active service in France and Italy, 1914–18. Reader in Commerce, University of London, 1920–5; Reader in Economics, 1925–6. Labour MP for Camberwell, 1924–9; for Bishop Auckland, 1929–31, 1935–59. Parliamentary Under-Secretary, Foreign Office, 1929–31. Chairman, National Executive of the Labour Party, 1936–7. Minister of Economic Warfare, 1940–2. President of the Board of Trade, 1942–5. Chancellor of the Exchequer, 1945–7; resigned over a Budget leak, 1947. Minister of Town and Country Planning, 1950–1. Created Baron, 1960.

[3] ARP: Air Raid Precautions.

close by. After some delay I got on to one of the Prime Minister's Private Secretaries. A moment later the Prime Minister himself came on.

PM 'Are you alone in the room?'

HD 'No, Prime Minister, but I soon can be.'

I signalled everyone out.

PM 'I am making, as you know, some changes in the Government, and I want to change your office.'

HD 'Where do you want me to go?'

PM 'I want you to take the Board of Trade.'

HD 'This is a bit of a surprise. Do you want an answer now? I am coming back tonight and shall be in London early tomorrow morning.'

PM 'I should like an answer soon, because I am making a number of changes, which all go together and one depends on another. Can you give me an answer in an hour?' That, I thought, was not much good. I had better decide at once.

HD 'I suppose the Board of Trade is a very full-time job?'

PM 'Yes, quite full-time. You will have many important duties, and you will have to do what you can with what remains of the trading community.'

HD 'So that would mean that I should give up all the other duties which I have got now?'

PM 'Yes, you would.'

HD 'Very well, I will take it, but on one condition. Can you tell me that you have confidence in my capacity to do it well?'

PM 'Yes, I have complete confidence in you and, after all, much of the work will not be very different from what you have been doing at MEW.'[1]

HD 'Very well. Thank you very much. I accept.'

Winston S. Churchill to General Sir Alan Brooke
(Churchill papers, 20/67)

22 February 1942
Secret and Private

Now that Mr Lyttelton, the Minister of State, is leaving Cairo, I contemplate somewhat different arrangements, namely:

---

[1] MEW: Ministry of Economic Warfare; this included Ministerial responsibility for the Special Operations Executive (SOE), which Churchill transferred to the Earl of Selborne, Minister of Economic Warfare from 1942 to 1945.

(a) General Auchinleck to be Supreme Commander over the three Services in his Command, Navy, Army and Air.

(b) A resident Cabinet Minister in Cairo, who would do all the work which Mr Lyttelton relieved him of, and in addition play a larger part in securing the proper handling of the rearward services.

2. It seems essential to find out why our forward servicing is so inferior to that of the enemy, and why such a small proportion of our tanks can be maintained in action.

3. Let me know your personal views in the next few days.

Winston S. Churchill to President Franklin D. Roosevelt
(Churchill papers, 20/70)

22 February 1942
Most Secret
Immediate

PACIFIC WAR COUNCIL

Pacific War Council met this evening

[...]

2. The Council note from paragraph 1 of General Wavell's telegram that:'Reinforcement of heavy American bombers from India has been stopped from Washington.'

The Council hope that, in view of the importance of making every effort to attack Japanese landing operations while the opportunity offers, the flow of American heavy bombers to Java may continue, until the Supreme Commander says that it is useless and must be stopped.

[...]

4. As regards the question in paragraph 5(b), the Council approve the immediate evacuation of the personnel mentioned in the first two sentences of paragraph 3. Thereafter, the policy should be:

(i) To evacuate technicians of all nationalities who no longer serve a useful purpose in the defence of the Island.

(ii) After this has been done, the Dutch General could evacuate:

(a) Wounded.

(b) Such men as become useless to the defence through loss of arms or equipment.

(c) After (a) and (b) it would be at discretion of Dutch General to decide when shipping must be evacuated to prevent its destruction by air attack. If there is time to load the ships before departure, he would decide who should go in them. The Council felt that our war effort must come first and therefore have not specifically mentioned women and children.

[...]

(6) The Council consider that the successful naval action off Bali reinforces their request for naval reinforcements to the ABDA area.

Winston S. Churchill to General Archibald Wavell
(Churchill papers, 20/70)

22 February 1942
Clear the Line
Personal and Secret

[...]

When you cease to command the ABDA area you should proceed yourself to India where we require you to resume your position as Commander-in-Chief to carry on the war against Japan from this main base.

It may be you will need a deputy Commander-in-Chief to take routine matters off your hands; but this can be settled when you get to Delhi. All other considerations are subsidiary.

2. I hope you realise how highly I and all your friends here, as well as the President and the Combined Staffs in Washington rate your admirable conduct of ABDA operations in the teeth of adverse fortune and overwhelming odds.

3. Australian Government have refused to allow their leading Division to take a hand at Rangoon. However, yesterday we turned the convoy Northward, being sure Australian Government would not fail to rise to the occasion. Convoy has now got so far North that it will have to refuel before going to Australia. So what about it? This gives three or four days for the Australian Government with its majority of one to think matters over in the light of the President's reiterated appeals, and it also enables us to see how the Hutton situation develops on the Burma front.

4. Many thanks for your kind wishes. I believe the nation is solid behind me here, and this would be a good thing considering the troubles we have to face.

Field Marshal Sir John Dill to Winston S. Churchill
(Churchill papers, 20/70)

22 February 1942
Most Immediate
Private

Hopkins has just told me that Curtin has refused President's appeal to let first Australian Division go to Burma.

Winston S. Churchill to John Curtin
(Churchill papers, 20/70)

22 February 1942
Most Secret

We could not contemplate that you would refuse our request, and that of the President of the United States for the diversion of the leading Australian Division to save the situation in Burma. We knew that if our ships proceeded on their course to Australia while we were waiting for your formal approval, they would either arrive too late at Rangoon or even be without enough fuel to go there at all. We therefore decided that the convoy should be temporarily diverted to the Northward. The convoy is now too far North for some of the ships in it to reach Australia without refuelling. These physical considerations give a few days for the situation to develop, and for you to review the position should you wish to do so. Otherwise the leading Australian Division will be returned to Australia as quickly as possible in accordance with your wishes.

Oliver Harvey: diary
('The War Diaries of Oliver Harvey', page 101)

22 February 1942

Winston has much to give and yet he has such disadvantages. His enormous courage and confidence, his hold over the country as a rallying force, his imagination and refusal to be bound by old ways – against that, his impulsiveness, his obstinacy in counsel, his refusal to give up full control of Defence. But the new Cabinet should be some improvement. The fresh mind of Cripps should wake it up – he is no 'yes' man and will get what he wants or leave. It is smaller and has shed the Beaver.[1]

[1] Lord Beaverbrook, who was sent to the United States to co-ordinate Allied supplies to the Soviet Union.

War Cabinet: Confidential Annex
(Cabinet papers, 65/29)

23 February 1942   10 Downing Street
6 p.m.

The Prime Minister informed the War Cabinet that the 7th Australian Division, now on its way back from Palestine to Australia, had touched at Colombo and was in the Indian Ocean. This Division was the only unit which could be diverted immediately to Burma, where, if it could arrive in time, it would be likely to turn in our favour the battle for Rangoon. If so diverted, it could have arrived on the 26th or 27th February.

It had therefore been suggested to the Australian Government that they should agree to this Division being diverted to Burma, in view of the critical nature of the fighting there and of the important strategic issue involved.

The Australian Government had refused this request. He had, however, thought it right to send another telegram to the Australian Government on 20th February urging them to change their mind. Sir Earle Page[1] had sent a strong telegram pressing them to adopt the same course. In view of the important issue involved, the Prime Minister had put the facts to President Roosevelt, who had then also sent a strong appeal to the Australian Government.

While awaiting a reply from the Australian Government to his second request, he (the Prime Minister) had taken upon himself the responsibility of ordering the convoy to turn North, so that, in the event of the Australian Government acceding to our request, no delay would be entailed.

The Prime Minister said that the Australian Government, after full consideration, had refused his second request. He read the following extract from telegram No. 139 from the Australian Government received on 21st February.

> 'In your telegram No. 233 it was clearly implied that the convoy was not (repeat not) proceeding to the Northwards. From your telegram No. 241 it appears that you have diverted the convoy towards Rangoon and had treated our approval to this vital diversion as merely a matter of form. By doing so you have established a physical situation which adds to the dangers of the convoy and the responsibility of the consequences of such divesion rests upon you.'

The Prime Minister said that on receipt of this reply the convoy had been ordered to proceed to Australia.

[1] Special Australian Envoy to the British War Cabinet, 1941–2.

The Prime Minister said that he took full responsibility for his action in changing the course of the convoy. As soon as the convoy had turned North, its escort had been increased, and this increased escort would continue to accompany the convoy. It so happened that some of the transports would now not have sufficient fuel to proceed to Australia without another call at Colombo to get fuel.

The Prime Minister said that he regretted that, owing to a misunderstanding, Sir Earle Page had not been informed when the convoy had been ordered to turn North. He also said that it had been hoped that the reply would be received from the Australian Government within a few hours. But the reply had not been received for nearly 30 hours.

Winston S. Churchill to John Curtin
(Cabinet papers, 20/70)

23 February 1942
Personal and Secret

Your convoy is now proceeding to re-fuel at Colombo. It will then proceed to Australia in accordance with your wishes.

2. My decision to move it northward during the few hours required to receive your final answer was necessary because otherwise your help, if given, might not have arrived in time.

3. As soon as the convoy was turned north, arrangements were made to increase its escort, and this increased escort will be maintained during its voyage to Colombo, and on leaving Colombo again for as long as practicable.

4. Of course I take full responsibility for my action.

President Franklin D. Roosevelt to Winston S. Churchill
(Churchill papers, 20/70)

23 February 1942
Personal
No. 84

In view of Curtin's final answer in the negative to our strong request I have sent him the following despatch in the hope that we can get the next contingent to help hold the Burma line.

2. Quote for Curtin. Thank you for yours of the twentieth. I fully understand your position in spite of the fact that I cannot wholly agree

as to the immediate need of the first returning division in Australia. I think that as of today the principal threat against the main bases of Australia and Burma, both of which must be held at all costs, is against the Burma or left flank, and that we can safely hold the Australian or right flank. Additional American fully equipped reinforcements are getting ready to leave for your area. In view of all this and depending of course on developments in the next few weeks, I hope you will consider the possibility of diverting the second returning division to some place in India or Burma to help hold that line so that it can become a fixed defence. Under any circumstances you can depend upon our fullest support. Roosevelt. Unquote.

3. I am working on additional plans to make control of Islands in Anzac Area more secure, and further to disrupt Japanese advances.

4. In Monday night's speech I am leaving out proposed reference to German ships running the Channel, because over here the first bad comments have about died down. All agree it is best not to stir up the controversy again. I hope you concur.

Oliver Harvey: diary
('The War Diaries of Oliver Harvey', page 101)

23 February 1942

Situation in Burma very bad. We've tried to get Curtin to agree to Australian Division on way home being diverted there as it is essential to hold this flank. But he has refused point blank in spite of personal approach from both PM and Roosevelt (latter is sending heavy US reinforcements to Australia).

Winston S. Churchill to General Hastings Ismay,
for the Chiefs of Staff Committee
(Churchill papers, 20/67)

23 February 1942
Secret

FAR EAST APPRECIATION: A REPORT BY THE CHIEFS OF STAFF

I doubt whether the internal security problem in India will become serious. The mass of the population will hold their breath, as usual, till the arrival of a new conqueror. There will, I think, be a healthy dread of the Japanese. [...]

Surely Fiji and New Caledonia ought not to be lost? They have already been garrisoned to such an extent as to require a substantial force to overrun them, and, if the United States fleet is regaining parity, it would be a tremendous risk for the Japanese to stretch out so far south when they are already so much spread in other directions. The United States should be warned.

At 4 p.m. on 23 February 1942, Churchill went to a reception at the Russian Embassy in Kensington Palace Gardens, London, to celebrate the anniversary of the Red Army's foundation, marking eight months of continuous fighting by the Red Army since the German invasion of the Soviet Union on 22 June 1941.

Winston S. Churchill to Josef Stalin
(Churchill papers, 20/70)

23 February 1942

The twenty fourth anniversary of the foundation of the Red Army is being celebrated today after eight months of a campaign which has reflected the greatest glory on its officers and men and has enshrined its deeds in history for all time.

On this proud occasion I convey to you, the Chairman of the Defence Committee of the Union of Soviet Socialist Republics, and to all members of the Soviet Forces, an expression of the admiration and gratitude with which the peoples of the British Empire have watched their exploits and of our confidence in the victorious end of the struggle which we are waging together against the common foe.

Winston S. Churchill

Winston S. Churchill: speech
(Hansard)

24 February 1942

WAR SITUATION

MINISTERIAL CHANGES

The Prime Minister (Mr Churchill): Since we last met here there has been a major reconstruction of the War Cabinet and among Ministers of Cabinet rank. There will be further changes, not only consequential changes, among the Undersecretaries, but these I have not yet had time to consider in all their bearings. After nearly two years of strain and struggle it was right and necessary that a Government called into being in the crash of the Battle of France should undergo both change and reinvigoration. I regret very much the loss of loyal and trusted colleagues, with whom I have come through so many hard times and who readily placed their resignations in my hand in order to facilitate a reconstruction of the Government. They had, of course, no greater share of responsibility than the rest of the Administration for the disasters which have fallen upon us in the Far East. Nevertheless, I am sure that we have achieved a more tensely-braced and compact Administration to meet the new dangers and difficulties which are coming upon us, and I believe that that is the general opinion of the House and of the country.

Attention is naturally concentrated upon the War Cabinet, and no doubt comparisons will be made with the War Cabinet of the last war. I have on previous occasions given my reasons why I do not believe that a War Cabinet entirely composed of Ministers without Departments is practicable or convenient. In other ways, however, the resemblance is fairly close. During most of the period from December, 1916, to November, 1918, the Lloyd George[1] War Cabinet consisted of six or seven Ministers, of whom one only had departmental duties, namely, Mr Bonar Law,[2] Chancellor of the Exchequer, Leader of the House, and Leader of the Conservative party. In addition, Mr Balfour, the Foreign Secretary, although not in name a member of the War Cabinet, was so to all practical purposes and was in fact a far more powerful politician than any of its members except the Prime Minister and the Chancellor of the Exchequer. The new War Cabinet consists of seven members, of whom three have no Departments. One is Prime Minister, one is Deputy Prime Minister with the Dominions Office, and one is Foreign Secretary. In the seventh case, the Minister of Labour and National Service replaces the

[1] David Lloyd George, 1863–1945. Educated at a Welsh Church school. Solicitor, 1884. Liberal MP for Caernarvon, 1890–1931. President of the Board of Trade, 1905–8. Privy Councillor, 1905. Chancellor of the Exchequer, 1908–15. An original member of the Other Club, 1911. Minister of Munitions, May 1915 to July 1916. Secretary of State for War, July–December 1916. Prime Minister, December 1916 to October 1922. Order of Merit, 1919. Independent Liberal MP, 1931–45. Created Earl, 1945.

[2] Andrew Bonar Law, 1858–1923. Born in Canada. Brought to Scotland at the age of 12. Conservative MP for Blackfriars and Hutchesontown division of Glasgow, 1900–6; for Dulwich, 1906–10; for Bootle, 1911–18; for Glasgow Central Division, 1918–23. Parliamentary Secretary, Board of Trade, 1902–5. Leader of the Conservatives in the House of Commons, 1911. Secretary of State for the Colonies, May 1915 to December 1916. Chancellor of the Exchequer, 1916–19. Lord Privy Seal, 1919–21. Prime Minister, 1922–3. Two of his four sons were killed in action in the First World War.

Chancellor of the Exchequer of the former model. I think this is right. In the last 25 years labour has made immense advances in the State, and it is desirable, both on personal and on public grounds, that this office, which serves all Departments, should be included.

There may prove to be other points of resemblance. It is now the fashion to speak of the Lloyd George War Cabinet as if it gave universal satisfaction and conducted the war with unerring judgment and unbroken success. On the contrary, complaints were loud and clamant. Immense disasters, such as the slaughter of Passchendaele, the disaster at Caporetto in 1917, the destruction of the Fifth Army after 21st March, 1918, all these and others befell that rightly famous administration. It made numerous serious mistakes. No-one was more surprised than its members when the end of the war came suddenly in 1918, and there have even been criticisms about the character of the peace which was signed and celebrated in 1919. Therefore we, in this difficult period, have other things to do besides that of living up slavishly to the standards and methods of the past, instructive and on the whole encouraging as they unquestionably are.

Let me explain how the duties are divided. The members of the War Cabinet are collectively and individually responsible for the whole policy of the country, and they are the ones who are alone held accountable for the conduct of the war. However, they have also particular spheres of superintendence. The Leader of the Labour Party,[1] as head of the second largest party in the National Government, acts as Deputy Prime Minister in all things, and in addition will discharge the duties of the Dominions Secretary, thus meeting, without an addition to our numbers, the request pressed upon us from so many quarters that our relations with the Dominions, apart from those between His Majesty's various Prime Ministers on which the Dominions are most insistent, shall be in the hands of a member of the War Cabinet.

The Lord President of the Council[2] presides over what is, in certain aspects, almost a parallel Cabinet concerned with home affairs. Of this body a number of Ministers of Cabinet rank are regular members, and others are invited as may be convenient. An immense mass of business is discharged at their frequent meetings, and it is only in the case of a serious difference or in very large questions that the War Cabinet as such is concerned. The Minister of State,[3] who will soon be returning from Cairo, has, as his sphere of superintendence, the whole process of production in

[1] Clement Attlee.
[2] Sir John Anderson.
[3] Oliver Lyttelton.

all its aspects. The White Paper which has been issued upon this subject is superseded and withdrawn, and I am not sure that the new arrangements will require to be defined so formally in a paper constitution. In these circumstances the Supplementary Estimate which was presented on 17th February for the purpose of asking this House to give financial effect to the arrangements set out in the White Paper of 10th February is no longer appropriate, and accordingly it is proposed, with the permission of the House, not to proceed with that Estimate. While the new revised arrangements now contemplated are taking shape, we shall arrange and see what are the best plans, financial and otherwise, appropriate to the altered circumstances. The special spheres of the remaining members of the War Cabinet are defined by the offices they hold.

My right hon. Friend the former Minister without Portfolio,[1] who has played a fine part in all affairs connected with this war, was busy with future plans for post-war reconstruction. The reduction in the size of the War Cabinet, which was held to be desirable in many quarters, has led to the elimination of this office. I must ask the House for a certain amount of time, though there will be no delay, before I am able to submit a scheme for this essential task of preparation for reconstruction. Even though we must now prepare ourselves for an evident prolongation of the war through the intervention of Japan, the whole of this preparatory work, of this preliminary work, for the post-war period must go forward, because no one can be sure that, as in the last war, victory may not come unexpectedly upon us. The seven members of the War Cabinet can sit together either as the War Cabinet of the United Kingdom of Great Britain and Northern Ireland, responsible to the Crown and to Parliament, or they can sit in a larger gathering with representatives from the Dominions and India. Both series of meetings will continue regularly, as before.

The Pacific War Council has also come into being, on which the representatives of the Dominions specially concerned, namely, Australia and New Zealand, of India and of the Netherlands, sit under my chairmanship or under that of my Deputy, the Dominions Secretary.[2] I am very glad to say that Generalissimo Chiang Kai-shek has just accepted an

---

[1] Arthur Greenwood, 1880–1954. Lecturer in Economics, Leeds University, and Chairman of the Yorkshire District Workers' Educational Association. Assistant Secretary, Ministry of Reconstruction, 1917–19. Labour MP for Nelson and Colne, 1922–31; for Wakefield, 1932–54. Parliamentary Secretary, Ministry of Health, 1924. Minister of Health, 1929–31. Privy Councillor, 1929; Deputy Leader of the Labour Party, 1935. Member of the War Cabinet, as Minister without Portfolio, 1940–2. Leader of the Opposition in the House of Commons, 1942–5. Lord Privy Seal, 1945–7. Chairman of the Labour Party, 1952.

[2] Viscount Cranborne.

invitation which I tendered him that a representative of China should join this Council. I recently explained to the House the relation of this body to the Chiefs of Staff Committee in London and the relation of both of these bodies to the combined Chiefs of Staff Committee in Washington. I can only say that all this inevitably complicated machinery, where many are concerned and oceans divide, is working swiftly and smoothly. The results, as I will presently explain, depend upon factors far more potent and massive than any machinery, however well devised, which we can immediately bring into being.

I will now, with the permission of the House, speak a little about my own part in it. At the time when I was called upon by the King to form the present Government we were in the throes of the German invasion of France and the Low Countries. I did not expect to be called upon to act as Leader of the House of Commons. I, therefore, sought His Majesty's permission to create and assume the style or title of Minister of Defence, because obviously the position of Prime Minister in war is inseparable from the general supervision of its conduct and the final responsibility for its result. I intended at that time that Mr Neville Chamberlain should become Leader of the House and take the whole of the House of Commons work off my hands. This proposal was not found to be acceptable. I had myself to take the leadership of the House as well as my other duties. I must admit that this Parliamentary task has weighed upon me heavily. During the period for which I have been responsible I find to my horror that I have made more than 25 lengthy speeches to Parliament in Public or in Secret Session, to say nothing of answering a great number of Questions and dealing with many current emergencies. I have greatly valued the honour of leading the House, which my father[1] did before me, and in which my public life has been spent for so long, and I have always taken the greatest trouble to give them the best possible service, and even in very rough periods I have taken most particular care of their rights and interests.

Although I feel a great sense of relief in laying down this burden, I cannot say that I do so without sorrow. I am sure, however, it is in the public interest, and I am also sure that my right hon. and learned Friend the Member for East Bristol (Sir S. Cripps), the new Lord Privy Seal, will prove to the House that he is a respecter of its authority and a leader capable of dealing with all the incidents, episodes and emergencies of

[1] Lord Randolph Henry Spencer Churchill, 1849–95. Third son of the 7th Duke of Marlborough. Secretary of State for India, 1885–6. Appointed Leader of the House of Commons and Chancellor of the Exchequer, June 1886. Resigned in December 1886 and received no further political office.

House of Commons and Parliamentary life. I shall, of course, as Prime Minister, remain always at the service of the House should the occasion require it, and I shall hope, from time to time, though I trust not too often, to seek their permission to give them a general appreciation of the progress of the war.

Let me now speak of the office, or title, which I hold as Minister of Defence. About this there seem to be many misunderstandings. Perhaps the House will bear with me while I explain the method by which the war has been and will be conducted. I may say, first of all, that there is nothing which I do or have done as Minister of Defence which I could not do as Prime Minister. As Prime Minister, I am able to deal easily and smoothly with the three Service Departments, without prejudice to the constitutional responsibilities of the Secretaries of State for War and Air and the First Lord of the Admiralty. I have not, therefore, found the need of defining formally or precisely the relationship between the office of Minister of Defence when held by a Prime Minister and the three Service Departments. I have not found it necessary to define this relationship as would be necessary in the case of any Minister of Defence who was not also Prime Minister. There is, of course, no Ministry of Defence, and the three Service Departments remain autonomous. For the purpose of maintaining general supervision over the conduct of the war, which I do under the authority of the War Cabinet and the Defence Committee, I have at my disposal a small staff, headed by Major-General Ismay, which works under the long-established procedure and machinery of the pre-war Committee of Imperial Defence and forms a part of the War Cabinet secretariat.

While, as I have said, I take constitutional responsibility for everything that is done or not done, and am quite ready to take the blame when things go wrong – as they very often do, and as they are very likely to do in future in many ways – I do not, of course, conduct this war from day to day myself; it is conducted from day to day, and in its future outlook, by the Chiefs of Staff Committee, namely, the First Sea Lord, the Chief of the Imperial General Staff, and the Chief of the Air Staff. These officers sit together every day, and often twice a day. They give executive directions and orders to the commanders-in-chief in the various theatres. They advise me, they advise the Defence Committee and the War Cabinet, on large questions of war strategy and war policy. I am represented on the Chiefs of Staff Committee by Major-General Ismay, who is responsible for keeping the War Cabinet and myself informed on all matters requiring higher decision. On account of the immense scope and complexity of the task, when fighting is going on literally all over the world, and when strategy and supply are so closely intermingled, the Chiefs of Staff Committee are assisted by a Vice-Chiefs of Staff Committee, which relieves them of a great mass of important questions of a secondary order. At the disposal of the Chiefs of Staff Committee and of the Vice-Chiefs Committee are the Joint Planning staffs and Joint Intelligence staffs of the three Services, consisting of specially-selected officers. In addition, there are the three General Staffs of the Army, Navy and Air Force, between whom constant collaboration proceeds at all levels where combined operations are involved. I think it necessary to put this matter in some detail before the House, because, although it sounds complicated, it is necessary to understand it.

Each of the three Chiefs of Staff has, it must be remembered, the professional executive control of the Service he represents. When, therefore, they meet together, they are not talking in vacuum, or in theory. They meet together in a position to take immediate and responsible action, in which each can carry out his share, either singly or in combination. I do not think there has ever been a system in which the professional heads of the Fighting Services have had a freer hand or a greater or more direct influence or have received more constant and harmonious support from the Prime Minister and the Cabinet under whom they serve. It is my practice to leave the Chiefs of Staff alone to do their own work, subject to my general supervision, suggestion and guidance. For instance, in 1941, out of 462 meetings of the Chiefs of Staff Committee, most of them lasting over two hours, I presided at only 44 myself. In addition, however, there are, of course, the meetings of the Defence Committee, at which the Service Ministers are present, as well as other Ministerial members, and there are the Cabinet meetings at which the Chiefs of Staff are present when military matters are discussed. In my absence from this country, or should I be at any time incapacitated, my Deputy has acted and will act for me.

Such is the machinery which, as Prime Minister and Minister of Defence, I have partly elaborated and partly brought into existence. I am satisfied that it is the best that can be devised to meet the extraordinary difficulties and dangers through which we are passing. There is absolutely no question of making any change in it of a serious or fundamental character as long as I retain the confidence of the House and the country. However tempting it might be to some when much trouble lies ahead to step aside adroitly and put someone else up to take the blows, the heavy and repeated blows, which are coming, I do not intend to adopt that cowardly course, but, on the contrary, to stand to my post and persevere in accordance with my duty as I see it.

I now turn to the general situation of the war. It had always been my hope that the United States would enter the war against Germany without Japan being immediately involved on the other side. The greatest forbearance was shown by both the English-speaking countries in the face of constant Japanese encroachments. These efforts proved vain; and, at a moment fixed by the war leaders in Japan, the sudden violent attacks were made upon Hawaii, the Philippines, the Dutch East Indies, and Malaya. Thereupon, an entirely new situation supervened. The conversion of the giant power of the United States to war purposes is only in its early stage and the disaster at Pearl Harbour and our own naval losses have given Japan for the time being – but only for the time being – the command of, or, at least, the superiority in, the Far Eastern seas.

Great Britain and the British Empire were engaged almost to their full strength, in their powers and in their equipment, with Germany in the Atlantic, with Germany as a potential invader and with Germany and Italy in the Libyan Desert, which protects Egypt and the Suez Canal. The shipping to nourish the large Armies we had in the Middle East has to go round the Cape and, as I said the other day, can make only three voyages in the year. Our shipping losses since the war began have been very heavy. In the last few months there has been a most serious increase in shipping losses, and our anti-U-boat flotillas and naval light forces of all kinds have been and are strained to the utmost limit, by the need of bringing in the food by which we live and the materials for the munitions with which we fight and the convoys which carry our troops so continually and in such great numbers to the various seats of war.

In addition to these actual burdens and perils, there remains the front, from the Levant to the Caspian, covering the approaches to India from the West, as well as the most important oilfields of Baku and Persia. A few months ago it seemed that this theatre would become dominant in our thoughts. At the same time, a heavy invasion enterprise was mounted by the enemy against Egypt. The extraordinary successes of the valiant Russian Armies, whose prowess we all honoured yesterday, has given us a breathing-space in both directions. As lately as October and November we were not only fully extended but, indeed, over-stretched, and I cannot imagine what our position would have been if we had yielded to the pressure which at one time was so vehement to open a new front in France or in the Low Countries.

Mr Gallacher (Fife, West): You would be in a strong position now.

The Prime Minister: Upon this situation, which I have so very briefly outlined to the House, there suddenly came the impact of Japan, a new combatant, long scheming and preparing, with a warlike population of 80,000,000, several millions of trained soldiers and a vast amount of modern material. This mighty impact fell upon our wide, prosperous but lightly-defended possessions and establishments throughout the Far East, all of which had, rightly, been kept at the very lowest level on account of the imperative requirements of the European and African theatres. I saw that some gentlemen who escaped from Penang announced to the world with much indignation that there was not a single anti-aircraft gun in the place. Where should we have been, I would like to know, if we had spread our limited anti-aircraft guns throughout the immense, innumerable regions and vulnerable points of the Far East instead of using them to preserve the vital life of our ports and factories here and of our fortresses which were under continuous attack and all our operations with the field Armies in the Middle East?

The House and the nation must face the blunt and brutal fact that if, having entered a war, yourself ill-prepared, you are struggling for life with two well-armed countries, one of them possessing the most powerful military machine in the world, and, then, at the moment when you are in full grapple, a third major antagonist with far larger military forces than you possess suddenly springs upon your comparatively undefended back, obviously your task is heavy and your immediate experiences will be disagreeable. From the moment that Japan attacked, we set in motion to the Far East naval forces, aircraft, troops and equipment on a scale limited only by the available shipping. All these forces and supplies were diverted from or came from theatres which already needed them, and both our margin of safety and the advance of our operations have been notably, though not, I trust, decisively, affected.

Before I left for the United States early in December most of the principal orders had been given, and in fact we managed to reinforce Singapore by over 40,000 men, together with large quantities of anti-aircraft and anti-tank artillery, all of which were withdrawn, as I have said, from other points where they were sorely needed or even actively engaged. This was especially true in regard to modern aircraft. Unfortunately, before enough of these latter could arrive in the Malay Peninsula, although there was no delay in giving orders and many daring expedients were adopted by the commanders, before they arrived in the Malay Peninsula, the airfields in Singapore Island were already under the fire of the Japanese artillery from Johore, from which we had been driven out. We were not therefore able to repeat the air fighting from an island base which has been so remarkable a feature of the prolonged defence of Malta, now under increasingly severe attack. Nevertheless, the speedy reinforcement of Singapore by no less than nine convoys would be judged a splendid achievement if the resultant defence had been crowned with success.

I have no news whatever from Singapore to give to the House. I have no information with which I can supplement such accounts – very scanty – as have appeared in the newspapers. I am therefore unable to make any statement about it, and for that reason, as I have no material for going into details, I do not propose to ask the House to go into Secret Session, and this Debate will be conducted throughout in public. I will, however, say this: Singapore was, of course, a naval base rather than a fortress. It depended upon the command of the sea, which again depends upon the command of the air. Its permanent fortifications and batteries were constructed from a naval point of view. The various defence lines which had been constructed in Johore were not successfully held. The field works constructed upon the island itself to defend the fortress were not upon a sufficiently large scale. I shall certainly not attempt at this stage to pass any judgment upon our troops or their commanders, 73,000 of whom are stated by the enemy to be prisoners of war – certainly larger numbers than that were in the fortress at the time of the attack. I shall not attempt, I say, to pass judgment. I think it would be a very unseasonable moment and a very ungracious task. We have more urgent work to do. We have to face the situation resulting from this great loss of the base, and the troops, and of the equipment, of a whole Army. We have to face the situation resulting from that and from the great new Japanese war which has burst upon us.

There is little more that I can usefully say at this juncture upon the progress of the general war. Certainly it would be very foolish to try and prophesy its immediate future. It is estimated that there are 26 Japanese divisions in the ABDA area, as it has been called, and we must remember that these divisions can be moved and supplied with far less tonnage, at far less expense, than is the case where European or United States troops are concerned. We have not so many. In the ABDA area I have mentioned the enemy have for the time being a waning command of the sea. They have the command of the air, which makes it costly and difficult for our air reinforcements to establish themselves and secure dominance. They are in many cases destroyed upon the ground before they can effectively come into action. We must, therefore, expect many hard and adverse experiences, which will be all the more difficult to bear because they are unaccompanied by the same sense of imminent national, domestic danger – that feeling of being in the business ourselves – which brought out all the best qualities of our people a year and a half ago.

If I were to dilate upon our hopes, these might soon be falsified, and I might be mocked by those who prove themselves wise by our failures. If, on the other hand, I painted the picture in its darkest hues, very great despondency might be spread among our ardent and growing Forces, and the enemy might be encouraged. I therefore say no more at this moment. Moreover, although it does not necessarily rest with me to do more than offer an opinion, I would deprecate a long series of speeches in the House censuring or explaining in detail the many tragedies which are occurring in the Far East, and I am not sure that we can afford to indulge ourselves too freely, having regard to the perils that beset us and to the ears that listen. On the other hand, if we look forward across the considerable period of immediate punishment through which we must make our way in consequence of the sudden onslaught of Japan – if we look forward through that and across that to the broad and major aspects of the war – we can see very clearly that our position has been enormously improved, not only in the last two years but in the last few months. This improvement is due, of course, to the wonderful strength and power of Russia and to the accession of the United States, with its measureless resources, to the common cause. Our position is in fact improved beyond any measure which the most sanguine would have dared to predict.

Beyond this phase of tribulation, which may be shorter or longer in accordance with our exertions and behaviour, there arises the prospect of ultimate victory for Britain, for the United States, for Russia and China, and indeed, for all the United Nations – victory complete over the foes that have fallen upon them. The ordeal through which we have to pass will be tormenting and protracted, but if everyone bends to the task with unrelenting effort and unconquerable resolve, if we do not weary by the way or fall out among ourselves or fail our Allies, we have a right to look forward across a good many months of sorrow and suffering to a sober and reasonable prospect of complete and final victory.

I will venture to end by repeating to the House the very words I used myself when I resigned from Mr Asquith's Government on 15th November 1915.[1] I apologise for quoting myself, but I have found comfort in

---

[1] Excluded in November 1915, for the first time since the outbreak of war, from the inner councils of war direction, Churchill resigned as Chancellor of the Duchy of Lancaster, and went to France, where for five months he commanded an infantry battalion on the Western Front.

reading them because of the occasion, because of what happened and because of our own position now. I said:

'There is no reason to be discouraged about the progress of the war. We are passing through a bad time now and it will probably be worse before it is better, but that it will be better, if we only endure and persevere, I have no doubt whatever. The old wars were decided by their episodes rather than by their tendencies. In this war the tendencies are far more important than the episodes. Without winning any sensational victories we may win this war. We may win it even during the continuance of extremely disappointing and vexatious events. It is not necessary for us, in order to win the war, to push the German lines back over all the territory they have absorbed or to pierce them. While the German lines extend far beyond their frontiers, while their flag flies over conquered capitals and subjugated provinces, while all the appearances of military success attend their arms, Germany may be defeated more fatally in the second or third year of the war than if the Allied army had entered Berlin in the first.'

Actually, as we now know, Germany was not defeated until the fifth year of the last war, and we are already far advanced into the third year of this present struggle, but, excepting in this respect, provided that you add Japan to Germany in each case, I find comfort in this passage which comes back to me like an echo from the past, and I commend it respectfully to the consideration of the House.

Winston S. Churchill to Ismet Inönü
(Churchill papers, 20/53)

24 February 1942

My dear Excellency,

Availing myself of the safe hand of the retiring Turkish Ambassador in London[1] who, in this capacity and as former Minister for Foreign Affairs, has served the interests of our two countries so wisely and so wholeheartedly, I take this opportunity to convey to Your Excellency my sincerest wishes for your own health and happiness and the prosperity and well-being of your country.

---

[1] Tevfik Rüstü Aras, 1883–1972. Born in Canakkale (Dardanelles). Graduated from the medical school in Beirut. A doctor in Ottoman Turkey, and a member of the Turkish Committee of Union and Progress. One of the founders of the Communist Party of Turkey, 1920. Member of the Turkish Parliament for Izmir, 1923–39. Minister of Foreign Affairs, 1929–37. Turkish Ambassador in London, 1939–42.

Fortune is never constant in war and today, as once before in the present conflict, we are passing through grim times. But when I look round and contemplate the prospect I am filled with confidence. We are not alone. We have staunch friends and allies and not the least amongst them is Turkey. I have been impressed by the firm and sagacious policy which Your Excellency, your Government and your warrior nation are pursuing: I have noted your resolution, to resist anyone who seeks to pass through your territory or violate your neutrality, a resolution expressed not merely in words but in positive acts of military preparation, and I am greatly heartened. I see in Turkey a barrier defended by stout hearts ready to withstand and hurl back the Nazi aggressor. I recall that in the dark days of 1940, when we faced peril immeasurably greater than that of today, there was no loosening in the bonds that bound our two countries together, for Turkey, as Your Excellency put it if I recollect aright, was no mere fair weather friend of this country. This loyalty and faith in our cause is an inestimable asset to our strength and I can assure you, Mr President, that my faith in Turkey grows stronger as each day she shows some new sign of her resolution in the face of peril.

No thoughtful man can doubt how this war is going to end and that the Germans are going to have a worse defeat than last time. When it will end is a more difficult question. It cannot, however, be supposed that Great Britain, the United States and the other United Nations will be exhausted by a prolonged struggle. On the contrary, in the coming years they will for the first time be thoroughly armed and marshalled for war, whereas those aggressor nations who started fully armed will not be able to increase their present effort. Then it will be that what is for the present a vision of the future will become reality. The world at last will be relieved from fear and brutal tyranny and the nations free to develop their lives in peace and security each according to its own genius.

Yours sincerely,
Winston S. Churchill

Winston S. Churchill to President Franklin D. Roosevelt
(Churchill papers, 20/70)

24 February 1942
No. 32

Warmest congratulations on your heartening declaration.[1]

[1] One of Roosevelt's 'fireside chats': a series of 30 evening radio broadcasts to the American people between 1933 and 1944. This one, given on 23 February 1942, to commemorate George Washington's birthday (on February 22), was one of Roosevelt's finest war speeches, including the words: 'Those

Note of a dinner conversation
(A. J. P. Taylor, 'Beaverbrook', page 517)

24 February 1942

Churchill and Beaverbrook met for dinner on 24 February. According to Beaverbrook's written account made at the time, Churchill again asked whether Beaverbrook would go to Washington. Beaverbrook said that he would, but as Churchill's personal representative and not to interfere with the organizations there. Churchill then said: 'I did not want you to leave the Government. Come back if you want to'. Beaverbrook: 'Let us leave things as they are'. Churchill went on that neither Attlee nor Bevin wanted to exclude Beaverbrook: 'I have assured them that you will not attack them'. Nor had Cripps raised any objections to Beaverbrook. Beaverbrook remained stubborn. On parting Churchill said 'We will gain in tranquillity but we will lose in activity.'

Sir Reginald Dorman-Smith to Winston S. Churchill
(Churchill papers, 20/88)

24 February 1942   Rangoon
6.30 p.m.

No important change, but if we can get Australians here we might effect radical change for the better. Obviously, it will be anxious business getting them, but I feel it is a risk well worth taking, as otherwise Burma is wide open for Japanese. Some of our troops scouting back across Sittang.

Sir Reginald Dorman-Smith to Winston S. Churchill
(Churchill papers, 20/88)

25 February 1942   Rangoon
11.20 p.m.

It is infinitely important to us to know whether Australian division will arrive. Please say yes or no.[1]

Americans who believe that we could live under the illusion of isolationism wanted the American eagle to imitate the tactics of the ostrich. Now, many of those same people, afraid that we may be sticking our necks out, want our national bird to be turned into a turtle. But we prefer to retain the eagle as it is – flying high and striking hard.' Roosevelt ended his broadcast: 'Tyranny, like hell, is not easily conquered; yet we have this consolation with us, that the harder the sacrifice, the more glorious the triumph.'

[1] Churchill sent copies of this telegram and Dorman-Smith's previous telegram to the Australian Prime Minister, John Curtin, with the note: 'I have of course informed the Governor of your decision' (*Churchill papers, 20/70*).

Winston S. Churchill to Sir Reginald Dorman-Smith
(Churchill papers, 20/70)

25 February 1942
Clear the Line
Personal and Secret

We have made every appeal, reinforced by President, but Australian Government absolutely refuses. Fight on.

War Cabinet: Confidential Annex
(Cabinet papers, 65/29)

25 February 1942
12 noon

The Chief of the Air Staff said at the present moment our Hurricane production was insufficient to meet the requirements of Russia and the Middle East. As a result our Hurricane squadrons in this country were already wasting.

Having regard to the information received as to the scale of Russian production of operational aircraft, it was to be doubted whether the Russians really attached much value to the monthly deliveries of fighter aircraft which we were making to them.

The Foreign Secretary said that he was afraid that this suggestion would create grave suspicion in the mind of the Russians, who would think that it was the beginning of a general falling off in our deliveries to them.

The Prime Minister said that, while he appreciated the view put forward by the Chiefs of Staff, he felt no doubt in his own mind that it was essential that there should be no interference with our supplies of Hurricane aircraft to Russia. He thought it was of importance that we should be in a position to state categorically and without qualification that we had punctually fulfilled our bargain in this matter.

General agreement was expressed with this view.

This led to some discussion on the position in the Middle East.

The Prime Minister said that we had been compelled to denude the Caspian–Levant front in order to reinforce the Far East; and, owing to shipping limitations, it was beyond our power to send sufficient re-inforcements to that area to stop a German break through.

The Foreign Secretary said that it seemed to him strategically unsound that we should be withdrawing troops from this vital area, where they could be used to support Turkey, and sending them to Australia, which was the area which the United States could most easily re-inforce.

The Prime Minister said that he was in agreement with this view, and proposed to take the matter up at a suitable opportunity with President Roosevelt, on broad, simple lines.

Winston S. Churchill to Sir Archibald Sinclair and
Air Chief Marshal Sir Charles Portal
(Churchill papers, 20/67)

26 February 1942
Secret

It is thought in many quarters that the Air news and propaganda defeats itself by the excessive recording of ordinary routine fighting. Many people turn off the wireless when the Air news is reached. There is perhaps an inevitable sameness about it, and one cannot see the wood for the trees. It is a pity, because fine exploits and exceptional occurrences do not always receive the distinction and attention which they deserve.

2. You would be well advised to adopt a much more highly selective process not only in the communiqués and on the broadcast, but in the reports made to the Cabinet. It has never been thought necessary to give an exact list of ordinary trench raids or skirmishes on the fronts of large armies. Fighting of a normal character in the different theatres should surely be summarised once a week, e.g., Malta has had a hard week (or a busy week) in the Air, so many sorties have been made, and so many enemy shot down, &c., instead of a daily laborious catalogue. If this were done, any event like 20 or 30 enemy aircraft being bowled over would make the right impression on the public. As it is, the Air Ministry's fine tale runs the risk of becoming a bore instead of an inspiration. Monotonous repetition should at all costs be avoided.

Winston S. Churchill to Sir Archibald Sinclair and
Air Chief Marshal Sir Charles Portal
(Churchill papers, 20/67)

26 February 1942

I am informed that many air accidents and failures to reach targets in bombing may be attributed to delay in obtaining the latest form of oxygen mask, for which orders were placed many months ago. Pray let me have the facts. If they are as stated, the question of expediting supplies should be taken up immediately.

Winston S. Churchill to General Claude Auchinleck
(Churchill papers, 20/70)

26 February 1942
Personal
No. 164

I have not troubled you much in these difficult days but I must now ask what are your intentions. According to our figures you have substantial superiority in the air, in armour and in other forces over the enemy. There seems to be danger that he may gain reinforcements as fast as or even faster than you. The supply of Malta is causing us increasing anxiety, and anyone can see the magnitude of our disasters in the Far East.

Pray let me hear from you. All good wishes.

General Claude Auchinleck to Winston S. Churchill
(Churchill papers, 20/70)

26 February 1942
Most Immediate
Personal and Most Secret

Very many thanks for your 164 (repeat 164).

Have refrained from bothering you till situation became clearer which it has now done. Have prepared draft appreciation which hope to telegraph to you tomorrow. Meanwhile instructions issued by me for action by 8th Army with maps showing present dispositions have been sent by air to CIGS.

Winston S. Churchill to General Archibald Wavell
(Churchill papers, 20/70)

26 February 1942
Personal and Secret

Pray consider whether key situation Ceylon does not require a first rate soldier in supreme command of all local services including civil government, and whether Pownall is not the man.[1] We do not want to have another Singapore.

---

[1] In March 1942, when Ceylon was the last remaining major source of natural rubber in Allied hands, Vice-Admiral Geoffrey Layton was appointed Commander-in-Chief, Ceylon, with powers over civilians and military alike, and with authority over the Governor, Sir Andrew Caldecott. General Pownall remained General Officer Commanding Forces in Ceylon.

Winston S. Churchill to Sir Samuel Hoare
(Churchill papers, 20/70)

26 February 1942
Personal and Secret

Government changes will I hope relieve special difficulties under which you suffer. There is no remedy for the rest but Victory, which will be long delayed but which is much more sure than when you went to Spain. Everyone must hold on.

Winston S. Churchill to Air Vice-Marshal Paul Maltby[1]
(Churchill papers, 20/71)

26 February 1942
Personal

I send you and all ranks of the British forces who have stayed behind in Java my best wishes for success and honour in the great fight that confronts you. Every day gained is precious, and I know that you will do everything humanly possible to prolong the battle.

Mary Churchill: diary
(Lady Soames papers)

26 February 1942

Home evening. Papa weary & sad. Mummie tired.

Lord Beaverbrook to Winston S. Churchill
(Churchill papers, 20/52)

26 February 1942
My dear Winston,

I am leaving this office today and going to the place I came from. And now I must tell you about twenty-one months of high adventure, the like of which has never been known.

---

[1] Paul (Copeland) Maltby, 1892–1971. Royal Welch Fusiliers, serving in India, 1911–14. Royal Flying Corps, France, 1915–18 (DSO, 1917). Royal Air Force, India, 1919–24. Commandant, Central Flying School (UK), 1932–4. Air Officer Commanding, RAF Mediterranean, 1935–8; 24 (Training) Group, UK, 1938–40; 71 Group, 1940–1; RAF Java, 1942. His elder son was killed in action in 1945. Serjeant-at-Arms, House of Lords, 1946–62.

All the time everything that has been done by me has been due to your holding me up.

You took a great chance in putting me in, and you stood to be shot at by a section of Members for keeping me here.

It was little enough I gave you compared with what you gave me. I owe my reputation to you. The confidence of the public really comes from you. And my courage was sustained by you. These benefits give me a right to a place in your list of lieutenants who served you when you brought salvation to our people in the hour of disaster.

In leaving, then, I send this letter of gratitude and devotion to the leader of the nation, the saviour of our people, and the symbol of resistance in the free world.

Yours affectionately,
Max

Winston S. Churchill to Lord Beaverbrook
(Churchill papers, 20/52)

27 February 1942

Thank you for all you say in yr splendid letter wh is a vy gt comfort & encouragement to me.

We have lived & fought side by side through terrible days, & I am sure our comradeship & public work will undergo no break. All I want you to do now is to recover yr strength & poise, so as to be able to come to my aid when I shall vy greatly need you.

Yr work during the crisis at MAP[1] in 1940 played a decisive part in our salvation. You shaped the Russian policy upon munitions [which] is all we can do for them. The figures of the Ministry of Supply[2] speak for themselves. You are one of our few fighting men of genius.

I am always your affectionate friend.

[1] Ministry of Aircraft Production, where Beaverbrook was the Minister from 2 August 1940 to 1 May 1941.
[2] Beaverbrook was Minister of Supply from 29 June 1941 to 4 February 1942.

Winston S. Churchill to James Stuart[1]
(Churchill papers, 20/66)

27 February 1942

QUINTIN HOGG[2]

He has been wounded [which] I regard as a high qualification in an MP.[3]

Winston S. Churchill to Sir Edward Bridges[4]
(Churchill papers, 20/67)

27 February 1942   Ditchley Park[5]

The Cabinet arrangements for next week should be as follows:

1. Monday, 5.30 p.m. at No. 10. General parade of the constant attenders, the Chiefs of the Staff and the Dominions and Indian representatives. Business: the general war situation, without reference to special secret matters such as forthcoming operations; and any other appropriate topics.

2. Tuesday, 6 p.m. at No. 10. Pacific Council.

3. Wednesday, 12 noon at House of Commons. War Cabinet only with yourself. We summon anyone we need for particular points.

4. Thursday, 12 noon at House of Commons. War Cabinet. (On both Wednesday and Thursday, if the business requires it, another meeting will be held at 6 p.m.).

5. Wednesday, 10 p.m. Defence Committee. This will consist of the Chiefs of the Staff, Service Ministers, India and Dominions if and as required, myself, the Deputy Prime Minister and the Foreign Secretary and probably Mr Oliver Lyttelton.

Let us see how this works.

[1] The Government Chief Whip.

[2] Quintin Hogg, 1907–2001. Barrister, Lincoln's Inn, 1932. Conservative MP for Oxford, 1938–50. On active service, 1939–45. Succeeded his father as 2nd Viscount Hailsham, 1950. First Lord of the Admiralty, 1956–7. Minister of Science and Technology, 1959–64. Disclaimed his peerage for life, 1963. Conservative MP, 1963–70. Secretary of State for Education and Science, 1964. Lord Chancellor, 1970–4, 1979–87 (his father, Secretary of State for War in 1931–5, had been Lord Chancellor in 1928–9 and 1935–8). Created Baron, 1970. Chancellor, University of Buckingham, 1983–92. Knight of the Garter, 1988.

[3] In August 1941, while serving as a Captain in the Rifle Brigade in the Western Desert, Quintin Hogg was wounded in the knee; the wound almost cost him his right leg.

[4] Edward Bridges, 1892–1969. Son of the Poet Laureate Robert Bridges. On active service, 1914–18 (Military Cross). Served in the Treasury, 1919–39. Secretary to the Cabinet, 1938–46. Knighted, 1939. Permanent Secretary, Treasury, 1945–56. Created Baron, 1957. Knight of the Garter, 1965.

[5] Ditchley Park, a country house north-west of Oxford, owned by Churchill's friend Ronald Tree, MP. The house was used by Churchill on wartime weekends when there was a full moon, when Chequers was considered vulnerable to German air attack.

Peter Fraser to Winston S. Churchill
(Churchill papers, 20/71)

27 February 1942
Most Secret, Personal

Major-General Puttick (NZ)[1] has just shown me a personal telegram he has received from the New Zealand Liaison Officer in London from which it appears that the joint planning commission in London, in considering the possible scale of attack on New Zealand, estimate it at 'sporadic raids by enemy cruisers and aircraft carriers' if Fiji and New Caledonia are held by us, and if Fiji and New Caledonia are lost, at 'one Brigade group with naval and air support'.

Candidly I must tell you that my colleagues and I are appalled by this attempt to think in terms of the past and if this line of thought is persisted in we must brace ourselves to meet the fate of Malaya and with infinite less reason or excuse. To suggest, as we must assume is the case, that an attack by a brigade group is all that New Zealand should prepare to meet seems to us to be unreal and dangerous to the last degree and we do beg you to ensure that if this kind of appreciation is to be laid before the Pacific War Council, it be accompanied by our very strongest protest and our most pointed reference to the appreciation contained in my telegram 91 of the 17th February which was and is fully concurred in by the NZ Chiefs of Staff.

[...]

If our Air Forces could attain a strength sufficient to be considerably superior, at or near to point of attack, to Jap Air Force of 4 carriers plus aircraft from warships then again invasion would appear to be improbable. But while these conditions are unfulfilled and while at the same time our land forces are only partially trained and are deficient in many important items of modern equipment I regard the scale of attack against which NZ must prepare and in fact is preparing is one Division supported by strong Naval Forces including 4 Aircraft Carriers and followed by a second division with reinforcing aircraft ferried by carriers.

---

[1] Edward Puttick, 1890–1976. A New Zealander, he served in the First World War in Samoa, Egypt, France, and Belgium (severely wounded, DSO). Commanded 4th New Zealand Infantry Brigade, New Zealand Expeditionary Force, Egypt, 1940–1; Greece, 1941. Commanded New Zealand Forces on Crete, May 1941. Major-General, 1941. Chief of the New Zealand General Staff, 1941–5. Lieutenant-General, 1942. General Officer Commanding New Zealand Forces, 1942–5. Knighted, 1946. Commanded the New Zealand contingent at the Victory March in London, 1946.

General Claude Auchinleck to Winston S. Churchill
(Churchill papers, 20/71)

27 February 1942   Cairo
Personal and Most Secret

To sum up my intentions for western front are:

1. To continue to build up armoured striking force in 8th Army forward area as rapidly as possible.

2. Meanwhile to make Gazala–Tobruk and Salum–Maddalena positions strong as possible and push railway forward towards El-Adem.

3. To build up in forward area reserves of supplies for renewal of offensive.

4. To seize first chance of staging limited offensive to regain landing grounds in area Derna–Mechili provided this can be done without prejudicing chances of launching major offensive to recapture Cyrenaica or safety of Tobruk area.

[...]

16. Am exploring all possibilities of releasing troops of all categories for duty in forward areas. Hope to secure services of brigade Sudanese troops and am pushing on with formation of garrison companies for guards and duties from labour units. Every use too will be made local levies in 9th and 10th Armies areas.

Winston S. Churchill to President Franklin D. Roosevelt
(Churchill papers, 20/71)

27 February 1942
No. 33

United Nations Declaration. I believe that a number of foreign individuals, organisations, or groups have recently told the United States Government, and in some cases they have told us as well, of their wish to accede to the United Nations Declaration as 'appropriate authorities' within the terms of the statement issued by the United States Government on January 6th. You will remember that this statement was devised for the Free French. Applications have been received, among others, from

Otto Strasser's[1] Free German movement, the Basque and Catalan émigré movements, King Zog[2] and the Latvian Minister at Washington.[3]

Halifax has told the State Department that the acceptance of statements of accession by these groups would be embarrassing to us and I understand that there is not in fact any question of such accessions being accepted. We may, however, shortly have to consider approaches from more welcome candidates such as Persia and Ethiopia and possibly Iraq and Saudi Arabia as well as the Free French.

2. My feeling is that it should be left to the country desiring to join to take the initiative, but that we should welcome the adherence of these particular countries. I am most anxious that you and we should keep in step and that no accession should be accepted without previous consultation between the two of us. As I understand that you are dealing personally with this question, I put my views directly to you.

3. Each particular case which arises can of course be discussed through the usual channels.

Mary Churchill: diary
(Lady Soames papers)

27 February 1942

Luncheon alone with Mummie & Papa at No. 10. Papa is at a very low ebb.

He is not too well physically – and he is worn down by continuous crushing pressure of events. He is saddened – appalled by events.

[1] Otto Johann Maximilian Strasser, 1897–1974. On active service with the German Army, 1915–18. Joined the Nazi Party, 1925; expelled for socialist tendencies, 1930. Fled to Austria, 1934 (after Hitler murdered his Nazi brother Gregor). Fled to Prague, 1938, then Switzerland, France, Portugal, and Bermuda. From 1941 in Canada, where he led a Free German movement. Denounced by Dr Goebbels as Nazi Germany's 'Public Enemy No. 1'.

[2] Ahmed Zog, 1895–1961. Son of the head of a leading Albanian clan. A Muslim. Educated in Constantinople. Fought against the Turks in 1913. On active service in the Austro-Hungarian Army, 1914–18. Albanian Minister of the Interior, 1920 and again in 1921. Commander-in-Chief of the Albanian forces, 1921. Prime Minister, 1921–4. After an attempt was made on his life, he retired with his colleagues to the mountains on the Serbian–Albanian border. Proclaimed Albania a republic, and elected President, 1925. Repressed the revolt of the northern Catholic tribes, 1926, and executed the Catholic priest who had inspired the revolt. Proclaimed King of Albania (as King Zog), 1928. Fled to Greece, 1939, after the Italian invasion; then to England. When Albania became Communist in December 1945, he went from England to Egypt, then to the United States, and finally to the South of France. He died in hospital in Paris.

[3] Alfreds Bilmanis, 1887–1948. Born in Riga, then part of the Russian Empire. Studied history at Moscow University, 1905–10. Officer in the Russian Army, 1914–17. Latvian Minister in Washington, 1935–48. In exile in the United States (where he died) after the Soviet incorporation of Latvia in 1945.

Oliver Harvey: diary
(*'The War Diaries of Oliver Harvey'*, pages 102–3)

27 February 1942

We hear that the view of the wiseacres in the lobbies is that the new Cabinet stocks are going up and those of the PM going down, and that before long the younger men, Cripps, AE and Lyttelton, will take over. Not unlikely I should say. PM does seem to be losing both grip and ground; he is exhausted by his superhuman efforts.

AE told me he would be quite happy to see Cripps at No. 10, if he himself could be Minister of Defence and run the war side. This surprised me. AE oscillates between wanting to be PM and wanting to stay where he is. I said whatever happened it was most important that he and Cripps should work together. But would the H of C agree to Cripps as PM and not a Tory? Of course if Cripps were PM now, AE could become the Tory PM later when parties divide again. But Cripps is still untried. I'm still afraid of the crank in him.

3.30 pm – AE had a long talk with Bracken early this afternoon: the PM's health was getting worse, the state of his heart was affecting his circulation and this in turn might affect his powers of coordination of thought and speech. It was essential, if he was to go on, that he should do less. He was already most depressed and said he could only go on for another month and then he would be finished.

B[1] said the only way of sparing the PM was for AE to become deputy Minister of Defence. AE was the only person in whom PM had confidence and to whom he might be persuaded to yield – he wouldn't let anyone else touch it. Would AE take it on if it were offered him and could he combine it with FO? AE said he would certainly be willing to do it and keep FO as well, but he didn't wish to press for it. He would do whatever the PM wished but he must leave it to B to put it to PM and for PM to make the first move.

[...]

We are all convinced that the PM cannot last much longer and the present is only a temporary arrangement which can at most go on for two or three months. But it will be far better than an abrupt change over.

---

[1] Brendan Bracken.

Winston S. Churchill to Josef Stalin
Cabinet papers, 20/71)

27 February 1942   Ditchley Park
Personal and Secret

The very great offensive power shown by Japan in her attacks on Malaya, Burma and the Dutch East Indies has made our situation for the time being much worse. Japan is attacking at her strongest, while the development of the far greater American power is necessarily slow. I cannot look for any marked improvement for a good many months, and meanwhile the defence of Burma and India and the maintenance of contact with China present most serious difficulties.

2. The above has led to withdrawals and diversions from the Levant–Caspian front of a decisive character. The three Australian Divisions are going home to defend their own country. The 18th British Division which was rounding the Cape was diverted to Singapore and has been captured there. The 17th British Indian Division which was to have gone from India to Persia is heavily engaged on the Burma front. The 70th British Division which was posted in Syria is moving as fast as possible to Burma and Ceylon. This leaves only 4 British-Indian Divisions, one incomplete Armoured Division spread over Syria, Palestine, Iran and Persia; that is to say only what is necessary to preserve local control and order. In addition to the troops we have had to send several hundred aeroplanes from the Middle East to Malaya, Burma and India. I feel bound to let Your Excellency know this so that you will not be counting on the forces we had hoped to place in the Levant–Caspian theatre to work in support of the left wing of the Russian Armies and to influence Turkey favourably. All this is the result of a new assault upon us by a first-class military, naval and air power when we are already fully extended elsewhere.

3. Shipping scarcity prevents the rapid movement of large reinforcements from this country. We are running monthly convoys of from forty to forty-five thousand men to the East, but the ships can only make three voyages in the year, and it will be possible to send at most three, and perhaps only two, additional divisions from home in the convoys which depart from here in March, April and May. These divisions may well be required to fight in Burma and India, and will not thus be available to replace the forces withdrawn from the Levant–Caspian area.

4. We are maintaining most strictly the monthly quotas of airplanes, tanks, etc. arranged with you at Moscow, and are taking special measures to protect the northern convoys.

5. The naval situation in the Atlantic is definitely improved, owing to the serious damage and disablement of the *Scharnhorst, Gneisenau* and *Prinz Eugen.*

6. I know that you never flinch from facing the hard facts.[1]

Winston S. Churchill to Anthony Eden
(Churchill papers, 20/67)

28 February 1942   Ditchley Park

DRAFT TELEGRAM TO STALIN[2]

My reaction is that it will be very dangerous, when announcing the total failure of effective fighting support, to make the new demand.[3] However, I have had the telegram fair-copied for consideration between us on Monday.

2. You should see the very bad telegram from Auchinleck proposing to do nothing till June. This is intolerable, and will be judged so by Stalin, Roosevelt, and everyone else.

3. I am sure it is not wise to tackle Stalin about going to war with Japan until we see what is the weight of the German spring offensive, and how he can stand up to it.

Winston S. Churchill to Sir Edward Bridges
(Churchill papers, 20/67)

28 February 1942   Ditchley Park

The India business[4] will be brought before the War Cabinet at noon on Tuesday. Thereafter, in consequence of the gravity of the decision, it will be necessary to consult certainly all the Ministers of Cabinet rank, and probably all the Under-Secretaries. Moreover, the King's assent must be obtained at an early date, as the rights of the Imperial Crown are plainly

---

[1] After Churchill had sent copies of this telegram to King George VI, General Ismay (for the Chiefs of Staff), and the Foreign Office, it was examined by the Chiefs of Staff Committee, and cancelled.

[2] On 28 February 1942 Sir Alexander Cadogan wrote in his diary: 'Found PM had sent a rather silly telegram to Stalin. Cancelled it (or held it up) and rang up A [Eden]. He agreed and I sent him down some modifications and additions' (*The Diaries of Sir Alexander Cadogan*, pages 437–8).

[3] On 1 March 1942, Sir Alexander Cadogan wrote in his diary: 'PM against asking anything of Stalin in Far East, but agrees to discuss the draft tomorrow' (*The Diaries of Sir Alexander Cadogan 1938–45*, page 439).

[4] A declaration that was to be made by the British Government about the future governance of India, and 'what answer should be given when we were asked in what way we hoped that the leaders of the principal sections of the Indian people would participate in the counsels of their country' (War Cabinet, 3 March 1942, *Cabinet papers*).

affected. You should bring this to the notice of the India Committee forthwith. The necessary meetings should be arranged during Tuesday and Wednesday.

I am favourably impressed by the draft, but we must not run the risk of a schism, and I must see the reaction upon a larger body than our present small group.

Winston S. Churchill to Brigadier Leslie Hollis
(Churchill papers, 20/67)

28 February 1942   Ditchley Park

It is a question whether, in view of the evacuation of Rangoon and the consequent restriction of the new communications, the 2nd Brigade of the 70th Division should not go to Ceylon. How soon could it get there?

2. Let me have a report about the RDF[1] installation and any proposed improvement, with dates.

3. I am relying upon the Admiralty to keep sufficient heavy ships at Trincomalee to ward off a seaborne expedition in the anxious fortnight or three weeks which must elapse before we are reinforced.

4. It will, I feel sure, be necessary for the *Indomitable* Squadrons to be off-loaded in Ceylon.

5. Let me have a list and timetable of the naval reinforcements and the building up of our fleet in the Indian Ocean during March, April and May.

Winston S. Churchill to Admiral Sir Herbert Richmond[2]
(Churchill papers, 20/59)

28 February 1942   Ditchley Park
Private and Confidential

My dear Admiral,

Thank you for your letter of February 11. I can assure you that you are not alone in your anxiety about Trincomalee. We are fully aware of the

---

[1] RDF: Radio Direction Finding (radar).

[2] Herbert W. Richmond, 1871–1946. Lieutenant, Royal Navy, 1893. Assistant Director of Naval Operations, Admiralty, 1913–15. Liaison Officer with the Italian Fleet, 1915. Commander, HMS *Commonwealth, Conqueror,* and *Erin* in the Grand Fleet, 1916–18. Director of Staff Duties and Training, Admiralty, 1918. Rear-Admiral, 1920. President of the Royal Navy War College, Greenwich, 1920–3. Commander-in-Chief, East Indies Squadron, 1924–5. Knighted, 1926. Commandant, Imperial Defence College, 1927–9. Admiral, 1929. Retired list, 1931. Author of many books on British naval history and strategy. Master of Downing College, Cambridge, 1936–46.

covetous eyes which the enemy must be casting at Ceylon. We are doing all that we can to strengthen Trincomalee as quickly as possible. No troops have been sent to New Zealand which could have gone to Ceylon.

Any help to Trincomalee must come from British sources, as distinct from Dutch, Australian or New Zealand. I cannot, therefore, see that the Pacific War Council could make much contribution to the problem.

Yours sincerely,
Winston S. Churchill

Winston S. Churchill to General Hastings Ismay
(Churchill papers, 20/67)

28 February 1942   Ditchley Park

Let me have the best estimate that can be made of the losses at sea and in aircraft sustained by the Japanese, together with the number of ships and aircraft in their possession at the outbreak of war.

There is no immediate hurry for this. A week is allowed.

Winston S. Churchill to General Hastings Ismay
(Churchill papers, 20/67)

28 February 1942   Ditchley Park

How are the supplies for Russia going through Archangel? Or is the port entirely closed?

Is there any congestion at Murmansk? Let me have a report on one sheet of paper.

Winston S. Churchill to Lord Moyne and to Brigadier Leslie Hollis,
for the Chiefs of Staff Committee
(Churchill papers, 20/63)

28 February 1942   Ditchley Park

THE DUKE OF WINDSOR[1]

The danger is of a kidnapping party from a submarine. The Germans would be very glad to get hold of the Duke and use him for their own pur-

---

[1] Edward Albert Christian George Andrew Patrick David, 1894–1972. Entered the Royal Navy as a Cadet, 1907. Prince of Wales, 1910–36. 2nd Lieutenant, Grenadier Guards, August 1914. Attached to Sir John French's Staff, November 1914. Served in France and Italy, 1914–18. Major, 1918. Succeeded his father as King Edward VIII, January 1936. Abdicated, December 1936. Duke of Windsor, 1936. At this point he was in the Bahamas, where he served as Governor for the duration of the war.

poses. In my opinion, continued protection against an attack by 50 men during darkness should be provided. Very considerable issues are involved.

Winston S. Churchill to Clement Attlee[1]
(Churchill papers, 20/67)

28 February 1942   Ditchley Park

REINVIGORATING EFFORTS IN EVERY BRANCH
OF THE ADMINISTRATION[2]

Would it not be better to be more precise? Everyone can agree they should reinvigorate their efforts, and that 'Traditional procedures which do not satisfy a rigorous test of efficiency' should be reconsidered. But what cases have you particularly in mind?

There is a lot of loose talk in the newspapers by people who lead comparatively easy lives and feel they are 'doing their bit' by representing the country as a mass of inefficiency and complacency. During the 31 months we have been at war most people have done a pretty good day's work every day, and, indeed, we have had to relax somewhat to provide for the leisure of workers and of Civil Servants.

The great thing is to find instances. I send you a cutting from *The Times* of today[3] which, if correct, is a very bad case. I should be very glad if you would find out for yourself how much truth there is in this statement which, after all, is made on the authority of 'shop Stewards,' who ought to know.

What are the 'traditional procedures' in the Admiralty, for instance, which ought to be abolished in, let us say, the Trade Protection Department? It would be a very good thing if you went and looked at one of the great Command Stations, like that at Liverpool, where the whole movement of shipping is regulated, or at one of the RAF Fighter Command centres, such as No. 11 Group at Uxbridge. This would be an easy journey from London, and you might even see Operations taking place on the 'board.'

Again, why do you not visit some of the big airplane and tank-production works, where you could see for yourself whether there was a great deal of slackness and inefficiency?

---

[1] Deputy Prime Minister

[3] Referring to a draft minute in which Sir Stafford Cripps suggested that the Prime Minister should circulate a memorandum on the need for reinvigorating efforts in every branch of the administration.

[3] 'Shop Stewards', *The Times*, 28 February 1942.

Lord Leathers could tell you much about the work which is being done at the ports. We have, in fact, in a single year halved the time taken in turning round many classes of ships.

You would, I am sure, find it very interesting to receive an account from the technical experts of all the developments which have been made in RDF in its many variants and night flying. This I can easily arrange for you.

Another series of attacks are made in the newspapers upon the Treasury, which is supposed to hamper production by insistence on 'red tape'. Here I think it would be very good if you had a talk with Sir Richard Hopkins,[1] after which you might be able to suggest some positive improvements.

Not only have people worked very hard in Britain during these 31 months, but a continued process of criticism – much of it unjust and ill-informed, but none the less stimulating, if only to rejoinder – has led to constant refinements.

There is much to be done, and many things can be done better. But mere general exhortations of the kind you suggest for a minute signed by me would not, I think, produce any effect at all.

Winston S. Churchill to Lord Woolton[2]
(Churchill papers, 20/67)

28 February 1942   Ditchley Park

I see you are reported as saying 'I am doubtful if anything short of penal servitude with the threat of flogging will frighten those people engaged in the Black Market.' I must tell you that I am entirely opposed to the use of flogging except for crimes of brutal violence. This position has been established by the evolution of British law and public opinion. Indeed, even in the cases of robbery with violence from females and weak people there is great reluctance to inflict the torture of the lash. The application of corporal punishment to cases of fraud in all its innumerable forms is wholly foreign to the humanitarian movement which characterizes our political thought. Although uninstructed persons may

---

[1] Richard Valentine Nind Hopkins, 1880–1955. Member of the Board of Inland Revenue, 1916; Chairman, 1922. Knighted, 1920. Controller of Finance and Supply Services, HM Treasury, 1927–32; Second Secretary, Treasury, 1932–42. Permanent Secretary, Treasury, 1942–5. Privy Councillor, 1945. Member of the Imperial War Graves Commission.

[2] Minister of Food.

cheer such a statement, or that which I regret to see the Solicitor-General[1] made about enforcing the death penalty, you may be quite sure that judges will not direct and juries will not convict if the penalties imposed are contrary to the ethical and social standards of the community.

2. Moreover, if flogging were used as a deterrent it would have to be applied in fact. The mere threat of it apart from its enforcement would not deter anyone. I hope therefore you will be careful not to be stampeded by the passing phases of Press agitation. The Press will be the first to desert you and leave you high and dry.

Air Vice-Marshal Maltby to Air Chief Marshal Sir Charles Portal
(Churchill papers, 20/71)

28 February 1942   Java
Important

Please convey thanks all of us to Prime Minister for his message and best wishes which all much appreciate. All will do their best to prolong the battle.[2]

Nellie Romilly[3] to Clementine Churchill
(Mary Soames, 'Clementine Churchill', page 314)

28 February 1942

[...]

These are as you say days of anguish for Winston, so full of strength & yet so impotent to stem this terrible tide from the Far East.

We must pray that the Country will show patience and constancy & then All may be Well.

---

[1] William Allen Jowitt, 1885–1957. Called to the Bar, Middle Temple, 1909; KC, 1922. Labour MP for The Hartlepools, 1922–4; for Preston, 1929–31; for Ashton-under-Lyne, 1939–45. Knighted, 1929. Privy Councillor, 1931. Solicitor General, 1940–2. Paymaster-General, 1942. Minister Without Portfolio, 1942–4. First Minister of National Insurance, 1944–5. Created Baron, 1945. Lord Chancellor, 1945–51. Created Viscount, 1947; Earl, 1951.

[2] Air Vice-Marshal Maltby, Air Officer Commanding Westgroup, Java, was taken prisoner by the Japanese in April 1942 and remained in Japanese captivity until August 1945.

[3] Nellie Hozier, 1888–1957. Clementine Churchill's sister. Served as a nurse in Belgium, 1914. Captured by the Germans in August 1914, but released almost immediately. In 1915 she married Colonel Bertram Romilly (1878–1940: Egyptian Camel Corps, 1914–17; Chief Instructor, Cairo Military School, 1925–8).

Winston S. Churchill to Lord Leathers, Lord Cherwell,
and Sir Edward Bridges
(Churchill papers, 20/67)

28 February 1942

DRAFT TELEGRAM TO PRESIDENT ROOSEVELT
ON SHIPPING NEEDS

It seems silly to invoke all this machinery, which cannot be often used, merely in order to get another 10,000 men out of 295,000 required by the end of June. The telegram should be reconceived in two parts. First, that 'Magnet' should be suspended after the present consignment have landed. Secondly, that 'Gymnast' is off for the present. Thirdly, we have great need to send another two divisions to the East besides the 5th Division going in the March WS Convoy.[1] Can he, and will he do this?

2. The second deals with our importation of food and munitions. We must know now what American ships we are going to have, month by month, till the end of the year. It is understood that the main weight of assistance cannot come till after June. We must aim at 26,000,000[2] in the calendar year 1942 as our very minimum.

3. Pray invite Mr Harriman[3] to join you on Monday, and let me have the best draft you can by Monday night, on which I will dictate either to the President or to Mr Hopkins.

---

[1] WS Convoys: convoys to the East from August 1940 to August 1943 (33 in all), via Cape of Good Hope. Known as 'Winston's Specials'. Setting off from the Clyde (Tail o' the Bank), they called at Freetown, Cape Town, Durban, Egypt, India, and, up to February 1942, had continued to Singapore.

[2] That is, 26 million Imperial deadweight tons (of imports from the United States), equivalent to 29.12 million short tons.

[3] William Averell Harriman, 1891–1986. Vice-President in Charge of Purchases and Supplies, Union Pacific Railroad, 1914–18. Chairman of the Board, Merchant Shipping Corporation, 1917–25. Chairman of the Board, Union Pacific Railroad, 1932–46. Member, Business Advisory Council, Department of Commerce, 1933–40. Division Administrator, National Recovery Administration, 1934. Roosevelt's emissary (Special Representative) in London, to negotiate Lend-Lease arrangements, March 1941. Accompanied Lord Beaverbrook on his mission to Moscow, with the rank of Ambassador, September 1941. Served on Combined Production and Resources Board, London, 1942. United States Ambassador to Moscow, 1943–6; to Britain, 1946. United States Secretary of Commerce, 1946–8. Special Assistant to President Truman, 1950–1. Chairman, NATO Commission on Defence Plans, 1951. Assistant Secretary of State, Far Eastern Affairs, 1961–3. United States negotiator, Limited Test Ban Treaty, 1963; Vietnam peace talks, Paris, 1968–9. In 1971, married Pamela Leland Hayward (Pamela Digby), Randolph Churchill's former wife.

March
1942

Winston S. Churchill to Brigadier Leslie Hollis,
for the Chiefs of Staff Committee
(Churchill papers, 20/67)

1 March 1942   Ditchley Park

GENERAL DE GAULLE'S PLAN FOR
THE CAPTURE OF MADAGASCAR[1]

I agree that Madagascar must still have a low priority.

2. Whatever happens, we must not have a mixed expedition. Either it must be Free French only, once they have been put ashore, or British Empire only.

3. I should not be in too great a hurry to reject de Gaulle's plan. Remember sixteen men took the French Cameroons.[2]

Winston S. Churchill to Air Chief Marshal Sir Charles Portal
(Churchill papers, 20/67)

1 March 1942   Ditchley Park

Let me have a note on the comparative ranges, so far as known, of Japanese and British fighter aircraft of all kinds.

---

[1] The Indian Ocean island of Madagascar had been ruled by France since 1896. In 1940 its colonial administration declared its allegiance to the Vichy Government in France. General de Gaulle proposed a military campaign to secure the island for the Free French.

[2] The Cameroons, formerly a German colonial territory, were divided in 1920 into two League of Nations Mandates, one French, one British. In June 1940 the French colonial administration of the French Cameroons declared its allegiance to Vichy. On 8 October 1940, de Gaulle's Free French Forces landed at Douala and secured the French Cameroons for the Free French. On 27 October, Free French forces crossed into Vichy-ruled French Equatorial Africa; on 12 November the Vichy forces capitulated.

We are repeatedly reading about long-range Japanese fighters, but the Air Ministry have always led me to believe no important advance in range was likely to be made.

Winston S. Churchill to Air Chief Marshal Sir Charles Portal
(Churchill papers, 20/67)

1 March 1942   Ditchley Park

The telegrams from the Middle East are always half-full of routine air fighting, which loads the wires and distorts the proportion. It would be better that routine matters of air skirmishing should be reported weekly, together with the number of planes in action or at short notice, the number of sorties made, tonnage of bombs dropped, and aircraft shot down, &c., and that Sitrep[1] messages should be reserved for important air events, or occurrences of a significant character.

Winston S. Churchill to General Hastings Ismay,
for the Chiefs of Staff Committee
(Churchill papers, 20/67)

2 March 1942   Ditchley Park
Secret

I am increasingly impressed with the disadvantages of the present system of having Naval, Army and Air Force officers equally represented at all points and on all combined subjects, whether in committees or in commands. This has resulted in a paralysis of the offensive spirit, due to the fact that the officers of the three Services together nearly always, except in the higher ranks, present the sum of their fears and difficulties.

2. It seems to me that we should move in the direction of appointing Supreme Commanders in particular areas and for special tasks. The Tasks Commander should be the new feature, who might sometimes be an Admiral, a General or an Airman. This would also be true of the staff work and joint planning. When any plan is to be studied, an officer of one or other of the three Services should be told to make a plan and the others to help him. Which Service so selected depends upon (a) the nature of the operation and which Service is predominant, and (b) the personality concerned.

3. I shall be obliged if you will give these matters your careful consideration.

[1] Sitrep: situation report.

Winston S. Churchill to Anthony Eden
(Churchill papers, 20/67)

2 March 1942
Secret

See A.[1] I never said anything of this kind, and I am sure Mackenzie King would repudiate the statement attributed to him.

As you know, I have thought it a good thing to have a window or loop-hole overlooking the Vichy courtyard, but this is very different from the statement attributed to me.

Winston S. Churchill to Air Chief Marshal Sir Charles Portal
(Churchill papers, 20/67)

2 March 1942

SHORTAGE OF FIGHTERS

All this[2] goes to show the enormous importance of making our night fighting squadrons available for dual purpose. Even though the results as day fighters might not be up to full standard, the squadrons could form a reserve and could be equipped with machines otherwise remaining in the ASUs.[3] It would be quite impossible to keep all these Beaufighter night squadrons idle perhaps for a whole year when we are so hard pressed. To keep them in their present position is another concession to the defensive.

2. A great effort must be made to increase the number of fighters by production.

Winston S. Churchill to the Duke of Windsor
(Churchill papers, 20/63)

2 March 1942
Most Secret

With present enemy submarine activity in Caribbean it is felt that Nassau is open to danger of attack by raiding parties from enemy submarines and that continuous protection against an attack by 50 men

[1] Secret report recounting conversation between William Mackenzie King and the French Minister to Ottawa on the subject of the Prime Minister's views regarding Canadian relations with Vichy.
[2] The reference is to a minute of 28 February 1942 reporting on the shortage of fighters.
[3] ASU: Air Storage Units (aircraft in storage).

during darkness should be provided. It has accordingly been decided that one company of British troops should be sent to Nassau as soon as possible and necessary arrangements are being made by Joint Staff Mission Washington who have been asked to communicate as regards details with Your Royal Highness direct.

Oliver Harvey: diary
('The War Diaries of Oliver Harvey', pages 103–4)

2 March 1942

I lunched with AE. He had heard no more from Bracken and we wondered what if anything had happened. He feels more and more that the present set-up by which the PM keeps all control over operations severely in his own hands can't last, altho' he sees himself saddled with a difficult if not impossible task if PM agrees to his being Assistant Minister of Defence. I tell him that this would only be a transitional stage which would prepare the country for the larger change if the PM drops out. In any case, I said, the present situation in which the management of the war is not being controlled or co-ordinated at all owing to the PM's spasmodic and hand-to-mouth methods cannot last. These are the vital months when the war may be won or lost and when we must play the few cards we have with the greatest skill and foresight if we are to reach the point in time when Allied production will enable us to overwhelm our enemies. He is going to talk it over with Cripps tonight and meanwhile find out from Bracken what happened over the weekend. It is fantastic that there should be no War Cabinet meeting daily to deal with the war, but only an occasional defence committee meeting at 10 o'clock at night once or twice a week at the whim of Winston. AE doesn't believe PM will ever agree to give up anything.

Later. Bracken reports that the PM didn't take too badly to the proposal that AE should become Assistant M of Defence but that their talk was interrupted.[1]

---

[1] Eden was not appointed Assistant Minister (or Deputy Minister) of Defence; indeed, the post never came into existence.

Sir Alexander Cadogan: diary
(*'The Diaries of Sir Alexander Cadogan'*, *page 438*)

2 March 1942

A[1] spoke to me of the general situation. He feels – as I do – that for the last fortnight there has been no direction of the war. War Cabinet doesn't function – there hasn't been a meeting of Defence Committee. There's no hand on the wheel. (Probably due to PM's health). Brendan and Cripps urge that A should be Deputy Defence Minister. This was my idea also. Hope he can keep the FO – and I can run it.

[...]

Cabinet 5.30 – over soon after 7. Nothing much. News from everywhere – except Russia – bad. There's something wrong with us, I fear.

Oliver Harvey: diary
(*'The War Diaries of Oliver Harvey'*, *page 104*)

3 March 1942

AE most depressed again this morning. A very long and unsatisfactory Defence Committee (old style) last night. 10 p.m. to 2 a.m. PM at his worst, discoursing, complaining, groaning. Lyttelton there, not Cripps. PM wished to send a snorter to Auchinleck. Lyttelton said generals were not to blame but the badness of our tanks (i.e. Beaverbrook's responsibility) which were definitely inferior to German tanks. This is what I always suspected.

PM's remedy is to suggest going out to Cairo with Beaverbrook and leave him there as M of State! AE in despair. I said I thought the only thing to do was to try and merge the Defence Committee in the new War Cabinet.

When the WC met on political questions, eg Russia and India, it was already working well and a great improvement on the old body, the PM no longer able to dominate it. It was important to get Cripps into the war discussions, and if he wasn't allowed in, he might very well present the PM with an ultimatum. I thought the new War Cabinet should insist on merging with the Defence Committee. AE thinks PM is determined to give up nothing, as he had always feared. A tragic situation. The PM has still such vitality and drive and yet it all spends itself in futile action.

[1] Anthony Eden.

But yet on India the Cabinet are about to take immense step, an offer of complete independence like a Dominion after the war. This idea originated with the PM himself who cut across the obstructionism of the Viceroy and the India Office and it has been pushed on by the new War Cabinet – an excellent example of what this Cabinet can do if it is allowed.

Winston S. Churchill to Sir Edward Grigg[1]
(Churchill papers, 20/53)

3 March 1942

My dear Ned,

It has been found necessary to have a representative of the Labour Party in the Ministerial team at the War Office. Comment has been made that no single Labour man is associated with a Department under whom so many millions are serving. I am very sorry indeed, therefore, to have to ask you to place your Office of Joint Parliamentary Under-Secretary of State at my disposal.[2]

If there is any way in which I can serve you, pray let me know. Your distinguished career would make your acceptance of a Peerage most welcome and appropriate.[3]

Yours very sincerely,
Winston S. Churchill

[1] Edward William Macleay Grigg, 1879–1955. Educated at Winchester and New College, Oxford. Editorial staff of *The Times,* 1903–5, 1908–13. Served in the Grenadier Guards, 1914–18 (Churchill shared his front-line dugout in November 1915). Military Secretary to the Prince of Wales, 1919. Knighted, 1920. Private Secretary to Lloyd George, 1921–2. National Liberal MP for Oldham, 1922–5. Governor of Kenya, 1925–31. Elected to the Other Club, 1932. National Conservative MP for Altrincham, 1933–5. Parliamentary Secretary, Ministry of Information, 1939–40. Financial Secretary, War Office, 1940. Joint Parliamentary Under-Secretary of State for War, May 1940 to March 1942. Minister Resident in the Middle East, 1944–5. Privy Councillor, 1944. Created Baron Altrincham, 1 August 1945. Editor of the *National Review,* 1948–55. His son, the journalist and historian John Grigg, was one of four peers to disclaim their titles in 1963, as permitted by the Peerage Act of that year.

[2] The new Joint Parliamentary Under Secretary of State for War was Arthur Henderson, 1893–1968 (son of the Labour leader Arthur Henderson). On active service, 1914–18. Labour MP for Cardiff South, 1923–4, 1929–31; for Kingswinford, 1935–50; for Rowley Regis and Tipton, 1950–66. QC, 1939. Joint Parliamentary Secretary of State for War, 1942–3; Financial Secretary, War Office, 1943–5. Parliamentary Under-Secretary of State, India Office, and Burma Office, 1945–7. Privy Councillor, 1947. Minister of State for Commonwealth Relations, 1947. Secretary of State for Air, 1947–51. Created Baron Rowley, 1966.

[3] Grigg declined a peerage, and also Cabinet office as First Commissioner of Works, as it was dependent on his acceptance of a peerage. In November 1944 Churchill appointed Grigg Minister Resident in the Middle East.

Lord Beaverbrook to Mary Catherine Inge [1]
(Lord Beaverbrook papers)

3 March 1942

Hannen Swaffer[2] is a very fine fellow – there is a great deal to be said in praise of him. But if he has been gossiping unfavourably about the Prime Minister, then he is misinformed.

The Prime Minister is an austere man, who works night and day. It is said that he drinks. But this is not true. I drink every day, or have in the past taken more to drink every day than the Prime Minister – yet I am known as an abstemious man.

I do not know a fault in his life, save only too strong a devotion to his friends.

His home life is excellent. His relations with Mrs Churchill might be told in story form as an example of a lifetime of domestic content.

I left him because of my asthma. I do not deny there was a difference of policy which did damage our close co-operation to a small degree. But resistance came from his colleagues rather than from the Prime Minister himself. And I was not entirely satisfied with my position as Minister of Production. But I showed that quite clearly in my speech in the Lords.

Baldwin once said that I was a man of power without responsibility. As Minister of Production I was carrying on my shoulders a great deal of responsibility without sufficient power.

Oliver Harvey: diary
('The War Diaries of Oliver Harvey', page 105)

3 March 1942

AE had rather touching interview with PM this evening when he showed him the list of Under-Secretaries. 'Anyone can have my job. Anything may happen to me at any time now. But remember if it does, you are the one who must succeed.' AE urged that Cripps should become a member of Defence Committee but PM did not respond.

---

[1] Mary Catherine Spooner, 1880–1949. Daughter of the Archdeacon of Maidstone. Married Dean Inge in 1905. An authority on the costume of the eighteenth century. Author of *The Secrets of My Successful Marriage* (1930).

[2] Hannen Swaffer, 1879–1962. Journalist. Joined *Daily Mail*, 1902. Invented 'Mr Gossip' for the *Daily Sketch*, 1913. Dramatic critic, *Daily Express*, 1926–31; *Daily Herald* from 1931.

Winston S. Churchill to General Hastings Ismay
(Churchill papers, 20/67)

4 March 1942

I was assured that the second American convoy would contain 17,000 or 18,000 men and that 3,000 Canadians would be added. This convoy was originally to sail from Halifax about the 8th or 9th February.

I agreed to the postponement until the 19th. Let me see the back papers about this. Which is the convoy in which the 3,000 Canadians (Armoured Division) are to come?

Winston S. Churchill to General Hastings Ismay,
for the Chiefs of Staff Committee
(Churchill papers, 20/67)

4 March 1942

Let me again set out the reinforcement story for the Indian theatre. The leading brigade of the 70th Division must reach Ceylon at the earliest moment (?When). Also the big convoy of AA[1] and AT.[2] Then come the two Brigade Groups, 16th and 17th, of the Australian 6th Division. These ought to stay seven or eight weeks, and the shipping should be handled so as to make this convenient and almost inevitable. Wavell will then be free to bring the remaining two brigades of the 70th Division into India and use them on the Burma front, additional to all other reinforcements on the way. The knowledge they are coming should make him freer to use the British Internal Security Battalion on the Burma front.

2. The *Indomitable*'s two squadrons should reach Ceylon 6th instant, and this with the existing air elements should give good protection both to the two Australian Brigade Groups (when they come) and to the two 'R' class battleships in the harbour, having regard to the fact that enemy air attack can only be from a carrier. Before the end of the month *Indomitable* should be armed for war and *Warspite* not far away. Some cruisers and a considerable flotilla, nearly 20, will be gathered. Thereafter the situation improves steadily, as *Formidable* will arrive and *Valiant* may not be many weeks away.

3. Pray let me know if we are all agreed about this, as cross purposes and misunderstanding on points of detail add greatly to our burdens.

---

[1] AA: anti-aircraft weapons.
[2] AT: anti-tank weapons.

Winston S. Churchill to the Chiefs of Staff Committee
(Churchill papers, 20/67)

4 March 1942

I have agreed with the Foreign Secretary that in view of the changes in the situation it is better not to give this bitter medicine to Russia at this juncture. They have probably found out for themselves what is going on. We may, therefore, delay any specific message.[1]

Winston S. Churchill to General Hastings Ismay,
for the Chiefs of Staff Committee
(Churchill papers, 20/67)

4 March 1942

I do not understand this attitude on our part. Sir Earle Page had pressed most strongly at your desire for the stopping off of Australian troops in Ceylon, to enable the island to be secured. The Australian Government have now agreed. I understood you needed troops in Ceylon most urgently. Now you turn round and ask General Wavell whether he wants them, observing 'it would be very difficult politically to decline this offer.' Surely you need these men. I only put the matter to you because of the fitting in of ships, &c. I propose to send the attached telegram to Mr Curtin.[2]

Winston S. Churchill to General Hastings Ismay,
for the Chiefs of Staff Committee
(Churchill papers, 20/67)

4 March 1942

Presumably ships carrying the two Australian Brigade Groups to Ceylon would discharge there and return for elements of 9th Australian Division from Suez, which they would carry to Australia direct, then returning to Ceylon to pick up the two Brigade Groups stopped off there. How long would this give the two Brigade Groups in Ceylon? Let this be calculated, or is there some other quite different arrangement for the shipping?

---

[1] About the impossibility of an Anglo-American 'Second Front' in 1942 against the Germans in western Europe.

[2] Winston S. Churchill to John Curtin (*Churchill papers, 20/71*), 4 March 1942. 'Most Secret. We thank you most cordially for your proffered help, which will make the position much better during these critical weeks.'

Winston S. Churchill to Clement Attlee
(Churchill papers, 20/67)

4 March 1942

I do not see much use in pumping all this pessimism throughout the Empire.[1] It is the fashion here: but it will do great harm wherever else it goes. Has it gone? Altogether there is too much talk. A very different picture and mood may be with us in a couple of months.

Winston S. Churchill to General Archibald Wavell
(Churchill papers, 20/71)

4 March 1942
Most Immediate
Clear the Line
Personal

Australia has offered as temporary reinforcement Ceylon garrison to stop off 16th and 17th Australian Brigade Groups, which can arrive about 20th. Australian Government stipulate adequate Air support. This should be forthcoming by the 6th, when *Indomitable* discharges her two squadrons at Ceylon. We are therefore accepting Australia's offer with cordiality. This should enable you to use the two later brigades of the 70th Division in India or on the Burma front if you so decide.

Winston S. Churchill to Peter Fraser
(Churchill papers, 20/71)

4 March 1942
Most Secret and Personal

Estimate you refer to is leakage at a very early stage of examination of question for which you asked, and in no way represents views of Chiefs of Staff, who have not yet even been consulted. This shows that there are disadvantages as well as advantages in liaison between your Officers and ours in initial stages of Staff study.

2. I agree with you that whatever is likely to invade New Zealand will not be a Brigade Group. Your telegram will be shown to the Planning Staff at the same time that any reports from their Juniors are considered.

---

[1] Churchill was commenting on a Dominions Office telegram to all United Kingdom High Commissioners in the Dominions about the situation in the Far East.

3. I am aiming at three large measures for New Zealand security. First, inducing the United States Navy to give effective protection in the Anzac area. Secondly, their reinforcement of Fiji and New Caledonia which we arranged at Washington, and thirdly, the sending of American troops into New Zealand as an alternative to recalling the New Zealand Division from the Middle East, thus saving shipping and needless movement.

4. It is impossible to say with certainty that the Japanese will not attack New Zealand in force, but there are many other far more tempting objectives for them and their resources are not unlimited. I am hoping that the recovery of sea power during May by the United States and our own naval developments in the Indian Ocean, may alter the strategic values which at present exist.

5. I am doing everything in my power to get you the weapons and munitions for which you have asked.

All good wishes,
Churchill

Winston S. Churchill to President Franklin D. Roosevelt
(Churchill papers, 20/71)

4 March 1942
No. 34

We are earnestly considering whether a declaration of Dominion Status after the war carrying with it if desired the right to secede should be made at this critical juncture. We must not on any account break with the Moslems who represent a hundred million people and the main army elements on which we must rely for the immediate fighting. We have also to consider our duty towards thirty to forty million Untouchables and our treaties with the Princely States of India, perhaps eighty millions. Naturally we do not want to throw India into chaos on the eve of invasion.

2. Meanwhile I send you in my immediately following telegram two representative messages I have received and a summary of a memorandum by the Military Secretary, India Office.[1]

3. I will keep you informed.

[1] The memorandum noted that the 'Pakistan scheme' being put forward by Mohammed Ali Jinnah (President of the Moslem League 'and the accepted head of the most powerful Moslem organisation in India') 'contemplates the creation of separate Moslem States in the Moslem majority areas independent of the rest of India, except so far as they accept joint control negotiating as separate political entities'.

Winston S. Churchill to President Franklin D. Roosevelt
(Churchill papers, 20/71)

4 March 1942
No. 36

Since my return to this country I have been giving much attention to the shipping situation, which is likely to impose severe limitations upon our efforts throughout 1942. There are two main aspects. First – military movements. You know we are moving very large numbers, including an Australian corps of three Divisions and the 70th British Division, from the Middle East across the Indian Ocean. To make good the depletion of the Middle East and to send large reinforcements both land and air to India and Ceylon, we should like to ship from the United Kingdom 295,000 men in the months February, March, April and May. A convoy of 45,000 men sailed in February. Another convoy of 50,000 including the 5th Division and seven squadrons of aircraft, will sail in March. Two further convoys totalling 85,000 men will sail in April and May. To achieve this we are scraping together every ton of man-lift shipping we can lay our hands on and adopting every expedient to hasten the turn-round and increase the carrying capacity of the shipping. Even so, we shall fall short of our aim by 115,000 men.

This is the situation in which I turn to you for help.

I think we must agree to recognise that 'Gymnast'[1] is out of the question for several months. Taking this factor into account can you lend us the shipping to convoy to the Indian Ocean during the next critical four months a further two complete Divisions (say 40,000 men), including the necessary accompanying MT,[2] guns and equipment. This would mean that we would like the shipping to load in UK during April and the first half of May. The combat loading ships now allocated to 'Magnet' might provide for 10,000 of this total and these and any other ships you are able to find could bring such a substantial proportion of 'Magnet' on their way to the UK that we could defer the balance of that movement.

Further the cargo shipping at our disposal has not only to maintain the flow of essential imports to the United Kingdom but also to keep up supplies to Russia and to meet increasing demands for the supply and maintenance of our troops in the East. Ships are having to be withdrawn from importing service to carry supplies to the East not only from this

---

[1] 'Gymnast': the Anglo-American plan for a major amphibious landing in French North Africa, eventually carried out as Operation Torch in November 1942.

[2] MT: Motor Transport.

country, but also from USA as many of the American ships that have been helping with the latter task are being diverted to other urgent duties. These developments with other consequences of the Far Eastern war are having a very serious effect on our importing capacity. During the first four months of this year we expect imports of only 7¼ million tons and recently sinkings have greatly increased.

This will mean a serious running down of stocks during the first part of the year, which cannot be continued and which must be made good by a substantial improvement in the rate of importation in the later months. We have made a careful analysis of the imports which we must secure during 1942, in order to maintain our full effort and to make sure that our stocks shall not be run down below the danger line by the end of the year, and are satisfied that it is not reasonable to aim at anything less than 26 million tons of non-tanker imports. This will certainly not be realised without very substantial additions to our shipping resources; it would therefore be a very great help to us in connection with all our plans if you could let me know to what extent we can expect assistance for our imports and for carriage of our equipment from US to the Middle East to be made available from your shipbuilding programme month by month as vessels come increasingly into service.

Sir Charles Wilson: diary
('Winston Churchill, The Struggle for Survival', page 32)

4 March 1942

The PM tells me that 640,000 tons of merchant shipping have been sunk in the last two months in what he calls 'American waters.' I have been finding out that wherever he goes he carries in his head the monthly figures of all sinkings, though he never talks about them. He is always careful to consume his own smoke; nothing he says could discourage anyone. When I say the PM never talks, I am not quite accurate. There are times – this does not happen very often – when I fancy I serve as a safety valve. Occasionally, too, I may pick up by chance a stray hint of what is going on in his head.

One day when things at sea were at their worst, I happened to go to the Map Room. There I found the PM. He was standing with his back to me, staring at the huge chart with the little black beetles representing German submarines. 'Terrible,' he muttered. I was about to retreat when he whipped round and brushed past me with his head down. I am not sure he saw me. He knows that we may lose the war at sea in a few months and that he can do nothing about it. I wish to God I could put out the fires that seem to be consuming him.

Winston S. Churchill to General Charles de Gaulle
(Churchill papers, 20/53)

4 March 1942

My dear General,

It is with profound regret that I have learnt of the loss of the Free French Submarine *Surcouf* and of her gallant crew, who must now all be presumed lost with their ship.[1]

This is a sad blow to the Free French Navy, as it is also to the Navies of the nations united in the fight for freedom against the Axis.

Pray accept my deep sympathy.

Yours very sincerely,
Winston S. Churchill

Winston S. Churchill to Admiral Emile Muselier[2]
(Churchill papers, 20/53)

4 March 1942

My Dear Admiral,

It is with profound regret that I have learnt of the loss of the *Surcouf* and of her gallant crew under the command of Capitaine de Fregate Blaison.[3]

You must share the sadness I feel in that the *Surcouf* was sunk not in action but by an accident when on her way to fight the enemy in the Pacific. Had she been spared I feel sure that she would have continued her fine work against the enemy in the best traditions of the French Navy.

Pray accept my deep sympathy.

Yours very sincerely,
Winston S. Churchill

---

[1] The *Surcouf*, then the largest submarine in the world (3,300 tons), sailing without lights – for security reasons – in the Caribbean Sea, collided with the American cargo ship *Thomas Lykes* on 19 February 1942. All 105 members of the crew, and its captain, Georges Blaison, were killed.

[2] Commander-in-Chief of the Free French Naval Force.

[3] Georges Blaison, 1906–42. Entered France's Naval College, 1925. Having retired from the French Navy in 1940 for health reasons, joined the Free French Naval Forces. Posthumously awarded the Medal of Knight of the Legion of Honour (1945) and the Medal of the Resistance (1947).

Winston S. Churchill to Admiral of the Fleet Sir Dudley Pound
(Churchill papers, 20/53)

4 March 1942
Private

My dear Pound,

You are in a different position to the other two Chiefs of the Staff because you are conducting the Naval war over its whole spread in direct contact with the enemy, and are in fact a Super Commander-in-Chief. I must say I consider this your first duty as First Sea Lord. Now that the war has invaded so many theatres and the work of the COS Committee has been so vastly extended and complicated I am clearly of opinion you should lighten your load. If therefore you represented this to me I would arrange for Brooke, as it is the Army's turn, to preside over the COS Committee so that you could attend or not as you chose and for the rest manage the movements of the Fleet and all the other aspects of Admiralty business confided to you. You know I have the greatest confidence in your judgement and in your handling of the Fleet.

2. I consider that Mountbatten[1] should join the COS Committee as an equal member while retaining control of the Commandos, etc., and assuming the title of Chief of Combined Operations. The rank of this office would be raised appropriately in all three Services, but not personally to the individual.

3. Pray give these matters your careful consideration.

Yours sincerely,
Winston S. Churchill

---

[1] Prince Louis Francis Albert Victor Nicholas of Battenberg (His Serene Highness Prince Louis of Battenberg), 1900–79. Second son of Prince Louis of Battenberg (Churchill's First Sea Lord, 1911–14), who in 1917 was created Marquess of Milford Haven and assumed the surname of Mountbatten. Naval cadet, 1913–15. Midshipman, 1916. Commander, 1932. Naval Air Division, Admiralty, 1936. Captain, 1937. Commanded HMS *Kelly* 1939 (despatches twice). Chief of Combined Operations, 1942–3. Supreme Allied Commander, South-East Asia, 1943–6. Created Viscount Mountbatten of Burma, 1946. Viceroy of India, 1947. Created Earl, 1947. Governor-General of India, 1947–8. First Sea Lord, 1955–9. Admiral of the Fleet, 1956. Chief of the Defence Staff, 1959–65. Murdered by terrorists of the Irish Republican Army (IRA), 27 August 1979, while fishing in a boat on a lake in the Irish Republic. Also killed were Nicholas Knatchbull, Mountbatten's elder daughter's 14-year-old son, and Paul Maxwell, a local 15-year-old youth who was a crew member. The Dowager Lady Brabourne, the 83-year-old mother-in-law of Mountbatten's elder daughter, died from her injuries the following day.

Winston S. Churchill to Admiral of the Fleet Sir Ernle Chatfield
(Churchill papers, 20/53)

4 March 1942
Secret

Dear Chatfield,

I noticed that you inquired in the Lords about the reasons for the delay of the capital ships which were building when you left the Admiralty.

It has not been possible for reasons of policy to make much progress with the *Lion* and *Temeraire*, as the construction effort has been concentrated on vessels likely to reach the line earlier.

The five King George V Class, for the design of which you were responsible, were first of all delayed by the lack of a decision as to what type of gun to install.

When progress upon this had been made you decided upon a further change, and substituted a 2-gun turret for the 4-gun super-imposed gun turret. This again involved the design of a new turret with all its thousands of drawings, and was the cause of at least another year's delay in every ship of the Class. The five ships were already under-gunned compared with the contemporary American vessels. Their present weight of broadside compares with them as follows:

King George V Class
Ten 14″ guns at 1,590 pounds equals   15,900 pounds

American warships
Nine 16″ guns at 2,700 pounds equals   24,300 pounds

(Difference 8,400 on the broadside)

As designed these ships were sadly lacking in anti-aircraft defences and before completion some 800 tons had to be added to their designed displacement on account of the unforeseen additions which were required. This necessarily detracted from the ships' performance. As you probably know, the underwater strength of these ships as compared with those of the enemy is now the subject of an independent investigation at the Admiralty.

It has always seemed to me a very great pity that these five ships when voted by Parliament were not armed either with the 15″ or 16″ gun. They are of course most useful ships, and we are very glad to have them as they come out. We could have had them two years earlier in each case, but for the reasons I have given above.

I much regret that it is not possible to make a reply to you in public on these most secret matters, but I do not think you should be left in any doubt of what the nature of the reply would be.

Yours sincerely,
Winston S. Churchill

Air Chief Marshal Sir Charles Portal to Winston S. Churchill
(Premier papers, 3/11/3)

5 March 1942
Secret

You will recollect that in November last the Cabinet considered the intensity of air operations being undertaken by Bomber and Fighter Command and decided that we should adopt a policy of 'conservation' throughout the winter. On the 14th February you authorized the resumption of full bombing of Germany, subject always, of course, to our not incurring heavy losses owing to bad weather and enemy resistance combined. The directive to Fighter Command, however, still emphasises the need for conserving resources in order to build up strong forces both for the needs of Home and overseas.

2. I think that present conditions demand a change in this principle of conservation of our fighter force. Intelligence information indicates that because of the heavy strain imposed upon its resources, especially by the fighting on the Russian Front, the GAF[1] is now much weaker than it has been at any stage of the war. This particularly applies to fighters. The Germans are clearly making great efforts to reduce wastage and to consolidate in order to build up their forces for a strong offensive in the spring; there is evidence that recuperation has already begun.

3. One of the ways in which we could best help the Russians would be to weaken the German fighter force and so reduce the adequacy of the air support given to the German armies. If by our air operations in the West, we can succeed in further weakening the GAF or at least preventing its recovery, the chances of the enemy launching a successful offensive against Russia and particularly towards the Caucasus or Iraq will be reduced.

4. I therefore recommend that we should renew our daylight 'Circus' operations over France.[2] The bombers would be sent to attack important

[1] GAF: German Air Force.

[2] The Royal Air Force began what were known as 'Circus' operations in January 1941, sending a force of bombers, escorted by a large number of fighters, with the aim of drawing German fighters into combat in circumstances favourable to the RAF. The first 'Circus' operation, on 10 January

objectives with the object of inducing German fighters to accept combat with our own fighter forces. We would hope to inflict casualties in the fighting and the additional flying that would be forced upon them should increase their normal wastage considerably.

5. May I have your authority to issue the necessary orders?[1]

Winston S. Churchill to President Franklin D. Roosevelt
(Churchill papers, 20/71)

5 March 1942
No. 37[2]

When I reflect how I have longed and prayed for the entry of the United States into the war, I find it difficult to realise how gravely our British affairs have deteriorated by what has happened since December 7. We have suffered the greatest disaster in our history at Singapore, and other misfortunes will come thick and fast upon us. Your great power will only become effective gradually because of the vast distances and the shortage of ships. It is not easy to assign limits to the Japanese aggression. All can be retrieved in 1943 and 1944, but meanwhile there are very hard forfeits to pay. The whole of the Levant–Caspian Front now depends entirely upon the success of the Russian Armies. The attack which the Germans will deliver upon Russia in the spring will I fear be most formidable. The danger to Malta grows constantly and large reinforcements are reaching Rommel in Tripoli en route for Cyrenaica.

2. Since we last talked I have not been able to form a full picture of United States plans by sea, air and land against Japan. I am hoping that by May your naval superiority in the Pacific will be restored and that this will be a continuing pre-occupation to the enemy. We expect by the middle of March in addition to the four 'R' Class battleships to have two of our latest aircraft carriers working with *Warspite* in the Indian Ocean and that these will be reinforced by a third carrier during April and by *Valiant* during May. This force will have available four modern cruisers and a number of older ones and about twenty destroyers. Based upon

---

1941, was against an airfield near Calais. The early operations were not a success, as the German fighter pilots were veterans who had fought over Spain, France, and Britain.

[1] On 8 March 1942, Churchill noted by hand on the bottom of Portal's minute: 'You are terribly short of fighter a/c: But it pays us to lose plane for plane. If you consider "Circus" losses will come within that standard it wd be worth while. But beware of the future. Please report again.'

[2] Churchill sent a digest of this telegram to the Dominion prime ministers and to Generals Wavell and Auchinleck on 22 May 1942.

Ceylon, which we regard as the vital point now that Singapore is gone, it should be possible to prevent oversea invasion of India unless the greater part of the Japanese Fleet is brought across from your side of the theatre, and this again I hope the action and growing strength of the United States Navy will prevent.

We hope that a considerable number of Dutch submarines will have escaped to Ceylon and these together with the only two submarines we have been able to spare from the Mediterranean should be able to watch the Malacca Straits.

As we understand your submarines from the ABDA area will be based on Fremantle for the purpose of patrolling the Sunda Straits and other exits through the Dutch Islands, we should not only get notice of but be able to take a toll of any Japanese forces breaking out into the Indian Ocean.

The next fortnight will be the most critical for Ceylon, and by the end of March we ought to be solidly established there, though by no means entirely secure.

3. With the *Tirpitz* and *Scheer* at Trondheim our Northern Force has not only to watch the Northern passages but also to guard the Russian convoys. The tension is however temporarily eased by the disabling of the *Scharnhorst*, *Gneisenau* and *Eugen*, the latter severely, we believe, and we are taking the opportunity of refitting *Rodney*. *Rodney* and *Nelson* should be ready for service in May but *Anson* will not be in fighting trim until August.

4. I should be glad to have from you a short statement of the dispositions and plans for the American Air Force. We have both suffered heavy casualties on the ground in Java and I was most grieved to see the untoward sinking of the *Langley* with her invaluable consignment.[1] Particularly I shall be glad to know to what point your plans for operating from China or the Aleutian Islands have advanced. We also hope that United States bombers based in North East India may operate in force against enemy bases in Siam and Indo-China.

5. You will realise what has happened to the army we had hoped to gather on the Levant–Caspian front, and how it has nearly all been drawn off to India and Australia, and you will see at once what our plight will be should the Russian defence of the Caucasus be beaten down. It would certainly be a great help if you could offer New Zealand the support of an American Division as an alternative to their recalling their own New

---

[1] The USS *Langley*, the first aircraft carrier of the United States Navy (converted from the collier *Jupiter* in 1922) had just been scuttled – with the loss of all her aircraft – after being disabled by the Japanese.

Zealand Division, now stationed in Palestine. This also applies to the last Australian Division in the Middle East. One sympathises with the natural anxiety of Australia and New Zealand when their best troops are out of the country, but shipping will be saved and safety gained by the American reinforcement of Australia and New Zealand rather than by a move across the oceans of these Divisions from the Middle East. I am quite ready to accept a considerable delay in 'Magnet' to facilitate your additional help to Australasia. Finally, it seems of the utmost importance that the United States main Naval Forces should give increasing protection in the ANZAC area, because this alone can meet the legitimate anxieties of the governments there and ensure the maintenance of our vital bases of re-entry.

6. Everything however turns upon shipping. I have sent you a separate telegram No. 36 about the import programme into Great Britain in the current calendar year 1942. It will certainly require a considerable allocation of the new American tonnage in the third and fourth quarters of the year. The immediate and decisive concern however is the provision of troop-carrying tonnage. I am advised that we have at the present time a total man-lift of 280,000 men, but of course at least half of this will be returning empty of troops from very long voyages. You have a comparable man-lifting power of 90,000 men and what has most alarmed me has been the statement that even by the summer of 1943 the American man-lift will only be increased by another 90,000.

If this cannot be remedied there may well be no question of restoring the situation until 1944, with all the many dangers that would follow from such a prolongation of the war. Surely it is possible by giving orders now to double or treble the American man-lift by the summer of 1943? We can do little more beyond our 280,000 and losses have been very heavy lately in this class of vessel. I should be most grateful if you would relieve my anxieties on this score. I am entirely with you about the need for 'Gymnast', but the check which Auchinleck has received and the shipping stringency seem to impose obstinate and long delays.

7. We are sending from 40 to 50 thousand men in each of our monthly convoys to the East. The needs of maintaining the Army and of building up the Air and anti-aircraft forces in the Indian theatre will at present prevent us from sending more than three Divisions from here in the March, April and May convoys, these arriving two months later in each case. It seems to me that all these troops may be needed for the defence of India, and I cannot make any provision other than that suggested in paragraph 5 for the Trans-Caspian front and all that that means.

8. Permit me to refer to the theme I opened to you when we were together. Japan is spreading itself over a very large number of vulnerable points and trying to link them together by air and sea protection. The enemy are becoming ever more widely spread and we know this is causing anxiety in Tokio. Nothing can be done on a large scale except by long preparation of the technical and tactical apparatus. When you told me about your intention to form Commando forces on a large scale on the Californian shore I felt you had the key. Once several good outfits are prepared, any one of which can attack a Japanese-held base or island and beat the life out of the garrison, all their islands will become hostages to fortune. Even this year, 1942, some severe examples might be made causing great perturbation and drawing further upon Japanese resources to strengthen other points.

9. But surely if plans were set on foot now for the preparation of the ships, landing-craft, aircraft, expeditionary divisions, etc., all along the Californian shore for a serious attack upon the Japanese in 1943 this would be a solid policy for us to follow. Moreover, the strength of the United States is such that the whole of this Western party could be developed on your Pacific coast without prejudice to the plans against Hitler across the Atlantic we have talked of together. For a long time to come it seems your difficulty will be to bring your forces into action and that the shipping shortage will be the stranglehold.

Winston S. Churchill to General Archibald Wavell
(Churchill papers, 20/71)

5 March 1942
Personal and Secret

All your activities and energy excite warmest admiration here.[1] Pray let me know if there is any way in which we can help you or strengthen your hands.

---

[1] Wavell had resumed his earlier post as Commander-in-Chief, India and Burma, on 2 March 1942 and had ordered defensive efforts to be intensified as the Japanese pushed forward in Burma. On March 3 he had discussed a co-ordinated British and Chinese strategy in Burma with Chiang Kai-shek, and appointed General Alexander to take command of the troops in Burma. That same day, a new British brigade reached Rangoon to reinforce its defences. On March 5, the day of Churchill's telegram, Wavell endorsed General Alexander's order for a counter-offensive to close the existing gap between the 1st Burma and 17th Indian Divisions.

Winston S. Churchill to Admiral of the Fleet Sir Dudley Pound
(Churchill papers, 20/53)

5 March 1942

My dear Pound,

Many thanks for your letter. It would be agreeable to me if you were yourself to suggest to me that the Army might have a turn in the Chair of the COS Committee.

Since the war began the Air have had a year and the Admiralty about a year and a half. The Army I believe have not presided for many years past. There is also the fact of your own special work as virtual Commander-in-Chief over the whole of the Fleets, in addition to purely Staff duties.

Should you send me such a letter, I would reply suitably and bring it before the COS Committee.

2. About Mountbatten, as I see it he would be de-navalized, and would not represent you in your absence or be in any way your Deputy. He tells me he feels very much the need for some honorary Air Force and Military rank, and this I think would be appreciated by the Services with which he comes into contact. He would also, in my view, keep the full Executive Command of the Combined Operations organization now brought into being, though he would have to devolve a good deal upon a Deputy. Following your train of thought about his being called in on certain subjects and becoming for the purposes of discussion a full Member without embarrassment of seniority, I have asked Ismay to make an analysis of the business of the COS Committee under a number of heads, so that I can indicate the kind of sphere I think he should fill. For instance, I want him to exercise influence upon the war as a whole, upon future planning in its broadest sense; upon the concert of the three Arms and their relation to the main strategy; upon Combined Operations in the largest sense, not only those specific Operations which his own organization will execute. I am quite prepared to proceed step by step, and see how we get on.

3. One of the difficulties is the mass of detail, much of it of a deadly character, affecting movement and action, with which the COS Committee is burdened. This makes it difficult for long-term views to be formed. Everything possible should I think be devolved upon the Vice-Chiefs, so long as the Chiefs of Staff keep complete control of the handling of the machine. I am asking Ismay for some suggestions which I might afterwards put before your Body.

Yours very sincerely,
Winston S. Churchill

Sir Alexander Cadogan: diary
(*'The Diaries of Sir Alexander Cadogan'*, page 440)

5 March 1942

Trouble in Cabinet. Winston having agreed in War Cabinet to Indian plan, puts it to other Ministers with a strong bias <u>against</u>, and finds them unanimously of that way of thinking! Talk – only talk – of resignations from War Cabinet – who met again at 6. Poor old Winston, feeling deeply the present situation and the attacks on him, is losing his grip, I fear.

Oliver Harvey: diary
(*'The War Diaries of Oliver Harvey'*, page 105)

5 March 1942

PM is now having a revulsion about India and doesn't wish to broadcast personally the new Declaration or to let it be announced at all until next week. AE reasoned with him last night and got him a little better but before going any further he wishes to submit the whole thing to the junior Ministers of the Government as well.

This happened today with disastrous results! PM put the plan to the assembled ministers with such an ill grace that beginning with Kingsley Wood the reactionary Tories all piped up strongly against it in spite of the fact that it had been approved by the War Cabinet. PM then said he must consider it again.

AE says the War Cabinet has been made to look ridiculous – which it has – and Cripps says he won't go on unless it is accepted. They are going to tackle the PM again today.

Here is a further example of the PM's lack of grip. We are now getting the worst of both worlds by drifting between two policies.

Oliver Harvey: diary
(*'The War Diaries of Oliver Harvey'*, pages 105–6)

6 March 1942

PM dined with AE last night. Now at last PM has come round about Russia. He says he agrees that we should accept Stalin's demand for recognition of 1941 frontiers and that Roosevelt must be pressed to agree or let us agree; he promises to send a personal message to Roosevelt to back up Winant's representations there. (Winant is just about arriving at Washington.) Meanwhile he will send a personal message to Stalin saying that Lyttelton has now taken over Beaver's work and he has instructed him to continue supplies to Russia on same scale as before. So bitten is he now with need for making progress with Stalin that he is actually thinking of setting off to meet Stalin himself, say in Teheran or Astrachan, accompanied by Beaverbrook, clearing up Cairo on the way. This from a man afflicted with heart who may collapse at any minute. What courage and what gallantry, but is it the way to do things? The statesman or even the opportunist would have realised the necessity for meeting Stalin like this months ago or at least when AE was sent to Moscow. But now as in so many other cases we are late, too late if we are to extract any benefit. We've roused Stalin's suspicions by delay and only come forward when it is obvious our Far Eastern situation forces us to be compliant.

But on India the PM has swung in the opposite direction. He says he won't announce the plan now, he will merely tell India he has a plan, which he'll produce after the war. This is hopeless. Yet, as AE reminded him, it was Winston who originated the idea of imaginative appeal to India on the broadcast. AE said Cripps would resign and the PM gave the impression that he would welcome it! Cripps is going anyway to Chequers for the weekend and may make him see sense. But talking last night, and perhaps in his cups, Winston said if the Labour leaders did not resign too, the Government could go on without Cripps, but if they resigned, then PM would resign too and advise King to send for AE! Lyttelton who was there, said he didn't think anyone would resign, not even Cripps.

Robert Barrington-Ward[1] at a Parliamentary Lobby lunch
(Donald McLachlan, 'In the Chair, Barrington-Ward of The Times')

6 March 1942

At a Lobby lunch at the Savoy on 6 March he saw Winston who was the principal guest, looking unwell. The speech he made off the record to this select and critical gathering – the political correspondents of the

---

[1] Robert Robin McGowan Barrington-Ward, 1891–1948. Joined the staff of *The Times*, 1913. Brigade Major, 1914–18 (Military Cross, DSO, despatches thrice). Assistant Editor, *Observer*, 1919–27. Assistant Editor and Chief Leader Writer, *The Times*, 1927–34; Deputy Editor, 1934–41. Supported Neville Chamberlain and appeasement, writing in his diary at the time of Munich: 'Most of this office is against Dawson and me!' Succeeded Geoffrey Dawson as Editor of *The Times*, 1 October 1941. Retired owing to ill-health, 1947.

national and provincial press with their editors, assistant editors and in some cases proprietors as guests – was rather on the defensive. He appealed against unfair criticism in the Press and said in effect that 'We lost at Singapore the reputation for fighting quality gained in the Battle of Britain and under bombing, and must recapture it.'

Winston S. Churchill to General Hastings Ismay,
for the Chiefs of Staff Committee
(Churchill papers, 20/67)

6 March 1942

I have received the attached letter from the First Sea Lord, and, in consequence, I appoint the CIGS as Chairman of the COS Committee. At the same time I wish to place on record my appreciation of the very great service which the First Sea Lord has rendered to the COS Committee and to His Majesty's Government, and my admiration of the manner in which he has been able to combine these ever-growing duties with his very direct responsibility in regard to the Fleet.

2. I am anxious that the COS Committee should endeavour to secure at least two sittings a week, which could be devoted to the general aspects of the war, large forward planning and other major issues. This might be possible if a further effort were made to devolve upon the Vice-Chiefs Committee a larger instalment of routine business.

3. I desire that Lord Louis Mountbatten, while retaining command of the existing Combined Operations forces and organisation, should attend the meetings of the COS Committee whenever larger issues are in question, and when his own Combined Operations or any special matters in which he is concerned are under discussion. His title will be Chief of Combined Operations, and his position upon the COS Committee when present will be that of full and equal membership irrespective of rank. However, in order to assist him in his present and new duties, he should be given the acting rank of Vice-Admiral in the Navy, with corresponding Honorary rank in the Army and the Air Force, thus making it clear that he has a combined function and in no way clashes with the special responsibilities of the Heads of existing Services.

4. No publicity will be given at present to any of these changes.

William Mackenzie King to Winston S. Churchill
(Churchill papers, 20/71)

6 March 1942
Secret

The Canadian Government heartily welcomes the statement of policy laying down the steps it is proposed to take for the earliest possible realization of complete self-government in India. We attach the highest importance to its early issue and believe it is in the interest of all the United Nations that the utmost expedition should be exercised in promulgating the new programme. We believe that a fully self-governing India has a great part to play in free and equal association with the other Nations of the British Commonwealth and that a free India fighting alongside the other free peoples of the world will strengthen immeasurably the common cause. We have had under consideration from time to time advisability of exchanging representatives with the Government of India and would be glad to make an early appointment of a High Commissioner for Canada in India if it was thought that such action on our part would help to signalize India's emergence as an equal member of the Commonwealth.

John Curtin to Winston S. Churchill
(Churchill papers, 20/71)

6 March 1942

We congratulate you upon the text of proposed statement foreshadowing a new Indian Union to become an associated British Dominion.

The Government's attitude towards the question was expressed by the Minister for External Affairs in the House of Representatives[1] on February 25th last in the following terms: 'We are aware of the great struggle of the Chinese people to maintain their integrity and re-build their nation, just as we recognize and sympathise with the aspirations of the Indian people to become one of the self-governing British nations and as such to take part in the defences of the Allied cause in Asia'.

---

[1] Herbert Evatt.

Winston S. Churchill to Clare Sheridan[1]
(Churchill papers, 20/53)

6 March 1942

My dear Clare,

I have made enquiries of the Admiralty about Lieutenant Thomas Brinsley Sheridan[2] but I am afraid that there is no information that I can give you beyond what you already know, namely, that he was one of the survivors from HMS *Prince of Wales* and went to Singapore. Since it fell there has, I am afraid, been no news from Singapore. But I see no reason to assume that he is not a prisoner of war.

Yours affectionately,
W

Averell Harriman to President Franklin D. Roosevelt
('Special Envoy to Churchill and Stalin', pages 126–7)

6 March 1942

Dear Mr President,

I have been worried about the Prime Minister – both his political status and his own spirits. He did not take well the criticism he found on his return from Washington. The criticism was not directed at him personally but against certain policies and against various individuals. Unfortunately, he bared his chest and assumed the blame for everything and everybody – politicians and soldiers alike. The natural effect of this was to turn the criticism against himself.

He was forced, obviously reluctantly, to make changes, thus failing to get full credit. He has, however, quieted things for the present. His opponents have found that he has an Achilles heel and will undoubtedly attack again. It is curious how, when criticism starts, a coalition government suffers from lack of party loyalty and support.

Although the British are keeping a stiff upper lip, the surrender of their troops at Singapore has shattered confidence to the core even in

[1] Clare Consuelo Frewen, 1885–1970. Churchill's cousin. Daughter of Moreton Frewen and Clara Jerome. Educated in Paris and Germany. Sculptress and writer. European correspondent of the *New York World*, 1922. Her husband, Wilfred Sheridan, whom she married in 1910, was killed in action in France in September 1915 (his elder brother had been killed in action in the Boer War). Her only son died in 1937, aged 21.

[2] Gerald Thomas Brinsley Sheridan, 1920–85. Clare Sheridan's nephew, son of her husband's brother, Maurice Overing Sheridan. Lieutenant (later Captain) Royal Marines. Survived the war in Japanese captivity.

themselves but, more particularly, in their leaders. They don't intend to take it lying down and I am satisfied we will see the rebirth of greater determination. At the moment, however, they can't see the end to defeats. Unfortunately Singapore shook the Prime Minister himself to such an extent that he has not been able to stand up to this adversity with his old vigour.

A number of astute people, both friends and opponents, feel it is only a question of a few months before his Government falls. I cannot accept this view. He has been very tired but is better in the last day or two. I believe he will come back with renewed strength, particularly when the tone of the war improves.

There is no other man in sight to give the British the leadership Churchill does.

Lord Linlithgow to Winston S. Churchill
(Churchill papers, 20/71)

6 March 1942
Private and Personal
Most Secret

Draft declaration on India has clearly now reached its final stage. I have no wish to worry you with details. I do however beg you to insert pledge to minorities in declaration. Many of our best fighting men come from minority communities and (corrupt group) pledge is all we can now do towards mitigation of disquiet, of a falling off in recruitment and of strong urge among serving soldiers here and overseas to get back to their villages before communal trouble begins. I am telegraphing to Amery[1] who will be able to put point at issue concisely to you.

Lord Linlithgow to L. S. Amery
(Churchill papers, 20/71)

6 March 1942

Following is brief summary of Commander in Chief's[2] views. Present percentage of composition of Indian armies. Hindu 41, Moslem 35,

---

[1] L. S. Amery, Secretary of State for India, May 1940 to August 1945.
[2] General Sir Alan Hartley.

Sikh 10, Gurkha 8 and half, others 5 and half. The Punjab supplies 50 percent of whole.

2. (A) Taken by itself knowledge future right to secede[1] would probably have no immediate effect if properly put out: but declaration of local option would have immediate effect of great unsettlement which will probably become dangerous as communal struggle over these proposals develops. Local option will be interpreted as acceptance of Pakistan and effect will be particularly bad on Punjab. Moslems of all ranks from provinces not likely to accede will ask how non-accession provinces will be governed: will they have army of their own, and if not how will they defend themselves against rest of India or against own minorities eg Sikhs? In result the minds of all will definitely be taken off task of fighting our enemies: as a sequel recruitment will be gravely imperilled.

(B) General tendency would be to discourage martial races but bring forward large numbers from non-martial classes who would be worthless against external enemies and only desire to be armed against internal enemies.

In any case if as seems probable, widespread communal disturbances develop in India, task of suppressing them with Indian troops will be impossible. A possibility of communal warfare in Indian army cannot be excluded.

(C) Probable effect on States[2] forces not clear.

(D) Serving Gurkhas unlikely to be affected.

(E) Effect on British Officer is likely to be dispiriting while his difficulties are increased. Number of volunteers for Indian army from England is likely to diminish.

3. Summing up Commander in Chief considers that generally effect of contemplated announcement on fighting services would be disastrous. He is quite certain contemplated announcement will take soldier's mind sooner or later off fighting our enemies and start him looking over his shoulder. Finally present time when things are going wrong would be particularly unhappy for such announcement.[3]

---

[1] I.e. from the British Empire. The 'local option' referred to describes the option to remain separate from the Indian Central Union. See further Churchill's note to Mackenzie King of March 8, reproduced below (page 362).

[2] The Indian Princely States.

[3] Churchill sent a copy of this telegram to Roosevelt on 6 March 1942 with the introductory note: 'Following has just reached me. I send it to you so that you may know how the situation is developing at the moment' (*Churchill papers, 20/88*).

Winston S. Churchill to President Franklin D. Roosevelt
(Churchill papers, 20/71)

7 March 1942
Personal and Secret
No. 41

In pursuance of my plan of keeping you informed about our Indian policy, and in continuation of my telegram No. 39 in which I gave you Wavell's views. I now send you telegram from the Viceroy,[1] just received, as well as one from the Governor of the Punjab.[2] These are not, of course, the only opinions on these matters, but they are very serious when the enemy is battering at the gate and when the Punjab supplied 50% of all fighting troops which can take part in the defence of India. We are still persevering to find some conciliatory and inspiring process, but I have to be careful that we do not disturb British politics at a moment when things are increasingly aquiver.

General Archibald Wavell to Winston S. Churchill
(Churchill papers, 20/71)

7 March 1942
Most Secret
Personal

Communication with Burma has been subject to long delays in last two days, wireless seems to have broken down altogether and I am without any message from Alexander.[3] I gather from naval message received this morning that decision was suddenly taken about midnight last night to abandon Rangoon, turn back convoys en route and carry out demolitions. Wired Alexander at once to enquire situation but have had no reply. Will inform you as soon as I have official news.

Winston S. Churchill to President Franklin D. Roosevelt
(Churchill papers, 20/71)

7 March 1942
Personal and Secret
No. 40

If Winant is with you now he will no doubt explain the Foreign Office view about Russia. The increasing gravity of the war has led me to feel

[1] The Marquess of Linlithgow.
[2] Bertrand Glancy.
[3] General Alexander, General Officer Commanding Burma, 1942.

that the principles of the Atlantic Charter ought not to be construed so as to deny Russia the frontiers she occupied when Germany attacked her. This was the basis on which Russia acceded to the Charter, and I expect that a severe process of liquidating hostile elements in the Baltic States, etc., was employed by the Russians when they took these regions at the beginning of the war. I hope therefore that you will be able to give us a free hand to sign the treaty which Stalin desires as soon as possible. Everything portends an immense renewal of the German invasion of Russia in the spring and there is very little we can do to help the only country that is heavily engaged with the German armies.

2. With regard to your conversation with the Staffs about my long telegram, I should like to tell you, for yourself alone, that I am by no means excluding an effort from here to take the weight off Russia once Hitler is definitely committed to the attack. I do not want to discuss this with the Combined Staffs at all at the present time. I hope it can remain secret between us.

3. I am keeping you informed about India so that you may see the difficulties I have to face. The weight of the war is very heavy now, and I must expect it to get steadily worse for some time to come.

Sir Bertrand Glancy[1] to L. S. Amery
(Churchill papers, 20/71)

7 March 1942

Following are my views on effect on Punjab of immediate declaration that India will at future date be given right to secede from Empire. Reasonable section of Moslems who are majority hold unshakeable view that until constitution acceptable to Moslem India is devised, Britain must continue to hold the ropes. They will certainly be worried that constitution on lines contemplated would place power in hands of Hindus whom they already suspect of pro-Japanese tendencies. They will therefore be diverted from working for defence of India as a whole and seek to align themselves elsewhere. Unprecedented intensification of bitterness between Sikhs and Moslems, between whom relations are already dangerously strained, will result.

All communities will wish to keep their own men at home to defend their own interests and recruitment will as a result be very seriously

[1] Bertrand James Glancy, 1882–1953. Joined the Indian Civil Service, 1905. Served in the Foreign and Political Department of the Government of India. Knighted, 1935. Political Adviser to the Crown Representative, 1938–41. Lieutenant-Governor of the Punjab, 1941–6.

affected. Disorders will be inevitable and present greatly reduced scale of security troops likely to be insufficient. Moslem League will probably greatly increase strength in the Punjab and will use influence ruthlessly for purpose of disruption. Premier of Punjab will probably resign with most or all of his Ministers. This would have very serious effect as no-one else could help in the war and hold the Punjab together as present Premier has done.

Declaration that provinces will have local option of acceding to Central India Union will not counteract effect of declaration that India will have right to secede from Empire dealt with above. Punjab is not homogeneous but composed of communities antagonistic to each other and internal trouble would be unavoidable. Punjab would probably not accede to Union. Moslem community would tend to form bloc with co-religionist neighbours.

Winston S. Churchill to William Mackenzie King
(Churchill papers, 20/71)

8 March 1942
Most Secret
Personal and Secret

There is danger of communal position in Punjab being misunderstood at home and following considerations are therefore put forward with particular reference to proposal for local option to remain separate from Central Union.

Punjab Moslems if they remained united could no doubt ensure exercise of option to remain separate in case of Punjab, but for following reasons their own communal apprehensions must be allayed. Sikhs would be alarmed at prospect of predominantly Moslem and separate Punjab and would begin to prepare themselves for trouble. Certainty of such trouble arising would cause Punjab Moslems to look to their own defences. Idea of a separated Punjab would therefore still keep both sides embittered. Number of arms known to be hidden in Punjab gives cause for additional anxiety. Further inflammation of communal passions can only be prevented by guarantee that we will ensure moderation and peace either in a separate or federated Punjab.

Latest routine report from Governor of Punjab refers to serious deterioration in public morale as result of bad news from Far East, and to growing mutual distrust and strain in relations between Moslems and Sikhs.

Winston S. Churchill to William Mackenzie King
(Churchill papers, 20/71)

8 March 1942
Personal and Secret

The matter is far more complicated than it appears. See especially telegrams from Commander-in-Chief and Viceroy. There is no difference between us on policy of a declaration but question of timing is greatly affected by our defeats in the East and imminent fall of Rangoon.

2. For your own information, Chiang was blissfully ignorant about Indian affairs, and seemed to think that Gandhi and Nehru were the only people who mattered in India.

3. In my opinion proposals will certainly be rejected by Congress and become the starting-point for new demands.

Winston S. Churchill to Sir Stafford Cripps[1]
(Churchill papers, 20/67)

8 March 1942

I held last year a number of 'Tank Parliaments,' at which all the Divisional Officers were present. They seemed a very fine lot. But, of course, the experiences we have gained at the front should make continual changes. The reference at 'A'[2] is probably to General Hobart.[3] It was with the greatest difficulty that I secured this officer's reinstatement. Prejudice against him is very strong, and but for my personal intervention he would be a corporal in the Home Guard. I have spoken about his case several times to General Brooke. You would find his opinion, I think, distinctly adverse to any startling promotion. I must put a good deal of confidence in General Brooke.

---

[1] Sir Stafford Cripps had entered the Cabinet as Lord Privy Seal on 19 February 1942. He was also Leader of the House of Commons.

[2] In a letter to Sir Stafford Cripps from Captain J. Hall, about tank warfare.

[3] Percy Cleghorn Stanley Hobart, 1885–1957. Joined the Royal Engineers, 1904. Served on the North-West Frontier of India, 1908. On active service on the Western Front, 1915, and in Mesopotamia, 1916–18, when he was wounded and taken prisoner. Military Cross, DSO (1916), OBE (1918). Served in Palestine, 1918; in Waziristan, 1921. Joined the Royal Tank Corps, 1923; Inspector, Royal Tank Corps, 1933–6. Commander, Tank Brigade, 1934–7. Deputy Director of Staff Duties, War Office, 1937. Major-General, 1937. Director of Military Training, War Office, 1937–8. Raised 7th Armoured Division, Egypt, 1938–9. Pushed into early retirement, 1940, by Maitland Wilson and Wavell, largely because of his unconventional views on tank warfare. Reinstated by Churchill. Raised 11th Armoured Division, 1941–2; 79th Armoured Division, 1942 (commanding it in north-western Europe, 1944–5). Knighted, 1943. His sister married (in 1927) Bernard Montgomery (later Viscount Montgomery of Alamein).

I am not at all sure that speed is the supreme requirement of tanks, certainly not of all tanks. Armour and gun-power decide the matter whenever tank meets tank. Anti-tank weapons are advancing fast in power, and thin-skinned animals will run ever-increasing risks.

I see no reason why you should not show the letter to the Secretary of State for War, stipulating for immunity for your correspondent, whose letter does not impress me.

President Franklin D. Roosevelt to Winston S. Churchill
(Churchill papers, 20/71)

8 March 1942
No. 113[1]

We have been in constant conference since receipt of your message of March 4 to ensure that nothing is left unexplored which can in any way improve our present prospects. We recognize fully the magnitude of the problems confronting you in the Indian Ocean and are equally concerned over those which confront us in the Pacific particularly since the United States assume a heavy responsibility regarding measures for the defence of Australia, New Zealand, and the guarding of their sea approaches. You on the other hand will recognize the difficulties under which we labour in deploying and maintaining in unprepared and distant positions the considerable forces which will be required to meet this critical situation. I know that you will also appreciate that success in holding this region depends largely upon the adequacy of shipping and the availability of munitions and aircraft for arming Dominion forces. The magnitude of the effort which may be put forth by the United States in the Southwest Pacific has a direct relation to the magnitude of the air offensive which the United States will be able to undertake from United Kingdom bases.

2. The United States is now operating a large part of the Pacific Fleet, in the Anzac region for the defence of Australia and New Zealand for preserving a base area for a future decisive offensive against Japan and for containing Japanese naval and air forces in the Pacific. Provided their bases in the west of Australia can be kept secure United States submarines will continue to operate in the ABDA area against Japanese supply lines and against naval forces that exit to the Indian Ocean.

---

[1] Churchill sent a digest of this telegram to the Dominion prime ministers and Generals Wavell and Auchinleck on 22 March 1942.

3. While Japan is indeed extending herself over a large area it must be admitted that the deployment has been skilfully executed and continues to be effective. The energy of the Japanese attack is still very powerful. It is only through a greater energy, skill and determination that Japan can be halted before she attains a dominating position from which it would prove most difficult to eject her. The United States agrees that the Pacific situation is now very grave and if it is to be stabilised requires an immediate concerted and vigorous effort by the United States, Australia and New Zealand. To establish the many defended bases now planned and to transport to them their garrisons together with enough amphibious troops for even minor offensives requires the movement there of some of our amphibious forces and the use of all our combat loaded transports which are not urgently needed at home for elementary training of additional amphibious formations. The loan to the British of transports for further troop movement to India requires the use of combat transports for carrying United States garrisons to positions in the Pacific and thus seriously reduces present possibilities of offensive action in other regions.

4. We concur in your estimate of the importance of the Indian and Middle East areas and agree the reinforcements are required. We also agree that the Australian and New Zealand Divisions now in that region should remain. The Forty First Division is leaving United States by the 18th of this month reaching Australia about April 10th. As a replacement for Australian and New Zealand Divisions allotted to the Middle East and India, the United States is prepared to despatch two additional Divisions one to Australia and one to New Zealand. A convoy of one-half a Division could leave about April 15th and the remainder of this Division about May 15th. Another United States Division can also leave for the Southwest Pacific about May 15th. It should be understood that our willingness to despatch these two Divisions over and above the Forty First which is already set up to go is based on the necessity for economizing in shipping and the continuing security of the Middle East, India, and Ceylon. It is therefore dependent upon the retention of a similar number of Australian and New Zealand Divisions in those theatres. The above movements in the Southwest Pacific can be accomplished provided that some twenty five cargo ships are withdrawn for one voyage from those engaged in transport of Lend-Lease material to the Red Sea and to China and scheduled to sail in April and May.

5. United States can furnish shipping to move two Divisions (40,000 men) with their equipment from the United Kingdom to the Middle East

and India. The first convoy consisting of all the United States shipping and the *Aquitania* can depart for United Kingdom about April 26th and the remainder about May 6th. The supplying of these ships is contingent upon acceptance of the following during the period they are so used:

(a) 'Gymnast'[1] cannot be undertaken.

(b) Movements of United States troops to the British Isles will be limited to those which these ships can take from the United States.

(c) Direct movements to Iceland (c) cannot be made.

(d) Eleven cargo ships must be withdrawn from sailings for Burma and Red Sea during April and May. These ships are engaged in transportation of Lend-Lease material to China and the Middle East.

(e) American contribution to an air offensive against Germany in 1942 would be somewhat curtailed and any American contribution to land operations on the Continent of Europe in 1942 will be materially reduced. It is considered essential that United States ships used for the movement of the two British Divisions be returned to us upon completion of the movement.

6. In addition to considerable United States air anti-aircraft and auxiliary troops there is now in Australia one Division intended for defence of New Caledonia which contributes directly to Australian security. As stated above the Forty First Division is scheduled to sail to Australia on March 18. With the arrival of this Division United States ground and air forces in Australia and New Caledonia will total some 90,000 men. Samoa has been garrisoned and a US Pursuit Squadron has been sent to Suva. With the line from Samoa held New Zealand in its retired position south thereof is not thought to be in danger of serious attack.

7. Personnel Shipping. The present shipbuilding programme seems to be about the maximum that can be attained and any increases would not be available until after June 1944. Included in the programme are 30 C-4 ships each having a lift of 3,675 men and 20 P-2 ships each having a lift of 5,750 men. Thus under construction we now have troopships that will carry 225,250 men. It is understood that the British do not plan to increase their total of troop-carrying ships. Shipping now available under the US flag will lift a total of about 130,000 men. Increases from conversions during 1942 are estimated at least 35,000 men. By June 1943 new construction will give an additional 40,000, by December 1943 an additional 100,000, and by June 1944 an additional 95,000. Thus neglect-

---

[1] 'Gymnast': The proposed Anglo-American amphibious landings in Vichy-controlled French North Africa.

ing losses the total troop-carrying capacity of US vessels by June 1944 will be 400,000 men.

8. Air. The deployment of the American Air Forces which at this stage must be regarded as wholly tentative including Army and shore based Naval aviation will be in accordance with the following strategic concept, offence against Germany using maximum forces, defense of the general area Alaska Hawaii Australia using necessary forces in support of the United States Navy in that area and in maintaining essential sea communication in all US areas, defense of North and South America using essential forces. Tentative distribution by the end of 1942 of first line strength is as follows:

A. Alaska: Army, one Group (30-5) heavy bombers and one Group (80) Pursuit Navy 48 VPB.

B. Hawaii and North Pacific Islands: Army, Two Groups (70) Heavy bombers three Groups plus two Squadrons (290) Pursuit one Squadron (13), Light bombers Navy one two six VPB forty eight VSO 90 VF 90 VSB.

C. South West Pacific and Australia: Army two Groups (70) Heavy bombers two Groups Medium bombers (114) One Group Light bombers (57) five Groups and one Squadron (425) Pursuit Navy 90 VPB, 24 VSO, 81 VSB, 81 VF.

D. Caribbean Area: Army two Groups (70). Heavy Bombers one Group (57). Medium bombers one Group (57) Light bombers four Groups (320) Pursuit Navy 108 VPB, 60 VSO.

E. China–India–Burma Area: Army one Group plus two Squadrons Heavy bombers (60) one Group Pursuit (80) exclusive of AVG.

F. Outposts on lines of communications: Army one Squadron Heavy bombers (8) two Squadrons Medium bombers (26) seven Squadrons Pursuit (175) Navy 48 VPB, 12 VSO.

G. Army Air Forces available for offensive against Germany:

1. By July 1942 three Groups Heavy Bombers (105) One Group Medium Bombers (57) three Groups Light Bombers (171) five Groups Pursuit (400).

2. By October 1943 eleven Groups Heavy Bombers (386) three Groups Medium Bombers (171) five Groups Light Bombers (285) seven Groups Pursuits (560).

3. By January 1943 fifteen Groups Heavy Bombers (525) seven Groups Medium Bombers (399) seven Groups Light Bombers (399) 13 Groups Pursuits (1040). Note Pursuit to be used as Fighter escort for daylight bombing and for offensive sweeps.

9. This does not include airplanes in depot reserve and those essential for operational training. As much as possible as this force is essential in United Kingdom if a concerted offensive against German military strength and resources is to be made in 1942. The above dispositions include forces previously set up for 'Gymnast' and 'Magnet'.[1]

10. In confiding thus fully and personally to you the details of our military arrangements I do not mean that they should be withheld from your close military advisors. I request however that further circulation be drastically reduced.

11. I am sending you a personal suggestion on Sunday in regard to simplification of area responsibilities.

12. This may be a critical period but remember always it is not as bad as some you have so well survived before.

Winston S. Churchill to General Claude Auchinleck
(Churchill papers, 20/71)

8 March 1942
Personal and Secret

The situation disclosed by your appreciation is very serious and not likely to be adjusted by correspondence. I should be glad therefore if you would come home for consultation at your earliest convenience, bringing with you any officers you may require, especially an authority on the state of the tanks and their servicing.

General Claude Auchinleck to Winston S. Churchill
(Churchill papers, 20/71)

9 March 1942

Am certain that I cannot repeat not leave Middle East in present circumstances.

Situation is entirely different to that obtaining last July and I am not repeat not prepared to delegate authority to anyone while strategical situation is so fluid and liable to rapid changes. I can give no more information regarding tank situation than I have already given nor would my coming home make it more possible to stage an earlier offensive.

---

[1] 'Magnet': Anglo-American operations to move United States ground forces into Northern Ireland as part of the build-up for subsequent operations on the European mainland.

I earnestly ask you therefore to reconsider your request. If you desire it I will gladly send senior staff officer who can explain tank situation in more detail.

War Cabinet: Confidential Annex
(Cabinet papers, 65/29)

9 March 1942
12 noon

INDIA

The War Cabinet first considered the revise of the draft Declaration which was approved.

The timing of its issue was next considered.

The Prime Minister said that events had shown that the immediate issue of the Declaration, without any preliminary sounding of public opinion in India, would be most unwise. This course would probably lead to the rejection of the Declaration by Congress, and would give rise to divisions of opinion here. In the circumstances, he thought that the right course was to accept the very generous offer made by the Lord Privy Seal[1] to visit India and discuss matters with the leaders of the main Indian political parties. The whole War Cabinet were greatly indebted to the Lord Privy Seal for this offer, and he would go with the fullest confidence of all of them. The Lord Privy Seal would take with him the draft Declaration as the plan which he would discuss with the leaders of Indian opinion, with a view to seeing whether it met with the measure of acceptance vital to its success.

The next question concerned the date of the announcement of the Lord Privy Seal's mission. In discussion, Wednesday 11th March was regarded as the most appropriate day.

The Prime Minister read to the War Cabinet a first draft of the statement which he proposed should be made.

This met with general approval.

Importance was attached to this statement making it clear that the Lord Privy Seal was taking out to India a specific scheme approved by the War Cabinet. Otherwise, it would be said that he was going out to negotiate.

---

[1] Sir Stafford Cripps.

Winston S. Churchill to Sir John Anderson[1]
(Churchill papers, 20/67)

9 March 1942

I must by Thursday next be in a position to announce the new arrangements for the Office of Minister of Production.

Mr Lyttelton has been exploring matters with Sir Edward Bridges and the various Heads of Departments concerned. In principle, the White Paper is the basis, and I have asked him to make the amendments in it which are now possible. It is hoped that it can be shortened and simplified.

When we see it in its new form, we can decide whether it will be necessary to lay it before Parliament. In any case, there will have to be a debate on the subject some time after the present week.

I shall be obliged if you will sit with Mr Lyttelton today and tomorrow, and endeavour to make me the final recommendations.

The Minister of Production is to have full effective powers to concert the action of the Departments concerned, except as reserved to the Admiralty, and to supervise and superintend their work, including the function of both correction and initiative. He is to have effective control of the allocation of raw materials, &c., and the assignments of priorities in accordance with the policy of the War Cabinet. He will conduct all American and foreign business. He will not have a separate Department, but he will be equipped with an adequate secretariat and staff for all these purposes.

Taking the above as a guide, pray let me have your assistance.[2]

Winston S. Churchill to Josef Stalin
(Churchill papers, 20/71)

9 March 1942
Personal and Secret

I have sent a message to President Roosevelt urging him to approve our signing the agreement with you about the frontiers of Russia at the end of the war.

2. I have given express directions that the supplies promised by us shall not in any way be interrupted or delayed.

---

[1] Lord President of the Council.
[2] Churchill sent copies of this minute to Sir Stafford Cripps and Oliver Lyttelton.

3. Now that the season is improving we are resuming heavy air offensive both by day and night upon Germany. We are continuing to study other measures for taking some of the weight off you.

4. The continued progress of the Russian Armies and the known terrible losses of the enemy are naturally our sources of greatest encouragement in this trying period.

Winston S. Churchill to A. V. Alexander[1] and
Admiral of the Fleet Sir Dudley Pound
(Churchill papers, 20/67)

10 March 1942

Is it credible that the Japanese have at present nine capital ships and two large aircraft carriers all building simultaneously?[2] If so, the future is indeed serious. On what evidence does this statement rest? What would be the amount of armour-plate, steel, and modern fittings of all kinds required for the completion of such an enormous fleet within two years from now? What yards are available for the simultaneous construction of so many ships? When is it supposed they were laid down? What is known of the ordnance industry of Japan? There may be other questions which should be asked. Pray let me have a considered reply.

We must on no account underrate the Japanese. Facts are, however, what is needed.

2. While not at present being completely convinced by the above assumptions, I cordially approve the development of shore-based torpedo-aircraft.

Winston S. Churchill to General Sir Alan Brooke
(Churchill papers, 20/67)

10 March 1942
Personal and Most Secret

In case we reach a complete deadlock with General Auchinleck, it would be right to consider the claims of Lord Gort,[3] who has not been

---

[1] First Lord of the Admiralty.

[2] Defence Committee papers, DO23 of 1942, 'Air Requirements for the Successful Prosecution of the War at Sea, Appendix 1, Capital Ships, Present and Prospective Strengths'.

[3] John Standish Surtees Prendergast Vereker, 1886–1946. Succeeded his father as 6th Viscount Gort, 1902. Educated at Harrow and Sandhurst. 2nd Lieutenant, 1905; Captain, 1914. On active service, 1914–18 (despatches nine times, Victoria Cross, Military Cross, DSO, and two

very well treated by fortune or otherwise. Perhaps you would speak to me about this.[1]

What also is your opinion of General Wilson?[2]

2. General Macfarlane[3] is wasted in Russia. He should be replaced by someone of the staff officer type and brought home to some Command. The Lord Privy Seal, who knows him well, speaks of him in the highest terms, and also thinks he is ill-placed in Russia.

Winston S. Churchill to Sir Archibald Sinclair and
Air Chief Marshal Sir Charles Portal
(Churchill papers, 20/67)

10 March 1942

I am not at all convinced by Fighter Command's defence of their accident rate, and am not prepared to remain satisfied with it. Considering the great plethora of pilots, the training can be extended, and properly trained pilots coming from long courses of instruction ought not to be represented as undisciplined boys.

I must request a continuance of severe pressure from the Air Ministry upon all Commands.

Let me have a weekly return by Groups from the Fighter Command of the accidents, together with the sorties.

I should be glad to receive proposals for increasing the length of the runways with a view to assigning a higher priority for the supply of materials, &c.

bars). General, 1937. Chief of the Imperial General Staff, 1937–9. Commander-in-Chief of the British Field Force, 1939–40. Inspector-General to the Forces for Training, 1940. Governor and Commander-in-Chief, Gibraltar, 1941–2; Malta, 1942–4. Field Marshal, 1943. High Commissioner and Commander-in-Chief, Palestine, 1944–5.

[1] In August 1942, General Auchinleck was replaced as Commander-in-Chief Middle East Command by General Sir Harold Alexander and as General Officer Commanding 8th Army by Lieutenant-General William Gott, who was killed in Egypt before taking up command. On Gott's death, Lieutenant-General Bernard Montgomery was appointed commander of the 8th Army.

[2] General Maitland Wilson, Commander-in-Chief, Persia–Iraq Command, 1942–3.

[3] Frank Noel Mason-MacFarlane, 1889–1953. On active service, 1914–18, France, Belgium, and Mesopotamia; Afghan War, 1919. Military Attaché, Budapest, Vienna, and Berne, 1931–4; Berlin and Copenhagen, 1937–9. Director of Military Intelligence, British Expeditionary Force, France, and Belgium, 1939–40; Gibraltar, 1940. Head of British Military Mission to Moscow, 1941–2. Governor and Commander-in-Chief, Gibraltar, 1942–4. Knighted, 1943. Chief Commissioner, Allied Central Commission, Italy, 1944. Colonel Commandant, Royal Artillery, 1944. Labour MP for North Paddington, 1945–6.

Winston S. Churchill to Lord Cherwell
(Churchill papers, 20/67)

10 March 1942

I agree with the general outline of your minute.[1] In particular, I am opposed to the heavy taxation of entertainments. It would be well worth while rationing bread moderately in order to bring in the more nourishing Lend-Lease foods. It would be better to ration than to let the stocks run down. Bread is scandalously wasted now and often fed to pigs and chickens. The great thing is to keep the price down, so that the poorest can buy their full ration.

I deprecate the policy of 'Misery first,' which is too often inculcated by people who are glad to see war-weariness spread as a prelude to surrender.

The value of all the various self-strafing proposals should be estimated in tonnage of imports. If there is a heavy economy to be achieved on any article, let us effect it; but it would be unwise to embark upon a lot of fussy restrictions in order to give, or try to give, satisfaction to the Fleet Street journalists who are exempted from military service, have no burden of responsibility to bear, and live in the restaurants of the Strand.

You should draft something for me couched in more decorous form.

Winston S. Churchill to Lord Linlithgow
(Churchill papers, 20/71)

10 March 1942
Action this Day
Personal and Secret

I agree with you that to fling out our declaration without knowing where we are with the Indian Parties would be to court what you rightly call a flop and start an acrimonious controversy at the worst possible moment for everybody. Yesterday before I was shown your 16U we decided not to publish any declaration now but to send a War Cabinet Minister out to see whether it could be put across on the spot because otherwise what is the use of having all the trouble? Stafford Cripps, with great public spirit, volunteered for this thankless and hazardous task. He will start almost immediately. In spite of all the differences in our lines of approach, I have entire confidence in his over-riding resolve to beat

---

[1] Opposing further restrictions on civilian food consumption.

Hitler and Co. at all costs. The announcement of his mission will still febrile agitation and will give time for the problem to be calmly solved or alternatively proved to be, for the time being, insoluble.

2. The document on which we have agreed represents our united policy. If that is rejected by the Indian Parties for whose benefit it has been devised, our sincerity will be proved to the world and we shall stand together and fight on it here, should that ever be necessary.

3. I hope therefore that you will await Lord Privy Seal's arrival and go into the whole matter with him. He is of course bound by the draft declaration, which is our utmost limit. Moreover, he will give full weight to the military and executive position in which India is now placed.

4. It would be impossible, owing to unfortunate rumours and publicity, and the general American outlook to stand on a purely negative attitude and the Cripps Mission is indispensable to prove our honesty of purpose and to gain time for the necessary consultations.

5. My own position is that nothing matters except the successful and unflinching defence of India as a part of the general victory, and this is also the conviction of Sir Stafford Cripps. Do not therefore think of quitting your post at this juncture, for this might be the signal for a general collapse in British Indian resistance with serious rupture of political unity here. We have a very bad time immediately ahead but nothing like so bad as what we have already forced our way through. The Secretary of State will apprise you further by official telegram.

Winston S. Churchill to John Curtin
(Churchill papers, 20/71)

10 March 1942
Personal and Most Secret

In response to various suggestions and requests which I made to the President for the common conduct of the war against Japan, I have received a message containing the following passage[1]:

'We concur in your estimate of the importance of the Indian and Middle East areas and agree the reinforcements are required. We also agree that the Australian and New Zealand Divisions now

[1] See Roosevelt's telegram No. 113 of 8 March 1942 (pages 364–8).

in that region should remain. The Forty First Division is leaving United States by the 18th of this month reaching Australia about April 10th. As replacement for Australian and New Zealand Divisions allotted to the Middle East and India, the United States is prepared to despatch two additional Divisions one to Australia and one to New Zealand. A convoy of one-half a Division could leave about April 15th and the remainder of this Division about May 15th. Another United States Division can also leave for the Southwest Pacific about May 15th. It should be understood that our willingness to despatch these two Divisions over and above the Forty First which is already set up to go is based on the necessity for economizing in shipping and the continuing security of the Middle East, India, and Ceylon. It is therefore dependent upon the retention of a similar number of Australian and New Zealand Divisions in those theatres. The above movements in the Southwest Pacific can be accomplished provided that some twenty five cargo ships are withdrawn for one voyage from those engaged in transport of Lend-Lease material to the Red Sea and to China and scheduled to sail in April and May.'

2. Our 5th British Division is about to sail from the United Kingdom. The President has also promised to give me the shipping to move two additional British Divisions (40,000 men) in April and May, and we are sending further British Divisions in our own ships during the next few months. How these Divisions will be disposed between the Middle East and India must depend upon how things are going when they have rounded the Cape. We have also postponed for an indefinite period the completion of the movement of various United States Divisions into Northern Ireland and Iceland (C) on which we had counted, in order to facilitate all the above movement of troops to the East and Far East.

3. You may be sure that the presence of considerable United States forces in the Anzac area will emphasise to the United States the importance of protecting that area by its main sea power and also of accelerating the equipment of existing Australian forces for which I am pressing.

4. I hope in these circumstances you will feel able to leave the 9th Australian Division in the Middle East where its presence is most sorely needed. We will send on the Brigades of the 6th Division, which you agreed might be stopped off for a while at Ceylon, as soon as the minimum arrangements for this all-important point can be made.

Winston S. Churchill to Peter Fraser
(Churchill papers, 20/71)

10 March 1942
Personal and Most Secret

3.[1] It is certain in view of the shipping position that an American division can reach New Zealand sooner than the New Zealand division can be withdrawn from the Middle East, and that a more economical use can be made of our resources and a more rapid deployment against the enemy. Moreover you may be sure that the presence of considerable United States forces in the Anzac area will emphasise to the United States the importance of protecting that area by its main sea power, and also of accelerating the equipment of existing New Zealand forces for which I am pressing.

4. You have never asked for the withdrawal of your Division and we have admired the constancy of spirit and devotion to the cause which has animated your Government and people. All the more do I feel this promised aid from the United States will be gratifying. I hope therefore you will empower me to accept the offer and to thank the President on your behalf. It would of course be very good if you cared to cable him yourself.

Winston S. Churchill to Sir John Miles[2]
(Churchill papers, 20/53)

10 March 1942

Dear Sir John Miles,

I am complimented that the Fellows of Merton should have remembered my father's connection with their College.[3]

I am very glad to accept the offer of an Honorary Fellowship which you have been so good as to extend to me on their behalf, and I shall prize this mark of distinction as a tribute to my father's memory.

Yours very faithfully,
Winston S. Churchill

---

[1] The first section of this telegram was identical to the first two paragraphs of the previous telegram to John Curtin.

[2] John Charles Miles, 1870–1963. Tutor at Merton College, Oxford, 1899–1930. Legal Assistant, Ministry of Munitions, 1915–18. Solicitor, Ministry of Labour, 1918–19. Knighted, 1919. Senior Research Fellow, Merton, 1930–6; Warden, 1936–47.

[3] Lord Randolph Churchill was an undergraduate at Merton College, Oxford, from 1867 to 1870.

Winston S. Churchill: statement
(Hansard)

11 March 1942   House of Commons
12 noon

SIR STAFFORD CRIPPS' MISSION TO INDIA

The crisis in the affairs of India arising out of the Japanese advance has made us wish to rally all the forces of Indian life, to guard their land from the menace of the invader. In August, 1940, a full statement was made about the aims and policy we are pursuing in India. This amounted, in short, to a promise that, as soon as possible after the war, India should attain Dominion status, in full freedom and equality with this country and the other Dominions, under a Constitution to be framed by Indians, by agreement among themselves and acceptable to the main elements in Indian national life. This was, of course, subject to the fulfilment of our obligations for the protection of minorities, including the depressed classes, and of our treaty obligations to the Indian States, and to the settlement of certain lesser matters arising out of our long association with the fortunes of the Indian subcontinent.

However, Sir, in order to clothe these general declarations with precision and to convince all classes, races and creeds in India of our sincere resolve, the War Cabinet have agreed unitedly upon conclusions for present and future action which, if accepted by India as a whole, would avoid the alternative dangers either that the resistance of a powerful minority might impose an indefinite veto upon the wishes of the majority or that a majority decision might be taken which would be resisted to a point destructive of internal harmony and fatal to the setting-up of a new Constitution. We had thought of setting forth immediately the terms of this attempt, by a constructive British contribution, to aid India in the realisation of full self-government; we are, however, apprehensive that to make a public announcement at such a moment as this might do more harm than good. We must first assure ourselves that our scheme would win a reasonable and practical measure of acceptance, and thus promote the concentration of all Indian thought and energies upon the defence of the native soil. We should ill serve the common cause if we made a declaration which would be rejected by essential elements in the Indian world, and which provoked fierce constitutional and communal disputes at a moment when the enemy is at the gates of India.

Accordingly, we propose to send a member of the War Cabinet to India, to satisfy himself upon the spot, by personal consultation, that the conclusions upon which we are agreed, and which we believe represent a just and final solution, will achieve their purpose. My right hon. and learned Friend the Lord Privy Seal and Leader of the House has volunteered to undertake this task. He carries with him the full confidence of His Majesty's Government, and he will strive in their name to procure the necessary measure of assent, not only from the Hindu majority, but also from those great minorities, amongst which the Moslems are the most numerous and on many grounds pre-eminent.

The Lord Privy Seal will, at the same time, consult with the Viceroy and the Commander-in-Chief upon the military situation, bearing always in mind the paramount responsibility of His Majesty's Government by every means in their power to shield the peoples of India from the perils which now beset them. We must remember that India has a great part to play in the world's struggle for freedom and that her helping hand must be extended in loyal comradeship to the valiant Chinese people, who have fought alone so long. We must remember also that India is one of the bases from which the strongest counter-blows must be struck at the advance of tyranny and aggression.

My right hon. Friend will set out as soon as convenient and suitable arrangements can be made. I am sure he will command in his task the heartfelt good wishes of all parts of the House and that, meanwhile, no word will be spoken or Debates be held, here or in India, which would add to the burden he has assumed in his mission, or lessen the prospects of a good result. During my right hon. and learned Friend's absence from this House, his duties as Leader will be discharged by my right hon. Friend the Foreign Secretary.

Henry Channon: diary
('Chips', page 324)

11 March 1942

Winston rose and without a preliminary cheer announced that important decisions had been made about India and that Cripps was going there at once (which I knew). The House appreciated the solemnity of the moment, and that our great Empire of India was perhaps to be bartered away.

Winston S. Churchill to Sir John Anderson
(Churchill papers, 20/67)

11 March 1942

FURTHER RESTRICTION OF CIVIL CONSUMPTION

Before we decide upon all or any of the measures proposed in your paper, we should have detailed estimates of the amount of shipping and of man-power which each will save. We must know precisely what the gains are and whether they are large enough to justify imposing further burdens which may produce war-weariness and undermine the will to victory.

The public may be willing to make sacrifices, not realising that the effect of these may be to sap their staying power later; the journalists, who lead comparatively sheltered lives, do not always fairly represent public feeling.

I am altogether opposed to the heavy taxation of entertainments.

Will you consider whether it would be worth while to impose a moderate restriction on bread consumption, in order to enable us to bring in the more nourishing Lease-Lend foods awaiting shipment?

If bread were included in the points rationing scheme at a fairly low price in points, the poorest classes and those accustomed to consume more bulky food than the average man could get what they require, while there would be a check upon the scandalous waste of stale bread now so common.

If there is a heavy economy to be achieved on any article, let us effect it; but it would be unwise to embark on a lot of fussy restrictions to satisfy a misguided clamour for sacrifice.

President Franklin D. Roosevelt to Winston S. Churchill
(Cabinet papers, 66/22)[1]

11 March 1942
Purely personal
No. 116

I have given much thought to the problem of India and I am grateful that you have kept me in touch with it. As you can well realize, I have felt

---

[1] Churchill circulated Roosevelt's telegram to the War Cabinet as War Cabinet paper WP 118.

much diffidence in making any suggestions, and it is a subject which, of course, all of you good people know far more about than I do.

I have tried to approach the problem from the point of view of history and with a hope that the injection of a new thought to be used in India might be of assistance to you. That is why I go back to the inception of the Government of the United States. During the revolution, from 1775 to 1783, the British Colonies set themselves up as thirteen States, each one under a different form of government, although each one assumed individual sovereignty. While the war lasted there was great confusion between these separate sovereignties, and the only two connecting links were the Continental Congress (a body of ill-defined powers and large inefficiencies) and second the Continental Army which was rather badly maintained by the thirteen states.

In 1783, at the end of the war, it was clear that the new responsibilities of the thirteen sovereignties could not be welded into a Federal Union because the experiment was still in the making and any effort to arrive at a final framework would have come to naught. Therefore, the thirteen sovereignties joined in the Articles of Confederation, an obvious stopgap Government, to remain in effect only until such time as experience and trial and error could bring about a permanent union. The thirteen sovereignties, from 1783 to 1789, proved, through lack of a federal power, that they would soon fly apart into separate nations.

In 1787 a Constitutional Convention was held with only 20–5 or 30 active participants, representing all of the States. They met, not as a parliament, but as a small group of sincere patriots, with the sole objective of establishing a federal government. The discussion was recorded but the meetings were not held before an audience. The present constitution of the United States resulted and soon received the assent of two thirds of the States.

It is merely a thought of mine to suggest the setting up of what might be called a temporary government in India, headed by a small representative group, covering different castes, occupations, religious and geographies – this group to be recognized as a temporary dominion government. It would, of course, represent existing governments of the British Provinces and would also represent the Council of Princes, but my principal thought is that it would be charged with setting up a body to consider a more permanent government for the whole country – this consideration to be extended over a period of five or six years or at least until a year after the end of the war. I suppose that this central temporary governing group, speaking for the new dominion, would have certain executive and administrative powers over public services, such as finances, railways, telegraphs and other things which we call public services.

Perhaps the analogy of some such method to the travails and problems of the United States from 1783 to 1789 might give a new slant in India itself, and it might cause the people there to forget hard feelings, to become more loyal to the British Empire, and to stress the danger of Japanese domination, together with the advantage of peaceful evolution as against chaotic revolution.

Such a move is strictly in line with the world changes of the past half century and with the democratic processes of all who are fighting Nazism. I hope that whatever you do the move will be made from London and that there should be no criticism in India that it is being made grudgingly or by compulsion. For the love of Heaven don't bring me into this, though I do want to be of help. It is, strictly speaking, none of my business, except insofar as it is a part and parcel of the successful fight that you and I are making.

Roosevelt

Winston S. Churchill to General Hastings Ismay,
for the Chiefs of Staff Committee
(Churchill papers, 20/67)

12 March 1942
Action this Day
Most Secret

It is necessary to study with urgent attention 'Bonus'.[1] For this purpose it should be assumed: (1) that Force H[2] moves from Gibraltar; (2) that its place is taken by the American tank force mentioned by First Sea Lord today. I would ask the President about this tomorrow, if desired; (3) that the 4,000 men and ships mentioned by CCO[3] at the same meeting should be employed; (4) that zero should be about the 30th April; (5) that in the event of success the Commandos should be relieved by garrison troops at the earliest moment. The Foreign Secretary has suggested

[1] 'Bonus': the plan to seize Vichy-held Madagascar (later called Operation 'Ironclad').

[2] Force H: a British naval formation created in 1940 to replace French naval power in the western Mediterranean that had been removed by the French armistice with Nazi Germany. Force H was based at Gibraltar, the base of the Flag Officer Commanding, North Atlantic, but the commanding officer of Force H reported directly to the First Sea Lord.

[3] CCO: Chief of Combined Operations (Admiral Lord Louis Mountbatten).

that their place could be taken by Belgian troops from the Congo, which are said to be good and numerous and would readily be forthcoming. Some British or South African elements could no doubt be found. The question of allowing Free French troops to come in on strictly limited terms after the fighting is over in order to conciliate French opinion should be considered. The advantage of the Americans being stationed at Gibraltar *pro tem* is considerable in itself and would, as First Sea Lord pointed out, probably prevent bombing reprisals for 'Bonus' being taken on the harbour.

All the above seems to form a harmony. Pray let me have a plan of action or, alternatively, reasons against it. We shall need some of these Commandos in the East anyhow.

Winston S. Churchill to General Claude Auchinleck
(Churchill papers, 20/71)

12 March 1942
Personal and Most Secret

Last week I proposed to the President that he should send an additional United States division to Australia (over and above the Forty First already sailed) and another one to New Zealand bracket three in all bracket provided that to save shipping the New Zealand Division and Ninth Australian Division were left in Middle East. He readily consented and I have made the offer to Australia and New Zealand. Should they accept, as their interest urges, position in Levant–Caspian theatre would be eased. Furthermore, President has granted my request for American shipping to carry two British divisions to Middle East or India as situation may require. Finally we are moving in British shipping another three divisions from UK (one of which, the Fifth, sails shortly), interspersed with drafts and details in the next five convoys including March. Total British divisions to move is thus five during period March to July. I consider this a very great improvement especially if Australians and New Zealanders agree.[1]

---

[1] On 14 March 1942 General Auchinleck replied to Churchill: 'This is splendid news and should help to ease situation considerably' (*Churchill papers, 20/71*).

Winston S. Churchill to Admiral Sir Geoffrey Layton[1]
(Churchill papers, 20/71)

12 March 1942
Immediate

It may no doubt be prudent to order women and non-combatants to leave discreetly, but why is it necessary to proclaim this fact to the enemy, thus adding to your dangers and giving the impression to the world of undue alarm? This report should never have been allowed to circulate outside Ceylon. Make sure you put the strictest censorship on every message leaving the island and let nothing out that does not indicate and inculcate high morale.[2]

Winston S. Churchill to Harry Hopkins
(Churchill papers, 20/71)

12 March 1942
Personal and Secret

I am most deeply concerned at the immense sinkings of tankers west of the 40th meridian and in the Caribbean Sea. In January, 18 ships totalling 221,000 dead-weight tons were sunk or damaged; in February the number rose to 34, totalling 364,941 dead-weight tons; in the first 11 days of March 7 vessels, totalling 88,449 dead-weight tons have been sunk. Yesterday alone 30,000 tons were reported as sunk or damaged. Thus in little over two months, in these waters alone, about 60 tankers have been sunk or damaged, totalling some 675,000 dead-weight tons. In addition to this several tankers are over due.

2. By re-arrangement of Atlantic convoy duties a considerable number of American destroyers have been released from escort duties on the cross-Atlantic routes for other services. We have handed over 24 AS Trawlers,[3] of which 23 have now reached you.

3. The situation is so serious that drastic action of some kind is necessary, and we very much hope that you will be able to provide additional

---

[1] Commander-in-Chief, Ceylon.

[2] Admiral Layton replied on 22 March 1942: 'Your message of 12th March received. My intention was to give a definite ruling regarding evacuation in order to remove the existing state of uncertainty and undercurrent of alarmist talk which was prevailing. My notice has had desired effect locally but I regret very much that I omitted to take precautions with censorship to stop its being sent out by Reuters' ('Personal and Secret', 22 March 1942, *Churchill papers, 20/72*).

[3] AS Trawlers: anti-submarine trawlers.

escort forces to organize immediate convoys in the West Indies–Bermuda area by withdrawing a few of your destroyers from other services, even if this means temporarily weakening your destroyer strength in the Pacific, until the 10 Corvettes we are handing over to you come into service.

4. The only other alternatives are, either, to stop temporarily the sailing of tankers which would gravely jeopardise our operational supplies, or to open out the cycle of Halifax–UK convoys thus for a period releasing sufficient escort vessels to make up the West Indies convoys. It must be realised, however, that not only will this further reduce our imports by about 30,000 tons a month, but will also take some little time to become effective.

5. I should like these alternatives to be discussed on the highest naval level at once.

If through opening out convoy cycle we were forced to reduce our imports for a time, this would have to be taken into consideration by you in helping us out with new tonnage in the last half of the year. Please let me know whether you think it well to bring all this before the President straight away.

6. I am enormously relieved by the splendid telegrams I have had from the President on the largest issues. It is most comforting to feel we are in such complete agreement of war outlook.

Please convey my personal greetings to King, Marshall and Arnold and say (quote) Happy days will come again (unquote). Trust you are well. Kindest regards to you and Diana.[1]

Lord Beaverbrook to Winston S. Churchill
(A. J. P. Taylor, 'Beaverbrook', page 523)

12 March 1942

It is my understanding that I will act in America as a line of communication from you to the President. I will not be expected to take any part in the organisation and machinery of the Washington agencies of the British Government.

---

[1] Hopkins' youngest daughter.

Winston S. Churchill to the Chiefs of Staff Committee
(Churchill papers, 20/67)

13 March 1942   Chequers
Most Secret

DISTRIBUTION OF FORCES, FAR EAST

On this lay-out of Japanese forces it seems very unlikely that an immediate full-scale invasion of Australia could take place. You are now making an appreciation for Australia of her position and this disposition of Japanese forces might well be the starting-point.

2. It seems to me that if the Japanese encounter difficulties in moving through Assam and if the Ceylon situation becomes solid for us, they will be more likely to turn northwards upon China.

Winston S. Churchill to Admiral of the Fleet Sir Dudley Pound
(Churchill papers, 20/67)

13 March 1942   Chequers
Most Secret

Where is *Centurion*[1] now? Can she not play any part in our combinations? If she were at Colombo, for instance, she could help shield a warship and make the enemy think we had one more. Think how much better off we should have been if she had been properly sunk at the mouth of Tripoli harbour.

2. Will you also kindly let me have a report on the air attack on *Tirpitz*, explaining how it was that twelve of our machines managed to get no hits as compared with the extraordinary efficiency of the Japanese attack on *Prince of Wales* and *Repulse*. Was *Tirpitz* under an air umbrella at the time, or not?

---

[1] HMS *Centurion*, a King George V class battleship, launched in November 1911 (when Churchill was First Lord of the Admiralty). Present at the Battle of Jutland, 1916. In the Black Sea, supporting the British intervention in Russia, 1919. Decommissioned, 1924. Fitted with a false superstructure to resemble a new battleship, 1941. Simulated an operational battleship in the eastern Mediterranean, June 1942. Stationed off Suez as an anti-aircraft ship, 1942–4. Deliberately sunk as a breakwater off the Normandy coast after D-Day, June 1944. Hit by German shore batteries: the Germans claimed that all but 70 of its several hundred crewmen had been killed; in fact the 70 seen leaving the ship were its entire crew.

Winston S. Churchill to Admiral of the Fleet Sir Dudley Pound
(Churchill papers, 20/67)

13 March 1942   Chequers
Secret

I noticed that when *Tirpitz* was attacked unsuccessfully by our torpedo aircraft she turned away behind a smoke-screen. Why was this manoeuvre not open to Admiral Phillips?[1] Had he the means of making smoke? Could not his destroyers have put up a smoke-screen? Or were they afraid of spoiling the shooting of his AA guns?

Winston S. Churchill to Oliver Lyttelton
(Churchill papers, 20/67)

13 March 1942   Chequers

COMMENT BY THE MINISTER OF STATE
ON A MEMORANDUM ON THE MIDDLE EAST
BY AN OFFICER OF THE IRISH GUARDS[2]

An officer of the Irish Guards might well be serving in some unit other than his own battalion. I do not know who the officer is, but it seems to me that the points he makes ought to be considered. The thing is to be sure where we are; therefore I never disdain unpalatable information.

---

[1] Commander-in-Chief of the Eastern Fleet, drowned when his flagship, the *Prince of Wales*, was sunk by Japanese torpedo bombers on 10 December 1941.

[2] 'Colonel Harvie Watt's Minute to the Prime Minister: Notes on the Middle East by an Officer of the Irish Guards', 2 March 1942 (*Foreign Office papers, 954/15A/5526*). These notes set out their author's view of problems in the Middle East. The main topics are: Egyptian King Farouk's attempt 'to play the British Embassy off against the Army' on the understanding that the Empire would not take over Egypt during the war, and poor treatment of British troops, e.g., exorbitant prices charged to British troops; extra work time for British; GHQ giving promotions only to those who operate at GHQ despite lack of experience; poor intelligence; late pay of officers and troops; slow mail delivery; and differences in pay between British and Dominion troops. The writer conludes: 'The feeling that the Services today have, is that the war is a political racket, in spite of all publicity to the contrary. England and Empire are not fighting total war, but that the English and Dominion Politicians and Political Parties are out for themselves and power after the war, and the mass are looked on as sheep for the use of a Politician...these notes are a summary of [the] thoughts which the Authorities never hear about.

Winston S. Churchill to Sir Archibald Sinclair and
Air Chief Marshal Sir Charles Portal
(Churchill papers, 20/67)

13 March 1942   Chequers
Secret and Private

TORPEDO-CARRYING AIRCRAFT

The attached papers[1] represent opinions which I hear repeated from all quarters. Pray let me have your answer to the principal points raised, not for communication in that form to my correspondent, but in order that the position shall be made clear. Afterwards it will have to come before the Defence Committee.

2. You need not argue the value of bombing Germany, because I have my own opinion about that, namely, that it is not decisive, but better than doing nothing, and indeed is a formidable method of injuring the enemy. I am aware also that a considerable conversion into torpedo-bombers has taken place, and that torpedoes are perhaps a bottle-neck: also that many have been sent to the Eastern Mediterranean: others will be needed in the Bay of Bengal, &c. Let me, however, have all the figures of what has been done and what is now planned. I certainly consider that shore-based torpedo-bombers should have priority over high-level bombers. Evidently they are a great defence against invasion.

3. I hope you realise how very widely the existing policy of the Air Ministry is challenged by opinion. For instance, the Archbishop of Canterbury[2] yesterday spoke to me for half an hour at luncheon on the failure of high-level bombing. He seemed to know a great deal about it, and said these were the opinions he heard on every side in the elevated circles in which he moves.

4. There are also great complaints that the Navy has not been given a fair share of the aircraft it needs, both fighters and torpedo-bombers, and that it has been overlain by the Air Ministry. I do not want lengthy explanations, but the dominant facts.

[1] Letter from Major G. Owen, MP, enclosing a memorandum by a friend on torpedo-carrying aircraft.

[2] Cosmo Gordon Lang, 1864–1945. Educated at Glasgow University and Balliol College, Oxford. Fellow of All Souls, 1889–93. Dean of Divinity, Magdalen College, Oxford, 1893–6. Honorary Chaplain to Queen Victoria from 1899 to her death in 1901; assisted with her funeral arrangements. Bishop of Stepney, 1901–8. Archbishop of York, 1908–21. Privy Councillor, 1909. Archbishop of Canterbury, 1921–42. In a broadcast on Sunday, 13 December 1936, three days after the Abdication, he criticized Edward VIII for having 'sought his happiness in a manner inconsistent with the Christian principles of marriage, and within a social circle whose standard and way of life are alien to all the best instincts and traditions of his people'. Knighted, 1937. Created Baron, 1942. Retired, 31 March 1942.

5. The question of putting the Coastal Command under the Admiralty is one, which will have to be faced in the near future.

General Sir Alan Brooke: diary
('War Diaries, Field Marshal Lord Alanbrooke', page 239)

13 March 1942

Considered Auchinleck's refusal to come home at this morning's COS. Drafted letter to PM about it, however he called up from Chequers and I had to tell him about it. He was infuriated and at once again suggested relieving him of his command! Would not agree to Auchinleck's suggestion that I should go out with CAS.

[...]

In afternoon another telephone call from Chequers, PM saying that he would now send telegram to Auchinleck! I shudder at what he may put in it, and we shall have to vet it tomorrow morning![1]

Winston S. Churchill to General Hastings Ismay,
for the Chiefs of Staff Committee
(Churchill papers, 20/67)

13 March 1942   Chequers
Most Secret

OPERATION 'BONUS': SEIZURE OF MADAGASCAR

I am much concerned at this delay, which may be fatal. Why cannot two battalions of the 5th Division be made available to support the Commandos, all going in the same convoy together? A delay of two or three weeks cannot be accepted. Besides, this would require a new convoy from England to Gibraltar. Moreover, the American naval movement must begin at once, and I must telegraph to the President on the subject. Every day you wait the place will be strengthened. There has been so much talk about the matter in the Press and from Vichy sources that very likely something is going on. See also Washington 1417 of today.

---

[1] In a subsequent letter to Auchinleck, Brooke referred to the trouble that his refusal to return home for consultation was causing and to the Chiefs of Staff's decision to send out General Nye, the Vice-Chief of the Imperial General Staff, to report. Brooke was anxious that Auchinleck should feel he was being supported from home. 'I hope', he wrote of Nye's impending visit, 'you will give him a full picture of your existing situation with its difficulties and prospects. Without such a full picture it will be very hard to make the PM understand reasons for delays' (*Turn of the Tide*, page 338).

Pray meet together this afternoon and have a further try. The sooner it is done the more certainly can the Commando forces be brought back here for other purposes.

Winston S. Churchill to President Franklin D. Roosevelt
(Churchill papers, 20/71)

14 March 1942 Chequers
Personal and Most Secret
No. 44

We have decided to do 'Bonus', and as it is quite impossible to weaken our Eastern Fleet we shall have to use the whole of Force H now at Gibraltar. This will leave the western exit of the Mediterranean uncovered, which is most undesirable.

Would it be possible for you to send say two battleships, an aircraft carrier, some cruisers and destroyers, from the Atlantic, to take the place of Force H temporarily? Force H would have to leave Gibraltar not later than March 30 and could hardly reach Gibraltar again before the end of June. We have not planned any operation for Force H inside the Mediterranean between April 1 and the end of June. It is most unlikely that French retaliation, if any, for 'Bonus' would take the form of attacking United States ships by air.

Moral effect of United States ships at Gibraltar would, in itself, be highly beneficial on both sides of the straits. Operation 'Bonus' cannot go forward unless you are able to do this. On the other hand, there are the greatest dangers in leaving 'Bonus' to become a Japanese base. We are not telling anyone about our plans and assaulting troops mingle quite easily with our March convoy to the east. A separate telegram will explain the meaning of 'Bonus'.

Winston S. Churchill to President Franklin D. Roosevelt
(Churchill papers, 20/71)

14 March 1942 Chequers
Personal and Secret
No. 45

For 'Bonus' read Madagascar now renamed 'Ironclad'.

Winston S. Churchill to Field Marshal Sir John Dill[1]
(Churchill papers, 20/71)

14 March 1942   Chequers
Personal

Your 104, para. 6. It is true that the agreed grand strategy was based on security of United Kingdom and USA, but surely we need not emphasise this at the present time when our chief problems are to secure our sea communications and to escape the shipping stranglehold which prevents us from sending away troops and equipment to distant theatres, and when it is certain that we shall not be able to send half what we should like during the present year. Your (C) is of course all right. (D) depends mainly on Russian resistance but it is essential that we should help ourselves in Middle East and Indian Ocean (See (C) below).

2. Would not the essentials be better stated as:

   A. Assumption of offensive against Japan by attacks on her captured islands and homeland and by harrying her communications, thus regaining the initiative, since defence of so many vulnerable points is impossible to either side.

   B. Taking the weight off Russia during the summer by the heaviest Air offensive against Germany which can be produced having regard to other calls on our air power, and anything else we can think of.[2]

   C. British mastery of the Indian Ocean, thus protecting India from seaborne invasion and our communications in the Middle East from attack. Such mastery is only possible if the offensive activities of the United States in the Pacific hold a large part of the Japanese fleet in those waters.

3. Chiefs of Staff agree.

---

[1] Chief of the British Joint Staff Mission, Washington.

[2] Dill replied to this point on 16 March 1942: 'Of course, I do not know to what you refer when you say "anything else we can think of". If some land offensive on a considerable scale in Europe were possible, then of course nothing would better help the Russians and the cause generally. But the facts that German fighting machine is still intact and that we are short of shipping in general and landing craft in particular militate against any useful landing being undertaken' (*Churchill papers, 20/71*).

Winston S. Churchill to John Curtin
(Churchill papers, 20/71)

14 March 1942
Most Secret   Chequers

I fully realise your urgent need of equipment and most strenuous efforts are being made to give you everything we can spare and to secure for you the largest possible share of American production. Immediately on receipt of your telegram, a cable was sent to our representatives in Washington instructing them to consult with your representatives there and to take all steps to ensure that there should be no delay in the shipment of munitions assigned from March production together with any material previously assigned but not shipped. We also instructed them to secure, if possible, additional releases of Army equipment which would, in the normal course, have come out of April's production.

2. Your paragraph 3 causes me to think that you misunderstand the procedure governing the making of assignments from American production. The whole output of American Army equipment is regarded as a single pool and at the monthly meeting in Washington, the needs of all claimants are considered on an equal footing. Your requirements are put forward on instructions from London where full consultation with your representatives takes place to ensure that your full requirements are known and that the strongest possible case is made for their fulfilment. It is open to your representatives in Washington to be present at the meeting and to reinforce the arguments put forward on behalf of the Australian case by our representatives. It is thus not a question of giving you allocations from our quota and of getting you allocations from the American quota; it is rather a question of securing you the maximum share of the whole pool which your needs, as compared with those of other claimants, justify. You can be sure that no effort on our part is spared to press your claims at this anxious time and to prevent the retention in non-active theatres of an undue amount of material. Your representatives here are in the closest consultation all the time.

3. You have been informed of the assignments of anti-aircraft guns, tanks, etc., which have been made and which are projected. There are unfortunately acutely conflicting demands which have to be carefully balanced.

4. The air equipment picture is slightly different in that a tentative agreement for the division of the United States output was reached

in January to cover the rest of the year. We have given earnest consideration to your needs for Kittyhawks[1] and Vengeances.[2] We have now decided to raise the number of Kittyhawks to be allocated to you from our quota from 125 to 205 and the Chiefs of Staff have instructed their representatives in Washington to press for the release in March and April of Kittyhawks from the American quota so as to take advantage of the shipping available.

5. The provision of Vengeance aircraft is more difficult as there is a most pressing demand for this type for squadrons in India. The relative priority between these two conflicting needs has been referred to the Combined Chiefs of Staff in Washington. At the same time, our representatives will press for the release to you of Vengeances from the American quota. The American decision on these points will, no doubt, be influenced by the fact that considerable numbers of American air units are already in Australia or on the way there. But we will press your claims to the limit and we will inform you of the result.

Winston S. Churchill to Peter Fraser
(Churchill papers, 20/71)

15 March 1942   Chequers
Personal and Most Secret

I am very glad to learn from your No. 141 that you welcome the President's offer, and I am telling him so today as the matter is most urgent. I have not yet heard from Australia.

2. You are quite right in supposing that shipping is the stranglehold. We are sending nearly fifty thousand men a month from the United Kingdom round the Cape to the East. The five monthly convoys beginning in March carry in these totals three British divisions from the United

---

[1] Kittyhawk: the Curtiss P-40 Warhawk (the first version of which was the Tomahawk, the second and more powerful version of the Kittyhawk) was a United States single-engined, single-crew-member fighter aircraft manufactured by the Curtiss-Wright Corporation in Buffalo, New York State. It was used by, among other Allied air forces, the USAAF, the RAF, and the Royal Canadian, Royal Australian, and South African air forces. It first saw combat with the British Commonwealth Desert Air Force in the Western Desert in June 1941. From 1942 to 1945 it was active in Eastern Europe, Italy, South-East Asia, and Alaska.

[2] Vengeance: The Vultee A-31 Vengeance, an American single-engined dive bomber with a crew of two (pilot and navigator/gunner) was built mostly in Nashville, Tennessee, originally, in 1940, for overseas sales. It was used by Commonwealth air forces from May 1942 to July 1944. As its vulnerability to fighter attack made it unsuitable in the Western Desert, it saw service primarily in Burma and with the Indian Air Force.

Kingdom. In addition I have obtained from the President the shipping to carry two additional divisions in May, making five in all from this country. This absolutely exhausts all shipping possibilities from our end for the period in question.

3. It is true these forces will have to be sent according to need, either to the Middle East or to India. We have to fear a German break-through in the Caucasus should the Russian defence weaken. We have also to defend India. Of course if you or Australia were actually invaded in force we should come to your aid at all costs.

4. We hope however to regain our sea power in the Indian Ocean in the next two or three months, and this should enable minor offensive action to be taken by us against the Japanese-conquered islands.

5. At the same time the United States Fleet is regaining its strength and is already a powerful protection for the Anzac area. It would be a very serious enterprise for the Japanese to start a heavy invasion over the immense distances to New Zealand or Australia. Not only has a landing to be effected but the invasion has to be nourished when set on shore. The Japanese are already completely spread about their conquests. Only nine divisions are left in Japan. Twenty have to be kept opposite Russia in Manchukuo. They have China on their hands. After only three months of war food troubles have already begun in Japan itself. New Zealand or Australia may well be attacked in order to draw large bodies of Allied troops from other quarters, but I doubt very strongly whether anything in of the nature of a serious invasion will be attempted. In any case there is no possibility of any troops reaching you sooner than the American division which is offered, whose departure I will endeavour to hasten in every way.

6. Our great aim must be to regain even a partial initiative which will make the enemy fearful of every place he holds, instead of our trying to be safe everywhere, for that is utterly impossible.

Winston S. Churchill to General Claude Auchinleck
(Churchill papers, 20/71)

15 March 1942   Chequers
Personal and Secret

Your appreciation of 27/2 contained in your 1723 cipher continues to cause deepest anxiety here, both to the Chiefs of Staff and Defence Committee. I therefore regret extremely your inability to come home for consultation. The delay you have in mind will endanger safety of Malta. Moreover there is no certainty that the enemy cannot reinforce faster than you, so that after all your waiting you will find yourself in relatively the same or even a worse position. Your losses have been far less than the enemy who nevertheless keep fighting. For instance the 7th Armoured Division was withdrawn to the Delta to rest although its losses were far less than those of the 15th and 21st German armoured divisions who came back at you with so much vigour. A very heavy German counterstroke upon the Russians must be expected soon, and it will be thought intolerable that the 635,000 men ex Malta on your ration strength should remain unengaged preparing for another set-piece battle in July.

2. A limited offensive to Derna of which you hold out some prospect would have the advantage at any rate of coming to grips with the enemy and forcing him to consume lives, munitions, tanks and aircraft. In that case if he beat your armour you would have to retire to your defensive zone. But if you beat his armour no one here understands why you should not press your advantage and go farther.

3. In your 1723 Susan para. 8. You estimate possible by March 1 that enemy may have in Libya 475 Medium Tanks and by April 1st 630. We now know from special sources CX/MSS/793/T4[1] that on March 11 Panzer Army Africa had in the forward area 159 Tanks serviceable and Italians 87, total 246, or barely half the number you credited them with by March 1. Moreover this includes the German type of Light Tank. Against this War Office report that on March 2 you had serviceable in Western Desert, Cruisers British Crusader, American M.3 Medium and American M.3. Light 174, Serviceable in the Delta 197, New Arrivals not yet issued 167, total 538. And I Tanks additional, including 6 being unloaded, 252. Total serviceable 790. On your own estimate Susan 1723 para. 9 by April 1 you will have ready for battle in forward area 330 Medium Tanks and 100 Valentines,[2] total 430. This takes no account of the large number of unserviceable but repairable.

[1] An Enigma decrypt.

[2] Valentine: the infantry tank produced in United Kingdom. In service 1940–5, used by the British Army and Red Army. Designed by Vickers-Armstrongs in 1938; manufactured by Vickers-Armstrongs and others, 1940–4. In all, 7,300 were built. Weight: 16–17 tonnes; length: 5.41 metres. Three members of crew. Armour: 8–65 mm. Primary armament: Mk I–VII: QF 2-pounder; Mk VIII–X: QF 6-pounder; Mk XI: QF 75 mm.

4. I greatly admired your action in throwing out Cunningham[1] and I was very glad when you got rid of Godwin-Austen.[2] I have done everything in my power to give you continuous support at heavy cost to the whole war. It would give me the greatest pain to feel that mutual understanding had ceased. In order to avoid this, I have asked Sir Stafford Cripps to stop for a day in Cairo about 19th or 20th on his way to India, and put before you views of the War Cabinet. He will be joined by General Nye,[3] who is proceeding separately, and is fully possessed of the Chiefs of Staff's opinion. It is impossible for CIGS to leave the centre at this moment.

Josef Stalin to Winston S. Churchill
(*Churchill papers, 20/71*)

15 March 1942   Kuibyshev[4]
Most Secret

I am very grateful to you for your message handed in at Kuibyshev on March 12th.

I express to you the appreciation of the Soviet Government for your communication regarding measures you have taken to insure supplies

---

[1] Alan Gordon Cunningham, 1887–1983. On active service, 1914–18 (DSO, Military Cross, mentioned in despatches five times). Major-General, 1938. General Officer Commanding the East Africa Forces, 1940–1. His offensive against the Italians in East Africa started with the occupation of the Indian Ocean ports of Kismayu and Mogadishu, the Italians having fled into the interior of Somalia. On 6 April 1941, Cunningham's forces entered Addis Ababa; his successful campaign resulted in the taking of 50,000 prisoners and the loss of only 500 of his men. This success led to Cunningham's knighthood, and to his appointment to command the newly formed 8th Army in North Africa, August 1941. His immediate task was to lead Auchinleck's Libyan Desert offensive, which began on 18 November 1941. Early losses led Cunningham to recommend the offensive be curtailed. This advice was rejected by Auchinleck, who relieved Cunningham of his command. Commandant of the Staff College, Camberley, 1942–3. General Officer Commanding-in-Chief in Northern Ireland (1943) and Eastern Command (1944). General, 1945. High Commissioner, Palestine, 1945–8.

[2] Commander XIII Corps, Western Desert, 1942.

[3] Archibald Edward Nye, 1895–1967. Entered the Army as a private soldier, 1914. On active service, 1914–18. Lieutenant, 1916. Major-General, 1940. Director of Staff Duties, War Office, 1940. Lieutenant-General, 1941. Vice-Chief of the Imperial General Staff, 1941–6. Knighted, 1944. Governor of Madras, 1946–8. High Commissioner for the United Kingdom in India, 1948–52; in Canada, 1952–6.

[4] With the start of the German advance on Moscow in October 1941, the Soviet Government institutions, the Communist Party, and the foreign diplomatic missions had moved to the city of Kuibyshev (formerly Samara) on the east bank of the Volga. On 5 March 1942, Shostakovich's Seventh Symphony was first performed in Kuibyshev's Opera and Ballet House. Moscow was restored as the Soviet Union's active capital city in the summer of 1943. Kuibyshev was named after V. V. Kuibyshev, the head of the State Planning Commission (Gosplan), who died in 1935.

to Union of Soviet Socialist Republics and to intensify air attacks on Germany.

I express the firm conviction that the combined actions of our troops, in spite of incidental reverses, will in the end defeat the forces of our mutual enemy and that the year 1942 will be decisive in the turn of events at the battle front against Hitlerism.

As regards the first point of your letter dealing with frontiers of Union of Soviet Socialist Republics I think that it will still be necessary to exchange views regarding the text of a respective [sic:? suitable] agreement, in the event of its being accepted for the signature by both parties.[1]

Oliver Harvey: diary
('The War Diaries of Oliver Harvey', page 109)

15 March 1942

A most tiresome situation is developing over the Russian frontier question. Roosevelt has seen Litvinov and told him squarely US opinion would disapprove of anything affecting the Baltic States and he can't agree to any treaty in respect of definite frontiers until the war is won, tho' US would support 'legitimate measures of security' for Russia; he also made it quite clear he resented Stalin talking to HMG and not to Roosevelt direct. This as a result of our suggestion of tripartite discussions on the subject!

Whilst FDR can legitimately claim that we should decide nothing without consultation with him, he cannot properly claim that he can over-rule our foreign policy or deny us a foreign policy at all. Russia and we were allies before USA came in. We are both Europeans and nearer the German menace. We must wait and see what Stalin replies.

Meanwhile Maisky[2] has received a message from Stalin for delivery to PM and AE together. PM is staying at Chequers over Monday. (He has

---

[1] The British Ambassador to the Soviet Union, Sir Archibald Clark Kerr, added at this point: 'The last paragraph is an exact rendering of the Russian.'

[2] Ivan Mikhailovich Maisky (1884–1975). Born in Omsk, the son of a Jewish doctor and a non-Jewish mother. A Menshevik, he was exiled by the Tsarist regime in Siberia, but escaped to Germany, and took a degree in economics at Munich University. Lived in London, 1912–17. Returned to Russia during the Revolution. Became a Bolshevik, 1922. Counsellor at the Soviet Embassy in London, 1925–7. Soviet Ambassador to Britain, 1932–43. A Deputy Foreign Minister, 1943–5. Soviet member of the Reparations Committee, 1945–8. Arrested during one of Stalin's anti-Jewish purges, 1949. Imprisoned, 1949–53. Worked at the Soviet Academy of Sciences from 1957 until his death, writing his memoirs and preparing various historical studies.

had some mysterious minor operation.) AE and Maisky are to go there to lunch tomorrow.

Sir Alexander Cadogan: diary
('The Diaries of Sir Alexander Cadogan', page 441)

16 March 1942

Cabinet 5.30.[1] Not much news, except of fearful sinkings – nearly all on American coast. Americans <u>do</u> certainly seem to be terrifyingly inefficient. And we have lent them about 40 naval vessels!

[...]

Winston has had a small operation.

Oliver Harvey: diary
('The War Diaries of Oliver Harvey', pages 109–10)

17 March 1942

Maisky gave his message to PM and AE yesterday. It turned out to be both agreeable and anodyne, a friendly acknowledgement of our present difficulties and confidence in the future, pleasure at our continuing supplies and reference to need of farther exchanges of views before treaty is signed. Maisky did not in any way confirm the pessimistic view which we took of the Litvinoff–Roosevelt talk. We must now await Stalin's own reaction to Roosevelt. On the whole AE favours our going on with the Anglo-Russian Treaty on our own. It is noticeable that opinion seems to be veering more and more in favour of meeting the Russians (eg Bruce[2] says the Australian Government is strongly in favour, R. A. Butler[3] is in favour).

PM is amazing. He is still proposing to go off to Cairo at the end of the month and clear up the military situation there, then to go on and

[1] Churchill was not present at this Cabinet: he was still at Chequers, recuperating from his small operation.

[2] Stanley Melbourne Bruce, 1883–1967. Born in Melbourne, Australia. On active service, Europe, 1914–17 (twice wounded, mentioned in despatches, Military Cross). Prime Minister of Australia and Minister for External Affairs, 1923–9. Minister without Portfolio, 1932–3. Australian Representative at the League of Nations, 1932–8. President of the Council of the League of Nations, 1936. High Commissioner for Australia in London, 1933–45. Representative of Australia in the British War Cabinet, and on the Pacific War Council, 1942. Minister for Australia to the Netherlands Government-in-Exile, London, 1942–5. Created Viscount, 1947. Chairman of the World Food Council, 1947–51.

[3] Richard Austen Butler, Minister of Education, 1941–5.

meet Stalin at somewhere like Baku. He told Maisky this yesterday and asked him if he thought Stalin would come to meet him. M said he was sure he would. But what courage!

Winston S. Churchill to General Claude Auchinleck
(Churchill papers, 20/71)

17 March 1942
Personal and Secret

I ought to have added the following to my No. 168 Susan of March 15. If as the result of all discussions it is decided that you must stand on the defensive until July, it will be necessary at once to consider the movement of at least 15 Air Squadrons from Libya to sustain the Russian left wing in the Caucasus.

Winston S. Churchill to President Franklin D. Roosevelt
(Churchill papers, 20/71)

17 March 1942
Personal and Secret
No. 46[1]

1. I have been earnestly considering yours of March 10. Although I sent a paraphrase of the operative parts of your proposals to Australia and New Zealand, I have not yet heard from them. It may be that Australia is relying on the discussions you will have with Dr Evatt who should now be with you.

2. I have also had the proposals examined by our Chiefs of Staff. In principle we see great merits in the simplification resulting from the American control of the Pacific sphere and the British control of the Indian sphere, and indeed there is no other way. There are however certain issues, some fundamental, which I must place before you.

3. Nothing must prevent the United States and British Navies from working to a common strategy from Alaska to Capetown. The immense distances and the practical facts require them to act in widely separated theatres, but they must operate with a single purpose, an exact timing, and upon closely co-ordinated plans.

[1] Churchill sent a digest of this telegram to the Dominion prime ministers and Generals Wavell and Auchinleck on 22 March 1942.

4. We are building up and shall presently have a respectable force which will be based in the Central Indian Ocean. This force already consists of five battleships, two of our latest aircraft carriers, four modern cruisers and several older ones, and thirteen destroyers; all under the command of Admiral Somerville[1] who has done well in a great deal of fighting in the Mediterranean. The remnants of the Dutch Navy are reforming with our assistance and wish to work under our command. In one month the modern aircraft carrier *Illustrious,* in two months the *Valiant* and in six months, we hope, the *Queen Elizabeth* will reinforce our Eastern Fleet. On completion of the refits of *Nelson, Rodney* and *King George V,* and should the situation permit, we should consider sending either *Nelson* or *Rodney* or possibly both to join the Eastern Fleet.

5. The British Eastern Fleet, composed as it is to a great extent of old ships with short-range guns, could only deal with a certain number of the Japanese Fleet. Similarly, a general Fleet engagement between the whole Japanese Fleet and the American Pacific Fleet would be a close-run thing.

6. Therefore it seems to us that all our naval forces must be directed from a single standpoint, and their problems viewed as a whole. This can only be done by the machinery of the Combined Chiefs of the Staff Committee, acting directly under you and me in constant contact and agreement. All other arrangements for separate Commands in the Pacific and Indian spheres must be effectively subordinated to this Supreme Command. I feel sure I am right in reading your proposals in this sense.

7. On this basis we welcome your proposal that an American should be appointed Commander-in-Chief of all Allies and of all three Services in the Pacific Area, with local Commanders in Australia, New Zealand, etc.

8. We also agree that the American Chiefs of the Staff under your direction should decide day to day operational questions affecting the action of this American Commander-in-Chief in the Pacific Area.

9. We suggest however that Staff Officers from Australia, New Zealand, the Dutch and the Chinese should be available in Washington to serve the American Staffs on operational matters as may be necessary. These officers might also be the technical advisers of the members of the Pacific Council in Washington to which I refer in para. 11 below. We have such an arrangement successfully working in London now.

[1] James Fownes Somerville, 1882–1949. Entered the Royal Navy, 1898. On active service at the Dardanelles, 1915 (despatches, DSO). Officer Commanding the Destroyer Flotillas, Mediterranean Fleet, 1936–8. Commander-in-Chief, East Indies, 1938–9. Retired list, 1939. Knighted, 1939. Officer Commanding Force H, 1940–2. Commander-in-Chief, Eastern Fleet, 1942–4. Head of the British Admiralty Delegation, Washington, 1944–5. Admiral of the Fleet, 1945.

10. So much for the executive conduct of the Pacific war. I now come to the advisory bodies which will have to be consulted on larger issues. Owing to geography they must be duplicated and have the same composition on each side of the Atlantic Ocean. There will in fact be two Pacific Councils. The one in Washington, lying as it will in close touch with the American executive machinery in the Pacific Area, will naturally have more practical and more effective influence upon events than its reproduction in London. It is not possible to draw a line between strategic and political maters, as these are interwoven at the top.

11. As we see it, our Pacific Council in London would discuss the whole state of the war against Japan and we would send our opinions from time to time to the similar body in the United States. The executive conduct of the Pacific war against Japan would remain the integral responsibility of the United States acting through the American Chiefs of the Staff and the American Commander-in-Chief, subject always to the co-ordination of naval effort as stated in para. 3 and to the decisions on grand strategy which are the function of the Combined Chiefs of the Staff and the Heads of Governments. Similarly the executive conduct of operations in the Indian theatre would remain the integral responsibility of the British War Cabinet acting through the Commander-in-Chief Eastern Fleet and the British Chiefs of the Staff, but the Pacific Council in Washington would send us their opinions when they thought fit.

12. It follows from the above that the United Kingdom should have a representative on the Pacific Council in Washington and that you should have a representative on the Pacific Council in London. Equally we would keep your representative informed of the course of affairs in the Indian Ocean, which also forms a large part of the sphere of the London Pacific Council. The Dutch, for instance, are full of ideas for counter-attacks on the Japanese captured places, which we will do our best to further before the summer is far advanced.

13. Turning back again to the highest war direction, the present arrangement centres upon the Combined Chiefs of the Staff Committee in Washington. The three British representatives in Washington act in accordance with the instructions of the British Chiefs of the Staff Committee in London. Do you wish that American representatives, say Admiral Stark and General Chaney,[1] should sit in on Japanese matters from time to time with our three Chiefs of the Staff here.

[1] James Eugene Chaney, 1885–1967. Second Lieutenant of Infantry, 1904. Served as a Major on the United States Air Service Staff, Europe, 1918. Head of Air Defense Command, 1940. An observer of the German Blitz, England, October–November 1940. Head of the Special United States Army

14. I have now heard from New Zealand that they welcome your kindly offer to send an American division at the dates mentioned into New Zealand. They have at no time asked for the withdrawal of their division from the Middle East, and they do not ask now. At the same time they do not wish to engage themselves never to ask for such return. If, for instance, they were heavily invaded their men abroad would feel deep distress about their homes and families and desire to go home and defend them. However, I do not think they are going to be heavily invaded, and anyhow the matter would be governed by shipping. Therefore let us take it as settled that you send a United States division to New Zealand and the New Zealand division remains in the Middle East, at any rate for many months to come. You will probably know from Dr Evatt[1] as soon as I from Mr Curtin what the Australian position is. It would certainly be most unfortunate if the last Australian division left the Middle East on the eve of the German offensive against the Caucasus.

15. On the supreme and general outlook in the Pacific, we are both agreed on the paramount importance of regaining the initiative against Japan and making all the captured places their hostages to fortune, as they were formerly ours. We assume that any large-scale methods of achieving this would be capable of being discussed by the Combined Chiefs of the Staff Committee in Washington and would not be settled out of hand by the American Chiefs of the Staff and their American Commander-in-Chief. We should naturally consult similarly on large-scale methods in our area.

16. There are a few points of detail. In your telegram of March 10 you say (quote) India would not be occupied by American troops or planes (unquote), but in your earlier message to me, No. 113, in which you set out American Air dispositions overseas for 1942, you allocated 60 heavy bombers and 80 pursuit aircraft for the China–India–Burma area. We hope this proposal holds good.

Observers Group, England, May 1941. Commanding General, United States Army Forces in Britain, January–June 1942. Commanding General, United States First Air Force, based in New York State, 1942–4. Commander, all United States forces (Army, Navy, Air Force, and Marines) on Iwo Jima, March–August 1945. Commanding General, Western Pacific, August 1945.

[1] Herbert Vere Evatt, 1894–1965. Born in Australia. Member of the New South Wales Legislative Assembly (Labour), 1925–9. KC, 1929. Justice of the High Court of Australia, 1930–40. Attorney-General and Minister for External Affairs, 1941–9; Deputy Prime Minister, 1946–9. Member of the Advisory War Council, 1941–5; of the Australian War Cabinet, 1941–6. Australian Representative in the UK War Cabinet, 1942 and 1943. Australian Member of the Pacific War Council, 1942–3. Leader of the Australian Delegation at the UN General Assembly, 1946 and 1947. Chairman of the United Nations Palestine Commission, 1947. In 1945 he received the Freedom of the City of Athens for defending the interests of small nations. Leader of the Parliamentary Labour Party, Australia, 1951–60.

17. Furthermore in detail, we would rather have the American light bombers and fighters which you think of sending to England by July sent to the Middle East, where American aircraft of these types are already operating. We are very short of these types in the Middle East and cannot increase what we are sending from here. By sending American types direct you would save the double lift and thus shipping. We have had to bleed the Middle East so much in order to help India, Ceylon and Burma that I am very anxious about our Air position in that area.

18. We have agreed on a line dividing the Pacific and Indian spheres, but naturally this line would be elastic, dependent on the movement of the enemy or tasks we might appoint for our forces. We must not have anything so rigid as to hamper planning or manoeuvre. The First Sea Lord is anxious that I should put the following point to you. (Begins) As the naval responsibility for dealing with sea-borne raids on the north-west and west coasts of Australia will be British, we assume that under your proposals, in which there are only two areas in the east, the boundary between them will generally follow the line of the Dutch Islands, modified as necessary to give room for your submarine patrols to the south of these islands (ends). Perhaps this could be taken care of in the final drawing of the line.

19. I have not attempted to discuss in this telegram your proposals for the joint control of the North and South Atlantic area. Pound is making some suggestions to King for a co-ordination of effort in the event of a break-out of German ships.

20. To sum up, I feel that your proposals as I have ventured to elaborate and interpret them will achieve the double purpose, namely (a) integrity of executive and operational action, and (b) opportunity of reasonable consultation for those whose fortunes are involved.

Winston S. Churchill to President Franklin D. Roosevelt
(Churchill papers, 20/72)

17 March 1942
Personal and Secret
No. 48

Your Nos. 119 and 120. If *Tirpitz* comes out only the fastest heavy ships are of any use. We must therefore keep two King George V's and *Renown*[1]

---

[1] HMS *Renown* was a battlecruiser of the Royal Navy, built in 1916. Upon completion, the *Renown* and her sister ship the *Repulse* (sunk in December 1941 along with the *Prince of Wales*) were the fastest capital ships in the world. *Renown* was sold for scrap in 1948.

in North working with our only remaining fast aircraft carrier on this station. *Tirpitz* has gone north to strike at our joint munition convoys to Russia and action may easily arise. Texas Class[1] could not play any part in such fighting. They could not therefore release corresponding force to go to Gibraltar.

2. In view of your help we could send to Gibraltar one eight inch cruiser and four destroyers (British) from the Home Fleet and makeshift with that while Force Hypo[2] is away.

3. We should greatly welcome your sending to Home Fleet one or two heavy cruisers, not less than four destroyers, and above all please a fast carrier invaluable to join *Victorious* in catching *Tirpitz.*

4. We assume any ships you will send will be under operational orders of C-in-C, Home Fleet.

5. Your points about sinkings and Atlantic convoys are being gone into separately, and a further signal will be made from Pound to King.

General Sir Harold Alexander to Winston S. Churchill
(Churchill papers, 20/72)

17 March 1942[3]
Personal and Secret

General Stilwell[4] arrived here yesterday 14/3 and stated that Generalissimo[5] had issued orders stopping the movement of Fifty Army to Toungoo area. This is serious in view of possible early advance of Japanese on this front and it is of urgent importance to transfer one Burdiv. to Prome area as agreed with China.

---

[1] Texas Class: two United States battleships of the Dreadnought class, built on the eve of the First World War.

[2] Force Hypo: Force H, the British naval formation based at Gibraltar that had been formed in 1940 to replace French naval power in the western Mediterranean.

[3] Originally sent by Alexander from Burma on 15 March; included by Churchill as part of his telegram No. 49 to Roosevelt of 17 March, reproduced at pages 404–5 below.

[4] Joseph ('Vinegar Joe') Warren Stilwell, 1883–1946. On active service in France, 1918 (DSM). Served three tours of duty in China between the wars, becoming fluent in Chinese. Military Attaché, United States Legation, Peking, 1935–9. Organised and trained the 7th Infantry Division, California, 1939–41. Appointed to command the Allied invasion of North Africa (Operation Torch) but sent as a matter of urgency to China as commander of the China–Burma–India Theatre for all Lend-Lease supplies going to China. Deputy Supreme Allied Commander, South-East Asia Command (under Admiral Lord Louis Mountbatten), August 1943 to October 1944, when he was recalled by Roosevelt, in part because of the high American casualty rate in Burma. Commander, Army Ground Forces, US 10th Army, in the closing battle for Okinawa, 1945.

[5] Chiang Kai-shek.

17 Div. alone in present state will have difficulty in holding up enemy advance on oilfields. Stilwell has wired Generalissimo on this subject and meanwhile is giving orders for certain moves to proceed. Dennys[1] (since killed) has also gone to Chungking to clarify situation.

Two. Stilwell also states Generalissimo has placed him in independent command of Chinese Troops in Burma which until 14/3 were under me. Have had no other notification. This arrangement appears very unsatisfactory as Stilwell has not necessary staff or local knowledge to take command and his other duties must inevitably interfere. We have built up supply organisation for China who have no supply units and also complete liaison organisation down to divisions which Stilwell cannot replace.

Winston S. Churchill to President Franklin D. Roosevelt
(Churchill papers, 20/72)

17 March 1942
Personal and Secret
No. 47

We are delighted MacArthur has arrived in Australia and that he has been appointed Supreme Commander with general acclamation.

You will by now have received my long reply to your No. 115 about the division of responsibility against Japan. I am cabling you tonight about Burma command.

Winston S. Churchill to President Franklin D. Roosevelt
(Churchill papers, 20/72)

17 March 1942
Personal and Secret
No. 49

Your message of March 15 about military command in Burma and Southern China. We do not think that suggestion that General Stilwell

---

[1] Lancelot 'Lance' Ernest Dennys, 1890–1942. Served in the First World War with the 5th Sikhs, Indian Army, in Egypt and on the North-West Frontier of India (Military Cross and bar). General Staff Officer, Intelligence, and later Training, between the wars. Major-General, 1st Punjab Regiment, Indian Army, 1940. British Military Attaché, Chungking, and Head of the British Military Mission with the Chinese, 1942. Killed in an air crash on 15 March 1942. Buried after the war in the Sai Wan War Cemetery in Hong Kong.

should have a separate military command in Burma as well as in Southern China would work well. I cannot do better than send you the message just received by me from General Alexander.[1]

[...]

Would it not be better for Stilwell to be under general directions of Alexander in respect of troops moving actually in British territory where we are responsible for supply and will have constantly increasing forces? Alexander is one of our best officers and cut his way out of the Rangoon area with great determination.

Winston S. Churchill to John Curtin
(Churchill papers, 20/88)

17 March 1942

I had not realised till I saw Sir Earle Page's cable to you that he had led you to expect a telegram from me in addition to the summary which was sent you of the President's proposals for dividing the commands. I was not in a position to send you definite advice till our Staffs had considered the proposals, and I had myself clarified some points with the President. I was expecting to receive your impressions, and have only now learned that you were expecting to hear further from me. However, no time has been lost, because it was necessary to examine these proposals very carefully. I have now telegraphed to the President on the main issue as appended.

2. I wish here and now, however, to make the following plain to you. The fact that an American commander will be in charge of all the operations in the Pacific area will not be regarded by His Majesty's Government as in any way absolving them from their determination and duty to come to your aid to the best of their ability, and if you are actually invaded in force, which has by no means come to pass, and may never come to pass, we shall do our utmost to divert British troops and British ships rounding the Cape, or already in the Indian Ocean, to your succour, albeit at the expense of India and the Middle East.

---

[1] General Alexander to Winston S. Churchill, 17 March 1942: reproduced at page 403 above.

Lord Beaverbrook to Winston S. Churchill
(A. J. P. Taylor, 'Beaverbrook', pages 523–4)

17 March 1942

For twenty-one months that I was a member of your Government I made a practice of submitting my resignation. It became a deliberate act of promoting. The object was 'urgency and speed'.

It was in storm over delays, protests on account of procrastinations, hostility and opposition to government by committee, fortified and strengthened by threats of resignation, that I tried to accomplish all the many tasks that you entrusted to me.

[...]

But the time came when I reached the conclusion that I would be more effective as an outsider because I had exhausted all my methods within the Government.

[...]

My refusal to do or say anything that might embarrass you over policy issues should not, however, interfere with my continuing to press these questions on your attention.

I do so, of course, as a private citizen.

And the gravity of the issues and the acuteness of the differences that arose between some of my colleagues and me make it imperative that I should press the points to the furthest extent within my power and subject to the limitations that I have imposed on my conduct.

What is it that I seek to persuade your Government? To:

(1) Make a decision to recognize the 1941 Russian frontiers including that with Finland but excluding that with Poland, irrespective of the decision of the United States.

(2) The increase in shipments to Russia of 500 tanks and 500 aircraft for which I first asked on 3rd December. Further, the shipment forthwith of the necessary aircraft spares which must be supplied if the Hurricanes are to fight in Russia in the spring.

(3) An expedition into Europe on the lines of your Antwerpattack, a strategy which you have brilliantly defended in volume I of the 'World Crisis'. The exact form of this expedition is, of course, a matter for the soldiers to determine. I used to urge an attack on Trondhjem or on Brest. But another sector would have to be selected now.

This three-fold issue stands between us and a complete understanding with Stalin. But there is one other matter I should mention.

Stalin has suffered many vexations. Numerous trials of temper are probably not within your knowledge. Some are certainly outside our influence. Unhappily, other incidents making serious friction have arisen in our ranks.

Winston S. Churchill to President Franklin D. Roosevelt
(Churchill papers, 20/72)

18 March 1942
Personal and Secret
No. 50

Pound has just informed me that he has received a very nice message from King in which the latter says he will do all he can to keep the Japanese interested in the Pacific, whilst we are building up our strength in the Indian Ocean.

2. King also mentions that he was considering sending your two new battleships to the Pacific when my request to you to put a force at Gibraltar was received. We had no idea that your new ships were ready for service, and therefore only had in mind two of your Texas Class.

3. We greatly appreciate your willingness to send your new ships to us but, knowing how urgent it is that you build up your Pacific Fleet, I think we should be wrong to accept your generous offer, thereby postponing this great reinforcement to your Fleet. If you can send us the ships I mentioned in my No. 48 we can manage, and shall be most grateful.

President Franklin D. Roosevelt to Winston S. Churchill
(Churchill papers, 20/72)

18 March 1942
Priority
Immediate
Personal and Secret
No. 122

You probably have heard of the good go we had at them out in New Guinea the other day. A substantial task force was in the Salamoa–Lae area apparently waiting to protect a good sized troop convoy. Our task force steamed into the Gulf of Papua on the opposite side of the Peninsula to a point some one hundred and twenty five miles distant from Salamoa.

105 of our planes took off from a carrier and caught the enemy completely by surprise inflicting the following damage. Two heavy cruisers sunk. One light cruiser believed sunk. One destroyer probably sunk. Two destroyers badly damaged and possibly sunk. Five transports of store ships sunk or badly damaged by fire. Two patrol craft burned possibly sunk. One minelayer left burning probably sunk. One seaplane tender seriously damaged. It was good coordination with our shore based aircraft who followed our naval planes the next day. These planes, Australian and American bombers, attacked the convoy as well as making further attack in the Salamoa–Lae area. All in all it was a good days work because we got away with the loss of only one plane and our information indicates that the Japs still don't know how they were hit.

It was by all means the best day's work we have had.

Winston S. Churchill to President Franklin D. Roosevelt
(Churchill papers, 20/72)

18 March 1942
Personal and Secret
No. 51

I am delighted to receive this splendid news. We have not been able to form any impression here of such events, except from the vague accounts in the newspapers, in which one cannot see the wood for the trees. It would be a great help if we could be told more. Could not some channel be arranged? Once more all my thanks and congratulations.

President Franklin D. Roosevelt to Winston S. Churchill
(Churchill papers, 20/72)

18 March 1942   Washington DC
Personal and Secret
No. 123

We will send departing about March 23rd detachment under command of Wilcox[1] comprising one new battleship, two heavy cruisers, one

---

[1] John W. Wilcox, Jr. Graduated from the United States Naval Academy, 1905. Rear-Admiral, appointed Commander Battleships, Atlantic Fleet, 18 March 1942. Washed from the decks of his flagship, USS *Washington*, in the North Atlantic, off Sable Island, and lost at sea, 27 March 1942.

carrier, five or six destroyers to report for temporary duty to Ghormley[1] to be under operational orders of C in C Home Fleet.[2]

We will keep ready on this side similar detachment in position suited to head off enemy when he comes into open Atlantic. We feel that you can include battleship in your replacement for force 'Hypo' and otherwise make it more nearly adequate.

Roosevelt

Winston S. Churchill to William Mackenzie King
(Churchill papers, 20/71)

18 March 1942
Private and Personal

Your No. 79. Question which has to be solved is not one between British Government and India, but between different sects or nations in India itself. We have resigned ourselves to fighting our utmost to defend India in order, if successful, to be turned out. Congress have hitherto definitely refused Dominion Status. Moslems, a hundred millions, declare they will insist upon Pakistan, i.e. a sort of Ulster in the North. We have our Treaties which must be respected with Princes in India, over ninety millions. There are forty million Hindu Untouchables to whom we have obligations. These are the grim issues which Cripps is valiantly trying to settle. There can be no question of our handing over control during the war. This would break up the Indian Army, 85 per cent. of which cares nothing for Congress and is loyal only to the King-Emperor. It would render the defence of India impossible. I should strongly recommend your awaiting developments till we see how the Cripps Mission goes. I have shown your telegram to Amery.

---

[1] Robert Lee Ghormley, 1883–1958. Graduated from the United States Naval Academy, 1906. On active service, Atlantic, 1916–18. Commanded the battleship *Nevada*, 1935. Rear-Admiral, 1938. Director of War Plans, Navy Department, 1938. Assistant Chief of Naval Operations, 1939. Special Naval Observer, London, 1940–1. Vice-Admiral, 1941. Commander, South Pacific Forces and South Pacific Area, 1942. Commander, Hawaiian Sea Frontier, 1943–4. Commander, United States Naval Forces in Germany, 1944–5. Chairman, General Board, Navy Department, Washington, 1946.

[2] Admiral of the Fleet John Cronyn Tovey.

Oliver Harvey: diary
(*'The War Diaries of Oliver Harvey'*, page 110)

18 March 1942

MacArthur has been got out of Philippines[1] and is to command Australian Pacific sphere. That is to the good. He and our Alexander in Burma should be a vast improvement on the old duds there before.

Meanwhile the dispute between Auchinleck and the PM as to whether the former should attack or wait still rages. Cripps and Nye are looking into it on the spot and the PM threatens to go himself at the end of the month.

A[2] says his tanks are less numerous and inferior to the enemy's.

President Franklin D. Roosevelt to Winston S. Churchill
(*Premier papers, 3/486/3*)

18 March 1942

Dear Winston,

I am sure you know that I have been thinking a lot about your troubles during the past month. We might as well admit the difficult military side of the problems; and you have the additional burdens which your delightful unwritten Constitution puts your form of government into in war-time just as much as in peace-time. Seriously, the American written Constitution, with its four-year term, saves the unfortunate person at the top a vast number of headaches.

Next in order is that delightful god which we worship in common, called 'the Freedom of the Press'. Neither one of us is much plagued by the news stories, which, on the whole, are not so bad. But literally we are both menaced by the so-called interpretative comment by a handful or two of gentlemen who cannot get politics out of their heads in the worst crisis, who have little background and less knowledge, and who undertake to lead public opinion on that basis.

My own Press – the worst of it – are persistently magnifying relatively unimportant domestic matters and subtly suggesting that the American rôle is to defend Hawaii; our east and west coasts do the turtle act and wait until somebody attacks our home shores. Curiously enough, these

---

[1] General MacArthur had left the Philippines (which the Japanese had invaded on 22 December 1941) on orders of President Roosevelt, while American troops were still fighting there, with no hope of holding back the Japanese. Making a perilous escape by sea to Australia, MacArthur declared on arrival: 'I shall return.'

[2] General Auchinleck.

survivors of isolationism are not attacking me personally, except to reiterate that I am dreadfully overburdened, or that I am my own strategist, operating without benefit of military or naval advice. It is the same old story. You are familiar with it.

Here is a thought from this amateur strategist. There is no use giving a single further thought to Singapore or the Dutch Indies. They are gone. Australia must be held, and, as I telegraphed you, we are willing to undertake that. India must be held, and you must do that; but, frankly, I do not worry so much about that problem as many others do. The Japanese may land on the seacoast west of Burma. They may bombard Calcutta. But I do not visualise that they can get enough troops to make more than a few dents on the borders – and I think you can hold Ceylon. I hope you can get more submarines out there – more valuable than an inferior surface fleet. I hope you will definitely reinforce the Near East more greatly than at present. You must hold Egypt, the Canal, Syria, Iran, and the route to the Caucasus.

Finally, I expect to send you in a few days a more definite plan for a joint attack in Europe itself.

By the time you get this you will have been advised of my talk with Litvinov, and I expect a reply from Stalin shortly. I know you will not mind my being brutally frank when I tell you that I think I can personally handle Stalin better than either your Foreign Office or my State Department. Stalin hates the guts of all your top people. He thinks he likes me better, and I hope he will continue to do so.

My Navy has been definitely slack in preparing for this submarine war off our coast. As I need not tell you, most naval officers have declined in the past to think in terms of any vessel of less than two thousand tons. You learned the lesson two years ago. We still have to learn it. By May 1st I expect to get a pretty good coastal patrol working from Newfoundland to Florida and through the West Indies. I have begged, borrowed, and stolen every vessel of every description over eighty feet long – and I have made this a separate command with the responsibility in Admiral Andrews.[1]

---

[1] Adolphus Andrews, 1879–1948. Beginning in February 1939 he participated in a three-week simulated battle in the South Atlantic and Caribbean. The exercise was described at the time as the most elaborate naval operation ever staged in American waters. Andrews commanded 'Black Force'. Vice-Admiral, Eastern Sea Frontier, 1942, with responsibility for United States naval defences from the Canadian Atlantic coast border to south Florida. By 1 April 1942, he had 23 large and 42 small Coast Guard cutters and 14 armed British trawlers, 3 United States Navy Patrol Craft, and 170 United States Army and Navy aircraft under his command. In 1944, when a Vice-Admiral (retired), he was a Member of the Navy Court of Inquiry, held at the Navy Department, Washington, into the circumstances of the Japanese attack on Pearl Harbor.

I know you will keep up your optimism and your grand driving force, but I know you will not mind if I tell you that you ought to take a leaf out of my notebook. Once a month I go to Hyde Park for four days, crawl into a hole, and pull the hole in after me. I am called on the telephone only if something of really great importance occurs. I wish you would try it, and I wish you would lay a few bricks or paint another picture.

Give my warm regards to Mrs Churchill. I wish much that my wife and I could see her.

As ever yours,
Franklin D. Roosevelt

PS. Winant is here. I think he is really a most understanding person.

Winston S. Churchill to Sir Stafford Cripps
(Churchill papers, 20/72)

19 March 1942   Cairo
Secret and Personal

We can speak together by telephone from Cairo though line is open. Great care must therefore be taken. For convenience in speaking cryptically Auchinleck will be No. 17, Nye 22, Monckton[1] 25, Lampson[2] 30, Ritchie 34 and Gott 39.

Winston S. Churchill to President Franklin D. Roosevelt
(Churchill papers, 20/72)

19 March 1942
Personal and Secret
No. 52

We are deeply grateful for your sending a force in which is included one of your new battleships to join C in C Home Fleet.

---

[1] Walter Turner Monckton, 1891–1965. Educated at Harrow and Balliol College, Oxford. President of the Oxford Union, 1913. On active service, 1915–19 (Military Cross). Called to the Bar, 1919. KC, 1930. Attorney-General to the Prince of Wales, 1932–6. Knighted, 1937. Director-General of the Press Censorship Bureau, 1939–40. Director-General, Ministry of Information, 1940–1; of British Propaganda and Information Services, Cairo, 1941–2. Solicitor-General, 1945. Conservative MP for Bristol West, 1951–7. Minister of Labour and National Service, 1951–5. Minister of Defence, 1955–6. Paymaster-General, 1956–7. Created Viscount, 1957.

[2] Miles Wedderburn Lampson, 1880–1964. Entered the Foreign Office, 1903. British Minister to China, 1926–33. Knighted, 1927. High Commissioner for Egypt and the Sudan, 1934–6; Ambassador to Egypt and High Commissioner for the Sudan, 1936–46. Privy Councillor, 1941. Created Baron Killearn, 1943. Special Commissioner in South-East Asia, 1946–8.

This will enable us to send a force which will include the *Renown* to Gibraltar. We will get in touch with Ghormley where your ships should proceed.

When the time is approaching for your new battleships to go to the Pacific please give us sufficient warning to enable readjustments to be made in British dispositions.

Winston S. Churchill to Harry Hopkins
(Churchill papers, 20/72)

19 March 1942

Max is off tomorrow and I shall be grateful if you will impress upon the President that though he is for the time being out of office at his own wish, we remain close friends and intimate political associates.

General Archibald Wavell to Winston S. Churchill
(Churchill papers, 20/72)

19 March 1942
Most Secret
Most Immediate

CGS[1] has lately returned from Burma and I have been at Calcutta discussing defence of NE India so you may like to have our general ideas on situation.

Two. I do not think we can count on holding Upper Burma for long if Japanese put in determined attack. Many troops still short of equipment and shaken by experiences in Lower Burma and remaining battalions of Burma Rifles of doubtful value. There is little artillery. Reinforcements in any strength impossible at present. Chinese cooperation not easy they are distrustful of our fighting ability and inclined to hang back. Not certain that they will compete with Japanese jungle tactics any more successfully than we have. Alexander can however be relied on to put up good fight and Japanese difficulties must be great. Dennys is great loss as he had Chinese confidence.

Three. There may come stage when we shall have to decide whether forces in Upper Burma shall withdraw north east into China uncovering Indian Frontier or northwest losing touch with Chinese. It seems to me

[1] General Hutton.

we should keep touch with Chinese at all costs and I propose to instruct Alexander accordingly.

Four. I am putting all we can into defence of NE India in spite of risks external and internal in remainder of India but even so we shall be thin on ground. You will have realised vital necessity of strengthening air force in India at once.

Five. Hartley returns from Ceylon today and I shall probably go [to] Burma towards end next week.

President Franklin D. Roosevelt to Winston S. Churchill
(Churchill papers, 20/72)

20 March 1942   Washington DC
No. 124

Reference your message concerning command in Burma. I have recently requested the Generalissimo[1] to continue reinforcing the Burma front and to permit Stilwell to make co-operative arrangements relative [to] command according to the principles laid down in his original directive approved by the combined Chiefs of Staff. Recent messages from Stilwell indicate that he and Alexander can continue to work effectively together but that the urgent need is for additional Chinese troops. The Generalissimo has placed Stilwell in command of the fifth and sixth Chinese Armies but unfortunately will not permit completion of their transfer to Burma pending clarification of the command situation. Stilwell has not only urgently requested the Generalissimo to recede from this position but has actually ordered additional units southward in the hope that the Generalissimo will approve. Despite command complications Stilwell provides a means of assuming complete co-operation whereas a Chinese commander might make the situation impossible for General Alexander. Stilwell is not only an immensely capable and resourceful individual but is thoroughly acquainted with the Chinese people, speaks their language fluently, and is distinctly not a self seeker. His latest telegram states 'Have arranged with General Alexander for co-operation and matter of command need not affect conduct of operations. Have asked Generalissimo to start another three divisions toward Burma.'

Under the circumstances I suggest we should leave the command status at that for the present. I feel that Generals Alexander and Stilwell will co-operate admirably. Strange that these two who were

---

[1] Chiang Kai-shek.

originally intended to meet at 'Super-Gymnast'[1] should in fact meet at Maymyo.

Roosevelt

President Franklin D. Roosevelt to Winston S. Churchill
(Churchill papers, 20/72)

20 March 1942
No. 125

Your interest in steps to be taken to combat the Atlantic submarine menace as indicated by your recent message to Mr Hopkins on this subject impels me to request your particular consideration of heavy attacks on submarine bases and building and repair yards thus checking submarine activities at their source and where submarines perforce congregate.

Winston S. Churchill to President Franklin D. Roosevelt
(Churchill papers, 20/72)

20 March 1942
Personal and Secret
No. 53

Your No. 124. We cordially accept the arrangement you propose and instructions have been sent to Generals Wavell and Alexander accordingly.

2. Your 125. The highest importance is attached by us to bombing U-boat construction yards and bases and they will play a leading part in our spring bombing offensive. All is in readiness for this, including a vastly improved method of finding our way to the target, first tried at Essen a fortnight ago. We have been only held back by weather, which is the worst experienced for bombing purposes in 15 years, just as last year was the best. It would be improvident to lose 15 or 20 bombers, as we have sometimes done, returning to fog-bound airfield in this island, when better conditions are certainly approaching. No chance will be lost.

3. We are also studying the attack by long-range aircraft upon U-boats coming from Bordeaux to the Caribbean. It is a question of competing claims.

[1] 'Gymnast' and 'Super-Gymnast': the Anglo-American plan for an amphibious landing in French North Africa in the spring of 1942 (later developed into 'Torch', the landings that took place from 8 to 16 November 1942).

Winston S. Churchill to John Curtin
(Churchill papers, 20/72)

20 March 1942
Immediate
Most Secret and Personal

I have to acknowledge your 207 informing us of the arrangements which you propose to make with the United States on the subject of Air co-operation between the United States and Australia.

2. Your 208. We note the opinions you have expressed and fully understand your point of view. It would not be possible for us as you suggest to uncover the whole of our sea communications with the Middle East, on which the life of the considerable armies fighting there depends. Neither would it be possible for us to neglect the security of Ceylon so far as it is in our power to preserve it, or to deprive ourselves of the means of reinforcing or defending India. The dispatch to the Pacific of three out of four of our fast armoured aircraft carriers would, as you perceive, leave any battleships we have placed or may place in the Indian Ocean entirely unprotected from Air attack and consequently unable to operate. This would expose all our convoys to the Middle East and India averaging nearly fifty thousand men a month to destruction at the hands of two or three fast Japanese cruisers or battle-cruisers, supported by perhaps a single aircraft carrier. While admiring the offensive spirit of your memorandum and sharing your desire for an early acquisition of the initiative, we do not feel that we should be justified in disregarding all other risks and duties in the manner you suggest.

3. These matters will however no doubt form part of the discussions which will take place in Washington when agreement has been reached upon the new organization proposed by the President upon which I have sent you the views which His Majesty's Government in the United Kingdom have transmitted to the President.

4. A more detailed commentary will be telegraphed when your proposals have been further studied by the Staffs.

Winston S. Churchill to Josef Stalin
(Churchill papers, 20/72)

20 March 1942
Personal and Secret

Many thanks for your reply of the 14th to my latest telegram. Beaverbrook is off to Washington where he will help smooth out the Treaty question with the President in accordance with the communications which have passed between us and between our Governments.

2. Ambassador Maisky lunched with me last week and mentioned some evidences that the Germans may use gas upon you in their attempted Spring offensive. After consulting my colleagues and the Chiefs of the Staff, I wish to assure you that His Majesty's Government will treat any use of this weapon of poison gas against Russia exactly as if it was directed against ourselves. I have been building up an immense store of gas bombs for discharge from aircraft, and we shall not hesitate to use these over all suitable objectives in Western Germany from the moment that your Armies and people are assaulted in this way.

3. It is a question to be considered whether at the right time we should not give a public warning that such is our resolve, as the warning might deter the Germans from adding this new horror to the many they have loosed upon the world. Please let me know what you think about this, and whether the evidence of German preparations warrants the warning.

4. There is no immediate hurry, and before I take a step which may draw upon our cities this new form of attack I must of course have ample time to bring all our anti-gas precautions to extreme readiness.

5. I trust you will give our new Ambassador[1] the opportunity of presenting this message himself, and the advantage of personal discussion with you. He comes, as you know, almost direct from close personal contact with General Chiang Kai-shek, which he has maintained during the last four years. He enjoyed, I believe, the General's high regard and confidence; I hope and believe that he will equally gain yours. He is a personal friend of mine of many years' standing.

---

[1] Archibald Clark Kerr, 1882–1951. Entered the Diplomatic Service, 1906. Envoy Extraordinary and Minister Plenipotentiary to the Central American Republics, 1925–8; to Chile, 1928–30; to Sweden, 1931–4. Knighted, 1935. Ambassador to Iraq, 1935–8. Ambassador to China, 1938–42; after the British consulate in Chungking was almost completely destroyed by Japanese bombing in 1940, and other diplomatic missions left the city, Clark Kerr kept the Union Flag flying on the Embassy building, close to Chinese Government buildings. Ambassador to the Soviet Union, February 1942 to February 1946. Privy Councillor, 1944. Special British Envoy to Java, 1946. Created Baron Inverchapel, 1946. Ambassador to the United States, 1946–8.

Winston S. Churchill to General Hastings Ismay,
for the Chiefs of Staff Committee
(Churchill papers, 20/67)

21 March 1942
Most Secret

Notes dictated subsequent to a Conference with the First Sea Lord and CAS. Night of March 20–21, 1942.

Part I.

The Far East. To concentrate the whole Eastern Fleet at Port T[1] and the whole shore-based air protection at Ceylon is a questionable policy. We should not distribute our air protection throughout Ceylon, but concentrate the bulk at Colombo with the minimum detachments from Trincomalee and certain airfields. If we were able to make Scapa Flow so formidable to the attacks of the main German shore-based air force that these have been discontinued for more than two years, we ought to be able to protect Colombo and make it a secure base for HM ships against Japanese air attacks necessarily limited to seaborne aircraft. Much progress has already been made in RDF, AA and Hurricane fighter strength.

2. Since the harbour at Colombo will not accommodate the whole Eastern Fleet, the Naval Staff are requested to consider whether *Warspite* and the two aircraft carriers, and later on *Valiant,* should not work from Colombo, while the slower 'R' Class cruise around Port T as their fuelling base. In this way, at any rate for the next two or three months, it should be possible either to act east of Ceylon and India with the fast division against a more weakly supported invasion, or, if superior Japanese forces approach, to rendezvous with the 'Rs' to the westward of a line Colombo–Port T.

3. Such dispositions would require the provision as fast as possible of up to, say, 25 Catalinas working from Colombo and refuelling at Port T. These reconnaissance craft ranging over the whole of the approaches from the east, and northwards into the Bay of Bengal, should, together with two British and four Dutch submarines watching the Malacca and Sunda Straits, give timely warning of heavy seaborne enemy approach across the broad waters. The provision at the earliest possible moment of 40, or better still 60, Wellingtons, based probably on Calcutta, would, at the discretion of the Commander-in-Chief, India, and Commander-in-Chief, Eastern Fleet, working in concert, either extend the reconnaissance of the Bay of Bengal southward to form contact with the

[1] Port T: Trincomalee.

Catalinas, or attack an invading fleet or flotilla working along in-shore from Rangoon to Calcutta, or, lastly, bomb enemy air bases or keypoints on land.

4. Meanwhile the strengthening of the RDF, AA and Hurricane defences of Colombo, and thereafter as far as possible, on a lower scale and priority, of Trincomalee and the Ceylon airfields, would steadily proceed according to the best dispositions to be made locally, the object being to provide a sure and safe base at Colombo from which our fast ships can act against weaker enemy naval forces. Meanwhile also the airfield at Port T should be completed and furnished with a squadron of Hurricanes, at the same time as the AA guns and RDF which can gradually be found for Port T are installed.

5. All the above arrangements seem appropriate for the immediate two or three months which lie before us, and can, of course, be reviewed constantly. It is not possible to defend Ceylon from seaborne invasion except by naval and air power securely based at Colombo, and dispersion of forces throughout an island 300 miles long should, of course, be avoided. These seem to be the best sea and air provisions which can be made for the Eastern front. I desire them to be examined by the Naval Staff and the COS Committee, and, if agreed in principle, a timetable of execution should be prepared.

Part II.

6. The arrangements for 'Ironclad'[1] are proceeding subject to:

(a) The interception and arrest of any French reinforcements from Dakar.

(b) The use of *Illustrious* as well as *Argus* and *Hermes* to support the Landing in case *Eagle* is retained at Gibraltar. This last measure seems necessary in view of the bitter need to feed Malta with Spitfires.

(c) The provision which should be made for a second reinforcement of the assaulting forces, in case they should be brought to a standstill after their existing reserves have been employed. Such an additional reserve of perhaps a brigade (three in all) might be available ten days after zero. The operation should not be delayed solely on account of it.

7. No difference exists between the Admiralty and the Air Ministry upon the scale of air defence to be provided on the coasts of Egypt and

[1] 'Ironclad' (formerly 'Bonus'): the invasion of Madagascar to replace the Vichy administration there with Free French rule.

Libya against oversea invasion now that we have no battle fleet. The most we can hope to do is to make up from United Kingdom the heavy drains upon Middle East caused by the approved requirements of the Far Eastern theatre.

Part III.

8. Home Waters. The Catalinas which have been or are being taken from the North-Western Approaches must be replaced by aircraft of approximately equal range, or as near as possible, and the total numbers must not fall below the December level. Outstanding points about the range and performance of the replacing aircraft must be resolved by conference between the Naval and Air Staffs. Calculations of range should be given both in sea and land miles.

9. The new naval proposal for a standing air patrol of the deboches from the Bay of Biscay will be further examined in a Naval and Air conference to be held by me on Friday, March 27, at 11.30 a.m. Whether this new plan involving four Squadrons of Wellingtons is justified depends entirely upon damage it is likely to do to the enemy. Three or four U-boats a month would be entirely profitable, but anything less than two would have to be balanced against the consequential serious diminution of our bombing effort against Germany.

10. The bombing offensive against Germany is our main effort, and at present, apart from munitions, our sole means of helping Russia. The competing needs of bombing oil refineries and submarine building works or bases are acute, and the latter target has been emphasized in importance by the request of the President.

11. Plans should be prepared to reinforce the British Coastal Command with additional torpedo bombers in the autumn in order to increase security against invasion, especially in the Narrow Waters.

Winston S. Churchill to John Curtin
(Churchill papers, 20/72)

21 March 1942
Personal and Secret
Most Immediate

You are reported to have stated in an interview yesterday with the British United Press quote We all admire Mr Churchill's brilliance although we have sometimes doubted the wisdom of the decisions he has imposed. Thus the campaign in Greece was opposed by Australia because she felt that the flank in North Africa was left open. Subsequent events proved we were correct. Unquote.

This is not borne out by any facts known to us. Mr Menzies as Premier of Australia was a party to all the decisions taken and was present at the discussions. The decision was not 'imposed' by me, but taken by the Cabinet on the advice of Generals Wavell and Dill on the spot in the Middle East and with the agreement after discussion of the Acting Prime Minister of Australia and his colleagues.

2. You are also reported to have said 'He, Mr Curtin, could understand why many people were puzzled when they saw reinforcements pouring into the British Isles which he hardly considered had been in imminent danger since last Autumn.'

This statement taken by itself is likely to mislead the public both in Australia and the United Kingdom. You were informed a fortnight ago in my No. 311 of the other troop movements which are in progress from the United Kingdom and you know that far more than double as many British troops are leaving for the East as are coming in from the United States in the same period.

3. It is far from my wish to be involved in controversy with you but such statements when put forth on your authority will probably be raised in the House of Commons, when I should be forced to reply.

Winston S. Churchill to President Franklin D. Roosevelt
(Churchill papers, 20/72)

21 March 1942
No. 55

I have now had very careful consideration given to your most secret telegram No. 113 by my close military advisers.

2. Your generous offer to lend us American shipping and, in addition, to release the *Queen Mary*, *Queen Elizabeth* and *Aquitania*[1] for our use is most welcome and I gladly accept the conditions set out in your para. 5. Thanks to your help we should now be able to send one more Infantry Division and one Armoured Division to the East making five in all in the next three months. We would have preferred to keep the monster liners, particularly *Queen Elizabeth*, on the long and safer journeys, but the need is so pressing that we must, I think, accept the risks of the Atlantic for them. There is a small point in your para. 5 (c). It would suit us better if

---

[1] Three pre-war ocean liners that had been converted to troop ships.

you could send a further 9,000 American troops to Iceland (C), even at the expense of Northern Ireland. Perhaps you would consider whether this could be managed.

3. <u>Personnel Shipping</u>. I am delighted to learn that your man-lift is so much better than I had been advised. We shall need it all.

4. <u>Air</u>. I am immensely impressed by your lay-out which should dominate the future and by the bold strategic outlook on which it is based. I am however, as you know, very anxious about the Levant–Caspian front. Even with United States contributions of aircraft for the RAF we ourselves can do little for that theatre. I therefore ventured to ask in para. 17 of my No. 46 whether you would consider sending to the Middle East instead of to the UK, all the light bombers and as many as possible of the fighters listed in your para. 8 G(1).

Sir Stafford Cripps to Winston S. Churchill
(Churchill papers, 20/72)

21 March 1942　　　　　　　　　　　　　　　　　　　Iraq[1]
Most Secret and Personal
Most Immediate

I am very satisfied with the atmosphere at Cairo after our talks. Last night I had long and most friendly talk with Auchinleck, Nye, Tedder, Cunningham's deputy and Monckton at which I went through my telegram to you in detail. They were all most helpful and cooperative. When I first arrived I felt a rather prickly atmosphere which was also apparent on Nye's arrival. That has now completely disappeared and everyone including Nye was most happy when we left at early (?word omitted)[2] this morning. I do not think there will be any need for you to trouble to come out and I think you would find journey long and (?word omitted). I hope you will get all additional detail you want from Nye before he returns home. I have no doubt as to (word of 10 letters[3] omitted)'s offensive (?determination) but I think his Scottish caution and desire not to mislead by optimism cause him to (?over) stress in statement the difficulties and uncertainties of situation. I am convinced of his determination to face these and am sure that it will help him very much if he can now be made to feel that all misunderstandings are at an end and there is no more questioning of his desire to take offensive.

---

[1] Cripps was on his way from Cairo by air to India, to take up his mission there.
[2] The question marks are in the text as deciphered.
[3] Auchinleck.

If you accept situation as detailed in my long telegram as I much hope you will, it would I am sure help if you could send Auchinleck a short friendly telegram expressing your satisfaction that he will have all possible help from you to hit the target at the appointed time.

Sir Stafford Cripps to Winston S. Churchill
(Churchill papers, 20/72)

21 March 1942
Most Secret and Personal

As a result of long talks with Auchinleck, Cunningham and Tedder and consultation with Nye I have come to the following conclusions.

2. At present time neither our strength in tanks nor in air is such as to give any chance worth considering of a successful offensive. Excluding infantry tanks which cannot be used as primary weapon in a tank battle we shall have by end of this month in front line armoured formations comprising about 250 tanks ready for operations as against German and Italian units comprising 350 (on best estimate available).

In air, due largely to heavy diversions to East, we have had a period of weakness resulting in loss of air superiority, and are today just beginning to be able to re-assert ourselves, our fighter strength in front line having risen again from 4 to 10 Squadrons. Owing to the fact we are no longer able to operate Wellingtons from Malta, our ability to interfere with enemy communications to and from Tripoli has been seriously diminished. Moreover transfer to East has gravely weakened our light bomber force.

3. New tank units are now being equipped with Grants which are coming forward well after initial difficulty due to necessity for various adjustments and additions shown necessary by experience and also fact that during transport here by sea certain vital parts got rusted up which has taken 2 to 8 days to put right for each tank. For these tanks moreover a new training of individual tank crews is essential as guns and operation differ from our tanks and also formation training is essential owing to difference in type of tank. I have visited one of the principal depots where these tanks are being prepared and am satisfied they will shortly come forward at a rate of about 40 repeat 40 a week. This should give by the middle of May an effective and trained tank force of 450 at the front with sufficient reserves in addition to the 150 infantry tanks.

4. In about a month's time the air strength should have been built up sufficiently to undertake and maintain intensive operations.

5. The question arises as to what the enemy strength is likely to be by that time. The two limits in tanks are 350 repeat 350 and 650 repeat 650. The latter is considered the most gloomy possible. The number they can build up will of course depend upon how far we can interfere with their communications.

6. This raises the important question of bomber power. Apart from one (repeat one) Liberator[1] (repeat Liberator) there is now nothing here or in Malta which can touch Tripoli, the most important point, and the Baltimores[2] are not yet available to bomb Benghazi by day. It is vital that there should be made available at the earliest possible moment heavy bombers capable of reaching Tripoli, and more Baltimores. I am confident heavy bombers can be used to better purpose here than against Germany and indeed they are essential if there is to be a chance of the reinforcements reaching the enemy.

7. Auchinleck takes the view that it is unlikely that anything can be done before about mid May (repeat mid May) and I agree that an attempt to make an attack before that would be to take an unwarrantable risk. This is subject of course to enemy not making some earlier move which would give us an opportunity which might occur.

He thinks that there should be good opportunity of attack about mid May and is working to that date, but all necessary help must be given with the urgent requirements which I detail at the end of this telegram. This attack if successful should reach Derna and as the railway should be completed by the beginning of June to Eladem subsequent further advance should then be facilitated. He considers that the battle may not be followed by a rapid advance but by a slow progress and it might well be two months before Benghazi could be reached.

8. The advance to Derna if it takes place would materially ease the Malta situation and would enable it to hold out longer. Meanwhile as you are aware efforts are being made to maintain Malta, but it is essential that the remainder of the Spitfires now in Gibraltar should be sent to Malta as quickly as possible to maintain fighter defence until Spitfires are available for reinforcements from the East.

[1] Liberator: the Consolidated B-24 Liberator, with a crew of between seven and ten, was an American heavy bomber designed by Consolidated Aircraft of San Diego, California. It was used by all branches of the United States armed forces and by several Allied armed forces and navies. In all, 18,482 were produced between 1940 and 1945, making it the most produced Allied heavy bomber in history.

[2] Baltimore: the Martin 187 Baltimore, with a crew of four, was a two-engined light attack bomber, built by the Glenn L. Martin Company in the United States. Originally ordered by France, its production was diverted to Britain from June 1940. Not used by the United States, it served with British, Canadian, Australian, South African, and Greek air forces. In all, 1,575 were built.

9. The danger of which Auchinleck is apprehensive is that an attack should develop in Syria, the North, via Caucasus or Turkey, or upon Cyprus, while the operation was on in the Western desert in which event it would be necessary to withdraw a considerable proportion of the air forces from the Western desert and surrender air superiority. This would mean abandoning the battle with extremely serious results. In my view this is a risk which must unfortunately be taken unless we are to abandon all hope of an offensive till the autumn.

10. I therefore suggest that the mid May date be accepted as the target and that everything possible be done to prepare for that date both here and at home. I am not suggesting that there is any want of effort here as I am sure there is not, but merely that an effort should be organised for that particular location. In this respect the urgent requirements for action at home are as follows:

(a) Despatch to Malta of the remaining Spitfires now in Gibraltar.
(b) Immediate despatch of heavy bombers capable of reaching Tripoli.
(c) Expediting of light bombers from USA by every possible means so as to arrive at earliest date.
(d) Sending out of fitters by air who could be taken from other less urgent work and put to build up the reserve of tanks which will be vital factor and deal with repairs when the offensive starts.
(e) Cessation of any further demands upon this front to send aircraft to India or elsewhere.

11. Nye will be able to send you any detailed explanation of cost based on the questionnaire formerly approved.

12. I have shown this telegram to Auchinleck, Tedder and Norman[1] (acting for Cunningham) and they agree with its contents as also does Monckton.

Winston S. Churchill to Sir Stafford Cripps
(Churchill papers, 20/72)

22 March 1942
Personal and Secret

Your Cairo telegrams do not convince me. The atmosphere may have been satisfactory, but the prospect is unremedied. Staffs are examining situation. Meanwhile, I have told Nye to remain and obtain precise

[1] (Horace) Geoffrey Norman, 1896–1972. On active service at sea, 1914–18. Captain, 1938. Deputy to Admiral Cunningham, Mediterranean, 1942. Rear-Admiral, 1947. Chief of Staff to Commander-in-Chief, Mediterranean, 1948–50.

answers to his 20 questions. There is no question of my approving passivity of army at present stage of discussion. Thank you very much for all the trouble you took.

2. I grieve to hear that your mother-in-law[1] has just died. Lady Cripps is going over to Fulmer this afternoon. We all send you our best wishes in momentous task now opening.[2]

Winston S. Churchill to General Archibald Nye[3]
(Churchill papers, 20/72)

22 March 1942
Personal and Secret

I have heard from the Lord Privy Seal.[4] I do not wonder everything was so pleasant considering you seem to have accepted everything they said and all we have got to accept is the probable loss of Malta and the army standing idle while the Russians are resisting the German counter-stroke desperately, and while the enemy is reinforcing himself in Libya faster than we are.

2. Do not hasten your return, but go into the questions of tank serviceability, armament, and the use of manpower in Middle East searchingly.

3. Also let me have precise answers to your 20 questions by cable in good time before you leave so that we can comment on them here.

4. Finally, try to form an opinion about possibility of enemy offensive, either from the West, or across the sea from Greece, the latter, A by air, or B by ships. This of course would alter the picture altogether.

Winston S. Churchill to General Hastings Ismay
(Churchill papers, 20/67)

22 March 1942

Let me have a report on the situation about gas masks for the civil population in Germany, so far as is known.

---

[1] Amy Swithinbank (née Eno), 1858–1942, Lady Cripps' mother, and widow of Commander Harold Swithinbank RN. Her father was the inventor of 'Eno's Fruit Salt', a popular effervescent drink (and patent medicine) for hangovers and digestive trouble.

[2] Cripps' mission to India. Cripps arrived in Karachi later that day, 22 March 1942, and reached Delhi the following day.

[3] Vice-Chief of the Imperial General Staff.

[4] Cripps.

Winston S. Churchill to Brendan Bracken
(Churchill papers, 20/67)

22 March 1942
Most Secret

The larger scope[1] was certainly intended by the Cabinet, and neutral nations should therefore be included.

2. It should surely be possible to point out to the newspaper proprietors or to the editors that before articles are printed advocating specific operations or drawing attention to the dangers attaching to particular places, the Military Adviser to the Ministry of Information should be consulted. General Lawson[2] is fully capable of giving guidance. For instance, suppose it were desirable for us to occupy Bear Island or Spitzbergen, articles advocating this would make the operation far more dangerous to our troops. Or, alternatively, articles pointing out that Thursday Island or Christmas Island was a very important strategic point and that strenuous efforts should be made to retain it, or that great alarm prevailed in the local population, or that special measures had been taken to enforce a black-out, would tend to concentrate the enemy's attention upon these places and increase the danger. It is not intended that the rule should be hard and fast so as to paralyse speculation, but reasonable consultation beforehand is most desirable. No other country tells the enemy all they are likely to do beforehand, or where they feel most vulnerable.

3. A much larger case is that of the invasion of the Continent. An agitation in the British Press to invade the Continent maintained throughout the Spring would certainly lead to the loss of many British lives through the improved preparations and fortifications made against it should such an operation ever be undertaken. I realise this is hard upon the Press. It is also hard upon the men who would be killed, and their dependants,

---

[1] Of press censorship. Churchill is responding to a minute from Bracken of 20 March, commenting on Cabinet conclusions of 18 March 1942 on the subject of the press (*Cabinet papers, 65/25*). The Cabinet had agreed that no material published within Britain could henceforth be cabled abroad that was '(i) calculated to give information of value to the enemy; or (ii) containing speculations as to future operations; or (iii) which might compromise the relations of this country with foreign Powers; or (iv) calculated to create ill-feelings between the United Nations themselves, or between them, or any one of them, and a neutral country'.

[2] Edward Frederick Lawson, 1890–1961. Member of the Levy-Lawson family, owners of the *Daily Telegraph*. On active service in Palestine, 1917 (DSO, Military Cross, despatches three times). Colonel, 1918. Worked under his uncle, Viscount Burnham, on the *Daily Telegraph*, 1919–39; General Manager, 1928–39. Vice-Chairman, Newspaper Proprietors' Association, 1934. Brigadier-General, in charge of the final defence perimeter around Dunkirk, May 1940. Major-General commanding the Yorkshire Division, 1941. Director of Public Relations, War Office, 1942–5. Succeeded his father as 4th Baron Burnham, 1943. Managing Director of the *Daily Telegraph*, 1945–61. In 1955 he published *Peterborough Court* (the story of the *Daily Telegraph*).

should action be taken. Surely points like this can be put with your authority and influence to the proprietors and editors.

4. When operations are intended or in progress, surmise is just as bad as leakage. The enemy does not know that it is not leakage. Promising operations may actually have to be abandoned because of Press discussion about them.

5. I regard all this as most serious if we are to embark upon a period of offensive operations. I get little comfort from your theory that so much is written that the significance cancels itself out. The enemy is very intelligent, and these newspapers reach him in a few days via Lisbon. All is carefully sifted and collated with other knowledge.

Winston S. Churchill to James Stuart[1]
(Churchill papers, 20/67)

22 March 1942

The attached[2] makes me ask you why can you not organize a band of, say, twenty competent and loyal MPs to counter-attack the handful of misfits and discards who are deliberately trying to injure the war effort?

Whenever possible they should be attacked in their constituencies by Members of their own Parties. Arrangements should be made to have these Members present in the House at Question time or during debates, so as to intervene with repartee and rejoinder to attacks upon the Government. All the fighting is one way now. Our great majority remains like a helpless whale attacked by swordfish, with the exception that it never even gives a lash of its tail. It seems to me a very serious omission in our arrangements that nothing of this kind is organized. There ought to be a fair 'give and take'.

Please speak to me about this, and let me know what you can do.

John Curtin to Winston S. Churchill
(Churchill papers, 20/67)

22 March 1942   Australia
Most Secret and Personal

In reply to your Winch No. 16 I have had no interview with British United Press and I have made no statements in any circumstances anywhere of the nature quoted by you as published by them.

---

[1] Government Chief Whip.
[2] A letter forwarding the report of a speech by Richard Stokes MP at Ipswich Warships Week.

Regarding Greece, I was leader of the Opposition at the time of Greece campaign and although without responsibility was not without knowledge. The fact that I have given no supposed warrant for this press report until now is evidence that I never said anything about Greece.

Regarding paragraph 2 of your telegram, this is published in third person. I utterly deny any statement which would warrant its publication. I am too concerned for safety of troops to discuss their movements.

I may have views which I put to you frankly. You may have views which similarly you put to me. Neither of us can help the other by accepting as reliable any but the direct version.

Winston S. Churchill to John Curtin
(Churchill papers, 20/67)

22 March 1942
Personal and Secret

I am very glad to know that reports in question are fabrications and I thank you cordially for putting my mind at ease upon the subject.

2. In the event of any question being put to me in Parliament I shall state that you have made no such public statements and given no such interview. If not pressed I shall not refer to the matter.

3. Do you not think however that either you or I should take the matter up with the BUP?[1] We have a very hard row to hoe and we must help each other all we can. You may be sure I shall not be behind hand if I can help it.[2]

Winston S. Churchill to Oliver Lyttelton
(Churchill papers, 20/53)

22 March 1942

OLIVER LYTTELTON'S PROPOSED SPEECH TO
THE HOUSE OF COMMONS

My dear Oliver,

I think the speech is very good, and I have only a few comments to make.

The first is: page 7. I had not contemplated the setting up under you of a permanent body consisting of the three Service Ministers and the three Production Ministers. If matters attained such proportions and the

---

[1] BUP: British United Press (press agency).
[2] Churchill deleted these last two sentences before sending this telegram.

issues were so high, they would have to be resolved by the Minister of Defence or by the Defence Committee, to which the Production Chiefs might also be invited. On the other hand, I see advantages in the body indicated at 'Y' on page 7, and this I presume is the one over which Walter Layton[1] (see page 8) will preside.

Pages 7 and 8 do not I think do justice to the existing organisation. It is no good announcing at this late hour as a great discovery that supply and strategy are interwoven, and that there ought to be effective connection between the Production and Service Ministries. Such connection exists on a vast scale, not only at the summit but in every grade. The connections between the Air Ministry and MAP,[2] or between the War Office and the Ministry of Supply, or between the Naval Staff and the Controller's Department of the Admiralty, are of the most intimate and omnipresent character. I should advise your finding out and stating what the present system is, and then showing how you propose to improve it. I have frequently defined the relationship of Production to the Service Departments as that of a shopkeeper to customers. The Chiefs of the Staff's Committee and the Defence Committee make the plans: the Production Departments under you make the tools to execute them. Of course a knowledge of what tools are makeable, and in what numbers, governs the plans; but this can be easily found out by the Planning authority.

Again on page 8, in regard to Tanks. As I told you, many thousands of Tanks will be required here and not have to be transported. Tank landing craft are no measure of Tank production. The bulk of the Tanks are carried in ordinary ships and landed at regular harbours, and this will continue to be the case. A vast production of Tank landing craft is however on foot in the United States. General Ismay will show you various requests I have made to the President setting forth and urging this idea. They began in June last year. We have also designed various types of landing craft and ships that discharge into floats or landing craft through holes cut in their sides, or by special ramps from their decks down which the Tanks can run into the landing craft. You had better know about all this vast business and how far it has proceeded before

[1] Walter Thomas Layton, 1884–1966. Taught economics at Cambridge, 1908–14. Worked at the Ministry of Munitions, 1915–18. CH, 1919. Editor of the *Economist*, 1922–38. Knighted, 1930. Chairman, *News Chronicle*, 1930–50. Director General of Programmes, Ministry of Supply, 1940–2. Chief Adviser on Programmes and Planning, Ministry of Production, 1942–3. Head of the Joint War Production Staff, Ministry of Production, 1942–3. Director, Reuters, 1945–53. Created Baron, 1947. Deputy Leader of the Liberal Party in the House of Lords, 1952–5.

[2] MAP: Ministry of Aircraft Production.

giving an impression to the House that it has only just occurred to any of us. General Ismay will come to see you tomorrow (Monday) at any time and show you the papers.

With regard to your general knowledge of the strategic plans, these must as far as possible be kept secret and not spread over the wide area of the Supply Departments. It is bad enough how many have to know about them now. You should tell the House that you are a Member of the Defence Committee. Here is where you will learn and participate in the decisions about broad strategy as well as about the special Operations affecting Production, and you will thus be able to give your directions to the Production Chiefs and make the necessary allocations and priorities with full knowledge, which need not however be imparted to all concerned. Perhaps you will try your hand at remodelling this part of the Statement.

All the rest is excellent.

Yours ever,
Winston S. Churchill

*Winston S. Churchill to General Hastings Ismay
and Brigadier Leslie Hollis
(Churchill papers, 20/67)*

23 March 1942
Secret

OPERATION 'SLEDGEHAMMER'[1]

Some of these arguments are strange to me. How do we 'deceive' the enemy if we lead them to believe that we are going to do something which, in fact, we <u>are</u> going to do? Do we want them to know and be fully prepared to meet us? There would be point in this if we decided against 'Sledgehammer.'

2. No air battles are less advantageous to us than those fought tip and run over coastal towns. We have a greater advantage the farther inland the raiders come.

---

[1] 'Sledgehammer': an American plan for an Allied landing of limited aims against northern France to take Cherbourg and the Cotentin Peninsula in the autumn of 1942 (later amended to 1943), in the event that either the Soviet Union or Germany seemed in danger of imminent military collapse. The plan was proposed by the United States Army strategic planning department under Major Dwight D. Eisenhower. In August 1942 it was decided to set it aside in favour of the North African landings (Operation Torch).

3. Sir Harold Wernher,[1] whom I have known for many years, would not in my opinion be suitable for this task. The appointment would cause surprise, and might lead to comment for various reasons.

4. Let me have a short note on what is entailed in bringing the South Coast ports into operation. Surely, however, we ought to know the scale of the expedition before we take any decision. It would not seem very convenient to marshal it in the most obvious places under the constant short-range attacks of the enemy's air force.

Winston S. Churchill to Anthony Eden
(Churchill papers, 20/67)

23 March 1942
Secret

It seems to me that in replying to the President's telegram about his relations with Vichy we should take the lines:

(a) That we do not mind his sending very limited quantities of supplies of food to French North Africa, provided the American observers can penetrate the country freely, and

(b) That we value his contacts with Vichy; but

(c) Nothing must interfere with operation 'Ironclad' to which we are now committed, and no assurances offered by the French should be accepted by the United States in such a way as to enable them to complain of a breach of faith.

This also would be the moment to ask the President whether, when 'Ironclad' comes off, he would allow explanations to be made by dropping leaflets on the place concerned that the expedition was British-American, and not British only. This might perhaps diminish opposition. If he gets himself tied up with assurances from Vichy that they would defend all French territory, this might be impossible.

Pray let me have your views.

---

[1] Harold Augustus Wernher, 1893–1973. On active service, 1914–18 (despatches). Chairman of Electrolux, 1926–63. Colonel, 5th Battalion, Beds and Herts Territorial Regiment, 1928. Knighted, 1930. Acting Brigadier, 1941. Acting Major-General, 1943. One of his two sons, Captain George Wernher, Royal Armoured Corps, was killed in action in the Western Desert on 4 December 1942.

Winston S. Churchill to Sir James Grigg[1]
(Churchill papers, 20/65)

23 March 1942
Personal and Private

I think a message on the following lines should be sent by you officially:

Major Randolph Churchill, MP was sent home on duty nine weeks ago to arrange certain matters affecting his branch of the Middle East Intelligence, then under Major-General Shearer.[2] He completed his work seven weeks ago, and has since been anxious to return. Meanwhile he has received orders, first, to await the arrival of Colonel Jehu[3] who, it appears had nothing to say to him, and secondly, not to return at present.

This Officer is a Member of Parliament, and his position is the subject of public attention on account of his being the Prime Minister's son. It is not known here that he was sent home on duty and not on leave, and that he is remaining here under orders. Consequently hostile comment is excited, and Parliamentary questions may be asked at any time. Major Randolph Churchill is thus being placed in a false position, and I shall be obliged if you will make up your mind as soon as possible what further orders are to be given to him.

You will of course check the facts, and advise me before dispatch.

In the meanwhile, should a question be asked in the House, I shall advise Randolph to make a personal statement, as he is being treated in an intolerable manner.

---

[1] Percy James Grigg, 1890–1964. Educated at Bournemouth School and St John's College, Cambridge. Entered the Treasury, 1913. Served in the Royal Garrison Artillery, 1915–18. Principal Private Secretary to successive Chancellors of the Exchequer, 1921–30. Chairman, Board of Customs and Excise, 1930; Board of Inland Revenue, 1930–4. Knighted, 1932. Finance Member, Government of India, 1934–9. Elected to the Other Club, 1939. Permanent Under-Secretary of State for War, 1939–42. Secretary of State for War, 1942. Privy Councillor, 1942. National MP, East Cardiff, 1942–5. British Executive Director, International Bank for Reconstruction and Development, 1946–7. Subsequently Chairman of Bass, and a director of Imperial Tobacco, the Prudential Assurance Company and other companies.

[2] Eric James Shearer, 1892–1980. Entered the Indian Army, 1911. On active service in Europe, 1914–18 (despatches, Military Cross). On active service, Iraq rebellion, 1919 (despatches); Malabar rebellion, 1922. General Staff, War Office, 1924–9. Retired, and joined Fortnum and Mason; Joint Managing Director, 1933–8. Returned to the Army, 1939. Director of Military Intelligence, Middle East, 1940–2. Military Spokesman, Cairo, 1941–2. Retired, 1942. Managing Director and Chairman of several trading and transport companies, including London and Overseas Freighters, 1961–6.

[3] Ivor Stewart Jehu, 1908–1960. A journalist and war correspondent in India, 1932–8. Director of Public Relations, Defence Department Government of India, 1940–2 (with the rank of Lieutenant-Colonel). Brigadier, in charge of Inter-Services Public Relations Directorate, India Command, 1942. Middle East Intelligence, Cairo, 1942–4. Editor, *Times of India*, 1945–8. Chief Information Officer, Ministry of Supply, 1952–9; Ministry of Aviation, 1959–60.

Sir James Grigg to General Claude Auchinleck
(Churchill papers, 20/65)

23 March 1942
Personal

I cannot allow your MS/7134 of 23rd March[1] to pass without comment. This officer was sent home on duty over two months ago to
arrange certain matters affecting his Branch of Middle East intelligence.
He completed his work seven weeks ago and has since been anxious
to return. Arrangements were finally made for his return a fortnight
ago, but these were cancelled as a result of your DMI's telegram of 10th
March ordering him to remain where he was pending further instructions which would be sent on your return to Cairo. This prolonged delay
has placed the officer in a very false position for the fact that he was the
Prime Minister's son has provoked the comment that he was using his
position to avoid returning to duty. You have now ordered him to return
by the first available transport without vouchsafing any explanation of
the delay or any indication of the duties for which he is now required.
I should like to know what in fact the explanation is and what you have
in mind for him.

President Franklin D. Roosevelt to Winston S. Churchill
(Churchill papers, 20/72)

23 March 1942
Secret and Personal
No. 127

I am greatly disturbed at the publicity coming out of the Casey business.[2] It seems to me to be getting attention all out of proportion to its
importance. I am particularly disturbed at what I learn from the papers,
that Curtin, on the one hand, may be going to publish a detailed White
Paper and that you, on the other, feel that you may have to discuss the
matter publicly in Parliament. It seems to me that all of this plays right
into the hands of our enemies and if there is any way that all further
public discussion of it could cease it would be desirable all around. I

[1] General Auchinleck had been critical of Randolph Churchill's failure to return to Cairo from
London.
[2] At Churchill's urging, Richard Casey (Australian Minister to the United States, 1940–2) had been
appointed British Minister of State Resident in the Middle East (based in Cairo) and a Member of
the British War Cabinet.

have had a long talk with Evatt about this and he is sending to Curtin the substance of what I am cabling to you. The Casey appointment, I realize, is but an incident. The more important matter is the basic relationship of Great Britain to Australia. I sense a growing feeling in this country of impatience at what appears publicly to be a rather strained relationship between Australia and the United Kingdom at this critical time. I am simply wondering how something might be done in the immediate future to change all that to an atmosphere of good will which is so essential to the unity of our military efforts directed against the enemy. I confess at the moment that I have nothing to propose although I am going to direct my mind towards it and if I think of anything I will let you know. I say this to you because I feel myself greatly responsible for the turn of events. I told Casey quite frankly that I hoped he would take the job in the Middle East because he would be a person in the area who would know both the American and Australian angles as well as the British, and I still think the decision for Casey to go to the Middle East is a wise one.

Winston S. Churchill to President Franklin D. Roosevelt
(Churchill papers, 20/72)

23 March 1942
Personal and Secret
No. 56

Your No. 127. You have no doubt seen the correspondence between me and Curtin, which speaks for itself. I accepted his agreement and waited five days before making the announcement.

2. The matter is complicated by Australian party politics which proceed with much bitterness and jealousy regardless of national danger. The present Labour Government in Australia, with a majority of one, contains various personalities, particularly Evatt and Beasley,[1] who have made their way in local politics by showing hostility to Great Britain. The failure of sea power to protect Australia from Japan brings this sentiment to a head. I am very glad you encouraged Casey to take up the appointment.

3. I shall be most interested to know your personal impressions of Evatt and how you get on with him.

[1] John Albert Beasley, 1895–1949. Assistant Minister for Industry and External Affairs, Australia, 1929–31. Leader of the Non-Communist Labour Party in the Federal Parliament, 1940–1. Minister of Supply and Shipping, 1941–5. Minister of Defence, 1945–6. Resident Australian Minister in London, 1946. High Commissioner for Australia in London, 1946–9.

John Curtin to Winston S. Churchill
(Churchill papers, 20/72)

23 March 1942
Secret and Personal
Immediate

I am in receipt [of] your Winch 17 and note its contents with pleasure. I shall take matter up with British United Press. While on this subject may I say that as soon as I get time to consider matter fully I shall make proposals to you regarding way in which matters relating [to] Australian security and therefore total security are broadcast to Australia. For example on Saturday night I heard BBC outline what British commentators consider to be the strategy which General MacArthur will employ. True or untrue these prognostications cannot help Allies but might aid the enemy. I am aware that we have a similar problem here which I will do my utmost to handle.

Winston S. Churchill to John Curtin
(Churchill papers, 20/72)

23 March 1942
Secret and Personal

I entirely agree. Cabinet have decided that a far stiffer control must be made here of all out-going and in-coming news, including expressions of opinion or descriptive matter. Similar control will be applied to the broadcasts. A small section of the foreign or overseas correspondents make a speciality of decrying the British war effort to America and Australia. At the same time the consequential critical responses in America and Australia are cabled back here and given prominence by all who wish to rock the boat. Thus we are all got into a mood where we claw each other instead of the enemy. We cannot afford this indulgence. The war is not fought to amuse the newspapers but to save the peoples.

Winston S. Churchill to John Curtin
(Churchill papers, 20/72)

23 March 1942
Personal and Secret

I have now for first time seen telegrams interchanged between you and Casey. It seems to me that publication of his telegram to you S.10 of March 15 would be deeply resented by the President, as revealing advice which he gave confidentially. You will I am sure in the interests of Australia seek the President's permission before bringing him in. I have had a very serious telegram from him on the whole subject, and on the danger to the Allied Cause of the 'strained relations' as he puts it prevailing between Australia and Great Britain. I do not expect any debate or trouble here.

Sir Alexander Cadogan: diary
('The Diaries of Sir Alexander Cadogan', page 442)

23 March 1942

Cabinet at 6. Lot of time taken up by Winston explaining his correspondence with Curtin and Casey. Sinkings continue as bad as ever. We seem to have had quite a good naval action putting a convoy into Malta.

Winston S. Churchill to Sir James Grigg and General Sir Alan Brooke
(Churchill papers, 20/67)

24 March 1942

Please let me have a report upon the steps you are taking to revise downwards the scales of Mechanical Transport and the frillings of all kinds by which our standard divisional units are encumbered.

I hope also the excessive expansion and complication of the armoured divisions will be searchingly scrutinised.

Winston S. Churchill to A. V. Alexander
(Churchill papers, 20/67)

24 March 1942
Most Secret

DRAFT NEW NAVAL CONSTRUCTION PROGRAMME, 1942

This programme seems to me well balanced and adapted to our needs. I should like, however, to be informed what type the destroyers will be, and how long they will take to construct. Numbers and speed of delivery are still the overriding requirements.

2. Let me have the proposed dates of completion of the fleet aircraft carriers and the intermediate aircraft carriers. How long will Fiji's take? Why have you not ordered the 8-inch gun cruisers authorised in the 1940 Supplementary Programme? Give me a description of 'Heavy Support Craft.'

3. I take exception to the opening sentence of paragraph 7. First, there are no grounds for taking modern or modernised ships as the basis. If you think the older battleships are worth risking men's lives in, they ought to be counted. Secondly, it is absurd to rate the Italian ships on the same level as the British.

I see you anticipate that there will be 'a slight preponderance of enemy strength until 1944, when United States building may possibly enable us to draw ahead'. In your recent paper about Japan and the need of increasing aircraft for the Fleet, exactly the opposite tendency was dwelt upon, namely, that the Axis Powers would be catching us up year after year. These arguments are mutually destructive. In any case, it was not necessary to use them, as you do not propose to proceed with *Lion* and do not ask for any battleship construction. I highly approve getting on with the 16-inch gun mountings.

4. More important even than new construction is the acceleration of existing vessels. Merely choking the firms with orders which they cannot execute is no service to anyone. I should like to be assured that laying down new cruisers or aircraft carriers will not delay the finishing of those already advanced. How about the extra effort that was to be made upon *Anson* and *Howe*? Can nothing be done to bring *Vanguard* into 1943?

5. After the Cabinet have pronounced upon this new programme it will still be necessary to know how it can be fitted into our existing approved production, and what sacrifices it will entail in other directions. These points can only be decided when their extent emerges. I have not yet had the financial statement, to which reference is made.

What is the merchant shipbuilding programme which you contemplate running step-by-step with warship building?

Winston S. Churchill to Sir James Grigg
(Churchill papers, 20/67)

24 March 1942

GENERAL GODWIN-AUSTEN

This officer enjoys the distinction of being the only British General who was beaten by the Italians. I consider the action leading to the evacuation of British Somaliland in 1940 very discreditable, and only the appeals which were made to me not to burden General Wavell with the matter on the eve of his offensive in November 1940, prevented the enquiry into General Godwin-Austen's conduct on which I was resolved.

I very much regretted to see this officer, who had so overrated the Italian fighting-power in Somaliland, placed in command of the 13th Corps in these all-important Libyan operations. I certainly felt no confidence in him.

Now this new episode has arisen where he is again found to be on the turn away and retirement side of things, contrary to the view of the Army Commander and also of General Auchinleck. He seems extremely touchy where he himself is concerned. The message, which he describes as 'objectionably overbearing' in his letter does not bear that construction in my eyes. On the contrary, it is a singularly mild effort to spur him into a combative mood.

In these circumstances I cannot agree to his having any further appointment. Surely, we have got enough younger officers coming on to enable us to let men who have failed in this way fall back into civilian forms of war service.[1]

Winston S. Churchill to Field Marshal Jan Smuts[2]
(Churchill papers, 20/72)

24 March 1942
Most Immediate
Most Secret and Personal

OPERATION IRONCLAD (MADAGASCAR)

We have decided to storm and occupy Diego Suarez as arrival of Japanese there would not be effectively resisted by the Vichy French and would be disastrous to the safety of our Middle East convoys and most menacing to South Africa. Operation is we believe on a sufficiently large scale to be successful. Assaulting force leaves tonight, intermingled with a convoy of 50,000 men, for the East.

---

[1] Godwin-Austen received no further active military appointment. He served as Principal Administrative Officer, India Command, New Delhi, 1945–6. After retirement and a knighthood, he returned to Britain. He was Chairman of the South-Western Division of the National Coal Board, 1946–8.

[2] Jan Christian Smuts, 1870–1950. Born in Cape Colony. General commanding Boer Commando Forces, Cape Colony, 1901. Colonial Secretary, Transvaal, 1907. Minister of Defence, Union of South Africa, 1910–20. Second-in-Command of the South African forces that defeated the Germans in South-West Africa, July 1915. Honorary Lieutenant-General commanding the imperial forces in East Africa, 1916–17. South African Representative at the Imperial War Cabinet, 1917 and 1918. Prime Minister of South Africa, 1919–24. Minister of Justice, 1933–9. Prime Minister again, 1939–48. Field Marshal, 1941. Order of Merit, 1947. In 1917 he was made an honorary member of the Other Club. One of Churchill's last public speeches was at the unveiling of Smuts' statue in Parliament Square in 1956.

2. Operation will be referred to in future by name that will be communicated to you later. Special naval escort requires movement of Gibraltar Squadron and various aircraft carriers and tank landing craft, all of which has been arranged. In order to facilitate this President Roosevelt is sending his latest battleship and several other important vessels to strengthen our Home Fleet, from which Gibraltar replacements will be made.

3. We cannot allow the island in question to be reinforced by French troops from Dakar. There has been no leakage of our plans, but the strategic significance of this island harbour is obvious and of course no one can prevent German-Vichy suggestions or British newspaper surmises. None the less, if we stop this Dakar crowd we can get there first and an enormous advantage will be gained, if the operation is successful.

4. Although our plans have been studied for many weeks, we could not take decision till President Roosevelt had given us the naval replacements we needed. This was only settled late last week and I have been seeking an hour in which to tell you about it all. Naturally I do not go into technical details myself, but I know that great pains have been taken and confidence is felt by the Chiefs of Staff that the powerful forces employed will make good work of the local garrison. We have carefully considered all the reactions with Vichy. I do not think they will be so much upset as they were about the bombing of the Paris workshops,[1] which after all they swallowed.

5. I must beg you therefore to favour this enterprise and facilitate our indispensable arrest of the French ships, should it be necessary to catch them at the Cape. Every possible consideration will be used but of course they cannot go to the island in question on any account.

6. I am having a very rough time now, but look how much better things are than a year ago, when we were alone. We must not lose our faculty to dare, especially in dark days.

---

[1] On the night of 3–4 March 1942, 235 aircraft of Bomber Command attacked the Renault factory at Boulogne-Billancourt, just to the west of Paris, where 18,000 lorries a year were being made for the German Army. As a result of the raid, production was halted for four weeks, but 367 French civilians had been killed, twice the number of civilian that had yet been killed in any British bombing raid on Germany.

Winston S. Churchill to Admiral Sir Andrew Cunningham
(Churchill papers, 20/72)

25 March 1942

I shall be glad if you will convey to Admiral Vian[1] and all who sailed with him the admiration which I feel at this resolute and brilliant action by which the Malta convoy was saved. That one of the most powerful modern battleships afloat[2] attended by two heavy and four cruisers and a flotilla should have been routed and put to flight with severe torpedo and gun fire injuries in broad daylight by five British light cruisers and destroyers constitutes a naval episode of the highest distinction and entitles all ranks and ratings concerned, and above all their Commander, to the compliments of the British nation.[3]

Winston S. Churchill to Harold Laski
(Churchill papers, 20/72)

25 March 1942
Private

My dear Laski,

It is entirely beyond my share of life and strength to deal with all the issues which your letter raises. In my view we ought to win the war first, and then in a free country the issues of Socialism and Free Enterprise can be fought out in a constitutional manner. I certainly should think it very undemocratic if anyone were to try to carry Socialism during a

[1] Philip Vian, 1894–1968. Joined the Royal Navy as a cadet, 1907. Captain, 1934. On 17 February 1940, commanding the destroyer *Cossack*, he boarded the German raider supply ship *Altmark* and rescued 299 British merchant seamen. For this feat he was awarded the DSO; a bar followed for attacking a German convoy in October 1940, and a second bar for his 'mastery, determination and skill in action against the German Battleship Bismarck' (*London Gazette*, 14 October 1941). Rear-Admiral, 1941. Commanded 15th Cruiser Squadron, Mediterranean, 1941–2, including escorting the convoys to Malta, for which he was knighted. Commanded Eastern (British) Task Force, Normandy invasion, 1944. Vice-Admiral commanding the Carrier Force, British Pacific Fleet, taking part in the assault on Okinawa, April 1945. Fifth Sea Lord, 1946. Commander-in-Chief, Home Fleet, 1950–2. In 1960 he published his memoirs, *Action This Day*.

[2] The Italian battleship *Littorio*, built in Genoa, commissioned in 1940. After the war she was taken by the United States as war compensation, but was scrapped in 1948.

[3] The 2½-hour naval Battle of Sirte was fought on 22 March 1942, north of the Gulf of Sirte and east of Malta, when the escorting warships (four light cruisers, one anti-aircraft cruiser, and 18 destroyers) of a British convoy of four merchant ships sailing from Alexandria to Malta frustrated the attack of a large Italian naval force (one battleship, three heavy cruisers, one light cruiser, and eight destroyers).

Party truce without a Parliamentary majority. I have always accounted you a friend rather than a follower. I think it would be a pity to break up the national unity in the war and that I believe is the opinion of the mass of the people.

Yours sincerely,
Winston S. Churchill

Henry Channon: diary
('Chips', page 325)

25 March 1942

The PM arrived at the 1922 Committee today,[1] looking shrunken and almost apologetic; yet I was surprised by the warmth of his reception, and he seemed much touched by it. I noticed that he saw I was not applauding – his eyes are often on me – and I hurriedly beat the table with my fist. The PM spoke for over half an hour and apart from attacking the *Daily Mirror* (and I am with him there) told us very little. He wound up well; and made a dramatic bid for more loyal support. Indeed I was almost moved.

Sir Stafford Cripps to Winston S. Churchill
(Churchill papers, 20/72)

25 March 1942
Most Immediate
Personal and Very Secret

I have had a discussion this morning with C in C,[2] and AOC in C,[3] as regards defence of North Eastern India. They are both sending back their views the former to you the latter to the Air Ministry. I fully realise the difficulties that you have in spreading the very small ration of butter over the large piece of bread but in the next few weeks the position in this country will be most critical from the morale point of view and if Calcutta is bombed – as it may be in a few days time – without any effective defence the result on the people may well be disastrous.

---

[1] The 1922 Committee of Backbench Conservative MPs invited Churchill as their guest for luncheon at the Savoy Hotel.

[2] Commander-in-Chief, India and Burma, General Sir Archibald Wavell.

[3] Air Officer Commanding-in-Chief, India, Air Chief Marshal Sir Richard Peirse.

There is already a great deal of criticism and a good deal of comment on the lines of what is the good of upsetting the Japanese by an ineffective defence and if this ineffectiveness is made clear over Calcutta and (?the) industries are lost or their output gravely diminished it will have very serious repercussions throughout the country. In these circumstances we must weigh up the relative needs of Great Britain, Middle East and Ceylon to see if anything can be spread. Planes can be flown from Takoradi if they can be taken there by carrier either from SA,[1] or Great Britain, and could then possibly arrive in time. Alternatively if the Middle East target date remains mid-May it might be possible to divert one or two squadrons during the next week or so. AOC in C, takes the view that seeing what our problem is Ceylon is over insured at the moment and that some might be spared from there. The need here is certainly desperate and urgent and I hope that by one or all of these methods a few squadrons of up to date fighters can be spared. They must be up to date if they are to deal with the Japanese fighters.

Winston S. Churchill to Sir Stafford Cripps
(Churchill papers, 20/72)

26 March 1942
Personal and Most Secret

We fully share your anxiety; and we have done, and are doing, all we can to help. On our information there should be 100 Hurricanes in India (excluding Ceylon) within the next few days. 70 more should arrive in April.

2. Nothing we can send from here could affect your situation for at least two months. The only aircraft-carrier with the Home Fleet could obviously not be filled up with fighters and sent to Takoradi but in point of fact it would not help the situation since 160 Hurricanes are already on the sea for that port.

3. I agree with Chiefs of Staff that Ceylon is by no means over-insured. To detach fighters from there to Calcutta would merely tend to make ourselves weak everywhere. If Calcutta were bombed and our defences proved ineffective, the consequences would be very serious. But the loss of Ceylon would cripple our whole war effort in the Middle East as well as India. The Chiefs of Staff have asked Wavell and Somerville to consult

---

[1] SA: South Africa.

together on that basis and advise them as to the possibility of withdrawing some fighters from Ceylon to NE India.

4. As to the possibility of further air reinforcements from the Middle East, Peirse has no doubt told you that he reported on 16th March that in his judgement 'minimum force to provide some security' in NE India was 2 squadrons fighters and 2 squadrons light bombers, and that Tedder[1] immediately promised him more than he had asked for, namely, 40 Hurricanes and 40 Blenheims with crews. Tedder emphasised that this involved 'risks which can and must be accepted' but that 'any further diversion in present circumstances would render situation here dangerous.' Nevertheless CAS[2] has again wired to Peirse and Tedder to consult together and see if latter can possibly do any more for India.

5. Wavell, in para. 4 of his 321 of 25/3, said he understood that Eastern Fleet would be unable to afford assistance to Akyab in the event of a sea borne landing escorted by cruisers. First Sea Lord has today telegraphed to Somerville asking what his intentions would be in this contingency.

Winston S. Churchill: speech[3]
(Churchill papers, CHAR 9/157)

26 March 1942   Caxton Hall
12.15 p.m.   London

A year, almost to a day, has passed since I addressed you here. We had then made our great recovery after the collapse of France. Our Air Force had won the Battle of Britain. We had endured, and were still enduring, the full fury of the German air raids. The position in Egypt was secure, and we were cheered by the long series of victories by which General Wavell destroyed the Italian armies in North Africa. But perhaps you will remember that I went out of my way to warn you that we could not expect to have successes unchequered by reverses.

Since then we have had an almost unbroken series of military misfortunes. We were driven out of Cyrenaica, and have now only partly re-established ourselves there. We were driven out of Greece and Crete. We have been attacked by a new, and most formidable antagonist in the Far East. Hong Kong has fallen; the Malay Peninsula and the possessions

---

[1] Air Officer Commanding-in-Chief, Mediterranean.
[2] Chief of the Air Staff, Sir Charles Portal.
[3] To the Central Council of the Conservative Party.

of the brave Dutch in the East Indies have been overrun. Singapore has been the scene of the greatest disaster to British arms which our history records. The Allied squadrons in the Netherlands East Indies have been virtually destroyed in the action off Java. Burma is invaded; Rangoon has fallen; very hard fighting is proceeding in Upper Burma. Australia is threatened; India is threatened. The Battle of the Atlantic, upon which all the time our power to live and carry on the war effort depends, after turning markedly in our favour for five or six months, has now for the time being – but only for the time being – worsened again.

Can you wonder that such a melancholy tale, which I do not fear to tell or to face, should have caused widespread distress and anxiety through-out our country and Empire? Yet it is in such moments that fortitude and courage are the only means of safety. I cannot offer this morning any guarantee that we are at the end of our misfortunes. We were engaged in a deadly grapple with two heavily armed opponents, both of whom had been preparing for years, and bending their whole national life to the fulfilment of a gospel of war. Beginning as we did, ill-prepared, we had gathered and engaged and employed all our resources to make head against these two Powers, Germany and Italy, when suddenly a third great Power, armed to the teeth, with a population of 80,000,000, with three or four millions of trained soldiers formed into an army of at least two millions, with a powerful, efficient navy and air force and a heavy outfit of munitions – I say outfit and not output – fell upon our eastern possessions, which our bitter needs in the West had forced us to leave so insufficiently guarded. In such a situation it would be foolish for us not to be prepared for further heavy blows, and I am not here to speak smooth words or make cheering promises. But this I will venture to say, that just as last year I warned you that you could not expect to have suc-cesses unchequered by reverses, so now in 1942 we need not expect to have reverses unrelieved by successes.

There is another side to the picture, there is another column in the account which has to be added up. When we look back over the sombre year that has passed, and forward to the many trials that lie before us, no one can doubt for a moment the improvement in our war position. A year ago we were alone: now three of the greatest nations in the world are sworn to us in close alliance, and are fighting at our side in all their growing power. Whereas a year ago all we could do was to fight stubbornly and doggedly on, as we had done when we were alone in former wars – and not without ultimate success – we have now at our side mighty allies. Whereas when we met here last year it was impossible to state any definite method by which we could come out victorious, except our confidence that that would be the end, it now seems very likely that we and our allies of the United Nations cannot lose this war, and with it all that makes life worth living, except through our own fault or their own fault, through failure to use our combined strength, overwhelming strength when fully mobilised and organised, and to use the multiplying opportunities which, as the months pass by, will present themselves to us. We must therefore examine searchingly and repeatedly our own conduct and the character and quality of our war effort in every form and direction. We must make sure our fellow-countrymen and our allies have the best service from us that we can give.

We are certainly aided by a great volume of criticism and advice from which it will always be our endeavour to profit in the highest degree. Naturally when one is burdened by the very hard labour of the task and its cares, sorrows, and responsibilities, there may sometimes steal across the mind a feeling of impatience at the airy and jaunty detachment of some of those critics who feel so confident of their knowledge and feel so sure of their ability to put things right. If I should be forced – as I hope I shall not be – to yield to such a temptation, I hope you will remember how difficult it is to combine the attitude of proper meekness and humility towards assailants at home with those combative and pugnacious qualities, with the spirit of offensive and counter-attack, which we feel were never more needful than now against the common enemy.

We have succeeded in preserving our traditional free institutions, free speech, full and active Parliamentary government, a free Press. We have done that under conditions which at times were more strained and convulsive than have ever beset a civilised State. But there is one limit which I must ask shall be respected. I cannot allow, while I bear the responsibility, a propaganda to disturb the Army, which is now so strong and solid; or to weaken the confidence of the country and the armed forces in the quality and character of our devoted corps of officers, guard or line, staff or regimental, to whom we must all look, not only as the leaders of audacious enterprises abroad but as our indispensable weapon against invasion here at home.

I am perpetually asked to devote more time and attention to the rebuilding of the post-war world, and measures, some of them elaborate and all of them carefully thought out, have been taken to prepare by study and planning for that most important and longed-for period. But as you will, I am sure, agree, we must be, above all things, careful that nothing diverts or distracts our thoughts or our fullest energies from the task of national self-preservation and of inter-allied duty which will require the total concentration for an indefinite period of all that we can give.

I will not therefore enter on these subjects today, except to say that a few weeks ago one of our leading intellectuals, a great thinker – and as the father of our new President once said, one of the great difficulties about great thinkers is that they so often think wrong – asked in public whether I was working for the new England or the old. It is an easy question to answer, for you as well as for myself: we are working for both. The new England, or the new Britain, for we have our Welsh and Scottish friends represented [a voice: 'And Northern Ireland!'] – and Northern Ireland which we never forget – the new Britain and the old Britain have always dwelt side by side in our land, and it is by the union and inter-play of the new impulses and the great traditions both working together that we have managed to solve peacefully, yet finally, problems which have ruined for ever the unity of many a famous State.

It is by this dual process that we have contrived to build up over generations that basis of life with its rights and tolerances, its individual freedom, its collective associations, and, above all, its infinite power of self-improvement and national progress, that decent way of life which the broad masses of our people share and for which they now show themselves prepared to fight, and if need be to die.

This is a very hard war. Its numerous and fearful problems reach down to the very foundations of human society. Its scope is world wide, and it involves all nations and every man, woman, and child in them. Strategy and economics are interwoven. Sea, land, and air are but a single service. The latest refinements of science are linked with the cruelties of the Stone Age. The workshop and the fighting line are one. All may fall, all will stand together. We must aid each other, we must stand by each other.

We must confront our perils and trials with that national unity which cannot be broken, and a national force, which is inexhaustible. We must confront them with resilience and ingenuity which are fearless, and above all with that inflexible will-power to endure and yet to dare for which our island race has long been renowned. Thus, and thus alone, can we be worthy champions of that grand alliance of nearly thirty States and nations which without our resistance would never have come into being, but which now has only to march on together until tyranny is trampled down.

In all this the Conservative Party has a vital part to play. Now is the time for all its characteristic qualities to come increasingly into action. Now is the time for it to impart to our affairs and our national life those elements of stability and firmness, that power to plough through the evil days till the whole result is gained. Now is the time, and without this aid it might be that all the strength of embattled democracy would be cast away. The time has not come to form judgments about the past: all our thoughts, all our will-power must be concentrated on what lies around us and before us. Yet, as your leader, I shall hope that when the whole story has been told it will be said of the Conservative Party in Parliament and throughout the land: They strove for peace too long, but when war came they proved themselves the main part of the rock on which the salvation of Britain was founded and the freedom of mankind regained.

Winston S. Churchill to General Hastings Ismay,
for the Chiefs of Staff Committee
(Churchill papers, 20/67)

27 March 1942

Various telegrams about air reinforcements for India. Let us be clear about Ceylon. What we want there is the integrity of the defences of the naval base. This is because we want the Fleet to operate from there into the Bay of Bengal, and not have to go 800 miles away to Port T.[1] Nothing must be taken from Ceylon which endangers the naval base or deters the Fleet from using it. If, however, Admiral Somerville can do nothing in the Bay of Bengal under present conditions, then the defence of Colombo becomes less important. We ought, therefore, to know what Admiral Somerville thinks is possible in the way of offensive action in the Bay of Bengal before any squadrons are removed from Ceylon.

2. One had hoped that *Warspite* and two armoured carriers would be able to play an important part in the Bay of Bengal. It seemed a great loss to have to send one of these fast carriers to Port T. to guard the fairly useless 'R' Class. If they are no use and only an encumbrance, why don't they get out of the way, say to Aden or cruising, and give the aircraft carriers their chance? Two of them together are much more than twice one, and three together more than twice two.

[1] Port T: Trincomalee.

Winston S. Churchill to Herbert Morrison[1] and Brendan Bracken[2]
(Churchill papers, 20/67)

27 March 1942
Action this Day

Here is Baume[3] out again. Cannot this rascal be told to leave the country? Surely everything in para. 7 is contrary to powers which we have now assumed. It is intolerable that bad blood should continue to be made between Great Britain and Australia in this way. Pray consult together this day.

Winston S. Churchill to President Franklin D. Roosevelt
(Churchill papers, 20/72)

27 March 1942
Personal and Secret
No. 59

Your 126. I asked the Foreign Office to send you a note on the details of your project which I hope may be considered. We do not mind your sending very limited quantities of supplies to French North Africa provided the American observers can penetrate the country freely especially if you could get compensating advantages in securing the control of strategic materials now going to Germany. We value your contacts with Vichy and it is well worth paying a certain price for them but please[4]

2. Nothing must interfere with operation 'Ironclad'[5] to which we are now committed and no assurances offered by the French about defending their Empire like they did Indo-China should be accepted by the United States in such a way as to enable them to complain of a breach of faith.

[1] Herbert Stanley Morrison, 1888–1965. Began work as an errand boy at the age of 14. Secretary to the London Labour Party, 1915–40. Mayor of Hackney, 1920–1. Member of the London County Council, 1922. Labour MP for South Hackney, 1923–4, 1929–31, 1935–59. Minister of Transport, 1929–31. Instrumental in winning the London County Council for Labour, 1934. Minister of Supply, May–October 1940. Home Secretary and Minister of Home Security, 1940–5 (Member of the War Cabinet, 1942–5). Lord President of the Council (responsible for economic planning and co-ordination) and Leader of the House of Commons, 1945–51. Organizer of the Festival of Britain, 1951 (in 1999 his grandson Peter Mandelson, Secretary of State for Trade and Industry, had responsibility for the Millennium Dome). Created Baron (Life Peer), 1959.

[2] Churchill sent a copy of this memorandum to Clement Attlee, the Secretary of State for Dominion Affairs.

[3] Frederick Ehrenfried (Eric) Baume, 1900–67. New Zealand-born journalist, author, and broadcaster. His parents were of German Jewish ancestry. In August 1939 an Australian newspaper appointed him its London correspondent; he took up residence in the Savoy Hotel. A war correspondent at Arnhem, 1944. Returned to Australia in 1945, becoming a freelance commentator for press and television.

[4] Sic.

[5] The landings on Madagascar, to end Vichy French rule on the island.

3. Our operation has been carefully planned. It comprises two strong and well-trained Brigades with a third in case of a check together with tank landing craft and two carriers as well as a battleship and cruisers. All these are additional to our Eastern Fleet which is now growing in size and balance. It would be a great help if we could give the impression by dropping leaflets at the moment of attack that the expedition was Anglo-American. Please consider whether you can let us do this or anything like it.

Winston S. Churchill to General Archibald Wavell
(Churchill papers, 20/72)

27 March 1942
Immediate
Personal

FIGHTER STRENGTH: INDIA

[...]

3. You do not state present strength of fighter aircraft in India. In addition to the 24 already in the country excluding fighters in Burma, 50 should have arrived recently at Karachi. Besides these 77 more are on the way by sea and 30 by air.

4. We do not think it right at present to denude Middle East further than what has already been arranged or may result from Peirse–Tedder consultation.

Commander Charles Thompson[1] to Winston S. Churchill
(Churchill papers, 20/57)

27 March 1942
PM.

Mr Sam Goldwyn[2] recommended that you should see the film *The Princess and the Pirate.*[3]

I sent a message thanking him for doing this but you may care to mention it to him at luncheon today & say that you enjoyed it.

---

[1] 'Tommy' Thompson, Personal Assistant to Churchill as Minister of Defence.

[2] Samuel Goldwyn, 1882–1974. Born (Szmuel Gelbfisz) in Warsaw. Emigrated to the United States, 1920. Founding partner in Goldwyn Picture Corp. (later Metro-Goldwyn-Mayer), 1916. An independent film producer from 1923. Presidential Medal for Freedom, 1971.

[3] Bob Hope's second film for Samuel Goldwyn. A technicolour extravaganza, it was nominated for two Academy Awards. Most quoted lines: *Princess:* 'I hear there are pirates in these waters.' *Sylvester (Bob Hope):* 'Yeah? Well, let them stay in the water, they're dangerous on ships!' Although the Churchill Archive dates this note as from 27 March 1943, the date is likely 27 March 1945. *The Princess and the Pirate* was not released in the US until November 1944 and would have taken several more months to reach UK theatres.

Josef Stalin to Winston S. Churchill
(Churchill papers, 20/73)

27 March 1942
Important
Personal and Secret

I thank you for the message recently transmitted to me by Sir A. Clark Kerr. I have had a long talk with Sir A. Clark Kerr and I am convinced that our joint work will proceed in an atmosphere of perfect mutual confidence.

2. I wish to express to you the Soviet Government's gratitude for the assurance that the British Government will look upon any use by the Germans of poison gas against the USSR in the same light as if this weapon had been used against Great Britain, that the British Air Force will immediately use against suitable objectives in Germany the large stocks of gas bombs held in England.

3. According to our information poison gas may be used against the USSR by the Finns as well as the Germans. I should like what you say in your message, about retaliatory gas attacks on Germany, to be extended to include Finland as well in case the latter should use poison gas against the USSR.

4. I think that it would be most expedient if the British Government were, in the near future, to issue a public warning to the effect that England would consider the use of poison gas against the USSR by either Germany or Finland as an attack upon England herself, and that she would reply by using gas against Germany.

5. It is, of course, understood that, if the British Government so wishes, the USSR is prepared in its turn to issue an analogous warning to Germany, in consideration of the possibility of a German gas attack on England.

6. The Government of the USSR considers that if the British Government issues such a warning to Germany it should do so not later than the end of April or beginning of May.

7. The Soviet Government would be most grateful if the British Government could help the USSR to obtain from England certain chemical means of defence, which it now lacks, and also certain materials for use in chemical counter-attack, in case of a German chemical attack on the USSR. If there is no objection on your side I could send a specialist in these matters to England in the near future.

Lord Desborough[1] to Winston S. Churchill
(Churchill papers, 2/464)

28 March 1942   Panshanger Park
                                                 Hertford
                                                 Hertfordshire

My dear Winston,

I must write one line to say how much I admired your last speech – The good temper, dignity and steadfastness with which you face the anxieties of these terrible times is an inspiration to us all, and has won you a place not to be shaken in the hearts of the people, who feel confident that whatever may happen you will pull us through –

Please do not think of answering this[2] –

Yours ever,
Desborough

Winston S. Churchill to General Hastings Ismay,
for the Chiefs of Staff Committee
(Churchill papers, 20/67)

29 March 1942

I think it would be wrong not to let General Auchinleck know the truth, but perhaps the word 'reluctance' might be substituted for 'great regret,' as 'regret' has some smack of censure about it.

2. There is no question of my sending any 'friendly telegram' at the present time. I have sent him several when he has been in misfortune through his plans miscarrying, but I could not honestly give him the impression that I am satisfied with his refusals either to act or to come home and discuss matters. Perhaps later on, when it is seen that he is intending to take the offensive, I might reconsider this suggestion. The situation is too grave for empty compliments.

---

[1] William Henry Grenfell, 1855–1945. Liberal MP for Salisbury (1880–2, 1885–6), for Hereford (1892–3); Conservative MP for Wycombe, 1900–5. Member of the Tariff Commission, 1904. Created Baron Desborough, 1905. President, British Imperial Council of Commerce. President, Association of Volunteer Regiments. He and his wife Ethel were close friends of Churchill. Their two sons were both killed in the First World War.

[2] Churchill replied by telegram: 'Thank you so much, Winston' (*Churchill papers, 2/464*).

Winston S. Churchill to General Hastings Ismay
(Churchill papers, 20/67)

29 March 1942

You should write to Lord Hankey as follows:

'In view of the statements which you made in the House of Lords about late sittings on defence matters,[1] the Prime Minister had the question examined.

'In the last six months the total is 19, or about 3 a month. At least 50 per cent. of these meetings ended before midnight.

'As the Prime Minister will probably make some reference to your remarks in the future, he thinks it is right to let you know what are the facts.'

Winston S. Churchill to Brigadier Leslie Hollis
(Churchill papers, 20/67)

29 March 1942

SECRECY

I cannot understand how you should have sent this paper other than in a locked box to be opened by me alone. Pray make sure forthwith that no paper relating to this or future special operations passes to and fro between those concerned otherwise than in a locked box.

Sir Stafford Cripps to Winston S. Churchill
(Churchill papers, 20/72)

29 March 1942   New Delhi
Most Immediate
Personal and Very Secret

It looks at the moment pretty certain that critical issue will arise tomorrow Sunday on question of defence responsibility. I have made it clear that under no circumstances can we give up any of responsibility for defence of India. A very considerable number of persons and interests have on the other hand stressed the need to raise the keenness of Indians to defend their country.

---

[1] Speaking in the House of Lords on 29 March 1942, Lord Hankey said that 'late night meetings should be reserved for emergencies'. He also quoted Cicero that 'armies can signify but little abroad unless there be counsel and wise management at home'.

2. The Viceroy Commander-in-Chief and myself have discussed this and want to do our utmost to deprive Congress of any excuse for refusal under this head. In order to get rid of possible implication in present draft that it is not for Indians to defend India we unite in urging the immediate acceptance – which I must have by 3 p.m. Indian Standard Time tomorrow March 29th to be effective in publication – of following paragraph in lieu of first portion of paragraph (e) down to 'desire and invite'.

<u>Begins</u>: (e) during the critical period which now faces India and until the new constitution can be framed His Majesty's Government must inevitably bear the full responsibility for and retain the ultimate control and direction of defence of India as part of the World War effort, but the task of organising to the full the military moral and material resources of India must be the responsibility of Government of India with the co-operation of the peoples of India. His Majesty's Government desire and invite. <u>Ends</u>.

3. If your agreement is received in time we will substitute this in agreed text for publication.

Winston S. Churchill to Sir Stafford Cripps
(Churchill papers, 20/72)

29 March 1942
Personal and Secret

There is no time to convene Cabinet, or even to consult colleagues, but since you assure me that Viceroy and Commander-in-Chief unite with you in urging proposed amendment of clause (e) I authorise you to act accordingly.

2. It would be better to omit the adjective 'full' before the word 'responsibility' and the adjective 'ultimate' before the word 'control'. Cable most immediate final text.

3. I am very glad you have made it clear that your mission in no way extends to Ceylon.

Sir Stafford Cripps to Winston S. Churchill
(Churchill papers, 20/72)

29 March 1942   New Delhi

Am inserting proposed amendment of paragraph (e) in final text with omission of 2 words requested in your paragraph No. 2. Full text of amended paragraph follows.

(e) During the critical period which now faces India and until the new Constitution can be framed His Majesty's Government must inevitably bear the responsibility for and retain control and direction of the defence of India as part of their world war effort, but the task of organising to the full the military moral and material resources of India must be the responsibility of the Government of India with the co-operation of the peoples of India. His Majesty's Government desire and invite the immediate and effective participation of the leaders of the principal sections of the Indian people in the counsels of their country, of the Commonwealth and of the United Nations. Thus they will be enabled to give their active and constructive help in the discharge of a task which is vital and essential for the future freedom of India.

On 29 March 1942 the British Government's proposals for Indian constitutional reform were published. India was to be granted full Dominion status after the war; until then, defence was to remain under British control.

Winston S. Churchill to President Franklin D. Roosevelt
(Churchill papers, 20/72)

29 March 1942
Personal and Secret
No. 60

In order to cope with future U-Boat hatchings, we are emphasising bombing attacks on U-Boat nests, and last night went to Lübeck with 250 bombers including 43 heavy. Results are said to be the best ever.[1] This is in accordance with your wishes expressed in your No. 125.

2. As I mentioned in my No. 53 replying to your No. 125, Admiralty and Coastal Command, RAF have evolved a plan for a day and night patrol over the debouches from the Bay of Biscay. Biscay ports are the

[1] With bombs aimed at the narrow streets and old half-timbered houses of the Old Town, 30 percent of Lübeck's built-up area was destroyed in a firestorm, with more than 3,000 residential buildings destroyed or severely damaged. At least 312 (possibly 320) German civilians were killed.

shortest and best departure points for U-Boats operating in Caribbean and American Coasts. German present practice is to proceed submerged by day and make speed on the surface at night. We hope that night attacks and menace by aircraft will hamper their night passage and force increasing exposure by day. Essential therefore to menace both by day and night thus increasing length of voyage and diminishing operational spell on your side. This advantage would be additional to any killings or maimings, some of which might be hoped for each month since there are never less than six U-Boats going or coming through the area to be patrolled.

3. In view of the very heavy sinkings still occurring on your side to which convoy when organised can only be partial remedy, Admiralty are pressing to allocate four and later on six Bomber Squadrons to this new Biscay patrol. On merits I am most anxious to meet their wish.

4. On the other hand the need to bomb Germany is great. Our new method of finding targets is yielding most remarkable results. However our bombing force has not expanded as we hoped. We have had a heavy disappointment in a structural defect with the wing tips of the Lancasters which requires laying up four squadrons of our latest and best for several months. Just at the time when the weather is improving, when Germans are drawing away flak from their cities for their offensive against Russia, when you are keen about our bombing U-Boat nests, when the oil targets are especially attractive, I find it very hard to take away these extra six squadrons from Bomber Command in which Harris[1] is doing so well.

5. Arnold[2] had arranged at your orders to send the first instalment of US Bomber groups to England arriving in July. Can you not manage to expedite this? Never was there so much good work to be done and so few to do it. We must not let our summer air attack on Germany decline into a second-rate affair. Everything is ready for your people here and there are targets of all kinds, from easy to hard, to work up on in contact with the enemy. Even a hundred American heavy bombers working from this country before the end of May would lift our air offensive to

[1] Arthur Travers Harris, 1892–1984. Known as 'Bomber Harris'. On active service, 1914–18 (AFC) with the Royal Flying Corps (later Royal Air Force). Served in India, 1921–2; Iraq, 1922–4; Egypt, 1930–2. Director of Plans, Air Ministry, 1934–7. Air Officer Commanding 4 Bomber Group, 1937. Head of RAF Mission to United States and Canada, 1938. Air Officer Commanding, Palestine and Transjordan, 1938–9. Air Vice-Marshal, 1939. Deputy Chief of the Air Staff, 1940–1. Head of the Royal Air Force Delegation to the United States, 1941. Air Marshal, 1941. Knighted, 1942. Commander-in-Chief, Bomber Command, 1942–5. Air Chief Marshal, 1943. Marshal of the Royal Air Force, 1945.

[2] General Henry Arnold, Commanding General of United States Army Air Forces.

the proper scale and enable me to spare the six squadrons now for the Biscay patrols.

Winston S. Churchill to General Wladyslaw Sikorski[1]
(Churchill papers, 20/72)

29 March 1942
Most Immediate
Secret

Arrangements for the evacuation from Uzbekistan of all your soldiers for whom Russians cannot provide rations are now being made by local Polish and British authorities. The first batch should arrive at Pahlevi on the 28th March. You will realise the arrival of such large numbers as the Russians propose to send out at such short notice will throw a very great strain upon our administrative machinery. But you may be sure no effort is being spared by us for the reception of your countrymen.

2. General Auchinleck proposes to concentrate the Polish Forces evacuated, together with the Carpathian Brigade, in Southern Palestine where suitable accommodation and conditions exist, and where they will be organised and equipped.

3. We are straining every nerve to send forces from United Kingdom to Middle East but are very severely limited by shortage of shipping: it therefore seems wrong to bring excellent soldiers to this country, where we have plenty of men, from Middle East, where we are so short, and where they can be most usefully employed.

4. I propose therefore that we should bring back only the men required for the Polish Naval and Air Force units and a minimum for your Armoured Division. Please let me know whether you agree with this policy and the minimum numbers which we should bring home in order to put it into effect.

---

[1] Wladyslaw Sikorski, 1881–1943. Organizer of pre-1914 Polish Military Organization, 1909. Lieutenant-Colonel, Polish Legions, 1914–18. Commanded two Army corps in the defence of Poland against the Bolsheviks, 1920. Prime Minister of Poland, 1922–3. Minister of Military Affairs, 1923–5. Commander, Lwow Army Region (which he had defended against the Ukrainians in 1919), 1926–8. On half-pay, 1928–39. Recalled to service, 1939. Prime Minister of the Polish Government-in-Exile (first in Paris, then in London) and Commander-in-Chief of the Polish Army from the fall of Poland until his death in an air crash at Gibraltar on 4 July 1943.

Winston S. Churchill to Randolph S. Churchill
(Churchill papers, 20/72)

29 March 1942
Personal and Secret

Please tell Colonel 4th Hussars[1] how much I value being Colonel of the Regiment, and thank him for his congratulations saying I have received similar congratulations from fifteen officers of the Regiment who are prisoners of war in Germany.

I send my best wishes to all ranks and hope they may soon have a chance of getting some of their own back. Say also that I keep in close touch with General Barnes[2] on matters affecting the Regiment at home.

Lord Halifax to Winston S. Churchill
(Churchill papers, 20/73)

29 March 1942   Washington DC
Secret and Personal

Evatt addressed private meeting on March 26th. Influential people.

One who was there tells me that after stressing Australian situation and needs he said 'but do not misunderstand me. If I had to choose whether Australia or Great Britain should go down I would wish *to save* Great Britain, for Great Britain is the bastion of us all'.

The audience much impressed.

---

[1] Lieutenant-Colonel R. B. Sheppard, DSO, OBE. Commanding Officer, 4th Hussars, Western Desert, May 1941 to August 1942. Retired from the Army, 1947.

[2] Reginald Walter Ralph Barnes, 1871–1946. Entered the Army, 1890. Lieutenant, 4th Hussars, 1894; one of Churchill's close Army friends. Went with Churchill to Cuba, 1895. Captain, 1901. Lieutenant-Colonel commanding 10th Hussars, 1911–15. Colonel, 1914. Brigadier-General, commanding 116th Infantry Brigade and 14th Infantry Brigade, 1915–16. Commanded 32nd Division, 1916–17, and 57th Division, 1917–19. Major-General, 1918. Knighted, 1919.

Winston S. Churchill to General Hastings Ismay,
for the Chiefs of Staff Committee
(Churchill papers, 20/67)

30 March 1942
Most Secret

It is of the greatest importance that de Gaulle's people should be misled about 'Ironclad'.[1] Once they know, the secret will be out, as in the case of Dakar. It is for this reason we have had to exclude their participation until after all is over.

2. It should be possible, through General Smuts, to lead them to believe that very secret South African preparations are being made by the Union Government. They might perhaps even be associated with these. The attack would not be timed to take place until the beginning of June. This is only a suggestion. Perhaps, however, some better plan of cover or deception may be developed. The matter should be considered in all its bearings. Major Morton[2] will represent me.

Winston S. Churchill to Admiral of the Fleet Sir Dudley Pound
and the Chiefs of Staff Committee
(Churchill papers, 20/67)

30 March 1942
Secret

OPERATION 'PERFORMANCE'[3]

What chance have these ships of getting away (see paragraph 4)? Surely, they will be just picked up as and when the Germans find it convenient.

[1] The imminent operation against the Vichy French administration on Madagascar.

[2] Desmond Morton, 1891–1971. 2nd Lieutenant, Royal Artillery, 1911. Converted to Roman Catholicism shortly before the First World War. Shot through the heart while commanding a field battery at the Battle of Arras, April 1917, but survived the wound. Later awarded the Military Cross. ADC to Sir Douglas Haig, 1917–18. Seconded to the Foreign Office, 1919. Head of the Committee of Imperial Defence's Industrial Intelligence Centre, January 1929 to September 1939, its terms of reference being 'to discover and report the plans for manufacture of armaments and war stores in foreign countries'. A member of the Committee of Imperial Defence sub-committee on Economic Warfare, 1930–9. Principal Assistant Secretary, Ministry of Economic Warfare, 1939. Personal Assistant to Churchill throughout the Second World War. Knighted, 1945. Economic Survey Mission, Middle East, 1949. Seconded to the Ministry of Civil Aviation, 1950–3.

[3] 'Performance': the breakout on 1–4 April 1942 from the Swedish port of Gothenburg, where they were interned, to the United Kingdom, of ten Norwegian merchant ships, supported on the second day of the breakout by six British destroyers and RAF Fighter and Coastal Command. Five of the merchant ships were sunk by the Germans in the Skagerrak, one was so badly damaged that British destroyers sank her, two returned to Gothenburg, and only two reached the United Kingdom.

If there is no chance whatever of their escaping, is it worth while running all the other risks? The situation seems quite different to when they got away last time, for then there was surprise.

Winston S. Churchill to Sir Andrew Duncan[1]
(Churchill papers, 20/67)

30 March 1942

As you know, I have always taken a special interest in Colonel Jefferis's experimental establishment known as MD1.[2] When you were there before you kindly agreed to have the Section attached to the Ministry of Supply for 'Pay and Rations', but free to devote their attention to new technical ideas in any field of military activity, reporting from time to time to me as Minister of Defence. It seems that there was some difficulty about this in the period of office of Lord Beaverbrook, who wished to make the Department responsible, as regards its research and development, to Mr Oliver Lucas.[3] I hope you will see no objection to continuing on the previous lines. Colonel Jefferis would, as regards his experimental work, be responsible to Lord Cherwell as my representative, who would report directly to you and to me; your officials would look after the administrative side on the lines which I believe have been agreed between Sir William Douglas[4] and Sir Edward Bridges; production would, of course, remain with you, and Jefferis would keep in close touch with your production side as hitherto.

Jefferis has worked, and is working, for the Navy and the Air Force, as well as for the Army and SS,[5] so that some such arrangement seems

---

[1] Andrew Rae Duncan, Minister of Supply.

[2] MD1: Ministry of Defence 1, an experimental establishment located at Whitchurch, 12 miles north of Chequers.

[3] Oliver Lucas, a director of Joseph Lucas, electrical component makers who supplied the car and aircraft industries. Director-General of Tank Research, Ministry of Supply, 1940–3. A member of the Supply Council, and Director of Design and Development at the Tank Board. Involved in the development of the jet engine during the war. After the war, engaged at Joseph Lucas in research on combustion, development of the fuel system, and manufacture of the relevant equipment for the jet engine.

[4] William Sholto Douglas, 1893–1969. On active service, 1914–18 (despatches thrice, Military Cross, DFC). Commanded 43 and 85 (Fighter) Squadrons, 1917–18. Assistant Chief of the Air Staff, 1938–40. Deputy Chief of the Air Staff, 1940. Air Officer Commanding-in-Chief, Fighter Command, 1940–2; Middle East Command, 1943–4; Coastal Command, 1944–5. Knighted, 1941. Air Officer Commanding the British Air Forces of Occupation, Germany, 1945–6. Governor, British Zone of Germany, 1946–7. Created Baron, 1948. Chairman, British European Airways, 1949–64.

[5] SS: The Secret Service.

perfectly logical. Although he has only a very small establishment, he has produced new weapons which have been well thought of and often ordered in very large numbers by the various services. It would seem a pity to interfere with arrangements which have worked so satisfactorily up to date.

Winston S. Churchill to General Sir Alan Brooke and
Lieutenant-General Sir Bernard Paget[1]
(Churchill papers, 20/67)

30 March 1942
Most Secret

GERMAN TANK LANDING CRAFT

If we are to believe the latest estimates of the Combined Intelligence Centre, all the stories about 800 specially constructed vessels and the deductions founded upon them as to the scale of invasion are obsolete. I was always sceptical about these 800 vessels, and have repeatedly questioned the trustworthiness of the rumours.

I hope all our calculations are kept up-to-date.

Winston S. Churchill to Sir John Anderson
(Churchill papers, 20/67)

30 March 1942

I was not aware you had taken decisions on this matter, and that they would be given effect without the Cabinet or myself being consulted. I am not at all convinced we should be wise to pull the Army to pieces at the present time. When did the Secretary of State for War agree to this proposal, and what are the classes of men serving in the Army at home who are fit enough to go down the pits and yet not able to take their places in the Field Force, which is already under strength.

---

[1] Commander-in-Chief, Home Forces.

Winston S. Churchill to Oliver Lyttelton
(Churchill papers, 20/67)

30 March 1942
Secret

PRODUCTION OF ANTI-AIRCRAFT GUNS

The point at 'A'[1] requires your attention. The advantages of the 5.25-inch AA guns would have to be very marked to justify the serious loss in numbers. With the war spreading ever more widely and new claims for flak protection constantly coming in, the emphasis should be on numbers. Take Turkey, for instance. A couple of hundred 3-7s might have enormous influence upon her action.

A loss of 4-1 requires very exceptional justification. Pray let me know your views.

Robert Barrington-Ward:[2] note by his biographer[3]
(Robert Barrington-Ward papers)

30 March 1942

B-W presented his host[4] with a photographed copy of a letter, found in *The Times* archives, dated 1898 and signed 'Winston S. Churchill' in which the writer regretted that he had been prevented by Kitchener[5] from acting as correspondent of the paper in the Sudan. This memento of his youth seemed to give pleasure. After reviewing the good news of the St. Nazaire Raid[6] and of American operations in the Pacific and agreeing that the collapse in Singapore was inexplicable, they passed on to the question of the *Daily Mirror*.

[1] Minute of 25 March 1942 from General Ismay replying to a query raised by the Prime Minister about the production of anti-aircraft guns.

[2] Editor of *The Times*.

[3] Donald McLachlan.

[4] Winston S. Churchill.

[5] In 1898, Kitchener was commanding the Khartoum Expeditionary Force, to which Churchill was eventually attached as a soldier, taking part in the charge of the 21st Lancers at the Battle of Omdurman. In his book *The River War* (1899), Churchill was critical of Kitchener's harsh attitude towards the wounded Dervish enemy.

[6] On the night of 27–8 March 1942, a combined raid by the Royal Navy, the Army, and the Royal Air Force was carried out against the dry dock in St Nazaire, on the Bay of Biscay, using the obsolete destroyer HMS *Campbeltown* to ram the main dock gate. The loss of the dry dock would force any large German warship in need of repairs, such as the *Tirpitz*, to return to home waters rather than having a safe haven available on the Atlantic coast. After the raid only 228 men returned to Britain; 169 were killed and 215 became prisoners of war. German casualties were more than 360 dead, mostly killed after the raid when *Campbeltown* exploded. In recognition of the bravery of the raiding party, 89 decorations were awarded to its members, including five Victoria Crosses.

Robert Barrington-Ward: diary
(Robert Barrington-Ward papers)

30 March 1942

I said no Minister had yet named the conductors of that paper[1] nor insisted on the impropriety of anonymous holdings (bank nominees) in newspapers – irresponsible control. If they closed down a paper with 1,800,000 circulation, there would be a widespread grousing and they would have a wolf by the ears.

Then control of outgoing cables. I suggested that to extend censorship generally to outgoing opinion raised an issue of principle and was wrong. Right course was to deprive a Dominion journalist persistently sending defamatory despatches of his cable facilities. (Some of them have been deliberately and shamefully mischievous.) Winston much excited and taken with this suggestion. Insisted that Bracken should inquire into his powers and report. (Incidentally I knew that the Empire Press Union would prefer this course.)

Then Winston got on to the Press generally (which he has rather on the brain.) Thinks *Daily Mirror, Daily Mail* and *Daily Herald* campaigns were calculated to undermine the Army. Makes no complaint of *TT*[2] *or Manchester Guardian*: 'sober reasoned criticism.' Hopes we can give him a hand from time to time to keep things steady. I said people wanted some vision of the future, some hope. British would always fight best when fighting for more than their skins.

'What do you want me to say?' I said I wouldn't offer an off-hand reply but should be prepared to draft something. 'Get it on a few sheets of paper and send it to me.' I most gladly undertook to do so.

He went on to the importance of preserving free enterprise. Nationalisation of the railways – no difficulty about that. But profit was 'not an ignoble motive.' I said it was all a matter of determining where the profit motive could still usefully function and where it could not.

Winston said 'I am an old man (he didn't sound it), not like Lloyd George coming out of the last war at 56 or so. I may be 70 before this war ends.' This was taking refuge in the view that reconstruction would be for someone else to take up in the future. He cannot see what the assurance, and in some measure the accomplishment, of it means to public confidence and war energy <u>now</u>. 'No man has had to bear such disasters as I have.' I said the nation had taken them very well.

[1] The *Daily Mirror*.
[2] *The Times* newspaper.

Far from storming he bore my candour and listened most patiently. Not quite as fit and sparkling as at our last lunch. A very impressive person with strong limitations. His utter absence of pomposity is engaging. He was wearing his one-piece 'siren suit.' Ate heartily.

Winston S. Churchill to John Curtin
(Churchill papers, 20/73)

30 March 1942
Most Immediate
Most Secret and Personal

During the latter part of April and the beginning of May, one of our armoured divisions will be rounding the Cape. If by that time Australia is being heavily invaded I should certainly divert it to your aid. This would not apply in the case of localized attacks in the North or of mere raids elsewhere. But I wish to let you know that you could count on this help, should invasion by say eight or ten Japanese divisions occur. This would also apply to other troops, of which we have a continuous stream passing to the East. I am still by no means sure that the need will arise, especially in view of the energetic measures you are taking and the United States help.

Winston S. Churchill to Sir Stafford Cripps
(Churchill papers, 20/73)

30 March 1942
Immediate
Personal

Your No. 817-S. It would be natural and possibly useful to collect information about Singapore from the sources you mention, though I do not see why the Viceroy should be involved. An Officer of the Intelligence Staff could quite well do the work. I am entirely opposed to anything in the nature of an inquiry during the war, and I have no doubt this position can be maintained in Parliament. I should also be very glad to receive a report from General Wavell, but on no account must the past be allowed to burden the present and future.

2. Everything on the home front is easier. We are all waiting anxiously for the Indian reaction to our proposals. All good wishes and congratulations on progress so far.

3. Your No. 835-S.[1] I am telling the India Office and Home Office to confer at once. You will realize no material can reach you for several months. Advisers can however be sent by Air.

General Sir Alan Brooke: diary
('War Diaries, Field Marshal Lord Alanbrooke', page 243)

30 March 1942

After dinner had to go round to see PM at 10.30 p.m.
[...]
was kept up till 1 a.m. discussing possibilities of some kind of offensive in Northern France to assist Russia in the event of German attack being successful, as it probably will be. A difficult problem – this universal cry to start a western front is going to be hard to compete with, and yet what can we do with some 10 divisions against the German masses? Unfortunately the country fails to realise the situation we are in.

Lady Leslie[2] to Winston S. Churchill
(Churchill papers, 1/368)

31 March 1942   Glaslough
                                                        County Monaghan
                                                                      Eire

Oh! My dearest Winston,

I am indeed touched by your wire saying you value a letter from me – It is difficult to write – 'à coeur ouvert' these days – what with censors & delayed posts – but I feel that my ardent thoughts – and prayers for you really make a link between us –

I am so convinced that the Powers Above watch over you and inspire you & – & will continue to lead you – as long as you can hear & follow their promptings – What would have become of the Empire but for your Help these last 3 years? – A spiritual Revival seems to be gradually permeating us all – and one feels confidence in the Future as long as we stand together – and aid each other – as you said at Caxton Hall the other day –

---

[1] A detailed report from Cripps about the serious lack of air raid precautions and firefighting equipment in the main Indian cities.

[2] Leonie Blanche Jerome, 1859–1943. Sister of Churchill's mother, Lady Randolph. Married Colonel John Leslie in 1884. Their younger son Norman had been killed in action on 18 October 1914.

I hope Dear you have a peaceful Easter with as many of the family as can get Leave – It is splendid the way they are all serving – There are still many simple joys one can enjoy – I sometimes feel ashamed of having our comforts here – & not to be able to share them with those who are in need & want – Lionel[1] feels the same – he has just married a very Charming young widow & is very happy, but says he knows he ought to be fighting with the Russians instead of honeymooning! – However he need not worry – his turn will come – he is in Cameron Highlanders – & has a special job –

Give my love to dear Clemmie & the others –

Yr. very devoted old Venerable Aunt –
Leonie[2]

War Cabinet: Confidential Annex
(Cabinet papers, 65/29)

31 March 1942
12.30 p.m.

The Home Secretary and Minister of Home Security reported the steps which he was taking to arrange for reports to be submitted by all the Civil Departments on their anti-gas preparations. He hoped that a Report covering the whole ground would be available in the following week.

The Prime Minister emphasised that preparations on this matter should fall into two stages. The first stage would be the steady over-haul of civilian anti-gas preparations in this country, which should be conducted without any publicity. When this stage had been completed, (which he hoped would be about the 18th to 20th April), there should be a broadcast to the public on the matter, which would include a statement to the effect that if gas was used by the enemy against Russia or against ourselves, we should retaliate. This aspect of the matter should for the moment, be regarded as most secret.

The War Cabinet's Conclusions were as follows:

---

[1] Lionel Alistair David Leslie, 1900–87. Churchill's first cousin. Fourth son of Sir John and Leonie Leslie. Educated at Eton. Captain, Cameron Highlanders; on active service, 1939–45 (despatches). He had married Barbara Enever on 12 January 1942.

[2] Churchill replied by telegram: 'Thank you so much dearest Leonie for your charming letter, Winston'.

(1) The unobtrusive inquiry into the state of readiness of the civilian anti-gas preparations should be pressed forward, with a view to a Report being submitted to the War Cabinet in the course of the following week.

(2) The Home Secretary[1] was asked to arrange with the Minister of Information for a notice to be issued to the Press, explaining that a steady overhaul of our anti-gas preparations was being carried out unobtrusively, but that for the present no mention of the matter should be made in the Press.

(3) The Secretary of State for Foreign Affairs should be asked to inquire into the possibility of sending to the USSR certain chemical means of defence.

(4) It would be undesirable for the Foreign Office to send a reminder at this juncture to the two countries (Hungary and Finland) which had not answered the questions put to them as to whether they would abide by the Gas Protocol.

[1] Herbert Morrison.

April
1942

Winston S. Churchill to General Hastings Ismay,
for the Chiefs of Staff Committee
(Churchill papers, 20/67)

1 April 1942

FALKLAND ISLANDS[1]

It would be a very serious thing to lose the Falkland Islands to the Japanese, and no comfort to say that it would hurt the United States more than ourselves. The 'penny packet' argument applies to the Americans as much as to ourselves. The islands are a British possession and responsibility. Hitherto I was told there was no shipping and that it would be much easier for the United States to reinforce them than for us. It is clear this is not so.

In these circumstances a British battalion should certainly be found, but let me know first how this could be done and what dislocation it involves.

The Falkland Islands are very well known, and their loss would be a shock to the whole Empire. They would certainly have to be retaken. The object of the reinforcement would be to make it necessary for the Japanese to extend their attacking force to a tangible size. This might well act as a deterrent.

---

[1] An archipelago of 778 islands in the South Atlantic Ocean, the largest being East Falkland and West Falkland. The Falkland Islands are located more than 250 nautical miles east of the coast of mainland South America. Against competing French, Spanish, and Argentine claims, British control was re-established there in 1833, and a permanent British colony established in 1840.

Winston S. Churchill to General Sir Harold Alexander
(Churchill papers, 20/73)

1 April 1942
Personal

We are watching with warmest admiration your skilful and resolute conduct of this most difficult campaign, and I also congratulate you on success of your visit to Generalissimo.[1]

Winston S. Churchill to President Franklin D. Roosevelt
(Churchill papers, 20/73)

1 April 1942
Personal and Secret
No. 61

Air attack on Malta is very heavy. There are now in Sicily about 400 German and 200 Italian fighters and bombers. Malta can only now muster 20 or 30 serviceable fighters. We keep feeding Malta with Spitfires in packets of 16 loosed from *Eagle* carrier from about 600 miles west of Malta.

This has worked a good many times quite well but *Eagle* is now laid up for a month by defects in her steering gear. There are no Spitfires in Egypt. *Argus* is too small and too slow and moreover she has to provide the fighter cover for the carrier launching the Spitfires and for the escorting force. We would use *Victorious* but unfortunately her lifts are too small for Spitfires. Therefore there will be a whole month without any Spitfire reinforcements.

2. It seems likely from extraordinary enemy concentration on Malta that they hope to exterminate our air defence in time to reinforce either Libya or their Russian offensive. This would mean that Malta would be at the best powerless to interfere with reinforcements or armour to Rommel, and our chances of resuming offensive against him at an early date ruined.

3. Would you be willing to allow your carrier *Wasp* to do one of these trips provided details are satisfactorily agreed between the Naval Staffs. With her broad lifts, capacity and length, we estimate that *Wasp* could take 50 or more Spitfires. Unless it were necessary for her to fuel *Wasp* could proceed through the Straits at night without calling at Gibraltar until on the return journey as the Spitfires would be embarked in the Clyde.

[1] General Alexander had flown to Chungking to discuss with Chiang Kai-shek the possible withdrawal of British forces from both Burma and China.

4. Thus instead of not being able to give Malta any further Spitfires during April a powerful Spitfire force could be flown into Malta at a stroke and give us a chance of inflicting a very severe and possibly decisive check on enemy. Operation might take place during third week of April.

Winston S. Churchill to President Franklin D. Roosevelt
(Churchill papers, 20/73)

1 April 1942
Personal and Secret
No. 62

Delighted by your letter of March 18 just received. I am so grateful for all your thoughts about my affairs and personal kindness. Our position here has always been quite solid but naturally with nothing but disaster to show for all one's work people were restive in Parliament and the Press. I find it very difficult to get over Singapore but I hope we shall redeem it ere long.

2. Dickie's[1] show at St. Nazaire, though small in scale, was very bracing. For your personal and secret eye I have made him Vice-Admiral, Lieutenant-General and Air-Marshal some few weeks ago, and have put him on the Chiefs of Staff Committee as Chief of Combined Operations. He is an equal member attending whenever either his own affairs or the general conduct of the war are under consideration. He will be in the centre of what you mention on the second page of your letter, para. 3. I am looking forward to receiving your plan. We are working very hard here, not only at plans but at preparations.

3. Your last paragraph on page 1. Speaking as one amateur to another, my feeling is that the wisest stroke for Japan would be to press on through Burma northwards into China and try to make a job of that. They may disturb India, but I doubt its serious invasion. We are sending 40 to 50 thousand men each month to the East. As they round the Cape we can divert them to Suez, Basra, Bombay, Ceylon or Australia. I have told Curtin that if he is seriously invaded, by which I mean six or eight enemy divisions, we will come to his aid. But of course this could only be at the expense of the most urgent needs in the other theatres. I hope you will continue to give Australia all possible reinforcement and thus enable me to defend Egypt, the Levant and India successfully. It will be a hard task.

[1] Lord Louis Mountbatten.

4. We cannot send any more submarines from the Mediterranean to the Indian Ocean and dispose only of two British and four Dutch. We are much stronger now at Ceylon and are fairly well equipped with garrisons, Hurricanes, some torpedo planes and RDF, together with pretty stiff flak. Admiral Somerville's fleet is growing to respectable proportions, and it may be an opportunity of fighting an action will occur. Meanwhile operation 'Ironclad' is going ahead. This also concerns Dickie a good deal. Altogether I hope we shall be better off in the Indian Ocean in a little while, and that the Japanese will have missed their opportunity there.

5. It seems important to make the Japanese anxious for their numerous conquests and prevent them scraping together troops for further large excursions. I should be very glad to know how your plans for Californian Commandos are progressing. I see some hints that Donovan[1] is working at them.

6. All now depends upon the vast Russo-German struggle. It looks as if the heavy German offensive may not break till after the middle of May or even the beginning of June. We are doing all we can to help and also to take the weight off. We shall have to fight every convoy through to Murmansk. Stalin is pleased with our deliveries. They are due to go up 50 per cent after June and it will be very difficult to do this in view of the new war and also of shipping. Only the weather is holding us back from continuous heavy bombing attack on Germany. Our new methods are most successful. Essen, Cologne and above all Lübeck were all on the Coventry scale.[2] I am sure it is most important to keep this up all through the summer, blasting Hitler from behind while he is grappling with the Bear. Everything that you can send to weight our attack will be of the utmost value.

At Malta also we are containing, with much hard fighting, nearly 600 German and Italian planes. I am wondering whether these will move to the South Russian front in the near future. There are many rumours of an air-borne attack on Malta, possibly this month.

---

[1] Head of the United States Office of Strategic Services.

[2] In the German bombing of Coventry on 14 November 1940, one-third of the city's factories were completely destroyed or severely damaged, as was the Cathedral, and 568 British civilians were killed. In the Cologne raid on 13–14 March 1942, several factories were badly damaged and 62 German civilians killed. In the Essen raid on the night of 25–6 March 1942, much of the bombing effort was drawn off by decoy fires; five citizens were killed. The Lübeck raid took place on the night of March 28–9; it was the first major success of Bomber Command, with 30% of the city's built-up area destroyed and 312 (or, according to another account, 320) people killed, the heaviest death toll in a raid on a German city thus far.

7. Having heard from Stalin that he was expecting the Germans would use gas on him, I have assured him that we shall treat any such outrage as if directed upon us, and will retaliate without limit. This we are in a good position to do. I propose at his desire to announce this towards the end of the present month and we are using this interval to work up our own precautions. Please let all the above be absolutely between ourselves.

8. Averell[1] is a great help here. He had a remarkable success with the House of Commons Committee three hundred strong in a most powerful, convincing speech. We shall be very glad to have Winant back, everybody is inspired by him. I am personally extremely well, though I have felt the weight of the war rather more since I got back than before.

My wife and I both send our kindest regards to you and Mrs Roosevelt. Perhaps when the weather gets better I may propose myself for a weekend with you and flip over. We have so much to settle that would go easily in talk.

Sir Stafford Cripps to Winston S. Churchill
(Churchill papers, 20/73)

1 April 1942   New Delhi
Most Immediate
Personal

I understand from Hindu press that difficulties are still in mind of Congress as to question of responsibility for Defence of India.

I have done what I could to clarify this point but as I think it would be a tragedy if negotiations were to break down upon any misunderstanding of the position I should like to suggest that I should ask Commander-in-Chief to meet yourself and Pandit Jawahar Lal Nehru with myself in order that he may explain fully to you the (?technical) difficulties of the situation and in order that you may make to him any suggestions you wish as to division of responsibilities in this sphere of government.

Unfortunately he is at the moment away in Calcutta but he is expected back on Saturday next at the latest (and possibly earlier). If you consider this a helpful suggestion – as I hope you will – I will ask him the moment he returns whether he will be prepared to attend such a meeting and I do not anticipate that there will be any difficulty about it.

I am sure you will realise that I do not want to be met with an impasse if there is any reasonable way out.

[1] Averell Harriman.

Sir Stafford Cripps to Winston S. Churchill
(Churchill papers, 20/73)

1 April 1942   New Delhi
Most Immediate
Personal

From all appearances it seems certain that Congress will turn down the proposals. There are a multitude of currents and cross currents but they are selecting the question of defence as their main platform for opposition.

2. The Moslem League who are prepared to accept will no doubt if Congress refuse also find some reasons for refusal as well as all the other sections of opinion.

3. There has been an almost unanimous protest from representatives including the European community as to the complete retention of the existing control of defence by HMG. (I should however add that the Viceroy doubts whether this is representative of the attitude of Europeans in Bengal). This protest arises partly from a misunderstanding of the position which I have tried to clarify in successive stages and partly because people feel that the maximum of appeal must be made to the Indian people by their leaders if they are to be galvanised to their defence, and that unless those leaders can claim some control over their defence of India they cannot make their appeal effective to the Indian people.

4. Except in the Punjab and the North West Frontier the present situation as to morale amongst the Indian and in many cases the European population is deplorable. The Anti-British feeling is running very strong and our prestige is lower than it has ever been owing to the events in Burma and more particularly in Singapore. The stories circulating on all sides as to Malaya and Singapore convey an impression of incompetence which is indeed alarming.

5. Unrest is growing among the population and unemployment is developing in certain centres. The food situation is causing disquiet and refugee problem in view of complaints of discrimination against the Indians, of which the administration is accused, and which I have asked the Viceroy to look into is a source of serious intensification of Anti-British feeling.

6. The outlook so far as internal situation goes is exceedingly bad and if we cannot persuade Indian Leaders to come in now and help us we shall have to resort to suppression which may develop to such a scale

that it may well get out of hand even though we use for this purpose a part of our frail military resources.

7. I give you this picture so that you may judge as to the importance from a Defence point of view of getting Indian Leaders into job of controlling, encouraging and leading Indian people. This cannot be done under existing circumstances by any appeaser.

8. The present situation as to Defence Minister is that new words which were drafted by Viceroy were put into paragraph (e) with full consent of Commander-in-Chief who consulted with Viceroy upon this point without my being present.

9. An explanatory letter was sent to main community containing following material paragraph: 'It must be clearly understood that final definition of division of responsibilities between HMG and Government of India is as stated in paragraph (e) of document. The Viceroy would be prepared to consult with Indian Leaders on this basis to see whether it were possible to designate an Indian to some office connected with Government of India Defence responsibilities without in any way impinging upon functions and duties of Commander-in-Chief either in his capacity as supreme commander of armed forces in India or as member of Executive Council in charge of Defence'.

10. I have consequently addressed a letter (text in my immediately succeeding telegram) suggesting interview with Congress Leaders with Commander-in-Chief.

11. If some adjustment can be so arrived at will you give me full authority subject to agreement of Commander-in-Chief and Viceroy.

Winston S. Churchill to Sir Stafford Cripps
(Churchill papers, 20/88)

1 April 1942

I cannot give you any authority to compromise on defence without submitting issue both to Cabinet and Ministers above the line. I will bring your telegram before Cabinet tomorrow. Everyone admires the manner in which you have discharged your difficult mission, and the effect of our proposals has been most beneficial in the United States and in large circles here.

General Archibald Wavell to Winston S. Churchill
(Churchill papers, 20/73)

1 April 1942
Most Immediate
Personal

Arrived Maymyo yesterday evening and had discussions with Governor, Alexander and Stillwell today. Visiting Chinese and British Headquarters tomorrow and returning [to] Delhi April 2nd or April 3rd.

2. Situation at both Toungoo and Prome appears unfavourable and complete command of air by the enemy sets Commanders extremely difficult task.

3. Governor is unable under Govt. of Burma Act to remove civil servants who have been found ineffective and send them out of Burma. I consider it urgent Military necessity that he should at this crisis have full powers to send (?out of) Burma any officials who are not up to the situation. I appreciate that this may require amendment to Govt. of Burma Act but cannot believe this is insuperable.

Winston S. Churchill to Dr Herbert Evatt[1]
(Churchill papers, 20/73)

1 April 1942
Personal and Most Strictly Secret

Following on a suggestion which I heard you had made I have telegraphed to Mr Curtin telling him that the 2nd British Infantry Division will be rounding the Cape during the latter part of April and early May and that the 8th Armoured Division will be following one month later. I have told him that if by that time Australia is being heavily invaded I should certainly divert either or both of these divisions to her aid. This would not apply in the case of localised attacks in the north or mere raids elsewhere but that he could count on this help should invasion by say eight or ten Japanese divisions occur.

2. We must be careful not to direct our limited reserves to theatres where there will be no fighting. No one knows yet whether Japanese will strike at Australia or India or, even more likely, South China. They have enough for a considerable operation in any one of these directions but surely not in all of them at once. I am by no means convinced that

[1] Australian Minister for External Affairs.

Australia is the chosen target. Once the enemy shows his hand decisions can be made.

3. I hold entirely to my promise of August 1940 quoted by you. This dealt with facts and not with possibilities. However, we have already left the Mediterranean denuded of all heavy ships and carriers in order to build up a naval force in the Indian Ocean which is already respectable. Not a day passes when we do not think of Australia.

4. It would be a mistake for the Commonwealth Government to recall the 9th Australian Division now. The two Brigades you kindly lent us for Ceylon can come on to you as soon as shipping is found. We have now got more consolidated there.

5. It is not possible to divert the whole flow of British production for six weeks as you suggest. Ships are loaded, plans are made and everything is moving to destinations of utmost urgency. I am trying to see whether more can be done about Bofors[1] RDF etc.

6. I hope you will come over here as soon as you can. You will find us very ready to lay everything before you. I look forward to meeting you.

Winston S. Churchill to General Hastings Ismay,
for the Chiefs of Staff Committee
(Churchill papers, 20/67)

2 April 1942
Most Secret

OPERATION 'IRONCLAD': MADAGASCAR

How do our plans stand for leaflets and propaganda on the Vichy garrison? It is reported that, while the navy is anti-British, the French troops are rather anti-Vichy. We must not neglect this side. I have telegraphed to the President, asking whether we may say it is an Anglo-American enterprise. Anyhow, we ought to let the garrison know that we shall take the place only to keep out the Japanese and restore it to France after the Axis is defeated. Have the leaflets been written? Let me see them, if so. If not, there is still time to have them printed through General Smuts, at Capetown. Let them therefore be drafted. I should be quite

---

[1] Bofors: the Bofors gun was a 40-mm aircraft auto-cannon, designed by the Swedish firm Bofors and first produced in 1935. The initial orders were from Belgium, Poland, Norway, and Finland. It was one of the most popular and widely used medium-weight anti-aircraft systems used by the Allies in the Second World War. At the Battle of Alamein, the Bofors guns were used to fire tracer rounds horizontally to mark safe paths for units through the German minefields. Six Bofors guns were landed in Normandy on D-Day on Sword Beach, where they shot down 17 German planes.

prepared, unless we have an absolute veto from the President, to take the Americans' name in vain and say that the island is under the joint guarantee of Great Britain and the United States until France is liberated. The Foreign Office should be consulted.

2. Would it not be possible, while the landing operation is taking place at the back, for a launch with a white flag to steam into the harbour and offer the most tempting terms for capitulation in the face of overwhelming force? All this must be carefully studied. CCO[1] should consider.

Winston S. Churchill to Admiral of the Fleet Sir Dudley Pound
(Churchill papers, 20/67)

2 April 1942
Most Secret

NEW NAVAL CONSTRUCTION PROGRAMME

Yours of 1st April, paragraph 1. Let me have the details of the 2,250-ton destroyers which you propose to build. I do not understand how they will be a screen against torpedo-carrying aircraft comparable to that which could be afforded by fighter aircraft working from carriers. Does all this arise out of the *Prince of Wales–Repulse* disaster? How far away from the battle fleet to be protected are the screening destroyers to lie? Let me have the argument set forth.

2. I am naturally prejudiced against destroyers which take 21 months to build, at a time when the multiplication of U-boats requires above all things numbers and speed of construction. On general grounds, an unarmoured vessel of 2,250 tons, i.e., practically a 'Scout' Class cruiser, like the 'Sentinel' Class, is a divergence from sound principles of naval construction. You make a ship which is neither a cruiser nor a destroyer, which is hunted by U-boats rather than being their hunter, and which exposes, I imagine, 180 officers and men to destruction at the hands of any light cruiser, without the slightest armour protection.

3. If these two flotillas of very large destroyers were converted into more destroyers of the class capable of being completed in a year, how many of them could we get?

4. It is a great mistake to blur types. The navy successfully resisted the temptation to multiply the old *Swift*.[2]

---

[1] Chief of Combined Operations, Lord Louis Mountbatten, appointed on 18 March 1942.

[2] HMS *Swift*, a destroyer launched in 1910, was sold to be broken up in 1921. Her class was intended to be a large ocean-going destroyer capable both of the usual destroyer requirements and

5. The fact that you have to construct these immensely powerful and costly (to the war effort) destroyers to protect the battle fleet is another point telling against the whole conception of the battleship, which must now move out of shore-based aircraft range, under heavy aircraft carrier protection, and surrounded by torpedo boats as large as small cruisers.

6. You speak of 'the 8-inch-gun cruiser,' but in your printed paper you mention four 8-inch-gun cruisers. Which is it?

President Franklin D. Roosevelt to Winston S. Churchill
(Churchill papers, 20/73)

2 April 1942
No. 129

As I have completed survey of the immediate long range problems of the military situations facing the United Nations, I have come to certain conclusions which are so vital that I want you to know the whole picture and to ask your approval. The whole of it is so dependent on complete co-operation by the United Kingdom and United States that Harry and Marshall[1] will leave for London in a few days to present first of all to you the salient points. It is a plan which I hope Russia will greet with enthusiasm and, on word from you when you have seen Harry and Marshall, I propose to ask Stalin to send two special representatives to see me at once. I think it will work out in full accord with trend of public opinion here and in Britain. And, finally, I would like to be able to label it the plan of the United Nations.

Winston S. Churchill to President Franklin D. Roosevelt
(Churchill papers, 20/73)

2 April 1942
Personal and Secret
No. 63

Your No. 129. Delighted Harry and Marshall are coming. Looking forward to their arrival and the sooner the better. Considering that

---

of high-speed scouting duties. Despite being the prototype for her class, no others were built: her weak armament, lack of speed, and high cost led the class to be abandoned. On the night of 20–1 April 1917, with one other destroyer, she engaged a force of six German destroyers in the Battle of Dover Strait. After two German ships were sunk, one by a torpedo from *Swift*, the remainder fled. *Swift* pursued them, but took several hits and was compelled to slow down.

[1] Harry Hopkins and General George C. Marshall.

everything turns on availability of naval forces and shipping we should greatly welcome King coming too.

On 3 April 1942 the Japanese bombed Mandalay, killing 2,000 people and setting fire to most of the town.

Winston S. Churchill to General Hastings Ismay,
for the Chiefs of Staff Committee
(Churchill papers, 20/67)

3 April 1942
Most Secret

DEFENCE AND SURVIVAL OF MALTA

This serious report[1] should be considered with a view to action. It seems odd that the SAA[2] position should be unsatisfactory, having regard to the fact that there has been no rifle or machine-gun fighting.

Are we to understand from paragraph 1(c) that they are entirely meat-less; or have they cattle they can kill, and if so, how many?

What are the plans for the April convoy?

2. We certainly have not got 'large quantities of transport aircraft', but what can be done with additional large submarines or fast ships of the 'A' type? What a pity we did not get hold of the *Surcouf*[3] and keep her on this job. How much can a submarine carry? What about sending in vitamins and other concentrates?

---

[1] Telegram of 31 March 1942 from the Governor of Malta regarding supply shortages on the island.

[2] SAA: Small arms ammunition.

[3] The *Surcouf*, then the largest submarine in the world (3,300 tons), and under the Free French flag, had been taken away from convoy duties following the outbreak of war with Japan, and was ordered to Sydney, Australia, via Tahiti. She left her convoy escort base, Halifax, Nova Scotia, on 2 February 1942 for Bermuda, leaving there in turn on February 12, bound for the Panama Canal.

*Winston S. Churchill to Sir Andrew Duncan, Oliver Lyttelton, and
General Hastings Ismay, for the Chiefs of Staff Committee*
(Churchill papers, 20/67)

3 April 1942
Secret

TANK PRODUCTION

A.22.[1] Our policy must be reviewed. There are 1,185 tanks delivered, of which about 900 are in the hands of troops. In the next six months we can either make 1,000 new ones, with all the improvements up to date and all mounting the 6-pounder gun, or make 500 new ones and rework 500 of the 1,185. The pros and cons of this have to be very carefully weighed.

2. In any competitive peace-time business no one would worry about the 1,185, but would pass rapidly on to new improved production. If we do this, we get the 1,000 new, plus the 1,185. All the new have the 6-pounder; all the 1,185 have the 2-pounder. Total 2,185. If we rework the 1,185 to the detriment of new production, we get 500 new, 500 reworked and 685 of the original unimproved. Total 1,685.

3. By this second method we lose 500 tanks, and we have to throw away 500 2-pounder turrets for which no use is at present proposed. This seems a dead loss. Decision turns upon the quality of the 1,185. What exactly is their unimproved value? They cannot be called useless. There is only one under repair for every two in service with troops. This is about the same proportion as the Matildas,[2] and compares as 2 to 1 *versus* 3 to 1 with the various Cruiser types.[3] Is it not better to have the 1,000 new 6-pounder A.22s and make the best we can of the 1,185? I am going to enquire myself into the possible uses of the 1,185. Two or three hundred of the worst could very likely be used for defence of aerodromes. The rest could be reworked gradually *without prejudice to new production*.

4. Meanwhile, care might be taken in handling the rest of the 1,185. Some could be used for training. The Canadian AT[4] Brigade speak well of them, and say that in the hands of tractor-practised drivers breakdowns are greatly reduced. Can we not, by bonuses, &c., and greater practice, induce similar proficiency in the British drivers? The Commanding Officers must be asked about this. Another question to put to them is whether the breakdowns in A.22s choke the field repair shops unduly. If

---

[1] A.22: Tank, Infantry, Mk IV, known as the Churchill tank.

[2] Matildas: A11 and A12, Tank, Infantry, Mk I and Mk II.

[3] Cruiser tanks: included Tank, Cruiser, Mk V, the Covenanter; and Mk VI, the Crusader. Other Cruiser tanks were the Cavalier, Centaur, Cromwell, and Challenger.

[4] AT: anti-tank.

this is so, some of them might be laid up temporarily as new 6-pounder A.22s arrive. The full equipment of the armoured units might be delayed accordingly, having regard to the receding of immediate invasion danger. Arrangements can be made to make sure that none of the 1,185 are employed outside this country.

5. Reflecting on the whole matter, the argument for leaving the 1,185 unimproved and making the best of them and their 2-pounder guns, and going ahead full speed on the new type, seems overwhelming. Pray let this be considered by the Ministry of Supply and the General Staff before the conference on Monday at Eastbourne.

Winston S. Churchill to Sir Archibald Sinclair
(Churchill papers, 20/67)

3 April 1942

HONOURS

I will, of course, consider your various recommendations. Surely Lord Riverdale[1] has already received a peerage and other honours at different times. What further reward do you suggest for him now? What special service has he rendered lately other than as an eminent industrialist?

2. Dr Jones's[2] claims in my mind are not based upon the Bruneval raid[3] but upon the magnificent prescience and comprehension by which in 1940 he did far more to save us from disaster[4] than many who are glitter-

[1] Arthur Balfour, 1873–1957. Master Cutler of Sheffield, 1911–12. Member of the Royal Commission on Railways, 1913. Member of his namesake Arthur Balfour (Lord Balfour)'s Committee on Commercial and Industrial Policy After the War, 1916. Member of the Manpower Committee, 1916. Member of the Advisory Council for Scientific and Industrial Research, 1916, 1929, 1933, 1935; Chairman, 1937–46. President of the Association of British Chambers of Commerce, 1923. Created Baronet, 1929; Baron Riverdale, 1935. Chairman of the United Kingdom Air Mission to Ottawa, 1940. In June 1942 he was appointed Knight Grand Cross of the Order of the British Empire (GBE) 'For services to the Empire Air Training Scheme'.

[2] Reginald Victor Jones, 1911–97. Air Ministry Scientific Officer, 1936 (seconded to the Admiralty, 1938–9). Assistant Director of Intelligence, Air Ministry, 1939–45; Director, 1946. CBE, 1942. CB, 1946. Professor of Natural Philosophy, University of Aberdeen, 1946–81. Director of Scientific Intelligence, Ministry of Defence, 1952–3. CH, 1994.

[3] Bruneval raid: a British Combined Operations raid carried out on the night of 27–8 February 1942 on a German radar installation in Bruneval, northern France. The radar equipment and the German radar technician the commandos brought back to Britain enabled British scientists to understand German advances in radar and to create counter-measures to neutralise those advances.

[4] In the summer of 1940, when Assistant Director of Intelligence at the Air Ministry, Dr Jones had discovered the method (of intersecting radio beams) whereby the Germans were directing their bombs against specific targets in Britain. As a result of his discovery, it was possible to deflect many of the German bomber missions away from their targets. Jones was awarded a CBE for his work, in the same honours list in which Lord Riverdale was appointed GBE.

ing with trinkets. The Bruneval raid merely emphasized and confirmed his earlier services. I propose to recommend him for a CB.

Winston S. Churchill to Sir Stafford Cripps
(Churchill papers, 20/73)

3 April 1942

War Cabinet and India Committee this morning considered your telegrams 859, 860 and 866S. We entirely approve your inviting Azad[1] and Nehru to talk Defence question over with you and Commander-in-Chief and asking them to state their proposals. We feel however, that we must know what these proposals are before you are in any way committed to their acceptance. I must, as I told you, consult not only the Cabinet but the Ministers above the line.

2. Cabinet showed itself disinclined to depart from the published text of the Declaration or to go beyond it in any way. It has made our position plain to the world and has won general approval. We all reached an agreement on it before you started and it represents our final position.

The restatement of paragraph (e) together with your explanation in paragraph 9 of 859S has made it plain that, as long as the Commander-in-Chief retains his position on the Viceroy's Council and as long as his existing control and direction of the defence of India are not in any way weakened, there is no objection in principle to the appointment by the Crown of a new Indian member on the council to co-operate in the sphere of military organisation.

3. If Congress leaders have some better way of providing for Indian association with defence, as safeguarded by you in your 859S, and if they assure you that subject to this they are prepared to accept the whole scheme, then some more precise interpretation to meet this outstanding point would be worthy of consideration. But are you satisfied that this is the actual position? Up to the present Congress spokesmen appear to have avoided anything which could be constructed as even a conditional acceptance of the post-war proposal.

---

[1] Abul Kalam Azad (known as Maulana Azad), 1888–1958. An Indian Muslim scholar and poet, imprisoned by the British (1915–20) for editing a nationalist newspaper. An active supporter of Gandhi's Non-Cooperation Movement; imprisoned a second time, 1930–4. A leading supporter of Muslim–Hindu unity, he opposed the partition of India on Muslim–Hindu lines. President of the Indian National Congress, 1923, 1940–5. Inaugurated the 'Quit India' movement, 7 August 1942; imprisoned for a third time, 1942–5. Opposed the creation of a separate Pakistan, 1947. Education Minister in independent India, 1947–52.

Winston S. Churchill to Stanley Bruce[1]
(Churchill papers, 20/53)

3 April 1942
Secret

My dear Bruce,

Thank you for letting me see your telegram, and for your help in these matters. I must however point out that in your Sub-section (2) you use the expression 'if Australia is in deadly peril', whereas what I said and mean is 'if Australia is being heavily invaded'. And again, in Sub-section (4) you use the expression 'a major threat to Australia'. I have never said anything about diverting troops to meet threats. We cannot do so while they are most urgently needed on fronts where heavy fighting is proceeding.

Please also see the words of my pledge of August 11, 1940, where the expression is 'If . . . Japan set about invading Australia or New Zealand on a large scale'. It is very important there should be no misunderstanding about this, as Dr Evatt from his telegrams clearly holds that Australia is 'in deadly peril' and that 'a major threat' has developed.

Yours sincerely,
Winston S. Churchill

President Franklin D. Roosevelt to Winston S. Churchill
(Churchill papers, 20/53)

3 April 1942

The White House
Washington DC

Dear Winston,

What Harry and Geo. Marshall will tell you all about has my heart and <u>mind</u> in it. Your people and mine demand the establishment of a front to draw off pressure on the Russians, and these peoples are wise enough to see that the Russians are today killing more Germans and destroying more equipment than you and I put together. Even if full success is not attained, the <u>big</u> objective will be.

Go to it! Syria and Egypt will be made more secure, even if the Germans find out about our plans.

Best of luck – make Harry go to bed early and let him obey Dr Fulton, USN, whom I am sending with him as super nurse with full authority.

As ever,
FDR

[1] Stanley Melbourne Bruce, High Commissioner for Australia in London, 1933–45, and Representative of Australia in the British War Cabinet and on the Pacific War Council, 1942.

President Franklin D. Roosevelt to Winston S. Churchill
(Churchill papers, 20/73)

3 April 1942   The White House
No. 130   Washington DC

Proposal in your number 61 of March 31[1] does not mention availability of *Furious*[2] which is scheduled to leave United States April third for the Clyde via Bermuda and whose plans show elevators large enough for Spitfires. Admiral King will advise Admiral Pound through Ghormley that *Wasp* is at disposal as you request if our estimate as to *Furious* should be incorrect.

President Franklin D. Roosevelt to Winston S. Churchill
(Churchill papers, 20/73)

3 April 1942   The White House
No. 131   Washington DC

OPERATION 'IRONCLAD' (MADAGASCAR)

Relative to your number 59 and the operation to which you are committed I feel that it would be unwise to identify the expedition in the manner indicated by your (word missing?). My reason for this is that we are the only nation that can intervene diplomatically with any hope of success with Vichy and it seems to me extremely important that we are able to do this without the complications which might arise by the dropping of leaflets or other informal methods in connection with your operation. I do hope that you will agree with this.[3]

---

[1] Document dated 1 April 1942 above (page 469).

[2] HMS *Furious*: a British 'large light cruiser' (a form of battlecruiser), launched in 1916 and converted into an early aircraft carrier. During trials on 2 August 1917, the first aircraft to land on a moving ship landed on *Furious*. In 1925 she was recommissioned with a new flush deck. In the Second World War she took part in the Arctic raid on Kirkenes and Petsamo (July 1941); Operation 'Pedestal', carrying aircraft to Malta (August 1942); Operation 'Torch', the North Africa landings (November 1942); and attacks on the *Tirpitz* (1943). She was placed in reserve in September 1944.

[3] In reply, Churchill telegraphed to Roosevelt: 'Fully agree' (Winston S. Churchill to President Franklin D. Roosevelt, No. 64, *Churchill papers, 20/73*).

Winston S. Churchill: recollection
(Remarks at the British Embassy, Washington,
quoted in Leonard Birchall, 'Battle for the Skies')

4 April 1942

The most dangerous moment of the War, and the one which caused me the greatest alarm, was when the Japanese Fleet was heading for Ceylon and the naval base there. The capture of Ceylon, the consequent control of the Indian Ocean, and the possibility at the same time of a German conquest of Egypt would have closed the ring and the future would have been black.[1]

Winston S. Churchill to General Hastings Ismay,
for the Chiefs of Staff Committee
(Churchill papers, 20/67)

4 April 1942   Chequers

Directions should be given to make effective the agreement about single responsibility for planning.

2. The selection of Task Commanders and Supreme Commanders in particular areas must be judged according to the circumstances of each case. No rules can be laid down restricting the action of Task Commanders and Supreme Commanders once they have been appointed to their particular operation or theatre. There is no risk of an officer selected for his all-round experience and outstanding qualities thrusting himself into tactical details of a Service other than his own. On the contrary, the danger is in the direction of undue diffidence leading to the paralysis and negation which are so much criticized in our operations.

---

[1] Just before dusk on 4 April 1942, a Catalina flown by Squadron Leader Leonard Joseph Birchall sighted a large Japanese fleet 400 miles south of Ceylon. His radio operator managed to transmit the location of the fleet before their aircraft was shot down by six Japanese Zero fighters from the carrier *Hiryu*. Shortly after first light, when the Japanese fleet had reached a position 200 miles south of Ceylon, a force of 125 aircraft was launched under the command of Mitsuo Fuchida of the *Akagi*, who had led the attack on Pearl Harbor. Unbeknown to the Japanese, the Royal Navy had concentrated its forces at Addu Atoll in the Maldives some 500 miles to the west, and the only warships in Colombo were the cruisers HMS *Dorsetshire* and HMS *Cornwall*, which rapidly put to sea following the report from Birchall's Catalina. A turning point in Britain's favour came on 5 April 1942, Easter Sunday, with the air battle over Colombo, but the threat of a Japanese invasion remained.

Winston S. Churchill to Air Chief Marshal Sir Charles Portal
(Churchill papers, 20/67)

4 April 1942   Chequers
Secret

Have you seen the figures which Sir Arthur Street[1] has sent me about the relative aircraft production, actual and prospective, of the two sides in this war? If these are true – and he vouches for them on the authority of the Air Staff – it looks as if the surplus of pilots will soon be reversed. The figures certainly justify you in forming new squadrons, not only to replace those sent abroad, but additional.

2. The extreme importance of pressing the enemy in the next six months and forcing him to use up his dwindling air power, is obvious. Could you let me have some figures to show the estimated wastage on both sides? The Axis must be more fully deployed and engaged than the Allies because so great a part of the British and American Air Forces cannot be applied to the fighting front, whereas Germany is fighting in Russia, before Malta, and in Libya; and Japan on all fronts simultaneously. Our interest is to engage wherever and whenever possible. Our problem will be to apply the broadest superficies of attack. Here again Transportation rears its ugly head.

3. Let me know what you feel about the great numbers of pilots massed together in the Bournemouth hotel. All these men will be wanted quite soon if American production opens out as promised.

---

[1] Arthur William Street, 1892–1951. On active service, Hampshire Regiment and Machine Gun Corps, 1914–18 (Egypt, Sinai, Palestine; wounded, despatches, Military Cross). Principal Private Secretary, Minister of Agriculture and Fisheries, 1919; First Lord of the Admiralty, 1919–22. Accompanied the First Lord to Constantinople during the Chanak crisis, 1922. Secretary, Royal Commission on Superior Civil Services in India, 1923–4. Second Secretary, Ministry of Agriculture and Fisheries, 1936–8. Deputy Under-Secretary of State for Air, 1938–45. Chairman, Anglo-French Co-ordinating Committee for Aircraft Production and Supply, 1939–40. Knighted, 1941. Permanent Secretary, Control Office for Germany and Austria, 1945–6. Deputy Chairman, National Coal Board, 1946–51. One of his three sons was killed on active service with the Royal Air Force in 1944.

Sir Stafford Cripps to Winston S. Churchill
(Churchill papers, 20/73)

4 April 1942   New Delhi
Most Immediate
Personal and Very Secret

The time has now arrived when a final decision must be arrived at as to how far we are prepared to go on the chance of getting a settlement. My best estimate of the situation is as follows.

2. The Moslem League are satisfied and prepared to accept scheme as it stands.

3. Congress reaction you know from my telegram No. 875-S of April 2nd. According to best information I can get as to internal stresses there are at least three sections of opinion. The Gandhi wing of non-violence who are against scheme altogether. They are indifferent as to what happens in the war and regard Great Britain as defeated and unimportant so far as future of India is concerned. They are definitely a minority. The remainder are all in favour of fighting the Japanese and would participate in war given conditions which in their view could make their participation effective.

4. This remainder falls into two main groups – those who consider defects (Non-Accession and Indian State representation) as fatal quite apart from the Defence question and those who would unwillingly swallow the rest of the scheme if they were satisfied on Defence.

5. It is impossible to estimate relative strength of the two groups, but the latter might if satisfied be able to swing working Committee particularly if offer on Defence were sufficiently favourable to make any refusal on that ground look ridiculous.

6. Nothing can be done to meet Congress on the points other than Defence. The first point upon 'Independence' is not a vital one. The second as to Indian States cannot be met without upsetting seriously the States' Rulers which I could not recommend at this stage. The third on Non-Accessions is vital to get Moslem League in and any change in that now would only result in losing their support and we should be no better off.

7. The only point therefore for negotiation is our Clause (E) which as you know was purposely left vague apart from general principle of retention of defence.

8. I must make it clear that so far as this point is concerned, the demand for transfer responsibility has come from all sides except Moslem League and Sikhs. Many Moslems have demanded it individually

e.g. Prime Minister Bengal. General trend of press is that it is a universal demand and if Congress refuse on this point whatever their actual views may be all other communities including Moslem League will probably point to it as a reason for refusal.

9. I must point out that if Congress do not accept no one will dare to state that they will accept scheme. I should expect it to be turned down by all sections including Moslems already although they have in fact passed a unanimous resolution accepting it in their Working Committee.

10. In the event of acceptance by Congress I am informed from a good source that non violent group will probably retire from all participation in Working Committee during the war and will leave other leaders (Maulana Azad, Nehru and Rajagopalachari[1]) to carry on.

11. These three are (?combatant) and Working Committee under their control. I am satisfied that if once they come in they will go all out to maximise Indian resistance to Japan and will fight with courage and determination to galvanise Indian people to action. They have told me that there would be no question whatever of any separate peace and I am certain this can be relied upon.

12. Estimates will differ as to how far their coming in will or can help in the actual prosecution of the war.

The two main factors in my view are: first that they will be able to assist greatly in preventing panic and maintaining morale amongst the great masses of civilian population and organising them in civil defence of all kinds, and second the Moslems also will come in and throw their weight into the war.

13. In addition I think that general psychological effect on Allied cause will be good especially in all eastern theatres of war including the Near and Middle East.

[1] Shrinivas Prasonna Rajagopalachari, 1883–1963. Known as 'Rajaji'. Advocate, High Court, Madras, 1906. Joined the Indian National Congress and participated as a delegate in the Calcutta session, 1906. Joined the Mysore Civil Service, 1906; Assistant Private Secretary to the Maharajah of Mysore, 1919–27. After Gandhi joined the Indian independence movement in 1919, became one of his followers, participating in the Non-Cooperation Movement and giving up his law practice. Elected to the Congress Working Committee, 1921, and served as General Secretary to the Congress. Imprisoned by the British, 21 December 1921 to 20 March 1922. Home Minister and Vice-President, Executive Council, Gwalior State. Prime Minister of Madras, 1937–9; introduced the Temple Entry Authorization and Indemnity Act 1939, under which restrictions were removed on Untouchables entering Hindu temples. Opposed India's entry into the war and imprisoned, 1940–1. Opposed the Quit India movement, 1942. Knighted, 1945. Minister for Industry, Supply, Education, and Finance, 1946–7. Governor of West Bengal, 1947–8. Acting Governor-General of India, 10–24 November 1947, in the absence of the Governor-General, Lord Mountbatten, who was in London for the wedding of his nephew Prince Philip and Princess Elizabeth. Succeeded Mountbatten as Governor-General of India, 1948–50. Government Director, Central Board, Imperial Bank of India, 1949–53. Indian Minister of Home Affairs, 1950–1. Chief Minister of Madras, 1952–4.

14. There will of course be risks of differences between His Majesty's Govt. and Indian Government, but these seem to me to be unimportant in view of major considerations stated in paragraphs 12 and 13.

15. If they do not accept, then situation will in my view become very difficult as we shall be attempting to carry on the war in at best a neutral atmosphere and at the worst a hostile one; a great deal of suppression will be necessary and this will again exacerbate nationalist feeling and no section of the people will be prepared to come out in open support of HM Govt.

16. It is in these circumstances that we must decide how far we can go with safety in giving to an Indian Minister control of defence.

[...]

27. In the event of acceptance, there will of course be difficulties as to apportionment of seats when Viceroy comes to form his new Government and I would propose in that event to stay till new Government is formed.

28. It is a matter of urgency to decide as to how we propose to proceed and I ask you to consider question most urgently as I am convinced we must make some offer to meet the situation.

Winston S. Churchill to General Hastings Ismay,
for the Chiefs of Staff Committee
(Churchill papers, 20/67)

4 April 1942   Chequers
Most Secret

Now that we have consolidated our position in Ceylon and our Eastern Fleet is growing in power, we ought to frame plans for a counter-offensive on the Eastern front in the summer or autumn.

2. Our first need is to secure effective sea and air command of the Bay of Bengal, especially its northern and north-western waters. For this purpose, American long-range bombers based on India, together with shore-based torpedo-carrying aircraft on the eastern coast of India, are required, all operating from airfields well protected by flak, fighters and RDF. Having regard to the approaching numerical superiority in the air of the Allied Powers, it should be possible in July, August or September to gain complete mastery of the north-eastern corner of the Bay of Bengal. A scheme should be worked out showing what naval, air and anti-aircraft forces would be necessary, on the assumption that our

naval forces will not have to act except under an effective shore-based air or carrier-borne umbrella.

3. When the requirements have been set out, we must see how soon we can work up to them.

4. Meanwhile we must expect that the northward advance of the Japanese armies through Burma towards and into China will continue and that General Alexander's greatly reduced forces will fall back into China with the Chinese armies. The Japanese would be well advised to press this attack into China, since by driving China out of the war they could obtain a major decision greater than any other open to them this year.

5. However, all this should take time, and it may well be that July, August, or even September, will still find a Chinese–Allied front south of Chungking and in Yunnan. Our counter-attack could then be brought to bear in a most effective manner across the enemy's line of communication northwards from the Malay Peninsula and Siam. For this purpose we should set ourselves to reconquer Rangoon, as our main and principal objective. This being done, and adequate air forces established thereabouts, we should follow the enemy up and along the Irrawaddy and the Burma Road, shielding ourselves with our right hand and compelling him to defend both the rear and the western flank of his communications in this theatre with China. In this way the weight will be taken off Chiang Kai-shek, and possibly the whole northward movement against China brought to a standstill.

6. Before putting any of this to General Wavell, I wish the plans to be worked out in detail, first, as regards the resources necessary, and, secondly, the dates at which they can be made available.

Winston S. Churchill: note
(Churchill papers, 20/56)

5 April 1942
Private Office

It would be wise to reduce the definite complaints to a short list which I can send with a covering letter not involving Jock[1] in any way.

---

[1] John Colville, the former Assistant Private Secretary in Churchill's Private Office (1940–1), who had written on 22 February 1942 to Clementine Churchill, from Pretoria, where he was doing pilot training with the Empire Air Training Scheme, with a series of complaints about the scheme. His letter ended: 'Please give my respects and my love to the PM. Nothing is more important to us than his continued strength and health.'

Winston S. Churchill to Sir Archibald Sinclair
(Churchill papers, 20/56)

5 April 1942
Private

I attach a note of complaints received from a recruit who has recently gone to South Africa under the Empire Air Training Scheme. He is a friend of mine whose judgment and morale I know to be very good and I am sure that his only intention in making these representations is to improve the efficiency of our arrangements.

Pray let his points be considered and please make no attempt to find out who he is.

Winston S. Churchill: note
(Churchill papers, 20/56)

5 April 1942

The discomforts of the voyage to South Africa could only be treated as a joke or else they would have been intolerable. Nearly 300 men had to sling their hammocks in a hold which could have held 50 comfortably. They had to feed on narrow tables beneath the hammocks on which they slept, and it would be difficult to say whether it was more disagreeable in the tropics or in the rough North Atlantic while everyone was being violently sick. There was a great deal of ill-feeling among the troops, both Army and RAF, which might have been lessened if the exigencies of the Battle of the Atlantic had been properly explained to them before they left.

2. There was much bitterness owing to the fact that the officers were using up a great deal of space and living the lives of the first class passengers in a peace time luxury liner.

3. There was a marked shortage of food.

4. There was a scarcity of washing facilities.

5. On arrival in South Africa there is a six weeks course of ground-work, covering everything already done in England and culminating in a series of somewhat daunting exams, before starting to fly. As some of the men have already been kicking their heels for over a year this has caused much dissatisfaction. Little attempt is made to meet or understand the men's feeling of impatience, and as a result enthusiasm evaporates and the sentiment 'the sooner I get home the better' is all too often heard.

Winston S. Churchill to Sir Stafford Cripps
(Churchill papers, 20/73)

5 April 1942   Chequers
Most Immediate
Secret

India Committee and War Cabinet will consider your proposals Monday evening. I hope by then we shall have heard from Viceroy and C-in-C. It would be a great help if we knew exactly what functions it would be proposed to hand over as matter cannot be decided purely on principle.

2. Ceylon news seems good and it is lucky we did not withdraw fighter forces.

3. Your wife is with us and sends following message.

'Begins. All my love and undaunted confidence. All friends send deepest support in your courage and handling. Greetings to you all. Ends.'

On 6 April 1942, Easter Monday, the Japanese bombed India for the first time. Their aircraft attacked two ports in Madras Presidency, Coconada and Vizagapatam, and also sank several British merchantmen in the Indian Ocean. Churchill, who was at Chequers that day, returned to London in the late afternoon for a 6.30 War Cabinet on India.

Oliver Harvey: diary
('The War Diaries of Oliver Harvey', page 114)

6 April 1942

Late Cabinet about India. Cripps reports that all parties have fixed on question of control of Defence now as vital, and efforts are being made to meet this as far as possible without endangering Wavell's control as C-in-C. But it is difficult. I fear it looks tho' that the Indians don't mean to accept the Plan anyhow and are manoeuvring for a specious ground to break on. A pity! It was a generous offer.

Sir Archibald Sinclair to Winston S. Churchill
(Churchill papers, 20/56)

6 April 1942

Your Minute dated yesterday about the experiences of a recruit on his way to South Africa under the Empire Air Training Scheme has just come into my hands. You asked me not to try and find out who he is but I must tell you at once that I know. It so happens that Jock wrote Louis Greig[1] a letter in which he made all these points.

I sent copies at once to the Air Members of Council concerned. It was an excellent letter and it will do him no harm in this Service to have written it. We are grateful for such information and for such measured and serious criticisms.

The criticism relating to the congestion of the ship accommodation is only too well founded. This is the unavoidable result of the decision of the Defence Committee that, in order to increase the carrying capacity of our convoys, many more men must be carried on each ship.[2]

Winston S. Churchill to General Hastings Ismay,
for the Chiefs of Staff Committee
(Churchill papers, 20/67)

7 April 1942
Action this Day
Most Secret

I cannot help feeling concerned about the condition of the Burma forces in view of the total absence of air support, and the telegrams of the Governor and General Alexander, and General Wavell's replies. Please let me have a short restatement of what we are doing to feed Wavell. Also please consider again the movement of six fighter squadrons from General Auchinleck to India. It is easy to see how bad it is to throw in forces piecemeal into Burma. The disintegration of General Alexander's army would also be very bad, especially having regard to the importance of China.

---

[1] Louis Greig, 1880–1953. Royal Marine Brigade, on active service in France, 1914. Staff Surgeon, Dover Patrol, 1914. Royal Air Force, 1918 (Major). Surgeon Commander, 1919. Gentleman Usher in Ordinary to King George V, 1924–36. Knighted, 1932. Personal Air Secretary to the Secretary of State for Air, Sir Archibald Sinclair, 1940–5.

[2] The rest of Sinclair's letter assured Churchill that all John Colville's complaints were appreciated, and were 'already being investigated'.

2. Let me also know the exact condition of the American heavy bombers which have arrived in India, or are on the way. So much has been said about these, and now it appears they are few and ill-equipped.

Winston S. Churchill to General Hastings Ismay,
for the Chiefs of Staff Committee
(Churchill papers, 20/67)

7 April 1942

ARMY REQUIREMENTS FOR TRANSPORT AIRCRAFT

The requirements of the General Staff for the Army appear to be out of all proportion to existing or prospective resources, and if satisfied would be destructive of the principle of an independent Royal Air Force. In this respect it would appear that the Air Ministry DO (42) 34[1] requires careful consideration and comment by the General Staff with a view to accepting fair points and minimising differences. Considering that the General Staff are well aware of the actual facts and what has happened, and that the disposition of existing resources was made with General Staff agreement, I do not see the justification for the observations in paragraph 1, sub-sections A and B, of COS (42) 164.[2] We surely none of us need to be taught these truisms. Painful and obvious as they are, they have arisen from the need to choose between various theatres in a woeful shortage of supplies.

2. Neither can paragraph 2, sub-section B, be guaranteed in all circumstances, however desirable it may be. There would be enormous dangers in tethering an immense proportion of our Air Force to Army units, most of which will be waiting about for months, and perhaps years, without becoming engaged with the enemy. I do not see at the present time any likelihood of our being able to go beyond the proposals in paragraph 40 of DO (42) 34. Paragraphs 8, 31 and 37 of DO (42) 34 seem to require the comments of the General Staff.

3. The General Staff request for 2,484 specially designed transport aircraft seems to be beyond all immediate possibilities. I am, however, most anxious to increase the air-borne forces to the utmost limit as soon

[1] On 'Air Forces for Co-operation with the Army and Navy'.

[2] In a memorandum on Army air requirements, the General Staff complained that ground forces were not receiving adequate air support, noting with particular bitterness that the promised support from No. 2 Bomber Group had not been forthcoming, the group having 'practically disintegrated' (*Cabinet papers, 80/35*).

as possible. A scheme should be prepared for converting all bombers as they fall obsolete to troop-carrying purposes, either parachute or ordinary. It should not make great demands upon production to fit new compartments to existing machines, but a special Conversion Branch should be set up and a good plan made.

4. I am sceptical of the Ministry of Aircraft Production assertion that it would be 'at least four years before a new machine could be made available in quantity for transport purposes'. Considering how very low and simple is the standard of performance required, all the elements of this problem must be known. A variety of patterns might be adopted to work in discarded engines and other material. It is only necessary to make flying buses, and uniformity is not essential as long as safety is secured. As a long-term project the United States might be willing to make and share a class of specially designed transport aircraft. What are they doing about it now?

5. Meanwhile, I hope proposals may be made here for increasing the airborne transportation programme. It is not necessary to have these worked out as if we were making a lady's dressing-case. The existing proposals of the Air Ministry in paragraph 49 of DO (42) 34 are exactly fitted to the tactical units they are to carry. The additions which we must make should consist, in the first instance at any rate, of anything that can be improvised to carry men or stores. Let me see the establishments proposed for an air-borne division. I trust simplicity and avoidance of fancy frillings will be sedulously sought for. A note on what the Germans do would be very helpful.

6. I am glad to see there is a considerable measure of agreement between the Admiralty and Air Ministry. See also my minute written after conference with First Sea Lord and CAS. We still await the President's reply to our request for the accelerated despatch of bomber groups to this country.

Winston S. Churchill to General Hastings Ismay,
for the Chiefs of Staff Committee
(Churchill papers, 20/67)

7 April 1942
Most Secret

Having regard to the promises made to Mr Curtin, it is necessary that the composition, and perhaps even the packing, of the April and May convoys should be considered, so as to render possible a diversion of the 2nd Division and later of the Armoured Division, should Australia actually be heavily invaded. This is only a precaution, as the danger certainly now seems less than the Australians anticipated. But you must know how to disentangle the ships, if need be.

Winston S. Churchill to President Franklin D. Roosevelt
(Churchill papers, 20/73)

7 April 1942
Personal and Secret
No. 65

According to our information five and possibly six Japanese Battleships, probably including two of sixteen-inch guns, and certainly five aircraft carriers, are operating in the Indian Ocean. We cannot of course make head against this force, especially if it is concentrated. You know the composition of our Fleet. The four R-class battleships[1] were good enough, in combination with the others, to meet the three Kongos,[2] which was all we believed were over on our side. They cannot of course cope with modernized Japanese ships. Even after the heavy losses inflicted on the enemy's aircraft in their abortive attack on Colombo, we cannot feel sure that our two carriers would beat the four Japanese carriers concentrated south of Ceylon. The situation is therefore one of grave anxiety.

2. It is not yet certain whether the enemy is making a mere demonstration in the Indian Ocean or whether these movements are the prelude to an invasion in force of Ceylon. In existing circumstances our naval forces are not strong enough to oppose this.

3. As you must now be decidedly superior to the enemy forces in the Pacific, the situation would seem to offer an immediate opportunity to the United States Pacific Fleet which might be of such a nature as

[1] R Class battleships: Revenge Class, also listed as Royal Sovereign Class. Five battleships launched in the First World War. They could use both coal and oil, and mounted eight 15-inch guns. Two fought in the Battle of Jutland, 1916, one of which, *Royal Oak*, was torpedoed in Scapa Flow on 14 October 1939 with the loss of 833 of her crew.

[2] Kongo Class (Japanese) battleships: four in all were built between 1913 and 1915, designed by a British naval architect (*Kongo* was completed in a British shipyard by Vickers). They carried eight 14-inch guns. Two acted as fleet escorts in the attack on Pearl Harbor; two supported the attack on Singapore. All four took part in the Battles of Midway and Guadalcanal, where two were sunk. *Kongo* fought at the Battle of Leyte Gulf, and was later sunk by an American submarine, with the loss of 1,200 of her crew. *Haruna* was sunk in an American air attack in late July 1945.

to compel Japanese naval forces in the Indian Ocean to return to the Pacific, thus relinquishing or leaving unsupported any invasion enterprise which they have in mind or to which they are committed. I cannot too urgently impress the importance of this upon you.

4. Looking forward to receiving Harry.

Winston S. Churchill to President Franklin D. Roosevelt
(Churchill papers, 20/73)

8 April 1942
Action this Day
No. 66

Since I sent you my No. 65 of 7th I have received the following from Deputy C-in-C at Colombo.[1] Begins: (Quote) Captain of *Gandara* and survivors of *Gandara* and *Dardanus* report ships were sunk by two heavy and one light cruiser, modern type.[2] Previously reported as two battleships and one cruiser. Position 16° N 82°20′ E at 0220Z on the 6th. Further particulars to confirm identity are being sought (Quote) Ends.

2. Position therefore seems somewhat easier. Will keep you informed of every change. Both *Dorsetshire* and *Cornwall*, 10,000-ton 8″ cruisers, were sunk same day south of Ceylon by from 40 to 60 fighter dive bombers each armed with one large bomb. There are 1,100 survivors.[3]

3. Hoping to see Harry and Marshall today.

Winston S. Churchill to General Hastings Ismay,
for the Chiefs of Staff Committee
(Churchill papers, 20/67)

8 April 1942

PLANS FOR A COUNTER-OFFENSIVE IN THE INDIAN OCEAN

I had not contemplated that any forces not now in or destined for the Far East would be involved in the counter-offensive which I have asked should be studied. Actually more forces would be required to maintain

---

[1] Rear-Admiral Palliser, Deputy Commander-in-Chief, Naval Forces, ABDA Command (based in Colombo).

[2] Two British merchant ships, the 5,281-ton *Gandara*, built in 1919, and the 7,832-ton *Dardanus*, built in 1923, were sunk by one light and two heavy Japanese cruisers off Golconda.

[3] HMS *Cornwall* and HMS *Dorsetshire* were sunk in the Indian Ocean within ten minutes of each other, both by the Japanese cruiser *Tone*. *Cornwall* lost 190 men, *Dorsetshire* 234.

a passive defensive from Assam to Ceylon without the command of the western part of the Bay of Bengal than would be needed to attack Rangoon if we had regained that command. It will be the poorest economy not to seek command of these waters and every effort must be made to obtain it at the earliest. Of course, if the enemy continues to use a large proportion of his naval and carrier-borne air strength in these waters, we shall have to struggle on as we do now, liable to be hit at a dozen places. But the enemy may change his disposition in consequence of American action, in which case we should be ready to profit therefrom. Also, if he invades Australia in force, we shall have to divert British divisions now destined for the Far East to Australia. But he may not do this. I still think he will not. In these circumstances the problem will not be one of making additional detachments from home or from the Middle East, but of the utilization in offensive action of the sea, land and air forces available in India and in Indian waters.

2. There is, of course, an intimate connection between what is possible in the Indian theatre and what happens in the Middle East or on the Levant–Caspian front, but I do not see the same close connection except in a very small number of landing craft, most of which are already in or can be improvised in the Eastern theatres, and the operation which we shall discuss with General Marshall. If it were a case of choosing between one or the other, this could only be settled on a survey of the entire war situation. Even if 'Sledgehammer'[1] were a certainty, which is far from being the case, it would be only prudent to have plans worked out for the operation I have outlined in the Bay of Bengal.

3. In addition to the enormous waste of force entailed in standing on the defensive on the Eastern front, there is the danger of the collapse of China. Should this occur, very large Japanese forces would immediately become available for major enterprises, and the scale of Indian defence would rise to impossible proportions. I should be very glad to receive the reports promised in paragraphs 2 and 3 of Brigadier Hollis's note, but unless these cover the points made in my minute of 4.4.42 I hope my wishes therein expressed will be complied with.

---

[1] 'Sledgehammer': an American plan for an Allied landing of limited aims against northern France, should either the Soviet Union or Germany seem in danger of imminent military collapse.

Harry Hopkins: note
('*The White House Papers of Harry L. Hopkins*', page 528)

8 April 1942

At dinner at 10 Downing Street: Churchill, Marshall, Attlee, General Brooke and Hopkins. Eden came in after dinner. We dined at 10 Downing Street as the guests of the Prime Minister, but the conversation was in the main social. Churchill, displaying his talents as a military historian, spent most of the evening discussing the Civil War and the (First) World War and never really came to grips with our main business, although General Brooke got into it enough to indicate that he had a great many misgivings about our proposal. Brooke made an unfavourable impression on Marshall, who thinks that although he may be a good fighting man, he hasn't got Dill's brains.[1] While at dinner, Churchill got word from the Bomber Command they were sending 350 bombers over Germany tonight.[2]

Winston S. Churchill to Anthony Eden
(*Churchill papers, 20/67*)

8 April 1942
Action this Day

I had a long talk with Selborne[3] after dinner tonight. He is quite willing that you should assume full responsibility for all SOE activities in neutral countries and will take your directions about them. I hope you will see him and make friendly arrangements with him about this. He has, of course, only been in office five weeks,[4] and the death of his father has forced him to give some attention to private affairs. I thought

---

[1] On 8 April 1942, General Sir Alan Brooke wrote in his diary: 'Finally 8.30 pm dinner with PM at 10 Downing St to meet Marshall and Harry Hopkins. Attlee also there and Anthony Eden came after dinner. Neither Hopkins nor Marshall disclosed their proposed plans for which they have come over. However it was an interesting evening and a good chance to get to know Marshall. But did not get back until 1.30 am!!' (*War Diaries, Field Marshal Lord Alanbrooke*, pages 245–6).

[2] On the night of 8–9 April 1942, the largest Bomber Command mission thus far, 272 aircraft, bombed Hamburg. The raid was a failure: only 14 aircraft bombed Hamburg, with 17 civilian deaths and no serious damage. Many bombs were dropped in error on Bremen, destroying a factory where four U-boats were being built. That same night, 24 aircraft of Bomber Command laid mines off Heligoland and 16 dropped propaganda leaflets over Belgium and France.

[3] Roundell Cecil Palmer, 1887–1971. Conservative MP (as Viscount Wolmer), for the Newtown Division of South-West Lancashire, 1910–18, and for Aldershot, 1918–40, when he succeeded to the Earldom of Selborne. Assistant Director of War Trade, 1916–18. Assistant Postmaster-General, 1924–9. Privy Councillor, 1929. Director of Cement, Ministry of Works and Buildings, 1940–2. Minister of Economic Warfare, 1942–5 (appointed 22 February 1942). CH, 1945. President of the Church Army, 1949–61.

[4] Actually six weeks: he was appointed on February 22.

you and he would be able to work together agreeably and that is why I made the change.

2. With regard to activities in enemy countries, it is of the utmost importance that SOE and SIS should work in the closest harmony. I have asked Selborne to see Menzies and put an end to the friction there is between the two branches. Selborne tells me he is in friendly relations with the General Staff, but I do not think it would be a good plan to put these important activities under military control without Ministerial guidance. You must, of course, be consulted as far as you wish to be.

3. Selborne tells me he is quite ready to have an investigation into his Department as he found it if you desire it. In that case I think a judge like Singleton J would be the man. But I hope this may not be necessary after the talks which I have suggested above.

On 9 April 1942, in the continuing battle for Ceylon, the Japanese attacked the harbour at Trincomalee and the British ships off Batticaloa. HMS *Hermes*, HMAS *Vampire*, and the corvette HMS *Hollyhock* were sunk, *Hermes* with the loss of 307 of its crew. The RAF lost at least eight Hurricanes and the Fleet Air Arm one Fairey Fulmar. The Japanese lost five bombers and six fighters, one in a suicide attack on the Trincomalee fuel tanks. Seven hundred civilians lost their lives in the attack on Trincomalee.

Winston S. Churchill: speech[1]
(Churchill papers, 9/157/83)

9 April 1942   10 Downing Street
3 p.m.

FREE DENMARK

I am very glad you devoted your munificent contribution to the Air Force, because that is the part of our armed attack which is most

---

[1] Given to acknowledge the gift of £38,000, for the purchase of aircraft, made by Danes in London to mark the second anniversary of their country's invasion by Germany (9 April 1940).

constantly in contact with the enemy. We have, as it seems, a very long road to trek. The arrival of a new enemy fresh, and very powerful, has prolonged the journey which Europe must travel, but has also brought us new friends far more powerful, once they have been given the time to realise their strength.

Therefore, I feel I may say with very good confidence that the day of the liberation of Europe can be looked and hoped for by all whose nations are in bondage at the present time. We shall never give in. We shall never weary. It is not seen how we can easily be destroyed. When we look at the times through which we have passed, we can see how much more we are now in power to continue our unrelenting struggle against the vile, dark, criminal forces which have laid their foul grip on Western Europe and on Christian civilisation.

We shall never pause in our struggle, nor will our great American and Russian allies, and I have very little doubt that the day will come – perhaps sooner than it would be prudent or sensible to hope – when Denmark will be free from the grip in which she has been held, and when she will resume her independent, honoured, and ancient place among the free peoples and States of Europe.

We here in England who hope to take part in the work of liberation and are resolved to do so, shall always be particularly grateful for the assistance we have received from the Danes and the moral support we have from the Danish nation, because of our connexion with the beautiful Queen Alexandra,[1] who was for so many years the object of admiration, the cynosure of the British nation.

We never have forgotten those days, nor have we forgotten the longer days in the past when our armies served together. We shall do our utmost to repay your country with good results. Good weather is needed to turn this splendid cheque for £38,000 into the first heavy thunder drops of the storm which has to beat upon this odious tyranny.

---

[1] Princess Alexandra of Denmark, 1844–1925. Daughter of Prince Christian of Schleswig-Holstein-Sonderburg-Glücksburg. Born in Copenhagen (her father became King Christian IX of Denmark in 1863). Married Edward, Prince of Wales, 1863. Princess of Wales, 1863–1901. Supported Denmark after the Prussian invasion of 1864, in contrast to Queen Victoria's support for Prussia. Her brother George became King of the Hellenes (Greece), 1864. Her sister Dagmar was later Empress of Russia. During the Boer War, Princess Alexandra founded the Queen Alexandra's Imperial Military Nursing Service (later Queen Alexandra's Royal Army Nursing Corps). In 1901 she became the first woman to be made a Lady of the Garter since 1495. Queen-Empress consort, 1901–10. Queen Mother, 1910–25. Deeply distrustful of her nephew, the German Kaiser Wilhelm II (Queen Victoria's grandson), she was a strong supporter of her son, King George V, in the First World War.

Sir Stafford Cripps to Winston S. Churchill
(Churchill papers, 20/73)

9 April 1942   New Delhi
Personal and Secret

Largely owing to very efficient and wholehearted help of Col. Johnson,[1] President Roosevelt's personal representative, I have hopes scheme may now succeed.

I should like you to thank the President for Col. Johnson's help on behalf of HMG, and also personally on my own behalf.

Winston S. Churchill to Sir Stafford Cripps
(Churchill papers, 20/73)

9 April 1942
Clear the Line
Personal

Colonel Johnson is not President Roosevelt's personal representative in any matter outside the specific mission dealing with Indian munitions and kindred topics on which he was sent. I feel sure President would be vexed if he, the President, were to seem to be drawn into the Indian constitutional issue. His message to me, just received from Mr Hopkins, who is with me as I write, was entirely opposed to anything like US intervention or mediation.

Winston S. Churchill to Sir Stafford Cripps
(Churchill papers, 20/73)

9 April 1942
Personal and Secret

Cabinet will study your latest formula immediately. Meanwhile you must not commit us in any way, as at first sight it seems most difficult to understand. Before coming to any decision we must of course have the independent and unprejudiced opinions of Viceroy and Commander-in-Chief.

---

[1] Louis Arthur Johnson, 1891–1966. Began practising law in Virginia, 1912. Captain, US Army, on active service, 1917–18. Lieutenant-Colonel, Infantry Reserve. Assistant Secretary of War, 1937–40. Personal Representative of President Roosevelt in India, March–December 1942. Secretary of Defense, 1949–50.

Oliver Harvey: diary
('The War Diaries of Oliver Harvey', page 115)

9 April 1942

Indian negotiations at critical stage – issue now is the formula describing functions of Indian Minister of War and his relation to Wavell as C. in C. Roosevelt's representative Louis Johnson has become an active intervener with Cripps and Nehru to the dismay of the Viceroy. What we don't seem to know is whether if we can reach agreement over the Defence question in the intermediate period, Congress etc. will accept our plan for the future. Cabinet today on all this.

Winston S. Churchill to Josef Stalin
(Churchill papers, 20/73)

9 April 1942
Personal and Secret

Yours of March 27.

At the beginning of May I will make the announcement warning the Nazis about our retaliating with poison gas for similar attacks on you. Warning will of course be applied to Finland equally and they will be mentioned though I do not see how we get at them.

2. Please send your specialist in chemical means of defence and counter-attack to explain exactly what materials the Soviet Government require from this country. We will then do our best to meet his wishes.

3. We could certainly let you have at least 1,000 tons of Mustard and 1,000 tons of bleaching by the first available ship if necessary in advance of your expert's report. There is more danger to troops in the open field from mustard spray than to people in towns.

Margot, Countess of Oxford and Asquith, to Winston S. Churchill
(Churchill papers, 20/59)[1]

10 April 1942   Savoy Hotel
London

Dearest Winston,

I think you should make Sir Frederick Leith-Ross[2] succeed Sir Horace Wilson.[3] He has a <u>1st class</u> brain, tho' he lacks all personal ambition. Nevertheless, he would be very useful to you, and <u>very</u> loyal.

Yours,
Margot

Henry[4] had the highest opinion of 'Leithers' as we called him.

Anthony Eden: diary
('The Eden Memoirs, The Reckoning', page 325)

10 April 1942

Saw Winston after luncheon. We spoke of American plan.[5] He feared General Staff would say 'Yes' and make this a pretext for doing less elsewhere.

General Sir Alan Brooke: diary
('War Diaries, Field Marshal Lord Alanbrooke', page 247)

10 April 1942   Chequers

[...] in evening had another COS meeting to discuss Joint Planning Staff report on Marshall's scheme for invasion of Europe. Then out to

---

[1] This letter was handwritten.

[2] Frederick William Leith-Ross, 1887–1968. Entered the Treasury, 1909. Deputy Controller of Finance, 1925–32. Member of the Economic Committee of the League of Nations (sometime Chairman), 1932–9. Knighted, 1933. Chief Economic Adviser to the Government, 1932–46. Director-General, Ministry of Economic Warfare, 1939–42. Chairman of the Inter-Allied Post-war Requirements Committee, 1941–3. Deputy Director-General, United Nations Relief and Rehabilitation Administration (UNRRA), 1944–5. Governor of the National Bank of Egypt, 1946–51. Deputy Chairman, National Provincial Bank, 1951–66.

[3] Horace John Wilson, 1882–1972. Entered the Civil Service, 1900; Permanent Secretary, Ministry of Labour, 1921–30. Knighted, 1924. Chief Industrial Adviser to the Government, 1930–9. Seconded to the Treasury for special service with Stanley Baldwin, 1935–7, and with Neville Chamberlain, 1937–40 (when he had a room at 10 Downing Street). Permanent Secretary to the Treasury and Head of the Civil Service, 1939–42. He was succeeded by Sir Richard Hopkins.

[4] H. H. Asquith, Prime Minister from 1908 to 1915, under whom Churchill served as President of the Board of Trade (1908–10), Home Secretary (1910–11), and First Lord of the Admiralty (1911–15).

[5] Operation Sledgehammer.

Chequers for dinner and the night. Harry Hopkins and Marshall there, also three Chiefs of Staff. We were kept up till 2 a.m. doing a world survey, but little useful work.

King George VI to Winston S. Churchill
(Churchill papers, 20/52)[1]

10 April 1942   Buckingham Palace

My dear Prime Minister,

Many thanks for your letter. I am so glad Wednesday evening will suit you for our dinner. I have asked Mr Hopkins & General Marshall to lunch with me on Wednesday so I shall already have seen them. But do please ask them to dinner if you like. I am sure we shall appreciate their presence, & it will be a compliment to them.

I am afraid the Indian situation has been a worry to you all this week. The loss of so many of our ships in the Indian Ocean is concerning me a great deal.[2]

Hoping to see you at lunch next Tuesday.

Believe me
Yours very sincerely
George R.I.

Sir Stafford Cripps to Winston S. Churchill
(Churchill papers, 20/73)

10 April 1942   New Delhi
Most Immediate
Personal and Secret

Following is text of formula on basis of which I am now negotiating. It incorporates alterations desired by Viceroy and Commander-in-Chief, and I understand that it substantially meets their views. It is outcome of long series of discussions in which Johnson has been invaluable as an intermediary and I urge most strongly that this formula should be agreed to. Without it there is no prospect of success but on this basis as follows now considerable chance.

---

[1] This letter was handwritten.
[2] Referring to the losses of HMS *Cornwall* and HMS *Dorsetshire*, and the two British merchant ships, SS *Gandara* and SS *Dardanus*, all sunk by Japanese aircraft on April 5.

2. Formula <u>begins</u>. (a) The Defence Department shall be placed in charge of a representative Indian member, but certain functions relating to conduct of the war will be exercised by Commander-in-Chief who will control the armed forces in India, and who will be the member of Executive Council in charge of the War Department. (b) This Department will take over such Governmental functions as are to be exercised by Commander-in-Chief as war member. A list of such functions has been prepared and is attached. (c) The Defence member shall be in charge of all other matters relating to Defence in Defence Department and those now dealt with by Defence Co-ordination Department in addition to other important matters closely related to defence. (d) In the event of any new functions falling to be discharged in relation to defence or any dispute arising as to allocation of any old functions it shall be decided by HMG. Formula <u>ends</u>

List of functions of War Member. <u>Begins</u>. The War Department, (?executive) for Governmental relations of General Headquarters, Naval Headquarters and Air Headquarters which include: (1) Examining and sanction (?ing of) all proposals emanating from GHQ's, Naval HQ's and Air HQ's.[1] (2) Representing policy of Government on all questions connected with the war which originate in or concern GHQ, NHQ or AHQ. (3) Acting as channel of communication between Government of India and HMG on all such questions. (4) Acting as liaison between these Headquarters and other departments of the Government and Provincial Governments. List <u>ends.</u>

3. Transfer in form of Defence Department is essential feature of this formula and gives much better chance than creation of Defence Co-ordination Department. In fact however effect is the same in content as proposal put in my letter to Azad see my telegram No. 930-S of April 7th. List of functions of War Member was drafted by Government of India experts and I am satisfied that it will retain for the Commander-in-Chief all the necessary functions. I understand the Viceroy and Commander-in-Chief agree that it meets their requirements but am asking them to telegraph their views separately as desired.

4. With reference to the point raised in paragraph No. 1 of telegram No. 441 dated April 6th I have throughout emphasised that existing legal and constitutional position must remain unchanged.

5. As I expect to receive the views of Congress on the proposed formula tomorrow it is essential that I should have the War Cabinet's authority to proceed on this basis not later than tomorrow evening. If on the

[1] General Headquarters, Naval Headquarters, and Air Headquarters, India.

basis of this formula they are ready to enter the reconstructed Executive Council I shall make it clear that this can only happen on the basis of the issue of the declaration as a whole by HMG. We cannot expect that any party will endorse the declaration as a whole as each will take exception to different points. If Congress agree to come into a National Government I feel confident that the Moslem League will do so also. Hindu Mahasabha[1] have already agreed subject to reservations on the long-term policy and I have no doubt that the Sikhs and the Depressed Classes would also come in.

Winston S. Churchill to Sir Stafford Cripps
(Churchill papers, 20/73)

10 April 1942   Chequers[2]
Most Immediate
Personal and Secret

Paras. 13 and 14 of your 973 S. There can be no question of want of confidence and we sympathize with you in your difficulties, but we have our responsibilities as well as you. We feel that in your natural desire to reach a settlement with Congress you may be drawn into positions far different from any the Cabinet and Ministers of Cabinet rank approved before you set forth.

2. The Viceroy has cabled us that while willing to help you in every way 'responsibility for any working difficulties does not rest with him'. We have not heard a word from General Wavell. We do not know for instance whether the Viceroy and you propose that there should be no European on the Council except the Commander-in-Chief. We have been told nothing about the character and composition of the new Council or National Government you think should be formed. We do not know whether the Home Department or Finance are to be placed in the hands

[1] Akhil Bharatiya Hindu Mahasabha (All-Indian Hindu Assembly), founded in 1915 as a counterweight to the Muslim League and the (non-sectarian) Indian National Congress. Its leaders included Lala Lajpat Rai, Bal Gangadhar Tilak, and Sri Aurobindo, who, during the Second World War, described Hitler as a dark and oppressive force, supported the Allies, and donated money to the British Government.

[2] With Churchill and his wife at Chequers on the weekend of Friday 10 April to Monday 13 April 1942 were Harry Hopkins and General Marshall. They arrived on Friday evening 'to stay weekend'. Sir Dudley Pound, Sir Alan Brooke, Sir Charles Portal, and General Ismay came to 'dine and sleep Friday'. Lord Leathers came 'to luncheon Saturday' and Lord Cherwell to 'luncheon Saturday and dine'. Sir Sholto Douglas came to 'dine Saturday'. Oliver Lyttelton, General Nye, Lord Louis Mountbatten, and Admiral Cunningham dined and slept Saturday night, to 'lunch and dine' on the Sunday. Averell Harriman, General Paget, and A. V. Alexander came to 'dine and sleep' on Sunday. Air Marshal Harris and General Eaker (US Army Air Forces) came 'to dine Sunday'. The Duke and Duchess of Marlborough came to 'luncheon Sunday'.

of Congress nominees. We have not heard what personalities the Viceroy has in mind for submission to the King-Emperor. We have received no assurance that there is any acceptance by India as a whole or by any of the principal Parties of the declaration which we drew up together.

3. We are concerned about the Viceroy's position. You agreed with his definition of his powers in 912.S (including retention of powers of over-riding the Executive Council) and we must definitely reject suggestion of a convention which would restrict them.

In your para. 13 you speak of carrying on negotiations. It was certainly agreed between us all that there were not to be negotiations but that you were to try to gain acceptance with possibly minor variations or elabora-tions of our great offer which has made so powerful an impression here and throughout the United States. As a fair-minded man you will I am sure try to realise how difficult it is for us to see where our duty lies amid all these novel proposals and in the absence of clear and simple explanations.

Sir Stafford Cripps to Winston S. Churchill
(Churchill papers, 20/73)

10 April 1942   New Delhi
Most Immediate

I have tonight received long letter from Congress President stating that Congress is unable to accept proposals. Rejection on widest grounds and not solely on Defence issues although it indicates that while Congress would agree that Commander-in-Chief should have freedom to control conduct of the war and connected activities as Commander-in-Chief and War Member proposed Formula left functions of Defence Member unduly restricted. Main ground of rejection is however that in the view of Congress there should be immediately a National Government and that without constitutional changes there should be 'definite assurances in conventions which would indicate that new Government would function as a free Government and Members of which would act as Members of a Cabinet in a constitutional Government'. Letter also states that picture of proposed immediate arrangements is not essentially different from old ones 'the whole object which we have in view that is to create a new psychological approach to the people to make them feel that their own national freedom had come, that they were defending their new won freedom, would be completely frustrated when they saw this old picture again which is such that Congress cannot fit into it'.

2. There is clearly no hope of agreement and I shall start home on Sunday.

Sir Stafford Cripps to Winston S. Churchill
(Churchill papers, 20/73)

11 April 1942
Most Immediate
Private and Personal

You will have heard of refusal of Congress upon what is almost a new point. But difficulties cannot be explained by telegram.

We have done our best under the circumstances that exist here and I do not think you need worry about my visit having worsened the situation from the point of view of morale or public feeling. In the last few days the temper has I think been better. My own view is that despite failure the atmosphere has improved quite definitely.

Nehru has come out in a fine statement for total war against Japanese; Jinnah has pledged me unwavering support of Moslems and Sikhs, and other Minorities will be on the whole relieved, and I hope to some extent reassured. The real difficulty has been the internal feelings in Congress itself, hence their long discussions and the veering of indications of their decisions.

There is a chance if we handle the situation wisely and without recrimination the All-India Congress Committee on April 21st may give an indication of a changing spirit as it is much more representative than Working Committee.

We are not depressed though sad at the result. Now we must get on with the job of defending India. I will tell you as to this on my return.

All good wishes. Cheerio. Stafford.

Winston S. Churchill to Sir Stafford Cripps
(Churchill papers, 20/73)

11 April 1942   Chequers
Most Immediate
Personal and Secret

You have done everything in human power and your tenacity, perseverance and resourcefulness have proved how great was the British desire to reach a settlement. You must not feel unduly discouraged or disappointed by the result. The effect throughout Britain and in the United States has been wholly beneficial. The fact that the break comes on the broadest issues and not on tangled formulas about defence is a great advantage. I am very glad you are coming home at once, where a most cordial welcome awaits you. Even though your hopes have not been fulfilled you have rendered a very important service to the common cause and the foundations have been laid for the future progress of the peoples of India.

Winston S. Churchill to Sir John Anderson[1]
(Churchill papers, 20/67)

11 April 1942

There is general agreement about the proposals in your paper about coal, except for the transfer of 7,000 trained soldiers from the Field Army to the pits. These 7,000 men, if they produce the same as the average mine-workers, might hew 2 million tons of coal in a year. The effect of such a dislocation in the Army at this critical time is so serious that I hope all other alternatives to find these 2 million tons will be exhausted. There are many alternatives, it seems to me at first sight, which are less injurious to our general war effort:

   (a) Drawing from the coal reserve of 12 million tons.
   (b) Economies might be effected by a system of allocating coal to various users such as obtains in other raw materials.
   (c) Further economies in the War Production Departments.
   (d) Reduction in industrial users other than munitions.
   (e) A possible reduction in the Export Programme.
   (f) Monetary rewards to miners for surrender of a portion of their customary coal allowance.
   (g) Directing a large number of untrained youths of 18–19 years into the pits.
   (h) Persuading or allowing a proportion of ageing men to work for another year.
   (i) Possible expansion in outcrop working.
   (j) Get miners to work an extra 15 minutes a week.

With all these possibilities in view, each of which might mean nearly 1 million tons a year, there should be no difficulty in finding the 2 million tons, and thus avoiding the injury to the Army.

2. Further help will be given by all your long-term projects, including the financial point about relating EPT[2] to tons mined.

---

[1] Lord President of the Council, a member of the War Cabinet.
[2] EPT: Export Programme Targets.

3. Meanwhile, the War Office are to specify how many miners they have in the Metropolitan Field Force, what proportion are face-workers, and how many of them are with the fighting formations; that is to say, excluding Transport, RASC,[1] RAOC,[2] and other ancillary services. The War Office will, of course, find the 5,000 men out of the 12,000 asked for, which are to be given from ADGB[3] and other Field Force branches.

4. I hope all these possibilities will enable us to round the corner without taking the very grave step at this juncture which would derange the solidity of the Army.

Clementine Churchill to Winston S. Churchill
(Baroness Spencer-Churchill papers)

11 April 1942

My Darling,

Please don't think I am indifferent because I was silent when you told me of Randolph's cable to Pamela saying he was joining a parachute unit [...] but I grieve that he has done this because I know it will cause you harrowing anxiety, indeed, even agony of mind.

I feel this impulse of Randolph's [...] is sincere but sensational. Surely there is a half-way house between being a Staff-Officer and a Parachute Jumper. He could have quietly & sensibly rejoined his Regiment & considering he has a very young wife with a baby[4] to say nothing of a Father who is bearing not only the burden of his own country but for the moment of an un-prepared America it would in my view have been his dignified & reasonable duty

I think his action is selfish & unjust to you both [...]

My Darling – Do you think it would be any use my sending an affectionate cable begging him on your account to re-join his Regiment

---

[1] RASC: Royal Army Service Corps.

[2] RAOC: Royal Army Ordnance Corps.

[3] ADGB: Air Defence of Great Britain.

[4] Winston Spencer Churchill, 1940–2010. Born 10 October 1940, the son of Randolph and Pamela Churchill. Educated at Eton and Christ Church, Oxford. A newspaper correspondent from 1963 (Yemen, Congo, Angola). In 1964 he published *First Journey*. Author, with his father, of *The Six Day War* (1967). Conservative MP for Stretford, 1970–83, and for Davyhulme, 1983–97. Parliamentary Private Secretary to the Minister of Housing and Construction, 1970–2; to the Minister of State, Foreign and Commonwealth Office, 1972–3. Conservative Party front-bench spokesman on defence, 1976–8. Author of *Defending the West*, 1981. Member of the Select Committee on Defence from 1983. A Governor of the English-Speaking Union, 1975–80. Among his published books are *Memories and Adventures*, 1989 and a biography of his father, *His Father's Son*, 1996.

& give up this scheme in which if he begins one feels he must perhaps persevere?

[...]

Winston S. Churchill to Randolph S. Churchill
(Churchill papers, 20/65)

12 April 1942
Personal

Please let me know what your employment is, as naturally I like to follow your fortunes. Acknowledge.

Randolph S. Churchill to Winston S. Churchill
(Churchill papers, 20/65)

12 April 1942
Personal

Am joining detachment of Special Air Service under Major David Stirling.[1] I think I will find the work interesting and agreeable, as I shall be with a number of friends with whom I served in No. 8 Commando prior to its disbandment.

President Franklin D. Roosevelt to Winston S. Churchill[2]
(Churchill papers, 20/73)

12 April 1942

INDIA

[...] every effort must be made by us to prevent a break-down.

I hope most earnestly that you may be able to postpone the departure from India of Cripps until one more effort has finally been made to prevent a break-down of the negotiations.

---

[1] (Archibald) David Stirling, 1915–90. Served in the Scots Guards, 1939–40 (evacuation of Dunkirk). No. 3 Command, Brigade of Guards, Middle East, 1941–2 (DSO, 1942). As commander of the Long Range Desert Group, later the First Special Air Service (SAS) Regiment, 1942–3, he organised deep penetration raids behind enemy lines, destroying 250 enemy aircraft on their aerodromes. Known in the Western Desert as the 'Phantom Major'. Captured early in 1943 by a unit of German soldiers specially trained in anti-SAS operations. Prisoner of war, 1943–5; his numerous attempts at escape ended with his being sent to Colditz. OBE, 1946. Knighted, 1990.

[2] This telegram was sent by President Roosevelt to Harry Hopkins, with a note that it should be given to Churchill 'immediately'.

I regret to say that I am unable to agree with the point of view contained in your message to me, that public opinion in the United States believes that negotiations have broken down on general broad issues. Here the general impression is quite the contrary. The feeling is held almost universally that the deadlock has been due to the British Government's unwillingness to concede the right of self-government to the Indians notwithstanding the willingness of the Indians to entrust to the competent British authorities technical military and naval defence control. It is impossible for American public opinion to understand why if there is willingness on the part of the British Government to permit the component part of India to secede after the war from the British Empire, it is unwilling to permit them to enjoy during the war what is tantamount to self-government.

I feel that I am compelled to place before you this issue very frankly, and I know you will understand my reasons for doing this. Should the current negotiations be allowed to collapse because of the issues as presented to the people of America and should India subsequently be invaded successfully by Japan with attendant serious defeats of a military or naval character for our side, it would be hard to over-estimate the prejudicial reaction on American public opinion. Would it not be possible, therefore, for you to have Cripps' departure postponed on the ground that you personally transmitted instructions to him to make a final effort to find a common ground of understanding? According to my reading, an agreement appeared very near last Thursday night. If you could authorize him to say that he was personally empowered by you to resume negotiations as at that point with the understanding that both sides would make minor concessions, it appears to me that an agreement might be yet found.

As I expressed to you in an earlier message, I still feel that if the component groups in India could be given now the opportunity to set up a Nationalist Government in essence similar to our own form of government under the Articles of Confederation with the understanding that following the termination of a period of trial and error they would be enabled then to determine upon their own form of constitution and to determine, as you have promised them already, their future relationship with the British Empire, probably a solution could be found. If you were to make such an effort and if Cripps were still unable then to find an agreement, at least you would on that issue have public opinion in the United States be satisfied that the British Government had made a fair and real offer to the Indian people and that the responsibility for such failure must be placed clearly, not upon the British Government, but upon the Indian people.

Winston S. Churchill: reflection
('The Hinge of Fate', pages 194–5)

[12 April 1942]

I was thankful that events had already made such an act of madness impossible. The human race cannot make progress without idealism, but idealism at other people's expense and without regard to the consequences of ruin and slaughter which fall upon millions of humble homes cannot be considered as its highest or noblest form.

The President's mind was back in the American War of Independence, and he thought of the Indian problem in terms of the thirteen colonies fighting George III at the end of the eighteenth century. I, on the other hand, was responsible for preserving the peace and safety of the Indian continent, sheltering nearly a fifth of the population of the globe. Our resources were slender and strained to the full. Our armies had surrendered or were recoiling before the devastating strokes of Japan. Our Navy had been driven out of the Bay of Bengal, and indeed out of most of the Indian Ocean. We had apparently been outmatched in the air. Still, there was the hope and the chance that all could be repaired and that we should not fail in our duty to preserve from hideous and violent destruction the vast, ancient Indian society over which we had presided for nearly two hundred years. Without the integrity of executive military control and the power to govern in the war area hope and chance alike would perish.

This was no time for a constitutional experiment with a 'period of trial and error' to determine the 'future relationship' of India to the British Empire. Nor was the issue one upon which the satisfying of public opinion in the United States could be a determining factor. We could not desert the Indian peoples by abandoning our responsibility and leaving them to anarchy or subjugation. That was at least a policy, but a policy of shame. It was our bounden duty to send all possible aid to Indian defence, and if this were so we should have betrayed not only the Indian peoples but our own soldiers by allowing their base of operations and the gallant Indian Army fighting at their side to disintegrate into a welter of chattering politics and bloody ruin.

Happily I had all my principal colleagues who had studied the Indian problem in agreement with me. Had this not been so, I would not have hesitated to lay down my personal burden, which at times seemed more than a man could bear. The greatest comfort on such occasions is to have no doubts. Nor, as will be seen as this account proceeds, were my convictions and those of the War Cabinet without their vindication.

Winston S. Churchill to President Franklin D. Roosevelt
(Churchill papers, 20/73)

12 April 1942
Personal and Secret
No. 68

I have read with earnest attention your masterly document about future of the war and the great operations proposed. I am in entire agreement in principle with all you propose, and so are the Chiefs-of-Staff. We must of course meet day to day emergencies in the East and Far East while preparing for the main stroke. All the details are being rapidly examined and preparations where action is clear have already begun. The whole matter will be discussed on evening of Tuesday, the 14th, by Defence Committee, to which Harry and Marshall are coming, and I have no doubt that I shall be able to send you our complete agreement.

2. I may say that I thought the proposals made for an interim operation in certain contingencies this year met the difficulties and uncertainties in an absolutely sound manner. If, as our experts believe, we can carry this whole plan through successfully, it will be one of the grand events in all the history of war.

3. About 3 a.m. this morning, the 12th, when contrary to your instructions[1] Harry and I were still talking, the text of your message to me about India came through from London. I could not decide such a matter without convening the Cabinet, which was not physically possible till Monday. Meanwhile Cripps had already left and all the explanations have been published by both sides. In these circumstances Harry undertook to telephone to you explaining the position, but owing to atmospherics he could not get through. He is going to telephone you this afternoon and also cable you a report.

4. You know the weight which I attach to everything you say to me, but I did not feel I could take responsibility for the defence of India if

[1] About looking after Harry Hopkins' health by not keeping him up late.

everything has again to be thrown into the melting pot at this critical juncture. That I am sure would be the view of Cabinet and of Parliament. As your telegram was addressed to Former Naval Person I am keeping it as purely private, and I do not propose to bring it before the Cabinet officially unless you tell me you wish this done. Anything like a serious difference between you and me would break my heart and would surely deeply injure both our countries at the height of this terrible struggle.

Winston S. Churchill to Admiral of the Fleet Sir Dudley Pound
(Churchill papers, 20/67)

12 April 1942
Secret

Can you give me details of the method of supplying Malta by submarine? I understand that removal of certain batteries greatly increases the carrying capacity of the submarine, and I would like to inform the United States authorities of these details for use in supplying Corregidor.[1]

Winston S. Churchill to Clement Attlee and others[2]
(Churchill papers, 20/52)

12 April 1942
(Please return to me)

Attached is a most secret document handed to me by Mr Hopkins.[3]

I am circulating this copy to those Ministers named above, for their personal information, and should be obliged if you would pass it on in

---

[1] With the fall of Bataan on 9 April 1942, the only United States forces still fighting were on the highly fortified island bastion of Corregidor, where 14,000 United States and Filipino troops faced 75,000 Japanese troops. In a radio message to President Roosevelt on 6 May 1942, Lieutenant-General Jonathan Wainwright declared: 'There is a limit of human endurance, and that point has long been passed.' Wainwright surrendered the Corregidor garrison that afternoon. After more than three years as a prisoner of war of the Japanese, he was on board the USS *Missouri* to witness the Japanese surrender; he then returned to the Philippines to receive the surrender of the local Japanese commander.

[2] The order in which Churchill circulated this document was: Dominions Secretary (Clement Attlee), Foreign Secretary (Anthony Eden), First Lord of the Admiralty (A. V. Alexander), Secretary of State for War (Sir James Grigg), and Secretary of State for Air (Sir Archibald Sinclair).

[3] Secret memorandum from Roosevelt to Churchill, entitled 'Operations in Western Europe', proposing joint policy and invasion plans for 1942. Hopkins and Marshall gave this document to Churchill when they dined with him at 10 Downing Street on 8 April 1942.

the above order, marked in each case 'Immediate: To be opened personally by . . . .'

Please send on <u>within a few hours</u>.

Henry Channon: diary
('Chips', page 325)

13 April 1942   5 Belgrave Square

At the re-opening of Parliament, the PM, uneasy, halting, almost inarticulate, made a short, and far from comprehensive, or eloquent statement about Singapore, Cripps and the recent loss of ships. He has lost his self-confidence and the House listened rudely.

House of Commons: Questions
(Hansard)

13 April 1942   House of Commons
BUSINESS OF THE HOUSE

Mr Arthur Greenwood: Is it the Prime Minister's intention to make a statement on the War Situation, and will it be possible at an early date to deal with the question of Malaya and Singapore, which is very much on the mind of the House? May I also ask whether, in view of the unfortunate end of the discussions in India and the early return of the Lord Privy Seal, the right hon. Gentleman could this week publish a White Paper on the history of the proceedings to clear the ground for what I think the House will hope will be an early Debate on the question on the Lord Privy Seal's return?[1]

The Prime Minister (Mr Churchill): It was thought convenient that I should deal with several points that were raised in the course of Questions in a brief statement at the end of them. With regard to the conversations in India and the mission of the Lord Privy Seal, it would be better to await the return of the Lord Privy Seal, who may be in a position to make a personal report to the House upon the very important mission with which he was charged. I will consider whether a White Paper can be laid, although a great deal of the information has been made public already by both parties to the negotiations.

[1] Sir Stafford Cripps' return from India.

I have a Question which was asked by the hon. Member for South Croydon (Sir H. Williams) about the loss of the two 10,000 tons 8-inch gun cruisers *Dorsetshire* and *Cornwall* in the Indian Ocean. On 4th April superior Japanese naval forces which had entered the Indian Ocean were observed steering towards Ceylon. These forces comprised at least three battleships, including one of the modernised 16-inch Nagato type[1] and five aircraft carriers, together with a number of heavy and light cruisers and destroyer flotillas. Severe air attacks were delivered on the harbours of Colombo and Trincomalee. As has been announced, the attacking aircraft suffered heavy losses at both places from the British fighter protection and anti-aircraft batteries. We also suffered to a lesser extent, but seriously, in our aircraft, and damage was done to shore establishments and to the few ships which remained in harbour. Besides these losses, the two 8-inch gun cruisers *Dorsetshire* and *Cornwall* and the aircraft carrier *Hermes*, which had left harbour before the attack, were sunk at sea by enemy aircraft. The naval operations were under the command of Admiral Sir James Somerville, an officer who for the last two years has been commanding in the Western Mediterranean and has almost unrivalled experience of the conditions of modern naval war. Without giving the enemy useful information, I cannot make any statement about the strength of the forces at Admiral Somerville's disposal or of the reasons which led him to make the dispositions of his fleet, for which he was responsible. Nothing in these dispositions and the consequences which followed from them have in any way weakened the confidence of the Admiralty in his judgment. I may, perhaps, add that it is quite impossible to afford continuous air protection by shore-based or carrier borne aircraft to all His Majesty's ships at sea. Many scores are at sea every day without such protection, and unless these risks are taken, there is no means of carrying on the immense business of convoy and sea war which falls upon the Royal Navy.

---

[1] The Nagato class Japanese battleships (the first in the world with 16-inch guns) were commissioned in 1920 and reconstructed with anti-torpedo bulges, 1934–6. The one in the Indian Ocean force was *Nagato*, the ship that had sent the 'Climb Mount Niitaka [...]' signal that committed the Carrier Strike Force to the attack on Pearl Harbor. The only Japanese battleship to survive the Second World War, she was destroyed in 1946 in a United States atomic bomb test. A life-size replica of her was made for the film *Tora! Tora! Tora!*. Her sister ship *Mutsu* was sunk by an internal explosion of a magazine on 8 June 1943, while moored in an anchorage in the Inland Sea of Japan, with the loss of 1,121 of her crew and visiting cadets. A top-secret official report concluded that the cause of the explosion was most likely a suicidal crewman who had recently been accused of theft.

I have had a Question also by the hon. Member for South Croydon[1] and the hon. Member for Central Southwark (Mr Martin)[2] about the course of events in Malaya and Singapore, and this Question is reinforced by what has fallen from my right hon. Friend opposite. Major-General Gordon-Bennett's[3] report has now been received. It is not suitable for publication. His Majesty's Government are, however, collecting information wherever it can be obtained. Thus, Sir Archibald Wavell has been instructed to appoint an officer to collect such information as is of value from persons who have escaped from Singapore to India and to send it to this country. Moreover, Sir Archibald Wavell, as supreme commander of the United Nations Forces in the ABDA area during the major part of the operations in Malaya, will, no doubt, furnish a report or despatch on what took place, but I cannot expect him to divert his attention from the immediate conduct of the war on the Eastern frontiers of India at the present time. All the available information is being and will be examined in order to make sure that none of the lessons to be learned from the fighting in Malaya are neglected. I cannot, however, hold out any expectation that any report or White Book about the fighting in Malaya will be published within any foreseeable period. Still less would it be appropriate to attempt to pronounce judgment while many of those who took part in these events are prisoners of war and are not able to give their accounts of what happened. I may add, however, that I will seek an opportunity during the next fortnight or so to make a statement to the House on the present course of the war. This will have to be in Secret Session.

---

[1] Herbert Geraint Williams, 1884–1954. Educated at the University of Liverpool. Electrical and marine engineer. Secretary, Machine Tool Trades Association, 1911–28. Secretary, Machine Tool Department, Ministry of Munitions, 1917–18. Conservative MP for Reading, 1924–9; for South Croydon, 1932–45; for Croydon East, 1950–4. Parliamentary Secretary, Board of Trade, 1928–9. Knighted, 1939. Member of the House of Commons Select Committee on Expenditure, 1939–44. Chairman, London Conservative Union, 1939–48; National Union of Conservative and Unionist Associations, 1948. Created Baronet, 1953.

[2] John Hanbury Martin, 1896–1983. On active service, 1914–18 (wounded). Member of the London Insurance Committee, 1936–45. Labour MP for Central Southwark, 1940–8. Secretary of the Franco-British Parliamentary Association, 1943–8.

[3] Henry Gordon-Bennett, 1887–1962. Born in Australia. On active service at Gallipoli, 1915 (wounded), and on the Western Front, 1916. Brigadier-General, commanding the 3rd Infantry Brigade, 1917–18. Major-General, 1930. Commander, 8th Division, Malaya, February 1941. Left Singapore at the surrender and made his way through Sumatra to to Java and then to Australia, arriving in Melbourne on 2 March 1942. Lieutenant-General commanding III Corps, Perth, 1942–4. His account of the Malayan campaign, *Why Singapore Fell* (1944), was critical of General Percival and other British officers.

I have one announcement to make which may be of interest to the House, and I mention it, first of all, to the House as I am present here today. On 19th October, 1941, my hon. and gallant Friend the Member for North Portsmouth (Sir R Keyes) was succeeded in charge of combined operations by Captain Lord Louis Mountbatten, GCVO, DSO, RN, with the title of Adviser on Combined Operations (ACO), and the rank of Commodore, First Class. On 18th March, 1942, Captain Lord Louis Mountbatten was appointed Chief of Combined Operations (CCO), which office carries with it the acting rank of Vice-Admiral and the honorary ranks of Lieutenant-General and Air Marshal. The Chief of Combined Operations attends the meetings of the Chiefs of Staff committee as a full member whenever major issues are in question and also when his own combined operations, or any matters in which he is concerned, are under discussion.

Mr Greenwood: The Prime Minister, in the first part of his reply, suggested that the House and the public had been fairly fully informed about the course of events in India, but we have had no authoritative statement, and I submit that the House really does not know what were the proposals which were made to the Indian representatives. Nor do we know, nor are we in a position to analyse, the causes of the breakdown. Some of us feel that a White Paper published before the Debate would clear the minds of Members and perhaps avoid a good deal of wasted discussion in the House. Would it not be better if the House had before it, in a reasonable form, an authoritative statement on the course of the discussions which have taken place?

The Prime Minister: I am quite ready to see what papers could be collected. It would be convenient to have even the papers that have already been published included in a comprehensive document. I will see what other matters can be included, but naturally I shall have to refer by telegraph to the Lord Privy Seal, who is on his way home, in order that he shall be consulted on the particular points which he thinks of special importance. I should feel, however, that really it would be much better after the White Paper has been published, if the material exists for it, to allow the Lord Privy Seal to state the position in his own words.

I take this opportunity, which I am sure the House will approve, of saying how much we have admired the tenacity and ingenuity and patience with which he conducted these negotiations, and although I have no doubt he feels stricken a most cruel blow by the fact that success was not achieved, that does not in any way lessen the fact that we highly approve of his mission and his conduct of these difficult negotiations.

Sir Percy Harris: Will the Prime Minister make clear whether his statement on the progress of the war will include as full an account as possible of what happened in Singapore, even if it has to be made in Secret Session?

The Prime Minister: Of course, I could not give an account of the war in Secret Session without referring to that most grave and disastrous episode, which has dominated the immediate course of affairs in the Indian and Malayan theatres, but I shall be careful myself not to prejudge those issues, on which, I think, our opinion should be suspended until at least we have the reports from various sides before us.

Sir John Wardlaw-Milne: May I say first that the House quite understands the difficulty of getting any account of what has happened in the fighting which took place on the island of Singapore? May I ask the Prime Minister, however, whether he is prepared to give the House by means of the commission for which he has been asked information as to the causes of the disaster, which have nothing to do, as the signatories see it, with the immediate fighting in Singapore or with the reports which would be received from people who have escaped from Singapore? What the House wants an inquiry into is the question of the causes which led up to it, and those cases can only be inquired into by means of a commission. Therefore I ask the Prime Minister whether he will consider the matter from that point of view.

The Prime Minister: I think it would not be in the general interest to have an inquiry by commission into all these matters. It would, I believe, put a serious burden upon all who might be called before such a commission and all who are concerned, and I am not prepared, after very careful consideration, to afford the slightest encouragement to the suggestion of my hon. Friend.

Sir Hugh O'Neill: In regard to the loss of the *Dorsetshire* and the *Cornwall* can the right hon. Gentleman say whether our Air Forces were able to carry out an attack on Japanese aircraft-carrying ships, and, if so, in what force and with what result?

The Prime Minister: It is quite true that while the attack on Colombo was being delivered by the Japanese our torpedo aircraft sallied out to attack the carriers from which the Japanese attack had been delivered, but owing to thunderstorms and low cloud in that vicinity, they did not make contacts on that day. The weather in the other parts of the Indian Ocean was not subject to those conditions of cloud and thunderstorms in which the Japanese carriers had shrouded themselves. Very valiant attacks were made by the torpedo aircraft that we possessed and also by the fighter bomber aircraft which were on the spot in such numbers as were available. As has already been published, one of the Japanese carriers is said to have had near misses, but whether any damage was done I have no knowledge. I know this, however, that practically all our aircraft taking part in the attack were either shot down or seriously injured or rendered unserviceable. That was the result, and I think it has already been announced. If not, I am glad to give the information now.

Mr Ammon:[1] With regard to the loss of the *Dorsetshire* and the *Cornwall*, is the Prime Minister aware that the statement he has made differs very little, if at all, from the previous statements with regard to the other disasters, and that it is not calculated to increase confidence but indicates rather that we have learned nothing from what has happened? There seems to have been no air cover at all. Surely there should be wider co-operation between the two arms?

The Prime Minister: I really have nothing to add to the statement I have made on the subject.

Sir H Williams: With regard to my question about a White Paper on Malaya, will my right hon. Friend reconsider the matter with a view to stopping the circulation in this country of most undesirable rumours?

The Prime Minister: I have already answered that.

[...]

Mr Gallacher: Has the right hon. Gentleman any information about the reason for the police breaking up the anti-Fascist, anti-Japanese demonstration in Penang three weeks before it was surrendered; and will he find out why the anti-Fascists who offered to form guerillas in Singapore were refused arms or assistance of any kind?

The Prime Minister: I have not heard about the episode referred to at Penang, nor have I any information at present upon the question which is asked about Singapore. My impression is, however, that a number of Chinese came down and helped to organise Chinese guerillas, and every assistance was given to them by the authorities.

Mr Henderson Stewart: According to Press reports, Major-General Gordon-Bennett is said to have stated in Australia that to say that 70,000 troops were in Singapore was a gross exaggeration. Is that so, and is the number of British prisoners in Japanese hands a good deal fewer than we feared?

[1] Charles George Ammon, 1873–1960. Educated at public elementary schools. Worked for the Post Office for 24 years. Labour MP for North Camberwell, 1922–31, 1935–44. Labour Party Whip, 1923. Parliamentary Secretary, Admiralty, 1924, 1929–31. Member, Select Committee on National Expenditure, 1939–44. Created Baron, 1944. Privy Councillor, 1945. Government Chief Whip and a Deputy Speaker, House of Lords, 1945–58. Chairman, Parliamentary Mission to China, 1947.

The Prime Minister: I cannot take any responsibility for various statements that are made by Major-General Gordon-Bennett. I have, I think, mentioned some figure in the past, and I am pretty confident that the closest examination of the figures will show that what the Government have said is correct.

Mr Stokes: With regard to Malaya and Singapore, is not the Prime Minister well aware that the general concern in the country is very much regarding the conditions precedent to the fall of Malaya and Singapore; and in view of the fact that the Government have reports from the Chancellor of the Duchy of Lancaster,[1] and must have had reports from Sir Archibald Wavell and, presumably, from Sir Shenton Thomas,[2] surely it must be possible to have a discussion on the conditions precedent to the fall? Does the right hon. Gentleman realise that the feeling in the country is such that people will not be content with a secret Debate and will insist on an open discussion?

The Prime Minister: Of course, in the period before Japan declared war there were a number of reports of great length and in great detail from the officers in that theatre. There were also at least three or four conferences, some secret, to which the Dutch and other Powers were invited. There is an immense mass of technical material upon the subject, but all of it bears very intimately upon our war arrangements, and I cannot think that any advantage – in fact there would be great disadvantage – would attach to its publication. It would certainly show, speaking very generally, that an immense amount of study and discussion preceded these lamentable events, but study and discussion are not in themselves sufficient to prepare against attack by a superior force of the enemy, and the difficulty under which we have suffered has been to search for the necessary forces to make head against the new attack to which we have been subjected.

[...]

Mr Glenvil Hall:[3] In the Debate later will the Prime Minister deal with what appears to be a reversal of the old-fashioned but sound policy of not sending capital ships into waters where the enemy have enormous pre-

---

[1] Alfred Duff Cooper.

[2] Governor of the Straits Settlements and High Commissioner for the Malay States, 1934–42. Interned by the Japanese, February 1942 to August 1945.

[3] William Glenvil Hall, 1887–1962. Barrister-at-law. On active service, 1914–18 (wounded, despatches). Labour MP for Portsmouth Central, 1929–31; for Colne Valley, 1939–62. Financial Secretary to the Treasury, 1945–50. British Representative, United Nations General Assembly, 1945, 1946, 1948; Consultative Assembly, Strasbourg, 1950, 1951, 1952. Privy Councillor, 1947. Chairman, Parliamentary Labour Party, 1950, 1951.

ponderance? Would not the best policy be, as heretofore, to use armed raiders and submarines rather than risk ships unnecessarily?

The Prime Minister: When you have the Pacific Ocean and the Indian Ocean, and the Japanese occupy an intermediate situation between the two, it is possible for them to use a large force on one side and a lighter force on the other, or vice versa. Consequently, the positions of our ships have to be related as far as possible to the information which we derive as to where the enemy's main strength lies. Certainly it would be impossible to carry on the immense business of convoy without His Majesty's ships – not capital ships in this case – being from time to time in situations where they have not got that support against air attack which everyone sees is eminently desirable.

Mr Rhys Davies:[1] Will the Prime Minister bear in mind that a number of people are seriously concerned at the fact that we have never won the loyalty of the native population in Malaya?

The Prime Minister: All my information is to the effect that the people of Malaya were thoroughly friendly.

Sir A. Southby:[2] I understood my right hon. Friend to say that the Government were making every effort to obtain information about Singapore. Will he keep an open mind on the question whether that end would not be achieved rather better if the inquiry were made by a commission?

The Prime Minister: I have already answered that in terms which I should have thought would have carried a clear impression to the minds of hon. Members.

Mr Maxton:[3] Would the right hon. Gentleman delay his final decision until the projected Debate has taken place? After all, if President Roosevelt can grant such a thing in similar circumstances, it seems to me there can be no objection to democratic Britain making such an investigation.

The Prime Minister: I have considered this matter carefully, and I cannot encourage any expectation that the decision which has been

---

[1] Rhys John Davies, 1877–1954. After elementary school, he began his working life as a farm servant. Later a coal miner in the Rhondda Valley. An official of the Distributive Workers' Union from 1906. Served on Manchester City Council, 1911–21. Labour MP for Westhoughton, Lancashire, 1921–51. Under-Secretary for the Home Department, Labour Government, 1924.

[2] Conservative MP for Epsom.

[3] James Maxton, 1885–1956. Organiser in Scotland for the Glasgow Federation of the Independent Labour Party, 1919–22. Labour MP for the Bridgeton Division of Glasgow from 1922 until his death. Chairman of the Independent Labour Party, 1926–31, 1934–9. Biographer of Lenin. A few weeks before Maxton died, Churchill wrote to him: 'I have been thinking a lot about you lately. I always say of you, "The greatest gentleman in the House of Commons"' (*Maxton papers*, quoted in Gordon Brown, *Maxton: A Biography*, London, 1986, page 294).

deliberately taken by His Majesty's Government will be in any way altered on that particular point.

Captain Duncan:[1] With regard to the last announcement of the Prime Minister, which will be welcomed not only by the Navy but by the other Services, may I ask how the staff is made up for the combined operations, and whether Lord Louis will be responsible only for Commando raids or for something bigger in future?

The Prime Minister: I think that is really covered by my answer, but in so far as it is not, I am not particularly anxious to go into details.[2]

Sir Stafford Cripps to Winston S. Churchill
(Churchill papers, 20/73)

13 April 1942   Karachi
Most Immediate
Personal and Secret

Last night I reviewed defence situation with Wavell at length, also with Peirse,[3] Viceroy and Governor Bengal.[4] They are all deeply (?word omitted) and anxious, and Wavell showed me at airport this morning a report from Alexander which is not encouraging.

However it is air and naval situation which is so disastrously dangerous at present. Our naval forces must avoid all contact with Japanese aircraft carriers and we have nothing with which latter can be attacked with effect. Our effort off Trincomalee with Blenheims shows they are of no use for this purpose. We have not planes to reconnoitre with hence loss of all merchant ships evacuated from Calcutta a few days ago. It was believed coast was clear but we had no means of seeing and therefore sailed the ships to a certain doom. The same may happen if we try again with further convoys as long as we cannot reconnoitre in advance.

---

[1] James Alexander Lawson Duncan, 1899–1974. On active service, Scots Guards, 1917–20, 1940–5. Conservative (Unionist) MP for Kensington North, 1931–45; Liberal Unionist MP for South Angus, 1950–64. Created Baronet, 1957.

[2] On 16 April 1942, Oliver Harvey wrote in his diary: 'More and more evidence comes in of the deplorable behaviour of all responsible in Singapore. No preparations, troops (British and Australian) refusing to fight, looting by troops, petty squabbling between officials, officials leaving their posts – 60,000 British troops beaten by 5,000 Japs! It must be hard to beat as a national disgrace. Many disturbing resemblances with the fall of France' (*The War Diaries of Oliver Harvey*, page 117).

[3] Air Officer Commanding-in-Chief, India, 1942–3.

[4] John Arthur Herbert, 1895–1943. Educated at Wellington School and Harvard University. Lieutenant, Royal Horse Guards, 1916. ADC to the Viceroy of India (Lord Irwin), 1926–8. Conservative MP for Monmouth, 1934–9. Assistant Whip, 1934–9. Knighted, 1939. Governor of Bengal from 1939 until his death.

Apart from our lack of protection against landings and Japanese aircraft carriers and battleships we are without any possibility of bombing their bases. Under existing circumstances they may well search out our naval units one by one until they all disappear and nothing is left between Cape Town and Hawaii north of Australia.

Under these circumstances I suggest an immediate reconsideration of our whole bombing policy must be made. The only thing that can hold the situation in India and eventually help to right it is long range bombers and reconnaissance machines which can search out aircraft carriers and at least frighten them away if they cannot be destroyed. If worst came to the worst and we lost India these planes could be used on coast of East Africa.

If we contemplate war continuing a long time we must reconsider types and we must substitute long range fighters to out distance Japanese machines, and long range torpedo carrying bombers.

Meanwhile it is a matter of the utmost immediate urgency to decide whether we are to allow the Eastern Fleet to be wiped out from air bit by bit and then India to fall in order to maintain nightly bombing of Germany.

Peirse whose experience qualifies him to express an opinion is certain our existing heavy bombers could be easily and quickly adapted to Indian conditions, that monsoon will not affect their capacity to continue flying with full loads, and that they could now be used in India to (?vital) purpose.

I beg you will consider this once again even if you have already considered it many times as after all my talks I believe only heavy bombers in reasonable numbers that (?word omitted) prevent arrival of Japanese in Persian Gulf, not as an Army but as destructive raiders. You will see from Governor Bengal's telegram the disastrous consequence likely to follow if Bengal is invaded. We have so little in India and it is impossible to see how it can be held once the Japanese have unlimited access for aircraft carriers to all and any points around its coast. We are powerless to discover where attack is likely to come if we cannot reconnoitre. This is I consider now the central strategical question of the war and we must make up our minds whether we are going to try to hold India or not. If we are then we cannot do it without heavy bombers and reconnaissance machines.

War Cabinet:[1] conclusions
(Cabinet papers, 65/26)

13 April 1942   10 Downing Street
5.30 p.m.

CONVOYS TO RUSSIA

The Prime Minister thought it was important that we should make the Russian Government realise the extent of the risks which were being run, and the efforts which were being made, in maintaining the northern supply route to Russia.

It was agreed that the Foreign Secretary should make representations, through the diplomatic channel, explaining the seriousness of the risks which we were running, and the importance of the fullest co-operation from the Russian air and naval forces in the protection of the convoys.

The Prime Minister undertook to send a telegram in the same sense to M Stalin.

General Sir Alan Brooke: diary
('War Diaries, Field Marshal Lord Alanbrooke', page 248)

14 April 1942

[...] back to Downing Street for a Defence Committee attended by Hopkins and Marshall. A momentous meeting at which we accepted their proposals[2] for offensive action in Europe in 1942 perhaps, and in 1943 for certain. They have not begun to realise all the implications of this plan and all the difficulties that lie ahead of us! The fear I have is that they should concentrate on this offensive at the expense of all else! We have therefore been pressing on them the importance of providing American assistance in the Indian Ocean and Middle East.

Winston S. Churchill: recollection
('The Hinge of Fate', pages 160–1)

9–10 April 1942

The experiences of the last few days had left no doubt in anyone's mind that for the time being Admiral Somerville had not the strength to fight a general action. Japanese success and power in naval air warfare were

---

[1] In addition to the War Cabinet (including for the first time Richard Casey as Minister of State), both Harry Hopkins and General Marshall were among those present.

[2] Operation Sledgehammer.

formidable. In the Gulf of Siam two of our first-class capital ships had been sunk in a few minutes by torpedo aircraft. Now two important cruisers had also perished by a totally different method of air attack – the dive-bomber. Nothing like this had been seen in the Mediterranean in all our conflicts with the German and Italian Air Forces. For the Eastern Fleet to remain near Ceylon would be courting a major disaster. The Japanese had gained control of the Bay of Bengal, and at their selected moment could obtain local command of the waters around Ceylon. The British aircraft available were far outnumbered by the enemy. The battle fleet, slow, outranged, and of short endurance, except for the *Warspite*, was itself at this moment a liability, and the available carrier-borne air protection would be ineffective against repeated attacks on the scale of those which had destroyed the *Dorsetshire* and *Cornwall*. There was but little security against large-scale air or surface attacks at the Ceylon bases, and still less at Addu Atoll.

On one point we were all agreed. The 'Rs' should get out of danger at the earliest moment. When I put this to the First Sea Lord, there was no need for argument. Orders were sent accordingly, and the Admiralty authorised Admiral Somerville to withdraw his fleet two thousand miles westward to East Africa. Here it could at least provide cover for the vital shipping routes to the Middle East. He himself, with the *Warspite* and his two carriers, would continue to operate in Indian waters in defence of our sea communications with India and with Persian Gulf. For this purpose he intended to base himself in Bombay. His actions were promptly approved by the Admiralty, whose thoughts in the grave events of the past few days had followed almost identical lines. These new dispositions were brought into effect forthwith.

There now arose one of those waves of alarm, which sometimes spread through High Commands. The vital point was to keep Ceylon.

Defence Committee: minutes
(Cabinet papers, 69/4)

14 April 1942

The Prime Minister said that the Committee had met to consider a momentous proposal which Mr Hopkins and General Marshall had brought over, and which had now been fully discussed and examined by the Staffs. For himself, he had no hesitation in cordially accepting the plan. The conception underlying it accorded with the classic principles of war – namely, concentration against the main enemy. One broad reservation must however be made – it was essential to carry on the defence of India and the Middle East. We could not possibly face the loss of an army of 600,000 men and the whole man power of India. Furthermore, Australia and the island bases connecting that country with the United States must not be allowed to fall, as this would inevitably prolong the war. This meant that we could not entirely lay aside everything in furtherance of the main object proposed by General Marshall. It would, of course, be impossible to ensure complete secrecy for the preparations. The true objectives could, however, be obscured in a cloud of rumours.

General Marshall said that it was a great relief to him to know that there was a basic agreement on general principles. All were in complete agreement as to what should be done in 1943. All were in complete agreement as to the necessity for developing the strongest air offensive against Germany and of expanding the programme of raids. The latter were of great importance, not only as diversions, but also to maintain the morale of the troops and give them battle experience. The effect of a nucleus of troops in the American Army who had actually taken part in operations against the enemy would be great.

[...]

The Prime Minister said that the fact must he recognised that we were unable, for the next two or three months, to cope unaided with the naval strength which the Japanese could develop in the Indian Ocean. At the moment, he had no sure knowledge of the United States' naval intentions and movements in the Pacific, but the move of the *Washington*[1] and other warships to join the British Home Fleet at Scapa was a striking and significant event. Coupled as it was with the retention of the *North Carolina*[2] on the Atlantic Station, it seemed to indicate that the United States Navy were not thinking of pressing matters on a large scale in the Pacific. From this a harmonious plan might result. For example, it might be possible for the *North Carolina* to move over to Scapa thus, perhaps, enabling us to release the *Duke of York* to go to the Indian Ocean. The first essential

[1] USS *Washington*: the second of two battleships in the North Carolina class. Launched on 1 June 1940 in the New York naval shipyard. In 1942 she was at Scapa Flow to fill in for British warships redeployed around Madagascar. Served as long-distance cover for several Iceland–Murmansk Arctic convoys. Participated in the Pacific battles, 1942–5, when she became the only American battleship in the Second World War to sink an enemy battleship (the Japanese *Kirishima*) in a one-to-one surface engagement. Badly damaged when she rammed the battleship USS *Indiana*, but returned to active service in the Pacific for the last year of the war. Sold for scrap, 1961.

[2] USS *North Carolina*: built in the Brooklyn Navy Yard, with nine 16-inch guns, and launched on 13 June 1940. She was the first new-construction United States battleship to see active service in the Second World War. In 1942, after two months at Scapa Flow, she sailed to the Pacific in time to support the US Marine landings on Guadalcanal. In action throughout the subsequent Pacific battles, and in naval operations against the Philippines and the Japanese home islands. Since 1962 she has been a battleship memorial in Wilmington, North Carolina.

in that area was to get superiority over the Japanese in seaborne aircraft. We ourselves would very shortly have three aircraft carriers in the Indian Ocean, and these might be joined in due course by the *Furious*. If, say, two or even three more could be provided by the United States, we would have a force of aircraft carriers which would entirely change the situation. We would not only regain security in the Indian Ocean, but we should be able to master the Bay of Bengal and might intervene against the Japanese advance Northwards through Burma. Thus the provision of these naval reinforcements would do more than the arrival in India of very large armies, and would be surest way of keeping China in the war. At the same time, it would be the best possible means of ensuring that the great project on the Continent of Europe could go forward without interference.

Sir Dudley Pound said that the Naval Staff were engaged in working out detailed proposals on the lines indicated by the Prime Minister, and they hoped to have these ready the following day.

General Marshall said that he would convey to the President and to the U.S. Naval Authorities the case which had been stated by the Prime Minister. He thought that it would interest the Committee to know that he had that day sent instructions through the War Department to General Stilwell, that he was to place General Brereton under the operational control of the British Authorities in India. This would enable the bombers under his command to be used to the best advantage. Certain fighters would also be available, allowing for the prior commitment to build up the American Volunteer Group to operational strength.

The Prime Minister expressed grateful appreciation for General Marshall's action.

[...]

Lord Louis Mountbatten said that the United States plan altered the whole picture of combined operations against the Continent. The plans which we had been at present evolving all fell short in one way or another for lack of essential resources. This would all be changed when the great flow of American forces began, and we should be enabled to plan that real return to the Continent, without which we could not hope to bring the war to a successful conclusion. From the point of view of combined operations, he welcomed the plan unreservedly.

The Prime Minister, summing up the discussion, said that, although it remained to work out the details of the plan, it was clear that there was complete unanimity on the framework. The two nations would march ahead together in a noble brotherhood of arms.

He would prepare a message to the President, conveying to him the conclusions which had been reached. He would also put forward to him a request for the vital requirements of the Indian Ocean, without which the whole plan would be fatally compromised. The details of this request would also be communicated to the Combined Chiefs of Staff in Washington. Full preparations could now start and we could go ahead with the utmost resolution. It would gradually become known that the English speaking peoples were resolved on a great campaign for the liberation of Europe, and it was for consideration whether a public announcement to this effect should in due course be made. He could assure Mr Hopkins and General Marshall that nothing would be left undone on the part of the British Government and people which could contribute to the success of the great enterprise on which they were about to embark.

[...][1]

General Marshall said that all were in complete agreement as to what should be done in 1943 and upon developing the strongest air offensive against Germany. The availability of troops presented no problem. The main difficulties would be found in providing the requisite tonnage, the landing-craft, the aircraft, and the naval escorts.

There were two points of doubt, which had arisen in his discussions with the British Chiefs of Staff. The first was whether sufficient material would be available from the United States for the support of the Middle East and India. The second was on the practicability of making a landing on the Continent, other than a large-scale raid, in 1942. We might be compelled to do this, and we must in any case prepare for it. He thought that the difficulties should not be insoluble, as we should have a great measure of air control. The size of our joint air programmes showed that this would be so, particularly as the German campaign against Russia would absorb great resources and thus reduce the hazards of our operations. Thus it would be the Germans who would have a taste of fighting without air support. There had not been much time before he left the United States to study the problem of operations in 1942 and, on the data available, he had concluded that they could not be undertaken before September. If they had to be done before then the United States contribution would be modest; but whatever was available in the way of American forces over here at the time could be used to the full. The President had particularly emphasised that he wished his armed forces to share to the greatest extent possible in whatever might be undertaken.

[1] The remainder of this extract from the minutes of the Defence Committee meeting of 14 April is reproduced in *The Hinge of Fate*, pages 284–6.

Sir Alan Brooke said that the Chiefs of Staff were in entire agreement with General Marshall on the project for 1943. Operations on the Continent in 1942 were governed by the measure of success achieved by the Germans in their campaign against Russia. We had felt that matters would come to a head before September.

The Chiefs of Staff entirely agreed that Germany was the main enemy. At the same time, it was essential to hold the Japanese and to ensure that there should be no junction between them and the Germans. If the Japanese obtained control of the Indian Ocean not only would the Middle East be gravely threatened, but we should lose the oil supplies from the Persian Gulf. The results of this would be that Germany would get all the oil she required, the southern route to Russia would be cut, Turkey would be isolated and defenceless, the Germans would obtain ready access to the Black Sea, and Germany and Japan would be able to interchange the goods of which they stood so much in need.

Mr Churchill then added that we were unable for the next two or three months to cope unaided with the naval strength which the Japanese could develop in the Indian Ocean. At the moment we had no sure knowledge of the United States' naval intentions and movements in the Pacific. The first essential in that area was to get superiority over the Japanese in seaborne aircraft. We ourselves would very shortly have three aircraft-carriers in the Indian Ocean, and these might be joined in due course by the *Furious*.

Mr Hopkins said that if public opinion in America had its way the weight of American effort would be directed against Japan. Nevertheless, after anxious discussion the President and the American military leaders had decided that it would be right to direct the force of American arms against Germany. It should not be thought however that there was any misunderstanding in the minds of the American Government as to the position in the Middle East and on the other great fronts, such as Russia, Australia, and the Pacific. The American decision had been governed by two main considerations. First, the United States wished to fight not only on the sea, but on land and in the air. Secondly, they wished to fight in the most useful place, and in the place where they could attain superiority, and they were desirous above all of joining in an enterprise with the British. If such an enterprise were to be launched this year the United States wished to make the greatest contribution that was possible, whenever it might take place. When they had suggested September as the earliest date for moving they had been largely influenced by the fear of promoting an enterprise in which they could not play an adequate part.

He had sensed public opinion both in America and in the United Kingdom, and had found it disturbed as to what the United States Navy was doing. There should be no doubt on this point. The Navy would join with the British to the full in bringing the enemy to action. They were only anxious that they should fight in favourable circumstances.

With regard to the Australian and other theatres, the United States would certainly discharge their obligations, but their whole heart would be fully engaged, in the great plan now proposed. The American nation was eager to join in the fight alongside the British.

Sir Charles Portal said that it was necessary to bear in mind the difference between air operations across Channel and the landing of an Expeditionary Force. The former could be continued or stopped at will. In the latter case however we could not take as much or as little as we liked. We should have to maintain the air effort for as long as the troops remained on the Continent. If therefore we launched an Expeditionary Force we must be sure that the air resources were sufficient to enable operations to be carried through to the end.

In conclusion, Mr Churchill said that, although it remained to work out the details of the plan [for the cross-Channel invasion of 1943], there was complete unanimity on the framework. The two nations would march ahead together in a noble brotherhood of arms. He would prepare a message to the President, conveying to him the conclusions which had been reached, and also put forward to him a request for the vital requirements of the Indian Ocean, without which the whole plan would be fatally compromised. Full preparations could now start, and we could go ahead with the utmost resolution. It would gradually become known that the English-speaking peoples were resolved on a great campaign for the liberation of Europe, and it was for consideration whether a public announcement to this effect should in due course be made.

Winston S. Churchill to General Hastings Ismay,
for the Chiefs of Staff Committee
(Churchill papers, 20/67)

14 April 1942

The attached telegrams[1] seem to show a mood of needless alarm. We must make every effort and run great risks to hold Ceylon. Admiral

---

[1] From Admiral James Somerville, Commander-in-Chief, Eastern Fleet (Command formed December 1941 through union of East Indies Command and China Station).

Somerville is well posted for the time being at Bombay. Why should he assume that Ceylon and Southern India are going to be lost in so short a time that Bombay will soon become unsafe? This is going to extremes with a vengeance. He should surely be told not on any account to propose evacuation of staff from Ceylon. Meanwhile I have drafted the telegram attached to the President for your consideration.

Winston S. Churchill to President Franklin D. Roosevelt
(Churchill papers, 20/73)

14 April 1942[1]
No. 69

I must revert to the grave situation in the Indian Ocean mentioned in my No. 65, arising from the fact that the Japanese have felt able to detach nearly a third of their battle fleet and half their carriers, which force we are unable to match for several months. The consequences of this may easily be:

(a) The loss of Ceylon.

(b) Invasion of Eastern India with incalculable internal consequences to our whole war plan and including the loss of Calcutta and of all contact with the Chinese through Burma.

But this is only the beginning. Until we are able to fight a fleet action there is no reason why the Japanese should not become the dominating factor in the Western Indian Ocean. This would result in the collapse of our whole position in the Middle East, not only because of the interruption to our convoys to the Middle East and India, but also because of the interruptions to the oil supplies from Abadan, without which we cannot maintain our position either at sea or on land in the Indian Ocean area. Supplies to Russia via the Persian Gulf would also be cut. With so much of the weight of Japan thrown upon us we have more than we can bear.

2. We had hoped that by the end of April the American Pacific Fleet would be strong enough to re-occupy Pearl Harbour and offer some menace to the Japanese which they would have to consider seriously. At present there seems to be no adequate restraint upon Japanese movements to the west. We are not sure moreover whether owing to the great distances even the re-occupation of Pearl Harbour in force by the United States battle fleet would necessarily exercise Command. We are deeply conscious of the difficulties of your problem in the Pacific area.

[1] Drafted by Churchill on 14 April 1942, this telegram was sent on April 15.

3. If you do not feel able to take speedy action which will force Japan to concentrate in the Pacific, the only way out of the immense perils which confront us would seem to be to build up as quickly as possible an ample force of modern capital ships and carriers in the Indian Ocean. By substituting one of the 4 'R' Class now at Kilindini for *Malaya* in 'Ironclad'[1] it will be possible to send her back to Gibraltar and for *Renown* to reach Admiral Somerville before the end of May. If you would consider sending *North Carolina* and *Ranger*[2] from Task Force 22 to join Somerville temporarily, he would soon be provided with a force of three long range capital ships and four carriers as well as the four Rs. In eight or nine weeks barring accidents we shall be better off. *Illustrious* should have joined Somerville by the middle of May and *Valiant* in June. *Nelson* and *Rodney* will be on the way from England. Thus we shall grow continually stronger and regain the power to fight an action in the Indian Ocean against any detachment Japan may dare to make from the Pacific.

4. Alternatively if you preferred to place *North Carolina* alongside *Washington* in Scapa we could send *Duke of York* to join Somerville in the Indian Ocean and *Ranger* could go direct to Capetown to meet her. The first method improves our position a fortnight earlier, when days may count.

5. We are most grateful to you for sending *Washington* and her consorts to help us and for the invaluable work *Wasp* is now doing.

6. It is also most important to have some American heavy bombers in India. There are at present about 14, and 50 more are authorised. But none of these was able to attack the Japanese naval forces last week. We have taken everything from Libya which is possible without ruining all prospects of a renewed offensive. We are sending every suitable aircraft to the East which can be efficiently serviced out there, but without your aid this will not be sufficient. Might I press you, Mr President, to procure the necessary decisions?

7. I am sending you a separate message about our memorable meeting with your envoys lat night. We have established the most intimate contacts with the United States Army and Air Force but as Harry will tell you we are not nearly so closely linked up on the Naval side. Yet all depends on this being successfully handled in unison. I am therefore

---

[1] 'Ironclad': the amphibious landings in Madagascar.

[2] USS *Ranger*: the first United States aircraft carrier to be designed and built from the keel up as an aircraft carrier. She was launched in 1933. On Neutrality Patrol, operating out of Bermuda, 1939–41. Flagship, US Atlantic Fleet, 1942. Her structural strength was poor, and she was used mostly for ferry and training duties. She did, however, see action twice: when she launched her aircraft off Casablanca during Operation Torch, November 1942; and against German shipping in Norwegian territorial waters in 1943. From 1944 to 1945, operating out of Pearl Harbor, she trained pilots for combat duty.

sending the First Sea Lord back with General Marshall and Harry in order that he may discuss with you and Admiral King the whole position and make long-term plans. I hope however that if you agree with either of the suggestions for naval movements made in Paragraphs 3 and 4 of this message you will be able to have the necessary orders given without waiting for his arrival. We cannot afford to lose any time.

Winston S. Churchill to A. V. Alexander and
Admiral of the Fleet Sir Dudley Pound
(Churchill papers, 20/67)

14 April 1942

Let me have the estimated aircraft of different patterns borne on each of the five Japanese aircraft carriers in the Indian Ocean and in our *Indomitable, Illustrious, Formidable.* Let me also have the tonnage on both sides.

What is the explanation why the Japanese are able to carry so many more aircraft than we do? What is the explanation why ships like *Illustrious, Formidable* and *Indomitable* should be described as not fully trained considering they have not been engaged for over a year and have been working up for several months? What are the aircraft for the *Formidable* which were left behind at Colombo? What steps have been taken to replenish her and arm *Indomitable* with Martlets?[1] These issues are causing very considerable concern.

Winston S. Churchill to Sir Archibald Sinclair
(Churchill papers, 20/67)

14 April 1942
Secret

We are placing great hopes on our bomber offensive against Germany next winter, and we must spare no pains to justify the large proportion of the national effort devoted to it. The Air Ministry's responsibility is to make sure that the maximum weight of the best type of bombs is

---

[1] Marlet: The Grumman F4F Wildcat was an American carrier-based fighter aircraft that began service in 1940 with both the United States Navy and the Fleet Air Arm (as the Martlet). It had a maximum speed of 310 miles per hour and an effective range of 390 miles. Armed with four machine guns, it was of particular service on convoy escort duties. Its first combat victory was on Christmas Day 1940, when a land-based Martlet destroyed a Junkers Ju 88 bomber over the Scapa Flow naval base. This was the first combat victory by a US-built fighter in British service in the Second World War. In 1942, the Wildcat was the only effective fighter available to the United States Navy and Marine Corps in the Pacific.

dropped on the German cities by the aircraft placed at their disposal. Unless we can ensure that most of our bombs really do some damage, it will be difficult to justify the pre-eminence we are according to this form of attack. The following seem to be needful for success:

(1) To make sure that crews are practised in the use of blind bombing apparatus, which should be installed by this autumn in most of our night bombers.

(2) To discover any difficulties which navigators may find in the use of sextants for astro-navigation, overcome them, and make sure they employ this method to get them within 12 to 15 miles of the target, after which the blind bombing equipment comes into play.

(3) To make certain that the large number of bombers we expect to get will not be immobilised by bad weather. This will entail preparing adequate runways, homing devices and possibly fog clearing gear on the aerodromes, and de-icing and blind landing equipment, &c., on the planes.

(4) To insist that a sufficient supply of incendiary and high charge-weight ratio bombs is available, even if this implies relaxing the penetration specifications. I raised this matter last July and was assured there would be no shortage, but I gather that the 1,000-lb. and 500-lb. bombs, which form the bulk of our loads, are still of the old inefficient type.

We must expect that the enemy will improve his defences, both ground and air. Various counter-measures are, I understand, in sight, which we are quite properly holding up for the time being. No doubt you will see that everything is concerted so that we can install and use each of them immediately [if] it is deemed desirable.

Winston S. Churchill to Sir Stafford Cripps
(Churchill papers, 20/73)

14 April 1942
Most Immediate
Personal and Most Secret

Parliament has asked for White Paper which we propose to lay containing (1) my statement of March 11th; (2) draft Declaration as published; (3) Congress resolution rejecting proposals with Azad's covering letter; (4) your reply in form of letter to Azad; (5) Azad's further reply; (6) Moslem League resolution rejecting proposals. Only texts we have on official record are (1), (2) and (4). We are telegraphing to India for remainder.

2. We understand from India that in Sunday morning's press Congress published not only correspondence but also formulae on defence, last of which was described as Cripps–Johnson formula, but not modifications in that formula suggested by Viceroy to which Congress agreed orally. We propose to include in White Paper various formulae followed by this note: 'Certain amendments in the last formula were suggested to the Congress leaders on April 10th and accepted orally by them. The final formula as amended was as follows'. Then would follow final formula as contained in your telegram 971-S of 10th April. Please telegraph whether you concur. Message ends.

Winston S. Churchill to Sir Stafford Cripps
(Churchill papers, 20/73)

14 April 1942
Most Immediate

Your cipher 13/4 from Karachi. In my immediately following telegram I send you a note on this subject prepared by the Air Ministry. We can discuss it all when you come home. Meanwhile I am making sure that everything in human power is being done.

2. I hope you will not let it be thought that we here are not deeply concerned with the prolonged inaction of the Libya Army. It seems to me quite possible that Rommel will grow stronger at a greater rate than our people. Now that one submarine flotilla has to go from the Mediterranean to the Indian Ocean and the air attack on Malta makes it impossible to station Bombers there, the route from Italy to Tripoli will be not much obstructed. Besides this the Middle East air will be increasingly drawn upon for the Indian emergency. There is no use pressing a General beyond his better judgement but I should like you to know that my opinion and that of the Staffs here is unaltered.

3. Kind regards. I have kept Lady Cripps fully informed of the way things ended at Delhi.

Winston S. Churchill to Sir Stafford Cripps
(Churchill papers, 20/73)

14 April 1942
Most Immediate
Personal and Most Secret

AIR REINFORCEMENTS FOR INDIA

My immediately preceding telegram. The following is the position given me by Air Ministry. Begins. Despatch of individual heavy bombers and crews would of course be possible, but until spares and unit equipment were available in India they could contribute nothing. Moreover no four-engined British bomber is yet free from teething troubles which demand constant attention from parent firms. Halifax[1] is first British type likely to be fit for tropical service, and we are urgently considering how necessary equipment and ground parties could arrive India most quickly. It is questionable whether Liberator,[2] which is a well-tried type, would not be ready as soon and give better service.

Despite great importance of bombing Germany as means of weakening German offensive against Russia, this has not been allowed to influence reinforcement of India. Ends.

Winston S. Churchill to John Curtin
(Churchill papers, 20/73)

15 April 1942
Personal and Secret

I am very much obliged to you for your decision to allow the Australian 9th Division to remain in Middle East for the present. All the contents of your telegram are being studied by the Chiefs of Staff. It is fully understood, and was certainly my wish, that United States forces should go to Australia unconditionally, and you have always been and will be perfectly free to decide the movement of all your troops.

---

[1] Halifax: the Handley Page Halifax was a British front-line, four-engined bomber, which made its first flight on 24 September 1939. Its first operational raid was against Le Havre on the night of 11–12 March 1941. During April and May 1942, Halifax bombers took part in a number of raids on the German battleship *Tirpitz* in Fættenfjord near Trondheim, Norway. The Halifax bombers flown by Bomber Command flew 82,773 operations, dropped 224,207 tons of bombs, and lost 1,833 aircraft. The 6,000 built between 1939 and 1945 were used by the Royal Air Force, and by the Canadian, New Zealand, Australian, Free French, and Polish Air Forces during the Second World War.

[2] Liberator: the Consolidated B-24 Liberator, an American heavy bomber (see note on page 424 above).

2. We are of course trying to build up as fast as possible a strong naval force in the Indian Ocean. The very considerable detachment which the enemy has presumed to make from his main fleet for the Indian Ocean and the Bay of Bengal makes it undesirable for us to seek a Fleet action for the time being, but these conditions will change rapidly in the next few months. *Valiant* should join Admiral Somerville in June, *Illustrious* in May, and we are planning still larger reinforcements of which I will inform you soon. Meanwhile of course we are anxious both about Ceylon and Calcutta.

General Sir Alan Brooke: diary
('War Diaries, Field Marshal Lord Alanbrooke', page 249)

15 April 1942

[...] dined 10 Downing Street [where the] King had been invited to meet Marshall and Harry Hopkins, also Pound, Portal, Mountbatten, Ismay and Hardinge[1] and self. After dinner heated discussion as to possible future of German plans. I propounded possible German move through Eastern Mediterranean with sea and airborne attacks against Cyprus and Syria. I suggested this might be an alternative if Germany did not feel strong enough to attack Russia. The King very interested and this resulted in good argument with Winston.

King George VI: diary
(Royal Archives)

15 April 1942   Buckingham Palace

I dined with Winston, where I met Gen. Marshall, Mr Hopkins, the Chiefs of Staff & Dickie M., Ismay & Alec[2] were also there. We had an interesting evening. Marshall explained his plan to send over here his trained & equipped divisions to fight in France if we were able to open up a Western Front. This has been discussed by the Defence Committee. Later Winston asked what Hitler would do if he did not attack Russia? Alan Brooke thought he could hold Russia, & strike south to the oil via Syria & Persia, thence to the Persian Gulf. Rommel on south would reach Egypt & the Canal, while the Italian fleet would escort troops via the Mediterranean. Naturally we should oppose this attack, & it would take a long time, but it might be Hitler's idea.

[1] Private Secretary to King George VI.
[2] Sir Alexander Hardinge.

Winston S. Churchill to Clement Attlee[1]
(Churchill papers, 20/67)

16 April 1942

SUGGESTED REVIEW AIR POLICY,
IN ORDER TO SEND BOMBER REINFORCEMENTS TO INDIA

These views are certainly fashionable at the moment. Everybody would like to send Bomber Command to India and the Middle East. However it is not possible to make any decisive change. All that is possible is being done. I should be very glad if you would see CAS[2] and hear what he has to say. The question is one of precise detail. It is no use flying out squadrons which sit helpless and useless when they arrive. We have built up a great plant here for bombing Germany, which is the only way in our power of helping Russia. From every side people want to break it up. One has to be sure that we do not ruin our punch here without getting any proportionate advantage elsewhere. You should see the telegram which the Chiefs of Staff have sent to Wavell. I pressed CAS very hard and I am pretty sure that he has done his best.

President Franklin D. Roosevelt to Winston S. Churchill
(Churchill papers, 20/73)

17 April 1942
No. 133

[...]

I wish to emphasize the following:

1. In my opinion it would be very unwise to curtail the planes now en route to General Stilwell. I have received from the Generalissimo a very despondent message and I feel that considerations of high policy call for aviation help to the Burma area immediately as the position of the Chinese must be sustained.

2. Plan 'A' of our Staff I think is by far the better.

3. A Japanese land attack on Ceylon in my opinion won't be made for several weeks' time.

4. It is my hope that shipping of the United Nations will be kept out of the Bay of Bengal.

5. I also hope that for the time being British warships will remain under the umbrella of land-based planes while they are in the vicinity of Ceylon and Southern India.

[1] Secretary of State for the Dominions, and a member of the War Cabinet.
[2] CAS: the Chief of the Air Staff, Sir Charles Portal.

6. The easiest and quickest way to increase air strength in the Indian theatre is to permit us to send all possible planes now here earmarked for the account of the British so that Brereton[1] may be brought up to strength. From the time we hear from you this large movement can start in forty-eight hours.

President Franklin D. Roosevelt to Winston S. Churchill
(Churchill papers, 20/73)

17 April 1942
No. 134

Your secret No. 69. We have been and are continuing studies of immediate needs. I hope you will read our Air Force suggestions sent to Marshall for your consideration. This would be much the quickest way of getting planes to India though they would be land based planes and for the time being would compel you to keep your fleet under their coverage. On the other hand this plan would do the most good to prevent Japanese landing at Ceylon, Madras or Calcutta. In other words they would definitely improve the general military situation in India area. These planes however involve use of *Ranger* as a ferry boat and prevent her use as carrier with her own planes. The *Ranger* is of course best suited for ferrying as we are not proud of her compartmentation and her structural strength. Measures now in hand by Pacific Fleet have not been conveyed to you in detail because of secrecy requirements but we hope you will find them effective when they can be made known to you shortly. I fully appreciate the present lack of naval butter to cover the bread but I hope you will agree with me that because of operational differences between the two services there is a grave question as to whether a main fleet concentration should be made in Ceylon area with mixed forces. Partly because of this and partly because of my feeling that for the next few weeks it is more important to prevent Japanese landing anywhere in India or Ceylon that we are inclined to give greater consideration to temporary replacement [of] your Home Fleet units rather than mixing units in Indian Ocean.

---

[1] Lewis Hyde Brereton, 1890–1967. US flying and fighting General who fought on most fronts in the Second World War. Commander-in-Chief, United States Far East Air Force, 1941. Commander, United States Middle East Air Force (based in India), 1942. Commander, United States 9th Air Force (Western Desert), 1942–3. In October 1943, transferred to UK to build up the 9th Air Force into a formidable tactical air unit in preparation for Operation Overlord, the Normandy Landings of 1944. From August 1944, Commander, 1st Allied Airborne Army (including for Operation 'Market Garden' – Arnhem).

It is my personal thought that your fleet in Indian Ocean can well be safeguarded during next few weeks without fighting major engagement in the meantime building up land based plane units to stop Japanese transports. I hope you will let me know your thought in regard to the air force measures indicated above. We could put them into effect at once.

Winston S. Churchill to President Franklin D. Roosevelt
(Churchill papers, 20/73)

17 April 1942
Secret and Personal
No. 70

Your envoys will take back with them a full note of our memorable meeting last Tuesday and a detailed commentary on your proposals by our Chiefs of Staff. I think, however, that you would wish to have at once a short account of the conclusions which were reached.

2. We wholeheartedly agree with your conception of concentration against the main enemy, and we cordially accept your plan with one broad qualification. As you will see from my 69 of the 15th April, it is essential that we should prevent a junction of the Japanese and the Germans. Consequentially, a proportion of our combined resources must, for the moment, be set aside to halt the Japanese advance. This point was fully discussed at the meting, and Marshall felt confident that we could together provide what was necessary for the Indian Ocean and other theatres, and yet go right ahead with your main project.

3. The campaign of 1943 is straightforward, and we are starting joint plans and preparations at once. We may, however, feel compelled to act this year. Your plan visualized this, but put mid-September as the earliest date. Things may easily come to a head before then. Marshall explained that you had been reluctant to press for an enterprise that was fraught with such grave risks and dire consequences until you could make a substantial air contribution; but he left us in no doubt that if it were found necessary to act earlier, you, Mr President, would earnestly wish to throw in every available scrap of human and material resources. We are proceeding with plans and preparations on that basis. Broadly speaking, our agreed programme is a crescendo of activity on the continent starting with an ever-increasing air offensive both by night and day and more frequent and larger scale raids, in which United States troops will take part.

4. I agree with the suggestion in your telegram No. 129 of 2nd April that you should ask Stalin to send two special representatives to see you at once about your plans. It will in any case be impossible to conceal the vast preparations that will be necessary, but with the whole coast of Europe, from the North Cape to Bayonne open to us, we should contrive to deceive the enemy as to the weight, the timing, the method and the direction of our attacks. It is indeed for consideration whether it would not be right to make a public announcement that our two nations are resolved to march forward into Europe together in a noble brotherhood of arms on a great crusade for the liberation of the tormented peoples. I will cable you further on this last point.

Winston S. Churchill to Robert Barrington-Ward
(Churchill papers, 20/53)

17 April 1942
Private and Confidential

My dear Barrington Ward,

I am taking away your Memorandum to study if I can at the weekend. But they are pressing me to make a speech on the war to the House in Secret Session next week and this may take what spare thought I have to give. I will do my best.

Have you thought out the details of this campaign you are running for what is called the Great General Staff? There seem to be a number of questions which you and your correspondents are not facing. A professional chief without a department or Service is to be appointed CGGS.[1] Presumably he can give directions to the three Chiefs of Staff. What happens if they or any of them do not agree with him? As he would be inevitably the product of one of the three Services this is a very likely chance.

Next, what is to happen to the Service Ministers? They have a constitutional position which entitles them to access to the Cabinet and to circulate papers. In all probability they would make common cause with their own professional adviser and so would their whole office. It would then be my duty to advise the Cabinet and to induce them to decide whether the CGGS was right or the Admiralty, War Office or Air Ministry. I fear I should be provided not with solutions but with a whole series of new disputes.

---

[1] Chief of the (proposed) Great General Staff.

Any of these disputes might be fatal either to the CGGS or the department concerned with which the other Chiefs of Staff might make common cause.

Again, have you anybody in your mind? Is he to be retired or serving? Old and sagacious or young and dynamic? Who is your man? Should he belong to the Army, Navy or Air Force? Have we any officer who has three-fold qualifications? It is very easy to suggest some unknown genius should be found on whom the Cabinet can dump their responsibilities to win the war and whom the Services will obey; but I think you ought to name the animal.

These are only a few of the difficulties which would arise. It would be a very good thing if you first of all made yourself acquainted with the existing organization and of the very large degree of fuzing which has already been achieved at the second and third levels of the Staffs. I shall be quite ready to let General Ismay give you the fullest particulars of this and I believe he would convince you of the difficulties of taking the kind of change you have in mind.

Yours sincerely,
Winston S. Churchill

Averell Harriman: recollection
('Special Envoy to Churchill and Stalin', pages 133–4)

[19–21 April 1942]

Churchill told me that 'Sledgehammer' was impossible, disastrous.[1]
[...]
He was gravely concerned that the British, with their limited resources and the limited support we could at that time give them, would have another setback. He was fearful that the divisions they landed would be destroyed – and this would undermine Britain's ability to launch future operations. I believe that General Marshall may have overestimated the state of readiness of the twenty to thirty British divisions in the United Kingdom. My information was that they were not up to strength and were seriously under-equipped.

I was going to jump on a plane and warn Roosevelt that there had been a serious misunderstanding. It was clearly impossible to explain this in a written message. But I had to go to bed and while I was out of action Churchill decided to go to Washington himself. So I left it to him.

[1] For Churchill's own commentary on his thinking at this time, see the extract from *The Hinge of Fate*, pages 288–9, reproduced at page 554 below.

Winston S. Churchill to General Archibald Wavell
(Churchill papers, 20/88)

19 April 1942

Naturally we have been working continually at your problems. According to our reckoning you have at the moment in India and Ceylon about 230 fighters and 80 bombers. There are already on the way to you with further reinforcements to follow about 200 fighters and 60 bombers. We have persuaded Americans to arrange to send about 46 heavy and medium bombers which are already in or nearing India and we are transferring aircraft to them from our U.S. allocations to bring their bombardment squadrons in India up to full strength in the near future. They have about 50 fighters in or en route to India and more may be sent shortly to West Africa for India in an American carrier.

2. Thus apart from losses your totals at the end of April should be 310 fighters and 160 bombers, at the end of May 410 fighters and 235 bombers, at the end of June 490 fighters and 295 bombers.

3. I am assured that this is really all that can be done for you in this period. The settled opinion of the Air Ministry and the Chiefs of Staff about the sudden sending to you of a large number of British heavy bombers has been conveyed to you in COS telegram OZ 29, 16/4/42. This view has been tested from every angle.

4. We are trying to build up a naval force in the Indian Ocean strong enough to require a larger detachment from the Japanese main fleet than they would care to provide. For this purpose I have asked the President to send the *North Carolina* to join the *Washington* at Scapa Flow. These are their two latest battleships. We will then release the *Duke of York* for Indian Ocean. *Renown* will accompany her. *Illustrious* should be with Somerville in May. *Valiant* should be ready in June. Thus we shall quite soon have three fast capital ships plus three of our largest armoured carriers. Steps are being taken to make them as prolific in aircraft as possible. Thus in eight to ten weeks Admiral Somerville's fleet, growing continually stronger, should become powerful. Especially is this so as we have reason to believe the United States main fleet will become more active and a greater pre-occupation to the enemy than hitherto.

5. But all this gathering of a naval force will be futile if Ceylon, particularly Colombo, is lost in the meanwhile. We must therefore consider the defence of Colombo by flak and aircraft as an object more urgent and not less important than the defence of Calcutta. As to the long Indian coastline between Calcutta and Ceylon, it is not possible in the near future to provide Air forces either to repel landings or to

afford an umbrella for naval movements. But do you really think it is likely the Japanese would consider it worth while to send four or five divisions roaming about the Madras Presidency? What could they do comparable to the results obtainable by capturing Ceylon or by pressing up north into China and finishing off Chiang Kai-shek? In China alone can a major decision be obtained by them in the present year. My thought therefore is that your treatment of the problem must be selective, and that the naval base at Colombo and the link with China via Calcutta have pre-eminence.

6. In my immediately following telegram I send you extracts from a telegram which I have received from General Chiang Kai-shek. Now that you know what Air Forces will be on the way, you will no doubt be able to decide whether anything can be done for him. I must point out that the collapse of China would liberate at least 15 and perhaps 20 Japanese divisions, and that thereafter a major invasion of India would indeed become a possibility.

Winston S. Churchill to President Franklin D. Roosevelt
(Churchill papers, 20/73)

19 April 1942
Personal and Secret
No. 71

I hope you will send *North Carolina* over to join *Washington* at Scapa. This will enable us to send *Renown* immediately and *Duke of York* as soon as possible afterwards to join our Eastern Fleet in the Indian Ocean. This force should prove a strong deterrent to Japanese attacks upon our convoy route to Egypt and India. There is no question of our seeking battle against superior forces, but we do not want to be sought out and found at a disadvantage. Admiralty information concurs with yours that there are indications that Japanese carriers have gone eastwards to replenish with aircraft after their severe losses at Colombo and Trimcomalee. All the more is there reason to use this lull to get into a sounder position.

2. As regards air reinforcements from Burma India and Ceylon Portal has drafted the note in my immediately following telegram after full discussion with Marshall and his officer.[1] On this basis therefore we

---

[1] In this note, Air Chief Marshal Portal stated: 'The air force suggestions referred to in the President's telegram to the Prime Minister No. 134 have been discussed by me with Marshall after careful joint examination by our respective staff officers. I agree that the quickest and soundest means of

welcome use you propose for *Ranger* and hope movement may go forward at full speed as you kindly suggest.

3. I also have had a long painful message from the Generalissimo[1] but I do not know what can be done beyond the measures now set on foot including especially the replenishment of AVG.[2] Alexander has done very well but his force is now little more than 10,000 effectives and if the Japanese continue to land new divisions it is only a question of time before they enter China from the South.

Winston S. Churchill to Francis Beattie[3]
(Churchill papers, 20/53)

19 April 1942

Dear Mr Francis Beattie,

I hope you will receive every support from the Electors of the Cathcart Division in your by-election.[4] At this critical time in the affairs of our country I ask all to vote for you as the Government candidate, irrespective of their Party affiliations. The Government in its waging of the war is supported by the Unionist, the Labour and the Liberal Parties, and I ask the Electors by voting for you now to demonstrate the national unity in our fight for life and freedom. To win we must have a united effort. A democratic government can do nothing without the support of the people. With that whole-hearted support great achievements can be obtained.

building up an air striking force is to bring US bombardment squadrons now in India up to full strength. It is welcome news to hear of 30 American Fortress and Liberator and 16 B25 aircraft already in or nearing India. To provide this force with a full reserve for immediate purposes I have agreed to transfer 34 heavy and medium bomber aircraft from British allocations. I have asked that these should be returned to us as early as possible as we ourselves are shortly forming 2 Liberator squadrons in India and another 3 either in Middle East or India as soon as possible afterwards. Nearly all the Liberator aircraft we are getting will be required for this purpose' (*Churchill papers, 20/73*).

[1] A request from Chiang Kai-shek for immediate and substantial air reinforcements.

[2] The 1st American Volunteer Group, known as the Flying Tigers, composed of pilots from the United States Army Air Forces, United States Navy, and United States Marine Corps, recruited under presidential sanction and commanded by Claire Lee Chennault (a retired US Army Air Corps officer who had worked in China since August 1937, first as military aviation adviser to Chiang Kai-shek in the early months of the Sino-Japanese War, then as director of a Chinese Air Force flight school). In action in China between 20 December 1941 and 14 July 1942. Their painted shark-faced fighters were among the most recognizable combat aircraft of the war. At a time of low morale in the United States, their victories over Japanese aircraft were a strong morale-raiser.

[3] Francis Beattie, 1885–1945. A baker; chairman of various bread bakeries in Scotland. Educated at Glasgow University. On active service, 1914–18. Member of the Sea Fish Commission, 1933–6. Director of Emergency Bread Supplies and Trade Adviser on Bread for Scotland, Ministry of Food, 1939–42. Conservative MP for the Cathcart Division of Glasgow from 1942 until his death.

[4] The by-election was occasioned by the death of the Conservative incumbent, Sir John Train (1873–1942). Beattie won the by-election and held the seat at the general election on 5 July 1945. He died in a road accident on 28 December 1945.

The Government must continue on its determined course until victory is won, knowing that it has that support to the full. All the world must know that the people of Scotland and Great Britain are whole heartedly behind the Government in our struggle at this time against barbarism and evil.

You will, I know, be a worthy representative of the Cathcart Division of Glasgow in the House of Commons. You know Glasgow's needs and the needs of the people and industries of the Clyde. You have already given valuable help to the national effort.

I look forward to welcoming in the House of Commons the reinforcements of your knowledge and experience and public spirit. They will be an asset to Parliament, both for the waging of war and for the solving of economic and social problems at home.

Yours sincerely,
Winston S. Churchill

Winston S. Churchill to Anthony Eden, and to General Hastings Ismay,
for the Chiefs of Staff Committee
(Churchill papers, 20/67)

19 April 1942
Secret

A large number of German and Italian prisoners of war are at present in Egypt and substantial numbers in India. Those in Egypt are a burden on the Army and a danger to internal security. In particular, there are 8,000 Germans who must now be well fed and truculent, and large numbers of troops are required to guard them.

2. Mr Hopkins suggested that the United States might gladly take these prisoners if asked. A start should certainly be made on the 8,000 Germans. There are many American ships returning empty from the Red Sea ports which might well carry them. No special escort would be necessary.

3. Pray let this matter be examined and proposals made for action. General Auchinleck should be consulted.[1]

---

[1] German and Italian prisoners of war were taken by ship to both the United States and Canada, where they remained for the duration of the war.

Winston S. Churchill to President Franklin D. Roosevelt
(Churchill papers, 20/73)

20 April 1942
Secret and Personal
No. 73

The Ambassador and the Heads of our Missions in Washington tell me that it may be necessary to create some combined bodies for dealing with supplies in addition to those we set up at Christmas. One example is food while our long range programmes of war production are also not yet covered by the existing machinery.

But if to the existing Raw Materials and Shipping Combined Boards we add two or three additional bodies, it appears that some means of pulling together all the inter-allied groups (other than the Chiefs of Staff) in order to get overall direction may be needed. I find that Harry Hopkins and our representatives are agreed about the need for a central focus of this kind.

We must in any case make some fresh appointments in connection with our various supply organisations in Washington. If, on your hearing Harry Hopkins' report of his talks with us, you agree about the desirability of setting up a single controlling body over the Combined Boards, I would at once appoint a representative with the appropriate status to work with your nominee.

Winston S. Churchill to President Franklin D. Roosevelt
(Churchill papers, 20/73)

20 April 1942
Personal and Secret
No. 74

Will you kindly consider whether you should not now make an offer to Pétain and or Darlan of British and American support if they will carry the French Fleet to Africa? Should you favour such a policy I will cable you exactly what we could put in on invitation to Morocco unopposed, and at what dates. It seems to me they ought to be offered blessings as well as cursings.

Winston S. Churchill to General Claude Auchinleck
(Churchill papers, 20/73)

20 April 1942
Personal and Secret

Have you seen the puff-balls[1] used against Tanks? I witnessed a demonstration last week which was most impressive. I understand you have 50,000. Is this so?

General Claude Auchinleck to Winston S. Churchill
(Churchill papers, 20/74)

21 April 1942   Cairo

Had useful demonstration[2] here a few days ago. Consider most effective especially against tank concentration.

RAF here have 17,000 and a further 50,000 en route.

Winston S. Churchill to A. V. Alexander and
Rear-Admiral Arthur Lumley Lyster[3]
(Churchill papers, 20/67)

21 April 1942

I am much obliged to you for your most interesting and full reply to my questions. Pray now let me have the best proposals possible for carrying *Illustrious* and *Formidable* to the highest pitch of efficiency in the shortest possible time.

Admiral Somerville's fleet is not seeking contact with the enemy at the present time, and it should be possible for intensive training to go forward in the calm waters in which he is now cruising and at the same time to meet replenishing aircraft sent round the Cape. If necessary, I could ask the President for an additional gift of Martlets.

[1] Puff-balls: aerial anti-tank bombs, invented by Colonel Jefferis.

[2] Of the 'puff-balls' referred to in the preceding document.

[3] (Arthur) Lumley Lyster, 1888–1957. On active naval service at Gallipoli, 1915, and in Italy, 1916–18 (DSO). Director of Staff Duties and Training, Admiralty, 1936–7. Rear-Admiral, 1939. Served at Scapa Flow, in Norwegian waters (despatches) and in Aircraft Carriers, Mediterranean Fleet (Battle of Taranto, CB), 1939–40. Fifth Sea Lord and Chief of Naval Air Services, 1941–2. Vice-Admiral, 1942. Flag Officer, Aircraft Carriers, Home Fleet, 1942–3 (CBE). Knighted, 1943. Flag Officer, Carrier Training, 1943–5.

Winston S. Churchill to General Hastings Ismay
(Churchill papers, 20/67)

22 April 1942

FORCE COMMANDERS FOR 'SLEDGEHAMMER'
(CHERBOURG LANDING)

These appointments should not have been made without my being consulted beforehand. My own idea is that, if General Alexander is free from Burma in the near future, as is likely on account of the shrinkage of his Command, he should be Supreme Commander of all the forces employed upon the task. Moreover, I am not convinced that Admiral Ramsey[1] is the best selection, though his position at Dover is convenient. General Marshall spoke to me very earnestly about the need of his being consulted before a decision was taken.

I think, therefore, these appointments must be considered provisional.

President Franklin D. Roosevelt to Winston S. Churchill
(Churchill papers, 20/74)

22 April 1942
No. 137

In reply to your Nos. 71 and 72 all plans have been completed for movement of agreed upon air planes to India at the earliest possible moment. Bad weather held up assembly of pursuit airplanes for shipment on *Ranger* but this movement is completed and *Ranger* should leave on Tuesday, April 21. Your approval of the utilization of Liberators (B-24) makes it possible for us to install ASV[2] equipment on these airplanes prior to movement to India. This will prove a great help in reconnaissance missions over the Bay of Bengal or the Indian Ocean. Seven Flying Fortresses should leave the United States within forty eight hours. Twenty four additional Libera-

---

[1] Bertram Home Ramsay, 1883–1945. Entered the Royal Navy, 1898; commanded Monitor 25, Dover Patrol, 1915; HMS *Broke*, 1916–18. Chief of Staff, China Station, 1929–31. On the Staff of the Imperial Defence College, 1931–3. Commanded HMS *Royal Sovereign*, 1933–5. Rear-Admiral and Chief of Staff, Home Fleet, 1935. Retired, 1938. Recalled, 1939. Flag Officer, Dover, 1939–42. Knighted, 1940. Flag Officer, Expeditionary Force, 1942. Naval Commander, Eastern Task Force, Mediterranean, 1943. Allied Naval Commander-in-Chief, Expeditionary Force, 1944–5. Killed in an aeroplane accident in France, January 1945. His 'finest hour' was as the naval officer in command of Operation 'Dynamo', the evacuation of the Dunkirk beachhead, in June 1940.

[2] ASV: Air to Surface Vessel, radar for maritime patrol aircraft. A British invention, ASV radar was first flown successfully on 17 August 1937. It could locate submarines from the air at a distance of 10–15 miles. It had a range above water of up to 36 miles. After initial difficulties with maintenance and training, on 17 March 1942 an improved version was flown in a Halifax bomber.

tors (B-24) should leave the United States shortly after May 10. This delay essential to provide them with satisfactory nose armament.

The twenty one B-25 which we took over from you should leave the United States during the coming week. This delay caused by additional equipment not on your airplanes such as automatic pilots being installed prior to this movement. Aircraft carrier *Ranger* will be available for further ferrying additional airplanes to India via Africa on its return from West Africa. To what extent and with what equipment it will be loaded will be determined after present movement starts. Availability of aircraft pilots and the time for turn around will all determine load and destination of second trip if it is made.

AVG for the time being has a total of 247 airplanes already at Karachi or east of Karachi or en route by air or by sea.

I assure you that everything possible is being done to meet requirement of AVG in China and your forces in India.

President Franklin D. Roosevelt to Winston S. Churchill
(Churchill papers, 20/74)

22 April 1942
Priority
Secret and Personal
No. 139

OPERATIONS IN WESTERN EUROPE

Replying to your No. 70, I am delighted with the agreement which was reached between you and your military advisers and Marshall and Hopkins. They have reported to me of the unanimity of opinion relative to the proposal which they carried with them and I appreciate ever so much your personal message confirming this.

I believe that this move will be very disheartening to Hitler and may well be the wedge by which his downfall will be accomplished. I am very heartened at the prospect and you can be sure that our army will approach the latter with great enthusiasm and vigour.

I would like to think over a bit the question of a public announcement. I will let you know my feeling about this soon.

I believe that any junction between Japanese and Germans is going to take a great deal of doing but realize that the remote prospect of this is something that must be watched.

In the meantime as you will have seen in the Press we have had a good crack at Japan by air and I am hoping that we can make it very difficult for them to keep too many of their big ships in the Indian Ocean. I will have a talk with Pound about this in a day or two.

I have a cordial message from Stalin telling me that he is sending Molotov[1] and a General to visit me. I am suggesting that they come here first before going to England. Will you let me know if you have any other view about this. I am quite pleased about the Stalin message.

While our mutual difficulties are many I am frank to say that I feel better about the war than at any time in the past two years.

I want to thank you for your cordial reception of Marshall and Hopkins.

Winston S. Churchill: reflection
('The Hinge of Fate', pages 288–9)

[22 April 1942]

Let me now set out my own view, which was persistent, of what had so far been decided and of what I thought should be done.

In planning the gigantic enterprise of 1943 it was not possible for us to lay aside all other duties. Our first Imperial obligation was to defend India from the Japanese invasion, by which it seemed it was already menaced. Moreover, this task bore a decisive relation to the whole war. To leave four hundred millions of His Majesty's Indian subjects, to whom we were bound in honour, to be ravaged and overrun, as China had been, by the Japanese would have been a deed of shame. But also to allow the Germans and Japanese to join hands in India or the Middle East involved a measureless disaster to the Allied cause. It ranked in my mind almost as the equal of the retirement of Soviet Russia behind the Urals, or even of their making a separate peace with Germany. At this date I did not deem either of these contingencies likely. I had faith in the power of the Russian armies and nation fighting in defence of their native soil. Our Indian Empire however, with all its glories, might fall an easy prey. I had to place this point of view before the American envoys. Without active British aid India might be conquered in a few months. Hitler's subjugation of Soviet Russia would be a much longer, and to him more costly, task. Before it was accomplished the Anglo-American command of the

[1] Vyacheslav Mikhailovich Scriabin, 1890–1986. Used the underground name 'Molotov'. Took part in the first Russian Revolution of 1905 as a student; arrested and deported to Siberia. Secretary of *Pravda*, 1911. Exiled for a second time, 1915. Member of the Executive of the Petrograd Soviet, 1917. Chairman of the Council of People's Commissars, 1930–41. People's Commissar for Foreign Affairs, 1939–46. Deputy Chairman of the State Defence Committee, 1941–5. Took part in the Teheran, Yalta, and Potsdam conferences, 1943–5. Foreign Minister, 1946–9, 1953–6. First Deputy Chairman, Council of Ministers, 1953–7. Soviet Ambassador to Mongolia, 1957–60; to the International Atomic Energy Agency, Vienna, 1960–2.

air would have been established beyond challenge. Even if all else failed this would be finally decisive.

I was in complete accord with what Hopkins called 'a frontal assault upon the enemy in Northern France in 1943'. But what was to be done in the interval? The main armies could not simply be preparing all that time. Here there was a wide diversity of opinion. General Marshall had advanced the proposal that we should attempt to seize Brest or Cherbourg, preferably the latter, or even both, during the early autumn of 1942. The operation would have to be almost entirely British. The Navy, the air, two-thirds of the troops, and such landing-craft as were available must be provided by us. Only two or three American divisions could be found. These, it must be remembered, were very newly raised. It takes at least two years and a very strong professional cadre to form first-class troops. The enterprise was therefore one on which British Staff opinion would naturally prevail. Clearly there must be an intensive technical study of the problem.

Nevertheless I by no means rejected the idea at the outset; but there were other alternatives which lay in my mind. The first was the descent on French North-West Africa (Morocco, Algeria and Tunisia), which for the present was known as 'Gymnast', and which ultimately emerged in the great operation 'Torch'. I had a second alternative plan for which I always hankered and which I thought could be undertaken as well as the invasion of French North Africa. This was 'Jupiter' – namely, the liberation of Northern Norway.

[...]

The attempt to form a bridgehead at Cherbourg seemed to me more difficult, less attractive, less immediately helpful or ultimately fruitful. It would be better to lay our right claw on French North Africa, tear with our left at the North Cape, and wait a year without risking our teeth upon the German fortified front across the Channel.

Josef Stalin to Winston S. Churchill
(Churchill papers, 20/74)

22 April 1942
Most Secret
Most Immediate

Recently the Soviet Government received from Mr Eden the drafts of two agreements between the USSR and Great Britain which differed in some material respects from the text of agreements which were under discussion while Mr Eden was in Moscow. In view of the fact that these drafts reveal fresh divergences of opinion which it would be difficult to solve by correspondence the Soviet Government have decided, despite all the obstacles, to send Mr Molotov to London in order, by means of personal discussion, to dispose of all the matters which stand in the way of the signing of the agreements. This is all the more necessary because question of opening a second front in Europe (which was raised in the last message addressed to me by President of the United States in which he invited Mr Molotov to go to Washington to discuss this matter) calls for a preliminary exchange of views between representatives of our two Governments.

Accept my greetings and my wishes for success in your fight against the enemies of Great Britain.

Winston S. Churchill to Robert Barrington-Ward
(Churchill papers, 20/53)

22 April 1942

My dear Mr Barrington-Ward,

Thank you very much for your letter, which certainly enables me to see to some extent what you have in mind.

At present I am advised by the Chiefs of the Staff Committee, of whom Sir Alan Brooke is Chairman. The advantage of dealing with the responsible executive heads of the Service Departments is that they have the great handling machinery in their control and can give immediate effect to what is decided. I do not quite understand what relationship the new 'Chief Professional Adviser' would have with the Chiefs of the Staff. Would he be able to give them directions? If so, they and their Ministers would certainly appeal to the Cabinet, as they are fully entitled to do.

Again, should I not run the risk of having conflicting advice given me by the 'Chief Professional Adviser' on the one hand and the Chiefs of the Staff Committee on the other? What happens if I do not agree with the advice of the 'Chief Professional Adviser', and the Cabinet when appealed to agrees with me?

As at present informed I am bound to say I do not see how such a scheme could possibly work, but perhaps you will be able to explain it more fully to General Ismay when he comes to see you this afternoon.

Yours v. sincerely,
Winston S. Churchill

Harold Nicolson: diary
('Harold Nicolson, Diaries and Letters', page 223)

22 April 1942

CONVERSATION WITH MALCOLM MACDONALD[1]

Malcolm had been lunching today with Winston. He said that the latter has no illusions at all about the decline in his popularity. 'I am like a bomber pilot', he said 'I go out night after night, and I know that one night I shall not return.' Malcolm is in fact rather appalled by the slump in Winston's popularity. A year ago he would have put his stock at 108, and today, in his opinion, it is as low as 65. He admits that a success will enable it to recover. But the old enthusiasm is dead for ever. How foul is public life and popular ingratitude!

Josef Stalin to Winston S. Churchill
(Churchill papers, 20/74)

23 April 1942
Personal and Secret

I thank you for the readiness expressed by you to address early in May to Germany and Finland a warning regarding the use by England of poison gases should Germany and Finland resort to this weapon in the war against the USSR.

I express my gratitude to you for your readiness to supply 1,000 tons of iprite and 1,000 tons of chlorine. But seeing that the USSR has a greater need of other chemical products, the Soviet Government would like to receive 1,000 tons of hypochloride of calcium and 1,000 tons of chloramine in place of the above mentioned products, or 2,000 tons of liquid chlorine in carboys should it prove impossible to supply these latter products.

[1] Malcolm John MacDonald, 1901–81. Son of Ramsay MacDonald. Educated at Bedales and Queen's College, Oxford. Labour MP for Bassetlaw, 1929–31 (National Labour 1931–5); for Ross and Cromarty, 1936–45. Parliamentary Under-Secretary, Dominions Office, 1931–5. Privy Councillor, 1935. Secretary of State for Dominion Affairs, 1935–8, 1938–9; Colonial Secretary, 1935, 1938–40. Minister of Health, 1940–1. High Commissioner, Canada, 1941–6. Governor-General of Malaya, Singapore, and British Borneo, 1946–8. Commissioner General for South-East Asia, 1948–55. High Commissioner, India, 1955–60. Governor-General of Kenya, 1963–4; High Commissioner, 1964–5. British Special Representative in East and Central Africa, 1965–6; in Africa, 1966–9. Order of Merit, 1969.

The Soviet Government propose to send the Deputy [?Peoples] Commissar of Chemical Industry, Andrei Georgiyevich Kasatkin,[1] to London in the capacity of their expert in questions of chemical defence and counter-attack.

Winston S. Churchill: Secret Session speech
('Secret Session Speeches', pages 46–75)

23 April 1942   House of Commons

THE WAR SITUATION

Since Japan became our enemy and the United States our Ally after December 7, the weight of the war upon us has become far more severe and we have sustained a painful series of misfortunes in the Far East. Apart from the stubborn and brave defence of the Bataan Peninsula by the United States, the brunt of the Japanese attacks has fallen almost entirely upon us and the Dutch. The United States fleet has not yet regained the command of the Pacific which was lost after Pearl Harbour: and while we are at war with Germany and Italy, we do not possess the naval resources necessary to maintain the command of the Indian Ocean against any heavy detachment from the main Japanese fleet. Before the Japanese entered the war, we were already fully extended in the North Sea, Atlantic, and Mediterranean theatres by sea, land, and air. We have drawn all possible forces to meet our new, fresh, and most formidable antagonist. But in spite of all we could do and the risks we ran and are running, we have been and are at present out-numbered by the sea, land, and air forces of Japan throughout the Far Eastern theatre. This fact must be faced by all who wish to understand what has happened and what is going to happen.

From the beginning of our struggle with Hitler, I have always hoped for the entry of the United States; and although the ideal was to have America in while Japan remained out, I did not think that the injuries Japan would certainly inflict upon us in our ill-guarded and even denuded Eastern theatre would be too heavy a price to pay for having the immense resources and power of the United States bound indissolubly to our side and to our cause. That is still my feeling. But I frankly admit that

---

[1] Andrei Georgiyevich Kasatkin, 1903–63. One of the organisers of the Soviet chemical industry. Deputy People's Commissar of Chemical Industry, 1941–5. At the time of his death he was First Vice-President of the State Commission of Standards, Measures and Measuring Instruments. Holder of, among other orders, the Order of Lenin, the Order of the Red Banner of Labour, and the Order of Merit.

the violence, fury, skill, and might of Japan has far exceeded anything that we had been led to expect. The Japanese military performances in China had not seemed remarkable. The Chinese had always been a weak nation, divided, and traditionally unwarlike. We knew that they were very ill-armed and ill-supplied, especially with every weapon that matters in modern war. And yet for four and a half years the Japanese, using as many as a million men at a time, had failed to quell or conquer them. This seemed to give a line as to form. The event was different. Neither, of course, were we prepared for the temporary eclipse and paralysis of the United States sea power in the Pacific, which followed from the disaster at Pearl Harbor. The combination of these two factors has been very adverse to us.

Our military position at the outbreak of the Japanese war was as follows. I had obtained from President Roosevelt in October last shipping sufficient to carry two divisions additional to our ordinary heavy convoys from this country to the Middle East. The first of these divisions, the 18th, was rounding the Cape in the early days of December. It was destined for the Levant–Caspian front, which it then seemed so necessary to reinforce, and the 17th Indian Division was already preparing to move from India to this same theatre, where the dangers of 1942 seemed mainly to lie. Both these divisions were immediately diverted to the Malay Peninsula. In the few days before I left for the United States we set in motion to India or Malaya other very considerable forces which we had on the water, including six antiaircraft and antitank units and two hundred and fifty aircraft. All these factors were sorely needed either in Libya, where General Auchinleck's offensive was at its height, or on the threatened Levant–Caspian front. The fact that they, and many other forces that have followed them, were turned to meet the new antagonist in no way lessens the need for them in the Middle East. This may become painfully apparent should the magnificent Russian defence of the approaches to the Caucasus be beaten down, or General Rommel be able to assume the offensive against Egypt in superior strength.

The House must face the position squarely. Not only have we failed to stem the advance of the new enemy, but we have had to weaken seriously the hopeful operations we were carrying on against the old. In all, in the first two months of the Japanese war, up to the time of the fall of Singapore, we had landed in the Malay Peninsula, or moved from India into Burma, 70,000 troops, 300 guns, a certain number of tanks, and 350 aircraft – all of which, I repeat, were taken away from actual fighting operations elsewhere. At the same time we began to move the Australian Army away from the Levant–Caspian front to sustain the Dutch in the

East Indies or, as has since turned out, for a large number of them, to defend the homeland of Australia.

The valiant and hitherto successful resistance of Russia has alone rendered these highly dangerous diversions possible without disastrous consequences so far. In spite of the results up to date, I remain convinced that the broad strategic dispositions which we made of our forces prior to the Japanese attack, and the redistributions made after that attack, were the best in our power. Sometimes, though not always, people are wise after the event, but it is also possible to be wise before the event and yet not have the power to stop it happening. In war misfortunes may come from faults or errors in the High Command. They may also come from the enemy being far too strong, or fighting far too well. It is easy when the tide is adverse to contend that alterations in the structure of the war direction would have made or will make amends for the vast and gaping lack of men and resources or power of transportation. It is easy, but it may not be true.

During these anxious times a series of unexampled losses fell upon the Royal Navy. On September 27 the *Nelson* had had her bows blown in by a torpedo and was put out of action for six months. On November 13 the *Ark Royal* was sunk in the Mediterranean by a single torpedo – a feature most disquieting to our naval constructors. On November 25 the *Barham* foundered off Libya from a volley of torpedoes, with a loss of 800 men. Here again chance played a hard part.

The *Prince of Wales* and the *Repulse* arrived at Singapore on December 2. This seemed to be a timely moment. It was hoped that their presence there might be a deterrent upon the war party in Japan, and it was intended that they should vanish as soon as possible into the blue. I have already explained to the House how they became involved in a local operation against Japanese transports in the Gulf of Siam which led to their destruction. On the night of December 9, in view of the news we had received about the heavy losses of the American fleet at Pearl Harbor, I proposed to the Chiefs of the Staff that the *Prince of Wales* and *Repulse* should join the undamaged portion of the American fleet in order to sustain the position in the Pacific. The matter was to be further considered next day, but in the morning arrived the news of the loss of both these great ships.

We had now no modern or modernized capital ships in the Indian Ocean. The remnants of the American Battle Fleet from Pearl Harbour were withdrawn a further two thousand miles or more to the Californian bases. Since then from San Francisco to Aden or Capetown, distances of about fourteen thousand miles, there has been no surface fleet capable of fighting a general action with the navy of Japan.

A further sinister stroke was to come. On the early morning of December 19 half a dozen Italians in unusual diving suits were captured floundering about in the harbour of Alexandria. Extreme precautions have been taken for some time past against the varieties of human torpedo or one-man submarine entering our harbours. Not only are nets and other obstructions used, but underwater charges are exploded at frequent irregular intervals in the fairway. Nonetheless, these men had penetrated the harbour. Four hours later explosions occurred in the bottoms of the *Valiant* and *Queen Elizabeth*, produced by limpet bombs fixed with extraordinary courage and ingenuity, the effect of which was to blow large holes in the bottoms of both ships and to flood several compartments, thus putting them both out of action for many months. One ship will soon be ready again, the other is still in the floating dock at Alexandria, a constant target for enemy air attack. Thus, we had no longer any battle squadron in the Mediterranean. *Barham* had gone, and now *Valiant* and *Queen Elizabeth* were completely out of action.

Both these ships floated on an even keel, they looked all right from the air. The enemy were for some time unaware of the success of their attack, and it is only now that I feel it possible to make this disclosure to the House, even in the strictness of a Secret Session. The Italian fleet still contains four or five battleships, several times repaired, of the new Littorio[1] or of the modernized class. According to pre-war notions and indeed all paper calculations, there was no reason why a large German and Italian army should not have been ferried across to invade not merely Libya or Palestine or Syria, but Egypt itself. The sea defence of the Nile Valley had to be confined to our submarine and destroyer flotillas with a few cruisers and, of course, to shore-based air forces. For this reason it was necessary to transfer a part of our shore-based torpedo-carrying aircraft from the south and east coasts of England, where they were soon to be needed, to the North African shore. This movement was justifiable because of the absence of any preparation for immediate invasion

---

[1] Littorio: Italian battleship class, also known as the Vittorio Veneto class. The most modern battleships used by Italy in the Second World War, and among the fastest European battleships. Three were built: *Vittorio Veneto*, hit by an aerial torpedo at the Battle of Matapan (27–9 March 1941) and interned by the Allies in September 1943; *Littorio*, sunk in shallow water at the Battle of Taranto (11–12 November 1940), later raised, also interned by the Allies in September 1943; and *Roma*, sunk by German air-launched anti-ship missiles while sailing into Allied internment in September 1943 (the first major warship to be sunk by guided missiles). A fourth Littorio class battleship, *Imperia*, was never completed, and was scrapped after the war.

apparent on the enemy's side of the Channel and because of his evident preoccupation with Russia. We may say these arrangements for the defence of Egypt have so far been successful.

The very opportune and brilliant action by Admiral Vian when, favoured by a happy slant of wind for his smoke screen, he made the Italian battleship turn tail in broad daylight by a mere attack of light cruisers and destroyers has been rightly applauded. It has, it will now be seen, a significance of a special character. We were, of course, left very bare in home waters. However, I have no doubt other resources will be at hand before the main German armies can again be transported to the west, and the invasion danger again become imminent.

These events and their sequence, which I have mentioned to the House in Secret Session, have a bearing upon the escape of the *Scharnhorst* and *Gneisenau* from their uncomfortable station at Brest. I have been impressed by the shock, which the passage of these two ships through the Channel gave to the loyal masses of the British nation. Personally, with my special knowledge, I thought it a very annoying incident but not comparable at all to the other happenings I have just described. Our torpedo-carrying aircraft were depleted by the needs of Egypt. As to the Navy, we do not for obvious reasons keep capital ships in the narrow seas. Attention has, however, also been drawn to the fact that there were only six destroyers capable of attacking the German battle cruisers. Where, it is asked, were all the rest of our flotillas? The answer is that they were and are out on the approaches from the Atlantic, convoying the food and munitions from the United States without which we cannot live.

However, there is a good plan which, should invasion again become imminent, will very rapidly multiply the flotillas in the narrow waters. The photographic reconnaissance of the enemy harbours, basins, and river mouths, made daily when the weather permits, should keep us well advised of any gathering of barges similar to that which took place in the summer and autumn of 1940. Moreover, in 1940 an invading force of perhaps 150,000 picked men might have created mortal havoc in our midst. But now our home army and Home Guard have grown and improved to such an extent that it would not be much use an invader coming with less than six or seven hundred thousand men and six or seven armoured divisions with many thousands of vehicles. The enormous shipping movements and air activities which would be the indispensable prelude to this would certainly be detected. We therefore feel entitled to use the flotillas to the utmost on feeding the island and escorting the outward-bound troop and Russian convoys, and we also felt entitled to send to the African shore a considerable proportion of our coastal torpedo-carrying aircraft after the disappearance of our battle fleet in the Mediterranean. We hold ourselves answerable in the gravest manner to watch and handle judiciously this invasion danger, and I do not think you will ever have to run again the frightful hazards through which we passed in 1940.

I will digress for a moment from my general theme to comment further upon the passage of the *Scharnhorst* and *Gneisenau* up the Channel and through the Straits of Dover. Most people thought this very astonishing and very alarming. They could have broken south and perhaps got into the Mediterranean. They could have gone out into the Atlantic as commerce raiders. They could have gone north about and tried to reach their own home waters by the Norwegian fiords. But the one way which seemed impossible to the general public was that they could come up the Channel and through the Straits of Dover. I will therefore read an extract from the Admiralty appreciation which was written on the 2nd February, ten days before the cruisers broke out, and when their exercise and steam trials and arrival of escorting German destroyers showed what they had in mind:

'At first sight this passage up the Channel appears hazardous for the Germans. It is probable, however, that, as their heavy ships are not fully efficient, they would prefer such passage, relying for their security on their destroyers and aircraft, which are efficient, and knowing full well that we have no heavy ships with which to oppose them in the Channel. We might well, therefore, find the two battle cruisers and the eight-inch cruiser with five large and five small destroyers, also, say, twenty fighters constantly overhead (with reinforcements within call), proceeding up Channel.

'Taking up all factors into consideration, it appears that the German ships can pass east up the Channel with much less risk than they will incur if they attempt an ocean passage to Norway, and as it is considered the Germans will evade danger until they are fully worked up, the Channel passage appears to be their most probable direction if and when they leave Brest.'

I have read this document to the House because I am anxious that Members should realize that our affairs are not conducted entirely by simpletons and dunderheads as the comic papers try to depict, and in particular that the Admiralty, which I regard as an incomparable machine for British protection, in spite of all the misfortunes and accidents that have happened, deserves a very broad measure of confidence and gratitude. Considering their knowledge and foresight and the intense, indefatigable care which has brought us thus far safely on this hard voyage, I think they deserve to be regarded with respect. Any featherhead can have confidence in times of victory, but the test is to have faith when things are going wrong for the time being, and when things happen which cannot be explained in public.

I now return to my narrative and general argument. The House will see that in November and December last year in a few weeks we lost or had put out of action for a long time seven great ships or more than one-third of our battleships and battle cruisers, and that this happened at a time when we were fully extended and had to meet the attack of a new fresh and tremendous enemy and while our great Ally was temporarily entirely crippled at sea. It is upon this background and with this accompaniment that I will make a very few observations about the tragedy and disaster of Singapore.

On December 7, 1941, there were in Singapore and the Malay Peninsula about sixty thousand British, Australian, and Indian troops, and immediately after the declaration we set in motion to Malaya, as I have described, between forty and fifty thousand others, including a high proportion of technical arms. After a long rear-guard action down the Malay Peninsula, there were, according to the War Office figures, about one hundred thousand men gathered in the island of Singapore by the morning of February 3. On the night of February 8 about five thousand Japanese made a lodgement on the north-western corner of the island and were gradually reinforced by landings from other points until perhaps thirty thousand men had been landed.

After five or six days of confused but not very severe fighting, the army and fortress surrendered. The Japanese have not stated the number of prisoners they have taken, but it does not seem that there was very much bloodshed. This episode and all that led up to it seems to be out of harmony with anything that we have experienced or performed in the present war. Many explanatory factors are mentioned: the absence of the Air Force, owing to the enemy's domination of our airfields; the dispiriting effects of the long retreat upon the troops engaged in it; the enervating effects of the climate upon all Europeans; the fact that some of the reinforcements had been a long time on board ship; and, above all, the embarrassment to the defence caused by it being intermingled with a city containing at that time upwards of one million human beings of many races and conditions.

In all these circumstances I do not at all wonder that requests should be made for an inquiry by a Royal Commission, not only into what took place upon the spot in the agony of Singapore but into all the arrangements which had been made beforehand. I am convinced, however, that this would not be good for our country, and that it would hamper the prosecution of the war. Australian accounts reflect upon the Indian troops. Other credible witnesses disparage the Australians. The lack of any effective counterattack by the 18th Division, which arrived in such high spirits and good order, and never seem to have had their chance, is criticized. The generalship is criticized.

Here is an endless field of recrimination. Most of those concerned are prisoners. General Wavell, who was in charge of the whole ABDA[1] area from January 15 onwards, is far too busy grappling with new perils. We, too, have enough trouble on our hands to cope with the present and the future, and I could not in any circumstances consent to adding such a burden, for a heavy burden it would be, to those which we have to bear. I must ask the House to support the government in this decision, which is not taken in any ignoble desire to shield individuals or safeguard the administration, but solely in the interests of the state and for the successful prosecution of the war. The premature fall of Singapore led to failures of the resistance in Java and Sumatra. But this might have happened in any case in view of the decisive Japanese superiority in numbers and organization.

What has happened in Burma? About two divisions of Indian and Burmese troops, with a very few British battalions, have resisted and delayed the northward advance of powerful Japanese forces for over two months. West of the Sittang River they were reinforced by a brigade of tanks drawn from General Auchinleck's command, and by other British reinforcements. The remains of this force, which altogether had comprised perhaps the equivalent of three divisions, were driven back on Rangoon and were surrounded there. About this time, General Alexander arrived by air from England and infused new vigour into the wearied and outnumbered troops. Having very thoroughly destroyed the facilities of the city and harbour, he cut his way out to the north with his whole force and all their transport after hard fighting. Meanwhile a number of Chinese divisions had been slowly making their way southward and gradually came into line upon our eastern flank. These Chinese divisions are about as strong as British brigade groups, but they seem very capable of fighting the Japanese with constancy and courage.

A long, thin front was established diagonally facing southwards, and this front is being slowly driven north towards Mandalay and Lashio.

[1] ABDA: American, British, Dutch, Australian (in the Far East and Pacific).

The Japanese have been greatly aided by disloyal Burmese, and both Siamese and Burmese contingents are fighting with them. The British Imperial forces are astride the Irrawaddy and the main Rangoon–Burma road and railway. They are outnumbered by the Japanese who are being steadily reinforced from Rangoon, where at least one and possibly two fresh divisions have lately been landed.

General Wavell has been receiving in India all the aircraft we can transport and service, to the temporary detriment of General Auchinleck's operations in Libya. The United States are sending powerful air reinforcements, both in India and China. All this takes time, and the number of airfields at our disposal in Burma and the protection which it was possible to afford to them have not been sufficient to enable the British Air Force to maintain itself, and successive reinforcements have been wiped out, many of them on the ground as they arrived. General Wavell has also to consider the defence of north-eastern India, which may at any time be gravely menaced. He is not therefore at present in a position to denude himself to any large extent, and he must not fritter away his resources. The difficulty is to get established on a sufficiently large scale and to maintain supplies and services in the test of Japanese superiority. Without this it is like throwing good money after bad, or throwing snowballs into a furnace to keep down the temperature. Efforts are being made to re-equip the American Volunteer Group working with the Chinese under the American general, General Stilwell, who has in every way shown himself a fine soldier and good comrade, and who has established the closest relations with General Alexander.

At the present time there is very little air support for our troops or for the Chinese, and Generalissimo Chiang Kai-shek has complained to me that he was promised air support which is not forthcoming when he ordered his divisions to march south into Burma. Mandalay and other towns have been the subjects of very severe air raids with great slaughter, and a huge flight of refugees is moving northward towards China, or westward in the hopes of reaching India over extremely primitive and half-constructed roads. Typhus and cholera have made their appearance behind our harassed front. Treachery and infiltration are rife. A tragic fate impends upon the mass of refugees collected to the north of Mandalay. In the midst of these scenes of indescribable misery and ruin, the Governor-General,[1] whom we know so well in this House as Minister of Agriculture a couple of years ago, and his devoted wife have been a fountain of courage and inspiration.

[1] Reginald Dorman-Smith.

The advance of the enemy has been greatly slowed down by the exertions of General Alexander and his American colleague and by the very brave fighting of the British, Indian, and Chinese troops still on the front. Our Imperial forces are however reduced to very small proportions. There is no means of bringing reinforcements to them by sea: the Japanese hold complete command of the Bay of Bengal, and only trickles of men and supplies can come over the mountain roads and tracks from Assam. General Wavell has the duty of distributing his resources to the best advantage, and we are sending him everything we can, having regard to our other responsibilities, which are neither few nor easy.

I cannot encourage the House to expect good news from the Burma theatre. The best that can be hoped for is that the retreat will be as slow as possible and give time for other factors to make their weight tell.

At this point we may consider what Japanese strategy is likely to be. So far as we know, the Japanese have seventy-two field divisions with some additional brigades and a mass of trained soldiers which is certainly not less than two million additional behind them. Of these seventy-two divisions, twenty-seven are in the so-called ABDA area including Burma, fifteen are in China, twenty are opposite Russia in Manchuria, and only ten are left in Japan. The Japanese Army in the ABDA area threatens simultaneously Australia, India, and, through Burma, China. They have conquered the whole of Malaya, the Philippines, and the Dutch East Indies. They have destroyed or captured the following divisions of the Allies or their equivalent. British and Indian, six; Dutch, three; United States, two; Filipinos, three or four. Total fourteen or fifteen. They may have lost a hundred thousand killed and wounded, but none of their divisional formations has been destroyed, and I make no doubt they can easily replace all casualties. They cost about a quarter to feed and carry of what British and still more American troops require. They certainly show no inferiority when they get to the spot.

The Japanese armies, navy, and air force, working in close harmonious combination, being absolutely fresh after their many years of preparation and inculcation of war as the highest art and duty, having brought their plans up to date by fullest information and closest study of the German victories in Europe, and having added their own jungle craft thereto, have established themselves in little more than four months in the whole of these wide regions, which they call their Asiatic Co-Prosperity Sphere, from Luzon to Rangoon, and from the northern approaches of Australia to the southern approaches of China. In this vast area they have forces largely superior to any that we can bring to bear for a long time. They are no doubt sprawled and spread widely, but they are consolidating their positions to the full extent of their saved-up resources.

Which way will they go? Where will they strike next? Australia naturally fears immediate invasion, and the United States, which has accepted responsibility for everything east of a line drawn west of Australia, has sent and is sending continuous strong reinforcements. We have transported back to Australia a large part of the Australian Imperial forces from the Middle East. We do not see here that the Japanese would get great advantages by invading Australia in force. By so doing they would commit themselves to a very formidable campaign, at a great distance from home, with American sea power, as it regains its strength, operative on their communications. No doubt the Japanese will do their utmost to threaten and alarm Australia and to establish lodgments and bases on the northern part of Australia in order to procure the greatest locking up of Allied forces in that continent. We have done and will continue to do everything in our power to sustain our kith and kin. I have also procured from President Roosevelt a substantial reinforcement of United States troops for New Zealand, whose attitude and morale have been admirable. But neither Great Britain nor the United States must be drawn into immobilizing in Australia undue numbers of the limited forces which they can transport across the sea within any given period.

Alternatively, the Japanese may invade India. There is no doubt of their ability, if they chose to concentrate their efforts, to invade and overrun a large part of India, to take Calcutta and Madras, and certainly to make very cruel air raids upon defence-less Indian cities.

The Japanese have not told us what they intend to do, so I can only make a guess, which I do under all reserves, knowing well the fallibility of human foresight in the fog of war. It would seem, however, looking at it from their point of view, that their best plan would be to push right ahead northwards from Burma into China, and try to finish up Chinese resistance and the great Chinese leader, Generalissimo Chiang Kai-shek. We have not noticed any Japanese movement lately, which is inconsistent with this idea, but there are several, which support it. Certainly by driving China out of the war and possibly installing another puppet government in China, which would be their ally, Japan would seem to be greatly furthering her own interests.

China is the only place where Japan can obtain a major decision in her favour in 1942. Moreover, let me point out, this process, if successful, would be to Japan one of contraction and not of further perhaps excessive expansion. It would be entirely in harmony with a Japanese attack on

Russia, for which many preparations have been made. It would certainly release a good many Japanese divisions for further enterprise in a subsequent year. Of course, this appreciation may be wrong, but it is what seems most in the interests of the enemy and therefore most to be feared.

Before I leave the Far Eastern theatre with its dark panorama of ruin, actual, and prospective, I will deal with the naval situation and the air situation as it affects naval operations in the Indian Ocean and the Bay of Bengal.

The surprise of Pearl Harbour threw the American Pacific Fleet, on which so much depended, out of action for the time being; and though the losses have been largely made good, the American fleet has remained separated from the enemy by the vast distances of the Pacific, and has been mainly concerned with maintaining communications with Australia, along which considerable forces are passing. The Japanese Navy lies in the centre of the scene, and like the Japanese Army it can strike in either direction. Our Eastern Fleet in the Indian Ocean cannot tell with any certainty what size or strength of Japanese vessels will emerge from the Malay Archipelago, through the Straits of Malacca or the Straits of Sunda. We cannot tell how far the Japanese preoccupations about the American Navy will force them to retain the bulk of their naval power in their home waters or in the Eastern Pacific. We do not know whether the Japanese wish to fight a battle with any American naval forces which may be operating in the islands between the American continent and Australia.

Obviously, if the main part of the Japanese Navy comes west into the Indian Ocean we, with our other tasks on hand, would not be able to fight the fleet action. On the other hand, when and in proportion as they get tied to the American sphere by the reviving strength of the American Navy, our control of the Indian Ocean will improve, provided of course we are not brought to action and defeated in the meantime. The fact, however, that the Japanese have at present a move either way, and can undoubtedly move our way in largely superior strength, confronts the Admiralty and the Commander-in-Chief of our Eastern Fleet with most vexatious and difficult problems, not capable perhaps for some months of a satisfactory solution.

After virtual annihilation of British, Dutch, and United States light forces in Javanese waters and the loss of Singapore, Java, and Sumatra, we naturally considered Ceylon as a key point we have to hold. This cannot be done without adequate shore-based aircraft and ample antiaircraft artillery. Our resources were limited and there are, as I have said, many clamant calls upon them. However, casting aside a great many other needs, we did manage to give a considerable measure of protection to Colombo and Trincomalee, and also to place in Ceylon military forces sufficient to require a substantial invading army to overcome them. All through March we were most anxious about Ceylon because of our weak condition there. But by the end of March we began to feel a little more comfortable; and this feeling persists so far.

In the last days of March, Admiral Somerville, who commands our Eastern Fleet, and who, as I said, is fresh from two years of almost continuous fighting in the Mediterranean and has conducted at least twenty extremely tricky and hazardous operations there – who is perhaps more familiar than any other man except Admiral Cunningham with the conditions of modern air attack on ships of war, who has run many convoys into Malta, raided Genoa, and taken part in all kinds of actions – formed the impression, from what scraps of information he could pick up, that a Japanese incursion into the Bay of Bengal was probable. It was also thought that there might well be a certain number of aircraft carriers supported by three Kongo battle cruisers. These are old battle cruisers modernized like every other large ship in the Japanese Navy (we, of course, only modernized a few of ours) and they carry fourteen-inch guns.

I am not, of course, going to tell what our naval strength was, is, or will be in these waters, but I will go as far as to say that we should have been happy to fight an action with a force of this kind. Accordingly, Admiral Somerville took station southeast of Ceylon, where he would be most likely to encounter the enemy, and our Catalina aircraft, which were on the spot, made far-ranging reconnaissances. There was no sign of the enemy and it became necessary for the fleet to go back to refuel. The Admiral came to the conclusion that the intelligence which had led him to expect the Japanese naval advance into the Indian Ocean was faulty. The whole work of the Navy has to be carried on. One of his two eight-inch gun cruisers, the *Cornwall*, was needed for an Australian troop convoy, and the other had to undergo certain necessary repairs. He sent both to Colombo. The *Hermes*, one of our oldest aircraft carriers, also had a mission to perform, and had to pick up various essentials at Trincomalee. No sooner had the Admiral dispersed his concentration than what he had formerly expected came to pass. A report was received of a large Japanese fleet steering northwestward towards Ceylon. The reconnaissance Catalina aircraft was shot down before it could describe exactly the composition of the enemy fleet.

Immediately Admiral Somerville, who had by now completed refuelling, issued orders to concentrate his ships. He expected to meet the three Kongos and perhaps two aircraft carriers together with ancillaries, and though he saw he could not intercept them before they attacked Colombo, he hoped to bring them to action should they tarry or should any of them be crippled by the counterattack of our shore-based bombers. He therefore fixed a rendezvous for his forces, told the *Dorsetshire* and *Cornwall* to get out of Colombo harbour and join him at this sea point, and he told *Hermes* at Trincomalee to go to sea and keep out of the way. The Admiralty did not interfere at all in these dispositions. When they put one of their best admirals in charge of a fleet and a theatre, they do not stand over him with a stick, jogging his elbow. It is only very rarely when they possess exceptional knowledge that they override the judgment of the man on the spot. If the Admiralty does too much of that they simply destroy the whole initiative and responsibility of the admirals at sea. Such a bad habit, only acquired through wireless telegraphy, would be entirely contrary to the traditions of the Royal Navy. But, of course, if the House thinks fit, it may blame me for whatever went wrong.

At daylight on April 5 the Japanese Air Force attacked Colombo. All was in readiness for them. The harbour was largely cleared of ships; the *Cornwall* and *Dorsetshire* were, as Admiral Somerville thought, safe at sea; the anti-air-raid precautions worked well; our fighters were in the air; and the enemy was beaten off with the loss of probably two-thirds of the aircraft they used in the attack. The counterattack by our Blenheims upon the enemy's aircraft carriers returned without finding them, but later in the day a Japanese reconnaissance plane sighted the *Cornwall* and *Dorsetshire* on their way to join Admiral Somerville's fleet. Both these ships were sunk in about a quarter of an hour by attacks of from forty to sixty fighter aircraft carrying one single large bomb each. Three-quarters of the ships' crews were, however, saved.

Here is another example of the formidable quality of the Japanese seaborne Air Force. Our cruisers have on many occasions in the Mediterranean been exposed to prolonged attacks by German and Italian aircraft and, though often damaged, have rarely been sunk, and in two cases only have they been sunk without all their anti-aircraft ammunition having been used up. The fact that the Japanese, in spite of their heavy losses in the morning, could provide so large a force to attack the cruisers made it clear that they were employing a greater number of aircraft carriers than had been expected. In fact, there were found to be no fewer than five. In these circumstances it would have been wrong to force a fleet action, and Admiral Somerville, with the full approval of the Admiralty, withdrew into the wastes of the Indian Ocean.

The way was now open for any Japanese seaborne invasion of Ceylon. However, this did not take place. Instead the Japanese raided Trincomalee, where they were again severely rebuffed. They caught the *Hermes*, which had been ordered to clear out of the harbour, and inflicted very heavy losses, nearly one hundred thousand tons, upon our shipping in the Bay of Bengal.

It seems now that the enemy has retired to replenish his aircraft carriers after their heavy losses, and that his incursion into the Bay of Bengal was a foray and demonstration with an intention to bring off a Pearl Harbor surprise at Colombo.

I am not able to tell the House what we are doing in this lull. I can speak of the past, but not even in Secret Session of the present and future, but it ought not to be assumed that we are doing nothing. On the contrary, we have every hope that we shall presently be stronger in the Indian Ocean than hitherto. The unpleasant fact remains that for the present the enemy has effective command of the Bay of Bengal. Ceylon is the objective, which would be most valuable to him, and it is there that we are most prepared.

I now leave the lesser war – for such I must regard this fearful struggle against the Japanese – and come to the major war against Germany and Italy. I will begin with the gravest matter, namely, the enormous losses and destruction of shipping by German U-boats off the east coast of the United States. In a period of less than sixty days, more tonnage was sunk in this one stretch than we had lost all over the world during the last five months of the Battle of the Atlantic before America entered the war. Most of all has this loss been heavy in tankers; indeed, the loss has been so severe that we have for some time past been withdrawing our own ships from the route. Our oil reserves are happily large, though the utmost economy must be practised.

We have done our best to aid the Americans in establishing a convoy system, and this will soon be brought into being. At their request, to assist the Americans we have sent over a number of our officers most experienced in anti-U-boat warfare, and upwards of thirty corvettes and antisubmarine craft from our own hard-pressed store. The figures for the last two months on the American coast, plus those in the Indian and Pacific Oceans from the Japanese attacks, constitute totals of monthly losses which are most alarming and formidable and comparable to the worst I have witnessed either in the last war or in this.

On the other side, it must be remembered that the United States brought into the pool of Allied shipping upwards of nine million gross tons, so that the tonnage at the disposal of the Allies today is substantially greater than at this time last year, though at the same time the calls on our fleets are also increased. Moreover, I feel confident that the counter-measures which are being taken will be successful as they have been in the Battle of the Atlantic, and that the sinkings will presently be reduced to manageable proportions. I must, however, repeat that tonnage sink-ings and the multiplication of U-boats constitute my greatest anxiety. It is only by the expansion of tonnage over losses, which will occur when the shipbuilding power of the United States makes itself felt, that easement will be given on the oceans which separate the United States from the rest of the world and the strength of the great Republic be enabled to come increasingly into action.

It is only by shipping that the United States or indeed ourselves can intervene, either in the Eastern or the Western theatre. People speak airily of moving armies hither and thither. They do not know how harsh is the tonnage stringency, especially for ships of a suitable speed to carry troops, and how rigorous are the limitations which time and numbers impose upon our actions. Nevertheless, since the new war started we have actually moved from this country or from the Middle East across the sea against Japan more than 300,000 men, and we have over a hundred thousand on salt water at the present time. All these great convoys have hitherto been carried through the perils of mines and U-boat attacks without any appreciable loss of any kind since the beginning of the war. I regard this as a prodigy of skill and organization on the part of all those responsible for it.

I now come to the Middle East. Our strongest and best-equipped army overseas stands in close contact with the enemy in Cyrenaica. Twice have we hunted the enemy out of the Benghazi triangle and twice have we been chased back ourselves. The very severe battle, which General Auchinleck fought last year just missed being a decisive victory. By what narrow margins, chances, and accidents was the balance tipped against us no one can compute.

When I last spoke on this subject I said: 'If not a victory, it was a highly profitable transaction.' That is true. We inflicted three times the loss on the enemy that we suffered ourselves. We have fifty per cent more prison-ers in our hands than we lost from all causes. Tobruk, after its stubborn defence, was relieved and is now a valuable supply base. The Gazala posi-tion, strongly fortified and strongly held, is one hundred and fifteen miles west of the starting point of our advance and two hundred and forty miles from our old lines at Mersa Matruh. Sollum Halfaya Pass and all that are in our hands. Our advancing railway runs through Fort Capuzzo and approaches El Adem. We maintain and manoeuvre considerable forces in this region. It is no use speculating what General Auchinleck or the enemy will try to do. Both sides have repaired their strength after the battle and the numbers, which might engage are considerably larger than before.

But the fact that we do not possess Benghazi has a serious bearing upon the defence of Malta, because we cannot give continuous daylight air protection to our convoys to Malta from Egypt. For now nearly two years Malta has stood against the enemy. What a thorn it has been in their side! What toll it has taken of their convoys! Can we wonder that a most strenuous effort has been made by Germany and Italy to rid themselves of this fierce, aggressive foe. For the last six weeks over four hundred and fifty German first-line strength in aircraft and perhaps two hundred Italian have been venting their fury on Malta. An unending, intermittent bombardment has fallen upon the harbour and city, and sometimes as many as three hundred aircraft have attacked in a single day. The terrific ordeal has been borne with exemplary fortitude by the garrison and people.

Very heavy losses have been inflicted upon the enemy's air strength. Malta is the first instance of an air force being maintained at odds often of ten to one from so few airfields all under constant bombardment. We replenish Malta with aircraft by all means in our power. The President has helped us with one of his best aircraft carriers, which has just completed a successful operation. We are stronger now than we have been, but the struggle is very hard and the question of supply and replenishment dangerous, difficult, and costly. The supply of food and ammunition is our constant care and our increasing anxiety.

If you add the air forces facing us in the Mediterranean to those which face us across the Channel and the North Sea, or are detained in Germany to meet our bomber offensive, we account for two-thirds of the German fighter strength and more than one-third of their bomber strength. We are also detaining in the Mediterranean area more than a thousand Italian first-line aircraft. Evidently this is a solid help to Russia. Both across the Channel and in the Malta fighting we have this year inflicted considerably heavier losses of aircraft than we have ourselves sustained. It is our interest to engage the enemy's air power at as many points as possible to make him bleed and burn and waste on the widest fronts and at the utmost intensity, and it pays us to lose machine for machine. We have done much better than that. Therefore, every day that the air battle for Malta continues, grievous as it is to the island, its defenders and its gallant inhabitants, it plays its part in our general war effort and in helping our Russian allies. It may be that presently the German Air Forces attacking Malta will have to move eastward to sustain the impending offensive against southern Russia. If so, we shall have topped the ridge. Meanwhile the struggle at Malta is very hard. It is too early to say how it will end. But all the time we watch with admiration and with gratitude this protracted, undaunted, heroic conflict.

No one will accuse me of glozing over[1] with a smooth and thin veneer the ugly realities of our situation. On the contrary, I thought the House would wish to have its darkest features underlined. But I would not have dared to do this if my confidence in our power to come through safe and victorious was in any way diminished, and I will now proceed to that part of my argument which will give reasons for this. If we are anxious about the sea, our enemies must be more anxious about the air. The gigantic American shipbuilding program, with our own comparatively modest contribution of twelve hundred thousand tons a year, will in 1943 give a very large favourable balance over sinkings, calculated even at a rate of half a million tons a month.

We shall be very tight this year, but we ought to be a good deal better off next year. On the other hand, the Axis air power, upon which the enemy has so largely relied and by which so many of his triumphs have been gained, is certainly falling behind in the race. The recent estimates of American aircraft production, which seemed so extravagant, have so far been not only made good, but exceeded. It is calculated that by July, 1942, the American, British, and Russian production of aircraft will be nearly three times that of Germany, Italy, and Japan.

Now, of course, it takes some months for an impulsion of this character to be felt upon the fighting fronts. Transportation rears her ugly head. But it is only a matter of six or nine months before a marked preponderance of air power should manifest itself upon our side. At present there are more pilots than aircraft, but we have in no way slackened off our training of pilots. On the contrary, we are stimulating it because quite soon – in fact, during this autumn, we hope – the flood of aircraft will overtake and bear forward on its crest the very great numbers of pilots who are being trained.

In particular, the air position of Japan deserves scrutiny. According to our information, the Japanese losses and wastage greatly exceed and perhaps are nearly double their output, and the Japanese are separated by vast distances from any assistance by their confederates. One cannot

[1] Disguising, explaining away.

tell where the various fronts of the Japanese war will be stabilized. But that we and the United States will presently be very much stronger in the air on all those fronts may be soberly but confidently expected. As this process goes on it will make a great deal of difference to the war in the whole Asiatic theatre.

What has been lost wholesale may be regained bit by bit, and after that perhaps more quickly. Our hope is that it will not be long before we have a fleet in the Indian Ocean well supported by seaborne and shore-based aircraft, which will be sufficiently powerful to challenge any major detachment of the Japanese Navy. At the same time the United States fleet in the Pacific will gain very large accessions of strength and, apart from the hazards of war, which we must never forget, will become even before the end of this year markedly superior to the whole Japanese Navy. The islands and bases, which the Japanese have lightly acquired will become very heavy hostages to fortune. All this is carefully weighed and calculated out and various important enterprises are afoot. The aircraft carriers which are being built or rapidly adapted are numbered not by dozens but by scores, and it may well be that even before the end of this summer Japanese cities will begin to feel the weight of an air attack of which they on Sunday morning received only a foretaste – and squealed well. On no account let any word be spoken in disparagement of the war effort and war impulse of the United States. Our lives depend upon the growing application of their power.

Thus we may look to a fairly rapid acquisition of general air superiority, to a solid re-establishment of sea power both in the Indian and Pacific Oceans and, though this has to be toiled for, to the expansion in spite of losses of our transportation by sea.

But it is in Europe that the immediate main clash impends. Everything goes to show that perhaps even before the end of May Hitler will hurl a renewed offensive upon Russia, and there are no indications which contradict the general impression that his main thrust will be towards the Caspian and the Caucasus. We do not know what reserves the Russians have gathered. Everybody has always underrated the Russians. They keep their own secrets alike from foe and friends. The renewed German onslaught will start this year perhaps somewhat earlier and certainly a good deal farther east than last year. But this time there will be no surprise on the Russian side. Terrible injuries have been inflicted during the winter by the Russian armies, not only upon the German military power, but biting and searing deep into the whole life of the Nazi regime. With all its power and organization, it is a haggard Germany that Hitler leads into this new, ferocious, and sanguinary campaign, against Russia. Behind lies a Europe writhing with hatred and thirsting for revolt.

What can we do to help Russia? There is nothing that we would not do. If the sacrifice of thousands of British lives would turn the scale, our fellow countrymen would not flinch. But at this present time there are two important contributions we can make. The first is the supply of munitions to the utmost extent, which our shipping can carry. We have hitherto not failed in any way in the immense undertakings which we made to Stalin. It is not, however, only a question of giving up what we need ourselves, but of carrying it there safely and punctually. Our northern convoys are a task of enormous difficulty and hazard. For the next few weeks the ice drifts lower and lower, and the channel between the ice floes and the North Cape becomes narrower. We convoy not only our own contribution but that of the United States, which to a large extent is taken from what the United States would otherwise have given us. Our ships and their escorts, the heaviest we have ever used, are pressed by the ice ever nearer to the shores of Norway, and large numbers of German U-boats and powerful air forces can strike continually at the merchant ships and their guardians.

There is a further serious complication – the *Tirpitz*, the *Scheer* and the *Hipper* lie in Trondheim fiord. Every British–American convoy to Russia is liable to attack by swift, heavy, modern German surface ships. Battleship escort has to be provided on every occasion. The enemy has great opportunities, by threatening attack upon the convoys and laying traps of U-boats, of inflicting vital losses upon our fleet. Serious risks are run by our great ships – so few, so precious – only one where in the last war there was a squadron of eight – every time they go north on this perilous duty; at any time the Admiralty or even the Minister of Defence may have to account to you for some loss which would take five years to replace. I cannot speak of our naval dispositions further than to say that the United States are with us on this. It is a grim and bitter effort amid fearful gales and ceaseless perils, but if it be in human power we will carry our tanks, our aircraft, and all the other essential supplies to our heroic ally in his sublime struggle.

There is another immediate way in which we can help. While the German armies will be bleeding copiously upon a two-thousand-mile front in the East we shall be on their backs in the German homeland. The British bombing offensive upon Germany has begun. Half a dozen German cities have already received the full measure that they meted out to Coventry. Another thirty or more are on the list. We have improved methods of finding the targets and built-up areas by night. The wastage of bombs has been reduced, perhaps by half. Daylight thrusts far into the heart of Germany, striking with deadly precision at the most sensitive industrial spots – such as the immortal feat of arms on Friday last[1] – will be launched upon the enemy. Presently – indeed, quite soon – heavy United States formations will be established here in England and will work at our side. This summer and autumn – aye, and winter, too – Germany will experience scientific and accurate bombing of a weight and upon a scale and frequency which none of the nations they have maltreated has ever endured. We must not let false guides divert our minds from these major and terrible strokes of war, or tempt us to fritter away the solid mass of our endeavour. I heard a pretended British voice on the German radio the other night, which said:

'We should know better than anyone that the "bombardment" of towns can't bring the end of the war nearer. London withstood about as heavy a bombardment as could be launched – something compared with which the raid on Tokyo can't have been more than a pinprick. The proper use of aircraft is to support land forces in the actual battle zone, and as the RAF isn't large enough to fulfil all its tasks, it should be reserved for this purpose only. A daylight raid on Augsburg, for instance, may be spectacular, but its practical value is negligible. They say we had six hundred planes up yesterday. It's a pity they weren't up over Burma, defending our stricken forces there.'

Plausible – but is it disinterested?

All this leads me to the final point I have to make. When I went to the United States in December last I proposed to the President the preparation of a combined British and American invasion of German-occupied Europe for the liberation of its enslaved peoples and for the ultimate destruction of Hitlerism.

The war cannot be ended by driving Japan back to her own bounds and defeating her overseas forces. The war can only be ended through the defeat in Europe of the German armies, or through internal convulsions in Germany produced by the unfavourable course of the war, economic privations, and the Allied bombing offensive. As the strength of the United States, Great Britain, and Russia develops and begins to be realized by the Germans, an internal collapse is always possible, but we must not count upon this. Our plans must proceed upon the assump-

---

[1] A daytime bombing raid of a diesel engine factory in Augsburg, Germany. It was in fact a miserable failure: seven of twelve bombers were shot down, one of which was the 1,000th kill for Jagdgeschwader 2, nicknamed 'Richthofen' after the Red Baron.

tion that the resistance of the German Army and Air Force will continue at its present level and that their U-boat warfare will be conducted by increasingly numerous flotillas.

We have, therefore, to prepare for the liberation of the captive countries of western and southern Europe by the landing at suitable points, successively or simultaneously, of British and American armies strong enough to enable the conquered populations to revolt. By themselves they will never be able to revolt, owing to the ruthless countermeasures that will be employed: but if adequate and suitably equipped forces were landed in several of the following countries, namely, Norway, Denmark, Holland, Belgium, and the French Channel coasts and the French Atlantic coasts, as well as Italy and possibly the Balkans, the German garrisons would prove insufficient to cope both with the strength of the liberating forces and the fury of the revolting peoples.

It is impossible for the Germans, while we retain the sea power necessary to choose the place or places of attack, to have sufficient troops in each of these countries for effective resistance. In particular, they cannot move their armour about laterally from north to south or west to east: either they must divide it between the various conquered countries – in which case it would become hopelessly dispersed – or they must hold it back in a central position in Germany, in which case it will not arrive until large and important lodgements have been made by us from overseas.

We had expected to find United States attention concentrated upon the war with Japan, and we prepared ourselves to argue that the defeat of Japan would not spell the defeat of Hitler, but that the defeat of Hitler left the finishing off of Japan merely a matter of time and trouble. We were relieved to find that these simple but classical conceptions of war, although vehemently opposed by the powerful isolationist faction, were earnestly and spontaneously shared by the government and dominant forces in the United States. The visit of General Marshall and Mr Hopkins was to concert with us the largest and the swiftest measures of this offensive character. It will no doubt become common knowledge that the liberation of the Continent by equal numbers of British and American troops is the main war plan of our two nations. The timing, the scale, the method, the direction of this supreme undertaking must remain unknown and unknowable till the hour strikes and the blows fall. More than that I cannot say – except that in the early hours of this morning I received a message from the President of which, since we are in Secret Session, I will read the material part:

'I am delighted with the agreement which was reached between you and your military advisers and Marshall and Hopkins. They have reported to me of the unanimity of opinion relative to the proposal, which they carried with them and I appreciate ever so much your personal message confirming this.

'I believe that this move will be very disheartening to Hitler and may well be the wedge by which his downfall will be accomplished. I am very heartened at the prospect and you can be sure that our army will approach the matter with great enthusiasm and vigour.

'While our mutual difficulties are many, I am frank to say that I feel better about the war than at any time in the past two years.'

Testing, trying, adverse, painful times lie ahead of us. We must all strive to do our duty to the utmost of our strength. As the war rises remorselessly to its climax, the House of Commons, which is the foundation of the British life struggle – this House of Commons which has especial responsibilities – will have the opportunity once again of proving to the world that the firmness of spirit, sense of proportion, steadfastness of purpose which have gained it renown in former days, will now once again carry great peoples and a greater cause to a victorious deliverance.

Harold Nicolson: diary
('Harold Nicolson, Diaries and Letters', pages 223–4)

23 April 1942

Secret Session in the House. I am not allowed, even in my diary, to give all the details of what passed, but I can at least give the outline.

Cripps, on his return from India, was received with a cheer stronger than that accorded to Winston. The latter when he rose (and after all the strangers had been spied and harried from the House) adopted his stolid, obstinate, ploughman manner. He tells of Singapore, where the conduct of our large army 'does not seem to have been in harmony with the past or present spirit of our forces'. He tells us of the Naval position in the Indian Ocean, and how the ships came to be lost. He tells us of the Middle East and what happened at Alexandria. He tells us of our present dangers and prospects and dwells at length upon the heavy sinkings which we are sustaining in the eastern Atlantic. It is a long and utterly remorseless catalogue of disaster and misfortune. And as he tells us one thing after another, gradually the feeling rises in the packed House. 'No man', Members begin to feel in their hearts, 'no man but he could tell us of such disaster and increase rather than diminish confidence.' He has the psychological force of a supreme specialist who tells one that there are signs of tuberculosis, that one may become very ill, but that cure is certain. And as this feeling rises, there rises with it a feeling of shame at having doubted him. He ends without rhetoric, but with a statement about our aircraft production which is encouraging. The House gives him a great ovation and the debate thereafter peters out.

I go to the St George's Day pageant organised by the *Daily Express* at the Albert Hall. Winston is there in the royal box. He gives the V-sign to an audience which does not greet him with any tumultuous applause.

Henry Channon: diary
('Chips', page 327)

23 April 1942

The House went into Secret Session at noon, and Winston at once rose majestically and began his long review of recent events. He painted a magnificent and vast canvas. I went up to the gallery and [...] looked down on the crowded House. Every seat was taken. Black coated dullards, they looked, with only a light sprinkling of khaki among them. For nearly two hours the PM spoke with almost no interruption; it was a tour de force. No humour or tact, little oratory, no *mea culpa* stuff, but straightforward, brilliant and colourful, a factual résumé of the situation. Only at 1.50 when MPs began to think of their stomachs, was there any restlessness. His account of the situation was definitely encouraging and heartening, and we left the Chamber confident that the War would, after all, be won, thanks chiefly to the stupendous American production.

General Sir William Dobbie[1] to Winston S. Churchill
(Churchill papers, 20/74)

23 April 1942   Malta

My [telegram] 1828 of 21/4 to Chiefs of Staff pointed out that if Malta is to be held drastic action (repeat action) to gain and maintain air superiority here is needed. Since then much has happened – 47 Spitfires arrived

---

[1] William George Sheddon Dobbie, 1879–1964. On active service in South Africa, 1899–1902, and on the Western Front, 1914–18 (despatches seven times, Mons ribbon, DSO). Inspector of the Royal Engineers, 1930–5. General Officer Commanding Malaya, 1935–9. Governor and Commander-in-Chief, Malta, 1940–2. Lieutenant-General, 1940. Knighted, 1941. One of his two sons was killed in action in the Second World War.

and in the two and a half days which have elapsed since then, 357 tons and 122 tons bombs have been dropped on the two aerodromes where they are accommodated. Some of them were in the air within 90 minutes of arrival when the first heavy attack came, but in spite of this and all other efforts on our part 17 have been destroyed on the ground or in the air and 29 more damaged on the ground and many more in combat.

We can at the moment only put six Spitfires into the air. AOC is doing his best to abate the nuisance by attacking aerodromes in Sicily. Last night the same Wellingtons made no less than seven attacks on Comiso – but we have not yet succeeded in stopping the enemy. Until we can succeed in doing so we cannot hope to revictual the place and supplies are dangerously low – as well as the vital AA ammunition.

If Malta is to be held, it must be revictualled, and to do so we must (repeat must) gain a good measure of local air superiority. We can deal with invasion – but enemy need not attempt that if he can maintain air blockade as at present. Situation demands most drastic action and we must think in quite different numbers of Spitfires than we have envisaged heretofore.

General Archibald Wavell to Winston S. Churchill
(Churchill papers, 20/74)

23 April 1942   Ceylon
Personal
Most Immediate

[...]
Things seem to be going well in Ceylon and all in good heart.

George Harvie-Watt to Winston S. Churchill
(Sir George Harvie-Watt papers)

24 April 1942

The outstanding feature of the week was your Speech in Secret Session. It is generally considered to have been a 'superb performance'. Even critics such as Clem Davies[1] and Henderson Stewart considered it

---

[1] Clement Davies, 1884–1962. An expert on agricultural law. Liberal MP for Montgomeryshire from 1929 until his death. President of the Welsh Liberal Federation, 1945–8. President of the Parliamentary Association for World Government, 1951. One of his two sons and his only daughter were killed in action in the Second World War.

was the 'biggest Parliamentary thing' you have done. As a result of the widespread approval, the Debate tended to collapse [...]

Lord Privy Seal,[1] in winding up, expressed surprise that none of the usual critics had taken part in the Debate. The advantage of a Secret Session, in his opinion, was that the critics could get a more detailed and frank reply from the Government. Such a reply was sometimes impossible in public session. Shinwell, in pressing for a Public Debate, considered that the speech of the Lord Privy Seal was provocative. He said that it had not been the House which had asked for a Secret Debate, but the Government, and that you had said little that could not have been said in public. He expressed the view that a good deal of what had been said about American Production, particularly with regard to shipping, was merely ballyhoo. Sir Edward Grigg and Lord Winterton also pressed for a Public Debate in view of the deep anxiety in the country and in the Services about the present position. A further contribution was made by General Jeffreys[2] who raised the question of the construction of the 'Churchill' and other tanks. I feel however that there is little pressure left in the demand for an enquiry into the fall of Singapore and that those who are clamouring for a Public Debate are divided in what they want to say. Grigg, for example, wishes to raise the question of a Chief of Combined Staffs. This could well be done on an ordinary Supply day, as could the other points, which the critics wish to raise.

[...]

There has been considerable comment in the Lobby regarding the Treaty with Soviet Russia and especially the provisions dealing with the Baltic States. This subject has apparently leaked out and many Members are making adverse comments to the effect that (i) This is Munich over again, but worse (ii) We are acquiescing in an aggression (iii) Why have a Treaty now? Why not wait to see the result of the German Spring offensive when Russia may not be in such a strong bargaining position and (iv) Is it true that America is not a party to or in favour of such a Treaty? It is felt by many Members that publication of the Treaty will not be received

---

[1] Sir Stafford Cripps.

[2] George Darell Jeffreys, 1878–1960. On active service with the Grenadier Guards, Nile Expedition, 1898 (including the Battle of Khartoum); South African War, 1900–2; France and Flanders, 1914–18 (including the retreat from Mons). Churchill's Commanding Officer when Churchill was in training with the 2nd Battalion Grenadier Guards, December 1915. Commanded the 19th Division (severely wounded), 1917–18 (despatches nine times). Major-General, 1922. Commanded London District, 1920–4. Knighted, 1924. General Officer Commanding-in-Chief, Southern Command, India, 1932–6. Chairman, Hampshire County Council Civil Defence Committee, 1938–54. County Organizer, Hampshire Home Guard, 1940. Conservative MP for Petersfield, 1941–51. Created Baron, 1952. Colonel, Grenadier Guards, 1952–60. His only son was killed in action in France.

kindly by our Allies and especially the Poles. The subject was discussed at the meeting of the Foreign Affairs Committee when deep concern was expressed. It was decided that a Deputation should wait upon the Foreign Secretary and that he should be urged to address the Committee. This is a matter which may well develop into a major crisis.[1]

Winston S. Churchill to President Franklin D. Roosevelt
(Churchill papers, 20/74)

24 April 1942
Secret and Personal
No. 75

OPERATION 'IRONCLAD' (MADAGASCAR)

In your No. 131 of 3rd April you said that you felt that it would be unwise to do anything which would give the impression that 'Ironclad' was a joint Anglo-American enterprise. In the situation which then existed I agreed with you: but now that Laval[2] has come into power at Vichy and you have withdrawn Leahy,[3] are not things different?[4]

In these changed circumstances, would you be prepared to reconsider your previous decision, and allow us to drop leaflets both at 'Ironclad' and in France which would give the impression that America was associated with the expedition, and that, conjointly with Great Britain, she guaranteed the return of 'Ironclad' to France after the war.

---

[1] Churchill sidelined this whole paragraph, and noted in the margin: 'Foreign Secretary to see. WSC. 26.4'.

[2] Pierre Laval, 1883–1945. A lawyer. Deputy for the Seine, 1914–19 (as a Socialist) and 1924–7 (as an Independent). Independent Senator, 1927–44. Minister of Public Works, 1925; of Justice, 1926; of Labour, 1930, 1932. Prime Minister and Foreign Minister, 1931–2, 1935–6. Foreign Minister, 1934–5. Deputy Prime Minister and Minister of Information (under Pétain), July–December 1940. Prime Minister (under Pétain), April 1942 to August 1944 (also Foreign Minister, Minister of the Interior, and Minister of Information and Propaganda). Arrested by the Gestapo, 1944, and interned, 1944–5. Tried in Paris for treason: his trial began on 4 October 1945; he was sentenced to death on October 10 and executed on October 15.

[3] William D. Leahy, 1875–1959. Commissioned in the United States Navy, 1899. Admiral, 1936. Chief of Naval Operations, 1937. Governor of Puerto Rico, 1939. American Ambassador to Vichy France, 1940–1. Chief of Staff to the President and to the Joint Chiefs of Staff, 1942–9. Honorary knighthood, 1945. In 1950 he published his memoirs, *I Was There.*

[4] Churchill is suggesting that with Laval (who openly supported German victory) in office and Leahy, who had maintained good relations with Pétain, no longer in post in Vichy (the US Embassy in Vichy France would formally come to an end in November 1942), US–French relations were deteriorating to the point where their preservation was no longer a reason to avoid joint Anglo-American operations.

Winston S. Churchill to General Sir William Dobbie
(Churchill papers, 20/74)

24 April 1942
Personal and Secret

DEFENCE OF MALTA

Your 158 and 159 to Colonial Secretary.[1] You may be quite sure that there shall be no intrigue where you are concerned. Nothing but the public interest must be considered. Mountbatten has not been consulted or had the slightest influence on War Cabinet discussions. His telegram quoted in your 159 had no authority.

2. Naturally we are gravely anxious about Malta. I am therefore sending Lord Cranborne at once by air to talk everything over with you. He will be accompanied by a Q[2] Staff Officer to go into your needs in stores in detail.

3. In all circumstances you may be confident of the gratitude of your countrymen.

General Sir William Dobbie to Winston S. Churchill
(Churchill papers, 20/74)

24 April 1942
Personal and Secret

Many thanks for your telegram of 24th. Entirely agree only public interest must be considered. You can rely on me doing all I can to further it with no thought of personal considerations. Will welcome Cranborne.

Winston S. Churchill to General Sir William Dobbie
(Churchill papers, 20/74)

24 April 1942
Personal and Secret

Cabinet thought better to send Mr Casey Minister of State, who is on way to Cairo. He hopes to start tomorrow night. All our hearts are with you in your hard battle.

---

[1] Dobbie had complained to the Colonial Secretary, Lord Cranborne, that Mabel Strickland, Editor of *The Times of Malta* and the daughter of a previous Prime Minister of the island, was conspiring to have him removed from the Governorship, blaming him for a lack of co-ordination to which she attributed the shipping losses incurred by the most recent supply convoy to Malta.

[2] Q: Quartermaster supplies for the army, under the Quartermaster-General to the Forces, responsible for the supply of equipment, provisions, and munitions.

Winston S. Churchill to Sir Walter Monckton[1]
(Churchill papers, 20/74)

24 April 1942

Casey is starting for Malta to report to Cabinet stop Governor has complained of Strickland[2] intrigue stop Matter is one of high importance. You should remain in Cairo.

Winston S. Churchill to President Franklin D. Roosevelt
(Churchill papers, 20/74)

24 April 1942
Personal and Secret
No. 76

In my immediately following telegram is a note drafted by me on 22nd for Defence Committee and accepted by them. It should explain to you how we are planning to act. I beg that this may be for you and Admiral King alone.

2. I am deeply anxious about Malta under the unceasing bombardment of 450 first-line German aircraft. If the island fortress is to hold out till the June convoy, which is the earliest possible, it must have a continued flow of Spitfires. The last flying off from *Wasp* was most successful, although unhappily the enemy's attack broke up many after they had landed. We are using *Eagle* to send in 15 or so at a time. I shall be grateful if you will allow *Wasp* to do a second trip. We will of course escort with *Renown* as before. I do not think enemy have the slightest idea *Wasp* has been in and out of the Mediterranean. Without this aid I fear Malta will be pounded to bits. Meanwhile its defence is wearing out the enemy's air force and effectively aiding Russia.

3. We cordially accept the proposals which Admiral King has made to the First Sea Lord about dispositions of American heavy ships in the Atlantic.

---

[1] Walter Monckton was serving as Director-General, British Propaganda and Information Services, Cairo.

[2] Mabel Strickland, 1899–1988. Daughter of the pre-war Prime Minister of Malta, Lord Strickland. In the Second World War she was Editor of *The Times of Malta*. One of Malta's political leaders during UK–Maltese integration talks, 1956–7; elected in 1962 to the Maltese Parliament; in 1964 she opposed Maltese independence.

Winston S. Churchill to President Franklin D. Roosevelt
(Churchill papers, 20/74)

24 April 1942
Personal and Secret
No. 77

No satisfactory solution of the Malta problem is available in May. The island must therefore hold out till the June dark period. This should be possible if rigorous severity of rationing is imposed from now and the supply of Spitfires by *Wasp* and *Eagle* is maintained.

2. We must not be deterred from 'Ironclad', for which such long preparations have been made, by the changes in the French Government. However, it would be wise to have both *Renown* and *Duke of York* handy either at Gibraltar or in home waters till we see the reactions upon Vichy France.

3. The month gained by Malta holding out till the middle of June and the dropping of the idea of a convoy from the West (a) eases the strain upon the Commander-in-Chief, Home Fleet by narrowing the gap between *Rodney* and *Nelson* being ready for action and any departure of *Duke of York*: (b) enables the May convoy to Russia to be run thus relieving a most dangerous congestion and avoiding failing Stalin at the most critical juncture.

4. All the above is very convenient in the West but is gained at the expense of the Command of the Indian Ocean. However, we were not going to get that anyhow until late in June. It is suggested therefore that the assembly of the Eastern Fleet should be fixed for 30th June, by which date, barring accidents, *Duke of York*, *Renown*, *Warspite*, *Valiant*, and three armoured aircraft carriers and the four R's should all be present. Here would be a fleet which, if not strong enough to fight the Japanese Navy, would be at any rate capable of dealing with a very heavy detachment. We may have to pay forfeits in the Indian Ocean in consequence of enemy action, but we are perforce running these risks now and would have to anyhow for five weeks to come. We shall have to go on running the risks for another four.

5. What should Admiral Somerville do in the meanwhile? First he is to cover 'Ironclad', for which he is not ill-equipped with the three carriers, *Warspite* and the four R's. This is all provided for in his orders and he is already on the way via Colombo.

6. After 'Ironclad' is over, it is hoped about the 10th May, he should work his way north to fuel at Aden in the early days of June. By this time

we shall know what has happened to General Auchinleck's offensive. If he has got Martuba or Benghazi, the chances of a Malta convoy getting through from the East will be greatly improved. We shall also know how much of the German Air Force has been drawn away from the Mediterranean to the South Russian Front, the actual moves that have taken place or are in progress. We can also judge the situation in the Indian Ocean as it then appears, observing that we cannot fight a fleet action anyhow except against a minor detachment. The decision can then be taken whether or not to escort the convoy in strength from the East through the Mediterranean or sail Southwards again to meet *Duke of York* and *Renown* and pick up *Valiant* for the Eastern Fleet assembly on June 30th.

7. Should the decision be to make a dart into the Mediterranean and see the convoy through in style, Admiral Somerville should proceed with all three aircraft carriers and *Warspite* with ancillaries through the canal where the convoy should be assembled. This convoy must be worthy of the effort and risk required to put it through. At least seven supply ships can now be loaded at Alexandria. If all goes well, there will still be time for Admiral Somerville to come back through the canal and make the general fleet rendezvous on 30th June at Colombo or Port T[1] or wherever is convenient.

Winston S. Churchill to President Franklin D. Roosevelt
(Churchill papers, 20/74)

24 April 1942
Cypher
No. 78

With regard to what you say in your telegram No. 139 about Molotov's journeyings, I have had message from Stalin saying he is sending M. here to discuss certain divergences in draft texts of our agreement, which he wants settled as soon as possible. He may even be already on his way. You will understand that I cannot now suggest to him a change in the order of his visits. If and when, therefore, Molotov bears down upon us, I propose to agree to a discussion of our drafts and would hope to clear main difficulties out of the way. But I will suggest to him that he should then go on to Washington and see you before anything is finally signed.

---

[1] Port T: Trincomalee.

Winston S. Churchill to Josef Stalin
(Churchill papers, 20/74)

24 April 1942
Cypher

I am very grateful to you for your message of April 23rd, and we shall of course welcome Monsieur Molotoff, with whom I am confident we shall be able to do much useful work. I am very glad that you feel able to allow this visit which I am sure will be most valuable.

Winston S. Churchill to William Mackenzie King
(Churchill papers, 20/88)

24 April 1942

We have now reviewed afresh the question of the maintenance of relations between the Canadian Government and the Vichy Government in the light of Laval's recent statement of policy and of the decision of the Union Government to sever relations with Vichy.

2. You will have noted that Laval repeatedly said that he would seek a policy of understanding and reconciliation with Germany, and that he went out of his way to deliver a bitter attack upon Great Britain.

3. The further clarification of the situation for which Mr Welles[1] asked you to wait has thus, it seems to us, now been given, and our advice would be that the time has come for the Canadian Government to terminate their relations with Vichy. The maintenance of these relations is only really of benefit to Vichy.

4. We are apprehensive lest Laval, whose skill is remarkable, may succeed in persuading the United States Government to maintain an attitude of tolerance towards him. We have accordingly instructed Halifax to put in a word of warning at Washington, although we are not actually pressing the United States Government to break off relations for the present at any rate.

5. There is, of course, the further disadvantage that Canada would be the only part of the Empire still maintaining relations with Vichy.

---

[1] (Benjamin) Sumner Welles, 1892–1961. A relative by marriage of Franklin Roosevelt. United States Foreign Service, 1914–25. During Roosevelt's presidential election campaign in 1932, Welles provided foreign policy expertise and was a major financial contributor. Special Envoy to Cuba, 1933. Under-Secretary of State, 1937–43. Visited Italy, Germany, and England to discuss peacemaking proposals, February–March 1940. He was known for his frequent use of the phrase 'No comment'.

Anthony Eden: recollection
('The Eden Memoirs, The Reckoning', page 326)

24 April 1942

[...] about 5 p.m. to Winston who had just woken up. He was in tearing spirits. Said he could not remember where he was on waking, he had had such deep sleep and he was striding about his room in vest and drawers with cigar in his mouth, whisky and soda at his side and calling for Nellie to produce his socks! We spoke of Government and I urged him to bring as many of Cabinet into his plans as he could. He agreed though arguing this must slow up machine. However Cripps, Oliver and I he thought pretty powerful with himself.

Winston S. Churchill to John Curtin
(Churchill papers, 20/74)

24 April 1942

Following for Prime Minister from Prime Minister. Begins. Greetings to you on Anzac Day.[1] We can never forget the great comradeship of Gallipoli with its imperishable memories.

Winston S. Churchill: recollection
('The Hinge of Fate', page 274)

[25 April 1942]

Disturbing news in April arrived about General Dobbie. Up to this moment he had been magnificent, and from all parts of the Empire eyes were turned on him – a Cromwellian figure at the key point. But the long strain had worn him down. I received this news with very deep regret, and I did not at first accept what I was told. However, a successor had to be chosen. I felt that in Lord Gort, the Governor of Gibraltar, would be found a warrior of the truest mettle. Mr Casey was flying out via Gibraltar to take up his appointment in Cairo as Minister of State, and I entrusted him with full explanations to Gort.

---

[1] Anzac Day: 25 April, the anniversary of the landings in 1915 on the Gallipoli Peninsula, where Australian and New Zealand Army Corps (ANZAC) forces, together with British, Newfoundland, and French, fought against the Turks.

Winston S. Churchill to Sir Walter Monckton
(Churchill papers, 20/67)

25 April 1942
Secret

You will have seen the telegrams exchanged with the President and have memorised the position. You take with you an *aide-mémoire* for Gort. You may explain the general picture to him, and tell him about the Malta position. I am sending you a letter from me to give him, so that he may be preparing himself for the duty which will be required of him in the event of Dobbie coming home.

2. If, on the other hand, when you get to Malta you decide to recommend Dobbie staying on, he must be given adequate powers over the Service Commanders, and you will no doubt recommend to us the form that it should take.

3. The dominant reason why I favour running the convoy from the East is because only one carrier would be available in the West, and three carriers working together give an enormous measure of mutual protection and protection to the convoy. We cannot obviously settle now the decision we shall have to take in the early days of June whether to send Somerville into the Mediterranean or not. That must depend on the Indian Ocean position. If we do not do so, Malta's plight will be very serious. On the other hand, you may take it that I shall press very hard to save Malta and to run all the necessary risks.

4. You have, I presume, seen the principal telegrams interchanged with General Auchinleck about the renewed offensive in Libya, and also General Nye's answers to the twenty questions. If not, you should ask Ismay to give them to you to read on the way down, but do not take them with you on the plane. Copies will be found in Cairo.

Winston S. Churchill to Lord Gort
(Churchill papers, 20/53)

25 April 1942
Secret

My dear Gort,

I avail myself of the Minister of State's[1] journey through Gibraltar and Malta to send you these few lines. It may be that – as he will explain to you

---

[1] Richard Casey, Minister Resident in the Middle East.

– a change will be required at a most critical juncture in the Command of Malta. If this should be so, we all feel you are the man of all others to render this vitally important service. You may be sure that I shall do everything in my power to carry a heavy convoy of supplies into Malta in the latter part of June, and that meanwhile the supply of Spitfires from the West will be continual.

I am delighted with all the reports we get of the splendid way in which you have organized Gibraltar and maintained the high morale of its garrison. Should you be required for this further service, you will be equipped with ample powers and will carry with you the full confidence of His Majesty's Government and of

Your sincere friend,
Winston S. Churchill

Winston S. Churchill to Field Marshal Jan Smuts
(Churchill papers, 20/74)

25 April 1942
Most Secret and Personal

OPERATION 'IRONCLAD' (MADAGASCAR)

Entirely agree desirability of occupying Tamatave and Majunga at earliest: but we do not think we have got sufficient troops or tackle to take these simultaneously with Diego Suarez. If this is so, we should have to take Tamatave and Majunga by amphibious operations, after we have established ourselves at Diego. Chiefs of Staff have asked Sturges[1] and Syfret[2] for their views. It is more a matter for the judgment of the former than of the latter.

Most grateful for your welcome offer of bomber squadron.

We are examining whole question of subsequent garrison of 'Ironclad', including provision of aircraft, and will cable again.

---

[1] Robert Grice Sturges, 1891–1970. Entered the Royal Navy, 1908; transferred to the Royal Marine Light Infantry, 1912. On active service, 1914–18 (including Gallipoli). Major-General, commanding operations in Iceland, 1940; in Madagascar, 1942. Officer Commanding Commando Group, 1943 (wounded, despatches twice; DSO). Lieutenant-General, 1945. Knighted, 1945.

[2] Edward Neville Syfret, 1889–1972. Entered the Royal Navy, 1904. Captain, 1929. Naval Secretary to the First Lord, 1939–41. Rear-Admiral, 1940. Commanded Force H, 1941–3. Knighted, 1942. Vice-Admiral, 1943. Vice-Chief of the Naval Staff, 1943–5. Commander-in-Chief, Home Fleet, 1945–8. Admiral, 1946.

President Franklin D. Roosevelt to Winston S. Churchill
(Churchill papers, 20/74)

25 April 1942
Personal and Secret
No. 140

Refer to your secret Number 76 addressed to me and am pleased to say that *Wasp* is to be made available for the second trip with Spitfires for Malta. It is good to know that the arrangements for dealing with enemy heavy ships in the North Atlantic are satisfactory. Your secret Number 77 to me gives us clear idea of planned movement in Indian Ocean and with respect to convoy from eastward into Malta. Time is definitely running in our favour just now. Best of luck.

Winston S. Churchill to President Franklin D. Roosevelt
(Churchill papers, 20/74)

25 April 1942
No. 79

Your 140. Thank you so much.

Winston S. Churchill to Josef Stalin
(Churchill papers, 20/74)

26 April 1942
Personal and Secret

Many thanks for your message of April 22nd.[1] His Majesty's Government will of course be very happy to receive M Kasatkin and will do their best to supply your requirements after discussion with him.

John Curtin to Winston S. Churchill
(Churchill papers, 20/74)

26 April 1942

The people of Australia very greatly appreciate your Anzac day message which you so thoughtfully sent on an Anniversary which this year has so much significance to us.

---

[1] Dated 23 April in the document reproduced above (page 557).

Winston S. Churchill to Chiang Kai-shek
(Churchill papers, 20/74)

26 April 1942
Personal and Secret

I am grateful to you for your frank telegram of the 17th April about the state of affairs in Burma. I value your opinion greatly and hope that you will always let me know what you feel, whether or not it makes pleasant reading.

The main point in your telegram is the lack of air support. How grievous this can be we know to our cost in many bitter experiences in this war. In no part of our war effort have we laboured so hard, to no part of our programme have we devoted so much of our resources as we have to the building up of air superiority. We began the war with a long handicap to overtake. There is nothing to which we look forward more confidently or with greater satisfaction than the day when we shall be able to submit the enemy to the punishment from the air from which we have ourselves suffered. That day will surely come.

Our air forces are greater in strength and are incomparably stronger than they were when war started but the circumstances of the Campaign have made it impossible for us to bring Air Forces to the support of your troops and ours in Burma to the extent which we should have wished.

The distance between our factories and the battlefield of Burma makes the sending out of aircraft a long and difficult task. You will know too that the lines of communication which supply India and Burma have also to supply our Forces in the Middle East. Then again, we have been gravely hampered by the fact that we have, for the time being, lost control of the sea in the Far East. In order to maintain essential sea communications, we have to provide some aircraft to protect and support our surface craft and ensure the security of Ceylon which is now our key base in the Indian Ocean.

Again, you know how difficult it is to build up from few and improvised landing grounds an air force in a country such as Burma against an enemy who has once established air superiority, and how easily small reinforcements melt away before the enemy's greater strength.

It is these difficulties, and others of which you are aware, which have prevented us from sending you the air force which we would have wished. I and all my officers agree with what you say about the importance to us all of the battle in Burma. We are doing, and we shall continue to do, all we can to help you. Both we and the United States are sending air forces from our two countries to General Wavell in increasing numbers as fast as possible. We shall do all in our power to sustain the Allied land forces in the Burma campaign.

I am sending a copy of Your Excellency's message to the Governor of Burma. He has had great difficulties to contend with. You know that you can rely on him to do all that is possible to sustain the cause of the Allies.

Winston S. Churchill to General Claude Auchinleck
(Churchill papers, 20/88)

26 April 1942

Your CS/938 of 25th instant attributes to enemy in Eastern Cyrenaica German tanks 265 runners plus 45 in workshops, whereas the special information[1] which has been sent to you states that on 21st there were only 161 German tanks serviceable in the forward areas. I should be glad to know how this important correction strikes you.

Winston S. Churchill to Mrs J. S. Courtauld[2]
(Churchill papers, 20/53)

26 April 1942

Dear Mrs Courtauld,

It was a great shock to read of the death of your husband. I knew him for many years; he served his country and the House faithfully and well, and we shall all miss him greatly. Private sorrow is especially difficult to bear in these hard times, and you have my heartfelt sympathy.

Yours sincerely,
Winston S. Churchill

---

[1] Derived from an Enigma decrypt.

[2] Henrietta Barbara Courtauld (née Holland), 1883–1959. Her husband, Major John Sewell Courtauld (1889–1942), had died on 20 April 1942. He had served in the First World War, being awarded the Military Cross, and was MP for Chichester from 1924 until his death.

Winston S. Churchill to Air Chief Marshal Sir Charles Portal
(Churchill papers, 20/67)

27 April 1942
Most Secret

Please make me proposals for increasing the number of discarded bombers which can be placed rapidly at the disposal of the Airborne Corps. At least 100 should be found within the next three months. We cannot go on with 10,000 keen men and only 32 aircraft at their disposal.

Winston S. Churchill to Admiral of the Fleet Sir Dudley Pound
(Churchill papers, 20/67)

27 April 1942
Most Secret

What forces exactly is Admiral Somerville going to use for 'Ironclad'? If he has three carriers available, why should he not use them all? Here surely also the 'Rs' would be useful in bombarding. There is a great deal to be said for a strong display of force, which may minimise opposition at the outset. If the forces are available, ought they not to be used?

President Franklin D. Roosevelt to Winston S. Churchill
(Churchill papers, 20/74)

27 April 1942
Priority
No. 141

I have seen your cable to Harry this morning relative to the shipments to Russia. I am greatly disturbed by this because I fear not only the political repercussions in Russia but even more the fact that our supplies will not reach them promptly.

We have made such a tremendous effort to get our supplies going that to have them blocked except for most compelling reasons seems to me a serious mistake.

I realize in talks I have had with Pound and again with Little[1] this morning and my own Naval advisers that the matter is extremely difficult

---

[1] Charles James Colebrooke Little, 1882–1973. Naval cadet, 1897. Commanded the submarines of the Dover Patrol, 1914–16; the Grand Fleet Submarine Flotilla, 1916–18. Deputy Chief of the

and I do not want for a moment to underrate those difficulties. On the other hand would it not be better for us to make all our plans in the immediate future on the basis of future experience. It may be that the next convoy will move through easier than we expect and that the difficulties which we now foresee may not be insurmountable and the losses which we may have to undergo may well be worth the risk.

I do hope particularly that you can review again the size of the immediate convoys so that the stuff now backed up in Iceland can get through and I hope that in any conversations that Eden may have with the Russian Ambassador they be confined to telling him the difficulties and urging their cooperation in bringing the convoys in rather than any flat statement about the limit to the number of ships that can be convoyed.

I can and will make some immediate adjustments at this end but I very much prefer that we do not seek at this time any new understanding with Russia about the amount of our supplies in view of the impending assault on their armies. It seems to me that any word reaching Stalin at this time that our supplies were stopping for any reason would have a most unfortunate effect.

Winston S. Churchill to John Curtin
(Churchill papers, 20/74)

27 April 1942
Most Secret

[...]

V. <u>Near Future</u>

Unknown factor is degree American action in Pacific will contain Japanese effort, but Japanese squadron recently operating in Indian Ocean was superior to our anticipated strength in next three months.

VI. <u>Future Policy</u>

(a) To build up and train the Eastern Fleet with all resources that can be spared. Until then to adopt policy of weaker Fleet, which is to evade and remain in being while raiding whenever practicable enemy lines of communication.

(b) To augment with American assistance shore based air strength in India and Ceylon.

Naval Staff, 1932–5. Knighted, 1935. Commander-in-Chief, China Station, 1936–8. Admiral, 1937. 2nd Sea Lord and Chief of Naval Personnel, 1938–41. Head of the Joint Staff Mission, Washington, 1941–2. Commander-in-Chief, Portsmouth, 1942–5.

(c) Next three months will be critical but when (a) and (b) have been completed it is hoped that Eastern Fleet will be able to adopt offensive policy in Indian Ocean, but action against Malaya barrier involving large scale combined operations beyond our resources until Germany has been defeated.

Anthony Eden: diary
('The Eden Memoirs, The Reckoning', page 326)

27 April 1942

Luncheon with Winston alone. He was in better form than I have known him for ages. We spoke of painting and pictures, the light on the Horse Guards, the right tactics in politics and so forth.

He strongly impressed upon me the importance of not being afraid to drop out for a bit. He ought to have gone for a tour of the Empire when he was out of office. It was a mistake to believe that if one had once played a great part one would be forgotten. I said that I thought Ll. G had made a mistake in not retiring after the last war. He recalled a conversation he had with Ll. G about it early in 1919 when motoring in France. Lothian[1] had advised him to retire and he had asked Winston's opinion. Winston had recalled his obligations to those who had worked with him.

Winston S. Churchill to Sir James Grigg
(Churchill papers, 20/67)

28 April 1942
Most Secret

REORGANISATION OF ARMOURED
AND INFANTRY DIVISIONS

I have carefully studied the new organisation of the Armoured Divisions and of the Infantry Divisions which is now proposed, and I need scarcely say, in view of opinions I have expressed from time to time, how cordially I agree with it. The intimate, harmonious mingling of armoured forces and infantry is essential if the infantry is to regain its rights as the leading arm upon the battlefield. The emphasis placed upon artillery relatively to

[1] Philip Henry Kerr, 1882–1940. Educated at the Oratory School, Birmingham, and New College, Oxford. Worked as a civil servant in South Africa, 1905–8. Editor, *The Round Table*, 1910–16. Secretary to Lloyd George, 1916–21. Secretary of the Rhodes Trust, 1925–39. Succeeded his cousin as 11th Marquess of Lothian, 1930. Chancellor of the Duchy of Lancaster, 1931. Chairman of the Indian Franchise Committee, 1932. Ambassador in Washington from 1939 until his death.

the German establishment in the Armoured Divisions also seems to me wise. In short, it seems that both Armoured and Artillery Divisions will be the gainer by the changes. I cannot believe that any General, having the choice between an existing Infantry Division and a new division with its armoured element, would hesitate to choose the new one. The Armoured Divisions also can easily be grouped together when it is desirable to use mass formations of armoured troops in the same way as Cavalry Brigades and Divisions have been used in the past to form a Cavalry Corps. Such an organisation would rise naturally out of the tactical requirements of a particular operation or a particular theatre, and need not have a permanent cadre or fixed establishment prescribed beforehand.

2. Let me see the strengths and composition of the Home Field Army before and after the reorganisation under the following heads:

1. Infantry battalions.
2. Number of guns in the Field Artillery (including howitzers).
3. Flak and A/T Units.
4. Machine guns of all kinds.
5. Armoured fighting vehicles of all types.
6. Non-fighting vehicles of all types.
7. Staffs of all kinds.
8. Numbers of supply transport and Administrative Services of all kinds.
9. And the total of officers and men of all ranks.

3. In comparing these new tables with those of the German system, it would be worth while to test our new organisation by comparing the percentage of Staffs, Divisional and Brigade, to the numbers of men in the division. This might also be applied to Signals, Postal Units, &c. It does not follow that the Germans are right, but I think it will be found that they serve more fighting men with fewer overheads.

Winston S. Churchill to President Franklin D. Roosevelt
(Churchill papers, 20/74)

28 April 1942
Personal and Secret
No. 80

ARCTIC CONVOYS TO RUSSIA

Your No. 141.

Eden has been dealing with this for me in consultation with First Sea Lord and Leathers. Following is the position. Voyage of each of these convoys now entails major fleet operation. With the best will in the world cycle of convoys cannot be more than three in two months. One convoy (PQ15), limited to 25 merchant ships, has just sailed. In view of what you tell me we are ready to consider, in the light of the experience gained in this convoy, whether the number of merchant ships in future convoys can be increased to as many as 35. Convoy should reach North Russian ports in about ten days' time. Meanwhile we are arranging for 35 merchant ships to be loaded for the next convoy (PQ16) due to leave Iceland (C) on the 17th May. But 35 is the absolute maximum number which it is safe to risk without further experience of the scale of enemy attack.

It is not clear from your telegram whether you had seen the contents of Leathers' letter to Harriman of 25th April, which were telegraphed to Hopkins the same day. This explains that even if the size of the convoys is limited to 25 merchant ships each, there will be 75 ships carrying supplies to Russia every two months, of which 24 are sufficient to lift Protocol supplies[1] from the United Kingdom, leaving 51, including tankers, available to carry supplies from the USA in each two-monthly period. We estimate that, apart from food, the Protocol calls for about 150,000 short tons per month from the USA. Deducting 10,000 tons from this for deliveries via the Persian Gulf, and proceeding on the assumption that each ship will carry on the average 6,000 short tons, not more than 24 ships per month (i.e. 48 in the two months) would be required to lift your quotas, leaving a margin of two or three for tankers and food supplies.

But the assumption that each ship can carry on the average 6,000 short tons presupposes that the cargo is stowed in such a way as to ensure that the highest priority goods are loaded into a much smaller number of ships than is now employed. Hitherto ships have been carrying about half this tonnage. This is a waste we can neither of us afford. The only possible course to adopt in order to work off the present accumulation at Iceland (C) is therefore to bring to the United Kingdom most of the 16 ships now waiting there, and also some of the 50 American and Russian ships which are on their way across the Atlantic. These would be discharged and restored. In our view this is the only possible course if the most important cargo is to reach Russia in the largest possible volume at an early date.

I hope this may meet your views. We are at our utmost strain for convoy escorts.

---

[1] The reference is to agreements between the United States, United Kingdom, and Soviet Union by which the former two countries agreed to make supplies available to the latter. Such protocols typically included schedules of the goods to be supplied, specified by type and quantity.

Winston S. Churchill to President Franklin D. Roosevelt
(Churchill papers, 20/74)

28 April 1942
Personal and Secret
No. 81

OPERATION 'IRONCLAD' (MADAGASCAR)

We have given further thought to 'Ironclad', and we feel that, in order to reduce to a minimum the risk of warlike reaction by Vichy, it is essential that you should come in fully behind us immediately [when] the operation has taken place.

What we would ask is that in addition

(1) To authorising leaflets as proposed in my telegram No. 59, you should

(2) if possible send a token United States detachment to join the occupying forces as soon as possible:

(3) in any event inform the Vichy Government immediately the operation has taken place that the operation has your approval and support, and

(4) immediately make public that such a communication has been made to Vichy.

If I might make a suggestion, your communication to Vichy (which might be made to the French Ambassador in Washington on the morning of zero day) might be on the following lines:

'The United States Government wish to inform the French Government that the occupation by British forces of "Ironclad", which has been undertaken to forestall occupation by the enemy, has the full approval and support of the United States Government. In order to make this plain, the United States Government will take an early opportunity to send United States forces to participate in the occupation. The United States and British Governments jointly undertake to restore "Ironclad" to France after the war. The United States Government also wish to make it plain that any warlike act committed by Vichy against Great Britain in consequence of the occupation would be regarded by the United States Government as an attack upon the United Nations as a whole, from which the United States Government would draw the necessary consequences and take the appropriate action.'

Winston S. Churchill to Lord Linlithgow[1]
(Churchill papers, 20/74)

28 April 1942
Personal and Secret

In view of the strenuous efforts which I have been making to provide additional squadrons for the defence of India, I am gravely concerned to learn from telegram No. 1102 S of 21st April of the poor progress which is being made with the construction of the aerodromes from which these squadrons will need to operate.

It is clear that unless immediate and very energetic steps are taken aircraft will arrive in India before the aerodromes are ready for them and in that event my position vis-à-vis the President, through whose good offices a large proportion of the aircraft are being obtained, will be difficult indeed.

I would therefore ask you personally to look into the civil aspects of this question, especially labour supply, railway priorities and the commandeering of lorries so that progress may be accelerated to the utmost.

Meanwhile, the suggestions in paragraph 6 of your telegram will be urgently examined here by the Departments concerned.

Winston S. Churchill to President Franklin D. Roosevelt
(Churchill papers, 20/74)

29 April 1942
Personal and Secret
No. 82

Most grateful for your telegram about 'Ironclad', for which all goes forward. Also for allowing *Wasp* to have another good sting.

2. I am highly interested in escape of General Giraud[2] and his arrival in Vichy. This man might play a decisive part in bringing about things of which you had hopes. Please tell me anything you know.

3. We have made two desperate attacks on *Tirpitz* at Trondheim. Results of first, no damage, but second is more hopeful. Will let you know when photographs are developed late tonight. We are keeping the Air fighting

[1] Viceroy of India.

[2] Henri-Honoré Giraud, 1879–1949. Military Governor of Metz and commander of the 6th Military Region, 1936–40. Commanded French 7th Army, based on Dunkirk, 1940; advanced into Holland, 10 May 1940. Taken prisoner May 1940, but escaped in 1942; brought out of Vichy France by a British submarine. Commander-in-Chief of the United French Armed Forces, 1943–4.

up at full intensity. German retaliation strikes at towns near the coast which have no flak. Numbers are moderate and pilots sometimes make second journeys. Monday night we got three out of 20 on Norwich, and last night five out of 20 on York, all shot down by night fighters.

4. I have had a telegram from Curtin saying that General MacArthur has asked him to request me 'to divert to Australia the 2nd British Infantry Division which will be rounding the Cape during the latter part of April and the beginning of May, and also the Armoured Division which is to round the Cape one month later. The diversion, he says, would be of a temporary nature, and these forces would remain in Australia only until such time as the 9th Australian Imperial Force Division and the remainder of the 6th Division are returned.' I should not be able to send these forces to Australia unless it is definitely invaded by 8 or 10 Japanese Divisions. They are all urgently needed in India. I fear this is a prelude to the recall of the Australian 9th Division.

5. General MacArthur also asks for a British aircraft carrier, pointing out that it is wasteful to operate an unbalanced naval force. He further requests an additional allocation of shipping on the Australian–American run, stating that the present amount of 250,000 tons is quite inadequate to complete requisite defence strength apart from offensive action.

6. I should be glad to know whether these requirements have been approved by you or the Washington Pacific Defence Council, and whether General MacArthur has any authority from the United States for taking such a line. We are quite unable to meet these new demands which are none the less a cause of concern when put forward on General MacArthur's authority.

President Franklin D. Roosevelt to Winston S. Churchill
(Churchill papers, 20/74)

29 April 1942
No. 142

In regard to 'Ironclad' I am saying in my speech tonight as follows:

'Recently we have received news of a change in what we used to know as the Republic of France – a name dear to the hearts of all lovers of liberty – a name and an institution which we hope will soon be restored to full dignity.

'Throughout the Nazi occupation of France we have hoped for the maintenance of a French Government which would strive to regain independence to re-establish the principles of "Liberty, Equality and Fraternity" and to restore the historic culture of France. Our policy has been consistent from the very beginning. However, we are now concerned lest those who have recently come to power may seek to force the brave French people to submission to Nazi despotism.

'The United Nations will take measures if necessary to prevent the use of French territory in any part of the world for military purposes by the Axis powers. The good people of France will readily understand that such action is essential for the United Nations to prevent assistance to the armies or navies or air forces of Germany, Italy and Japan. The overwhelming majority of the French people understand that the fight of the United Nations is fundamentally their fight, that our victory means the restoration of a free and independent France – and the saving of France from the slavery which would be imposed upon her by her enemies and her internal traitors.

'We know how the French people really feel as we know that a deep-seated determination to obstruct every step in the Axis plan extends from Occupied France through Vichy France to the people of their colonies in every ocean and on every continent. Our planes are helping in the defence of French colonies today and soon American Flying Fortresses will be fighting for the liberation of the darkened continent of Europe.'

I fully approve your third and fourth suggestions and will get this to the French Ambassador on the morning of zero day and will add that if for the defeat of the Axis powers it is desirable that American troops or ships use 'Ironclad' in the common cause of the civilized peoples we shall not hesitate to do so at any time.

Winston S. Churchill to William Mackenzie King
(Churchill papers, 20/74)

29 April 1942
Secret

We are all cheered and fortified by the memorable decision[1] which Canada has taken at what may well be the hinge of the war.

---

[1] Canada's decision to introduce conscription.

Lady Leslie to Winston S. Churchill[1]
(Churchill papers, 20/74)

29 April 1942   Glaslough
                                                County Monaghan

Dearest Winston.

Looking through old letters I came across an early one from you describing your first visit to New York. I enclose a copy, as it will amuse you to read of your first impressions. How little you could foresee that 45 years later you would return there, and that the attention of the whole US would be focused on you. I don't remember who was travelling with you[2] – you write 'we', nor can I think why you sign yourself so pompously to me, except that you were very serious for a boy of twenty.[3] Nowadays most of my mail consists of letters praising you and extolling you to the skies, and abusing the people who heckle you and criticize your work, and they always end 'how proud you must be of him'. Well, so I am dear. We were cheered by the subdued tone of Hitler's speech.[4] I listened to him – his voice was no longer truculent and his German less flowery. I feel he has lost something.

We have Lady Reading[5] coming here on Sunday. It will be a great joy to see her again – so few of my friends ever come across the Channel now. I see nobody and letters are unsatisfactory, what with delays and censors. There will be wailing and gnashing of teeth in US over the reduction of incomes – the fair ladies will not have such smart clothes! I buy nothing new till you have won your victory (oh I had to buy galoshes for it rains every day!).

My love to darling Clemmie
Yr. Devoted old
Leonie[6]

[1] This letter was handwritten.

[2] It was Churchill's fellow officer, Reginald ('Reggie') Barnes.

[3] Churchill had signed his letter to his aunt with his full name: 'Winston S. Churchill'.

[4] On 6 April 1942, in the course of a speech in the Reichstag, Hitler declared: 'In my eyes, the year 1942 already has behind it the most fateful trial of our people. That was the winter of 41 to 42. I may be permitted to say that in that winter the German people, and in particular its Wehrmacht, were weighed in the balance by Providence. Nothing worse can or will happen. That we conquered that winter, that "General Winter", that at last the German fronts stood, and that this spring, that is, early this summer, we were able to proceed again, that, I believe, is the proof that Providence was content with the German people [...] You do not realize what is hidden beneath these words in the way of human heroism, and also of human pain, and suffering, and we may say, often anxiety too, naturally, deathly anxiety on the part of all those who, especially for the first time, are placed before the trial of God in this highest court.'

[5] Stella Charnaud, 1894–1971. Married the 1st Marquess of Reading (Rufus Isaacs) in 1931. Widowed, 1935. Vice-Chairman, Imperial Relations Trust, 1936–68. Governor of the BBC, 1946; Vice-Chairman of the BBC, 1947–51.

[6] Churchill replied to his aunt by telegram: 'Thank you so much. Best Love, Winston.'

On 30 April 1942, HMS *Edinburgh,* on convoy escort duty, was damaged by a U-boat in the Arctic.

President Franklin D. Roosevelt to Winston S. Churchill
(Churchill papers, 20/74)

30 April 1942   Washington DC
No. 143
ARCTIC CONVOYS TO RUSSIA

King is communicating with Pound today relative to the urgent necessity of getting off one more convoy in May in order to break the log jam of ships already loaded or being loaded for Russia.

I am very anxious that ships not be unloaded and reloaded in England because I believe it would leave impossible and very disquieting impression in Russia.

Our problem is to move 107 ships now loaded or being loaded in the United Kingdom and the United States prior to June first. I hope you will agree to the proposal King is making because I think on balance that this is the most important thing we can use our escorts for.

We would watch our loadings from here out so that the agreed upon number leaving Iceland after June first would fall within the possibilities of our convoy system. I know that this is a difficult enterprise but I think it is so important that I hope you will examine King's proposal with Pound carefully.

Roosevelt

Winston S. Churchill to General Hastings Ismay,
for the Chiefs of Staff Committee
(Churchill papers, 20/67)

30 April 1942
Secret
OPERATION 'IRONCLAD': (MADAGASCAR)

Too much stress should not be laid on 'gaining control of the whole island.' It is 900 miles long, and all that really matters are the two or three principal centres and, above all, Diego Suarez. We are not setting out to subjugate Madagascar, but rather to establish ourselves in key positions to deny it to a far-flung Japanese attack. A principal object must be to get our good troops forward to India and Ceylon at the earliest moment, replacing them with garrison battalions from East or West Africa. Getting this place is meant to be a help and not a new burden. The true defence of Madagascar will be the Eastern Fleet when based with adequate air on Colombo and Port T. There is no need to alter the telegram, but I should be glad that this point of view should be recognised.

Winston S. Churchill to General Claude Auchinleck
(Churchill papers, 20/88)

30 April 1942

Later, most secret,[1] information which you have received confirms your estimate in CS/938, 25th April. You will also have noticed[2] reinforcements completing 12,000 to reach Africa Army by the end of May.

Winston S. Churchill to John Curtin
(Churchill papers, 20/74)

30 April 1942
Personal and Secret

Please see my Winch No. 20 which defines the conditions in which alone we should be justified in diverting divisions to Australia as they round the Cape. Since then no signs have appeared of a heavy mass invasion of Australia, although attacks at Port Moresby and Port Darwin are possible. The danger to India has been increased by the events in Burma as well as by an inevitable delay due to needs in home waters in building up the Eastern Fleet. We should certainly be judged to have acted wrongly if we sent to an uninvaded Australia troops needed for an invaded India. The most noticeable strategic movement of Japanese forces has been the reinforcement by three divisions of their army of twenty divisions in Manchuria towards Siberian Russia. We must continue to decide where to send our limited reinforcements according to the situation.

2. The arrangements General MacArthur proposes of sending the 2nd Division and the Armoured Division to Australia temporarily pending

---

[1] Derived from Enigma decrypts.
[2] From another Enigma-based message.

the return of the remainder of the 6th Australian Division and the 9th Australian Division would seem to involve the maximum expenditure and dislocation of shipping and escorts.

3. We hope to relieve the Australian troops in Ceylon by 2 Brigade Groups of our 5th Division which is now in the Indian Ocean, at about the end of May.

4. None of the three armoured aircraft carriers, *Illustrious, Formidable* and *Indomitable,* can be taken from the Eastern Fleet. To remove one would be to destroy its chances of fighting a Fleet action this summer. The small carrier *Hermes* which we had hoped to send you has been sunk, and no other carrier is available.

5. I cannot hold out any prospect of our being able to increase the British allocation of shipping on the Australian–American run. The whole of our tonnage is engaged to the utmost in transporting munitions to Russia, in the heavy troop convoys of about 50,000 men a month we are sending round the Cape, and in the very sharply straitened supply to this island.

6. Nevertheless you may be sure that General MacArthur's recommendations will continue to be studied here, and I have also reported them to the President in case he may feel able to take any further action. I am also looking forward to discussing the position with Dr Evatt, who will soon be here.

Winston S. Churchill to General Archibald Wavell
(Churchill papers, 20/74)

30 April 1942
Personal and Secret

Your No. 10319 and other messages on the same point. It is natural and indeed your duty to see things from your own point of view, but we have the painful task of assigning priorities for our limited reinforcements among various urgent and serious claims.

2. I send you in my immediately following telegram (OZ 119) the appreciation of C-in-C Home Fleet which gives solid reasons why we are unable to make the full concentration before June.

3. I also send you in my OZ 120 the latest I have received from Mr Curtin, from which you will see that he is using General MacArthur to claim the 2nd Division and Armoured Divisions which will be rounding the Cape at the beginning of May and in the early days of June respectively.

I do not intend to agree to this unless Australia is at that time actually invaded by 8 or 10 Japanese divisions. This seems to be most unlikely.

4. Both these telegrams will give you an idea of the calls upon us.

5. The proposed attempt to relieve Malta cannot be decided upon till the early days of June. If the operation is thought too dangerous or if the situation in the Indian Ocean is critical, the decision will be adverse. You realize I suppose that this would seal the fate of Malta and its large garrison. It is a question of balancing risks and evils, and this can only be done at close quarters with them.

6. Perhaps you would convey the substance of this communication to the C-in-C Ceylon who has also protested from the Ceylon angle.

May
1942

Winston S. Churchill to Oliver Lyttelton
(Churchill papers, 20/67)

1 May 1942

I note from DC (S) (42) 34[1] that the output of aircraft is still far below programme. Heavy bombers are one-fifth down, light bombers nearly one-half. This is most disappointing in a long month after we had been promised that these were truly realistic forecasts. I hope you will be able to find out what is the real limiting factor, so that it can be put right.

Neither the programme of labour requirements, which has been outstanding for a long time, and which you asked for at your last meeting, nor the report on specialised machine tools with a statement about double shifting and the types in short supply has yet been presented.

Can we rely absolutely upon sufficient allocations of magnesium from America in the second half of this year? According to DC (S) (42) 34, our supplies will only be 10,600 tons as against requirements of 14,900 tons.

I observe that aircrews are not mentioned in this monthly Report. Last autumn the position was held to be disquieting, and from WP (42) 181 it appears that the difficulties have not been overcome. This is a most serious matter and every effort must be made to put it right immediately.

Winston S. Churchill to Air Chief Marshal Sir Charles Portal
(Churchill papers, 20/67)

1 May 1942
Most Secret

Let me have by tomorrow the proposed policy for bombing during May together with a list of the principal objectives at which it is desired

[1] The Aircraft Programme: Monthly Progress Report for March 1942 by the Minister of Aircraft Production (Colonel John Jestyn Llewellin from February to November 1942).

to strike. I realise, of course, that the weather governs our actions from day to day, but give me the plan apart from weather.

2. You have no doubt seen General Dobbie's appeal for an intervention by Bomber Command in Sicily. It might be this would be necessary in order to keep down the attack just before a wave of Spitfires was landed. How would you do it? Could the Wellingtons[1] fly from England to bomb Sicily, land on the possibly cratered airfields of Malta, and return home the next night, dropping another load of bombs? If not Wellingtons, what aircraft would you use? It is quite understood this would be very costly if it had to be done. Pray let me have the best plan possible.

3. Will a PRU[2] be sent over *Tirpitz* again today? This might reveal tugs in position round her. It is most important to get information.

President Franklin D. Roosevelt to Winston S. Churchill
(Churchill papers, 20/74)

1 May 1942
Personal and Secret
No. 144

It seems probable to me that the request made upon you by Mr Curtin for two divisions and for additional marine assistance was made upon his own responsibility although probably based upon conversations with General MacArthur. The directive under which General MacArthur holds his command provides that the United States Chiefs of Staff will constitute the executive agency through which orders are to be passed to him and we had assumed that any request of his for reinforcement would be directed here. However the command set up in Australia is complex and understandings in certain details are reached only as they arise and it is therefore possible that both Mr Curtin and General MacArthur felt it proper to make request for British assistance directly upon the British Government.

We have previously replied to a message from General MacArthur informing him that additional airplane carriers are not now available for assignment to the South West Pacific. Only today we received another

---

[1] Wellington: The Vickers Wellington was a British-designed and British-built twin-engine, long-range medium bomber, introduced into the RAF in 1938. It was used widely early in the war as a night bomber, and throughout the war on anti-submarine duties. It saw action in Europe and the Mediterranean with the RAF, Fleet Air Arm, Royal Canadian Air Force, and Polish Air Force. More than 11,000 were built during the Second World War.

[2] PRU: Photographic Reconnaissance Unit (Royal Air Force).

request for a number of ships desired for coastwise and local transportation in Australia but we had no knowledge of any special need for additional trans-Pacific shipping nor for the two British Divisions now at sea.

I agree with you these should go to India and I hope Mr Curtin's request is not a mere preliminary to an insistence upon the return home of the Ninth Australian Division. As you know in accepting some time ago your suggestion that we send an additional Division to the Australians we did so in the hope that they would then feel able to leave one of their own in the Middle East. We will instruct General MacArthur immediately that his future requests for reinforcements except for routine supply which should follow accustomed channels will be processed to the United States Chiefs of Staff. Where your forces are concerned we will then communicate with the British Chiefs of Staff.

With this arrangement definitely prescribed and understood you will know that any request reaching you from Mr Curtin is made upon his own responsibility. If you think it advisable I will express the hope to Mr Curtin that he will not ask the return of any of his troops from the Near East.

This despatch is in reference to your number eight two.

Roosevelt

Winston S. Churchill to President Franklin D. Roosevelt
(Churchill papers, 20/74)

1 May 1942
Personal and Most Secret
No. 84

OPERATION 'IRONCLAD' (MADAGASCAR)

Thank you for your telegram No. 142 which is of great help to us. We have drafted terms which we propose that the Force Commander should, if he can, put to the Governor at the earliest possible moment. After stating that the territory cannot be allowed to suffer the fate of Indo-China and that it should be made available to those forces which are fighting to restore freedom of the world and secure the liberation of France and French territory, the Governor is summoned to surrender the territory unconditionally and is given the following assurances. The territory will remain French. Those who elect to return to France will be repatriated as opportunity offers. The salaries and pensions of all officials who elect to co-operate will be provided for. Trade with the United Nations will be restored and the territory will receive all the economic benefits accorded to those French territories which have already joined the United Nations.

2. In view of your telegram, I am including a statement that the operation has the full approval of the Government of the United States, unless I hear from you that you see objection to this.

3. In addition to your communication to the French Ambassador at Washington I would urge that it is essential that the same message should also be delivered to Pétain or Laval at the earliest possible moment in order that they may know what is afoot before the news reaches Vichy from 'Ironclad'. I would suggest that you telegraph the text of your communication *en clair* to Mr Tuck[1] as soon as you hear from us that the Operation has been launched. This will be done by code-word through Field Marshal Dill, and if all goes well the news should reach you between 8 p.m. and 11 p.m. Eastern Standard time on Monday, 4th May. This will mean that your man at Vichy will have to act any time after 3 a.m. Tuesday, 5th May Vichy local time.

4. If for any reason, such as weather, the Operation has to be postponed, the Force Commander will naturally maintain wireless silence and we shall receive no news for 24 or perhaps even 48 hours.

Winston S. Churchill to General Archibald Wavell
(Churchill papers, 20/74)

1 May 1942
Personal and Secret

I have given immediate personal consideration to your 10577 C. The two Brigades of 6th Australian Division will not move from Ceylon until they are relieved by two of the Brigades of 5th Division. The remaining brigade of that Division and divisional troops are moving straight on to India. As soon as arrangements can be made to replace the 29th Independent Brigade Group which is one of our best and most highly trained Brigades in 'Ironclad' by inferior troops, it will also come forward to you. The whole of the 2nd Division should also be with you by June 8 unless Australia is actually heavily invaded, meanwhile, in which case India's danger would be diminished. As against this the second in order of the

---

[1] Somerville Pinkney Tuck, 1891–1967. Also known as S. Pinkney Tuck. United States Foreign Service Officer. Consul in Alexandria (1919), Samsun (1921), Vladivostok (1922–3), Geneva (1924–8). Counsellor, United States Embassy at Vichy (appointed October 1941). Minister to Egypt, 1944; Ambassador to Egypt, 1946–8.

two African Brigades you were expecting, one of which you already have, will have to go to garrison 'Ironclad' if operation is successful.

2. Operation 'Ironclad' on which War Cabinet is resolved date of which will be cabled separately, involves 29th Independent Brigade Group plus one Commando and one Brigade of the 5th Division. A second Brigade of the 5th Division is standing by at sea as a potential reserve. It is however hoped that the delay to this Brigade will be short, as Vichy garrison of 'Ironclad' is reported to consist only of local native troops with about two hundred French officers, against which we are putting eleven thousand of our best troops.

3. India has a real interest in 'Ironclad' as a Japanese fleet established there would paralyse our communications with India.

4. We are sorry about the need of moving the two Australian Brigades from Ceylon, but it was always understood with the Commonwealth Government that they were only stopped off temporarily to meet emergency. You had no grounds for counting on them as a permanency. Of course, if an actual attack took place before they left it would not be possible to let them go even though their reliefs had arrived.

5. We fully understand and share your anxieties but except for a short delay in respect of two Brigades of the 5th Division and the withholding of the second African Brigade you should be stronger and not weaker than you had been led to expect.

[...]

Winston S. Churchill to Field Marshal Jan Smuts
(Churchill papers, 20/53)

1 May 1942
Personal and Secret

I send this by Mr Waterson[1] to give you my warmest wishes.

I am very glad you will be on the spot at the time mentioned. All our hopes are centred upon the successful engagement of the Army. The fate of Malta depends upon our gaining ground to the westward, and the hazards of battle ought, in my judgment, to be accepted. If this opportunity is lost, the enemy will probably grow stronger the more we wait. I should be very glad to know your personal independent opinion after you have

---

[1] Sidney Frank Waterson, 1896–1976. Educated at Westminster School. On active service, 1915–19 (Salonika and France). Moved to South Africa after the First World War; a member of the Union of South Africa Parliament, 1929–38. High Commissioner for the Union of South Africa in London, 1939–42. Returned to South Africa to become Minister of Economic Development, 1943–8; of Mines, 1945–8; of Transport, 1948.

been into the whole situation with Auchinleck and with Casey, who can tell you how we feel here. Please wire me as fully as possible.

I shall also look forward to speaking to you on the telephone from Cairo. Although we cannot deal with secret matters, it will be a joy to me to hear your voice again.

I hesitate very much to suggest your coming here, because I know how great are your preoccupations in South Africa and how precious is your safety to the Empire and the Cause. Nevertheless if you could come via Takoradi and visit us, it would have a splendid effect and Cabinet and Parliament would welcome you with the utmost enthusiasm. If you should decide on this, I will make every arrangement for the safety and comfort of your journey. You alone must judge whether it is expedient.

Before you get this, 'Ironclad' will be over. I feel quite hopeful that with the heavy forces employed the capture of the main harbour should be sure and speedy. It will be of the utmost importance to move these specially trained troops forward to India without the slightest delay and to replace them by holding forces. We are so straitened at the present time that we could not afford to take on an additional burden of this kind. I hope however that if all goes well and we are given additional breathing-space, we may establish ourselves so strongly at Colombo that 'Ironclad' will be well shielded from the war. Anything you can do to send in extra troops and aircraft from South Africa will be of the greatest assistance.

With every good wish,
Believe me,
Winston S. Churchill

Winston S. Churchill to General Hastings Ismay,
for the Chiefs of Staff Committee
(Churchill papers, 20/67)

2 May 1942

OPERATION 'IRONCLAD' (MADAGASCAR)

At first we thought only of taking DS,[1] but later on General Smuts emphasised the importance of T[2] and A,[3] and we instructed our Commanders to extend their plans.

---

[1] DS: Diego Suarez.

[2] T: Tamatave: the one port on the Indian Ocean coast of Madagascar.

[3] A: Antananarivo: the capital and largest town in Madagascar, 100 miles from the Indian Ocean.

2. Great care must be taken, however, not to let these new objectives delay the movement of British troops to India. There can be no question of spreading our forces out in the island at the outset. DS is the only thing that matters, and the tidying up can be done any time in the next three months.

3. Of course, all may go quite easily, but it must be made clear to the Commanders that three out of the four British brigades must be on their way to India within forty-eight hours of the capture of DS. Portsmouth could be held with the enemy in Caithness, and so DS with hostile forces still in A and T.[1]

4. A message should be sent on the following lines:

'As soon as DS has been captured, all British troops except the 29th Brigade Group must resume their voyage to India with the utmost urgency. Tidying up of the rest of the island must await convenience and, if necessary, arrival of other forces.'

Pray consider the above.

Winston S. Churchill to President Franklin D. Roosevelt
(Churchill papers, 20/88)

2 May 1942
Personal and Secret

With very great respect, what you suggest is beyond our power to fulfil. Admiral King has expressed opinion that our Transatlantic escorts are already too thin. Reduction proposed would dislocate convoy system for eight weeks, during which, if enemy switched from your east coast to mid-ocean, disastrous consequences might follow to our main life line.

2. Moreover, difficulty of Russian convoys cannot be solved merely by anti-submarine craft. Enemy heavy ships and destroyers may at any time strike. Even on this present QP Convoy[2] we have been attacked by hostile destroyers, which were beaten off with damage to one of ours. *Edinburgh*,[3] one of our best 6-inch cruisers, has been badly damaged by

---

[1] It is 400 miles from Diego Suarez in northern Madagascar to Antananarivo in central Madagascar; 573 miles from Caithness in northern Scotland to Portsmouth in southern England.

[2] Convoy QP 11 left Murmansk on 28 April 1942 and arrived in Reykjavik on 7 May 1942. Its 13 merchant ships flew the British (4), American (4), Panamanian (4), and Russian (1) flags.

[3] The cruiser HMS *Edinburgh* (launched 1938), having joined Convoy QP 11 after loading a large quantity of gold at Murmansk, was torpedoed on 30 April 1942 while taking station ahead of the convoy. She was being towed towards Murmansk (as reported by Churchill) when she was torpedoed again (her stern being blown off) on 2 May 1942; 58 of her crew were drowned. The gold was salvaged in the early 1980s. The Russian merchant ship, the *Tsiolkovsky*, was also sunk.

U-boats and is being towed to Murmansk, where *Trinidad*,[1] damaged last convoy, is still penned. Just now I have received news that *King George V* has collided with our destroyer *Punjabi*,[2] *Punjabi* being sunk and her depth charges exploding have damaged *King George V*. Difficulty of Russian convoy escorts is therefore at least as much surface ships of high fighting quality as of anti-submarine craft. We have made desperate attacks on *Tirpitz*, in Trondheim, but, alas, although near the target, have not achieved any damage.

3. I beg you not to press us beyond our judgment in this operation, which we have studied most intently, and of which we have not yet been able to measure the full strain. I can assure you, Mr President, we are absolutely extended and I could not press the Admiralty further.

4. Six ships from Iceland have already arrived at the Clyde and their reloading ought to begin forthwith. Three convoys every two months, with either 35 or 25 ships in each convoy, according to experience, represent extreme limit of what we can handle. Pound is cabling separately to Admiral King.

General Archibald Wavell to Winston S. Churchill
(Churchill papers, 20/74)

2 May 1942   India
Personal and Most Secret

Fully appreciate your anxieties as regards Malta, naval strength in Home waters and Australian claims, and most difficult decisions which you have to take in these matters. Do not feel, however, that I am kept sufficiently in picture to make forward planning easy. I gave some examples in my telegram, but by no means all.

2. I recognise that changes of plan are inevitable in war, but feel that forewarning might have saved me some shocks and dangers. It must,

---

[1] The cruiser HMS *Trinidad* (launched 1938), while escorting the Reykjavik–Murmansk convoy PQ 13, was struck by her own malfunctioning torpedo while seeking to engage a German U-boat in March 1942; 32 of its crew were killed. She was later damaged in a German air attack, and scuttled (15 May 1942).

[2] The destroyer HMS *Punjabi* (launched 1937) was sunk on 1 May 1942 in a collision in dense fog with *King George V* while both were part of a screen providing distant cover for Reykjavik–Murmansk Convoy PQ 15; 49 of her crew of 209 were drowned. Churchill did not know at that point, and thus could not tell Roosevelt, that the American battleship USS *Washington*, also part of the screen, had to sail between the halves of the sinking destroyer and suffered slight damage from the detonation of the destroyers' depth charges.

for instance, surely have been known beforehand that R repeat R class battleships were incapable of facing Japanese fleet and I should not repeat not have been led to believe that strong fleet was available by end of March.

3. I have not repeat not been consulted on 'Ironclad', which has obvious repercussions on defence of India, and do not repeat not know arguments for it, but should have thought that with our present weak forces, concentration was better policy than dispersion.

4. As regards 5th Division WO telegram 80090 of 2/4 definitely gave whole Division as due India, and nothing indicated any change till 85243 was received. I have been making number moves to clear accommodation for whole division in India, and have based plans on its being available. WO telegram 74696 of 6/3 stated that Australian Brigades would be removed only when sufficient naval and air reinforcements had arrived which is certainly not yet. I had therefore every reason to expect I should have Australian Brigades and 5th Division during critical period when no fleet may be available.

5. If whole of 2nd and 5th Divisions and 29th Brigade eventually reach me, I may be up to expected strength, but this will not be before July, and my experience of commitments such as 'Ironclad' is that they grow and absorb troops, rather than diminish. During critical months of May and June I shall be much weaker than expected, and events are moving very fast in Burma.

6. Do not rpt not think it is appreciated at home how long moves take in India, and therefore how far ahead they have to be planned. It has taken one month to move Brigade from Abbotabad to Assam, and move of 23rd Division of two brigades only from Ranchi to Assam will take 3 to 4 weeks.

7. Will do our best with what you provide, but feel it my duty to represent above.

Winston S. Churchill to Randolph S. Churchill
(Churchill papers, 1/369)

2 May 1942   10 Downing Street
Personal

I send this letter by DMI,[1] hoping it will make a swift passage. The papers say that you have rejoined the Commandos. Of course I do not wish

---
[1] The Director of Military Intelligence, Francis Davidson.

to hamper you in any way, but I am told that parachuting becomes much more dangerous with heavy people. This no doubt will be considered. I notice that David Stirling has been recalled home, but I hope that you will have found other friends and that the life will be to your liking.

I was very glad to hear from Stafford Cripps that he had met you dining at the Embassy, so I suppose all is put right there.

Things are better here for the time being. I made a speech of an hour and fifty minutes in Secret Session, which opened the eyes of the House so much to the vast panorama of the war and its many grievous dangers, that the debate utterly collapsed and we are not to have one on the war till just before Whitsuntide.

People here are greatly heartened by our Air offensive over Germany. Lübeck and Rostock[1] were practically destroyed, and one German city after another will get during this summer the worst punishment that has yet been inflicted in this war. There are many signs that the Germans will be gravely affected by the prolonged, severe Air bombardment coming upon their homes at the same time that they will be bleeding on the 2,000-miles Russian front. As the summer progresses the weakness of all the Axis Powers in the Air will become increasingly apparent, and it is our interest to force the Air fighting at every point. Our improved methods of dealing with the very puny retaliatory attacks which they have been forced to make on this country, reached their climax last night when we shot down 11 out of less than 50. We have a lot of other things going forward which will become noticeable in due course.

The depression following Singapore has been replaced by an undue optimism, which I am of course keeping in proper bounds.

We had a bad day yesterday on the home front, losing both Wallasey[2] and Rugby[3] to our local hostile – .[4] There is no doubt that at these by-elections, the only people who will really take the trouble to go to the poll are those who have a grudge against the Government. Only about 35 per cent. vote, and the loyal majority are busy with their war work. Both

---

[1] On the night of 26–7 April 1942, more than a hundred bombers of Bomber Command struck at Rostock: 60 percent of the town centre was destroyed and 204 German civilians killed. In reporting the raid, German radio used the term 'terror raid' for the first time. Dr Goebbels noted in his diary that 'community life in Rostock is practically at an end'.

[2] At the Wallasey by-election on 29 April 1942, George Leonard Reakes, a former Mayor of Wallasey (1937–8) and Labour supporter, who was working in the postal censorship, won (uncontested) a traditionally Tory seat, calling out when the results were announced: 'It is a victory for Churchill!'

[3] At the Rugby by-election on 29 April 1942, William John Brown stood (uncontested) as an Independent candidate, and was elected. In the 1945 general election he held the seat against both Conservative and Labour challengers, but came third in the general election of 1950.

[4] Word missing in Churchill's copy of this letter.

the victorious candidates (Independents) proclaimed their allegiance to me personally, and of course they all clamour for more vigorous war. There is no sort of pacifism or war-weariness to be discerned in any of these fights. The days when Party chairmen could have a safe walk-over are however ended.

Max will be back in a day or two, and I am looking forward to hearing his account of the American scene.

Averell has been quite seriously ill, it seems with a kind of typhoid, but he is definitely better these last few days. Pamela will no doubt tell you more about this, as she and Kathleen[1] are watching over him, assisted by the best doctors and nurses. I earnestly hope he will be better soon, for he is a true friend of our country, and I have taken a great personal liking to him.

Mary has become a Sergeant, and is much counted on in her Battery. She tells me that she has written to you. Your Mother has been suffering from tiredness as a result of her Russian Fund and other activities. She has had a sore throat, which is now better.

I went to Chartwell last week, and found Spring there in all its beauty. The goose I called the naval aide-de-camp and the male black swan have both fallen victims to the fox. The Yellow Cat[2] however made me sensible of his continuing friendship, although I had not been there for eight months.

Pamela seems very well, and is a great treasure and blessing to us all. Winston was in the pink when I saw him last. He has not so far grown old enough to commit the various forms of indiscretion which he would be expected to inherit from his forebears. Sarah[3] and Diana are both well and lively, and send their love.

---

[1] Kathleen Harriman, 1917–2011. Averell Harriman's younger daughter. When her father was in London (1941–2), she served as a reporter for the International News Service, and later for *Newsweek*. Accompanied her father to Moscow (1943–5), sending her newspaper reports from there, and to the Yalta Conference (1945). In 1947 she married Stanley Mortimer Jr, an heir to the Standard Oil fortune. Her father died in 1986. In 1994, she was one of a group of her father's heirs who sued his second wife, Pamela Harriman (Randolph Churchill's former wife), charging that she and her associates had squandered tens of millions of dollars of their inheritance through high-risk investments. The suit was settled in 1995; the terms of the settlement were not disclosed.

[2] This was Tango. Grace Hamblin, who worked at Chartwell from 1932 to 1939 and was Clementine Churchill's private secretary throughout the war, writes: 'All cats were made much of, and ginger was the favoured colour – or "tango"' (letter to the author, 22 December 1997). When Chartwell passed into the hands of the National Trust after Churchill's death, the family requested that a marmalade cat named Jock (after Churchill's own last cat, a birthday gift from Sir John Colville) always be kept in residence.

[3] Sarah Millicent Hermione Spencer Churchill, 1914–83. Dancer and actor. Born while her father was returning from the siege of Antwerp, 7 October 1914. Married Vic Oliver in 1936 (divorced, 1945). Appeared on stage in Birmingham, Southampton, Weston-super-Mare, and London, 1937–9; on tour with Vic Oliver in the play *Idiot's Delight*, 1938; in London in *Quiet Wedding*, 1939, and in

Casey will be out soon, and I have no doubt will get into touch with you. He is a very good man and will, I am sure, do well.

Winston S. Churchill to Robert Graves[1]
(Churchill papers, 20/53)

2 May 1942

My dear Robert Graves,

I am sorry to remember that I have deferred so long in writing to tell you how much I enjoyed 'Sergeant Lamb of the Ninth' and 'Proceed Sergeant Lamb'.[2]

I have read very few books during this war, in fact I think only six or seven altogether. I find sometimes a book dwells with me for several months, and I read a chapter or two at a time.

I greatly enjoyed these books of yours, as indeed I have all your pictures of the past which you have a wonderful gift of recalling. Also I am a great lover of narrative, in which art you excel.

Once more thanking you,

Believe me,
Yours sincerely,
Winston S. Churchill

J. M. Barrie's *Mary Rose*, 1940. Appeared in the film *Spring Meeting*, 1940. Entered the Women's Auxiliary Air Force, October 1941. Assistant Section Officer (later Section Officer) at the Photographic Interpretation Unit, Medmenham, 1941–5. Accompanied her father (as ADC), to the conferences at Teheran (November 1943) and Yalta (February 1945). In 1949 married Anthony Beauchamp, who died in 1957. In 1951 appeared on the US stage in *Grammercy Ghost*. In April 1962 married the 23rd Baron Audley, MBE, who died in July 1963. Published *The Empty Spaces* (poems) in 1966, *A Thread in the Tapestry* (recollections) in 1967, *Collected Poems* in 1974, and *Keep on Dancing* (further recollections) in 1981.

[1] Robert von Ranke Graves, 1895–1985. Writer. Educated at Charterhouse and St John's College, Oxford (Honorary Fellow, 1971). Though a pacifist, he served in France during the First World with the Royal Welch Fusiliers. Bronze Medal for Poetry, Olympic Games, Paris, 1924. Professor of English Literature, Egyptian University, 1926. Clark Lecturer, Trinity College Cambridge, 1954. Gold Medal of National Poetry Society of America, 1960. Professor of Poetry, University of Oxford, 1961–6. Arthur Dehon Little Memorial Lecturer, Massachusetts Institute of Technology, 1963. Gold Medal for Poetry, Cultural Olympics, Mexico, 1968. Queen's Gold Medal for Poetry, 1968. His books (over 137) and manuscripts are on permanent exhibition at Lockwood Memorial Library, Buffalo, NY. In 1968 the village of Deya, Mallorca, where he had lived since 1929, recognised him as an adoptive son.

[2] The fictional life of Roger Lamb, a young Irishman serving in the American War of Independence. The novel was first published in two parts (in 1940), because of wartime paper shortage, as *Sergeant Lamb of the Ninth* and *Proceed, Sergeant Lamb*.

Winston S. Churchill to General Hastings Ismay,
for the Chiefs of Staff Committee
(Churchill papers, 20/67)

3 May 1942
Secret

I have approved paragraph 4 of Colonel Price's[1] minute[2] which has been telephoned for immediate action. The scale on which Diego Suarez should be fortified as a naval base depends on whether we are able to re-establish ourselves at Colombo and Port T.[3] At present this is hoped to be about mid-July. In the interval there is the question of the Malta convoy. One does not, therefore, see how the Fleet will be able to base itself on DS to any important extent in the near future. The same is true of Kilindini.

2. Nevertheless a proportion of AA guns should be set up at DS, and it should be developed as a reserve base as our means allow. Do the Chiefs of Staff agree with the view that DS should rank before Kilindini so far as <u>additions</u> are concerned? Anyhow, for the next two months Colombo must continue to have first priority in AA.

3. Should we again be comfortable in the Bay of Bengal and in Ceylon waters, we must look forward to building up Port T as a strong base with proper AA and shore-based torpedo squadrons and reconnaissance craft. But it is not necessary to consider this immediately.

4. I agree with CIGS's proposals,[4] but I think paragraph 4 should be pressed with the utmost energy. The Foreign Secretary told me the Belgians would readily give these troops. Alternatively, if this fails, there is a West African Brigade. We shall need three Brigades to hold 'Ironclad,' and the whole of the 5th Division is to go forward to India at the earliest moment after the operation. It is also most important to relieve the 29th Brigade Group and send it to India as soon as suitable relief can be provided. It will probably be necessary to have a certain number of white troops in DS in addition to gunners, &c., but these need not be mobilised field troops organised in brigades. Battalions will suffice. SA[5] might find a couple.

---

[1] Lieutenant-Colonel C. R. Price, RE, of the War Cabinet Secretariat under Cabinet Secretary Sir Edward Bridges.

[2] On the air and other forces to be used in holding Madagascar if captured.

[3] Port T: Trincomalee.

[4] Memorandum by General Sir Alan Brooke (Chief of the Imperial General Staff) recommending the transference of two brigade groups from East Africa.

[5] SA: South Africa.

Winston S. Churchill to Sir Reginald Dorman-Smith[1]
(Churchill papers, 20/74)

3 May 1942
Most Immediate
Secret

BURMA

If and when you feel you cannot do any good by remaining as seems to be the case you should return by air to India and report from there to Secretary of State. You should make best arrangements possible for your staff. Every effort will be made to send Blenheim or other aircraft. The above is to be taken as an order.

Sir Reginald Dorman-Smith to Winston S. Churchill
(Churchill papers, 20/74)

3 May 1942
Most Immediate
Private and Personal   Myitkyina

With a very heavy heart I will obey your orders. I can do no more good here and will leave dawn May 5th.

Richard Casey[2] to Winston S. Churchill
(Churchill papers, 20/74)

3 May 1942   Malta
Hush
Most Secret
Immediate

I arrived Gibraltar 29th April was weather bound there for two days and reached here late night of May 1st. I leave for Cairo tonight.

2. I talked with Gort in Gibraltar and spent yesterday getting to know Dobbie, Lieut. Governor and three service commanders here.

3. I have no doubt that Dobbie should be replaced by Gort as soon as possible.

4. Dobbie is man of courage and high character who has set example of steadiness and devotion to duty. He has gone out of his way to make my task easy for me by his generous attitude. I hope his services and high quality will be publicly recognised.

[1] Governor of Burma.
[2] Minister Resident in the Middle East.

5. But the team here are not working together and the main reason is that Dobbie is no longer capable of vigorous leadership. He has little grasp of the situation or power of decision and lacks the knowledge and drive which would enable him to guide and where necessary impose his will on the forceful commanders under him. Although respected by the civil population he is not giving them adequate lead and has failed to get anything like the maximum out of them. For example with population of 300,000 it should have been possible to organise large body of adult male labourers to work under discipline in support of services. Accomplishment in this field has been totally inadequate. Situation today is regrettable. It would become menace if shortage food or threat of invasion put population under further strain. Dobbie's departure will be regretted by people of Malta but his own view with which I agree is that it will not be more than 9 days wonder.

6. Service Commanders assure me they have every confidence in one another. Account they gave me of service unity may be a little rose coloured (see next paragraph) but they certainly seem to have come to proper understanding about control in event of invasion. Task of resisting attempt at invasion would fall principally on General Beak[1] as enemy would presumably begin by neutralising RAF and there is no naval strength. Admiral Leatham[2] and AVM Lloyd[3] have agreed in circumstances to place all their personnel at disposal of General Beak who appears to be robust fighting soldier determined to make utmost possible resistance with forces available.

7. There is of course inevitable strain and criticism at lower level. It is agreed there is lack of plan on air defence: naval staff are considered weak but they have little to do. Such matters Gort will make his care.

8. My chief doubt relates to office of Lieutenant Governor. Service chiefs have no faith in Sir Edward Jackson[4] its present occupant. He is

[1] Daniel Marcus William Beak, 1891–1967. Commander, Royal Naval Volunteer Reserve, 1914–18 (Victoria Cross, Military Cross and bar, DSO). His Victoria Cross was awarded for his actions on the Western Front on 21–5 August and 4 September 1918. General Officer Commanding, Malta, 1942.

[2] Ralph Leatham, 1886–1954. Entered the Royal Navy as a cadet, 1900. Rear-Admiral, 1st Battle Squadron, 1938–9. Commander-in-Chief, East Indies Station (and Senior Naval Officer, Basra), 1939–41. Knighted, 1942. Flag Officer in Charge, Malta, 1942–3; Deputy Governor of Malta, 1943. Commander-in-Chief, Plymouth, 1943–5. Governor and Commander-in-Chief, Bermuda, 1946–9.

[3] Hugh Pughe Lloyd, 1894–1981. On active service, 1914–18 (DFC, Military Cross). Air Officer Commanding, Malta, 1941–2. Knighted, 1942. Commander, Allied Coastal Air Forces, Mediterranean, 1943–4. Commander, Commonwealth Bomber Force, Okinawa, 1944–5. Senior Instructor, Imperial Defence College, 1946–7. Commander-in-Chief, Air Command, Far East, 1947–9. Air Officer Commanding-in-Chief, Bomber Command, 1950–3.

[4] Edward St John Jackson, 1886–1961. Called to the Bar, Inner Temple, 1910. Attorney-General, Nyasaland Protectorate, 1918; Tanganyika Territory, 1924–9; Ceylon, 1929–36. Knighted, 1933.

a lawyer turned administrator and it is said he cannot forget his former craft. He did not impress me very favourably but he has considerable ability and there is no-one here to replace him. I think therefore question whether he should be retained in office must await Gort's arrival. One possibility is to abolish the post of Lieutenant Governor and appoint a Civil Secretary to Governor-General. Colonial Office might be asked to consider urgently whom they could find for such a post if Gort wanted a man quickly.

9. It is important Gort should come here without delay. I know from my talks with him that he will of course be ready to do so. But in fairness to him it ought to be placed on record that he is being sent here late in the day when there may be no longer time for him to influence defence plans.

10. Gort will be as Dobbie is C-in-C as well as Governor General but it will be necessary to make clear he is in fact supreme Commander on all matters in the Island. I propose to discuss implication of this with C-in-Cs in Cairo and will telegraph again on this question and relation of Malta to Middle East as soon as possible after arrival there.

11. It occurred to me that public reaction to change of Governor would be helped if Gort brought with him George Cross awarded to Malta.[1]

12. This telegram deals only with personalities. My immediately following telegrams deal with strategic and supply positions.

President Franklin D. Roosevelt to Winston S. Churchill
(Churchill papers, 20/74)

3 May 1942   Washington DC
Secret and Personal
No. 145

I refer to your personal and secret despatch No. 85 and feel that, following exchange of despatches between Admiral Pound and Admiral King, it is now essential for us to acquiesce in your views regarding Rus-

Legal Secretary to the Government of Malta, 1937–40. Lieutenant-Governor of Malta, 1940–3. Chief Justice of Cyprus, 1943–51. Chief Judge, British Zone of Germany, 1953. UK Member of the Mixed Board to review sentences for war crimes in Germany, 1955–7; to determine the deconcentration of the German coal and steel industries, 1959–60.

[1] The George Cross (the civilian equivalent of the Victoria Cross) had been awarded to the island of Malta by King George VI in a letter of 15 April 1942 to the Governor of Malta, Lieutenant-General Sir William Dobbie, to 'bear witness to the heroism and devotion of its people'. The George Cross is now an integral part of the Flag of Malta. With the award, Malta's official name became Malta GC.

sian convoys but continue to hope that you will be able to keep convoys at strength of 35 ships.

Propose to press Russians to reduce requirements to absolute essentials on grounds that preparations for 'Bolero'[1] will require all possible munitions and shipping.

Winston S. Churchill to General Archibald Wavell
(Churchill papers, 20/74)

3 May 1942
Most Secret
Most Immediate

You will have seen my telegram about the Governor of Burma. I am also anxious about Alexander. There is no sense in his remaining to command a force reduced to little more than a brigade. He is needed for very important business. Whenever you consider that his command has fallen to the level of a division or less and that no important military advantage can be gained by his retention of it you should order him to return to India by air leaving him no option. This is what we did to Gort before Dunkirk.[2]

General Archibald Wavell to Winston S. Churchill
(Churchill papers, 20/74)

4 May 1942   India
Most Secret
Most Immediate

Alexander's headquarters are already moving between Yeu and Kalewa, and there is no landing ground or means by which I can extract him before he reaches Kalewa.

In any event, consider he should remain with force at present. When he reaches Kalewa will get him back as soon as situation permits.

---

[1] 'Bolero': the administrative preparations for the opening of a 'second front' in north-west Europe, involving the movement of United States ground forces and equipment across the Atlantic to Britain.

[2] Field Marshal Lord Gort VC commanded the British Expeditionary Force in Belgium and France at the time of the Dunkirk evacuation (26 May to 3 June 1940). As the Dunkirk perimeter dwindled, he was ordered back to Britain. Ironically, it was to Alexander that he handed over command for the final phase of the Dunkirk evacuation.

Winston S. Churchill to A. V. Alexander and
Admiral of the Fleet Sir Dudley Pound
(Churchill papers, 20/67)

4 May 1942
Secret

It is probable that we shall not have the use of *King George V* for at least three months, after which I suppose a long period of working up will be required. Pray examine therefore the following plan to tide us over this most critical interlude.

2. Let the whole of the *King George V* crew go on leave simultaneously for a fortnight or whatever is the proper period. Meanwhile let the *Anson's* crew be transferred to *King George V,* and the *King George V* men go as a complete, integral, highly trained unit to the *Anson,* which is an identical ship in almost every respect. Thus the working up of the *Anson* would consist almost entirely of testing her material qualities. This change ought to save at least a month's or six weeks' delay in the ship being ready for battle.

Winston S. Churchill to Lord Gort[1]
(Churchill papers, 20/74)

4 May 1942

You should proceed forthwith to Malta and assume command as Governor, Commander-in-Chief and Supreme Commander in the island. Every effort must be made to prolong the resistance of the fortress to the utmost limit. We recognise you are taking over a most anxious and dangerous situation at a late stage. We are sure that you are the man to save the fortress and we shall strive hard to sustain you.

Winston S. Churchill to General Sir William Dobbie
(Churchill papers, 20/74)

4 May 1942

Pursuant on the report received from Minister of State we have decided that your long and gallantly borne vigil at Malta entitles you

---

[1] At Churchill's request, this telegram was despatched to Lord Gort in Gibraltar through 'C' (Colonel Sir Stuart Menzies, head of the Secret Intelligence Service).

to relief and throws new honour on the Island's record. Lord Gort has been ordered to take over from you at the earliest. I take this occasion of expressing on behalf of His Majesty's Government the high regard in which your conduct of this historic defence stands at home. I shall take the opportunity immediately upon your return of submitting your name to His Majesty for a signal mark of his favour.[1] Let me also thank you for the selfless and high minded spirit in which you have viewed the situation including your own and for your devotion to the public interest.[2]

General Sir Alan Brooke: diary
('War Diaries, Field Marshal Lord Alanbrooke', pages 254–5)

4 May 1942

PM then invited all the Chiefs of Staff to lunch at 10 Downing Street, where he arrived a little later from Chequers. He was in good form and said he felt elated, I think probably mainly with excitement at thought of attack on Madagascar!

Winston S. Churchill to General Archibald Wavell
(Churchill papers, 20/74)

5 May 1942
Most Secret
Immediate

Measures will be taken forthwith to make sure you are kept more fully informed in future not only of what affects India directly but of whole picture. General Ismay will assume responsibility for this. I have asked War Office for a report about the African Brigades.

2. Operation 'Ironclad' is of high importance to India because if Japanese by-pass Ceylon and establish themselves there with French connivance as they did in Indo-China, the whole of our communications with you and ME would be imperilled if not cut. There is of course the danger of our getting hung up there and of the place becoming a burden

---

[1] On his return to London, General Dobbie was decorated by the King with the GCMG. The citation referred to 'the steadfast and gallant bearing of the garrison and civil population' under his guidance and leadership.

[2] General Dobbie replied to Churchill on 5 May 1942: 'Your telegram of 4th [May] received. Very grateful for your kind words which I deeply appreciate. Trust I may report to you personally on my return' (*Churchill papers, 20/74*). On May 6 Churchill invited Dobbie to do so.

and not a help. We hope to have minimized this risk by the use of strong forces and severe, violent action. As soon as DS[1] is taken everything will be pushed on to you as fast as possible. We hope to garrison 'Ironclad' with two African Brigades and one from the Belgian Congo or West Coast. The two African Brigades are already under orders and the first begins movement on June 1. They may just as well be in 'Ironclad' as in Africa. The 5th Division moves on at once independently.

3. Long before the Japanese entered the war the Admiralty were endeavouring to build up our naval strength in the Indian Ocean while maintaining the minimum force necessary for security in the North Atlantic. The Rs were the first ships available and were sent primarily as escorts for convoys against Japanese cruiser raiders, which were the most we hoped to have to deal with. The damage to the US Fleet at Pearl Harbour altered the situation and it was necessary to build up a force capable of dealing with a more powerful eruption by the Japanese. *Warspite, Indomitable* and *Formidable* were consequently sent to join the R class.

4. Though the concentration which was effected at the end of March was one of considerable strength, at no time did we give any indication that it could be looked upon as a strong fleet as it was obviously lacking in modern capital ships. I was quite clear myself in the situation around April 5 that an engagement with the three modern Japanese battleships and their four carriers acting together would not have been to our advantage. It was noticeable however that the Japanese on their part did not appear to seek an action with our forces and this may well have been due to the presence of the R class battleships which according to the Naval Staff would have a definite value in a general engagement provided they had good air protection. They certainly cannot be ruled out as a factor in the Eastern Fleet.

5. Since my last to you we have had the misfortune to have *KGV* damaged by a collision with destroyer *Punjabi* whose depth charges exploded too near the battleship. This makes it necessary to send her in for refit which was already overdue, and will prevent *Duke of York* from going East. Instead of this Admiralty will send the two 16-inch *Nelson* and *Rodney*, and *Valiant* should be ready early in July.

6. Situation would be most favourably altered if we could damage *Tirpitz*, and Air attacks with desperate courage are being made upon her in Trondheim. While she is there the burden on the northern convoys to Russia is cruel upon the Fleet, and in all my experience I have never seen the strain so great.

[1] DS: Diego Suarez.

7. I agree with you that the months of May and June must be most anxious for us in the East, but I have every hope you will get the 5th Division in May and the 2nd Division in June. These at any rate are our resolves subject to the incalculable hazards of war.

8. For the moment the strain on Malta seems to have lessened, and Hitler has had to shift both a Fighter and Bomber Group eastward for his offensive against Russia. He is even more strained in the Air than we are at sea and this condition will increase rapidly month by month.

Winston S. Churchill to General Claude Auchinleck
(Churchill papers, 20/74)

5 May 1942
Personal and Secret

COS Paper OZ-75 was prepared on the British principle of facing the worst which, when applied in the House of Commons in Secret Session, had a most exhilarating and heartening effect.

2. Moreover situation has improved in the fortnight which has passed since Paper was written. The next two months are no doubt very dangerous in the Indian and Pacific Oceans as no one can predict with certainty what the next Japanese move will be. The Australians naturally think they are going to be invaded in great force. It certainly looks as if the Japanese would menace or attack Port Moresby and Darwin with a view no doubt <u>inter alia</u> of making us lock up as many troops as possible in Australia. Most significant movement is however three Japanese divisions from the remaining ten in Japan being sent to reinforce the twenty on the Russian–Manchurian front. It would clearly be in Japanese interests to finish off China, and the strong thrusts they are making northwards would seem to favour that idea.

3. One thing is certain – they cannot do everything at once. They did not like what they got at Colombo and Trincomalee and all their Carriers went back to Japan or Formosa to make good heavy losses in aircraft. If they were going to invade Ceylon and or India in strength, it is odd they did not do it as early as possible after the fall of Java or at any rate when they made their strong naval and air raid into the Indian Ocean in early April. We know of no special grounds for assuming that a heavy invasion of India is at this moment imminent or certain.

4. Meanwhile our position is strengthening. Ceylon is now in much better trim than in March or early April. Admiral Somerville's Fleet has

been strengthened by arrival of *Illustrious. Valiant* is nearer her completion date, and we are sending the two 16-inch battleships *Nelson* and *Rodney* at earliest to join his Eastern Fleet. It is hoped the Eastern Fleet may be fully formed in early July.

5. We hope today to occupy Diego Suarez for which strong forces have been assembled. Thereafter the whole 5th British Division proceeds to India arriving during May, followed by 2nd British Division arriving India during June. The 8th British Armoured Division rounds the Cape early in July and will be available to go either to India or the Middle East or to Australia if that country were invaded in force.

6. It looks as if the crisis of the air attack on Malta has for the time being passed. One German Bomber and one German Fighter Group have moved to the Eastward and there are indications that a second and third Bomber Group and a second Fighter Group are about to follow.[1] But the Island is still in grave peril owing to shortage of supplies and it is essential to make sure that food and ammunition reach them during the June dark period at latest. A successful offensive in Libya would be the most certain method of ensuring this.

7. While therefore we are grateful to you for your offer to denude the Middle East further for the sake of the Indian danger, we feel that the greatest help you could give to the whole war at this juncture would be to engage and defeat the enemy on your Western front. All our directions upon this subject remain unaltered in their purpose and validity and we trust you will find it possible to give full effect to them about the date which you mentioned to the Lord Privy Seal.

General Archibald Wavell to Winston S. Churchill
(Churchill papers, 20/74)

5 May 1942 India
Most Immediate

Air Ministry Special Cypher Section

I thank you for your most valuable explanation in your OZ.144 and realise all your difficulties. I hope that 'Ironclad' will go well and not involve us in any unforeseen commitments.

2. My Staff are examining best and most economical way to carry out the relief of Australian Brigades in Ceylon if necessary. We must (?) try

[1] The information in this sentence was derived from Enigma decrypts.

to avoid dangerous congestion of shipping in Colombo Harbour and to reduce time taken to load and unload.

3. I am off to Assam tomorrow for few days. Sudden collapse of Chinese in Burma was disappointing and has upset time programme I was working to. We are short of news at moment as everyone is on move in difficult country but I hope withdrawal is proceeding successfully. We are working hard at getting back wounded and refugees etc. from Myitkyina by air and at forming front on Assam border to relieve Burma troops who will want time to rest and refit. Stillwell's staff suggest that up to 20,000 Chinese may withdraw to India but my latest advices indicate that majority will make for China.

4. Have ordered Alexander back as soon as he gets to Kalewa cannot get touch with him earlier.

5. Our defence of India is very thin at present but we will make it (?) look as thick as possible and are grateful for help you are giving.

Winston S. Churchill to General Hastings Ismay
(Churchill papers, 20/67)

6 May 1942

PUFF BALLS[1] FOR THE MIDDLE EAST

This is very unsatisfactory. The whole object was to give the Middle East a supply in time for any battle they might fight. Now we have just enough in both places not to be an important feature in any operations that may occur. I made some efforts to get these out to Middle East before the November battle, and even so it has not been possible to bring them into action in any appreciable numbers.

Winston S. Churchill to Admiral Sir James Somerville
(Churchill papers, 20/67)

6 May 1942
Personal and Secret

Your No 18. Should be glad if you would address yourself particularly to (a) improved reciprocal defence by three carriers in company as compared to one alone, (b) special dangers of an attack by enemy aircraft

---

[1] 'Puff ball': A 9lb aerial anti-tank bomb.

before dawn and how best to meet them, and (c) what would be the best proportion of fighters and torpedo planes for each aircraft carrier to carry, and what would your three carriers have available for the occasion.

2. We shall know several important things by 1st June now hidden, and we must then survey the whole scene and count the cost and risk either way.

3. All good wishes.

Winston S. Churchill to Sir Archibald Sinclair
(Churchill papers, 20/67)

6 May 1942

I am glad to learn that the numerous matters raised in my Minute of 14th April are in hand.

I hope that a really large order for H2S [1] has been placed and that nothing will be allowed to stand in the way of getting this apparatus punctually. If it fulfils expectations it should make a big difference in the coming winter.

Your statement that MAP [2] cannot supply MC [3] bombs in quantity before the end of this year is most surprising. Last July I wrote to you on this subject and you replied that they had been promised at an early date. Now it seems that they are still awaiting hammer tests, &c. Surely it would be better to drop plenty of HE [4] in any thin-walled container than waste so large a proportion of our bombing effort.

Although all the essential matters are being dealt with, there are so many facets of the task, which have to be completed at the proper time that it might be a good thing to appoint some one man to be responsible for taking the necessary action by the proper dates and rendering a monthly report. I have heard Sir Robert Renwick [5] mentioned as a man of drive and business experience who has already rendered valuable

---

[1] H2S: an airborne, ground-scanning radar system, developed for the Royal Air Force, designed to identify targets on the ground for night and all-weather bombing. H2S radar was first used by RAF bombers for navigation on 30 January 1943. Fitted to Stirling and Halifax bombers, it initially provided ground mapping for navigation and night bombing.

[2] MAP: Ministry of Aircraft Production.

[3] MC: Medium capacity.

[4] HE: High explosive.

[5] Robert Renwick, 1904–73. Educated at Eton and Trinity College, Oxford. Chairman of the London Electric Supply Company. Created Baronet, 1937. Controller of Communications, Air Ministry, and Controller of Communications Equipment, Ministry of Aircraft Production, 1942–5. Knighted, 1946. Chairman of the Institute of Directors. Created Baron, 1964.

service in connection with Gee.[1] Perhaps you might think he is a good man for this purpose. It would be most unfortunate if we found later on that the bombing programme was held up because one or other of the items was lagging behind.

Josef Stalin to Winston S. Churchill
(Churchill papers, 20/74)

6 May 1942   Kremlin
Personal and Secret   Moscow

I have a request of you. Some 90 steamers loaded with various important war materials for the USSR are bottled up at present in Iceland or in the approaches from America to Iceland. I understand there is a danger that the sailing of these ships may be delayed for a long time because of the difficulty to organise convoy escorted by the British Naval Forces.

I am fully aware of the difficulties involved and of the sacrifices made by Great Britain in this matter. I feel however incumbent upon me to approach you with the request to take all possible measures in order to insure the arrival of all the above mentioned materials in the USSR in the course of May as this is extremely important for our front.

Accept my sincere greeting and best wishes for success.

Stalin

Richard Casey[2] to Winston S. Churchill
(Churchill papers, 20/74)

6 May 1942   Cairo
Most Secret

C-in-Cs[3] are telegraphing to the Chiefs of Staff today on the subject of the fate of the projected land operations in Cyrenaica. This subject

---

[1] Gee: a radio navigation system used to increase the destructiveness of Royal Air Force bombing raids. The first operational Gee mission took place on the night of 8–9 March 1942 when a force of about 200 aircraft attacked Essen. The system was installed on a Wellington of 115 Squadron. Krupp, the principal target, escaped bombing, but bombs did hit the southern areas of the city. In total, 33 percent of the aircraft reached the target area, an enormous advance over earlier results. The first completely successful Gee-led attack was carried out on the night of 13–14 March 1942 against Cologne.

[2] Minister of State Resident in the Middle East (based in Cairo), and a member of the British War Cabinet.

[3] The three Commanders-in-Chief, Middle East: General Auchinleck, Air Marshal Tedder, and Vice-Admiral Pridham-Wippell.

was discussed at the Defence Committee today at which I presided for the first time. I have been in Cairo for only 48 hours and have been busy getting acquainted with the principal individuals with whom I will be associated and trying to get an appreciation of the size and shape of the problems here.

C-in-Cs only finished the considered (?) appreciation of the factors affecting the date of the Cyrenaican operations last night and I did not become aware of the result (which is contained in their telegram today to the Chiefs of Staff) until this morning. I feel in these circumstances that my personal observations on this most important subject would not have much value at this stage and in consequence I have suggested that their telegram should go as from themselves and without my being a party to it. The telegram of course mainly reflects Auchinleck's view as the man primarily concerned but I should make it clear that Tedder and Pridham Wipple[1] accept his view if not without question certainly with complete confidence that every possible alternative has been considered. All three are fully alive to the fact that there are many intangible factors which affect the problem in addition to the mere counting of tanks on either side and they feel as I do that the presentation of their telegram is somewhat inadequate. On the other hand Auchinleck feels that superiority in armour is such a vital factor as to outweigh all other considerations. He has just got the latest figures of German strength from sources that he believes to be reliable and these confirm the estimates here that the Germans have succeeded in bringing their armoured divisions up to strength.

In these circumstances while fully aware of the advantage to Malta of getting Cyrenaica he is clearly convinced that it would be at serious risk to launch his offensive before the date now given by C-in-Cs. Auchinleck does not go so far as to say that to attack in mid May would necessarily mean disaster but he clearly does believe that at the best it would be an extremely hazardous enterprise while at the worst failure might endanger the subsequent safety of Egypt.

He thinks it most unlikely that anything can happen within the next 10 days to alter this situation for the better. I asked Auchinleck a great many questions on the proposed postponements and was unable to shake

[1] Henry Daniel Pridham-Wippell, 1885–1952. Midshipman, 1901. A destroyer commander, 1914–1918, Gallipoli, Adriatic, Palestine coast (despatches). Officer Commanding Home Fleet Destroyer Flotillas, 1936–8. Director of Personnel Services, Admiralty, 1938. Second-in-Command, Mediterranean Fleet, 1940–2 (acting Commander-in-Chief, May 1942). Vice-Admiral, 1941. Knighted, 1941. Flag Officer Commanding, Dover, 1942–5. Admiral, 1944. Commander-in-Chief, Plymouth, 1945–7.

him in any way at all as regards his firmly held view as to the necessity for postponement. He clearly believes that a very grave risk would be run by having the Eighth Army engage the enemy prematurely. All that I feel able to say at this very early stage in my time here is that Auchinleck appears to have taken all ascertainable factors as well as the imponderables into account and that on net balance the conclusion that he and his (?) colleagues have come to seems to be inescapable unless of course it is decided that the general situation warrants the risks being taken that the Commanders-in-Chief believe to exist. I have seen no evidence on the part of the Commanders-in-Chief of lack of appreciation of the urgency of the task ahead. I know quite well your strongly held desire that this operation should be carried out on or near the Target date. On the other hand, the only concrete evidence that I have to weigh as to the practicability of the operation is that provided for me today by Auchinleck and his colleagues.

I have as yet no other background although I will provide this for myself as rapidly as possible. I am meeting OC 8 Army[1] here tomorrow and am making three day visit to Western Desert Front beginning on May 12 principally to meet Corps, Divisional and Brigade Commanders.

Winston S. Churchill to General Claude Auchinleck
(Churchill papers, 20/74)

7 May 1942
Personal and Secret

Your CC/36 of 6/5[2] raises the gravest issues and is being considered by Chiefs of Staff and War Cabinet. Expect to telegraph you tomorrow. Meanwhile all preparations for offensive as previously contemplated should continue.

Please show this telegram to the Minister of State.[3]

---

[1] Lieutenant-General Ritchie.
[2] In which Auchinleck explained his arguments for postponing operations in Cyrenaica.
[3] Richard Casey.

Winston S. Churchill: statement
(Hansard)

7 May 1942   House of Commons

MADAGASCAR OPERATIONS (FRENCH SURRENDER)

The Prime Minister (Mr Churchill): I thought the House might wish to know at once the latest news from Madagascar. In order to prevent bloodshed as far as possible, very strong forces of all arms were employed, and preparations were made extending over the last three months. The landings were, as has already been made public, successfully accomplished, and by Tuesday evening our troops were in contact with the French forces in and before Diego Suarez, before the promontory of Antsirane and the promontory of Oronjia. The first assault on Antsirane at dawn yesterday was repulsed with losses which may have exceeded 1,000 men, but Major-General Sturges, of the Royal Marines, who commanded the troops on the island, attacked again during last night and captured the promontory. The French naval and military commanders surrendered and the town of Diego Suarez was also occupied.

Early this morning a further attack was made on the Oronjia batteries, which command the entrance to the harbour. These have now surrendered, and a Protocol is now being drawn up between the commanders on either side. The minesweepers of the powerful covering fleet under Admiral Syfret which had been assembled have already begun their work, and it is expected that the Fleet will enter the harbour of Diego Suarez at about 3.30 this afternoon.

These operations, which were not without risks of various kinds, have been carried out with great dash and vigour. The French also fought with great gallantry and discipline. We grieve that bloodshed has occurred between the troops of our two countries whose peoples at heart are united against the common foe. We trust that the French nation in time will come to regard this episode as a recognisable step in the liberation of their country, including Alsace-Lorraine, from the German yoke.

Henry Channon: diary
('Chips', page 316)

7 May 1942

[...]

Winston suddenly appeared in the House, and rose at the end of the division and made a colourful statement about the British seizure of the

Island of Madagascar, which capitulated today. He was cheered. I think he only comes to the House now when searching for kudos.

Sir Alexander Cadogan: diary
('The Diaries of Sir Alexander Cadogan', page 450)

7 May 1942

Cabinet at 12 about Russia. Everyone (except Cripps, who was late) was – quite rightly – against A[1] giving watered down terms to the Russians. This would be <u>fatal</u>. Just what we shouldn't do. PM evidently hopes the Treaty is off the map. 'We must remember that this is a <u>bad</u> thing. We oughtn't to do it, and I shan't be sorry if we don't.' Agreed PM should include in his Sunday broadcast a warning about gas. Auk[2] says he can't attack! But I don't think PM will stand this.

Oliver Harvey: diary
('The War Diaries of Oliver Harvey', page 122)

7 May 1942

A very serious situation in Middle East. Auck. doesn't now wish to attack till July which spells the loss of Malta because it can no longer be supplied without the use of the Cyrenaica aerodromes. PM very upset and told AE that he thought of replacing Auchinleck by Alexander – a good fighter if there was one. AE was told a disconcerting story of his friend General Gott[3] being in favour of hanging on at Benghazi before, and General Auchinleck having wished to go right back to Matruh. We shan't win wars with such generalship as that.

Winston S. Churchill to General Hastings Ismay,
for the Chiefs of Staff Committee
(Churchill papers, 20/67)

8 May 1942

It is of importance that the 17th and 13th Brigade Groups of the 5th Division should resume their voyage to India at the earliest. If possible, they should start within three days.

---

[1] Anthony Eden.
[2] General Auchinleck.
[3] Lieutenant-General William Gott, Officer Commanding XIII Corps, 1942.

2. The 29th Brigade Group and the Commando should be capable of holding Diego Suarez while we are looking round and considering the next step. The Commanders on the spot should be asked on this basis what the next step should be, and how urgent they consider it.

3. General Smuts' handsome offer of a South African Brigade Group should be accepted, and I should like to telegraph to him accordingly. (NB – He started at dawn this morning for Cairo. When will he get there?) Meanwhile we should ascertain from South Africa how soon the South African Brigade Group could arrive in Diego Suarez. It could then take over from the 29th Brigade Group, which could in whole or part form striking columns for Majunga, Tamatave and Antananarivo. By the time these are cleared up the first of the South African Brigade should have arrived, and one would hope that the 29th Brigade Group plus the Commando could move on to India, where it would be good to have it by July.

4. When is the 2nd African Brigade to leave Mombasa and when does it arrive in Madagascar? What has been settled about the Brigade from West Africa – Belgian or Nigerian?

5. What arrangements will be made for holding the batteries?

6. The capture of Diego Suarez should now cut out Kilindini as a subject for AA and AC defence definitely. Colombo remains first priority, Trincomalee second, but there ought to be some flak mounted at Diego. Please let me know what provision can be made, and when.

7. What is to happen to the naval forces? Admiral Syfret will presumably stand by until the mopping up of other centres of resistance is completed. Would it not be a good thing for Admiral Somerville to put in an appearance with his fast ships at Colombo on his way to Aden where the decision about the Malta convoy must be taken in the light of other matters which are pending in Libya?

8. Lastly, what is to be done about air in Madagascar? Some support will be needed for the remaining operations. But we cannot long tie up one of our best Carriers. General Smuts has promised to send us a Squadron or more from South Africa. What is to happen to the four Catalinas which were borrowed from Ceylon, and which will, I expect, be needed back there soon?

I shall be glad to know what the Chiefs of Staff recommend on these points, and on any others which may not have occurred to me.

Winston S. Churchill to Sir James Grigg,
General Sir Alan Brooke, and Oliver Lyttelton
(Churchill papers, 20/67)

8 May 1942
Secret

HOME GUARD[1]

It seems very important to raise the figure of 60 rounds per rifle to 100 at the earliest. This should be possible by the middle of June. The position at the present moment is serious, and every effort should be made to relieve it.

2. What arrangements are made now for practice? How much ammunition have the Home Guard been allowed to fire? It is more important to build up the reserve than to train them under present hard conditions. Let me know what has been done, and what is proposed in the future as things improve.

3. In the footnote to Flag 'B', 1,700,000 is the figure given for men in the Home Guard. My latest figure is 1,450,000, of which only 840,000 have rifles. Of course, those with rifles are relieved by those without, and they all ought to be trained, but surely the emphasis should be on getting a number trained in shooting equal to the rifles issued. Let me know what is the plan about this.

4. I still think that, in view of the immense quantities of .30 ammunition now being produced in America, 319 million rounds in March, for instance, we ought to try to get another 100 millions over to improve holdings of the Home Guard and for practice. I should be willing to make an effort for this.

5. Let me have a return showing the equipment of the Home Guard, including rifles, American machine-guns and Tommy guns, and also the British weapons of this kind which they may have. I suppose machine-gun accounts for two or three men to only one? Also, how many sporting and shotguns are available with Home Guard? How many are there without firearms of any kind? We cannot afford to let the whole of this vital fac-

---

[1] The Home Guard (initially the Local Defence Volunteers or LDV – popularly called 'Look, Duck, Vanish'), maintained from 1940 to 1944, consisted of one and a half million local volunteers otherwise ineligible for military service, mostly because of their age, intended as a secondary defence force in the event of a German invasion. It guarded the coastal areas of Britain as well as airfields, factories, and explosives stores. It had its origin in a letter written by Churchill on 8 October 1939, when First Lord of the Admiralty, to Sir Samuel Hoare, the Lord Privy Seal, calling for the formation of a Home Guard force of half a million men over the age of 40. It was not, however, until 14 May 1940 that Anthony Eden, then Secretary of State for War, gave a radio broadcast announcing the formation of the LDV and called for volunteers to join the force.

tor in our defence fall into twilight because for the moment invasion is not obviously threatened.

Winston S. Churchill to President Franklin D. Roosevelt
(Churchill papers, 20/74)

8 May 1942
No. 86
Personal

Delighted to hear your good news from the Solomons.[1]

War Cabinet: Confidential Annex
(Cabinet papers, 65/30)

8 May 1942
3 p.m.

The War Cabinet had before them a telegram from the Commanders-in-Chief, Mediterranean and Middle East, dated 6th May (No. CC36), circulated as WP(42)193.

In this telegram the Commanders-in-Chief set out the pros and cons for launching an offensive in the Western Desert during the next three months. Their arguments were largely based on a numerical comparison of the armoured forces on both sides and the conclusion which they reached was that an offensive would not be justified before the 15th June.

The Prime Minister read to the Cabinet an interim reply which he has sent saying that the Commanders-in-Chief telegram raised grave issues, which were being carefully considered by the Chiefs of Staff, Defence Committee and War Cabinet; in the meantime, preparations should continue for an offensive on the date originally contemplated. A telegram had been received in reply from the Commander-in-Chief,

---

[1] The Battle of the Coral Sea was fought between 4 and 8 May 1942 off the Solomon Islands, 500 miles north-east of Australia, between the Japanese naval forces and the naval forces of the United States and Australia. It was the first naval battle in which aircraft carriers were in action against each other, and the first naval battle in which neither side's warships saw, or fired directly on, the warships of the adversary. In terms of numbers of ships sunk, the battle was a victory for Japan, but the American–Australian force brought a halt to the Japanese plan to invade Port Moresby (Papua New Guinea) and use it as a base for bombing Australia. In addition, during the battle two Japanese fleet carriers were damaged and thus unable to take part in the Battle of Midway (4 to 7 June 1942), thereby facilitating an American victory at Midway.

Middle East,[1] saying that preparations were proceeding in accordance with previous plans.

The Chief of the Imperial General Staff[2] said that the telegram did not deal with two very important factors: first, the bearing which operations in Cyrenaica would have on the Malta situation; secondly, the possibility of German offensive action, which, by all indications, might take place at the end of May. It seemed strange that the Commander-in-Chief had not taken into account the possibility of upsetting the Axis plans by timing his (General Auchinleck's) offensive so as to take advantage of the offensive contemplated by General Rommel.

The Chief of the Imperial General Staff handed round a Paper setting out the present Orders of Battle in Libya and the numbers of tanks available to both sides. The main point was that, on the best estimates available, excluding 250 Infantry tanks, on the 1st June we should have 566 tanks to 521 of the enemy, whereas on the 15th June we should have 748 to 590 of the enemy. The Chiefs of Staff felt that, in view of the opinion expressed by the Commanders-in-Chief, it would be wrong to give General Auchinleck a direct order to attack on, say, the 15th May. At the same time, the Chiefs of Staff thought it would be right to tell General Auchinleck that his attack should be carried out in such a way as to provide the maximum support for the convoy to Malta in the June dark period. The Chiefs of Staff favoured putting these views to General Auchinleck and seeing whether he agreed with them.

The Chief of the Air Staff[3] said that he had received no recent appreciation from the Middle East of the air position. He had telegraphed a request for such an appreciation to be furnished. He gave particulars of a comparison drawn up by the Air Staff in this country, of our forces in the Middle East, with the enemy forces in North Africa, Crete, the Dodecanese and Greece, but excluding Sicily. The position was as follows:

First Line Strengths

	Enemy Forces	British Forces
15th May	685 (325 Italian)	716
15th June	770 (350 Italian)	734

Available Aircraft

15th May	469 (247 Italian)	893
15th June	532 (260 Italian)	980

[1] General Auchinleck.
[2] Sir Alan Brooke.
[3] Sir Charles Portal.

The air position was thus definitely favourable to us; the enemy could, of course, reinforce their air forces in this area more quickly than we could, but only at the cost of drawing off forces from other theatres.

The Chief of the Naval Staff[1] said that, from the Naval point of view, it would be much better if we could capture Benghazi before the Malta convoy started in June rather than that the attack, regarded from the point of view of the Malta convoy, should be merely a diversion.

The Prime Minister then invited the views of Ministers individually.

There was a general consensus of opinion on the part of Ministers in that, looking at the matter from the point of view of our war strategy as a whole, the advantages to be gained by postponing the offensive until the 15th June were more than offset by the disadvantages of delay until that date. In this connection great importance was attached to the position at Malta.

The following particular points were made in discussion:

(1) The Lord Privy Seal[2] said that the crucial part of the telegram was paragraph 9. General Auchinleck feared the effect on the defence of the Delta of an unsuccessful offensive. He was also nervous of being called on to defend Syria or the Northern Frontier while attacking in the Western Desert. He therefore wanted to see something approaching a certainty of success before he attacked, and was anxious that the risks of a partial success or failure should be appreciated here.

(2) The Secretary of State for Dominion Affairs[3] thought that it would pay us to attack as soon as practicable.

(3) The Minister of Production[4] pointed out the great value which would accrue from the capture of the Martuba aerodrome from the point of view of the June convoy to Malta. This pointed to an offensive at the very beginning of June. The Prime Minister said that the disadvantage of this date was that 12,000 Germans were due to arrive in Libya by the beginning of June.

(4) The First Lord of the Admiralty[5] said that, looking at the situation from the Naval point of view, it appeared that the enemy was intensifying the investment of Malta, in order to prevent interference with the despatch of reinforcements to Libya. Taking a long view it seemed, therefore, that delay would make our ultimate task more difficult.

[1] Sir Dudley Pound.
[2] Sir Stafford Cripps.
[3] Clement Attlee.
[4] Oliver Lyttelton.
[5] A. V. Alexander.

(5) The Minister of Labour and National Service[1] thought that the enemy might intend a simultaneous attack in Libya and Russia, and drew attention to the advantages of anticipating the enemy attack.

(6) The Secretary of State for War[2] thought that the real purpose behind the telegram of 6th May was that General Auchinleck wanted to be sure whether he was taking the military responsibility of advising that an offensive should be undertaken on a given date, with good chances of success. If the War Cabinet decided to take the responsibility of saying that an attack ought to be carried out before the date now suggested, he thought that General Auchinleck would be willing to fall in with this suggestion.

(7) The Secretary of State for Air[3] was in favour of an attack being launched before the June dark period, in order to give us a chance of obtaining possession of vital aerodromes. The choice of the actual date should, however, be left to the Commander-in-Chief.

The Prime Minister said that battles were not won by arithmetical calculations of the strength of the opposing forces. From this point of view, the telegram of 6th May was somewhat disappointing and difficult to understand, more particularly since it included no mention of the very serious consequences if we failed to relieve Malta. The Commanders-in-Chief must, however, have had the Malta situation in mind, and the explanation might be that the telegram had been deliberately confined to an account of the strength of the opposing armoured forces, in order to concentrate attention on the stark facts of the position.

In conclusion, the Prime Minister said that he thought the dates discussed, namely the 15th May and the 15th June, had no particular significance except in relation to the Malta convoys. He thought that a telegram should be sent to the effect that the War Cabinet were of opinion that an attack ought to take place in the latter half of May. The telegram should not give General Auchinleck a positive order, but should make it clear that the War Cabinet were prepared to assume full responsibility for the consequences if an attack took place and was not successful. The importance of a successful offensive from the point of view of relieving Malta should be mentioned.

The War Cabinet agreed with the Prime Minister's view of the action to be taken.

[1] Ernest Bevin.
[2] Sir James Grigg.
[3] Sir Archibald Sinclair.

The Chief of the Imperial General Staff agreed, but suggested that the telegram should also give General Auchinleck the opportunity, if he so desired, of taking advantage of a German offensive in early June to launch a counterstroke.

The War Cabinet agreed with these views. A telegram was thereupon drafted by the Prime Minister to give effect to the decision reached and was approved.

Winston S. Churchill to General Claude Auchinleck
(Cabinet papers, 20/75)

8 May 1942
Personal and Secret
Hush – Most Secret
Most Immediate

The Chiefs of Staff, the Defence Committee and the War Cabinet have all earnestly considered your telegram No. CC/36 in relation to the whole war situation having particular regard to Malta, the loss of which would be a disaster of first magnitude to the British Empire and probably fatal in the long run to the defence of the Nile Valley.

2. We are agreed that in spite of the risks you mention in para. 9, you would be right to attack the enemy and fight a major battle if possible during May, and the sooner the better. We are prepared to take full responsibility for these general directions, leaving you the necessary latitude for their execution. In this you will no doubt have regard to the fact that the enemy may himself be planning to attack you early in June and is trying to be ready by then.

3. Please hand a copy of this message to Minister of State and also ask him to show it to General Smuts on arrival.

Winston S. Churchill to Admiral Edward Syfret
and General Robert Sturges
(Churchill papers, 20/75)

9 May 1942
Immediate
Most Secret

I congratulate you cordially upon the swift and resolute way in which your difficult and hazardous Operation was carried through. Pray give all ranks my best wishes and tell them that their exploit has been of real assistance to Britain and the United Nations. Ends.

Add for 29th Brigade <u>only</u>: I was sure when I saw you at Inverary[1] nine months ago that the 29th Brigade Group would make its mark.

Winston S. Churchill to Josef Stalin
(Churchill papers, 20/75)

9 May 1942
Personal and Most Secret
Immediate

I have received your telegram of May 6th and thank you for your message and greetings. We are resolved to fight our way through to you with the maximum amount of war materials. On account of *Tirpitz* and other enemy surface ships at Trondheim the passage of every convoy has become a serious Fleet operation. We shall continue to do our utmost.

2. No doubt your Naval advisers have pointed out to you the dangers to which the convoys are subjected from attack by enemy surface forces, submarines and air from the various bases in enemy hands which flank the route of the convoy throughout its passage.

3. Owing to adverse weather conditions the scale of attack which the Germans have so far developed is considerably less than we can reasonably expect in the future.

4. We are throwing all our available resources into the solution of this problem, have dangerously weakened our Atlantic convoy escorts for this purpose, and as you are no doubt aware have suffered severe Naval casualties in the course of these operations.

5. I am sure that you will not mind my being quite frank and emphasising the need of increasing the assistance given by the USSR Naval and Air Forces in helping to get these convoys through safely.

6. If you are to receive a fair proportion of the material which is loaded into ships in the United Kingdom and the United States, it is essential that

---

[1] Churchill had visited the commando training centre at Inverary (in Argyll, Scotland, on the western shore of Loch Fyne) on 27 June 1941. During his visit he watched the demolition of barbed wire entanglements and a demonstration of beach assault and landing techniques. His son Randolph had earlier been in training at Inverary.

the USSR Naval and Air Forces should realise that they must be largely responsible for the convoys, whether incoming or outgoing, when to the Eastward of the meridian of longitude 28° East in waters which are out of sight of Murman Coast.

7. The ways in which further assistance is required from the USSR forces are as follows:

(a) Increased and more determined assistance from USSR surface forces.

(b) Provision of sufficient long range bombers to enable the aerodromes used by the Germans to be heavily bombed during the passage of the convoys in the North Cape Areas.

(c) Provision of long range fighters to cover the convoys for that part of their voyage when they are approaching your coast.

(d) Anti-submarine patrols both by aircraft and surface vessels.

8. When broadcasting tomorrow (Sunday) night I propose to make the declaration warning the Germans that if they begin gas warfare upon the Russian Armies we shall certainly retaliate at once upon Germany.

John Martin: diary
(Sir John Martin papers)

9 May 1942

Day off; but much at No. 10 over completion of draft Honours List.[1] Excellent film 'One of Our Aircraft is Missing'.[2]

---

[1] The King's Birthday Honours List, issued on 11 June 1942, included a barony for John Maynard Keynes, whom Churchill had brought into the Treasury in 1925 to try to persuade the senior officials there not to support a return to the Gold Standard (he did not succeed); and knighthoods for Alexander Korda, who in 1935 had commissioned a film script from Churchill on the reign of King George V, and whose films Churchill much admired, and for Robert Watson-Watt, whose researches on radar in the mid-1930s Churchill had strongly supported, against official scepticism.

[2] The film *One of Our Aircraft is Missing*, not officially released until 27 June 1942, tells the story of the crew of an RAF Vickers Wellington bomber who are forced to bail out over the Netherlands, and of how Dutch patriots help the crew despite the dangers to themselves. Directed and produced by Michael Powell and Emeric Pressburger, the film was edited by David Lean. Throughout the film the Germans spoke German. The actors included Eric Portman, Bernard Miles, and Googie Withers. It was the first feature film (of more than 60) in which Peter Ustinov appeared.

Middle East Defence Committee to Winston S. Churchill
and the Chiefs of Staff
(Churchill papers, 20/75)

9 May 1942   Cairo
Most Secret
Most Immediate

Reference personal and secret telegram OZ 175 of 8/5 from Prime
Minister to General Auchinleck.

2. We realise you can view situation as a whole, and are therefore in
much better position than we to assess value of results likely to accrue
from earlier offensive in Libya, and therefore the risks which it is justifiable to run to gain these results. Nevertheless, we feel that we must
once again bring to your notice certain considerations which we are
not repeat not sure we have adequately stressed.

3. First in regard to Malta. We realise its importance, but do not
repeat not, in the light of the most recent information in our possession, consider that its fall (much though this would be deplored)
would necessarily be fatal to security of Egypt for a very long period
if at all, provided our supply lines through the Indian Ocean remain
uninterrupted. In its present almost completely neutralised state, Malta
has very little influence on the enemy maintenance situation in North
Africa, though it is containing large enemy air forces. The regaining
of Cyrenaica by us, though it would greatly assist the movement of our
ships to and from Malta in the Eastern Mediterranean can not repeat
not of itself guarantee the restoration to Malta of its offensive power
in the event of the enemy continuing to devote large air forces to its
neutralisation. This is merely an expression of opinion.

4. Secondly. It would be most dangerous to assume that, having
launched an offensive in the latter half of May, we can count on being
able to operate aircraft from landing grounds near Benghazi before
the end of June or even later, depending on the degree of resistance
offered by the enemy, and the tactical results obtained on the battlefield, neither of which can be foreseen.

We do not rpt not need to stress the fact that the rate of progress of
any offensive undertaken against a well led, well armed and determined
enemy, without the measure of superiority which experience has proved
to be desirable, can not repeat not be foretold with any degree of

accuracy. For supply reasons alone it is most unlikely that we can establish ourselves firmly in Cyrenaica within two months of starting an offensive, and it may well need a longer period than this.

5. Thirdly. We feel that to launch an offensive with inadequate armoured forces may very well result in the almost complete destruction of those troops, in view of our experience in the last Cyrenaican campaign. We can not rpt not hope to hold the defensive positions we have prepared covering Egypt however strong we may be in infantry against a serious enemy offensive unless we can dispose of a reasonably strong armoured force in reserve, which we should not rpt not then have. This also was proved last December, and will always be so in terrain such as the Western Desert, where the southern flank of any defensive position west of the El Alamein–Dattara depression position must be open to attack and encirclement. In this connection we invite your attention to Para. second of personal telegram CS/849 for COS from VCIGS sent from Cairo on 22nd March 1942. We still feel that the risk to Egypt incurred by the piecemeal destruction of our armoured forces which may result from a premature offensive may be more serious and more immediate than that involved in the possible loss of Malta, serious though this would be.

6. Fourthly. You mention the possibility of an enemy offensive against us early in June. There are certain though not repeat not very definite indications of this from the information at our disposal, and we are naturally watching it closely and continually. We would point out that if the enemy could be induced to attack us with the forces now at his disposal in our existing strong positions, while we retain our existing armoured forces in reserve behind them, it might very well be the best thing that could happen. We are not rpt not afraid of this eventuality and hope that if it materialises we can so damage his armoured forces as to give us a good chance of passing to the counter offensive, and possibly thereby achieving our object, which is to destroy his forces, and particularly his armoured forces, in Cyrenaica before he can withdraw them westwards and so continue to threaten Egypt.

7. Conclusion. We ask you once more to give these points your consideration.

Winston S. Churchill to General Claude Auchinleck
(Cabinet papers, 65/30)

10 May 1942
Personal and Most Secret

Reference Middle East Defence Committee Telegram No. CC/42 of 9/5.

The Chiefs of Staff, the Defence Committee and the War Cabinet, have again considered the whole position. We are determined that Malta shall not be allowed to fall without a battle being fought by your whole army for its retention. The starving out of this fortress would involve the surrender of over 30,000 men, Army and Air Force, together with several hundred guns. Its possession would give the enemy a clear and sure bridge to Africa with all the consequences flowing from that. Its loss would sever the air route upon which both you and India must depend for a substantial part of your aircraft reinforcements. Besides this, it would compromise any offensive against Italy and future plans such as 'Acrobat'[1] and 'Gymnast'.[2] Compared with the certainty of these disasters, we consider the risks you have set out to the safety of Egypt are definitely less, and we accept them.

2. We therefore reiterate the views expressed in Paragraph 2 of our OZ 175 with this qualification – that the very latest date for engaging the enemy which we could approve is one which provides a distraction in time to help the passage of the June dark-period convoy.

3. This telegram, like our No. OZ 175 is addressed to you as Military Commander-in-Chief, the Air having been placed under your general direction for the purposes of major operations.

Winston S. Churchill to the Very Reverend Spencer Carpenter[3]
(Churchill papers, 20/53)

10 May 1942

My dear Dean of Exeter,

I was much grieved when I heard of the loss of life and damage at Exeter,[4] and I greatly admire the fortitude with which the people of the City have borne their trials.

---

[1] 'Acrobat': the planned advance from Cyrenaica into Tripolitania.

[2] 'Gymnast': the Anglo-American plan to land in French North Africa.

[3] Spencer Cecil Carpenter, 1877–1959. Chaplain to King George V, 1929–35. Dean of Exeter, 1935–50. Among his 20 books were *A Parson's Defence* (his first, 1912), *Faith in Time of War* (1940), and *Exeter Cathedral* (1942).

[4] Air raid warning sirens were sounded at Exeter at 1.36 a.m. on 4 May 1942 as 20 German bombers approached from the English Channel and the estuary of the River Exe. The first bombs (sticks

I should like, if I possibly can, to come down some time to visit Exeter, as you kindly suggested in your letter of May 7, but it is impossible for me, I am afraid, to undertake any definite commitment. You can be sure however that I will bear the matter in mind if a suitable opportunity occurs.

I have received letters urging me to remove the embargo on the news about the damage to Exeter Cathedral, but the advice of the responsible Departments is against making exceptions in individual cases to the rule that names of damaged buildings are not released until twenty-eight days after the raid, and I have felt bound to accept their advice.

Yours very faithfully,
Winston S. Churchill

Winston S. Churchill to Sir James Grigg
(Churchill papers)

10 May 1942

ANTI-AIRCRAFT COMMAND

The greatest problem in AA Command today seems to be personnel. It appears indefensible to maintain 280,000 men waiting for an attack that may never develop, if other means can be found to man the weapons. I realise that the Home Guard can never man weapons required in working hours. Light AA regiments must therefore be manned by whole-time soldiers. I am sure however that rocket batteries and heavy AA searchlights, in varying proportions, could be manned, wholly or in part, by Home Guard and ATS.[1] How is the scheme of mixed batteries getting on? I am told women are not volunteering in sufficient numbers.

2. General Pile[2] should be asked to state a ceiling for Home Guard and ATS, and to estimate how many men he could release for use with the Field Army if this ceiling were reached. Ways and means can then

of incendiaries) fell at 1.51 a.m. The 'all clear' sounded at 2.50 a.m. In the air raid, 123 people were killed or died soon afterwards. Among them were 29 fireguards, 11 firewatchers, four air raid wardens, and one fireman; 26 youngsters under 16 lost their lives, including four babies. Almost 400 shops, almost 150 offices, 50 warehouses and stores, and 36 pubs and clubs were destroyed. Of the 20,000 houses in the city, 1,500 were destroyed and 2,700 seriously damaged.

[1] ATS: Auxiliary Territorial Service.

[2] Frederick Alfred Pile, 1884–1976. Entered the Army, 1904. On active service, 1914–18 (despatches, DSO, Military Cross). Colonel, 1928. Succeeded his father as 2nd Baronet, 1931. Major-General, 1937. Commander, 1st Anti-Aircraft Division, Territorial Army, 1938–9. Lieutenant-General, 1939. General Officer Commanding-in-Chief, Anti-Aircraft Command, 1939–45. General, 1941. Knighted, 1941. Director-General, Ministry of Works, 1945. In 1949 he published *Ack-Ack: Britain's Defence Against Air Attack During the Second World War.*

be examined for making this exchange. He has been most helpful in releasing and diluting.

Winston S. Churchill to Captain[1] and Ship's Company, USS 'Wasp'[2]
(Churchill papers, 20/75)

10 May 1942

SPITFIRES TO MALTA

Many thanks to you all for timely help. Who said a wasp couldn't sting twice?

Winston Churchill[3]

Chequers Guard to Winston S. Churchill
(Churchill papers, 20/56)

10 May 1942

All Ranks of No. 2 Company Holding Bn. Coldstream Guards presently stationed at Chequers and entrusted with the honour and duty of guarding the Prime Minister while in residence here, do respectfully send their congratulations to him on the second anniversary of his taking office.

We are filled with unbounded admiration and deep gratitude for the fighting way you have led our country during this time. Our confidence in you is absolute and that you will lead us through to victory there is no shadow of doubt. You are indeed described by the motto of our regiment – NULLI SECUNDUS.[4]

---

[1] Forrest Percival Sherman, 1896–1951. US Naval Academy class of 1918. In May 1942, appointed Captain of USS *Wasp* (on ferry duty supplying Malta, then transferred to the Pacific; disabled by a Japanese submarine and scuttled, 15 September 1942). Awarded the Navy Cross for his 'extraordinary heroism' in command of *Wasp*. Chief of Staff to the Commander, Air Force, Pacific Fleet, 1942–3. Deputy Chief of Staff to the Pacific Fleet Commander (Admiral Nimitz), 1943–5. Vice-Admiral, and Deputy Chief of Naval Operations, 1946. Commander, US Operating Force, Mediterranean, 1948–9. Admiral, and Chief of Naval Operations, 1949–51.

[2] A United States aircraft carrier, launched in 1939. The sole ship of her class.

[3] On 18 May 1942 Churchill received the following telegram: 'Captain, Officers and ships company of USS *Wasp* thank the Prime Minister for his gracious message which they much appreciate' (*Churchill papers, 20/75*).

[4] Second to None.

Winston S. Churchill: broadcast
(BBC Written Archives Centre)

10 May 1942
9 p.m.

I have now served for two years exactly to a day as the King's First Minister. Therefore I thought it would be a good thing if I had a talk to you on the broadcast, to look back a little on what we have come through, to consider how we stand now, and to peer cautiously, but at the same time resolutely, into the future.

The tremendous period through which we have passed has certainly been full of anxieties and exertions; it has been marked by many misfortunes and disappointments. This time two years ago the Germans were beating down Holland and Belgium by unprovoked brutal, merciless invasion, and very soon there came upon us the total defeat of France and the fatal surrender at Bordeaux. Mussolini, the Italian miscalculator, thought he saw his chance of a cheap and easy triumph, and rich plunder for no fighting. He struck at the back of a dying France, and at what he believed was a doomed Britain. We were left alone – our quarter of a million Dunkirk troops saved, only disarmed; ourselves, as yet unarmed – to face the might of victorious Germany, to face also the carefully saved-up strength of an Italy which then still ranked as a first-class Power.

Here at home in this island, invasion was near; the Mediterranean was closed to us; the long route round the Cape, where General Smuts stands on guard, alone was open; our small, ill-equipped forces in Egypt and the Sudan seemed to await destruction. All the world, even our best friends, thought that our end had come. Accordingly, we prepared ourselves to conquer or to perish. We were united in that solemn, majestic hour; we were all equally resolved at least to go down fighting. We cast calculation to the winds; no wavering voice was heard; we hurled defiance at our foes; we faced our duty, and, by the mercy of God, we were preserved.

It fell to me in those days to express the sentiments and resolves of the British nation in that supreme crisis of its life. That was to me an honour far beyond any dreams or ambitions I had ever nursed, and it is one that cannot be taken away. For a whole year after the fall of France we stood alone, keeping the flag of freedom flying, and the hopes of the world alive. We conquered the Italian Empire, we destroyed or captured almost all Mussolini's African army; we liberated Abyssinia; we have so far successfully protected Palestine, Syria, Persia and Iraq from German designs. We have suffered grievous reverses in going to the aid of the heroic Greeks; we bore unflinching many a heavy blow abroad, and still more in our cities here at home; and all this time, cheered and helped by President Roosevelt and the United States, we stood alone, neither faltering nor flagging.

Where are we now? Can anyone doubt that if we are worthy of it, as we shall be, we have in our hands our own future? As in the last war, so in this, we are moving through many reverses and defeats to complete and final victory. We have only to endure and to persevere, to conquer. Now we are no longer unarmed; we are well armed. Now we are not alone; we have mighty allies, bound irrevocably by solemn faith and common interests to stand with us in the ranks of the United Nations. There can only be one end. When it will come, or how it will come, I cannot tell. But, when we survey the overwhelming resources which are at our disposal, once they are fully marshalled and developed – as they can be – as they will be – we may stride forward into the unknown with growing confidence.

During the time that we were all alone, we were steadily growing stronger. He would have been a bold man, however, who in those days would have put down in black and white exactly how we were going to win. But, as has happened before in our island history, by remaining steadfast and unyielding – stubborn, if you will – against a Continental tyrant, we reached the moment when that tyrant made a fatal blunder. Dictators, as well as democracies and parliamentary governments, make mistakes sometimes. Indeed, when the whole story is told, I believe it will be found that the Dictators, for all their preparations and prolonged scheming, have made greater mistakes than the Democracies they have assailed. Even Hitler makes mistakes sometimes. In June last, without the slightest provocation, and in breach of a pact of non-aggression, he invaded the lands of the Russian people. At that time he had the strongest army in the world, trained in war, flushed with incredible unbroken success, and equipped with limitless munitions and the most modern weapons. He had also secured for himself the advantages of surprise and treachery. Thus he drove the youth and manhood of the German nation forward into Russia.

The Russians, under their warrior chief, Stalin, sustained losses which no other country or government has ever borne in so short a time and lived. But they, like us, were resolved never to give in. They poured out their own blood upon their native soil. They kept their faces to the foe. From the very first day to the end of the year, and on till tonight, they fought with unflinching valour. And, from the very first day when they were attacked, when no one could tell how things would go, we made a brotherhood with them, and a solemn compact to destroy Nazidom and all its works. Then Hitler made his second grand blunder. He forgot about the winter. There is a winter, you know, in Russia. For a good many months the temperature is apt to fall very low. There is snow, there is frost, and all that. Hitler forgot about this Russian winter. He must have been very loosely educated. We all heard about it at school;[1] but he forgot it. I have never made such a bad mistake as that. So winter came, and fell upon his ill-clad armies, and with the winter came the valiant Russian counter- attacks. No one can say with certainty how many millions of Germans have already perished in Russia and its snows. Certainly more have perished than were killed in the whole four and a quarter years of the last war. That is probably an understatement. So besotted is this man. In his lust for blood and conquest, so blasting is the power he wields over the lives of Germans, that he even blurted out the other day that his armies would be better clothed and his locomotives better prepared for their second winter in Russia than they were for their first.

There was an admission about the length of the war that struck a chill into German hearts as cold as the icy winds of Russia. What will be the sufferings of the German manhood in this new bloodbath? What is there in front of Hitler now? Certain it is that the Russian armies are stronger than they were last year, that they have learnt by hard experience to fight the Germans in the field, that they are well-equipped, and that their constancy and courage are unquenched. That is what is in front of Hitler. What is he leaving behind him? He leaves behind him a Europe starving and in chains; a Europe in which his execution squads are busy in a dozen countries every day; a Europe which has learned to hate the Nazi name as no name has ever been hated in the recorded history of mankind; a Europe burning for revolt whenever the opportunity comes.

But this is not all he has left behind. We are on his tracks, and so is the great Republic of the United States. Already the Royal Air Force has set about it; the British, and presently the American, bombing offensive against Germany will be one of the principal features in this year's world war. Now is the time to use our increasingly superior air strength, to strike hard and continually at the home front in Germany, from which so much evil has leaked out upon the world, and which is the foundation of the whole enormous German invasion of Russia. Now, while the German armies will be bleeding and burning up their strength against

---

[1] Churchill's schoolboy poem 'The Influenza', written when he was 15, contained the lines: 'O'er miles of bleak Siberian plains / Where Russian exiles toil on chains'.

the two-thousand-mile Russian line, and when the news of casualties by hundreds of thousands is streaming back to the German Reich, now is the time to bring home to the German people the wickedness of their rulers, by destroying under their very eyes the factories and seaports on which their war effort depends.

German propaganda has been constantly appealing of late to British public opinion to put a stop to these severe forms of warfare, which, according to the German view, should be the strict monopoly of the *Herrenvolk*. Herr Hitler himself has not taken at all kindly to this treatment, and he has been good enough to mingle terrible threats with his whinings. He warns us, solemnly, that if we go on smashing up the German cities, his war factories and his bases, he will retaliate against our cathedrals and historic monuments – if they are not too far inland. We have heard his threats before. Eighteen months ago, in September 1940, when he thought he had an overwhelming Air Force at his command, he declared that he would rub out – that was the actual expression, rub out – our towns and cities. And he certainly had a good try. Now the boot is on the other leg. Herr Hitler has even called in question the humanity of these grim developments of war. What a pity this conversion did not take place in his heart before he bombed Warsaw,[1] or massacred twenty thousand Dutch folk in defenceless Rotterdam,[2] or wreaked his cruel vengeance upon the open city of Belgrade![3] In those days, he used to boast that for every ton of bombs we dropped on Germany, he would drop ten times, or even a hundred times as many on Britain. Those were his words, and that was his belief. Indeed, for a time we had to suffer very severely from his vastly superior strength and utter ruthlessness.

But now it is the other way round. We are in a position to carry into Germany many times the tonnage of high explosives which he can send here, and this proportion will increase all the summer, all the autumn, all the winter, all the spring, all the summer, and so on, till the end! The accuracy of our bombing has nearly doubled, and, with continued practice, I expect it will improve still more. Moreover, at the same time, our methods of dealing with his raiders over here have more than repaid the immense

---

[1] In the first week of September 1939, 10,000 Polish civilians were killed in the German bombing raids on Warsaw.

[2] In the bombing of the Dutch city of Rotterdam on 14 May 1940, the death toll in the city was actually 814 (many civilians had already left upon the ultimatum of surrender or bombing; also, the bombing was called off before completion). Nevertheless, rumours put the figure at 20,000, even 30,000.

[3] In the bombing of the Yugoslav capital, Belgrade, on 6 April 1941 (Easter Sunday), 17,000 civilians were killed, the largest number of civilian deaths in one day in 20 months of war.

care and science bestowed upon them, and the very large scale upon which they are applied. During the month of April we have destroyed one-tenth of all the raiding aircraft, which have assailed our island; whereas, acting on a scale several times as big, the losses which we have suffered have been proportionately far smaller. We have waited long for this turning of the tables, and have taken whatever came to us meanwhile.

You will remember how the German propaganda films, seeking to terrorise neutral countries and glorying in devastating violence, were wont to show rows of great German bombers being loaded up with bombs, then flying in the air in battle array, then casting down showers of bombs upon the defenceless towns and villages below, choking them in smoke and flame. All this was represented from the beginning of the war to neutral countries as the German way of making war. All this was intended to make the world believe that resistance to the German will was impossible, and that subjugation and slavery were the safest and easiest road. Those days are gone. Though the mills of God grind slowly, yet they grind exceeding small. And for my part, I hail it as an example of sublime and poetic justice that those who have loosed these horrors upon mankind will now in their homes and persons feel the shattering strokes of just retribution.

We have a long list of German cities in which all the vital industries of the German war machine are established. All these it will be our stern duty to deal with, as we have already dealt with Lübeck, with Rostock, and half-a-dozen important places. The civil population of Germany have, however, an easy way to escape from these severities. All they have to do is to leave the cities where munitions work is being carried on – abandon their work, and go out into the fields, and watch their home fires burning from a distance. In this way they may find time for meditation and repentance; there they may remember the millions of Russian women and children they have driven out to perish in the snows, and the mass executions of peasantry and prisoners-of-war which in varying scales they are inflicting upon so many of the ancient and famous peoples of Europe. There they may remember that it is the villainous Hitlerite régime which is responsible for dragging Germany through misery and slaughter to ultimate ruin, and learn that the tyrant's overthrow is the first step to world liberation.

We now wait in what is a stormy lull, but still a lull, before the hurricane bursts again in full fury on the Russian front. We cannot tell when it will begin; we have not so far seen any evidences of those great concentrations of German masses which usually precede their large-scale offensives.

They may have been successfully concealed, or may not yet have been launched eastward. But it is now the tenth of May, and the days are passing. We send our salutations to the Russian armies, and we hope that the thousands of tanks and aeroplanes which have been carried to their aid from Britain and America will be a useful contribution to their own magnificently developed and reorganised munitions resources.

There is, however, one serious matter which I must mention to you. The Soviet Government have expressed to us the view that the Germans in the desperation of their assault may make use of poison gas against the armies and people of Russia. We are ourselves firmly resolved not to use this odious weapon unless it is used first by the Germans. Knowing our Hun, however, we have not neglected to make preparations on a formidable scale. I wish now to make it plain that we shall treat the unprovoked use of poison gas against our Russian ally exactly as if it were used against ourselves, and if we are satisfied that this new outrage has been committed by Hitler, we shall use our great and growing air superiority in the West to carry gas warfare on the largest possible scale far and wide against military objectives in Germany. It is thus for Hitler to choose whether he wishes to add this additional horror to aerial warfare. We have for some time past been bringing our defensive and precautionary arrangements up to date, and I now give public warning, so that there may be no carelessness or neglect. Of one thing I am sure: that the British people, who have entered into the full comradeship of war with our Russian ally, will not shrink from any sacrifice or trial which that comradeship may require.

Meanwhile, our deliveries of tanks, aircraft and munitions to Russia from Britain and from the United States continue upon the full scale. We have the duty of escorting the northern convoys to their destination. Our sailors and merchant seamen face the fearful storms of the Arctic Circle, the lurking U-boats and shore-based aircraft, as well as attacks by German destroyers and surface craft, with their customary steadfastness and faithful courage. So far, though not without some loss both to the supply ships and their escorts, every convoy has successfully fought its way through, and we intend to persevere and fight it out on this northern route to the utmost of our strength.

Is there anything else we can do to take the weight off Russia? We are urged from many quarters to invade the continent of Europe and so form a second front. Naturally, I shall not disclose what our intentions are, but there is one thing I will say:

I welcome the militant, aggressive spirit of the British nation so strongly shared across the Atlantic Ocean. Is it not far better that in the thirty-second month of this hard war we should find this general desire to come to the closest grips with the enemy, than that there should be any signs of war-weariness? Is it not far better that demonstrations of thousands of people should gather in Trafalgar Square[1] demanding the most vehement and audacious attacks, than that there should be the weepings and wailings and peace agitations which in other lands and other wars have often hampered the action and vigour of governments? It is encouraging and inspiring to feel the strong heartbeats of a free nation, surging forward, stern and undaunted, in a righteous cause. We must not fail them, either in daring or in wisdom.

This week, two islands have been in our minds – one is very large, the other very small – Madagascar and Malta. We have found it necessary to take precautions to prevent Madagascar falling into enemy hands, by some dishonourable and feeble drifting or connivance by Vichy, like that which injured us so much in Indo-China. It is three months since the decision was taken, and more than two months since the expedition left these shores. Its first task was to secure the splendid harbour of Diego Suarez, in the northern part of Madagascar, which, if it had fallen into Japanese hands, might have paralysed all our communications with India and the Middle East. While the troops were on the sea, I must tell you I felt a shiver every time I saw the word 'Madagascar' in the newspapers. All those articles with diagrams and measured maps, showing how very important it was for us to take Madagascar and forestall the Japanese, and be there 'first for once,' as they said, filled me with apprehension. There was no question of leakage, or breach of confidence. As they say, great minds think alike. But shrewd surmise may be as dangerous as leakage. And it was with considerable relief that I learned the difficulties of our soldiers and their losses had been exaggerated, and that the operation had been swiftly and effectually carried out.

We hold this island in trust; we hold it in trust for that gallant France which we have known and marched with, and whose restoration to her place among the great Powers of the world is indispensable to the future of Europe. Madagascar rests under the safeguard of the United Nations. Vichy, in the grip of the Germans, has been made to bluster and protest. The France that rose at St Nazaire,[2] and will one day rise

[1] A series of protest meetings had been held in Trafalgar Square, calling for a 'Second Front Now', in support of the Soviet Union. Lord Beaverbrook's *Daily Express* was at the forefront of that campaign.

[2] In support of the British raid on the dry dock at St Nazaire on 27–8 March 1942.

in indescribable fury against the Nazis, understands what we have done and gives us its trust.

The smaller island is Malta, a tiny rock of history and romance. Today we welcome back to our shores General Dobbie, for nearly two years the heroic defender of Malta. The burden which he has borne so honourably and for so long entitles him to release and repose. In Lord Gort we have a new impulse. His work at Gibraltar has been of the highest order. It was not his fault that our armies did not have their chance in France. He is a grand fighter. For the moment the terrific air attack on Malta has slackened. It looks as if a lot of enemy aircraft had moved eastward. I wonder why? If so, another intense air battle for Malta, upon which the enemy have concentrated such an immense preponderance of strength, and for which they have sacrificed so many of those aircraft which they now have to count more carefully every day – another intense air battle will have been definitely won. But other perils remain, and I know of no man in the British Empire to whom I would sooner entrust the combating and beating-down of those perils than Lord Gort.

If we look back today over the course of the war as it has so far unfolded, we can see that it seems to divide itself into four very clearly defined chapters. The first ended with the overrunning by the Nazis of Western Europe and with the fall of France. The second chapter, Britain alone, ended with Hitler's attack upon Russia. I will call the third chapter which then began, 'the Russian glory.' May it long continue! The fourth chapter opened at Pearl Harbour, when the military party in Japan treacherously attacked the United States and Great Britain in the Far East. That is where we are now.

The aggression of Italy in 1940 had carried the war from Europe to Africa. The aggression of Japan has involved all Asia, including unconquerable China, and in one way or another has drawn in, or will draw in, the whole of the American Continent. Thus the struggle has become worldwide, and the fate of all states and nations and their future is at stake. This latest chapter – universal war – confronts us with many difficulties and immense complications. But is there any thoughtful sensible person who cannot see how vastly and decisively the awful balances have turned to the advantage of the cause of freedom? It is true that the Japanese, taking advantage of our preoccupations elsewhere, and of the fact that the United States had striven for so long to keep the peace, have seized more easily and more quickly than they expected their lands of booty and desire in the East Indian Archipelago. Henceforward they will find resistance stiffening on all their widely spread fronts. They can ill afford losses such as those they have sustained in the naval action of the Coral Sea; so far we have no detailed accounts, but it is obvious, if only from the lies the Japanese have felt compelled to tell about the sinking of a battleship of the Warspite class, that a most vigorous and successful battle has been fought by the United States and Australian naval forces.

The Japanese warlords cannot be indifferent to the losses of aircraft inflicted upon them at so many points, and particularly off the northern coasts of Australia, and in their repulse at Colombo and Trincomalee. At the start the pent-up, saved-up resources of Japan were bound to prevail in the Far Eastern theatre; but the strength of the United States, expressed in units of modern war power, actual and potential, is alone many times greater than the power of Japan. And we also shall make our contribution to the final defeat and punishment of this ambitious and greedy nation. Time will, however, be needed before the true strengths on either side of the Eastern war become manifest. I am not prone to make predictions, but I have no doubt tonight that the British and American sea power will grip and hold the Japanese, and that overwhelming air power, covering vigorous military operations, will lay them low. This would come to pass, of course, very much sooner, should anything happen to Hitler in Europe.

Therefore tonight I give you a message of good cheer. You deserve it, and the facts endorse it. But be it good cheer or be it bad cheer will make no difference to us; we shall drive on to the end, and do our duty, win or die. God helping us, we can do no other.

Peter Fraser to Winston S. Churchill
(Churchill papers, 20/75)

11 May 1942

Please accept my warmest congratulations on your speech which struck an immediate response in every New Zealand heart.[1]

---

[1] Churchill replied at once: 'Thank you so much.'

Lord Halifax to Winston S. Churchill
(Churchill papers, 20/75)

11 May 1942   Washington DC

Welles[1] spoke in enthusiastic terms to me this evening about your speech and said reaction here had been splendid. This is supported by universal comment reaching me. It was exactly what was wanted.

Winston S. Churchill to Miss G. Lamont[2]
(Churchill papers, 20/53)

11 May 1942

My dear Miss Lamont,

I was much touched by the kind thought which prompted you to give me a 'birthday cake' yesterday.[3] I was sorry that in the rush I was not able to thank you personally but it was on the dinner table at No. 10 last night after my broadcast and Mrs Churchill and I both enjoyed it very much.

During these last two years I have been down to Chequers very often and you have been unfailing in your kindness and in the trouble you have taken for our comfort, and I am very grateful.

Yours very sincerely,
Winston S. Churchill

Winston S. Churchill to Captain James Drummond-Hay[4]
(Churchill papers, 20/56)

11 May 1942

My dear Captain Drummond-Hay,

Please convey to all Ranks of No. 2 Company, Holding Battalion, Coldstream Guards, my warm thanks for their message of congratulation.

It gives me great pleasure to note when I come down to Chequers that the high standard of soldierly bearing and smartness of your Regiment is so well maintained by the Companies of the Holding Battalion which are stationed there from time to time.

Yours sincerely,
Winston S. Churchill

[1] Sumner Welles, United States Under-Secretary of State.

[2] Grace Lamont, Curator of Chequers.

[3] A cake in honour of Churchill's second anniversary as Prime Minister.

[4] James Drummond-Hay, 1905–81. Inherited the estate of Seggieden, Perthshire, 1928. Married the daughter of the 13th Duke of Hamilton, 1930. Captain, later Major, Coldstream Guards, 1939–45. Served in Germany, 1945–8.

Winston S. Churchill to Anthony Eden
(Churchill papers, 20/67)

11 May 1942

The suggestion at (a) is most dangerous.[1] I hope you will give the firmest refusal, amounting to a diplomatic rebuff, to discuss any of these suggestions.

Winston S. Churchill to General Archibald Wavell
(Churchill papers, 20/75)

11 May 1942
Personal and Secret
Immediate

We should be glad to have Alexander back from Burma as soon as operations permit. Let me know how he is in health and whether he is much knocked about. I am sorry you cannot have him for Southern Command in India. We shall have need of him ourselves.[2]

Winston S. Churchill to President Franklin D. Roosevelt
(Churchill papers, 20/75)

12 May 1942
Personal and Secret
No. 87

The evidence at present available shows that Japanese carriers are equipped with striking forces of fighter dive-bombers in large numbers. Hitherto we have assessed our fighter strength as that necessary to meet the torpedo-carrier or large dive-bomber, of which a considerably lesser number can be operated by the enemy. It is necessary to increase our own fighter aircraft strength in Eastern Fleet carriers.

2. Your very generous help in the delivery of fighter aircraft will permit us to operate a large increase for a time but, owing to our quota ending this September and not re-starting until 1943, we cannot continue to

---

[1] Telegrams Nos 953 and 954 from Angora (Ankara) reported a suggestion from the Secretary-General of the Turkish Ministry for Foreign Affairs that Britain and Germany should negotiate: (a) refers to a proposal that the British Air Attaché should fly to London to lay these views before the Prime Minister.

[2] General Alexander returned to Britain from Burma and was given command of the 1st Army, which was to take part in the North African landings (Operation Torch) in November 1942. But on 8 August 1942 he was flown to Cairo to replace General Auchinleck as Commander-in-Chief, Middle East Command.

operate the fighter strength desired. A loan of 200 Martlets (which are the ideal aircraft for the purpose) has been asked for through the MAP,[1] to be delivered between now and December 1942. I should be very grateful for your help in this matter, which I regard as most important and urgent.

3. There is another urgent matter to which I would like to draw your attention, namely the early supply of transport aircraft for our airborne forces. As you know we hope to use our airborne forces in operations this summer but our ability to do so depends largely on the supply of transports from the United States. Without this help, our airborne forces can only be lifted at the cost of the bombing offensive against Germany.

4. Under Portal's Agreement with Arnold,[2] we have already been promised a considerable number of transports but the most useful types will arrive too late for our purpose. Our immediate need, therefore, is to receive the largest possible number of American transports within the next few weeks at the expense, if necessary, of supplies later in the year. I therefore ask whether you could let us have 200 American transports as early in June as possible.

5. In this connection I would like also to suggest that American airborne units should be sent at the same time to train and operate alongside our own in this country. Should this suggestion meet with your approval I need hardly say that we should be delighted to have your troops with us and that they would be assured of a warm welcome from our own airborne forces which Marshall reviewed with me when he was over here.

Randolph S. Churchill to Winston S. Churchill
(Churchill papers, 1/369)

12 May 1942   Cairo

Warmest congratulations[3] and love.

Randolph Churchill

Winston S. Churchill to Randolph S. Churchill
(Churchill papers, 1/369)

12 May 1942

Thanks and love.

Father

[1] MAP: Ministry of Aircraft Production.
[2] Henry Arnold, Commanding General of United States Army Air Forces.
[3] On his father's broadcast of Sunday, 10 May.

J. J. Tinker[1] to Winston S. Churchill
(Churchill papers, 20/61)

12 May 1942

Dear Mr Churchill,

On Sunday evening in your excellent broadcast you dealt with the use of poison gas and said that if Hitler used it against the Russians we should not hesitate to do the same with the Germans. Thinking this over it struck me that Hitler would much rather prefer gas to high explosive bombs over his cities because gas would not do so much damage and with this thought in his mind he would at once use gas against the Russians to cause Britain to carry out your pledge and do the same with Germany.

My knowledge of gas warfare is this – It is mainly effective when the contending armies are face to face but it will have little effect in bombing places where they are prepared for it – gas masks, etc. No, my view is, bomb Germany with high explosives and smash her up that way.

Yours sincerely,
J. J. Tinker

Winston S. Churchill: draft answer to J. J. Tinker
(Churchill papers, 20/61)

12 May 1942

Say in 3 p.

You may be sure we shall give them what they like least – but we cannot fail in our comradeship with Russia.[2]

Oliver Harvey: diary
('The War Diaries of Oliver Harvey', page 123)

12 May 1942

PM has opened out to AE about his idea of sending the Beaver[3] to Washington in place of Halifax. He wants to recall H because he is a flop

---

[1] John Joseph Tinker, 1875–1957. A miners' agent in Lancashire. Labour MP for Leigh, 1923–45. Parliamentary Private Secretary to the Secretary of State for War (Stephen Walsh), 1924.

[2] The letter, as sent by Leslie Rowan, of Churchill's Private Office, read: 'Dear Sir, The Prime Minister has seen your letter of 12th May and has asked me to thank you for it and to say that you may be sure that we shall give the Germans what they like least, but that we cannot fail in our comradeship with Russia. Yours truly, TLR.'

[3] Lord Beaverbrook.

and make him leader of the H of L (Bobbety's[1] health won't permit of
his going on with this as well as CO) and to make the Beaver Ambassador
where he says he will put our case across, get the aeroplanes we want out
of America and have daily touch with Roosevelt. AE not at all keen, he
told PM he thought it would be unpopular here, and he was not at all
sure that Roosevelt would welcome it. As Ambassador, B would be very
difficult to control and to work with. He finally got PM to agree to send
a personal wire to Harry Hopkins to ask him, as a friend and 'off the
record', what he feels about it.

Winston S. Churchill: remarks
(*'Winston S. Churchill, His Complete Speeches'*, *volume 6, page 6635*)

12 May 1942   Outside House of Commons
6.00 p.m.

ADDRESS TO THE PARLIAMENTARY HOME GUARD

When France fell out of the war two years ago and we were left alone,
we were in imminent danger of invasion, and at that time we were not
only destitute of an Army but we were an unarmed people. But at the
same time that we reorganised our Army the Home Guard sprang into
existence, and now we have the best part of 1,750,000 men trained to
the use of arms, conscious of their military character and accustomed
readily and rapidly to come together at any point, fixing their minds
upon the possibilities of contact with the enemy, which are never to be
excluded. This body, engaged in work of national importance during
all the hours of the day, and often of the night, is nevertheless an invaluable addition to our armed forces and an essential part of the effective
defence of the Island.

More especially is this true in view of the fact that airborne invasion
becomes more and more a possibility and a feature of modern war. If
in 1940 the enemy had descended suddenly in large numbers from
the sky in different parts of the country, he would have found only
little clusters of men, mostly armed with shotguns, gathered round our
searchlight positions. But now, whenever he comes – if ever he comes
– he will find, wherever he should place his foot, that he will immediately be attacked by resolute, determined men who have a perfectly

---

[1] Lord Cranborne, Colonial Secretary since 22 February 1942.

clear intention and resolve, namely, to put him to death or compel his immediate surrender.

Therefore, to invade this island by air, apart from the difficulties of facing the Royal Air Force by daylight, is to descend into a hornet's nest. And I venture to think that there is no part of that nest where the stings are more ready and their effective power to injure more remarkable than here in the ancient Palace of Westminster, where, rifle in one hand and sometimes speech notes in the other, we conduct the essential work of the Mother of Parliaments, and make clear that neither bombardment nor invasion will prevent our institutions functioning steadily, unbrokenly, throughout the storms of war.

Winston S. Churchill to Anthony Eden
(Churchill papers, 20/67)

13 May 1942
Action this Day
Secret

MUNITIONS TO TURKEY

The following seems to me to be the policy of munitions to Turkey:

Nothing much can be done this summer or before the Russian campaign decides itself more clearly. Nor do we ask anything more of the Turks than to keep intruders out. But as soon as the Russian front shuts down with the winter an effort should be made, for which preparations must be begun forthwith, to give them a substantial packet of tanks, AT guns and flak. By that time there should be an immense flow of munitions in the United States and our own output running higher. The figures mentioned in America are enormous, and there should be no difficulty in sparing 1,000 tanks and 1,000 AT and AA guns. No doubt older Marks might form the bulk.

2. If a plan is prepared on this sort of scale and deliveries begin in November, the promise will make the Turks stand faithful during the summer, keeping neutral, and the arrival of these weapons which they can train upon during the winter may make them our Allies in the spring.

3. If you think well of this, let us take it up with Production here and in the United States.

Winston S. Churchill to John Llewellin[1]
(Churchill papers, 20/67)

13 May 1942
Action this Day

Let me have a report on Flag C of your latest return, Column 5. This shows that you have 1,797 'in preparation.' These are presumably in addition to the 649 ready, and ready within four days. The shortage of aircraft at the present moment is acute. Now is the time for you to bring forward this reserve of 1,797, which are presumably defective in this or that spare part.

Lord Beaverbrook in 1940 gained great advantages for us by a searching analysis and scrutiny of the machines in the ASUs.[2] What we want now is <u>more aircraft in the front line</u>. Get at it and bite at it.

2. Give me therefore the following reports:

(a) The corresponding figures to 649 and 1,797, week by week, for the last two years, and

(b) Make me a proposal to bring forward into the squadrons 500 of the 1,797 by 15th July. It may well be that there are some additional spare parts with the RAF at home surplus to immediate requirements, which would make some of these machines alive. I am told the Beaufighters in particular could be brought forward, and are urgently needed. There are 280 of these on your hands. Let me have a separate return, showing what is holding back the 100 most promising Beaufighters.

3. I presume you have an exact record of each of these types of machines, and can say exactly what is needed to bring any one of them forward to the fighting line. If so, let me see it. If not, you ought to have. You need not give any explanation about the 363 Wellingtons; I am already aware of it.

---

[1] Minister of Aircraft Production.
[2] ASUs: Air Support Units.

Winston S. Churchill to Richard Casey
(Churchill papers, 20/75)

13 May 1942
Immediate
Most Secret

REQUEST FROM CAIRO FOR AMERICAN BOMBERS
IN MIDDLE EAST

Consequent on decisions taken during Marshall's visit, allocation American Heavy Bombers and disposition of American Units has been agreed. It has been decided that American Heavy Bombers Units shall be concentrated in United Kingdom. All American Heavy Bombers are either required for Coastal Command and to equip the five British Heavy squadrons to be formed overseas this year as you already know, or else they are needed to meet purely American requirements. To approach President as you suggest would, therefore, only be regarded as departure from agreed plans for offensive action in Western Europe.

Josef Stalin to Winston S. Churchill
(Churchill papers, 20/75)

13 May 1942
Personal

I have received your message of the 11th May,[1] and am writing to thank you for the promise to arrange for maximum delivery of war materials to the USSR. We quite understand the difficulties which Great Britain is overcoming, and those heavy sea losses which you are suffering while accomplishing this big task.

As for your suggestion for the Air Force and Navy of the USSR to take more effective measures for protection of transports in the area mentioned by you, you may not doubt that on our part all possible measures will be taken immediately. It is necessary, however, to take into consideration the fact, that our Naval Forces are very limited, and that our Air Forces in its vast majority are engaged at the battlefront.

Please accept my sincere greetings.

---

[1] Reproduced at page 646 above, dated 9 May.

Churchill later wrote in his war memoirs: 'At last, on April 1, it became possible for the United States Navy to make a start with a partial convoy system. At first this could be no more than daylight hops of about a hundred and twenty miles between protected anchorages by groups of ships under escort, and all shipping was brought to a standstill at night. On any one day there were upwards of a hundred and twenty ships requiring protection between Florida and New York. The consequent delays were misfortune in another form. It was not until May 14 that the first fully organised convoy sailed from Hampton Roads for Key West. Thereafter the system was quickly extended northward to New York and Halifax, and by the end of the month the chain along the east coast from Key West northward was at last complete. Relief was immediate, and although the U-boats continued to avoid destruction the shipping losses fell'.[1]

Winston S. Churchill to General Sir Alan Brooke
(Churchill papers, 20/67)

14 May 1942
Secret

What are the standing instructions for dealing with 'infiltration'? In Burma we have had loosely held fronts of several hundred miles; small parties of Japanese – sometimes only two or three hundred men – penetrate, and the whole front has to retire. Surely the way to deal with infiltration is to kill the infiltrators. This can be done by forming small mobile groups of highly-trained officers and men capable of travelling quite light and closing on the infiltrators as soon as they make themselves manifest. It ought to be possible to form such bodies and equip them with whatever weapons and transport may be needed.

The principle of attacking the infiltrators rather than withdrawing the front is surely a vital one.

---

[1] *The Hinge of Fate*, pages 106–7.

George Harvie-Watt to Winston S. Churchill
(Sir George Harvie-Watt papers)

14 May 1942

There was a meeting of the Foreign Affairs Committee on Tuesday with Wardlaw-Milne in the Chair: about 25 Members were present. The Chairman reported the result of the recent Deputation to the Foreign Secretary on the Anglo-Russian Agreement. The Deputation felt that:

1. The Government was apparently committed to the proposals and

2. Russia was for some reason making a special point of the recognition of the Baltic States.

The Foreign Secretary[1] put a formidable case for the Agreement, but the Deputation was not satisfied with his explanations. The Lord Privy Seal[2] had subsequently seen Victor Cazalet and had again put to him the points very strongly and very fairly. Cazalet stated however that the Lord Privy Seal's persuasive argument had failed to convert him. There is a feeling in the Committee that this is an attempt by the Russians to separate us from the United States. Stalin, some Members think, does not wish to see at the Peace Conference a strong Anglo-American bloc. It is felt that we should have obtained the consent of America before agreeing to any recognition of frontiers. The Committee is not, in any way, hostile either to the Foreign Secretary or to the Government in its criticism, but it considers they are doing a service to the Government in drawing attention to the strong feeling that exists. It would not be sufficient, the Committee felt, for the Agreement when signed, but subject to ratification, to be then submitted for approval to the House. Sir Malcolm Robertson[3] said he was horrified that such an Agreement should have been contemplated and that we should ever consent to be a party to giving away the independence of other nations. The strongest possible protest should be made on the subject as no country in the world could trust us after this Agreement was made public. It was felt that the position now reached was unfortunate as (1) if Russia wins then she would be so strong that we could do nothing about these States; (2) if she loses, the matter does not arise; (3) it is wrong for one ally to make a separate agreement, as they like, with another. Why shouldn't Roosevelt agree to give away

[1] Anthony Eden.

[2] Sir Stafford Cripps.

[3] Malcolm Arnold Robertson, 1877–1951. Entered the Foreign Office, 1898. British High Commissioner, Rhineland, 1920–1. Consul-General, Tangier, 1920–5. Knighted, 1924. Ambassador to the Argentine, 1927–9. Chairman of Spillers Ltd, 1930–47. Conservative MP candidate for Mitcham, Surrey, 1940–5. Chairman of the British Council, 1941–5.

Malaya to China? Sir Ralph Glyn[1] thought that the Government should take steps to find out what the feeling in the House is now and not wait for ratification. The general view of the Committee was that the result in the country would be disastrous and that the Foreign Secretary should be asked to go to the Committee and hear what Members feel about it. The Foreign Secretary, on my last report on the subject, appeared to think I had exaggerated the position, but there is no exaggeration on this subject. Members are feeling strongly about it and it is likely to give rise to difficulties for the Government in the future.[2]

Harry Hopkins to Winston S. Churchill
(Churchill papers, 20/75)

15 May 1942

I thought your last Sunday's speech was one of the best you have yet delivered. I will reply to your private message in a day or two.

Winston S. Churchill to A. V. Alexander and
Admiral of the Fleet Sir Dudley Pound
(Churchill papers, 20/67)

15 May 1942
Secret

This is not a very helpful telegram. It would seem to involve an immense dispersion of our limited aircraft and AA. I do not think we could accept the views of Admiral Somerville[3] as governing the strategic mission of the Eastern Fleet. He is hardly justified, in paragraph 9, in speaking of 'the whittling down of the proposed reinforcements,' since instead of *Duke of York* and *Renown* he gets the two 16-inch gun ships. He seems to me to be asking for everything and giving the least possible. I should be glad to discuss this with you and the Naval Staff after you have considered it carefully and before any answer is sent.

---

[1] Ralph George Campbell Glyn, 1885–1960. Educated at Harrow and Sandhurst. Joined the Rifle Brigade, 1904. Unsuccessful Conservative Parliamentary candidate, 1910. On active service at the Dardanelles, in France and in the Balkans, 1914–18. Conservative MP for Clackmannan and Eastern Stirlingshire, 1918–22, and for Abingdon, 1924–53. Parliamentary Private Secretary to Ramsay MacDonald, 1931–7. Created Baronet, 1934. Created Baron, 1953.

[2] Churchill marked this document for Eden to read.

[3] Commander-in-Chief, Eastern Fleet, 1942–4.

2. See paragraph 6. The Admiral is no judge of whether the French will invite the Japanese to come into Madagascar. I cannot see why the fact we have a garrison and an Air Force in Diego Suarez makes Madagascar 'an additional commitment'. Most people would think it would be a deterrent requiring a considerable Japanese expedition.

3. Nothing could be more foolish than to squander our resources over all the places he mentions, and not have one that is strong and safe and well protected. I see he is asking for further 'military reinforcements' for Ceylon, which is the opposite of what General Wavell has in mind.

Winston S. Churchill to Anthony Eden
(Churchill papers, 20/67)

15 May 1942
Secret

SUPPLY OF MUNITIONS TO TURKEY

There is no need to unsay anything we have said, but the fact remains that, should Turkey be attacked in the summer or autumn of 1942, there are practically no forces that we could send to her aid, and even if we had large forces the communications from Syria do not lend themselves to their movement. Something, no doubt, will be done under the pressure of the event.

2. We have made certain promises of minor allocations of munitions during the summer and autumn. These should be kept so far as is physically possible.

3. My idea was to make a large, simple offer to the Turks operative from November on. Your last sentence leads swiftly to our usual conclusion, viz., to do nothing. I should not propose to work the policy I have set out through the Joint Assignments Board, but to persuade the President to join with me in making a promise to Turkey which, if they and others survive the summer, would give them effective hope of being in a strong position by the spring of 1943. Something on the lines I have suggested might play a very important part in encouraging Turkey through these anxious months and in enabling her to participate in the 1943 campaign, should our affairs in these regions prosper.

Winston S. Churchill to Admiral Edward Syfret
(Churchill papers, 20/75)

15 May 1942
Most Immediate
Most Secret

I want you to see clearly our picture of the Madagascar operation. It must be a help and not a hindrance. It must be a security and not a burden. We cannot lock up active Field Army Troops there for any length of time. The 13th and 17th Brigades must go on to India almost immediately. If you could take Tamatave and Majunga in the next few days they could help you in this, but they have got to go on anyhow.

2. Since 'Ironclad' was conceived and executed the Indian Ocean situation has changed to our advantage. Time has passed. The Japanese have not yet pressed their attack upon Ceylon or India. On the contrary these dangers look less near and likely than before. We gave them a rebuff at Colombo and Trincomalee at the beginning of April. In the early days of July we hope to form the whole of the Eastern Fleet, namely: *Nelson, Rodney, Warspite* and *Valiant* with the three Carriers and the four Rs and to base this Fleet upon Colombo and Port T.

3. If and when this is accomplished, Madagascar will be very far behind the front line. One can hardly imagine the Japanese trying to take Diego Suarez with less than ten thousand men in transports with battleship and Carrier escort involving a very large part of their limited Fleet. They have to count every ship even more carefully than we do in view of numerical inferiority. I doubt very much whether they will attempt to establish lodgements or submarine bases in Madagascar now that we have the key point.

4. Therefore your problem is one of holding the place with the least subtraction from our limited resources. You should make up your minds whether you can do this by taking Tamatave and Majunga in the next few days and then sending on to India the 13th and 17th Brigades (which would also have the advantage of releasing the Naval Forces now employed in the Madagascar Area which are so urgently required elsewhere), or whether you will make yourselves comfortable at Diego Suarez and try to wangle things with the French and with the natives pending arrival of the Union Brigade and the first of the two African Brigades, after which the 29th Brigade must move on.

5. It may be however you will think it better to let matters simmer down and make some sort of *modus vivendi* with the French Authorities.

Money and trade facilities should be used. Here at home we have had to indicate that the Free French will be associated with Madagascar, but this is for the sake of keeping the Movement going and it must be several months before Free French Representatives arrive – if ever. Anyhow the local situation will not be ruined by orders from home for their sake.

6. The way you can help the war best is to get the 13th and 17th Brigades on to India at earliest and the 29th Brigade within the next two months. Everything else is subordinate to this except of course holding Diego Suarez, which must on no account be hazarded. Cable fully but do not delay any action on which you may decide.

7. This telegram is agreed by COS Committee and supersedes where necessary previous instructions.

Winston S. Churchill to General Archibald Wavell
(Churchill papers, 20/75)

15 May 1942
Personal and Secret
Immediate

Operation 'Ironclad' went off well and nothing that matters to you should be hung up there for very long. The leading Brigade of the 5th Division should reach you on the 17th May. The 17th and 13th Brigades will be re-embarked as soon as they are relieved by the Union Brigade Group which General Smuts has handsomely offered us and a KAR Brigade from East Africa. The former ought to arrive by the end of this month and the latter by about 6th June. The 29th Brigade must remain for a while to tidy up Majunga and Tamatave but we hope that when the second Brigade from East Africa arrives in July the 29th Brigade can be released and come on to you. This will be your pure gain.

2. I presume that amid your present anxieties you are also thinking of the future. If all goes well in various quarters I hope that before the middle of July we may assemble at Colombo and Port T,[1] assuming that the defences of Ceylon have been completed and those of Port T sufficiently progressed, the whole Eastern Fleet comprising *Warspite, Valiant,* the two 16-inch battleships, the three Carriers and the available Rs, together with cruisers and flotillas. From then on the battle area of the Eastern Fleet will be the waters south and east of Ceylon but as the year advances and your shore-based air force is established on the eastern

[1] Port T: Trincomalee.

shores of India, we must aim at recovering effective control of the Bay of Bengal. By that time you would have the 2nd and 5th British Divisions and the 29th Brigade and possibly a complete Armoured Division with two other Divisions from home if they are not drawn off to the Middle East or Australia.

3. Should these dispositions be possible, would you not be able to take offensive action against the Japanese communications through Burma and particularly by attacking Rangoon by an amphibious operation. In this way help would be given to Chiang Kai-shek and hope to encourage him to hold out. By now you will have had the Chiefs of Staff's first thoughts on these possibilities (Telegram No. COS (India) 55 of 9/5).

4. In outlining these objectives to you, I cannot be sure that events will render them possible. But it seems to me that it would be well worthwhile working out offensive schemes on the above assumptions.

John Martin: diary
(Sir John Martin papers)

16 May 1942

Visit to Leeds – factories, triumphal drive through streets, speech from Town Hall steps to crowd of 25/30,000. Visited 9th Armoured Division, Laken Heath (Newmarket).

Winston S. Churchill: speech
('Winston S. Churchill, His Complete Speeches', volume 6, page 6636)

16 May 1942   Town Hall Steps
                                                          Leeds

In the height of the second great war, it is a great pleasure to come to Leeds and bring to the citizens a word of thanks and encouragement in all the work they are doing to promote the common cause of many nations and in many lands. That cause appeals to the hearts of all those in the human race who are not already gripped by tyranny or who have not already been seduced to its insidious voice. That cause is shared by all the millions of our cousins across the Atlantic who are preparing night and day to have their will and rights respected. It appeals to the patient millions of China, who have suffered long from cruel aggression and still fight with faithful stubbornness. It appeals to the noble manhood of Russia, now at full grips with the murderous enemy, striking blow for blow and repaying better ones for blows struck at them. It appeals to all the people of Britain, without discrimination of class or party. It appeals to all the peoples of the British Empire throughout the world, and I have here at my side Dr Evatt[1] from Australia.

I voice on behalf of this vast gathering of men and women of Leeds our warmest message of good will and comradeship to our kith and kin in Australia, who, like ourselves, lie under the menace of imminent enemy attack, and who, like ourselves, are going to strike a heavy and successful blow on all who spring upon us.

You have had your test in battle,[2] but lately the enemy has not been so ready to come to this island: first, because a large portion of his air force is engaged against our Russian allies, and secondly because he knows that our arrangements for meeting him, thanks to the assistance of hundreds and thousands of active, willing minds and hands, are improving in power and efficiency every day. I have seen some of your factories this morning, though not as many as I should have liked to have seen, and I know well the great contribution which Leeds is making to the whole forward and upward thrust of the War.

We have reached a period in the War when it would be premature to say that we have topped the ridge, but now we see the ridge ahead. We see that perseverance, unflinching, dogged, inexhaustible, tireless, valiant, will surely carry us and our Allies, the great nations of the world, and the unfortunate nations who have been subjugated and enslaved, on to one of the most deep-founded movements of humanity which have ever taken place in our history. We see that they will come to the top of the ridge, and then they will have a chance not only of beating down and subduing those evil forces which have withstood us so long, which have twice let ruin and havoc loose on the world, but they will have that further and grander prospect that beyond the smoke of battle and the confusion of the fight we shall have the chance to settle our countries and the whole world together, moving forward together on the high road. That is the prospect that lies before us if we do not fail. And we shall not fail.

Here in the 33rd month of the War none of us is weary of the struggle. None of us is calling for any favours from the enemy. If he plays rough

---

[1] Australian Representative in the British War Cabinet, and Australian Member of the Pacific War Council.

[2] Leeds had received its worst bombing raid on the night of 14–15 March 1941, when 4,500 houses were damaged, 100 beyond repair. At the height of the raid, more than 4,000 wardens, 1,845 firemen, and 77 ambulance crews were on duty. By the time the all clear sounded at 3.12 on the morning of 15 March, 65 people were dead or dying, eight of them children.

we can play rough too. Whatever we have got to take we will take, and we will give it back in even greater measure. When we began this war we were a peaceful and unarmed people. We had striven hard for peace. We had even gone into folly over our desire for peace, and the enemy started all primed-up and ready to strike. But now, as the months go by and the great machine keeps turning and the labour becomes skilled and habituated to its task, we are going to be the ones who have the modern scientific tackle. It is not now going to be a fight of brave men against men armed. It is going to be a fight on our side of people who have not only the resolve and the cause, but who also have the weapons.

We shall go forward together. The road upwards is stony. There are upon our journey dark and dangerous valleys through which we have to make and fight our way. But it is sure and certain that if we persevere – and we shall persevere – we shall come through these dark and dangerous valleys into a sunlight broader and more genial and more lasting than mankind has ever known.

Winston S. Churchill and Chiefs of Staff to Admiral Edward Syfret
(Churchill papers, 20/75)

16 May 1942
Most Secret
Most Immediate

Operations for capture of Tamatave and Majunga are to be abandoned for the present and your task is to make Diego Suarez secure with the minimum forces. Guidance about effecting a *modus vivendi* with French Authorities will be sent as soon as possible. In the meanwhile no commitment should be taken on.

2. One Brigade of the 5th Division should be released at once. The remaining Brigade of 5th Division should go on to India as soon as the first of the garrison brigades arrives from Union or East Africa.

3. 29th Brigade and Commando should be released as soon as the second garrison brigade arrives, if the situation then permits.

4. Separate instructions will be sent about the release of naval forces.

Winston S. Churchill to General Hastings Ismay,
for the Chiefs of Staff Committee
(Churchill papers, 20/67)

17 May 1942 Chequers
Most Secret

Not only Premier Stalin, but President Roosevelt will object very much to our desisting from running the convoys now. The Russians are in heavy action and will expect us to run the risk and pay the price entailed by our contribution. The United States ships are queueing up. My own feeling, mingled with much anxiety, is that the convoy ought to sail on the 18th. The operation is justified if a half gets through. The failure on our part to make the attempt would weaken our influence with both our major allies. There are always the uncertainties of weather and luck, which may aid us. I share your misgivings, but I feel it is a matter of duty.

2. I presume all the ships are armed with AA guns and that not more than 25 will be sent.

3. I will bring the question before the Cabinet tomorrow (Monday) in your presence, but meanwhile all preparations should proceed.

Winston S. Churchill to General Hastings Ismay
(Churchill papers, 20/67)

17 May 1942 Chequers
Secret

Let me have a report twice weekly on the progress of the studies and preparations for 'Sledge-Hammer.'[1]

Winston S. Churchill to Anthony Eden and Lord Leathers[2]
(Churchill papers, 20/67)

17 May 1942

Have we thanked the Americans properly for the allocation of 70 tankers? This seems to me to have been a very open-handed action on

---

[1] 'Sledgehammer': the Anglo-American amphibious landing, of limited aims, against northern France, planned to take place in the autumn of 1942 (later amended to 1943), should either the Soviet Union or Germany seem in danger of imminent military collapse.

[2] Minister of War Transport.

their part, considering the losses they have suffered. No doubt thanks is conveyed departmentally, but should I not make some reference to this in one of my telegrams to the President? If so, let me have the materials.

Winston S. Churchill to A. V. Alexander and
Admiral of the Fleet Sir Dudley Pound
(Churchill papers, 20/67)

17 May 1942
Secret

Dr Evatt, who has become much more friendly, has made me the strongest appeals about an aircraft-carrier. We had, of course, promised them the *Hermes*,[1] but she was sunk on our business before being sent to them. You now tell me that they had said they did not want her. Have you seen, however, the long telegram which Dr Evatt has received from Mr Curtin, in which the need of two aircraft-carriers is stressed? I carefully avoided making the slightest promise, but I have been wondering whether the *Furious* could be spared. Will you let me know what are your plans for her?

2. Why should the *Victorious* require a refit now? How long has she been with the Fleet? I should have thought less than a year. What is the nature of the defects which require her withdrawal at this critical juncture? I recognise the fact that the Americans have withdrawn *Wasp* and that this makes our position more difficult, and, of course, *Wasp* is a reinforcement for the Pacific. We have to consider our permanent relationship with Australia, and it seems very detrimental to the future of the Empire for us not to be represented in any way in her defence.

---

[1] HMS *Hermes*, the world's first purpose-built aircraft carrier, launched in 1919. Participated in the blockade of Dakar, June 1940. Supported British Commonwealth troops in Italian Somaliland, February 1941. Joined the Eastern Fleet in Ceylon, February 1942. Sunk by Japanese aircraft on 9 April 1942, while preparing to participate in Operation 'Ironclad' against Madagascar; 307 of her crew of 566 were drowned.

Winston S. Churchill to Field Marshal Jan Smuts
(Churchill papers, 20/75)

17 May 1942
Personal

You will see from our signal of May 16 to SO Force 'F' (appended)[1] that we have had to put off for the time being clearing up Tamatave and Majunga as the movement of the 5th Division to India must be completed at the earliest moment. We are greatly obliged to you for sending the Union Brigade Group, and I hope you will not be vexed because we are not able to dominate the Island completely as proposed.

2. It seems to me that there ought to be materials for a *modus vivendi* at the present time. All we want is to make sure the Japanese do not have facilities in the remaining Madagascan harbours. For this purpose it might be sufficient if we had agents in the principal ports by agreement with the Vichy French there. We have much to give in the way of trade, and money too may be used. We are of course making ourselves strong at Diego Suarez.

3. It has occurred to me that perhaps the High Commissioner, Ormsby-Gore,[2] might visit Diego Suarez and give general political guidance to the people on the spot and see what kind of a temporary settlement is possible with the French. After all they do not want us to attack them. Pray let me have your views.

4. I have been hoping to hear from you ere now on the points mentioned in my letter which Mr Waterson[3] carried but I see you have been moving about in the Western Desert in order to see for yourself. I wish I were with you.

---

[1] Not printed here.

[2] William George Arthur Ormsby-Gore, 1885–1964. Educated at Eton and New College, Oxford. Conservative Unionist MP for Denbigh, 1910–18; for Stafford, 1918–38. Intelligence Officer, Arab Bureau, Cairo, 1916. Assistant Secretary, War Cabinet, 1917–18. Member of the British Delegation (Middle East Section) to the Paris Peace Conference, 1919. British Official Representative on the Permanent Mandates Commission of the League of Nations, 1920. Under-Secretary of State for the Colonies, 1922–4, 1924–9. Privy Councillor, 1927. First Commissioner of Works, 1932–6. Secretary of State for the Colonies, 1936–8. Succeeded his father as 4th Baron Harlech, 1938. High Commissioner, South Africa, 1941–4. Chairman of the Bank of British West Africa, 1951–61; of the Midland Bank, 1952–7. A Trustee of the Tate and National Galleries.

[3] Sidney Waterson, High Commissioner of South Africa in London.

President Franklin D. Roosevelt to Winston S. Churchill
(Churchill papers, 20/75)

17 May 1942
Personal and Secret
No. 146

It now appears that delivery of carrier fighters will fail to meet our minimum requirements in 1942 so that the loaning of the Martlets to you would merely mean that our own carriers were to the same degree not equipped. I am putting every pressure on delivery of carrier fighters and hope our production rate can be increased.

Plans are being pushed to train, equip and move air transport units to the UK as rapidly as possible. The present schedule and the probability is: for June two groups of 52 planes each; for July two additional groups, making a total of 208 transport planes. This is an advance of one month on the original schedule. It is planned to augment this air transport force by four additional groups by November 1942, providing a grand total of 416 planes. Transport groups on reaching England will be made available to assist the British forces both in operations and training.

The importance of airborne troops in operations is fully appreciated and we are doing everything possible to accelerate the rate at which air transport can be made available in England.

I welcome the invitation for our parachutists and airborne troops to train in the UK alongside yours: a battalion of parachutists will be sent in June, the remainder of the first armoured Division and the first serial of General Spaatz's[1] eighth air force will complete the June shipment. I am particularly anxious to start our air units operating with you on the offensive and to bet some of our ground troops trained in amphibious operations against the possibility of any emergency operations this summer.

---

[1] Carl Spaatz, 1891–1974. Entered West Point Military Academy, 1910. Served with the American Expeditionary Force, France, 1917–18. United States observer in Britain during the Battle of Britain, 1940. Officer Commanding US 8th Air Force and Commanding General of the United States Army Air Forces, European Theatre, 1942; North-West African Air Force, 1943. Commanding General, Strategic Bombing Force, operating against Germany, 1944. Honorary knighthood, 1944. Commanding General, US Strategic Air Forces in the Pacific, supervising the final strategic bombing of Japan, 1945. Commanding General, US Army Air Forces, 1946–7. Chief of Staff, US Air Force, 1947–8.

Winston S. Churchill to General Claude Auchinleck
(Churchill papers, 20/75)

17 May 1942
Most Secret
Personal

It is necessary for me to have some account of your general intentions in the light of our recent telegrams.

Winston S. Churchill to General Hastings Ismay,
for the Chiefs of Staff Committee
(Churchill papers, 23/10)

18 May 1942
Most Secret

THE AUTUMN CAMPAIGN OF 1942 IN THE INDIAN OCEAN

We should aim at assembling the Eastern Fleet at Kilindini by the 7th July at the latest, and at basing this Fleet on Colombo or/and Trincomalee by the 15th July. All arrangements, including AA, Fighter and Torpedo Aircraft, moorings &c, for the protection and accommodation of the Fleet at either of these stations, should be pressed forward with the utmost urgency.

2. The movement of the four modernised ships and the three Carriers to Ceylon harbours should not be prevented for the sake of including the four Rs. Otherwise we shall see another case of their low fighting quality and obsolete character becoming an actual hindrance rather than a help to our operations. Based upon Diego Suarez they can, at this great distance from the enemy and with strong naval forces established in Ceylon, afford protection to the convoy route. When the accommodation in Ceylon is prepared for their reception, they may, if desired, move there.

3. We must resist the temptation to disperse our Anti-Aircraft resources between Colombo and Trincomalee. Whatever is necessary should be given to one port, and the other should make shift with what is left pending further improvement. We must make up our mind which. Until we have one invincibly defended base in Ceylon, we cannot provide for Addu Atoll, which can play its part as indicated in paragraph 9 of Admiralty No. 1419B/May 16. Remember the Scotch say 'ain guid house and weel plenished'.

4. As between Kilindini and Diego Suarez, the priority for AA defences should go to Diego Suarez, which should be developed as a stronghold against all forms of attack, <u>and advertised as such to an even greater extent</u>. As it is highly improbable that any attack will be made upon it or upon any part of Madagascar by the Japanese, the forces and resources employed there must remain, as proposed by the COS Committee, on an altogether secondary level.

5. The task of Commander-in-Chief, Eastern Fleet, 'to deter the Japanese from operating in the Bay of Bengal except by a superior force', is admirably defined in Admiralty No. 1419B/May 16. Let us stick to this, <u>and make other ideas conform to it.</u>

6. The probability of the Japanese sending into the Indian Ocean a fleet superior to the Eastern Fleet (less the four Rs) appears small. Their narrowly measured resources in capital ships and regular Aircraft Carriers enforces upon them extreme care. It does not seem that they would be anxious to seek a battle with so substantial a force as the Eastern Fleet (even less the four Rs), provided – and provided only – (a) that our Aircraft Carriers have their full equipment of Martlets or other fast Fighters, and (b) that we keep as much as possible within the range of our shore-based torpedo aircraft. If the losses in a fleet action were anything like equal, the result to Japan would be irreparable disaster. Nothing in the Japanese strategy has hitherto shown them willing to risk any part of their battle-fleet. Their incursion into the Bay of Bengal was very carefully conducted. Their abandonment of their expedition after the action in the Coral Sea shows the stringency of the Aircraft Carrier problem with them. Therefore we need not expect them to seek a trial of strength in the Indian Ocean with a detachment only of their fleet. To send the main fleet would be for them a most adventurous decision.

7. Every effort should be made to reach the full quota of shore-based aircraft (Reconnaissance, Bomber and Torpedo) required to give protection to the Eastern Fleet when operating in the Bay of Bengal, and to dominate the shore-based aircraft of the enemy which he must be expected to be building up on the territories he has conquered in that region. The combination of sea and air power which we should seek to establish there by the end of September should be sufficient, not only to prevent seaborne invasions of India, but to enable us to take oversea action of our own. In this theatre, as in others, it pays us to force the air fighting and to lose machine for machine.

8. All military reinforcements to India are, of course, dependent upon the fortunes of war in Libya, in the Caucasus and in Australia. Assuming,

however, that the course of events is not unfavourable to us, we should be able to send the 8th Armoured Division and at least one British Infantry Division, besides the 2nd and 5th Divisions, to arrive in India by the end of September. This would give General Wavell the 70th, 2nd, 5th, 44th and 8th Armoured Divisions, together with the British Indian Army and garrisons of (say) 4 Divisions. Total, 9 Divisions. In October, therefore, conditions should permit his assumption of a general offensive against the Japanese in Burma.

9. It is absolutely necessary that this offensive should be planned from now on, and every effort made, subject to events, to carry it into effect. Landing craft must be prepared locally and a proportion sent from home. British and American air reinforcements must be gathered to the utmost limit permissible by other needs. The attack upon the Japanese lines of communication might be vital to the continued resistance of China. We ought also to hold out the prospect to Chiang Kai-shek, under all necessary reservations, of such an attack, in order to keep him fighting. Everything goes to show the correctness of the judgment we formed, that the drive against Chungking is the first Japanese objective, apart, of course, from Russia, which depends upon how the battle in the west develops. A general amphibious British air and land offensive from Moulmein to Assam must be the aim we set before ourselves for the autumn and winter of 1942.

War Cabinet: Confidential Annex
(Cabinet papers, 65/30)

18 May 1942
5.30 p.m.

The Prime Minister said that the Chiefs of Staff had raised the question whether the next convoy to Russia should sail, in view of the substantially increased risk of air attack from Norway.

With the ice barrier in its present position the convoy must sail for 6–7 days within range of enemy bombers based in Norway. The Germans had about 100 bombers in this area, of which 69 were long-range bombers; and they had a very good system of air reconnaissance. The scale and duration of the air attack on the next two convoys was likely to be greater than any yet experienced. The Chiefs of Staff feared that, unless the weather conditions were particularly unfavourable for air operations, it was likely that our losses would be considerable.

In addition to the loss of merchant vessels, we had also to take into account the risks to which the escorting vessels would be subjected.

In these circumstances the question arose whether it would be expedient to cancel the convoys due to sail in May and June, and increase the size of the convoys sailing after the beginning of July, when it would be possible to take a more northerly route which, for the greater part of the voyage, would lie outside the range of JU87s and JU88s.

The main points raised in discussion were:

(a) If the May and June convoys were cancelled, how far would it be possible to make up the deficit by increasing the quantity of supplies sent thereafter.

After the beginning of July the Admiralty would be prepared to take the risk of increasing the size of the convoy to 50 ships. But, if no convoys sailed until July, the congestion of shipping destined for Russia would be very large. And, if the supplies which had been dammed up were released too rapidly, a great strain would be thrown on the port facilities in Russia.

(b) It was recognised that the Navy would be relieved of a heavy responsibility, and a substantial risk, if these sailings could be deferred until after the end of June. On the other hand, it would not be easy to convince either Premier Stalin or President Roosevelt.

(c) It was suggested that the position should be explained to Premier Stalin, who might be asked to say whether he was in such immediate need of these supplies that he would wish an attempt made to get through the May and June convoys during those months, even though, say, half the amounts shipped might well be lost en route, rather than to face postponement until July, when conditions would be easier.

In reply to this suggestion, it was pointed out that the decision was one which we must take ourselves, and ought not to place on other shoulders. In any event, Premier Stalin was almost certain, if the point was put to him, to reply that an attempt should be made to force through these supplies, at whatever cost.

(d) The Prime Minister expressed the view that it was our duty to fight these convoys through, whatever the cost. The Russians were engaged in a life and death struggle against our common enemy. There was little we could do to help them, except by maintaining the flow of supplies by this northern route. In the last convoy, 22 out of 25 ships had got through, in spite of our apprehensions: and this time we might again do better than we feared.

The effect on war comradeship between the United Nations, of cancellation of the May Convoy would, he feared, be very serious.

(e) It was not thought that any appreciable advantage would be gained by confining the convoy to faster vessels. On the whole the First Sea Lord thought that if the convoy was to sail, we might as well send 35 ships.

The War Cabinet decided as follows:

(1) The May convoy, due to leave that night, should sail as arranged.

(2) Premier Stalin should be informed that we had given orders for this convoy to sail, notwithstanding the additional risk to which it would be subject. He should be strongly urged to send heavy bombers to attack the aerodromes in Norway from which the German aircraft were operating, and warned that it might be necessary to cancel the sailing of the June convoy.

(3) The question whether the June convoy should sail should be decided by the War Cabinet in the light of the losses sustained by the May convoy.

General Archibald Wavell to Winston S. Churchill
(Churchill papers, 20/75)

18 May 1942
Most Immediate
Most Secret

Alexander will leave Imphal area about 20/5. I shall probably meet him [in] Calcutta on my way to Manipur to see Burma troops. Liaison Officer reports him in excellent health and spirits. Do you want him back at once? I want him to write account of Burma campaign before he leaves.

2. Troops from Burma collected Imphal area will probably be about 20,000. They are reported tired and disorganised but in quite good spirits. I will decide after seeing them whether to reorganise them in forward areas or bring back further into India. Propose send home few representative personnel from Burma campaign for propaganda purposes.

3. No repeat no news yet of Stilwell's whereabouts nor of Chinese troops of whom it is now repeat now reported considerable numbers may make for India.

4. Authoritative account of results [of] Coral Sea battle would be of greatest value here both from morale point of view and to assess effect on Japanese Navy. At present no one here has much idea what happened.[1]

---

[1] The Battle of the Coral Sea (4–8 May 1942) marked the United States' first naval victory against the Japanese. In a battle fought entirely from the air, the Americans lost one aircraft carrier, one destroyer and one tanker, while the Japanese lost seven major warships, rendering their invasion fleet unable to continue its mission.

Oliver Harvey: diary
('The War Diaries of Oliver Harvey', page 125)

18 May 1942

[...]

More defeatism from the Chiefs of Staff. They wish to terminate the Madagascar operation (which they were kicked into) with the occupation of the North bit only, whilst concluding a *modus vivendi* with the Vichy governor as regards the rest. AE up in arms against this, is pointing out to PM that Vichy can never be trusted. Their first reaction was to appeal to Japs against us and they will now provide nests for German and Italian agents. AE wishes to clear the rot out and put in a good Free French Governor (General Legentilhomme[1]). The trouble is the PM now so loathes de Gaulle, he almost prefers Vichy itself – as the Americans do.

Winston S. Churchill to Anthony Eden
(Churchill papers, 20/67)

19 May 1942

The telegrams seem to be growing longer and longer. For a while, after you issued some warning, there was an improvement. The waste of time and energy involved in these long codings and decodings is most serious. I quite understand they all want to help the war by increasing their output. In fact, they clog and hamper.

Winston S. Churchill to Josef Stalin
(Churchill papers, 20/75)

19 May 1942
Personal and Most Secret

A convoy of 35 ships sailed yesterday with orders to fight their way through to you. The Germans have about a hundred bombers in wait for these ships and escort. Our advisers think that, unless we are again favoured with weather which hampers the German air force, we must

[1] General Paul-Louis le Gentilhomme, 1884–1975. Commander of the French troops on the Somali coast, 1940, with his headquarters at Jibuti. One of only two French commanders and Governors-General (the other being General Catroux in Indo-China) who maintained their opposition to Vichy. Unable to persuade his subordinates to remain in the war, in April 1941 he led seven battalions of Free French troops against the Vichy forces in Syria, continuing in action himself despite being severely wounded. A member of the Free French National Committee, 1941, in charge of the War Department.

expect that a large proportion of the ships and of the war materials contained in them will be lost.

2. As I mentioned in my telegram of the 9th May, much will depend on the extent to which your long-range bombers can bomb the enemy aerodromes, including that at Bardufoss, between the 22nd and 29th of this month. I know that you will do your utmost.

3. If luck is not with us and the convoy suffers very severe losses, the only course left to us may be to hold up further convoys until we get more sea room when the ice recedes northward in July.[1]

General Claude Auchinleck to Winston S. Churchill
(Churchill papers, 20/75)

19 May 1942
Personal
Most Secret
Immediate

Your OZ 244 17/5.

My intention is to carry out the instructions in paragraph two of your OZ 192 10/5.

2. I am assuming that your OZ 192 10/5 is not (not) meant to imply that all that is required is an operation solely to provide a distraction to help the Malta convoy but that the primary object of an offensive in Libya is still to be the destruction of the enemy forces and the occupation of Cyrenaica as a step toward the eventual expulsion of the enemy from Libya. If I am wrong in this assumption then I should be so informed at once as plans for a major offensive differ entirely from those designed merely to produce a distraction. I am proceeding as if my assumption is right (right).

3. Assuming that a major offensive is to be carried out but that its inception must be so timed as to provide distraction to help the Malta convoy, the actual moment of the launching of the offensive will be governed by three considerations – First, the sailing date of the convoy; second, enemy action between now and then; third, the relative air strength of the enemy and ourselves. All these are under close and continuous examination here.

[1] The Russian Deputy Chief of the Naval Staff had expressed 'great satisfaction at our decision to send the May convoy. The Russians were going to treat the arrival of this convoy as a special operation. 200 aircraft of the Red Army would be employed on protection measures' (War Cabinet, 21 May 1942, *Cabinet papers, 65/26*).

4. There are strong signs that the enemy intends to attack us in the immediate future. If he does attack, our future action must be governed by the results of the battle and cannot be forecast now (now).

5. Assuming that the enemy does not attack us first, it is my intention that General Ritchie shall launch his offensive in Libya on the date which will best fit in with the object of providing the maximum distraction for the Malta convoy, and at the same time, ensure the fullest degree of readiness in the forces carrying out the offensive. These considerations are mutually conflicting as you will realise, and entail a certain degree of compromise which it will be my responsibility in consultation with the other Commanders-in-Chief to determine. The importance of avoiding an abortive attack has already been fully set out in No. CS/36 of 6/5 from Commanders-in-Chief to Chiefs of Staff and does not (not) need further explanation from me.

6. In conclusion may I ask your consideration of the fact that owing to the narrowness of our margin of superiority over the enemy both on the land and in the air, the success of a major offensive cannot (not) be regarded as in any way certain, though everything will be done to make it as certain as possible. In any event success is not (not) likely to be rapid or spectacular as progress will probably have to be methodical owing to the special nature of the problem.

7. I feel therefore that it is of the greatest importance that in the first instance no publicity at all should be given to our intention to carry out a major offensive even after it has been launched. Still less should the public be led to hope for a speedy and striking success.

8. This telegram has been seen by the Minister of State,[1] C in C Mediterranean[2] and AOC-in-C[3] who agree with it.

Winston S. Churchill to Anthony Eden
(Churchill papers, 20/67)

19 May 1942

See 'A.'[4] I quite understand the French resisting when we attacked them at Oran, Dakar, Syria and Madagascar, under the present unhappy conditions. But this wanton attack by them on our aircraft so far out at

---

[1] Richard Casey.

[2] Admiral of the Fleet Sir Andrew Cunningham.

[3] Air Marshal Sir Arthur Tedder.

[4] Paragraph 7 of Central War Room Record No. 989 of 19 May 1942: an attack by a French fighter aircraft on a Catalina on anti-submarine patrol from Gibraltar.

sea seems to stand on a different footing. We have never accepted their 20-mile notification, and anyhow this was probably outside that limit. Can we not do something about it?

Winston S. Churchill to General Claude Auchinleck
(Churchill papers, 20/75)

20 May 1942
Personal and Secret
Immediate

Your CS/1010.

Your paragraph 2. Your interpretation of the instructions contained in my OZ 192 of May 10 is absolutely correct. We feel that the time has come for a trial of strength in Cyrenaica and that the survival of Malta is involved.

2. The greatest care will be taken to prevent newspaper speculation here about attacks either way in Cyrenaica. If and when a battle begins public will merely be informed heavy fighting is in progress. You must impose the same restriction at your end and we can consult together about any definite pronouncement.

3. Of course we realise that success cannot be guaranteed. There are no safe battles. But whether this one arises from an enemy attack and your forestalling or manoeuvring counterstroke, or whether it has to be undertaken by you on its own, we have full confidence in you and your glorious Army, and whatever happens we will sustain you by every means in our power.

4. I should personally feel even greater confidence if you took direct command yourself as in fact you had to do at Sidi Rezegh. On this however I do not press you in any way.

5. Ought not the New Zealand Division to be nearer the battlefront? If you want any help in dealing with the New Zealand Government pray recur to me.

Harold Nicolson: diary
('Harold Nicolson, Diaries and Letters', page 226)

20 May 1942

The House is in a bad mood and the debate consists of one long stab and dig at Winston. The difficulty is that serious people do not like getting up to defend Winston on strategical grounds. The critics always know some small detail which sounds damaging and which can only be answered by disclosing information of value to the enemy. Hore-Belisha[1] makes a particularly damaging attack. Cripps[2] winds up well and strongly, but I fear that Winston's position in the House (in spite of his triumph in the secret session) is not a strong one. This fills me with dismay.

Winston S. Churchill: recollection
('The Hinge of Fate', page 296)

21 May 1942

Molotov did not arrive until May 20, and formal discussions began the following morning. On that day and at the two following meetings the Russians maintained their original position, and even brought up specifically the question of agreeing to the Russian occupation of Eastern Poland. This was rejected as incompatible with the Anglo-Polish Agreement of August 1939. Molotov also put forward a case for the recognition in a secret agreement of Russia's claims on Roumania. This also was contrary to our understanding with the United States. The conversations at the Foreign Office, which Mr Eden conducted, though most friendly, therefore moved towards a deadlock.

Lord Beaverbrook to Henry Luce and Clare Boothe Luce[3]
(Lord Beaverbrook papers)

21 May 1942

PUBLIC DEMAND FOR A SECOND FRONT

The Government will be judged by the speed with which it acts. And should it fail in urgency, not even the prestige of Churchill will save it from condemnation.

---

[1] *Hansard*, 20 May 1942, Volume 380, columns 251–61.

[2] *Hansard*, 20 May 1942, Volume 380, columns 324–38.

[3] Henry Robinson Luce, 1898–1967. Born in China, the son of an American missionary there. On active service with the American Army in France, 1917–18. Founder (1923), Editor and Publisher of *Time*, of *Fortune* (1928), and (1936) of *Life*, becoming a multi-millionaire. Evolved the cinema programme *The March of Time* (1935). Organized United China Relief, 1940. His wife Clare Boothe Luce, a pre-war friend of Randolph Churchill, was later United States Ambassador to Italy.

The Prime Minister's position today is unchallenged. It is true that those who in the House of Commons formerly were careful to distinguish between him and his Government have now come out into the open in criticism of him. But the agitation to remove him from his position as Minister of Defence finds no support outside a small group of Tories. And by the public he is regarded with undiminished admiration and affection. They believe in his leadership, and they have no faith in his critics.

War Cabinet: conclusions
(Cabinet papers, 65/26)

21 May 1942   10 Downing Street
5.30 p.m.

The Prime Minister informed the War Cabinet that M Molotov had arrived in this country on the previous day, <u>en route</u> to the United States. M Molotov was most anxious that no information should be given of his arrival in this country. Should the news leak out, no confirmation should be issued. He had said that there were two matters which he wished to discuss: first, the Political Treaty; secondly, the Second Front question. A first Meeting had been held at 11.30 that morning. As regards the Political Treaty, M Molotov had said that he must have as a minimum the Russian frontier as at the time of Hitler's aggression on Russia in June, 1941. He had used language which seemed to imply that he would not be able to make any concession on the point of difference between the two drafts. He had added, however, that if it was not possible to reach agreement, he thought it would be better to defer signature altogether for some time. He also said that he attached more importance to the Second Front than to the signature of the Treaty.

[...]

The Prime Minister said that a Meeting would be held on the following morning, attended by representatives of the Chiefs of Staff, at which the Second Front question would be dealt with. He invited the Vice-Chief of the Imperial General Staff to prepare a short Note on the prospects of 'Sledgehammer'.

War Cabinet: Confidential Annex
(Cabinet papers, 65/26)

21 May 1942　　　　　　　　　　　　　　　　　10 Downing Street
5.30 p.m.

[...]

Dr Evatt also quoted from a telegram which had been sent to the Prime Ministers of Australia and New Zealand on 11th August, 1940, in which the Prime Minister had said:

> 'If however contrary to prudence and self-interest, Japan set about invading Australia or New Zealand on a large scale, I have the explicit authority of the Cabinet to assure you that we should then cut our losses in the Mediterranean and proceed to your aid, sacrificing every interest except only the defence and feeding of this Island on which all depends.'

Dr Evatt emphasised that, notwithstanding the fact that according to our grand strategy the defeat of Germany was our prime objective, all these documents emphasised the importance of ensuring the security of Australia, as a base of operations against Japan.

The Prime Minister said that he entirely stood by the assurance given in the cable to Mr Menzies quoted by Dr Evatt. The contingency of invasion on a large scale had not yet arisen, however, and he hoped that it would never arise. If it did arise, one British Armoured Division, (the 8th) and one Infantry Division (the 44th), which would be rounding the Cape in the course of the next few weeks, could be diverted to Australia more quickly than forces from any other theatre.

Continuing, the Prime Minister said that, since Japan had come into the war, Australia had made a direct appeal for help from the United States, and we had fallen in with Australia's wishes in this matter. The line of demarcation which had been drawn in the Pacific put Australia into the United States sphere. Notwithstanding this demarcation of spheres, we did not, of course, regard our obligations to do what we could to help Australia as being lessened in any way. The position must be, however, that while we would do all in our power to come to Australia's help if she was invaded, we could not afford to lock up in any theatre (Australia included) sufficient troops to meet all possible invasion risks. Our strategy must be to use our available forces to meet the main enemy effort, whenever it might be made. At the moment it was not easy for us to forecast where Japan would strike next. There were a number of possibilities. Before long we should see in what direction Japan's threat developed. We would, however, do what we could to give Australia more air support.

We were encountering difficulties ourselves with the Americans over the allocation of aircraft. They had made proposals under which they would keep for themselves 5,000 aircraft which had been allocated to us. These were enough to equip 100 new Squadrons, the personnel for which had been provided for. He was not unmindful of the fact that there were 7 squadrons in this country manned by Australians, and we would like some of these squadrons to be sent to Australia. He had asked the Chief of the Air Staff on the previous day to consider the despatch from this country to Australia of three Spitfire squadrons.[1]

[...]

The Prime Minister asked the Chief of the Air Staff to draw up a paper explaining shortly the measures proposed for the despatch of these three squadrons to Australia. This should for a basis for a communication to be made by Dr Evatt to the Australian Government. No communication should be sent in the meantime by the United Kingdom authorities on the matter.

Dr Evatt expressed his gratitude to the War Cabinet for the decision reached. He hoped that it would be understood that the despatch of the two Australian squadrons was a decision of the United Kingdom Government, and that it would not be said that the Commonwealth Government had asked for their recall.

The Prime Minister assented and added that, notwithstanding our own difficulties, we would take all possible steps to see that nothing was lacking which would ensure the successful operation of these squadrons in Australia.

Dr Evatt also asked that the decisions taken should not be regarded as affecting Australian applications for allocations of aircraft to the South West Pacific.

The Prime Minister assented, pointing out that the three squadrons were a special contribution to Australia in an emergency.

Winston S. Churchill to President Franklin D. Roosevelt
(Churchill papers, 20/75)

21 May 1942
Personal and Secret
No. 88

We understand and respect the generous impulse which inspires the United States Air Force to engage American lives in the conflict at the

---

[1] Two Australian squadrons and one British.

earliest moment. God knows we have no right to claim undue priority in the ranks of honour. Let us each do our utmost. So may it be to the end.

2. The sole objective must be the optimum air impact on the enemy, month by month. We have both of us to find the highest fulfilment of this irrespective of whether British or United States pilots man the aircraft.

3. For this purpose a common expansion plan is necessary, and a ruthless scrutiny of reserves, discrepancies or anything clogging the pipelines. Please send Arnold and Towers[1] at the earliest possible moment. We shall lay everything before them. Portal will return with them [and if necessary I will come myself[2]].

4. I ought to tell you however that as we understand it, General Arnold's proposals for revision of the allocations of American aircraft to the Royal Air Force mean the loss of nearly 5,000 aeroplanes to us this year. The effect would be to reduce by over 100 squadrons (nearly 2,000 first line aeroplanes) the force which we had planned to have in action by the Spring of 1943. Dependent on your expected deliveries we have already taken into service and are now training pilots, crews and mechanics for this plan, and ancillary equipment of all kinds will be available for it. Indeed, we have in active theatres of war awaiting aeroplanes at this moment about 30 squadrons, some of them veteran units which have lost their equipment in action.

5. I hope Mr President you will not take any final decision without considering how these hundred squadrons are to be replaced by American units on the various battle-fronts by the dates expected. Without your assurance on these points the whole structure of our plans would collapse, and an entirely new view of the war would have to be taken.

Winston S. Churchill to General Archibald Wavell
(Churchill papers, 20/75)

21 May 1942
Private and Secret

Your 12211/C. Certainly keep Alexander to write his report. Give him my regards.

---

[1] John Henry Towers, 1885–1955. US Naval Academy class of 1906. A naval aviator. Assistant Naval Attaché, London, 1914–15. In charge of naval aircraft procurement, 1939–42 (when the air arm of the US Navy grew from 2,000 planes to 39,000). Vice-Admiral, Commander Air Force, Pacific Fleet, 1942–5 (appointed October 1942). Commander-in-Chief, Pacific Fleet, 1946–7.

[2] Words deleted by Churchill before the telegram was sent.

2. No clear account of Coral Sea action has reached us. Japanese had one Carrier sunk and one badly damaged and possibly sunk and thereupon abandoned their project against Port Moresby or Darwin for which about twenty transports were being escorted. Action was fought only by aircraft on both sides. Americans had two Carriers damaged but expect both will survive. This last is most secret, and for you and the Viceroy alone. Admiralty think main Japanese fleet is at Truk in Caroline area. There are very good reasons for believing that operations against Midway Island are certain, against Aleutian Islands very probable, and against Hawaii probable.

3. I feel much more hopeful that you will get through the next two months than I did two months ago. The end of July if all goes well should see you more comfortable. We are thinking hard here about your affairs and how to help you.

Minutes of a meeting
(Churchill papers, 20/75)

22 May 1942   10 Downing Street
11 a.m.

Mr Churchill welcoming M Molotov and his advisers, said that he understood that M Molotov was anxious to place before British Government the views held by the Soviet Government on the subject of an invasion of the Continent.

M Molotov said that he had been charged by the Soviet Government to come to London to discuss the question of the establishment of a 'Second Front'. This was no new problem. It had first been raised nearly ten months ago and now, more recently, the impetus had come from President Roosevelt, who had suggested to M Stalin that he (M Molotov) should go to the United States to discuss this question. Although, therefore, the initiative for the present enquiry had come from the United States, the Soviet Government had thought it right that he should proceed to the United States via London, since it was upon Great Britain that the main task for organising the 'Second Front' would initially fall.

Speaking generally, M Molotov said that the Soviet Government considered this to be a most urgent and pressing problem, in which both Great Britain and Russia were vitally concerned. It was indeed a matter for discussion with complete frankness, as becoming conversations between Allies. On the Russian Front, operations of the greatest intensity and importance were now impending and the weeks and months which lay immediately ahead were fraught with the most serious consequences to the Soviet Union and their Allies. During last winter, the Soviet Army had got the better of Hitler's Army, and had immediately set about preparing for the campaign of 1942. Nevertheless, the Soviet Government contemplated a fierce and bitter struggle in which the Germans would not yield easily or quickly. In this battle, the main weight would fall upon the Soviet Army. They were proud of this honour. On both sides, immense forces, backed by mighty armaments, were ranged against each other. The material aid rendered by Great Britain and the United States was highly prized and appreciated by the Soviet Government. Nevertheless, the most urgent issues were involved in the establishment of a 'Second Front'.

The object of his (M Molotov's) visit was to learn how the British Government viewed the prospects of drawing off some of the weight from Russia, where it seemed that, at the present time, the balance of advantage in armed strength lay with the Germans. It should be remembered that Hitler could call upon vast resources seized from the subjugated and enslaved peoples scattered over a large part of Europe.

In concrete terms, the proposal he had to make was that Russia's Allies, and Great Britain in the first place, should aim at containing 40 enemy divisions in Western Europe. If this could be done, the doom of Hitler was sealed, if not in 1942, at any rate very soon afterwards.

Mr Churchill said that, in all previous wars, control of the sea had given the Power possessing it the great advantage of being able to land, at will, on the enemy's coast, since it was impossible for the enemy to be prepared at every point to meet seaborne invasion. The advent of air power had altered the whole situation. For example, in France and the Low Countries the enemy could move his Air Forces in a few hours to threatened points anywhere along the coast; and bitter experience had shown that landing, in the teeth of enemy air opposition, was not a sound military proposition. The inescapable consequence was that large portions of the Continental coastline were denied to us as places for disembarkation. We were forced, therefore, to study our chances at those parts of the coast where our superior fighter force would give us control in the air. Our choice was, in fact, narrowed down to the Pas-de-Calais, the Cherbourg 'tip' and part of the Brest area.

The problem of landing a force this year in one or more of these areas was being studied, and preparations were being made with the utmost energy. Our plans were being based on the assumption that the landing of successive waves of assault troops would bring about air battles which, if continued over a week or ten days, would lead to the virtual destruction of the enemy's air power on the Continent. Once this was achieved and the air opposition removed, landings at other points on the coast could be effected under cover of our superior sea power. The crucial point in making our plans and preparations was the availability of the special landing craft required for effecting the initial landing on the very heavily defended enemy coastline. Unfortunately, our resources in this special type of craft were, for the time being, strictly limited.

As far back as last August, at the Atlantic meeting, he (Mr Churchill) had impressed upon President Roosevelt the urgent need for the United States to build as large a number of tank landing and other assault craft as possible. Later, in January of this year, the President had agreed that the United States should make an even larger effort to construct these craft. We, for our part, for more than a year, had been turning out as large a number of assault craft as our need for constructing ships for the Navy and Mercantile Marine, which had suffered grievous losses, permitted.

In April, President Roosevelt had sent Mr Hopkins and General Marshall to London with the proposal that the United States should join with Great Britain, at the earliest date, in taking the greatest possible weight off Russia. We had immediately agreed to this proposal, and joint studies were proceeding apace. It could not be expected, however, that United States forces would be available till very late in 1942, or that the landing craft we so urgently required would be available in large numbers this year.

By 1st August we should have only 383 landing craft: by 1st September 566. In 1943, very much larger numbers would be available, and we could descend on the enemy coast at five or six points, anywhere between the North Cape and Bayonne. It was, however, the earnest resolve of the British Government to see what could be done this year to give the much needed support to the valiant Russian armies, who were confronting so large a part of Germany's military might, and had already inflicted such deep wounds upon it.

Two points should, however, be borne in mind. First, with the best will and endeavour, it was unlikely that any move we could make in 1942, even if it were successful, would draw off large numbers of enemy land forces from the Eastern Front. In the air, however, the position was different; in the various theatres of war we were already containing about one-half of the Fighter and one-third of the German Bomber strength. If our plan for forcing air battles over the Continent proved successful, the Germans might be faced with the choice either of seeing the whole of their fighter air force in the West destroyed, or of making withdrawals from their air strength in the East.

The second point related to M Molotov's proposition that our aim should be to draw off (including those now in the West) not less than 40 German divisions from Russia. It should be noted that, at the present time, we had confronting us in Libya 11 Axis divisions, of which 3 were German, the equivalent of 8 German divisions in Norway, and 25 German divisions in France and the Low Countries. These totalled 44 divisions.

But we were not satisfied with that, and if any further effort could be made or plan devised, provided it was sound and sensible, for drawing the weight off Russia this year, we should not hesitate to put it into effect. Clearly, it would not further either the Russian cause or that of the Allies as a whole if, for the sake of action at any price, we embarked on some operation which ended in disaster and gave the enemy an opportunity for glorification at our discomfiture.

Thus, to sum up, we and the United States would do everything that was physically possible to meet the wishes of the Russian Government and Nation in this matter.

M Molotov enquired whether the views expressed by Mr Churchill were shared by the United States Government on the subject of the second front.

Mr Churchill said that the United States Government shared to the full our resolve to operate on the Continent with the largest possible forces at the earliest possible moment. This was their ardent desire, and in 1943 our joint plans contemplated the landing of a force of up to 1.5 million United States–British troops on the Continent.

The United States were anxious to take their share in any operations carried out this year, but their contribution in the near future would not be on any considerable scale. As an earnest of their intent, we had with us now in London a number of American officers who were collaborating closely with our staffs in the preparation of plans: and more were on their way.

M Molotov then asked whether it was possible and appropriate to make an estimate of the percentage of British troops, including those on all fronts, employed on active operations against the enemy, at any given date during the last three months.

Mr Churchill said that the proportion of British troops on all fronts actually at grips with the enemy was naturally small. He went on to explain in general terms the dispositions of our forces; up to 50,000 men a month were leaving our shores for the Middle and Far East theatres.

M Molotov said that he had no doubt that Great Britain genuinely wished for the success of the Soviet Army against the Germans this summer. What, in the view of the British Government, were the prospects of Soviet success? Whatever their views might be he would be glad to have a frank expression of opinion – good or bad.

Mr Churchill said that, without detailed knowledge of the resources and reserves on both sides, it was difficult to form a firm judgement on this question. Last year the military experts, including those of Germany, had thought that the Soviet Army might be borne down and overcome. They had proved quite wrong. In the event the Soviet forces had defeated Hitler and nearly brought his army to disaster. Consequently Russia's Allies felt great confidence in the strength and ability of the Soviet Army.

The Intelligence available to the British Government did not indicate the massing of vast German forces at any particular point on the eastern front. Moreover, the full-scale offensive heralded for May now seemed unlikely to take place before June. In any event, it did not seem that Hitler's attack this year could be as strong or so menacing as that of 1941. In making this statement he (Mr Churchill) did not wish it to be inferred that we were asking our guests for information which they might be reluctant to disclose.

M Molotov, in reply, agreed that nobody could be expected to make accurate prophecies about the future. The great Russian country and people believed in their own strength, but they also believed in facing up to the worst possibilities. Supposing the Soviet Army failed to hold out against the maximum effort, which Hitler would undoubtedly exert during 1942, how would the British Government view the position in which they would then be placed?

Mr Churchill said that if the Russians were defeated or the Soviet military power was seriously reduced by the German onslaught, Hitler would, in all probability, move as many troops and air forces as possible back to the West, with the object of invading Great Britain. He might also strike down through Baku to the Caucasus and Persia. This would expose us to the gravest dangers, and we should by no means feel satisfied that we had sufficient forces to ward off the latter thrust. Therefore, our fortunes were bound up with the resistance of the Soviet Army. Nevertheless, if, contrary to expectation, they were defeated, and the worst came to the worst, we should fight on, and with the help of the United States, hope to build up overwhelming Air superiority, which, in the course of the next 18 months or 2 years would enable us to put down a devastating weight of air attack on the German cities and industries. We should, moreover, maintain the blockade and make landings on the Continent against an increasingly enfeebled opposition. Ultimately, the power of Great Britain and the United States would prevail. It should not be overlooked that after the fall of France Great Britain had stood alone for a whole year with but a handful of ill-equipped troops between her and Hitler's victorious and numerous divisions.

But what a tragedy for mankind would be this prolongation of the war, and how earnest was the hope for Russian victory and how ardent the desire that we should take our share in conquering the evil foe. He, Mr Churchill, wished M Molotov to realise that it was the dearest wish of the British nation and Army to come to grips with the enemy at the earliest moment and so to aid the gallant fight of the Russian Army and people.

In conclusion, Mr Churchill asked M Molotov to bear in mind the difficulty of overseas invasions. After France fell out of the war, we in Great Britain were almost naked – a few ill-equipped divisions, less than 100 tanks and less than 200 Field guns. And yet Hitler had not attempted an invasion, by reason of the fact that he could not get command of the air. The same sort of difficulties confronted us at the present time. He suggested that General Isayev[1] and Admiral Kharlamov[2] should meet Lieutenant-General Nye and Vice-Admiral Lord Louis Mountbatten that afternoon, in order that they might be told the exact position as regards the special landing craft necessary for overseas operations.

M Molotov agreed. He thanked Mr Churchill, for what he had said. He would carefully report to his Government. In conclusion, he would like to say that the Russian people also believed in their strength and in the strength of their Allies.

Winston S. Churchill to Anthony Eden
(Churchill papers, 20/67)

22 May 1942

MILITARY ASSISTANCE TO TURKEY

I did not say, as you will see if you will be so kind as to read my minute again, that doing nothing was 'your' usual conclusion. On the contrary, I said 'our' usual conclusion.

---

[1] Major-General Fedor Mikhailovich Isayev, 1896–1967.
[2] Admiral Nikolay Mikhaylovich Kharlamov, 1905–83.

2. I have made no proposals for 'using promises for the future as a happy pretext for ignoring undertakings already given for the present.'

3. I have made a proposal, however, which I am prepared to back which would for the first time give you a practical and hopeful policy towards Turkey, and I should be grateful if you would address your mind to this.

Winston S. Churchill to Lord Cranborne
(Churchill papers, 20/67)

22 May 1942

REQUEST FROM GOVERNOR OF CYPRUS[1] CONCERNING
EVACUATIONS OF CYPRUS IN THE EVENT OF INVASION

I think you should reply as follows:
'There is no question of such a situation arising, and no advantage in discussing it beforehand. If it were to arise, instructions would be sent you in time.'

General Claude Auchinleck to Winston S. Churchill
(Churchill papers, 20/75)

22 May 1942
Personal

Thank you very much for your OZ 261 of 21/5 and for confirmation of your instructions contained in OZ 192 of 10/5. I am now absolutely clear as to my task and I will do my utmost to accomplish it to your satisfaction.

2. Thank you too for your arrangements regarding publicity which will be scrupulously followed by me here.

3. Am most grateful for your most generous expression of confidence in the Army I command and in myself and for the assurance of your support, the measure of which has been proved to us so often and so amply in the past.

4. Much as I would like to take command personally in Libya I feel that it would not repeat not be the right course to pursue. I have considered the possibility most carefully and have concluded that it would

---

[1] Charles (Campbell) Woolley, 1893–1981. On active service, 1914–18; Captain, South Wales Borderers, in action in France, Salonika, the Caucasus (mentioned in despatches, Military Cross). Ceylon Civil Service, 1921–35. Colonial Secretary, Jamaica, 1935–8. Chief Secretary, Nigeria, 1938–41. Governor and Commander-in-Chief, Cyprus, 1941–6. Knighted, 1943. Governor and Commander-in-Chief, British Guiana, 1947–53.

be most difficult for me to keep a right sense of proportion if I became immersed in tactical problems in Libya. I feel that a situation may arise almost at any time when I shall have to decide whether I can continue to reinforce and sustain the Eighth Army without serious hindrance or whether I must hold back and consider the building up of our Northern Front which I am now weakening in order to give General Ritchie all the help possible. On balance I think my place is here but you can rely on me I hope to adapt myself to the situation and to take hold if need arises. I am in very close touch with General Ritchie and he is fully in my mind. I hope all will be well.

5. I have considered fully the desirability of bringing the New Zealand Division out of Syria into Egypt. Apart from the political aspect which I am sure you could settle as you so kindly offer to do there are other considerations. I am loathe to denude Syria of troops just now partly because of the uneasy political situation in the country itself and partly because of the possible effect on the Turks of whose attitude I am not repeat not too sure. I feel they mean well but circumstances may be too strong for them and it is most important that they should not get the idea that we are weakening or becoming unable to support them.

I am already bringing 10th Indian Division, a well trained formation, from Iraq to reinforce Eighth Army should need arise and have meanwhile sent up a Brigade of 4th Indian Division as an interim reinforcement. With these reinforcements the Eighth Army will almost reach saturation point so far as power to provide the Army with food and water is concerned. Water especially is a very serious problem. Moreover the NZ Division has been severely denuded by the Government of Senior Officers who are needed to command newly raised troops in New Zealand and it is now training officers to replace these. I am watching the whole situation very closely and if I have to put the rest of 4th Indian Division into Cyprus to provide against a possible threat to the Island I should probably have to bring the NZ Division down to Egypt but I would rather not move it at present.

6. Once more I thank you for your most sustaining message. There will be hard fighting as there was before. I have great confidence in our troops and in our dispositions. I have a firm hope of victory and pray that it may lead to greater things.

General Archibald Wavell to Winston S. Churchill
(Churchill papers, 20/75)

22 May 1942
Personal
Most Secret
Most Immediate

Met Alexander today, who is in very good shape. Am flying tomorrow to Dinjan, where hope to meet Stilwell and hear whether any of his Chinese are coming [to] India. Shall then go Imphal to see troops from Burma.

2. Alexander has performed fine feat in bringing back Army. Will let you have full story later. Total numbers about 30,000, of whom approx. half fighting troops. Fighting troops are: British 5,000, Indians 9,000, Burmese 1,000. Above very rough figures only. Will cable in more detail later.

3. All fighting troops have rifles, light automatics and other personal weapons and equipment. Ten 25-pounders brought back. Fourteen 3.7 Hows, four (?AP)[1] guns, no AA guns, about 70 lorries brought back, all tanks and remaining motor transport lost owing to sudden rise Chindwin River, and difficulties of ferrying. AA guns had to be abandoned owing impossibility of embarking on ferry boats, same applies to tanks, which were anyway near end mechanical life. All animal transport brought back.

4. Believed all sick and wounded evacuated either by air, or with retiring column.

Winston S. Churchill to Josef Stalin
(Churchill papers, 20/75)

23 May 1942

We have greatly enjoyed receiving M Molotov in London and have had fruitful conversations with him on both military and political affairs. We have given him a full and true account of our plans and resources. As regards the Treaty, he will explain to you the difficulties, which are mainly that we cannot go back on our previous undertakings to Poland, and have to take account of our own and American opinion.

I am sure that it would be of the greatest value to the common cause if M Molotov could come back this way from America. We can then continue our discussions which I hope will lead to the development

[1] AP: possibly 'anti-personnel', but in view of the question mark in the original document there may have been an error in transmission here.

of close military co-operation between our three countries. Moreover, I shall then be able to give him the latest developments in our own military plans.

Finally I hope that the political discussions might also then be carried a stage further. For all these reasons I greatly hope that you will agree that M Molotov should pay us a further visit on his way home to you.

Josef Stalin to Winston S. Churchill
(Churchill papers, 20/75)

24 May 1942
Personal and Secret

I have received your message which was delivered in Kuibyshev and in which you inform me that 35 ships carrying the war materials for the USSR are presently on the way to the Soviet ports. I thank you for your message on the sailing of the ships. On our part our naval and air forces will do their utmost for the protection of these transports on the section of the route which was indicated in your message to me on 9th May.

Winston S. Churchill to Brendan Bracken
(Churchill papers, 20/67)

24 May 1942

Surely you should do something, first of all to correct the pessimism in the BBC, and secondly to let the public know the harm that is done by this kind of thing.[1]

Winston S. Churchill to Sir James Grigg
(Churchill papers, 20/67)

24 May 1942

The 'hate' topic seems to me to have been handled in the worst way. First, a foolish system is allowed to grow up at a battle school. It is

---

[1] Telegram No. 756 from the British Embassy in Madrid reported on the bad effect in Spain of press reports and broadcasts from London critical of the Government.

advertised as widely as possible in the Press, who are encouraged to take photographs and write lurid articles on the subject. After abut a month or six weeks of this the Churches are disturbed, and then General Paget goes to the other extreme and writes a letter which will certainly give offence in Russia and will excite scorn in America. If he felt like this about it, it was his duty to give an order to put an end to the objectionable teaching when he first heard of it. He having failed to do this, it would have been well if you had given the needed political guidance, for which he should certainly have asked.

2. I shall be glad if you will ask General Paget when he first heard of the kind of training that was being given, and why he did not take steps to correct it.

3. Will you kindly also let me know whether General Paget consulted you before he wrote his letter?

[...]

Josef Stalin to Winston S. Churchill
(Churchill papers, 20/75)

24 May 1942
Personal and Secret

I received your last message on 24th of May. Viacheslav Molotov as well as I feel that it might be for him advisable on the return journey from the USA to stop in London to complete the negotiations with the representatives of the British Government on the questions in which our countries are interested.

Winston S. Churchill to Lord Beaverbrook
(Churchill papers, 20/55)

24 May 1942
Private and Confidential

My dear Max,

I am sure it would never do for you to make a statement on these lines.[1] Everything which passes in the Defence Committee is governed by

---

[1] On 23 May 1942 Beaverbrook had sent Churchill a draft statement: 'On 27 February 1941, the Air Ministry informed me that they did not intend to place any further orders for dive bombers in the United States. I asked Captain Margesson, Secretary of State for War,

Cabinet secrecy, and every War Cabinet Minister is bound by collective responsibility. For one man to go away and to give his own account of what happens in these secret conversations would be very hardly judged by the public and would also be prejudicial to the whole conduct of business in time of war.

When a Minister resigns from a Government, Parliament expects him to give the reason and it is the duty of the Prime Minister to advise The King to permit all the necessary revelations which fair play requires. But the Dive Bomber story had nothing to do with your much-regretted departure, and I could not ask The King to give you the liberty you have suggested.

If of course you are attacked in public for anything you did or did not do during your tenure of office, you have a right to expect me to defend you, which in this matter would be very easy.

Yours very sincerely,
Winston S. Churchill

Winston S. Churchill to Oliver Lyttelton and Lord Portal[1]
(Churchill papers, 20/67)

25 May 1942

When driving through South London today I noticed a great many private houses damaged by air raids, which appear structurally all right, but are nevertheless unrepaired and uninhabitable. In view of certain accessions of populations which we are to receive from abroad, we shall surely need every habitable dwelling-house, and it would seem that some relief might be had from a vigorous policy in this direction.

---

if the Army would order any of these machines. He replied that it was for the Air Ministry and not the War Office to place the order. On Air Ministry advice, he was satisfied that there would be sufficient dive-bombers for the Army for a considerable time to come so that no useful purpose could be served by raising a new demand. In September, in reply to a case stated by Air Chief Marshal Freeman, I reported to the Defence Committee that the Air Ministry opposed the project of buying additional dive-bombers for the army and that Captain Margesson accepted their advice. The Defence Committee was invited by me to direct the Air Ministry to order additional dive-bombers' (*Churchill papers, 20/55*).

[1] Wyndham Raymond Portal, 1885–1949. On active service, 1914–18 (DSO). Succeeded to his father's baronetcy, 1931. Chairman of the Coal Production Council. Created Baron, 1935. Regional Commissioner for Wales, Civil Defence Scheme, 1939. Additional Parliamentary Under-Secretary, Ministry of Supply, 1940–2. Minister of Works and Planning, 1942–4 (succeeding Lord Reith on 22 February 1942). Created Viscount, 1945. President of the Olympic Games, 1948. The Ministry of Works and Buildings had been changed after 11 February 1942 to the Ministry of Works and Planning. In February 1943 it became the Ministry of Works.

Please let me have a report upon the numbers of houses in this condition, and whether you think a useful policy could be developed with resultant economy of labour and material.

Sir Edward Spears[1] to Winston S. Churchill
(Churchill papers, 20/60)

25 May 1942   British Legation
Personal   Beirut

Dear Winston

The two photographs of you arrived a few days ago, and I am very glad indeed to have them. They are a present inspiration to me and it is quite extraordinary the effect they have on local people who see them. Their faces light up at once. Your speeches are recalled and become revivified in their minds and one sees their courage rising. It would be good propaganda to distribute as many photographs of you as possible here, and this I am endeavouring to do.

It is an absolute fact that you are the linch-pin of the whole of our war machine, and this is more apparent in these parts even than it could be at home. By comparison Roosevelt is a distant and nebulous figure, far less real than Stalin, which is perhaps not astonishing as the latter is so much closer and Russian resistance seems so much more real to the people here than the American war effort.

Yours ever,
E Louis Spears

---

[1] Edward Louis Spears, 1886–1974. Joined the Kildare Militia, 1903. Captain, 11th Hussars, 1914. Four times wounded, 1914–15 (Military Cross). Liaison Officer with French 10th Army, 1915–16. Head of the British Military Mission to Paris, 1817–20. Brigadier-General, 1918. National Liberal MP for Loughborough, 1922–4; Conservative MP for Carlisle, 1931–45. Churchill's Personal Representative with the French Prime Minister, May–June 1940. Head of British Mission to de Gaulle, 1940. Head of Mission to Syria and the Lebanon, 1941. First Minister to Syria and the Lebanon, 1942–4. Knighted, 1942. Created Baronet, 1953. Chairman of Ashanti Goldfields 1945–71. Chairman (1948–66) and later President of the Institute of Directors.

Winston S. Churchill to Dr Emil Oprecht[1]
(Churchill papers, 20/53)

25 May 1942

My dear Sir,

Thank you so much for sending me an inscribed copy of the German translation of 'Into Battle'.[2]

I have been told of the great difficulties which you have to encounter in publishing books in English on behalf of the Ministry of Information in Switzerland, and I should like to say how much I and the authorities concerned here value the work which you are doing.

Yours very faithfully,
Winston S. Churchill

War Cabinet: Confidential Annex
(Cabinet papers, 65/30)

25 May 1942

The Prime Minister and he[3] had spent Friday evening with the Soviet Delegation. The Prime Minister had given the Delegation an account of the world position, and had finished up by referring to the suggested Treaty of Mutual Assistance.

At the Meeting on Saturday afternoon, the text of the draft Treaty of Mutual Assistance had been handed to M Molotov.

Anthony Eden: diary
('The Eden Memoirs, The Reckoning', page 329)

25 May 1942

Winston and I had long talk with Molotov and Maisky[4] who arrived at 10 p.m. W spoke of progress of war and told them of Libya and our

---

[1] Emil Oprecht, 1895–1952. Born in Zürich. A Swiss publisher and bookseller. After 1933 he published the books of many German writers in exile in Switzerland.

[2] Churchill's book of speeches, *Into Battle* (published in Britain by Cassell on 2 February 1941) was published in the German language by Emil Oprecht's firm Europa Verlag: 'it was translated in England, printed in unoccupied France, bound in Switzerland, published under the Putnam imprint, and released by Europa Verlag in Zyrich. Churchill received his copy of the work via the Press Attaché of the British Legation in Berne and the Ministry of Information on 16 April 1942' (Ronald I. Cohen, *Bibliography of the Writings of Sir Winston Churchill*, London and New York, 2006, Volume I, p. 552). Europa Verlag published an edition under its own name in 1947.

[3] Molotov.

[4] The Soviet Ambassador to Britain.

production and other matters, Molotov drew plans of the most anxious sectors of the front for Russia, Leningrad, Moscow and Kharkov. We also spoke of Treaty, when he said that he had received authority to sign. We discussed drafts together. Winston talked America to them, rather too much I thought. Anyway I put in that our war production was still greater than theirs (the United States'), for Winston spoke almost as though we were doing scarcely anything.

After they left Winston congratulated me most warmly on Treaty developments. He said that if it came off it would be much the biggest thing I had done. He was particularly delighted that we should have thought of second draft.

War Cabinet: Confidential Annex
(Cabinet papers, 65/30)

26 May 1942   10 Downing Street
1 p.m.

The Prime Minister said that M Molotov had now informed us that the USSR accepted the alternative draft Treaty of Mutual Assistance. Subject to Cabinet approval the Treaty would be signed that afternoon.

The Foreign Secretary said that the amendments proposed in the text as circulated (see WP (42) 218) were quite minor in importance, and it was hardly necessary for him to bring them before the War Cabinet. The wording of the second paragraph of Article IV had been amended on the lines indicated to the War Cabinet on the previous day, and the title of the Treaty had also been altered.

The Foreign Secretary added that he had seen the Turkish Ambassador and the representative of the Polish Government in this country, and had informed them of what was proposed. They had both expressed themselves as pleased.

The Prime Minister said that M Molotov had asked that the Treaty should be kept secret until he had returned to Russia after his visit to the United States. He (the Prime Minister) thought that there would be advantage in publishing the Treaty while M Molotov was in the United States. But this was an aspect of the matter on which we must defer to Russian wishes, and all practicable steps must be taken to ensure secrecy.

The Prime Minister said that the War Cabinet were greatly indebted to the Foreign Secretary for his skilful handling of the negotiations and for the very satisfactory result which had been achieved.

The Foreign Secretary thanked all his colleagues, and particularly the Prime Minister, for the help and support which they had given him in the matter.

The War Cabinet:

Authorised the Foreign Secretary to sign the Treaty that afternoon.

Winston S. Churchill to Josef Stalin
(Churchill papers, 20/75)

27 May 1942

We are most grateful to you for meeting our difficulties in the Treaty as you have done. I am sure the reward in the United States will be solid and our three great Powers will not be able to march together united through whatever has to come. It has been a great pleasure to meet Monsieur Molotov and we have done a great beating down of barriers between our two countries. I am very glad he is coming back this way for there will be more good work to be done.

2. So far all has been well with the convoy[1] but it is now at its most dangerous stage. Many thanks for the measures you are taking to help it in.

3. Now that we have bound ourselves to be Allies and friends for twenty years I take occasion to send you my sincere good wishes and to assure you of the confidence which I feel that victory will be ours.

---

[1] Arctic convoy PQ 16 consisted of 21 American, eight British, four Soviet, one Dutch, and one Panamanian-registered merchant ships. Its close escort from Iceland to Northern Russia consisted of 15 warships, led by the destroyer HMS *Ashanti*, with the destroyers ORP (Okret Rzeczypospolitej Polskiej [Ship of the Polish Republic]) *Garland*, HMS *Volunteer*, HMS *Achates*, and HMS *Martin*, the anti-aircraft gunship *Alynbank*, four Flower class corvettes, one minesweeper, and four armed trawlers. Among the two cover support groups was a Distant Covering Force of the battleships HMS *Duke of York* and USS *Washington*, the carrier HMS *Victorious*, the cruisers HMS *London* and USS *Wichita*, and 13 Allied destroyers. On 30 May 1942, after five days of air attacks during which eight ships were sunk, 17 ships reached Murmansk, and eight reached Archangel. The convoy was such a success in terms of the war stores delivered to the Soviet Union that the Germans made greater efforts to disrupt the following convoys. The heavy lift ships from PQ 16 including SS *Empire Elgar* stayed at Archangel and Molotovsk (now Severodvinsk) unloading convoys for more than a year.

Winston S. Churchill to Lord Selborne[1]
(Churchill papers, 20/67)

27 May 1942

I commend to your notice a recent book by John Steinbeck,[2] *The Moon is Down*,[3] published this year by The Viking Press of New York.

In addition to being a well-written story, it stresses, I think quite rightly, the importance of providing the conquered nations with simple weapons such as sticks of dynamite, which could be easily concealed and are easy in operation.

Winston S. Churchill to Sir James Grigg
and General Sir Alan Brooke
(Churchill papers, 20/67)

27 May 1942
Secret

A company of a Young Soldiers Battalion of Corps Troops, Buffs, were detailed for my protection when I visited Chartwell this weekend. I naturally inspected it, and asked questions about its equipment. I was told that they were short of Bren gun carriers and very short of Bren guns. The output of Bren guns and Bren gun carriers has been very good for some time. I was not aware that there was any deficiency in these two items.

2. I also noticed there were in the battalion two different marks of Lee Metford rifles. Even some platoons were half and half. The sighting of these rifles is different, although of course they take the same ammunition. Could you let me have a note on this, stating whether any other units are in a similar condition.

3. I request that no trouble should be caused to the company or the battalion, as I am responsible for asking the questions which it was the duty of those concerned to answer.

---

[1] Minister of Economic Warfare.

[2] John Ernst Steinbeck, 1902–68. Born in California. His first novel, *Cup of Gold*, was published in 1929. US war columnist overseas, 1943. Nobel Prize in Literature, 1962.

[3] Written to inspire the resistance movements in the German-occupied countries of Europe, it tells the story of the military occupation of a small coastal town in northern Europe by the army of an unnamed nation at war with England and the Soviet Union. Clandestine translations were distributed in Denmark, France, Italy, the Netherlands, and Norway.

Winston S. Churchill to President Franklin D. Roosevelt
(Churchill papers, 20/75)

27 May 1942
Personal and Secret
No. 89

We have done very good work this and last week with Molotov and as Winant will no doubt have informed you we have completely transformed the Treaty proposals. They are now in my judgment free from the objections we both entertained and are entirely compatible with our Atlantic Charter. The Treaty was signed yesterday afternoon with great cordiality on both sides.

2. Molotov is a Statesman and has a freedom of action very different from what you and I saw with Litvinov.[1] I am very sure you will be able to reach good understandings with him. Please let me know your impressions.

3. So far all has gone well with the Northern Convoy but the dangers on the next two days must necessarily be serious.

4. I had an opening talk with Arnold and Towers and both are coming to me for the weekend. I am arranging for them to meet all our Air Chiefs and they will go into every detail together. I have hope that a good arrangement will be possible. The two principles seem to be:

(a) Optimum impact on the enemy and

(b) Maximum American contribution thereto.

5. Mountbatten and Lyttelton will come together but former's visit must be short on account of our common work with which he is charged.

6. I am fully aware of your preoccupations in the Pacific at the present time and if you considered it necessary to withdraw *Washington* at once we should quite understand. It is, however, most important to complete our concentration in the Indian Ocean of *Warspite*, *Valiant*, *Nelson* and *Rodney* by the middle of July. This can be done if we can retain *Washington* until *King George Fifth* finishes refitting at the end of June.

7. The introduction of convoys between Key West and Hampton Roads has evidently had the good effects we all expected, but the Caribbean and Gulf of Mexico are still very sore spots. King and Pound have been in communication about this and I hope it may be found possible even by running risks elsewhere, to provide sufficient escort craft to deal with these areas.

[1] Maxim Litvinov, Commissar for Foreign Affairs, 1930–9 (when Stalin dismissed him in favour of Molotov). Soviet Ambassador in Washington, 1941–3.

8. I must express my gratitude for your allocation of seventy tankers to build up United Kingdom stocks of oil. Without this help our stocks would have fallen to a dangerous level by the end of the year. This action is the more generous considering recent heavy American tanker losses and the sacrifices involved in releasing so many ships.

Winston S. Churchill to President Franklin D. Roosevelt
(Churchill papers, 20/75)

27 May 1942
No. 90

I am venturing to send you a collection of the books I have written, which I have had bound up, hoping you will find a place for them in your shelves.[1] Kindest good wishes.

Former Naval Person

President Franklin D. Roosevelt to Winston S. Churchill
(Churchill papers, 20/75)

27 May 1942
No. 148

I believe it is desirable to have Mountbatten come for a short visit if he can be spared. I am having your Nassau friends[2] to lunch next Monday. Looking forward to seeing Lyttelton. All well here. Take care of yourself.

Richard Casey to Winston S. Churchill
(Churchill papers, 20/75)

27 May 1942   Cairo
Personal and Secret
Important
Most Secret

As you will know, the enemy have started offensive in Cyrenaica. All three Cs-in-C have made all preparations in their power, and express

---

[1] In the President's Study at Hyde Park are 17 of Churchill's published books, in seven boxes, each one bound in red leather with Roosevelt's coat of arms stamped in gold on the cover and in red slip-cases with 'From/W.S.C./to/F.D.R./1942 embossed on the spine.

[2] The Duke and Duchess of Windsor (the Duke was Governor of the Bahamas, and was living in the capital, Nassau).

themselves as welcoming the action. Before active operations get into their stride, I would like to report on some other matters of consequence to which I have been giving considerable attention since I last telegraphed you.

I am in course of trying to get a concise list of the principal current and prospective deficiencies in Army and RAF equipment, which I hope to be able to telegraph you in brief within the next week, in the hope that you may be able to do something about it.

I have been going into the manpower position in Middle East, and hope to telegraph you concisely about it within 48 hours.

Auchinleck is about to move all officers and other ranks of GHQ out of their present living quarters (houses, flats and hotels) in Cairo into a tented camp near the Pyramids, although they will continue to work in present GHQ in Cairo. He believes that health and efficiency will be promoted thereby, and at the same time the obvious disparity with Western Desert service conditions will be lessened. He is also seeking to reduce numerical strength of GHQ by ten percent.

On supply side we have had anxieties about corn in Egypt. Egyptian Administration is pretty hopeless, and it looked as if they would fail to get control of harvest now being gathered. Ambassador[1] has been very helpful with the Egyptians who have now agreed to Anglo-Egyptian board to supervise purchase of wheat. I hope that, with British help, the machine will be made to work. There is similar problem in Syria, and I have sent an energetic and forceful British businessman up there to help Spears.

Coal is another anxiety. Heavy shipments are needed, much of which has now to come from UK. We are pressing the Egyptians to convert locomotives to oil burning as fast as possible. Cutting down of imports of all kinds continues reasonably satisfactorily. I will send figures in my next report.

We have been discussing with all concerned, including Americans who are very helpful, best means of increasing industrial production, particularly in Egypt and Syria. We hope to have a scheme shaped up very shortly.

Problem of refugees, particularly Greeks and Poles, is becoming formidable, and Army are very naturally jibbing at having to help feed these people. I am arranging for a single office to handle this under guidance on policy of a War Council Committee.

[1] Sir Miles Lampson.

Walter Monckton left here by air via Lagos 26th May, and if not delayed is due in London on 2nd June. He has not (not) resigned, and I hope may be induced to return here shortly to act as assistant or even deputy to myself. It would be of considerable assistance if he would do so and you would agree to his doing so.

I had a useful three days' visit to the Western Desert front ten days ago, and have since spent a day at Alexandria with the Navy. I propose making a series of such short trips to other countries as opportunity allows. Please let me know whether this is the kind of report you want.

President Franklin D. Roosevelt to Winston S. Churchill
(Churchill papers, 20/75)

27 May 1942
No. 149

The visitor[1] is expected tonight but will not discuss 'Bolero'[2] until Thursday. A short summary of what you and he said to each other about 'Bolero' is desired quickly. It would aid me to know.

Roosevelt

Winston S. Churchill to Cyril Lakin[3]
(Churchill papers, 20/53)

27 May 1942
My dear Lakin,

The tragic death of that esteemed Member and fine sportsman, Patrick Munro,[4] while taking part in a Home Guard exercise at the House of Commons, came as a shock to his many friends in the House and in the Llandaff and Barry Division.

---

[1] Molotov.

[2] 'Bolero': the administrative preparations for the opening of a 'second front' in north-west Europe, involving the movement of United States ground forces and equipment across the Atlantic to Britain.

[3] Cyril Harry Alfred Lakin, 1893–1993. A Welsh farmer and barrister. On active service, 1915–18; South Wales Borderers, France, and Salonika. Assistant Divisional Commissioner, Ministry of Food, 1918. Assistant Editor, *Daily Telegraph*, 1929–33. Literary Editor, *Sunday Times* and *Daily Telegraph*, 1933–7. Conservative (National Unionist) MP for Llandaff and Barry, 1942–5.

[4] Patrick Munro, 1883–1942. Rugby International for Scotland, 1905, 1906, 1907, 1911. Colonial Civil Servant, 1907–29; Governor of Khartoum Province, 1925–9. Conservative MP for Llandaff and Barry, 1931–42. Assistant Whip, 1937. He died on 3 May 1942.

His place in Parliament must now be filled and I hope that all his friends and supporters in the Division will rally to your support in the forthcoming by-election.

Let there be no doubt in the minds of the electors that you are the candidate who stands for the completion and execution of the plans for victory that have been developed by the National Government which it has been my duty to lead during the past two perilous years.

You come before the constituency, of which you are a native, as a National Government candidate, and the political principles for which you stand are plain to all. You believe with me that the Government and the nation should concentrate their life-energies on cleansing the world from Hitlerism and that when victory has been won the future of this country should be planned in harmony and combined action with other like-minded peoples in accordance with the principles of the Atlantic Charter.

If your opponents are opposed to this policy, they should say so, [or else explain to the people of Llandaff and Barry the personal idiosyncracies which lead them to advertise themselves at this anxious time].[1]

I urge every elector, man and woman, to grasp the opportunity open to them to use their votes to further the prosecution of the war. To abstain from voting at such a time as this is to neglect the prime duty and to sacrifice the time-honoured privilege of a Briton. [Welshmen may be sure that if Hitler had a vote he would not fail to put his cross (Swastika) against the Government that spells his doom.][2]

Yours sincerely,
Winston S. Churchill

Winston S. Churchill to President Franklin D. Roosevelt
(Churchill papers, 20/75)

27 May 1942[3]
No. 91

I send in my immediately following[4] report of our formal conversation, which covers 'Bolero', 'Sledgehammer' and 'Super Round-Up'.[5]

---

[1] Words in brackets deleted by Churchill before the letter was finally sent.

[2] Sentence deleted by Churchill before the letter was finally sent.

[3] The typed-out telegram is dated '28.5.42'. However, Churchill refers in it to 'Tomorrow 28th'.

[4] Transcript of the discussion between Churchill and Molotov on 22 May 1942: see pages 697–702 above.

[5] 'Super Roundup': the final development of Operation 'Roundup', involving a substantial Allied landing in northern France as soon as possible after Operation 'Torch' (scheduled for the summer of 1943). Eventually postponed in January 1943 in favour of Operation 'Husky' against Sicily.

Additional private conversation improved atmosphere but did not alter substance. We made great progress in intimacy and goodwill.

2. We are working hard with your Officers and all preparations are proceeding ceaselessly on the largest scale. Dickie[1] will explain to you the difficulties of 1942 when he arrives. I have also told the Staffs to study a landing in the north of Norway, the occupation of which seems necessary to ensure the flow of our supplies next year to Russia. I have told Molotov we would have something ready for him about this to discuss on his return here. We did not go deeply into it in any way. Personally I set great importance upon it if a good plan can be made.

3. So far our Northern convoy is fighting its way through having lost five ships, sunk or turned back, out of thirty five. Tomorrow 28th we ought to be getting under the Russian air umbrella if any has been provided. Otherwise two more days of this.

4. Auchinleck's news tonight indicates that the battle in Libya has begun. This may be the biggest encounter we have ever fought. General Smuts who has visited the whole front expresses high confidence in the result. I am sure all American hearts will be with us. The issue seems to depend on the armoured fighting on the desert flank. Personally I welcome the trial of strength and am glad if it has come about by Rommel's attack.

5. We must never let 'Gymnast'[2] pass from our minds. All other preparations would help if need be towards that.

President Franklin D. Roosevelt to Winston S. Churchill
(Churchill papers, 20/75)

28 May 1942
Secret
No. 150

I am inclined to favour the idea of inviting General Smuts to come to Washington to see me and stay for a few days, more in a personal than in a formal capacity. I have known him ever since 1918 and correspond with him occasionally. Also I think it may be of help to him in his home problems to get a picture of the general situation from a fellow Dutchman like me. I would not set any especial date but merely suggest some time this summer. Please let me know what you think.

---

[1] Lord Louis Mountbatten.
[2] 'Gymnast': the Anglo-American plan to land in French North Africa.

I also have an idea that if I were to invite our friend John Curtin to come here for a very short visit, but at a different time from Smuts visit it might do much good in a wholly different way. From all I hear he is thoroughly honest and sincere person but has had little opportunity to appreciate the world situation outside his own sphere. There are also matters regarding command and operational problems in the Southwest Pacific on which I should like to try my hand at indoctrination.

I wish you would let me have your personal thought on this matter also.

Winston S. Churchill to President Franklin D. Roosevelt
(Churchill papers, 20/75)

28 May 1942
Personal and Secret
No. 93

I can see nothing but good in either or both of the visits you mention. General Smuts may be coming here in the near future and a good opportunity would arise then. Shall I mention your idea to him as an additional incentive? We have been good friends for nearly forty years and I regard him as one of the greatest living men. As to Curtin, a visit could do nothing but good. I have got on very well with Evatt.

Josef Stalin to Winston S. Churchill
(Churchill papers, 20/75)

28 May 1942   Kremlin
                                                        Moscow

I thank you very much for friendly feelings and good wishes expressed by you in connection with the signature of our new Treaty. I am sure this Treaty will be of the greatest importance for the future strengthening of friendly relations between the Soviet Union and Great Britain as well as between our countries and the United States of America and will secure the close collaboration of our countries after the victorious end of the war. I hope also that your meeting with Molotov on his way back from the United States will present the opportunity to bring to an end that part of the work which was left uncompleted.

With regard to the measures concerning protection of convoys you may be rest assured that in this respect everything possible on our side will be done now and in the future.

Please accept my most sincere good wishes as well as my fullest confidence in our complete joint victory.

Stalin

Winston S. Churchill to Field Marshal Jan Smuts
(Churchill papers, 20/75)

28 May 1942
Personal and Most Secret

Yor 930 will be studied deeply by us. I am encouraged by your paragraph 1.[1] The battle has now begun.

2. Your paragraph 2. We are of course agreed in principle. Much of what you recommend is being done. *Nelson, Rodney, Warspite, Valiant,* with the three best armoured aircraft carriers, *Illustrious, Indomitable, Formidable,* should be around Colombo by the end of July. About the same time Wavell should have the 70th, 5th and 2nd British Divisions in full equipment and good order as well as three <u>trained</u> Anglo-Indian Field Divisions apart from garrison troops and <u>two further Anglo-Indian Divisions which will not be trained until late Autumn.</u> This is more than the Japanese have yet encountered. <u>By that date there should be at the disposal of the C in C India a total of 27 operationally fit Squadrons for the defence of India and Ceylon a proportion of which he will undoubtedly allot to the East Coast.</u>

3. My own belief is that Japanese will strike north and try to finish off Chiang Kai-shek but the distances are very great and <u>we are examining urgently the possibility of striking</u> eastward at the Japanese communications through Burma in the autumn. For this purpose it will be necessary to have naval and air command of the western half of the Bay of Bengal and a good umbrella of shore-based aircraft in its northern quarter. Ceylon is the naval key-point of all this.

4. It will be difficult to find resources to meet really heavy German attack by the Caucasus and Caspian on the assumption that the Russian Front breaks to the southward. There is no reason however at present

[1] In the first paragraph of his Telegram No. 930 Smuts wrote: 'I have no doubt of our success whether it is defensive or offensive. My only doubt is whether we can finally dispose of enemy before he once more falls back on Ageila and leaves us to hold lengthened line with larger forces which may be badly wanted further East. ... Our men are thoroughly imbued with offensive spirit and with daring strategy success should be within our grasp this time. I have a very high opinion of Auchinleck himself. ... Facilities communications and services in the rear impressed me very favourably. Lyttelton's work in preparing for adequate Middle East base has been outstanding and rear position is very different from what it was a year ago.'

to assume such disaster. Anyhow the year is advancing and the Germans have much to conquer and a long way to go before this occurs.

5. We have had a very good week with Molotov and completely transformed the original draft of the Treaty which is now in my opinion quite inoffensive to the United States. You will receive detailed accounts from the Dominions Office. This is a great relief to me.

6. I am delighted to hear there are good prospects of your coming here. I look forward to your naming the date.

Sir Miles Lampson[1] to Winston S. Churchill
(Churchill papers, 20/65)

28 May 1942   Cairo
Important

Randolph was involved in a motor car accident this morning and is now at Territorial General Hospital Alexandria where according to medical authorities he will probably have to stay about a week. He suffers from contusion on chest but X-ray has revealed no broken bones. He is conscious.

Is there anything in particular you would like me to do? Or any message for him?

Winston and Clementine Churchill to Randolph S. Churchill
(Churchill papers, 20/65)

29 May 1942
Action this Day

Much distressed darling Randolph to hear of your accident but relieved that no bones broken. Much Love

Papa and Mummie

Sir Miles Lampson to Winston S. Churchill and Pamela Churchill
(Churchill papers, 20/65)

29 May 1942

Report on Randolph this evening says that apart from chest discomfort and being forbidden to smoke he is making good progress.

---

[1] Ambassador to Egypt and High Commissioner for the Sudan.

Winston S. Churchill to General Henry Arnold
(Churchill papers, 20/53)

29 May 1942

My dear General Arnold,

General Chaney[1] has been good enough to pass on to me the case of oranges. Oranges are all too rare at present and it was most kind of you to think of sending them to me. Thank you so much.

Yours sincerely,
Winston S. Churchill

Winston S. Churchill to Herbert Morrison
(Churchill papers, 20/53)

29 May 1942

My dear Herbert,

I must congratulate you on the spirited manner in which you faced our critics at the Labour Conference and recalled the main body of the Party to its duty. You showed great courage in all this, and I am sure the Labour Movement will appreciate what you did as much as I do.

I was much complimented by the Chairman's[2] message to me, and I shall send him a public message.

Yours very sincerely,
Winston S. Churchill

PS I had written this <u>before</u> seeing you at Cabinet.

Winston S. Churchill to John Curtin
(Churchill papers, 20/75)

30 May 1942
Personal and Secret

I am most grateful to you for your telegram. Evatt's visit has been a great success and he has made many friends over here. I feel I shall have another friend in Australia. Evatt has also repeatedly assured me of your goodwill. This will be a great help in the many difficulties we have to face together.

[1] Commanding General, United States 1st Air Force, based in New York State.

[2] Walter Henry Green, 1878–1958. Left elementary school to be apprenticed in the engineering trade. Councillor, Deptford Borough Council, 1909; Mayor of Deptford, 1921, 1922. Member of the Executive of the London Labour Party, 1923–43. Member of the National Executive of the Labour Party, 1935. Labour MP for Deptford, 1935–45. Chairman of the Labour Party, 1941–2.

On the night of 30–1 May 1942, the Royal Air Force carried out the first 1,000-bomber raid over Germany. It was against Cologne: 1,047 aircraft took part (602 Wellington bombers, 131 Halifaxes, 88 Sterlings, 79 Hampdens, 73 Lancasters, 46 Manchesters, and 28 Whitleys); 41 aircraft were lost (a record high) and 1,455 tons of bombs were dropped, causing 2,500 separate fires and totally destroying 3,300 buildings (including nine hospitals and 17 churches). The German death toll was also a record for the RAF: 411 civilians and 58 military personnel, mostly members of anti-aircraft units.

Sir Alexander Cadogan: diary
(*'The Diaries of Sir Alexander Cadogan'*, page 456)

31 May 1942

Heard on wireless about our 1,000-plane raid on Germany. Grand! Can't make out what's happening in Libya battle, but nothing seems to have gone irretrievably wrong yet. The convoy seems to have got through to Russia with loss of 7 out of 35. No naval losses reported.

Winston S. Churchill to Oliver Lyttelton
(*Churchill papers, 20/67*)

31 May 1942

STEN GUN[1] AMMUNITION

I am glad to learn that you are trying to get the United States to make Sten cartridges in larger quantities, for it would be a pity to have all these guns starved of ammunition. They would be ideal weapons to give to oppressed peoples, so that we should always be able to find a use for them.

---

[1] Sten gun: a British sub-machine gun. Its name is an acronym formed from the names of its chief designers, Major – later Colonel – Reginald **S**hepherd and Harold **T**urpin, and **EN**gland (post-war evidence of Colonel Shepherd to the Royal Commission on Awards to Inventors). It was manufactured from 1941, and could fire some 500 rounds a minute. More than three and a half million were made.

Winston S. Churchill to Lord Linlithgow[1]
(Churchill papers, 20/75)

31 May 1942
Personal and Secret

During his last visit here Mr Hopkins expressed himself in scathing terms about Johnson who carries no special weight with President. I have already telegraphed once to Hopkins warning him about Johnson,[2] and I am sending another telegram today asking definitely he should not return to India. Good wishes.

Winston S. Churchill to Harry Hopkins
(Churchill papers, 20/75)

31 May 1942
Personal and Secret

There are rumours that the President will invite Pandit Nehru to the United States. I hope there is no truth in this, and that anyway the President will consult me beforehand. We do not at all relish the prospect of Johnson's return to India. The Viceroy is also much perturbed at the prospect. We are fighting to defend this vast mass of helpless Indians from imminent invasion. I know you will remember my many difficulties.

Winston S. Churchill to General Claude Auchinleck
(Churchill papers, 20/75)

31 May 1942
Private

I am very thankful for the way in which the battle has gone so far. My confidence is based not only on your excellent reports but on the Special Intelligence[3] which I am having sent you very fully.

I shall certainly be asked to make some statement about the battle at noon on Tuesday so let me have anything you have got which is publishable by 8 a.m. that day. All good wishes.

[1] Viceroy of India.

[2] Personal Representative of President Roosevelt in India, March–December 1942.

[3] During 1942, Churchill received details of several thousand German top-secret military and air signals, sent by Enigma and other encrypted radio circuits. Details of any of the decrypts that bore on German intentions and actions in the Middle East were sent to the relevant British Commander-in-Chief, enabling them, again and again, to anticipate a German move, or to take advantage of a German shortage or deficiency.

Winston S. Churchill to General Archibald Wavell
(Churchill papers, 20/75)

31 May 1942
Personal

We have been working here as you know at plans for a counter-stroke upon Japanese communications through Burma so as to help Chiang Kai-shek and encourage him to hold out. Chiefs of Staff have not yet considered reports from Planning Committee but will do so speedily. Meanwhile you have been asked to prepare plans and have told us you were already making them on your own. I hope we shall hear from you as soon as possible what you think you can do, when you can do it and what you want in order to do it. My personal hope was that you would try to retake Rangoon about the end of September.

2. Alexander is needed here and should start as soon as convenient. Regards to you both.

3. The battle in Libya goes well, and we hope soon to pass to the counter offensive.

Winston S. Churchill to Richard Casey
(Churchill papers, 20/75)

31 May 1942
Personal

The value of heavy bombers in the Mediterranean is fully realised by us all but I am afraid that the position is still as stated in the telegram OZ 35 of 17/4, sent by the Chiefs of Staff to the Commanders-in-Chief, Middle East. The two Halifax squadron equipments are on their way but cannot arrive until the end of July. By then we hope that the Halifax may be fit to operate for short periods away from England.

The first Liberators are intended for India and a few should have left us and reached Egypt before the middle of June. However, as you know, the Liberator maintenance equipment and personnel have now been sent to India with the result that the aircraft could not operate efficiently in Egypt, even if any of them could be made ready for operations before the date of the convoy. I am afraid therefore that there would be no value in holding them for a time in Egypt to help you.

The AOC-in-C will have to do the best he can with his Wellingtons. CAS has signalled to ask him how he proposes to divide their employment between the different types of target available.

Richard Casey to Winston S. Churchill
(Churchill papers, 20/75)

31 May 1942
Personal

Auchinleck is reporting daily and quite fully on the battle and will no repeat no doubt seek to sum it all up before long.

My impression is that the enemy seriously underestimated our strength which caused him to undertake a very bold enterprise in which he has failed and we have won.

Relative casualties cannot yet be estimated although I shall be very surprised if balance of advantage is not repeat not appreciably on our side apart from setback to state of mind of enemy which retreat must involve. Follow up is now being organised.

June
1942

War Cabinet: Confidential Annex
(Cabinet papers, 65/30)

1 June 1942   10 Downing Street
6 p.m.

The Prime Minister said that owing to another operation, not specified to the War Cabinet (the relief of Malta), it would be necessary to postpone the next convoy to Russia for ten days or a fortnight. He thought that the question of getting extra air support to accompany the convoy should be considered.

The Chief of the Naval Staff[1] said that the postponement for ten days or a fortnight would still make it possible for us to adhere to the schedule of three convoys in two months. We simply could not provide escorts simultaneously for the Russian convoy and the Malta convoy.

The Foreign Secretary[2] said that if the convoy was to be postponed, it would help matters very much if we could send some additional tanks over and above the normal quota.

The Secretary of State for War[3] said that if the convoy was postponed he might be able to make available some additional A22s.[4]

The Prime Minister said that a definite decision should be taken to postpone the next convoy by ten days or a fortnight, and the Admiralty should have the necessary latitude in this matter. The Secretary of State for War should report what he could do in the way of making available an additional consignment of A22's, and the Secretary of State for Foreign Affairs should inform the Soviet Government of the decisions which we had reached when we knew what we could do in the way of making available an additional consignment of tanks.

[1] Admiral Sir Dudley Pound.
[2] Anthony Eden.
[3] Sir James Grigg.
[4] A22: The Churchill tank.

Winston S. Churchill to General Hastings Ismay,
for the Chiefs of Staff Committee
(Churchill papers, 20/67)

1 June 1942
Most Secret

OPERATION 'JUPITER'[1]

This must be considered as an alternative to a medium 'Sledgehammer' this year.

2. High strategic and political importance must be attached thereto. It may be all that we have to offer to the Russians. In studying it the Planners need not burden themselves with such questions as (a) would not the Russians prefer to use the shipping for more munitions, or (b) would they not prefer us to do 'Sledgehammer.' Let us look at it on its merits.

3. About 70 German bombers and 100 fighters established in the north of Norway in only two airfields, protected by about ten or twelve thousand effective fighting men, are denying us all entry into Norway and taking a heavy toll of our convoys. If we could gain possession of these airfields and establish an equal force there, not only would the northern sea route to Russia be kept open, but we should have set up a second front on a small scale from which it would be most difficult to eject us. If the going was good, we could advance gradually southward, unrolling the Nazi map of Europe from the top. All that has to be done is to oust the enemy from the airfields and destroy their garrisons.

4. Surprise can easily be obtained because the enemy could never tell till the last moment whether it was an ordinary convoy at sea or an expedition.

5. It must be assumed that the Russians will support this movement, though they certainly will not do so until they know that any form of 'Sledgehammer' is off. The effects on Sweden and on Finland may also be important.

6. It is essential to plan this operation so as not to put an undue strain upon the Fleet or upon our anti-U-boat vessels. For this purpose the expedition must be entirely self-contained. The troops must be based on the ships which carry them there, they will draw their supplies from them, and in the winter the great bulk of them will live in these ships. We must expect that the enemy will probably destroy the hutments he has erected. After the Navy has convoyed and landed the expedition, the German U-boats will come out to cut its communications. But if the

---

[1] 'Jupiter': Operations in northern Norway, including an attempt to secure Petsamo in combination with Soviet forces.

expedition carries three or four months' supplies with it, the U-boats will get tired of waiting and a refresher convoy may have a safe passage. We shall know whether they are there or not.

7. The first step is to establish in Murmansk six squadrons of fighters and two or three squadrons of bombers. This will only be renewing on a larger scale the help we may have already given at this end of the northern flank of the Russian line, and the enemy would not necessarily attach significance to it.

8. The second step is the landing of a storm party equal to a division in the Petsamo area. This is a fierce and hazardous operation, but small beer compared with what we are talking about in 'Sledgehammer.' Simultaneously with the above, the airfield at the head of the Parsangerfjord must also be mastered by the equivalent of a brigade group.

9. The British aircraft from Murmansk would then establish themselves on the airfields, and the question to be decided is how they could be expelled therefrom. We should no doubt arrange heavy Russian pressure in the north of Finland, and our operation would be associated with this.

10. There would have to be two waves. First, the fighting expedition; the second, a week later, the supplies. Thereafter the expedition would fend for itself for at least three months. How would the coming of winter affect our position? Would it make it easier for the enemy to attack us, or harder? This should be patiently thought out. During the winter the new snow tanks should be brought to the scene. Whether we should go south to attack Tromso need not be decided except in harmony with the main war situation.

Winston S. Churchill to General Hastings Ismay,
for the Chiefs of Staff Committee
(Churchill papers, 20/67)

1 June 1942
Most Secret

Your last paragraph really does not bear on the question of the Western Theatre versus the attack on Japan. I have never suggested sending any further troops to the East than those now on the sea or under orders. The most that would be asked would be aviation, certain landing craft, and any special tackle that may be required. Should we gain success in

Libya, we must review the whole position, and by then I hope General Wavell will have let us know his views, what he would like to do and what he wants to do it with. There is no need to take any decision about the 8th Armoured and 44th Infantry Divisions until we see what the situation is as they round the Cape. Neither are we committed to any attack on the Japanese communications through Burma this year until the moment when it is launched. But, having regard to the immense disaster which the falling out of China would spell, it seems only prudent to get everything moving to the aid of the Chinese, subject to the progress of the war. Of course, if the Russian southern front crumbles, there could be no question of our pushing hard in the Far East. In any case, I repeat, it is only the use of the troops now assigned to the Eastern theatre that would be involved.

2. We must not acquiesce too easily in the many delays which hamper the assembly of the Eastern Fleet. There is a good deal in Admiral Somerville's telegrams which favours the idea of his playing a passive rôle, avoiding 'frittering away' his strength in the Bay of Bengal, &c. No satisfactory explanation has been given by this officer of the imprudent dispersion of his forces in the early days of April, resulting in the loss of *Cornwall*, *Dorsetshire*, and *Hermes*. I have protected him in Parliament because I felt he was trying hard, but he should be made to realize that it is his duty, once his fleet is assembled and based on Ceylonese harbours, to prevent any seaborne invasion of Eastern India unless escorted by markedly superior Japanese strength. Also, when our shore-based air is established on the east coast of India in adequate strength, he may have to escort an amphibious expedition of our own. I entirely agree that the air will be the key to movement here. Let us therefore wait (a) the results of the battle in Libya, and (b) Wavell's ideas.

3. As they advance, the Japanese will be spread about enormous areas of wild country in Burma and South China, and will be in contact with the Chinese. They have only five or six divisions in these regions, and their supply problem will become one of great difficulty, ragamuffins though they be. We cannot afford to have idle troops or idle aircraft anywhere, and as the summer advances we may be able to re-establish ourselves at Akyab and make them wear out their air force by fighting at continually closer quarters. No one can tell whether the conditions which would render an amphibious stroke possible will establish themselves, but it would be most improvident not to have everything ready so as to take advantage of such a situation should it arise. We shall know a lot by August that we do not know now.

Winston S. Churchill to Air Chief Marshal Sir Charles Portal
(Churchill papers, 20/67)

1 June 1942
Action this Day
Secret

We have heard some talk of the time it would take, even after Martuba airfield was recovered, to convert it into an advance fuelling base. This is all nonsense. A good plan should be made, having for its object the immediate refuelling, for one or two occasions only, of the Beaufighters[1] which would be pushed off there to cover the Malta convoy. The fate of Malta may depend on this.

Pray let me have the best plan you can make so that I can then put it up to Auchinleck and Tedder.

All we want is a temporary refuelling point. The convoy will be upon us very soon. The matter is of the utmost urgency.

Winston S. Churchill to Anthony Eden
(Churchill papers, 20/67)

1 June 1942
Secret

MADAGASCAR

Please see the attached from the Chiefs of Staff. The policy is set out in my telegram to Admiral Syfret, which the Chiefs of Staff concurred in, and which you saw before it was sent. We cannot depart from this policy. The troops must move on to India without delay. The ships are already dispersed and it will not be easy to find naval forces in the near future for the operations which General Smuts desires. In these circumstances, we ought certainly to establish a <u>modus vivendi</u> with the Vichy authorities. This agreement must give us the necessary security against any part of the island being used as a submarine base, or any intrigue between the Madagascar-Vichy authorities and the Japanese. More than that we do not need; and more than that we cannot get without fighting.

---

[1] Beaufighter: the Bristol Type 156 Beaufighter ('the Beau') was a British long-range heavy fighter, a development of the Bristol Aeroplane Company's earlier Beaufort torpedo bomber design. The name Beaufighter derives from 'Beaufort' and 'fighter'. Operational from 27 July 1940, it was used first as a night fighter, then as a fighter–bomber, and finally as a replacement for the Beaufort as a torpedo bomber. Almost 6,000 were built. Their main users were the Royal Air Force and the Royal Canadian and Royal Australian Air Forces. It had a crew of two (the pilot and the observer).

The only reason why I assented to your holding telegram was that an answer is due to Smuts before any agreement is made which would preclude our taking Tamatave and Majunga, &c., at a later date. I propose now to send the attached telegram to Smuts.[1] Let me have your views.

Richard Casey to Winston S. Churchill
(Churchill papers, 20/65)

1 June 1942
Personal

31st May hospital reports your son's condition shows continued improvement. He has been examined by Brigadier Small,[2] consulting physician to Middle East Forces, who is quite satisfied with him.

Casey

Winston S. Churchill to President Franklin D. Roosevelt
(Churchill papers, 20/75)

1 June 1942
Personal and Secret
No. 96

Like you I am anxious about Russia and also China in the next few months. It is often easier to see dangers gathering than to have the power to ward them off, and very often they don't happen.

2. Mountbatten will explain to you some of the practical difficulties as we see them here of a medium-scale operation this year. We are still working at it and trying to make plans to overcome them. All preparations should go forward with the utmost speed, and I am having your new convoy proposals examined by the Chiefs of Staff and the Admiralty.

3. I had some very pleasant talks with Arnold, though I am still much troubled on the subject.

4. I hope you were pleased with our mass air attack on Cologne. There is plenty more to come, and I look forward eagerly to the arrival of your Bombing Groups.

5. The battle in Libya goes well, and I expect considerable results or even possibly a complete decision.

---

[1] Sent on 4 June 1942: see page 744 below.

[2] William Douglas Denton Small, 1889–1964. Lieutenant in Royal Army Medical Corps at outbreak of war in 1939. Colonel, 1940. Brigadier and Consultant Physician Middle East Forces, 1942. CBE, 1943.

General Claude Auchinleck to Winston S. Churchill
(Churchill papers, 20/76)

1 June 1942
Personal

You may care to add the CS/1168[1] something on following lines.
Begins.

The skill, determination, and pertinacity shown by General Ritchie
and his corps commanders, Lieutenant Generals Norrie and Gott,
throughout this difficult and strenuous week of hard and continuous
fighting have been of the highest order.

2. You may also like to mention, if security reasons do not rpt not forbid,
excellent performance of Grant tanks, with which users are well pleased,
and also 6 pounder anti-tank gun which has done great execution.

3. The story of General Messervy's[2] capture, deception of the enemy
and escape, and resumption of command of 7th armoured division all
within a few hours is a good one. I sent it to CIGS.

President Franklin D. Roosevelt to Winston S. Churchill
(Churchill papers, 20/75)

1 June 1942
Secret

I am thrilled at the thought of the books and shall always cherish
them.

2. I have sent invitations to Smuts and Curtin, the latter not expected
until after he has seen Evatt.

---

[1] CS/1168: Auchinleck's communiqué about the battle in Libya. Churchill had asked Auchinleck
if he (Churchill) could read it out in the House of Commons on 2 June 1942.

[2] Frank Walter Messervy, 1893–1974. Educated at Eton and Sandhurst. 2nd Lieutenant,
Indian Army, 1913. On active service, 1914–18 (France, Palestine, Syria); 1919 (Kurdistan).
Colonel, commanding Gazelle Force, Sudan, 1941; 9th Indian Infantry Brigade, Keren, 1941.
DSO, 1941. Major-General, commanding 4th Indian Division, Western Desert, and Cyrenaica,
1941–2; 1st Armoured Division, Cyrenaica, 1942. Taken prisoner, but escaped, 1942. Com-
manded 7th Armoured Division, Western Desert, 1942; 43rd Indian Armoured Division, 1942–3.
Commanded 7th Indian Division, Arakan, and at Kohima, 1944; IV Corps, Burma (Tamu to
Rangoon), 1944–5. Bar to DSO, 1944. Knighted, 1945. Lieutenant-General, 1945. General
Officer Commanding-in-Chief Malaya Command, 1945–6; Northern Command, India, 1946–7.
Commander-in-Chief, Pakistan Army, 1947.

3. Molotov's visit is I think a real success because we have got on personal footing of candour and as good [a] friendship as can be acquired through an interpreter. His departure will be delayed two or three days more.

4. He has made very clear his real anxiety as to the next four or five months, and I think this is sincere and not put forward to force our hand. I have a very strong feeling that the Russian position is precarious and may grow steadily worse during the coming weeks.

5. Therefore I am more than ever anxious that 'Bolero'[1] proceed to definite action beginning in 1942. We all realise that because of weather conditions the operations cannot be delayed until the end of the year.

6. After talking with our Staff, I believe the German air forces cannot be defeated or indeed brought to battle to an extent which will bring them off the Russian front until we have made a landing. I have great confidence in the ability of our joint air forces to gain complete control of the Channel and enough of the land for appropriate bridgeheads to be covered. This will result either:

(a) Pulling German air forces away from the Russian front with effort to destroy it on our part, or

(b) If German air force fails to come out the ground troop operation can be increased with objective of establishing permanent positions.

7. United Staffs are now working on proposal to increase shipping for use in 'Bolero' by cutting out a large portion of materials for Russia, other than munitions which can be used in battle this year. This ought not to diminish supplies of munitions like planes, tanks, guns, ammunition which Russians could use in combat this summer. I think we can cut further on Murmansk-Archangel convoys and send more ready to use munitions via Basra. This would make your Home Fleet task easier particularly destroyers.

8. I will telegraph you when Molotov leaves, and I am especially anxious that he carry back some real results of his mission and that he will give a favourable account to Stalin. I am inclined to think that at present all the Russians are a bit down in the mouth. But the most important thing is that we may be and probably are faced with real trouble on the Russian front and must make our plans to meet it.

Roosevelt

---

[1] 'Bolero': the administrative preparations for the opening of a 'second front' in north-west Europe, involving the movement of United States ground forces and equipment across the Atlantic to Britain.

Sir Alexander Cadogan: diary
('The Diaries of Sir Alexander Cadogan', page 456)

1 June 1942

6. Cabinet. Libya battle seems to have quite good possibilities. Portal couldn't add much to what is already published about the great raid. Sinkings bad.

[...]

We're planning to send another large bombing force over the Ruhr tonight.[1]

[...]

As PM said, 'We've had worse weekends.'

Winston S. Churchill: statement
(Hansard)

2 June 1942   House of Commons
12 noon

The Prime Minister (Mr Churchill): I thought the House would wish to have some news of the important and very severe battle which has now been proceeding for a week in the Libyan desert. Accordingly, I asked General Auchinleck for a statement. I do not think I can do better than read it out in his actual words.[2] [...]

General Auchinleck ends by repeating that the battle is not yet over, and the issue still remains to be decided, but he says that the spirit and morale of our men in Libya, both Army and Air Force, whether they come from India, South Africa, the United Kingdom or elsewhere in the British Commonwealth, and that of our most gallant Allies, the Free French, is magnificent.

In a further telegram the Commander-in-Chief adds:

'The skill, determination and pertinacity shown by General Ritchie and his Corps Commanders, Lieutenant-Generals Norrie and Gott,

[1] On the night of 1–2 June 1942, a second 'thousand bomber' raid was carried out, this time over Essen: 956 bombers took part. Haze and low cloud made accurate bombing impossible. Eleven houses were destroyed and 15 German civilians killed. Bombs intended for Essen fell on ten nearby towns, including Oberhausen (killing 83 people), Duisburg (52 killed), and Mülheim (15 killed).

[2] At this point Churchill read in full Auchinleck's communiqué (CS/1168) describing Rommel's attack of May 26 and the measures taken to counter it. These included successful RAF bombing runs against the routes to be used by the Nazis, known to British forces from captured documents. Nazi counter-attacks in the air were largely unsuccessful, and ground attacks were repelled or advanced only at heavy cost. There was, Auchinleck asserted, 'no shadow of doubt that Rommel's plans for his initial offensive have gone completely awry', though not without cost in British armour and aircraft.

throughout this difficult and strenuous week of hard and continuous fighting, have been of the highest order.'

He further dwells upon the excellent performance of the American Grant tanks, with which all users are well pleased, and says that our new heavy anti-tank gun has done great execution.

That finishes the message from General Auchinleck. From all the above it is clear that we have every reason to be satisfied, and more than satisfied, with the course which the battle has so far taken and that we should watch its further development with earnest attention.

I ought not to sit down without referring to the mammoth air raid delivered by the Royal Air Force on the Cologne region during the night of 30th–31st May. In this triumph of skill, daring and diligence against the enemy, all previous records of night bombing have been doubled and excelled. On that occasion no fewer than 1,130 British-manned aircraft operated across the sea. The results have been of a devastating character, but accurate photography has so far been hampered by the pall of smoke which hung over the smitten area. Last night, also, 1,036 machines of the Royal Air Force visited the Continent. Nearly all of these operated on the Essen region, and the first reports received indicate numerous and widespread conflagrations. From this second large-scale raid 35 of our bombers are missing.

I do not wish it to be supposed that all our raids in the immediate future will be above the four-figure scale. Methods of attack will be continually varied according to circumstances. On the other hand, these two great night-bombing raids mark the introduction of a new phase in the British air offensive against Germany, and this will increase markedly in scale when we are joined, as we soon shall be, by the Air Force of the United States. In fact, I may say that as the year advances German cities, harbours and centres of war production will be subjected to an ordeal the like of which has never been experienced by any country in continuity, severity or magnitude.

I am sure the House will wish me to express its compliments to Air Marshal Harris and the officers, non-commissioned officers and men of the Bomber Command, including the efficient and devoted maintenance staffs, upon the work which they are doing and the results achieved. Congratulations upon these encouraging events are also due to my right hon. Friend the Secretary of State for Air,[1] to the Chief of the Air Staff[2] and to the Air Ministry upon the activities of those committed to their charge.

[1] Sir Archibald Sinclair.
[2] Air Chief Marshal Sir Charles Portal.

War Cabinet: Confidential Annex
(Cabinet papers, 65/30)

2 June 1942　　　　　　　　　　　　　　　Prime Minister's Room
12.30 p.m.　　　　　　　　　　　　　　　House of Commons

The Prime Minister thought that there were grave risks in allowing General de Gaulle to go to French West Africa, where he might make statements very unfavourable to this country. He thought it was much better that he should remain here until a proper Free French Council had been formed, and that gentle, but firm influence should be brought to bear on him to stay here on the ground that he was greatly needed in this country.

Winston S. Churchill to Ernest Bevin
(Churchill papers, 20/67)

2 June 1942

Thank you for your note of the 14th May.[1]

I agree that we have done well to draft two million people into the Forces, Civil Defence, industry and services, especially when it is remembered that the unemployed have also been absorbed and that so many have been transferred from civil employment to the Forces and other Government work.

We are rapidly approaching the limits of manpower which can be devoted directly to the war. It will be for the Minister of Production[2] and the Supply Departments to endeavour to increase efficiency of management, and to achieve the best distribution of effort in the Government sector, as between constructional and production work, and as between the three services and the various weapons. This may have to be modified in some degree by the American entry into the war.

---

[1] An analysis of the manpower position at this point compared with before the war.
[2] Oliver Lyttelton (since 12 March 1942).

Winston S. Churchill to Brigadier Francis Davidson[1]
(Churchill papers, 20/67)

2 June 1942
Secret

Let me have a report, on not more than two pages, about the patriotic activities in Yugoslavia; and the relative position of the German and Italian invaders.

Winston S. Churchill to Air Chief Marshal Sir Charles Portal
(Premier papers, 3/18/2)

2 June 1942

I presume General Pile[2] and all others concerned have been keyed up to expect a German retaliation for our raids.[3]

Winston S. Churchill to Brendan Bracken
(Churchill papers, 20/67)

2 June 1942

I am sorry that you regard this extract from the War Cabinet Minutes as derogatory.[4] I remember many cases in my experience of a small Cabi-

---

[1] Francis Henry Norman Davidson, 1892–1973. Entered the Army, 1911. On active service, 1914–18 (wounded, despatches four times, Military Cross and bar, DSO). Corps Commander Royal Artillery, I Corps, British Expeditionary Force, 1939–40. Director of Military Intelligence, War Office, 1940–4; Major-General, British Army Staff, Washington, 1944–6.

[2] General Officer Commanding-in-Chief, Anti-Aircraft Command.

[3] The British bombing raid of 28–9 March 1942 on the historic German city of Lübeck prompted retaliatory attacks on British historical and cultural centres, known as the 'Baedeker raids' after the German Baedeker tourist guide to Britain. Exeter, Bath, Norwich, and York had been attacked in late April and early May; Canterbury would be targeted on June 2 and June 6. Portal replied: 'All concerned are fully alive to the possibilities of German retaliation for our raids. Special gun dispositions have been made at the Baedeker towns. Mobile balloon barrages are at present disposed at Norwich and Canterbury. A third will be operational at Salisbury by tonight. Each night possible areas of attack are reviewed in the light of the meteorological information, and a close watch is kept on beam activity and information from special sources. Starfish have been used to a greater degree with success. Their use has been extended to cover many of these towns. The Air Staff are in close touch with the Ministry of Home Security, and estimates of likely scales of attack have been sent to the appropriate Regional Commissioners' (*Premier papers, 3/18/2*). Starfish, first used in the autumn of 1940, were decoy flares, designed to resemble German bombing markers and thus to lure German bombers away from their designated targets.

[4] Churchill is responding to a minute of 1 June 1942 from Brendan Bracken (Minister of Information) about the Cabinet decision of 29 May 1942 appointing the Secretary of State for Dominion Affairs (Clement Attlee) and the Chancellor of the Exchequer (Sir Kingsley Wood) to inquire into the working of press censorship.

net Committee being invited to discuss with the Head of a Department some proposal of his, or matter of administration. It is a method that I first heard of at the time of Mr Balfour's administration. The alternative is for the Prime Minister to thrash it out himself. I was too tired and too occupied to do this that day.

2. However, since you take it amiss, I have told Bridges to remove the passage from the records, and I am telling the two Ministers concerned that they need not go into the matter, as you prefer to make your own inquiry and report.

3. With regard to the Minister of Information being present at the War Cabinet at its private sittings, this raises the difficulty of others wanting to come too. You know how strong the feeling has been in the country in favour of there being a small executive. Surely, when a D notice[1] was put out about Molotov's visit the subject matter of the veto was made known to you? We were asked by the Soviet Government to take every step to maintain secrecy in regard to Molotov's name. Let me know in what form the D notice request reached you.

4. Now please leave off scolding me on paper, and, if you have any griefs, come and beat me up personally. You know perfectly well that you can see me almost any time.

Winston S. Churchill to Anthony Eden
(Churchill papers, 20/67)

2 June 1942

The Admiralty view of the Diego Suarez incident is that a Japanese midget submarine was brought by a larger Japanese submarine which also carried a reconnaissance plane to within striking distance of the harbour. After doing their work and being hard pressed, the two Japanese who formed the crew of the midget submarine scuttled her and got ashore, where they were presently shot by our patrols. Their papers are in Japanese, and an interpreter is being flown to read them.

2. If this theory is correct, the Vichy-Madagascar French are not necessarily involved.

3. When I get the notes which I have told Ismay to prepare, I will tomorrow draft a new telegram to Smuts, which I will discuss with you. We must tidy this business up.

---

[1] D-notice: Defence Notice; a formal request to the media not to publish material deemed to be sensitive in defence terms. Though not legally enforceable, it carried the weight of an official instruction.

Winston S. Churchill to Field Marshal Jan Smuts
(Churchill papers, 20/76)

2 June 1942
Most Secret and Personal

In view of the growing importance of British West Africa as a vital link in communications and as source of essential supplies, we have been considering whether we could improve the co-operation of all services, civil and military, throughout the area. We have come to conclusion that there would be advantage in present circumstances in establishing a special authority to ensure unity of direction while maintaining continuity of local control. We are accordingly considering possibility of appointment in West Africa of a Resident Minister of Cabinet rank not War Cabinet, who would be responsible for co-ordination between civil and military authorities and all West African Governments concerned. His powers would be somewhat similar to those of Minister of State in Cairo. We have not yet reached a final decision, and of course a lot depends on finding the right man, but I wanted you to know in good time the way our minds are working.

Winston S. Churchill to General Claude Auchinleck
and Air Marshal Sir Arthur Tedder
(Churchill papers, 20/76)

2 June 1942
Personal and Most Secret

There is no need for me to stress the vital importance of the safe arrival of our convoys at Malta and I am sure you will both take all steps to enable the air escorts and particularly the Beaufighters to be operated from landing grounds as far west as possible. I hope that you have prepared a plan for bringing Martuba into use as an advance refuelling base immediately it is in our possession including arrangements for guards, AA protection and possibly the transport by air of aviation petrol, oil and ammunition for operations by our fighters. Even two refuellings might make a decisive difference. Other points will no doubt occur to you both. Let me know as soon as possible that all arrangements are complete.

Winston S. Churchill to General Hastings Ismay,
for the Chiefs of Staff Committee
(Churchill papers, 20/67)

3 June 1942
Most Secret

This[1] is a good example of how resources can be frittered away and dispersed in an unending process of passive defence. It is no use being afraid of getting into trouble because an enemy raiding party turns up at some unguarded spot. The defence of all these places can only be maintained by naval power based on Ceylon harbours, with adequate seaborne air and shore-based air protection. In case anything slips through the naval defence, a mobile force with amphibious equipment should be prepared, organised and kept in Egyptian theatre. This force, which might be a suitably equipped brigade group, would proceed to the attack of the raiders after their descent had been made and inflict a salutary punishment upon them. But while this force is organised on paper, and even sometimes, if occasion serves, exercises as a tactical unit, it must, of course, be earmarked from existing resources in the Middle East, and should take part in all the fighting whenever it is needed. This seems to me a good opportunity for impressing upon these Commanders-in-Chief the fallacy of trying 'to be safe everywhere.' There are not enough troops in the world to meet these kinds of demands.

Winston S. Churchill to Sir Horace Wilson[2]
and General Hastings Ismay
(Churchill papers, 20/67)

3 June 1942

The attached[3] makes me desirous of raising again the question of having some other honour besides the VC which is posthumous. The DSO naturally is in my mind. Pray advise me how this matter should be ripened. I mentioned it to The King yesterday and he seemed interested.[4]

---

[1] Telegram No. CC/55 of 2 June 1942 from Commanders-in-Chief, Middle East, to the Chiefs of Staff, asking for extra forces to meet possible Japanese raids in the Arabian Sea area.

[2] Head of the Civil Service.

[3] A letter from Sir Charles Portal about awards to fighter pilots in auxiliary fighter catapult ships (converted merchant ships).

[4] The posthumous DSO was introduced shortly after Churchill's meeting with the King. It was awarded later that year to Lieutenant-Commander Malcolm David Wanklyn VC, DSO, and bar, who by the end of 1941 had sunk nearly 140,000 tons of enemy shipping, including a destroyer and troopships, tankers, and supply and store ships. He and his crew were killed in April 1942 on

Winston S. Churchill to Sir James Grigg
(Churchill papers, 20/67)

3 June 1942

It seems to me a pity to move Riddell-Webster[1] after only seven months in the highly complicated Middle Eastern theatre: and in the middle of a battle too. In wartime moves of officers must not be governed by rotation but by the most effective accomplishment of particular tasks.

2. I expect to be consulted, as I have always been by your predecessors and by the other Service Departments, in high appointments and moves of this character. Very pleasant relations have existed between me and your predecessors and other Service colleagues in my discharge of my general responsibilities. I should be very sorry to see any change in this respect.

3. The War Cabinet Ministers have a perfect right to discuss among themselves or with me any question of a departmental character. It is no more than their duty and should not in any circumstances be described as going 'behind your back.' I thought you understood the conditions of War Cabinet Government at the time you were appointed Secretary of State.

Winston S. Churchill to Admiral of the Fleet Sir Dudley Pound
(Churchill papers, 20/67)

4 June 1942
Secret

As you know, I do not think that the arrangement of commands is the best that could be made. I thought that Cunningham should command the Home Fleet, Admiral Noble[2] should go to Washington, and that Admiral Tovey[3] should go to Liverpool and manage the Western Approaches. I am sure that this is what the true interests of the Service and the war require, and I hope it may soon be brought about.

their 25th patrol. Wanklyn was posthumously awarded a second bar to his DSO. Another recipient was Lieutenant Albert Michael Sinclair ('The Red Fox') of the King's Royal Rifle Corps, who had made several escape attempts while in German captivity, including from Colditz, where he pretended to be a German sergeant-major in the 'Franz Josef' escape attempt on 19 May 1943, and was shot and wounded. Shot dead on 25 September 1944 after trying to escape over the wire from the park (the only prisoner of war to be killed while attempting to escape from Colditz), he was awarded a posthumous DSO for his persistent efforts to escape.

[1] Lieutenant General in Charge of Administration, Middle East (Cairo), 1941–2 (despatches). Quartermaster-General to the Forces, War Office (London), 1942–6.

[2] Percy Lockhart Harnam Noble, 1880–1955. Entered the Navy as a boy cadet, 1894. Served in the Grand Fleet, 1914–18. Captain, 1918. Vice-Admiral, 1935. Knighted, 1936. Commander-in-Chief, China Station, 1938–40. Admiral, 1939. Officer Commanding-in-Chief Western Approaches, 1941–2. Head of the British Naval Delegation, Washington, 1942–4.

[3] Commander-in-Chief, Home Fleet, 1940–3. Commander-in-Chief, the Nore, 1943–6.

2. However, I think there are advantages in Admiral Cunningham paying a short visit to the United States as they will pay great attention to what he says on account of his having actually handled ships against the enemy so frequently on so large a scale. I hope that in say a couple of months he will be put in his rightful place as the head of the Home Fleet. All that you say about him shows how wrong it is to send him off out of the war. You know well that all important Anglo-American decisions are taken between the First Sea Lord and Admiral King.

3. I could not agree to the course you propose of making Admiral Cunningham deputy to Field-Marshal Dill. Dill's position is exceptional. Admiral Cunningham has been appointed by you merely to fill Little's place.[1] If he is treated exceptionally, the Air Force will demand a similar rise for Air Marshal Evill.[2] In fact they have a better case as far as the importance of their business actually transacted in the United States is concerned.

4. In deference to your wishes, I have, on reconsideration submitted Admiral Cunningham's name to The King for a Baronetcy.[3]

Winston S. Churchill to Field Marshal Jan Smuts
(Churchill papers, 20/76)

4 June 1942
Most Secret and Personal

Thank you for your messages in High Commissioner's telegrams 948 of May 28th and 967 of June 1st. I want to put clearly before you how we stand in Madagascar.

2. As I told you in my OZ 245 to Cairo we had reluctantly to put off clearing up Tamatave and Majunga as it was necessary for the 5th Division to get on to India at the earliest moment. We therefore instructed General Sturges[4] to make Diego Suarez secure with the minimum forces, and gave him authority to try to make some sort of arrangement with the Governor at Tananarive.

3. On the 27th May a British subject of the name of Barnett arrived at Diego Suarez from Tananarive with the story that he had been asked by a member of the Governor's staff to try to find a basis of agreement between

---

[1] Admiral Cunningham was appointed Head of the British Admiralty Delegation in Washington, replacing Admiral Little on the latter's appointment as Commander-in-Chief at Portsmouth.

[2] Head of the Royal Air Force delegation in Washington, 1942. Vice-Chief of the Air Staff, 1943–6.

[3] Admiral Cunningham received a baronetcy on 7 July 1942.

[4] Major-General Sturges, commanding the troops on Madagascar.

Tananarive Government and British forces which would safeguard the honour, sovereignty and neutrality of Madagascar Government and put an end to bloodshed. Thereupon Sturges sent him an aide memoire, the text of which is given in my immediately following telegram. We do not care for all these proposals as they stand and doubt whether the Governor will make acceptable counter-proposals. We have directed Sturges not to carry negotiations any further pending the Governor's reply which he is to telegraph to us immediately, together with his comments in the light of the existing military situation. So much for the political side of the story.

4. The military picture is as follows:

(a) The Naval forces which took part in the Madagascar operations have already been dispersed. The carriers have joined Somerville's Fleet and the destroyers have gone to help in the Mediterranean.

(b) The assault shipping and landing craft are still in East African waters and can be reassembled.

(c) Army. The 13th British Brigade has already left Madagascar and arrived in India. The 22nd East African Brigade is due at Diego Suarez this week and the 17th British Brigade of the 5th Division will then move on to India. The Brigade which you are so very kindly providing is to go forward as soon as shipping is available, and the 27th East African Brigade is due at Diego Suarez on approximately the 24th July. The 29th Brigade will then move on to India and the Commando will probably return home.

(d) Air Forces at present consist of your composite bomber-reconnaissance squadron (one flight Marylands[1] and two flights Beauforts);[2] one RAF flight (six Lysanders); and a few Lodestars.[3]

5. General Sturges reported on the 14th May that one Brigade and one Commando would be required for the capture of either Tamatave

[1] Maryland: the Martin Maryland, with a crew of three, was an American light bomber that first flew in 1939. Used by the Royal Air Force for photo-reconnaissance operations in North and Eastern Africa, and sometimes as a bomber, being faster and better armed than the Blenheim; but since it was a 'rare bird', its role was mainly reconnaissance missions. It was a Maryland bomber that was sent to take photographs of the Italian Fleet before and after the Battle of Taranto (11 November 1940); the pilot of that Maryland was Adrian Warburton, who scored his five confirmed kills with the Maryland's forward-firing guns, the only person ever to achieve ace status in a bomber. It was also a Maryland that brought back the photographs that alerted the British to the German battleship *Bismarck* having left harbour on 22 May 1941.

[2] Beaufort: the Bristol Beaufort, a British torpedo bomber that first saw service with Coastal Command and then with the Fleet Air Arm. Flying from Britain, and also based in Egypt and on Malta, Beauforts operated as torpedo bombers, conventional bombers, and mine-layers until 1943, when they were used as training aircraft, flying (between 1939 and 1945) more hours in training than on operational missions; more were lost through accidents and mechanical failures than were lost to enemy fire. Declared obsolete in 1945.

[3] Lodestar: the Lockheed Model 18 Lodestar, a passenger transport aircraft, first introduced in March 1940. It had a crew of three, and could carry up to 30 passengers.

or Majunga; that since almost all the assault shipping would be required for each attack, it would not be possible to carry out the two operations simultaneously; and that the naval forces required would be of the order of one aircraft carrier, one cruiser, six destroyers, three corvettes, minesweepers, etc. General Sturges also estimated that, in view of the decision that the Free French should be associated with us in the administration of Madagascar, Tamatave and Majunga would each require a Brigade Group as a permanent garrison. I do not accept the view that such large forces would be required merely to garrison these places after resistance had been overcome, and I consider that the evil effects of Free French participation, though real, are exaggerated.

6. From this, however, you will see that General Sturges regards the capture of Tamatave and Majunga as fairly formidable operations. It would be vexatious to have a failure and get entangled. Our experience has been that the Vichy French are apt to fight hard unless attacked by obviously superior forces, and are particularly bitter when the Free French are involved.

7. If no arrangement is possible with the local Government and we still want to clear up Tamatave and Majunga, the best opportunity would be after the arrival of the 27th East African Brigade on July 24th and before the departure for India of the 29th Brigade, and the Commando. It is, however, impossible to say so far ahead of the time whether the necessary naval forces could be made available.

8. We should be very ready to be guided by your views. Would you care to have General Sturges fly to see you, or could you go to Diego Suarez yourself?

Winston S. Churchill to Field Marshal Jan Smuts
(Churchill papers, 20/76)

4 June 1942
Most Secret and Personal

My immediately preceding telegram. Following are contents of Aide Mémoire.

The British forces have only one objective to deny island of Madagascar and naval base of Diego Suarez to Japanese and to protect island from attack.

2. The objective is wholly strategic and British forces will be withdrawn at the end of the war or at an earlier date if strategy allows.

3. The first step towards this objective has been to take measures for defence of Diego Suarez. This is being done and British Commander pays a high tribute to co-operation and public spirit of French community in that place.

4. The next step must be to take measures for defence of neutrality of remainder of Madagascar. The Commander of the British forces would of course prefer that these measures should be taken in full collaboration with French naval and military authorities and that French naval and military personnel should combine in practical measures to be conducted in defence of port and air fields. But if this were unacceptable British Commander would ask an assurance that full permission to take such measures as were necessary should be granted by French Authorities. These should include use of all ports and airfields and should be accompanied by a bona fide offer of full co-operation excluding actual employment of French forces but including use of the French coast defences and AA armaments wherever British forces should deem it necessary.

5. The French flag would be flown as it is today. The British forces would respect French sovereignty throughout island. They would recognize Monsieur Annet as Governor General of Madagascar acting on behalf of France and would be happy to co-operate in any way with his present administration of island. French Courts would be respected and French civil administration assisted in every way.

6. The British Commander would ask that French troops other than those who might be allowed to collaborate in defence of ports and airfields should be maintained at a strength necessary for the safeguarding of internal security in island. The location of these troops would form part of a subsequent agreement. In the event of agreement on this the British Commander would not (repeat not) wish to maintain British troops in the capital and would suggest retention there of a British Mission of Liaison whose members would be unarmed (Americans might be included).

7. The British Commander would wish to ensure economic prosperity of island and with this aim would recommend conclusion of an economic agreement whereby Madagascar would receive supplies necessary for her welfare and whereby main products of island would be purchased by British or allied concerns. (Both these measures have already been taken at Diego Suarez).

8. The British Commander would extend to a limited number in rest of island the facilities for repatriation already granted to those officials at Diego Suarez whose consciences did not (repeat not) allow them to co-operate with British Authorities.

9. If agreement could be reached on lines indicated in preceding paragraphs hostilities would cease.

10. It is felt that if at a very early date an official representative of the Governor General submitted proposals and terms based on the above reasonable anticipation of early agreement could be enjoyed but it must not be inferred that foregoing para has any official aspect or that thereby is complied any undertaking to abstain in meantime from a further military action.

Winston S. Churchill to President Franklin D. Roosevelt
(Churchill papers, 20/76)

4 June 1942
No. 99

I must tell you that we received invaluable help from Winant[1] during our Russian negotiations. He made the Russians understand, as no one else could do, how injurious to good relations between us three, must have been the American reaction to the old treaty. I have no doubt that his intervention and plain speaking were largely instrumental in helping us to secure a treaty which fulfilled our own ideals. We are all most grateful for this help.

Winston S. Churchill to General Hastings Ismay,
for the Chiefs of Staff Committee
(Churchill papers, 20/67)

5 June 1942
Secret

I did not intend advocating sending any part of 'Ironclad' forces to Australia and I am obliged to you for showing me that this was the natural inference from my note. What I am after is this: I want to have a punch available against the Japanese lines of communication and also for diversionary action in the ABDA area. It seems to me very tiresome to have to drag back assault ships and assault landing craft all round the Cape to Britain. As you know I do not think there is much doing on the French coast this year. Anyhow, what is brought back would not be decisive even this year and would only be a drop in the bucket in 1943. However, these forces might be invaluable in the Eastern theatre. They would be the steel tip to the lance out there instead of a mere make-weight at home.

---

[1] The United States Ambassador to Britain.

2. Would you please discriminate between '"Ironclad" assault ship-ping' on the one hand, and 'Assault landing craft' on the other. How many are there of each and what is involved?

3. It seems questionable to cart No 5 Commando of 450 men all the way to Diego Suarez and then bring it back against the tide. They might do wonders in the East.

4. I am all for the 29th Division going to Wavell as arranged. I am counting on this brigade for future operations of an offensive character and I am in full accord with the Chiefs of the Staff view about this.

Winston S. Churchill to Sir James Grigg
and General Sir Alan Brooke
(Churchill papers, 20/67)

5 June 1942

In all communiqués, Indian divisions having three British battalions and British artillery should be called British Indian divisions in order to prevent the impression that there are hardly any British troops fighting. Unless you disagree, pray convey this to Middle East Command. Let me also have the composition of the 5th and 10th Indian Divisions, or British Indian Divisions, showing the British elements and numbers.

Winston S. Churchill to Anthony Eden
(Churchill papers, 20/67)

5 June 1942
Secret

I am quite willing to see de Gaulle one day next week, and can talk to him as at 'A.'[1] The exploits of his troops at Hacheim[2] furnish a good occasion.

---

[1] Minute of 4 June 1942 from the Foreign Secretary (PM/42/125) saying that General de Gaulle had consented to postpone his visit to Africa and the Near East, and asking that in return he should be consulted in regard to present and future events. There is in fact no record of Churchill and de Gaulle having met the following week, or indeed at any time before Churchill's departure for Washington on June 17.

[2] Bir Hacheim (also Bir Hakeim), a remote oasis in the Libyan desert. From 26 May to 11 June 1942, a 3,600-strong force of the 1st Free French Division under General Marie-Pierre Kœnig defended the oasis against 45,000 attacking German and Italian troops under Rommel, holding off the much larger Axis force for 16 days. Tobruk was taken ten days later by Rommel's troops, after which Rommel continued to advance against the British until halted at the First Battle of El Alamein in July 1942. Ten days into the battle, Rommel received orders from Hitler to kill all enemy soldiers in battle or shoot them when captured; in Hitler's view the Free French troops were partisans, not regular soldiers, who had among their number political refugees from Germany. Rommel ignored this order and took Free French soldiers as regular prisoners of war. As to the importance of the battle, in an interview in 1991 General Bernard Saint-Hillier said: 'A grain of sand had curbed the Axis advance, which reached El Alamein only after the arrival of the rested

Winston S. Churchill: War Cabinet memorandum[1]
(Churchill papers, 23/10)

5 June 1942   10 Downing Street
Secret

FRANCO-GERMAN CO-OPERATION IN NORTH AFRICA ETC.

Whatever our feelings of well-placed scorn and distrust of the Vichy Government may be, we ought not to forget that it is the only Government which may perhaps give us what we want from France, namely, the Toulon Fleet and the entry into the French North African provinces. One has therefore to consider what, if any, are the chances of this. They do not seem to me entirely negligible. The Vichy Government under Darlan, Laval or perhaps Doriot[2] must, of course, pay its way from week to week with its German masters. Their only alternative is the installation of a Gauleiter and complete occupation. From my own personal observation of what has happened, I do not feel that the Vichy Government have done anything more than was absolutely necessary to stave off this second alternative. They have borne Oran, Dakar, Syria, Madagascar, the British blockade and British air raids with the least possible show of anger. This attitude has been forced upon them by sentiment against Germany of the vast majority of the French nation, both in occupied and unoccupied France, and by the French conviction that they must not sever the future of France from the United States.

2. The cardinal question not only for Vichy but for France is who will win the war? At first there seemed no possibility of defeating Germany. But the campaigns in Russia, the entry of the United States, the enormous staying power of Great Britain, our evident growing preponderance in the Air, have brought back hope to virile French hearts and affected ever wider circles in France. The Germans are not sure even of the tools they tolerate at the head of French affairs. They know that it is the interest

British divisions: this grain of sand was Bir Hakeim.' (As a captain in the French Foreign Legion in 1942, Saint-Hillier had taken part in the battle; in 1962 he was French military representative to the European Allied Command.)

[1] War Cabinet Paper 239 of 1942.

[2] Jacques Doriot, 1898–1945. A labourer at St Denis, near Paris, from an early age. On active service, 1917; taken prisoner of war. Active in the French Communist Party, 1920–34 (when he was expelled). Elected Mayor of St Denis, 1931. Formed the ultra-nationalist Parti Populaire Français (PPF), 1936, organising it along Italian Fascist and German Nazi lines. Supported the German occupation of northern France, 1940. One of the founders, in 1941, of the Légion des Volontaires Français (LVF), a French unit of the German Army. Fought with the LVF on the Eastern Front. Awarded the Iron Cross, 1943. Living in southern Germany from 1943, he set up a radio station, Radio-Patrie, and published a newspaper, *Le Petit Parisien*. Killed in southern Germany on 22 February 1945, when his car was strafed by Allied fighters.

even of such creatures to join the winning side once they are sure which it is, and that they have a gift to give to the Allies of inestimable value.

3. I have always been ready to take rough action against Vichy, and have always been sure that Vichy would in one shape or another put up with it. I look forward to a time in the war, which I cannot fix but may not be far off, when the great change of heart which has taken place in the French masses and the apparent certainty of an Allied victory will produce a sudden, decisive change in the action of the Vichy Government.

Winston S. Churchill to Ivan Maisky[1]
(Churchill papers, 20/53)

5 June 1942

My dear Ambassador,

Thank you so much for your letter asking about Randolph. It was very good of you to make this enquiry. His injuries to his chest were more serious than first indicated. Pneumonia supervened, but I am assured he is progressing favourably.[2]

Yours sincerely,
Winston S. Churchill

Winston S. Churchill to General Archibald Wavell
(Churchill papers, 20/76)

5 June 1942
Secret and Personal

Your 13523/C 3rd June. Please send me as soon as possible your plan for counter offensive in Upper Burma, together with your estimate for the forces and tackle which you will require. We can then compare your ideas with our own appreciation of the problem. If the monsoon makes Rangoon impossible before November we must bow to the inevitable, but the sooner we can get on the move the better.

2. Reference your para 5: You will by now have received the maturely considered Admiralty message to Admiral Somerville (OZ 343 of 3rd June) with which I am in cordial agreement.

[1] Soviet Ambassador to Britain.
[2] On receiving further information from General Auchinleck in Cairo, Churchill deleted the words from 'I am glad...' and replaced them with: 'His injuries to his chest were more serious than first indicated. Pneumonia supervened, but I am assured he is progressing favourably.'

3. I do not understand why Admiral Somerville has not kept you informed of his movements and plans. You have a naval liaison officer at your HQ for this purpose. I hope that a better liaison will be arranged when your OGS meets him at Colombo.

4. I am disturbed that the news of the accident to *Ramillies*[1] should have reached you at all, since strict orders had been given that it was to be kept absolutely secret. How did you get it? If the accident had had any effect on your immediate plans, we should of course have let you know.

5. Reference your para 6: Full details of our intentions about the landing craft used in 'Ironclad' were sent to you in Telegram 2245B of 14th May. There was never any intention of adopting Admiral Somerville's recommendation that all these craft and troops should be sent to Australia.

6. I am very sorry to hear that the 13th Brigade contracted bad Malaria in Madagascar. There is all the more reason for getting the rest of the British troops there to India as soon as possible.

General Sir Alan Brooke: diary
(*'War Diaries, Field Marshal Lord Alanbrooke', page 263*)

5 June 1942

At this morning's COS we discussed again the various possibilities of helping Russia by proceeding to France, either as a lodgement or as raid. Prospects not hopeful. We then turned to examine the PM's pet attack on Northern Norway which appears even more impossible, except possibly for limited operations to secure Petsamo in combination with the Russians. Monty[2] came to lunch and I discussed with him his large exercise which he has just completed to try out the new divisional organization.

---

[1] The battleship HMS *Ramillies*, which had been instrumental in the successful operation to take control of Madagascar, was severely damaged by submarine attack in Diego Suarez harbour on 30 May 1942.

[2] Bernard Law Montgomery, 1887–1976. Educated at St Paul's School. Entered the Army, 1908. On active service, 1914–18 (despatches, DSO). Major-General, 1938. Commanded 3rd Division (retreat to Dunkirk), 1940. Commanded 8th Army (North Africa, Sicily, Italy), July 1942 to January 1944. Knighted, 1942. Commander-in-Chief, British Group of Armies and Allied Armies, northern France, 6 June 1944 (Normandy Landings); Commanded 21st Army Group, northern Europe, June 1944 to May 1945. Field Marshal, 1944. Commanded British Army of Occupation on the Rhine (BAOR), 1945–6. Created Viscount, 1946. Deputy Supreme Allied commander, Europe, 1951–8.

Winston S. Churchill to R. J. Hunt[1]
(Churchill papers, 20/53)

5 June 1942

My dear Mr Hunt,

I am glad to learn that you have been selected to stand as the National Government candidate in the Maldon by-election caused by the death of my old colleague, Sir Edward Ruggles-Brise.[2]

It is still my convinced opinion that in these days when the future of our country, and indeed of all civilization, is in the melting-pot, by-election fights are completely out of keeping with the gravity of the times. I hope therefore that no one will show such levity of mind as to provoke an unnecessary and meaningless contest.

The electors of Maldon know well that they have every reason to place full confidence in you as their representative in the House of Commons. They have seen the value of your work on the County Council for the past ten years. You are known as one of themselves. You have a wide business experience which enables you to appraise at their true worth the value to the nation both of individual effort and of national organization. As an agricultural engineer you are familiar with the difficulties and also the achievements of the farming community who have responded so readily, and so effectively, to every call that has been made upon them during the war.

If an election contest is challenged, then I urge the electors to return you to Parliament by an ample majority, in proof of their unshakable resolve to carry the war to a victorious end and of their confidence in the National Government which I have the honour to lead.

Yours sincerely,
Winston S. Churchill

[1] Reuben James Hunt, 1888–1970. Born in Earls Colne, Essex. Educated at a local grammar school. Company director. Knighted, 1953. During the 1942 by-election campaign, he declared that Britain's reverses in Libya were due to 'our too-heavy arms shipments to Russia'. This gave the Independent candidate Tom Driberg the opportunity to accuse Hunt of making a 'wretched alibi for the incompetence of brass hats'. Hunt was not elected; Driberg was.

[2] Edward Archibald Ruggles-Brise, 1882–1942. Educated at Eton and Trinity College, Cambridge. On active service, 1914–18 (Military Cross). Landowner, land agent, and farmer. Conservative MP for Maldon, 1922–3 and from 1924 until his death. Created Baronet, 1935. He died on 12 May 1942.

Winston S. Churchill to General Hastings Ismay,
for the Chiefs of Staff Committee
(Churchill papers, 20/67)

6 June 1942
Most Secret

SPITZBERGEN: OPERATION 'JACKPOT'[1]

This disquiets me considerably. The Chiefs of the Staff, after mature consideration, advised this small enterprise for which I obtained the approval of the War Cabinet. All orders have been issued, and preparations have been proceeding. Ships are actually being loaded.

2. The Commander-in-Chief,[2] whose whole attitude is negative and who would have stopped the last convoy to Russia had his advice been taken, has now furnished more reasons for doing nothing. On this, the whole of the advice previously given by the Chiefs of the Staff is stultified, and we are assured that Spitzbergen is of no importance.

3. As one of the reasons for delaying the Russian convoy for a fortnight, the fact that we had to carry the expedition to Spitzbergen was stressed. Now that the Russian convoy has been postponed, Spitzbergen is dropped.

4. Now it may well be that the Germans will occupy Spitzbergen, and once they have got there we shall be told by the Commander-in-Chief that an additional impediment has been placed on carrying supplies to Russia. The occupation of Spitzbergen by the enemy will be considered most unfortunate both in Britain and in Russia. Surely it at least doubles the range of the German aircraft, which can be refuelled at their base at Spitzbergen and sally out with good radius against us the farther our route lies to the north.

5. I must have the Cabinet consulted before an enterprise, undertaken and prepared so deliberately, is discarded. In the meanwhile, the loading should not be stopped.

---

[1] 'Jackpot': a British landing on Norway's largest island, Spitzbergen, bordering the Arctic Ocean, the Greenland Sea and the Norwegian Sea. Spitzbergen was not then occupied by the Germans (who had conquered Norway in May–June 1940). In August 1941 a ten-day combined British, Canadian and Norwegian commando raid had destroyed the German installations on the island.

[2] Vice-Admiral Tovey, Commander-in-Chief, Home Fleet, 1940–3, whose responsibilities included the Murmansk and Archangel convoys.

Winston S. Churchill to Lord Cranborne
(Churchill papers, 20/67)

6 June 1942
Most Secret

SOUTHERN IRELAND

The situation has changed very much in our favour since this question was last considered. Very large United States forces are coming into Ireland. The Germans are deeply involved on the Eastern Front. It is <u>we</u> who are making preparations now to invade the Continent. There is therefore very little likelihood of the weapons which it is now proposed to give to Southern Ireland being used against anybody but ourselves in case we have need of these bases.

I cannot consider the matter as in any way urgent. I hope therefore that it may be reconsidered when we see how the fighting goes in Russia.

Winston S. Churchill to Admiral of the Fleet Sir Dudley Pound
(Churchill papers, 20/67)

6 June 1942

RUSSIAN CONVOYS

I do not think these telegrams do the Commander-in-Chief[1] much credit, and I think he took advantage of your speech to emphasise his naturally negative and unenterprising attitude of mind. Reading them reinforces in my mind all I said to you in my recent minute. I am keeping telegrams which you have sent me.

Winston S. Churchill to Sir Edward Bridges
(Churchill papers, 20/67)

7 June 1942

LORD LONDONDERRY'S[2] MEMOIR

Quite a lot of this deals with a period which has ceased to count, and much of it is eight, nine, ten years away. There are many precedents for

---

[1] Vice-Admiral Tovey.

[2] Charles Stewart Henry Vane-Tempest-Stewart, 1878–1949. Churchill's second cousin. Educated at Eton and Sandhurst. As Viscount Castlereagh, Conservative MP for Maidstone, 1906–15. Succeeded his father as the 7th Marquess of Londonderry, 1915. Served briefly on the Western Front as Second-in-Command, Royal Horse Guards, 1915. Under-Secretary of State for Air, 1920–1. Minister of Education and Leader of the Senate, Government of Northern Ireland, 1921–6. Returned to Westminster as First Commissioner of Works, 1928–9 and 1931; and as Secretary of State for Air and Lord Privy Seal, 1931–5. He published *Wings of Destiny* in 1943.

earlier publication about the political relations of Ministers. I cannot judge the character of the references you make without the book. Please send it to me, with flagged pages.

2. The principle that permission must be obtained is also modified by the maxim 'permission should not be unreasonably withheld'. I think the pre-war years should count, at any rate from 1935, and special attention should be paid to them. Private letters are of course protected by the existing copyright law, by which the ownership of the letter is vested in the recipient and the copyright in the writer. But this is not our affair. With regard to quotations from official documents or Cabinet proceedings, you should mark all those which have to be excluded in the public interest and let Lord Londonderry know that they would have to be excised or stated in a different way. But a <u>bona fide</u> interpretation of the public interest must prevail.

3. The precedents in favour of a fairly free publication <u>after</u> the war is over are very numerous. See my own voluminous writings – Lord Fisher,[1] Mr Asquith, Mr Lloyd George, Sir William Robertson,[2] Sir Henry Wilson's diaries,[3] and so on.

4. Our real point is that we must not be hampered in the conduct of the war until it is won. Whatever liberties are given to Lord Londonderry should be given to Lord Chatfield. But I really think pre-1935 is ancient history.

---

[1] John Arbuthnot Fisher, 1841–1920. Known both as 'Jackie' and, because of his somewhat oriental appearance, 'the old Malay'. Entered the Navy, 1854. First Sea Lord, 1904–10. Admiral of the Fleet, 1905. Created Baron, 1909. Retired, 1911. Head of the Royal Commission on Fuel and Engines, 1912–14. Re-appointed First Sea Lord at Churchill's urging, 1914. Resigned, in protest at Churchill's Dardanelles plans, 1915. Successfully encouraged Churchill to call for his reinstatement, 1916, but in vain. His *Memoirs* were published in 1919.

[2] William Robert Robertson, 1860–1933. Entered the Army as a private soldier, 1877. Chief of the Imperial General Staff, 1916–18. Created Baronet, 1919. Appointed Field Marshal on Churchill's intervention. The first soldier in the British Army to rise from the lowest to the highest rank. In 1921 he published *From Private to Field Marshal*.

[3] Henry Hughes Wilson, 1864–1922. Entered the Army, 1882. Suppported Unionist officers in the so-called 'Curragh Mutiny' of 1914. Chief of the Imperial General Staff, 1918. Field Marshal, 1919. Created Baronet, 1919. Assassinated by the IRA. In 1927, Major-General Sir C. E. Caldwell published *Field Marshal Sir Henry Wilson: His Life and Diaries*.

Winston S. Churchill to General Hastings Ismay,
for the Chiefs of Staff Committee
(Churchill papers, 20/67)

7 June 1942

This paper[1] requires your earnest consideration. All our difficulties will be aggravated if China is forced out of war. By far the best and easiest way to defend India is to attack the Japanese lines of communication through Burma. The proposals I have put before you on the subject, stressing the urgency of this, have not yet made any headway. There will have to be a meeting of the War Cabinet and the Defence Committee combined on Thursday next, and I propose to keep the whole morning clear for that from 11 o'clock onwards. It will be necessary to examine, first, our Far Eastern campaign of 1942; secondly, the progress of 'Sledgehammer,' &c.

2. I have not yet received any outline of 'Imperator'.[2] Pray let me have this.

3. In order to survey this ground beforehand, I should like to see the three Chiefs of the Staff on Monday night (8th June) in the Cabinet Room at Downing Street at 10:30 pm.

4. We can discuss 'Jackpot' then.

Winston S. Churchill to Brendan Bracken
(Churchill papers, 20/67)

7 June 1942

You had better let Sir Stafford Cripps know that I shall myself be making my broadcast on coal economy and my appeal to the miners that very Sunday night, 14th June. Should we not be trespassing too much upon the public temper to give them two broadcasts on the same subject on the same day, by Members of the same Government?

2. Broadcasts by Ministers ought to be fairly evenly distributed. I think that if Sir Stafford Cripps gives too many broadcasts his colleagues will complain.

---

[1] WP(42) 236 ('Free China').

[2] 'Imperator': a plan – in response to the repeated Soviet calls for a second front – to land an army division and armoured units on the Channel coast of France, to carry out a two- or three-day raid and then to re-embark.

Winston S. Churchill to Sir Archibald Sinclair
(Churchill papers, 20/67)

7 June 1942

I have learnt with pleasure that the preliminary trials of H2S[1] have been extremely satisfactory. But I am deeply disturbed at the very slow rate of progress promised for its production. Three sets in August and twelve in November is not even beginning to touch the problem. We must insist on getting, at any rate, a sufficient number to light up the target, by the Autumn, even if we cannot get them into all the bombers, and nothing should be allowed to stand in the way of this.

I propose to hold a meeting to discuss this next week and to see what can be done. The relatively disappointing results of our second big raid make it doubly urgent.

I am glad you have arranged with the Minister of Aircraft Production[2] for Sir Robert Renwick[3] to make a personal effort to accelerate production of the needed radio equipment. But I hope you will not let him disperse his efforts on too many bits of apparatus. The main thing is to hit the target, and this we can do with H2S. All the other items are, of course, useful, but nothing like so urgent.

It is most necessary that training, aerodromes, runways and bombs should all be synchronised, and it was for this reason that I suggested it might be well to put Sir Robert Renwick in charge of the whole thing. The difficulty of co-ordinating all these matters is obvious, but the urgent need is clear. If you do not wish Sir Robert Renwick to undertake it, I trust you will appoint some other individual to be responsible for ensuring that everything marches in step, so that we are not faced at the end by some missing item. I do not think it is sufficient to leave this matter to the ordinary processes of departmental organisation.

As to the bombs, you told me in your minute of 19th July, 1941, that a production order had been placed for 500-lb MC[4] bombs, and that you were proceeding with the design of a larger one. It has been stated at several meetings that you entirely agreed they were superior to the

---

[1] H2S: an airborne, ground-scanning radar system designed to identify targets on the ground for night and all-weather bombing.

[2] Colonel Llewellin.

[3] Controller of Communications, Air Ministry, and Controller of Communications Equipment, Ministry of Aircraft Production.

[4] MC bomb: a 'medium case' or 'medium capacity' bomb, dropped by aircraft, with a combined blast, penetration, and fragmentation effect similar to that of the GP (general purpose) bomb, but with a higher ratio of explosive material to metal, increasing the damage it could inflict and reducing the likelihood of its not exploding on impact.

GP bomb,[1] and I am disappointed that such a large proportion of our effort should still be applied to carrying bombs with only half the blasting power they might have.

Winston S. Churchill to Sir James Grigg
(Churchill papers, 20/67)

7 June 1942
Secret

You should bring this matter[2] before the War Cabinet, circulating a Very Secret paper to them, including Auchinleck's letter and your Annex II. I do not know what they will say. My own feeling is that to carry this legislation there would have to be a great sense of emergency, in which very serious figures could be disclosed. The figures do not seem to be serious at the present time if we leave out the Australians and Cypriots. It will be well to apprise the Cabinet of the position well in advance.

2. The Australian papers show conclusively how disastrous it would be to the Empire to have an inquiry about Singapore. It is all bound to come out sooner or later, but the later the better.

President Franklin D. Roosevelt to Winston S. Churchill
(Churchill papers, 20/76)

7 June 1942
No. 155

I delivered to Molotov our Joint Protocol of supplies from July 1, 1942, to June 30, 1943. I amended the general statement somewhat but in no important degree. A copy of the Protocol and of the preliminary statement has been given to the appropriate British representatives here. I was greatly pleased with the visit. He warmed up far more than I expected and I am sure that he has a far better understanding of the situation here than when he arrived. I confess that I view with great concern the Russian Front and am going to wire you in a day or two a specific proposal which I have in mind.

The business in the Pacific is going well and I am sure we are inflicting some very severe losses on the Jap Fleet. The outcome, however, is still inde-

---

[1] GP bomb: general purpose bomb, dropped by aircraft, with a combined blast, penetration, and fragmentation effect.

[2] The reintroduction of the death penalty for desertion in the field and cowardice in the face of the enemy (minute of 5 June 1942 from Sir James Grigg, Secretary of State for War).

cisive but we should know more before the day is over. I am sure our aircraft are giving very good account of themselves. I will keep you informed.

Roosevelt

Winston S. Churchill to Lord Selborne
(Churchill papers, 20/60)

7 June 1942

My dear Selborne,

Colonel Walter Elliot,[1] as an ex-Secretary of State for Scotland, has indicated that he intends to raise in the House of Commons the statements which you made in the Debate of June 4 in the House of Lords about setting up independent Scottish and Welsh Parliaments, etc. I have read the passages to which he no doubt intends to refer, and I note that you were 'speaking entirely for yourself'. Doubtless it will be possible for me in reply to a Question to point to this, and to say you had no ministerial authority whatever for making such statements or referring to such a matter. All the same, I must say I think that to fly balloons of this kind when we are in our present troubles, without consulting me or any other of your colleagues or even the Secretary of State for Scotland[2] who is directly concerned, does not in any way lighten the burden we all have to bear. No Minister gains the right to open large questions of policy merely by prefixing his speech with the words 'speaking personally'.

[1] Walter Elliot, 1888–1958. On active service, 1914–18 (Military Cross and bar). Conservative MP for Lanark, 1918–23, for Kelvingrove 1924–45, for the Scottish Universities, 1946–50, and for Kelvingrove again from 1950 until his death. Minister of Agriculture and Fisheries, 1932–6. Secretary of State for Scotland, 1936–8. Minister of Health, May 1938 to May 1940. Director of Public Relations, War Office, 1941–2. In 1951 Churchill wanted to offer him the Ministry of Education, but he was away from his telephone when the call came from Downing Street. His second wife, Katherine Tennant, Chairman of the Women's National Advisory Committee of the Conservative Party, 1954–7, was created Baroness Elliot of Harwood after failing to win her late husband's seat (Glasgow Kelvingrove) at the by-election following his death in 1958. She died in 1994.

[2] Thomas Johnston, 1881–1965. An early Scottish socialist. Editor of *Forward* (which he helped to launch), 1906–33. In 1909 he published a book, *Our Scots Noble Families*, with the aim of discrediting the Scottish landed aristocracy. Labour MP for Stirling and Clackmannan West, 1922–4; Dundee, 1924–9; Stirling and Clackmannan West, 1929–31, 1935–45. Under-Secretary of State for Scotland, 1929–31. Privy Councillor, 1931. Lord Privy Seal, 1931. Regional Commissioner for the Scottish Civil Defence Region, April 1939 to May 1940. Secretary of State for Scotland, February 1941 to May 1945. A long-standing supporter of the Home Rule movement, he persuaded Churchill to counter nationalism north of the border by creating an All-Party Scottish Council of State and a Scottish Council of Industry, thereby devolving some power away from Whitehall. Chairman of the Scottish National Forestry Commission, 1945–8. President of the Scottish History Society, 1950–2. Represented Scottish interests in the council appointed to devise the Festival of Britain, 1951. Chancellor of Aberdeen University from 1951 until his death. Chairman of the Broadcasting Council for Scotland, 1955–6. Director, Independent Television Authority in North-East Scotland, 1961–5.

I shall be glad if you will let me know what you wish me to say when the Question is raised.

I think your view about the 'balance of power' at the head of the last paragraph of Column 174 of the official report is erroneous, and I do not think you have considered where the opposite theory would lead you. Obviously on your principles we ought to have worked with Germany against the rest of Europe from the beginning of the present century. I was certainly not aware that this was your view. The genius of Britain has for 400 years led her to ally herself with the second strongest Continental power. In this way we have avoided the fate of the jackal who goes hunting with the tiger. To make your statement correct in fact, you should add after the word 'another' in the 6th line of the aforesaid paragraph – 'from which we have emerged victorious, carrying with us the liberties of Europe'.

Yours very sincerely,
Winston S. Churchill

Anthony Eden: diary
('The Eden Memoirs, The Reckoning', page 331)

7 June 1942

Winston rang up twice in morning. First about Libya battle, as to which we agreed that reports were disappointing. We were both depressed by extent to which Rommel appears able to retain offensive. 'I fear that we have not very good generals,' said W. He was also depressed by Chiefs of Staff sudden decision to cancel their own previous plans to take certain place in north.[1] I had not heard of this change. W feared it had to do with Tovey's extreme reluctance to continue Russian convoys. 'The politicians are much abused, but they get little help or inspiration from their service advisers,' was W's comment and it can hardly be denied.

Later he spoke about China. There also he wants us to plan ahead for offensive action to relieve Chiang who is obviously hard pressed. Military appear to take a leisurely view and I undertook to raise political issue with him to emphasize urgency. Then at least we can get examination.

---

[1] Petsamo (Operation Jupiter).

Winston S. Churchill to General Hastings Ismay,
for the Chiefs of Staff Committee
(Churchill papers, 20/67)

8 June 1942
Most Secret

OPERATIONS ON THE CONTINENT IN 1942

The plan 'Imperator,' which I have seen only in outline, proposes to land on the Continent a division and armoured units to raid as effectively as possible during two or three days, and then to re-embark as much as possible of the remnants of the force. This is to be our response to a 'cri de coeur' from Russia in the event of things going very wrong there. Certainly, it would not help Russia if we launched such an enterprise, no doubt with world publicity, and came out a few days later with heavy losses. We should have thrown away valuable lives and material, and made ourselves and our capacity for making war ridiculous throughout the world. The Russians would not be grateful for this worsening of the general position. The French patriots who would rise in our aid and their families would be subjected to pitiless Hun revenge, and this would spread far and wide as a warning against similar imprudences in case of larger-scale operations. Many of those who are now egging us on would be the first to point all this out. It would be cited as another example of sentimental politics dominating the calm determination and common sense of professional advisers.

2. In order to achieve this result, we have to do the two most difficult operations of war: first, landing from the sea on a small front against a highly prepared enemy, and, second, evacuating by sea two or three days later the residue of the force landed. It may be mentioned that this force would certainly encounter near the place proposed superior German armour and good German troops, by whom it would be accompanied on its inland excursion. When we see in Libya that it is only evenly, if evenly, that we fight with German armour, we must regard the stay on shore of the landed force as very hazardous and costly. The arrangements for bringing off the wounded would alone open up a vista of Q problems,[1] unless they are to be left where they fall virtually unattended.

---

[1] Q: Quartermaster (supply) problems.

3. However, all this is to be regarded as 'bait' to draw the German fighters into combat with British air fighter superiority. The idea is presumably that the German fighter Air Force will feel bound to face extermination rather than let British armoured units go as far as Lille or Amiens. Would they be wise to make this sacrifice? Surely, having regard to the great superiority which they possess in armour and ground troops compared to the force proposed, the farther they let them get into France and the more closely and deeply they let them become involved the better. They could therefore afford to use their Air Force with great restraint, avoiding action, and thus frustrating what they will divine was our main purpose.

4. Of course, if this were one of a dozen simultaneous operations of a similar kind, very different arguments would hold. Such large establishments might be built up and disturbances caused in France as to confront the enemy with a major danger and cause him to use his whole air power, or even to bring back squadrons from the East. But a single foray of this kind would not have that effect on the mind of the German General Headquarters, and, even if it did, as we are only staying a few days there would be no time for any movements to take place. In fact, the result on the fourth day, when our remnants returned to Britain à la Dunkirk, would be that everyone, friend and foe, would dilate on the difficulties of landing on a hostile shore. A whole set of inhibitions would grow up on our side prejudicial to effective action in 1943.

5. I would ask the Chiefs of the Staff to consider the following two principles:

(a) No substantial landing in France unless we are going to stay; and

(b) No substantial landing in France unless the Germans are demoralised by another failure against Russia.

It follows from the above that we should not delay or impede the preparations for 'Sledgehammer' for the sake of 'Imperator'; secondly, that we should not attempt 'Sledgehammer' unless the Germans are demoralised by ill-success against Russia; and, thirdly, that we should recognise that, if Russia is in dire straits, it would not help her for us to come a nasty cropper on our own.

6. It would seem wise that all preparations should go forward for 'Sledgehammer' on the largest scale possible at the dates mentioned, but that the launching of 'Sledgehammer' should be dependent not on a Russian failure, but on a Russian success and consequent proved German demoralisation in the West.

Winston S. Churchill to Lord Swinton[1]
(Churchill papers, 66/25)[2]

8 June 1942   10 Downing Street
Secret

THE MINISTER RESIDENT IN WEST AFRICA

You have been appointed Cabinet Minister Resident in West Africa. You will serve under, and report direct to, the War Cabinet, through its Secretary. The main purpose of the appointment will be to ensure the effective co-operation, in the prosecution of the war, of all Services, Civil and Military, in West Africa. For this purpose you will convene and preside over a War Council, the constitution of which will be a matter on which you will submit recommendations to His Majesty's Government.

2. On the Civil side you will work through the Governors and the existing organisation of the Governors' Conference, presiding over the latter when you think fit.

3. In the political sphere you will give broad political guidance to the Commanders-in-Chief. You will also take steps to maintain the best possible relations in the civil and military side with the Free French and Belgian authorities in West Africa and watch developments in Free French and Belgian territories. For this purpose His Majesty's Consuls-General at Leopoldville and Brazzaville and His Majesty's Consul at Duala will be instructed to send you copies of their reports. You will, however, bear in mind that both the Belgian Government and the Free French National Committee are extremely sensitive about any suggestion of British tutelage over their African territories and that they have insisted (and we have agreed) that all questions of policy, military, political or economic, shall be dealt with in London, where their central administrations are established, and that they leave very little latitude in these matters to

[1] Philip Cunliffe-Lister, 1884–1972. On active service, 1914–17 (Military Cross). Joint Secretary, Ministry of National Service, 1917–18. Conservative MP for Hendon, 1918–35. President of the Board of Trade, 1922–3, 1924–9, 1931. Secretary of State for the Colonies, 1931–5. Created Viscount Swinton, 1935. Secretary of State for Air, 1935–8 (when he advocated a larger Air Force expansion than the Government was prepared to accept). Brought back into Government on the outbreak of war as Chairman of the United Kingdom Commercial Corporation, responsible for pre-empting purchases of supplies and materials overseas that were needed by the German war machine. Appointed by Churchill in May 1940 to be Chairman of the Security Executive, concerned with measures against sabotage in Britain and overseas. Organized the supply route to the Soviet Union through the Persian Gulf, 1941–2. Cabinet Minister Resident in West Africa, 1942–4. Minister for Civil Aviation, 1944–5. Minister of Materials, 1951–2. Secretary of State for Commonwealth Relations, 1952–5. Created Earl of Swinton, 1955. His elder son died of wounds received in North Africa in 1943.

[2] Printed for the War Cabinet as War Cabinet Paper No. 245 of 1942.

their local colonial authorities. Similarly, you will take steps to ensure the prompt settlement of problems arising out of the ever-increasing interests of the United States in your sphere.

4. It will be your special duty to see that the resources and needs of all territories in your sphere are, so far as possible, dealt with as a whole, in order to ensure the most effective use of those resources for the war effort. You will pay particular attention to transportation questions.

5. You will also maintain contact with the Officers in your sphere engaged on propaganda, subversive and economic warfare, in order to ensure that these activities are conducted in harmony with general Government policy.

6. Your functions will also include the prompt settlement of matters within the policy of His Majesty's Government, more particularly where several authorities or Departments are concerned.

7. You will be fully informed of the approved policy of His Majesty's Government on all major issues affecting your responsibilities. If any question arises on which you require special guidance, you will, provided that there is time, refer the matter home. You will, in any case, report from time to time to His Majesty's Government and will receive their directions.

8. Your normal channel of communications will be through the Secretary of State for the Colonies. On Departmental matters your telegrams will, when necessary, be addressed to the Ministers concerned through that channel. You will also address personal telegrams to the Prime Minister and Minister of Defence on defence matters. In general, except where an immediate decision is required, you will consult the home authorities on any proposed action before it is taken if it is not clearly in accordance with approved or accepted policy. When on grounds of urgency you act on any important matter without prior consultation with London, you will report the circumstances as soon as possible.

9. Your sphere includes the following territories: Nigeria, the Gold Coast, Sierra Leone, the Gambia, Liberia, Fernando Po, and (subject to what is said in paragraph 3) French Equatorial Africa, the French Cameroons and the Belgian Congo. Your appointment does not, of course, in any way impair the existing responsibilities of the Commanders-in-Chief, the Governors, or His Majesty's Representatives in these territories, or their special relationships with their respective Departments at home, with whom they will continue to correspond direct.

10. You should submit to His Majesty's Government a recommendation as to your place of residence in West Africa. You should also report

as soon as possible on the above instructions, and on your requirements
of staff to implement them.

Winston S. Churchill to General Claude Auchinleck
(Churchill papers, 20/76)

9 June 1942
Most Secret and Personal

I have been continually thinking about your great battle and how we
can best sustain your army, so that it may be fought to a victorious end.
Here is some good news.

2. The 8th Armoured Division is now at the Cape and the 44th Division
is nearing Freetown. We have deliberately kept an option on the ultimate
destination of these divisions until we could see our way more clearly.

3. Some time ago I promised the Australian Government that if Australia were seriously invaded we should immediately divert both these
Divisions to their assistance. Australia up to date has not repeat not been
seriously invaded, and in view of the naval losses which Japanese have
sustained in the battles of the Coral Sea and off Midway Island,[1] we regard
a serious invasion in the near future as extremely improbable.

4. We were also prepared, though we have never promised Wavell, to
send both these Divisions to India if it looked as though the Japanese
had an invasion of India in mind. This also seems extremely improbable at the moment and India have already got the 2nd, 5th and 70th
British Divisions.

5. We have therefore decided, with the full agreement of the Chiefs
of Staff, that the 8th Armoured Division and the 44th Division should
be sent to you unless Australia is threatened with serious invasion within
the next few days. You may therefore make your plans for the battle on
the assumption that the 8th Armoured Division will reach Suez at the
end of June and the 44th Division by mid-July.

6. Thereafter, depending on the general situation then prevailing, you
should be prepared to send to India one of your Indian Divisions and

---

[1] In the Battle of Midway, fought between 4 and 7 June 1942, the United States won a decisive
victory over Japan. American cryptographers, who had broken the Japanese naval code, learned in
advance the date and location of the attack and the complete Japanese order of battle, enabling
the United States Navy to set up an ambush. All four Japanese aircraft carriers and a heavy cruiser
were sunk for the loss of one American aircraft carrier and one destroyer. Losses in manpower were
also disproportionate: 307 United States deaths and 3,057 Japanese deaths. After Midway, Japanese
shipbuilding and pilot-training programmes were unable to keep pace in replacing their losses while
the United States began steadily to increase its shipbuilding and pilot training.

the 252nd Indian Armoured Brigade. Pray let us have your proposals so that we may tell General Wavell.

7. A detailed account of the exact state of the 8th Armoured Division and of the technical preparedness of its tanks, together with the exact loading on the various ships and their dates of arrival, is being sent you separately. You can thus make the best possible plans for disembarking, organising and bringing it into action in the most effective manner with the least delay. We feel that with this rapidly approaching reserve behind you, you will be able to act with greater freedom in using your existing resources. All good wishes.

Anthony Eden: diary
('The Eden Memoirs, The Reckoning', page 330)

9 June 1942

Molotov and Maisky dined with Winston, Clem[1] and I also there. Long talk after dinner, mainly an explanation by W of second front problems. I think that this did much good. At least it helped to increase confidence. Party broke up after 1 am.

Winston S. Churchill to Sir James Grigg
(Churchill papers, 20/67)

10 June 1942

RE-EMPLOYMENT OF GENERAL CUNNINGHAM

Paragraph 4 of General Auchinleck's first letter of 25th November seems to me decisive. It was to this, I think, that Lyttelton[2] was referring when the matter was mentioned in Cabinet. I cannot myself see any reason for employing this officer again. You yourself admit that you would not employ him in a fighting Command.

Employment is not a right in the higher sphere and should be given on grounds of public interest, and not through kind-heartedness towards individuals.

A flow of promotion to the upper ranks is of the utmost importance, and in modern war battle casualties among British generals are rare.

However, if you wish to bring the matter up in Cabinet, you are very welcome to do so. The discussion was not completed last time, as you

[1] Clement Attlee.
[2] Oliver Lyttelton, the Minister of Production (since 12 March 1942).

wanted to find which was the letter to which Lyttelton referred. You may bring it up when Lyttelton returns, but to the War Cabinet only. My own view remains that the public interest does not require the employment of this officer and would not be served thereby.

Winston S. Churchill to Admiral of the Fleet Sir Dudley Pound
(Churchill papers, 20/67)

10 June 1942
Secret

ESTIMATED JAPANESE LOSSES IN THE BATTLE OF MIDWAY

The loss of these four aircraft carriers, &c., sensibly improves our position in the Indian Ocean and Bay of Bengal. For instance, Addu Atoll, which can only be attacked by seaborne aircraft, becomes pretty secure and is worthy of attention. There still remain shore-based aircraft at the Andamans, but these are not very numerous, and the distance is great from there to Colombo or Trincomalee. It seems to me that severe restraint is imposed upon the Japanese by their need to husband their large naval units. Perhaps you will consider what further instructions should be given to Admiral Somerville. General Wavell also should be informed.

PS – What about A/S[1] and A/Midget[2] nets and devices at Colombo and other harbours?

Winston S. Churchill to Anthony Eden
(Churchill papers, 20/67)

10 June 1942

CO-ORDINATION OF BRITAIN'S POLICY TOWARDS AUSTRIA
WITH UNITED STATES' POLICY

I do not propose to subject myself to any special inhibition about Austria. I certainly took forward to its liberation and thereafter to its re-establishment, either as a separate State or as the centre of a mid-Europe confederation.

---

[1] A/S: Anti-submarine.
[2] A/Midget: Anti-midget-submarine.

Oliver Harvey: diary
('The War Diaries of Oliver Harvey', pages 131–2)

10 June 1942

Molotov has pressed very hard for a Second Front in 1942. Roosevelt encouraged him to do so, although the whole burden this year must fall on us. PM very firm on the limitations of what was possible for us this year: he would not authorise any large-scale operation which didn't offer fair prospect of success, since a failure would not help Russia either. Roosevelt had calmly told Molotov he would be prepared to contemplate a sacrifice of 120,000 men if necessary – <u>our</u> men. PM said that he would not hear of it.

Sir Alexander Cadogan: diary
('The Diaries of Sir Alexander Cadogan', page 457)

10 June 1942

[. . .] at 7, to No. 10 for a farewell to the Russians. Broached a bottle of champagne of which I drank only a compulsory sip in a toast. Russians left just before 8. I said goodbye – A has got to see them off at Chedding-ton (in Buckinghamshire) at midnight! (Maisky made no bones about indicating to me that that was expected!). What savages! PM in quite good form – and in his rompers!

Winston S. Churchill to General Claude Auchinleck
(Churchill papers, 20/76)

11 June 1942
Personal and Secret

Many thanks for your facts and figures. They seem to me quite good. Although of course one hopes for success by manoeuvre or counter-stroke, nevertheless we have no reason to fear a prolonged <u>bataille d'usure</u>. This must wear down Rommel worse than Ritchie[1] because of our superior communications. More especially is this true in view of what is coming towards you as fast as ships can steam. Recovery work is most encouraging, and reflects credit on all concerned. Please give my compliments to Ritchie and tell how much his dogged and resolute fighting is admired by the vast audience which follows every move from day to day.

[1] General Neil Ritchie, Commander of the 8th Army.

General Claude Auchinleck to Winston S. Churchill
(Churchill papers, 20/89)

11 June 1942

Thank you very much for your most encouraging and understanding telegram of June 11.

Our losses have been heavy, and I am afraid in one engagement avoidably so, but, as you say, our resources are greater than his and his situation is not enviable.

I have passed your message to General Ritchie, who will, I know, be deeply gratified by it.

War Cabinet: Confidential Annex
(Cabinet papers, 65/30)

11 June 1942
11 a.m.

The Prime Minister gave the War Cabinet a general review of the state of planning in all theatres.

(1) Continental Operations.

The Prime Minister explained that he had made a most careful examination, in consultation with the Chiefs of Staff, of the action which we could take in 1942 and 1943 to help Russia.

As a result of this study, he had reached the conclusion, with which the Chiefs of Staff were in full agreement, that operations in 1942 should be governed by the following two principles:

(i) No substantial landing in France in 1942 unless we are going to stay: and

(ii) No substantial landing in France unless the Germans are demoralised by failure against Russia.

He had handed the previous evening an Aide Memoire (attached)[1] to M Molotov summarising the action which we proposed to take and this had been well received.

Broadly speaking, the operations divided themselves into three phases: first, the immediate future; next, what we could do in the Autumn of 1942 and finally, the operations for 1943.

(a) 'Rutter'.[2]

[1] Published here as the next document.

[2] Operation 'Rutter' (later Operation 'Jubilee'): a British and Canadian landing at Dieppe, planned in April 1942, for implementation at the end of June, and eventually carried out on 19 August 1942.

This would take place shortly. It was a 'butcher and bolt' raid on the Continent of about 24 hours' duration, employing some 6,000 to 7,000 men.

(b) 'Sledgehammer'.

This was a large scale operation employing six Divisions, or possibly more, if circumstances were favourable. The carrying out of this operation was entirely dependent on the situation on the Russian front, and was only considered to be practicable if German morale had started to crack. It would take two months to assemble the necessary shipping and September would be the last month in which it could be carried out, owing to weather conditions. It had been explained to M Molotov that a landing on the Continent this year which was doomed to failure, and resulted in another Dunkirk with considerable slaughter, would do nothing to help the Russians and would, moreover, prejudice the larger scale operations planned for 1943.

The Prime Minister emphasised that in his talks with the Russians he had not committed us in any way to do 'Sledgehammer'. The conditions in which he might undertake the operation had been clearly explained to and understood by them. In his own view, it seemed unlikely that these conditions would obtain, but it was clearly right that all preparations for the operation should go ahead.

In the ensuing discussion, there was general agreement

(a) That we should not attempt any major landing on the Continent this year, unless we intended to stay there.

(b) That all plans and preparations for 'Sledgehammer' should be pressed forward with the greatest vigour, on the understanding that the operation would not be launched, except in conditions which hold out a good prospect of success.

(c) That the Chiefs of Staff should have authority to ask for the necessary shipping to be taken up for 'Sledgehammer' on the 1st July, without further reference to the War Cabinet.

(c) 'Imperator'.

This operation had been planned as a large scale raid to follow 'Rutter'. The forces employed were to have amounted to one division and some armoured units, which were to remain in the Continent for three or four days. Their objective was to have taken Abbeville or Amiens, and it had been hoped to bring on an air battle in which we might subject the German Air Force to considerable wastage.

The Prime Minister said that he was strongly opposed to this operation. He had explained his views to the Chiefs of Staff and the latter had expressed their complete agreement with them. The operation had therefore been cancelled. This decision met with general approval as being in accordance with the policy set out under (b).

(d) 'Roundup'.[1]

This operation was one of grand conception involving an assault on the Continent employing no less than one million American troops, together with about twenty-one British Divisions, of which six or seven would be armoured. The enemy coast line would be assaulted in force at many points. There was no limit to the scope or objectives.

The operation would probably not be begun at the date contemplated in the original Marshall Plan, ie 1st April 1943. It was unlikely that the American forces would be trained in time. Some hold-up in training would be occasioned by the preparations for 'Sledgehammer,' and the weather would be much better a little later in the Spring. Moreover, by postponing the date of the assault from the 1st April to the 1st May, we should have by the later date, nearly 50 per cent. more landing craft available.

There was general agreement that 'Roundup' should not take place before the 1st May.

(e) Northern Norway.

The Prime Minister said that he had given much thought to an operation in Northern Norway. Clearly we could not do 'Sledgehammer' and a Norway operation at the same time. Nevertheless, as in his view it was unlikely that 'Sledgehammer' would take place, it was all the more important to give careful study to what could be done in this strategically important area in the far North. A firm foothold in Northern Norway would immensely increase the security of our Russian Convoys and would open the highway to the South and enable us to start to unroll Hitler's map of Europe from the top. The chief bar to action at the present time was the presence of a considerable German air force in Northern Norway which was menacing our sea communications round the North Cape to Russia. If we could get ashore and obtain the use of the aerodromes for ourselves, the tables would be turned.

Continuing, the Prime Minister thought we must not be unduly influenced by our experiences in the 1940 Norway campaign. Even then we had landed and re-embarked a considerable force with little or no Anti-Aircraft defences. A successful operation in Northern Norway would have great effect on opinion in Finland and Sweden. The Prime Minister asked the Chiefs of Staff to give the most earnest consideration to the possibility of a landing in Northern Norway on the broad lines that he had suggested.

[1] 'Roundup': plan for the liberation of France in 1943.

(f) 'Jackpot'.

The Prime Minister said that the Chiefs of Staff had now reconsidered the situation and were of the opinion that an occupation of 'Jackpot' was not essential for the protection of our convoys to Russia. He outlined the circumstances leading up to the present situation and explained that the survivors of Dr Sverdrup's[1] expedition were now prepared, provided they could obtain certain reinforcements, to evict a small German party now installed in one of the fiords. The proposal was that the Norwegians should provide this reinforcement.

It was reported that the Norwegians had not shown themselves very taken with this idea, and it had therefore been agreed that, if necessary, British volunteers should be called for to augment the Norwegian expedition. Every effort must be made to give the small force all necessary equipment, particularly LAA[2] guns.

(2) Middle East.

The Prime Minister read out to the War Cabinet a telegram which he had sent to General Auchinleck (OZ420 of 9/6) offering him the 8th Armoured and 44th British Divisions for the Middle East, and General Auchinleck's reply (CS/1230 of 10/6).

He mentioned that it had been suggested to the Commander-in-Chief, that, on the arrival of the 8th Armoured Division and 44th Division, he might send back to India one Indian division and an Indian armoured brigade. No final decision need, however, yet be taken on the latter movement.

The War Cabinet were informed that the question of sending one or possibly two more divisions to the Middle East after the 51st Division had left at the end of this month, was being considered. This could be done without any serious prejudice to 'Roundup'.

(3) Assistance to China.

The Prime Minister said that he had recently given much thought, in consultation with the Chiefs of Staff, to measures to assist China and, in particular, to the possibility of offensive operations in the late summer or autumn to re-open the supply line through Burma. There were now in India, or shortly would be, three entirely British Divisions.

---

[1] Otto Neumann Knoph Sverdrup (1854–1930), a Norwegian sailor and Arctic explorer. His fourth and last expedition had taken place in 1921.

[2] LAA: light anti-aircraft guns, a valued component of British fighting forces. In 1942 the 3rd LAA Battery formed part of the Rangoon Garrison until the British evacuated the city on 7 March 1942; it joined the fighting retreat of British forces in Burma, reaching India two months later.

Future allocation of troops to India would depend on whether the Russian Front held or broke. If the former, then more troops could be sent to General Wavell.

(4) Malta.

The Prime Minister said that General Marshall had now agreed that a force of about 20 American Liberators, which had been sent to the Middle East for a specific operation which was due to take place that day, could be used for attacking the Italian Battlefleet, if they should attempt to interfere with the Convoys Harpoon and Vigorous.[1] This was most satisfactory, particularly as the negotiations had been carried through on the Staff level and it had not been necessary to invoke the President's assistance.

The War Cabinet were informed of the general scope of Harpoon and Vigorous.

(5) 'Bolero'.

The Minister of Labour and National Service said that valuable time was being lost in making ready for the reception of the American forces in this country because the plans for their accommodation had not yet been settled. If advantage was to be taken of the fine weather and long hours of daylight, it was of great importance that the plans should be completed as a matter of urgency, so that the construction arrangements for the camps, etc., could proceed without further delay.

War Cabinet: aide-memoire
(Cabinet papers, 65/30)

11 June 1942

After a most thorough and comprehensive examination of all possible steps which we could take to draw the weight of Russia, we have reached the following conclusions:

(i) In accordance which our agreement, we will, to the best of our ability, continue to send supplies of aircraft, tanks and other war equipment to Russia by the hazardous Northern route and by the Persian route.

---

[1] Harpoon was a British supply convoy of six merchant ships, sailing from Gibraltar to Malta (5–15 June 1942). To divide German and Italian attention and offensive capability, it sailed at the same time as Vigorous, a supply convoy of 11 supply ships, sailing from Alexandria to Malta (11–16 June 1942). Harpoon reached Malta despite two of its destroyer escort being put out of action by Italian warships. Vigorous, after one cruiser and three destroyers of its escort had been sunk by German aircraft and Italian torpedo boats, was ordered by Admiral Harwood to return to Egypt.

(ii) In the air we are already containing in the various theatres of war about one half of the German fighter strength and one third of their bomber strength. With a view to forcing the Germans to make further withdrawals from their air strength in the East, we shall continue our bombing of German towns and industry, and also our day bomber and fighter offensive over Occupied France.

(iii) We have despatched, and will continue to despatch, considerable reinforcements to Libya, where we have confronting us 11 Axis Divisions, including two German Armoured Divisions and one German Motorised Division. We intend to keep the enemy fighting hard in this theatre. Malta has for the last four months contained considerable German air forces in Sicily. At one time they had over 400 first-line aircraft pounding the Island. We have sent, and will continue to send, large fighter reinforcements to keep the air battle going there.

(iv) We shall continue our policy of raids against selected points on the Continent. These raids will increase in size and scope as the summer goes on. By this means we are preventing the Germans from transferring any of their 33 Divisions in Western Europe to their Eastern front, and keeping them constantly on the alert, never knowing at what point the next attack may come.

(v) We are making preparations for a landing on the Continent in August or September 1942. As already explained, the main limiting factor to the size of the landing force is the availability of special landing craft. Clearly, however, it would not further either the Russian cause or that of the Allies as a whole if, for the sake of action at any price, we embarked on some operation which ended in disaster and gave the enemy an opportunity for glorification at our discomforture. It is impossible to say in advance whether the situation will be such as to make this operation feasible when the time comes. We can therefore give no promise in the matter, but, provided that it appears sound and sensible, we shall not hesitate to put our plans into effect.

(vi) We are prepared, if the idea appeals to the Russian Government, to send a force of 4 fighter and 2 fighter-bomber squadrons to Murmansk, with a view to releasing Russian air forces for operations on other parts of the Russian front. The British squadrons could arrive about the end of July. Does this project appeal to our friends?

(vii) Is the Russian Government still attaching any importance to a combined Russian–British operation in the Petsamo area, such as has been previously suggested? If so, we should be pleased to start conversations with the Russian Staff on this subject.

(viii) Finally, and most important of all, we are concentrating our maximum effort on the organisation and preparation of a large scale invasion of the Continent of Europe by British and American forces in 1943. We are setting no limit to the scope and objectives of this campaign, which will be carried out in the first instance by over a million men, British and American, with air forces of appropriate strength.

Winston S. Churchill to Oliver Lyttelton
(Churchill papers, 20/76)

11 June 1942
Personal

Your MS 14. It was not possible to come to grips with the Russians on the points you mention but relations have become much more intimate and we will do our best. The best opinion here does not anticipate any smooth or rapid advance for the Germans into the Caucasus. The Russians, though anxious, are in very good heart and the forces on either side seem well matched. You will, I am sure, be relieved by the new direction we have given to our reinforcements. All good wishes.

Winston S. Churchill to Field Marshal Jan Smuts
(Churchill papers, 20/76)

11 June 1942

I am repeating to you General Sturges' telegrams PO/65, 66, 67 and 68, in which he reports and comments on the proposals received from Vichy circles in Tananarive.

2. I must, in fairness to Sturges, explain that in sending his aide-mémoire to the Madagascan French Government he was acting in accord with instructions which I sent him (see my No. 1022 dated 4th June, paragraph 2). In the military sphere he has shown himself to be a resolute and resourceful commander.

3. We have instructed Platt[1] to proceed to Diego Suarez as soon as possible and thereafter to visit you with Sturges. We shall be grateful for your recommendations in regard to future action in Madagascar in the light of your consultation with them.

4. Meanwhile the position as we see it is as follows:

[1] General Officer Commanding-in-Chief, East African Command.

There are three possible courses:

(i) That we capture the whole of Madagascar;

(ii) that we remain in Diego Suarez and its vicinity and take our chance of mischief from the Vichy authorities, who will for their part be afraid of our attacking them; and

(iii) that we make terms with Vichy authorities.

5. The advantages of (i) are that we should clear up a potentially dangerous situation, that our action would have a vigorous aspect, and that we would have the valuable products of Madagascar at our disposal.

6. The disadvantages are that we have very pressing reasons for wishing to reduce to the minimum our continuing military commitments in Madagascar. Sturges estimates that after the capture of Tamatave and Majunga he would still require five Brigade Groups to garrison the whole island. This estimate is, of course, a matter of opinion. Such a commitment could not be met in view of the urgent requirements in other theatres. The capture of Tamatave and Majunga would involve the concentration of a fairly large naval force, including at least one aircraft carrier, and the reassembly of the assault shipping. The operation could not take place before the end of July.

7. The advantage of course (ii) is that we would have to use a minimum of troops. The disadvantage is that we would remain in a position of insecurity, with a possibility of Vichy making trouble for us with the help of the Japanese.

8. The advantages of course (iii) are that there would be less risk of our having to undertake a campaign, and that there would be a slight decrease in our insecurity at Diego Suarez. The disadvantages are that troops would be required for garrison purposes jointly with the French, that French officers and officials who take their orders from Vichy cannot be wholly trusted, and that our action would irritate or depress the Free French.

9. You will see from Sturges' telegram No. 67 that he has not succeeded in getting any indication of the Governor's view on his aide-mémoire or of Vichy's views. Nor is there any assurance that the French, who are responsible for the counter-proposals, are representative of the Tananarive authorities and that they have been authorised to speak for them. The suggested amendments brought back by Barnett[1] were, however, of a

---

[1] Barnett, the British man who arrived at Diego Suarez from Tananarive on 27 May 1942 stating that he had been asked by a member of the Governor of Madagascar's staff to try to find a basis of agreement between the Vichy Government and British forces which would safeguard the honour, sovereignty, and neutrality of the Madagascar Government and put an end to bloodshed.

precise nature and may have received official consideration. Sturges has pointed out that neither Annet[1] nor any responsible official will move without reference to Vichy, and past experience shows that we can expect little satisfaction by negotiation with Vichy. You probably noticed that the Tananarive radio on the 6th June denied that the Vichy authorities had any intention of negotiating and declared that previous contacts were only to exchange prisoners and collect information and wounded. None the less, in view of our imperative reasons for wishing to reduce to the minimum our continuing military commitments in Madagascar, we should have been disposed to regard the overtures made by Barnett as offering the basis for negotiation of a possible settlement had we been satisfied that they were prompted by the French Governor and authorities in the island.

Proposed additions as follows:

1. Agreement made with the French Commander at Diego Suarez regarding temporary military occupation recognised by French thereby putting an end to hostilities.

2. Madagascar to maintain attitude of resistance to all foreign attack from whatever quarter.

3. No sabotage by French of ports, factories, railways, &c.

4. Assurance regarding feeding population in Diego Suarez and exchange local products.

5. Uninterrupted communication between local Government and French Metropolitan Government regarding cables, wireless codes, &c.

6. Free seaborne traffic with France, control by approved organisation (Navicerts).[2]

7. Uninterrupted coastal traffic.

8. French administration to continue at Diego Suarez, including control of budget revenue and expenditure.

9. French forces continue role of defence and security.

10. Freedom of flight for French military and commercial aircraft except over Diego Suarez.

11. No British interference in police or courts or appointment officials. Comments.

---

[1] Armand Léon Annet, 1888–1973. Born in Paris. Governor of French Somaliland, 1935–7. Lieutenant-Governor of Dahomey, 1938–40. Vichy Governor-General of Madagascar from 1941 to 1942. Starting on 5 May 1942, he defended the island with about 8,000 troops. On 5 November 1942, Annet surrendered his remaining forces near Ihosy, on the south of the island. He died in Paris.

[2] Navicert: a document allowing a neutral ship to cross a blockade line in wartime.

I shall await your instructions before allowing Barnett to return, but hope you will give me latitude to keep door open for next stage. I consider this should be an intimation that so long as an accredited French official arrives with definite request to negotiate there are some hopes of agreement.

Barnett had no authority to consult Carter,[1] but I think I was right to do so. You may wish to use Carter now and to ask his intervention in <u>pourparlers</u> either at this stage or later. (?He is) reputed to be most sympathetic and helpful to British interests and told Barnett that our proposal formed ground agreement. I believe his co-operation would be valuable.

At the same time I recommend there should be no delay in sending Barnett back, and I therefore ask for immediate reply.

Winston S. Churchill to Alexis Leger[2]
(Churchill papers, 20/76)

11 June 1942
Personal and Secret

I wish you could see your way to accept General de Gaulle's invitation to join the Free French National Committee over here. I am sure your presence would be most serviceable to the common cause, and it would be a great pleasure to me to be working with you again. Great events are going to happen in France in the next twelve months. You must bear your part in them.

General Sir Alan Brooke: diary
('War Diaries, Field Marshal Lord Alanbrooke', page 264)

11 June 1942

PM in good form and carried Cabinet with him in his proposed policy that we do not land in France in strength except to stop there, and we do not go there unless German morale is deteriorating.

---

[1] James Garneth Carter, 1877–1949. Born in Brunswick. Glynn County, Georgia. Merchant tailor; letter carrier; newspaper manager. US Consul in Tamatave, 1906–16; Tananarive, 1916–27; Calais, 1927–40; Bordeaux, 1940. US Consul General in Tananarive, 1941–2.

[2] (Marie-René) Alexis Leger (pseudonyms, as writer and poet: St-John Perse and Saint-Leger Leger), 1887–1975. Joined the French Foreign Service, 1914. Chef de Cabinet, Ministry of Foreign Affairs, Paris, 1925–32. Honorary knighthood, 1927. Secretary General, Ministry of Foreign Affairs, Paris, 1933–40. Left France for the United States, 1940. Consultant on French Literature, Library of Congress, 1941–5. Nobel Prize in Literature, 1960.

Winston S. Churchill to General Archibald Wavell
(Churchill papers, 20/76)

12 June 1942
Secret and Personal

Your No 13968/C. COS Committee are working at your affairs but meanwhile the following is purely personal from me and is not in any sense a directive:

Your paragraph 2. All these minor operations are very nice and useful nibbling. What I am interested in is the capture of Rangoon and Moulmein and, thereafter, striking at Bangkok. For this we should first have to fight our way along the coast amphibiously from Chittagong via Akyab, and at the right time launch an overseas expedition of forty or fifty thousand of our best British troops with suitable armour across the northern part of the Bay of Bengal. The object of this would be to carry the war back into Southern Burma and Malaya, and strike at the Japanese communications passing northwards into Southern China. This would be seizing the initiative and making the enemy conform instead of being, through no fault of your own, like clay in the hands of the potter. It would be war on a large scale, and the movement of reserves from Britain would be regulated accordingly. For anything like this I could leave you Alexander.

2. There would be no possibility of any large operation if the Russian southern front is beaten in and the Caucasus, &c., are overrun, or if Auchinleck were beaten back by Rommel. No large offensive from India is possible unless all goes well in both these theatres.

3. The Japanese naval losses, particularly in aircraft carriers, are severe, and they now have to count their capital units on their fingers. This will impose increasing caution upon their navy. Reports indicate recent movement of 250 aircraft back from Malaya, &c., northwards towards Manchuria and Japan itself. This also shows strain. Its significance is enhanced by the reinforcement of Japanese army opposite Russia by four divisions in the last three months, reducing Japanese divisions in Japan to only six. If Russia stumbles in the west, Japan will no doubt fall upon her in Siberia. Meanwhile, as I have repeatedly pointed out, the most natural, prudent and fruitful course for Japan is to press on against Chiang Kai-shek.

4. In thinking over the large offensive from India which I have mentioned, you should assume that the Fleet and the Air Force would be

used with resolution in your support, and that the necessary tackle would be provided. Let me know how you stand in relation to these ideas.[1]

President Franklin D. Roosevelt to Winston S. Churchill
(Churchill papers, 20/76)

12 June 1942

Grand. The quicker the better including the receiver's wife.[2]

Roosevelt

Winston S. Churchill to General Hastings Ismay,
for the Chiefs of Staff Committee
(Churchill papers, 20/67)

13 June 1942   Chequers

The following note on 'Jupiter' should be read by the Planning Committee in conjunction with my previous paper on the subject. The Planners should set themselves to making a positive plan and overcoming the many difficulties, and not concern themselves with judging whether the operation is desirable or not, which must be decided by higher authority.

General Macfarlane[3] should be consulted by the Planners, and it is possible Russian troops might be used to come in behind a British high-class landing force.

I must have a preliminary report by next Tuesday.

---

[1] In his reply to Churchill on 14 June 1942, Wavell wrote: 'We can now begin definitely to plan recapture of Burma which has been in my mind ever since it became obvious that I was likely to lose it. In view of limited resources likely to be at my disposal I initiated as first stage plans for reoccupation of Upper Burma.' He also wrote: 'I consider I have enough troops now to initiate operations against both Upper and Lower Burma but further reserves would be required to exploit success. I am however very far from satisfied with state of training of troops and all Indian formations require about another six months training. British formations require acclimatisation and specialised training' ('Secret and Personal', *Churchill papers, 20/76*).

[2] This is a reply to Churchill's suggestion that he visit Roosevelt. He departed on June 17, returning on June 26. Mrs Churchill did not accompany him.

[3] General Mason-MacFarlane, Head of British Military Mission to Moscow, 1941–2.

Winston S. Churchill: note
(Churchill papers, 20/67)

13 June 1942　　　　　　　　　　　　　　　　　　Chequers

OPERATION 'JUPITER'

There are two important differences between 'Imperator' and 'Jupiter.'
First, in 'Jupiter' we can certainly bring superior forces to bear at the point
of attack and in the whole region invaded; secondly, if successful, we get
a permanent footing on the Continent of constant value to the passage
of our convoys and capable of almost indefinite exploitation southwards.
In fact, we could begin to roll the map of Hitler's Europe down from the
top. Once we have established ourselves with growing air power in the
two main airfields, we can attack by parachute and other means under air
cover the airfields to the southward and make ourselves masters of this
northern region, so that with the Spring of 1943 other landings could be
made, Tromso and Narvik taken, then Bodo and Mo, by combinations
of seaborne landings under shore-based air. No great mass of the enemy
could be brought to bear upon them, except by inordinate efforts over
bad communications. The population would rise to aid us as we advanced,
and only as we advanced. All this would be a convenient prelude and
accompaniment to 'Round-up'. The distraction caused to the enemy's
movements would far exceed the employment of our own resources. The
reactions upon Sweden and Finland might be highly beneficial. Here
is the best way of acting in the autumn of this year as an alternative to
'Sledgehammer' if we judge that the Germans in France are not by then
sufficiently demoralized for us to take the plunge.

2. It has come to be accepted by us as an axiom that it is impossible to
land anywhere against opposition, including air opposition, however limited, without superior air strength. This is a hard saying, which limits all
use of sea power to the very small portions of the French coast which are
under home-based fighter protection, and consequently to those points
on the enemy's coasts where his best troops are concentrated and in the
highest state of readiness. Without in any way disputing the desirability
of having superior air power and fighter cover, it may be questioned
whether it is indispensable if the objective is of sufficient value and there
is no other way. The lessons of the Norwegian campaign in the Spring of
1940 must not be overstressed. We had practically no anti-aircraft artillery and we exposed many scores of vessels for a month to the enemy's
air attack without any compensating air defence. There were scarcely a
dozen anti-aircraft guns available to us on shore. We landed over 20,000
men at Namsos and Andelsnes and brought them off again without undue

loss, and the reason we came off was as much the military strength of the enemy as his air power. It is not intended to press this argument too far, but there is no doubt that even merchant ships which have very powerful Oerlikon[1] and other flak defence can, for a while and for an adequate need, carry out an operation without total destruction. The last Russian convoy was attacked continuously for four or five days with a loss of 20 per cent. It is a question whether it is better to land without fighter cover at a point where the enemy are very weak in armour and troops, or with fighter cover at a point where the enemy are very strong in armour and ground troops. It is a question of emphasis and proportion.

3. Lately Mid-East Command gave us detailed calculations of the number of sorties likely to be expected against 'Vigorous'.[2] The estimate may be right or wrong, but it is, anyhow, the way to look at these problems. They must be faced in detail instead of our bowing to a general taboo. Let us take September or October and examine the number of sorties possible by the German Air Force at Murmansk and Petsamo against an expedition of, say, forty ships with escort which was approaching the coast. The armada would probably be sighted at dawn of D, minus one, and would have to make the final approach during the dark hours of that day, assaulting before dawn of Day 0. The protection of the armada during the daylight advance would be by four or five auxiliary aircraft carriers, and every ship would have six or seven Oerlikons or other flak on their decks. The protection at the moment of landing and of the ships when anchored or beached would be by six or seven beach defence ships with their trained floating flak. These would also take part in the protection during the approach. Similarly, the flak of the transports would be used in their own defence on arrival. With all this, it seems unlikely that more than one-fifth or one-sixth of the transports and covering craft would be sunk. A military attack is not ruled out simply because a fifth of the soldiers may be shot on the way, provided the others get there and do the job.

---

[1] Oerlikon: the Oerlikon 20mm cannon, designed in Germany at the beginning of the First World War, and used in both world wars. It had a rate of fire of 300 rounds a minute. In 1924, following the restrictions on German arms manufacturing in the Treaty of Versailles, the Oerlikon firm, named after the Zurich suburb in which was based, acquired all rights to the weapon, plus the manufacturing equipment and the employees of the German firm that had manufactured it hitherto. Second World War versions had an effective range against low-flying aircraft (high explosive rounds) of 1,600 yards. A few weeks before the fall of France, the Oerlikon factory approved manufacture of their gun in the United Kingdom, under licence. The Royal Navy managed to smuggle out the necessary drawings and documents from Zurich. The production of the first British-made Oerlikon guns started in Ruislip, at the end of 1940; the first guns were delivered to the Royal Navy in spring 1941. From 1942, Oerlikon guns were used on United States Navy ships.

[2] Vigorous: The British supply convoy to Malta from Alexandria (11–16 June 1942).

4. Naturally, during the approach, British and/or Russian forces from Murmansk would heavily attack any enemy airfields within range, and this should further minimize the losses of the armada.

5. The business of landing and assaulting and of capturing the airfields and other key-points is a matter for Combined Operations, and need not be touched upon here.

6. It is intended at the moment that the transports carrying the troops should also carry a large part of their stores, and should also serve as the habitations and bases of the troops, in so far as these cannot be found ashore. It is essential that the expedition should be self-contained for three months, so that the Navy is liberated from all need of convoys. Let me have calculations as to the strength of the forces required, say, 25,000 men of high quality; of the number of ships required to carry them; of the most convenient size of the said ships; and of the quantity of stores which they would have to carry for the three months' reserves. Also, whether it would be better to send them altogether in one armada, or wait till the first lot have made a landing and then send a second wave.

7. As soon as the airfields are in our hands, our fighter aircraft from Murmansk must occupy them. This may have to begin before our own flak is in position. We have to fight our way into the air as well as on to the shore. But special arrangements to bring portable flak to the airfields at the earliest moment would be necessary. Three batteries of mobile or portable Bofors would be needed for each airfield, and these should be in position in the first two days. The heavier flak should come in as soon as possible. As we should only have two airfields to work from at the beginning, it is essential that these should bristle with guns.

8. As soon as the airfields are established with flak and fighter protection, the heavy bombers would be flown from Scotland and would operate from these airfields against the enemy airfields to the south.

Winston S. Churchill to President Franklin D. Roosevelt
(Churchill papers, 20/76)

13 June 1942   Chequers
Personal and Secret

Very many thanks for your No. 156. I had a long talk with Mountbatten last night and, in view of the impossibility of dealing with correspondence with all the many difficult points outstanding, I feel it is my duty to come to see you. I shall hold myself ready to start as weather serves from Thursday 18th onwards and will advise you later. I shall bring CIGS, General Brooke, whom you have not yet met, with me, also General Ismay. My own personal group will be: Tommy[1] and John Martin.[2] Colonel White[3] thanks you very much for the invitation, by which she is complimented, but thinks she had better stay here on account of her Russian Fund.

Please let plan be secret till we arrive.

This is the moment for me to send you my heartiest congratulations on the grand American victories in the Pacific, which have very decidedly altered the balance of the naval war.

All good wishes to you and friends.

Winston S. Churchill to General Claude Auchinleck
(Churchill papers, 20/76)

13 June 1942   Chequers
Personal and Most Secret

Your decision to fight it out to the end most cordially endorsed. We shall sustain you whatever the result. Retreat would be fatal. This is a business not only of armour but of will power. God bless you all.

John Martin: diary
(Sir John Martin papers)

14 June 1942   Chequers

Last night we had the film about *The Young Mr Pitt*.[4] Interesting resemblances with the present.

---

[1] Charles Ralfe 'Tommy' Thompson, Churchill's Naval ADC and Personal Assistant as Minister of Defence.

[2] Churchill's Principal Private Secretary.

[3] Clementine Churchill's codename.

[4] Directed by Carol Reed: the story of Pitt the Younger, who became Prime Minister at the age of 24. Pitt was played by Robert Donat, his political rival, Charles James Fox, by Robert Morley, and Napoleon by Herbert Lom. It was formally released on 21 September 1942.

Winston S. Churchill: message[1]
('The Times', 15 June 1942)

14 June 1942

UNITED NATIONS DAY CEREMONY, LONDON

In a Proclamation to the people of the United States our great friend, President Franklin D. Roosevelt, has reminded them that for many years it has been the American custom to set aside June 14 in honour of their flag, the emblem of their freedom, their strength, and their unity as an independent nation under God. He has told them that as a nation they are fighting not alone, but shoulder to shoulder with the valiant peoples of the United Nations, the massed angered forces of common humanity, and he has asked them that on their Flag Day, June 14, they should honour not only their own Colours but also the flags, and, through the flags, the peoples of the United Nations.

Outside the United Kingdom these are the peoples whose names today make up the great Roll of Honour. The United States of America, the Union of Soviet Socialist Republics, China, Australia, Belgium, Canada, Costa Rica, Cuba, Czechoslovakia, the Dominican Republic, El Salvador, Free France, Greece, Guatemala, Haiti, Honduras, India, Luxembourg, Mexico, the Netherlands, New Zealand, Nicaragua, Norway, Panama, Poland, the Union of South Africa and Yugoslavia.

I join my voice to his in honouring today the forces of the United Nations. Let us pay this tribute to the valour and sacrifice of those who have fallen and to the courage and endurance of those who fight today. Let us remember every one, man, woman and child, who in the oppressed and tortured countries works for the day of liberation that is coming.

In this ceremony we pledge to each other not merely support and succour till victory comes, but that wider understanding, that quickened sense of human sympathy, that recognition of the common purpose of humanity without which the suffering and striving of the United Nations would not achieve its full reward.

---

[1] United Nations Day, 14 June 1942, was marked by a ceremony in front of Buckingham Palace, where this message from Churchill was read out.

Winston S. Churchill to Anthony Eden
(Churchill papers, 20/67)

14 June 1942
Secret

I only circulated my paper because you seemed to be giving considerable currency to various French documents not of very high authority but tending to work up an extra hate against Vichy and renewed enthusiasm for de Gaulle. I was anxious that the Cabinet should not become unduly biased by what is such an easy and popular case to state.

2. For thirty-five years I have been a friend of France, and have always kept as closely in touch as possible with the French people. I therefore have a certain instinct about them on which I rely. It is very easy to make the kind of case you have set down out of all the shameful things the Vichy Government have said. But this does not make sufficient allowance for the unnatural conditions prevailing in a defeated country with a Government living on the sufferance of the enemy. It does not alter in any way my wish or extinguish my hope to have the French Fleet sail to Africa, and to get an invitation for British or American troops to enter French North Africa. Nor does it alter the fact that, at any rate, for some time to come, Vichy is the only party who can offer these good gifts. At a certain stage it will not only be in their interests to offer them, but their lives may depend upon it. President Roosevelt has the same feeling as I have about all this, and so, I believe, have the Chiefs of Staff. The position is so anomalous and monstrous that very clear-cut views, such as you are developing, do not altogether cover it. There is much more in British policy towards France than abusing Pétain and backing de Gaulle.

3. I do not think there are any serious differences between us, but rather a shade of emphasis. Certainly circulate your paper if you wish to have the matter thrashed out in Cabinet. I will weigh in with de Gaulle's 'traitor' telegram,[1] which I think will convince most people that he had better stay here in England under our control. Imagine what he would do if free to fulminate from Brazzaville.

---

[1] On 10 June 1942 General de Gaulle wrote to two members of his staff, Generals Eboué and Leclerc, expressing his mistrust of British and American 'imperialist' plans and his plans to benefit from the inevitable capitulation of the 'Anglo-Saxon' powers.

Winston S. Churchill to L. S. Amery
(Churchill papers, 20/67)

14 June 1942
Secret

If Gandhi tries to start a really hostile movement against us in this crisis, I am of opinion that he should be arrested, and that both British and United States opinion would support such a step. If he likes to starve himself to death, we cannot help that.[1]

I think you should mention the matter to the Cabinet tomorrow (Monday) at our principal weekly meeting.

Winston S. Churchill to Sir John Anderson
(Churchill papers, 20/67)

14 June 1942

REPAIR OF DAMAGED HOUSES

Your minute does not altogether meet the need as I see it. If by the expenditure of fifteen or sixteen million pounds we can get 158,000 new serviceable houses, we shall be in a far better position to cope with the movement consequent upon the great influx that is to be expected from the United States, and it would be very cheap in money and labour at the price. I am astonished that more has not been done already.

2. The return of Government Departments to London should also be emphasized. To what extent are evacuated children coming back? They are in no more danger in London, where the defences are so strong, than in the country.

Winston S. Churchill to Anthony Eden
(Churchill papers, 20/67)

14 June 1942
Secret

I am asking the Chief of the Air Staff and Bomber Command to consider bombing two, or perhaps even three, villages in Germany as a reprisal for the cruel obliteration of the Czech village of Lidice.[2]

---

[1] Gandhi made several statements to the press in late May and early June 1942 hinting at his plans to start 'something' soon in India that 'may be very big if the Congress and people are with me'. This would be the 'Quit India' movement, launched in August 1942. On several occasions Gandhi engaged in hunger strikes as a way of protesting against British rule in India.

[2] One of several SS reprisal actions for the assassination of Reinhart Heydrich, Protector of Bohemia and Moravia. The War Cabinet minutes for 15 June 1942 note: 'Reference was made to the action

As you are the keeper of our conscience on these matters, perhaps you will let me know before tomorrow's Cabinet what you think.

Winston S. Churchill to General Claude Auchinleck
(Churchill papers, 20/76)

14 June 1942
Personal and Secret

Your No. CS/1248, Para 2. To what position does Ritchie want to withdraw the Gazala troops? Presume there is no serious question in any case of giving up Tobruk. As long as Tobruk is held no serious enemy advance into Egypt is possible. We went through all this in April 1941. Do not understand what you mean by withdrawing to 'old frontier'.

2. Am very glad you are bringing New Zealand Division into the Western Desert. Let me know dates when it can be deployed, and where.

3. CIGS agrees with all this. Please keep us informed.

Winston S. Churchill to Baron de Cartier de Marchienne[1]
(Churchill papers, 20/53)

14 June 1942
My dear Ambassador,

With your letter of May 14 you were kind enough to send me a Note urging that permission be granted for the despatch through the blockade of vitamins and milk products for children and expectant mothers in Belgium.

My colleagues and I have given very close and sympathetic consideration to this proposal, particularly as we well understand the importance which the Belgian Government attach to it; but, with great regret, I must inform you that we do not feel able at this stage to modify our blockade policy in the manner you suggest.

of the Germans in destroying the whole of the village of Lidice in Czechoslovakia, the men being killed and the women and children taken away. The question was raised whether, as an act of counter-retaliation, we should destroy a number of German villages by air attack. The main point made in discussion was that such action could only be carried out effectively by a considerable number of aeroplanes, on a clear moonlight night. Action on the lines suggested would therefore mean the use of forces which would otherwise be employed against objectives of greater importance. The War Cabinet decided that this suggestion should not be followed up' ('War Cabinet: Conclusions', 15 June 1942, 5.30 p.m., *Cabinet papers, 65/26*).

[1] Emile-Ernest de Cartier de Marchienne, 1871–1946. Entered the Belgian Diplomatic Service, 1892. Minister to China, 1910; to the United States, 1917. Ambassador to the United States, 1920. Ambassador to Britain, 1927–46. Honorary knighthood, 1934.

You will, I am sure, agree that our policy has to be determined by the best interests of our allies and ourselves, and by our common resolve to defeat the enemy as rapidly as possible. I am only too well aware of the suffering caused in Belgium and elsewhere by the German occupation; but as you know, we cannot permit the enemy to draw any contribution from outside towards the maintenance of the occupied countries as a source of strength to his war machine, nor can we admit his claim to transfer to the United Nations the task of feeding them. By her acts of aggression against Belgium and other countries Germany has made herself responsible for supplying them; and I am sure that it is in the interests of none of us to weaken this principle by any concession which could postpone, even for a single day, our common victory.

Yours v. sincerely,
Winston S. Churchill

Winston S. Churchill to Lord Beaverbrook
(Churchill papers, 20/53)

14 June 1942

My dear Max,

The fact that Mr Driberg[1] and Mr Frank Owen[2] are standing as Independent candidates in two by-elections will of course be taken by everyone as indicating that you are running election candidates against the Government. This would be a great pity from many points of view.

Yours ever,
W

---

[1] Thomas Edward Neil Driberg, 1905–76. Educated at Lancing College and Christ Church, Oxford. Joined the Communist Party when he was 15. From 1928, worked on the *Daily Express*, where he became the widely read columnist 'William Hickey'. In the 1942 by-election he took the previously Conservative-held seat of Maldon, defeating the Conservative candidate by 12,219 votes to 6,226. Labour MP for Maldon, 1942–59; for Barking, 1959–74. Expelled from the Communist Party, 1941. Took the Labour Whip, 1945. Television and radio critic, *New Statesman*, 1955–61. Chairman of the Labour Party, 1957. Select Preacher before the University of Oxford, 1965. Created Baron Bradwell shortly before his death. In his autobiography, *Ruling Passions*, published the year after his death, he described the three passions that drove his life: his homosexuality, his left-wing political beliefs, and his allegiance to the High Church wing of the Church of England.

[2] (Humphrey) Frank Owen, 1905–79. Journalist, author, and broadcaster. Liberal MP for Hereford, 1929–31. Writer on the *Daily Express*, 1931–7. Editor, *Evening Standard*, 1938–41. Unsuccessful Parliamentary candidate, 1942. Served with the Royal Armoured Corps, 1942–3; South-East Asia Command, 1944–6 (Lieutenant-Colonel, OBE). In 1946 he published *The Campaign in Burma*. Editor, *Daily Mail*, 1947–50.

Winston S. Churchill to President Franklin D. Roosevelt
(Churchill papers, 20/53)

14 June 1942

My dear Mr President,

For a long time I have watched with grateful admiration the vast stream of gifts which from the first days of the War has been flowing from America to Great Britain for the relief of suffering and the succour of distress, and in a volume which has barely lessened as a result of the advent of war to America, though a considerable diminution of it was well to be expected. The generosity of these gifts, each one of which represents a personal sacrifice by an individual, is overwhelming and without precedent. I am therefore anxious in the first place to express to you, Mr President, the profound gratitude of the British people, and shall be glad if there is some way in which you may see fit to pass my feelings along to the American public.

My second purpose in addressing you today is unhappily one of informing you that we now feel under the necessity of asking that this brotherly flow of material shall be diminished. It is not that the gifts are not desired – indeed they have constantly been ingeniously devised to meet our real needs and the parcels from America have become a familiar and welcome feature in all the misfortunes which have overtaken our civilian population. The request which I am now compelled to make is due to additional demands on shipping resulting from the enormously increased flow of war materials for which ocean transport has to be provided. We shall have therefore to assign to goods of a more warlike character the shipping space which has hitherto been available for the relief of our people – a sacrifice which we will make here without complaint, but not without very great regret.

As to the method of procedure, we have a Committee here – the American Gifts Committee – which hitherto has endeavoured to ensure that gifts from America shall only be of a character that shall meet some real need. The Committee will now have to extend its activities and try to control the actual volume of gifts. A statement will shortly be issued to the press indicating the lines along which it is hoped to proceed.

I cannot conclude this letter, Mr President, without affirming once again our gratitude for the comfort in days of suffering and of trial that was brought to us by the people of America, and our desire to make known our thanks.

Yours v sincerely,
Winston S. Churchill

Winston S. Churchill to Admiral of the Fleet Sir Dudley Pound
(Churchill papers, 20/67)

14 June 1942
Secret

Let me have a report about the sinkings in the Mozambique Channel.[1] Where are the Japanese submarines or U-boats based, and what measures are you proposing?

General Sir Alan Brooke: diary
('War Diaries, Field Marshal Lord Alanbrooke', page 265)

14 June 1942

A Sunday disturbed by many calls from the PM who was much disturbed at bad turn taken by operations in the Middle East. Rommel certainly seems to be getting the better of Ritchie and to be out generalling him.

Winston S. Churchill to General Hastings Ismay,
for the Chiefs of Staff Committee
(Churchill papers, 20/67)

15 June 1942

MURMANSK

It looks very much as if the Germans were preparing for a sea-borne and air-borne attack on Murmansk. The steady movement of tank-landing craft up the coast of Norway and the recent visit of Hitler to General Mannerheim are among recent indications. What are we going to do about this, and what are the Russians going to do? All this bears on 'Jupiter.'[2]

---

[1] On 12 June 1942 the *Mercury* newspaper (Hobart, Tasmania) reported a message from Lourenço Marques, in Portuguese East Africa, that 'three freighters sunk by torpedo in the Mozambique Channel recently were British, Czech and Greek. The Czech boat, from which 20 members of the crew were later picked up, was said to have been 180 miles from Beira. No survivors have been picked up from the other ships. Portuguese rescue planes sighted the submarine, which was not identified, but was presumed to be Japanese.'

[2] German activity elsewhere in the Soviet Union was also under scrutiny at this time. 'The Germans had started a definite offensive in the Kharkov area and claimed to have crossed the Donetz River. The Russians claimed to have knocked out 250 German tanks. There were indications of a German

Winston S. Churchill to General Hastings Ismay
(Churchill papers, 20/67)

15 June 1942

[...]

2. The preparations of 'Sledgehammer' and 'Round-up' should be separated from Commander-in-Chief, Home Forces. He has enough to do in other directions. Pray show me how this can be achieved.

Winston S. Churchill: memorandum
(Churchill papers, 20/67)

15 June 1942
Most Secret
OPERATION 'ROUND-UP'

For such an operation, the qualities of magnitude, simultaneity and violence are required. The enemy cannot be ready everywhere. At least six heavy disembarkations must be attempted in the first wave. The enemy should be further mystified by at least half a dozen feints which, if luck favours them, may be exploited. The limited and numerically inferior Air Force of the enemy will thus be dispersed or fully occupied. While intense fighting is in progress at one or two points, a virtual walk-over may be obtained at others.

2. The second wave nourishes the landings effected, and presses where the going is good. The fluidity of attack from the sea enables wide options to be exercised in the second wave.

3. It is hoped that 'Jupiter' will be already in progress. Landings or feints should be planned in Denmark, in Holland, in Belgium, at the Pas de Calais where the major air battle will be fought, on the Cotentin Peninsula, at Brest, at St. Nazaire, at the mouth of the Gironde.

4. The first objective is to get ashore in large numbers. At least ten armoured brigades should go in the first wave. These brigades must accept very high risks in their task of pressing on deeply inland, rousing the populations, deranging the enemy's communications, and spreading the fighting over the widest possible areas.

5. Behind the confusion and disorder which these incursions will create, the second wave will be launched. This should aim at making

offensive in the Kursk sector. The Germans appeared to be suffering heavy casualties in their attack on Sebastopol' (War Cabinet: Conclusions, 15 June 1942 at 5.30 p.m., *Cabinet papers, 65/26*).

definite concentrations of armour and motorised troops at strategic points carefully selected. If four or five of these desirable points have been chosen beforehand, concentrations at perhaps three of them might be achieved, relations between them established, and the plan of battle could then take shape.

6. If forces are used on the above scale, the enemy should be so disturbed as to require at least a week to organise other than local counter-strokes. During that week a superior fighter air force must be installed upon captured airfields, and the command of the air, hitherto fought for over the Pas de Calais, must become general. The RAF must study, as an essential element for its success, the rapid occupation and exploitation of the captured airfields. In the first instance these can only be used as refuelling grounds, as the supreme object is to get into the air at the earliest moment. Altogether abnormal wastage must be expected in this first phase. The landing and installation of the flak at the utmost speed is a matter of high consequence, each airfield being a study of its own.

7. While these operations are taking place in the interior of the country assaulted, the seizure of at least four important ports must be accomplished. For this purpose at least ten brigades of infantry, partly pedal-cyclists, but all specially trained in house-to-house fighting, must be used. Here again the cost in men and material must be rated very high.

8. To ensure success, the whole of the above operations, simultaneous or successive, should be accomplished within a week of Zero, by which time not less than 400,000 men should be ashore and busy.

9. The moment any port is gained and open, the third wave of attack should start. This will be carried from our Western ports in large ships. It should comprise not less than 300,000 infantry with their own artillery plus part of that belonging to the earlier-landed formations. The first and second waves are essentially assaulting forces, and it is not till the third wave that the formations should be handled in terms of divisions and corps. If by Zero 14, 700,000 men are ashore, if air supremacy has been gained, if the enemy is in considerable confusion, and if we hold at least four workable ports, we shall have got our claws well into the job.

10. The phase of sudden violence irrespective of losses being over, the further course of the campaign may follow the normal and conventional lines of organisation and supply. It then becomes a matter of reinforcement and concerted movement. Fronts will have developed, and orderly progress will be possible. Unless we are prepared to commit the immense forces comprised in the first three waves to a hostile shore with the certainty that many of our attacks will miscarry, and that if we fail the whole

stake will be lost, we ought not to attempt such an extraordinary operation of war under modern conditions.

11. The object of the above notes is to give an idea of the scale and spirit in which alone they can be undertaken with good prospects of success.

Winston S. Churchill to Air Chief Marshal Sir Charles Portal
(Churchill papers, 20/67)

15 June 1942
Secret

In conversation with Air Marshal Harris, on Saturday last, I learned with pleasure that he is keen upon using the June moon for another edition of 'Arabian Nights'.[1] I hope you will approve of this, unless there is some very serious reason to the contrary.

Meanwhile, I have asked the Admiralty to make sure that they do not prevent Coastal Command from playing its part. I understand Joubert[2] had 250 machines ready, but that the Admiralty stopped their use.

Pray let me know if I can assist you.

Winston S. Churchill to General Claude Auchinleck
(Churchill papers, 20/76)

15 June 1942
Personal and Secret

We are glad to have your assurance that you have no intention of giving up Tobruk. War Cabinet interpret paragraph 1(b) of your telegram to mean that, if the need arises, General Ritchie would leave as many troops in Tobruk as are necessary to hold the place for certain.

---

[1] Arabian Nights: the 'Thousand Bomber' raids.

[2] Philip Bennet Joubert de la Ferté, 1887–1965. Educated at Harrow and Woolwich. Royal Field Artillery, 1907. Royal Flying Corps, 1913. On active service, as a pilot, in France, Egypt, and Italy, 1914–18 (DSO, despatches six times). Transferred to the Royal Air Force, April 1918. Lieutenant-Colonel Commanding the Royal Air Force in Italy, 1918. Air Officer Commanding No. 35 Group, 1929. Commandant, RAF Staff College, Andover, 1930. Air Officer Commanding No. 11 Group, 1936. Air Officer Commanding-in-Chief, Coastal Command, 1936–7. Officer Commanding Royal Air Force, India, 1937–9. Knighted, 1938. Assistant Chief of the Air Staff, 1930–41. Air Chief Marshal, 1941. Officer Commanding-in-Chief, Coastal Command, 1941–3; introduced Planned Flying and Maintenance and a torpedo-carrying version of the Beaufighter. Inspector General, Royal Air Force, 1943. Deputy Chief of Staff for Information and Civil Affairs, South East Asia Command, 1943–5. Director of Public Relations, Air Ministry, 1946–7. Published *The Fated Sky: An Autobiography* in 1952.

George Harvie-Watt to Winston S. Churchill
(Churchill papers, 20/55)

15 June 1942

You may be interested to know that Winterton[1] has seen Baldwin recently and Baldwin had said 'If you ever have a chance of a chat with Winston, tell him he has all my affection, support and sympathy in his tremendous task.'[2]

General Sir Alan Brooke: diary
('War Diaries, Field Marshal Lord Alanbrooke', page 265)

15 June 1942

5.30 p.m. Cabinet meeting and very gloomy owing to bad news from Libya and from Malta convoys. Lasted till 7.30 p.m.

After dinner 1 hour's hard work before 10.30 meeting with PM at 10 Downing St. Just back at 1.20 a.m!! And we did <u>nothing</u> except meander round from Burma to France and back. Also discussed upcoming meeting to Washington, and nearly decided to start tomorrow morning at 11 a.m!! Now postponed to Wednesday at any rate!

Winston S. Churchill to General Claude Auchinleck
(Churchill papers, 20/76)[3]

16 June 1942
Personal and Secret

It certainly looks as if the enemy will himself attack you soon. I fully share your view that this would give 8th Army its best chance. Although many famous victories have been won by the repulse of an assailant followed by a counter-stroke, I cannot help thinking at this time of Napoleon's preconceived rupturing counter-stroke at Austerlitz. We have often been inclined to think that Germans are particularly vexed when some well thought out plan on which they are working is upset by the unexpected. This would seem to apply all the more in these days when the unimpeded initiative is of special value to armoured forces. In short the picture of two separate battle plans, theirs and ours, clashing upon

---

[1] Lord Winterton, Chairman of the Inter-Governmental Committee for Refugees, 1938–45.

[2] Churchill noted on this letter: 'Mrs C to see'.

[3] Churchill passed this draft to General Smuts, noting that he had not sent it 'for fear of deranging plans at the last moment'.

each other makes a powerful appeal to the mind. Special intelligence seems to give us opportunities for timing a blow upon the enemy at his most vulnerable moment.[1]

2. Pray excuse these rudimentary thoughts upon an approaching episode which you have been studying so long. Your affairs are so much in my mind that I could not resist.

Winston S. Churchill to King George VI
(Royal Archives)

16 June 1942

Sir,

In case of my death on this journey I am about to undertake, I avail myself of Your Majesty's gracious permission to advise that you should entrust the formation of a new Government to Mr Anthony Eden, the Secretary of State for Foreign Affairs, who is in my mind the outstanding Minister in the largest political party in the House of Commons and in the National Government over which I have the honour to preside, and who I am sure will be found capable of conducting Your Majesty's affairs with the resolution, experience, and capacity which these grievous times require.

I have the honour to remain,

Your Majesty's faithful and devoted servant and subject,
Winston S Churchill

Winston S. Churchill to General Hastings Ismay,
for the Chiefs of Staff Committee
(Churchill papers, 20/67)

16 June 1942

All this[2] shows quite clearly the need of getting busy on 'Anakim'.[3] It seems to me that the Joint Intelligence Staff might well be asked to

---

[1] 'On 6 June Rommel had asked for 6,000 men immediately. On 9 June he ordered every fit man to the front, and further decrypts spoke of 15th Panzer Division's desperate need for replacements. By 11 June . . . Enigma has established that what had arrived were four battalions of general replacements each a thousand strong.

'On 11 June, in light of this evidence, GS Int GHQ ME produced an appreciation of the German intentions which was largely accurate and which envisaged an all-out attack on Tobruk' (F. H. Hinsley et al., *British Intelligence in the Second World War*, Volume II: *Its Influence on strategy and Operations*, London, 1981, pages 381–2).

[2] A report on the worsening situation on the Sino-Japanese front.

[3] 'Anakim': the plan to recapture Burma, beginning with a seaborne invasion in early 1943, and re-open the overland supply line to China.

make a plan of their own, or possibly even confer with the Joint Planners, impressing upon them the need of action. I have repeatedly stated that the danger of the collapse of Chiang Kai-shek is one of the greatest we have to face at the present time.

Winston S. Churchill to A. V. Alexander and
Admiral of the Fleet Sir Dudley Pound [1]
(Churchill papers, 20/67)

16 June 1942
Action this Day

It will be necessary to make another attempt to run a convoy into Malta. This can only be from Gibraltar, though a feint from Alexandria will be useful. The fate of the island is at stake, and if the effort to relieve it is worth making, it is worth making on a great scale. Strong battleship escort capable of fighting the Italian battle squadron and strong aircraft carrier support would seem to be required. Also at least a dozen fast supply ships, for which super-priority over all civil requirements must be given.

2. The improved situation in the Indian Ocean enables a delay to be accepted in the movement of *Rodney*. In any case 'Anakim' does not happen till later on in the year.

3. I shall be glad to know in the course of the day what proposals can be made, as it will be right to telegraph to Lord Gort, thus preventing despair in the population. He must be able to tell them: 'The Navy will never abandon Malta.'

Winston S. Churchill to Josef Stalin
(Churchill papers, 20/76)

16 June 1942
Personal and Secret

We have reported to you various indications that the Germans are reinforcing the north of Norway and Finland and sending invasion craft thither. This might portend an attack upon Murmansk, accompanied by the basing of heavy surface ships in the extreme north, with the intention of cutting our supply line to you. Pray let me know what you think about joint operations between us in those parts and particularly whether

[1] Also sent to General Ismay, for the Chiefs of Staff Committee.

you wish for the six Squadrons of the Royal Air Force mentioned in my aide-mémoire to Monsieur Molotov.

Winston S. Churchill to General Claude Auchinleck
(Churchill papers, 20/76)

16 June 1942
Personal and Secret

I am thankful you have succeeded in regrouping the 8th Army on the new front in close contact with your reinforcements, and the Cabinet was very glad to know that you intended to hold Tobruk at all costs. Let us know whether much stores fell into enemy's hands.

2. We cannot of course judge at the present time battle tactics from here. Certainly it would seem however that advantage would be gained if the whole of our forces were engaged together at one time and if the initiative could be recovered. It may be the new situation will give you this opportunity, especially if the enemy, who is evidently himself hard-pressed is given no breathing space. Armoured warfare seems to favour the offensive because it allows a design to be unfolded step by step, whereas the defensive, which was so powerful in the last war, has to yield itself continually to the plans of the attacker. All good wishes.

Winston S. Churchill to Captain Charles Mott-Radclyffe[1]
(Churchill papers, 20/53)

16 June 1942

Dear Captain Radclyffe,

I am glad to learn that you are standing as the Conservative candidate and supporter of the National Government in the forthcoming by-election in the Windsor Division.

Your opponent, undeterred by the recent experiences of political free-lances who have provoked by-elections, challenges your return. He

[1] Charles (Edward) Mott-Radclyffe, 1911–92. His father, a Lieutenant-Colonel in the Rifle Brigade, was killed in action on the Western Front in 1915. Educated at Eton and Balliol College, Oxford. Diplomatic Service (Athens and Rome), 1936–8. Commissioned in the Rifle Brigade, 1939. Member of the Military Mission to Greece, 1940–1. Liaison Officer, Syria, 1941. Conservative MP for Windsor, 1942–70. On active service, Middle East and Italy, 1943–4. Parliamentary Private Secretary to Secretary of State for India (L. S. Amery), December 1944 to May 1945. Junior Lord of the Treasury, May–July 1945. Conservative Whip, 1945–6. Chairman, Conservative Parliamentary Foreign Affairs Committee, 1951–9. Knighted, 1957. Captain, Lords and Commons Cricket, 1952–70.

proclaims himself my ardent supporter and in the same breath condemns those responsible for the handling of our domestic and military affairs. The electors may rest assured that I utterly repudiate the support of men who have not the courage to attack me but concentrate their fire upon my colleagues.

Those who believe with me that, while we are waging war against a powerful and ruthless enemy, we should wage it whole-heartedly with a National Government of all parties supported by a united nation, will vote for the man who stands without question as the National Government candidate.

As a soldier who has seen service on three fronts and has been wounded in action, you worthily represent the younger generation that will bear the brunt of building up the new Britain in the years that will follow victory.

We are at war to defend our way of life, the life of a free democratic people. I hope that every elector will go out on polling day and exercise his – or her – democratic right to vote. Your return to the House of Commons by a resounding majority will be a message of encouragement to the National Government and provide yet another proof of the nation's undeviating resolve to make victory certain.

Yours sincerely,
Winston S Churchill

Shortly before midnight on 17 June 1942, Churchill left Stranraer in Scotland by flying boat for Washington and his second visit to President Roosevelt. Although the battle in the Western Desert was at its height, the journey was undertaken with the approval of the War Cabinet in the recognition that the Prime Minister and the President had 'business of the highest importance to the general strategy of the war' to conduct, including matters that 'could only be achieved by personal discussions' between them.[1] It was during this visit that the two men reached an agreement, of the utmost secrecy, whereby the United States and Britain would share 'as equal partners' their respective researches into the creation and manufacture of an atom bomb.

---

[1] Churchill, *The Hinge of Fate*, pages 334, 336.

Winston S. Churchill: recollection
('The Hinge of Fate', pages 337–8)

17 June 1942

Although I now knew the risks we had run on our return voyage flight from Bermuda in January, my confidence in the chief pilot, Kelly Rogers, and his Boeing flying-boat was such that I asked specially that he should take charge. My party was completed by Brigadier Stewart,[1] the Director of Plans at the War Office (who was later killed when flying back from the Casablanca Conference), Sir Charles Wilson, Mr Martin, and Commander Thompson. We left Stranraer on the night of June 17, shortly before midnight. The weather was perfect and the moon full. I sat for two hours or more in the co-pilot's seat admiring the shining sea, revolving my problems, and thinking of the anxious battle. I slept soundly in the 'bridal suite' until in broad daylight we reached Gander. Here we could have refuelled, but this was not thought necessary, and after making our salutes to the airfield we pursued our voyage. As we were travelling with the sun the day seemed very long. We had two luncheons with a six-hour interval, and contemplated a late dinner after arrival.

For the last two hours we flew over the land, and it was about seven o'clock by American time when we approached Washington. As we gradually descended towards the Potomac River I noticed that the top of the Washington Monument, which is over five hundred and fifty feet high, was about our level, and I impressed upon Captain Kelly Rogers that it would be peculiarly unfortunate if we brought our story to an end by hitting this of all other objects in the world. He assured me that he would take special care to miss it. Thus we landed safely and smoothly on the Potomac after a journey of twenty-seven flying hours. Lord Halifax, General Marshall, and several high officers of the United States welcomed us. I repaired to the British Embassy for dinner. It was too late for me to fly on to Hyde Park that night. We read all the latest telegrams – there was nothing important – and dined agreeably in the open air. The British Embassy, standing on the high ground, is one of the coolest places in Washington, and compares very favourably in this respect with the White House.

[1] Guy Milton Stewart, 1900–43.

John Martin: diary
(Sir John Martin papers)

17 June 1942

Left at midday for Stranraer, from which we took off about 11.30 p.m. by RMA *Bristol* (Capt Kelly Rogers).

Party consists of PM, CIGS (Brooke), Ismay, Brig GM Stewart (Director of Plans), Tommy, Kinna,[1] and Sawyers.

General Sir Alan Brooke: diary
('War Diaries, Field Marshal Lord Alanbrooke', page 266)

17 June 1942

Travelled up to Stranraer in PM's special – very comfortable. Had meals alone at table with him and thus able to settle many points in anticipation of talk with Roosevelt. Arrived Stranraer about 10.30 p.m., where news was telephoned through to PM. Then went by motor boat to the Boeing Clipper. Huge flying boat beautifully fitted up with bunks to sleep in, dining saloon, stewards, lavatories etc.

Winston S. Churchill to Brigadier Leslie Hollis,
Clement Attlee, and Anthony Eden
(Churchill papers, 20/67)

17 June 1942
Most Secret
Private

The First Sea Lord has given me four alternative schemes for a further attempt to victual Malta from the West. You should obtain this paper from him. Of these schemes the first is the most satisfactory, but it depends upon American help, for which I will ask the President. Meanwhile, I have told the First Sea Lord to begin loading the ten supply ships.

---

[1] Patrick Francis Kinna, 1913–2009. His father, Captain Thomas Kinna, had been decorated for his part in the relief of Ladysmith (28 February 1900), in which Churchill had also taken part. An accomplished shorthand typist, after eight years at Barclays Bank he won the All-England championship for secretarial speeds. Joined the Intelligence Corps in 1939; posted to Paris as clerk to Major-General HRH the Duke of Windsor. Recommended by the Duke's staff to Churchill. Churchill's shorthand clerk, 1941–5. In addition to his Pitman shorthand speed of 150 words per minute, Kinna could take dictation straight on to a manual typewriter at 90 words per minute. In 1945 he turned down the opportunity to stay with Churchill after the war, and from 1945 to 1951 he worked for the Foreign Secretary, Ernest Bevin. Joined the timber firm Montague Meyer, 1951, rising to become personnel director.

2. Will you please sit with the First Lord and the First Sea Lord and press this matter forward to the utmost. Apparently Admiral Harwood[1] has a plan for a further attempt from the East during the next ten days, provided the American Liberators can be made available. Let me have details of this and what is thought of it, so that I can put the point to the President if there is value in it. At first sight it seems rather a forlorn hope with the forces available after what happened last time.

3. We are absolutely bound to save Malta in one way or the other. I should not myself exclude sending two or three of the carriers and *Warspite* and *Valiant* through from the Indian Ocean in the middle of July, if there is no other way. This was the original plan which we reluctantly abandoned owing to the objections of the First Sea Lord. Owing to the Japanese losses in the Pacific, the situation in the Indian Ocean has become less urgent, and a further delay could be accepted in forming the Eastern Fleet. Admiral Cunningham has written, at the request of the First Sea Lord, a paper on this scheme, for which you should also ask. You should, if necessary, see him.

Now that the Italians have shown a readiness to bring their battle-fleet down to arrest a convoy reaching Malta from the East, an opportunity of bringing them to battle might be found, which would have far-reaching effects.

4. I am relying upon you to treat the whole question of the relief of Malta as vitally urgent, and to keep at it with the Admiralty till a solution is reached. Keep me advised so that I can do my best with the President.

Winston S. Churchill to President Franklin D. Roosevelt
(Churchill papers, 20/76)

17 June 1942
Secret and Personal

Hope arrive Baltimore Thursday.[2] Portal is much occupied here but he can come over later if necessary. Looking forward to seeing you keenly.

---

[1] Henry Harwood, 1888–1950. Entered the Royal Navy, 1903. Specialised in torpedoes. Commodore, commanding the South American Division of the America and West Indies Station, and Commanding Officer HMS *Exeter*, 1936. Rear-Admiral, commanding squadron in action against the *Admiral Graf Spee* at the Battle of the River Plate (December 1939). Knighted, 1939. Lord Commissioner of Admiralty and Assistant Chief of the Naval Staff, December 1940 to April 1942. Vice-Admiral and Commander-in-Chief, Mediterranean Station, 1942–5. Flag Officer Commanding the Orkneys and Shetlands, 1945.

[2] Thursday, 18 June 1942.

Winston S. Churchill to General Douglas MacArthur
(Churchill papers, 20/58)

17 June 1942

My dear General MacArthur,

I have been glad indeed to have the opportunity of getting first-hand news of you from Wilkinson[1] whom I have asked to take back this letter.

It bears with it every good wish for you and your Command. Your doings have won the admiration of my countrymen, and we expect great news of you when the time comes to turn upon the enemy.

Sinkings of our ships remain heavy, and the Germans are beating on Murmansk, Kharkov, Sebastopol and Tobruk, but we are making all efforts to send you supplies.

For very many months my thoughts have turned perpetually to the Far East and the Pacific, and I render daily thanks that His Majesty's Australian subjects have a fighting soldier of your quality to guard them and guide them through these historic times.

Yours sincerely
Winston S. Churchill

Winston S. Churchill to Colonel Sir Courtauld Thomson[2]
(Churchill papers, 20/53)

17 June 1942

My dear Sir Courtauld,

I greatly appreciate your wish to give me the Russian gold medal, which I admire so much, but I feel I should prefer to buy it myself. Please accept my thanks for your kind thought, and also for all the help you have given my Wife in connection with her Russian Fund.

---

[1] Gerald Hugh Wilkinson, 1909–65. Reported for MI6 in Philippines on Japanese movements, 1940. Became Churchill's liaison with General MacArthur, often serving on island of Corregidor and in Australia, 1941–3. Reported directly to WSC. Served with British Security Coordination in New York, 1943–5.

[2] Courtauld Greenwood Courtauld-Thomson, 1865–1964. Educated at Eton and Magdalen College, Oxford. On several hospital boards. Knighted, 1912. British Red Cross Commissioner, France, 1914–15; Malta, Italy, Egypt, Macedonia, and the Near East, 1915–19 (attached to GHQ Staff; despatches five times). Chairman, Princess Christian's Nursing Home, Windsor, 1920–46. Chairman of the Irish Civil Service Commission, 1921–6. Chairman, University College Hospital, 1937–48. In 1942, he presented his country house Dorney Wood (Dorneywood) – the house, its contents, and an endowment – to the nation. Created Baron, 1944.

I much enjoyed the hours I spent at Dorney Wood[1] last Saturday. It is a beautiful property and will, I feel, play a notable part in the domestic and social life of future Governments.

I have sent Lord Portal[2] a copy of your note about it and asked him to get in touch with you. You may therefore expect shortly to hear from him on the subject.

Yours very sincerely,
Winston S Churchill

Lord Alanbrooke: recollection
('Turn of the Tide', page 399–400)

17 June 1942

I find that I did not mention two little episodes in my diary which nevertheless have remained very clear in my memory as being typical of Winston. We were walking down the quay to embark in the motor-boat to take us to the Clipper. He was dressed in his zip-suit and zip-shoes, with a black Homburg hat on the side of his head and his small gold-topped malacca cane in his hand. Suddenly, almost like Pooh-Bear, he started humming, "We are here because we're here – We're here because we're here!" This little song could not have been more appropriate. It was at a time when the Atlantic had not been so very frequently flown, we were both somewhat doubtful why we were going, whether we should get there, what we should achieve while we were there, and whether we should ever get back. We were facing a journey of twenty-seven hours in the air, and might reasonably have some doubts as to whether we should reach our destination.

The next incident was on our arrival in the flying-boat. He sent for the steward and said to him: 'The clock is going to do some funny things while we are in the air; it is either going to go backwards or forwards, but that is of little consequence, my stomach is my clock and I eat every four hours!' As I had to share every one of these meals with him, and, as they were all washed down with champagne and brandy, it became a little trying on the constitution[...].

[1] Dorney Wood: also Dorneywood, a Queen Anne-style house built in 1920 near Burnham in Buckinghamshire. Among those who have occupied it were Anthony Eden and James Callaghan (when Foreign Secretary) and John Major (when Chancellor of the Exchequer). It is the Prime Minister of the day who decides which Cabinet Minister is to live in the house. It has been occupied more recently by John Prescott (as Deputy Prime Minister) and Alistair Darling (as Chancellor of the Exchequer).

[2] Minister of Works and Planning.

[. . .]

Our departure had been especially delayed till after dark owing to the danger of meeting a German Focke-Wulf plane, apt to cruise over the Western Approaches. I have a most vivid memory of the thrill of the start of that flight. Looking out over a sea of cotton-wool clouds with a pink tinge from the red sky and the silver wings of the Clipper reflecting this glorious colour, and with it all the wonderful feeling of sailing out into the boundless spaces of the Atlantic.

Lord Ismay: recollection
('The Memoirs of General The Lord Ismay', page 251)

17 June 1942

We were in the air for over twenty-six hours at a stretch, but the time passed quickly and pleasantly. When we were about four hours from Washington, the Prime Minister looked at his watch. 'It is nearly eight o'clock, Tommy. Where's dinner?' Tommy explained that he was engaged to dine at the British Embassy, and that it was only about 4.30 p.m. according to sun time. The Prime Minister retorted that he didn't go by sun time. 'I go by tummy time, and I want my dinner.' He had it – and so did we all – and a very good dinner it was! We landed on the Potomac River three or four hours later, and assembled at the British Embassy in time for a second meal.

General Sir Alan Brooke: diary
('War Diaries, Field Marshal Lord Alanbrooke', page 266)

18 June 1942

Had long morning in bed as the clock was going back and breakfast was not available till 11 a.m. (about 8 a.m. real time). Still flying over blankets of cloud till about 12.30 when we found the sea again and shortly afterwards flew over a large convoy of some 35 ships. PM in tremendous form and enjoying himself like a schoolboy! As we waited to embark he was singing a little song to himself 'We're here because we're here'. As I write we are over the Atlantic and within about an hour's flying time of Newfoundland.

Itinerary
(Franklin D. Roosevelt papers)

18 June 1942   The White House
                                                     Washington DC

The Prime Minister arrived in Washington by <u>air</u> June 18. The President being in Hyde Park, the PM spent night in Washington and flew to New Hackensack and airfield near Hyde Park, (Navy plane).

Winston S. Churchill to Field Marshal Jan Smuts
(Churchill papers, 20/76)

18 June 1942
Most Secret and Personal

I have been giving the most careful thought to how we can best help you with air forces for the defence of the Union in response to the message which you sent me through Waterson[1] on 5th June.

2. I realise that your most pressing need is for reconnaissance and bomber aircraft to deal with the threat of attacks against shipping by armed merchantmen and surface raiders. To meet this the Air Staff feel that they cannot do better than hasten the despatch of the 36 Ventura bombers[2] which are allocated to you in the United States and to back these up with aircraft from our own allocations of Venturas – say 36 to start with, making an initial total of 72. We have carefully examined every other possibility and I am satisfied that this is the best arrangement. Fifteen aircraft are at Miami loaded with spares ready to go and the remainder will follow as quickly as possible. Delivery will be via Natal, Liberia, Accra and Khartoum, where I understand the South African Air Force have made arrangements to collect them.

3. As a further help, a Catalina squadron should be ready for operations at Mombasa by the end of June under the operational control of C-in-C, Eastern Fleet, and this will, of course, be available to co-operate with you in carrying out long-range reconnaissance off the East Coast of Africa.

---

[1] South African High Commissioner in London.

[2] Ventura: the Lockheed Ventura, an American built two-engine bomber. In February 1940 the Royal Air Force ordered 675 Venturas; they were delivered from mid-1942. A further 550 were ordered in August 1941. Their first combat mission was on 3 November 1942, on a low-level raid against a factory in the Netherlands; of the 47 that took part, nine were shot down. They were then switched to medium altitude raids. The Ventura's last bombing mission was on 9 September 1943. A number were then modified and served in Coastal Command.

4. Meanwhile I realise that you are also in need of fighters. These could only be provided immediately by withdrawing them from the flow of reinforcements to the Middle East. Bearing in mind the heavy toll which the battle in Libya is taking [on] our fighters I feel that you will agree that we cannot afford to withhold them from that theatre at this critical juncture. The moment the situation improves it will, however, be possible to divert a number of Kittyhawks[1] to you. They could normally be unloaded in South Africa within a week to 10 days of the order being given.

Winston S. Churchill: recollection
('The Hinge of Fate', pages 338–9)

19 June 1942

Early the next morning, the 19th, I flew to Hyde Park. The President was on the local airfield, and saw us make the roughest bump landing I have experienced. He welcomed me with great cordiality, and, driving the car himself, took me to the majestic bluffs over the Hudson River on which Hyde Park, his family home, stands. The President drove me all over the estate, showing me its splendid views. In this drive I had some thoughtful moments. Mr Roosevelt's infirmity prevented him from using his feet on the brake, clutch, or accelerator. An ingenious arrangement enabled him to do everything with his arms, which were amazingly strong and muscular. He invited me to feel his biceps, saying that a famous prize-fighter had envied them. This was reassuring; but I confess that when on several occasions the car poised and backed on the grass verges of the precipices over the Hudson I hoped the mechanical devices and brakes would show no defects. All the time we talked business, and though I was careful not to take his attention off the driving we made more progress than we might have done in formal conference.

The President was very glad to hear I had brought the CIGS with me. His field of interest was always brightened by recollections of his youth. It had happened that the President's father[2] had entertained at Hyde Park

---

[1] 'Kittyhawk' was the name given by the British and Commonwealth air forces to the later models of the Curtiss P40 Warhawk, an American single-engine, single-seat, all-metal fighter and ground attack aircraft that first flew in 1938. In front-line service until the end of the war. It was the third most-produced American fighter, after the P-51 and P-47; by November 1944, when production of the P-40 ceased, 13,738 had been built.

[2] James Roosevelt Sr, 1828–1900. A businessman with coal and transportation interests. Vice-President, Delaware and Hudson Railway. President, Southern railway security Company. Recurring heart problems turned him into an invalid.

the father[1] of General Brooke. Mr Roosevelt therefore expressed keen interest to meet the son, who had reached such a high position. When they met two days later he received him with the utmost cordiality, and General Brooke's personality and charm created an almost immediate intimacy which greatly helped the course of business.

I told Harry Hopkins about the different points on which I wanted decisions, and he talked them over with the President, so that the ground was prepared and the President's mind armed upon each subject. Of these 'Tube Alloys'[2] was one of the most complex, and, as it proved, overwhelmingly the most important.

Winston S. Churchill to Josef Stalin
(Churchill papers, 20/76)

19 June 1942

STATEMENT FOR PUBLICATION ON EVENING OF 22 JUNE 1942

As the Soviet Union enters the second year of the war I, as Prime Minister of Great Britain, which in a few months time will enter on its fourth year of war, send to you, the leader of the great allied Soviet peoples, a renewed expression of our admiration for the magnificent defence of your armed forces, guerrilla bands, and civilian workers during the past year, and of our firm conviction that those achievements will be equalled and surpassed in the coming months.

The fighting alliance of our two countries and of our other allies to whom there has now been joined up the vast resources of the United States, will surely bring our enemies to their knees. You can count on us to assist you by every means in our power.

During the year which has passed since Hitler fell upon your country without warning, friendly relations between our two countries and peoples have been progressively strengthened. We have thought not only of the present but of the future and our Treaty of Alliance in the war against Hitlerite Germany and of collaboration and mutual assistance in the post-war period, concluded during M Molotov's recent visit to this country has been welcomed as sincerely by the British people as I know it has been welcomed by the Soviet people. That Treaty is a pledge that

---

[1] Victor Alexander Brooke, 1843–1891. 3rd Baronet. Educated at Harrow. Lived mostly in France, at Pau, where his son Alan was born. Died of pneumonia in Pau at the age of 48. A keen naturalist; his work on antelopes was unfinished at the time of his death.

[2] 'Tube Alloys': codename for British work on what would become the atomic bomb, which from late 1941 had involved British and Canadian scientists working in collaboration with counterparts in the United States.

we shall confound our enemies and when the war is over, build a sure peace for all freedom loving peoples.

Winston S. Churchill: recollection
('The Hinge of Fate', pages 341–2)

20 June 1942   The White House
                                                Washington DC

Our talk took place after luncheon, in a tiny little room which juts out on the ground floor. The room was dark and shaded from the sun. Mr Roosevelt was ensconced at a desk almost as big as the apartment. Harry sat or stood in the background. My two American friends did not seem to mind the intense heat.

I told the President in general terms of the great progress we had made, and that our scientists were now definitely convinced that results might be reached before the end of the present war. He said his people were getting along too, but no one could tell whether anything practical would emerge till a full-scale experiment had been made. We both felt painfully the dangers of doing nothing. We knew what efforts the Germans were making to procure supplies of 'heavy water' – a sinister term, eerie, unnatural, which began to creep into our secret papers. What if the enemy should get an atomic bomb before we did! However sceptical one might feel about the assertions of scientists, much disputed among themselves and expressed in jargon incomprehensible to laymen, we could not run the mortal risk of being outstripped in this awful sphere.

I strongly urged that we should at once pool all our information, work together on equal terms, and share the results, if any, equally between us. The question then arose as to where the research plant was to be set up. We were already aware of the enormous expense that must be incurred, with all the consequent grave diversion of resources and brain-power from other forms of war effort. Considering that Great Britain was under close bombing attack and constant enemy air reconnaissance, it seemed impossible to erect in the Island the vast and conspicuous factories that were needed. We conceived ourselves at least as far advanced as our Ally, and there was of course the alternative of Canada, who had a vital contribution herself to make through the supplies of uranium she had actively gathered.

It was a hard decision to spend several hundred million pounds sterling, not so much of money as of competing forms of precious war-energy, upon a project the success of which no scientist on either side of the Atlantic could guarantee. Nevertheless, if the Americans had not been willing to undertake the venture we should certainly have gone forward on our own power in Canada, or, if the Canadian Government demurred, in some other part of the Empire. I was however very glad when the President said he thought the United States would have to do it. We therefore took this decision jointly, and settled a basis of agreement. I shall continue the story in a later volume. But meanwhile I have no doubt that it was the progress we had made in Britain and the confidence of our scientists in ultimate success imparted to the President that led him to his grave and fateful decision.

Winston S. Churchill to President Franklin D. Roosevelt
(Franklin D. Roosevelt papers)

20 June 1942

The continued heavy sinkings at sea constitute our greatest and most immediate danger. What further measures can be taken now to reduce sinkings other than those in actual operations, which must be faced? When will the convoy system start in the Caribbean and Gulf of Mexico? Is there needless traffic which could be reduced? Should we build more escort vessels at the expense of merchant tonnage, and if so to what extent?

2. We are bound to persevere in the preparation for 'Bolero', if possible in 1942, but certainly in 1943. The whole of this business is now going on. Arrangements are being made for a landing of six or eight divisions on the coast of Northern France early in September. However, the British Government do not favour an operation that is certain to lead to disaster, for this would not help the Russians whatever their plight, would compromise and expose to Nazi vengeance the French population involved, and would gravely delay the main operation in 1943. We hold strongly to the view that there should be no substantial landing in France this year unless we are going to stay.

3. No responsible British military authority has so far been able to make a plan for September 1942 which had any chance of success unless the Germans became utterly demoralised, of which there is no likelihood. Have the American Staffs a plan? At what points would they strike? What landing-craft and shipping are available? Who is the officer prepared to command the enterprise? What British forces and assistance

are required? If a plan can be found which offers a reasonable prospect of success His Majesty's Government will cordially welcome it, and will share to the full with their American comrades the risks and sacrifices. This remains our settled and agreed policy.

4. But in case no plan can be made in which any responsible authority has good confidence, and consequently no engagement on a substantial scale in France is possible in September 1942, what else are we going to do? Can we afford to stand idle in the Atlantic theatre during the whole of 1942? Ought we not to be preparing within the general structure of 'Bolero' some other operation by which we may gain positions of advantage, and also directly or indirectly to take some of the weight off Russia? It is in this setting and on this background that the French North-West Africa operation should be studied.

General Hastings Ismay: note[1]
('The Hinge of Fate', pages 344–5)

20 June 1942   The White House
                                                Washington DC

Plans and preparations for the 'Bolero' operation in 1943 on as large a scale as possible are to be pushed forward with all speed and energy. It is however essential that the United States and Great Britain should be prepared to act offensively in 1942.

2. Operations in France or the Low Countries in 1942 would, if successful, yield greater political and strategic gains than operations in any other theatre. Plans and preparations for the operations in this theatre are to be pressed forward with all possible speed, energy, and ingenuity. The most resolute efforts must be made to overcome the obvious dangers and difficulties of the enterprise. If a sound and sensible plan can be contrived we should not hesitate to give effect to it. If, on the other hand, detailed examination shows that, despite all efforts, success is improbable, we must be ready with an alternative.

3. The possibilities of French North Africa (Operation 'Gymnast') will be explored carefully and conscientiously, and plans will be completed in all details as soon as possible. Forces to be employed in 'Gymnast' would in the main be found from 'Bolero' units which have not yet left the United States. The possibility of operations in Norway and the Ibe-

---

[1] Of a discussion between Churchill, Roosevelt, General Brooke, and Harry Hopkins at the White House, 20 June 1942. This document is one of several sent by Ismay to Churchill when Churchill was preparing his memoirs.

rian peninsula in the autumn and winter of 1942 will also be carefully considered by the Combined Chiefs of Staff.

4. Planning of 'Bolero' will continue to be centred in London. Planning for 'Gymnast' will be centred in Washington.

Clementine Churchill to Winston S. Churchill
(Baroness Spencer-Churchill papers)

20 June 1942　　　　　　　　　　　　　　10 Downing Street

My Darling,

Yesterday evening when you called me on the telephone, your voice sounded quite close – as if you were speaking in the next room. I do hope your conversations with the President will be fruitful – Hyde Park sounds lovely & I suppose there June is 'Flaming June'. Yesterday I had just returned from a long day in Birmingham where I 'opened' a large Social Centre (YWCA)[1] for Birmingham Munition Workers. After which I had luncheon with the Lord Mayor[2] in the Town Hall. I was encouraged by Max sending me £1,000 for the YWCA, also, Mr Simon Marks[3], so I feel I may raise the necessary money to help the poor little ATS & WAAF.[4] The 'Wrens' I feel are more or less all right for as you have remarked to me 'The Navy always travels first class'.

I wish the President would give me a Slogan for my 1943 YWCA Calendar! I mean to sell 1 million copies & make 30,000. I think I have snaffelled Chiang Kai-shek – Stalin will come along later, & I can torture you at my leisure for some opposite tho' not prophetical remark.

Jack[5] & I are proceeding to Chartwell where we intend to feed your fish & your Cat.

　　　　　　　Tender love from your own PUSSIE.
　　　　　　　[drawing of a cat]Purrr-rrr-rr

The Lord Mayor of Birmingham informed me that Max was coming there today to address 20,000 people in the City Square. To open the 'Second Front' I expect!

---

[1] YWCA: Young Women's Christian Association.

[2] Norman Tiptaft, 1883–1970. Born in Birmingham. Served as a Cadet in the Royal Flying Corps. Stood unsuccessfully for the Birmingham Handsworth parliamentary seat as an Independent in 1918 and 1922. Elected Councillor for Handsworth, 1919. Lord Mayor of Birmingham, 1941–2.

[3] Simon Marks, 1888–1964. Educated at Manchester Grammar School. Chairman and Joint Managing Director, Marks & Spencer Ltd. Knighted, 1944, Created Baron, 1961.

[4] ATS, WAAF: the Auxiliary Territorial Service (the women's branch of the British Army) and the Women's Auxiliary Air Force.

[5] Churchill's younger brother, John Strange Spencer-Churchill.

Josef Stalin to Winston S. Churchill
(Churchill papers, 20/76)

20 June 1942
Personal and Secret

I received your message with a warning that the Germans have intention to organise invasion from the Northern Norway and Finland. I fully
share your view on the desirability of our joint operations in these regions
but I would like to know whether it is contemplated the participation of
the British Naval and Land Forces and in what numbers. Many thanks
for your promise to send six squadrons to the Murmansk area. Could
you tell me when they will arrive?

Stalin

Itinerary
(Franklin D. Roosevelt papers)

20 June 1942   The White House
                                                Washington DC

On the night of June 20, the President accompanied by Mr Churchill
and staffs, drove to Highland, West Shore, New York Central rr,[1] took
special train to Washington. Left Highland 11:00 p.m., arriving Arlington
Cantonment, Washington, 9:00 a.m., June 21. Route: West Shore NYC rr
to Weehawken, N.J., thence Baltimore and Ohio rr to Arlington Cantonment.[2] The PM occupied stateroom in President's private car.

Winston S. Churchill: recollection
('The Hinge of Fate', pages 343–4)

21 June 1942   The White House
morning   Washington DC

Late on the night of the 20th the Presidential train bore us back to
Washington, which we reached about eight o'clock the next morning.
We were heavily escorted to the White House, and I was again accorded
the very large air-conditioned room, in which I dwelt in comfort at about
thirty degrees below the temperature of most of the rest of the building. I
glanced at the newspapers, read telegrams for an hour, had my breakfast,

---

[1] rr: railroad.
[2] See map on page 1593.

looked up Harry across the passage, and then went to see the President in his study. General Ismay came with me. Presently a telegram was put into the President's hands. He passed it to me without a word. It said, 'Tobruk has surrendered, with twenty-five thousand men taken prisoners.' This was so surprising that I could not believe it. I therefore asked Ismay to inquire of London by telephone. In a few minutes he brought the following message, which had just arrived from Admiral Harwood at Alexandria:

> Tobruk has fallen, and situation deteriorated so much that there is a possibility of heavy air attack on Alexandria in near future, and in view of approaching full moon period I am sending all Eastern Fleet units south of the Canal to await events. I hope to get HMS *Queen Elizabeth* out of dock towards end of this week.

This was one of the heaviest blows I can recall during the war. Not only were its military effects grievous, but it had affected the reputation of the British armies. At Singapore eighty-five thousand men had surrendered to inferior numbers of Japanese. Now in Tobruk a garrison of twenty-five thousand (actually thirty-three thousand) seasoned soldiers had laid down their arms to perhaps one-half of their number. If this was typical of the morale of the Desert Army, no measure could be put upon the disasters which impended in North-East Africa. I did not attempt to hide from the President the shock I had received. It was a bitter moment. Defeat is one thing; disgrace is another. Nothing could exceed the sympathy and chivalry of my two friends. There were no reproaches; not an unkind word was spoken. 'What can we do to help?' said Roosevelt. I replied at once, 'Give us as many Sherman tanks[1] as you can spare, and ship them to the Middle East as quickly as possible.'

The President sent for General Marshall, who arrived in a few minutes, and told him of my request. Marshall replied, 'Mr President, the Shermans are only just coming into production. The first few hundred have been issued to our own armoured divisions, who have hitherto had to be content with obsolete equipment. It is a terrible thing to take the weapons out of a soldier's hands. Nevertheless, if the British need is so great they must have them; and we could let them have a hundred 105-mm self-propelled guns in addition.'

---

[1] Sherman: the M4 Sherman (formerly the Medium Tank, M4) was the main battle tank used by the United States forces in the Second World War, in service from June 1942. Its main gun was mounted on a fully traversing turret. More than 50,000 were built. It was named after the American Civil War general William Tecumseh Sherman. When first deployed in the Western Desert it was more powerful than the German tanks that faced it. The later German tanks had heavier armour and more powerful guns.

To complete the story it must be stated that the Americans were better than their word. Three hundred Sherman tanks with engines not yet installed and a hundred self-propelled guns were put into six of their fastest ships and sent off to the Suez Canal. The ship containing the engines for all the tanks was sunk by a submarine off Bermuda. Without a single word from us the President and Marshall put a further supply of engines into another fast ship and dispatched it to overtake the convoy. 'A friend in need is a friend indeed.'

Winston S. Churchill: recollection
('The Hinge of Fate', pages 345–6)

21 June 1942   The White House
early afternoon   Washington DC

On June 21, when we were alone together after lunch, Harry said to me, 'There are a couple of American officers the President would like you to meet, as they are very highly thought of in the Army, by Marshall, and by him.' At five o'clock therefore Major-Generals Eisenhower[1] and Clark[2] were brought to my air-cooled room. I was immediately impressed by these remarkable but hitherto unknown men. They had both come from the President, whom they had just seen for the first time. We talked almost entirely about the major cross-Channel invasion in 1943, 'Roundup' as it was then called, on which their thoughts had evidently been concentrated. We had a most agreeable discussion, lasting for over an hour. In order to convince them of my personal interest in the project I gave them a copy of the paper I had written for the Chiefs of Staff on June

[1] Dwight David Eisenhower, 1890–1969. Graduated from West Point Military Academy, 1915. Drafted the War Department's study and plans for industrial mobilisation, 1929–33. Assistant Military Adviser to the Commonwealth of Philippine Islands, 1935–40. Assistant Chief of Staff, in charge of the Operations Division, War Department, General Staff, Washington, 1941. Officer Commanding US Forces in England (for European operations), 1942. Commander-in-Chief, Allied Forces in North Africa, November 1942 to January 1944. Honorary knighthood, 1943. Supreme Commander, Allied Expeditionary Force in Western Europe, January 1944 to May 1945. Honorary Order of Merit, 1945. Commander, American Zone of Occupation, Germany, 1945. Chief of Staff, American Army, 1945–8. Supreme Commander, North Atlantic Treaty Organisation (NATO) Forces in Europe, 1950–2. President of the United States, 1953–61.

[2] General Mark (Wayne) Clark, 1896–1984. Known to Churchill as 'the American Eagle'. On active service with United States Army, 1917–18. Chief of Staff for United States ground forces in England (for European operations). Made a secret visit by submarine to North Africa in preparation for the November 1942 landings (Operation 'Torch'). Commander 5th Army, Anglo-American invasion of Italy, 1943, and capture of Rome, June 1944. Honorary knighthood, 1944. In April 1945 received the surrender of 230,000 German troops in Italy, the Tyrol, and Salzburg. United States High Commissioner and Commanding General, Austria, 1945–7. Deputy Secretary of State, 1947.

15, two days before I started, in which I had set forth my first thoughts of the method and scale of such an operation. At any rate, they seemed much pleased with the spirit of the document. At that time I thought of the spring or summer of 1943 as the date for the attempt. I felt sure that these officers were intended to play a great part in it, and that was the reason why they had been sent to make my acquaintance. Thus began a friendship which across all the ups and downs of war I have preserved with deep satisfaction to this day.

A month later, in England, General Eisenhower, evidently anxious to prove my zeal, asked me if I would send a copy of my paper to General Marshall, which I did.

Winston S. Churchill: recollection
('The Hinge of Fate', page 346)

21 June 1942   The White House
evening   Washington DC

In the evening, at 9.30 p.m., we had another conference in the President's room, at which the three American Chiefs of Staff were present. There were some discussions about the naval position and the alarming U-boat sinkings off the east coast of America. I strongly urged Admiral King to extend the convoy system to the Caribbean and the Gulf of Mexico at once. He was in full agreement, but thought it better to wait until he had adequate escort vessels available. At 11.30 p.m. I had yet another talk with the President, with Marshall, King, Arnold, Dill, Brooke, and Ismay present. The discussion centred round the deterioration of the situation in the Middle East, and the possibility of sending large numbers of American troops, starting with the 2nd Armoured Division, which had been specially trained in desert warfare, to that theatre as soon as possible. It was agreed that the possibility should be carefully studied with particular reference to the shipping position, and that in the meanwhile I should, with the full approval of the President, inform General Auchinleck that he might expect a reinforcement of a highly trained American armoured division, equipped with Sherman or Lee[1] tanks, during August.

---

[1] Lee: the M3 Lee (Medium Tank M3), known as the 'General Lee' after the Civil War general Robert E. Lee. A modified version, built to British specifications, was known as 'General Grant' after the Civil War general Ulysses S. Grant. More than 6,000 were produced between August 1941 and December 1942, but as soon as the better-performing M4 Sherman became available in large numbers, the M3 Lee was withdrawn.

Anthony Eden: recollection
('The Eden Memoirs, The Reckoning', page 331)

22 June 1942   London
5 a.m. UK time

The highlight of this tragic period was the surrender of Tobruk on June 21st. News of this reached the Prime Minister while he was in conference with President Roosevelt in Washington. He felt the humiliation bitterly. A few hours later he telephoned to me, at what was five in the morning, our time. He asked for news of the position at home. The New York newspapers, he said, were full of the impending fall of the Government. I told him that I had heard not one word of this. Of course there was much grief. No doubt there would be blame for the Government, but so far nothing had happened to shake us.

General Auchinleck, who took over direct operational command of the Eighth Army[1] on June 25th, decided that it was not possible to make a final defence at Mersa Matruh and chose instead the Alamein position.

Winston S. Churchill to General Claude Auchinleck
(Churchill papers, 20/77)

22 June 1942   Washington DC

Your telegrams of 20th and 21st instant and Minister of State's No. MS/20 of 21st received, also Cabinet's telegram No. OZ. 544 in reply to your No. CC/68, CIGS. Dill and I earnestly hope stern resistance will be made on the Sollum frontier line, special intelligence has shown stresses which enemy has undergone. Very important reinforcements are on their way. A week gained may be decisive; we do not know exact dates of deployment New Zealand Division, but had expected it would be by the end of the month. 8th Armoured and 44th are approaching and near. We agree with General Smuts that you may draw freely upon 9th and 10th Armies, as the danger from north is more remote. Thus you can effect drastic roulement with the 3 Divisions now east of the Canal.

2. I was naturally disconcerted by your news, which may well put us back to where we were 18 months ago, and leave all the work of that period to be done over again. However, I do not feel that the defence of the Delta cannot be effectively maintained, and I hope no one will be unduly impressed by the spectacular blows which the enemy has struck at

[2] From General Ritchie.

us. I am sure that, with your perseverance and resolution and continued readiness to run risks, the situation can be restored, especially in view of the large reinforcements approaching.

3. Here in Washington the President is deeply moved by what has occurred and he and other high United States Authorities show themselves disposed to lend the utmost help. They authorise me to inform you that the second United States Armoured Division, specially trained in desert warfare in California, will leave for Suez about 5th July and should be with you in August. You need not send the Indian Division and 288th Indian Armoured Brigade back to India, as proposed. Measures are also being taken, in addition to those described in the Chiefs of Staff telegram No. COS (ME) 275, to divert India-bound aircraft to the Libyan theatre. The 'Halpro' Force[1] is remaining and will be brought up to full strength. I have told CAS to give you his schedules of deliveries, including the 4 Halifax Squadrons, unless he has already done so.

4. The main thing now is for you to inspire all your forces with an intense will to resist and strive and not to accept the freak decisions produced by Rommel's handful of heavy armour. Make sure that all your man-power plays a full part in these critical days. His Majesty's Government is quite ready to share your responsibilities in making the most active and daring defence.

Oliver Harvey: diary
('The War Diaries of Oliver Harvey', pages 133–4)

22 June 1942

AE spoke to PM on the telephone and told him he ought to come back at once. PM appeared peevish and reluctant and implied he was doing most important things over there. Very little information yet about the disaster but AE thinks we were both outmanoeuvred and outweaponed. Yet this was the situation which Auchinleck wanted; he wanted to be attacked, not to attack.

[1] In June 1942, a specially trained United States bomber unit, commanded by Colonel Harry A. Halverson, with 23 Liberator bombers, reached the Middle East. The Halpro Force (**Hal**verson **Pro**visional Detachment) was made up of members of the 98th Bombardment Group (Heavy), consisting initially of 23 B-24D Liberator heavy bombers with hand-picked crews, and was on its way to the Far East to be used by the 10th Air Force in China for bombing raids on Tokyo. However, after the fall of Rangoon the Burma Road was cut, making it impossible to give the detachment logistical support in China. It was therefore kept in Egypt to help stem the German advance there. Halpro's first mission was flown on 12 June 1942 against Romanian oil facilities at Ploesti. On 15 June it assisted the RAF in attacking an Italian fleet. Halpro then flew in support of British Commonwealth forces fighting in the deserts of Egypt and Libya.

The PM has sent a strong and stirring telegram to Auchinleck urging him to display the utmost vigour in holding the frontier and telling him he can count on full support of HMG. He has got Roosevelt to agree to send American armoured troops to reinforce. PM evidently just about to start home.

Winston S. Churchill: recollection
('The Hinge of Fate', page 346)

22 June 1942   The White House
                                                       Washington DC

Meanwhile the surrender of Tobruk reverberated round the world. On the 22nd Hopkins and I were at lunch with the President in his room. Presently Mr Elmer Davis,[1] the head of the Office of War Information, arrived with a bunch of New York newspapers, showing flaring headlines about 'Anger in England', 'Tobruk fall may bring change of Government', 'Churchill to be censured', etc.

I had been invited by General Marshall to visit one of the American Army camps in South Carolina.[2]

General Sir Alan Brooke: diary
('War Diaries, Field Marshal Lord Alanbrooke', page 270)

23 June 1942

Went to office in the morning and at 2.30 p.m. on to the White House to attend meeting of President, PM, Harry Hopkins, Marshall, Arnold, Pug Ismay and self. We discussed what could be done to reinforce Middle East rapidly by diverting USA Air Force from India to ME and also details concerning sailing of an armoured division from this country.

---

[1] Elmer Holmes Davis, 1890–1958. Born in Indiana. Educated at Queen's College, Oxford. On the staff of the *New York Times*, 1914–24. Member of Council, Authors' League of America, 1926–41. News Analyst, Columbia Broadcasting System (CBS), 1939–42. Director, Office of War Information, 1942–5.

[2] Fort Jackson, established in 1917: a United States Army Training Centre. It covers more than 52,000 acres, with more than 100 ranges and field training sites.

Lord Ismay: recollection
('The Memoirs of General The Lord Ismay', page 256)

23 June 1942

In the course of the next twenty-four hours, three conferences were held in the President's room; but everyone's thoughts were on the disaster in the Egyptian Desert, and the discussions centred round the steps which should be taken to restore the situation. The problem of a Second Front in North-West Africa, which the Prime Minister had come to Washington to settle, was scarcely mentioned.

The British and American newspapers were filled with stories of our crushing defeat and criticisms of the Prime Minister. The American papers carried banner headlines. 'Churchill faces stormy session when house convenes', 'British ire is high. Churchill under fire'. Many organs of the British Press were equally critical. It is hard for a leader who is representing his country abroad on a mission of vital importance to be pilloried by his own countrymen, and Churchill was not altogether joking when he said that he was the unhappiest Englishman in America since General Burgoyne on the day of his surrender at Saratoga. But he refused to be stampeded into rushing home at once, and insisted on carrying out his visit to Fort Jackson in South Carolina.

Itinerary
(Franklin D. Roosevelt papers)

23–5 June 1942
                                                      The White House
                                                      Washington DC

Trip to Camp Jackson, SC.

The Prime Minister accepting an invitation from the Army to witness training activities at Camp Jackson, near Columbia, SC, left Arlington Cantonment by special train 10:30 p.m., June 23, arrived Camp Jackson 10:45 a.m., June 24; left Camp Jackson that evening, arriving Arlington early morning, June 25. This move over the Southern Railroad into Camp Jackson, returning same route. The PM used the President's private car on this trip.

Lord Ismay: recollection
(*'The Memoirs of General The Lord Ismay'*, pages 256–7)

23 June 1942

It was an interesting and instructive day. In the morning we saw a battalion do a parachute drop. This was a competent, professional performance. In the afternoon we were shown a brigade of young soldiers doing a field firing exercise with ball ammunition. The troops were obviously very green; and in reply to a question by the Prime Minister, I ventured the opinion that it would be murder to pit them against continental soldiery. Churchill agreed that they were still immature, but added that they were magnificent material who would soon train on. The battles which they fought in Europe two years later showed how right he was.

Winston S. Churchill: recollection
(*'The Hinge of Fate'*, pages 346–7)

23 June 1942

We were to start by train with him[1] and Mr Stimson[2] on the night of June 23. Mr Davis asked me seriously whether, in view of the political situation at home, I thought it wise to carry out the programme, which of course had been elaborately arranged. Might it not be misinterpreted if I were inspecting troops in America when matters of such vital consequence were taking place both in Africa and London? I replied that I would certainly carry out the inspections as planned, and that I doubted whether I should be able to provoke twenty members into the Lobby against the Government on an issue of confidence. This was in fact about the number which the malcontents eventually obtained.

Accordingly I started by train next night for South Carolina, and arrived at Fort Jackson the next morning. The train drew up, not at a station, but in the open plain. It was a very hot day, and we got out of the train straight on to the parade ground, which recalled the plains of India in the hot weather. We went first to an awning and saw the American armour and infantry march past. Next we watched the parachute exer-

---

[1] General Marshall.

[2] Henry Lewis Stimson, 1867–1950. Born in New York City. Admitted to the Bar, 1891. Secretary of War, 1911–13 (under President Taft). Colonel, American Expeditionary Force, France, 1917–18. Governor-General of the Philippines, 1927–9 (under Coolidge). Secretary of State, 1929–32 (under Hoover). Member of Panel, Permanent Court of Arbitration, The Hague, 1938–48. Secretary of War (under Roosevelt), 1940–5. No other politician has served in the Cabinets of two Republican and two Democratic presidents.

cises. They were impressive and convincing. I had never seen a thousand men leap into the air at once. I was given a 'walkie-talkie' to carry. This was the first time I had ever handled such a convenience.

In the afternoon we saw the mass-produced American divisions doing field exercises with live ammunition. At the end I said to Ismay (to whom I am indebted for this account), 'What do you think of it?' He replied, 'To put these troops against German troops would be murder.' Whereupon I said, 'You're wrong. They are wonderful material and will learn very quickly.' To my American hosts however I consistently pressed my view that it takes two years or more to make a soldier. Certainly two years later the troops we saw in Carolina bore themselves like veterans.

Henry Channon: diary
('Chips', page 332)

23 June 1942

I walked, in the heat, to the House and I found an atmosphere of disappointment, bewildered rage and uneasiness.

[...] towards the end of a wild barrage, John Wardlaw-Milne rose and demanded that the debate should take place immediately, suggesting Thursday as an appropriate day. Attlee refused, and intimated that it would be better to await the arrival of facts before trying to find out who was guilty, and that next week would be time enough. Obviously playing for time until the Prime Minister could get back. Wardlaw-Milne then threatened a Vote of Censure, and the House was electrified and cheered. The Lobbies soon hummed, and everyone I saw was suddenly as excited as an aged virgin being led to her seducer's bed.

Everybody agreed that Winston should cease to be Minister of Defence, and Belisha[1] said to me 'When your doctor is killing you, the first thing to do is to get rid of him'.

Ernest Brown[2] admitted that it was extremely difficult for 'those in the family' as he described the Government, to be loyal to Winston. The House was in a ferment.

---

[1] Leslie Hore-Belisha.

[2] Ernest Brown, 1881–1962. A Baptist lay preacher. On active service in Italy, 1916–18 (Military Cross). Liberal MP for Leith, 1927–31; National Liberal, 1931–45. Parliamentary Secretary, Ministry of Health, 1931–2. Secretary to the Mines Department, 1932–5. Privy Councillor, 1935. Minister of Labour, 1935–40 (and National Service, May 1939 to May 1940). Secretary for Scotland, 1940–1. Minister of Health, 1941–3. Chancellor of the Duchy of Lancaster, 1943–5. Minister of Aircraft Production, 1945. CH, 1945.

Winston S. Churchill: speech
(Press cutting in Churchill papers, 9/158)

24 June 1942   Fort Jackson
                                                   South Carolina

I am enormously impressed by the thoroughness and precision with which the formation of the great war-time army of the United States is proceeding. The day will come when the British and American armies will march into countries, not as invaders, but as liberators, helping the people who have been held under the cruel barbarian yoke.

That day may seem long to those whose period of training spreads across the weeks and months. But when it comes, it will make amends for all the toil and discipline that has been undergone. Also, it will open the world to larger freedom and to life, liberty, and the pursuit of happiness, as the grand words of your Declaration of Independence put it.

General Claude Auchinleck to Winston S. Churchill
(Churchill papers, 20/77)

24 June 1942   Cairo
Personal and Most Secret

[...]

I deeply regret that you should have received this severe blow at so critical a time as a result of the heavy defeat suffered by the forces under my command. I fear that the position is now much what it was a year ago when I took over command except that the enemy now has Tobruk which may be of considerable advantage to him not only from the supply point of view but because he has no need to detach troops to contain it as was the case last year.

4. We are deeply grateful to you and to the President of the United States for the generous measure of help which you propose to give us and for the speed with which you are arranging to send it. The second United States Armoured Division will indeed be a welcome reinforcement as will the Grant and Lee tanks diverted from India. Your assurance that the Indian infantry division and the Indian armoured brigade need not now be sent back to India will greatly ease my difficulties in regard to the internal security problem in Iraq and Persia, especially in the oilfield areas. Air Marshal Tedder informs me that the diversion of

aircraft to this theatre and the permission to retain the Halpro force here will strengthen our hands immensely while the Halifax squadrons will greatly increase our offensive power in the air.

5. With regard to your para 4, I believe that practically without exception the troops in the 8th Army are as determined to beat the enemy as ever they were which is saying much and that their spirit is unimpaired. As to accepting decisions brought about by enemy action we will do all we can by improving tactics and leadership to prevent their recurrence but as you know we are trying to train an army and use it on the battle-field at the same time. We are catching up but have not caught up yet. As to using all my manpower I hope I am doing this but infantry cannot win over battles in the desert as long as the enemy has superiority in armour and nothing can be said or done to change this fact. Guns and armour and just enough infantry to give them and their supply organisation local protection are what is needed. Masses of infantry are no use without guns and armour. We can not have too many guns or too many tanks and the tanks must be American medium tanks, which can stand up to German tanks and not Crusaders with only two pounder guns in them, though Crusaders with six pounder guns should be all right. I thank you personally and most sincerely for all your help and support during the past year and deeply regret the failures and setbacks of the past month for which I accept the fullest responsibility.

Henry Channon: diary
('Chips', page 333)

24 June 1942   London

The House is still in a turmoil, and people intrigue in corners. Ward-law-Milne will put down his motion, and the Government will survive, but scared and shaken.

[...]

[...] the PM is flying back, today I believe, to take charge of the crisis. It will be a battle, certainly, but one always gets back to the old problem, there is no alternative to Winston.

Winston S. Churchill to General Claude Auchinleck
(Churchill papers, 20/77)

25 June 1942   Washington DC
Personal

Do not have the slightest anxiety about course of affairs at home. Whatever views I may have about how the battle was fought or whether it should have been fought a good deal earlier, you have my entire confidence, and I share your responsibilities to the full.

2. I have just shown your message to the President, who was strongly moved and means to come to our aid. The difficulties about shipping the American Armoured Division, which are considerable, are in process of being flattened out. The Americans are also trying to send a large number of a new kind of anti-tank rocket gun, of which they have great hopes. Meanwhile you have heard of the American air reinforcements which are already being directed to the Middle East. Plans are being formed to send another large wave, perhaps 100, long-range bombers as fast as possible; also to hurry out to you further-improved Grant tanks. I shall propose to President tomorrow placing an American General under your Command, with a seat on the Middle East War Council, observing that he would speak both for American Air and Army Units.

3. Please tell Harwood[1] that I am rather worried about reports of undue despondency and alarm in Alexandria and of the Navy hastening to evacuate to the Red Sea. Although various precautionary moves may be taken and *Queen Elizabeth* should be got out at earliest, I trust a firm, confident attitude will be maintained. The President's information from Rome is that Rommel expects to be delayed three or four weeks before he can mount heavy attack on the Mersa Matruh position. I should think the delay might well be greater.

4. I hope the crisis will lead to all uniformed personnel in the Delta and all available loyal manpower being raised to the highest fighting condition. You have over 700,000 men on your ration strength in the Middle East. Every fit male should be made to fight and die for victory. There is no reason why units defending the Mersa Matruh position should not be reinforced by several thousands of officers and administrative personnel ordered to swell the battalions or working parties. You are in the same kind of situation as we should be if England were invaded, and the same intense drastic spirit should reign.

---

[1] Vice-Admiral and Commander-in-Chief, Mediterranean Station, 1942–5.

Winston S. Churchill: recollection
('The Hinge of Fate', pages 349–50)

25 June 1942

On the 25th I met the representatives of our Dominions and India, and attended a meeting of the Pacific War Council. That evening I set out for Baltimore, where my flying-boat lay. The President bade me farewell at the White House with all his grace and courtesy, and Harry Hopkins and Averell Harriman came to see me off. The narrow, closed-in gangway which led to the water was heavily guarded by armed American police. There seemed to be an air of excitement, and the officers looked serious. Before we took off I was told that one of the plain-clothes men on duty had been caught fingering a pistol and heard muttering that he would 'do me in', with some other expressions of an unappreciative character. He had been pounced upon and arrested. Afterwards he turned out to be a lunatic. Crackpates are a special danger to public men, as they do not have to worry about the 'get away'.

We came down at Botwood[1] the next morning in order to refuel, and took off again after a meal of fresh lobsters. Thereafter I ate at stomach-time – i.e. with the usual interval between meals – and slept whenever possible. I sat in the co-pilot's seat as, after flying over Northern Ireland, we approached the Clyde at dawn, and landed safely. My train was waiting, with Peck,[2] one of my personal secretaries, and a mass of boxes, and four or five days' newspapers. In an hour we were off to the South. It appeared that we had lost a by-election by a sweeping turnover at Maldon.[3] This was one of the by-products of Tobruk.

This seemed to me to be a bad time. I went to bed, browsed about in the files for a while, and then slept for four or five hours till we reached London. What a blessing is the gift of sleep! The War Cabinet were on the platform to greet me on arrival, and I was soon at work in the Cabinet Room.

---

[1] Botwood, Newfoundland. In 1940, its relatively fog-free airport was chosen to be a reconnaissance base for Catalina flying boats. Tens of thousands of troops passed through Botwood during the Second World War. When Bob Hope and his troupe were stormbound at Botwood in 1943, they performed for the Royal Canadian Air Force Command personnel stationed there. By 1945, Botwood had been superseded by Gander as Newfoundland's main transatlantic staging post.

[2] John Howard Peck, 1913–95. An Assistant Private Secretary to the First Lord of the Admiralty (Lord Stanhope), 1937–9; to the Minister for Co-ordination of Defence (Lord Chatfield), 1939–40; to the First Lord of the Admiralty (Churchill), April–May 1940; to the Prime Minister (Churchill), 1940–5. Transferred to the Foreign Service, 1946. Ambassador to Senegal, 1962–6; to Mauritania, 1962–5. Under-Secretary of State, 1966–70. Ambassador to the Republic of Ireland, 1970–3. Knighted, 1971. Published his memoirs, *Dublin from Downing Street*, in 1978.

[3] The Maldon by-election was held on 25 June 1942, when the Independent candidate Tom Driberg defeated the Conservative candidate R. J. Hunt, gaining 61.3% of the vote.

Winston S. Churchill to General Claude Auchinleck
(Churchill papers, 20/77)

25 June 1942
Most Secret

I told you in my 'Googly'[1] No. 13 that President proposed to send you the Second United States Armoured Division and that it would leave from Suez about 5th July. We find that the shipping of this Division within the next month presents very grave difficulties and would involve serious interference with WS 21[2] and WS 22.[3]

2. General Marshall has therefore put forward a proposal which CIGS considers even more attractive from your point of view, since you will be getting a generous hamper of the most modern equipment and your reinforcements from England are not affected. We have therefore accepted following proposal:

3. The Americans will send 300 Sherman (M.4) tanks and 100 self-propelling 105-mm gun howitzers to the Middle East as an urgent move. These equipments will sail for Suez about 10th July in two sea-trains taken from the Havana sugar traffic, doing 15 and 13 knots respectively, and their passage will be expedited by every possible means. A small number of American key personnel will accompany the tanks and guns.

4. We think it probable that you will have sufficient trained personnel to man these equipments. Please let us know exactly how you stand. If you cannot find the men we would propose to send the personnel of an armoured brigade to you in WS 21. We would try to arrange for these men to have one or two weeks' training on American-type in North Ireland.

---

[1] 'Googly': the prefix for telegrams from Churchill to Auchinleck.

[2] WS Convoys (known as Winston's Specials) sailed from the United Kingdom to India and the Far East. WS 21, with 12 merchant ships, left the Clyde on 29 July 1941, reaching Freetown on August 10 and leaving five days later, with five extra merchant ships. The convoy continued – with further accessions of American merchant ships reaching it from the United States – to St Helena, Cape Town, Durban, Aden, and Bombay. It was escorted, in different sections of its voyage, by a total of two battleships, four aircraft carriers, two cruisers, and 16 destroyers.

[3] The 19 merchant ships of WS 22 sailed from Liverpool on 28 August 1942 (and from the Clyde a day later) for Gibraltar, Freetown, Takoradi, Cape Town, Durban, Mombasa, Aden, Bombay, and Karachi.

Winston S. Churchill to Henry L. Stimson
(Churchill papers, 20/53)

25 June 1942

My dear Stimson,

May I offer to yourself and General Marshall my best thanks for the most interesting and instructive day which you have permitted me to spend with your troops. My only regret is that the time at my disposal did not allow a longer visit.

I have had considerable experience of such inspections and I can say that I have never been more impressed than I was with the bearing of the men whom I saw. The undemonstrative, therefore grim, determination which was everywhere manifest not only in the seasoned troops but in the newly-drafted, bodes ill for our enemies.

I should be grateful if you would convey my thanks to General Eichelberger[1] and all who were concerned in making the many detailed arrangements which such a visit at short notice required. I very much appreciated their concern for my comfort and convenience.

Yours sincerely
Winston S Churchill

Winston S. Churchill to Theodore F. Wilson[2]
(Churchill papers, 20/53)

25 June 1942

My dear Wilson,

May I again thank you for the services rendered to me by your Agents.

As on the occasion of my last visit, everything which could contribute to my comfort and convenience was anticipated and arranged.

Yours v faithfully,
Winston S Churchill

---

[1] Robert Lawrence Eichelberger, 1888–1972. Graduated from the United States Military Academy (West Point), 1909. Superintendent, United States Military Academy, 1941. Commanded the United States I Corps in Australia, 1942. At the Buna front in Papua, New Guinea, led I Corps to the first Allied victory against Japanese ground forces, December 1942. Took I Corps to a further victory at Hollandia, April 1944. Commanded the newly formed 8th Army from September 1944, in action in the southern Philippines, Leyte, and Luzon. Took the surrender of 50,000 Japanese troops on Luzon alone. On board USS *Missouri* to witness the Japanese surrender. Commanded the first occupation forces in Japan.

[2] Director of Personnel, United States Treasury.

Lord Ismay: recollection
('The Memoirs of General The Lord Ismay', page 257)

25–6 June 1942

The next night we took off from Baltimore in the Boeing Clipper. Churchill was in splendid form. 'Now for England, home, and – a beautiful row,' was his farewell remark to Hopkins. His last act before leaving the White House had been to send Auchinleck a message of encouragement. 'You have my entire confidence, and I share your responsibilities to the full.' Would many Prime Ministers facing a Vote of Censure have been so considerate, loyal and generous to the commander whose defeat had caused this political storm?

General Claude Auchinleck to Winston S. Churchill
(Churchill papers, 20/77)

26 June 1942   8th Army HQ
Personal and Most Secret

Most grateful your Googly 27 25/6 and for your generous support. The news of American determination to aid us and their efforts to speed up the movements of reinforcements both ground and air are most heartening. We all realise the shipping difficulties. Any tank-destroying device such as the new American rocket gun will be more than welcome and will be given fullest opportunity. The increased strength of long-range bombers made available by you is magnificent. Is already having its effect and the news that many more are coming is magnificent. An American general on the Middle East War Council speaking for both Army and Air would, I am sure, help us tremendously and be warmly welcomed by me. Your message was passed to Admiral Harwood last night. Air Marshal Tedder and I are in close touch with him regarding possibilities of intensified air attacks on ports. Impossible to gauge enemy intentions at present, but consider it at least probable that he will try to exploit his success by early resumption of attack. His administrative difficulties must be considerable, however, and we know his German units have suffered heavily. Every day or week gained is an advantage to us. Your instructions regarding fighting manpower will be carried out and are in fact being observed. Working parties in El Alamein portion are being reinforced from base depôts in Delta so far as maintenance limitations and especially water supply will permit. Consider have sufficient infantry in Matruh position already and all available artillery has been deployed. As more becomes available it will be sent up. We will do our best.

Winston S. Churchill to Harry Hopkins
(Churchill papers, 20/77)

27 June 1942
Personal and Secret

President would be interested to see following extracts from Auchinleck's reply to my telegram from Washington telling him that the President was much moved by position in Middle East and determined to help them by all the means in his power.

'The news of American determination to aid us and their efforts to speed up the movements of reinforcements both ground and air are most heartening. We all realise the shipping difficulties. Any tank-destroying device, such as the new American Rocket Gun, will be more than welcome and will be given fullest opportunity. The increased strength of long-range bombers made available by you is magnificent. Is already having its effect and the news that many more are coming is magnificent. An American General on the Middle East War Council speaking for both Army and Air would, I am sure, help us tremendously and be warmly welcomed by me.

'Impossible to gauge enemy intentions at present, but consider it at least probable that he will try to exploit his success by early resumption of attack. His administrative difficulties must be considerable, however, and we know his German units have suffered heavily. Every day or week gained is an advantage to us.'

War Cabinet: conclusions
(Cabinet papers, 65/26)

27 June 1942   10 Downing Street
5.30 p.m.

THE PRIME MINISTER'S VISIT TO THE UNITED STATES

The Prime Minister gave the War Cabinet an account of his visit to the United States and of the Conferences which had taken place. The defeat of our forces in the Middle East, and, perhaps even more, rumours of its effect on the political situation in this country, had figured largely in the American Press. The attitude of the Administration had, however, been very staunch.

The Prime Minister outlined the help which the United States had arranged to send to the Middle East.

[...]

The Prime Minister mentioned a suggestion which had been made that an international commission should be set up by the United Nations, under high judicial authority, to collect evidence of atrocities committed by the enemy. He had told the President that he agreed with the scheme in principle, though the details required further examination.

The War Cabinet took note of this statement.

War Cabinet: Confidential Annex
(Cabinet papers, 65/30)

27 June 1942   10 Downing Street
5.30 p.m.
Most Secret

The Prime Minister gave the War Cabinet a resumé of his visit to the United States.

He gave details of the invaluable help which they were sending to the Middle East. This comprised 300 Sherman tanks, which were an improvement on the General Grant tanks, and 100 self-propelled 105 mm guns. General Auchinleck had expressed his gratification at these reinforcements, which should reach Suez by the end of August.

The Americans had also promised generous help in the air, and, all being well, we should have over 100 bombers in the Middle East shortly. The *Ranger*[1] would off-load 62 Kittyhawks of improved performance at Takoradi, and these would be in action within a month. General Auchinleck had accepted the proposal that an American General should be appointed to the Middle East to command the United States forces in that area.

The Air agreement had been settled in a manner more favourable to us than had been expected.

The Prime Minister read to the War Cabinet a memorandum which he and the President had agreed about our strategy in the West for 1942–1943.

The Chief of the Imperial General Staff gave the War Cabinet an account of his discussion with the Combined Chiefs of Staff and his impressions of certain American units which he had visited.

The first few days had been taken up in clearing up certain misunderstandings which had arisen. General Marshall was bent on concentrating on the 'Bolero' plan. Other very high quarters in Washington were, how-

---

[1] USS *Ranger*: the first purpose-built United States aircraft carrier.

ever, apprehensive that if we concentrated on 'Bolero' to the exclusion of any other projects, either in 1942 or 1943, there was a danger that, if 'Bolero' was not practicable, large bodies of American troops would be locked up in Great Britain and remain indefinitely inactive.

Winston S. Churchill to General Claude Auchinleck
(Churchill papers, 20/77)

28 June 1942
Secret and Personal

I am very glad you have taken Command. Do not vex yourself with anything except the battle. Fight it out wherever it flows. Nothing matters but destroying the enemy's armed and armoured force. A strong stream of reinforcements is approaching. We are sure you are going to win in the end.

Winston S. Churchill to Richard Casey
(Churchill papers, 20/77)

29 June 1942
Personal and Secret

Many thanks. Your full account of campaign in Egypt will be most interesting, and I wonder how Rommel's tanks will get on amongst the irrigation canals. Make sure that every man in uniform is made to fight. All good wishes.

General Claude Auchinleck to Winston S. Churchill
(Churchill papers, 20/77)

29 June 1942
Personal and Most Secret

Will do my best to carry out your orders and so will every one in 8 Army. Your efforts to send us help thoroughly appreciated. We are doing everything possible here.

Winston S. Churchill to Sir Charles Wilson[1]
(Churchill papers, 20/53)

29 June 1942

My dear Sir Charles,

Thank you so much for your great kindness in coming with me to Washington at such short notice and, I fear, at no little personal inconvenience.

It was a great comfort to have you there and I am more than grateful.

I was almost sorry not to be able to provide you with some work. But your presence kept the marauder away.

Yours very sincerely,
Winston S Churchill

Winston S. Churchill to Sir John Wardlaw-Milne
(Churchill papers, 20/53)

30 June 1942

Dear Wardlaw-Milne,

I brought your letter[2] of June 30 before the War Cabinet this morning, and they desired me to inform you that in view of the challenge to the competence and authority of the Government which has now for some days been spread throughout the world, it is imperative that the matter should go forward to an immediate issue, and for this all arrangements have been made.

Yours very truly,
Winston S. Churchill

[1] Churchill's doctor. This was his first journey overseas with Churchill.

[2] Sir John Wardlaw-Milne, Chairman of the House of Commons Select Committee on National Expenditure and Conservative MP for Kidderminster, placed before the War Cabinet a Vote of Censure against the Government, with the intention of forcing Churchill out of office with a vote of no confidence.

Winston S. Churchill to Richard Casey
(Churchill papers, 20/77)

30 June 1942
Personal and Secret

Further to my OZ 601, I wished to let you know how much I appreciate the part you have played not only in the main situation, but also in the change of command, which I have long desired and advocated. While Auchinleck fights at the front, you should insist upon the mobilisation for battle of all the rearward services. Everybody in uniform must fight exactly like they would if Kent or Sussex were invaded. Tank hunting parties with sticky bombs and bombards, defence to the death of every fortified area or strong building, making every post a winning post and every ditch a last ditch. This is the spirit you have got to inculcate. No general evacuation, no playing for safety. Egypt must be held at all costs.

July
1942

Winston S. Churchill: Written Answers
(Hansard)

1 July 1942   House of Commons

The Prime Minister (Mr Churchill): I have carefully considered this matter, and I have had at no time any doubt but that if an appeal were made on the grounds of the urgency and seriousness of the situation the Debate would be postponed. But, after all, this Vote of Censure has been on the Order Paper for some time, and it has been flashed all over the world. When I was in the United States, I can testify to the lively excitement which was created by its appearance, and, although we in this country may have our own knowledge of the stability of our institutions and of the strength of the Government of the day, yet that is by no means the opinion which is shared or felt in other countries. Now that this has gone so far, and this matter has been for more than a week the subject of comment in every part of the world, it would be, in my opinion, even more injurious to delay a decision than to go forward with this issue.

Winston S. Churchill to the War Cabinet
(Cabinet papers, 66/26)

1 July 1942   10 Downing Street

I circulate, for consideration by my colleagues, a Memorandum giving effect to a suggestion of mine for the appointment of a United Nations Commission on Atrocities which was handed to me by Mr Hopkins at our last meeting, on the 25th June. I told the President that I agreed with the scheme in principle, though the details required further examination.

A UNITED NATIONS COMMISSION ON ATROCITIES.

An authoritative presentation of the atrocities committed by the Germans and Japanese in Lidice, Poland, Nanking, Hong Kong and other places should:

(a) Help to keep the people of the United Nations informed of the nature of our enemies, spurring us to renewed efforts to defeat them; and

(b) Serve to deter those committing the atrocities by naming their names and letting them know that they are being watched by the civilised world, which will mete out swift and just punishment on the reckoning day.

2. Such an authoritative presentation could be made by a United Nations Commission on Atrocities, headed by someone like former Chief Justice Hughes, and including outstanding representatives of the other United Nations, such as Tolstoy of Russia, Del Vayo of Spain, Sforza of Italy, Holdsworth of England, and Dr Wu of China. To avoid any implications of propaganda, the personnel of the Commission should not officially represent their Governments, though they should be satisfactory to them. They should be persons of a world-wide reputation for integrity and an ability to appraise the evidence.

3. The Commission should –

(a) Investigate the atrocities by taking depositions, interrogating eye-witnesses and assessing all other available or obtainable evidence; and

(b) Report to the United Nations, from time to time, on the shooting and maiming of hostages and prisoners, the beating and torturing of women and children, and the other violations of the fundamental rights of human beings. The report to the United Nations should, wherever possible, name the persons who are responsible for the atrocities.

Harold Nicolson: diary
(*'Harold Nicolson, Diaries and Letters', page 231*)

1 July 1942   London

To the House for the first day of the debate on the Vote of Censure. Wardlaw-Milne is an imposing man with a calm manner which gives the impression of solidity. He is in fact rather an ass, and the position he has

acquired as one of the leaders of the back-benches has caused his head
to swell badly. He begins well enough, but then suddenly suggests that
the Duke of Gloucester[1] should be made Commander-in-Chief. A wave of
panic-embarrassment passes over the House. For a full minute the buzz
goes round, 'but the man must be an ass.' Milne pulls himself together
and recaptures the attention of the House, but his idiotic suggestion has
shaken the validity of his position and his influence is shattered.

Roger Keyes seconds. He is a very dull speaker, and most people troop
out to luncheon. Keyes denies that the PM ever interfered with Service
chiefs. In fact he complains that he never overrides their advice. They
are all for caution, and the result was that when we might have won the
battle of the Mediterranean, we hesitated and fumbled, and now it was
too late.

Winterton rises to speak, and the PM strolls out deliberately with
bowed shoulders. Bob Boothby makes an admirable speech supporting
the Government, but I notice that in *The Times* it is not even mentioned.
The debate goes on till after midnight.

Henry Channon: diary
('Chips', page 334)

1 July 1942

John Wardlaw-Milne moved his much publicised Vote of Censure in
strong and convincing language today, and I watched the front bench
squirm with annoyance. Winston looked harassed and everyone was
emotional and uneasy. I thought it all rather horrible. Wardlaw-Milne
held the House well, he was fair, calm and dignified, and he was listened
to with respect, until he made an unfortunate suggestion, that the Duke
of Gloucester should be made Commander-in-Chief of the forces. The
House roared with disrespectful laughter, and I at once saw Winston's
face light up, as if a lamp had been lit within him and he smiled genially.
He knew now that he was saved, and poor Wardlaw-Milne never quite
regained the hearing of the House.

---

[1] Prince Henry William Frederick Albert, 1900–74. Third son of King George V and Queen Mary.
Educated at Eton, the Royal Military College, and Trinity College, Cambridge. Created Duke of
Gloucester, March 1928. Chief Liaison Officer, British Expeditionary Force, 1939–40; Home Forces,
1940–1. His elder son was killed in an aeroplane crash in 1972.

House of Commons: Debate
(Hansard)

2 July 1942

Sir John Wardlaw-Milne (Kidderminster): I beg to move, with the leave of the House, 'That this House, while paying tribute to the heroism and endurance of the Armed Forces of the Crown in circumstances of exceptional difficulty, has no confidence in the central direction of the war.'

Mr A. Bevan (Ebbw Vale): I beg to second the Motion.

The Hon. Members who put their names to this Motion and I were rebuked yesterday by hon. Members in some parts of the House for having done so. They rebuked us on two grounds – one, that a Motion of this nature moved at this time would have a bad effect upon the morale of the troops; and the other that it would have a bad effect upon the morale of the country. I want to reply to these two charges at the beginning. I believe it would have been a very bad thing indeed for the reputation of the House of Commons if this Motion had not been moved. It is the duty, as I understand it, of Members of Parliament to try and reproduce in the House of Commons the psychology which exists in the country, and there can be no doubt that the country is deeply disturbed by the movement of events at the present time. Having put the Motion on the Order Paper, it would have been a great disservice to the country if we had withdrawn it. I do not know whether hon. Members have received many letters in the last few days, but if they have they will have realised that there are far more people supporting the Motion outside the House than are represented by the names on the Order Paper.

With regard to the morale of the troops, my hon. Friends and I would be loath indeed to do anything here which might have the effect of undermining the courage and resolution of our troops in battle. It is not, however, what we say in this House, it is not the speeches we make that bring home to the soldiers the defects in the direction of the war; it is what they experience themselves in battle. It would be a serious thing if the soldiers in the field could not hear any voices raised in their behalf in the House of Commons. I believe that nothing would more nerve our Forces to greater efforts and arouse their enthusiasm than the knowledge that their representatives in the House of Commons were doing their best to see that they are given the right weapons with which to fight. It will never be possible for us, in this war, to move a Vote of Censure on the Government at a time when no battle is in progress. Battles are going to be continuous throughout the war, and, therefore, we must take the opportunity, when we think it is proper, to move a Vote of Censure upon the Government, although it may happen that at that very moment a series of grave battles is in progress.

The Prime Minister has decided to wind up the Debate, and I understand he proposes to talk for something like an hour and a half. I am bound to point out to the House that I think a very serious disservice is being done to the House and the country by the fact that the Prime Minister did not see fit to open the Debate. He has the right to choose when he will speak. Of course he has, but the Prime Minister is also Minister of Defence, and the House had the right to be put in possession of the facts of the case, so that the Debate might have proceeded upon an examination of those facts. I know that it is better debating tactics for the Prime Minister to wind up the Debate. In that way, he will win the Debate. But the country is now more concerned with the Prime Minister winning the war than with his winning a Debate in the House of Commons. The Prime Minister wins Debate after Debate and loses battle after battle. The country is beginning to say that he fights Debates like a war and the war like a Debate. It would have been much more dignified for the Prime Minister and of much greater service to the House, if he had opened the Debate yesterday and allowed one of his Ministers to wind up. Indeed, the Prime Minister could have opened the Debate and wound it up as well. He has done so before. But that would have been undignified for other Members of the Government, because it would give the impression once more to the world that there was only one man in the Government.

So, because of that situation, the House of Commons is in the difficulty of having to await the Prime Minister's reply before it is able to consider the merits of the Government's case. Furthermore, yesterday we were at a disadvantage in having had a speech from the Minister of Production. Rather it was the Government's disadvantage, not ours. I have heard some members of the Government complain about the right hon. Gentleman's speech. I do not see why they should complain, because, had the right hon. Gentleman made himself more clear, the Government's case would have suffered more damage. What, in fact, did the right hon. Gentleman say? What was the main case made by him? It was that we had had no time in which to produce new weapons and that, therefore, our troops in Libya had to fight with weapons which were designed before the war. That was his main case – that we could not change the designs in time, that there are new designs in production, but that they could not be put on the battlefield because we had to continue with the old types. What then becomes of the Prime Minister's statement last December that at last we were meeting the enemy on equal terms with modern weapons?

I would also refer to a speech which was made yesterday in another place. Ministers are all concerned to prove that they were right and that they made no mistakes when in office. I recommend hon. Members to read the speech made in another place, because that is another answer to the Government. Ministers are trying to absolve themselves by putting the blame somewhere else. I hope to show that the blame rests squarely upon the Government's own shoulders. I, therefore, believe that it is the duty of hon. Members to state their minds clearly and independently upon this matter. The House may not agree with me, but when I sit down, there should be no misunderstanding about what I think.

It seems to me that there are three things wrong. First, the main strategy of the war has been wrong; second, the wrong weapons have been produced; and third, those weapons are being managed by men who are not trained in the use of them and who have not studied the use of modern weapons. As I understand it, it is strategy that dictates the weapon and tactics that dictate the use of the weapon. The Government have conceived the war wrongly from the very beginning, and no one has more misconceived it than the Prime Minister himself. The nature of the weapons used by the enemy has not been understood by the Prime Minister ever since the beginning of the war. I will read to the House what the right hon. Gentleman said on 19th May, 1940:

'It would be foolish to disguise the gravity of the situation. It would be still more foolish to lose heart or courage, or to suppose that well-trained, well-equipped armies, numbering 3,000,000 or 4,000,000 of men, can be overcome in the space of a few weeks or even months, by a super-raid of mechanised vehicles, however formidable.'

That is precisely what did happen in a few weeks. No one was more Maginot minded than the Prime Minister himself. I have read all his speeches very carefully, and I say that no one has thought of this war in terms of the last war more than the Prime Minister himself. That is contained in the statement to which I refer. He also said: 'We may look forward with confidence to the stabilisation of the front in France'. Fancy, after Poland and in the opening weeks of the Battle of France, speaking about stabilisation of the front in France. No Russian general, no German general speaks about the stabilisation of the front. The front cannot be stabilised in modern war, and Rommel is proving it today. The Prime Minister went on to say: 'and to the general engagement of the masses which will enable the qualities of the French and British soldiers to be matched squarely against those of their adversaries: For myself, I have invincible confidence in the French Army and its leaders.'

The Prime Minister (Mr Churchill): Ought I to have said the opposite?

Mr Bevan: It is a case of what the right hon. Gentleman ought not to have said. He ought not to have used language which, on the face of it, reveals quite clearly that the Prime Minister had not penetrated to the heart of the methods that were being used by the Germans or were going to be used in this war. It is that primary misconception of the war which has been responsible for the wrong strategy of the Government, and, the strategy being wrong, the wrong weapons were produced. The chief evidence of that is the case of the dive-bomber. The second chief evidence of that is the complete failure to equip the British Army with transport planes. Take the situation in Libya. The right hon. Gentleman the Minister of Production yesterday said that according to modern methods of warfare 'islands' of troops had been made in the desert behind fortifications. We had one in Bir Hacheim, fought with distinguished gallantry by the Free French. This has been one of the most heroic episodes in the whole war, and I am informed that they had not even two-pounder guns in Bir Hacheim. Having seen for more than two years that we should be fighting a desert war in Libya, we still have not provided any transport planes, and had to send a tank brigade through with supplies, whereas the Germans have supplied strong points and islands of resistance in Russia right throughout the winter by transport planes.

I say that if the war had been properly conceived, if the Prime Minister had understood it, we should have had both dive-bombers and transport planes, so that wherever we organised a strong point, whether in the desert or elsewhere, transport plans would have been available to supply our troops. Further, had we produced transport planes in any quantity, we should have been able right through the campaign there to use them for carrying a great deal of material instead of having to send all supplies 14,000 miles by sea. I ask the House seriously whether that condition of affairs reveals any deep penetration by the Government into the nature of the war we have to fight. A lot has been said about dive-bombers. Even now the Government have not made up their minds upon them. The Secretary of State for War says that discussions are proceeding. I would remind hon. Members of a letter, from Mr Westbrook, which they have probably read for themselves, which was published in *The Times*. He was at the Ministry of Aircraft Production and went out to the Near East in charge of supplies, or at least as one of the higher officials, and he came home from the Near East for reasons that it is not politic to state in public. He says: 'Just lately many confusing and conflicting statements have been made about the lack of dive-bombers. The true facts are that the Air Ministry decided before the war against the use of them.' Against the use of them before the war. Where was our Intelligence Service? For the last five or six years I have heard the Prime Minister making eloquent speeches about the German military preparations. His reputation to this day rests upon those speeches. The affectionate regard the country still has for him arises out of gratitude because he warned the country at that time. But he warned the country about them quantitatively; the qualitative position he left aside. He gave us the figures, but there was no insight behind the figures. He has been in charge of this war really for three years. He must have known the nature of the weapons that the Germans were making. Dive-bombers were not a secret. The Czechs knew of them and had prepared to resist them. Czech military strategy was based upon the use of the dive-bomber. The letter from Mr Westbrook goes on: 'Probably this was correct until we had the mastery of the air or sufficient capacity to enable their production without detriment to the more important types.' There, of course, is the official defending his decisions. The fact remains that a prototype was never developed, that the Government could not even make up their mind then, because they fell between two stools. Mr Westbrook says further: 'Both Lord Beaverbrook and I thought they were necessary, so he obtained a request from Mr Eden, then at the War Office, and a quantity to a new design were ordered from America in the summer of 1940. These are now in production. There were, however, delivery delays, as the British Air Commission in America were never allowed to give them any form of priority.' That is a most serious statement. We have no right to complain against America. If America did not want to give them priority, why should America do so when we ourselves said they were no use? We did not ask for priority for them. The result is that after three years of war the British Army is not equipped with dive-bombers. I say that at once reveals that the Prime Minister and his Government have not gone to the heart of this modern war-making, and I say that it is disgraceful that the lives of British soldiers should be lost because of the absence of this elementary knowledge at the top.

We ourselves, here, must accept responsibility for it. After all, the Government are responsible to us, and if the House of Commons refuses to exercise its independence against the Government, the House of Commons must accept responsibility for the result. It is we, not party machines, not secret meetings upstairs of Members on any side of the House, but we in this House who are responsible for sending British soldiers on to the battlefield with improper weapons, and hon. Members, when they go back to their constituencies, should not hide behind any formality of Parliamentary debate but face squarely up to the facts. When the mothers and fathers of British soldiers ask why their boys go into battle worse equipped than the enemy, for heaven's sake say, 'We are responsible, and nobody else.'

Sir Granville Gibson (Pudsey and Otley): The hon. Member was for seven years. He always voted against any increase in armaments for seven years.

Earl Winterton (Horsham and Worthing): What about the Government? What about the Home Secretary?

Mr Bevan: I will face the issue squarely. I do not run away from it. This House of Commons gave the Government unlimited power to rearm this country in 1935, and Ministers still in this Government were responsible at that time. The right hon. Gentleman has picked them for his Government. Do not throw the jeer back at me; it belongs over there. It is the Prime Minister who has cast the mantle of his benediction on the shoulders of those guilty Ministers. They are still there sitting on that front Bench, so do not throw the jeer at me. In any case, even if the rearmament of Britain before the war was quantitatively lacking, there is no excuse for its having been qualitatively inefficient. There may be an excuse for a lack of will, but not for a lack of brains, and our brains were wrong and the brains are still wrong.

I will not talk about guns, because they were exploded yesterday – almost all day. We know the situation as regards guns. We know that the guns supplied to our troops did not answer the Prime Minister's description. They were not modern weapons. The Spanish Republicans were using an 8-pounder anti-tank gun in 1936. The Germans learned the lesson in Spain and made the gun immediately afterwards in Germany. We were rearming then, we were supposed to be rearming. We had two White Papers on rearmament. But, of course, the Government of that day were too much occupied in trying to destroy the Republican Government in Spain to learn any military lessons from the campaign in Spain. That was the situation. I shall not deal further with that aspect of it, because I am going on to another matter.

Why is the strategy wrong? I say, first, that it is because the Prime Minister, although possessing many other qualities, sometimes conceives of the war, it seems to me, in medieval terms, because he talks of it as if it were a tourney. But the strategy is wrong because the Prime Minister has a wrong instrument of Government. We have been at war for three years. Over and over again I have heard the Prime Minister speak most eloquently about the defects of the machinery of Government. Look at it for a moment. There is a War Cabinet of seven. One of them I rule out, the Lord President of the Council.[1] I do not want to be offensive, he is a most distinguished man, but I have always looked upon him rather as a Civil servant than as a politician. So I rule him out. I do not believe that the guidance of the right hon. Gentleman on matters of high political principle differs from that he would get from any Government Department. Then there is the Secretary of State for Foreign Affairs, burdened by a complicated office. There is the Minister of Labour, with a most distinguished career, a most dynamic personality. He has a most complicated Department, a huge Department with a large staff. Also, he speaks every weekend. How can he master documents about the war? I do not think the right hon. Gentleman has ever claimed to understand much about war – this is a serious matter – and in any case he has not got the time.

There is the Minister of Production.[2] He is a member of the War Cabinet. The Minister of Production was, I understand, a business man of distinction, but he has no political experience worth speaking about, as was revealed yesterday. I say with all respect that in his own sphere he is a most eminent man. [AN HON. MEMBER: 'And a soldier.'] This place is full of soldiers. Stalin was not a soldier, but he is a very good general. The Minister of Production is at the head of the most vital Department of all. He has no time to attend to matters of strategy, so he is no use in the War Cabinet for this purpose. Then there is the Deputy Prime Minister.[3] We had a Debate the other day. There was no Vote of Censure then. The Government had an overwhelming Vote of Confidence. Every newspaper in the country, every critic in the House of Commons, including men of long standing such as the right hon. Member for Carnarvon Boroughs (Mr Lloyd George), all advised that we should have a small War Cabinet of six Ministers without Portfolio. The Prime Minister made a few changes. He threw out the only Minister in the War Cabinet who did not have a portfolio, and gave a portfolio to the Deputy Prime Minister. Before then the Deputy Prime Minister did not have a Department. Now he has one.

[1] Sir John Anderson.
[2] Oliver Lyttelton.
[3] Clement Attlee.

That foolish instrument exaggerates all the natural weaknesses which are the accompaniments of the Prime Minister's strategy. The Prime Minister has qualities of greatness – everybody knows that – but the trouble is that he has too much to do. He has not around him colleagues to whom he can delegate any of this matter concerning the central direction of the war. The result is that all these defects which he possesses are made dangerous, because the Prime Minister, among all his other qualities, has a gift of expression which is exceedingly dangerous. He very often mistakes verbal felicities for verbal inspiration. The Prime Minister will, in the course of an evening, produce a whole series of brilliant improvisations, but he has not the machinery to carry them through.

It is the absence of support as much as anything else which is responsible for the situation. I seriously suggest to the House that whatever they may do about this Motion, they should for Heaven's sake insist, at this grave hour, that the Prime Minister be kept under the clamp of strong men who have got no Departmental interests. The House knows that that is the correct thing to do, the country knows it, and every responsible man in public affairs in this country outside the Government knows that it is the right thing to do. Why does not the House of Commons exert its dignity and force the Prime Minister to do it? Even an inadequate man giving his full attention is better than a clever man who cannot give any attention. It would be a most improper thing for me to suggest that the members of the War Cabinet are men of no stature. But in this matter the country is entitled to their full services in the central direction of the war, and I suggest that we should insist upon that being done.

Under the War Cabinet I suggest that you must have a far better co-ordination between the Services than now exists. There must be a central staff, presided over by one man who can have immediate access to the War Cabinet and who can ultimately be responsible for central strategy. I do not disagree with the Prime Minister having no Minister of Defence; I do not see how on earth, in war-time, the Prime Minister could delegate responsibility for the war to anybody else. He could not do that, but what he could do would be to have around him a number of Ministers who could assist him in that matter, and the War Cabinet as a whole could see the Chiefs of Staff instead of the Prime Minister.

The Prime Minister: They do.

Mr Bevan: Instead of the Prime Minister seeing them before the War Cabinet sees them, because then the Prime Minister goes into the War Cabinet defending his own decisions.

The Prime Minister: That is not true.

Mr Bevan: I am sorry, but the right hon. Gentleman will have his opportunity of correcting me later. It is the strategy that is wrong, and the production of weapons. Again, I should like to remind hon. Members that this is not a new story; we have been saying this for two years. All over the country the working classes have been deeply disturbed by the failures of production. Talk about not being able to change over to new types – even now there are aircraft factories idle in this country, changing over to new long-range bombers which may be available in two years' time. The country is bored with hearing of the production of long-range bombers. They know very well that the long-range bomber is not a decisive weapon of war, whatever else it may be. Therefore it is foolish at this moment to be changing to new types of long-range bombers which may not be available at the decisive moment.

On Tuesday the right hon. Gentleman the Minister of Production told us that he had now appointed regional controllers. The Trades Union Congress, the trade unions of Britain separately, the Production Engineers Institute and this House of Commons asked for regional boards over two years ago. We have been trying to get the decentralisation of production controls for over two years, and the Prime Minister fought a successful rearguard action against us. He has been fighting rearguard actions against the House of Commons all the time, making concessions all the while to buy off the political situation, not to create a machine for war-making.

So much for production. Then there is the actual use of the weapons in the field. I speak in this matter without authority at all; I have never fought in a battle, I do not know what it is to use weapons in the field, so I have to speak with diffidence in this. Nevertheless, we are responsible, we have to make up our minds. We are as responsible as the Government. I am informed – the Prime Minister will correct me if I am wrong – that even today the staff colleges of the Army have no textbook on the coordination of air and land forces. Even today, our Chiefs of Staff and our war captains are not being educated in the co-ordination of those two weapons. I do not know what hon. Members think of that, but it frightens me. It frightens me to think that after three years of war there is no textbook in our staff colleges on this most urgent and important matter. Why, even the small nations of Europe had it years ago, and we have not got it yet.

We have in this country five or six generals, members of other nations, Czechs, Poles and French, all of them trained in the use of these German weapons and this German technique. I know it is hurtful to our pride, but would it not be possible to put some of those men temporarily in charge in the field, until we can produce trained men of our own? Is there anything wrong in sending out these men, of equal rank with General Ritchie? Why should we not put them in the field in charge of our troops? They know how to fight this war; our people do not, and I say that it is far better to win battles and save British soldiers' lives under the leadership of other members of the United Nations than to lose them under our own inefficient officers. The Prime Minister must realise that in this country there is a taunt, on everyone's lips, that if Rommel had been in the British Army, he would still have been a sergeant. Is that not so? It is a taunt right through the Army. There is a man in the British Army – and this shows how we are using our trained men – who flung 150,000 men across the Ebro in Spain, Michael Dunbar. He is at present a sergeant in an armoured brigade in this country. He was chief of staff in Spain; he won the battle of the Ebro, and he is a sergeant in the British Army. The fact of the matter is that the British Army is ridden by class prejudice. You have got to change it, and you will have to change it. If the House of Commons has not the guts to make the Government change it, events will. Although the House may not take any notice of me today, you will be doing it next week; remember my words next Monday and Tuesday. It is events which are criticising the Government. All that we are doing is giving them a voice, inadequately perhaps, but we are trying to do it.

Therefore, you have to change that business; you have to purge the Army at the top. It will have to be a drastic purge, because the spirit of the British Army has to be regained. I have spoken to men from other nations who have been around the British Army, and they say that never in the history of Great Britain has better human material been provided in the British Army. But it is badly led, not by men without courage – there is no lack of courage in the British Army at any point, at the top or at the bottom – but it is not trained, or is wrongly trained. Therefore, if you are going to give the new weapons which the Minister of Production talked about yesterday, you must give them into the hands of men who know how to use them and who believe in them. You must do that with the dive-bombers; if you have dive-bombers, you must purge from the Air Ministry those men who do not believe in dive-bombers, because the man who does not believe in his own weapon cannot use it. So you will have to purge them.

Furthermore – and I said I was going to be quite frank – if the Prime Minister wants to restore confidence in the British Army, he will have to change his Secretary of State for War.[1] Why on earth he appointed him I do not know. I am not trying to be offensive; the right hon. Gentleman has been in the War Office for five years, and he is picked out of a respectable obscurity and is pushed into an office. Nobody, no soldier in the British Army knows him. All they know is that he has been at the War Office for five years, and they have no confidence in the War Office. They do not believe in the War Office, and the Prime Minister's political sagacity is so great that he picks out an official from the War Office and makes him Secretary of State for War. I say that the Prime Minister has great qualities, but obviously picking men is not one of them, and he does not know what the reaction is to these men in the country as a whole.

Now I come to my conclusion. Here is our situation; how are we going to face it? If this Debate resulted in causing demoralisation in the country in the slightest degree, I would have preferred to cut my tongue out. We do not want to do that. I believe that there is only one way in which we can recover ourselves. Our weapons are not what they ought to be, but they are the weapons we have got, and Hitler is not going to call the war off until we produce better ones; the war is going on, and we shall have to fight with the weapons we have. This country can fight. If the Government think that there is any dismay in the country, they are wrong; there is anger in the country. This is a proud and brave race, and it is feeling humiliated. It cannot stand the holding out of Sebastopol for months and the collapse of Tobruk in 26 hours. It cannot stand the comparison between these lost battles, not lost by lack of courage, but by lack of vision at the top. It cannot stand this; it is a proud and valiant country, and it wants leadership. It is getting words, not leadership, at the moment from the Government. There is only one way: Fight the enemy in Libya, for Heaven's sake fight him, wherever you can get at him.

The country expects, and declarations have been made – I can speak freely about this, though I understand that the Prime Minister cannot – that in a very short time, at a time and place to be decided by the Government, we shall launch an attack upon the enemy in a theatre of war nearer to this country. I do beg and pray the Government, when they make that decision, to make it out of considerations of strategical propriety and not as a consequence of political propaganda. Nevertheless, we have to do it. We can not postpone it until next year. Stalin expects it; please do not misunderstand me, for Heaven's sake do not let us make the mistake of betraying those lion-hearted Russians. Speeches have

---

[1] Sir James Grigg.

been made, the Russians believe them and have broken the champagne bottles on them. They believe that this country will act this year on what they call the second front. Molotov said so; they expect it and the British nation expects it. I say it is right, it is the correct thing to do, and the Government have practically said so. Do not on these high matters speak with a twisted tongue; do not use words with double meanings; do not use sentences with hidden purposes. On these high matters, speak truthfully and simply, so that the people can understand and trust. Let the Government, for Heaven's sake, make their political dispositions. In the meantime, let them change the direction of the war. Purge the Army and the Air Force of the elements which are not trusted at the moment. Get at the enemy where he really is – 21 miles away, not 14,000 miles away.[1] Get him by the throat. If this country at this moment were downhearted, it would be a very good thing. Send some politicians out. It has been done before: it was done in the Afghanistan campaign. Send some of us out, and let us risk our lives. When the troops land in Europe, and you go to rouse Europe, as Europe can be roused, send some of us out with the landing troops.

Petty-Officer Alan Herbert (Oxford University): You must be trained first.

Mr Bevan: If, by the deaths of some of us, we can rouse the British nation, is it not worth while? Some went out to Spain untrained. Training is needed; but we have grand human material, and there is an opportunity in Europe for us. Let us get rid of this defeatist complex. This nation can win; but it must be properly led, it must be properly inspired, and it must have confidence in its military leadership. Give us that, and we can win the war, in a fashion which will surprise Hitler, and at the same time hearten our friends.

Lieutenant-Colonel Elliot (Glasgow, Kelvingrove): We have at last heard the authentic voice of a Vote of Censure, the voice in which a Vote of Censure should be supported in such a Debate. Yesterday the Mover and the Seconder spoke in uncertain tones. Now an attack is launched with the will and intention of oversetting the Government – because only in order to overset the Government is such a speech justified. It was a speech which obviously sounds the ring of the enormous enthusiasm which we always knew the hon. Member for Ebbw Vale (Mr Bevan) possessed. It sounds, in a way, an encouraging note for the nation, because, if it is true, as he says, that in the blocks of opinion for which he has

---

[1] That is, across the English Channel, not in the Far East.

spoken in the past – blocks of opinion which in the past were spiritually opposed to war and battle – these humiliations of which he spoke have sunk down, and if they are willing to take the forward-looking path, both in the direction and the conduct of the war, which he suggested, we may get a fusion of many elements in the war which was not available in the past, and which may be of the greatest value in the future. But untrained enthusiasm is not enough. The hon. Member's own speech shows that. It was a powerful speech, a well-informed speech, and, especially at the end, a cogently-argued speech, but parts of it ran counter to what he has urged on the Government.

Mr Bevan: I was talking in terms of spiritual inspiration. I am not suggesting that untrained men would be of any use. All I suggested was that we should send politicians with the troops, as that might inspire the others.

Lieutenant-Colonel Elliot: But he said, 'Do not act on political considerations.' With that the House agreed. He said that decisions should be made on strategical considerations. That ran counter to other parts of his speech. Strategic decisions must not be influenced by other considerations. As the hon. Member said, nothing would be more fatal than to launch men on to the Continent in answer to some popular urge, and to find a greater Dunkirk. Think of the shame and humiliation, and of the responsibility of this House. As the hon. Member said, when soldiers go, it is at the bidding of this House: when they die, it is at the bidding of this House. It is our serious and grave responsibility to see that everything possible is done before we send these men.

I do not complain – none of us complains – about the Motion being brought forward or about its being supported in the bitter and astringent terms which the hon. Member used. A Vote of No Confidence must mean the overthrow of the Government – although in part of the hon. Member's speech he was arguing for a change, not in the central direction, but in what I might call the peripheral direction, the inner circle, of the Army. Let him look at the inner history of past revolutions, and see how often they have to be guided and led by the enthusiasm of professional soldiers. Take the French Revolution. Time after time the French generals were men trained and inspired in not only the traditions but the technical skill of the old Army.

The Mover and the Seconder yesterday seemed to speak in terms which suggested that they did not wish to push the Motion of No Confidence to the Vote. The Seconder's professional record and personal qualities, and the gallant record in war both of himself and of his family, must be appreciated and respected in this House. His wish was not to get rid of the central director of the war, the Prime Minister. He paid most glowing tributes to the Prime Minister. [An HON. MEMBER: 'As Prime Minister.'] Yes, as Prime Minister. The Mover, I am not sure in his speech, but certainly in an article in a Sunday paper, seemed to press strongly for the retention of the Prime Minister if the solution could be adopted of appointing another Minister of Defence.

But the hon. Member for Ebbw Vale rejected that solution altogether. He said, 'How can you divorce the Prime Minister, who has the full responsibility, from the conduct of the war?' Indeed, I find it very difficult to see how that could be done. That was the solution Mr Asquith rejected. If it was not good enough for Mr Asquith, does anybody suppose that it would be good enough for the present Prime Minister? Correspondence passed between Mr Asquith and the right hon. Gentleman the Member for Carnarvon Boroughs (Mr Lloyd George) about how a solution which would bring the Prime Minister out of the direction of the war could be adopted. Mr Asquith said in a letter to the right hon. Gentleman the Member for Carnarvon Boroughs that the suggested arrangement was to the following effect: 'The Prime Minister to have supreme and effective control of war policy. The agenda of the War Committee will be submitted to him; its Chairman will report to him daily; he can direct it to consider particular topics or proposals, and all its conclusions will be subject to his approval or veto. He can, of course, at his own discretion attend meetings of the Committee.' He wrote that to the right hon. Gentleman the Member for Carnarvon Boroughs, and that same afternoon he wrote: 'After full consideration of the matter in all its aspects, I have come decidedly to the conclusion that it is not possible that such a Committee could become workable and effective without the Prime Minister as Chairman.' My hon. Friend the Member for Kidderminster (Sir J. Wardlaw-Milne) maintained his contention that a divorce of this kind could be effected. Yet under much more favourable circumstances a man with admittedly far less experience in war than the present Prime Minister, and a far more judicial frame of mind, in the space of time between a morning and afternoon turned down the solution which has been urged upon the House.

The fact is that this is not a true Vote of Censure. So far we have not heard that authentic note, not even, I think, in the speech of the hon. Member for Ebbw Vale. That is what marks this Debate sharply off from the great Norway debate, when the Vote of Censure was put and gained the general acceptance of the House. No one could say that all the speeches showed a desire to retain the services of Mr Chamberlain as

Prime Minister – 'Go, go, go,' they shouted. That is far different from the attitude with which this Motion is approached at the present time. The House is still fundamentally and instinctively grateful to the Prime Minister, and desires to retain his services as Prime Minister; and I contend that while his services are retained as Prime Minister his services as Minister of Defence will have to be retained also. It is not only in this country that such a situation exists. In Russia Stalin has control of his Armies. Take the United States, where the President of the Republic is constitutionally Commander-in-Chief of the Army. The hon. Member for Kidderminster said that the President does not administer it. I am not sure how far he takes part in the day-to-day direction of the war, but the responsibility of actually being Commander-in-Chief is on his shoulders, and except by delegation he cannot move from that position.

Mr A. Edwards[1] (Middlesbrough East): Will the right hon. and gallant Gentleman deal with the point which has been the main point? Did Stalin or Roosevelt tolerate failures without taking some action? I think that is the point.

Lieutenant-Colonel Elliot: That, if I may say so, is the administration of the war. Admittedly there is disquiet in the House on that. I think we all agree that changes should be made. The House does not know and has naturally a difficulty in recommending what those changes should be, but I contend that it stands for changes on the periphery and the inner circle and not at the centre, and it is the centre at which this Motion is directed. That is the reason why I shall vote against the Motion. We are in the midst of one of the most difficult of war tasks. We are attempting to run an Empire in a great war on a democratic basis, a task which the Greeks said was impossible. It will require all the energy and the resolution as well as the brains and ingenuity of this House before it can survive that fight. I do not wish to delay the House unduly, but I say that the essence of the position of Defence Minister is the right of access of the chief staff officers to the highest political authority, nor will it ever be possible to divorce that. The Defence Minister is the heir and successor of the Prime Minister in his position as Chairman of the Committee of Imperial Defence. The essence of the Committee of Imperial Defence was that the technical chiefs sat in the room with, and had direct access to, the main director. In time of war the danger of intermediate Ministers is that they merely insert cogs in the wheel but do not shorten consid-

---

[1] Alfred Edwards, 1888–1958. MP for Middlesbrough East, 1935–50 (Labour, 1935–48; expelled from the party in 1948 when he opposed Labour's nationalization of the steel industry; joined Conservative Party in 1949).

eration of the problems under discussion. The solution which has been put forward of a Defence Minister is a solution which cannot and will not be adopted.

Then we have to say, 'Are you satisfied with the central direction of the war, taking the war in its broadest sense?' Can we leave out when we are considering, as the hon. Member for Ebbw Vale was considering, the presence of Departmental Ministers in the War Cabinet itself, the direction of the war in its political aspects? We cannot. In its home aspects you cannot. He spoke of the difficulties of production. On that we are all, of course, very greatly concerned. But can we leave out the achievement, let us say in the feeding of the nation, in the health of the nation, the great achievements in the rationing of the nation, the bringing of equality into fields where otherwise it would have been utterly absent? The equalitarian feeling of rationing has a great effect in steadying the nerves of the nation. I remember in the last war somebody saying how wonderful it was that the Minister of Food himself could not get a quarter of an ounce of butter more than the speaker could. That is a very great and difficult thing to put through. It is part of the direction of the war.

When the Minister of Labour[1] is blamed for not having prevented strikes, let us remember the tremendous power he has exercised, and has had to exercise, in the direction of labour. We all remember in the last war the leaving certificates, the trouble, the friction, the worry of these things. All that falls on the shoulders of the Minister of Labour in the direction of the war, and in the central direction of the war one is bound to take into account the feeling of solidarity which the Government have been able to inspire. That is shown by the fact that this Motion is signed by seven Labour and seven Conservative Members. It is a very unusual thing when a Motion such as that gains equal support on both sides of the House, and that would not have been the case had not the Govt. by its central direction of the war inspired a feeling of solidarity in the nation.

The idea of a small War Cabinet which will be removed from all Departmental duties has advantages, but it has great disadvantages also, and one is certainly the loss of the day-to-day touch which only someone like the Minister of Labour coming hot from the problem can put to his colleagues. We all remember the mutiny at Invergordon.[2] We all remember the small Cabinet at that time, from which the First Lord of the Admiralty

---

[1] Ernest Bevin.

[2] Mutiny by Royal Navy crews at Invergordon on 15–16 September 1931 in protest at wage cuts for public sector workers, including the military, introduced by the National Government in response to the Great Depression.

was excluded, and when an uproar was caused in the whole Fleet by mere inadvertence. If the First Lord had been in the Cabinet and had had the chance of explaining these things to his colleagues round the table, that episode and the effect it had would have been avoided. I think that the War Cabinet has certainly to its credit great positive achievements in the conduct of the war which we should remember on occasions like this when a Vote of Censure is brought forward. We lost the Anglo-French War, and started a new war, Britain against the Axis. To that great accessions of strength have come – Russia and America. They have been attacked by the Axis, but it was their truculent attitude towards the Axis which led the Axis to attack them, and that attitude was greatly inspired by the unflinching and stubborn stand which this country was making.

It is not enough to say that it was mere coincidence that the war against Russia should happen to break out at the same time as the war against Britain, or that the war against America should break out at the same time as the war of Britain against Germany. It was because the Axis Powers and dictators saw that the spirit of resistance to tyranny had been lit again in the world and that it would spread all over the world. It was lit while there was still time. If they had continued to pile up their resources and do nothing, it would have been too late. It was this country that nursed the flame, and it was the War Cabinet which was in charge of the flame in this country.

The hon. Member for Seaham (Mr Shinwell) on a previous occasion gave a very interesting account to the House of similar Debates which had taken place in previous Parliaments, when, over 100 years ago, we were faced with a great revolutionary force led by soldiers of genius sweeping over the Continent and doing great damage to the interests and to the prestige of this country. He quoted the remarkable fact that time after time the Younger Pitt succeeded in carrying tremendous weight in this House although he met with disaster in the field. I looked it up last night to see what the context really was, and it is not uninteresting especially in this Debate. 'Pitt was at the head of a nation engaged in a life-and-death struggle, a nation eminently distinguished by all the physical and mental qualities which make excellent soldiers [...] But the fact is that after eight years of war, after a vast expenditure of life and an expenditure of wealth far exceeding the expenditure of the American war, of the Seven Years' War, of the war of the Austrian Succession and of the war of the Spanish Succession, united, the English Army under Pitt was the laughing-stock of all Europe. It could not boast of a single brilliant exploit. It had never shown itself on the Continent but to be beaten, chased, forced to re-embark, or forced to capitulate.' That was the school in which the

Peninsular Army that fought under Wellington was being hammered and forged. It is possible that the House of Commons at that time knew quite as much about the circumstances about which Macaulay wrote in 1859, nearly half a century later. Then followed the passage quoted by the hon. Member for Seaham complaining that 'thus, through a long and calamitous period, every disaster that happened without the walls of Parliament, was regularly followed by a triumph within them. At length he had no longer an opposition to encounter, and in the eventful year 1799 the largest minority that could be mustered to vote against the Government was 25.' It is odd how history in some ways is repeated. It would be wrong to consider this Division as a complete absolution, or, to quote the inimitable phrase of my right hon. Friend the Prime Minister himself on a previous occasion, as a spontaneous ebullition of enthusiasm which can no longer be suppressed.

There are two points which make a sharp difference between the Napoleonic Wars and this war, and the first – and it is extraordinary that no reference is made to it in this Debate – is the need of that command of the sea. Here our position is much more like that of the earlier wars. There the loss of command of the sea led to the surrender of Yorktown and the loss of the American Colonies. The battle of the Atlantic remains the decisive battle of this war, for, if we retain the Western Ocean we win, and if we lose the Western Ocean we sink. Lose the Battle of the Atlantic, and we might hear far more of the priorities necessary for ships and ship-building. Balance this with tanks and dive-bombers. All these things have to be brought in. That the House of Commons should debate a war for two days without mention of sea-power is wrong. Sea-power remains, as always, decisive for our people. In the Mediterranean the Libyan position began to worsen when Rommel crossed the sea, and turned against us when the Navy could not interrupt his communications. When Admiral Vian was fighting battleships with light cruisers it was clear the Mediterranean Command was gravely impaired. The worsening of the situation in Libya is very closely linked up with the establishment of that clear, rapid line of communication bringing the whole weight of Italy and of industrial Germany at short range on to the desert of North Africa.

On all these things, however, the country says, 'We want more information. We want an inquiry. We want a report.' May I make this positive suggestion to the Government? There is a means to deal with all that by the publication of despatches. The Service chiefs have always had the right to send despatches and to have those despatches published. This Government began, it is true after a long delay, to publish despatches.

We must have some form of technical data upon which brilliant speakers and debaters such as the hon. Member for Ebbw Vale can base their conclusions. Without some technical information from the Army in the field I do not believe it will be possible for that informed opinion to be produced. Documents dealing with Libya and the defence of Calais which have been put out by the publication departments are of great interest, but they do not have the quality of a despatch written by the Commander-in-Chief himself. These are documents which will be of the greatest value to this country, and sooner or later, in some form or other, they ought to be produced.

The second aspect to which attention should be given is a point which has been stressed by almost every speaker in the Debate, and that is the aspect of engineering. This is an engineers' war. This is a point which the House could properly press upon the Government. The hon. Member for Ebbw Vale complained of lack of co-operation between the Army and the Air Force, but the hon. and gallant Member for East Aberdeen (Flight-Lieutenant Boothby) mentioned yesterday that he thought that the co-operation at the top was good but that the co-operation in the lower ranks was where the deficiency arises. That takes time. It is part of the turnover of the thought of this country from peace to war, which is far more important than the turnover of the production of this country from peace to war. It was the spiritual attitude towards war which led to the real disarmament of this country during the last 20 years, and it is not until we are reorganised in spirit as well as in the provision of weapons that we shall really be formidable to protect Europe against tyranny. They are the people who will have to be brought more and more into the foreground both in the Forces and outside. The Army is being milked, and has been milked in the past, for the Air Force, but surely we now see that that is all wrong. However important is the Air Force, the men who are standing up breast to breast against Rommel at this moment are as important as the men who are fighting his aeroplanes in the air. There is an old proverb in the cavalry which runs: 'Make much of your horses.' It enshrines the very profound truth that if you do not love a thing, you will not get the best out of it. If you say to the Army, 'We will purge you, weed you out, pluck you and pick you,' you will not get the best out of the Army, and none of us in this House has the conscience that we are yet getting the best out of the Army that can be obtained.

Some of the things said in the Debate yesterday were scarcely credible. It was said, for instance, that a tank turret was of such a size that a man could not get into it. I should have thought it would have been possible to make a wooden model. To take a thing from a drawing board is all very well, but surely it would have been a comparatively simple process to make a mock-up model of such a thing in order to see whether an ordinary man could operate it. It seems to me that the thought of the nation has not yet been concentrated upon this line. It will be necessary for us to obtain the thought of the nation if we are to get through our difficulties of today.

Mr Sloan[1] (South Ayrshire): It was said that all the guns were pointing one way.

Lieutenant-Colonel Elliot: That is not the case, but these are things which do not mean much to the man whose mind is not imbued with the spirit of what he is trying to do. Until we get that spirit, I am sure we shall not get the satisfactory weapons we require. This is a war of iron and steel and electricity. Iron is on top. We are being pushed about by machines. That is what we feel to be the greatest humiliation we are suffering. I remember at the time of Narvik a cartoon by Low, a terribly biting cartoon, which pictured a man in an iron-ore quarry while nosing along the valley came a great tank which had been made from this iron and, overhead, were flying machines of steel. It further showed that the man had dropped his barrow and that fetters had been put on him from behind. It was called 'the Iron comes back'. The domination of humanity by engines is the feeling we have now, and of which we must rid ourselves. This anger and humiliation we feel is healthy anger and a wholesome humiliation. It was through a valley of humiliation that another great hero came to a satisfactory end of his adventures, and I hope it may be so again. We want a transformation of the spirit of which the first flickers began to be evident in a quarter from which they had not been evident before – the speech and, still more, the thought, of the hon. Member for Ebbw Vale. I am encouraged and hopeful and, therefore, although I shall go into the Lobby with the greatest satisfaction and do my best to vote down the Motion to which he has put his name, I rejoice in having been able to ring my lance against his shield and in being able to say, 'Here is an adversary against whom anyone will be proud to tilt in the House of Commons.'

Wing-Commander Grant-Ferris[2] (St Pancras, North): I do not propose to talk in general terms of the Motion of Censure, but I wish to

[1] Alexander Sloan, 1879–1946. Secretary of the National Union of Scottish Mineworkers. Labour Member of Parliament for South Ayrshire from 1939 until his death.

[2] Robert Grant Grant-Ferris, 1907–97. Educated at Douai. Joined the Auxiliary Air Force, 1933. Unsuccessful Conservative candidate, 1935. Conservative MP for St Pancras North, 1937–45; for Nantwich, 1955–1974. Served in the RAF during the Second World War: Flight Commander, 1939; Wing

deal exclusively with the very vexed question of dive-bombers. There is a great deal of misunderstanding, not only in this House but throughout the country, about the use to which the dive-bomber can be put. There are several essentials which must be met before the dive-bomber can be used with any degree of certainty and any degree of satisfaction to the Power which is using it. First of all, you must have fighter cover, good substantial fighter cover, for your dive-bombers. Secondly, there must not be substantial fighter opposition to them, because otherwise they will be put off and will not be able to do their work properly. Thirdly, their effectiveness will be greatly minimised if there is strong, light anti-aircraft opposition to them from the ground. The House will remember a well-known figure in the Air Force, Air Commodore Basil Embry,[1] who has thrice won the D.S.O. Just after the war broke out, when he was a wing-commander, he escaped from a prison camp in occupied countries, and I met him here in company with my right hon. and gallant Friend the Minister of Fuel and Power.[2] He said that he had had a conversation with a colonel in the Luftwaffe, who told him that the only reason why Germany did so well with dive-bombers in France and the Low Countries was because British fighter opposition was too small to be effective and that our light 'Ack Ack' was practically negligible, with the result that their dive-bombers did tremendous execution. Those were the words of the German Luftwaffe colonel. You say that it was propaganda, but at that time this wing-commander was a prisoner, and it could not have been much use putting over propaganda to him.

Let us see how much the Junkers 87 was used in the Battle of Britain. I have taken care to ascertain correct figures, and I find that on three

Commander, 1941. In charge of the fighter defences of Malta, 1941–2. Parliamentary Private Secretary to the Minister of Town and Country Planning, 1944–5. Created Baron Harvington, 1974.

[1] Basil Edward Embry, 1902–77. Joined RAF, 1921. Appointed to a permanent commission in the rank of Flying Officer, 1926. AFC, 1926. Flight Lieutenant, 1927. Served in Indian Wing, 1934. Squadron Leader, 1935. DSO, 1938. Wing Commander, 1938. Served in France and Norway, 1939. Bar to DSO and second bar to DSO, 1940. Shot down and captured by German Army in Occupied France but escaped to England via Spain and Gibraltar, 1940. Air Officer Commanding RAF Wittering, 1940. Group Captain, 1941. Air Vice-Marshal, 1943. CB, 1945. DFC and third bar to DSO, 1945. Director-General of Training, 1945. KBE, 1945. Awarded Order of Dannebrog, Commander 1st Class, by Danish Government, 1947. Air Officer Commanding-in-Chief, Fighter Command, 1949–53. KCB, 1953. Commander-in-Chief, Allied Forces Central Europe, 1953–6. GCB, 1956.

[2] Gwilym Lloyd George, 1894–1967. Second son of David Lloyd George. Educated at Eastbourne College and Jesus College, Cambridge. On active service in France, 1914–19 (Major, Royal Artillery; despatches). Liberal MP for Pembrokeshire, 1922–4, 1929–50; for Newcastle North, 1951–7. Assistant Liberal Whip in the House of Commons, 1924. Parliamentary Secretary to the Board of Trade, 1931 and 1939–41. Parliamentary Secretary, Ministry of Food, 1941–2; Ministry of Fuel and Power, 1942–5; Ministry of Food, 1951–4. Secretary of State for the Home Department and Minister for Welsh Affairs, 1954–7. Created Viscount Tenby, 1957.

days 96 dive-bombers were shot down by our Fighter Command over our waters and this country. They were used for only a few more days. Afterwards the Germans ceased to use them simply because the cost was too great. Let us turn to the position in Libya. I cannot speak from practical knowledge of the desert itself, although I have served four months this year in Alexandria and have had an opportunity of speaking to those who took part in the battle which took place about Christmastime and the retreat which followed. We have heard a lot about the way in which Bir Hacheim was dive bombed. Well, I took the opportunity of checking this myself, and I can assure the House that the Free French there were not dive bombed successfully. Junkers 87 machines were used against them, and all were shot down out of the sky. A certain number of Junkers 88 had to be sent for – very good general purpose bombers and reasonably good dive-bombers – to help to do the job. But as a matter of fact dive-bombing was not responsible for the fall of Bir Hacheim.

Let us look for a moment at Tobruk itself. I do not think anybody, even the Government, knows very much about those hours when Tobruk was in our hands, just before its fall, but I can well visualise what the position would be there, having previously been in the neighbourhood, as it were. Our Air Force were falling back from Gambut, Gazala, El Adem and other places to their rear landing grounds. I am quite sure that at that time they were not in a position to operate against the hostile aircraft which were attacking Tobruk. Consequently, the Army was at a very great disadvantage, as the fighter protection which should have been there could not be forthcoming because the Air Force were not in a position to give assistance on that particular day for the reasons I have given.

Mr Molson[1] (The High Peak): Were the dive-bombers at Bir Hacheim shot down by anti-aircraft guns or by fighters?

Wing-Commander Grant-Ferris: I think my hon. Friend will remember the message of the Free French at that time; it was 'Merci pour le R.A.F.' We have heard a good real about the Stormovik which is alleged to be a Russian dive-bomber, but the Stormovik is not a dive-bomber in the essential sense of the word. It is a general purposes bomber like the Ju.88, and not like the Ju.87. Therefore, it is no good saying that dive-bombers qua dive-bombers have had great success on the Russian front.

[1] Arthur Hugh Elsdale Molson, 1903–91. President of the Oxford Union, 1925. Political Secretary, Association of Chambers of Commerce of India, 1926–9. Barrister-at-Law, Inner Temple, 1931. Conservative Member of Parliament for Doncaster, 1931–5; for the High Peak Division of Derbyshire, 1939–61. Served in the 36th Searchlight Regiment, 1939–41; Staff Captain, 11th Anti-Aircraft Division, 1941–2. Minister of Works, 1957–9. Created Baron, 1961. Chairman of the Council for the Protection of Rural England, 1968–71.

Mr Woodburn[1] (Clackmannan and Stirling, Eastern): Have we any general purposes bombers?

Wing-Commander Grant-Ferris: I will refer to that in a moment. The Minister of Production told us that the Government are, or very shortly will be, in possession of a considerable number of dive-bombers. Although I cannot speak officially, because I do not know, I would mention, from what talk I have heard unofficially, that the dive-bombers, as they are called, which we are getting are general purposes bombers, such as the Ju.88 or the Stormovik, which is really what we need, and not the dive-bomber pure and simple, as we have seen in the past. One must not confuse dive-bombers and dive-bombing. One can dive bomb with a number of aircraft; one can dive bomb to perfection only with a slow type such as the Ju.87, Ju.87 cannot be used against reasonable opposition.

One word more. I was in Newcastle the other day, and I went to a news film on which I saw pictures of the Libyan battle, the fighting, the bombs dropping; and mention was made by the commentator about the way in which the French at Bir Hacheim had been dive bombed, and he finished by saying, 'Would to God we had more of these dive-bombers.' That is the very worst propaganda to put out. It is absolutely ridiculous to talk like that. There is a proper function for dive-bombing. It can be used only when a situation exists such as I have already described. And let it be remembered that the men who fly the dive-bombers are the cream of the men who are available, and it is not right to use them – it is very bad policy to use them – if their lives are to be thrown away. I ask the House and the country to keep clearly in mind the difference between dive-bombers, and dive-bombing, to remember that first of all there have to be the fighters to protect them, that there have to be bombers to do the long-distance bombing, that when one is happy about that situation, one can go in for dive-bombing, and then, let them be of a general purposes type of aircraft. But they must be second to everything else, because their use is severely limited.

Major Furness[2] (Sunderland): I have wondered whether I ought to speak in this Debate. In the first place, it is a long time since I have been in the House, and when one is absent one gets out of touch with

[1] Arthur Woodburn, 1890–1978. An engineer, (iron foundry) administrator, author and economist. Labour MP for Clackmannan and East Stirling, 1939–70. Member of the Select Committee on National Expenditure, 1939–45. Parliamentary Private Secretary to the Secretary of State for Scotland, 1941–5. Secretary of State for Scotland, 1947–50.

[2] Stephen Noel Furness, 1902–74. MP for Sunderland, 1935–45. Junior Lord of the Treasury, 1938–40.

the situation and the cross-currents of political opinion. But perhaps in a Debate of this sort, when we are concerned with very fundamental issues, it is advantageous to have a fresh mind. Secondly, I was reluctant to speak because I felt that when an hon. Member in uniform speaks in the House, he is exposed to one or two great dangers. The fact that he is in uniform probably gives to his utterances a weight which his real position in the Army and his knowledge of military affairs do not warrant. An hon. Member who wears uniform because he is a member of a claims commission is no better informed on military matters – and indeed, probably is not as well informed, for he has not the time – than a member in civilian dress. On the other hand, if a Member in uniform has been lucky enough from time to time to have a job in which he serves under important men, he has to be very careful not to give away important secrets, or betray some confidence which has been imposed in him. In the Army I have had jobs of both sorts, and I shall try to avoid both those dangers.

I speak because I feel that these are extremely serious times. I have been quiet in the House since the outbreak of the war, and I feel that now, if in those three years of soldiering one has learned anything, one must speak and say what one thinks. The appalling military record of the British Army in this war – it is a most melancholy thing to have to say, but after all, it is our bounden duty in the House to speak frankly – the appalling record of the British Army is that it has won successes, and striking successes, against the Italians, but has never won a single campaign against the German Army. In Norway, Belgium, France, Greece and Crete, and now in Libya, its record is one of failure. It is high time that we began to look into the matter and inquire why these failures arise. If in this House we say that failure is inevitable, the sooner we pull down the shutters and close, the better. We dare not say failure is inevitable, and we have the duty to try to find out what is wrong.

There are certain unavoidable causes for our present situation, and I will state them briefly. I speak merely as a wartime soldier, but it is definitely a fact – one sees it now, although I certainly did not realise it before – that in peace-time this country did not think much of its Army or spend much money on it. We are suffering for that now. When the hon. Member for Ebbw Vale (Mr Bevan) rather sneers at professional soldiers, I would like to join issue with him. I am not a professional soldier, but I have met professional soldiers, and I must say that on the whole – of course, they are good, bad and indifferent, just as Members of Parliament are good, bad and indifferent – those I have met, and especially the staff officers, compare in ability with any Members of the House, and certainly they compare in devotion to duty. The Army today is an amateur army. In the battalion in which I served first, there was at the outbreak of the war only one Regular officer, and further back, at brigade headquarters, out of a staff of eight or ten, only two were Regular officers. As one goes further back and higher up, there are more and more Regular officers.

Generally speaking, even on the staffs of very big and important formations, there are today at least 50 per cent. who are war-time soldiers, and at staff colleges 50 per cent. of the students are war-time soldiers. That being so, it is bound to take time for amateurs like myself to learn. It is so easy to think that when an intelligent person is put into uniform he becomes a soldier. I used to think that, but I realise now how much there is to learn, and, indeed, there are some things which can never be learned at my age. Even very high officers have had no experience before the war in handling armoured formations, armoured corps, and armies. It is a very different thing moving an army and moving a division. In those days, such was our position, and so much had we cut down, that we had to have wooden models to represent tanks and guns. That is the first reason. The second reason is, as I have said, that we fought alone for a year against two enemies, and then a third enemy sprang upon us. The third reason is in relation to command of the sea. Command of the seas is no longer in our power in the same way as it was in the old days. We have the most vulnerable Empire. It is scattered all over the world, and it can be attacked piece by piece. In the old days it was kept going on the basis of unchallenged sea power. These are the reasons why shortcomings are inevitable, but I do not think they are a sufficient explanation for what has happened.

The right hon. and gallant Member for Kelvingrove (Lieutenant-Colonel Elliot) dealt very ably with the position of the Prime Minister in this matter. There is no doubt that the Prime Minister is running the war, as far as supreme control and direction of strategy are concerned, and there is no doubt in my mind that, so long as he is Prime Minister, he will go on doing so, and that you have either to get rid of him or allow him, as Prime Minister, to be responsible for the Service Departments. I am somewhat of a neutral in this matter. Before the war I was a junior Minister when the Prime Minister was not in office, and since he has been in office I have been away from the House. I certainly have no hopes of favours to come, or gratitude for past services. Thinking the matter over, and having regard to the fact that he was the man who kept us going when we fought alone, that he is the man who put us right with Russia and jumped in when Russia came into the war and allied ourselves with her, and with the knowledge that he does well in his office now that we are linked with America, I think we should be most unwise to make a change. If there is a desire to make a change, an alternative to his place must be brought forward. If an alternative is brought forward, I am willing to make my choice, but it seems to me that he is the only man, and that he must remain.

The fact that I am going to support him in the Lobby does not mean that I am satisfied with the conduct of the war. There are four points of criticism I wish to make in this respect. I have felt for some time, and I think one may say it is the general opinion held among officers of my standing in the Army, that our present bombing policy is entirely and fundamentally wrong. I think we are sacrificing our chances of winning this war by using the Air Force as an independent unit. The Germans have not bombed this country for quite a long time. Their bombing force has not been used against this country, but in Russia and in the Mediterranean. It is not because the Germans love our people – they would love to kill all our people – but that they are concentrating on one thing at a time and putting first things first. If in our offensive in Libya we had used our Air Force against Italy and stopped those supplies going to Rommel, we should now be in a very different position. When I read about certain air marshals saying we are going to try this experiment of heavy bombing, I say that we had better stop it now, because it has gone on too long, and we are sacrificing Army co-operation machines for heavy bombers. The sooner it is stopped the better, if we want to win the war.

My second criticism is in regard to equipment. The experience in the Army is that we delay so long in making new equipment that the Germans come out with it before us or that we rush something out, producing it in enormous quantities, with figures of 500,000 or more, which turns out to be no good. Obviously I cannot give figures to the House, but that is why we send out tanks with turrets which men cannot get into, or delay in bringing out new guns which the Germans produce before us. I feel very unhappy about the way in which we seem to shut our men up in places like Singapore and Tobruk, and then the general hauls down his flag. It is causing enormous harm in the Army, and it also has a psychological effect. It is quite all right to give ground, because that does not matter in war, but it seems the most appalling thing that 80,000 British soldiers at Singapore and 30,000 soldiers at Tobruk should go into captivity. It is something we cannot understand, and something which I implore the Government to think about, because of its psychological effect. I can assure the Government the psychological effects are bad for me, and I am certain it is worse in the case of the men serving in the ranks.

The last point I want to make is that we want some organisation in the Army where people have time to think. We have organisations for teaching, but what we want is some place in which you can shut up a certain number of intelligent people and say to them, 'Study the best use of this new war invention' or 'Study the best use of this particular combination of armoured divisions or corps formations.' At present we are learning by trial and error, but we should learn much more quickly if generals were unencumbered with details, as they are today, and could sit down and study these matters. Whatever may be wrong in this war, there are two sets of people who are not to blame. The first is the civilian population of the country. I think that ought to be said. They have delivered the goods, and, if the right goods have not been delivered, they are not the people at fault. It is not because our people have failed in blood, and toil, and sweat, but because the wrong goods have been ordered. The second class of people are the men in the ranks of the British Army. After being a Member of this House it has been a great experience to command a platoon. I know I may have failed, but these men have never failed, and I am sure, if properly led, they never will. If things go awry, it is our fault and our responsibility, and certainly it is not the responsibility of the people or the men we represent.

Sir Percy Harris (Bethnal Green, South West): I should like to congratulate the hon. and gallant Gentleman on his most interesting and well informed speech. He has made a valuable contribution to the discussion, and I am very glad that he has made a new maiden speech in his new capacity as an officer in the Army.

Let us be frank with ourselves. This Motion is an attack on the Prime Minister. It may be camouflaged by its wording, 'in the central direction of the war', but it is an attempt to undermine his position and, it logically and necessarily follows, to displace him by some other leader. I have very great sympathy with independence. I was for many years a free lance. In the War Parliament, of which I was a member, I was one of those wicked people who not only attacked the Government but exercised their right of voting against them in a very critical Division. Incidentally, it was the cause of the loss of my seat when an election took place. I would not suggest that that should influence anyone. On the contrary, at a time like this every Member of the House has the responsibility to exercise his own judgment and to do what he thinks right and proper for the successful prosecution of the war. I should like to congratulate the hon. Member for Ebbw Vale (Mr Bevan) on his very courageous speech. He has been a critic of every Government as long as I can remember. He has always been a free lance. He has voted against every Government and spoken against every combination, whatever its political label, whether a Conservative, National, Coalition or Labour Government. He was equally fearless in his criticism when he had a Government of his own political label. I believe it is the duty of every man who is convinced that the direction of the Government is wrong and that the Prime Minister of the day is a bad Prime Minister to vote against the Government, provided always that he sees a better man to take his place.

I do not know if these critics have visualised the kind of combination which is to displace the present Government. When there was a similar Debate on Norway we were quite clear in our minds. We saw a possible alternative, and when we took the great responsibility of forcing a Division we saw a new Government and a new Cabinet and a new Prime Minister. I have never regretted that vote, and I believe that most Members feel the same. But to blame the Prime Minister for all the shortage of material and lack of preparation comes very badly from men like the hon. Member for Kidderminster (Sir J. Wardlaw-Milne). I have a very vivid memory of my being responsible for putting on the Paper in September, 1938, an Amendment to the Address asking for the setting-up of a Ministry of Supply. We had a certain number of Members who exercised independent judgment. There were the right hon. Gentleman, now Under-Secretary of State for the Colonies,[1] the Minister of Information[2] and the Prime Minister. He made a very remarkable speech. He warned the country, he almost prophesied what would take place if we did not take drastic measures, and particularly if we did not set up a Ministry of Supply. He dealt with the problem of guns and tanks and the whole productive side of the war. It ill becomes those who then failed to exercise independence to attack him. After all, you cannot turn out guns like sausages from a machine. You cannot build tanks in a moment. If you change your mind in the light of experience, you have to have the blue

[1] (Maurice) Harold Macmillan, 1894–1986. Educated at Eton and Balliol College, Oxford. On active service, Grenadier Guards, 1914–18 (wounded three times). Conservative MP for Stockton-on-Tees, 1924–9, 1931–45. Author of *Reconstruction: A Plea for a National Policy* (1933), *Planning for Employment* (1935), *The Next Five Years* (1935), *The Middle Way* (1938), and *Economic Aspects of Defence* (1939). Parliamentary Secretary, Ministry of Supply, 1940–2. Privy Councillor, 1942. Minister Resident, Allied HQ, North-West Africa, 1942–5. Secretary for Air, 1945. Minister of Housing and Local Government, 1951–4. Minister of Defence, 1954–5. Secretary of State for Foreign Affairs, 1955. Chancellor of the Exchequer, 1955–7. Prime Minister, 1957–63. Chancellor of the University of Oxford, 1960. Created Earl of Stockson, 1984.

[2] Brendan Bracken.

prints, the jigs and tools and the factories and all the organisation. You cannot change that suddenly.

I am very glad that the Noble Lord the Member for Horsham (Earl Winterton) reminded the House that we have to thank the various Secretaries of State, and especially the Chancellor of the Exchequer[1] and his predecessor, who made the designs, prepared the blue prints and provided the factories and the necessary tools for the production of aeroplanes. The result was that it was possible to extend our supplies so rapidly that we won the Battle of Britain. But that did not apply to the War Ministry. It was the failure then to set up a Ministry of Supply to make the necessary preparations for the provision of tanks and guns which was responsible for our failure – and it is a failure – to meet the Germans on equal terms. Just before the time when the Prime Minister was warning the House and the country of the necessity for rearming the nation in preparation for war, in 1937, Germany had one armoured division. In 1938 she had three armoured divisions. In 1939 it had increased to nine armoured divisions. In 1940, at the time of the failure of France, they had 10 armoured divisions. On the other hand, in October 1939, we had only one. I understand that a former Secretary of State for War, the right hon. Gentleman the Member for Devonport (Mr Hore-Belisha), is to be the last speaker in support of the Motion. He is one of those who did nothing to support the proposal to set up a Ministry of Supply. The full responsibility was his for the rearming and the mechanisation of the Army, and it will want a lot of explanation to prove that the responsibility was not his. In 1938 the present Prime Minister warned the whole nation, and followed it up by a vote against his own party, of the necessity for rearming. We can all criticise. We know there have been faults. I think we ought to pay special attention to the junior Member for the Cambridge University (Professor Hill) in his insistence on the proper use of the scientific and technical knowledge of the country. This country could hold its own scientifically and technically with any country in the world, and we have been pioneers in many branches of technical and scientific experiment.

I agree with my hon. Friend in what he said about the position of the officers. We are proud of the traditions of our Army. It is a magnificent service, and the training of our officers is good. I am not one of those who criticise either Sandhurst, Woolwich or the Staff College, but they attract a somewhat limited number of people. Only a limited section of the population adopt the Army as a profession. Only a percentage of the

[1] Sir Kingsley Wood.

profession take it seriously, and the number of candidates for the staff colleges is very small. The competition is infinitesimal and, therefore, our choice is limited. In the last war we made proper use of our temporary officers. Many of them proved their ability in war and were promoted rapidly, not only to the rank of colonel but to commands in responsible positions. My hon. and gallant Friend the Member for Berwick-on-Tweed (Captain Grey) reminds me that his father, who was an old Territorial officer, did distinguished service in Mesopotamia and rose to the rank of major-general. There is not one officer in high rank, except one who has just been promoted to the Army Council, who is either a temporary or a Territorial officer. There is something radically wrong in a war, which is a mechanical war and depends on industrial and scientific skill for its organisation, when that is the case, and I suggest that the Government might well inquire into the whole system of promotion and the use of the undoubted talent that is in the Army drawn from the scientific and practical sections of the population.

I was interested in the change at the War Office. We have had three or four changes there. When the present holder of the office was promoted from being a civil servant to be made Secretary of State I was not one of the critics. I say, however, that a golden opportunity was lost to introduce new blood into the War Office. At one of the most critical periods in the last war there was a change in the War Office. My right hon. Friend the Member for Carnarvon Boroughs (Mr Lloyd George) was brought in like a breath of fresh air into the whole Department. He brought a new spirit. My right hon. Friend the Secretary of State for India[1] had something to do with it, and he will bear me out in saying that the appearance of my right hon. Friend the Member for Carnarvon Boroughs, with his new outlook and ideas, brought an entirely new spirit into the War Office. If we are to make the best use of the brains and ability of the country, we ought to introduce new men at the head and a new spirit right through the management of the Army. Nothing would do more to encourage those splendid men in the Army. I am talking with some knowledge when I say that they are the finest men we have ever had in the Army and compare most favourably with the men in the last war. Officers of experience confirm that. Nothing would encourage them more than to see some men who had risen from the ranks during the war in high commands and responsible positions. The generals in command of the Dominion troops are without exception amateur generals. The distinguished general in command of the Canadian Army in this country is in

[1] L. S. Amery.

the ordinary way an amateur general, as also are the generals in charge of the Australian and South African Forces. In the last war one of the most successful generals was General Monash, who was in charge of the Australians and in peacetime, I believe, was a dentist.

I believe that we shall give the Prime Minister today a great Vote of Confidence. His leadership has never been more necessary than now. He has never failed us at any critical moment of the war. Whether it was at the time of Dunkirk, or at the time of the entry of Russia into the war, or when he was at Washington after America had become our Ally, he has never failed us. We are confident in his leadership. Let him inquire into some of the organisation of the War Office personally and see whether he can introduce there some of that modern spirit that prevails in the Navy and Air Force, but is singularly lacking in the Army.

Mr Garro Jones[1] (Aberdeen, North): I must say at the outset that, like the right hon. Baronet the Member for South-West Bethnal Green (Sir P. Harris), I do not share the view which has been expressed by some hon. Members that it is in some way blameworthy to have put this Motion upon the Order Paper. I do not think that it renders a disservice to the country, and I am not sure that in the long run it will render any disservice to the Government. It is true that the putting down of the Motion has caused a certain amount of excitement abroad, but no one who has had the opportunity of studying the foreign Press and broadcasts can have any doubt that there is something which has caused a great deal more excitement abroad than the putting down of this Motion. That is the events of the last few weeks. This Debate has run on for 18 or 19 hours. Like a great many hon. Members, I have sat here throughout that time, and it has struck me as being one of the strangest Debates I have ever heard in this House. We have had declared backers of the Motion of No Confidence making speeches supporting the Government, and we have had declared supporters of the Government making speeches supporting the Motion, if not in express terms, at any rate by implication.

So far as the decided attitude of my hon. Friends is concerned, it is clear and single-minded and can be expressed in one short sentence – 'How can the happenings of the past be sifted ruthlessly and promptly and classified into lessons for the future?' That being our position, we shall vote against this Motion. We need be under no misapprehension that the Motion actually means calling upon the Prime Minister to resign

[1] George Morgan Garro Jones, 1894–1960. On active service, Royal Flying Corps, 1915–17. Advisory Officer to the United States Air Service, 1918. London Editor, *Daily Dispatch*, 1922–4. Liberal MP for South Hackney, 1924–9. Labour MP for Aberdeen North from 1935 until his death.

and to form a new Government – in what direction the Motion does not make clear. Confidence in the Government or in anybody else is a peculiar thing. When I read the Motion and noted the names attached to it, I could not help asking myself if these hon. Members who have no confidence in the Government have any confidence in one another. It is obvious to anyone who has been an attentive observer of the proceedings of this House that those who signed the Motion consist of people of the most diametrically opposed views on the fundamental issues of national policy. So far as the practical aspect of the matter is concerned, therefore, we can do no other than vote against the Motion. Nevertheless, it is to be hoped that the Prime Minister will not look upon today as an occasion for a Parliamentary triumph. During the course of the Debate some 150,000 words will be spoken. Much truth will be contained in them, and a great many errors and mistakes, and I am certain that it will be an easy task for the Prime Minister, by an over-refinement of the arguments, to discomfit all his critics, but if that should be the sole result, then it will be a barren consequence of our two days' proceedings.

As I am going to refer in a constructive way to the tactical handling of our Forces, which perhaps is the very spearhead of our war effort, I shall avoid as far as I can any reflection upon the skill of any individual general. We must all be grateful to our military leaders for their bravery and devotion, but it would surely be wrong to carry our loyalty to them to the point of disloyalty to our constituents and to our cause. I think that the most effective part of the speech made by the hon. Member for Ebbw Vale (Mr A. Bevan) was that in which he dealt briefly with the tactical handling of our troops. I hope the Prime Minister will not resent the speech made by the hon. Member for Ebbw Vale. I have listened to him making many speeches in this House, and have always told him that I hardly ever agree with everything he says, but that there is always a great deal of truth in it, and there was a great deal of truth in his speech today. It was a healthy piece of Parliamentary criticism, and if the Prime Minister resents it, he will be making a mistake. It is not only the critics of the Government who have taken this view about the tactical handling of our troops. The Minister of Production put it with delicate irony in his speech yesterday when he said: 'In peace-time it was not thought that the military art was one of those activities to which the consideration of the human mind should be given.' That is all too true, and I am not at all sure that it applies exclusively to some Members of this House. I have a feeling that it applies also to a great deal of the military organisation at the War Office for which we paid so expensively in pre-war years, because a mass of evidence leads to the conclusion that our greatest inferiority in relation to our enemies has been in the sphere of thought and planning. The hon. and gallant Member for Sunderland (Major Furness) said there was no single body throughout our war organisation, from the War Cabinet downwards, which was charged with the exclusive duty of thought upon the immediate strategical and tactical and equipment problems. I know that it is impossible to think in a vacuum, that there must be a certain link with the outside world, but there ought to be attached to the General Staff or to the Ministry of Defence some body whose sole duty should be to think and to plan in the realm of tactics and weapons for immediate and future needs.

We know what generally happens when a new committee is set up. It is what is known as the snowball system. It begins by taking a few more secretaries, a few more officers and in the end becomes buried beneath piles of papers and files. There is one aspect of our war effort which ought to be preserved and protected from that, and that is the part of our war effort in every sphere whose duty it is to think about our plans. The most important and direct necessity is in the realm of tactics and weapons. I would give such a body a name which would make it clear that its sole duty would be to think out these plans. I would call it something like the Joint Deliberative Staff for Tactics – and similarly for Equipment – and I would have one of those bodies in every theatre of the war. I should keep it free from operational and administrative duties. It seems to me wrong that the Chiefs of the General Staff, in addition to their enormous burden of thought and responsibility, should have at the same time heavy administrative duties. I know that they have been able to a certain extent to delegate them, but they all have heavy administrative duties in addition to those of thought and planning.

I do not propose to recapitulate what has been said about our guns – our 6-pounders and our 4.5 guns. I listened to a long controversy here yesterday about whether the 4.5 weapon was a gun or a howitzer when in fact there are a 4.5 gun, a 4.5 howitzer and a 4.5 anti-aircraft gun, three entirely different weapons. I mention that only to illustrate how easy it is to become involved in a tangle of technicalities.

But I propose to recite briefly the reasons why I think that in the sphere of thought we have been beaten all along the line throughout this war, beginning with the Battle of France. I am only going to refer to examples and not going into details. There was the attack on the Belgian forts – entirely new methods, and the element of surprise. There was the attack through the Ardennes, which were thought to be impassable for tanks and mechanised armies. The German army turned the neglect of that supposedly impassable region to their own advantage. Air-borne attack – never thought of in this country, certainly not prepared for. The transport of troops by air – 25,000 of them transported to Norway in a few days, a strategy which broke upon the world almost as a novelty. A simpler point, the sending of messages en clair. It was done in France and it is done in the desert. 'All aircraft to Armentières' – or to Tobruk or to Bir Hacheim. Our messages are sent in code. While we are busy decoding these messages the tide of the battle is turning.

It was said that in the desert the heat at this season would be too great for pitched battles, but the German army took forethought for that and prepared measures to reduce the temperature in their tanks. We who are supposed to have 'dominion over palm and pine' never saw that in the battle of the desert in summer an enormous advantage could be given to the troops which could reduce the temperature in their tanks by 10 or 15 degrees. Then there was the provision of this 88 mm gun. We have heard it said, and I dare say the Prime Minister will claim, that the weapons with which we are now fighting are weapons which were designed long ago, but that does not apply to the 88 mm gun. It is true that the gun itself, while I will not say it is stale, was designed a good many years ago, but what matters about that gun is its mounting – its all-round traverse, its self-propelled vehicle, and its general adaptation to use as an anti-tank gun. We could have done precisely the same thing with our 3.7 anti-aircraft guns. There is no technical reason, I am informed, why, if the factor of thought had operated on the British General Staff as well as it operated on the German General Staff, we should not have had a weapon corresponding to the 88 mm gun even before the Germans had it.

It was the same with the Japanese advance. The jungle North of Malaya was impassable. The Japanese adapted their troops, gave them Plimsoll shoes and light weapons, and they turned the jungle from being an obstacle to being an advantage to their troops. We know also how the Russian Army, by a hundred stratagems, turned the Russian winter from an enemy into a friend. All those stratagems are in the sphere of Army operations. On reflection, and I have thought long about it, I have hardly been able to think of a single decisive stratagem which has sprung from the brains of our own General Staff, and I invite hon. Members who have not already done so, to submit themselves to the same test.

I can think of many stratagems which have been imitated, but imitation in many walks of life enables people to get through without failure, and even with a moderate amount of success, but in war imitation is no substitute for thought. It means invariably that you are one move behind the enemy, and sometimes more than one move, and also completely deprived of the element of surprise. Unfortunately, imitation is often the resource of men who are not able to think and who use it as a cover for their incapacity. Therefore, it is of vital importance that if that is a weakness in our war effort we should remedy it.

In the air war I want to say that our record has been very much better, and that I think the nation has good cause to be grateful to those who prepared our Royal Air Force on its technical side – I am not saying on the production side. The 8-gun fighter and our detection system in the Royal Observer Corps were the salvation of this country in the days of our greatest peril. Many people ask why we did not send 200 bombers to Libya. I have always been against the long-range-bomber policy. I think the aircraft is too specialised, takes up too many man-hours in relation to smaller and more versatile types; but it is only fair to say it was not a practical proposition to send 200 bombers to Libya during the course of the battle. It is true that at that time we were making heavy attacks with 1,000 and more bombers on Cologne and other German cities, but it is not always remembered that if you send bombers you must also send bombs, and the bomb-lifting cranes and ammunition. The weight of bombs alone, to enable them to operate for three weeks is about 100 tons per machine in the case of a long-range-bomber, and they use petrol every hour they are in the air equal to that which would be used by 200 10 hp motor-cars running all at the same time. Therefore, we must be fair to the administration of the Royal Air Force and say that it was not possible without prolonged preparation. Where the staff of the Royal Air Force were to blame, in my view, was in the original decision to concentrate so largely upon long-range bombers and thus to reduce the strategic mobility of a great part of their striking force.

I am bound to say there is one respect in which the Air Staff has failed, and that is in regard to the dive-bomber. The story of the dive-bomber provides a dreadful example of the kind of obstinacy which loses wars. There is an unanswerable case for the dive-bomber, for everyone who approaches the matter with an impartial mind: France, Norway, Greece, Crete, Malaya, Bir Hacheim and Tobruk. We do not over-estimate the importance of the dive-bomber. We do not say that it is an absolutely decisive weapon. If you take the pilots in the Royal Air Force, they say that they would not mind sitting down under the dive-bomber, because they know what they can hit and what they cannot hit. They say that if people will only dig slit trenches and sit there until the machines have gone over they will be all right, but you cannot get that into the heads of the infantry, German or British, and it requires a prolonged period of training to bring them to that stage. We have never had dive-bombers even to accustom them, under suitable conditions, to that sort of thing.

We heard the statement the day before yesterday of the Secretary of State for War. It was a pathetic statement; it indicated a complete failure in the instrument of decision. After all these years he admitted that discussions were still going on with the Air Ministry in relation to the adoption of the dive-bomber. The great mistake that the Air Ministry have made was to make misleading statements, and condemn the dive-bomber on the basis of the original Stuka type, knowing all the time that immense technical improvements had been made in the performance of that weapon.

I will just give one more example of the lack of thought and decision. I am not going to say anything about the old controversy between generals, admirals and air marshals, though it is still going on. Admiral Cunningham, landing in the United States, said that it was too early yet to say that the battleship had been rendered obsolete by the aircraft. I really think it is time for the Government to come to some decision on that. The case of the *Scharnhorst* and the *Gneisenau* was a tremendous victory for the thinking power of the German staff. They accepted the certainty of discovery accompanied by air protection over those two battleships as against the chance of escape undiscovered with the certainty that there would be no air protection. That was a classic example of clarity of tactical thought, and I would like to know whether there is anybody exclusively engaged at the Admiralty on problems of that kind.

I want to conform to the desire of the House that speakers should be as brief as possible, and I am now going to say something very briefly about the central direction of the war. It is impossible, in my view, to separate the two offices, at any rate while one of them is held by the present Prime Minister, and further I think that for him to give up either of those two offices at the present time would be an abdication which would throw our war effort into confusion and disarray. Almost all his life has been a training for the responsibilities which rest upon him today. I do not believe that any job, however vast, is too big for one man. What restricts the capacity of any individual is not the size of the job but his capacity to delegate to a sufficient degree. I believe that it is in that direction that the Prime Minister has not hitherto succeeded. I believe that it is essential for him to divest himself of some of his duties. I do not say that with any sort of *arrière pensée*, or as any backdoor method of criticism. I mean it in all sincerity. He is doing too much. He appoints Ministers and public servants, he visits the operations rooms, he presides over the War Cabinet, the Defence Committee and sometimes the General Staffs Committee, he reads to the House the Army news, the Navy news, and sometimes the Air news. I really think that it is astonishing that the Prime Minister, with the whole world horizon of the war before him, should think it necessary if one ship is sunk to come and read a statement to the House about it, to the exclusion of the departmental Minister concerned. He also discharges innumerable duties of a civic and military character which we know little about. In all these things the strain is continuous. There is no holiday for the Prime Minister in war time. It is small wonder that, while he turns an unfaltering face of defiance to the enemy, he sometimes shows at home a little tenderness towards criticism and gratitude for praise.

But even assuming that the Prime Minister accurately divides up his precious time in answer to all the demands made upon him, who can tell how long the burden must be borne? I hope that he will not shrink from self-examination, and decide whether he is not trying to carry a burden which one day, despite all the Votes of Confidence, will unhappily bear him down, to the further damage of our war effort and our cause. I hope that the vivid writing on the wall, underlined by those of us who will support him in the Lobby, will not go unheeded or spurned. Frankly, we want and we need the Prime Minister and all that is best in his Government – that is our view – but we desire that he will accept the counsel of this House, for only by doing so can he retain its trust until the triumphant end.

Captain Profumo[1] (Kettering): I would like to thank the House for permitting me to intervene for a few minutes until such time as another right hon. Gentleman catches your eye, Mr Speaker. I had hoped to speak at some length in this Debate, but I will confine myself to asking hon. Members to regard the matter in front of us at this moment from the angle from which I, as a soldier and a very junior Member of Parliament, am looking at it myself. In an hour or so we shall be asked to give

---

[1] John Profumo, 1915–2006. Known as 'Jack'. Commissioned into Royal Armoured Corps as 2nd Lieutenant, 1939. Served in North Africa with Northamptonshire Yeomanry as Captain. Conservative MP for Kettering, 1940, becoming the youngest Member of Parliament. Voted against Chamberlain in the division of 8 May 1940 which precipitated the emergence of Churchill as Prime Minister. OBE, 1944. Conservative MP for Stratford-upon-Avon, 1950. Parliamentary Secretary to the Ministry of Civil Aviation, 1952. Married actress Valerie Hobson, 1954. Parliamentary Under-Secretary of State for the Colonies, 1957. Under-Secretary of State at the Foreign Office, 1958. Minister of State for Foreign Affairs, 1959. Secretary of State for War, 1960. In October 1963, upon the public revelation that in 1961 he had had an affair with a model, Christine Keeler, who had previously had an affair with Yevgeni Ivanov, Senior Naval Attaché at the Soviet Embassy, he resigned. CBE, 1975.

a Vote either of confidence or of no confidence in the central direction of the war, which means, virtually: Are we satisfied with the right hon. Gentleman who is now our Prime Minister or are we not? In so doing we must examine the alternatives. The critics who have spoken during this Debate have put their points of view most clearly and most strongly, but in my opinion have offered no possible alternative to the present constitution of our Government as it stands.

May I, as a serving officer, tell the House – and I can do so quite honestly – that there is great concern in the Forces about our present situation, but there is far greater concern about the habitual critics, who, after every reverse or setback, like lean and hungry dogs smell around for a bone to pick. Let us look at it a little closer. What effect has this Debate had, first, upon members of the Forces, and, secondly, upon the ordinary, uninformed public? Frankly, the effect must be to confuse them. The hon. Gentleman who opened the Debate put one point of view, and expressed opinions which were not always accurate. He told us at one moment that there were no tanks in Libya which had not been designed before the war. Strictly, that may be true, but every one of the tanks in Libya at the moment has got modifications and improvements which have been made since the war started. In comparison, there are no tanks in the German Army, in any of the Panzer divisions, which were not originally designed before the war. He then talked about the Tank Production Board and told us that it met only once a month. Is it fair for the public to get that picture of the Tank Production Board? Its members may meet only once a month, but it is not only their meetings which constitute their work. It is delving into the ideas of tank users themselves in the armoured divisions up and down the country and in the arenas of war; so that statement is not very fair. The hon. and gallant Member who seconded the Motion yesterday disagreed with the Mover. Then we had other speeches in disagreement, and at one moment yesterday a considerable argument about a 4.5 gun which added to the confusion, because not a soul who was arguing about it knew what he was talking about.

How can you expect the average soldier, sailor or airman to train himself to fight with a will, when we, the Legislative Assembly, are sitting here on our benches behind the lines, wrangling and discussing somewhat unimportant things like that? I do not want to give the House the impression that I am not in favour of criticism. I most certainly am. This is the first speech I have made in the House, in which I have supported the Government. My first speech, and my very first vote, went against the Government of the day on the occasion of the Debate on Norway. Therefore, I am as keen a critic as any hon. or right hon. Member. But I do feel profoundly at this moment that it is vital that every hon. and right hon. Member should use his vote at the end of this Debate. I have heard hon. Members saying that they are going to abstain. That is not fair. The country and the Armed Forces demand, at this moment, supreme confidence in the direction of the war by the right hon. Gentleman the Prime Minister. We will disagree afterwards – possibly we may disagree in private, but certainly we will disagree – and I have a great many criticisms which I hope the House will allow me to put on another occasion. But this awful moment in our war should be the signal for greater co-operation and more concerted effort for everybody to redouble their efforts and toe the line and pull together. How are we going to persuade the munition workers to make more guns when we have not decided whether they are of the right type or not; to make further aerodromes when we are debating whether the aeroplanes on them are the right ones; to go down the pits and produce the coal when we are arguing about it in Westminster? This is the moment for supreme unity.

Earl Winterton (Horsham and Worthing): We are doing exactly the same thing as the hon. and gallant Member did when he voted against the Government over Narvik.

Captain Profumo: Certainly, but the time was different and there was an obvious alternative. There is one other point I want to make. A great deal of the criticism made in this Debate has been made by people who are not in full possession of the facts. It very often is the case, but when the criticism reaches the public it reaches them in a different form from that in which it is made in this Chamber. There was one moment when the right hon. Gentleman the Minister for Production mentioned the Churchill tanks, and an hon. and gallant Member opposite, who calls himself the voice of the Army, said 'Where is the Churchill tank?' That is the voice of the Army. If he does not know where the Churchill tank is, then let the voice pipe down. That is the sort of thing that goes out to the public and causes confusion and lack of confidence.

Sir, my time is up; I wanted to say more, but I do feel strongly at this moment that it is time to shelve our own criticisms, large or small, and give the right hon. Gentleman the Prime Minister the confidence that is due to him for having taken us so far along the road to victory. This is going to be a long war like a boxing match. The boxer often has to take punishment. But if when he goes back to his corner, he is not fanned properly or given a sponge of vinegar to suck, that is not going to help him win. I ask all Members to vote in favour of the Government against this Motion, but in any case to use their votes so that they can go away confident that they have done their duty.

Mr Hore-Belisha (Devonport): I do not know whether my hon. and gallant Friend who has spoken so sincerely wishes to number me among the habitual critics of the Government. I hope not, for if he would do me the honour of reading the speeches I have made, I think he would find they are balanced, and have not, in any way, been over-critical. This, he said, is a moment when we should all cooperate, and of course I agree with him. But it is above all a moment for wise action, and it is for that reason we are holding this Debate today. Confronted with a catastrophe neither the character of which nor the dimensions of which were anticipated even dimly by His Majesty's Government, what is the proper course of action for Parliament to take? It seems to me that there are three alternatives. One is that we should remain silent and impotent while these great events unfold themselves. The current of war, however, is continuous, it is swift, and it is becoming turbulent. For us to stand aside, at this moment would be a confession of impotence. Another suggestion which has been made is that we should discuss the matter in some general way and at large, let us say upon the Adjournment. The time for indulgence in mere dialectics has passed. No Debate can be justified now unless it leads to a conclusion. The Government might, of course, have put down a Vote of Confidence in their conduct of operations. From such an act of immodesty we have, at any rate, spared them. The counterpart of a Vote of Confidence is a Vote of Censure, the purpose of which is to bring a subject to a clear-cut issue, and this is a time in which issues should be clear-cut.

It is said that our deliberations will have a bad effect abroad. If the outside world is to retain its confidence in us, it will be most likely to do so if it sees us frankly facing our own difficulties, analysing them, and eradicating them. It is said that the soldiers will be disturbed. Where else are they to look but to this representative assembly? Surely it would depress their morale beyond bearing if we were to ignore the conditions in which they have been, and still are, fighting. Finally, it is said that we break the unity of the nation. The nation well understands the difference between unity and uniformity. We all have one common aim, and we shall all share in the fate of our country, whatever it may be. I seem to remember an occasion, in fact I do remember an occasion, on which my right hon. Friend the Prime Minister, standing below the Gangway, said: 'If only 50 Members of the Conservative party went into the Lobby tonight to vote for this Amendment, it would not affect the life of the Government, but it would make them act. It would make a forward movement of real power, of real energy'. [Official Report, 17 November 1938; col. 1129, Vol. 341] Well and deeply do I appreciate the feelings of those Members who imagine that if this Motion were carried to its logical conclusion we should add a political upheaval to a military disaster. I understand their point of view, and I share it, but I repeat that if only 50 Members were to go into the Lobby today to vote for this Motion it would not affect the life of the Government, but it would make them act. It would make a forward movement of real energy. What my hon. Friends and myself who are associated with this Motion desire is that we should acquire a new realisation of the character of this war, and impart a new impulse to its conduct. Why do we criticise, my hon. Friends and myself, the central direction of the war? Not because we attribute to the central direction of the war all the shortcomings and all the deficiencies; not at all. The good and the bad must be put into fair balance, and we have no desire to do otherwise. Nor do we think that defeats should necessarily be made the cause of complaint, still less of Votes of Censure. We have had many defeats. I do not think my right hon. Friend the Prime Minister, or his colleagues, could complain of the tolerance of the House or of the country.

Every measure for which they have asked has been granted. On a number of occasions we have discussed the war in a friendly manner, as I hope we still are discussing it. But the suggestions that have been made over the last two days have been made before: the warnings that have been uttered have been uttered before. There must come a time when one should ask His Majesty's Government to act upon them. If defeats occur after reasonable risks have been taken, well and good: but if they are attributable to false appreciation, it is not well and good. If situations and prospects are consistently misjudged, neither the tactics nor the equipment can ever suffice to meet them. If you persist in under-estimating your enemy and in over-estimating yourself, you are courting disaster.

What is the situation in which we now find ourselves, and how have we been led into it? We are fighting for our sea power, our historic asset. The Government are very much to be congratulated upon the fact that within two months of the fall of France, which we were powerless to avoid, we had complete sea command of the Eastern Mediterranean. That fact was announced on 20 August, 1940. It was repeated at various intervals, and on 10th November last my right hon. Friend stated: 'Rather more than a year ago I announced to Parliament that we were sending a Battle

Fleet back into the Mediterranean for the destruction of the German and Italian convoys. The passage of our supplies in many directions through the sea, the broken morale of the Italian Navy, all these show that we are still masters there.' On 29 January my right hon. Friend said: 'This second front in the Western Desert afforded us the opportunity of fighting a campaign against Germany and Italy on terms, most costly to them. If there be any place where we can fight them with marked advantage, it is in the Western Desert and Libya because not only [...] have we managed to destroy two-thirds of their African Army and a great amount of its equipment and air power, but also to take a formidable toll of all their reinforcements of men and materials, and, above all, of their limited shipping across the Mediterranean, by which they are forced to maintain their supplies'. – [Official Report, 29 January 1942; cols. 1012–13, Vol. 377.] I see that Admiral Cunningham thinks we overestimated our success in that direction. He says that, in fact, the enemy got across rather more than we thought he did. We had then established command of the Eastern Mediterranean; and we held it until recently. But command of the Eastern Mediterranean depends upon Alexandria, the only major naval base East of Gibraltar which has been usable by the Fleet. I am going to ask my right hon. Friend, whether the German and Italian claims that the Germans have broken through our Alexandria defences are true? He might tell us when he comes to reply. I sincerely hope that it is not so. Upon Alexandria depends our position in the Eastern Mediterranean. He who holds Alexandria, holds Suez; and he who holds Suez holds the path to our Eastern Empire: he is astride Asia and Africa. Because we hold Suez, we have held our sway in those two Continents. We have acquired thereby our prestige among the Eastern peoples. Thereby also we have increased and multiplied our commerce. Indeed, our situation as a great Power, it would be no exaggeration to say, depends upon that fact. The Battle of the Atlantic and the Battle of the Mediterranean are one; for, should we be ousted from the Mediterranean, the Italian naval units will be free to move into other waters. The Axis Powers could send their transports freely to Syria and Palestine, Where they could maintain armies, and they could penetrate to Iraq. The oil for which the panzers and the Luftwaffe are thirsting would be theirs in abundance. They could attack Russia on a second front South of the Caucasus, and break our lines of communication with Russia through the Persian Gulf. That is the situation with which we are confronted, at its worst; but it is better to look at matters at their worst. If the worst should happen, we should be forced back upon this island.

That is the pass to which, if things go badly, we may come. Only a quick and complete reversal of our fortunes can avoid these consequences. We, as comrades and fellow-Members, must face that situation. How did it arise? General Wavell was, at one time, master in North Africa. He advanced to Benghazi. His advance was there halted. The position was judged to be completely safe. A Governor of Cyrenaica was appointed. We were called upon to send two, if not three, divisions to Greece. We had an obligation to Greece, which we were bound to honour. We were not bound to honour it in that way. The best service which we could have rendered to Greece, as I and other Members ventured to say at that time, would have been by smashing the Italian Empire completely and invading Southern Italy, rather than going into Northern Greece. Had General Wavell continued his advance from Benghazi, Rommel could never have entered North Africa. The decision was taken. We had a disaster in Greece. We had a worse disaster in Crete. It was held, despite all the experience of Norway, that Crete could withstand an invasion. We lost many ships from assault by shore-based aircraft. It was inevitable that we should. Our naval position was weakened. We lost 300,000 or 400,000 tons of shipping, and General Wavell lost all that he had gained in as many days as it had taken him weeks to acquire it.

When Rommel appeared in Africa his presence was discredited. It was stated that he was not there. Later it was said that he was there but was only in very small force. Either our Intelligence was at fault, as it had been in Norway, or the interpretation of it was inadequate. The Government, with great resolution, set themselves to retrieve this position. They gave priority in the war to Libya. They sent all the supplies possible to Suez and Alexandria. They were assisted by the Americans, who also despatched material, so much indeed, that we were told that the quay accommodation was insufficient. At length we were in a position to recover what we had lost, and on 20th November my right hon. Friend stated: 'The offensive has been long and elaborately prepared and we have waited for nearly five months in order that our Army should be well equipped with all those weapons which have made their mark in this new war [...] The object is the destruction of Rommel's Army [...] The Desert Army is now favourably situated for a trial of strength [...] It is far too soon to indulge in any exultation.' As indeed it was, for the offensive had hardly begun – '[...] This is the first time British troops have met the Germans at least equally well-armed and equipped and realising the part which a British Victory in Libya will play upon the whole course of the war'. – [Official Report, 20 November 1942; cols. 474 and 475, vol. 376.] It was on 20 November. There was an elaborately prepared offensive. We were going to meet the Germans at least on equal terms. On the same day a message was sent to all ranks of the Army. It was in these terms, and it was sent by the Prime Minister: 'I have command from the King to express to all ranks of the Army and the Royal Air Force in the Western Desert and to the Mediterranean Fleet His Majesty's confidence that they will do their duty with exemplary devotion in the supremely important battle which lies before them. For the first time British and Empire troops will meet the Germans with an ample equipment in modern weapons of all kinds. The battle itself will affect the whole course of the war. Now is the time to strike the hardest blow yet struck for final victory, home and freedom. The desert army may add a page to history which will rank with Blenheim and Waterloo. The eyes of all nations are upon you. May God defend the right!' Although we were only beginning, the next day, throughout the 24 hours, in every European language the BBC broadcast to the oppressed peoples in all the occupied countries that the Germans were now on the run in Libya and that Britain had smashed Rommel's panzer divisions. Never was an offensive initiated with so much panoply, with so much drum-beating and with so much bugle-sounding. Never were the expectations of the public roused to so high a pitch. On 11th December, after a number of, as it seems, extravagant claims had been made by military spokesmen in Cairo, my right hon. Friend identified himself completely with them. He went on to say that 'the Libyan offensive did not take the course which its authors expected though it would reach the end at which they aimed.' Having said that, he said later that he made it a rule never to prophesy. 'On 18 November General Auchinleck set out to destroy the entire armed forces of the Germans and Italians in Cyrenaica, and now on 11th December' – he said to an incredulous House – 'I am bound to say that it seems very probable he will do so.' Again: 'We had a superiority in armour and in the air [...] Some of the German tanks carried, as we know, a 6-pounder gun, which though it of course carries many fewer shots is sometimes more effective than the gun with which our tanks are mainly armed.' Our tanks were mainly armed with a 2-pounder, which the right hon. Gentleman did not say at the time. 'However, we had a good superiority in the numbers of armoured vehicles [...] Like other people concerned, I had hoped for a quick decision, but it may well be that this wearing down battle will be found in the end to have inflicted a deeper injury upon the enemy than if it had all been settled by manoeuvre and in a few days.' He then explained that we could hit the enemy more decisively in this theatre than in any other because we had command of the sea, and could isolate the battlefield. He continued: 'The enemy, who has fought with the utmost stubbornness and enterprise, has paid the price of his valour, and it may well be that the second phase will gather more easily the fruits of the first [...]' That is what my right hon. Friend said. He went to America immediately afterwards, and he reiterated there the statement that we had superiority in equipment, and he also said that if he were asked to explain why our arms had proved insufficient in Malay, he could only point to the victories of General Auchinleck in Libya. Very shortly afterwards General Auchinleck, who, like General Wavell, had stopped on the Gulf of Sidra and had not pursued his offensive, was back on the Gazala line. We started then with an ample supply of equipment. It became equipment of equal quality, and it had now become in Washington of superior quality. At the same time it was said that Singapore would be held. In Ottawa immediately afterwards my right hon. Friend said: 'This fighting in Libya proves that when our men have equal weapons in their hands and proper support from the air, they are more than a match for the Nazi hordes.' Again: 'The German Army is decisively beaten, but its power of resistance has not ceased." So that was the situation when my right hon. Friend was last in America. Did we in fact have equal equipment, or superior equipment, or anything like it? Every military correspondent concurs that we were out-gunned and that our armour was not as good as the armour of the German tanks. We chose to make this offensive, we initiated it. The hon. and learned Member for North Croydon (Mr Willink) asked me yesterday whether I was not in some way responsible for the qualitative inferiority of our tanks. Well, if I had been, that was a very long time ago, but I can give him an answer on that point which does not rest upon my opinion. I do not wish to refer to these matters, because they are completely irrelevant – we are dealing with statements of the Prime Minister that our equipment is superior – but if my hon. and learned Friend will look at the speech made by Lord Margesson on the last Army Estimates, he will see that our Noble Friend then stated: 'Before the war our tank and anti-tank gun, the 2-pounder, was, without doubt, the best in the world, and its worth was shown in the battles preceding the evacuation from Dunkirk.'

In a few sentences I think the sequence of that matter is this: We started the war with a 2-pounder gun which was the best in the world and which could penetrate the armour of the German tanks. This gun was captured in France, where we lost 750 tanks, and the Germans, who had a 37-mm gun on their tanks – roughly the same calibre as ours – studied our guns, saw that they would penetrate their armour and thickened the armour of their own tanks. The armour of their later models had more resistance than their earlier tanks, and they also improved their anti-tank guns. We are still using Matildas and Valentines and Cruisers, doubtless with certain improvements, but this is roughly the position.

What great advancement in our equipment had been made to justify the Prime Minister making these repeated statements? He says we have a 6-pounder gun. Yes, but we did not have it in a tank. We sent Mr Westbrook officially to report on equipment in Libya last summer, and he wrote: 'I reported home among other things – some done – that it was essential to have dive-bombers and 6-pounder guns if we were to defeat the enemy. We started last autumn without either and then flew a number of guns out to the middle of the battle.' He further said that his suggestions 'were frustrated by the indecision and regulations framed by those who are far remote from the difficulties they cause'. Well, that has never been unusual in dealing with Governments, either under my right hon. Friend or his predecessors. The fact is that we had nothing to justify the statements that we had superiority of equipment. What I am concerned with is the morale of the Army. If you convince our Army that it has to undertake an offensive with superior, or even equal, armour and you prepare for five months to smash German panzer divisions, and then that Army is utterly routed, confidence is shaken. You have no right to put the Army in that position. To blame generals as you do by inference when you say that your equipment was superior is ungenerous, to blame the Army is unworthy. But to blame your predecessors is contemptible.

While we are on this subject of equipment, I would like to refer to a question which was asked of me by my hon. and gallant Friend the Member for East Aberdeen (Flight-Lieutenant Boothby). He asked me why the Army had no dive-bombers. I would point out that if this offensive, which was so much belauded by the Prime Minister, had turned out well, I do not think the House of Commons would have stopped to pass me a resolution of thanks for the equipment, but I will answer his question about dive-bombers. He asked me whether I tried to get dive-bombers when I was at the War Office. I would not deal with any subject concerning my term of office – and I never have – unless it had been made public elsewhere. An attack was made upon me in another place because I tried to get an Army Air Force before the war and because I repeated my efforts, of course, while I was in the Government during the war. I do not think I make any revelation when I say that. The Army has no dive-bombers or any other planes – none at all. My whole case is that unless you give to a Service control over its own tactical instruments you will never get them properly developed. That is my case. I will proceed now to say a few words upon it, as I have done repeatedly during the last two years. What is the German view of this matter? The Germans continue to make Stukas. If they were guided by the Minister of Production, doubtless they would not do that.

The Minister of Production (Mr Lyttelton): I did not say that.

Mr Hore-Belisha: My right hon. Friend said that Stukas were not responsible for the fall of Bir Hacheim or Tobruk. Where then have they been used successfully? There is a reluctance to admit that the dive-bomber is any good. However, I am not making any attack upon the Minister. I think he made the best of a difficult case yesterday. If he had these difficulties, as I am sure he had, and had come to the House of Commons and said he could not get this superiority of equipment, the House would have sympathised with him. Instead of that he made speeches, like other Members of the Government, saying that we were producing material at such a spate that it had almost become uncontrollable. While in America he said that that country produced every week munitions worth as much as the cost of building the Panama Canal.

Mr Lyttelton: Every six months.

Mr Hore-Belisha: Every six months, then. That is the kind of astronomical picture that is being given to us. But I do not blame him, because I have great respect for him, and I wish him well. As to dive-bombers, this is the German view, the view of the man who is actually in charge of these operations in the Mediterranean – Air Marshal Kesselring: 'The Luftwaffe could never have achieved its task in the recent campaigns of movement had it not constantly paid attention to one factor throughout its training and development, namely, to become part of the Wehrmacht and then to fit itself unconditionally, mentally and practically into the battles of the land forces.' There is the great distinction between the German air force and our own. Unless you can get a land mentality, your Army will never have its needs supplied. The same applies to the Navy. The Japanese have developed the use of air power with their navy in the same way that the Germans have developed it with their army. If we had been as successful as the Japanese have been with this combination of air and sea power, we should not have lost the *Prince of Wales* and the *Repulse*. We should have sunk the *Prinz Eugen*, and our position in the Mediterranean would have been very different. Remember what Admiral Cunningham said: You cannot preserve your sea power without land-based aeroplanes and they should be given to the Navy forthwith.

I want to ask the Prime Minister whether he intends to do anything in that direction before it is too late. The principal justification for a Ministry of Defence, in my judgment, is that you should integrate these arms. If you allow these old differences to be perpetuated neither your Navy, your Air Force nor your Army can exert the influence upon which you rely. We have misjudged this situation, and we are in a serious plight. Even so, I should very much hesitate to press this Motion were not the process of misjudgement continuing. This is what Mr Samuel Rayburn, Speaker of the House of Representatives, said after the Prime Minister had addressed the leaders in the United States, in company with Mr Roosevelt: 'Mr Churchill indicated that Britain will hold and that there is no danger of losing Egypt.'

The Prime Minister: I must say that was a statement made by other lips than mine.

Mr Hore-Belisha: Of course, I withdraw unconditionally at once. Then I will say that my right hon. Friend the Foreign Secretary has since said it, and my right hon. Friend the Minister of Labour has since said it.

The Minister of Labour (Mr Ernest Bevin): Can my right hon. Friend quote?

Mr Hore-Belisha: If my right hon. Friend denies that, I will not press it at all. It is enough that my right hon. Friend the Foreign Secretary should have said it. What I am saying is that we may lose Egypt or we may not lose Egypt – I pray God we may not – but when my right hon. Friend the Prime Minister, who said that we would hold Singapore, that we would hold Crete, that we had smashed the German army in Libya, and further came down to the House to celebrate General Auchinleck's victory in the first phase, almost before it had begun – which gave me a quiver down my spine at the time, as it did many other hon. Members – when I read that he had said that we are going to hold Egypt, my anxieties became greater than they otherwise would have been. On his return to this country, a joint statement was issued by the Prime Minister and the President of the United States. 'There is no doubt,' said this statement, 'in our minds that the over-all picture is more favourable to victory than it was either in August or December of last year.' I want to ask the Prime Minister what he meant by that. Last December we had not lost Singapore, and my right hon. Friend did not anticipate we would lose it. Last December General Auchinleck was attacking and advancing, not retreating. What is meant by that statement? How can one place reliance in judgments that have so repeatedly turned out to be misguided? That is what the House of Commons has to decide. We are concerned less with the fate of the Government than with the fate of the country. It is not by over-confidence, not by boasting or arrogance or rhetoric, that we shall win this war. It is by a humble devotion to our task, with a knowledge of its magnitude and with a knowledge that if we fail, 1,000 years of British history are over. That is why my hon. Friends have put down this Motion. That is why they consider it unseemly that the peace-time practice of pressure or influence should be brought to bear on Members to tell them how to vote. Think what is at stake. In 100 days we lost our Empire in the Far East. What will happen in the next 100 days? Let every Member vote according to his conscience.

The Prime Minister (Mr Churchill): This long Debate has now reached its final stage. What a remarkable example it has been of the unbridled freedom of our Parliamentary institutions in time of war. Everything that could be thought of or raked up has been used to weaken confidence in the Government, has been used to prove that the Ministers are incompetent and to weaken their confidence in themselves, to make the Army distrust the backing it is getting from the civil power, to make the workmen lose confidence in the weapons they are striving so hard to make, to represent the Government as a set of nonentities over whom the Prime Minister towers, and then to undermine him in his own heart and, if possible, before the eyes of the nation. All this poured out by cables and radio to all parts of the world, to the distress of all our friends and to the delight of all our foes. I am in favour of this freedom, which no other country would use, or dare to use, in times of mortal peril such as those through which we are passing. But the story must not end there, and I make now my appeal to the House of Commons to make sure that it does not end there.

Although I have done my best, my utmost, to prepare a full and considered statement for the House, I must confess that I have found it very difficult, even during the bitter animosity of the diatribe of the hon. Member for Ebbw Vale (Mr Bevan), with all its carefully aimed and calculated hostility, to concentrate my thoughts upon this Debate and to withdraw them from the tremendous and most critical battle now raging in Egypt. At any moment we may receive news of grave importance. But the right hon. Gentleman the Member for Devonport (Mr Hore-Belisha) has devoted a large part of his speech, not to this immediate campaign and struggle in Egypt, but to the offensive started in Libya nearly eight months ago, and he, as did the Mover of the Motion of Censure, accused me of making misstatements in saying that, for the first time, our men met the Germans on equal terms in the matter of modern weapons. This offen-

sive was not a failure. Our Armies took 40,000 prisoners. They drove the
enemy back 400 miles. They took the great fortified positions on which
he had rested so long. They drove him to the very edge of Cyrenaica,
and it was only when his tanks had been reduced to 70 or perhaps 80
that, by a brilliant tactical resurgence, the German general set in motion
a series of events which led to a retirement I think to a point 150 miles
more to the West than that from which our offensive had started. Ten
thousand Germans were taken prisoner among those in that fight. I am
not at all prepared to regard it as anything but a highly creditable and
highly profitable transaction for the Army of the Western Desert. I do not
understand why this point should be made now, when, in all conscience,
there are newer and far graver matters which fill our minds.

The military misfortunes of the last fortnight in Cyrenaica and Egypt
have completely transformed the situation, not only in that theatre, but
throughout the Mediterranean. We have lost upwards of 50,000 men, by
far the larger proportion of whom are prisoners, a great mass of material,
and, in spite of carefully organised demolitions, large quantities of stores
have fallen into the enemy's hands. Rommel has advanced nearly 400
miles through the desert, and is now approaching the fertile Delta of the
Nile. The evil effects of these events in Turkey, in Spain, in France and
in French North Africa cannot yet be measured. We are at this moment
in the presence of a recession of our hopes and prospects in the Middle
East and in the Mediterranean unequalled since the fall of France. If
there are any would be profiteers of disaster who feel able to paint the
picture in darker colours, they are certainly at liberty to do so.

A painful feature of this melancholy scene was its suddenness. The
fall of Tobruk, with its garrison of about 25,000 men, in a single day was
utterly unexpected. Not only was it unexpected by the House and the
public at large, but by the War Cabinet, by the Chiefs of the Staff and by
the General Staff of the Army. It was also unexpected by General Auchinleck and the High Command in the Middle East. On the night before its
capture, we received a telegram from General Auchinleck that he had
allotted what he believed to be an adequate garrison, that the defences
were in good order, and that 90 days' supplies were available for the
troops. It was hoped that we could hold the very strong frontier positions,
which had been built up by the Germans and improved by ourselves,
from Sollum to Halfaya Pass, from Capuzzo to Fort Maddalena. From
this position our newly-built railroad ran backwards at right angles, and
we were no longer formed to a flank – as the expression goes – with our
backs to the sea, as we had been in the earlier stages of the new Libyan

battle. General Auchinleck expected to maintain these positions until the powerful reinforcements which were approaching, and have in part arrived, enabled him to make a much stronger bid to seize the initiative for a counter-offensive.

The question of whether Tobruk could be held or not is difficult and disputable. It is one of those questions which are more easy to decide after the event than before it. It is one of those questions which could be decided only with full knowledge of the approaching reinforcements. The critics have a great advantage in these matters. As the racing saying goes, they 'stand on velvet.' If we had decided to evacuate the place, they could have gone into action on 'the pusillanimous and cowardly scuttle from Tobruk', which would have made quite a promising line of advance. But those who are responsible for carrying on the war have no such easy options open. They have to decide beforehand. The decision to hold Tobruk and the dispositions made for that purpose were taken by General Auchinleck, but I should like to say that we, the War Cabinet and our professional advisers, thoroughly agreed with General Auchinleck beforehand, and, although in tactical matters the Commander-in-Chief in any war theatre is supreme and his decision is final, we consider that, if he was wrong, we were wrong too, and I am very ready on behalf of His Majesty's Government to take my full share of responsibility. The hon. Member for Kidderminster (Sir J. Wardlaw-Milne) asked where the order for the capitulation of Tobruk came from. Did it come from the battle-field, from Cairo, from London or from Washington? In what a strange world of thought he is living, if he imagines I sent from Washington an order for the capitulation of Tobruk. The decision was taken to the best of my knowledge by the Commander of the Forces, and certainly it was most unexpected to the Higher Command in the Middle East.

When I left this country for the United States on the night of 17th June, the feeling which I had, which was fully shared by the Chief of the Imperial General Staff, was that the struggle in the Western Desert had entered upon a wearing down phase, or a long battle of exhaustion, similar to that which took place in the autumn. Although I was disappointed that we had not been able to make a counter-stroke after the enemy's first onslaught had been, I will not say repulsed but rebuffed and largely broken, this was a situation with which we had no reason to be discontented. Our resources were much larger than those of the enemy, and so were our approaching reinforcements. This desert warfare proceeds among much confusion and interruption of communications, and it was only gradually that the very grievous and disproportionate losses which our armour sustained in the fighting around and south of Knightsbridge became apparent.

Here I will make a short digression on to a somewhat less serious plane. Complaint has been made that the newspapers have been full of information of a very rosy character. Several hon. Members have referred to that in the Debate, and that the Government have declared themselves less fully informed than newspapers. Surely this is very natural while a battle of this kind is going on? There never has been in this war a battle in which so much liberty has been given to war correspondents. They have been allowed to roam all over the battlefield, taking their chance of getting killed, and sending home their very full messages whenever they can reach a telegraph office. This is what the Press have always asked for, and it is what they got. These war correspondents, moving about amid the troops and sharing their perils, have also shared their hopes and have been inspired by their buoyant spirit. They have sympathised with the fighting men whose deeds they have been recording, and they have, no doubt, been extremely anxious not to write anything which would spread discouragement or add to their burdens.

I have a second observation to make on this minor point. The war correspondents have nothing to do except to collect information, write their despatches and get them through the censor. On the other hand, the generals who are conducting the battle have other preoccupations. They have to fight the enemy. Although we have always asked that they should keep us informed as much as possible, our policy has been not to worry them but to leave them alone to do their job. Now and then I send messages of encouragement and sometimes a query or a suggestion, but it is absolutely impossible to fight battles from Westminster or Whitehall. The less one interferes the better, and certainly I do not want generals in close battle, and these desert battles are close, prolonged and often peculiarly indeterminate, to burden themselves by writing full stories on matters upon which, in the nature of things, the home Government is not called upon to give any decision. After all, there is nothing we can do about it here while it is going on, or only at very rare intervals. Therefore, the Government are more accurately, but less speedily, less fully and less colourfully informed than the newspapers. That is the explanation. It is not proposed to make any change in this procedure.

To return to my general theme; when on the morning of Sunday, the 21st, I went into the President's room I was greatly shocked to be confronted with a report that Tobruk had fallen. I found it difficult to believe, but a few minutes later my own telegram forwarded from London, arrived. I hope the House will realise what a bitter pang this was to me. What made it worse was being on an important mission in the country of one of our great Allies. Some people assume too readily that, because a Government keeps cool and has steady nerves under reverses, its members do not feel the public misfortunes as keenly as do independent critics. On the contrary, I doubt whether anyone feels greater sorrow or pain than those who are responsible for the general conduct of our affairs. It was an aggravation in the days that followed to read distorted accounts of the feeling in Britain and in the House of Commons.

The House can have no idea how its proceedings are represented across the ocean. Questions are asked, comments are made by individual members or by independents who represent no organised grouping of political power, which are cabled verbatim, and often quite honestly taken to be the opinion of the House of Commons. Lobby gossip, echoes from the smoking room and talk in Fleet Street are worked up into serious articles seeming to represent that the whole basis of British political life is shaken, or is tottering. A flood of expectation and speculation is let loose. Thus I read streamer headlines like this: 'Commons demand Churchill return face accusers', or 'Churchill returns to supreme political crisis'. Such an atmosphere is naturally injurious to a British representative engaged in negotiating great matters of State upon which the larger issues of the war depend. That these rumours coming from home did not prejudice the work I had to do was due solely to the fact that our American friends are not fair-weather friends. They never expected that this war would be short or easy, or that its course would not be chequered by lamentable misfortunes. On the contrary, I will admit that I believe in this particular case the bonds of comradeship between all the men at the top were actually strengthened. All the same, I must say I do not think any public man charged with a high mission from this country ever seemed to be barracked from his home land in his absence – unintentionally, I can well believe – to the extent that befell me while on this visit to the United States, and only my unshakable confidence in the ties which bind me to the mass of the British people upheld me through those days of trial.

I naturally explained to my hosts that those who were voluble in Parliament in no way represented the House of Commons, just as the small handful of correspondents who make it their business to pour out damaging tales about our affairs to the United States, and I must add to Australia, in no way represent the honourable profession of journalism. I also explained that all this would be put to the proof when I returned by the

House of Commons as a whole expressing a responsible, measured and deliberate opinion, and that is what I am going to ask it to do today.

I noticed that it was stipulated that I should not be allowed to refer in any way in the statement I am now making, or in a statement about Libya, to the results of my mission in the United States. I suppose it was not wished that I should be able to plead any extenuating and correlative circumstances. But I must make it clear that I accept no fetters on my liberty of debate except those imposed by the rules of Order or by the public interest. I have a worthier reason, however, for not speaking at length about my American mission further than the published statement agreed upon between the President and me. Here is the reason. Our conversations were concerned with nothing, or almost nothing, but the movement of troops, ships, guns and aircraft and with the measures to be taken to combat the losses at sea and to replace, and more than replace, the sunken tonnage.

Here I will turn aside to meet a complaint which I have noticed that the Minister of Defence should have been in Washington when the disaster at Tobruk occurred. But Washington was the very place where he should have been. It was there that the most urgent future business of the war was being transacted, not only in regard to the general scene but also in regard to the particular matters that were passing. Almost everything I arranged in the United States with the President and his advisers is secret, in the sense that it must be kept from the enemy, and I have therefore nothing to tell about it, except this – that the two great English-speaking nations were never closer together and that there never was a more earnest desire between Allies to engage the enemy or a more whole-hearted resolve to run all risks and make all sacrifices in order to wage this hard war with vigour and carry it to a successful conclusion. That assurance, at least, I can give the House.

I hope there will be no disparagement of the United States shipbuilding programme. We are making considerable shipbuilding efforts ourselves. We could only increase our output at the expense of other indispensable munitions and services. But the United States is building in the present calendar year about four times as much gross tonnage – not dead weight but gross tonnage – as we are building, and I am assured that she will launch between eight and 10 times as much as we are building in the calendar year 1943. Shipping losses have been very heavy lately,[1] and the bulk has been upon the Eastern shores of America.

[1] On 3 July 1942 Churchill had received an Admiralty report, 'Merchant Tonnage Sunk by Enemy Action', that showed that a grand total of 3,738,000 tons of British and American, and British and Amer-

The most strenuous measures are being taken to curtail this loss, and I do not doubt that they will be substantially reduced as the masses of escort vessels now under construction come into service and the convoy system and other methods of defence come into full and effective operation. These measures, combined with the great shipbuilding effort of the United States and the British Empire, should result in a substantial gain in tonnage at the end of 1943 over and above that which we now possess, even if, as I cannot believe, the rate of loss is not substantially reduced. This we shall owe largely to the prodigious exertions of the Government and people of the United States, who share with us, fully and freely, according to our respective needs and duties in this as in all other parts of our war programme.

I have not trespassed very long on the United States aspect, although that is the most vital sphere, and I return to the Desert and to the Nile. I hope the House will realise that I have a certain difficulty in defending His Majesty's Government from the various attacks which have been made upon them in respect of materials and preparation, because I do not want to say anything that can be shifted, even by the utmost ingenuity of malice, into a reflection upon our commanders in the field, still less upon the gallant men they lead. Yet I must say that one of the most painful parts of this battle is that in its opening stages we were defeated under conditions which gave a good and reasonable expectation of success. During the whole of the spring we had been desirous that the Army of the Western Desert should begin an offensive against the enemy.

The regathering and reinforcement of our Army was considered to be a necessary reason for delay, but of course this delay helped the enemy also. At the end of March and during the whole of April, he concentrated a very powerful air force in Sicily and delivered a tremendous attack upon Malta, of which the House was made aware at the time by me. This attack exposed the heroic garrison and inhabitants of Malta to an ordeal of extreme severity. For several weeks hundreds of German and Italian aircraft – it is estimated more than 600, of which the great majority were Germans – streamed over in endless waves in the hopes of overpowering the defences of the island fortress. There has never been any case in this war of a successful defence against a superior air power being made by aircraft which have only two or three airfields to work from. Malta is the first exception. At one time they were worn down to no more than a dozen fighters, yet, aided by their powerful batteries, by the ingenuity

ican-controlled, merchant shipping had been sunk, of which the British total was 1,369,400 tons.

of the defence and by the fortitude of the people, they maintained an unbroken resistance. We continued to reinforce them from the Western Mediterranean as well as from Egypt by repeated operations of difficulty and hazard, and maintained a continuous stream of Spitfire aircraft in order to keep them alive, in spite of the enormous wastage, not only in the air but also in the limited airfields on the ground. As part of this, hundreds of fighter aircraft have been flown in from aircraft carriers by the Royal Navy, and we were assisted by the United States Navy, whose carrier *Wasp* rendered notable service on more than one occasion, enabling me to send them the message of thanks, 'Who says a wasp cannot sting twice?' By all these exertions, Malta lived through this prodigious and prolonged bombardment, until at last, at the beginning of May, the bulk of the German aircraft, already weakened by most serious losses, had to be withdrawn for the belated German offensive on the Russian front.

Malta had come through its fearful ordeal triumphant and is now stronger in aircraft than ever before. But during the period when this assault was at its height, it was practically impossible for the fortress to do much to impede the reinforcements which were being sent to Tripoli and Benghazi. This, no doubt, was part of the purpose, though not the whole purpose, of the extraordinary concentration of air power which the enemy had thought fit to devote to the attack. The enemy did not get Malta, but they got a lot of stuff across to Africa. Remember that it takes four months to send a weapon round the Cape and perhaps a week or even less to send it across the Mediterranean – provided it gets across. Remember also that the great number of these desertised Spitfires, if not involved in very severe fighting at Malta, would have been available to strengthen our Spitfire force in the battle which has been proceeding. Thus it may well be that we were relatively no better off in the middle of May than we had been in March or April.

However, the armies drew up in the Desert in the middle of May about 100,000 a side. We had 100,000 men, and the enemy 90,000, of whom 50,000 were Germans. We had a superiority in the numbers of tanks – I am coming to the question of quality later – of perhaps seven to five. We had a superiority in artillery of nearly eight to five. Included in our artillery were several regiments of the latest form of gun howitzer which throws a 55-pound shell 20,000 yards. There were other artillery weapons, of which I cannot speak, also available. It is not true, therefore, as I have seen it stated, that we had to face 50-pounder guns of the enemy with only 25-pounder guns. The 25-pounder, I may say, is one of the finest guns in Europe and a perfectly new weapon which has only begun to flow out since the war began. It is true that the enemy, by the tactical use which he made of his 88 mm anti-aircraft guns, converting them to a different purpose, and his anti-tank weapons gained a decided advantage. But this became apparent only as the battle proceeded. Our Army enjoyed throughout the battle and enjoys today superiority in the air. The dive-bombers of the enemy played a prominent part at Bir Hacheim and Tobruk, but it is not true that they should be regarded as a decisive or even as a massive factor in this battle. Lastly, we had better and shorter lines of communication than the enemy, our railway being already beyond Fort Capuzzo and a separate line of communications running by the sea to the well-supplied base and depot of Tobruk.

We were, therefore, entitled to feel good confidence in the result of an offensive undertaken by us, and this would have been undertaken in the early days of June if the enemy had not struck first. When his preparations for an offensive became plainly visible, it was decided, and I think rightly, to await the attack in our fortified positions and then to deliver a counter-stroke in the greatest possible strength.

Here, then, were these armies face to face in the most forbidding and desolate region in the world, under conditions of extreme artificiality, able to reach each other only through a peculiar use of the appliances of modern war. The enemy's army had come across a disputed sea, paying a heavy toll to our submarines, and except for the period when Malta was neutralised, to the Malta Air Force. The Imperial Forces had almost all come 12,000 miles through submarines which beset the British shores, and round the Cape to Suez or from South Africa and India. One may say that the forces assembled on both sides in this extraordinary situation represented a war effort which in other theatres would have amounted to three or four times their numbers. Such was the position when, on 26th May, Rommel made his first onslaught.

It is not possible for me to give any final account of the battle. Events move with such rapidity that there is no time to disentangle the past: one tale is good till another is told. Any hasty judgment would be more exciting than true. The main features may however be discerned. Rommel had expected to take Tobruk in the first few days, but the reception which he got deranged his plan. Very heavy losses in armour were sustained by both sides. However he held tenaciously to the inroad he had made, and we were so mauled in the struggle that no effective counter-stroke could be delivered. On 4th June an attempt was made, but was repulsed by a counter-attack with heavy loss by artillery. The battle then centred upon Bir Hacheim, where the Free French resisted with the utmost gallantry. Around this the struggle surged for eight or nine days. Finally it was decided to withdraw the garrison, and this was successfully accomplished, though with heavy losses.

Here, no doubt, was a turning point in the battle. Whether anything more could have been done we cannot tell. Certainly very large numbers of troops remained on fronts which were not engaged, and certainly Rommel and his Germans punched on unflaggingly day after day. After the fall of Bir Hacheim another five days of fighting occurred round the Knightsbridge and Acroma positions. Up till 13th June the battle was equal. Our recovery process had worked well. Both sides lost, I will not say evenly, but proportionately, because our numbers were greater, and we could expect to lose more while keeping even. But on the 13th there came a change. On that morning we had about 300 tanks in action, and by nightfall no more than 70 remained, excluding the light Stuart tanks; and all this happened without any corresponding loss having been inflicted on the enemy. Sir, I do not know what actually happened in the fighting of that day. I am only concerned to give the facts to the House, and it is for the House to decide whether these facts result from the faulty central direction of the war, for which of course I take responsibility, or whether they resulted from the terrible hazards and unforeseeable accidents of battle. With this disproportionate destruction of our armour Rommel became decisively the stronger. The battlefield passed into the hands of the enemy, and the enemy's wounded tanks could be repaired by his organisation while all our wounded tanks were lost to us.

Many evil consequences followed inevitably from this one day's fighting. There came the decision to withdraw from the Gazala position. The South African Division was withdrawn into Tobruk, and moved through Tobruk further East, without heavy loss. The main part of the 50th English Division extricated itself by a 120-mile journey round the Southern flank of the enemy. In the desert, everything is mobile and mechanised, and when the troops move they can move enormous distances forward or back. The old conceptions and measurements of war do not apply at all. One hundred miles may be lost or won in a day or a night. There followed the decision to hold Tobruk together with the Halfaya–Sollum–Capuzzo–Maddalena line, which I have already mentioned, and then the fall of Tobruk after only one single day of fighting.

This entailed withdrawal from the Sollum–Halfaya line to the Mersa Matruh position, which placed 125 miles of waterless desert between the 8th Army and its foes. Most authorities expected that 10 days or a fortnight would be gained by this. However, on the 5th day, on 26th June,

Rommel presented himself with his armoured and motorised forces in front of this new position. Battle was joined on the 27th along the whole front, and for the first time I am glad to say our whole Army, which had been heavily reinforced with new and fresh troops, was engaged all together at one time. Although we consider we inflicted very heavy damage upon the enemy the advance of the German Light Division together with the remainder of the Panzer Corps, 100 to 150 heavily armed tanks, which is about what it amounted to – led to our further retirement owing to the destruction of our armour. Naturally, I am not in a position to tell the House about the reinforcements which have reached the Army or which are approaching, except that they are very considerable, and after the lecture I have been read by the right hon. Gentleman apparently it is wrong even to say that we shall hold Egypt. I suppose one ought to say we are going to lose Egypt. But I will go so far as to say that we do not regard the struggle as in any way decided.

Although I am not mentioning reinforcements, there is one reinforcement which has come, which has been in close contact with the enemy and which he knows all about. I mean the New Zealand Division. The Government of New Zealand, themselves under potential menace of invasion, authorised the fullest use being made of their troops, whom they have not withdrawn or weakened in any way. They have sent them into the battle, where, under the command of the heroic Freyberg, again wounded, they have acquitted themselves in a manner equal to all their former records. They are fighting hard at the moment.

Although the Army in Libya has been so far overpowered and driven back, I must make it clear, on behalf of the challenged central direction of the war, that this was not due to any conscious or wilful grudging of reinforcements in men or material. Of course, the emergency of the Japanese war had led to the removal of a part of the Australian Forces to defend their homeland, and very rightly. In fact, it was I who suggested to them that they should not consider themselves bound in the matter, having regard to their own danger. Several important units of British troops had to go to India which, a little while ago, seemed threatened by invasion. Other Forces in India which were due to proceed to the Middle East had to be retained there. But extreme exertions have been made by the home Government for the last two years to strengthen and maintain the Armies in the Middle East. During that time, apart altogether from reinforcements to other theatres, there have gone to the Middle East from this country, from the Empire overseas and to a lesser extent from the United States, more than 950,000 men, 4,500 tanks,

6,000 aircraft, nearly 5,000 pieces of artillery, 50,000 machine guns and over 100,000 mechanical vehicles. We have done this in a period, let the House remember before they dismiss our efforts and our designs as inadequate to the occasion, when for a large part of the time we were threatened with imminent invasion here at home and during the rest of it were sending large supplies to Russia. So far as the central direction of the war is concerned, I can plead with some confidence that we have not failed in the exertions we have made or in the skill we have shown.

Now I come to the question of the quality of some of our material, to the design and armour of our tanks and to our anti-tank artillery. This was dealt with at some length yesterday by my right hon. Friend the Minister of Production, and by Lord Beaverbrook in another place. I agree with the hon. Member for Ebbw Vale that the House should read carefully that extremely masterly, intricate and authoritative statement of facts upon these matters. I do not attempt to go into them in detail here, as I should keep the House beyond the time they have so generously accorded me, but I must ask the House to allow me to place the salient points of the tank story before them.

The idea of the tank was a British conception. The use of armoured forces as they are now being used was largely French, as General de Gaulle's book[1] shows. It was left to the Germans to convert those ideas to their own use. For three or four years before the war they were busily at work with their usual thoroughness upon design and manufacture of tanks, and also upon the study and practice of armoured warfare. One would have thought that even if the Secretary of State for War of those days could not get the money for large scale manufacture he would at any rate have had full-size working models made and tested out exhaustively, and the factories chosen and the jigs and gauges supplied, so that he could go into mass production of tanks and anti-tank weapons when the war began.

When what I may call the Belisha period ended we were left with some 250 armoured vehicles, very few of which carried even a 2-pounder gun. Most of these were captured or destroyed in France. After the war began the designs were settled and orders on a large scale were placed by the right hon. Gentleman. For more than a year, until Hitler attacked Russia, the threat of invasion hung over us, imminent, potentially mortal. There was no time to make improvements at the expense of supply. We had to

---

[1] Almost certainly *Vers l'armée de métier* (1934), translated as *Towards a Professional Army* and *The Army of the Future*. In this book, published in English in 1940, de Gaulle writes about the importance of tanks and quick movements – not unlike *Blitzkrieg*. The book sold poorly in France, but much better in Germany, where it was allegedly read by Hitler.

concentrate upon numbers, upon quantity instead of quality. There was a major decision to which I have no doubt we were rightly guided.

Mr Hore-Belisha: May I interrupt? I should have thought that if my right hon. Friend wanted to make some reference to technical matters during my period he would have told me, so that I could have the facts. That being so I must inform the House that a very long time ago, in the Debate on Greece in May 1941, my right hon. Friend made certain charges about my period at the War Office in relation to tanks. I then had not the facts. I had to secure them from the War Office, and that I did on 23rd June, and I think in justice I must read this letter to the House:

'The Prime Minister was, I understand, intending to develop the argument that whereas in the last war tanks were slow in movement and designed to be proof against ordinary bullets only, it would have been natural to suppose that the preparations for this war would have included the energetic development of fast tanks which would also be sufficiently armoured to stand up against cannon fire. In so far as the Prime Minister's statement is capable of this interpretation, that you definitely ignored or rejected the advice of the General Staff to introduce tanks having both those qualities, it is not borne out by the fact. The Purple Primer[1] of 1931 was only concerned with advocating a tank capable of resisting armour-piercing bullets and not artillery fire.'

That is a direct contravention of an attack made upon me in May 1941. My right hon. Friend is now making another attack on technical grounds with reference to my period, and I think he might have notified me in advance so that I might have access to the facts for my defence.

The Prime Minister: I was only citing the facts as they are known to me; I have not been concerned to make a detailed attack upon the right hon. Gentleman's administration of the War Office. I am explaining that we had, at the time after Dunkirk, to concentrate upon numbers. We had to make thousands of armoured vehicles with which our troops could beat the enemy off the beaches when they landed and fight them in the lanes and fields of Kent or Norfolk.

When the first new tanks came out they had grievous defects, the correction of which caused delay, and this would have been avoided if the preliminary experiments on the scale of 12 inches to the foot – full scale – had been carried out at an earlier period. Is that a very serious attack? Undoubtedly delay would have been saved if we had had the

---

[1] A handbook on mechanised and armoured formations issued in 1929. In 1931 the 1st Brigade of the Royal Tank Corps was established, and its Commander, Charles Broad, demonstrated effectively the use of radio to control a tank formation.

model there and worked it. How do you make a tank? People design it, they argue about it, they plan it and make it, and then you take the tank and test and re-test it. When you have got it absolutely settled you go into production, and only then do you go into production. But we have never been able to indulge in the luxury of that precise and leisurely process. We have had to take it straight off the drawing board and go into full production, and take the chance of the many errors which the construction will show coming out after hundreds and thousands of them have been made.

Mr Hore-Belisha: What about the Churchill tank?

The Prime Minister: At the present moment I have not got there. At the present moment I am only dealing with the Matildas, Cruisers and Valentines, which I may say belong to the Belisha group. Nevertheless, I was about to say that in spite of the fact that there was this undoubted delay through no preliminary work having been carried as far as it should have been, it would be wrong in my opinion to write off as useless the Matilda, the Cruiser and the Valentine tanks. They have rendered great services, and they are today of real value. In Russia the Valentine is highly rated. Has the House any idea of the number of tanks we have sent to Russia? As I said, we have sent 4,500 altogether to the Nile Valley. We have sent over 2,000 tanks to Russia, and the Russians are using them against the German armour, with vigour and effect. Therefore, I am not prepared to say that it is right to dismiss these weapons – although their appearance was retarded by the circumstances which I have mentioned – as not effective and powerful weapons of war.

Shortly after the present National Government was formed, in June 1940, to be exact, I called a meeting of all authorities to design and make a new tank, capable of speedy mass production and adapted to the war conditions to be foreseen in 1942. In 1942 – that was the test. Of course I do not attempt to settle the technical details of tank design any more than I interfere with the purely tactical decisions of generals in the field. All the highest expert authorities were brought together several times and made to hammer out a strong and heavy tank, adapted primarily for the defence of this Island against invasion, but capable of other employment in various theatres. This tank, the A22, was ordered off the drawing board, and large numbers went into production very quickly. As might be expected, it had many defects and teething troubles, and when these became apparent the tank was appropriately re-christened the 'Churchill'. These defects have now been largely overcome. I am sure that this tank will prove, in the end, a powerful, massive and serviceable weapon of war. A later tank, possessing greater speed, was designed about a year after, and plans have been made to put it into production at the earliest moment.

Neither of these types has yet been employed against the enemy. He has not come here, and, although I sent the earliest two that were made out to Egypt to be tested and made desert-worthy, none has yet reached a stage where it can be employed at that distance. It must be remembered that to get a tank from this country, or a gun, into the hands of troops in the Nile Valley or in the desert takes about six months. Hon. Members will see that the date on which this battle began was a date before we could have got the new and improved weapon into the hands of the troops. For this battle – for the first battle I say the equipment was adequate – we tried to make up by numbers for an admitted inferiority in quality.

I have been asked by the hon. Gentleman who opened the Debate to speak about dive-bombers and transport aircraft. I can only say that the highest technical authorities still hold very strong opinions on either side of this question. Of course, you cannot judge whether we ought to have had dive bombers at any particular date without also considering what we should have had to give up if we had had them. Most of the Air-Marshals, the leading men in the Air Force, think little of dive-bombers, and they persist in their opinion. They are entitled to respect for their opinion, because it was from the same source that the 8-gun fighter was designed which destroyed so many hundreds of the dive-bombers in the Battle of Britain and has enabled us to preserve ourselves free and uninvaded.

Mr Bevan: The dive bomber in the Battle of Britain was adapted by the Germans for a use never intended for the dive bomber. The dive bomber was intended by German military strategy to be used in co-operation with troops. It was shot down over Britain because it was being wrongly used.

The Prime Minister: In what way does that affect the argument I am holding, namely, that if we had made dive-bombers instead of 8-gun fighter aircraft, we might not have had the 8-gun fighter aircraft to shoot down the JU87s when they came over? I remember well, 40 years ago, rising to interrupt the late Mr Balfour, and, after I had said what I had to say, he rebuked me by saying, 'I thought my hon. Friend rose to correct me on some point of fact, but it appears that he only wishes to continue the argument.' Now there is no doubt whatever that the Army desire to have dive-bombers, and, nearly two years ago orders were placed for them. They have not come to hand in any number yet. That is a detailed story which I certainly do not wish to press, if it should be thought in any way that we were throwing any blame off our shoulders onto those of the United States. On the point of priority, the case is clear, when you have, as you had then in the United States, an immense market, an immense productive sphere and no priority questions had arisen. The rate at which the product was evolved was not influenced by the priority position. It was influenced by various incidents – changes of design and so forth – which occurred.

The dive-bomber against ships at sea appears to me to be a still more dangerous weapon. I say that because this is my own opinion on the matter, but as to transport aircraft I wish, indeed, we had 1,000 transport aircraft; but if we had built 1,000 of these unarmed transport aircraft, it would have cut off our already far from adequate bomber force. I know there is a tendency to deride and disparage the bomber effort against Germany, but I think that is a very great mistake. There is no doubt that this bomber offensive against Germany is one of the most powerful means we have of carrying on an offensive war against Germany. We did not like it when the blitz was on, but we bore it. Everyone knows that it was the main preoccupation of the Government and the municipal authorities of that day, with factories being delayed in their work, ports congested and so forth. We, at any rate, had hope. We felt that we were on the rising tide. More was coming to us, and, moreover, we were buoyed up by the sympathy of the world – 'London can take it' and so on. No such consolations are available in Germany. Nobody speaks with admiration and says, 'Cologne can take it.' They say, 'Serve them right.' That is the view of the civilised world. In addition to that, they know that this attack is not going to get weaker. It is going to get continually stronger until, in my view, it will play a great and perfectly definite part in abridging the course of this war, in taking the strain off our Russian Allies, and in reducing the building and construction of submarines and other weapons of war. Of course, one would like to have had both, but at this moment, much though we need transport aircraft, I am not at all sure, if I were offered a gift of 1,000 heavy bombers or 1,000 transports, which I should choose. I should take advice.

To return to the main argument which is before the House, I will willingly accept, indeed I am bound to accept, what the Noble Lord has called the 'constitutional responsibility' for everything that has happened and I consider that I discharged that responsibility by not interfering with the technical handling of armies in contact with the enemy. But before the battle began I urged General Auchinleck to take the command himself, because I was sure nothing was going to happen in the vast area of the Middle East in the next month or two comparable in importance to the fighting of this battle in the Western Desert, and I thought he was the man to handle the business. He gave me various good reasons for not doing so, and General Ritchie fought the battle. As I told the House on Tuesday, General Auchinleck, on 25th June, superseded General Ritchie and assumed the command himself. We at once approved his decision, but I must frankly confess that the matter was not one on which we could form any final judgment, so far as the superseded officer is concerned. I cannot pretend to form a judgment upon what has happened in this battle. I like commanders on land and sea and in the air to feel that between them and all forms of public criticism the Government stand like a strong bulkhead. They ought to have a fair chance, and more than one chance. Men may make mistakes and learn from their mistakes. Men may have bad luck, and their luck may change. But anyhow you will not get generals to run risks unless they feel they have behind them a strong Government. They will not run risks unless they feel that they need not look over their shoulders or worry about what is happening at home, unless they feel they can concentrate their gaze upon the enemy. And you will not, I may add, get a Government to run risks unless they feel that they have got behind them a loyal, solid majority. Look at the things we are being asked to dare now, and imagine the kind of attack which would be made on us if we tried to do them and failed. In war time if you desire service you must give loyalty.

General Auchinleck is now in direct command of the battle. It is raging with great intensity. The *communiqué* which has been issued on the tape – I have not had any news myself – states that the attacks yesterday were repulsed. But the battle is of the most intense and serious character. We have assured General Auchinleck of our confidence, and I believe it will be found that this confidence has not been misplaced. I am not going to express any opinion about what is going to happen. I cannot tell the House – and the enemy – what reinforcements are at hand, or are approaching, or when they will arrive. I have never made any predictions except things like saying that Singapore would hold out. What a fool and a knave I should have been to say that it would fall. I have not made any arrogant, confident, boasting predictions at all. On the contrary, I have stuck hard to my blood, toil, tears and sweat, to which I have added muddle and mismanagement, and that, to some extent I must admit, is what you have got out of it.

I repudiate altogether the suggestion that I misled the House on June about the present campaign. All I said was that: '[...] it is clear that we have every reason to be satisfied, and more than satisfied, with the course which the battle has so far taken and that we should watch its further development with earnest attention.' – [Official Report, 2nd June; col. 533, vol. 380.] Nothing could be more guarded. I do not know what my critics would like me to say now. If I predict success and speak in buoyant terms and misfortune continues, their tongues and pens will be able to dilate on my words. On the other hand, if I predict failure and paint the picture in the darkest hues – I have painted it in pretty dark hues – I might safeguard myself against one danger, but only at the expense of a struggling Army. Also I might be wrong. So I will say nothing about the future except to invite the House and the nation to face with courage whatever it may unfold.

I now ask the House to take a wider survey. Since Japan attacked us six months ago in the Far East we have suffered heavy losses there. A peace-loving nation like the United States, confined by two great oceans, naturally takes time to bring its gigantic forces to bear. I have never shared the view that this would be a short war, or that it would end in 1942. It is far more likely to be a long war. There is no reason to suppose that the war will stop when the final result has become obvious. The Battle of Gettysburg proclaimed the ultimate victory of the North, but far more blood was shed after the Battle of Gettysburg than before. At the same time, in spite of our losses in Asia, in spite of our defeats in Libya, in spite of the increased sinkings off the American coast, I affirm with confidence that the general strength and prospects of the United Nations have greatly improved since the turn of the year, when I last visited the President in the United States. The outstanding feature is of course the steady resistance of Russia to the invaders of her soil, and the fact that up to now at the beginning of July, more than halfway through the summer, no major offensive has been opened by Hitler upon Russia, unless he calls the present attacks on Kharkov and Kursk a major offensive. There is no doubt that the Russian Government and nation, wedded by the ties of blood, sacrifice and faith to the English speaking democracies of the West, will continue to wage war, steadfast, stubborn, invincible. I make no forecast of the future. All I know is that the Russians have surprised Hitler before and I believe they will surprise him again. Anyhow whatever happens they will fight on to death or victory. This is the cardinal fact at this time.

The second great fact is the growth of air power on the side of the Allies. That growth is proceeding with immense rapidity and is bound to manifest itself as the months pass by. Hitler made a contract with the demon of the air, but the contract ran out before the job was done, and the demon has taken on an engagement with the rival firm. How truly it has been said that nations and people very often fall by the very means which they have used and built their hopes upon for their rising up.

For the last six months our convoys to the East have grown. Every month about 50,000 men with the best equipment we can make have pierced through the U-boats and hostile aircraft which beset these islands, and have rounded the Cape of Good Hope. That this should have been done so far without loss constitutes an achievement prodigious and unexampled in history. As these successive Armies, for they are little less, round the Cape we decide where they are to go. Some months ago Australia feared that an invasion was imminent. If so, our Forces would have gone to aid our kith and kin irrespective of the position in the Middle East. Personally, I have never thought that the homeland of Australia would be heavily invaded by Japan in the present year, and now that the Australian manhood is armed and in the field, and that a large American Army has arrived in Australia and in the island stepping stones across the Pacific as a feature of the central direction of the war, I am confident that the mass invasion of Australia would be a most hazardous and unprofitable operation for Japan. On the contrary, throughout the whole of the South-West Pacific the watchword of the Allies is now 'attack'.

In March and April last we were deeply anxious about India, which, before Japan entered the war, had been stripped almost bare of trained troops and equipment for the sake of other theatres. India has now been strongly reinforced. A far larger Army, British and Indian, stands in India under the command of General Wavell than ever before in the history of the British connection. Ceylon, which at one time appeared to be in great jeopardy, is now strongly defended by naval, air and military forces. We have secured a protective naval base in Madagascar. When I remember reading an article by the right hon. Gentleman headed, 'Take Madagascar Now' – I am not blaming the right hon. Gentleman, as he could not know that our troops had been some weeks on the sea – I really wonder whether he might not have found time to make some acknowledgment of the speed and efficiency with which his direction had been carried out.

All this improvement in the position of Australia, New Zealand and India has been effected in the main by the brilliant victories gained by the United States Navy and Air Force over the Japanese in the Coral Sea and at Midway Island. No fewer than four out of eight Japanese regular aircraft carriers – vessels which take four years to make – have been sunk, as well as one of their converted auxiliary carriers. When the Japanese came into the Bay of Bengal at the beginning of April with five carriers, we were caused great anxiety, but five are now at the bottom of the sea; and the Japanese, whose resources are strictly limited, are beginning to count their capital units on their fingers and toes. These splendid achievements have not received the attention they deserve in this island. Superb acts of devotion have been performed by the American airmen. From some of their successful attacks on the Japanese aircraft carriers only one aircraft returned out of 10; in others, the loss was more than half. But the work has been done, and the position in the Pacific has been definitely altered in our favour.

This relief has enabled important forces to be directed upon Egypt. The extraordinary valour and tenacity of the Russian defence of Sebastopol and General Timoshenko's massive strokes in the battles round Kharkov, together with the lateness of the season, have enabled us to concentrate our efforts on the destruction of Rommel's army. At this moment, the struggle in Egypt is gradually approaching its full intensity. The battle is now in the balance, and it is an action of the highest consequence. It has one object, and one object only, namely, the destruction of the enemy's army and armoured power. Important aid is now on the way, both from Britain and from the United States. A hard and deadly struggle lies before the Armies on the Nile. It remains for us at home to fortify and encourage their Commander by every means in our power.

I wish to speak a few words 'of great truth and respect' – as they say in the diplomatic documents – and I hope I may be granted the fullest liberty of debate. This Parliament has a peculiar responsibility. It presided over the beginning of the evils which have come on the world. I owe much to the House, and it is my hope that it may see the end of them in triumph. This it can do only if, in the long period which may yet have to be travelled, the House affords a solid foundation to the responsible Executive Government, placed in power by its own choice. The House must be a steady, stabilising factor in the State, and not an instrument by which the disaffected sections of the Press can attempt to promote one crisis after another. If democracy and Parliamentary institutions are to triumph in this war, it is absolutely necessary that Governments resting upon them shall be able to act and dare, that the servants of the Crown shall not be harassed by nagging and snarling, that enemy propaganda shall not be fed needlessly out of our own hands, and our reputation disparaged and undermined throughout the world. On the contrary, the will of the whole House should be made manifest upon important occasions. It is important that not only those who speak, but those who watch and listen and judge, should also count as a factor in world affairs. After all, we are still fighting for our lives, and for causes dearer than life itself. We have no right to assume that victory is certain; it will be certain only if we do not fail in our duty. Sober and constructive criticism, or criticism in Secret Session, has its high virtue; but the duty of the House of Commons is to sustain the Government or to change the Government, if it cannot change it, it should sustain it. There is no working middle course in war-time. Much harm was done abroad by the two days' Debate in May. Only the hostile speeches are reported abroad, and much play is made with them by our enemy.

A Division, or the opportunity for a Division, should always follow a Debate on the war, and I trust, therefore, that the opinion of the over-whelming majority of the House will be made plain not only in the Division, but also in the days which follow and that, if I may so call them, the weaker brethren will not be allowed to usurp and almost monopolise the privileges and proud authority of the House of Commons. The majority of the House must do their duty. All I ask is a decision one way or another.

There is an agitation in the Press which has found its echo in a number of hostile speeches to deprive me of the function which I exercise in the general conduct and supervision of the war. I do not propose to argue this today at any length, because it was much discussed in a recent Debate. Under the present arrangement the three Chiefs of the Staff, sitting almost continuously together, carry on the war from day to day assisted not only by the machinery of the great Departments which serve them, but by the Combined General Staff, and making their decisions effective through the Navy, Army and Air Forces over which they exercise direct operational control. I supervise their activities, whether as Prime Minister or Minister of Defence. I work myself under the supervision and control of the War Cabinet to whom all important matters are referred and whom I have to carry with me in all major decisions. Nearly all my work has been done in writing, and a complete record exists of all the directions I have given, the inquiries I have made and the telegrams I have drafted. I shall be perfectly content to be judged by them.

I ask no favours either for myself or for His Majesty's Government. I undertook the office as Prime Minister and Minister of Defence, after defending my predecessor to the best of my ability, in times when the life of the Empire hung upon a thread. I am your servant, and you have the right to dismiss me when you please. What you have no right to do is to ask me to bear responsibilities without the power of effective action, to bear the responsibilities of Prime Minister but clamped on each side by strong men. As the hon. Member said, if today, or at any future time, the House were to exercise its undoubted right, I could walk out with a good conscience and the feeling that I have done my duty according to such light as has been granted to me. There is only one thing I would ask you in that event. It would be to give my successor the modest powers which would have been denied to me.

But there is a larger issue than the personal issue. The Mover of this Vote of Censure has proposed that I should be stripped of my responsibilities for Defence in order that some military figure or that some other unnamed personage should assume the general conduct of the war, that he should have complete control of the Armed Forces of the Crown, that he should be the Chief of the Chiefs of the Staff, that he should nominate or dismiss the generals or the admirals, that he should always be ready to resign, that is to say, to match himself against his political colleagues, if colleagues they may be considered, if he did not get all he wanted, that he should have under him a Royal Duke as Commander-in-Chief of the Army, and finally, I presume, though this was not mentioned, that this unnamed personage should find an appendage in the Prime Minister to make the necessary explanations, excuses and apologise to Parliament when things go wrong, as they often do and often will. That is at any rate a policy. It is a system very different from the Parliamentary system under which we live. It might easily amount to or be converted into a dictatorship. I wish to make it perfectly clear that as far as I am concerned I shall take no part in such a system.

Sir John Wardlaw-Milne: I hope that my right hon. Friend has not forgotten the original sentence, which was 'subject to the War Cabinet'?

The Prime Minister: Subject to the War Cabinet against which this all powerful potentate is not to hesitate to resign on every occasion if he could not get his way. It is a plan, but it is not a plan in which I should personally be interested to take part, and I do not think that it is one which would commend itself to this House.

The setting down of this Vote of Censure by Members of all parties is a considerable event. Do not, I beg you, let the House underrate the gravity of what has been done. It has been trumpeted all round the world to our disparagement, and when every nation, friend and foe, is waiting to see what is the true resolve and conviction of the House of Commons it must go forward to the end. All over the world, throughout the United States, as I can testify, in Russia, far away in China and throughout every subjugated country all our friends are waiting to know whether there is a strong, solid Government in Britain and whether its national leadership is to be challenged or not. Every vote counts. If those who have assailed us are reduced to contemptible proportions and their Vote of Censure on the National Government is converted to a vote of censure upon its authors, make no mistake, a cheer will go up from every friend of Britain and every faithful servant of our cause, and the knell of disappointment will ring in the ears of the tyrants we are striving to overthrow.

Question put:

'That this House, while paying tribute to the heroism and endurance of the armed Forces of the Crown in circumstances of exceptional difficulty, has no confidence in the central direction of the war.'

The House divided: Ayes, 25; Noes, 475.

Henry Channon: diary
('Chips', page 334)

2 July 1942

Today Belisha made what proved to be a brilliant, eloquent and damning attack on the Government. He was skilful and deadly, and I admired his courage and accurate marshalling of the facts. Surely Churchill, I thought, could not answer him, but answer him he did, and for over an hour we had all the usual Churchillian gusto [...] But his magic had no magic for me, we might as well have Macaulay or even Caruso as Prime Minister. He skated around dangerous corners, and by clever evasion managed to ignore the question as to whether he had ordered Tobruk to be held. Nevertheless he had his usual effect of intoxicating his listeners. I left before he sat down and went to the library, put my head into my hands, took a deep breath and prayed for advice [...] The argument against voting against the Government is strong and, on balance, I decided I hadn't 'the guts,' so slowly walked into the very crowded Aye Lobby to the derision of the few abstainers, perhaps 20 in all. I saw Winterton and Archie Southby muttering to one another. They had abstained, as had Lady Astor, Megan Lloyd George and others who sat silent on the benches. I waited until the final figures were announced. 475 to 25, a Government majority of 450. The PM rose, looked up at the Speaker's Gallery, smiled at Mrs Churchill, and then walked out of the Chamber to go to the Smoking Room. As he left he received a polite but lukewarm ovation.

Harold Nicolson: diary
(*'Harold Nicolson, Diaries and Letters', page 231*)

2 July 1942   London

The second day of the Vote of Censure Debate. Aneurin Bevan opens with a brilliant offensive, pointing his finger in accusation, twisting and bowing. Then comes Walter Elliot and then Hore-Belisha.

Winston sits there with a look of sullen foreboding, his face from time to time flickering into a smile. He rises stockily, his hands in his trouser pockets. He makes a long statement which really amounts to the fact that we had more men and more tanks and more guns than Rommel, and that he cannot understand why we were so badly beaten. He gives no indication of how the battle of Egypt is likely to go. In the end, after one hour and thirty minutes, he is quite fresh and gay. He gets his vote of confidence by 476 [*sic*] to 25, plus a great ovation afterwards. But the impression left is one of dissatisfaction and anxiety, and I do not think it will end there. The only thing he could do is to bring back Wavell as CIGS. I feel deeply sorry for him. Every weapon he uses smashes in his hands.

President Franklin D. Roosevelt to Winston S. Churchill
(*Churchill papers, 20/77*)

2 July 1942   Washington DC

Number 160, Good for you.

Harry Hopkins to Winston S. Churchill
(*Churchill papers, 20/77*)

2 July 1942   Washington DC

Action of Commons today delighted me. These have been some of the bad days. No doubt there will be others. They who run for cover with every reverse, the timid and faint of heart, will have no part in winning the war. Your strength, tenacity, and everlasting courage will see Britain through and the President, you know, does not quit. I know you are of good heart for your military defeats and ours and our certain victories to come will be shared together. More power to you.

Harry Hopkins

Winston S. Churchill to Harry Hopkins
(Churchill papers, 20/77)

2 July 1942

Thank you so much my friend. I knew you and the President would be glad of this domestic victory. I hope one day I shall have something more solid to report.

Chiefs of Staff: memorandum
(Cabinet papers, 66/26)

2 July 1942
Most Secret

[...]

5. At the War Cabinet meeting on the 11th of June, the Prime Minister laid down, and the War Cabinet generally approved, that operations in 1942 should be governed by the following two principles:

(i) No substantial landing in France in 1942 unless we are going to stay: and

(ii) No substantial landing in France unless the Germans are demoralised by failure against Russia.

It seems to us that the above conditions are unlikely to be fulfilled and that, therefore, the chances of launching operation 'Sledgehammer' this year are remote.

6. It is true that there are certain military advantages in mounting 'Sledgehammer,' even though it is unlikely to be launched. In the first place, our preparations are bound to keep the Germans guessing. They may not force them to withdraw troops form their Eastern Front, but they are unlikely to weaken their Western Front, particularly in air forces. Secondly, the mounting of 'Sledgehammer' will be a useful dress-rehearsal for 'Round-up,' especially for Commanders and Staffs.

[...]

If we do not make active and serious preparations for 'Sledgehammer,' the Russians are almost bound to know very soon that we are not fulfilling our promise that we would do so.

Anthony Eden: diary
(*'The Eden Memoirs, The Reckoning', pages 332–3*)

2 July 1942

Winston wound up with one of his most effective speeches, beautifully adjusted to temper of the House.

Work at the Office. Then dined with him alone except for his brother. Much discussion of war situation. Winston said repeatedly that we had not done as well as we should. 'I am ashamed,' etc., and we discussed too the problems of the Army, its Trade Union outlook, paucity of talent, etc. I urged Winston to see Ralph[1] about his 'Churchill' tanks.

Then Winston broached possibility of another journey. I didn't like it and told him I thought he wouldn't be able to help and would be in the way. 'You mean like a great blue-bottle buzzing over a huge cowpat!' said Winston. I said this was just what I did mean! At this moment Brendan appeared and took up the running strongly against the project, especially on grounds of risk. But this W would not have. Anyway he had made his testament in my favour before he went to the United States and he was not indispensable. Argument was inconclusive.

On 3 July 1942, at a meeting in Downing Street, Churchill gave orders for 200 hundred operational sets of H2S ground-mapping radar to be operational by mid-October. This proved to be an essential preliminary to the preparations for a successful amphibious landing in Normandy in June 1944.

---

[1] Ralph Assheton, 1901–84. Conservative Member of Parliament for Rushcliffe, Nottinghamshire, 1934–45; for the City of London, 1945–50; for Blackburn West, 1950–5. Parliamentary Secretary, Ministry of Labour and Ministry of National Service, 1939–42; Ministry of Supply, 1942–3. Financial Secretary to the Treasury, 1943–4. Chairman of the Conservative Party Organization, 1944–6. Created Baronet, 1945. Chairman of the Public Accounts Committee, 1948–50; of the Select Committee on Nationalized Industries, 1951–3. Created Baron Clitheroe, 1955. Lord Lieutenant of Lancashire, 1971–6.

Oliver Harvey: diary
(*'The War Diaries of Oliver Harvey'*, page 137)

3 July 1942

PM made, as usual, a great speech yesterday and on the whole seems to have won the sympathy of the House. All were rather overawed by the issues being fought out in Africa and slightly ashamed of themselves.

AE dined with PM afterwards. He told me this morning he found the PM 'in the greatest heart' and planning to go off at once to Egypt himself by aeroplane! He told AE he had got the King's permission as well as that of Attlee and Bevin. AE and Bracken did their best to shake him out of such a mad idea which, tho' admittedly most heartening to the troops, would only hinder General Auchinleck. PM was like a naughty child. He went on to say to AE he had prepared his political testament which he would leave behind. 'You may like to know what is in it. You are in it.'

Battle yesterday still uncertain. Very hard fighting round Alamein. Late last night our most secret sources said that Rommel was talking of making 'one more attempt' to take the place today. That is encouraging.

Winston S. Churchill to General Claude Auchinleck
(*Churchill papers, 20/89*)

3 July 1942

On the 1st July we told you our special information that enemy, after feinting at your southern flank, would attack centre of your position, about where 18th Brigade lay, and thereafter turn northwards to cut off El Alamein strong point. This is exactly what he appears to be trying to do. Are you getting these priceless messages (which have never erred) in good time? Every MK telegram ought to be in your hands without a moment's delay.

2. How is the 8th Armoured Division getting on and when can it come wholly or partly into action? What is state and position of 9th Australian Division? Have they got all their guns?

3. Should be glad to have your opinion at leisure about how Rommel's tanks would get on among canals and irrigation of Delta.

4. Germans are enquiring whether inundations have been made. This was all planned two years ago with Wavell. Presume it has been carried out. Whole idea here is that Egypt should be defended just as drastically as if it were Kent or Sussex, without regard to any other consideration than destruction of the enemy.

5. Everyone here greatly heartened by your splendid fight. Overwhelming vote House of Commons confidence in Government and your Army.

Winston S. Churchill to General Bernard Freyberg
(Churchill papers, 20/77)

3 July 1942
Personal and Most Secret

Deeply moved to hear of your new wound and new glory. Trust that injury is not serious and that you will soon be back commanding your splendid Division.

All good wishes to you and to them.

Winston S. Churchill to John Curtin
(Churchill papers, 20/77)

3 July 1942
Personal and Most Secret

I am much obliged for your agreement to the diversion of your 42 Spitfires to the Middle East. I of course agree that the month's delay should not be allowed to affect the ultimate position and that you should therefore not lose the 15 Spitfires which would have been sent in July under the original arrangement.

Nevertheless, in order to give Egypt the maximum help during this critical period I would ask you to accept the July allocation for wastage in two instalments, 8 to be sent in July and 7 in August.

Thus shipments to you would be 6 in June, 50 in July, 22 in August, totalling 78 by end of August as before.

Winston S. Churchill to Dr Herbert Evatt
(Churchill papers, 20/77)

3 July 1942
Most Secret and Personal

I am so sorry about the delay in your Spitfires which I regard as your particular packet. The needs of battle are imperative and over-riding, but I am paying personal attention to meeting your wishes and fulfilling my promise.

Winston S. Churchill to President Franklin D. Roosevelt
(Churchill papers, 20/77)

3 July 1942   London
Personal and Secret
No. 104

Grateful for action you are taking. We consider that French ships must be made to obey the orders of the British Naval Commander-in-Chief under penalty of being sunk if and when he orders them to proceed through the Canal.

2. We agree that they should now be given the offer that on emerging from the Canal they will come into the protective custody of the United States under the conditions you outline. Admiral Godfroy[1] will be informed by Admiral Harwood that we have agreed to this.

3. Action will not be taken unless and until the land battle is definitely decided against us. Meanwhile control over French ships, personnel and supplies is to be strictly enforced.

Winston S. Churchill to Captain J. G. Morrison[2]
(Churchill papers, 20/54)

3 July 1942   10 Downing Street

Dear Captain Morrison,

As an old friend of your father[3], who so faithfully served the Salisbury Division in Parliament for many years, I send you my best wishes for your

[1] René Emile Godfroy, 1885–1981. French naval officer. Commander of 4th Cruiser Division in Far East, 1937. Commander of 2nd Cruiser Squadron, promoted to Vice-Admiral, 1940. Agreed to demilitarize French naval forces in Alexandria upon British request after French–German armistice. Joined Free French in 1943 and retired later that year.

[2] John Granville Morrison, 1906–96. Landowner and Conservative Party politician. Born 16 December 1906; son of late Hugh Morrison and Lady Sophia Castalia Mary Leveson-Gower, 2nd daughter of 2nd Earl Granville. Educated at Eton and Magdalene College, Cambridge. Married, 1928, Hon. Margaret Esther Lucie Smith (died 1980). Served with Royal Wilts Yeomanry, 1939–42. Conservative MP for Salisbury Division of Wiltshire, 1942–64; Chairman, 1922 Committee, 1955–64. Created 1st Baron Morgadale of Islay in the county of Argyll, 1964. Lord-Lieutenant of Wiltshire, 1969–81.

[3] Hugh Morrison, 1868–1931. Conservative Party politician. Born 8 June 1868, son of late Alfred Morrison and Mabel née Chermside of Fonthill in Wiltshire. Married, 1892, Lady Sophia Castalia

success as the National Government Candidate in the by-election which is now taking place in the constituency.

You yourself have youth and energy on your side. You are in peace time a farmer in a county of farmers, and in war-time a soldier among soldiers, who has seen service on many fronts since the first day of the war. All your experience has formed a fitting prelude to a parliamentary career and I look forward to welcoming you shortly in the House of Commons.

Yours sincerely,
Winston S. Churchill

War Cabinet: Confidential Annex
(Cabinet papers, 65/31)

3 July 1942   10 Downing Street
12 noon

The Prime Minister said that if Egypt was overrun, he thought that our attitude to the country should be the same as though the enemy invaded Kent and Sussex, namely, that the enemy should be fought ruthlessly and with Russian methods applied.

General Sir Alan Brooke: diary
('War Diaries, Field Marshal Lord Alanbrooke', page 276)

3 July 1942

[...] had about ¾ hour with Winston, first of all trying to convince him that he should not try to fly out by Gib and the Mediterranean in a Liberator. And secondly that he should wait till the situation consolidates a little more in Egypt before flying out.

Mary Leveson-Gower. Educated at Eton and Trinity College, Cambridge. High Sheriff of Wiltshire, 1904.

Winston S. Churchill to A. V. Alexander and
Admiral of the Fleet Sir Dudley Pound
(Churchill papers, 20/67)

4 July 1942
Most Secret

We must adapt ourselves to this rapidly changing scene. A great ease-ment has come to us in the Indian Ocean compared with the March–April position. At any time now the Japanese may involve themselves with Russia. India has been strongly reinforced. Ceylon is getting into good order.

2. The needs of Malta have diverted *Nelson* and *Rodney*, and delayed the formation of the Eastern Fleet. This could be accepted in view of the easement mentioned above.

3. Admiral King, wishing to press his offensive in the South-West Pacific, has asked us to take what looks to me to be very dangerous action towards Timor in August. I confess I feel great anxieties about commit-ting our three carriers, *Valiant* and *Warspite* to waters where the Japanese shore-based aircraft may be found too powerful.

4. There is another operation which ought to be considered. It depends entirely upon the course of the battle now in progress at Alamein. Should we be successful there, should Rommel be forced to retreat, as in that event he might be quite quickly, beyond Mersa Matruh, Alexandria would be freed from danger.

5. Ought we not then to reassert our sea power in the Eastern Mediter-ranean? Pray consider whether Admiral Somerville should not for the time being re-enter the Mediterranean through the Canal with one or two carriers, *Warspite* and *Valiant*, and thus make impossible any attempt to throw an enemy army across from Greece on to the Egyptian shore. It seems to me there is less risk in this operation than in the one for which Admiral King is pressing, and it could be given as a very good reason – i.e., our ships could not be accused of standing idle while the Americans were moving. See also Wavell's telegram of today showing how very long he will be before doing anything across the Bay of Bengal.

6. I am not suggesting the running of a convoy from Alexandria to Malta simultaneously with the Gibraltar effort; but even a feint would be a great help if we were strong in the Eastern Mediterranean at the same time *Nelson* and *Rodney* were entering from the other end with the convoy. At the very least the arrival of Admiral Somerville's fleet in the Mediterra-nean would be an invaluable distraction. It would steady things in Turkey and, coming on the heels of victory at Alamein, should we win that battle, it would very nearly restore our prestige in the Eastern Mediterranean.

7. I wish this to be examined by the Naval Staff most earnestly and in a forward spirit, so that should the Alamein battle turn in our favour we have our new view carefully considered beforehand.

8. In this connection the great increase in our long-range bombing power which should occur during July and at the beginning of August ought to give protection in the Eastern Mediterranean both against oversea invasion and for His Majesty's ships. The return of the British battle fleet to Alexandria would have a world-wide effect. There is no need to consider them tied there permanently. On the contrary, when we have consolidated our position on land it would be right to send them back to the Indian Ocean. According to our present plans they might well be back there at the end of September, which would be in plenty of time for any operation which General Wavell may design across the Bay of Bengal.

9. There are two special points which are separate from the above design, but on which I wish to receive a report:

(a) When the August convoy goes from Gibraltar, what are the possibilities and risks of sending *Nelson* and *Rodney* straight on through the Mediterranean to join Admiral Somerville? I do not press this at all, nor do I wish it to hamper the consideration of the larger scheme.

(b) If it is definitely decided not to run a convoy from Alexandria to Malta in August, which I assume must be taken as settled, is there not time to send half a dozen of the loaded merchantmen there round the Cape to crowd in with the Gibraltar party?

Winston S. Churchill to General Claude Auchinleck
(Churchill papers, 20/77)

4 July 1942
Personal and Secret

I cannot help liking very much the way things seem to be going. If fortune turns I am sure you will press your advantage, as you say, 'relentlessly.'

Winston S. Churchill to Air Marshal Sir Arthur Tedder
(Churchill papers, 20/77)

4 July 1942
Personal
Most Immediate

Here at home we are all watching with enthusiasm the brilliant, supreme exertions of the Royal Air Force in the battle now proceeding in Egypt. From every quarter the reports come in of the effect of the vital part which your officers and men are playing in this Homeric struggle for the Nile Valley. The days of the Battle of Britain are being repeated far from home. We are sure you will be to our glorious Army the friend that endureth to the end.

Winston S. Churchill to Harry Hopkins
(Churchill papers, 20/77)

4 July 1942
Personal and Secret

I send you my own personal return of shipping losses for the first six months of 1942. It is all very serious, particularly the remorselessly increasing losses of American and American-controlled shipping.

Winston S. Churchill to Field Marshal Jan Smuts
(Churchill papers, 20/77)

4 July 1942
Most Secret and Personal

I have been so much harried by the weaker brethren in the House of Commons since my return from America last week, that this is the first chance I have had of telling you how deeply I grieve for the cruel losses you have sustained in your gallant South African divisions, and how much I admire the indomitable manner in which you have inspired South Africa to face this heavy blow.

2. We have been through so much together and are so often in harmony of thought that I do not need to say much now about the lamentable events of the last three weeks. I am still hopeful that all can be retrieved. The President gave me three hundred of their latest Sherman tanks, which are far superior to the Grants, and one hundred 105 mm self

propelled gun-howitzers as anti-tank weapons. These should reach Egypt by the beginning of September. The President is also sending Liberators with those already there up to about one hundred, which should arrive during July. Two heavy Halifax bombing squadrons from England will be in action during the next ten days. Another sixty American fighters are being rushed across the Atlantic via Takoradi. All this is additional to our regular reinforcement of the air. As you probably know, the 8th Armoured Division with 350 tanks, mostly Valentines, is landing now. The 44th British Infantry Division should land July 23, and the 51st a month later. Whether these forces will be able to play their part depends upon the battle now proceeding at Alamein. I will send you in a separate message the Air Ministry's reply to your No. 1170.

3. I read your Q.0372 to the President. My own ideas are identical with yours. Two months ago I asked the Staffs here and General Wavell to prepare plans to strike at the Japanese lines of communication through Burma and Malaya by attacking Rangoon and Moulmein, aiming at Bangkok. They say this cannot be done till after the monsoon ends in October. General Alexander should arrive home in the next few days from General Wavell with the full plan, which I thought he would carry out himself if all goes well.

Every good wish.
Winston Churchill

Winston S. Churchill to President Franklin D. Roosevelt
(Churchill papers, 20/77)

4 July 1942
Personal and Secret
No. 105

The Boston Bomber is doing great work in Egypt. Auchinleck reported on 1st July that Boston attacks 'were regular as trains and most heartening to troops'. But battles of this intensity take a heavy toll. Apart from the replacements which will be needed, we have in Egypt the personnel of four light bomber squadrons without any aircraft at all.

2. Only ten Bostons will reach us in the Middle East during July. There are, however, in Iraq, en route to Russia, forty Bostons which are ready to fly, and behind them another seventy two as yet unerected. The Middle East

have made an urgent appeal to be allowed to have these forty aircraft as an immediate reinforcement. They could be in the battle within a week.

3. Would you consider allowing us to have these forty Bostons at once: and if so, would you approach Stalin and tell him that you will make them up to him as quickly as possible? With Russia in the thick of the battle, this is a hard request and I shall quite understand if you do not feel able to do as I ask. But our needs are great and there is no other way of getting the additional bombers into action at once.

Winston S. Churchill to Admiral Harold Stark[1]
(Churchill papers, 20/77)

4 July 1942

My dear Admiral,

I found your very kind letter and the gramophone records awaiting me on my return from the United States. I had them played last night, and enjoyed them immensely. It was so good of you to send them to me.

Yours sincerely,
Winston S. Churchill

Admiral of the Fleet Sir Dudley Pound to Admiral Louis Hamilton[2]
('The Hinge of Fate', page 235)

4 July 1942

CONVOY PQ17

9.11 p.m.
Cruiser Force withdraw to the westward at high speed.

9.23 p.m.
Owing to threat from surface ships, convoy is to disperse and proceed to Russian ports.

9.36 p.m.
Convoy is to scatter.[3]

---

[1] Commander, United States Naval Forces in Europe.

[2] Rear-Admiral Commanding the First Cruiser Squadron.

[3] Churchill wrote in his war memoirs: 'Admiral Pound would probably not have sent such vehement orders if only our own British warships had been concerned. But the idea that our first large joint Anglo-American operation under British command should involve the destruction of the two United States cruisers as well as our own may well have disturbed the poise with which he was accustomed to deal with these heart-shaking decisions. This is only my surmise from what I knew of my friend, for I never discussed the matter with him. Indeed, so strictly was the secret of these

Winston S. Churchill to General Hastings Ismay,
for the Chiefs of Staff Committee
(Churchill papers, 20/67)

5 July 1942
Most Secret

'Sledgehammer'[1] or one-third 'Bolero' as the Americans call it, is now at a point where a decision must be reached whether to take up shipping or not.

2. No responsible British General, Admiral or Air Marshal is prepared to recommend 'Sledgehammer' as a desirable or even as a practicable operation in 1942. No confirmation of the hopes of additional landing craft from the United States has been obtained. The three American divisions will not be here in time to be trained for the special amphibious work required. The chances of favourable conditions in the first part of September are dependent on the uncertain factors of wind and visibility during the limited period when moon and tides are suitable.

3. On the other hand, there is a price to be paid. The taking up of the shipping would cost us a loss in imports at the rate of 950,000 tons per annum and would derange the costal trade affecting winter coal. Far more serious is the fact that the interruption of the training of the troops, apart from the loss of a landing-craft, &c., would delay 'Roundup'[2] for at least two to three months, even if the enterprise were unsuccessful and the troops had to be withdrawn after a short stay.

4. In the event of a lodgment being effected and maintained, it would have to be nourished, and the bomber effort upon Germany would have to be greatly curtailed, if not entirely suspended. All our energies would be absorbed in defending the bridgehead. There would be no possibility of mounting a large-scale operation in 1943, as all our resources would be absorbed piecemeal on the very narrow front which alone is open. It may, therefore, be said that premature action in 1942, while probably ending in disaster, would decisively injure the prospects of well-organised, large-scale action in 1943.

5. If these views are accepted, we should tell the President and, when we have heard from him, tell the Russians, giving them all the reasons

---

orders being sent on the First Sea Lord's authority guarded by the Admiralty that it was not until after the war that I learned the facts' (*The Hinge of Fate*, pages 235–6).

[1] 'Sledgehammer': The planned Anglo-American amphibious landing of limited aims against northern France.

[2] 'Roundup': the plans for the liberation of France.

set out in the Chiefs of Staff Paper and the CCO's Appendix. There would, of course, be no public indication that the project was not going forward, as this would damage British and Russian morale and put the enemy at his ease.

6. The question of 'Gymnast'[1] will then come to the front, and must be taken up with the President. The question of 'Jupiter'[2] or some form of 'Jupiter', in concert with the Russians would also seem to be of great urgency from every point of view, military and political. Our whole power to help Russia in any effectual manner this year depends upon our driving the enemy aircraft from the northern airfields of Norway.

Winston S. Churchill to Anthony Eden
(Churchill papers, 20/67)

5 July 1942
Most Secret

The above[3] leaves me in doubt whether you want the three Polish divisions or not if you have to take with them this mass of women and children. Personally I want them. If we win the Alamein battle we ought to be able to handle them even with their encumbrances. If we don't win, the project will be impracticable.

2. Surely the telegram should be re-drafted to achieve this purpose, saying in short –

(a) We want the Poles with their belongings, making up our minds to overcome the 'insuperable difficulties'.

(b) For the sake of the *armour propre* of the Soviet Government, representing the transaction as a movement of fighting men, their families and dependants.

---

[1] 'Gymnast': the Anglo-American plan to land in French North Africa.

[2] 'Jupiter': planned operations in northern Norway.

[3] Draft telegram to Sir Archibald Clark Kerr, Ambassador to the Soviet Union, about Polish reinforcements from Russia for the Middle East.

Winston S. Churchill to Lord Cranborne
(Churchill papers, 20/67)

5 July 1942
Secret

Pray let me have some proposals about this.[1] The strength of opinion in the United States is very great, and we shall suffer in many ways there by indulging the British military authorities' and Colonial Office officials' bias in favour of the Arabs and against the Jews. Now that these people are in direct danger, we should certainly give them a chance to defend themselves. Colonel Orde Wingate should not be put on one side, but given a fair chance and proper authority.

It may be necessary to make an example of some of these anti-Semite officers and others in high places. If three or four of them were recalled and dismissed, and the reason given, it would have a very salutary effect.

Winston S. Churchill to H. G. Wells[2]
(Churchill papers, 20/54)

5 July 1942

My dear Wells,

Thank you very much for sending me a copy of your new book 'Phoenix.' I am so sorry to hear that you are unwell and unable to inscribe your books and I hope you will soon be quite recovered.

Yours sincerely,
Winston S. Churchill

---

[1] Minute of 3 July 1942 by the Prime Minister's Principal Private Secretary (John Martin), covering: (a) telegrams Nos 3539 and 3572 from Washington reporting an appeal to the Zionist leader Dr Chaim Weizmann for the formation of a Jewish force, possibly under Colonel Orde Wingate; (b) telegram from Rabbi Stephen Wise and other Zionist leaders in the United States asking that all available Jewish manpower in Palestine be immediately mobilised.

[2] Herbert George Wells, 1866–1946. A prolific writer, author of more than 70 books. One of his best-known works, *The Time Machine*, was published in 1895. In his *Men like Gods*, published in 1925, Churchill appears thinly disguised as Rupert Catskill, whose 'wild imaginings had caused the deaths of thousands of people'.

Air Chief Marshal Sir Arthur Tedder to Winston S. Churchill
(Churchill papers, 20/77)

5 July 1942
Personal and Most Secret
Most Immediate

On behalf of the RAF Middle East I thank you most sincerely for your inspiring message.

All of us are determined to do our utmost and more to help the Army to clear the enemy out of Africa.

Margot, Countess of Oxford and Asquith,[1] to Winston S. Churchill
(Churchill papers, 20/59)

5 July 1942   Savoy Hotel
London

Dearest Winston,

There is <u>nothing</u> so tiresome as advice, – nevertheless, you and I are old friends, and have had <u>many</u> happy days together. You were fond of Henry, and rock-climbed with Cys![2] – (now a Judge). I implore you to give General Wavell some sort of authority. All the soldiers I know <u>adore</u> him. In the <u>1st</u> official <u>German</u> communique, the writer said, – 'The British can never win this war, they have only one General to our hundreds – Wavell. The French can never win this war, they have only one General – de Gaulle.' Wavell is completely wasted where he is – why not use him?

Love to you both,
Yours,
Margot

---

[1] The former Margot Asquith, wife of H. H. Asquith, Prime Minister 1908–16.

[2] Cyril Asquith, 1890–1954. Barrister, judge, and Law Lord. The fourth son of H. H. Asquith, Prime Minister 1908–16 and later Earl of Oxford and Asquith. Educated at Winchester and Balliol College, Oxford; Hertford, Craven, and Ireland Scholarships, 1911; Eldon Scholar and Fellow of Magdalen College, 1913. Served as a Captain in Queen's Westminster Rifles, 1914–19. Married Anne Stephanie Pollock, 1918. Judge of High Court of Justice, King's Bench Division, 1938–46; a Lord of Justice of Appeal, 1946–51. Created Baron Asquith of Bishopstone, 1951. Member of Lord Chancellor's Law Reform Committee, 1952. Member of the Other Club.

Winston S. Churchill to President Franklin D. Roosevelt
(Churchill papers, 20/77)

6 July 1942
Personal and Most Secret

Our code-words need clarification. By 'Bolero' we British mean the vast arrangements necessary both in 1942 and 1943 for the operation against the Continent. The Joint Anglo-American Staffs committees are all working on this basis. They are not operational, but purely administrative. What you in the conversation have called 'One-third Bolero' we have hitherto been calling 'Sledgehammer'. The name 'Round-up' has been given to the 1943 operation. I do not much like this name, as it might be thought over-confident or over-gloomy, but it has come into considerable use. Please let me know whether you have any wishes about this. The 'Gymnast' you and I have in view is, I think, the variant called by your Staffs 'Semi-Gymnast'.[1] I also use the word 'Jupiter' to describe an operation in the Far North.

Winston S. Churchill to Anthony Eden
(Churchill papers, 20/67)[2]

6 July 1942
Secret

I will most certainly do everything to help Blum[3] if he desires to escape, though I agree with you that his name will not be one to conjure with

---

[1] 'Semi-Gymnast': the name chosen for the North African landings with French co-operation (which never took place).

[2] Churchill sent a copy of this minute to Major Desmond Morton, his adviser on governments-in-exile.

[3] Léon Blum, 1872–1950. Born in Paris, of Jewish parents. Chef de Cabinet to Minister of Public Works, 1914. Deputy for Paris, 1919. A leader of the 'Front Populaire', 1936. Prime Minister, June 1936 to June 1937. Vice-President of the Cabinet, 1937–8. Prime Minister and Finance Minister, March–April 1938. Interned in Germany, 1941–5. Prime Minister and Foreign Minister, December 1946 to January 1947. President of the French Socialist Party.

in post-war France. I hope, however, that Mandel,[1] and Reynaud[2] if he wishes, will also be assisted. I consider we have obligations toward these men, though particularly to Mandel, who never swerved.

2. I have asked Major Morton to read Blum's book. As it is a document of some value, there is no reason why it should not be set up in galley proof to make it easy for others to read.

3. I think it will be sufficient to repeat to Monsieur Blum the message which I sent to Monsieur Reynaud and General Georges.[3]

War Cabinet: conclusions
(Cabinet papers, 65/25)

6 July 1942   10 Downing Street
5.30 p.m.

The Prime Minister said that early consideration must be given to the arrangements for escorting future convoys to North Russia.

[...]

---

[1] Georges Mandel (born Louis Rothschild), 1885–1944. Borne near Paris, of Jewish parentage. Took the name of Georges Mandel as a journalist. Joined Clemenceau's Staff on *L'Aurore*, 1903. Chef de Cabinet to Clemenceau, 1906–9 and 1917–19 (during Clemenceau's two premierships). In charge of the trials dealing with treason and defeatism, 1917–18. Elected to the Chamber of Deputies, 1920. Minister of Posts and Telegraphs, 1934–6 (when he introduced the first French television broadcast, in November 1935). Minister of Colonies, April 1938 to May 1940. Minister of the Interior, May–June 1940 (when he arrested many Nazi sympathisers). Churchill's choice to lead a Free French movement in Britain, but refused to leave France, June 1940. Imprisoned in France, 1940–2; in Germany, 1943–4. Sent back to France, 4 July 1944. Assassinated by Vichy militia, 7 July 1944.

Edward Spears later recalled, of Georges Mandel's remarks: 'He said Daladier was fundamentally weak, but could be relied on not to make a separate peace, for such an act of cowardice would require courage of a kind, and even that debased kind of pluck was beyond him. "It is true then that the horns of the bull of Vaucluse are only those of a snail?" I asked. "No truer quip has been evolved in the Chamber," answered Mandel, who went on to say it was imperative that the English should take over the direction of the war, and, as this role was apparently beyond Chamberlain, the sooner Churchill was in charge the better' (*Prelude to Dunkirk*, London, 1954, pages 59–60).

[2] Paul Reynaud, 1878–1966. On active service, 1914–18 (twice decorated). Entered the Chamber of Deputies, 1919. Minister of Colonies, 1931–2. Minister of Justice, April–November 1938. Minister of Finance, 1930, November 1938 to March 1940. Prime Minister, 21 March to 17 June 1940 (Foreign Minister, 21 March to 18 May, 6–17 June 1940). Arrested by the Vichy Government, September 1940. Deported to Germany, 1943–5. Released, 1945. Minister of Finance, 1948. Deputy Prime Minister, 1953. President of the Finance Committee of the National Assembly, 1958.

[3] Joseph Georges, 1875–1951. Entered the French infantry, 1897. Chief of Staff to Marshal Foch, 1918. Head of the French Economic Service in the Ruhr, 1923. Chief of Staff to Marshal Petain, 1925–6. Chef de Cabinet in the Maginot Government, 1929. Commanded XIX Corps in Algeria, 1931. Wounded in Marseille at the time of the assassination of King Alexander of Yugoslavia, 1934. Created Generalissimo, 1934. Commander of the Forces and Operations in the North East, 1939–40. A member of the French Committee of National Liberation, 1943.

The Prime Minister said that he would consult with the Secretary of State for War with a view to submitting to the War Cabinet proposals defining the conditions which must be satisfied before any General Officer in the field was justified in surrendering, and emphasising the obligation on all units to continue fighting so long as possible.

Sir Alexander Cadogan: diary
('The Diaries of Sir Alexander Cadogan', page 461)

6 July 1942

[...] 5.30 Cabinet. Egypt seems better. The Russian convoy situation bad. I don't know <u>how</u> we can keep this up. Russian front not too good [...]. PM furious about Generals ordering surrender – and he's quite right. Says we ought to make it clear that any General ordering surrender will, after the war, be tried for his life and have to justify himself. The Gen. in Tobruk ordered surrender, it seems, to 'save bloodshed'. But how much blood did he let by doing so? Unfortunately, he's a S African, so <u>we</u> can't do anything about him.

Winston S. Churchill to Randolph S. Churchill
(Churchill papers, 20/65)

6 July 1942

Thrilled by your long letter. Hope you are making progress. Doctor's report not yet received. Would you like to be invalided to the Cape till you are fit again?[1]

Love.

---

[1] On 8 July 1942, Randolph replied from Cairo to his father: 'Thank you for cable. Making good progress and feel very well. Plans still uncertain, but hope to find sedentary employment here till fully recovered. Love' (*Churchill papers, 20/65*).

Winston S. Churchill to General Archibald Wavell
(Churchill papers, 20/77)

6 July 1942
Personal and Secret

Your No. 15736/C of 2nd July and your No. 15707/C of 3rd July. I am perplexed by the latter telegram. If you can do nothing until January, obviously alternative plans must be considered. I do not understand why, with trained regular troops, six months' specialised training is required before they can get in and out of landing-craft. In the 70th, 2nd and 5th British Infantry Divisions you have troops who have had over two years' intensive training in combined operations apart from getting in and out of boats.

2. We were proposing to give you the 29th Infantry Brigade of four battalions with a Commando of 400 affiliated thereto. This force is specially expert in amphibious warfare and could clear the way for easier landing by supporting troops. The whole Army does not have to scramble ashore under fire. The leading highly trained elements seize the landing places and the rest come in behind them.

3. Your No. 15707/C, paragraph 4. The conditions you prescribe render all action impossible. Why do you require 1,150 first-line air strength, involving probably double that number of machines, when as far as we can make out barely one-quarter of that number would be available to the Japanese in the theatre concerned? How many airfields do you require to operate 1,150 first line modern aircraft from, and what is your estimate of the ground personnel to sustain them?

4. Previously you have said that it is the monsoon, which is not over till November, which delays action. Surely for the calm weather period you can collect a number of native craft and improvise others capable of transporting troops under cover of the Fleet and the proportion of special landing-craft which will go on ahead. How many troops do you propose to carry in one hundred ships less than 500 feet in length and 24 feet in draught, and how many on the average in each ship, observing that once you have got possession of a harbour larger vessels can come in with three or four thousand men apiece?

5. Broadly speaking, your No. 15707/C seems to close all prospects of offensive action from India for a long time to come. However, General Alexander is expected here in a few days. He no doubt has your reason in more detail than you have given them to the Chiefs of Staff, and we will go into the whole matter with him.

Winston S. Churchill to Lord Leathers[1]
(Churchill papers, 20/67)

7 July 1942
Action this Day

Make sure that the Red Cross supplies to Russia are always distributed in at least six ships of any one convoy, and arrange with the Red Cross to facilitate this, while also taking care that the components of any one article are not separated. Report what action has been taken before the next convoy sails.

Winston S. Churchill to Admiral of the Fleet Sir Dudley Pound
(Churchill papers, 20/67)

7 July 1942

Is there any truth in the reports of slackness amongst Admiralty dockyard workers at Portsmouth and other centres?

As at any given time roughly one escort vessel is refitting, repairing, &c., for every three in service, a successful drive to speed up dockyard work would add appreciably to our effective fleet.

Winston S. Churchill to General Claude Auchinleck
(Churchill papers, 20/89)

7 July 1942
Personal and Secret

Your 20854 of 7th July. Quite understand your feelings, but message was released by your own military censors by the Cairo beam to London, which is audible to the German Listening Service before it reaches London.

2. Effect of message is that on Monday morning strong Allied columns moved in northerly direction behind Rommel's army making for two points on the coast between Alamein and Daba. It is stated they are not supported by tanks, but are strongly equipped by 2-pounder and 6-pounder anti-tank guns.

3. The censor who released this should surely be tried by court-martial and the correspondent who wrote it sent home round the Cape. I recommend you to hand this censorship business over to the Minister of

---

[1] Minister of War Transport.

State while you are busy fighting the battle. You cannot possibly blame the BBC as there is no second censorship here on your Cairo releases and no point in having one.

War Cabinet: Confidential Annex
(Cabinet papers, 65/31)

7 July 1942
5.30 p.m.

The Prime Minister summarised the outcome of the discussions which he had had with the Chiefs of Staff about Operations 'Sledgehammer', 'Round-up', 'Gymnast' and 'Jupiter'.

The conditions which would make this operation practicable in 1942 were now extremely unlikely to arise. These were that there should be no major offensive operations on the Continent in 1942 unless we intended to stay there, and unless a crack in German morale was evident. As to the operation itself, if it had been possible to force a lodgement in the heavily defended Pas-de-Calais area and, at the same time, to effect simultaneous landings at many other points on the French coast, the losses which would inevitably be incurred in the Pas-de-Calais would be compensated by our ability to make firm lodgements elsewhere. In present circumstances, however, operations on such a scale were out of the question in 1942.

The Chiefs of Staff's report dealt with the implications of mounting 'Sledgehammer'. Since the mounting process would take up to two months an immediate decision was necessary unless the operation was to be regarded as abandoned for 1942. The shipping implications, although considerable, were not intolerable, but the effect on 'Round-up' training would be very serious and would put back that operation for two or three months.

In the above circumstances, it seemed that the right policy would be not to abandon 'Sledgehammer' altogether, but only to make such preparations for it as would enable us to deceive the enemy, but not at the expense of interference with 'Round-up'.

The War Cabinet agreed with this view.

After further discussion, the War Cabinet:
(1) Gave general approval to the Note by the Chiefs of Staff dated 7th July (Appendix II).

(2) Agreed that, although the conditions which would make 'Sledge-hammer' a sound and sensible enterprise were very unlikely to occur, the operation should not be completely abandoned. Planning should proceed and a proportion of the necessary shipping, both ocean-going and coastwise, should be taken up: but, broadly speaking, preparations should be confined to those which would not seriously prejudice opera-tion 'Round-up'. In particular, training for 'Round-up' should not be interfered with.

(3) Agreed that, in view of the unlikelihood of 'Sledgehammer' being undertaken, the Americans should be encouraged to proceed with opera-tion 'Gymnast', and that we ourselves should undertake 'Jupiter', if by any means a sound and sensible plan could be devised.

(4) Invited the Prime Minister to inform President Roosevelt of the above conclusions, and to say that, in view of the unlikelihood of 'Sledgehammer' being undertaken, it was assumed that he would wish to proceed with operation 'Gymnast'. Meanwhile, we, for our part, were studying the possibility of an operation in Northern Norway, or, if this should prove impracticable, elsewhere.

(5) Invited the Prime Minister to reply to Premier Stalin's telegram of 20th June, 1942, and to say that we were greatly interested in the pos-sibility of combined operations with the Russians in the Petsamo–Benak area, and were prepared to use both naval and land forces if a good plan could be worked out. If he (Premier Stalin) was in favour of operations of this kind, perhaps he would permit discussions between the two Staffs.

(6) Invited the Chiefs of Staff to submit material for a reply to General Smuts' Telegram No. 1211 of the 7th July.

Note: With reference to Conclusion (3) above, it was decided sub-sequent to the meeting that General McNaughton[1] should be asked to undertake the preparation of a plan for 'Jupiter', to be carried out largely by Canadian troops.

---

[1] Andrew George Latta McNaughton, 1887–1966. Born in Canada. On active service, 1914–18 (wounded twice, despatches thrice). Chief of the Canadian General Staff, 1929–35. Commanded 1st Division, Canadian Overseas Force, 1939–40. Lieutenant-General, 1940. General Officer Com-manding the Canadian Corps, 1940–2. General Officer Commanding-in-Chief, 1st Canadian Army, 1942–4. General, 1944. President, Canadian Atomic Energy Control Board, 1946–9. His younger son, Squadron Leader, Royal Canadian Air Force, was killed in action over Germany in 1942. At the weekend of 11–12 July 1942, General McNaughton visited Chequers, where he and Churchill 'had a long talk in the garden' (*Hinge of Fate*, page 393).

Sir Alexander Cadogan: diary
(*'The Diaries of Sir Alexander Cadogan', page 461*)

8 July 1942

[...]

Very gloomy outlook and Cabinet yesterday seems to have been very depressing. Chiefs of Staff have no ideas and oppose everything. PM said 'We'd better put an advertisement in the papers, asking for ideas'!

War Cabinet: Confidential Annex
(*Cabinet papers, 65/31*)

8 July 1942
12.30 p.m.

The Prime Minister read to the War Cabinet the Personal telegram which he had sent to President Roosevelt informing him of the conclusions reached at the Meeting held on the previous day.

The Prime Minister then referred to the question of the appointment of a Supreme Commander for the American and British forces for the 'Round-up' Operation. On his last visit to America he had gathered that if the Supreme Command was offered to General Marshall, he would be very pleased to accept it. The Americans were proposing to employ 27 Divisions to our 21 in 'Round-up'. He thought that our interests would best be served by the appointment of an American as Supreme Commander. If General Marshall was appointed, he would, of course, receive loyal and effective aid and support from the Staffs in this country, who might be expected to exercise some influence over his views. An American Supreme Commander would also be in the best position to obtain the maximum resources and equipment from America for the expeditionary forces, and there could be no reproach, if any part of the operation was not successful, that this was due to there being a British Generalissimo. Moreover, the forces engaged in the operation would be so large that the local Commanders of the British forces would, of course, be British.

The Prime Minister also referred to a telegram received that morning from Field Marshal Dill (IZ 792) pointing to the advantages of an American Supreme Commander.

The Prime Minister read to the War Cabinet a draft telegram to the President which he had prepared, to the effect that we had been considering the question of Command, and that it would be agreeable to us if General Marshall would undertake this task.

In discussion, general agreement was expressed with the view that it would be desirable to invite the Americans to appoint General Marshall as Supreme Commander.

The War Cabinet [...] Authorized the Prime Minister to despatch a short telegram to the President to the effect that we had been considering the question of the appointment of a Supreme Commander for the 1943 operation, and that it would be agreeable to us if General Marshall would undertake this task.

Winston S. Churchill to President Franklin D. Roosevelt
(Churchill papers, 20/77)

8 July 1942
Personal and Secret
No. 107

No responsible British General, Admiral or Air Marshal is prepared to recommend 'Sledgehammer' as a practicable operation in 1942. The Chiefs of the Staff have reported: 'The conditions which would make "Sledgehammer" a sound sensible enterprise are very unlikely to occur'. They are now sending their paper to your Chiefs of Staff.

2. The taking up of the shipping is being proceeded with by us for camouflage purposes, though it involves a loss in British imports of perhaps 250,000 tons. But far more serious is the fact that, according to Mountbatten, if we interrupt the training of the troops, we should, apart from the loss of landing craft &c., delay 'Roundup' or 1943 'Bolero' for at least two or three months even if the enterprise were unsuccessful and the troops had to be withdrawn after a short stay.

3. In the event of a lodgement being effected and maintained it would have to be nourished and the bomber effort on Germany would have to be greatly curtailed. All our energies would be involved in defending the bridgehead. The possibility of mounting a large-scale operation in 1943 would be marred if not ruined. All our resources would be absorbed piecemeal on the very narrow front which alone is open. It may therefore be said that premature action in 1942, while probably ending in disaster, would decisively injure the prospect of well-organised large-scale action in 1943.

4. I am sure myself that 'Gymnast' is by far the best chance for effective relief to the Russian front in 1942. This has all along been in harmony with your ideas. In fact, it is your commanding idea. Here is the true

Second Front of 1942. I have consulted Cabinet and Defence Committee and we all agree. Here is the safest and most fruitful stroke that can
be delivered this autumn.

5. We, of course, can aid in every way, either by transfer of American
or British landing forces from the United Kingdom to 'Gymnast' and
with landing craft, shipping, &c. You can, if you choose, put the punch
in partly from here and the rest direct across the Atlantic.

6. It must be clearly understood that we cannot count upon an invitation or a guarantee from Vichy. But any resistance would not be comparable to that which would be offered by the German Army in the Pas de
Calais. Indeed, it might be only token resistance. The stronger you are
the less resistance there would be and the more to overcome it. This is
a political more than a military issue. It seems to me that we ought not
to throw away the sole great strategic stroke open to us in the Western
theatre during this cardinal year.

7. Besides the above, we are studying very hard the possibility of an
operation in Northern Norway, or, if this should prove impracticable,
elsewhere in Norway. The difficulties are great owing to the danger of
shore-based aircraft attack upon our ships. We are having frightful difficulties about the Russian convoys.[1] All the more is it necessary to try to
clear the way and maintain the contact with Russia.

Winston S. Churchill to President Franklin D. Roosevelt
(Churchill papers, 20/77)

8 July 1942
Personal and Secret
No. 108

My immediately preceding telegram No. 107. We have been deeply
considering the question of Command of maximum 'Bolero'. It would
be agreeable to us if General Marshall would undertake this supreme
task in 1943. We shall sustain him to the last inch.

2. The War Cabinet authorise me to convey the above to you.

---

[1] Arctic convoy PQ 17 consisted of 34 merchant ships, American, British, Soviet, Dutch, and
Panamanian-registered. On 27 June 1942 the ships sailed eastbound from Hvalfjord, Iceland, to
Arkhangelsk, northern Russia. The convoy was located by German forces on July 1, after which it
was shadowed continuously and subjected to a series of heavy enemy daylight attacks, which lasted
a week and resulted in the loss of 21 vessels. The disastrous outcome of the convoy demonstrated
the difficulty of passing adequate supplies through the Arctic, especially during the summer period
of perpetual daylight.

Winston S. Churchill to President Franklin D. Roosevelt
(Churchill papers, 20/77)

8 July 1942
Personal and Secret
No. 109

My immediately preceding Telegram No. 108.

I hope, Mr President, you will make sure that the appointment of a United States Commander over 'Bolero' 1943 does not prejudice operations of immediate consequence such as 'Gymnast'.

Winston S. Churchill to General Sir Alan Brooke
and the Chiefs of Staff Committee
(Churchill papers, 20/67)

8 July 1942

General McNaughton[1] should be entrusted with the preliminary study and planning of 'Jupiter', being given all the necessary assistance by the Chiefs of Staff Organization. Climate proclaims that the Canadian Army should undertake this task, if it is thought feasible. The decision whether or not to adopt the plan will be reserved.

Winston S. Churchill to Sir Andrew Duncan[2]
(Churchill papers, 20/67)

8 July 1942

The King told me yesterday that there was a shortage of silk[3] for VCs and other decorations. I could not believe that this minute requirement could not be met, and I consider it should have super priority. Please let me know.

---

[1] General Officer Commanding-in-Chief, 1st Canadian Army.
[2] Minister of Supply
[3] Silk was used principally for parachutes.

General Archibald Wavell to Winston S. Churchill
(Churchill papers, 20/77)

8 July 1942
Personal and Secret
Immediate

I am having suggestions in your telegram fully examined by Chiefs of Staff and when Alexander reaches you I hope we shall be able to get clear picture of possibilities and difficulties of this important operation which must in the words of the Marriage Service 'be entered into discreetly advisedly and soberly'.

2. Meanwhile I would remind you that my record in this War has shown no reluctance to take offensive whenever possible against considerable odds and difficulties. You can also I think trust me not to misrepresent situation or exaggerate difficulties as you seem to suspect.

3. During two years practically continuous fighting since June 1940 I have usually been in state complete inferiority to my opponents in the air. You can hardly blame me for seeking to have proper air support in extremely difficult combined operation in Lower Burma.

4. Actually only about 600 aircraft out of total of 1,100 will be available for offensive operations into Burma and this is only reasonable against enemy air force which may well number up to 600 and can be rapidly reinforced. Remainder are for defence Ceylon without which Navy will not operate, protection of shipping, coastal reconnaissance, transport, photography, etc. Alexander has details.

Winston S. Churchill to General Hastings Ismay
(Churchill papers, 20/67)

9 July 1942
Action this Day

Let me have a short report on the working of the Trans-Persian railway. How many trains are running each day? How many tons are being delivered each week on the Caspian shore? Who is in charge of the railway organization? Is there complete harmony between the port authorities under the Ministry of War Transport and the railway officials under the War Office?

2. What is the condition of the road and the road traffic?

3. Naturally I am wondering whether we can divert anything from the Arctic route.

Winston S. Churchill to Sir James Grigg and General Sir Alan Brooke
(Churchill papers, 20/67)

9 July 1942

Surely when the 300 Shermans and the 100 self-propelled guns, from which so much is hoped, reach Suez, they should be made to play a part in a decisive stroke. Instead of this, 193 Shermans only are to be used and 107 left lying in reserve. No provision has been made for the self-propelled artillery. The United States authorities will greatly resent the spectacle of their tanks, which it has cost them much to give, being frittered into action in this way.

It is very difficult to help the Army of the Middle East.

Winston S. Churchill to President Franklin D. Roosevelt
(Churchill papers, 20/77)

9 July 1942
Personal and Secret

We welcome the proposal in the first paragraph of your telegram that the French warships at Alexandria should proceed by way of the Canal to Martinique. We suggest the following additions to the proposed offer.

First, that the United States and British Governments will agree to the periodical relief and repatriation of the French crews from these ships after they have reached Martinique, on the same basis as proposed had the ships remained at Alexandria. Secondly, that the offer should be made irrespective of whether the fall of Alexandria becomes imminent, since they would in any case be in danger of enemy air attack there.

With regard to the last paragraph of your telegram we do not admit that these French warships are in any way within the scope of the Armistice Agreement.

Winston S. Churchill to President Franklin D. Roosevelt
(Churchill papers, 20/77)

9 July 1942
Personal and Secret

Thank you so much about the transfer of the Boston Bombers destined for Russia. We shall try to use them well.

Winston S. Churchill to Josef Stalin
(Churchill papers, 20/77)

9 July 1942

I have just heard from President Roosevelt that you have consented to the transfer to our forces in Egypt of the 40 Boston Bombers which had reached Basra on their way to you. This was a hard request to make to you at this time, and I am deeply obliged to you for your prompt and generous response. They are going straight into the battle, where our aircraft have been taking a heavy toll of the enemy.

President Franklin D. Roosevelt to Winston S. Churchill
(Churchill papers, 20/77)

9 July 1942   Washington DC

My dear Mr Prime Minister,

I have received your letter of June 14, 1942 in which you express the gratitude of the British people for the vast stream of gifts which from the first days of the war has been flowing from America to Great Britain for the relief of suffering. You ask that this expression be conveyed to the American public.

You say also that this flow of material must be diminished due to additional demands on shipping and that it will be necessary to assign to goods of a more warlike character the shipping space which has hitherto been available for the relief of the British people. You state further that the American Gifts Committee in Great Britain, which hitherto has endeavored to ensure that gifts from America shall meet some real need, will now try to control the actual volume of gifts.

I am gratified by your statement that the relief sent from this country has given comfort to the British people during their days of great trial, and I shall give the American people your expression of appreciation for the gifts they have provided. I am convinced that their action is indicative of the profound admiration felt in this country for the heroic stand of the British people against a barbarous foe.

You may be assured that we shall cooperate in every feasible way with the American Gifts Committee in order to meet the situation brought about by the increased demand for shipping.

Franklin D. Roosevelt

Sir Alexander Cadogan: diary
(*'The Diaries of Sir Alexander Cadogan'*, pages 461–2)

9 July 1942

[...]

PM arrived in high dudgeon, and enjoyed himself enormously. He devoted himself to attacking Cabinet decision, taken last Monday week in his absence to tell Americans that, as part of general plan for relief, we should be prepared to keep on 'a system of rationing after the war'. His line was: 'Are we to tell the British soldier, returning from the war, that he is to tighten his belt and starve, in order that Roumanians may batten on the fat of the land. I've never heard of such a thing.' In vain, A, Cripps, Attlee, Bevin and Co., told him that nor had they – that that was an outrageous proposition, but didn't happen to be the one that they had subscribed to. That didn't matter: Winston began again 'Are we, who alone saved the world during a whole year, to go short while Americans eat what they will, free of all restriction?' &c. &c. No arguing with that. Kingsley[1] was on velvet. He and PM the only ones against the rest of the Cabinet and Kingsley felt quite safe with such support. He kept interjecting comment – and got roundly smacked on the head. He insinuated that the B of T[2] had quickly sent off their instructions after the snap division in the Cabinet. Dalton, quick as lightning, said 'the B of T work quite quickly when not obstructed by the Treasury.' Great fun. And Winston enjoyed it more than anyone (except me).

[1] Sir Kingsley Wood, Chancellor of the Exchequer.
[2] B of T: Board of Trade.

Winston S. Churchill to Sir James Grigg and Lord Leathers
(Churchill papers, 20/67)

10 July 1942

I see that a beginning has been made in boxing vehicles shipped abroad from this country and that during May 1,126 (not 1,453 as originally stated) out of 7,517 were boxed. I trust the proportion will show a steady rise and that every effort is being made to improve the methods of packing and to devise means to crate the vehicles still outstanding.

2. Well over 1,000 vehicles, which could have been packed in this way, were not boxed on the ground that they were required for operations on arrival. Having regard to the immense importance of freeing shipping for imports this argument can only be accepted in really urgent cases. Over 850 small vehicles were not boxed because we are told that it would save no appreciable amount of shipping space. But every little helps.

3. When we remember that boxing 15 per cent of the vehicles has in one month saved about 80,000 tons of imports – as much as the quantity saved monthly by raising the milling ratio, clothes and soap rationing, and abolishing the basic petrol, all put together – the importance of carrying this policy to the limit of refinement both here and in America is evident.

4. I trust your Departments will co-operate in pursuing the matter vigorously and that there will be an improvement in the June return.

Richard Casey to Winston S. Churchill
(Churchill papers, 20/65)

10 July 1942
Most Immediate

Medical authorities have today invalided Randolph home after his recent accident. He wishes to return by air instead of long sea [?grp. omtd. ?voyage] [?route]. There is no difficulty about air passage and Doctors see no objection provided I accept formal responsibility.

I propose to agree unless I hear from you to the contrary urgently.

As at present arranged Randolph leaves on Monday.[1]

[1] 13 July 1942.

Winston S. Churchill to Richard Casey
(Churchill papers, 20/65)

10 July 1942   10 Downing Street
Private

RANDOLPH CHURCHILL

Thank you for your kind action. He has Parliamentary duties here, while medically unfit for active service.

Winston S. Churchill to Air Chief Marshal Sir Charles Portal
(Churchill papers, 20/67)

11 July 1942

It is vital that the use of Benghazi and Tobruk as supply ports should be denied to the enemy. They must be subjected to heavy and continuous bombing on the largest scale. Please let me know the resources Tedder will have available, and the use he intends to make of them. He should be informed of the great importance we attach to the destruction of these ports.

Winston S. Churchill to John Curtin and Peter Fraser
(Churchill papers, 20/77)

11 July 1942
Personal and Most Secret

(To Mr Curtin only.) I am very glad that the 9th Australian Division is now in action in the Western Desert, and I am most thankful to you for making it available for this vital keypoint of the war.

(To Mr Fraser only.) The Division which you consented to leave in the Middle East is doing splendid work in the Western Desert and has already brought fresh fame to New Zealand's arms at this vital keypoint of the war.

2. The unforeseeable tide of disaster which drove us from Gazala to Alamein with the loss of Tobruk and 50,000 men has now for the first time been stemmed. General Auchinleck has received strong reinforcements raising his Army to 100,000 men with another 20,000 well forward in the Delta behind them. He is thus about double Rommel in men. He has a fair equality in artillery, but is still somewhat weaker in armour to the enemy. This imposes prudence upon him for two reasons. First, a

retirement is much worse for him than for Rommel, who has nothing but deserts behind him, and, secondly, far more strength is coming to General Auchinleck than to the enemy.

3. For instance, the 8th Armoured Division with 350 Valentine tanks has landed and will soon be in action. About 400 tanks of all natures having been despatched before the battle began, will reach General Auchinleck in July and early August as replacements. The 44th British Infantry Division fully equipped, 15,000 strong with 72 guns, should have arrived by the end of July and the 51st British Infantry Division a month later.

4. It was very fortunate that four months ago I obtained from President Roosevelt the shipping to carry an additional 40,000 men to the East without deciding on their destination till they rounded the Cape. Without these the reinforcements now proved so needful by the hazards of war could not have been at hand.

5. When in Washington I obtained from the President 300 of the latest and finest tanks (Shermans) in the American Army. They were taken from the very hands of the American troops who eagerly awaited them, and were sent by special convoy direct to Suez. With them went one hundred 105 mm self-propelled guns which definitely outmatch the 88 mm, the whole being accompanied by a large number of American key men. These should arrive early September. Apart from the 8th Armoured Division and in addition to the two armoured and one army tank brigades now in action forward, we have in the Delta the personnel of four armoured brigades awaiting re-equipment. About half these men are desert trained in tanks. We should therefore be able to bring into action incomparably the most powerful and best-trained armoured division yet seen in the Middle East or, indeed, anywhere. But I hope the issue will be decided in our favour earlier. This is especially desirable because of dangers that may, though I do not say they will, develop on the northern approaches to Egypt.

6. Scarcely less important are the air reinforcements given me by the President on the morrow of Tobruk. As you know we have not been hitherto able for technical as well as military reasons to provide heavy bomber squadrons for the Middle East, though they have often asked for them. But now the President has assigned to the defence of Egypt the Halpro Group[1] of 20 Liberators which was on its way to India, after

---

[1] Halpro Group (**Hal**verson **Pro**ject = Halpro): the first American unit of the United States Army Air Forces to arrive in the Middle East in 1942, under the command of Colonel Harry A. Halverson. Halpro's primary mission became the interdiction of supplies to Rommel's army in North Africa by bombing strikes on Axis cargo ships at sea or in the ports of Tobruk and Benghazi.

bombing Roumanian oil-fields, 10 other Liberators which had already reached India, and a Group of 35 Liberators from the United States. These with our own Liberators make up about 85 of these heavy bombers, which should all be available this month. At the same time our two Halifax squadrons will come into action, making up to 117 heavy bombers in all. It is this force I rely upon to beat up the ports of Tobruk and Benghazi, hampering Rommel's reinforcements besides, of course, playing the part of a battle-fleet in preventing a sea-borne invasion of Egypt. We have great enterprises in preparation for the revictualling of Malta, but as these deal with future operations you will not, I am sure, wish me to mention details.

In addition to the above, the President sent about 70 of his latest Kittyhawks across in the Carrier *Ranger* which should soon be reaching West Africa.

7. Besides this, every preparation has been made to defend the Delta should the battles in the desert go against us. Here we have very large numbers of men all of whom have been ordered to take part in the defence of Egypt exactly as if it was England that was invaded. Cultivation and irrigation of the Delta make it literally the worst ground in the world for armoured vehicles, and armour as a factor would lose a great deal of its predominance. All ideas of evacuation have been repressed, the intention being to fight for every yard of ground to the end. As I have said, however, I do not think this situation will arise.

8. We are having a great struggle to carry supplies to Russia. One-fifth of the June convoy was sunk, and I fear less than one-half of the July convoy got through. The difficulties and dangers of this route are enormous, especially during the season of perpetual daylight. This is serious as it is almost the only thing we can do for our valiant Ally who is taking so heavy a toll of Hitler's armies and will, I am confident, endure to the end. To show you what a good comrade Premier Stalin is proving himself: they have offered us three divisions of partly-equipped Poles for the Levant–Caspian theatre, and have transferred to Egypt 40 Boston fighter bombers which were on the way to them through Basra. In this last matter the President was my intermediary.

9. The House of Commons has proved a rock in these difficult days as it did in the struggle against Napoleon, and I have also been greatly encouraged by the goodwill of your Government and people. I have never felt more sure that complete ultimate victory will be ours. But the struggle will be long and we must not relax for an instant.

10. (For Mr Fraser only.) We are looking forward to welcoming Mr Nash.[1]

Winston S. Churchill to Averell Harriman
(Churchill papers, 20/54)

11 July 1942

My dear Averell,

Thank you so much for your letter of July 9 informing me of the output of merchant ships in the United States for June 1942. You have undertaken an enormous task, but I am sure that it will not prove beyond your capacity.

Yours very Sincerely,
Winston S. Churchill

Winston S. Churchill to Field Marshal Sir John Dill[2]
(Churchill papers, 20/77)

12 July 1942
Personal

I have had the full text of the Staff paper sent to you by air. You should draw particular attention to Mountbatten's Note showing the mortal injury that would be done to 'Round-up' by 'Sledgehammer'. Apart altogether from this, no one is able to solve the problems of 'Sledgehammer' itself.

2. 'Gymnast' affords the sole means by which the United States forces can strike at Hitler in 1942. If 'Gymnast' were successful our resulting threat to Italy would draw important German air forces off Russia. 'Gymnast' does not interrupt the vast preparations and training for 'Round-up' now proceeding on this side. It only means that six United States divisions will be withdrawn intact from 'Round-up'. These might

---

[1] Walter Nash, 1882–1968. Member of New Zealand Parliament since 1929; Prime Minister, New Zealand, 1950–7 and 1960–3. Educated in St John's Church School. Member, National Executive, Labour Party, 1919–60; Minister of Social Security, 1938; Minister of Marketing, 1936–41; Minister of Finance and Customs, 1935–9; Minister of New Zealand in the United States, 1942–4; Member of New Zealand War Cabinet, 1939–45; Deputy Prime Minister of New Zealand, 1940–9. Member of Pacific War Council, Washington, 1942–4.

[2] Head of the British Joint Staff Mission in Washington.

surely be replaced by new U.S. divisions, which would be ready before the transportation schedule is accomplished.

3. However, if the President decides against 'Gymnast' the matter is settled. It can only be done by troops under the American flag. The opportunity will have been definitely rejected. Both countries will remain motionless in 1942, and will be concentrated on 'Round-up' in 1943.

4. There could be no excuse in these circumstances for the switch of United States effort which you mention in your last paragraph (please number your paragraphs in future), and I cannot think that such an attitude would be adopted.

Winston S. Churchill to General Hastings Ismay,
for the Chiefs of Staff Committee
(Churchill papers, 20/67)

12 July 1942
Most Secret

It is for the War Cabinet and Minister of Defence to prescribe the conditions under which the operation 'Anakim'[1] should be undertaken. This alone can afford to the Staffs the data on which to work. For instance, the calculations made by General Wavell's Staff in India cannot have any validity apart from the Japanese air, sea and ground strength in Malaya and Burma. They have tried to proceed on the assumption that all the available airfields will be occupied to capacity with Japanese aircraft, but this depends on whether these aircraft are available and what other business the Japanese have on hand.

2. If we take November, when the monsoon has ceased, as the date when all should be ready, we shall know by then whether the conditions are favourable for the launching of 'Anakim'. These main conditions are that:

(a) General Auchinleck beats Rommel.
(b) The Russian southern front holds, or Turkey stands true to her engagements, and Persia is not invaded.
(c) Japan is drawn into war with Russia in Siberia.

[1] 'Anakim': British plan for a seaborne invasion of lower Burma in spring 1943, with the aim of retaking Rangoon and thereby enabling an advance up the Irrawaddy River. This was intended as the first element in a threefold plan for the recapture of the whole of Burma.

(d) That (c) and the American–Australasian attacks northwards and around the islands captured by Japan cause continuous wastage of the Japanese Air Force.

(e) The naval situation in the Pacific and Indian Oceans continues to move in our favour.

3. Unless for these or other reasons the Japanese air force available for the regions affected by 'Anakim' is cut down to below its present level and their military forces similarly cannot be greatly reinforced, we need not commit ourselves to the enterprise. Nothing will have been risked or lost, and all the preparations will be helpful in the future.

4. In principle, the operation should comprise three parts. First, the engagement of the enemy front in Assam through our increasing pressure and also, if possible, by guerilla diversions in the Chin Hills. Secondly, the seizure of Akyab at a moment convenient to the growth of our air power in the Bay of Bengal and the rest of the plan. Thirdly, the attack upon Rangoon and Moulmein with the ultimate object of an advance towards Bangkok by an overseas expedition from India. For all these purposes, five divisions with two in reserve, or their equivalents expressed in more suitable formations, including the 29th Brigade from Diego Suarez, should be sufficient. If, however, the conditions set out in paragraph 2 are favourable, a further two divisions can probably be found from the Middle East. The air force should be supplied to the ratio of at least 2:1 to the believed air strength of the enemy, apart, that is to say, from the air forces required for reconnaissance and protection of the Eastern Fleet.

5. It is to be noted that if our preparations should draw much larger Japanese air and ground forces to the 'Anakim' theatre, this in itself, while preventing the operation, would be a sensible aid to Siberian Russia and to the American–Australasian offensive.

Winston S. Churchill to General Claude Auchinleck
(Churchill papers, 20/77)

12 July 1942
Personal

We are all only too well aware that the Japanese threat to India and our defeats in the Western Desert have stripped the northern front bare. You also no doubt realise that it is physically impossible to send six, or even four, additional divisions from home or from the United States to the northern theatre before the end of October. The only way in which a sufficient army can be gathered in the northern theatre is by your defeating or destroying General Rommel and driving him at least to a safe distance. If this were accomplished before the middle of September, the Australian and New Zealand divisions could return to their stations in Palestine and Syria and the 51st Division could be sent to the northern theatre direct. We will send the 56th Division in the August convoy and are preparing yet another division for the East. One British division might perhaps have to be withdrawn from India if the Russian southern flank showed signs of breaking.

2. It must be recognized, however, that, if you do not succeed in defeating and destroying Rommel, then there is no possibility whatever of making a sufficient transference to the north, and we shall continue to be entirely dependent on the Russian front holding. There is no need to assume that the Russian front will break, or that, if it does, any substantial forces could operate in Persia as early as October. Indeed, the General Staff's picture was that the advent of winter might prevent any serious threat before the spring of 1943, and even then it would be in terms of a maximum of seven divisions. The Germans would be running serious risks in advancing south-east while the main mass of the Russian armies is undefeated on their front and on the flank of their advancing spearhead.

3. If you beat Rommel decisively, as I am confident you will, and if the Germans do not beat the Russians sufficiently to break into Persia or Syria in 1942, 'Acrobat'[1] will again come under consideration.

Winston S. Churchill to General Thomas Corbett[2]
(Churchill papers, 20/77)

12 July 1942
Personal

General Auchinleck should not be troubled with these following matters, although they are of high importance, till there is a definite lull in the battle. Meanwhile you should reply fully.

---

[1] 'Acrobat': the planned advance from Cyrenaica into Tripolitania.

[2] Thomas William Corbett, 1888–1981. Indian Army officer, commissioned in 1908. Brigadier responsible for the Cavalry, Army Headquarters India, 1940. Inspector of Cavalry, Army Headquarters India, 1940–1. General Officer Commanding 31st Indian Armoured Division, 1941. Commander, IV Corps, Middle East, January–March 1942; Chief of Staff in the Middle East, 1942. General Officer Commanding 7th Indian Infantry Division in Burma until retiring in 1943.

2. I wish to know what use it is proposed to make of the 8th Armoured Division with 350 tanks, mostly Valentines,[1] which type has done so well against the Germans on the Russian front. Here is a regular trained British armoured division of 15,000 men, comprising two armoured brigades complete in every detail. When is it going to the front? I note you have had to draw 32 tanks away for the exigencies of battle. Besides 8th Armoured Division you have in Egypt six armoured brigades and one army tank brigade, of which three are forward and the remainder re-equipping. You should receive during July and early August about 400 additional tanks.

3. I am perplexed about what you propose to do with the American tanks which should arrive at the beginning of September. The President gave me these 300 latest Sherman tanks, which are magnificent weapons, superior to the Grant and probably to anything on the battlefield. They are the first 300 that have come to the American army, and it was a great sacrifice on their part to take them from their troops who were eagerly awaiting them. I asked that special arrangements should be made in Egypt to have the personnel complete and ready to receive the tanks as they arrive. All we have been told is that the 8th Armoured Brigade of the 10th Armoured Division will be equipped with them. What happens to the rest? Remember, I shall have to account for all this to the President. We have been assailed at home with abuse of the material with which the 8th Army has been supplied. Here, then, is superior material in superior quantities to the enemy. I trust it will be put to the highest and, indeed, a decisive use.

4. All this applies even more to the 100 105 mm self-propelled guns, which the American army consider the very latest and most powerful anti-tank weapon. How do you propose to man and use these?

5. I wish also to know what use it is proposed to make of the 44th British Division, which should be landed by the end of this month.

Winston S. Churchill to General Claude Auchinleck
(Churchill papers, 20/77)

12 July 1942
Personal

I am deeply concerned at your paragraph 4 about 'bad condition' of Valentines. Without burdening yourself, have detailed immediate report

[1] Valentine: infantry tank produced in the United Kingdom.

telegraphed, in order that, if enquiry shows that despatching authorities are to blame, severe measures may be taken.

Winston S. Churchill to Slobodan Jovanovitch[1]
(Churchill papers, 20/54)

12 July 1942

My dear Excellency,

You enquired in your letter No. 889 of June 12 whether facilities could be given for the despatch of 3,000 tons of foodstuffs through the blockade for relief of the civil population in your country.

This request has received the fullest consideration from His Majesty's Government, but I am sorry to say that deeply though we sympathise with the suffering which German occupation has brought to your country, we do not feel able to authorise a departure from the present policy regarding the blockade. This policy, as you know, does not exclude the despatch to occupied territories of foodstuffs which are obtainable in neutral European countries inside the blockade, provided that these are not of a kind which these countries are at the same time importing through our controls, and that they can be conveyed to their destination without infringement on our Naval blockade. But we are convinced that the principle of the blockade itself must be maintained. We have, indeed forsaken this principle in one single and wholly exceptional case but we cannot abandon it generally so as to relieve the enemy of his responsibility to provide for the countries which he has overrun. Still less, I fear, is it possible to seek to repair the consequences of deliberate robbery and oppression, while the power of the robber and oppressor remains unbroken. For so long as the enemy is master in Europe, he holds the people at his mercy whatever we may do, and we cannot hope to change his policy or frustrate its effects. I therefore firmly believe that the best and only means to bring relief to the sufferings of Europe is to maintain our pressure on the enemy unrelaxed in order that your country and the rest may be free from tyranny as quickly as possible.

Yours sincerely,
Winston S. Churchill

[1] Slobodan Jovanovitch, 1869–1958. Serbian jurist, historian, sociologist, journalist, and pro-Western politician. Graduated in law in Geneva, 1890; Professor of the University of Belgrade's Law School until 1941. Prime Minister of Yugoslav Government-in-Exile (11 January 1942 to 26 June 1943). In exile in London from 1941 until his death.

Winston S. Churchill to Sir Kingsley Wood
(Churchill papers, 20/67)

13 July 1942

Pray let me have the following information. What is the difference in yearly pay of a British soldier anywhere and an American soldier quartered in this country? You should take allowances into consideration and give me a simple block figure.

What would be the cost to the Exchequer of advancing the British pay (taking allowances, etc., into consideration) half-way up to the American level, on condition that the Americans reduced theirs to meet us and paid the surplus to their troops as a nest-egg in the United States?

I am deeply concerned about the troubles that will arise here and the tremendous demand that may be made upon you to equalise upwards. I therefore wish to explore the possibilities of equalising downwards. There is no need for you to argue the matter at this stage, because anyone can see the disadvantages. But let me know the figures. They may indeed be staggering.

Winston S. Churchill to Sir James Grigg
(Churchill papers, 20/67)

13 July 1942
Secret

We were told that one brigade of the 8th Armoured Division was tactically loaded in order that it might be brought into action immediately on disembarkation. We now hear from General Auchinleck that there will be a delay owing to the 'bad condition' of the tanks. I have asked him to let me have an immediate detailed report.

Meanwhile, a searching inquiry must be started at once. The responsibility for any negligence that there may have been at this end, from the time the orders were given for the despatch of the 8th Armoured Division up to the time it was shipped, must be resolved and severe measures taken against the delinquents.

Winston S. Churchill to A. V. Alexander and
Admiral of the Fleet Sir Dudley Pound
(Churchill papers, 20/67)

13 July 1942

Paragraph 2[1] might well be read in the sense that Admiral Tovey is not prepared to obey the orders he might receive from the Admiralty. It seems a pity to express matters this way in a telegram which is sent out of the country and will be seen by foreign staffs.

Winston S. Churchill to A. V. Alexander and
Admiral of the Fleet Sir Dudley Pound
(Churchill papers, 20/67)

13 July 1942

I am very much shocked to learn that *Valiant* will not be ready for service until mid-August. This is a month later than you have hitherto promised. I much regret I was not told when this grievous failure occurred. What is the cause of this new delay to *Valiant*?

2. I feel anxiety about the negative attitude we are adopting towards Admiral King and the American operations in the Pacific. I promised we would assist by making diversions in any way possible, but, of course, I did not commit us to any particular operation. We must now show a helpful attitude. I understand you have sent a telegram to Admiral Somerville asking him what he can do. I have not seen this telegram. He has two first-class carriers and the *Warspite*. He has been doing nothing for several months, and we cannot really keep this fleet idle indefinitely.

Winston S. Churchill to President Franklin D. Roosevelt
(Churchill papers, 20/77)

13 July 1942
Personal and Secret
No. 112

I directed that telegrams Nos. 108 and 109 should be sent through the Foreign Office, as I was not sure whether you would wish the American Embassy in London to be informed of subject matter. By a regrettable

---

[1] Of an Admiralty telegram to the British Naval Mission in Washington, sent on 11 July 1942.

mistake they were not delivered by British Embassy, Washington. They will be delivered by hand to you this morning. Naturally I was puzzled at not receiving an answer, so rang up Harry. All's well that ends well.

War Cabinet: conclusions
(Cabinet papers, 65/27)

13 July 1942   10 Downing Street
5.30 p.m.

[...]

SHIPPING LOSSES
INDIA

[...]

7. The War Cabinet were informed that recent enemy broadcasts about our shipping losses had included the names of certain ships which were still afloat. This showed that enemy's information was inaccurate. Such announcements might nevertheless be deeply disturbing to the families affected.

The Prime Minister thought that the right way of dealing with this matter would be for a public statement to be made giving an assurance that the next of kin were invariably and promptly informed when a ship had gone down. Relations of seamen should therefore ignore enemy propaganda statements on shipping losses. This suggestion was approved.

8. 00 [...] The Secretary of State for India said that, while the final Resolution of the Congress Working Committee referred to in telegram 5419 had not yet been textually agreed upon, the Resolution summarised in the former telegram was too serious to ignore. The Congress Working Committee, claiming the position of an authority parallel to that of the Government, deliberately instructed people to resist the Government's action in regard to measures such as the removal of boats or vehicles. This was an intolerable challenge, and was made worse when read together with paragraph 4 of the Resolution which said that 'All restrictions on organisation for self-protection should be disregarded'.

Continuing, the Secretary of State said that he thought it right to bring this Resolution to the immediate notice of the War Cabinet, who should authorise the Viceroy, if the terms of the Resolution were confirmed, to take such action as he thought necessary, including possibly the immediate arrest of Gandhi.

[...]

The Prime Minister said that we were responsible for the defence of India. It was essential that we should have the same facilities for the defence of India as we had for the defence of this country. He thought that it would be reasonable that the Secretary of State for India should give the Viceroy an immediate assurance that, if in the opinion of the Government of India the situation should make it necessary to take strong measures in order to ensure the same co-operation in the defence of India as we had in this country, they would receive the fullest support from His Majesty's Government.

The War Cabinet –

Approved this suggestion, and authorised the Secretary of State for India to send a telegram to the Viceroy on the lines proposed by the Prime Minister.

General Claude Auchinleck to Winston S. Churchill
(Churchill papers, 20/89)

14 July 1942

Of Valentines received with 8th Armoured Division first 67 inspected reveal that approximately 500 items required workshop attention. Time spent on each tank varied from 140 to 200 man-hours.

2. General condition of these tanks was better than those received earlier this year, but the performance of the engines was below standard. Some higher gears could not be engaged. In a number of cases the cylinder head gaskets were blowing. All engines required tuning and adjustments to steering gear had to be carried out. In most cases clutch withdrawal levers required adjustment. All 2-pounder guns required buffer piston clearances checked. This is a Middle East modification which must be done in United Kingdom. They were not marked, so checking had to be done.

3. Approximately 160 items of tank fittings were deficient, of which 120 were important, such as towing shackle, armament components, periscope components, power traverse control boxes. Some of these items may have been pilfered in transit.

4. There was no evidence of bad stowage or of serious damage in transit.

5. The general condition of the majority of the tanks is that to be expected after a long voyage which involves movement by road, rail and

sea under varying climatic conditions. Tanks cannot be battleworthy after such a voyage without attention.

Winston S. Churchill to President Franklin D. Roosevelt
(Churchill papers, 20/77)

14 July 1942
Absolutely Personal and Secret

Only four ships have reached Archangel with four or five more precariously in the ice off Nova Zembla out of the thirty-three included in Convoy PQ17. If a half had got through we should have persevered, but with only about a quarter arriving the operation is not good enough. For instance, out of nearly six hundred tanks in PQ17 little over one hundred have arrived and nearly five hundred are lost. This cannot help anybody except the enemy. The Admiralty cannot see what better protection can be devised, nor can they hazard battleships east of Bear Island. Stark[1] agrees with Admiralty view and that all possible was done by us last time. *Washington* has already been withdrawn for her task in the Pacific.

2. We therefore advise against running PQ18, which must start 18th at latest. If it were composed only of our merchant ships we should certainly not send them, but no fewer than twenty-two are your own American ships. We should therefore like to know how you feel about it.

3. Future prospects of supplying Russia by this northern route are bad. Murmansk has been largely burnt out and there are several signs of an impending German attack upon it. By the time that perpetual daylight gives place to the dark period Archangel will be frozen. Some additional supplies may be passed over the Basra route. This is being pressed, but it will not amount to much. Thus Russia is confronted at this anxious moment with a virtual cutting off of the northern sea communications. We wait your answer before explaining things to Stalin. The message which it is proposed to send to him, if you agree that the convoy is not to go, is being sent to you later today. Meanwhile the convoy is continuing to load and assemble.

4. Allied shipping losses in the seven days ending 13th July, including the Russian convoy, were reported at not far short of four hundred thousand tons for this one week, a rate unexampled in either this war or the last and, if maintained, evidently beyond all existing replacement plans.

---

[1] Admiral Harold Stark, Commander, United States Naval Forces in Europe.

Winston S. Churchill to A. V. Alexander and Sir Archibald Sinclair
(Churchill papers, 20/67)

14 July 1942

I understand that Coastal Command squadrons, with an initial establishment of 20 machines, are flying only about thirty hours a day, and that a substantial increase in the number of sorties per squadron could be obtained if the maintenance organisation were expanded and improved. Until everything possible has been done in this direction there can be no case for transferring additional squadrons from Bomber to Coastal Command.

It is true that the standard of serviceability in Coastal Command will fall off if the aircraft make more frequent sorties. But could not this be permitted without anxiety if a clear understanding were reached that Coastal Command could call on Bomber Command for help in case of sudden emergency?

Winston S. Churchill to President Franklin D. Roosevelt
(Churchill papers, 20/77)

14 July 1942
Personal and Secret

I am most anxious for you to know where I stand myself at the present time. I have found no one who regards 'Sledgehammer' as possible. I should like to see you do 'Gymnast' as soon as possible, and that we in concert with the Russians should try for 'Jupiter'. Meanwhile all preparations for 'Roundup' in 1943 should proceed at full blast, thus holding the maximum enemy forces opposite England. All this seems to me as clear as noonday.

Winston S. Churchill to Josef Stalin
(Churchill papers, 20/77)

14 July 1942
Most Personal and Secret

DRAFT

We commenced running small convoys to North Russia in August 1941 and, until December, the Germans did not take any steps to interfere with them. From February 1942, the size of the convoys was increased and the Germans then moved a considerable force of U-boats and a large number of aircraft to North Norway and made determined attacks on the convoys. By giving the convoys the strongest possible escort of destroyers and anti-submarine craft the convoys got through with varying but not prohibitive losses. It is evident that the Germans were dissatisfied with the results which were being achieved by means of aircraft and U-boats alone, because they commenced to use their surface forces against the convoys. Luckily for us, however, to start with they made use of their heavy surface forces to the westward of Bear Island and their submarines to the eastward. The Home Fleet was thus in a position to prevent an attack by enemy surface forces. Before the May convoy was sent off the Admiralty warned us that the losses would be very severe if, as was expected, the Germans employed their surface forces to the eastward of Bear Island. We decided, however, to sail the convoy. An attack by surface ships did not materialise, and the convoy got through with a loss of one-sixth, chiefly from air attack. In the case of PQ17, however, the Germans at last used their forces in the manner we had always feared. They concentrated their submarines to the westward of Bear Island and reserved their surface forces for attack to the eastward of Bear Island. The final story of PQ17 convoy is not yet clear. At the moment, only four ships have arrived, but four others are believed to be off the coast of Nova Zembla. The latter may, however, be attacked from the air at any time. At the best, therefore, only one-quarter will have survived and it is possible that the figure will only be one-eighth.

2. I must explain the dangers and difficulties of these convoy operations, when the enemy's battle-squadron takes its station in the extreme North. We do not think it right to risk our Home Fleet east of Bear Island or where it can be brought under the attack of the powerful German shore-based aircraft. If one or two of our very few most powerful battleships were to be lost or even seriously damaged while *Tirpitz* and her consorts, soon to be joined by *Scharnhorst*, remained in action, the whole command of the Atlantic would be lost. Besides affecting the food supplies by which we live, our war effort would be crippled; and above all the great convoys of American troops across the ocean, rising presently to as many as 80,000 in a month, would be prevented and the building up of a really strong second front in 1943 rendered impossible.

3. My naval advisers tell me that if they had the handling of the German surface, submarine and air forces, in present circumstances, they would guarantee the complete destruction of any convoy to North Russia. They are unable to hold out any hopes that convoys attempting to

make the passage in perpetual daylight would fare any better, even if as well, as PQ17.

It is therefore with the greatest regret that we have reached the conclusion that to continue to attempt further convoys to North Russia during the summer months could bring no benefit to you and would only involve grievous injury to our common cause.

4. PQ18 will therefore not sail to Archangel, but we are prepared to despatch immediately some of the ships of this convoy to the Persian Gulf. Selection of ships would be made in consultation with Soviet authorities in London in order that priorities of cargo may be agreed.

If fighter aircraft (Hurricanes and Airacobras[1]) are selected, can you operate and maintain them on the Southern Front? We could undertake to assemble them at Basra.

We hope to increase through clearance capacity of trans-Persian routes so as to reach 75,000 tons monthly by October and are making strenuous efforts to obtain a further increase. We are asking the United States Government to help us by expediting despatch of the rolling-stock and trucks.

An increased volume of traffic could be handled at once if you would agree to American trucks for USSR now being assembled in the Persian Gulf being used as a shuttle service for transporting goods by road between the Gulf and the Caspian.

In order to ensure full use of capacity, we agree to raise figure of loadings due to arrive September to 95,000 tons and October to 100,000 tons, both exclusive of trucks and aircraft.

5. All the above only emphasises the importance of combined Russo-British operations to drive the enemy out of the northern Norwegian airfields. We have been studying the possibility of these operations for some time, and if a good plan can be made between our officers we shall be prepared to help with sea, land and air forces to the best of our ability. For our direct attacks by landings from the sea we must wait till there is a reasonable amount of darkness, i.e., until October. The danger from enemy aircraft will then be much reduced. All this must be studied by your officers and ours. It would be better if you could send your officers

---

[1] Bell P-39 Airacobra: one of the primary American fighters produced by Bell Aircraft. An all-metal, low-wing, single-engine fighter with a tricycle undercarriage and an Allison V-1710 liquid-cooled Vee-12 engine. Uniquely, its engine was located behind the pilot, connected to the propellor by a long shaft. The lack of an efficient turbo-supercharger limited it to low-altitude work. Produced from 1940 to May 1944 and introduced into service in 1941. Used with great success by the Soviet Air Force, to whom large numbers were given under the Lend-Lease Agreement. Used also by the Free French and co-belligerent Italian air forces.

here, but if this is impossible, we will come to you. It may well be that this study will show that the difficulties are prohibitive.

6. In addition to a combined operation in the North, we are thinking of what we can do to help on your southern flank. If we can beat back Rommel, we might be able to send powerful air forces in the autumn to operate on the left of your line. The difficulties of maintaining these forces over the trans-Persian route will clearly be considerable, but the project is being most earnestly examined and I shall hope to put detailed proposals before you in the near future. We must, however, first beat Rommel, of which I have good hopes.

7. Let me once again express my thanks for the 40 Bostons. We are straining every nerve to beat Rommel out of Egypt, if not further. Large reinforcements are approaching General Auchinleck in a constant stream, and the impending arrival of strong British and American heavy armoured forces should give the necessary security to the Eastern Mediterranean, as well as obstructing Rommel's supply ports of Tobruk and Benghazi.

8. I am sure it would be in our common interest, Premier Stalin, to have the three divisions of Poles you so kindly offered join their compatriots in Palestine, where we can arm them fully. These would play a most important part in future fighting as well as keeping the Turks in good heart by the sense of growing numbers to the southward. I hope this project of yours, which we greatly value, will not fall to the ground on account of the Poles wanting to bring with the troops a considerable mass of their women and children who are largely dependent on the rations of the Polish soldiers. The feeding of these dependants in Palestine will be a considerable burden to us. We think it well worth while bearing that burden for the sake of forming this Polish army which will be used faithfully for our common advantage. We are very hard up for food ourselves in the Levant area but there is enough in India if we can bring it there. If we do not get the Poles we should have to fill their places by drawing on the preparations now going forward on a vast scale for the Anglo-American mass invasion of the Continent. I am glad to see that these preparations, so far as they have advanced, have already led the Germans to withdraw two heavy bomber groups from South Russia to the South of France. Believe me, my comrade, and friend, there is nothing that is useful and sensible that we and the Americans will not do to help you in your grand struggle. The President and I are ceaselessly searching for means to overcome the extraordinary difficulties which geography, salt water and the enemy's air power interpose.

Winston S. Churchill to Brigadier Leslie Hollis
(Churchill papers, 20/67)

15 July 1942

I fear that to change 'Roundup' would make the Americans think there was some change of purpose. Therefore we must stick to this boastful, ill-chosen name and hope it does not bring us bad luck.

2. I do not think we had better alter the President's wording in paragraph 2. We are not now dealing with policy, but only with nomenclature.

3. I agree about 'Festival'.[1]

4. Draft accordingly and promulgate after obtaining American agreement.

Winston S. Churchill to A. V. Alexander and
Admiral of the Fleet Sir Dudley Pound
(Churchill papers, 20/67)

15 July 1942
Action this Day
Secret

Although in order to ascertain the American reaction I have approved the draft telegram to Stalin attached to my 113 Personal and Secret to the President of yesterday, a further intense effort must be made to solve the problem of running convoys by the northern route. Let the following be examined:

Suspend the sailing of PQ18 as now proposed from 18th instant.

See what happens to our Malta operation. If all goes well, bring *Indomitable, Victorious, Argus,* and *Eagle* north to Scapa and collect with them at least five of the auxiliary aircraft carriers, together with all available 'Didos'[2] and at least 25 destroyers. Let the two 16-inch battleships go right through under this air umbrella and destroyer screen, keeping southward, not hugging the ice, but seeking the clearest weather, and thus fight it out with the enemy. If we can move our armada in convoy under an umbrella of at least 100 fighter aircraft we ought to be able

---

[1] 'Festival': probably a reference to projected US landings in West Africa, though this cannot be confirmed.

[2] Dido: Sixteen Dido class cruisers were built for the Royal Navy between 1940 and 1944. They were designed primarily as anti-aircraft cruisers, but had dual-purpose turrets that could also engage ships.

to fight our way through and out again, and if a Fleet action results, so much the better.

2. I was not aware until this morning that it was the cruiser *Admiral Hamilton* who ordered the destroyers to quit the convoy. What did you think of this decision at the time? What do you think of it now?

Winston S. Churchill to Brendan Bracken
(Churchill papers, 20/67)

15 July 1942

I certainly do not intend to apologise to these American Press Correspondents.[1] You should confront them with these extracts and emphasise the damage that was done by their portrayal of an insignificant and unrepresentative minority as representing Parliament as a whole.

General Sir Alan Brooke: diary
('War Diaries, Field Marshal Lord Alanbrooke', page 281)

15 July 1942

[...] the situation in the ME was not improving, the Auk was suggesting giving the 8th Army to Corbett. It was essential that I should go out to see for myself what was really wrong, and for that job I did not want Winston treading on my heels! Fortunately that lovely evening sitting in the garden of 10 Downing Street I found him in one of his amenable moods. I jumped in at once and to my joy got his approval[...]

Oliver Harvey: diary
('The War Diaries of Oliver Harvey', page 140)

15 July 1942

A difficult day with Maisky yesterday. M dined with PM and AE joined them again after. A message to Stalin is being drafted to show how hopeless it is to continue the North Russian convoys at present when over 2/3 go to the bottom. It may be possible to resume them later with aircraft carriers. Meanwhile we are trying to send more via Persia but capacity is

---

[1] Letter from the Association of American Correspondents in London complaining of the Prime Minister's remarks about American journalists in his statement in the House of Commons on 2 July 1942.

limited. PM very anxious that America should proceed with NW Africa plan. We learn that the President too is very keen but is being opposed by his soldiers – so like ours.

Winston S. Churchill to Lord Woolton
(Churchill papers, 20/67)

16 July 1942

Complaints reach me about your new plans for poultry rationing as they affect country-folk. The hen has been part and parcel of the country cottager's life since history began. Townsfolk can eke out their rations by a bought meal. What is the need for this tremendous reduction to one hen per person? Anyhow, the Cabinet ought to have been informed.

Winston S. Churchill to President Franklin D. Roosevelt
(Churchill papers, 20/78)

16 July 1942
Personal and Secret
No. 116

Further to my No. 113 and appended draft to Stalin. We are, as you know, running a heavily-guarded convoy to Malta soon, relying upon very strong sea-borne fighter protection. If this should succeed without serious losses it might render possible an attempt in September to run an even more powerfully mounted and protected convoy to Russia. Admiralty are studying this, and I do not propose in my message to Stalin to close the door, as is done in paragraph 3 of the draft in my No. 115 telegraphed to you. The Malta convoy will decide whether very strong sea-borne fighter protection is effective. That can only be proved by trial.

2. I am glad indeed you are sending our friends[1] over. I feel sure this was the only thing to do.
[Later]

3. Your 166 and 167 just received are covered by the foregoing. Many thanks.

---

[1] Marshall, King, and Hopkins.

Winston S. Churchill to President Franklin D. Roosevelt
(Churchill papers, 20/78)

16 July 1942
Clear the Line
Personal and Secret
No. 118

Am holding up long telegram to Stalin for another 24 hours, in hopes of being able to improve paragraph 3 a little. Should be grateful if you would say nothing to him meanwhile.

Winston S. Churchill to President Franklin D. Roosevelt
(Churchill papers, 20/78)

16 July 1942
Clear the Line
Personal and Secret
No. 117

Will convey our friends on arrival to usual weekend resort where British Chiefs of Staff await them. I wish I could guarantee the beauties and the weather of Hyde Park.[1]

Winston S. Churchill to Field Marshal Sir John Dill
(Churchill papers, 20/78)

16 July 1942
Most Secret and Personal
Immediate

I am very glad our friends are coming. Soldiers and statesmen here are in complete agreement.

---

[1] Roosevelt's country home on the Hudson River, New York State.

President Franklin D. Roosevelt to Winston S. Churchill
(Churchill papers, 20/78)

16 July 1942
No. 166

After consultation with King I must reluctantly agree to the position which the Admiralty has taken regarding the Russian convoy to the North and I think your message to Stalin is a good one. I assume you will send it at once.

In the meantime we must omit nothing that will increase the traffic through Persia.

A suggestion has been made that American railway men take over the operation of the railroad. Have you any opinion about this. They are first class at this sort of thing.

Roosevelt

Winston S. Churchill to Sol Bloom[1]
(Churchill papers, 20/54)

16 July 1942

My dear Mr Sol Bloom,

Lord Halifax has told me of your wish to possess one of the long cigars which I sometimes smoke. I am therefore sending one to you privately with an expression of my best wishes.

Yours sincerely
Winston S. Churchill

[1] Sol Bloom, 1870–1949. Entertainment and popular music entrepreneur. Member of the US House of Representatives for New York's 19th Congressional District from 1923 until his death. Son of Polish Jewish emigrants. A strong supporter of Zionism. Introduced to the production side of the theatre business in his early teens; graduated to theatre manager. Chaired the House Committee on Foreign Affairs, 1938. A delegate to the convention in San Francisco that established the United Nations. Represented the United States at the first meeting of the UN General Assembly in London, 1946.

Winston S. Churchill to Lord Somers[1]
(Churchill papers, 20/54)

16 July 1942

I first met 'BP'[2] many years before the birth of the Scout Movement. He was a man of character, vision and enthusiasm and he passed these qualities on to the Movement which has played and is playing an important part in moulding the character of our race. Sturdiness, neighbourliness, practical competence, love of country, and above all, in these times, indomitable resolve, daring and enterprise in the face of the enemy, these are the hallmarks of a Scout.

You have many practical difficulties under war-time conditions in carrying on your work but with persistence and ingenuity these can be surmounted in Scout fashion and I have no doubt that in your hands the Movement will carry on its task with the steadfast will and high courage with which it was founded. 'Be prepared to stand up faithfully for Right and Truth however the winds may blow'.

Winston S. Churchill

President Franklin D. Roosevelt to Harry Hopkins,
General George C. Marshall, and Admiral Ernest King
('The White House Papers of Harry L. Hopkins', pages 604–6)

16 July 1942

INSTRUCTIONS FOR LONDON CONFERENCE, 1942

1. You will proceed immediately to London as my personal representatives for the purpose of consultation with appropriate British authorities on the conduct of the war.

2. The military and naval strategic changes have been so great since Mr Churchill's visit to Washington that it became necessary to reach immediate agreement on joint operational plans between the British and ourselves along two lines:

(a) Definite plans for the balance of 1942.

---

[1] Arthur Herbert Tennyson Somers Cocks, 1887–1944. Educated at Mulgrave Castle; Charterhouse; New College, Oxford. Succeeded to barony, 1899. An Army officer during First World War. DSO, 1918. Military Cross. KCMG, 1926. Governor of the State of Victoria, Australia, 1926–31. Acting Governor-General of Australia, 1930–1. Lord Lieutenant of Hertfordshire, 1933. Red Cross Commission in the Middle East, 1940. Chief Scout for Great Britain and Chief Scout of the British Commonwealth, 1941.

[2] Robert Baden-Powell, 1857–1951. Entered the Army, 1876. Chief Staff Officer, Matabeleland, 1896–7. Commanded the defence of Mafeking, 1899–1900. Lieutenant-General, 1908. Founded the Boy Scouts and Girl Guides, 1908. Knighted, 1909. Created Baron, 1929. Order of Merit, 1937.

(b) Tentative plans for the year 1943, which of course will be subject to change in the light of occurrences in 1942, but which should be initiated at this time in all cases involving preparation in 1942 for operations in 1943.

3. (a) The common aim of the United Nations must be the defeat of the Axis Powers. There cannot be compromise on this point.

(b) We should concentrate our efforts and avoid dispersion.

(c) Absolute co-ordinated use of British and American forces is essential.

(d) All available US and British forces should be brought into action as quickly as they can be profitably used.

(e) It is of the highest importance that US ground troops be brought into action against the enemy in 1942.

4. British and American material promises to Russia must be carried out in good faith. If the Persian route of delivery is used preference must be given to combat material. This aid must continue as long as delivery is possible, and Russia must be encouraged to continue resistance. Only complete collapse, which seems unthinkable, should alter this determination on our part.

5. In regard to 1942, you will carefully investigate the possibility of executing 'Sledgehammer'. Such an operation would definitely sustain Russia this year. It might be the turning-point which would save Russia this year. 'Sledgehammer' is of such grave importance that every reason calls for accomplishment of it. You should strongly urge immediate all-out preparations for it, that it be pushed with utmost vigour, and that it be executed whether or not Russian collapse becomes imminent. In the event Russian collapse becomes probable, 'Sledgehammer' becomes not merely advisable but imperative. The principal objective of 'Sledgehammer' is the positive diversion of German air forces from the Russian front.

6. Only if you are completely convinced that 'Sledgehammer' is impossible of execution with reasonable chance of serving its intended purpose inform me.

7. If 'Sledgehammer' is finally and definitely out of the picture I want you to consider the world situation as it exists at that time, and determine upon another place for US troops to fight in 1942.[1]

It is my present view of the world picture that:

(a) If Russia contains a large German force against her 'Round-up' becomes possible in 1943, and plans for 'Round-up' should be immediately considered and preparations made for it.

[1] Underlining here and below by Roosevelt in original memorandum.

(b) If Russia collapses and German air and ground forces are released 'Round-up' may be impossible [for] fulfilment in 1943.

8. The Middle East should be held as strongly as possible whether Russia collapses or not. I want you to take into consideration the effect of losing the Middle East. Such loss means in series:

(1) Loss of Egypt and the Suez Canal.

(2) Loss of Syria.

(3) Loss of Mosul oil-wells.

(4) Loss of the Persian Gulf through attacks from the north and west, together with access to all Persian Gulf oil.

(5) Joining hands between Germany and Japan and the probable loss of the Indian Ocean.

(6) The very important probability of German occupation of Tunis, Algiers, Morocco, Dakar, and the cutting of the ferry route through Freetown and Liberia.

(7) Serious danger to all shipping in the South Atlantic, and serious danger to Brazil and the whole of the east coast of South America. I include in the above possibilities the use by the Germans of Spain, Portugal, and their territories.

(8) You will determine the best methods of holding the Middle East. These methods include definitely either or both of the following:

(a) Sending aid and ground forces to the Persian Gulf, to Syria, and to Egypt.

(b) A new operation in Morocco and Algeria intended to drive in against the back door of Rommel's armies. The attitude of French colonial troops is still in doubt.

9. I am opposed to an American all-out effort in the Pacific against Japan with the view to her defeat as quickly as possible. It is of the utmost importance that we appreciate that defeat of Japan does not defeat Germany and that American concentration against Japan this year or in 1943 increases the chance of complete German domination of Europe and Africa. On the other hand, it is obvious that defeat of Germany or the holding of Germany in 1942 or in 1943 means probable eventual defeat of Germany in the European and African theatre and in the Near East. Defeat of Germany means the defeat of Japan, probably without firing a shot or losing a life.

10. Please remember three cardinal principles – speed of decision on plans, unity of plans, attack combined with defence but not defence

alone. This affects the immediate objective of US ground forces fighting against Germans in 1942.

11. I hope for total agreement within one week of your arrival.

Franklin D. Roosevelt
Commander-in-Chief

President Franklin D. Roosevelt to Winston S. Churchill
(Churchill papers, 20/78)

17 July 1942
Personal
No. 168

I really think it better for our friends to go straight to London and not go to resort for a couple of days. They ought to orient themselves first before any general meeting. I know you will understand. Also I hope secrecy in regard [to] their visit can be maintained.

Winston S. Churchill to President Franklin D. Roosevelt
(Churchill papers, 20/78)

17 July 1942
No. 119

Certainly. Whatever you wish. We are always entirely at your service.

Oliver Harvey: diary
('The War Diaries of Oliver Harvey', page 141)

18 July 1942

AE tells me PM is ringing him up every morning now to discuss the night's news. I say how excellent this is. It enables him to guide the old gentleman a good deal. He hates bringing Attlee and all into his inmost counsels.

[...]

Peake[1] told me Halifax has been shocked on returning after a year to a meeting of the War Cabinet to find how the proceedings had deterio-

---

[1] Charles Brinsley Pemberton Peake, 1897–1958. Captain, Leicestershire Regiment; on active service, 1915–18 (despatches, Military Cross). Entered the Diplomatic Service, 1922. Head of the News Department, Foreign Office, and Chief Press Adviser, Ministry of Information, 1939. Personal Assistant to Lord Halifax in Washington, 1941. British Representative to the French National Com-

rated. Nothing but endless monologues from the PM. He was also struck by the poor display of Lyttelton and Cripps.

Winston S. Churchill to President Franklin D. Roosevelt
(Churchill papers, 20/78)

18 July 1942

Apart from minor verbal amendments the telegram to Stalin as sent today, Friday, differs only in the following respect from the draft sent in my No. 115:

2. (a) Last three sentences of paragraph 1 amended to read: 'At the moment only four ships have arrived at Archangel, but six others are in Nova Zembla harbours. The latter may, however, be attacked from the air at any time. At the best, therefore, only one-third will have survived.'

(b) Paragraph 3 and the first sentence of Paragraph 4 amended to read: 'My naval advisers tell me that if they had the handling of the German surface, submarine and air forces, in present circumstances, they would guarantee the complete destruction of any convoy to North Russia. They have not been able so far to hold out hopes that convoys attempting to make the passage in perpetual daylight would fare better than PQ17. It is, therefore, with the greatest regret that we have reached the conclusion that to attempt to run the next convoy, PQ18, would bring no benefit to you and would only involve dead loss to the common cause. At the same time, I give you my assurance that, if we can devise arrangements which give a reasonable chance of at least a fair proportion of the contents of the convoys reaching you, we will start them again at once. The crux of the problem is to make the Barents Sea as dangerous for the German Warships as they make it for ours. This is what we should aim at doing with our joint resources. I should like to send a senior officer of the RAF to North Russia to confer with your officers and make a plan.

'Meanwhile, we are prepared to despatch immediately to the Persian Gulf some of the ships which were to have sailed in the PQ convoy.'

(c) Paragraphs 5, 6, and 7.

'5. Your telegram to me on 20th June referred to combined operations in the North. The obstacles to sending further convoys at the present time equally prevent our sending land forces and air forces for operations in Northern Norway. But our officers should forthwith consider together

mittee, 1942–4. Political Adviser to General Eisenhower, Supreme Commander, Allied Expeditionary Force, 1944–5. Consul-General, Tangier, 1945–6. Ambassador at Belgrade, 1946–51. Knighted, 1948. Ambassador at Athens, 1951–7.

what combined operations may be possible in or after October when there is a reasonable amount of darkness. It would be better if you could send your officers here, but if this is impossible, ours will come to you.

'6. In addition to a combined operation in the North, we are studying how to help on your Southern flank. If we can beat Rommel, we might be able to send powerful air forces in the autumn to operate on the left of your line. The difficulties of maintaining these forces over the trans-Persian route without reducing your supplies will clearly be considerable, but I hope to put detailed proposals before you in the near future. We must, however, first beat Rommel. The battle is now intense.

'7. Let me once again express my thanks for the 40 Bostons. The Germans are constantly sending more men and aircraft to Africa: but large reinforcements are approaching General Auchinleck, and the impending arrival of strong British and American heavy bomber aircraft forces should give security to the Eastern Mediterranean, as well as obstructing Rommel's supply ports of Tobruk and Benghazi.'

(d) Last paragraph, words 'In Palestine' omitted from the fourth sentence and last sentence but two amended to read 'these preparations have already led the Germans to withdraw two heavy bomber groups from South Russia to France.'

3. I have added that I have shown this telegram to you.

Winston S. Churchill to Herbert Morrison
(Churchill papers, 20/54)

18 July 1942

My dear Herbert,

Thank you so much for the extremely kind reference which you made in your speech last week to the warnings I gave before the war.[1]

I hear from various quarters that your speech gave great satisfaction in the Services, especially in the Army.

Yours vy sincerely,
Winston S. Churchill

---

[1] Speaking at County Hall, London, Herbert Morrison said: 'We were all responsible for the treatment that the army received between the last war and this. I have condemned myself and accept my share of responsibility and blame as a citizen and a member of Parliament. I think that all political parties and phases of thought were responsible. But I would add a reservation about one man whose voice was pretty well a solitary one, though an urgent one, and that is the present Prime Minister. (Cheers.) He did warn us; he warned Parliament, but his warnings unhappily were not heeded' (*The Times*, 17 July 1942).

Winston S. Churchill to General Hastings Ismay,
for the Chiefs of Staff Committee
(Churchill papers, 20/67)

18 July 1942
Secret

The first part of this draft telegram[1] had better wait for a few days for the Chiefs of Staff's reply to my minute, about tidying up 'Ironclad', of today's date.

2. Before I could agree to the second paragraph, I should like to know how the tank position stands. We ought not, in this phase of the war, to accumulate large reserves of tanks behind the armoured formations in Great Britain. Invasion is unlikely, and these reserves can be accumulated in time for any offensive by us in 1943. The 300 Sherman tanks are a windfall, and the decision not to send PQ18 and possibly to suspend sendings to Russia during the daylight period certainly give us at least another 250 tanks. Moreover, tank production is expanding. There should be very large numbers of tanks available in 1943. I consider, therefore, that no case has been shown for not providing the tanks as promised for both South African divisions.

3. First, however, let me know what scale these divisions are to be upon. Are they to be on the new scale of one armoured brigade and one motorized brigade, in which case they only require 200 tanks apiece; or are they on the old 350 scale? I imagine the former as being correct, and, if so, there are only 400 tanks to be found altogether.

4. I recognise the force of the argument that we cannot withdraw the South African divisions for training in a different rôle at the present time; but the course of the battle and the arrival of other reinforcements may render this possible in, say, a couple of months. I should hope, therefore, that the promised dates and programme could be maintained.

Chiefs of Staff Committee: minutes
(Cabinet papers, 79/56)

18 July 1942
Evening

The discussion showed that there was complete agreement between the Prime Minister on the one hand and the Chiefs of Staff on the other.

[1] Draft reply to telegram 1211 (T.961/2) from General Smuts about the conversion to armour of the two South African Divisions in the Middle East.

In respect of the action in 1942, the only feasible proposition appeared to be 'Gymnast'. It would be much to our advantage to get a footing in North Africa cheaply, in the same way as the Germans got Norway cheaply, by getting there first.

'Gymnast' would in effect be the right wing of our Second Front. An American occupation of Casablanca and district would not be sufficient. The operations would have to extend to Algiers, Oran, and possibly farther east. If the Americans could not supply the forces for all of these, we might undertake the more easterly operations with British troops accompanied by small American contingents. It was probable that the United States would be unable to supply all the naval forces necessary for 'Gymnast' in addition to those necessary for their 'Bolero' convoys. In that event we should have to help them out.

General Sir Alan Brooke: diary
('War Diaries, Field Marshal Lord Alanbrooke', page 282)

18 July 1942

[...]

At 4 p.m. when I was getting near end of work and thinking of soon going home was informed that all the Chiefs of Staff were wanted at Chequers for the night!! Arrived there just in time for dinner. Pound, Portal, Mountbatten, Ismay, Cherwell and self. After dinner we had long sitting reviewing the whole war and relative advantages of various fronts. This lasted till 2 a.m. when we were taken to see a film! Finally to bed at 2.45 a.m.

Richard Casey to Winston S. Churchill
(Churchill papers, 20/78)

19 July 1942   Cairo
Personal

[...]

4. All possible steps have been taken as regards defence of the Delta if things were to go wrong. On the other hand, all arrangements have been made to enable a quick follow up to be made should the enemy break or be broken.

[...]

10. We have given close attention to programme of demolitions. In view of our special relations with Egypt, we wish to avoid as far as possible destruction of essential means of life of the people. But short of this programme provides for as complete a destruction as would be practicable of military and economic assets. No actual demolitions have as yet been carried out in the Delta.

11. We hoped to persuade Egyptian Government to hand gold reserve over to us for safety. Having so far failed to persuade them we are making most secret plans to remove gold forcibly if necessary.

[...]

20. The unexpected announcements in America and by the BBC of the negotiations (Martinique) with Vichy about the French Fleet caused me some anxiety because of the statement it contained that if the US offer were refused we should be justified in sinking the French ships. I succeeded in suppressing this part of the statement and the rest of the announcement has done good in that crews of French ships are said to be indignant that Vichy refused US offer. Meantime, most secret plans have been made for the sinking of the ships if the need arises.

Winston S. Churchill: note
('The Hinge of Fate', pages 401–3)

20 July 1942

I do not desire to discuss this morning the merits of the various grave major proposals which are before us, but rather to survey the general scene and suggest the most convenient method and sequence of our conferences. We must reach decisions, and though these affect the whole future of the war there is no reason why the process should be protracted.

The first question is 'Sledgehammer'. Should we do it or not? But here also arises immediately the question, in what form? Our visitors may be thinking of one thing, while we have been working mainly at another. If we have been unable to devise a satisfactory plan ourselves, we will give the most earnest, sympathetic attention to any American plan. It is most important that no one should come to these discussions with a closed mind, either for or against any particular project. It is of course necessary to consider not only whether a thing can be done, but whether on balance it would be a profitable use of our resources at the present time.

We must consider the effect of doing or not doing 'Sledgehammer' on the future of 'Round-Up', for which all the 'Bolero' preparations are proceeding. We are ardently in favour of 'Round-up'. But here again what is 'Round-up'? Is it necessarily confined to an attack upon the western seaboard of France? Is the idea of a second front necessarily confined within those limits? Might it not be extended even more widely, and with advantage? We have been inclined to think that 'Sledgehammer' might delay or even preclude 'Round-up'. On the other hand, it may be contended that the fortunes of 'Round-up' do not depend to any large extent on what we do, but on what happens in Russia.

We have hitherto discussed 'Sledgehammer' on the basis that Russia is either triumphant or crushed. It is more probable that an intermediate situation will confront us. The Russian battle may long hang in the balance; or, again, the result may be indeterminate, and the Russian front will be maintained, though somewhat farther to the east.

If 'Sledgehammer' is excluded what are we to do pending 'Round-up'? Or, if it is held that the exclusion of 'Sledgehammer' destroys 'Round-up', what are we to do anyway?

Here I will come to the second chapter, the operation 'Gymnast'. This should certainly be examined in all its various forms and from every angle. The Germans will probably not wait indefinitely before occupying the 'Gymnast' area and drawing Spain and Portugal into their system. Even though not strong enough to invade Britain with Russia still on their hands, they might easily find enough for that. We have to face the prospect of a German occupation of the North African and West African coasts. How serious would be the disadvantages of this?

The case for or against 'Gymnast' is powerfully affected by the course of the battle now raging in Egypt. Should General Auchinleck win his advance westward may be very rapid. 'Acrobat' might then again come into view, with possibilities of action against Sicily and Italy, and also of regaining the air control of the Southern Mediterranean, with all the saving of shipping that would result therefrom.

A wide gap now exists in our defences. The Levant–Caspian front is almost bare. If General Auchinleck wins the battle of Egypt we could no doubt build up a force of perhaps eight divisions, which, with the four Polish divisions when trained, would play a strong part in delaying a German southward advance. But if General Auchinleck cannot drive the enemy to a safe distance away from Egypt, or if, having driven them, he pursues them into 'Acrobat', then the only shield for the vital region south of the Caspian is the Russian southern armies. We cannot yet say how they will fare. It is far too early to assume that they will break. Even at the worst they should retire in force through the Caucasus and hold the mountain range through the winter and retain, possibly with our air assistance, the naval command of the Caspian Sea. These are great bulwarks. At present they are our only bulwarks. . . .

General Sir Alan Brooke: diary
('War Diaries, Field Marshal Lord Alanbrooke', page 282)

20 July 1942

[. . .] At 12.30 we went round to 12 Downing Street to meet American Chiefs of Staff with PM!

War Cabinet: Confidential Annex
(Cabinet papers, 65/31)

20 July 1942
5.30 p.m.

The Prime Minister said that the Cabinet would have to decide whether they should direct that the Chiefs of Staff should proceed with the 'Sledge-hammer' plan, notwithstanding the views which they held as to its feasibility. In his own (the Prime Minister's) view, the Cherbourg Peninsula was an attractive objective as part of a scheme which involved simultaneous landings on several parts of the French coast. If, however, no landings were made except in the Cherbourg Peninsula, we should find great difficulty in hanging on to territory which we had captured, and in maintaining our invading force, while the enemy brought all his Air Force to bear on a single small port. Moreover, even if we could maintain ourselves, the drain on our resources of men would be such that 'Round-up' would be indefinitely delayed in the following year. Again, there was nothing to prevent the enemy from building a strong defensive Line across the narrow neck of the Peninsula and bottling up our forces. On the other hand, we must not show ourselves too ready to raise difficulties [. . .]

The Chief of Combined Operations stated that he believed that the assault of the Cherbourg Peninsula would be feasible. Since March last he had taken the view that this was the one area of the coast on which we could stage a successful assault this year. Detailed planning for operation on this part of the coast, had, however, not been pursued, on the grounds that we should not help Russia by operations in the Cherbourg Peninsula, since we could not bring our strong Air Force fully to bear against the enemy's Air Force in this area. This we could only do in the Pas de Calais area.

The Prime Minister said that he had considered whether, if it was decided that we should say that we did not agree with the view put forward by the United States Chiefs of Staff in their Memorandum, we should say (a) that we were not in agreement with their view, or (b) that, while we did not share the American opinion, if they wished to conduct the operation we were prepared to carry it out with them. He saw danger in the second course, and thought that, on the whole, the wisest course, if we did not see our way to agree with the American proposal in regard to carrying out 'Sledgehammer' in 1942, was that we should ask the American Chiefs of Staff to report to the President that it had not been possible to reach an agreed plan for this operation.

The Prime Minister said that no discussions had yet taken place as to what alternative operation could be carried out if agreement was not reached to carry out 'Sledgehammer' in 1942. It had been decided that we should first reach a decision on 'Sledgehammer' before considering alternative operations. If Sledgehammer was abandoned, discussion of 'Gymnast' would at once be started. If it was decided not to carry out 'Sledgehammer' in 1942, planning for 'Round-up' in 1943 would, of course, continue.

The Chief of the Imperial General Staff agreed that if 'Sledgehammer' was abandoned for 1942, we should continue planning for 'Round-up'. It was relevant, in this connection, that it would not be until September that enough American troops would have arrived in this country to replace the forces that we had removed from Northern Ireland. The Chiefs of Staffs' view was that 'Gymnast' should be carried out before the end of 1942, since otherwise there was a risk that the enemy would anticipate us. 'Gymnast' would, therefore, be carried out many months before 'Round-up' could take place. But the repercussions of 'Gymnast' (or of 'Mohican',[1] which was a more powerful and extended version of 'Gymnast') on 'Round-up' had not yet been fully examined. He thought that, while there had been no definite discussion with the Americans on 'Gymnast', they were favourably impressed with the importance of the scheme, and that they had not hitherto taken into account the advantage which would accrue in the saving of shipping if the Mediterranean route could be re-opened.

---

[1] 'Mohican': original name of 'Torch', the landings in North Africa carried out from 8 to 16 November 1942.

The Prime Minister then read to the War Cabinet telegram No. 990, Private and Personal, dated 23rd July, from Admiral Cunningham to the First Sea Lord, on the advantage of 'Gymnast', and stressing the importance of the operation including, if possible, a surprise attack on Bizerta.

The Chief of the Naval Staff said that he greatly favoured operation 'Mohican'. If the Germans were to occupy the North African Atlantic littoral, our WS[1] convoys would have to go over to the American side of the Atlantic. As the result, the journey from Liverpool to Bombay would be lengthened from 12,000 miles to 15,500 miles, as compared with a figure of 7,300 miles by the route through the Mediterranean.

The Secretary of State for Foreign Affairs said that, on the political side, he thought that 'Sledgehammer' suffered from the serious disadvantage that it would be carried out too late this year to give any help, either morally or militarily, to Russia. He had not greatly favoured a project for landing at Casablanca alone, since he thought it would be a long time before troops landed at Casablanca could make their way along the North African coast. In the meanwhile the Spanish position might develop in an unpleasant way. These objections, however, did not apply to operation 'Mohican', which he understood included a landing at several points on the North African coast. The timing of the right plan, however, was of the utmost importance.

The Prime Minister then asked members of the War Cabinet for an expression of their views.

All expressed themselves in favour of making clear that we did not agree to operation 'Sledgehammer' being carried out in 1942, and favoured operation 'Mohican'.

The Prime Minister said that it was for consideration whether a Memorandum should be handed to the Americans in reply to the Memorandum dated 21st July which was handed to our Chiefs of Staff. On the whole, he thought that the right course was that a Memorandum should be prepared and kept for record, setting out our reasons against carrying out this operation, but should not be handed to the Americans unless they asked for such a document.

As regards the reply to be given, he thought that the United States Chiefs of Staff should be asked to inform the President that it had not been found possible to reach agreement on the proposed plan for 'Sledgehammer' in 1942. This would, he thought, open the way for discussion on the alternative operations with the least difficulty.

---

[1] WS ('Winston's Specials') Convoys sailed from the United Kingdom to India and the Far East.

The War Cabinet agreed with this conclusion, which General Ismay was instructed to convey orally to the United States Chiefs of Staff.

House of Commons: Oral Answers
(Hansard)

21 July 1942

GENERAL ELECTION

Mr De la Bère[1] asked the Prime Minister whether he can make a statement regarding the Government's intentions as to holding a General Election before the end of 1942?

The Prime Minister (Mr Churchill): It would be most unusual and in my view contrary to the best precedents for any statement to be made forecasting the advice which in hypothetical circumstances should be tendered to the King in respect of a Dissolution of Parliament.

Mr De la Bère: Is it not essential whilst perils press to reason calmly about holding a General Election? Would the Prime Minister impress on Lord Beaverbrook the necessity for calm reasoning?

The Prime Minister: I must embrace this opportunity of testifying my admiration for the principles of free speech and a free Press.

Mr Gallacher: Does that apply to the 'Daily Worker'?[2]

Winston S. Churchill to General Sir Alan Brooke
(Churchill papers, 20/67)

21 July 1942
Secret

Please take some opportunity of inquiring from the United States representatives what they propose to do if Japan attacks Russia, and

---

[1] Rupert de la Bère, 1893–1978. Captain, East Surrey Regiment; on active service, 1914–18 (including Mesopotamia). Seconded to Royal Air Force, 1918. Conservative MP for Evesham, 1935–50; for South Worcestershire, 1950–5. Sheriff of the City of London, 1941–2. Lord Mayor of London, 1952–3. Knighted, 1952.

[2] The newspaper of the Communist Party of Great Britain. The paper was extremely pro-Soviet and, prior to the USSR's entry into the war, heavily criticized the British Government's war policy. As a result it was suppressed by Home Secretary Herbert Morrison from 21 January 1941 to 7 September 1942. On 29 May 1942, in a memorandum to the War Cabinet entitled 'The position of the "Daily Worker"' (CAB 66/25), Morrison noted that 'the view that the ban on this newspaper should be lifted is not confined to M.P.'s who are on the political left', and that 'if prohibition were a regrettable necessity in December, 1940, it is no longer justifiable in the changed circumstances of today'. Nevertheless, he continued, 'any immediate requests for the lifting of the ban should, in my view, be resisted'.

what preparations they have made to utilize Russian bases. This might happen quite soon.

Winston S. Churchill to A. V. Alexander and
Admiral of the Fleet Sir Dudley Pound
(Churchill papers, 20/67)

21 July 1942
Secret

THE BATTLE IN EGYPT

I cannot help having the impression that Admiral Harwood and the Navy are doing very little in this fight, either in cutting off the enemy's supplies or in actively bombarding the enemy bases. Apart from one bombardment, the Navy seem to have played no part whatever.

If I am wrong, pray let me know.

Winston S. Churchill: memorandum
(Churchill papers, 23/10)

21 July 1942
Most Secret
To be kept under lock and key

A REVIEW OF THE WAR POSITION

The time has come to review the whole field of the war and place its salient features in their true proportion.

2. The first is the immense power of the German military machine. Because the German armies have been so long busy in Russia, we are apt to forget this terrible engine. When we feel what a couple of Panzer divisions and the 90th German Light Division can do in North Africa against our greatly superior numbers and resources, we have no excuse for underrating German military power in 1943 and 1944. It will always be possible for them to set up a holding front against Russia and bring back fifty or sixty, or even more, divisions to the West. They could make the transference with very great rapidity across the main railway lines of Europe. We have no right to count upon a collapse of German military power on the European Continent. In the event of the overthrow of the Nazi régime, it is almost certain that the power would pass to the Chiefs

of the German Army, who are by no means ready to accept the kind of terms which Britain and the United States deem essential to future world security.

3. The second main fact is seaborne tonnage. We can only get through this year by running down our stocks heavily. At the cost of much internal friction and disturbance, we may, by 'tightening the belt', save perhaps a million tons. Whether this should be done as a moral exercise, should be carefully weighed. It can, however, have no appreciable effect upon the problem of maintaining our war effort at home and abroad. There is no reason to assume that we cannot get through the present year or that the tonnage position in 1943 will not steadily improve as a result of the prodigious American shipbuilding. But we must be careful not to let our position deteriorate to an unmanageable degree before we have a clear understanding with the United States as to the future. With this object we must now in the next few weeks come to a solemn compact, almost a treaty, with the United States about the share of their new merchant ship building we are to get in 1943 and 1944. Up till the time when the United States entered the war, we had pretty well recouped ourselves for our losses by acquiring control of the shipping of Continental States as they were successively subjugated by the enemy. No more windfalls can be expected from this source. We can only expand our own building sensibly at dire expense to our war effort. Nothing we can do can change our minimum import requirements appreciably. The tonnage needed to guarantee these must be a first charge. We ought, therefore, to ask the United States to deliver to us during 1943 sufficient tonnage to occupy fully our available merchant crews. As it would be foolish to have large numbers of British life-trained merchant seamen and officers standing idle without ships while in the United States crews will have to be trained specially, our desire should not be deemed unreasonable.

4. On no account must we run our stocks down to a dangerous level for the sake of getting through 1942, without knowing where we stand in 1943. And the minimum stocks needed must not be written down unduly. Serious bombing of our ports might well hamstring our intake for considerable periods when we should be lost without something in the larder. Moreover, we should not start on the basis that the British should make a greater sacrifice of their pre-war standard of living than the American people. We should point out that any further curtailment of our imports taking 1942 and 1943 together can only be made through a definite curtailment of our munitions output. Already nearly three-quarters of British and British-controlled shipping is primarily employed

on the war effort, and only one-quarter is exclusively engaged in feeding and supplying this island.

5. It might be true to say that the issue of the war depends on whether Hitler's U-boat attack on Allied tonnage, or the increase and application of Allied Air power, reach their full fruition first. The growth of U-boat warfare and its spread to the most distant waters, as well as improvements in U-boat design, in a formidable degree must be expected. Against this may be set the increase of Allied anti-submarine craft and improvement in methods. But here is a struggle in itself.

6. On the other hand, we Allies have the Air power. In the days when we were fighting alone, we answered the question: 'How are you going to win the war?' by saying: 'We will shatter Germany by bombing'. Since then the enormous injuries inflicted on the German Army and man-power by the Russians and the accession of the man-power and munitions of the United States, have rendered other possibilities open. We look forward to mass invasion of the Continent by liberating armies, and general revolt of the populations against the Hitler tyranny. All the same, it would be a mistake to cast aside our original thought which, it may be mentioned, is also strong in American minds, namely, that the severe, ruthless bombing of Germany on an ever-increasing scale will not only cripple her war effort, including U-boat and aircraft production, but will also create conditions intolerable to the mass of the German population.

7. It is at this point that we must observe with sorrow and alarm the woeful shrinkage of our plans for Bomber expansion. The needs of the Navy and of the Middle East and India, the shortfall of our British production programmes, the natural wish of the Americans to fly their own bombers against the enemy, and the inevitable delay in these machines coming into action, all these falling exclusively upon Bomber Command, have prevented so far the fruition of our hopes for this summer and autumn. We must regard the Bomber offensive against Germany at least as a feature in breaking her war-will, second only to the largest military operations which can be conducted on the Continent, until that war-will is broken. Renewed, intense efforts should be made by the Allies to develop during the winter and onwards ever-growing, ever more accurate and ever more far-ranging Bomber attacks on Germany. In this way alone can we prepare the conditions which will be favourable to the major military operations on which we are resolved. Provision must be made to ensure that the bombing of Germany is not interrupted, except perhaps temporarily, by the need of supporting military operations. Having regard to the fact that Allied aircraft construction already outnum-

bers Axis aircraft construction by between two and three to one, these requirements should not be unattainable.

8. Although no expansion of ARP services can be accepted and, on the contrary, judicious pruning must still continue, we should be unwise to assume that heavy bombing attacks on Great Britain will not be renewed. At present over half of the German Bomber strength is occupied against Russia. By a transference to the West, the Germans could assemble during the next few months an equality in Bomber aircraft for our account. We have developed an elaborate, and indeed wonderful, system of scientific defence which has enabled us to await a renewal of the former 'blitz' with confidence. If anything should go wrong with this scientific system of defence, even though the enemy were similarly affected, then the reciprocal bombing of both countries would be conducted on very much the conditions of the winter of 1940–41. Should this develop, our advantage over Germany would have to be expressed by the ever-increasing numerical superiority of our Bomber aircraft and the bomb-content capable of being discharged by us.

Winston S. Churchill to President Franklin D. Roosevelt
(Churchill papers, 20/78)

21 July 1942
Personal and Most Secret
No. 121

I am anxious to do all I can to help you combat the U-boat.

As you are no doubt aware, there are some 300 BDEs[1] and DEs[2] building in United States at British request.

According to my information the twin screw corvettes building in Canada and the first BDEs and DEs complete at the same time.

The ocean-going minesweepers are a similar case.

2. We cannot tell which of us or where the enemy will strike in the different phases of the war. We must act according to circumstances. I would propose therefore that all the above-mentioned vessels and also the United Kingdom production should be thrown in the common pool

---

[1] BDEs: British Destroyer Escorts, small (1,140-ton), lightly armed ships of a design established by the Royal Navy on the basis of its experience in U-boat hunting. Used an all-welded steel hull, diesel engines, and mass production assembly methods.

[2] DE: Destroyer Escort, the classification for a small, lightly armed warship designed to be used to escort convoys of merchant marine ships. Employed primarily for anti-submarine warfare, but also provided some protection against aircraft and smaller attack vessels.

and assigned to the best common advantage according to needs. The machinery of the Combined Chiefs of Staff and the Munition Assignments Board is suited to the task. Decisions must be made in good time to allow the completing ships to receive United States or British equipment as the case may be. This procedure has already led to the transfer of 15 single screw corvettes to the United States Navy. It is in accordance with the general agreement about munitions and I urge that it should have our blessing.

As our need of the eight Fairmiles[1] is at this moment less urgent, the Admiralty are arranging their transfer now.[2]

Winston S. Churchill to General Hastings Ismay,
for the Chiefs of Staff Committee
(Churchill papers, 20/67)

22 July 1942

Special authority must be obtained from the COS Committee in respect of any mechanical vehicles shipped without being boxed. It may be convenient for the COS Committee to devolve this work either upon the Vice-Chiefs' Committee or to any one of the Vice-Chiefs of Staff selected for the purpose.

It is essential that, except where actual combat landings are to be prepared for, all mechanical transport should be boxed. The saving in shipping space achievable far exceeds the results of many galling restrictions on the life and food of the country.

I must ask for active and continuous help in this matter.

[1] Fairmile: Motor Torpedo Boat designed in 1942, armed with a 6-pound gun, 2 twin 0.5″ machine guns, Holman Projector, rocket flares, and two depth charges.

[2] Roosevelt replied to this telegram on 25 July 1942. His telegram No. 169 read: 'I agree that anti-submarine craft, whether British or American, should be assigned to operate in those areas where their services are most urgently needed as the intensity of the U-boat campaign shifts. It appears to me this disposition can best be decided upon from time to time by the combined Chiefs of Staff.

'Due to the need for active employment of all anti-submarine craft immediately upon being available after completion, it appears to me to be impracticable to establish a strategic pool of such craft if by this is meant a reserve pool of vessels not actually operating offensively against enemy submarines.

'In the allocation of anti-submarine craft prior to completion the primary consideration should be the expeditious completion of these craft for active operations. Such allocation should therefore be made in accordance with the prospective availability of essential equipment, whether British or American. Whether or not availability of equipment is the governing factor it would seem that allocation can best be accomplished through the machinery of the combined Chiefs of Staff. In other words I approve idea of the pool so long as everything in it is constantly employed' (*Churchill papers, 20/78*).

Lord Linlithgow to Winston S. Churchill
(Churchill papers, 20/78)

22 July 1942   New Delhi
Secret

Your fighter squadron 615 under command of Squadron Leader Duckenfield, AFC, is now operational and deployed in defence of Calcutta.

2. I am confident that it will fight as well over the Sundarbans in defence of India as it fought over the hop-fields of Kent in the Battle of Britain.

Winston S. Churchill to Lord Linlithgow
(Churchill papers, 20/78)

22 July 1942
Personal

Thank you so much. Please convey my good wishes to 615 Squadron. I am confident they will bring new distinction in India & Burma.

General Sir Alan Brooke: diary
('War Diaries, Field Marshal Lord Alanbrooke', page 283)

22 July 1942

Started COS at 10 a.m. and was sent for by PM at 10.45 to discuss proposed draft of telegram to hurry the Auk on to attack. I had telegram read to me by shorthand writer and asked to see it in type in order to save time and try and stop its despatch.

Oliver Harvey: diary
('The War Diaries of Oliver Harvey', page 142)

22 July 1942

PM on tenterhooks to know when Auck will launch his counter-offensive. Latter will never get more reinforcements than he has now, and Rommel will be getting more. PM wonders whether he should send A a telegram, but fears to hustle him.

Josef Stalin to Winston S. Churchill
(Cabinet papers, 65/31)

23 July 1942   Kremlin
Personal and Secret Moscow

I received your message of July 17. Two conclusions could be drawn from it. First, the British Government refuses to continue the sending of war materials to the Soviet Union via the Northern route. Second, in spite of the agreed communiqué concerning the urgent tasks of creating a Second Front in 1942 the British Government postpones this matter until 1943.

2. Our naval experts consider the reasons put forward by the British naval experts to justify the cessation of convoys to the northern ports of the USSR wholly unconvincing. They are of the opinion that with goodwill and readiness to fulfil the contracted obligations these convoys could be regularly undertaken and heavy losses could be inflicted on the enemy. Our experts find it also difficult to understand and to explain the order given by the Admiralty that the escorting vessels of the PQ17 should return, whereas the cargo boats should disperse and try to reach the Soviet ports one by one without any protection at all. Of course I do not think that regular convoys to the Soviet northern ports could be effected without risk or losses. But in war-time no important undertaking could be effected without risk or losses. In any case, I never expected that the British Government would stop despatch of war materials to us just at the very moment when the Soviet Union in view of the serious situation on the Soviet–German front requires these materials more than ever. It is obvious that the transport via Persian Gulf could in no way compensate for the cessation of convoys to the northern ports.

3. With regard to the second question, i.e., the question of creating a Second Front in Europe, I am afraid it is not being treated with the seriousness it deserves. Taking fully into account the present position on the Soviet–German front, I must state in the most emphatic manner that the Soviet Government cannot acquiesce in the postponement of a Second Front in Europe until 1943.

I hope you will not feel offended that I [have] expressed frankly and honestly my own opinion as well as the opinion of my colleagues on the questions raised in your message.

Winston S. Churchill: reflection
('The Hinge of Fate', page 242)

[23 July 1942]

These contentions are not well-founded. So far from breaking 'contracted obligations' to deliver the war supplies at Soviet ports, it had been particularly stipulated at the time of making the agreement that the Russians were to be responsible for conveying them to Russia. All that we did beyond this was a good will effort. As to the allegations of a breach of faith about the Second Front in 1942, our *aide-mémoire* was a solid defence. I did not however think it worth while to argue out all this with the Soviet Government, who had been willing until they were themselves attacked to see us totally destroyed and share the booty with Hitler, and who even in our common struggle could hardly spare a word of sympathy for the heavy British and American losses incurred in trying to send them aid.

The President agreed with this view.

Winston S. Churchill to General Hastings Ismay,
for the Chiefs of Staff Committee
(Churchill papers, 20/67)

23 July 1942
Most Secret
Action this Day

The following points seem to be important:

A re-emphasis of our intention to form a second front at the earliest possible moment, and continuance of all preparations for crossing the Channel, including the preliminary heavy reconnaissance raids.

2. Continuance of the WS convoys as arranged, namely: July, drafts; August, 56th Division; September, drafts; October, additional armoured division. This, with tanks and other material now on the way, should give General Auchinleck the following troops not yet engaged in the Western Desert:

10th Armoured Division, 2nd Brigade of 8th Armoured Division, 8th Armoured Brigade (4th Hussars and two RT Regiments), the additional armoured division, 44th, 51st, 56th Divisions, 5th and, if necessary, 2nd from India, one and a half Polish divisions, elements of two Indian divisions; in all at least ten divisions not yet engaged. It is not necessary to decide on sending more at present by WS convoys, apart from drafts, until we know how the battle goes in the Western Desert and how the Russian southern front fares. By the end of August we shall know far better how we stand in both quarters.

3. It is of the utmost importance to carry out 'Gymnast', with variants, at earliest possible. It seems very dangerous to delay beyond October. We should concert the whole plan with the United States authorities, offering them all the escorts and assistance in our power but pressing continually for speed.

4. Meanwhile, 'Bolero' should move steadily forward. It would seem necessary to replace with United States divisions in Great Britain by November the seven British divisions which will have sailed to the East. Over and above this, the full 'Bolero' programme should be pursued, subject only to impingement caused by 'Gymnast', &c. This impingement would fall for operational purposes in September and October and, for reinforcement of 'Gymnast', during November and December, by which time the American forces required for 'Gymnast' should have landed. Thereafter, unless we decide to move into Europe, only drafts and stores would be required. It should not be admitted that 'Gymnast', though it impinges temporarily on 'Bolero,' is at the expense of 'Roundup'.

5. If, however, we move from 'Gymnast' northward into Europe, a new situation must be surveyed. The flank attack may become the main attack, and the main attack a holding operation in the early stages. Our second front will, in fact, comprise both the Atlantic and Mediterranean coasts of Europe, and we can push either right-handed, left-handed or both-handed as our resources and circumstances permit.

6. For all these purposes we should strengthen 'Bolero' and 'Gymnast' with the largest transportations of United States troops that are possible. Meanwhile, we shall pin down the largest numbers possible of enemy troops opposite 'Bolero'. It is not wise to try now to look too far ahead. If, however, by June 1943 we have fifteen United States divisions and fifteen British ready to strike from Britain, and ten United States divisions, say, and four British available on which to draw for offensive action northward from the 'Gymnast' area, we shall be well placed.

7. It will be necessary to keep the 'Jupiter' threat continually effective by the making of plans and preparations. This will require some appearance of ships in the north, and the issue of the necessary snow equipment and training of some troops for Arctic service. The number to be available for combined operations with Russians would not exceed four

brigade groups. Thus the enemy may be kept in doubt of whether he will be struck in the north, the centre or the south.

8. In addition to the above, we ought to try to help Russia directly on her southern flank with air power. We have, hitherto, talked in terms of twenty squadrons, British and American, but it seems to me that we ought to aim jointly at at least forty by the end of the year, beginning with smaller numbers. With such a force, added to the divisions already available for this theatre, it should be possible to defend the Caspian Sea and the Caucasus Mountains, and to encourage Turkey to preserve neutrality, and thus shield the whole of the Levant–Caspian sector. The troops set out in paragraph 2 could then be regarded as capable of being used either to support the Levant–Caspian front or to move westwards into 'Acrobat', &c. In so vast and complex a scene above all it is specially desirable to have options open which allow of strategic manoeuvres according as events unfold.

Winston S. Churchill to Sir Kingsley Wood
(Churchill papers, 20/67)

23 July 1942

INDIA

Lord Keynes[1] mentioned to me the other night that we were incurring enormous indebtedness to India and to various Dominions and Colonies. Especially is this the case in regard to India. Are we, on the other hand, charging India for the defence services we are giving? Over 100,000 British troops are in India. The British Navy has sustained heavy losses in constantly guarding India. India has not yet been invaded. In my opinion all out-of-pocket charges by Great Britain for defending India or any other Colony must be set off against these book figures which are piling up.

How also does the case stand with the various Dominions? It is important that this question should be dealt with in good time, so that the Government of India know exactly what charges they are incurring with us. I wish the matter discussed at Cabinet.

---

[1] John Maynard Keynes, 1883–1946. Economist. Educated at Eton and King's College, Cambridge. Served at the India Office, 1906–8; the Treasury, 1915–19. Editor of the *Economic Journal*, 1911–44. Principal Treasury Representative at the Paris Peace Conference, 1919. Created Baron, 1942. Leader of the British Delegation to Washington to negotiate the American Loan, 1945. Among his publications were *The Economic Consequences of the Peace* (1919) and *The Economic Consequences of Mr Churchill* (July 1925).

Winston S. Churchill to Brigadier Francis Davidson[1]
(Churchill papers, 20/67)

23 July 1942

I always understood the proper terminology was:

    161 Brigade
    9th Division
    XII Corps
    Tenth Army.

On what principle are you working now?

2. On the Russian map it is important not to use arrows except to indicate attacks. Sometimes arrows are used to pull out the name of some Army, e.g., the Roumanian or Italian, which looks as if these large red panels were actually attacking. A small circle would be better instead of the arrowhead in these cases.

3. With regard to attacks of all kinds, there is nothing better than expressive arrows.

Winston S. Churchill to Stanley Bruce[2]
(Churchill papers, 20/54)

23 July 1942
Secret

Dear Mr Bruce,

I am sorry not to have thanked you sooner for the note on the Russian Convoys enclosed in your letter of July 7.

You no doubt realise that our margin in naval strength is so slight that if we either lose or have seriously damaged two or three units in the capital ship or large aircraft carrier classes we might lose control of our vital communications in either the Atlantic or Indian Ocean.

If we lost control of the Atlantic, not only would this country be paralysed but also Australia, and no more supplies would reach Russia via either Archangel or the Persian Gulf.

In the loss of the *Prince of Wales* and *Repulse* we have an example of what may happen to capital ships without fighter protection and the same thing might easily happen with Home Fleet in the Barents Sea as there are many days on which aircraft cannot be operated from carriers in these

[1] Director of Military Intelligence.

[2] High Commissioner for Australia in London and representative of Australia in the British War Cabinet.

Northern Waters, whereas shore-based aircraft can operate on any day on which their aerodromes are free from fog and make full use of the variations in visibility which so frequently occur in those latitudes.

The Midway Island battle also shows what may happen to capital ships and carriers when they pit themselves against shore-based aircraft. No doubt the Japanese ships were protected by fighters but this is no guarantee against a heavy attack by shore-based aircraft as if an attack is made by say 25 aircraft 20 may be shot down but the remainder will get in their attacks.

The Germans have sufficient aircraft in North Norway to deliver even heavier attacks than this, and indeed on this occasion they made a heavy attack on the convoy at 340 miles, and attacks on single ships at over 500 miles.

You remark that the passing of these Northern Convoys is vital but I am sure you will agree that it is much less vital than our control of sea communications. You speak of the risk that the Germans took in sending out the *Tirpitz* and suggest that we should be prepared to take equal risks. The cases are not however comparable. If we unreasonably risk the Home Fleet, we risk having our vital sea lines cut, whereas if the *Tirpitz* was sunk it would not affect Germany's position in the same way.

Naturally the Admiralty is trying to overcome these difficulties.

Yours sincerely,
Winston S. Churchill

General Sir Alan Brooke: diary
('War Diaries, Field Marshal Lord Alanbrooke', page 284)

23 July 1942

[...] Whilst lunching received message that PM wanted Chiefs of Staff to meet him at 3 p.m. Arrived there to be told latest developments in our negotiations with Americans. Roosevelt had wired back accepting fact that western front in 1942 was off. Also that he was in favour of attack in North Africa and was influencing his Chiefs in that direction. They were supposed to be working out various aspects with their staff and will probably meet us tomorrow. Winston anxious that I should not put Marshall off Africa by referring to Middle East dangers in 1943. Told him I must put whole strategic position in front of Americans. Foresee difficulties ahead of me!!

War Cabinet: Confidential Annex
(Cabinet papers, 65/31)

24 July 1942
5 p.m.

The Prime Minister reminded the War Cabinet that a telegram had been despatched to Premier Stalin on the 18th July[1] (No. 1073 from the Foreign Office to Kuibyshev) explaining that we had reached the conclusion, with the greatest regret, that to run the next convoy PQ18 would bring no benefit to the Russians and would only involve dead loss to the common cause. At the same time, if we could devise arrangements which would give a reasonable chance of a fair proportion of the convoys reaching Russia, we would start them again at once. In the meantime we would despatch immediately to the Persian Gulf some of the ships which were to have sailed in the PQ convoy.

The Prime Minister said that on the previous night M Maisky had handed to him the Russian reply. This was read out to the War Cabinet. (A copy is annexed to these Minutes as Annex A.) The Prime Minister also referred to a number of points in this telegram which were contrary to the facts. (See note appended to these Minutes as Annex B.)

It would be very easy for us to answer certain passages in this telegram; e.g., the statement that 'with good will and readiness to fulfil the contracted obligations, the convoys could be regularly undertaken'. But it was important that we should avoid a wrangle, which would be of no advantage to either of us. He had accordingly contented himself with saying to M Maisky that he would not have received a message in these terms but for the stern fight which the Russians were putting up against the Germans: that he would consult the Cabinet; but that his present view was that it would be better that Premier Stalin's telegram should be left unanswered: and that we would, of course, continue to do our utmost to help the Russians.

The Secretary of State for Foreign Affairs said that he had seen M Maisky that afternoon, and had expressed the view to him that it was a pity that an answer had been sent in these terms. He thought that, on the whole, it would be better that we should not answer Premier Stalin's telegram, as we could not do so without replying to the charges made in it. M Maisky had been disposed to agree with this view, more especially since Premier Stalin's telegram could perhaps be regarded as a reply to the Prime Minister's telegram of the 17th July. He had, however, sug-

[1] Actually sent on July 17.

gested that it would be very helpful if a full explanation could be given to him, and to his Naval Attaché, of the reasons why we had decided that we must discontinue sailing the convoys. Such a meeting might result in the Russians being persuaded that nothing could be done; or it might result in agreement that some action was possible. In any case it would result in a better understanding of each other's position, which would be something gained.

It was agreed that such an explanation should be given.

The Prime Minister said that M Maisky had also raised the point that apparently we had ceased heavy bombing attacks on Germany. He had replied that we had been doing all that was possible in bad weather; and that we had dropped more bombs in the preceding month on Germany than in any previous month. Further, we hoped to carry out some heavy bombing attacks in the approaching full moon period. He thought, however, that it would be desirable that a meeting should take place, at which an explanation could be given to M Maisky as to our bombing effort.

This course was agreed to.

[...]

The question was also raised as to Commando raids on the Continent, from the point of view of their effect on Russian morale. The Prime Minister said that he told M Maisky that heavy raids would be carried out in the near future.

The Prime Minister recalled that, at their Meeting two days earlier, it had been decided that the United States Chiefs of Staff should be asked to inform the President that it had not been found possible to reach agreement on the proposed plan for 'Sledgehammer' in 1942. General Marshall, however, had taken the line that he did not wish to report disagreement, and a telegram had been sent to the President by the United States Chiefs of Staff, to the effect that it had been agreed that there should be no 'Sledgehammer' operation in 1942.

On Thursday, the United States Chiefs of Staff had spent the whole day in discussion among themselves with United States Officers in this country. They had met our Chiefs of Staff that morning, and he understood that a most satisfactory conclusion had been reached, and had been embodied in a Memorandum.

[...]

The Chief of the Imperial General Staff then went through the Memorandum, and drew attention to the following points:

(i) Preparations for 'Sledgehammer' would be continued, for purposes of deception.

(ii) The Americans had expressed a desire to send an Armoured Division to the Middle East in British shipping, in substitution for an Armoured Division which we proposed to send to that theatre.

Winston S. Churchill to Sir James Grigg
(Churchill papers, 20/67)

24 July 1942

Inconvenience and unnecessary work is frequently caused by inaccuracies and inconsistencies in figures emanating from the War Office. MAP's[1] statistics have greatly improved since a strong Central Statistical Section, with high status and staff with first-rate qualifications, was set up. It may be that an equal improvement might be effected if the same were done in the War Office.

Pray make me proposals.

Winston S. Churchill to John Curtin
(Churchill papers, 20/88)

24 July 1942

I send you a minute which has been prepared by the Chiefs of Staff.

It had always been our intention to build up a considerable force in the Levant–Caspian area this summer, in order to provide against the possibility of a break on the Russian southern flank and a German advance through the Levant or Persia.

2. The extension of the war to the Far East compelled us:

(a) To divert to Malaya and India three British divisions (the 18th, 5th and 2nd) from the United Kingdom which would be otherwise have been available for the Middle East.

(b) To return from the Middle East to Australia two out of the three Australian Divisions.

(c) To send the 70th British Division from the Middle East to India.

(d) To despatch to Burma and Malaya certain British-Indian formations which were to have gone to Basra.

(e) To retain in India certain other British-Indian formations which were similarly destined.

---

[1] MAP: Ministry of Aircraft Production.

3. As a result, the Levant–Caspian front is now almost bare, and we entirely depend for the security of these vital regions on the Russian front holding. We estimate that, even if the Russians were to break, the Germans could not invade Iraq and Persia in great strength until the Spring of 1943; but if there were little or nothing there to stop them, they could push through with small forces at a much earlier date.

4. Much depends also upon the result of the battle now raging in Egypt. If we win, it may be possible to divert some of the forces now fighting in the Western Desert to secure the northern front; but these will be only a fraction of what is required.

5. We ourselves are doing everything we can to reinforce the Middle East. The 44th Division is just about to arrive; the 51st Division arrives next month; and the 56th Division is being prepared for despatch in August. This will probably be followed by a further armoured division from this country. In addition, we are prepared to move one, or even two, divisions from India, which is now less threatened.

6. Even, however, if General Auchinleck wins his battle and all the above reinforcements reach their destination, there will not be a man too many in the Middle East as whole. It is our considered opinion that to withdraw the 9th Australian Division at the present time, or, indeed, during this year (1942), would endanger the safety of the vital Abadan oilfields. Without them we cannot hope to maintain our position in the Middle East and the Indian Ocean. Some 60 per cent of Australia's oil requirements are supplied from this source, and, owing to heavy loss of tankers, could not be brought from elsewhere without the greatest difficulty, if at all.

7. Apart from the necessity on strategical grounds for retaining the well-seasoned 9th Australian Division in the Middle East, it must be remembered that its transportation to Australia, coupled with the transportation of a division to replace it, would involve an unjustifiable and dangerous shipping commitment.

Part II

I note the points you make about wastage and the difficulties you may find in despatching reinforcements from Australia. I very much hope that you will be able to overcome these difficulties and keep your fine Division, now gaining fresh distinction, up to strength. But should this prove impossible, I suggest that it would be necessary to fall back upon the expedient of making good wastage by breaking up ancillary units.

Anthony Eden: diary
('The Eden Memoirs, The Reckoning', page 337)

24 July 1942

Went to see Winston, who reported on a somewhat stormy interview with Maisky last night, when the latter brought a rough answer from Stalin [to the news of a convoy's postponement]. I told Winston that this was to be expected, but he was not to be easily soothed. Asked me to see Maisky, which I did, also Winant.

Last named was very critical of us for not starting up second front. I reminded him that his people did not suggest anything before October which would be useless for Russia and even then scale could not be enough, on American plan, to affect Eastern front. He had no arguments, but was obstinate and said we should ask Americans for what we wanted by given date and put it up to them. I told him I saw no use in this since we both knew American contribution must be of the smallest this year. I have never seen Winant so put out. He dislikes 'Gymnast'.

General Sir Alan Brooke: diary
('War Diaries, Field Marshal Lord Alanbrooke', page 285)

24 July 1942

At 4.30 p.m. we met PM and I put memorandum to him, he was delighted with it and passed it at once. At 5 p.m. Cabinet meeting first of all to discuss Stalin's reply to stopping Northern Convoy and intimation that western front was not possible. It was an unpleasant reply![1] Then PM got me to put up our memorandum to the Cabinet. From the start things went wrong! Anthony Eden and Cripps thought they saw a flaw in it, they began to argue about things they did not understand, others joined in, and very soon we had one of those situations I have now seen frequently in the Cabinet, where the real issue is completely lost in arguing out some detail which is misquoted and distorted in the discussion. I perspired heavily in my attempts to pull things straight and was engaged in heated arguments with Eden and Cripps with most of Cabinet taking sides. Bevin, John Anderson, Bruce and PM with me, Attlee, Oliver Lyttelton, Alexander against. In the end I triumphed and had the memorandum passed without a word being altered. Any changes would have

---

[1] Churchill wrote in his war memoirs: 'I need scarcely say I got a rough and surly answer' (*The Hinge of Fate*, page 241).

been fatal, the Americans have gone a long way to meet us, and I should have hated to have to ask them for more.

A very tiring week, but it is satisfactory to think that we have got just what we wanted out of the USA Chiefs. Have just been told that I am for Chequers tomorrow night!

Memorandum[1] to Kathleen Hill[2]
(Churchill papers, 1/371)

24 July 1942

Mr Plater of Harrods telephoned. Re the fish food that the PM wants for Chartwell, he finds that they do not deliver at all to Westerham, and not until next Friday at No. 10. Therefore unless he hears to the contrary, he proposes to bring the fish food with him on the day that the PM wants to meet him at Chartwell. If it is wanted before then, he will pop it in a taxi to No. 10 or send it by rail to Westerham.

He asks if you would be kind enough to acknowledge the visit which he paid to Chartwell the other day, for the records of Harrods, i.e. address the letter to Harrods, Ltd.

Winston S. Churchill to Admiral of the Fleet Sir Dudley Pound
(Churchill papers, 20/67)

25 July 1942

It was never intended to keep AS craft[3] idle in a pool, but only to treat the whole onflow of new construction as available for direction either to British or to American hands, the decision being taken on a forecast of the strategic situation at the time when the question of gun armament and other fittings had to be settled. Our use of the word 'pool' is perhaps unfortunate.

---

[1] The author of this note is named only as 'Joe'; it has not so far been possible to discover his surname or any further details about him.

[2] Rose Ethel Kathleen Hill, 1900–92. Chief Clerk, Automobile Association and Motor Union Insurance Company, Portsmouth, 1917–24. District Commissioner of Girl Guides, Bengal–Nagpur Railway, 1928–30. Secretary to the Chief Commissioner of Girl Guides for All-India, 1930–2. Broadcast as a solo violinist, Calcutta, Bombay, and Delhi, 1935–6. Returned to England, 1937. Churchill's first Residential Secretary, July 1937; lived at Chartwell from July 1937 to September 1939. Churchill's Personal Private Secretary from 1939 to 1946. MBE, 1941. Curator of Chequers, 1946–69. Kathleen sent the requested acknowledgement on 17 July 1942.

[3] AS: Anti-submarine.

Pray let me have a draft for the President, clearing the matter up. I was not aware there was shortage of equipment.

Winston S. Churchill to Peter Fraser
(Churchill papers, 20/78)

25 July 1942
Most Secret and Personal

General Auchinleck has raised question of keeping New Zealand Division up to strength. In asking you to consider ways and means of maintaining this splendid Unit on present basis, I cannot do better than quote Auchinleck's own words: 'Value of trained, acclimatized force, such as New Zealand Division, to Middle East is very great, and I view its possible reduction at present stage with great concern.'

2. Alternative to despatch of reinforcements for existing force would be (a) to break up New Zealand base organization with its training centres, schools of instruction, &c., or (b) gradual reduction of division in size.

3. I should be sorry to see either alternative adopted and hope they can be avoided by despatch of reinforcements from New Zealand.

4. I think you intended this month to review the possibility of moving your Army Tank Brigade to the Middle East. I certainly would not press for this if you decided to keep it in New Zealand for the present.

Winston S. Churchill to Field Marshal Jan Smuts
(Churchill papers, 20/78)

25 July 1942
Most Secret and Personal

Many thanks for your No. 1328.[1] All decisions are taken by the War Cabinet on the advice of the Chiefs of Staff's Committee, with both of which bodies I live in the closest association. Complete unity prevails inside this circle. This unity extends to the larger War Cabinet circle, which includes Dominions and Indian representatives and various additional Ministers of Cabinet rank, but, of course, it is not possible to initiate all war plans in so numerous a gathering. I can well believe there is fretfulness outside these two concentric circles. We are never likely to

---

[1] Telegram No. 1034/2 concerning the War Cabinet and Defence Committee.

run short of volunteers for the higher direction of the war. However, the political situation, both Party and Parliamentary, is quite solid, and, of course, it is well known that I would not continue to bear the responsibility without the modest directing powers I possess.

2. For the last week we have had General Marshall, Admiral King and Mr Hopkins from America with us, and have reached decisions which cover the whole field of the war. On these we have obtained complete unity between soldiers and statesmen and our two countries. With the war extending all over the world there are bound to be a great number of points of contact about which action must be taken, especially while the initiative remains with Germany and Japan. Moreover, the uncertainties of the great Russian battle and of the fighting in Egypt make it impossible to decide too far ahead.

3. I hope to send you shortly for your own personal and secret information an account of the policy we have settled. I am pretty sure you will like it.

Kindest regards. How I wish you were with us.

Winston S. Churchill to Air Vice-Marshal Hugh Lloyd
(Churchill papers, 20/78)

25 July 1942

I congratulate you on your brilliant fourteen months in Malta, and wish you continued success in your new important Command.[1]

Winston S. Churchill to Lord Selborne[2]
(Churchill papers, 20/54)

25 July 1942
Secret

My dear Top,

Thank you so much for sending me the Quarterly Progress Report of SOE activities. It is encouraging to learn of the steady increase in scale and in achievement of the work being done by these brave men.

Yours very sincerely,
Winston S. Churchill

---

[1] As Senior Air Staff Officer, HQ Middle East Command (appointed 15 July).
[2] Minister of Economic Warfare.

General Sir Alan Brooke: diary
('War Diaries, Field Marshal Lord Alanbrooke', pages 285–6)

25 July 1942

Was then sent for by PM who wanted to hear results of our morning meeting with Marshall and King. I told him that we had fixed up question of North Africa. USA to find Supreme Commander with British deputy. Under him two Task Force Commanders, one USA for Casablanca front, and one British for Oran front. I wanted Alexander for Task Force Commander. He wanted him to do both Deputy Supreme Commander and Task Force Commander! Had an hour's argument with him from 6 to 7 p.m. about, finally had to stop as it was time to start for Chequers!!

Arrived there at 8 p.m. Party consisted of PM, Mrs C, Marshall, King, Harry Hopkins, Harriman, 3 Chiefs of Staff, Pug, Martin and Tommy. After dinner American Chiefs were shown Cromwell's mask and Queen Elizabeth's ring. They then left by special [train] for Scotland to fly to America. After they left we were shown a good film, 'The Younger Pitt', and then 2 hours talk and bed at 2.45 a.m.! Dog tired and grateful this week is over.

John Martin: diary
(Sir John Martin papers)

26 July 1942   Chequers

An unusual evening on Friday, when we went down by river to Greenwich to a dinner given by the Admiralty in honour of certain visitors. Fortunately it was a fine day and the river and the Hospital looked their best in the soft evening light. I had not been down that way since before the outbreak of war and saw for the first time some of the blitz damage in the City and East End. Fortunately Greenwich Hospital itself has escaped serious damage and we were able to dine in the fine Painted Hall. I have never seen so many Admirals. Their Lordships gave us an excellent dinner, after which we went to the young officers' gunroom, where the PM toasted Admiral (Jackie) Fisher's grandson[1] who was one of them and happened to be celebrating his 21st birthday. Alexander, the First Lord, then sat down at the piano and for about an hour thumped out I should think every song in the Students' Song Book and conducted community

[1] John Vavasseur Fisher, 1921–. Educated at Stowe and Trinity College, Cambridge. Succeeded his father as 3rd Baron Fisher, 1955. Member, Eastern Gas Brigade, 1962–71; East Anglia Economic Planning Council, 1971–7. Director, Kilverstone Latin-American Zoo and Wild Life Park, 1973–91.

singing with great gusto. The room was crowded with sub-lieutenants, admirals and Wrens (who have a training course for officers at Green-wich), all singing at the tops of their voices (not excluding the PM), the most cheerful party I have seen for a long time. Altogether a memorable evening, which the Americans obviously enjoyed enormously. It ended with Auld Lang Syne and the two National Anthems.

Winston S. Churchill to General Hastings Ismay,
for the Chiefs of Staff Committee
(Churchill papers, 20/67)

26 July 1942

In view of 'Torch',[1] paragraph 5[2] may be affected. I consider it of great importance that 'Anakim' should not be turned down or hamstrung. Pray let me know what can be done to save the position; otherwise General Wavell's preparations will come to a standstill. Only the very gravest reasons should prevent General Wavell having the 'Ironclad' outfit of landing-craft. Let me know what these reasons are.

Winston S. Churchill to A. V. Alexander and
Admiral of the Fleet Sir Dudley Pound
(Churchill papers, 20/67)

26 July 1942

I am quite sure it would be unwise to make any such statement.[3] The Soviets have officially announced the safe arrival of the convoy, and we must respect their declaration. I do not think that the Royal Navy has much to fear from slanders of the kind you mention. At the same time, I await the report on the decision of Admiral Hamilton to withdraw the six destroyers from the convoy. Is it true that fifteen of the ships were sunk by U-boats, and only six by air?

The question of running a convoy in September must be studied, even if we cannot give it any more escort than last time. It may be *Tirpitz* will not be in the north and will have got tired of waiting at Narvik.

I recognize that 'Torch' is an additional complication.

---

[1] 'Torch': Allied invasion of French North Africa.
[2] Of Telegram No. 17502/C from Armindia (General Wavell) to Chiefs of Staff about 'Anakim'.
[3] Minute of 24 July 1942 from the First Lord of the Admiralty suggesting that a statement should be made on the recent convoy to Russia to counteract rumours that the Navy deserted the merchant ships.

Winston S. Churchill to Anthony Eden
(Churchill papers, 20/78)

26 July 1942
Most Secret and Personal

I am personally bound to Hopkins for the secrecy and privacy of this telegram,[1] which was sent largely at my desire. It is most important that Field-Marshal Dill should not be informed, on account of his exceptionally close relations with General Marshall. The President was vexed that Marshall told Dill before this visit the views of the American Chiefs of Staff, with which he, the President, did not agree. We must be very careful not to make bad blood between our American friends. I have therefore telegraphed as attached.

Winston S. Churchill to Anthony Eden
(Churchill papers, 20/67)

26 July 1942

Every effort should be made to prevent any such appeals[2] being made to Gandhi, who is at once debilitated and implacable.

We should make it clear both to the President and to the Generalissimo that we should strongly object to intervention of this kind.

Sir Ronald Campbell[3] to Winston S. Churchill
(Churchill papers, 20/78)

26 July 1942
Most Secret and Personal

In accordance with Foreign Office telegram No. 4485, Foreign Office telegram No. 4482 has been copied or shown by me to no-one except the President. In particular it has not been shown to Dill.

---

[1] Telegram No. 4482 of 25 July 1942 from Foreign Office to Washington: Mr Hopkins to President about operations in 1942 and 1943.

[2] Press report of a possible appeal to Gandhi by President Roosevelt and General Chiang Kai-shek.

[3] Ronald Ian Campbell, 1890–1983. Entered the Diplomatic Service, 1914. Minister Plenipotentiary, Paris, 1938–9. Minister at Belgrade, 1939–41. Knighted, 1941. Minister in Washington, 1941–5. Ambassador to Egypt, 1946–50. Director of the Royal Bank of Scotland, 1950–65.

Winston S. Churchill to President Franklin D. Roosevelt
(Churchill papers, 20/78)

27 July 1942
Personal and Most Secret

I was sure you would be as pleased as I am, indeed as we all are here, at the results of this strenuous week. Besides reaching complete agreement on action, relations of cordial intimacy and comradeship have been cemented between our high Officers. I doubt if success would have been achieved without Harry's invaluable aid.

2. We must establish a second front this year and attack at the earliest moment. As I see it this second front consists of a main body holding the enemy pinned opposite 'Sledgehammer' and a wide flanking movement called 'Torch' (hitherto called 'Gymnast'). Now that everything is decided we can, as you say, go full steam ahead. All depends on secrecy and speed and on having a regular schedule of political and military action. Every hour counts and I agree with you that October 30 is the latest date which should be accepted.

3. Secrecy can only be maintained by deception. For this purpose I am running 'Jupiter' and we must also work up 'Sledgehammer' with the utmost vigour. These will cover all movements in the United Kingdom. When your troops start for 'Torch' everyone except the secret circles should believe that they are going to Suez or Basra thus explaining tropical kit. The Canadian Army here will be fitted for Arctic service. Thus we shall be able to keep the enemy in doubt till the last moment.

4. Meanwhile I hope 'Bolero' processes will continue at full blast subject only to any necessary impingement upon them made by 'Torch', which impingement eventuates only in a certain delay. Thus we shall be able to strike left handed, right handed or both handed.

5. I talked to General Marshall about the scale of supplies and equipment at present laid down for United States forces in 'Bolero'. At 9 tons a man initial equipment and nine-tenths a ton a month maintenance this works out at 11,700,000 long tons for the first nine months and over 19 million for the second nine months, that is to say almost as much in 1943 for the American Expeditionary Forces, as we are planning for the whole importation of Great Britain both in food and raw materials. At present it is laid down that the first million Americans bring with them 175,000 motor vehicles or one for six men involving 175,000 drivers and probably as many more in the workshops for maintenance. According to

our joint shipping authorities, only two-thirds of the shipping required for such scales can be made available. It is, therefore, a case of coming with much fewer men or lighter scales. General Marshall promised to look into these scales with a view to cutting them drastically.

6. I have to draw so heavily on stocks this year to get through with 25 millions import, and even if this is achieved it is only one-half our pre-war import and 27 or 28 millions will be our minimum next year. It would be most imprudent to remain without any reserve stocks in case heavy bombing of the Mersey and Clyde begins again. I should be most grateful if you would examine this yourself. I am working here with Averill, Douglas and Leathers.

7. We were disappointed at not breaking Rommel's front last week though heavy losses were inflicted upon him in bitter fighting. We have far heavier reinforcements approaching and far better communications than he has and marked superiority in the air. The 8th British Armoured and 44th British Infantry Divisions are now landed, and the 51st British Infantry Division arrives in three weeks besides at least 40 or 50 thousand replacements flowing in steadily. The Shermans should arrive early in September and we hope to bring them into action during that month. Thus I feel confident we can defend Egypt and I trust Auchinleck may destroy this man where he now stands. I am delighted to have the United States Armoured Division and hope it may follow the 56th which lands early in October.

8. If Auchinleck beats Rommel we shall have about seven Divisions which can either be directed to follow up a victory in the Western Desert into 'Acrobat' or, should the Russian Southern Front give way, the Levant–Caspian theatre.

9. I still feel that in spite all other demands upon us we ought to try to place 20, 30, or even 40 Air Squadrons on the Russian Southern Flank thus helping them to hold the barrier formed by the Caspian, the Caucasus Mountains and a Turkey confirmed in neutrality. It also seems necessary to have something solid to offer Stalin. Whatever happens, however, nothing must interfere with 'Torch' or weaken Auchinleck before he has won.

Winston S. Churchill to General Hastings Ismay,
for the Chiefs of Staff Committee
(Churchill papers, 20/67)

27 July 1942
Most Secret

I am very much pleased with this proposal.[1] There should be no movement until General Auchinleck's battle is won, and no approach should be made to the Russians until I am in a position to address Premier Stalin personally on the subject. We need very much to make some definite proposal to him.

Please report further.

Winston S. Churchill to Oliver Lyttelton and others[2]
(Churchill papers, 20/67)

27 July 1942
Action this Day

We have at present made or are completing about 20,000 2.4-pounder T and A/T[3] guns. It is proposed in the next twelve months to make 20,000 more. This weapon is already out of date, and we shall be justly censured if we commit ourselves to a further enormous production of it. I understand that it is proposed to make a wide distribution to the infantry, so that every battalion may feel it can face enemy tanks. But the 2-pounder is not the weapon that we should make for this, as it cannot stop a tank except under the most favourable conditions. The Bombard or the Jefferis rifle rocket give better results and are much easier to make. Even the 6-pounder is now falling behind. In all these circumstances we must this week review the 2.4-pounder programme at a Defence (Supply) Committee, which I can preside over at 11.30 on Thursday morning, 30th July. We might also then consider the Tank supply position, including the progress made in improving the A 22s.

---

[1] To support the Russians with air forces based on Caucasia. Reference: IZ.968 (CC/88) 26.7.42 from Middle East.

[2] This minute was also sent to Sir James Grigg, Secretary of State for War; General Sir Alan Brooke, Chief of the Imperial General Staff; and Sir Andrew Duncan, Minister of Supply.

[3] T: tank; AT: anti-tank.

Winston S. Churchill to A. V. Alexander, Admiral of the Fleet,
Sir Dudley Pound, and General Ismay, for the Chiefs of Staff Committee
(Churchill papers, 20/67)

27 July 1942
Most Secret

When the decision was taken to drop the July convoy to Russia, it was thought that only one-quarter or perhaps one-eighth of the ships had got through. Now we know that one-third got in. This was achieved even in the most unfavourable circumstances. It is therefore necessary for us to consider running a September convoy, and I should like to be able to notify Premier Stalin of this at the earliest moment. I should myself prefer to await the results of 'Pedestal'[1] but in view of the tension in Russia it may not even be possible to do this before telling the Russians.

2. In view of the 'Torch', I no longer press for the movement northward of the 'Pedestal' ships. It would seem right to attach two auxiliary carriers to the convoy and every effort must be made to ward off attacks by surface ships. It may be that the interruption of the convoys may lead to a withdrawal of the *Tirpitz* more to the south. She has been out of dock a long time now. In any case, if the convoy attracted the *Tirpitz* over two lines of submarines we, on our side, should have a chance too. Pray let me, therefore, have your proposals as soon as possible.

3. It is essential that we should demand greater exertions from the Russians at the reception end. Is it possible to reinforce them by a squadron of heavy bombers from here? I should not propose to send the air personnel in this convoy.

4. We have now had a negative answer about combined operations in the North Russia. New proposals are being studied by the Chiefs of Staff about placing an Anglo-American air contingent on the Russian southern flank.

5. I should like to be able to announce both these intentions, i.e., the convoy and the southern flank air reinforcements in the same message.

6. The Minister of War Transport should make proposals for a September convoy.

---

[1] Convoy to Malta, August 1942.

Winston S. Churchill to General Claude Auchinleck
(Churchill papers, 20/78)

27 July 1942
Personal and Most Secret

I have not troubled you with messages while you have been so fiercely engaged, but you and your Army have never been out of our thoughts for an hour.

2. It seems to me you have the advantage of Rommel in the air, in communications and, above all, in the reinforcements which, luckily, we sent in good time.

3. I should be glad if you would let me know when the 44th Division will be able to go into action, and I hope you will find it possible to let it fight as a unit and not be forced to melt it down like so much else for the exigencies of battle.

4. Could you also reassure me about the Siwa Oasis on which I asked CIGS to send you a telegram? I have no doubt you have thought it all out.

5. CIGS is coming out to you early next week. He will be able to tell you about our plans, which are considerable. See my immediately following telegram, which should be deciphered by your personal staff.

Winston S. Churchill to General Claude Auchinleck
(Churchill papers, 20/78)

27 July 1942
Personal and Most Secret

To be deciphered by General Auchinleck's personal staff.

Reference paragraph 5 of my immediately preceding telegram, the following is for your eye alone.

Last week we had General Marshall, Admiral King, and Mr Hopkins with us here. Complete agreement has been reached by all concerned that the Americans and ourselves make a combined attack in October on the lines of 'Gymnast' expanded to cover the north as well as the west shores of that area. Everything is concentrated on this, and the President has given the order 'full steam ahead'. Secrecy and speed are vital. You will see how this, if successful, would fit in with 'Acrobat', if ever the Russian situation and your own achievements render such an enterprise possible.

War Cabinet: Confidential Annex
(Cabinet papers, 65/31)

27 July 1942
5.30 p.m.

The First Sea Lord said that the position regarding convoy PQ17 was as follows:

10 ships had reached Archangel.
1 was still on the way.
1 was unaccounted for.
21 had been sunk.

If the ship still in passage reached port safely, the convoy would have delivered to Russia 164 tanks, 896 vehicles of various kinds, 87 aircraft, in addition to general cargoes of considerable size.

The Prime Minister pointed out that practically one-third of the convoy had reached Archangel. This was better than we had at one time expected. There was much to be said for attempting to run a further convoy to North Russia in September. By that time, the Germans might have withdrawn their naval forces from North Norway. There would be great political advantage if we could tell the Russians that this was our plan.

The Secretary of State for Foreign Affairs strongly favoured the despatch of a convoy in September.

The First Lord of the Admiralty said that a number of loaded ships were being held up in Iceland. The crews of these ships were giving trouble, and the position would certainly deteriorate if they were left there until September. It was for consideration whether the ships should not be brought to this country.

The Prime Minister said that 6% of the merchant seamen in Convoy PQ17 had lost their lives. The remainder were in North Russia, and, after what they had gone through, it seemed unfair to call upon them to make the return journey until there was more darkness in Northern waters

Winston S. Churchill to John Curtin
(Churchill papers, 20/78)

27 July 1942
Most Secret and Personal

I am sorry to have to tell you that, owing to lack of suitable shipping facilities, we shall not be able to despatch during July the whole of the 50

Spitfires which we undertook to send you during the month. Only 12 will actually have left by the end of this month, but we are using a special ship which will sail about 5th August in order to send you as soon as possible the outstanding 38, and we will include also 8 of the August quota. The remaining 14 of the August quota will leave about 12th August.

Winston S. Churchill to Commander Stephen King-Hall[1]
(Churchill papers, 20/54)

27 July 1942
Private and Confidential

Dear Commander King-Hall,

Mrs Churchill has shown me your News-Letter[2] of July 23, and I think it might be a good thing if you had a talk with Air Marshal Harris, Commander-in-Chief Bomber Command. If you like this idea I will arrange a meeting, being convinced that you will use any confidential facts which may be disclosed to you with all discretion and propriety.

Our Bomber Command is making an intense effort at the present time, having regard to the inroads made upon it for the sake of Coastal Command, the Middle East, etc., and the proportion of sorties to machines is higher than ever before.

Yours sincerely,
Winston S. Churchill

President Franklin D. Roosevelt to Winston S. Churchill
(Churchill papers, 20/78)

28 July 1942   Washington DC
Secret

The Three Musketeers arrived safely this afternoon, and the wedding is still scheduled. I am of course very happy in the result, and especially in the successful meeting of minds. I cannot help feeling that the past week represented a turning-point in the whole war and that now we are on our way shoulder to shoulder. I agree with you that secrecy and speed are vital, and I hope the October date can be advanced. I will talk with

[1] Director of Factories Defence, Ministry of Aircraft Production, and founder of the weekly *King-Hall News Letter.*

[2] *News Letter* No. 315 of 23 July 1942 made reference to a statement issued by Roosevelt and Churchill the previous month which had said 'that the coming operations... will divert German strength from the attack on Russia' and noted the lack of any sign of this happening.

Marshall in regard to scale of supplies and equipment in terms of tonnage and in terms of the UK importations of food and raw materials. Also I will do my best to get the air squadrons on the Russian southern flank. I fully agree that this should be done.

War Cabinet: conclusions
(Cabinet papers, 65/27)

28 July 1942   10 Downing Street
5.30 p.m.

The Prime Minister said that our approach to the United States authorities must be put on the basis that sufficient shipping must be provided to enable us to import 25 million tons in 1942 and 27 million tons in 1943. These import programmes must be regarded as irreducible minima, and must have the first call on the shipping available.

Shipping for the 'Bolero' movement must rank second in priority to the requirements of this import programme, for the 'Bolero' requirements were subject to variation if not in quantity, at any rate in time. The completion date of the 'Bolero' movement could, if necessary, be postponed for one or two months if it became necessary to use the shipping which would be set free by such a postponement for fulfilling the needs of our minimum import programme.

[...]

The Prime Minister said that, as our Forces now had to fight overseas, it was essential that they should learn to travel light. It followed that further measures must be taken to cut down to the bare minimum the establishments of the rearward formations. There must be a searching enquiry into the use of man-power in the three Services with a view to reducing the numbers of ancillary and non-combatant personnel, thereby facilitating any necessary increases in combatant troops. An enquiry into this question should be held by a Committee of Cabinet Ministers.

Winston S. Churchill to Oliver Lyttelton
(Churchill papers, 20/67)

28 July 1942
Action this Day

I do not know whether you realise the extreme gravity of the incendiary bomb position. The shortage is so acute that it is forcing the

RAF to restrict the scale of fire-raising attacks planned for the next few months.

Are we going to get our fair share of the magnesium available from America this year? In your Minute of the 5th May, you told me you would take this matter up on the highest level if satisfactory assurances could not be obtained.

Is the development of substitutes for the use of magnesium (such as those described in DC (S) (42) 50) going ahead at full speed?

Pray let me know what supplies the RAF can expect in the coming autumn and winter.

William Mackenzie King to Winston S. Churchill
(Churchill papers, 20/65)

28 July 1942   Ottawa[1]

Have just had a delightful few hours with Randolph who honoured me with a visit today. He is looking exceedingly well and is most cheerful. All good wishes.

Mackenzie King

Winston S. Churchill to William Mackenzie King
(Churchill papers, 20/65)

28 July 1942

Thank you so much for receiving him so kindly.

Winston S. Churchill

Winston S. Churchill to Admiral Harold Stark[2]
(Churchill papers, 20/54)

28 July 1942

My dear Admiral,

Thank you so much for your letter. I think we shall always remember the very happy evening we had together at Greenwich.

---

[1] On 17 July 1942 Randolph Churchill had telegraphed to his father from the Gold Coast: 'Returning via Natal and United States. Longest way round is shortest way home. Love' (*Churchill papers, 20/65*).

[2] Commander, United States Naval Forces in Europe.

How kind of you to send me a record of 'Home on the Range'. I played it at Chequers and enjoyed it very much.

For Japan it might be reversed 'Range on the Home'.

Yours sincerely,
Winston S. Churchill

Sir Charles Wilson: diary
('Winston Churchill, The Struggle for Survival', pages 47–8)

28 July 1942

I was summoned this morning to No. 10 Downing Street, where I heard that we should soon be on the move. The PM has decided to fly to Cairo. From Gibraltar he will fly south to Takoradi on the Gold Coast, and so across Central Africa to Cairo. It means about five days in the air, landing at places where malaria and yellow fever are rife. The PM wanted my advice about inoculations. I did not like the plan and gave my reasons.

As I was leaving I met John Anderson.[1] He said that certain members of the Cabinet were concerned about the Prime Minister's travels and the dangers he was running in flying over hostile territory in an unarmed bomber. He and Cripps had arranged to see the PM this afternoon, and, as health might come up, he would like me to be there.

At the appointed hour I joined them in the Cabinet Room. I was most concerned with the actual risk of the protective measures against yellow fever. While we were discussing these problems, the door opened and the Prime Minister hurried in, beaming at us disarmingly – always a sign that he is up to mischief. He began to unfold a large map, spreading it on the table.

'Vanderkloot[2] says it is quite unnecessary to fly so far south. He has explained to me that we can fly in one hop to Cairo. Come here and look.'

Sir John knelt on a chair to get nearer the map, while Cripps leant over his shoulder. The PM, with a pencil, traced the route from Gibraltar across Spanish Morocco till he struck the Nile, where his pencil turned sharply to the north.

'This changes the whole picture,' the PM added confidently.

---

[1] Lord President of the Council.

[2] William J. 'Bill' Vanderkloot, 1915–2000. American pilot who flew for Churchill. Graduated from the Parks Air College, East St Louis, Illinois. Before the Second World War he worked as a commercial pilot flying DC-2s and DC-3s.

I ventured to ask who Vanderkloot was. It appeared that he had just crossed the Atlantic in a bomber, and it is in this machine that we are to fly to Cairo. I wondered why it was left to an American pilot to find a safe route to Cairo, but that did not seem a profitable line of speculation.

'You see, Charles, we need not bother about inoculations.'

Anderson and Cripps pored over the map like excited schoolboys, and the party broke up without a word of warning or remonstrance about the risks the PM was taking in flying over hostile territory in an unarmed bomber by daylight. The PM gets his own way with everyone with hardly a murmur.

President Franklin D. Roosevelt to Winston S. Churchill
(Churchill papers, 20/78)

29 July 1942
Personal and Most Secret

I agree with you that your reply to Stalin must be handled with great care. We have got always to bear in mind the personality of our Ally and the very difficult and dangerous situation that confronts him. No one can be expected to approach the war from a world point of view whose country has been invaded. I think we should try to put ourselves in his place. I think he should be told in the first place, quite specifically that we have determined upon a course of action in 1942. I think that, without advising him of the precise nature of our proposed operations, the fact that they are going to be made should be told him without any qualifications.

While I think that you should not raise any false hopes in Stalin relative to the Northern convoy, nevertheless I agree with you that we should run one if there is any possibility of success, in spite of the great risk involved.

I am still hopeful that we can put air-power directly on the Russian front, and I am discussing that matter here. I believe it would be unwise to promise this air-power only on condition that the battle in Egypt goes well. Russia's need is urgent and immediate. I have a feeling it would mean a great deal to the Russian Army and Russian people if they knew some of our Air Force was fighting with them in a very direct manner.

While we may believe that the present and proposed use of our combined Air Forces is strategically the best, nevertheless I feel that Stalin does not agree with this. Stalin, I imagine, is in no mood to engage in a theoretical strategical discussion, and I am sure that other than our major operation the enterprise that would suit him the best is direct air support on the southern end of his front.[1]

Winston S. Churchill to Lord Leathers
(Churchill papers, 20/67)

29 July 1942

SHIPPING LOSSES

The recent statement in America that our losses in the week beginning July 12th had been the worst since the outbreak of war was most unfortunate. It can only be understood if the American authorities work on a notification basis, and by some mischance were notified in this one week of losses which had actually occurred in the course of several weeks. Such a procedure naturally gives no true picture of the course of the war at sea.

We should try to work out with the Americans a common policy about publication of shipping losses. Perhaps you would take up with their authorities, if you have not already done so, the question whether any figures at all should be made public, and if so, what they should cover.

Pray let me know the result.

Winston S. Churchill to Clement Attlee
(Churchill papers, 20/67)

29 July 1942

Your paper[2] poses a great many questions, the answers to some of which you already know.

1. In no case have the Germans received more effective support from their air force than we have had from ours during the battle in Libya. It is not true that the dive-bomber conferred any important advantage on the enemy.

2. The reason we have not got air transport machines is that our factories from the beginning have been concentrated upon making fighters and bombers. We only had just enough fighters to come through the

---

[1] Churchill's response to this telegram in his memoir was: 'I therefore let Stalin's bitter message pass without any specific rejoinder. After all, the Russian armies were suffering fearfully and the campaign was at its crisis' (*The Hinge of Fate*, page 243).

[2] A memorandum of 10 July 1942 by Attlee posing certain questions with regard to the war effort.

Battle of Britain, and we have far too few bombers now to do justice to the targets presented in Germany. As you know, measures have been taken for six months past to develop a larger air transport service. I am sure it would be a mistake to cripple our bomber effort.

3. These criticisms have become commonplaces. There is no doubt we had not sufficient forces to withstand the attack of Japan while we were so heavily engaged with Germany and Italy.

4. I have no doubt that CIGS will give you a report upon these points.

5. I agree with you about Commandos, and I have myself rescued them from the orthodox school. Most British authorities hold that it is bad for an Army to differentiate between Storm Troops and the rest. Certainly the Germans have profited by it. One must take care, however, not to rot the Army by making out that only Commandos can fight.

6. It is easy to mix up cause and effect in these matters. The Germans had been preparing for war for at least ten years in the most active manner, while our Army was grudged and stinted in every way. Compulsory service was only introduced a few months before the outbreak. The career of an officer in the British Army was depressing compared to the attractions of civil life. Most of the rewards of British public life went to the politicians. That is no doubt why the standard is so high. It must also be remembered that Britain for the last twenty years was hagridden by pacifism and haunted by the craven fear of being great, while Germany was passionately preparing for a war of revenge and world dominion. I certainly have never claimed that we are as expert in land warfare as the Germans. We hold our own better in the air and on the sea.

7. The fighting organization of the division is about 15,000. The figure of 40,000 is obtained by adding its share of corps, army, line of communication troops and a host of other services of the rear. Tactically the division is a very well-proved unit, to which people have got accustomed. I agree with you that when the operations are on a small scale the brigade group is preferable. The new organisation of divisions in two infantry and one army tank brigade seems very good. It is certainly the result of the most modern thought and experience. I am assured that the Corps Command do a great deal of useful work, and it is noteworthy that the present battle in Egypt is being fought by two corps organizations, the 13th and 30th, which have apparently evolved themselves under the stress of continuous battle. The CIGS would give you particulars about the need of preserving Corps Commands in Great Britain, and why it has not been thought wise to go direct from the division to the Army.

8. I shall welcome any help you can give to reduce the present excessive standards of transport. The new Cabinet Committee, over which you preside, will give you opportunities for this and generally for cutting down redundant services of the rear. As you know, I have persistently worked to comb the tail in order to sharpen the teeth.[1] We are in full agreement about this.

9. You will no doubt bring this matter before the Cabinet Committee. I cannot think that our policy of a separate air force has been wrong. The great mass of our Army has not been engaged, and if we had had large numbers of squadrons bound to the Army we should not have had the fighter strength to save ourselves from destruction in the Battle of Britain. Naturally, the Army would like to have a great mass of air force and air transport planes permanently at its disposal, and the same is true of the Navy. But the real test must be the maximum air action against the enemy, which certainly could not be achieved by keeping large masses of the Air Force idle.

10. Continuous reflection leaves me with the conclusion that, upon the whole, our best chance of winning the war is with the big bombers. It certainly will be several years before British and American land forces will be capable of beating the Germans on even terms in the open field.

11. We have not built up land forces beyond the minimum necessary to defend this island, the Nile Valley, and India. Should the Germans turn from Russia against us, we should hardly have a division to spare.

12. We reinforced India with three divisions, and are now having to withdraw two of them to the Levant–Caspian front. I was not aware that you had wished to send British garrisons to Australia and South Africa. The United States have sent reinforcements to Australia, and South Africa is well protected by British sea power. The more we can bomb Germany, the better for all concerned.

13. The growth of Coastal Command at the expense of Bomber Command is a very marked feature. The only thing that is doing any good at the present time has been cut down to one-eleventh of our total first-line strength. It would be a disaster to cut them further. Personally, I increasingly feel that this is the most hopeful of our various methods of attack, though by no means the only one.

14. If these questions have not been considered already, I cannot conceive what the General Staff of the Army exists for.

---

[1] The image relates to the beaver, which has both sharp teeth to get its job done and a paddle-like tail to protect itself at the rear (see Linda Pickard, 'Using Animal Wisdom to Sharpen Leadership Acumen', MyLeadership website).

15. I should be glad if you would read my paper on artillery. Everything shows that artillery is coming back into its own on land. To withdraw our Bomber Force from the cities, factories, and seaports of Germany to be a mere handmaid of the Army, bombing airfields and railway junctions behind the hostile front, would be a great relief to the enemy.

16. I agree with this.

17. All the papers bearing on this discussion are available, and you should ask General Ismay for them.

18. I have no doubt that this has been studied, and I expect that preparations are made on a more than lavish scale. By all means discuss the matter with CAS. The Air Force establishments in the Middle East are terrifying in lavishness.

19. To some extent I agree with this, but General Auchinleck has been very close to the fighting. It is noteworthy that two Major-Generals commanding the 2nd Armoured Division were shot down in three days, so that they must have been somewhere near the fighting.

20. You might well discuss these points with CIGS.

21. It would be disastrous to destroy the characteristic of the Air Force in this way. We have only to remember what happened in the action in Egypt in June 1941 to see how inefficiently the Army can use the air in little umbrellas over the different columns. Everything I hear from the front in Egypt favours the existing system.

22. All these questions are the subject of constant study, and the answers to many of them can be given immediately and with precision. I do not understand your suggestion about one man being put over the Vice-Chiefs of Staff with authority over them. I should think that would raise difficulties with the Chiefs of Staff as to whose authority was to prevail.

23. Pray let me have any proposals you may have in mind with regard to our planning machinery. I am sure you are familiar with it.

24. I should suppose that this is the main task that General Wavell has in hand at the present time. General Alexander, who is home, could no doubt tell you what is being done to profit by the lessons learned in the Burma campaign.

Winston S. Churchill to President Franklin D. Roosevelt
(Churchill papers, 20/78)

29 July 1942
Most Secret

Campbell is being instructed to communicate to you Stalin's answer to my message of the 18th July.

2. I do not propose to embark on an argument, but Stalin will no doubt expect some account of our recent conversations here on the second front. Subject to what you may feel, I propose to refer Stalin to the Aide-Mémoire explaining our attitude handed to Molotov here just before he left for Moscow, which I showed you, and to say that it still represents our general position, but that we have agreed with you on certain action, although at present stage nothing can be said about time and place.

3. We might also say that we hope to resume convoys in September, if Russians can provide necessary air force to deny German surface ships use of Barents Sea, and that if the battle in Egypt goes well we should be able to make a firm offer of air support on the Russian southern flank.

4. What are your views?

5. In the meanwhile, we are explaining to Maisky in detail nature of problems of Russian convoys and latest position about bombing attacks on Germany and plans for Commando raids.

Anthony Eden: recollection
('The Eden Memoirs, The Reckoning', pages 337–8)

29 July 1942

On July 29th I dined with rest of the War Cabinet at No. 10 Downing Street to meet the King. I sat on the other side of the Prime Minister. He suggested that he should make a visit to Egypt. I did not pay much heed, for he had proposed this before. When the King had gone, however, Mr Churchill suddenly said at 1 a.m., 'Now, we'll have a Cabinet', and proposed that he should leave for Egypt two days later. Mr Attlee nodded his head. Nobody else said much, except Mr Bevin, who approved. I thought that they were all as surprised as I and only learnt afterwards that some of them were not. I asked whether the doctor approved, but I was also troubled by the risks of the journey, though it was clearly useless to speak to the Prime Minister about these; they would only whet his appetite.

Field Marshal Sir John Dill to Winston S. Churchill
(Churchill papers, 20/78)

30 July 1942
Private

Had a talk with President this evening. He is, of course, full out for 'Torch' and will press preparations here to utmost.

2. He had just had a talk with Litvinoff who, as the President said, can always be trusted to take a pessimistic view. Nevertheless President was somewhat disquieted by the views which Litvinoff expressed. He is just a little afraid that in their anguish Russians may say 'Britain and America do not love us or they would do more to help; what is there left to us except to make the best peace we can'. This is how the President put it in chatty conversation.

3. To show some love for Russia President is turning over two projects in his mind. First is to ask you to run another convoy, if only of twenty ships, by the northern route in September. And second is to give the Russians air support by way of Caucasia.

4. This is just to let you know how President's mind is working. If these ideas develop further he will of course telegraph you direct. He is off for a few days rest which he badly needs.

Anthony Eden: diary
('The Eden Memoirs, The Reckoning', page 338)

30 July 1942

Took the telegram[1] round to Winston and he jumped at it. W agreed to a Cabinet before luncheon.

At meeting he asked me what I thought. I said that on reflection I had liked less and less idea of his visit to Egypt. That I should have advised against journey for that alone. But that this new development seemed to me to put a different complexion on whole business, and if Joe were prepared to invite him I thought he should go. All this of course subject to doctor's all clear. The others agreed.

---

[1] Eden wrote in his memoirs: 'Cadogan showed me a personal telegram from Sir Archibald Clark Kerr, our Ambassador in Moscow, suggesting an early visit by the Prime Minister to Stalin. I wrote in my diary that "A meeting in Astrakhan, or even Moscow, with Joe (Stalin) at a time like this might indeed pay a dividend"' (*The Eden Memoirs, The Reckoning*, page 338).

Winston S. Churchill to President Franklin D. Roosevelt
(Churchill papers, 20/78)

30 July 1942
Personal and Most Secret

I have sent the telegrams which follow to Stalin and I hope you will authorize me to tell him what we have settled. I am sure I can state the case in all its bearings.

2. It was necessary for me on other grounds to go to Cairo. The CIGS will come with me in both cases. I am also asking Smuts and Wavell to come to Cairo.

3. The Admiralty are prepared to try to run another PQ convoy of 40 ships about September fourth.

4. I cannot give up any aircraft from the Middle East till Rommel is beaten but anything additional you can find for the Southern Russian front will be a God-send.

Winston S. Churchill to Josef Stalin
(Churchill papers, 20/88)

30 July 1942

We are making preliminary arrangements (see my immediately following message) to make another effort to run a large convoy through to Archangel in the first week of September.

2. I am willing, if you invite me, to come myself to meet you in Astrakhan, the Caucasus, or similar convenient meeting-place. We could then survey the war together and take decisions hand-in-hand. I could then tell you plans we have made with President Roosevelt for offensive action in 1942. I would bring the Chief of the Imperial General Staff with me.

3. I am starting for Cairo forthwith. I have serious business there, as you may imagine. From there I will, if you desire it, fix a convenient date for our meeting, which might, so far as I am concerned, be between the 10th and 13th August, all being well.

4. The War Cabinet have endorsed my proposals.

Oliver Harvey: diary
('The War Diaries of Oliver Harvey', page 145)

30 July 1942
Afternoon

It has now been decided that the PM should do both. He is to start tomorrow for Egypt, meanwhile to telegraph to Stalin proposing to visit him and to pick up Stalin's reply en route. AE's visit to America must wait. But what energy and gallantry of the old gentleman, setting off at 65 across Africa in the heat of mid-summer!

War Cabinet: Confidential Annex
(Cabinet papers, 65/27)

30 July 1942   10 Downing Street
12.45 p.m.

[...] The Secretary of State for Foreign Affairs said that, politically, a meeting between the Prime Minister and M Stalin would be of the greatest value, and, in his view, would be of far more value than a visit by the Prime Minister to Egypt. Against the advantages of such a visit there must, however, be put the risks to the Prime Minister's health which such a journey would involve.

The Prime Minister said that he believed it was his duty to go on this journey. The risk to health should not be over stressed, and he felt confident of his fitness to undertake the journey. His medical adviser, Sir Charles Wilson, would go with him, and he would take all due precautions. He proposed to telegraph to M Stalin to say that he was coming out to Egypt and that he would like to meet him at Astrakhan, or such other place as would suit M Stalin, in order to give him an account of our discussions with the United States authorities and of our plans for 1942. He would take to meet M Stalin the Chief of the Imperial General Staff, who was flying out to Egypt separately, and Sir Alexander Cadogan.

Sir Alexander Cadogan: diary
('The Diaries of Sir Alexander Cadogan', pages 464–5)

30 July 1942

[...] Martin[1] tells me PM's doctor, Attlee and Anderson trying to dissuade him from going! Heard later he insisted on doing so, but prob-

---

[1] John Martin, Churchill's Principal Private Secretary.

ably Saturday night[1] – not tomorrow night! [...] Bore not knowing one's plans. Don't know yet for sure, as PM has still to be tested tomorrow morning for 'high flying'.

Josef Stalin to Winston S. Churchill
(Churchill papers, 20/78)

31 July 1942   Kremlin
Absolutely Secret   Moscow

On behalf of the Soviet Government I invite you to the USSR to meet the members of the Government. I should be very grateful if you could come to the USSR to consider jointly the urgent questions of war against Hitler, as the menace from these quarters to Great Britain, the United States of America, and the USSR has now reached a special degree of intensity.

I think the most suitable meeting-place would be Moscow, as neither I nor the members of the Government and the leading men of the General Staff could leave the capital at the moment of such an intense struggle against the Germans.

The presence of the Chief of the Imperial General Staff would be extremely desirable.

The date of the meeting please fix yourself in accordance with the time necessary for completion of your business in Cairo. You may be sure beforehand that any date will suit me.

Let me express my gratitude for your consent to send the next convoy with the war materials for the USSR at the beginning of September. In spite of the extreme difficulty of diverting aircraft from the battle-front we will take all possible measures to increase the aerial protection of the convoy.

Winston S. Churchill to Josef Stalin
(Churchill papers, 20/78)

31 July 1942
Personal and Secret

My immediately preceding message.

We are making preliminary arrangements for sailing a convoy of forty ships during the first week in September. I must make it clear, however,

[1] 1 August 1942.

that there is little chance of even one-third of the ships getting through to you, as was the case in PQ17, unless the air threat to the German surface forces in the Barents Sea is such as to deter the latter from operating against the convoy. As you are no doubt aware the situation has been discussed with Maisky and I understand the latter has communicated to you what we consider the minimum air requirements.

Winston S. Churchill to President Franklin D. Roosevelt
(Churchill papers, 20/78)

31 July 1942
Absolutely Secret

I should be grateful for a decision about the command of 'Bolero', 'Sledgehammer', 'Round-up', and 'Torch'.[1] It would be agreeable to us if General Marshall were designated for the Supreme Command of 'Round-up', and that in the meanwhile General Eisenhower should act as his deputy here. We would appoint General Alexander as Task Force Commander in the first instance, to work with and under General Eisenhower. Both these men would work at 'Torch', and General Eisenhower would also for the time being supervise the 'Bolero'–'Sledgehammer' business. He will thus be able to draw for 'Torch' the necessary forces with the least injury to 'Bolero' and 'Round-up'. As soon as 'Torch' has taken shape he would command it, with Alexander and an American commander as Task Force Commanders of the two forces, starting from United Kingdom and United States. When this party starts out to do the job we should be glad if you would nominate either General Marshall or another [as] *locum tenens* to carry forward the work of 'Bolero', 'Sledgehammer', and 'Round-up'. We will supply him also with a deputy.

2. It seems important to act quickly, as committees are too numerous and too slow. If you prefer other arrangements pray let me know your wishes.

---

[1] This meant the 'Bolero', 'Sledgehammer', and 'Roundup' group; and 'Torch'.

Winston S. Churchill to General Claude Auchinleck
(Churchill papers, 20/78)

31 July 1942
Absolutely Secret

I hope to arrive in Cairo on Monday, August 3. The CIGS should arrive by a different route on the same day. I have asked Field-Marshal Smuts and General Wavell to try to come there during the same week. Let nothing take your eye off the ball.

Winston S. Churchill to President Franklin D. Roosevelt
(Churchill papers, 20/78)

31 July 1942
Personal and Secret

INDIA

We do not agree with Chiang Kai-shek's estimate of the Indian situation. The Congress Party in no way represents India and is strongly opposed by over 90 million Mohammedans, 40 million Untouchables and the Indian States comprising some 90 millions, to whom we are bound by Treaty. Congress represents mainly the *intelligentsia* of non-fighting Hindu elements, and can neither defend India nor raise a revolt. The military classes, on whom everything depends, are thoroughly loyal, in fact over a million have volunteered for the Army and the numbers recently volunteering greatly exceed all previous records. Their loyalty would be gravely impaired by handing over the Government of India to Congress control. The reckless declarations of Congress have, moreover, given rise to widespread misgiving, even among its own rank and file.

2. The Government of India have no doubt of their ability to maintain order and carry on government with efficiency and secure India's maximum contribution to the war effort whatever Congress may say or even do, provided, of course, that their authority is not undermined. His Majesty's Government here have no intention of making any offer beyond the sweeping proposals which Sir Stafford Cripps carried to India and in fact could not do so without creating grave internal trouble in India. So far as I am concerned, I could not accept responsibility for making further proposals at this stage. We have, however, only today in Parliament made clear that, while the specific proposals suggested by Cripps failed to secure agreement, we stand firmly by the broad intention of our offer, which is that India should have the fullest opportunity at the earli-

est possible moment after the war to attain to complete self-government under constitutional arrangements of her own devising. I earnestly hope therefore, Mr President, that you will do your best to dissuade Chiang Kai-shek from his completely misinformed activities, and will lend no countenance to putting pressure upon His Majesty's Government.

Winston S. Churchill to Field Marshal Sir John Dill
(Churchill papers, 20/78)

31 July 1942
Personal

I am sure that the President's wish is full steam ahead 'Torch' at earliest possible moment. We regard this as decided absolutely with overriding priority. No one here is thinking of anything else. You should ask to see President urgently.

Sir Alexander Cadogan: diary
('The Diaries of Sir Alexander Cadogan', page 465)

31 July 1942

Went to Cabinet War Room at 11 to pick up PM and we started for Farnborough about 11.30. PM and Mrs C[hurchill] in one car and I and [Sir] Charles Wilson in another. Our blood pressures were satisfactory, and we were put in the 'Chamber'. Taken up to 15,000 ft. and kept there ¼ hour (with a little oxygen). Felt no effects at all. Nor, apparently, did PM. We then came down and I, as usual, became very deaf, and slight pain in head. PM complained of pain, but we discovered that was due to clumsy adjustment of his oxygen mask, which was pressing. Clemmie peeked at him through port-hole. Blood-pressures good after [...] Arranged now we start tomorrow night.

August
1942

War Cabinet: conclusions
(Cabinet papers, 65/27)

1 August 1942   10 Downing Street
11.30 a.m.

The War Cabinet were informed that the First Lord of the Admiralty[1] thought that certain modifications should now be made in the programme of Naval construction approved by the War Cabinet in the previous April.

The main points were as follows:

(1) That nine intermediate aircraft-carriers should be laid down in addition to the four approved in the last new construction programme. This would mean that four cruisers, a mine-sweeper and two cargo liners would have to be cancelled; the cruisers would not have been completed for four years in any case. It would also involve delay to four other cruisers, six destroyers, some mine-sweepers and about twelve merchant vessels.

(2) It was also proposed to cancel four twin-screw corvettes and to replace them by seven single-crew corvettes. The Prime Minister said that he was in general agreement with these measures but thought that the First Lord of the Admiralty should, perhaps, go further and cancel the laying down of the very large type of destroyers, which would take two years to complete, the capacity thus released being used to build a larger number of smaller destroyers, which could be completed within about a year's time. He thought that there would be an overwhelming need for an increase in anti-submarine convoys in the following year.

The War Cabinet:

Agreed that this matter should be investigated by a Committee of Ministers, a report being made to the War Cabinet.

---

[1] A. V. Alexander.

War Cabinet: Confidential Annex
(Cabinet papers, 65/31)

1 August 1942   10 Downing Street
11.30 a.m.

The Prime Minister referred to a telegram from General Auchinleck (No. 30295 of 31st July) copies of which had been circulated to the War Cabinet, stating that he had reached the conclusion that an opportunity to resume offensive operations was unlikely to arise before the middle of September, depending on the enemy's ability to build up his tank force. This seemed to him (the Prime Minister) to be a very depressing account of the position. This telegram had made him all the more convinced that it was necessary that the position should be considered on the spot. He hoped that as the result of his visit he might be able to make arrangements which would result in a more vigorous handling of matters. He thought the time had now been reached when General Auchinleck could once more concern himself with the duties of Commander-in-Chief, Middle East, some other General being appointed to command the Eighth Army. The powers of this General would, of course, have to be very carefully considered.

The Prime Minister said that he was leaving that night, and hoped to be in Cairo in two days' time. He had arranged to meet General Smuts and General Wavell in Cairo, and if a meeting with M Stalin was arranged he would then go on to meet him, perhaps at Astrakhan. He read to the War Cabinet a copy of a telegram which he had sent to M Stalin, suggesting a meeting.

The Lord Privy Seal[1] said that he thought it might be desirable to inform the House, in Secret Session, that the Prime Minister had gone to Egypt, after word had been received of his arrival.

The Prime Minister said that he agreed with this course. Nothing, of course, should be said of a meeting with M Stalin, for the present.

The Prime Minister referred to a telegram from the Joint Staff Mission at Washington (JSM 326) reporting that the United States Chiefs of Staffs were clearly coming round to the view that the decision to undertake 'Torch' must be made now, at once, without waiting until the 15th September.

The Prime Minister said that a reply had been sent to General Dill making it clear that we entirely agreed with this view.

---

[1] Sir Stafford-Cripps.

The Prime Minister reminded the War Cabinet that on the 8th July it had been agreed that he should send a telegram to the President to the effect that it would be agreeable to us if General Marshall could be appointed to be Supreme Commander for the 1943 operations. No decision on the matter had yet been reached. He had now proposed to the President (in Personal Telegram No. T.1066/2) that General Eisenhower should be designated to act as General Marshall's deputy here, having command of the forces assigned for 'Torch' and also for 'Bolero' and 'Round-Up'. If this plan was adopted, he thought it might not be desirable to use so high-sounding a phrase as 'Supreme Commander'. Further, he thought that it would be undesirable that there should be any announcement on this matter, or discussion of it in the Press, at the present time. This point should be brought to the notice of the Minister of Information, who should be authorised to arrange for the issue of a 'D' Notice, if necessary.

General agreement was expressed with this view.

[...]

The Prime Minister outlined the main features of this Operation.[1] A crucial stage would be reached on the night before the convoy reached the narrow passage between Cape Bon and Sicily. In making the plan, the Admiralty had had to decide whether the heavy ship escort should carry the convoy right through to Malta at the risk of our two 16-inch battleships being heavily attacked by air or whether, during the final stage of the journey, escorting forces should be confined to cruisers and destroyers. If ill befell our heavy ships in the narrow waters approaching Malta, the whole balance of naval power would be affected. On the other hand, if it was decided not to risk the heavy ships during the final stage and the convoy suffered severe losses from attack by enemy surface ships, some searching questions would be asked. In view of the grave issues involved, he asked the War Cabinet to support any decision which might be taken.

[...]

After some discussion, the Prime Minister proposed that the plan advocated by the Admiralty – namely, that the heavy ships and aircraft-carriers should not go through with the convoy in the final stage – should be adopted.

---

[1] Operation 'Pedestal', the August supply convoy to Malta.

Winston S. Churchill to Clement Attlee and others[1]
(Churchill papers, 20/67)

1 August 1942   10 Downing Street

It would be better not to announce my arrival in Cairo to Parliament till Thursday next, and then to do it in Secret Session. Every effort should be made to hold the news at least till Friday. Of course, if it breaks earlier, other arrangements can be made. Meanwhile D notice holds.

2. No public reference should be made to Moscow till a communiqué is agreed between Stalin and me. Parliament may be told in secret as late as possible as follows:

The Prime Minister left this country last Saturday on his way to the Middle East and was accompanied by the CIGS. He is at present in Egypt, and he has been invited by M Stalin to proceed to meet him in Moscow. This invitation the Prime Minister has accepted. It is evidently desirable, on every ground, that absolute secrecy should be preserved as to his Russian movements, about which an agreed communiqué will be issued as soon as convenient. It is expected that he will be absent from this country for from 20 to 30 days.

Anthony Eden: recollection
('The Eden Memoirs, The Reckoning', page 338)

1 August 1942

On August 1st I had luncheon with the Prime Minister and Mrs Churchill, when Lord Beaverbrook and Mr Brendan Bracken, as well as the Prime Minister's brother, Major John Churchill, were the other guests. Both Beaverbrook and Bracken wanted to go with him. The Prime Minister and I walked up and down in Downing Street garden while we discussed whether either of them should do so. He felt the need for company, especially in Moscow, but finally decided to travel with Brooke and Cadogan, but with no other Minister.

---

[1] These others were Sir Stafford Cripps (Lord Privy Seal), Anthony Eden (Foreign Secretary), and Brendan Bracken (Minister of Information).

King George VI to Winston S. Churchill
(Churchill papers, 20/52)[1]

1 August 1942   Windsor Castle

My dear Prime Minister,

I must send you one line before you leave to wish you *bon voyage* and a safe return.

I know from what you have so often told me, that you have long planned this journey to find out for yourself the reason for the many difficulties and delays in the Middle East.

I feel that your visit East will be even more epoch-making than those you have paid to the West, not that I would wish to belittle the latter in any way, but because of two people with whom you will make personal contact, Smuts and Stalin. Two great men in their own spheres, utterly different in character, but with a single aim to win this war. You have this same aim and what could be better than that you should meet them at this moment. The results of your deliberations may be the turning point of the war, knowing what powerful forces are coming to help from the West.

You and I know what this country has done, is doing, and will continue to do towards the winning of the war. Your journey will not be too easy physically, so I pray you to take great care of yourself, though I know you have already taken steps to ensure this.

I shall follow your journey with the greatest interest and shall be more than delighted when you are safely home again.

As I have told you before, your Welfare means a great deal not only to the United Nations, but to me personally. With my very best wishes to you on your new venture,

Believe me
Your very sincere and grateful friend
George RI

Winston S. Churchill to King George VI
(Royal Archives)[2]

1 August 1942   10 Downing Street

Sir,

I am deeply touched by your Majesty's most kind and gracious letter. Always Sir you are very good to me. I wish indeed that it had been in my

[1] This letter was handwritten by the King.
[2] This letter was handwritten by Churchill.

power to bring about earlier and more decisive success. But the ultimate result is sure.

I trust indeed and pray that this journey of mine will be fruitful. Only my conviction that it is my duty has led me to it. I am shocked by Auchinleck's latest wire (about remaining on the Defensive till the middle of September). How strong will the enemy be by then! In Russia too the materials for a joyous meeting are meagre indeed. Still I may perhaps make the situation less edged.

I am looking forward to meeting my old friend Smuts again. His wisdom and his courage will be a comfort in these serious days that lie ahead.

I hope Your Majesty will have some rest and peace at Balmoral, and once more expressing my grateful thanks for all the kindness and friendship with which I have been honoured,

I remain,
Your Majesty's faithful and devoted servant,
Winston S. Churchill

Winston S. Churchill to General George C. Marshall
(Churchill papers, 20/78)

1 August 1942
Personal and Secret

Your No. 2712 to General Eisenhower for me. Harriman, Douglas, Leathers and Salter agree that any misunderstanding about tonnage estimates was not due to British Ministry of War Transport.

2. Confusion arises partly from lack of agreed vocabulary, but mainly from absence of sufficiently detailed information as to type and character of cargo.

3. I am very glad you are looking into vehicles. If we have too many we shall not be able to move at all. The latest figure received by the War Office is in advance of that I mentioned to you. It is the vehicles that take the shipping space out of all proportion to the other needs of the fighting men. I suggest starting at an arbitrary figure of 100,000 vehicles, pick the types most needed, and see what is the best army that can be built up on them in the given nine months.

4. This is all the more important because anyway there is a heavy deficit in shipping. I venture to suggest that the available shipping should be taken as the starting basis and that the Shipping Boards, hand in glove with the Military Authorities, should pack the best outfit possible

for the nine months from July 1 to March 31, 1943. I doubt very much whether anything in excess of what I have mentioned will be possible by the latter date.

5. Shipping Boards are cabling their agreed report for presentation to President. I am informing him that I strongly endorse their recommendations. This report should be read in conjunction with this message of mine. Thank you so much for cabling me and for the pains you are taking in this fundamental matter.

Winston S. Churchill to Josef Stalin
(Churchill papers, 20/78)

1 August 1942
Absolutely Secret

I will certainly come to Moscow to meet you and will fix the date from Cairo.

Field Marshal Sir John Dill to Winston S. Churchill
(Churchill papers, 20/78)

1 August 1942
Personal

President has gone [to] Hyde Park for short rest but before going he issued orders for full steam ahead 'Torch' at earliest possible moment. He has asked Combined Chiefs of Staff to tell him on 4th August earliest date when landing could take place (our JSM 329 refers). Risk of whittling to Pacific may still exist (Paragraph (E) (1) of CCS 94 frightened me), but President entirely sound on this point.

2. In American mind 'Round-up' in 1943 is excluded by acceptance of 'Torch'. We need not argue about that. A one-track mind on 'Torch' is what we want at present and I conclude you would accept Marshall for this Command if President so desired and not stipulate that he should be reserved for 'Round-Up' in spite of what you say in your telegram to President of 31/7. (FO 4578 to Washington).

3. May what you are at have the success which (word omitted) courage and imagination deserve.

Winston S. Churchill: recollection
('The Hinge of Fate', page 411)

2 August 1942

It had been arranged that Sir Alexander Cadogan should come with me to represent the Foreign Office. We started after midnight on Sunday, August 2, from Lyneham in the bomber 'Commando'. This was a very different kind of travel from the comforts of the Boeing flying-boats. The bomber was at this time unheated, and razor-edged draughts cut in through many chinks. There were no beds, but two shelves in the after cabin enabled me and Sir Charles Wilson, my doctor, to lie down. There were plenty of blankets for all. We flew low over the South of England in order to be recognised by our batteries, who had been warned, but who were also under 'Alert' conditions. As we got out to sea I left the cockpit and retired to rest, fortified by a good sleeping cachet.

Winston S. Churchill to General Hastings Ismay
(Churchill papers, 20/87)

2 August 1942   Gibraltar
Most Secret
Most Immediate
For those concerned only

German wireless announcement visit to Moscow odd and disquieting as more important matters may leak. Please make searching secret enquiry with object of future security for our plans.

2. My telegram to Roosevelt through British Embassy Washington sent off 3 a.m. Friday morning was sent by Campbell[1] to Sumner Welles,[2] who sent it by messenger that night to President at Hyde Park without any indication of urgency or importance. President did not read it until I rang him up at 5 o'clock yesterday. Had it been sent through Winant[3] it would not have touched State Department, and delivery possibly in three or four hours. As I do not wish to send every message through Winant essential Campbell should be instructed to deliver immediately personally important messages in former naval person series, and to make sure they are transmitted by special messenger by air if President away. Please get this cleared up.

[1] British Minister in Washington.
[2] United States Under-Secretary of State.
[3] United States Ambassador in London.

Winston S. Churchill: recollection
('The Hinge of Fate', pages 411–12)

2–3 August 1942

We reached Gibraltar uneventfully on the morning of August 3, spent the day looking round the fortress, and started at 6 p.m. for Cairo, a hop of 2,000 miles or more, as the détours necessary to avoid the hostile aircraft around the Desert battle were considerable. Vanderkloot, in order to have more petrol in hand, did not continue down the Mediterranean till darkness fell, but flew straight across the Spanish zone and the Vichy quasi-hostile territory. Therefore, as we had an armed escort till nightfall of four Beaufighters we in fact openly violated the neutrality of both these regions. No one molested us in the air, and we did not come within cannon-shot of any important town. All the same I was glad when darkness cast her shroud over the harsh landscape and we could retire to such sleeping accommodation as 'Commando' could offer. It would have been very tiresome to make a forced landing on neutral territory, and even descent in the desert, though preferable, would have raised problems of its own. However, all 'Commando's' four engines purred happily, and I slept sound as we sailed through the starlit night.

It was my practice on these journeys to sit in the co-pilot's seat before sunrise, and when I reached it on this morning of August 3 there in the pale, glimmering dawn the endless winding silver ribbon of the Nile stretched joyously before us. Often had I seen the day break on the Nile. In war and peace I had traversed by land or water almost its whole length, except the 'Dongola Loop', from Lake Victoria to the sea. Never had the glint of daylight on its waters been so welcome to me.

Now for a short spell I became 'the man on the spot'. Instead of sitting at home waiting for the news from the front I could send it myself. This was exhilarating.

Winston S. Churchill to Clement Attlee
(Churchill papers, 20/87)

3 August 1942   Cairo
Most Secret

We are all agreed that no public statement should be made. I realise your difficulties and I know how many rumours are cropping up everywhere. These are probably the result of surmise, but they may be from leakage from Washington or disclosure from Moscow. So long as we do not give official confirmation these rumours may increase in number and diversity and produce confusion. We found this to be the case in Molotov's journeyings when, against our own judgment, we yielded to Stalin's request for complete official secrecy. We could not, of course, in any case make any official announcement without first consulting Stalin.

2. Complete stop has been put on here, but that may be difficult to hold for more than 96 hours from this morning. Anyhow I am against officially publicly confirming right story, which may draw bombs on this neutral city, or anyhow may be afterwards alleged to have done so.

3. My wishes about Parliament stand though reference to place of meeting Moscow should be deleted. It is vital that all should be kept vague about these dates and movements.

4. Smuts is here and holds strongly there should be no official announcement until visits are over.

General Sir Alan Brooke: diary
(*War Diaries, Field Marshal Lord Alanbrooke', pages 289–90*)

3 August 1942   Cairo

After dinner, when I was dropping with sleepiness PM again called me in and kept me up till 1.30 a.m. Back to the same arguments that Auk must come back to the Command of the ME and leave the 8th Army. Exactly what I have always told him from the start! Then argued strongly for Gott to take over, whilst I know that Gott is very tired. Finally suggested that I should take it over!![1]

Clementine Churchill to Winston S. Churchill
(*Baroness Spencer-Churchill papers*)

4 August 1942   10 Downing Street

My Darling,

It was both dramatic & mysterious standing in the dark on that aerodrome while your monster bomber throbbing, roaring & flashing blue

---

[1] After the war, Viscount Alanbrooke wrote, at this point in his diary: 'Winston's suggestion that I should take over the 8th Army personally gave rise to the most desperate longings in my heart! I had tasted the thrill of commanding a formation in war whilst commanding II Corps in France. For sheer thrill and excitement it stood in a category by itself, and not to be compared to a Staff appointment. Even that of CIGS, when working for a man like Winston, must mean constant frustration, friction, and untold difficulties in achieving the results one was after' (*War Diaries, Field Marshal Lord Alanbrooke*, page 290).

light taxied away into the blackness. It seemed a long time taking off – Finally we saw its huge dim shape airborne against the row of 'glim' lights which I suppose are there as a guide to planes. I was assured that these are invisible from the air.

Yesterday the House went into Secret Session for a few minutes while Mr Attlee told the Members of your journey & its two-fold purpose. Colonel Harvie-Watt tells me that the statement was well received – Later in the evening I dined with him & his handsome dark wife who is about to have another baby. There were Sir Frederick Pile & Lady Pile,[1] she, a dark rather inspired looking little woman & the Gwylim Lloyd-Georges.

General Pile says there are now about 32,000 women in 'Ack Ack' – I told him that Mary had been recommended for a Commission by her Board. This week-end I go to Dytchley to stay with the Trees.[2] I have sent all the servants away for a week's holiday except the tall Housemaid Lena. She & 'Smoky' are looking after me. Last night at the Harvie-Watt dinner we had grouse! & delicious Burgundy. I think he is a gourmet!

I think much of you my Darling & pray that you may be able to penetrate & then solve the problem of the Middle East stultification or frustration or what is it?

This first part of your journey is less dramatic & sensational than your visit to the Ogre in his Den; but I should imagine it may be more fruitful in results.

Nancy Astor[3] has made an ungracious & clumsy (I was about to write 'ass of herself' – But I will not compare her to the animal which bore Christ in triumph) speech which has repelled everybody.

All my love & hopes go with this letter.

Your Clemmie
[Sketch of cat]

---

[1] Hester Mary Melba Phillimore, 1900–49. Daughter of George Grenville Phillimore. Married to Sir Frederick Pile, who was appointed head of the Anti-Aircraft Command of the RAF in July 1939. For the duration of the war she kept a diary giving a factual account of the progress of the war and recording many details concerning the war effort on the home front. This is now in the National Archives within the Phillimore papers.

[2] At Ditchley Park in Oxfordshire, the country house of Ronald Tree MP and his wife Nancy, which the Trees had put at the Prime Minister's disposal for weekends when the full moon rendered Chequers vulnerable to air attack.

[3] Nancy Witcher Langhorne, 1879–1964. Born in Virginia. Married first, in 1897, Robert Gould Shaw (divorced, 1903); second, in 1906, 2nd Viscount Astor. Conservative MP for Plymouth Sutton, 1919–45 (the first woman to take her seat in the Westminster Parliament). CH, 1937.

Winston S. Churchill to Clement Attlee
(Churchill papers, 20/87)

4 August 1942   Cairo
Most Secret and Personal

What line do you propose to take with Parliament about enemy reports of alleged Russian visit as reflection upon our power to keep secrets. Let me know as I may have some suggestions.

2. Smuts arrived yesterday sparkling with vitality and in pink of condition, having flown long distances very high without oxygen or ill-effects of any kind. He is delighted with 'Torch'. We are seeing people separately in relays and keeping in closest touch. I do not expect to make any recommendations to you for a few days.

General Sir Alan Brooke: diary
('War Diaries, Field Marshal Lord Alanbrooke', page 291)

4 August 1942   Cairo

Came back to Embassy at 5.45 p.m. for large conference under PM attended by Smuts, Auchinleck, Wavell, the Admiral, Tedder, Casey, Jacob and self. PM reviewed the whole situation and explained plans for offensive in North Africa with Americans, and its relation to western attack in ME. On whole he was fairly sound in most of his arguments. Finally cross questioned Auchinleck as to probable date of his offensive. I could see that he did not approve of his replies! He is again pressing for an attack before Auchinleck can possibly get ready! I find him almost impossible to argue with on this point. Conference lasted 2¾ hours!! Just had time to rush off for a bath before 9 p.m. dinner.

After dinner I was dragged off into the garden by PM to report results of my day's work. As I expected my work was not approved of! Montgomery could not possibly arrive in time to hurry on the date of the attack! I told him no one else could. He then pressed for Gott, I told him I had discussed him with Auchinleck, who did not consider him up to it, and also that he was too tired. I then told him about the project to move Wilson as too old. He then said that I was failing to make use of the two best men; Gott and Wilson. He then said that he knew neither of them but that Eden had told him so!! I got level with him this time by suggesting that it was not astonishing that Eden should select old Green Jacket officers! This went home all right and he saw the logic of it and was very nice. However he kept me arguing till 1 a.m.!! and we have got to get up at 4.45 a.m. tomorrow!!! Moscow party is growing – Wavell is coming and probably Harriman.

Henry Channon: diary
('Chips', page 335)

4 August 1942 London

I went to the House of Commons, which was in Secret Session, and Cripps clumsily announced to the astonished Chamber that Winston and Co are in the Middle East en route for Russia. Everybody gasped. The House of Commons is once more several laps behind London society, which is already well aware of the trip.

Winston S. Churchill to President Franklin D. Roosevelt
(Churchill papers, 20/88)

5 August 1942 Cairo

I should greatly like to have your aid and countenance in my talks with Joe. Would you be able to let Averell come with me? I feel that things would be easier if we all seemed to be together. I have a somewhat raw job. Kindly duplicate your reply to London. Am keeping my immediate movements vague.

President Franklin D. Roosevelt to Winston S. Churchill
(Churchill papers, 20/78)

5 August 1942
Immediate

I am asking Harriman to leave at earliest possible moment for Moscow. I think your idea is sound and I am telling Stalin Harriman will be at his and your disposal to help in any way.

Winston S. Churchill to Josef Stalin
(Churchill papers, 20/78)

5 August 1942 Cairo
Most Secret

We plan to leave here one day, arriving Moscow the next, with intermediate stops at Tehran.

2. Details will have to be arranged in part by our RAF authorities in Tehran in consultation with yours. I hope you may instruct latter to give the benefit of their assistance in every way.

3. I cannot yet give any indication regarding dates beyond what I have already suggested to you.

Winston S. Churchill: recollection
(*'The Hinge of Fate', pages 414–15*)

5 August 1942   Cairo

On August 5 I visited the Alamein position. I drove with General Auchinleck in his car to the extreme right flank of the line west of El Ruweisat, which was held by the Australian 9th Division. Thence we proceeded along the front to his headquarters behind the Ruweisat Ridge, where we were given breakfast in a wire-netted cube, full of flies and important military personages. I had asked for various officers to be brought, but above all General 'Strafer' Gott. It was said that he was worn down with his hard service. This was what I wanted to find out. Having made the acquaintance of the various Corps and Divisional Commanders who were present, I therefore asked that General Gott should drive with me to the airfield, which was my next stop. Objection was raised by one of Auchinleck's staff officers that this would take him an hour out of his way; but I insisted he should come with me. And here was my first and last meeting with Gott.

As we rumbled and jolted over the rough tracks I looked into his clear blue eyes and questioned him about himself. Was he tired, and had he any views to give? Gott said that no doubt he was tired, and that he would like nothing better than three months' leave in England, which he had not seen for several years, but he declared himself quite capable of further immediate efforts and of taking any responsibilities confided to him. We parted at the airfield at two o'clock on this afternoon of August 5. By the same hour two days later he had been killed by the enemy in almost the very air spaces through which I now flew.

At the airfield I was handed over to Air Vice-Marshal Coningham,[1] who, under Tedder, commanded all the air-power which had worked

---

[1] Arthur Coningham, 1895–1948. Born in Brisbane, Australia. Educated in New Zealand. Served with New Zealand forces in Samoa and Egypt, 1914–16. Joined Royal Flying Corps, 1916. Served in the European war, 1916–19 (despatches, Military Cross, DSO, DFC); in Kurdistan, 1923 (despatches). Flew from Cairo to Kano, October 1925, the first east–west crossing of Africa by air (AFC). During the Second World War, served with Bomber Command (CB) and with 8th Army in North Africa (KCB, 1942). Formed 1st Tactical Air Force, French North Africa, 1943. Operations, Sicily

with the Army, and without whose activity the immense retreat of five hundred miles could never have been accomplished without even greater disasters that we had suffered. We flew in a quarter of an hour to his headquarters, where luncheon was provided, and where all the leading Air officers, from Group Captains upwards, were gathered. I was conscious of an air of nervousness in my hosts from the moment of my arrival. The food had all been ordered from Shepheard's Hotel. A special car was bringing down the dainties of Cairo.

Winston S. Churchill to Clement Attlee
(Churchill papers, 20/87)

5 August 1942   Cairo

Just returned from a long but invigorating day with Eighth Army, visiting Alamein and Ruweisat and seeing South African and Australian troops, interviewing Generals Morshead,[1] Ramsden,[2] and Gott, spending morning with Auchinleck and afternoon with Tedder, Coningham, and the Royal Air Force. Troops were very cheerful, and all seem confident and proud of themselves, but bewildered at having been baulked of victory on repeated occasions. I propose to visit all the formations, both forward and rear, while pondering on the recommendations I shall have to make to the Cabinet.

2. I am discussing the whole situation with Smuts, who is a fount of wisdom. Wherever the fault may lie for the serious situation which exists, it is certainly not with the troops, and only to a minor extent with their equipment.

and Italy, 1943. Air Officer Commanding-in-Chief, 2nd Tactical Air Force, 1944–5. Air Marshal, 1946. Air Officer Commanding-in-Chief, Flying Training Command, 1945–7. Retired, 1947.

[1] Leslie James Morshead, 1889–1959. On active service with the Australian Imperial Forces, 1914–18 (Gallipoli and France, despatches six times, DSO). Commanded 18th Australian Infantry Brigade, Middle East, 1941–2; Commandant, Tobruk Garrison, 1941. General Officer Commanding Australian Imperial Force, Middle East, 1942–3. Commanded Commonwealth 9th Australian Division at El Alamein, 1942. Knighted, 1943. General Officer Commanding New Guinea Force, 1944. Task Force Commander, Borneo operations, 1945 (despatches thrice).

[2] William Havelock Ramsden, 1888–1969. Educated at Bath College and Sandhurst. Captain, East York Regiment, 1916. Served in France, 1917–18 (Military Cross). General Staff Officer (rank of Major), Weapon Training, 1926–30. Brevet Lieutenant-Colonel, 1933. East York Regiment (India), 1934. Lieutenant-Colonel, 1st Battalion Hampshire Regiment, 1936. On operations in Waziristan, 1936–7 (despatches, medal); Palestine, 1938–9 (despatches, medal; DSO). Colonel (antedated to 1936), and Temporary Brigadier, 1939. Commander, West Lancashire Area, 1939. Commander, 25th Infantry Brigade, France, 1939–40. Commander, 50th Division, Middle East, 1940–2 (despatches). Major-General, 1941; Commander, XXX Corps (Acting Lieutenant-General), Middle East, July–September 1942. Commander, 3rd Division, December 1942 to 1943. Commander, Sudan Defence Force and British troops, Sudan and Eritrea, January 1944 to June 1945; retired, September 1945.

3. I am purposely keeping my future movements vague. I am very glad the House was contented with the statement. This change and open air are doing me a great deal of good.

Winston S. Churchill to Clement Attlee
(Churchill papers, 20/87)

5 August 1942
Immediate

You should know that in order to confuse enemy false rumours are being spread through special channels both locally and to enemy about my movements.

General Sir Alan Brooke: diary
('War Diaries, Field Marshal Lord Alanbrooke', page 293)

6 August 1942   Cairo

One of the most difficult days of my life, with momentous decisions to take as far as my own future and that of the War was concerned.

Whilst I was dressing and practically naked, the PM suddenly burst into my room. Very elated, and informed me that his thoughts were taking shape and that he would soon commit himself to paper! I rather shuddered and wondered what he was up to! Ten minutes later he burst into my room again and invited me to breakfast with him. However, as I was in the middle of my breakfast by then he asked me to come as soon as I had finished my breakfast. When I went round he made me sit on the sofa whilst he walked up and down. First of all he said he had decided to split the ME Command in two. A Near East taking up to the canal, and a Middle East taking Syria, Palestine, Persia and Iraq. I argued with him again that the Canal was an impossible boundary as both Palestine and Syria are based administratively on Egypt. He partially agreed, and then went on to say that he intended to remove the Auk to the Persian Iraq Command as he had lost confidence in him. And he wanted me to take over the Near East Command with Montgomery as my 8th Army Commander! This made my heart race very fast!! He said he did not require an answer at once, and that I could think it over if I wanted. However I told him without waiting that I was quite certain it would be a wrong move. I knew nothing about desert warfare, and could never have time to grip hold of the show to my satisfaction before the necessity to attack became imperative.

Another point which I did not mention was that after working with the PM for close on 9 months I do feel at last that I can exercise a limited amount of control on some of his activities and that at last he is beginning to take my advice. I feel therefore that, tempting as the offer is, by accepting it I should definitely be taking a course which would on the whole help the war the least. Finally I could not bear the thought that Auchinleck might think that I had come out here on purpose to work myself into his shoes! PM was not pleased with this reply but accepted it well.

Winston S. Churchill to Clement Attlee
(Churchill papers, 20/87)

6 August 1942   Cairo
8.15 p.m.

As a result of such inquiry as I have made here, and after prolonged consultations with Field-Marshal Smuts and CIGS and Minister of State, I have come to the conclusion that a drastic and immediate change is needed in the High Command.

2. I therefore propose that the Middle East Command shall be reorganised into two separate Commands, namely:

(*a*) 'Near East Command', comprising Egypt, Palestine, and Syria, with its centre in Cairo, and

(*b*) 'Middle East Command', comprising Persia and Iraq, with its centre in Basra or Baghdad.

The Eighth and Ninth Armies fall within the first and the Tenth Army in the second of these Commands.

3. General Auchinleck to be offered the post of C-in-C the new Middle East Command. The title remains the same, but its scope is reduced. It may however become more important later. It also preserves General Auchinleck's association with India. It must be remembered that General Wavell's appointment as C-in-C India was for the duration of the war, and that the India Office have always desired that Auchinleck should return there if possible. I know of nothing that should prevent the eventual realisation of this plan, though of course no promise can be made in respect of events which are unforeseeable.

4. General Alexander to be Commander-in-Chief the Near East.

5. General Montgomery to succeed Alexander in 'Torch'. I regret the need of moving Alexander from 'Torch', but Montgomery is in every way qualified to succeed [him in that].

6. General Gott to command the Eighth Army under Alexander.

7. General Corbett to be relieved as CGS Near East.

8. General Ramsden to be relieved as GOC XXXth Corps.

9. General Dorman-Smith to be relieved as Deputy CGS.[1]

10. It will be necessary to find two Corps Commanders for the Eighth Army in the place of Gott and Ramsden. We have ideas for both these posts, but it would be better for the CIGS to discuss these and a number of junior changes which require to be made with Gott and Alexander when the last-named arrives.

[...]

12. The above constitute the major simultaneous changes which the gravity and urgency of the situation here require. I shall be grateful to my War Cabinet colleagues if they approve them. Smuts and CIGS wish me to say they are in full agreement that amid many difficulties and alternatives this is the right course to pursue. The Minister of State is also in full agreement. I have no doubt the changes will impart a new and vigorous impulse to the Army and restore confidence in the Command, which I regret does not exist at the present time. Here I must emphasise the need of a new start and vehement action to animate the whole of this vast but baffled and somewhat unhinged organisation. The War Cabinet will not fail to realise that a victory over Rommel in August or September may have a decisive effect upon the attitude of the French in North Africa when 'Torch' begins.

13. I hope I may receive Cabinet approval at the earliest possible moment, and that Alexander will start forthwith. It is necessary that he should reach here before I and the CIGS start for Russia. This I hope

---

[1] In 1954, General E.E. Dorman-Smith (later Dorman-O'Gowan) successfully sued Churchill for libel, causing the following footnote to be added to subsequent editions of *The Hinge of Fate*: 'The references to the Officers whose names figure in this list are factual only. Neither they nor my later remarks are to be taken as imputing personal blame to any individual. These were the principal changes in Commands and Staff at the time when General Auchinleck was replaced by General Alexander.

'Major-General Dorman-Smith only became Deputy Chief of Staff on 16 June 1942. He thus bears no responsibility for the fall of Tobruk or the defeats at Gazala. From June 25 to August 4 he acted as General Auchinleck's Principal Operations Officer at Headquarters Eighth Army during the operation described in Chapter 1. My appreciation in that Chapter of the handling of the Eighth Army is supported by Rommel's remarkable tribute.' See *Churchill Papers CHUR 4/58*, folio 312, document entitled 'Agreed Footnote'.

to do Sunday or Monday. The changes should become effective from Monday, and public announcements must follow at the earliest moment compatible with the interest of the fighting front. Meanwhile the utmost secrecy must be observed.

Winston S. Churchill to Clement Attlee
(Cabinet papers, 65/31)

7 August 1942   Cairo

Our proposal to divide the Command is made entirely on merits. I doubt if the disasters would have occurred in the Western Desert if General Auchinleck had not been distracted by the divergent considerations of a too-widely extended front – see especially his reply of 22.5.42. to my CS.1010 of 20.5.42. Paragraph 4 of this reply shows that he would have taken direct command of the battle which began at the end of May but for reluctance to become 'immersed in tactical problems in Libya'. This phrase in itself reveals the false proportion engendered by extraneous responsibilities. It is in fact 'the tactical problems of Libya' which dominate our immediate affairs.

2. The two Commands are separated by desert areas of 300 or 400 miles, and the only lateral communications between them by the railway through Turkey which we cannot use for the passage of troops, by motor tracks across the desert and by sea voyage round Arabia, taking nearly 14 days. Both Commands have entirely different bases of supply. The Near East from the Canal zone, the Middle East from the Persian Gulf ports leading up the Euphrates, and also by the Trans-Persian railway to the Northern fronts against invasion from the Caucasus or Caspian Basin. It would be more natural to associate Iraq and Persia with the India command, to which they are joined by short direct sea connection from Karachi and Bombay. General Wavell began this week by suggesting that they should be returned to the Indian sphere. The main reason why they were detached was because on the outbreak of war with Japan, General Wavell had to look eastward to Burma and Malaya, and we wished to relieve him of this distraction.

3. There is no natural unity between the two commands now proposed for Near and Middle East. It is quite true that battered war divisions from the Western Desert will be sent to recuperate in the new Middle East Command, but such transferences can be settled quite easily by the Chiefs of Staff in London in the same manner as they now settle the far

more important questions as to where divisions are to be sent as they round the Cape, or whether divisions are to be ordered back from India to the Persian theatre.

4. All the above views are considered by Field Marshal Smuts and CIGS. We are all convinced that the division now proposed is sound on geographical, strategic and administrative grounds.

5. It is quite a separate question who should fill the Iraq–Persia command and command the Tenth Army now formed or forming there. This Tenth Army is now commanded by General Quinan[1] who, it is agreed by all here, is not adequate to the task. I have no hesitation in proposing Auchinleck's appointment (?) to it. At the head of an army with a single and direct purpose he commands my entire confidence. If he had taken command of the Eighth Army when I urged him to I believe we should have won the Gazala battle, and many people here think the same. He has shown high-minded qualities of character and resolution. He restored the battle of Sidi Rezegh, and has only recently stemmed the retreat at Alamein. There is no officer here or in India who has better credentials. Only the need of making an abrupt and decisive change in the command against Rommel and giving the Army the sense of a new start has induced me to propose the re-distribution of Commands. I should be most reluctant to embarrass Alexander with remote cares at a moment when all our fortunes turn upon the speedy and decisive defeat of Rommel. Nor can I advise that General Auchinleck should be ruined and cast aside and unfit to render any further service. I am sure that if he accepts the directions which I seek Cabinet authority to give him, he will in no way have lost confidence in himself but, on the contrary, will address himself to his new task, with single-minded vigour. Here I must point out that when General Wavell was removed from the Middle East Command to India he in no way lost his reputation with the public at home or abroad, and this was proved by the fact that the President specially asked for him to be appointed Supreme Commander of the ABDA area in spite of the defeats he had sustained and some mistakes that he had made.

6. My recommendations stand as a whole, being conceived in their integrity solely from the point of view of the harmonious division of responsibilities and of the selection of the best men to discharge them. Indeed I think the nation will admire the array of our distinguished com-

---

[1] Edward Pellew Quinan, 1885–1960. Entered the Indian Army, 1905. Commanded the 9th (Jhansi) Infantry Brigade, 1934–8. Major-General, 1937. A District Commander, Waziristan, 1938. Lieutenant-General, 1941. General Officer Commanding Iran and Iraq, 1941. General, 1942. Knighted, 1942. Commander of the North-Western Army in India, 1943. Retired, 1943. Colonel, 8th Punjab Regiment, 1945.

manders Wavell Auchinleck and Alexander each facing their respective dangers on the vast front which extends from Cairo to Calcutta.

7. There is no difficulty in preserving a single Air Command over the existing Middle East area. We are all impressed with Air Marshal Tedder's work here. The fact that the new Command will be separate no more prevents him from exercising authority over the RAF in Iraq and Persia than it does in the entirely separate Command of General Platt in East Africa.

8. I earnestly hope that my colleagues will find themselves able on further consideration of this most difficult problem to authorise me to proceed as I propose. In all this I have the complete agreement of Smuts and CIGS. A decision has now become most urgent since Alexander has already started and Auchinleck has, of course, no inkling of what is in prospect. I must apprise him tomorrow.

9. I am most grateful for the agreement of the Cabinet to the other parts of my plan, grave though they be.

Oliver Harvey: diary
('The War Diaries of Oliver Harvey', page 147)

7 August 1942 London

PM telegraphed last night his proposals from Cairo. Smuts, the CIGS and Casey all concur. They are indeed slashing, a massacre of generals, tho' not of innocents.

Winston S. Churchill: recollection
('The Hinge of Fate', pages 418–19)

7 August 1942 Cairo

I spent all August 7 visiting the 51st Scottish Division, who had just landed. As I went up the stairs after dinner at the Embassy I met Colonel Jacob. 'This is bad about Gott', he said. 'What has happened?' 'He was shot down this afternoon flying into Cairo.' I certainly felt grief and impoverishment at the loss of this splendid soldier, to whom I had resolved to confide the most direct fighting task in the impending battle. All my plans were dislocated. The removal of Auchinleck from the Supreme Command was to have been balanced by the appointment to the Eighth Army of Gott, with all his Desert experience and prestige, and the whole covered by Alexander's assumption of the Middle East. What was to happen now?

[…]

It appeared that the War Cabinet had already assembled at 11.15 p.m. on August 7 to deal with my telegrams of that day, which had just been decoded. Discussion was still proceeding upon them when a secretary came in with my new messages, stating that Gott was dead, and secondly asking that General Montgomery should be sent out at once. I have been told this was an acute moment for our friends in Downing Street. However, as I have several times observed, they had been through much and took it doggedly. They sat till nearly dawn, agreed in all essentials to what I had proposed, and gave the necessary orders about Montgomery.

Winston S. Churchill to Peter Fraser
(Churchill papers, 20/78)

7 August 1942   Cairo
Most Secret and Personal
Decypher yourself

We are most deeply grateful for the reinforcements promised to your splendid division, which has already rendered the highest service here and played a notable part in stemming the adverse tide.

2. I am in Egypt on a tour of inspection. I saw General Freyberg yesterday, and hope to visit the New Zealand division in the near future. Please keep my whereabouts secret.

Harold Nicolson: diary
('Harold Nicolson, Diaries and Letters', page 238)

7 August 1942   London

I dine at Pratts and find Pug Ismay next to me. He is in a confidential mood.

[…] He talks about Winston. He calls him 'a child of nature'. He says that when things are going well, he is good; when things are going badly, he is superb; but when things are going half-well, he is 'hell on earth'. He says that Winston has the deepest veneration for the House of Commons. One day Pug found him in distress at having to prepare a speech. He said to him, 'But why don't you tell them to go to hell?' Winston turned round on him in a flash and said, 'You should not say those things: I am the servant of the House.'

Pug is very bitter about those who make Second Front capital for themselves. He fears that a weaker man than Winston might surrender to the popular clamour. He is furious with responsible people who do not understand that we cannot have unity of command with Russia, since the Soviets tell us nothing – nothing at all. He then goes off wearily to work for another four hours and I go to bed.

Sir Alexander Cadogan: diary
('The Diaries of Sir Alexander Cadogan', page 469)

7 August 1942   Cairo

Dinner was rather a frost. We assembled as usual at 9 but the PM didn't put in an appearance until 9.30, looking like a thunderstorm. Poor man, he had just heard that the key General, who was to be given the main appointment in the scheme of changes he had been arranging here, had been shot down while flying back from the Front to Cairo. It really is bad luck. So poor Winston sat speechless and desperate during dinner and had hardly recovered before the small hours. The American General Maxwell,[1] who sat next to him, and who didn't know what had happened, must have thought he was a frightful flop. I explained to him afterwards. It was delightful in the garden – quite a cool breeze. Winston kept me and Miles up until 2.30 discussing everything on earth. He was due to start off on a visit to a unit at 5.30 a.m.! But he put it off, and finally didn't go until 8.30.

Winston S. Churchill to General Claude Auchinleck
(Churchill papers, 20/54)

8 August 1942   Cairo
Most Secret and Personal

Dear General Auchinleck,

On June 23 you raised in your telegram to the CIGS the question of your being relieved in this Command, and you mentioned the name of General Alexander as a possible successor. At that time of crisis for the Army His Majesty's Government did not wish to avail themselves of your high-minded offer. At the same time you had taken over the effective command of the battle, as I had long desired and had suggested to you

---

[1] Major-General R. L. Maxwell, Commander, United States Forces in the Middle East.

in my telegram of May 20. You stemmed the adverse tide, and at the present time the front is stabilised.

2. The War Cabinet have now decided, for the reasons which you yourself had used, that the moment has come for a change. It is proposed to detach Iraq and Persia from the present Middle Eastern Theatre. Alexander will be appointed to command the Middle East, Montgomery to command the Eighth Army, and I offer you the command of Iraq and Persia, including the Tenth Army, with headquarters at Basra or Baghdad. It is true that this sphere is today smaller than the Middle East, but it may in a few months become the scene of decisive operations, and reinforcements for the Tenth Army are already on the way. In this theatre, of which you have special experience, you will preserve your associations with India. I hope therefore that you will comply with my wish and directions with the same disinterested public spirit that you have shown on all occasions. Alexander will arrive almost immediately, and I hope that early next week, subject of course to the movements of the enemy, it may be possible to effect the transfer of responsibility on the Western battlefront with the utmost smoothness and efficiency.

3. I shall be very glad to see you at any convenient time if you should so desire.

Believe me,

Yours sincerely,
Winston S. Churchill

PS Colonel Jacob, who bears this letter, is also charged by me to express my sympathy in the sudden loss of General Gott.

Winston S. Churchill to President Franklin D. Roosevelt
(Churchill papers, 20/78)

8 August 1942   Cairo
Most Secret
Personal

You will no doubt have seen the cables sent by the British Chiefs of Staff, London, to the combined Chiefs of Staff, Washington, about accelerating the date of 'Torch'. I am sure that nothing is more vital than this, and that superhuman efforts should be made. Every day counts. I have already telegraphed to London welcoming the appointment of General Eisenhower as Allied Commander-in-Chief for 'Torch', and the British Chiefs are co-operating with him to the full. [...]

2. I also wish to endorse the suggestion of the Admiralty about some United States submarines working from Gibraltar.

3. I have been busy here with a reorganisation of the High Command which was necessary. I am detaching Iraq and Persia from the Middle East Command and transferring General Auchinleck there. Alexander will succeed him as Commander-in-Chief Middle East. General Gott, who was to have been appointed to command Eighth Army under Alexander, was killed yesterday. I propose to appoint General Montgomery in his place. This will promote the utmost concentration upon the battle. A victory here might have a decisive effect upon the attitude of the French towards 'Torch'.

4. All these changes are of the utmost secrecy, and no announcement will be made until the Command has been definitely transferred. Pray therefore let this be for yourself alone.

5. I am giving my own personal attention in detail on the spot to the reception and utilization of the Shermans and 105's for which we are eagerly waiting. I am visiting the units tomorrow that are to receive these weapons.

6. Averell has just arrived, and we shall be off soon on our further quest. I will keep you informed.

7. I am also seeing Generals Maxwell[1] and Brereton.[2]

Colonel Ian Jacob:[3] diary
(General Sir Ian Jacob papers)

8 August 1942   Cairo

The Prime Minister was asleep. He awoke at six o'clock, and I had to recount to him as best I could what had passed between me and General Auchinleck. CIGS joined us ... The Prime Minister's mind is entirely fixed on the defeat of Rommel, and on getting General Alexander into complete charge of the operations in the Western Desert. He does not understand how a man can remain in Cairo while great events are occurring in the Desert and leave the conduct of them to someone else. He strode up and down declaiming on this point, and he means to have his way. 'Rommel, Rommel, Rommel, Rommel!' he cried. 'What else matters but beating him?'

---

[1] Commander, United States Forces in the Middle East.

[2] Commander, US Middle East Air Force.

[3] Edward Ian Claud Jacob, 1899–1993. 2nd Lieutenant, Royal Engineers, 1918. Military Assistant Secretary, Committee of Imperial Defence, 1938. Lieutenant-Colonel, 1939. Military Assistant Secretary to the War Cabinet, 1939–45. CBE, 1942. Retired from the Army, 1946, with the rank of Lieutenant-General. Controller, European Services, BBC, 1946. Knighted, 1946. Chief Staff Officer to the Minister of Defence, and Deputy Secretary to the Cabinet, 1952. Director-General of the BBC, 1952–60.

President Franklin D. Roosevelt to Winston S. Churchill
(Churchill papers, 20/52)

8 August 1942   Washington DC
Personal and Most Secret

Thanks so much for your news. I wholly agree date for 'Torch' should be advanced and I am asking three weeks advance over the selected date.

2. Announcement of Eisenhower Command I leave to discretion of Chiefs of Staff in London and Washington.

3. Best of luck to you and Averell on your great adventure.

Sir Alexander Cadogan: diary
('The Diaries of Sir Alexander Cadogan', page 468)

8 August 1942   Cairo

[...]

After tea, an Indian Prince arrived to call on the PM – a tall, inscrutable, impassive figure, beautifully dressed, with an immaculate turban and a great panache of gauze flowing from the top of it. The PM appeared in his rompers and what he calls his 10-gallon hat – a sort of Mexican affair... The Indian registered practically no surprise at all, but I don't know what he was thinking.

After that, the Army photographers and cinema operators were admitted to the garden to photograph Winston and Smuts playing with baby Victor![1] What England will think when the Film is released, I really cannot imagine. (I don't appear in the Film: I was standing behind the operators making suitable noises to attract Victor's attention).

[...]

---

[1] Victor Miles George Aldous Lampson, born 9 September 1941. Son of 1st Baron Killearn, GCMG, CB, MVO, PC, and his second wife, Jacqueline Aldine Leslie. Educated at Eton. Late Captain, Scots Guards. Succeeded his half-brother as 3rd Baron Killearn, 1996. Partner (1979–2001) and Director (1999–2003), AMP Ltd. Chairman, Henderson Global Investors (Holdings) Ltd, 2001–5. Managing Director, Corporate Finance, Cazenove & Co. Ltd, 2001–2. Non-executive Director, Maxis Communications Bhd, Malaysia, 2002. Shanghai Real Estate Ltd, 2002; Ton Poh Emerging Thailand Fund, 2005.

Winston S. Churchill to President Franklin D. Roosevelt
(Churchill papers, 20/78)

9 August 1942 Cairo
Secret and Personal

I hope you will let me see beforehand the text of any message you are thinking of sending me upon the anniversary of the Atlantic Charter on the 14th August. We considered the wording of that famous document line by line together and I should not be able, without mature consideration, to give it a wider interpretation than was agreed between us at the time. Its proposed application to Asia and Africa requires much thought. Grave embarrassment would be caused to the defence of India at the present time by such a statement as the Office of War Information has been forecasting. Here in the Middle East the Arabs might claim by majority they could expel the Jews from Palestine, or at any rate forbid all further immigration. I am strongly wedded to the Zionist policy, of which I was one of the authors. This is only one of the many unforeseen cases which will arise from new and further declarations.

2. Would it not be sufficient to dwell on the progress made in this memorable year, to the growth of the United Nations, to the continued magnificent resistance of Russia to aggression, to the success of the arms of the United States in the Pacific and to the growth of our combined air power? Finally, we could re-affirm our principles and point to the hope of a happier world after some preliminary intervening unpleasantness has been satisfactorily got over. I am sure you will consider my difficulties with the kindness you always show to me.

Winston S. Churchill to Anthony Eden
(Churchill papers, 20/87)

9 August 1942 Cairo
Most Secret and Personal

I emphatically agree with your proposed reply Tulip No. 69. I cannot see any advantage in making specific declarations on the spur of the moment. There is every advantage in keeping things vague and general. The Atlantic Charter was considered line by line by the President and me and I cannot be drawn into a new instrument without full consideration beforehand. I am telegraphing direct to President as well. See my immediately following message. Does he really mean that the Arabs by a majority should have the right to throw the Jews out of Palestine. Yet this is how they would read it. I should not be able to associate myself with any such declaration as is proposed. It is quite easy to send friendly messages pointing out the progress made since the Charter was signed.

General Sir Alan Brooke: diary
('War Diaries, Field Marshal Lord Alanbrooke', page 296)

9 August 1942   Cairo

Had settled to breakfast with PM on his terrace at 8.30 a.m. At 7.15 a.m. his valet woke me to inform me that the PM was awake and wanted to know when I should breakfast. I replied 8.30 a.m. as settled. The valet was horrified and replied, 'But Sir Alan, the Prime Minister likes to breakfast when he wakes up!' I replied that if that was so I regretted that he would have to breakfast alone as I intended to breakfast at 8.30, and turned round for another snooze! At 8.30 I went round. He had finished but bore me no ill will. We were expecting Alexander, and I wanted to see him badly before the PM got hold of him and had instructed for him to be brought round to my room. Unfortunately he arrived while I was having breakfast on verandah. The PM's flag lieutenant whispered in my ear that he had arrived, but PM overheard and had then to be told that Alex had gone to the lavatory! Finally I got an opportunity and dashed out to see him. I wanted to warn him as regards the PM's conception of the Command of the ME as opposed to that of the Eighth Army, which he mixes together...

Winston S. Churchill to Admiral of the Fleet Sir Dudley Pound
(Admiralty papers, 178/323)

9 August 1942   Cairo

I am deeply disappointed that Shermans cannot arrive before September 5. All yesterday I was inspecting four splendid brigades of armoured troops who only await these weapons to become the most formidable armed force in Africa. I am giving considerable attention to the synchronisation of the equipment of these brigades and to the acceleration of their training, but I do not see how they can come into action, except in emergency, before the third week in September. I had always counted on the Shermans arriving September 1. This would be forty-five days from sailing.

2. In view of the immense importance of beating Rommel as a prelude to 'Torch', I beg you will make a renewed effort to regain the lost

five days, all of which can be used. Pray cable what is present speed of convoy, and what you can do.

3. 51st Division was promised for August 13. Where is it, and will date be kept?

Winston S. Churchill to Sir Archibald Sinclair and
Air Chief Marshal Sir Charles Portal
(Special Operations Executive papers, 8/916)

9 August 1942   Cairo

I am most impressed with all that Tedder and Coningham have told me of the extreme importance of having out here a proportion, if only a small one, of the very latest types of fighter aircraft. Coningham declares he could make them desert-worthy himself. The fact that these machines are in the air keeps the enemy always wondering when he will meet them; the quality of our leadership in design makes the value out of all proportion to the number sent. Please make me proposals.

Lord Derby[1] to Beverley Baxter[2]
(Earl of Derby papers)

9 August 1942
Confidential

I confess that the one thing that has made me think whether it is right to keep complete silence is the news you tell me, and which of course I shall keep a profound secret, that the Prime Minister had gone off to meet some of the Allies. I wish he would realise the country won't stand

---

[1] Edward George Villiers Stanley, 1865–1948. Educated at Wellington College. Lieutenant, Grenadier Guards, 1885–95. Conservative MP for West Houghton, 1892–1906. Postmaster-General, 1903–5. 17th Earl of Derby, 1908. Director-General of Recruiting, October 1915. Under-Secretary of State at the War Office, July–December 1916. Secretary of State for War, December 1916–18. Ambassador to France, 1918–20. Secretary of State for War, 1922–4. Member of the Joint Select Committee on the Indian Constitution, 1933–4. In 1960 Randolph Churchill published *Lord Derby, 'King of Lancashire'*.

[2] Arthur Beverley Baxter, 1891–1964. Educated in Canada. Served as Lieutenant Infantry, Canadian Engineers, with Canadian Expeditionary Force, and with Royal Engineers, 1918. Joined London *Daily Express*, 1920. Managing Editor, *Sunday Express*, 1922; *Daily Express*, 1924. Editor-in-Chief, Inveresk publications, 1929. Editor-in-Chief and Director, *Daily Express*, 1929–33. Public Relations Counsel, Gaumont British Picture Corporation Ltd, 1933–5. Editorial Adviser, Allied Newspapers, 1938. Conservative MP for Wood Green, 1939–45, 1945–50; for Southgate from 1950 until his death. Fellow of the Royal Society of Literature. Knighted, 1954. Publications: *The Parts Men Play* (novel); *The Blower of Bubbles* (collection of short stories); *Strange Street* (autobiography); *Men Martyrs and Mountebanks, First Nights – and Noises Off* (collection of critical articles); *First Nights and Footlights* (collection of critical articles); *It Happened in September* (play).

for that. His duty is here and he has no right to go abroad at a moment like this. If he has not got anybody in the Government he can trust to send instead of himself, get a new Government. Don't for Heaven's sake let the country be as it is now without a Leader. There are plenty of difficulties on the Home front as well as on the Foreign front. He will have all his work cut out to keep his authority. He has got it to the full now because people think he is there directing things but if they know that he is off elsewhere I promise you you will find there would be a tremendous agitation against him.

Winston S. Churchill to General Hastings Ismay
('The Hinge of Fate', page 423)

10 August 1942   Cairo

General Auchinleck is disinclined to accept the command of the Iraq–Persia theatre . . . As however I am convinced that he is the best man for the job, I have given him a few more days to consider the matter further. I shall not press him unduly, but I am anxious that he should not take his decision while under the immediate effects of the blow, which he has accepted with dignity, but naturally not without distress.

Appropriate military authorities are studying the problem connected with the proposed institution of a separate command for Iraq and Persia and the administrative changes consequent thereupon. I should be glad if at the same time the Chiefs of Staff would also propose the best methods for giving effect to the policy. General Smuts has returned to South Africa, but CIGS and General Alexander share my conviction that this separation is desirable at the present time . . .

Winston S. Churchill to General Sir Harold Alexander
('The Hinge of Fate', between pages 654 and 655)

10 August 1942[1]   British Embassy
Most Secret   Cairo

Yr prime & main duty will be to take or destroy at the earliest opportunity the German–Italian Army commanded by Field Marshal Rommel together with all its supplies & establishments in Egypt & Libya.

---

[1] This message, written on August 10, was formally dated five days later (Martin Gilbert, *Churchill: A Life*, pb edn, London, 1992, page 726).

2. You will discharge or cause to be discharged such other duties as pertain to yr Command without prejudice to the task described in paragraph 1 wh must be considered paramount in His Majesty's interests.

Winston S. Churchill to General Claude Auchinleck
(Churchill papers, 20/54)

10 August 1942   Cairo
Secret

Dear General Auchinleck,

On my return journey I propose to hold a Conference at Baghdad on the 14th or 15th in order to discuss *inter alia* the machinery of an independent Command for Iraq and Persia. By that time I shall have received the report now being prepared here by the Minister of State with the assistance of the Joint Staffs. I shall also have received from London the observations of the Chiefs of Staff Committee.

By then I should like to know whether you feel able to undertake the very difficult and serious task which I proposed to you. If, as I hope will be the case, you feel wholeheartedly that you can take your station in the line I hope you will meet me in Baghdad, providing of course that the transference of Command has been effected here. General Wavell will be there; Peirse is coming from India and the Minister of State from Cairo, together perhaps with some other officers from both directions.

Believe me,
Yours very sincerely,
Winston S. Churchill

Winston S. Churchill to Clement Attlee
(Churchill papers, 20/87)

10 August 1942   Cairo
Most Secret
Most Immediate

It is indispensable to run further PQs[1] after September. I shall be asked about this and I must know. I cannot believe Admiralty resources will not admit of this as well as 'Torch'. Reply Moscow.

---

[1] PQs: supply convoys to Russia via the northern Arctic route.

Winston S. Churchill to Admiral of the Fleet Sir Dudley Pound
(Churchill papers, 20/87)

10 August 1942   Cairo
Most Secret and Personal

Shall be glad of early information about 'Pedestal' if it can be safely sent to Moscow, but do not send to Teheran.

Winston S. Churchill: recollection
('The Hinge of Fate', pages 426–7)

10–11 August 1942

Late on the night of August 10, after a dinner of notables at the genial Cairo Embassy, we started for Moscow. My party, which filled three planes, now included the CIGS, General Wavell, who spoke Russian, Air Marshal Tedder, and Sir Alexander Cadogan. Averell Harriman and I travelled together. By dawn we were approaching the mountains of Kurdistan. The weather was good and Vanderkloot in high spirits. As we drew near to these serrated uplands I asked him at what height he intended to fly them. He said nine thousand feet would do. However, looking at the map I found several peaks of eleven and twelve thousand feet, and there seemed one big one of eighteen or twenty thousand, though that was farther off. So long as you are not suddenly encompassed by clouds, you can wind your way through mountains with safety. Still, I asked for twelve thousand feet, and we began sucking our oxygen tubes. As we descended about 8.30 a.m. on the Teheran airfield and were already close to the ground I noticed the altimeter registered four thousand five hundred feet, and ignorantly remarked, 'You had better get that adjusted before we take off again'. But Vanderkloot said, 'The Teheran airfield is over four thousand feet above sea-level'.

Sir Reader Bullard,[1] His Majesty's Minister in Teheran, met me on arrival. He was a tough Briton, with long experience of Persia and no illusions.

---

[1] Reader William Bullard, 1885–1976. Acting Vice-Consul, Beirut, 1909–10. Served subsequently in the Consular Service, in Tbilisi, Trebizond, Erzerum, and Basra. Civil Adviser, Basra, 1914. Deputy Revenue Secretary, Mesopotamia (Iraq), 1919. Military Governor, Baghdad, 1920. Middle East Department, Colonial Office (under Churchill), 1921. Agent and Consul, Jedda, 1923–5. Consul, Athens, 1925–8; Addis Ababa, 1928. Consul-General, Moscow, 1930. Knighted, 1936. Minister, later Ambassador, Teheran, 1939–46. Director, Institute of Colonial Studies, Oxford, 1951–6.

We were too late to leap the northern range of the Elburz Mountains before dark, and I found myself graciously bidden to lunch with the Shah[1] in a palace with a lovely swimming pool amid great trees on an abrupt spur of the mountains. The mighty peak I had noticed in the morning gleamed brilliant pink and orange. In the afternoon in the garden of the British Legation there was a long conference with Averell Harriman and various high British and American railway authorities, and it was decided that the United States should take over the whole Trans-Persian railway from the Gulf to the Caspian. This railway, newly completed by a British firm, was a remarkable engineering achievement. There were 390 major bridges on its track through the mountain gorges. Harriman said the President was willing to undertake the entire responsibility for working it to full capacity, and could provide locomotives, rolling-stock, and skilled men in military units to an extent impossible for us. I therefore agreed to this transfer, subject to stipulations about priority for our essential military requirements. On account of the heat and noise of Teheran, where every Persian seems to have a motor-car and blows his horn continually, I slept amid tall trees at the summer residence of the British Legation about a thousand feet above the city.

Winston S. Churchill to Anthony Eden
(Churchill papers, 20/87)

11 August 1942   Moscow
Most Secret

I lunched with the Shah today at one of his small palaces with a very beautiful garden. I was much impressed with his intelligence and goodwill, both of which are in marked contrast to his brother-in-law.[2] He expounded

---

[1] Mohammad Reza Pahlavi, 1919–80. Shah (Emperor) of Iran from September 1941 until his overthrow by the Iranian Revolution on February 1979. The second and last monarch of the House of Pahlavi of the Iranian monarchy. Educated at Institute Le Rosey, Switzerland, until 1935. Came to power after forced abdication of his father, Reza Shah, by Anglo-Soviet invasion. Subsequent to his succession as Shah, Iran became a major conduit for wartime British and, later, American aid to the USSR. This massive supply effort became known as the Persian Corridor and marked the first large-scale American and Western involvement in Iran, which would continue to grow until the revolution against the Iranian monarchy in 1979.

[2] Farouk I (1920–65). The penultimate King of Egypt and Sudan and the tenth ruler from the Muhammad Ali Dynasty. Educated at the Royal Military Academy, Woolwich. Succeeded his father, Fuad I, in 1936. His sister Princess Fawzia Fuad was the first wife and Queen Consort of the Shah of Iran. Overthrown in the Egyptian Revolution of 1952 and forced to abdicate in favour of his infant son Ahmed Fuad. Died in exile in Italy.

the principles of the allied cause with the greatest vigour and explained why he was convinced that the interests of Persia lay wholly with Britain and the United States. Duke of Gloucester's visit had the best effect.

Clement Attlee to Winston S. Churchill
(Cabinet papers, 65/31)

11 August 1942   London
Most Secret

Your REFLEX No. 68 was considered by Cabinet and Defence Committee this morning.

1. It is quite impossible to do 'Torch' and PQ convoy at the same time, whatever risk is taken elsewhere. Hence if 'Torch' were to take place on 7th October we could not run a PQ convoy in October.

2. Even allowing for very generous assistance from the Americans, the requirements for 'Torch' for destroyers and other escort craft are so great that they can only be provided by ceasing to run the Sierra Leone and Gibraltar convoys and heavily cutting the escorts for Coastal convoys, with consequent loss of imports.

3. There seems considerable doubt, however, whether the Americans will be ready for 'Torch' by 7th October, and at the moment Eisenhower gives November 5th as the date, in which case it might just be possible to run an October PQ convoy.

4. Everyone is seized with the importance of carrying out 'Torch' at the earliest possible moment, and we are doing everything possible to persuade the Americans to work to an early date in October, in which case an October PQ convoy would not be possible.

5. It would be most unwise, therefore, to get committed to an October convoy as we should have to go back on our word if we found it interfered with 'Torch'.

6. PQ convoys after 'Torch' must depend on:

(a) Length and subsequent requirements of 'Torch' operations.

(b) Measure of success of 'Pedestal' and whether the latter will need to be repeated this year.

Winston S. Churchill: recollection
('The Hinge of Fate', pages 427–9)

12 August 1942

At 6.30 next morning, Wednesday, August 12, we started, gaining height as we flew through the great valley which led to Tabriz, and then turned northwards to Enzeli on the Caspian. We passed this second range of mountains at about eleven thousand feet, avoiding both clouds and peaks. Two Russian officers were now in the plane, and the Soviet Government assumed responsibility for our course and safe arrival. The snow-clad giant gleamed to the eastward. I noticed that we were flying alone, and a wireless message explained that our second plane, with the CIGS, Wavell, Cadogan, and others, had had to turn back over Teheran because of engine trouble. In two hours the waters of the Caspian Sea shown ahead. Beneath was Enzeli. I had never seen the Caspian, but I remembered how a quarter of a century before I had, as Secretary of State for War, inherited a fleet upon it which for nearly a year ruled its pale, placid waters. We now came down to a height where oxygen was no longer needed. On the western shore, which we could dimly see, lay Baku and its oil-fields. The German armies were now so near the Caspian that our course was set for Kubiyshev, keeping well away from Stalingrad and the battle area. This took us near the delta of the Volga. As far as the eye could reach spread vast expanses of Russia, brown and flat and with hardly a sign of human habitation. Here and there sharp rectilineal patches of ploughed land revealed an occasional State farm. For a long way the mighty Volga gleamed in curves and stretches as it flowed between its wide, dark margins or marsh. Sometimes a road, straight as a ruler, ran from one wide horizon to the other. After an hour or so of this I clambered back along the bomb bay to the cabin and slept.

I pondered on my mission to this sullen, sinister Bolshevik State I had once tried so hard to strangle at its birth, and which, until Hitler appeared, I had regarded as the mortal foe of civilised freedom. What was it my duty to say to them now? General Wavell, who had literary inclinations, summed it all up in a poem. There were several verses, and the last line of each was, 'No Second Front in nineteen forty-two'. It was like carrying a large lump of ice to the North Pole. Still, I was sure it was my duty to tell them the facts personally and have it all out face to face with Stalin, rather than trust to telegrams and intermediaries. At least it showed that one cared for their fortunes and understood what their struggle meant to the general war. We had always hated their wicked régime, and, till the German flail beat upon them, they would have watched us being swept out of existence with indifference and gleefully divided with Hitler our Empire in the East.

The weather being clear, the wind favourable, and my need to get to Moscow urgent, it was arranged to cut the corner of Kuibyshev and go on straight to the capital. I fear a splendid banquet and welcome in true Russian hospitality was thus left on one side. At about five o'clock the spires and domes of Moscow came in sight. We circled around the city by carefully prescribed courses along which all the batteries had been warned, and landed on the airfield, which I was to revisit during the struggle.

Here was Molotov at the head of a concourse of Russian generals and the entire Diplomatic Corps, with the very large outfit of photographers and reporters customary on these occasions. A strong guard of honour, faultless in attire and military punctilio, was inspected, and marched past after the band had played the National Anthems of the three Great powers whose unity spelt Hitler's doom. I was taken to the microphone and made a short speech. Averell Harriman spoke on behalf of the United States. He was to stay at the American Embassy. M Molotov drove me in his car to my appointed residence, eight miles out of Moscow, 'State villa No. 7'. While going through the streets of Moscow, which seemed very empty, I lowered the window for a little more air, and to my surprise felt that the glass was over two inches thick. This surpassed all records in my experience. 'The Minister says it is more prudent,' said Interpreter Pavlov.[1] In a little more than half an hour we reached the villa.

[1] Vladimir Pavlov, 1921–93. Ukrainian-Soviet diplomat and translator. Skilled in German, English, Spanish, and French. Appointed chief interpreter of the Soviet Foreign Ministry, 1939. First Counsellor with rank of Ambassador to the Soviet representative in Berlin, 1939 and 1940. In August 1939, participated as translator in the negotiation between Soviet Foreign Minister Molotov and German Foreign Minister Joachim von Ribbentrop that resulted in the so-called German–Soviet Non-Aggression Agreement (also known as the Ribbentrop–Molotov Pact); served as official translator for negotiations between Molotov and Hitler in Berlin in November 1940. Interpreter and director of the Central European Division in Soviet Foreign Ministry in Moscow, in charge of the Ministerial analysis and evaluation of Anglo-Soviet relations, from December 1940. Took part in most inter-Allied war conferences, 1942–5, translating in talks between Stalin, Churchill, and Roosevelt during Teheran (1943), Yalta (1945), and Potsdam (1945) conferences. Soviet delegate to founding conference of the United Nations in San Francisco, 1945. After the war, employed as one of the Soviet representatives in London and in the late 1940s as a counsellor at the Soviet Embassy in Paris. Soviet delegate to the Four Power Conference of Foreign Ministers in Paris, 1949.

Clementine Churchill to Winston S. Churchill
(Baroness Spencer-Churchill papers)

12 August 1942   10 Downing Street

My Darling,

Mrs Green has just received the romantic message saying that you are 'resting in this delightful Persian garden' for a few hours. I am glad you are having a short respite from trouble & anxiety. I am awaiting the announced letter. I hoped it would come in time for me to reply to it. But this note has to go in a few moments so I can wait no longer.

I'm giving today a little luncheon party to keep the Home Pot simmering: the Winants, Lord & Lady Leathers, Colonel Llewellyn[1] the 'Harry Kitten' & your Jack. Tomorrow the Wooltons Mrs Biddle[2] 'Pug' etc.

All my thoughts wishes & prayers.

Your loving

I spent last weekend at Dytchley.   CLEMMIE

Averell Harriman: recollection
(in conversation with Martin Gilbert, 18 July 1973)

12 August 1942

Winston decided to go to Moscow and take the news to Stalin personally about the decision not to attempt the invasion in 1942, and to explain why the Torch was the best we could do. Winston felt that the fact that he was willing to go personally to see Stalin would enable Stalin to accept the decision more easily. Both Winston and Roosevelt told me that their main objective in the Summer of 1942 was to keep Russia in the war, to prevent a collapse of the Red Army, and to have sufficiently good relations with the Russians to be able to concert their military operations to best advantage.

The Prime Minister was spending the night at his little cottage at Chartwell. As I came in the Russian Ambassador was leaving. Winston asked me to play bezique with him. He told me: 'It is not right for the Prime Minister to play bezique with one of His Majesty's subjects during a war, but it is all right with the President's Personal Envoy.'

---

[1] Colonel J. J. Llewellin, Minister of Aircraft Production.

[2] Margaret Biddle, wife of the American diplomat Anthony (Tony) Drexel Biddle. From 1941 to 1944 Biddle served as United States Ambassador to the Governments-in-Exile of Poland, Belgium, the Netherlands, Luxembourg, Norway, Greece, Yugoslavia, and Czechoslovakia (all in London).

The background of our discussion at Chartwell was this. Molotov had gone to the United States in the Spring of 1942 and had obtained a somewhat exaggerated view of the American Army's determination for a Second Front. The Communiqué issued after his discussion with Roosevelt went too far. General Marshall had objected to it but Roosevelt insisted upon it. Roosevelt wanted to give Hitler maximum concern which he thought would prevent the full deployment of Nazi forces on the Russian Front. He felt that if the Nazis could be made afraid of invasion they would keep the maximum number of troops in the West. Roosevelt also felt that the promise of a Second Front in 1942 would encourage the Russian Army and Russian people to have faith in the West – faith to continue the war. Winston was utterly opposed to this approach – utterly opposed to any promise of a Second Front in 1942. He argued that for the Americans, failure in opening a Second Front would be the loss of a single battle, whereas for Britain it would be a defeat. I myself was utterly convinced that a cross-channel operation would be impossible. I knew the condition of the British forces. They were very ill-trained and very ill-armed – particularly ill-armed. The best had been sent to the Middle East. I felt that Roosevelt was over-optimistic about the strength of the British Army.

After the Molotov Communiqué Eden had insisted that Molotov be given a memorandum which made it clear that whatever Russia might have said, the British did not regard the Communiqué as committing Britain to a Second Front in 1942. Eden's memorandum was completely fair and frank – it said there could be no promise of a cross-channel operation.

Churchill was always for the Mediterranean operation rather than the cross-channel. Roosevelt, when it became clear that the cross-channel was impossible in 1942, pressed for a European operation of some sort. He wanted the pressure to be taken out of the Far Eastern situation. So he fell in line with the North Africa plans. He believed that it was politically impossible for America to give most of its military effort to a situation in which there was not any military action. He was convinced under pressure from the public that the Japanese were our enemy. A large part of our country faced the Pacific – the war in Europe affected them less, the Navy's war was a Pacific war.

General Marshall feared that there would be an impossible situation in Europe if Hitler defeated the Russians. He therefore allowed Molotov to give Stalin the impression that America was much keener on the Second Front than Britain.

And so it was that I went to Chartwell. The Prime Minister was leaving for Moscow[1] on Wednesday. I told Eden some American ought to go with him, but Roosevelt said No, I don't want the Prime Minister to think I am trying to spy on him. But finally after pressure from Eden the Prime Minister telegraphed to Roosevelt who agreed that I should go to Moscow.

On the plane to Russia we never discussed the tactics of our talk with Stalin. Winston knew that I was opposed to a Second Front in 1942, and wanted me to make the point in my own way. On the first evening we discussed the progress of the war. Stalin was fascinated by the factual account which Winston gave him, and all seemed well for breaking the news to him. On the second evening Churchill prepared to tell Stalin of the decision. But to his surprise, at the outset of the meeting, Stalin attacked him in the most vicious way. A short while before there had been the disastrous Northern Convoy in which over twenty-five per cent of the ships had been sunk. Stalin referred to this and said: 'This is the first time in history the British Navy has ever turned tail and fled and from the battle. You British are afraid of fighting. You should not think the Germans are supermen. You will have to fight sooner or later. You cannot win a war without fighting'. Stalin was really insulting. It followed very closely what he had said to Max Beaverbrook and me during our visit of the previous year, when he told us that the sparsity of our support proved to his colleagues that we wanted to see the Red Army defeated.

Stalin was talking – and, remembering what he had told Max Beaverbrook and me, I passed a note to Winston: 'Don't take this too seriously – this is the way he behaved last year.'

Winston started to answer. In my view it was the most brilliant of his wartime utterances. He described what the British had done in the year they had stood alone, what they had achieved. But he forgot that to have anything interpreted accurately you had to say a few words, and then let them be interpreted. Winston went on and on. At one point the interpreter got so enthralled by Winston's speech that he put his pencil down.

When Winston finished, the interpreter translated. But as he tried to translate, Winston kept on pushing him: 'Did you tell him this?' 'Did you tell him that?' The interpreter stumbled along. Winston got angrier and angrier: 'Have you told him this? Have you made that clear?' Stalin began to laugh and then he said – not having heard a half of what Winston had

[1] Via Cairo.

wanted to be interpreted: 'Your words are not important, what is vital is the spirit.' In fact Winston's speech was never translated in full.

Winston then described to Stalin the 'Torch' operation, and Stalin seemed to get more and more interested in that. And then, totally without warning he said: 'I understood Ambassador Harriman is here to explain to you the American position.' Finally I was able to explain in detail what the actual condition of our troops and [equipment] was. The lack of landing craft – for General Marshall had told me the facts. The Prime Minister was very eloquent, as we drove home, in his gratitude. Anyone who had been attacked like he had wanted an ally. Stalin saw he could not drive a wedge between the allies.

I have often reflected on the violence of Stalin's attack and the extreme brilliance of Churchill's reply. Although he had been so provoked, Churchill didn't once say – Where was Russia when Britain stood alone – he didn't once mention the perfidious Molotov–Ribbentrop Treaty. His constraint under this fierce onslaught was remarkable – it was also wise, for there were certain things you couldn't question Stalin about.

After Churchill and I had given our answers, and had explained the 'Torch' to him, Stalin said: 'It is not for me to question what the British and American Governments have decided, I must accept their decision. But we will fight whatever they do.' One could not help but respect his dignity. He was of course concerned that if Stalingrad fell, the Germans would encircle Moscow and take the city. During my visit in 1941 he had told me that Hitler had made a great blunder in his three-pronged attack. If Hitler had concentrated on Moscow, Stalin said, he would have taken the city, the nerve centre of the nation. In that event, Stalin told me, the Russians would have continued to resist, but the fall of Moscow would have ended all possibility of a Russian offensive. Stalin told me that Hitler had avoided the Kaiser's mistake in 1914 and had driven direct to Paris – he had therefore expected him to drive direct to Moscow.

Stalin knew the dangers he was in as a result of our decision not to open a Second Front in 1942. But in all our discussions he never put himself in a pleading position. He was tough – critical beyond the degree of normal politeness – but he never went as far as the threat – which we feared he would make – that if we didn't invade German-occupied Europe, his Red Army would collapse. Stalin indicated to us with a good deal of dignity and pride – appropriate pride – that the Red Army would go on fighting regardless of what we did, or did not do.

As a result of Stalin's onslaught, Winston wanted to leave Moscow immediately. But Stalin persuaded him to stay over for the banquet on the following night. But although he went to the banquet he was still angered – that is why he went in his siren suit. This dressing down lecture from Stalin about the cowardice of the British Navy cut him pretty deeply – he was gravely annoyed. At the banquet he was a in a reserved mood – somewhere between grumpy and reserved.

On the following afternoon Winston went to see Stalin to say goodbye. Stalin asked him to stay to dinner. Winston stayed all night. They talked about everything in the world – from early in the evening to three in the morning. They discussed the Allied Intervention; the creation of the Collective Farms. Stalin's frankness removed from Churchill's mind the insult he had felt – the unforgivable rudeness of Stalin.

In making this demand for a Second Front throughout this period Stalin stated that the operation was an easy one. When it actually happened I went to see him. He said to me: 'The Normandy Landings and the opening of this Front is the most grandiose military operation in history. This is the operation that Napoleon and Hitler had contemplated but had not had the courage to undertake.' He was sympathetic and understanding – I could not help remembering his previous words about how easy it would be. But Stalin did not have the Anglo-Saxon necessity to be consistent.

I have never forgotten the intensity of Stalin's onslaught – indeed the insulting part of what he said was contained in a relatively few sentences: 'Never in history has the British Navy turned back. The Germans aren't supermen. If you fight them you will find they can be dealt with.'

Averell Harriman to President Franklin D. Roosevelt
('Special Envoy to Churchill and Stalin', pages 152–3)

12 August 1942   Moscow

Stalin took issue at every point with bluntness, almost to the point of insult, with such remarks as 'You can't win wars if you aren't willing to take risks' and 'You must not be so afraid of the Germans'. This phase of the discussion ended by Stalin stating abruptly, but with dignity, that he could not force action [by the Allies] but he did not agree with the arguments. He expressed the opinion, too, that grave difficulties confronted 'Round-up' and showed little interest in it. So far there had been no agreement on any point and the atmosphere was tense.

The Prime Minister then described the bombing activity over Germany and his hopes for substantial increase with American participation. Here came the first agreement between the two men. Stalin took over the argument himself and said that homes as well as factories should be destroyed. The Prime Minister agreed that civil morale was a military objective, but the bombing of working men's houses came as a by-product of near-misses on factories. The tension began to ease and a certain understanding of common purpose began to grow. Between the two of them, they soon had destroyed most of the important industrial cities of Germany.

The Prime Minister, with great adroitness, took the occasion of the more friendly interchange to bring the discussion back to the Second Front. He explained the decision regarding 'Torch' and its tactics, emphasizing the need for secrecy [...]

About this time the Prime Minister drew a picture of a crocodile and pointed out that it was as well to strike the belly as the snout.

Winston S. Churchill to President Franklin D. Roosevelt[1]
(Churchill papers, 20/88)

13 August 1942   Moscow

MEETING WITH STALIN ON 12 AUGUST 1942

Machine carrying Brooke, Cadogan, Wavell and Tedder was forced to return to Teheran, but Harriman and I arrived here comfortably at 5 p.m., 12th and were met by Molotov, Voroshilov and many others.

2. Not being at all tired, I began conference with Stalin at Kremlin at 7 p.m. This lasted nearly four hours. There were present only Stalin, Molotov, Voroshilov, myself, Harriman and our Ambassador with interpreter. The first two hours were bleak and sombre. I explained at length, with maps and arguments, why we would not do Sledgehammer. He said that he did not agree with our reasons. He argued the other way and everyone was pretty glum. Finally he said that he did not accept our view but we had the right to decide.

In this discussion I had, of course, explained 'Round-Up', which he passed over too lightly because it was remote and there were great difficulties in landing anywhere outside fighter cover. However, the figures of American arrivals in UK and our own proposed expeditionary force were told as solid facts.

3. We then passed on to the ruthless bombing of Germany, which gave general satisfaction: Monsieur Stalin emphasised the importance

---

[1] Churchill sent an identical telegram to Clement Attlee 'for the War Cabinet and others concerned' (Telegram of 13 August 1942, *Churchill papers, 20/87*).

of striking at the morale of the German population, and I made it clear that this was one of our leading military objectives. He said he attached the greatest importance to bombing and that he knew raids were having a tremendous effect in Germany. After this prolonged discussion, it seemed that all we were going to do was no 'Sledgehammer', no 'Round-up' and pay our way by bombing Germany. I thought it was best to get the worst over first. I did not try to relieve it, and I asked specially that there should be the plainest speaking between friends and comrades in peril. However courtesy and dignity prevailed.

4. This was the moment in the battle when I brought 'Torch' into action. As I told the whole story Stalin became intensely interested. His first question was what would happen in Spain and Vichy France. A little later on he remarked that the operation was militarily right but he had political doubts about effect on France. He asked particularly the timing, and I said not later than October 30th, but President and all of us were trying to pull it forward to October 7th. This seemed a great relief to the three Russians. At this point Monsieur Stalin said, according to the interpreter, 'May God prosper this undertaking'.

5. This marked the turning point in our conversation. He then began to raise various political objections fearing that the Anglo-American seizure of 'Torch' regions would be misunderstood in France. What were we doing about de Gaulle? I said if he were thought helpful he would be used, but at present we thought the American flag was a far better chance of an easy entry. Harriman backed this very strongly by referring to reports by American agents all over 'Torch' territories on which the President relies, and also Admiral Leahy's opinion. Presently Monsieur Stalin epitomized four main reasons for 'Torch'.

First. It would hit Rommel in the back.

Second. It would over-awe Spain.

Third. It would produce fighting in France between Germans and Frenchmen in France and,

Fourth. It would expose Italy to the whole brunt of the war.

This statement pleased me greatly as showing his swift and complete mastery of a problem hitherto novel. I added, of course, the fifth reason, namely shortening of the sea route through the Mediterranean. He was concerned to know whether we were able to pass through the Straits of Gibraltar. I also told him the changes of command in Egypt and our determination to fight a decisive battle there in late August or September. Finally, it was clear that they all liked 'Torch' though Molotov asked whether it could not be in September.

6. I then proceeded to open the prospect of our placing an Anglo-American Air Force on the southern flank of the Russian Armies to defend the Caspian and the Caucasian mountains and generally to fight in this theatre. I did not, however, go into details, as of course we had to win our battle in Egypt first and I had not the President's plan for the American contribution. If Stalin liked the idea who would set to work in detail upon it. He replied that they would be most grateful for this aid, but that the details of location, etc., would require study. As you know, I am very keen on this project because it will bring about more hard fighting between the Anglo-American air power and the Huns, all of which aids the gaining of mastery in the air under more fertile conditions than looking for trouble over the Pas de Calais.

7. Thus all ended cordially, and I expect I shall establish a solid and sincere relationship with this man and convince him of our ardent desire, shared by the President, to get into battle heavily and speedily to the best advantage. About the Russians, he said only that the Germans had produced more tanks and power than had been expected, that the news from the south was not good, and that the Russians had started diversion at Rshev, which was making progress.

8. I must tell you what a help Harriman was in this extremely serious, tense, and at one time critical discussion. He came in heavily in the name of the President, in everything about 'Torch', and his presence throughout was invaluable.

9. It is arranged that I see Monsieur Molotov today, when I can go more at length into the political sides of 'Torch' and reassure them about France and Vichy.

If, as I hope, Brooke and the others arrive this evening, the military authorities on both sides are to sit together and check up both on strategy and technical detail.

I told Stalin I should hold myself at this disposition should he wish to see me again. He replied that the Russian custom was that the visitor should state his wishes and that he was ready at any time. Accordingly I am going to propose another talk for this evening, perhaps at 10 p.m. He knows the worst, and we parted in an atmosphere of great goodwill. I am lodged in State Villa No. 7 where Stalin sometimes stays himself. It stands in the midst of a thick wood, is strongly guarded on every side, and has a spacious underground suite in case of air raids. The weather is beautiful, and what we should like best in England.

Josef Stalin to Winston S. Churchill: aide-memoire
(Cabinet papers, 20/79)

13 August 1942   Moscow

As a result of an exchange of views in Moscow which took place on August 12th, of this year, I ascertained that the Prime Minister of Great Britain, Mr Churchill, considered the organisation of a Second Front in Europe in 1942 to be impossible. As is well known, the organization of a Second Front in Europe in 1942 was pre-decided during the sojourn of Molotov in London, and it found expression in the agreed Anglo-Soviet communiqué published on June 12th last. It is also known that the organisation of a Second Front in Europe has as its object the withdrawal of German forces from the Eastern Front to the West and the creation in the West of a serious base of resistance to the German-Fascist forces, and the affording of relief by this means to the situation of the Soviet forces on the Soviet German front in 1942.

It is easy to grasp that the refusal of the Government of Great Britain to create a Second Front in 1942 in Europe inflicts a moral blow to the whole of Soviet public opinion, which calculates on the creation of a Second Front, and that complicates the situation of the Red Army at the front and prejudices the plan of the Soviet Command. I am not referring to the fact that the difficulties arising for the Red Army as a result of the refusal to create a Second Front in 1942 will undoubtedly be detrimental to the military situation of England and all the remaining Allies. It appears to me and my colleagues[1] that the most favourable conditions exist in 1942 for the creation of a Second Front in Europe, inasmuch as almost all the forces of the German Army and the best forces to boot, have been withdrawn to the Eastern Front, leaving Europe an inconsiderable amount of forces, and these of inferior quality. It is unknown whether the year of 1943 will offer conditions for the creation of a Second Front as favourable as 1942.

We are of opinion therefore that it is particularly in 1942 that the creation of a Second Front in Europe is possible and should be effective. I was however unfortunately unsuccessful in convincing Mr Prime Minister of Great Britain thereof, while Mr Harriman, the representative of the President of the United States, fully supported Mr Prime Minister in the negotiations held in Moscow.

---

[1] Churchill italicised the words 'and my colleagues' in reproducing this document in his published memoirs (*The Hinge of Fate*, page 441).

Winston S. Churchill: recollection
(*'The Hinge of Fate'*, *pages 436–7*)

13 August 1942

Late the next morning I awoke in my luxurious quarters. It was Thursday, August 13 – to me always 'Blenheim Day'. I had arranged to visit M Molotov in the Kremlin at noon in order to explain to him more clearly and fully the character of the various operations we had in mind. I pointed out how injurious to the common cause it would be if owing to recriminations about dropping 'Sledgehammer' we were forced to argue publicly against such enterprises. I also explained in more detail the political setting of 'Torch'. He listened affably, but contributed nothing. I proposed to him that I should see Stalin at 10 p.m. that night, and later in the day got word that eleven o'clock would be more convenient, and as the subjects to be dealt with would be the same as those of the night before would I wish to bring Harriman? I said 'Yes,' and also Cadogan, Brooke, Wavell, and Tedder, who had meanwhile arrived safely from Teheran in a Russian plane. They might have had a very dangerous fire in their Liberator.

Before leaving this urbane, rigid diplomatist's room I turned to him and said, 'Stalin will make a great mistake to treat us roughly when we have come so far.' For the first time Molotov unbent. 'Stalin,' he said, 'is a very wise man. You may be sure that, however he argues, he understands all. I will tell him what you say.'

[...]

We all repaired to the Kremlin at 11 p.m., and were received only by Stalin and Molotov, with their interpreter. Then began a most unpleasant discussion.

General Sir Alan Brooke: diary
(*'War Diaries, Field Marshal Lord Alanbrooke'*, *pages 299–300*)

13 August 1942   Moscow

The two leaders, Churchill and Stalin, are poles apart as human beings, and I cannot see a friendship between them such as exists between Roosevelt and Winston. Stalin is a realist if ever there was one; facts only count with him. Plans, hypotheses, future possibilities mean nothing to him, but he is ready to face facts, even when unpleasant. Winston, on the other hand, never seems anxious to face an unpleasantness until forced to do so. He appealed to sentiments in Stalin which do not, I think, exist. Altogether, I felt we were not gaining much ground.

General Sir Alan Brooke: notes
('Turn of the Tide', pages 460–1)

13 August 1942   Moscow

Personally I feel our policy with the Russians has been wrong from the very start [...] We have bowed and scraped to them, done all we could for them, and never asked them for a single fact or figure concerning their production, strength, dispositions, etc. As a result, they despise us and have no use for us except for what they can get out of us.

It had been a long and tiring flight lasting some fifteen hours. I was longing for a bath, light dinner and bed. It was not to be: as I stepped out of the plane I was handed a message from Winston to come at once to dine with him, to go on to the Kremlin at 11 p.m.

Tired as I was I would not have missed that meeting between Stalin and Winston for anything in the world. Everything of that meeting is still vivid in my memory. We were shown into a sparsely furnished room of the Kremlin, which reminded me of a station waiting-room. I think the only picture on the wall was that of Lenin. Stalin, Molotov and the interpreter entered and we sat at a long table.

We were soon involved in heated discussions concerning Western Second Front, and Winston had made it clear that such an offensive was not possible for the present but would be replaced by operations in North Africa. Stalin then began to turn on the heat and through the interpreter he passed a lot of abusive questions such as: 'When are you going to start fighting? Are you going to let us do all the work whilst you look on? Are you never going to start fighting? You will find it is not too bad if you once start!' etc., etc.

The effect on Winston was magnetic. He crashed his fist down on the table and poured forth one of his wonderful spontaneous orations. It began with: 'If it was not for the fighting qualities of the Red Army...' And then went on to tell Stalin exactly what his feelings were about fighting and a lot more.

Stalin stood up sucking at his large bent pipe, and with a broad grin on his face stopped Winston's interpreter and sent back through his own: 'I do not understand what you are saying, but by God, I like your sentiment.'

Looking back on that episode I am convinced that Stalin insulted Winston with the purpose of finding out what his reactions would be, and of sizing up what kind of a man he was. He very soon discovered what Winston was made of, and I am certain that this outburst of Winston's had impressed Stalin and started feelings of admiration for what he discovered was a true fighting man. At any rate, from that moment onwards the relations between the two improved and there grew up between them certain bonds of mutual admiration and appreciation based on the highly-developed fighting qualities which both of them possessed.

Winston S. Churchill to Clement Attlee
(Churchill papers, 20/87)

13 August 1942   Moscow

In my conversation last night with Monsieur Stalin I did not touch upon the PQ convoys as I did not want to harm 'Torch' (?) but this will have to be mentioned. I am certain only the plainest and most realistic dealing is helpful. I have, of course, no news of 'Pedestal' except Eagle[1] which is bad and TULIP 109 but you ought at least to be able to send sixty ships in the September PQ. Please reassure me about this. I must have something to say.

Sir Alexander Cadogan: diary
('The Diaries of Sir Alexander Cadogan', pages 471–2)

13 August 1942

The second meeting with Stalin took place after 11 p.m. that night, 13 August, in a sparsely-furnished chamber at the Kremlin. As in Beaverbrook's mission of the previous autumn, and Eden's of the winter, Stalin's line now hardened. He made gratuitously insulting remarks about the British Army's cowardice. Eventually the Prime Minister had had enough. He cracked his hand on the table, wound himself up almost audibly, and burst into a torrent of oratory. 'I have come round Europe in the midst of my troubles – yes, Mr Stalin, I have my troubles as well as you – hoping to meet the hand of comradeship; and I am bitterly disappointed. I have not met that hand.'

---

[1] On August 11, HMS *Eagle*, one of four aircraft carriers taking part in Operation 'Pedestal', was hit by four torpedoes and sank.

Tedder said that for about five minutes Churchill spoke 'in the most lucid, dramatic, forceful way I have ever heard anybody speak'. Both interpreters had failed to take a note. Only Cadogan had scribbled down the Prime Minister's words. He began to read them out but Stalin held up his hand. 'I do not understand the words, but by God I like your spirit.' The meeting ended at 2 a.m.

On the way back, Cadogan asked the Prime Minister: 'Shall I tell Stalin in confidence that you are hesitating whether to accept his invitation to dinner tomorrow after what has happened?'

'No, that is going too far, I think.'

Winston S. Churchill to President Franklin D. Roosevelt[1]
(Churchill papers, 20/79)

13 August 1942   Moscow
Secret and Personal
INDIA

I take it amiss Chiang should seek to make difficulties between us and should interfere in matters about which he has proved himself most ill informed which affect our sovereign rights.

Decision to intern Gandhi was taken by Executive of twelve, at which only one European was present. These Indians are as good Indian patriots and as able men as any of the Congress leaders. They have shown great courage and it is essential not to weaken their authority. All Chiang's talk of Congress leaders wishing us to quit in order that they may help the Allies is eye-wash. They are concerned with one thing only, namely, Congress supremacy. It occurred to me you could remind Chiang that Gandhi was prepared to negotiate with Japan on the basis of a free passage for Japanese troops through India in the hopes of their joining hands with Hitler. Personally I have no doubt that in addition there would been an understanding that the Congress would have the use of sufficient Japanese troops to keep down the composite majority of 90 million Moslems, 40 million untouchables and 90 million in the Princes' states. The style of his message prompts me to say 'Cherchez la femme'.

2. It may well be that the ensuing weeks will show how very little real influence the Hindu Congress has over the masses of India.

3. Averell and I are sending you full accounts of our conversation with Stalin, and up-shot of which is so far satisfactory.

[1] Churchill sent a copy of this telegram to the Secretary of State for India, Leo S. Amery, and the War Cabinet.

Winston S. Churchill to Harry Hopkins
(Churchill papers, 20/79)

13 August 1942　　　　　　　　　　　　　　　　　　　　　　Moscow

Harold Laski is asking approval for his going to the United States, quoting especially Mrs Roosevelt's invitation to attend some Youth Congress. Laski has been considerable nuisance over here and will I doubt not talk extreme left wing stuff in the United States. Although I liked his father[1] and maintained friendly relations with the son he has attacked me continually and tried to force my hand both in home and war politics. Unless therefore Mrs Roosevelt makes a personal point of it I should be glad if the invitation were not pressed. All good wishes.[2]

Winston S. Churchill: handwritten note
(Churchill papers, 20/87)

[14 August 1942]　　　　　　　　　　　　　　　　　　　　　[Moscow]

Tired as I was I dictated the following note before going to bed near dawn.

Winston S. Churchill to Members of the War Cabinet
(Churchill papers, 20/79)

14 August 1942　　　　　　　　　　　　　　　　　　　　　　Moscow
Personal and Most Secret

I visited Molotov at the Kremlin yesterday morning in order to explain to him more clearly and fully the character of the operations 'Sledgehammer', 'Round-Up', 'Bolero', 'Torch', and 'Jupiter'. I pointed out how injurious to the common cause it would be if, owing to recriminations about dropping 'Sledgehammer', we were forced to argue publicly against such enterprises. I also explained more fully the political setting

---

[1] Nathan Laski, 1863–1941. Educated at private school, Middlesbrough. Indian merchant for over 50 years; retired, 1930, and devoted himself to social work. Hon. MA, Manchester University. Justice of the Peace. Chairman, Manchester Jewish Hospital and Manchester and Salford Jewish Council. Chairman, Jewish Board of Guardians. Member of War Pensions Committee. Publications: *A Week in Palestine* (1924); *India as I Know It* (1928).

[2] On 28 August 1942 Harry Hopkins telegraphed to Churchill from Washington: 'Invitation from the United States for Laski to speak is not now being pressed and it is understood here that he is not coming' (*Churchill papers, 20/79*).

of 'Torch'. He listened affably but contributed nothing. I proposed to him that I should see Stalin at 10 p.m. that night, and later in the day got word that 11 o'clock would be more convenient and that as the subjects to be dealt with would be the same as those of the night before, would I wish to bring Harriman. I said 'yes', and also Cadogan, Brooke, Wavell and Tedder who had meanwhile arrived safely from Teheran in a Russian plane. They might have had a very dangerous fire in their Liberator.

2. Accordingly, we all repaired to the Kremlin at 11 p.m. and were received only by Stalin and Molotov with the interpreter. Then began a most unpleasant discussion. Stalin handed me the enclosed document to which see also my reply. When it was translated I said I would answer it in writing and that he must understand we had made up our minds upon the course to be pursued and that reproaches were vain. Thereafter we argued for about two hours, during which he said a great many disagreeable things, especially about our being too much afraid of fighting the Germans, and if we tried it like the Russians we should find it not so bad, that we had broken our promise about 'Sledgehammer', that we had failed in delivering the supplies promised to Russia and only sent remnants after we had taken all we needed for ourselves. Apparently these complaints were addressed as much to the United States as to Britain.

3. I repulsed all his contentions squarely but without taunts of any kind. I suppose he is not used to being contradicted repeatedly but he did not become at all angry or even animated. On one occasion I said, 'I pardon that remark only on account of the bravery of the Russian troops'. Finally he said we could carry it no further. He must accept our decision and abruptly invited us to dinner at 8 o'clock tonight.

4. Accepting the invitation I said I would leave by plane at dawn the next morning i.e. 15th. Joe seemed somewhat concerned at this and asked could I not stay longer. I said, certainly, if there was any good to be done, and that I would wait one more day anyhow. I then exclaimed there was no ring of comradeship in his attitude. I had travelled far to establish good working relations. We had done our utmost to help Russia and would continue to do so. We had been left entirely alone for a year against Germany and Italy. Now that the three great Nations were allied, victory was certain provided we did not fall apart, and so forth. I was somewhat animated in this passage and before it could be translated he made the remark that he liked the temperament (or spirit?) of my utterance. Thereafter the talk began again in a somewhat less tense atmosphere.

5. He plunged into a long discussion of two Russian trench mortars firing rockets which he declared were devastating in their effects and which he offered to demonstrate to our experts if they could wait. He said he would let us have all information about them, but should there not be something in return. Should there not be an agreement to exchange information of inventions. I said that we would give them everything without any bargaining except only these devices which, if carried in aeroplanes over the enemy lines and shot down would make our bombing of Germany more difficult. He accepted this. He also agreed that his Military authorities should meet our Generals and this was arranged for three o'clock this afternoon. I said they would require at least 4 hours to go fully into the various technical questions involved in 'Sledgehammer', 'Round-Up', 'Torch'. He then observed at one moment that 'Torch' was militarily correct but that the political side required more delicacy, i.e. more careful handling. From time to time he returned to 'Sledgehammer', grumbling about it. When he said our promise had not been kept, I replied 'I repudiate that statement. Every promise has been kept.' And I pointed to the aide memoire I gave Molotov. He made a sort of apology saying that he was expressing his sincere and honest opinions, that there was no mistrust between us but only a difference of view.

6. Finally I asked about the Caucasus. Was he going to defend the mountain chain, and with how many divisions. At this he sent for a relief model and with apparent frankness and knowledge he explained the strength of this barrier, for which he said 25 divisions were available. He pointed to the various passes and said they would be defended. I asked were they fortified and he said yes certainly. The Russian front line which the enemy had not yet reached is north of the main range. He said they would have to hold out for two months when the snow would make the mountains impassable. He expressed himself quite confident of his ability to do this, and also recounted in detail the strength of the Black Sea Fleet which was already at Batum. He expressed, however, suspicion of Turkish intentions and indicated that he did not trust them not to attack him in the rear. If they did he would smash them.

7. All this part of the talk was easier, but when Harriman asked about the plans for bringing American aircraft across Siberia, to which the Russians have only recently consented after long American pressing, he replied, curtly, 'Wars are not won with plans.' Harriman backed me up throughout and we neither of us yielded an inch nor spoke a bitter word.

8. It was arranged that Cadogan and Molotov should meet today to draw up a communiqué and to discuss publicity. Stalin assented to this

with a short laugh, remarking that they were the two who had drawn up the Anglo-American Russian communiqué issued in London.

9. He made his salute and held out his hand to me on leaving and I took it. In the public interest I shall go to the dinner tonight.

10. We asked ourselves what was the explanation of this performance and transformation from the good ground we had reached the night before. I think the most probable is that his Council of Commissars did not take the news I brought as well as he did. They perhaps have more power than we suppose and less knowledge. And that he was putting himself on the record for future purposes and for their benefit and also letting off steam for his own. Cadogan says a similar hardening up followed the opening of the Eden interview at Christmas, and Harriman says that this technique was also used at the beginning of the Beaverbrook mission.

11. It is my considered opinion that in his heart so far as he has one Stalin knows we are right and that six divisions on 'Sledgehammer' would do him no good this year. Moreover I am certain that his sure-footed and quick military judgment make him a strong supporter of 'Torch'. I think it not impossible that he will make amends. In that hope I persevere. Anyhow I am sure it was better to have it out this way than any other. There was never at any time the slightest suggestion of their not fighting on and I think myself that Stalin has good confidence that he will win.

12. When I thanked Stalin for the 40 Bostons he made a half-disdainful gesture, saying 'They were American planes. When I give you Russian planes then you may thank me.' By this he did not mean to disparage the American planes but said that he counted on his own strength. He stated his aircraft production at 1,800 a month plus 600 trainers.

13. I make great allowances for the stresses through which they are passing. Finally, I think they want full publicity for the visit.

Winston S. Churchill to Josef Stalin
(Churchill papers, 20/87)[1]

14 August 1942   Moscow

The best second front in 1942 and the only large scale operation possible from the Atlantic, is 'Torch'. If this can be effected in October, it will give more aid to Russia than any other plan. It also prepares the

---

[1] Churchill noted in his war memoirs that he prepared this telegram on the morning of 14 August 1942 'with the aid' of General Brooke and Sir Alexander Cadogan (*The Hinge of Fate*, pages 441–2).

way for 1943 and has the four advantages mentioned by Premier Stalin in the conversation of August 12th. The British and United States Governments have made up their minds about this and all preparations are proceeding with the utmost speed.

(2) Compared with 'Torch', the attack with 6 or 8 Anglo-American divisions on the Cherbourg Peninsula and the Channel Islands would be a hazardous and futile operation. The Germans have enough troops in the West to block us in this narrow peninsula with fortified lines and would concentrate all their air forces in the West upon us. In the opinion of all the British Naval, Military and Air authorities the operation could only end in disaster. Even if the lodgment were made it would not bring a single division back from Russia. It would also be far more a running sore for us than for the enemy, and would use up wastefully and wantonly the key men and the landing craft required for real action in 1943. This is our settled view. The CIGS will go into details with the Russian Commanders to any extent that may be desired.

(3) No promise has been broken by Great Britain or the United States. I point to paragraph 5 of my aide memoire given to Mr Molotov on the 10th June 1942 which distinctly says 'We can therefore, give no promise'. This aide memoire followed upon lengthy conversations, in which the very small chance of such plan being adopted was made abundantly clear. Several of these conversations are on record.

(4) However, all the talk about an Anglo-American invasion of France this year has misled the enemy and has held large air forces and considerable military forces on the French channel coast. It would be injurious to all common interests, especially Russian interests, if any public controversy arose in which it would be necessary for the British Government to unfold to the Nation the crushing arguments which they conceive themselves to possess against 'Sledgehammer'. Widespread discouragement would be caused to the Russian armies who have been buoyed up on this subject, and the enemy would be free to withdraw further forces from the West. The wisest course is to use 'Sledgehammer' as a blind for 'Torch', and proclaim 'Torch' when it begins as the second front. This is what we ourselves mean to do.

(5) We cannot admit that the conversations with Mr Molotov about the second front, safeguarded as they were by reservations both oral and written, formed any ground for altering the strategic plans of the Russian High Command.

(6) We reaffirm our resolve to aid our Russian allies by every practicable means.

Winston S. Churchill: recollection
('The Hinge of Fate', page 443)

14 August 1942

During the dinner Stalin talked to me in lively fashion through the interpreter Pavlov. 'Some years ago,' he said, 'we had a visit from Mr George Bernard Shaw and Lady Astor.' Lady Astor suggested that Mr Lloyd George should be invited to visit Moscow, to which Stalin had replied, 'Why should we ask him? He was the head of the intervention.' On this Lady Astor said, 'That is not true. It was Churchill who misled him.' 'Anyhow', said Stalin, 'Lloyd George was head of the Government and belonged to the Left. He was responsible, and we like a downright enemy better than a pretending friend.' 'Well, Churchill is finished finally,' said Lady Astor. 'I am not so sure,' Stalin had answered. 'If a great crisis comes the English people might turn to the old war-horse.' At this point I interrupted, saying, 'There is much in what she said. I was very active in the intervention, and I do not wish you to think otherwise.' He smiled amicably, so I said, 'Have you forgiven me?' 'Premier Stalin, he say,' said Interpreter Pavlov, 'all that is in the past, and the past belongs to God.'

Winston S. Churchill to President Franklin D. Roosevelt
and Clement Attlee
(Churchill papers, 20/88)

15 August 1942   Moscow

At a conference in Moscow on Saturday Voroshilov[1] and Shaposhnikov[2] met Brooke, Wavell, and Tedder, who offered detailed reasons about

[1] Klimenti Yefrimovitch Voroshilov (Voroshiloff), 1881–1969. An underground mineworker at the age of seven. Organised the first ever strike in his district at the age of 18. Worked under Stalin in Baku before the First World War. Chairman of the Committee for the Defence of Petrograd, November 1917. Commander-in-Chief of the defence of Tsaritsyn, 1918. People's Commissar for the Military Region of Kharkov, 1919. Defeated Wrangel in the Crimea, 1920. Quelled the Kronstadt uprising, 1921. Commander of the Moscow Region, 1924 (following the death of Lenin). People's Commissar for Naval and Military Affairs, 1925–34. People's Commissar for Defence, 1935–40. For a short while after the German invasion in June 1941, commanded the Leningrad Front; then sent to the Urals to organise the reserves. Head of the Control Commission in Hungary, 1947. Following Stalin's death in 1953, he became Chairman of the Praesidium of the Supreme Soviet (in effect, President of the USSR). Confessed to 'anti-Party sins', 1957. Published the memoirs of his early struggles, *Life Stories*, in 1968

[2] Boris Mikhailovitch Shaposhnikov, 1882–1945. Colonel in Russian Imperial Army and Red Army military commander. Marshal of the Soviet Union. Graduated from the Nicholas General Staff Academy in 1910. Colonel in Caucasus Grenadiers division during First World War. In 1917 supported

no 'Sledgehammer'. No impression was made, as the Russians, though entirely good-humoured, were acting under strict instructions. They did not even attempt to argue the matter in serious detail. After some time CIGS asked for details about the Caucasus position, to which Voroshilov replied he had no authority to speak on this point, but would ask for it.

Accordingly, in the afternoon a second meeting was held, at which the Russians repeated what Stalin had said to us, to the effect that twenty-five divisions would be assigned to the defence of the Caucasus mountain line and the passages at either end, and they believed they could hold both Batum and Baku and the Caucasus range until the winter snows greatly improved their position. However, CIGS is by no means reassured. For instance, Voroshilov stated that all the passes were fortified, but when CIGS had flown at 150 feet all up the west bank of the Caspian he only saw the northern line of defence being begun with anti-tank obstacles, pill-boxes, etc. In my private conversation with Stalin he revealed to me other solid reasons for his confidence, including a counter-offensive on a great scale, but as he asked me to keep this specially secret I will not refer to it further here. My own feeling is that it is an even chance they will hold, but CIGS will not go so far as this.

Winston S. Churchill: reflection
('The Hinge of Fate', page 445)

15 August 1942

I had been offended by many things which had been said at our conferences. I made every allowance for the strain under which the Soviet leaders lay, with their vast front flaming and bleeding along nearly 2,000 miles, and the Germans but fifty miles from Moscow and advancing towards the Caspian Sea. The technical military discussions had not gone well. Our generals had asked all sorts of questions to which their Soviet

the Russian Revolution and in 1918 joined the Red Army as one of few Red Army commanders with formal military training. On Red Army General Staff, 1921–5. Commander of the Leningrad military region, 1925; of the Privolzhsk and then Moscow military regions, 1928–32. Appointed Commandant of the Red Army's Frunze Military Academy, 1932. Returned to the command of the Leningrad region, 1935. Chief of the General Staff, 1937 to August 1940. Marshal of the Soviet Union, 1940. Reinstated as Chief of the General Staff at the time of the German invasion, 1941, remaining in post until November 1942. Also became Deputy People's Commissar for Defence, holding this post until 1943. Commandant of the Voroshilov Military Academy until his death in 1945. Despite his background as a Russian Imperial Army officer, Shaposhnikov won the respect and trust of Stalin. Stalin's admiration was shown by the fact that he always kept a copy of Shaposhnikov's most important work, *Mozg Armii* (The Brain of the Army) (1929), on his desk.

colleagues were not authorised to give answers. The only Soviet demand was for 'A Second Front NOW'. In the end Brooke was rather blunt, and the military conference came to a somewhat abrupt conclusion.

Winston S. Churchill: recollection
('The Hinge of Fate', pages 445–9)

15–16 August 1942

Our hour's conversation drew to its close and I got up to say good-bye. Stalin seemed suddenly embarrassed, and said in a more cordial tone than he had yet used with me, 'You are leaving at daybreak. Why should we not go to my house and have some drinks?' I said that I was in principle always in favour of such a policy. So he led the way through many passages and rooms till we came out into a roadway still within the Kremlin, and in a couple of hundred yards gained the apartment where he lived. He showed his own rooms, which were of moderate size, simple, dignified and four in number – a dining-room, working room, bedroom, and a large bathroom. Presently there appeared, first a very aged housekeeper and later a handsome red-haired girl, who kissed her father dutifully. He looked at me with a twinkle in his eye, as if, so I thought, to convey, 'You see, even we Bolsheviks have family life.' Stalin's daughter[1] started laying the table, and in a short time the housekeeper appeared with a few dishes. Meanwhile Stalin had been uncorking various bottles, which began to make an imposing array. Then he said, 'Why should we not have Molotov? He is worrying about the communiqué. We could settle it here. There is one thing about Molotov – he can drink.' I then realised that there was to be a dinner. I had planned to dine at State Villa Number Seven, where General Anders,[2] the Polish commander, was awaiting me, but I told my new

---

[1] Svetlana Iosifovna Alliluyeva Stalin (later Lana Peters), 1926–2011. The youngest child and only daughter of Josef Stalin and Nadezhda Alliluyeva (Stalin's second wife). Raised by a beloved nanny after her mother shot herself in 1932. Educated at Moscow University: studied fine arts and history. Became a naturalized United States citizen after defecting in 1967. Wrote *Twenty Letters To A Friend* (1967), *Only One Year* (1969), *Faraway Music* (1984).

[2] Władysław Anders, 1892–1970. Born in an area of Poland which at that time was part of the Russian Empire. Educated at Riga Technical University; member of the Polish student fraternity Arkonia. Served Tsar Nicholas II as an officer in the 1st Krechowiecki Lancers regiment during the First World War. Later joined the Polish Army as a commissioned officer in a cavalry regiment. In command of a cavalry brigade at the time of the outbreak of the Second World War. Wounded several times during the German invasion of Poland in September 1939 and the retreat to the east. Held prisoner in Lvov and later in Lubyanka prison, Moscow. Released by the Soviets with the aim of forming a Polish Army to fight alongside the Red Army. Continued friction with the Soviets over political issues led to the exodus of Anders' men – known as the Anders Army – together with a size-

and excellent interpreter, Major Birse,[1] to telephone that I should not be back till after midnight. Presently Molotov arrived. We sat down, and with two interpreters, were five in number. Major Birse has lived twenty years in Moscow, and got on very well with the Marshal, with whom he for some time kept up a running conversation, in which I could not share.

We actually sat at this table from 8.30 p.m. till 2.30 the next morning, which, with my previous interview, made a total of more than seven hours. The dinner was evidently improvised on the spur of the moment, but gradually more and more food arrived. We pecked and picked, as seemed to be the Russian fashion, at a long succession of choice dishes, and sipped a variety of excellent wines. Molotov assumed his most affable manner, and Stalin, to make things go, chaffed him unmercifully.

Presently we talked about the convoys to Russia. This led him to make a rough and rude remark about the almost total destruction of the Arctic convoy in June. I have recounted this incident in its place. I did not know so much about it then as I do now.

'Mr Stalin asks,' said Pavlov, with some hesitation, 'has the British Navy no sense of glory?' I answered, 'You must take it from me that what was done was right. I really do know a lot about the Navy and sea-war.' 'Meaning,' said Stalin, 'that I know nothing.' 'Russia is a land animal,' I said; 'the British are sea animals.' He fell silent and recovered his good-humour. I turned the talk on to Molotov. 'Was the Marshal aware that his Foreign Secretary on his recent visit to Washington had said he was determined to pay a visit to New York entirely by himself, and that the delay in his return was not due to any defect in the aeroplane, but because he was off on his own?'

Although almost anything can be said in fun at a Russian dinner, Molotov looked rather serious at this. But Stalin's face lit with merriment as he said:

able contingent of Polish civilians via the Persian Corridor into Iran, Iraq, and Palestine. In Palestine Anders formed and led the 2nd Polish Corps, fighting alongside the Western Allies. Commander of II Polish Corps in Italy 1943–6, capturing Monte Cassino in the Battle of Monte Cassino. Deprived of Polish citizenship and military rank in 1946 by the Soviet-installed Communist Government in Poland. Remained in exile in Britain as prominent member of Polish Government-in-Exile and Inspector-General of the Polish forces-in-exile. Died in London and was buried, in accordance with his wishes, among his fallen soldiers from II Polish Corps at the Polish War Cemetery at Monte Cassino, Italy. In 1989, after the collapse of Communism in Poland, Anders' citizenship and military rank were posthumously reinstated. Wrote *An Army in Exile* (1949).

[1] Arthur Herbert Birse, 1889–1967. A British subject, born in St Petersburg and raised in Russia. After the Revolution of 1917, left Russia and became a banker in Amsterdam and London. Registered with the Officers' Reserve in 1939. Transferred from Cairo to Moscow in 1941, and when the Foreign Office interpreter on whom Churchill normally relied fell ill, Birse was asked to take his place at Churchill's first meeting with Stalin. After the war, Birse went back to banking.

'It was not to New York he went. He went to Chicago, where the other gangsters live.'

Relations having thus been entirely restored, the talk ran on. I opened the question of a British landing in Norway with Russian support, and explained how, if we could take the North Cape in the winter and destroy the Germans there the path of the convoys would henceforward be open. This idea was always, as has been seen, one of my favourite plans. Stalin seemed much attracted by it, and, after talking of ways and means, we agreed we must do it if possible.

It was now past midnight and Cadogan had not appeared with the draft of the communiqué.

'Tell me,' I asked, 'have the stresses of this war been as bad to you personally as carrying through the policy of the Collective Farms?'

This subject immediately roused the Marshal.

'Oh, no', he said, 'the Collective Farm policy was a terrible struggle'.

'I thought you would have found it bad,' said I, 'because you were not dealing with a few score thousands of aristocrats or big landowners, but with millions of small men.'

'Ten millions,' he said, holding up his hands. 'It was fearful. Four years it lasted. It was absolutely necessary for Russia, if we were to avoid periodic famines, to plough the land with tractors. We must mechanise our agriculture. When we gave tractors to the peasants they were all spoiled in a few months. Only Collective Farms with workshops could handle tractors. We took the greatest trouble to explain it to the peasants. It was no use arguing with them. After you have said all you can to a peasant he says he must go home and consult his wife, and he must consult his herder.' This last was a new expression to me in this connection.

'After he has talked it over with them he always answers that he does not want the Collective Farm and he would rather do without the tractors.'

'These were what you call Kulaks?'

'Yes', he said, but he did not repeat the word. After a pause, 'It was all very bad and difficult – but necessary.'

'What happened?' I asked.

'Oh, well,' he said, 'many of them agreed to come in with us. Some of them were given land of their own to cultivate in the province of Tomsk or the province of Irkutsk or farther north, but the great bulk were very unpopular and were wiped out by their labourers.'

There was a considerable pause. Then, 'Not only have we vastly increased the food supply, but we have improved the quality of the grain beyond all measure. All kinds of grain used to be grown. Now no one is allowed to sow any but the standard Soviet grain from one end of our country to the other. If they do they are severely dealt with. This means another large increase in the food supply.'

I record as they come back to me these memories, and the strong impression I sustained at the moment of millions of men and women being blotted out or displaced for ever. A generation would no doubt come to whom their miseries were unknown, but it would be sure of having more to eat and bless Stalin's name. I did not repeat Burke's[1] dictum, 'If I cannot have reform without injustice, I will not have reform.' With the World War going on all round us it seemed vain to moralise aloud.

About 1 a.m. Cadogan arrived with the draft, and we set to work to put it into final form. A considerable sucking-pig was brought to the table. Hitherto Stalin had only tasted the dishes, but now it was half-past one in the morning and around his usual dinner hour. He invited Cadogan to join him in the conflict, and when my friend excused himself our host fell upon the victim single-handed. After this had been achieved he went abruptly into the next room to receive the reports from all sectors of the front, which were delivered to him from 2 a.m. onwards. It was about twenty minutes before he returned, and by that time we had the communiqué agreed. Finally, at 2.30 a.m. I said I must go. I had half an hour to drive to the villa, and as long to drive to the airport. I had a splitting headache, which for me was very unusual. I still had General Anders to see. I begged Molotov not to come and see me off at dawn, for he was clearly tired out. He looked at me reproachfully, as if to say, 'Do you really think I would fail to be there?'

Winston S. Churchill to Clement Attlee
(Churchill papers, 20/79)

16 August 1942[2]   Moscow

The dinner passed off in a very friendly atmosphere and the usual Russian ceremonies. Wavell made an excellent speech in Russian. I proposed

---

[1] Edmund Burke, 1729–97. Anglo-Irish statesman, author, orator, political theorist, and philosopher who, after relocation to England, served for many years in the House of Commons as a member of the Whig Party. He is mainly remembered for his opposition to the French Revolution. It led to his becoming the leading figure within the conservative faction of the Whig party, which he dubbed the 'Old Whigs' in opposition to the pro-French-Revolution 'New Whigs' led by Charles James Fox. Living before the terms 'conservative' and 'liberal' were used to describe political ideologies, Burke was prized by both conservatives and liberals in the nineteenth century. From the twentieth century he has generally been viewed as the philosophical founder of modern conservatism.

[2] Original document dated August 15, but written in the early hours of the following day.

Stalin's health and Alexander Cadogan proposed death and damnation to the Germans. Though I sat on Stalin's right I got no opportunity of talking about serious things. Pavlov, the little interpreter, was a very poor substitute for Maisky. Stalin and I were photographed together, also with Harriman. Stalin made quite a long speech proposing the quote Intelligence Service unquote in the course of which he made a curious reference to the Dardanelles in 1915, saying that the British had won and the Germans and Turks were already retreating but we did not know because the intelligence was faulty. This picture, though inaccurate, was evidently meant to be complimentary to me.

2. I left about 1.30 a.m. as I was afraid we should be drawn in to a lengthy film and was fatigued. When I said good-bye to Stalin he said that any differences that existed were only of method. I said we would try to remove even those differences by deeds. After a cordial handshake I then took my departure and got some way down the crowded room but he hurried after me and accompanied me an immense distance through corridors and staircases to the front door where we again shook hands.

3. Perhaps in my account to you of the Thursday night meeting I took too gloomy a view. I feel I must make full allowance for the really grievous disappointment which they feel here that we can do nothing more to help them in their immense struggle. In the up-shot they have swallowed this bitter pill. Everything for us now turns on hastening 'Torch' and defeating Rommel.

4. I have just had a long talk, with dinner lasting six hours, with Stalin and Molotov alone in his private apartment with a good interpreter. I will send you a fuller account later but we covered the whole ground and parted on most cordial and friendly terms. At this meeting the following communiqué was agreed and our Ambassador will be getting into touch with London about its publication on either 17 or 18 August. Communiqué reads. Begins.

Anglo-Soviet Communiqué

On the negotiations of the Prime Minister of Great Britain, Mr Winston Churchill, with the President of the Council of the People's commissars of USSR, J. V. Stalin.
Begins.

Negotiations have taken place in Moscow between President of the Council of the People's commissars of USSR, J. V. Stalin, and Prime Minister of Great Britain, Mr Winston Churchill, in which Mr Harriman representing the President of United States of America participated. There took part in the discussions – The People's Commissars for Foreign Affairs – V. M. Molotov, Marshal K. E. Voroshilov – from Soviet side; the British Ambassador, Sir A. Clark Kerr, CIGS, Sir A. Brooke and other responsible representatives of British armed forces, and the Permanent Under Secretary of State for Foreign Affairs, Sir A. Cadogan – from the British side.

A number of decisions were reached covering the field of the war against Hitlerite Germany and her associates in Europe. This just war of liberation both Governments are determined to carry on with all their power and energy until the complete destruction of Hitlerism and any similar tyranny has been achieved. The discussions, which were carried on in an atmosphere of cordiality and complete sincerity, provided an opportunity of re-affirming the existence of the close friendships and understanding between the Soviet Union, Great Britain and United States of America in entire accordance with the allied relationships existing between them. Ends.

CIGS met the Russian Military authorities twice yesterday 15th. He was much impressed with the demonstration of the mortar on the 14th. I am leaving at dawn today 16th and hope to reach Cairo morning 17th.

5. Note to Private Office. Please arrange transmission of this message through US Embassy from Former Naval Person to President Roosevelt.

Winston S. Churchill to President Franklin D. Roosevelt
(Churchill papers, 20/79)

15 August 1942

Your 178. Am much obliged to you for the form in which you have couched your message which is entirely agreeable to me. Fear it is too late for me to reply now.

2. Any consoling or heartening message you feel like sending to Stalin secretly would be helpful. You will have seen my full accounts. I do not know what I should have done without Averell.

President Franklin D. Roosevelt to Winston S. Churchill
(Churchill papers, 20/79)

15 August 1942

Mr Stalin's understanding of our difficulties and his cordiality have made me very happy.

I only wish that I might be with you both, as that would complete the party.

Give Mr Stalin my warmest regards and keep me in touch with developments.

Winston S. Churchill to Admiral of the Fleet Sir Dudley Pound
(Churchill papers, 20/87)

15 August 1942

Prolongation of life of Malta was worth the heavy cost.

Winston S. Churchill to Members of the War Cabinet
and President Franklin D. Roosevelt
(Churchill papers, 20/87)

[16 August 1942]   [Teheran]
Most Immediate
Decypher Yourself[1]

[...]

I went to wind up with M Stalin at 7 p.m. yesterday, and we had an agreeable conversation, in the course of which he gave me a full account of the Russian position, which seemed very encouraging. He certainly speaks with great confidence of being able to hold out until the winter. At 8.30 p.m., when I got up to leave, he asked when was the next time he was going to see me. I said that I was leaving at dawn. He then said, 'Why do not you come over to my apartment in the Kremlin and have some drinks?' I went, and stayed to dinner, to which M Molotov was also summoned. M Stalin introduced me to his daughter, a nice girl, who kissed him shyly, but was not allowed to dine. The dinner and the communiqué lasted till 3 a.m. this morning. I had a very good interpreter and was able to talk much more easily. The greatest goodwill prevailed, and for the first time we got on to easy and friendly terms. I feel that I have established a personal relationship which will be helpful. We talked a great deal about 'Jupiter', which he thinks essential in November or December. Without it I really do not see how we are going to be able to get through the supplies which will be needed to keep this tremendous fighting army equipped. The Trans-Persian route is only working at half

[1] As telegraphed: 'DEYOU'.

what we hoped. What he requires most of all are lorries. He would rather have lorries than tanks, of which he is making 2,000 a month. Also he wants aluminium.

[…]

On the whole, I am definitely encouraged by my visit to Moscow. I am sure that the disappointing news I brought could not have been imparted except by me personally without leading to really serious drifting apart. It was my duty to go. Now they know the worst, and having made their protest are entirely friendly; this in spite of the fact that this is their most anxious and agonising time. Moreover, M Stalin is entirely convinced of the great advantages of 'Torch', and I do trust that it is being driven forward with superhuman energy on both sides of the ocean.

General Archibald Wavell: poem
(War Diaries, Field Marshal Lord Alanbrooke, page 307)

16 August 1942   en route from Moscow to Teheran
Most Personal And Very Secret
Ballade Of The Second Front
PM Loquitur

1. I do not like the job I have to do. I cannot think my views will go down well. Can I convince them of our settled view; will Stalin use Caucasian oaths and yell?
   Or can I bind him with my midnight spell; I'm really feeling rather in a stew.
   It's not so hot a thing to have to sell; No Second Front in 1942.
2. I thought so, things are stickier than glue; they simply hate the tale I have to tell.
   Stalin and Molotov are looking blue; if I give in an inch they'll take an ell. I wonder if they'll put me in a cell, and deal with me like Hitler with a Jew.
   It's not so hot a thing to have to sell; No Second Front in 1942.
3. Come, things are taking on a rosier hue; the whole affair has got a better smell.
   I think that after all we'll put it thru; though not as merry as a wedding bell.
   The sound is now less like a funeral knell; another vodka for? Here's Fortune
   – Phew!

I've got away with what I come to sell; No Second Front in 1942.
Envoi
4. Prince of the Kremlin, here's a fond farewell;
   I've had to deal with many worse than you.
   You took it though you hated it like hell;
   No Second Front in 1942.

Winston S. Churchill to Josef Stalin
(Churchill papers, 20/79)

16 August 1942   Teheran

On arriving at Teheran after a swift and smooth flight I take occasion to thank you for your comradeship and hospitality. I am very glad I came to Moscow, firstly because it was my duty to tell the tale, and secondly because I feel sure our contacts will play a helpful part in furthering our cause. Give my regards to Molotov.

Sir Alexander Cadogan: diary
('The Diaries of Sir Alexander Cadogan', page 474)

17 August 1942   Teheran

The PM had set his heart on my seeing the Shah – I can't think why – so an audience had to be fixed and I just had time to have tea, unpack and have a bath and dash off to the Palace to be presented at 6. He's a nice and intelligent young man, but he mumbles so (though he speaks good French) that I only heard about 50% of what he said. (Flying always makes me deaf for an hour or two.) [...]

Today I spent a lazy day with nothing much to do. The PM talks of spending a week here, but I hope to push him off earlier.

Winston S. Churchill to A. V. Alexander and
Admiral of the Fleet Sir Dudley Pound
(Churchill papers, 20/87)

17 August 1942   Cairo
Most Secret and Personal

Please convey my compliments to Admirals Syfret, Burrough, and Lyster and all officers and men engaged in the magnificent crash through of supplies to Malta, which cannot fail to have an important influence on the immediate future of the war in the Mediterranean.

2. Papers here report thirteen enemy aircraft shot down, but this was only by the Malta force, and I have seen no mention of the thirty-nine additional shot down by the carriers, which puts a very different complexion on the air fighting.

Winston S. Churchill: broadcast to Moscow
('Winston S. Churchill, His Complete Speeches', volume 6, page 6662)

17 August 1942　　　　　　　　　　　　　　　　　Cairo

We are full of determination to continue the struggle hand in hand, whatever sufferings and hardships may await us, and to continue the struggle hand in hand as comrades and brothers until the last vestiges of the Hitlerite *régime* are turned to dust, remaining in the memory as an example and a warning for the future.

Winston S. Churchill to Sir Archibald Sinclair and
Air Chief Marshal Sir Charles Portal
(Churchill papers, 20/87)

17 August 1942　　　　　　　　　　　　　　　　　Cairo
Most Secret and Personal

Stalin attaches special importance to bombing Berlin and is going to start himself soon. Should be glad if we also struck hard as soon as darkness permits. Let me know what your intentions are. Operations should be concerted to avoid clashes over target.

Winston S. Churchill to Clement Attlee
(Churchill papers, 20/87)

17 August 1942　　　　　　　　　　　　　　　　　Cairo
Secret and Personal

Arrived here at eleven a.m. having covered distance from Moscow to Cairo in 15 flying hours, but we rested on the way for a night at Teheran.

2. Minister of State informs me that there is no doubt General Auchinleck does not wish to accept the Iraq–Persian command. He is seriously

upset by the turn of events and wishes to leave at once to join his wife in India where he will probably have a rest at some hill station. He is coming to take leave of me tomorrow.

3. We are meeting tomorrow 18, to consider Chiefs of Staff report and Local Committee report on separation of commands. General Alexander definitely does not want to have this burden of distant responsibility on his hands while he is centring all his thoughts upon Rommel. CIGS and I endorse this view. Question of making Iraq–Persia a separate command stands in a different light in view of Auchinleck's refusal. I am still of the belief the separation is right on the merits, but I now do not see the outstanding personality who can fill the gap. We shall also consider the return to India of the Iraq–Persia sector. General Wavell would like this, and as he has a deputy C-in-C, Hartley, in India he does not feel he would be over burdened. I shall have this alternative explored.

[. . .]

6. Meanwhile the Fifth British Division is arriving in the Tenth Army area. The Tenth Indian Division which is battle worn will be there soon to recuperate. The 56[1] and either a British or American Armoured Division are scheduled for this destination. Am most anxious not to move the Second British Division out of India at the present time and CIGS has arranged with General Wavell to substitute an Indian armoured brigade for it.

7. General Anders is coming here on the 20th and I am having the whole question of the formation and equipment of the Polish Divisions searchingly examined in order that they may be formed and equipped in Persia at the earliest possible moment.

8. I am having constant talks with General Alexander who has now assumed command. Likewise Montgomery. I am going to the former's headquarters at the front for Wednesday night, seeing troops both in the afternoon and following morning. General Alexander tells me that he (? word omitted) the Army scattered about in bits and pieces and that it requires drastic reorganisation. He favours the division rather than the brigade group organisation and is regrouping his forces for the approaching battle. He has good hopes it will take place in September but I cannot hurry the process beyond his judgement. He realizes the extreme urgency. I am more than ever convinced that the changes were absolutely necessary. There is no offensive punch in the army at the present moment. No mobile mass of manoeuvre and the troops had

---

[1] 56th Infantry Division.

undoubtedly lost confidence in the High Command including as far as they knew him at all General Auchinleck. Everything is being prepared with the utmost energy for what I trust will be a decisive stroke, certainly before 'Torch' begins.

Winston S. Churchill to Clement Attlee
(Churchill papers, 20/87)

17 August 1942   Cairo
Most Secret and Personal

As Auchinleck has definitely refused the Iraq–Persia Command, there is no reason for further delaying the announcement of the changes. Present situation cannot possibly continue and the Army must know who are leading them. Propose, therefore, that tomorrow 18th it should be announced that Alexander has relieved Auchinleck and Montgomery has assumed command of the 8 Army in succession to Ritchie.

The question of the Iraq–Persia Command will require a few days further study but is no longer affected by the movements of personalities.

Winston S. Churchill to Lord Linlithgow[1]
(Churchill papers, 20/79)

17 August 1942   Cairo
Most Secret and Personal

I must congratulate you upon the resolute and skilful manner in which you are grappling with the disorders fomented by Congress. I hope you will have seen my telegram to President Roosevelt in reply to his request for my observations on Chiang Kai-shek's telegram to him. If not Secretary of State will repeat it to you. My own conviction is that if this situation is handled with the poise and strength which the Government of India is showing under your guidance, it will soon demonstrate the very slender hold which the Congress have both upon the Indian masses and upon the dominant forces in India life and society.

2. General Wavell who will return to you shortly will give you a full account of my visit to Moscow and will also tell you about several other secret operational plans which are being concerted. These are for your information alone.

---

[1] Viceroy of India.

3. I have every reason to believe that it will be possible to avoid moving the Second Indian Division out of India at the present time towards the Caspian Front. CIGS will accept instead the other Indian Armoured Brigade. It seems to me that you need as much British strength as possible in these difficult times.

4. Every personal good wish.

King George VI to Winston S. Churchill[1]
(Churchill papers, 20/59)

17 August 1942

I am delighted that your talks with Stalin ended on such a friendly note. As a bearer of unwelcome news your task was a very disagreeable one, but I congratulate you heartily on the skill with which you accomplished it. The personal relationship which you have established with Stalin should be valuable in the days to come; and your long journey has, I am sure, been well worth while.

I hope that you are not too tired, and that you will be able to take things more easily now.

My best wishes for a safe and comfortable journey home when your business is completed.

General Sir Alan Brooke: diary
('War Diaries, Field Marshal Lord Alanbrooke', page 308)

18 August 1942

[...] I slept solidly from midnight to 8.30 a.m. Whilst dressing the PM breezed in in his dressing gown and told me he had been thinking over the urgency of the attack against Rommel. He then started producing all the arguments that I have so frequently battled against for speeding up the date. I had to point out that it was exactly 2 days!! ago that Alex had taken over and Monty arrived, and that there was a mess to be put right [...]

---

[1] This message was sent as a Most Secret cipher telegram to Cairo.

Winston S. Churchill to King George VI[1]
(Churchill papers, 20/59)

18 August 1942　　　　　　　　　　　　　　　　　　　　　　Cairo
Most Secret and Personal

Mr Churchill with his humble duty to Your Majesty, has been much encouraged by Your Majesty's most gracious message.

2. Mr Churchill hopes to deal with a number of important and urgent problems here during the present week. He is in the best of health and not at all tired. Your Majesty is always so kind, and these fresh marks of your confidence are most agreeable.

Winston S. Churchill to Clement Attlee
(Churchill papers, 20/87)

18 August 1942　　　　　　　　　　　　　　　　　　　　　　Cairo
2.30 p.m.
Most Secret and Personal

Pray look at the series of telegrams in this sequence, Reflex 132, Reflex 142, Tulip 169, Reflex 147. It is not proposed that General Lumsden[2] should be Commander of 30th Corps. He is reserved to command the mass of manoeuvre which is being formed. In my Reflex 148 I sent you the draft of the announcement, which mentioned Alexander and Montgomery and also McCreery,[3] CGS, but said nothing whatever about Lumsden. Do not however issue any contradiction at the moment.

2. I had also hoped that the disclosure of my visit to Cairo, which was forced by the Pretoria radio, would have been on a different day from these grave changes in the High Command. I thought this would have been

---

[1] Sent as a secret cipher telegram from Cairo.

[2] Herbert Lumsden, 1897–1945. Educated Royal Military Academy, Woolwich. 2nd Lieutenant RA, 1915. Served in First World War, 1915–18 (Military Cross). Lieutenant, 12th Royal Lancers, 1938–40. Served in Second World War, 1939–45 (despatches twice, DSO and bar, wounded). Colonel, 1940. Temporary Major-General, 1942. Temporary Lieutenant-General, 1943. Special representative with General MacArthur, 1943. Major-General, 1944. Commanded X Corps, 8th Army, 1942–3.

[3] Richard London McCreery, 1898–1967. On active service in France, 1914–18 (Military Cross); 1940 (DSO). Commander, 8th Armoured Division, Middle East, 1941–2; Tunisia, 1943. Chief of General Staff, Middle East, 1942. Knighted, 1943. Commanded 8th Army in Italy, 1944–5. General Officer Commanding-in-Chief, British Forces of Occupation in Austria, and British Representative as the Allied High Commissioner for Austria, 1945–6. General Officer Commanding-in-Chief, British Army of Occupation on the Rhine, 1946–8. British Army Representative, Military Staff Committee, United Nations, 1948–9. Retired, 1949. Colonel Commandant, Royal Armoured Corps, 1947–56.

more becoming and more in accordance with your wishes. I set all this out in my Reflex 147 which should have reached you in plenty of time.

3. You should announce General McCreery's appointment as CGS during 19th for papers of 20th.

4. Surely precedent required reference to His Majesty having been pleased to appoint, etc. see *Times* of July 2, 1941 for announcement of Wavell's supersession by Auchinleck.

Winston S. Churchill to Clement Attlee
(Churchill papers, 20/87)

18 August 1942   Cairo
10.30 p.m.
Most Secret and Personal

We propose release here tonight for publication in papers 19th account of my first visit to Cairo, and to meet your wishes will delay announcement of changes in Command till tomorrow 19th for publication 20th.

2. We now wish also to announce appointment of Major-General McCreery as CGS. It should be pointed out to the Press privately that he is a leading authority on tank warfare. Actual text of announcement of changes in command contained in my immediately following telegram. If you want any changes in form, there is still time if you cable.

3. No reference should be made to my second visit, but there is no reason why friends and the Press should not know discreetly that I am on my way home. We are already putting out misleading rumours that I have reached Khartoum.

Winston S. Churchill to Clement Attlee, Anthony Eden, and
Air Chief Marshal Sir Charles Portal
(Churchill papers, 20/87)

19 August 1942   Cairo
Most Secret and Personal

I agree that there is no possibility of influencing the situation in the next sixty days. I also agree that nothing can be moved before the decision here, which will certainly be reached in forty days, and may come much sooner.

2. Matter must be viewed as long-term policy; namely, to place on the southern flank of the Russian armies a substantial British and, later on, American Air Force,

    (a) in order to strengthen the Russian air-power generally;

    (b) in order to form the advance shield of all our interests in Persia and Abadan;

    (c) for moral effect of comradeship with the Russians, which will be out of all proportion to the forces employed. We must have the means to do them a friendly act, especially in view of the difficulties of PQ convoys after September; and

    (d) because this is no dispersion of forces, but a great concentration on the supreme Air Force target, namely, wearing down the German Air Force by daily fighting contact. We can fight them at more advantage in the ordinary conditions of the battle-front than by looking for trouble over the Channel. It pays us to lose machine for machine.

3. I have committed HMG to this policy in my talks with Stalin, and I must ask the Cabinet for support. See also, when it reaches you, the account of the military conversations in Moscow, and also my correspondence with the President on the matter, to which he attaches great importance.

4. CAS[1] should prepare a draft project for a movement of the kind outlined by Air Chief Marshal Tedder, which can be first sent to the President by me with a covering telegram. If his reply is satisfactory I will then make a firm offer to Stalin, which might not be operative till November, but which would enable immediate work to be started on surveying and preparing the landing-grounds and would give us access to the Russian sphere in Persia and the Caucasus. If things go well we will advance with the Russians' southern wing; if ill, we shall anyhow have to put forces of this order in North Persia. I wish to telegraph to the President before I leave here. Final decision can be taken at home when we hear what he says.

5. Everybody always finds it convenient to ease themselves at the expense of Russia, but grave issues depend upon preserving a good relationship with this tremendous army, now under dire distress. It will take a lot to convince me that action within the limits mentioned by Tedder will interfere with 'Torch'.

---

[1] Chief of the Air Staff, Air Chief Marshal Portal.

Winston S. Churchill: recollection
(*'The Hinge of Fate', pages 462–3*)

19 August 1942

On August 19 I paid another visit to the Desert Front. I drove with Alexander in his car out from Cairo past the Pyramids, about 130 miles through the desert to the sea at Abusir. I was cheered by all he told me. As the shadows lengthened we reached Montgomery's headquarters, at Burg-el-Arab. Here the afterwards famous caravan was drawn up amid the sand-dunes by the sparkling waves. The General gave me his own wagon, divided between office and bedroom. After our long drive we all had a delicious bathe. 'All the armies are bathing now at this hour all along the coast,' said Montgomery as we stood in our towels. He waved his arm to the westward. Three hundred yards away about a thousand of our men were disporting themselves on the beach. Although I knew the answer, I asked, 'Why do the War Office go to the expense of sending out white bathing drawers for the troops? Surely this economy should be made.' They were in fact tanned and burnt to the darkest brown everywhere except where they wore their short pants.

How fashions change! When I marched to Omdurman forty-four years before the theory was that the African sun must at all costs be kept away from the skin. The rules were strict. Special spine-pads were buttoned on to the back of all our khaki coats. It was a military offence to appear without a pith helmet. We were advised to wear thick underclothing, following Arab custom enjoined by a thousand years of experience. Yet now half-way through the twentieth century many of the white soldiers went about their daily toil hatless and naked except for the equal of a loin cloth. Apparently it did them no harm. Though the process of changing from white to bronze took several weeks and gradual application, sunstroke and heatstroke were rare. I wonder how the doctors explain all this.

After we had dressed for dinner – my zip hardly takes a minute to put on – we gathered in Montgomery's map wagon. There he gave us a masterly exposition of the situation, showing that in a few days he had firmly gripped the whole problem. He accurately predicted Rommel's next attack, and explained his plans to meet it. All of which proved true and sound. He then described his plans for taking the offensive himself. He must however have six weeks to get the Eighth Army into order. He would re-form the divisions as integral tactical units. We must wait till the new divisions had taken their place at the front and until the Sherman tanks were broken in. Then there would be three Army Corps, each under an experienced officer, whom he and Alexander knew well. Above all the artillery would be used as had never been possible before in the Desert. He spoke of the end of September. I was disappointed at the date, but even this was dependent upon Rommel. Our information showed that a blow from him was imminent. I was myself already fully informed, and was well content that he should try a wide turning movement round our Desert Flank in order to reach Cairo, and that a manoeuvre battle should be fought on his communications.

At this time I thought much of Napoleon's defeat in 1814. He too was poised to strike at the communications, but the Allies marched straight on into an almost open Paris. I thought it of the highest importance that Cairo should be defended by every able-bodied man in uniform not required for the Eighth Army. Thus alone would the field army have full manoeuvring freedom and be able to take risks in letting its flank be turned before striking. It was with great pleasure that I found we were all in agreement. Although I was always impatient for offensive action on our part at the earliest moment, I welcomed the prospect of Rommel breaking his teeth upon us before our main attack was launched. But should we have time to organise the defence of Cairo? Many signs pointed to the audacious commander who faced us only a dozen miles away striking his supreme blow before the end of August. Any day indeed, my friends said, he might make his bid for continued mastery. A fortnight or three weeks' delay would be all to our good.

Winston S. Churchill to Air Chief Marshal Sir Charles Portal
(Churchill papers, 20/87)

19 August 1942   Cairo
Most Secret and Personal

BOMBING POLICY

250 Heavies far exceeds weight and number of any previous attack on Berlin. What date will 500 be possible? Certainly no attack should be made – 'regardless of cost' but Harris mentioned to me before I left possibility of an attack in the August moon. Can you do it in September? I had always understood darkness was the limiting factor, not numbers.[1]

[1] The first daylight raid on Germany was attempted on 19 September 1942. Six Mosquitoes were involved. Two had to turn back owing to mechanical problems. Two bombed Hamburg, one bombed Berlin, and one was lost, presumed shot down.

Winston S. Churchill to General Hastings Ismay
(Churchill papers, 20/87)

19 August 1942
Most Secret and Personal

THE DIEPPE RAID[1]

Consider it would be wise to describe 'Jubilee' as 'Reconnaissance in force'.

Clementine Churchill to Winston S. Churchill
(Baroness Spencer-Churchill papers)

19 August 1942   10 Downing Street

My Darling,

I count the days & nights since you flew away in the dark – Eighteen –
I pray that all the work you have done will bear fruit. I suppose this will
reach you before you wing your way back?

I send you my dear love
CLEMMIE [Drawing of a cat]

Winston S. Churchill: recollection
('The Hinge of Fate', pages 464–5)

20 August 1942

On August 20 we sallied forth early to see the prospective battlefield
and the gallant troops who were to hold it. I was taken to the key point
south-east of the Ruweisat Ridge. Here, amid the hard, rolling curves
and creases of the desert, lay the mass of our armour, camouflaged,
concealed, and dispersed, yet tactically concentrated. Here I met the
young Brigadier Roberts,[2] who at that time commanded the whole of

---

[1] On 19 August 1942 a force of some 6,000 troops, mainly Canadian, with substantial RAF and
some Royal Navy support, mounted a raid on German-occupied Dieppe (Operation 'Jubilee').
Churchill considered the raid 'costly but fruitful' (*The Hinge of Fate*, page 459), yielding invaluable
lessons that helped pave the way for both Operation 'Torch' later in 1942 and Operation 'Overlord' two years later.

[2] George Philip Bradley Roberts, 1906–97. Known as 'Pip'. Educated at Marlborough and Royal
Military College, Sandhurst. Entered the Army as 2nd Lieutenant, Royal Tank Corps, 1926. Captain,
Royal Tank Regiment, 1939. Major, 7th Armoured Division, 1939. As Brigade Major, 4th Armoured
Brigade, took part in Battle of Sidi Barrani and defeat of Italian Army in Libya, 1941 (Military
Cross). Served on staff of 7th Armoured Division, June 1941; XXX Armoured Corps, November
1941. Officer Commanding 3rd Royal Tank Regiment, January 1942. Wounded in Battle of Gazala,
June 1942 (DSO). Officer Commanding 22nd Armoured Brigade, July 1942; took part in Battles
of Alam Halfa and El Alamein (bar to DSO). Led brigade into Tunis, May 1943 (2nd bar to DSO).

our armoured force in this vital position. All our best tanks were under him. Montgomery explained to me the disposition of our artillery of all natures. Every crevice of the desert was packed with camouflaged concealed batteries. Three or four hundred guns would fire at the German armour before we hurled in our own.

Although of course no gatherings of troops could be allowed under the enemy's continuous air reconnaissance, I saw a great many soldiers that day, who greeted me with grins and cheers. I inspected my own regiment, the 4th Hussars, or as many of them as they dared to bring together – perhaps fifty or sixty – near the field cemetery, in which a number of their comrades had been newly buried. All this was moving, but with it all there grew a sense of the reviving ardour of the Army. Everybody said what a change there was since Montgomery had taken command. I could feel the truth of this with joy and comfort.

We were to lunch with Bernard Freyberg.[1] My mind went back to a similar visit I had paid him in Flanders, at his battlepost in the valley of the Scarpe,[2] a quarter of a century before, when he already commanded a brigade. Then he had blithely offered to take me for a walk along his outposts. But knowing him and knowing the line as I did I declined. Now it was the other way round. I certainly hoped to see at least a forward observation post of these splendid New Zealanders, who were in contact about five miles away. Alexander's attitude showed he would not forbid but rather accompany the excursion. But Bernard Freyberg flatly refused to take the responsibility, and this was not a matter about which orders are usually given, even by the highest authority.

Instead we went into his sweltering mess tent, and were offered a luncheon, far more magnificent than the one I had eaten on the Scarpe. This was an August noonday in the desert. The set piece of the meal was a scalding broth of tinned New Zealand oysters, to which I could do no more than was civil. Presently Montgomery, who had left us some time before, drove up. Freyberg went out to salute him, and told him his place had been kept and that he was expected to luncheon. But 'Monty', as he was already called, had, it appeared, made it a rule not to accept hospitality from any of his subordinate commanders. So he sat outside in his car eating an austere sandwich and drinking his lemonade with all formalities. Napoleon also might have stood aloof in the interests of

Commanded 11th Armoured Division in Normandy, June 1944. Led troops liberating Belsen concentration camp, 1945. CB, 1945. Retired from the Army, 1949.

[1] General Officer Commanding New Zealand Forces.

[2] The Scarpe: a river that ran through the First World War battlefields of northern France around Arras, in the area where Freyberg fought with great distinction.

discipline. *Dur aux grands* was one of his maxims.[1] But he would certainly have had an excellent roast chicken, served him from his own *fourgon.* Marlborough would have entered and quaffed the good wine with his officers – Cromwell, I think, too. The technique varies, and the results seem to have been good in all these cases.

We spent all the afternoon among the Army, and it was past seven when we got back to the caravan and the pleasant waves of its beach. I was so uplifted by all I had seen that I was not at all tired and sat up late talking. Before Montgomery went to bed at ten o'clock, in accordance with his routine, he asked me to write something in his personal diary. I did so now and on several other occasions during the long war. Here is what I wrote this time:

Winston S. Churchill to General Bernard Montgomery
('The Hinge of Fate', pages 464–5)

20 August 1942   Western Desert

May the anniversary of Blenheim which marks the opening of this new Command bring to the Commander in Chief of the Eighth Army and his troops the fame and fortune they will surely deserve.

Winston S. Churchill

Winston S. Churchill to H. V. Morton[2]
(Churchill papers, 20/54)

20 August 1942   Cairo

My dear Mr Morton,

I have been reading your book 'I, James Blunt' and I was impressed by the powerful picture which you paint of what life would be like in this country under the Nazi yoke. It is an excellent thing that the horrors of a Nazi occupation should be brought home to the British people in this way.

The Minister of Information tells me that your book has had a wide circulation and I am glad to hear it. He also tells me that you have refused all payment for your work and I should like to offer you my appreciation of your generous gesture.

Yours very truly,
Winston S. Churchill

---

[1] *Dur aux grands*: 'hard on the great ones'.

[2] Henry Vollam Morton, 1892–1979. Born in Lancashire. Prolific journalist, novelist, and travel writer. His book *I, James Blunt,* a fictional account of what life in Britain would be like if the Nazis won the war, was first published in 1942.

Winston S. Churchill to Clement Attlee, for the War Cabinet[1]
(Churchill papers, 20/87)

21 August 1942   Cairo

As a result of conferences which we held in Teheran and Cairo with Mr Harriman and his American railway experts we are all agreed that I should accept the President's offer to take over the working of the Trans-Persian railway and the port of Khorramshahr. We cannot run it unless they provide 60 per cent of the total personnel required. Their offer is to take it over as a task, becoming our servants so far as all movement is concerned, but managing everything on American lines, with American personnel, military and civil. Transference would be gradual and spread over a good many months. When completed it will release about 2,000 British railway personnel, who will be urgently required on other parts of our military railway system. You will see my telegram to the President as it passes through.

Winston S. Churchill to Clement Attlee, for the War Cabinet[2]
(Churchill papers, 20/87)

21 August 1942   Cairo
Most Secret and Personal

Have just spent two days in the Western Desert visiting HQ Eighth Army. Brooke, Alexander, Montgomery, and I went round together, seeing 44th Division, 7th Armoured Division, and 22nd Armoured Brigade, and representatives of the New Zealand Division. I saw a great number of men and all the principal commanders in the XIIIth Corps area, also again Air Marshal Coningham, who shares headquarters with General Montgomery.

2. I am sure we were heading for disaster under the former régime. The Army was reduced to bits and pieces and oppressed by a sense of bafflement and uncertainty. Apparently it was intended in face of heavy attack to retire eastwards to the Delta. Many were looking over their shoulders to make sure of their seat in the lorry, and no plain plan of battle or dominating will-power had reached the units.

3. So serious did this appear that General Montgomery insisted on taking command of the Eighth Army as soon as he had visited the front, and by Alexander's decision the whole command in the Middle East was transferred on the 13th.

---

[1] Also sent on Churchill's instructions to General Ismay 'and others concerned'.
[2] Also sent on Churchill's instructions to General Ismay 'and others concerned'.

4. Since then, from what I could see myself of the troops and hear from their commanders, a complete change of atmosphere has taken place. Alexander ordered Montgomery to prepare to take the offensive and meanwhile to hold all positions, and Montgomery issued an invigorating directive to his commanders, of which I will circulate the text on my return. The highest alacrity and activity prevails. Positions are everywhere being strengthened, and extended forces are being sorted out and regrouped in solid units. The 44th and the 10th Armoured Divisions have already arrived in the forward zone. The roads are busy with the forward movement of troops, tanks, and guns. General Horrocks commands the XIIIth Corps. Ramsden remains with the XXXth Corps. General Lumsden is forming the Xth Corps for a mass of manoeuvre for the offensive battle towards the end of September. For this a bold and comprehensive plan has been made.

5. However, it seems probable that Rommel will attack during the moon period before the end of August. He has lost valuable shipments, on which he counted, and underrates our strength, but we must not underrate his. We must expect a very wide turning movement by perhaps 20,000 Germans and 15,000 Italians, comprising formations of two Panzer and four or five Axis motorised divisions. The ensuing battle will be hard and critical, but I have the greatest confidence in Alexander and Montgomery, and I feel sure the Army will fight at its best. If Rommel does not attack in August he will be attacked himself at greater relative disadvantage in September. This would fit in well with 'Torch'.

6. For an August battle we should have the front about 700 tanks, with 100 replacements, about 700 serviceable aircraft, 500 field guns, nearly 400 6-pounder and 440 2-pounder anti-tank guns; but as we have only 24 medium guns we are definitely weaker in medium artillery. As parachute descents must be expected on a large scale and Rommel will no doubt bid high for victory, the Army will be extended to the full.

7. To give the fullest manoeuvring power to the Eighth Army in the event of its being attacked next week, a strong line of defence is being developed along the Delta from Alexandria to Cairo. The 51st [Highland] Division is taking station there. I shall visit it tomorrow. I drew General Alexander's attention to the inundation plans which we made two years ago, and action has been taken at various points.

8. To sum up, while I and others would prefer the September to the August battle, because of our growing strength, I am satisfied that we have lively, confident, resolute men in command, working together as an admirable team under leaders of the highest military quality. Everything

has been done and is being done that is possible, and it is now my duty to return home, as I have no part to play in the battle, which must be left to those in whom we place our trust. I have still a good deal of business to settle. As you will see from other telegrams, Gort is here and Platt arrives tomorrow. CIGS and I plan to start Sunday night by a route which you will learn in a separate telegram. I hope to be available for my weekly luncheon with the King on Tuesday if that should be His Majesty's wish.

9. My general impression of 'Jubilee' [Dieppe] is that the results fully justified the heavy cost. The large-scale air battle alone justified the raid.

10. I thank you all most warmly for the support you have given me while engaged in these anxious and none too pleasant tasks.

Winston S. Churchill to Clement Attlee, for the War Cabinet[1]
(Churchill papers, 20/87)

21 August 1942   Cairo
Most Secret and Personal

PERSIA AND IRAQ (PI) COMMAND

Following is plan referred to in Reflex 175.

1. The Directive to General Alexander cannot be modified as he must at once be freed from all responsibility for Persia and Iraq.

2. The establishment of the Persia–Iraq Command, the expansion of the Tenth Army and the strategic study of the growing danger to these regions from the Caucasus is urgent.

3. Consequently a general must be appointed before I leave who will be responsible to His Majesty's Government for taking all the decisions affecting PI area which would otherwise have been taken by General Alexander.

4. This general will be designated as Commander in Chief PI area, and will build up a separate command as quickly as possible. He will have allocated to him forthwith the principal elements out of which the PI command and its headquarters will be formed. See Appendix A.[2]

5. In the first instance the C-in-C PI will have his headquarters in Cairo and he will be assisted by all the departments of the staff in Cairo exactly as if he was General Alexander himself. He will do this work without prejudice to the interests or authority of General Alexander who in all

---

[1] Also sent on Churchill's instructions to General Ismay 'and others concerned'.

[2] The Appendix listed the reinforcements being sent to the 10th Army: 79 Anti-Tank Regiment from Iraq, 17 Indian Infantry Brigade from Syria, the Polish Brigade from Syria, anti-aircraft artillery (204 guns in all), and 290 anti-tank guns.

matters of assignment has priority unless he waives it, or unless instructions are given from London.

6. As the work in paragraphs 4 and 5 develops, the C-in-C PI will form his advanced headquarters in Persia or Iraq and will move thither as soon as he considers it necessary. He will leave behind him in Cairo an organisation which will look after the interests of his Command in harmonious agreement with GHQ Middle East until such time as he can stand entirely on his own feet.

7. The C-in-C PI will take as his guide the report of the Committee setting up a separate Command for P and I. This may require some modifications as it works out. He or his representative will have a seat upon the War Council presided over by the Minister of State, the functions of the latter over the whole area will be in no wise affected except as proposed in the Committee's report.

8. The Air Forces in the PI area and their general standard of maintenance will be specified from time to time by HMG on advice of COS. These forces will remain under command of AOC-in-C Middle East[1] but once established at his headquarters C-in-C PI may with the approval of HMG announce that the conditions specified in Paragraph 4 of my Directive of October 1941 have arisen, and while this period of active operations continues he will have all the rights over the Air Forces within his assignment enjoyed by General Alexander in the Western Desert.

9. This arrangement is for three months only and meets a situation which cannot be foreseen. During this period a decisive battle may be expected in the Western Desert. A decision will be reached or the winter will have come in the Caucasus and on the Russian Front. Other considerable operations will have been launched by the Allies. The PI Command will have been formed and taken its station. The Air Contingent for the Caspian Theatre will either, if the Russians hold, have come into action on their Southern flank, or if fortune is adverse, will be serving with the Tenth Army in Persia.

10. CIGS and I propose General Sir Maitland Wilson as C-in-C PI Command under the conditions set forth above.

---

[1] Air Marshal Tedder.

Winston S. Churchill to Clement Attlee, for the War Cabinet[1]
(Churchill papers, 20/87)

21 August 1942   Cairo
Most Secret and Personal

After prolonged consultation and reflection I have prepared the plan for separating the Commands set forth by my immediately following telegram. CIGS has arranged with GHQ ME and with General Wavell for the movements of troops necessary to expand the Tenth Army. He and I are in complete agreement on all points including the choice of General Wilson. You will see that I have abandoned the Indian alternative in favour of the original solution. The report of the committee here is lengthy but is generally agreed as a working basis by all parties, including Minister of State's representative he, unfortunately, being ill.

2. Lightening the burden on General Alexander and beginning the expansion of the Tenth Army and large scale preparations to meet the enemy in Persia cannot be delayed even for a single day. I have, therefore, availed myself of the Cabinet consent in principle which was given to my previous proposals and have placed General Wilson in command as from tonight, and have directed that all shall go forward as planned on this temporary and emergency basis. I should be obliged if my colleagues will endorse my action.

Sir Alexander Cadogan: diary
('The Diaries of Sir Alexander Cadogan', pages 475–6)

21 August 1942   Cairo

The PM got back about 6 p.m. yesterday, and then had a conference from 7 to 9. He was in terrific form and had enjoyed himself like a schoolboy, having bathed twice. He held forth the whole of dinner, ragging everyone. Sir Charles Wilson, his 'Personal Physician', is one of his principal butts. To Winston's delight, poor CW fell ill of the usual local tummy complaint, and Winston now goes about saying to everyone 'Sir Charles has been a terrible anxiety to us the whole time, but I hope we'll get him through!' Last night at dinner Winston held forth to the whole table on medicine, psychology &c. (all Sir Charles' subjects) and worked himself up to a terrific disquisition. I suspect (and I inferred from Sir Charles' expression) that it was pretty good nonsense. And I think

---

[1] Also sent on Churchill's instructions to General Ismay 'and others concerned'.

Winston must have had an inkling of that too, as he ended up 'My God! I do have to work hard to teach that chap his job!'

Sir Charles Wilson to John Martin
(Sir John Martin papers)

21 August 1942 Cairo

My dear Martin,

All is well in health line. Nevertheless I believe as facts of trip get known, opinion in Cabinet will harden against such expeditions unless vitally necessary. In saying this, I don't mean that anything dramatic has happened. Apart from fact that I think everyone except PM, Rowan and Kinna have had a dose of the local tummy malady (e.g. CIGS, both Thompsons, CIGS's ADC, our hostess, CMW etc., etc.); that Casey has high fever from undiagnosed cause; that on two successive journeys the other Liberator had to turn back because a cable fused (Chief Air Fitter said airplane might easily have caught fire); that yesterday sleeping in desert, I found a scorpion under my bed – all very small items – it isn't really a job for a man of 67 or 68. Smuts has communicated to me from Pretoria his own misgivings and his hopes that I may be able to take action. I hope he is very well. I believe Cabinet will be reluctant to accept any responsibility for these trips when they reflect on what they mean. I am writing because I think it might be worth while saying to Cripps and Anderson that the PM contemplates fitting out a Liberator to take him over the Globe and that time to check this is <u>immediately on his return</u>. When they meet him they could say 'This has been well worth while but we have been very anxious about you and hope it is last trip unless absolutely necessary.' They must not bring me in or say they've had any report from me. He knows I'm not enthusiastic over these trips from his point of view and my position might become untenable if I push my opposition too far.

Smuts's line is not only concerned with these trips but with burden put on PM, and the inevitable consequences (in Smuts' opinion) unless it is made lighter. I talked to Anderson about his health as you know and he also said burden must be made lighter.

Climate has been nothing like as bad as it usually is at this time of year: we have been lucky. Moscow in pine woods was delightful. Teheran very pleasant. While working and sleeping as he does in air-conditioned room here, he has had very little to compete with climatically. But yesterday his day began 6.30 a.m. In 1½ hours he bumped over worst desert track I could imagine; stood in moving vehicle for a long time in clouds of desert dust and sand, made 2 speeches, bathed twice, much more travelling in car in middle of day, then flight home to Cairo just in time for a long conference lasting till dinner time, etc. etc. He was very tired. All right this morning. That is a pretty full day for 67 or 68. Moreover these long journeys in Liberator (so noisy you have to shout into a man's ear to be heard) are tiring 10½ to 12 hours on end. He said to me 'I never get into the plane without thinking I may be killed'.

I think I have given you enough – matter incoherently jotted down – to bring out my point. We are asking too much if we want him to last.

Yours,
Charles Wilson

Winston S. Churchill to President Franklin D. Roosevelt
(Churchill papers, 20/79)

22 August 1942   Cairo
Most Secret and Personal

I have delayed my reply until I could study the Trans-Persian situation on the spot. This I have now done, both at Teheran and here, and have conferred with Averell, General Maxwell, General Spalding and their railway experts. The traffic on the Trans-Persian Railway is expected to reach 3,000 tons a day for all purposes by the end of the year. We are all convinced that it ought to be raised to 6,000 tons. Only in this way can we ensure an expanding flow of supplies to Russia while building up the military forces which we must move into Northern Persia to meet a possible German advance.

2. To reach the higher figure it will be necessary to increase largely the railway personnel and to provide additional quantities of rolling-stock and technical equipment. Furthermore, the target will only be attained in reasonable time if enthusiasm and energy are devoted to the task and a high priority accorded to its requirements.

3. I therefore welcome and accept your most helpful proposal contained in your telegram, that the railway should be taken over, developed and operated by the United States Army. With the railway should be the ports of Khorramshahr and Bandarshahpur. Your people would thus undertake the great task of opening up the Persian Corridor, which will carry primarily your supplies to Russia. All our people here agree on the benefits which would follow your approval of this sugges-

tion. We should be unable to find the resources without your help, and our burden in the Middle East would be eased by the release for use elsewhere of the British units now operating the railway. The railway and ports would be managed entirely by your people, though the allocation of traffic would have to be retained in the hands of the British Military Authorities, for whom the railway is an essential channel of communication for operational purposes. I see no obstacle in this to harmonious working.

4. The changeover would have to be carefully planned to avoid any temporary reduction of effort, but I think it should start as soon as possible. Averell is cabling you detailed suggestions.

Winston S. Churchill: recollection
('The Hinge of Fate', page 468)

22 August 1942   Egypt

On August 22 I visited the Tura caves, near Cairo, where vital repair work was being done. Out of these caves the stones of the Pyramids had been cut some time before. They came in very handy now. The reader will have seen my perpetual complaints of the bad servicing and slowness of repairs of our aircraft and tanks. Everything looked very smart and efficient on the spot, and an immense amount of work was being done day and night by masses of skilled men. But I had my tables of facts and figures and remained dissatisfied. The scale was far too small. The original fault lay with the Pharaohs for not having built more and larger Pyramids. Other responsibilities were more difficult to assign. We spent the rest of the day flying from one airfield to another, inspecting the installations and addressing the ground staffs. At one point two or three thousand airmen were assembled. I also visited, brigade by brigade, the Highland Division, just landed. It was late when we got back to the Embassy.

General Sir Alan Brooke: diary
('War Diaries, Field Marshal Lord Alanbrooke', page 312)

22 August 1942   Cairo

It has all been intensely interesting, but very hard work when the background of constant contact with Winston is taken in to account! And yet nothing could have been kinder and more charming than he has been throughout this trip.

Winston S. Churchill to A. V. Alexander and
Admiral of the Fleet Sir Dudley Pound
(Churchill papers, 20/87)

23 August 1942   Cairo
Secret and Personal

Australia have lost their 8-inch cruiser *Canberra*.[1] It might have lasting effect on Australian sentiment if we gave freely and outright to Royal Australian Navy one of our similar ships. Please give your most sympathetic consideration to the project and be ready to tell me about it when I return. Meanwhile I am not mentioning it to anyone.[2]

Winston S. Churchill: recollection
('The Hinge of Fate', pages 469–70)

23 August 1942

We sailed off from the Desert airfield at 7.5 p.m. on August 23, and I slept the sleep of the just till long after daylight. When I clambered along the bomb-bay to the cockpit of the 'Commando' we were already approaching Gibraltar. I must say it looked very dangerous. All was swathed in morning mist. One could not see a hundred yards ahead, and we were not flying more than thirty feet above the sea. I asked Vanderkloot if it was all right, and said I hoped he would not hit the Rock of Gibraltar. His answers were not particularly reassuring, but he felt sufficiently sure of his course not to go up high and stand out to sea, which personally I should have been glad to see him do. We held on for another four or five minutes. Then suddenly we flew into clear air, and up towered the great precipice of Gibraltar, gleaming on the isthmus and strip of neutral ground which joins it to Spain and the mountain called the Queen of Spain's chair. After three or four hours' flying in mist Vanderkloot had been exact. We passed the grim rock-face a few hundred yards away without having to alter our course, and made a perfect landing. I still think it would have been better to go aloft and circle

---

[1] The 10,000-ton Australian Navy heavy cruiser *Canberra*, built in 1927 by John Brown & Co., was badly damaged on the night of 8–9 August 1942 by Japanese counter-attack during the first of the American offensives on the island of Guadalcanal, in the Solomons Group, designed to drive the Japanese from the chain of Pacific Islands. *Canberra*, commanded by Captain F. E. Getting, sank some hours later. Of the 816 people on board, 732 were rescued, of whom 109 were wounded; 84 people were killed, including Captain Getting.

[2] Churchill's suggestion was accepted, and the cruiser *Shropshire* presented to the Australian Government. See page 1130 below.

round for an hour or two. We had the petrol and were not pressed for time. But it was a fine performance.

We spent the morning with the Governor, and flew home in the afternoon, taking a wide sweep across the Bay of Biscay when darkness fell.

John Martin to Rosalind Ross[1]
(Sir John Martin papers)

24 August 1942

I went down in PM's special train with Mrs C. to meet him at an aerodrome 'somewhere in the south of England'.[2] We had become quite buddies during Winston's absence, for I used to go and see her most mornings to take the latest news of the travellers. So in the train we had a long heart to heart talk about her daughters. The arrival at the aerodrome was rather thrilling. It was dark, with clouds gathering overhead, and the first we knew was the drone of engines far above. Then a squadron of escorting Spitfires came down into sight and finally the big Liberator. The PM seemed remarkably fit and fresh and so were most of the rest of the party, though they must have had an exhausting time. Now he is back in the old routine again, apparently none the worse – and it is certainly a great relief to have him back.

King George VI to Winston S. Churchill
(Churchill papers, 20/59)

24 August 1942   Balmoral[3]
handwritten

I am delighted to hear of your return on the completion of a very successful and important journey. I have followed your movements and deliberations with the keenest interest, and I feel sure that you have done much to clear up the situation in the Middle East.

I have arranged to return to London on the morning of Thursday, September 3rd, and will be glad to see you for luncheon if convenient.

---

[1] Rosalind Julia Ross (1913–2005). Daughter of Sir David Ross, KBE. Met John Martin, Principal Private Secretary to the Prime Minister, in September 1941; they were married on 1 May 1943.

[2] Lyneham airport, near Swindon, in Wiltshire.

[3] John Martin delivered this message to Churchill by hand when he reached Lyneham airport.

If you can get your work done in London during this week, I should be delighted if you would come here for the weekend, arriving Saturday, August 29th. I hope you are not too tired. A little Scotch air would do you good.

Winston S. Churchill: recollection
(*'The Hinge of Fate', page 472*)

25 August 1942

When on August 24 I returned from Cairo to London much remained to be decided about the final shaping of our plans, and on the following day Generals Eisenhower and Clark came to dine with me to discuss the state of the operation.

I was at this time in very close and agreeable contact with these American officers. From the moment they arrived in June I had arranged a weekly dinner at Number 10 on Tuesdays. These meetings seemed to be a success. I was nearly always alone with them, and we talked all our affairs over, back and forth, as if we were all of one country. I set great value on these personal contacts. Irish stew turned out very popular with my American guests, and especially with General Eisenhower. My wife was nearly always able to get this. I soon began to call him 'Ike'. For Mark Clark[1] and Bedell Smith,[2] the latter of whom arrived early in September as Chief of Staff to Eisenhower, I coined the titles 'the American Eagle'

[1] General Mark (Wayne) Clark, Chief of Staff for United States ground forces in England (for European operations).

[2] Walter Bedell Smith, 1895–1961. Known as 'Beetle' and to Churchill as 'the American Bulldog'. Enlisted in as a private in the Indiana National Guard, 1911, aged 16. Graduated from Officer Candidate Training Camp at Fort Benjamin Harrison and commissioned a 2nd Lieutenant in the US Army Reserve, 1917. Served during the First World War with 4th Infantry Division (United States) in France; commissioned a 1st Lieutenant in the Regular Army. Adjutant for the 12th Infantry Brigade, 1922. Assistant in the White House Bureau of the Budget, 1925–9. Also served in War Department's Bureau of Military Intelligence and with 45th Infantry Regiment in the Philippines; at the Infantry School, Command and General Staff School and the Army War College. At the outbreak of the Second World War, appointed Secretary of the US Joint Chiefs of Staff and American Secretary of the Anglo-American Combined Chiefs of Staff. Went to England in 1942 to become Chief of Staff to General Eisenhower, with whom he remained to the war's end. Smith laid the basis for the negotiation of the Italian armistice of 1943 and arranged the surrender of the German forces in the west in May 1945. After the war, took leave from the Army to serve as US Ambassador to the Soviet Union, 1946–9. After resigning his ambassadorship, in March 1949 he was promoted to General and assumed command of the 1st United States Army at Fort Jay, New York. Selected as Director of Central Intelligence (head of the Central Intelligence Agency) by President Harry S Truman, 1950. Retired from Army and as DCI, 1953. Served as Under Secretary of State, 1953–4; involved in creation of the National Security Agency. Founder member of the Bilderberg Group, 1954–7.

and 'the American Bulldog'. You have to look at their photographs to see why. We also had a number of informal conferences in our downstairs dining-room, beginning at about ten o'clock at night and sometimes running late. Several times the American generals came for a night or a week-end to Chequers. Nothing but shop was ever talked on any of these occasions.

One of General Eisenhower's aides-de-camp, a friend from civil life, has suggested in his book that all these meetings were a great burden upon the already overworked American officers. If this be true they showed great politeness and address in concealing their feelings. Anyhow, I am sure these close relationships were necessary for the conduct of the war, and I could not have grasped the whole position without them.

Winston S. Churchill to King George VI
(Churchill papers, 20/59)

25 August 1942   10 Downing Street

I am deeply grateful to Your Majesty for your most kind message on my return from the Middle East.

I am also honoured by Your Majesty's invitation to come to Balmoral if I can get my work done in London during the week. Might I confirm this on Thursday, as I cannot tell how things will go? In any case I shall hope to attend upon Your Majesty on September the 3rd at the Abbey, and to come to luncheon afterwards.

I thank You Majesty for your inquiries. I am not at all tried. We had a wonderful journey back, only twenty-six hours from Cairo, of which five were spent having a bath and a rest at Gibraltar.

War Cabinet: conclusions
(Cabinet papers, 65/27)

25 August 1942   10 Downing Street
5.30 p.m.

The Prime Minister said that there were strong military reasons for providing an adequate air-mail service for our troops in the Middle East. It was essential that the morale of the troops should be maintained, and the War Cabinet should recognise the extent to which they depended on letters from home. He also stressed the need for improving the supply of books and periodicals for the troops in this theatre. In his view, Bomber

Command and Coastal Command should provide (in the proportions 3:2) the additional aircraft necessary to ensure a total weekly allocation of 6,000 lbs for mails for the Services on this route.

War Cabinet: Confidential Annex
(Cabinet papers, 65/31)

25 August 1942
5.30 p.m.

The Prime Minister gave the War Cabinet an account of the main impressions which he had formed during his visit to the Middle East and to Moscow.

In Egypt he had visited the front on two occasions and had seen all the principal Commanders. Before he left, there had been signs that the enemy very likely contemplated an attack in the next moon period i.e. in the immediate future. Since he had returned to this country, however, there had been some indications which pointed the other way, and it was not now so certain that the attack would take place. General Alexander had given orders that our Army should hold their present position pending an offensive. As a preparation for this offensive he was in process of regrouping the various formations which had been broken up into a number of small units. The armour was also being concentrated.

Should the enemy launch an offensive, it was General Alexander's intention that the battle should be fought out with the object of destroying the enemy's forces. For this purpose it might be necessary to uncover[1] Cairo, and he (the Prime Minister), with the agreement of the Chief of the Imperial General Staff, had agreed that should General Alexander find it necessary to uncover the Capital, General Wilson should be put in charge of the Capital, with plenary powers (see WP (42) 379). At the same time, there were 45,000 troops in the Delta, which was being put into a state of defence with preparations for demolitions and flooding.

The Prime Minister then gave details of the strength of our forces in guns and tanks, as compared with the enemy. In 25-pdrs we had a great superiority over the enemy. They, however, had some superiority in medium artillery. The air strength was, he thought, in our favour in about the proportion of 9 to 5.

The Prime Minister then referred to the reasons which had led him to recommend the changes in Command which had been made. He was

[1] 'uncover': remove air defences from.

greatly obliged to the War Cabinet for the support which they had given to his proposals. The changes made had had the full support of Field-Marshal Smuts and the Chief of the Imperial General Staff.

The Chief of the Imperial General Staff said that the steps taken to re-organise our forces had already shown good results, but would require some time for their full development. It was proposed to form a large mass of [word obliterated on page] Manoeuvre which could be used to exploit an advantage [word obliterated on page] opportunity offered. General Montgomery had obtained a quick grasp of the situation, and had clear ideas of what he would do if the enemy attacked him, or if he were in a position to launch an offensive. He had brought a number of units up from the rear nearer the front line, which would improve their tone. A decision had also been made to move GHQ (with the exception of the administrative branches) out of Cairo. He was sure that the combination of General Alexander and General Montgomery, who knew each other well and had complementary qualities, would be successful.

The Prime Minister then said that General Auchinleck had been unwilling to accept the Iraq–Persia Command which had been offered to him, for two reasons. In the first place, he did not think that the Iraq–Persia Command was a very good arrangement. Secondly, his confidence in himself had suffered a severe shock as the result of his supersession. There was no reason why he should not recover his confidence and render further good service later on. He had gone to India on leave, but this should not be made public at the present time.

The Prime Minister then turned to the Iraq–Persia area, and gave details of the forces which were at present available and would become available later on to form a front in this area should the Russians fail to hold the Caucasus line.

The Foreign Secretary said that he had seen the Turkish Ambassador that morning, whose attitude had shown a marked[1] change and revealed considerable anxiety as to the position. He said that Batum was an inadequate base for the Russian Fleet, and feared that, if things went badly for the Russians, great pressure would be put upon the Turks. He had made it clear that if Turkey were attacked she would fight, but had said that it would be of great assistance if Turkey could know definitely what assistance in armaments she could reckon on receiving from us by a given date. Thus, Turkey was particularly short of anti-tank guns. He (the Foreign Secretary) thought that it would be of great assistance if the Prime Minister would see the Turkish Ambassador.

[1] The word 'marked' has been crossed out in the copy.

The Prime Minister said that he would do so.

The Prime Minister then gave the War Cabinet some account of his talks with Premier Stalin. There was no doubt at all of the Russian determination to continue fighting. Although they had pressed us strongly to start a second front in Europe this year, they had not 'cried misery'. He thought that he had established relations with Premier Stalin which would facilitate co-operation between our two countries, and he had formed the highest opinion of Premier Stalin's sagacity. The Prime Minister also referred to his interviews with the Shah of Persia, who had made a favourable impression on him.

The Secretary of State for Dominion Affairs said that the War Cabinet were greatly indebted to the Prime Minister for having undertaken this long and arduous journey, and for the great services to the country which he had thereby rendered. All his colleagues rejoiced to have the Prime Minister safe home among them once more.

The Prime Minister thanked the War Cabinet warmly for what had been said, and for the support, which they had given to him.

Winston S. Churchill to Air Chief Marshal Sir Hugh Dowding[1]
(Churchill papers, 20/54)

25 August 1942

My dear Dowding,

Thank you for your letter and enclosure of August 10 which reached me here. It would have been in my opinion most wrong for you to publish the letter which the censor has stopped, and great harm would have been done to our country thereby.

There was no need for you take such a reckless step because you knew well from our relations that you had only to write to me to ensure that immediate attention would be given to what you said. I am calling for a report on the whole question[2] and will let you know when I have studied it.

---

[1] Hugh Caswall Tremenheere Dowding, 1882–1970. Educated at Winchester. Joined the Royal Artillery, 1900; Royal Flying Corps, 1914. On active service, 1914–19 (despatches). Director of Training, Air Ministry, 1926–9. Commanding the Fighting Area, Air Defence of Great Britain, 1929–30. Air Member for Research and Development, 1930–6. Knighted, 1933. Air Officer Commanding-in-Chief, Fighter Command, 1936–40. Mission to the United States for the Ministry of Aircraft Production, 1940–2. Created Baron, 1943

[2] Dowding had written an article advocating the use of mustard gas bombings in Germany. It was not approved by the Chiefs of Staff and was suppressed.

I am also enquiring into how it was your dispatch on the Battle of Britain was not published. I understood more than a year ago from the Chief of the Air Staff that it would be published.

Yours sincerely,
Winston S. Churchill

General Douglas MacArthur: message[1]
(Churchill papers, 20/58)

25 August 1942

If disposal of all the Allied decorations were today placed by Providence in my hands, my first act would be to award the Victoria Cross to Winston Churchill. No one of those who wear it deserves it more than he. A flight of 10,000 miles through hostile and foreign skies may be the duty of young pilots, but for a Statesman burdened with the world's cares, it is an act of inspiring gallantry and valour.

Winston S. Churchill: broadcast to Egypt
(BBC Written Archives Centre)

26 August 1942   London

During my stay in Egypt I have been gratified to learn of the valuable assistance which the British civilian community has rendered to the war effort. I know that very many of the community have joined his Majesty's forces, and that many others have been asked to forgo their desire to do so in order to carry on civilian work of real importance.

Of those who, for one reason or another, have not joined his Majesty's forces, many have volunteered for duty in local battalions or the RAC,[2] many again are doing excellent service in their spare time in hospitals, welfare centres, ARP organizations, and so forth. I know, too, that you have contributed in generous measure to the war funds of various kinds, and I have been specially pleased to learn of the success of your own community war fund which is doing so much for the welfare of his Majesty's forces in Egypt.

---

[1] Sent to Churchill by Stewart Menzies ('C'), who had received it from a member of General MacArthur's staff. It is not certain whether MacArthur himself intended his comment to be passed on.
[2] RAC: Royal Armoured Corps.

I am not surprised at this record: it is what one would expect of a community such as yours which can take a legitimate pride in past achievements.

And you can be no less proud of the present. You are privileged to be serving in your respective ways in a centre of vital importance to the victory of the United Nations, and it is only natural you should set a high example of loyal service to other British communities abroad.

When the enemy recently thrust forward into Egypt you were called upon to stand firm and face with fortitude whatever the future might bring. With few exceptions you responded to the call with the spirit one would expect of a community with such traditions as yours.

'Stay put and carry on with the good work you are doing' remains the order of the day for British residents in Egypt. This is not only the duty, but, as I have said, the privilege of every British resident, man and woman, who can do useful war work here; and it is in order to ensure that the best possible use is made of all available effort that the law applying compulsory national service for British subjects has been extended to Egypt.

Winston S. Churchill to President Franklin D. Roosevelt
(Churchill papers, 20/90)

26 August 1942
Personal and Most Secret

I am concentrating my main thought upon 'Torch' from now on, and you may trust me to do my utmost to make your great strategic conception a decisive success. It seems to me from talks I have had with Eisenhower, Clark and our own people here that the best, and indeed the only, way to put this job through is to fix a date for the party and make everything conform to that, rather than saying it will start when everything is ready. It would be an immense help if you and I were to give Eisenhower a directive something like this:

You will start 'Torch' on 14th October, attacking with such troops as are available and at such places as you deem fit.

This will alter the whole character of the preparations. Eisenhower will really have the power he should have as the Allied Commander-in-Chief. Endless objections, misgivings and well-meant improvements will fall back into their proper places, and action will emerge from what will otherwise be almost unending hummings and hawings. I think Eisenhower would like this, and it would, anyhow, give him a chance which he has not now got.

2. As I see this operation, it is primarily political in its foundations. The first victory we have to win is to avoid a battle. The second, if we cannot avoid it, to win it. In order to give us the best chances of the first victory, we must (*a*) present the maximum appearance of overwhelming strength at the moment of the first attack, and (*b*) attack at as many places as possible. This is an absolutely different kind of operation from the Dieppe business or any variants of 'Sledgehammer'. There we were up against German efficiency and the steelbound, fortified coasts of France. In 'Torch' we have to face at the worst weak, divided opposition and an enormous choice of striking-points at which to land. Risks and difficulties will be doubled by delay and will far outstrip increase of our forces. Careful planning in every detail, safety first in every calculation, far-seeing provisions for a long-term campaign, to meet every conceivable adverse contingency, however admirable in theory, will ruin the enterprise in fact. Anything later than the date I have mentioned enormously increases the danger of leakage and forestalment.

3. In order to lighten the burden of responsibility on the military commanders, I am of opinion that you and I should lay down the political data and take the risk upon ourselves. In my view, it would be reasonable to assume (*a*) that Spain will not go to war with Britain and the United States on account of 'Torch'; (*b*) that it will be at least two months before the Germans can force their way through Spain or procure some accommodation from her; (*c*) that the French resistance in North Africa will be largely token resistance, capable of being overcome by the suddenness and scale of the attack, and that thereafter the North African French may actively help us under their own commanders; (*d*) that Vichy will not declare war on the United States and Great Britain; (*e*) that Hitler will put extreme pressure on Vichy, but that in October he will not have the forces available to overrun the unoccupied France while at the same time we keep him pinned in the Pas de Calais, &c. All these data may prove erroneous, in which case we shall have to settle down to hard slogging. For this we have always been prepared, but a bold, audacious bid for a bloodless victory at the outset may win a very great prize. Personally, I am prepared to take any amount of responsibility for running the political risks and being proved wrong about the political assumptions.

4. It is evident that these assumptions would be greatly helped by a battle won in the Western Desert. Either Rommel attacks us by the August moon, or we shall attack him by the end of September. Either

way there will be a decision, and I feel very confident that the decision will be helpful.

5. I have refrained, as you know, from going into any details here because I feel it is a note that must be struck now of irrevocable decision and superhuman energy to execute it.

Winston S. Churchill to Admiral of the Fleet Sir Dudley Pound
(Churchill papers, 20/67)

26 August 1942
Most Secret

It is true that no one can tell how far an enterprise like 'Torch', once begun, will carry us. Nevertheless, we should now make plans to resume the PQ convoys late in October or the beginning of November. It may be that losses in 'Torch', or great and hopeful developments there, will force or induce us to concentrate all our efforts in the Mediterranean. But the results of battle explain themselves and we have to accept them.

2. Although I indicated in my conversations with Stalin, and it is upon the record, that 'Torch' would affect the PQs, I think it would be a great mistake at this crisis to send him news, which amounts to the fact that he will get nothing more after the September convoy this year. We should therefore get the utmost help we can from the President, and push ahead with plans for the PQs until or unless we have to give them up by main force. I still think means may be found to run them. If not, there will be overwhelming reasons for not doing so.

3. I shall be ready to talk to you sometime today or tomorrow about this.

Winston S. Churchill to Chiang Kai-shek
(Churchill papers, 20/79)

26 August 1942

I have received from Sir H. Seymour[1] an account of the conversation your Excellency was so good as to hold with him on 11th August about India. As you asked that this conversation should be conveyed to me, and as these views were stated to be your Excellency's personal views, I take this opportunity of replying directly and giving my own similar personal views in an earnest, sincere and friendly spirit.

---

[1] Ambassador to China.

2. I do not consider that Congress in any way represents India, which is a continent like Europe inhabited by many different races, nations, and religions. There are, for instance, 95 million Moslems, 45 million Untouchables and 90 million subjects of the Principalities, none of whom are represented by the Congress, which is almost entirely a Hindu organisation. If these large minorities are added together they comprise a substantial majority of all the people of India. Moreover, the Congress has nothing in common with the fighting races of India, of whom well over a million have volunteered for the army during the present war, there being no compulsory service in India. These brave Indian soldiers belong mainly to the Northern races, among whom Moslems predominate. If at any time in the future, as a result of the constitutional process to which we are committed, the British withdraw their troops from India, the Hindu parliamentarians would be rapidly dominated by the Moslem warriors. If Mr Gandhi could get a compact and adequate Japanese army placed at the disposal of the Congress for the purpose of holding down the Moslems, other non-Hindu elements and the States, furnished to him in return for assistance to the Japanese in making a free passage through India to try to join hands with Germans, then and then only would he be able to set up Hindu ascendancy all over India. It has been shown that he was ready to negotiate with the Japanese, but this would not by itself be enough for him. The Japanese would also have to lend him an army or he and his friends would speedily be overthrown by the martial races. It has occurred to me that your Excellency might be willing to reflect a little on some of these points.

3. I think the best rule for Allies to follow is not to interfere in each other's internal affairs. We are resolved in every way to respect the sovereign rights of China, and we have abstained even from the slightest comment when Communist–Kuomintang differences were most acute. I should, therefore, greatly regret if your Excellency were to be drawn into political correspondence with the Congress, or with individuals who are endeavouring to paralyse the war effort of the Government of India and to unsettle the internal peace and order of these vast regions. I am afraid that such an incident would lead to the estrangement from your Excellency of powerful sections of British opinion, who would naturally feel that our war burden against Germany, Italy and Japan had been increased by one whom we have long regarded as a hero and a friend.

4. With regard to the suggestion which your Excellency has made that His Majesty's Government should accept the mediation of the President of the United States regarding their relations with the Indian Congress and generally with India, I should like to place on record the fact that

no British Government of which I am the head, or a member, will ever be prepared to accept such mediation on a matter affecting the sovereign rights of His Majesty The King Emperor. I have, as your Excellency knows, the warmest feelings of friendship and admiration for the President and we are working together over the whole field of the war in the closest comradeship. I am sure he would not be willing to make any such proposal to me, because he is very well acquainted with the conviction I have about my duty to Crown and Parliament.

5. I was very glad to find when I visited Moscow that Premier Stalin was in such good heart and had so confident an outlook on the future of the war which he and the Russian people are waging with inflexible resolution. I am not unduly impressed by the gains which the Germans have made in Russia this summer. They have so far shown far less strength than they manifested when they first made their murderous onslaught in 1941. It now looks as if the Japanese are unwilling to attack Russia until they know the conditions under which the German and Russian fronts will reach the now-approaching winter. From the Russian point of view I am glad of this, but, of course, it may throw more burden on your Excellency and on the Chinese people as well as making the defence of India a more immediate and prominent task. However, I am persevering with the plans of which I spoke to Dr Wellington Koo[1] for an offensive upon the Japanese lines of communication along the Burma Road and other roads between Siam, Malaya and China. I asked General Wavell to meet me here in Cairo for the purpose of concerting these plans which have to be fitted in with other enterprises we have in mind. It is my earnest hope that we may be able to do something to relieve the pressure upon the Chinese people under your Excellency's inspiring leadership before many months have passed.

---

[1] Vi Kyuin Wellington Koo, 1888–1985. Chinese Minister to the United States, 1915. Member (and later head) of the Chinese Delegation to the Paris Peace Conference, 1919. Represented China on the Council of the League of Nations, Geneva, 1920–2. Minister of Foreign Affairs, Peking, 1922–4; Finance Minister, 1926; Prime Minister and Minister of Foreign Affairs, 1921–7 Ambassador in London, 1941–6; in Washington, 1946–56. Judge of the International Court of justice, 1957–67; Vice-President, 1964–7.

Winston S. Churchill to Lieutenant-General Sir Wilfrid Lindsell[1]
(Churchill papers, 20/54)

26 August 1942

Dear General Lindsell,

I want to send you my warm thanks for all the aid and assistance you have given me during my visits to Cairo. I made heavy calls upon your time which you answered most readily, and the information which you gave me was always useful and clear. I am also much obliged to you for the arrangements which you made for my visits to the front and elsewhere.

The service which I received from the car drivers, dispatch riders and the military police has been excellent, and I should be glad if you would convey to all of them my personal thanks.

Yours sincerely,
Winston S. Churchill

Winston S. Churchill to Michael Wright[2]
(Churchill papers, 20/54)

26 August 1942

Dear Mr Wright,

I have seen for myself, and all my staff have told me, how great has been the assistance you have given us during our two visits to Cairo. I

---

[1] Wilfrid Gordon Lindsell, 1884–1973. Educated at Birkenhead School, Victoria College, Jersey, and Royal Military Academy, Woolwich. 2nd Lieutenant, Royal Artillery, 1903; Lieutenant, 1906; Captain, 1914; Major, 1918. Served in France during the First World War with the British Expeditionary Force (MC, 1916; DSO, 1918). OBE, 1919. Appointed to Adjutant-General's staff at War Office, 1920. Instructor at School of Military Administration, 1921–3; at Staff College, Camberley, 1925–8. Brevet Lieutenant-Colonel, 1927; Brevet Colonel and Colonel, 1931. Commandant, Senior Officers' School, Sheerness, 1934–5. Commander, Royal Artillery, 4th Division, 1937–8. Major-General in Charge of Administration, Southern Command, 1938–9. On outbreak of Second World War, appointed Quartermaster-General of British Expeditionary Force. Temporary Lieutenant-General, 1940. KBE, 1940. Lieutenant-General, 1941. Lieutenant-General in charge of Administration in the Middle East, 1942–3. CB, 1942. Principal Administrative Officer to the Indian Command, 1943–5. Despatches thrice. KCB, 1943. GBE, 1946. American Legion of Merit, degree of Commander. LLD (Hon.) Aberdeen University. Publications: *Military Organisation and Administration* (1923); reissued as *Lindsell's Military Organisation and Administration* (1948).

[2] Michael (Robert) Wright, 1901–76. Educated at Winchester and Balliol College, Oxford. Entered the Diplomatic Service, 1926. British Embassy, Washington, 1926–30. Second Secretary, Diplomatic Service, 1930–6. British Embassy, Paris, 1936–40; Cairo, 1940–3; Washington, 1943–6 (CMG, 1945). Served on staff of Special Commissioner in South-East Asia, 1946–7. Assistant Under-Secretary of State, Foreign Office, 1947–50. Ambassador to Norway, 1951–4 (KCMG, 1951). Ambassador to Iraq, 1954–8 (GCMG, 1958). UK delegate to Conference for Cessation of Nuclear Tests, Geneva, 1959; to 10 Power and 18 Power Disarmament Conferences, Geneva, 1960 and 1962. Chairman, Atlantic Trade Study, 1966–72. Director, Guinness Mahon Holdings Ltd, 1964–73. Board Member, International Movement for Atlantic Union. Founder Member, British North American Committee, 1969. A Vice-President of the Royal Geographical Society, 1971–4. Member of Institute of Directors. Grand Cross, Order of St Olav (Norway), 1975.

know well how much work such visits entail and how great a strain it must have thrown upon you. I send you my warmest thanks and I hope you will accept this signed photograph as a memento of these two visits during which your help has been invaluable.

Yours sincerely,
Winston S. Churchill

Winston S. Churchill to President Franklin D. Roosevelt
(Churchill papers, 20/29)

27 August 1942
Personal and Secret
No. 139

We are all profoundly disconcerted by the memorandum sent us by the United States Joint Chiefs of Staff on the 25th instant about 'Torch'. It seems to me that the whole pith of the operation will be lost if we do not take Algiers as well as Oran on the first day. In Algiers we have the best chance of a friendly reception, and, even if we got nothing except Algeria, a most important strategic success would have been gained. General Eisenhower with our cordial support was in fact planning landings at Philippeville and Bone for Day 3. We cannot of course be sure of getting to Tunis before the Germans, but neither is it certain that the Germans would be well received by the French in Tunis even if Vichy gave them permission.

2. Strongly established in Algeria with Oran making good the communications, we could fight the Germans for Tunis, even if they got there. But not to go east of Oran is making the enemy a present not only of Tunis but of Algiers. An operation limited to Oran and Casablanca would not give the impression of strength and of widespread simultaneous attack on which we rely for the favourable effect on the French in North Africa. We are all convinced that Algiers is the key to the whole operation. General Anderson,[1] to whom this task has been assigned by Eisenhower, is

[1] Kenneth Arthur Noel Anderson, 1891–1959. Born in India. Educated at Charterhouse and Royal Military College, Sandhurst. Entered the Army as 2nd Lieutenant in the Seaforth Highlanders, 1911. Served in France, 1914–16 (wounded; Military Cross), and Palestine, 1917–18. Captain, 1915. Major, 1923. Graduated from Staff College, 1928. Served on North-West Frontier, 1930 (despatches) and Palestine, 1930–2. Lieutenant-Colonel, 1930. Colonel, 1934. Commanded 11th Infantry Brigade, 1938–40. Commanded 3rd Division during final phase of evacuation from Dunkirk. Major-General, 1940. CB, 1940. Home Forces, 1940–2, commanding 1st Division, 8th Corps and Eastern Command. Commanded 1st Army during Operation 'Torch', 1942. Commanded 2nd Army, 1943–4, during preparations for Normandy landings. KCB, 1943. Transferred to Eastern Command, 1944. Gen-

confident of his ability to occupy Algiers. The occupation of Algeria and the movement towards Tunis and Bizerta is an indispensable part of the attack on Italy which is the best chance of enlisting French co-operation and one of the main objects of our future campaign.

3. We are all agreed about Oran, and of course we should like to see Casablanca occupied as well, but if it came to choosing between Algiers and Casablanca it cannot be doubted that the former is incomparably the more hopeful and fruitful objective. Inside the Mediterranean landings can be made in October on four days out of five. On the Atlantic shores of Morocco the proportion is exactly reversed, only one day in five being favourable.

4. Nevertheless, if the operations at Oran and Algiers yield good reactions and results, entry might easily be granted to a force appearing off Casablanca, and a feint would certainly be justified. It is, however, by far the most difficult point of attack and the one most remote from the vital objectives in the Mediterranean. Casablanca might easily become an isolated failure and let loose upon us for a small reward all the perils which have anyway to be faced in this great design. So far as Algiers is concerned, all we ask from you is an American contact team to show the flag. We cannot, however, do Algiers and Oran at the same time. If therefore you wish to do Casablanca on a large scale with all its risks, it is indispensable that United States forces should continue to be directed on Oran as now planned by the Allied Commander-in-Chief.

5. A complete change in the plans such as the memorandum suggests would of course be fatal to the date and thus possibly to the whole plan. In October Hitler will not have the power to move into Spain or into Unoccupied France. In November and with every week that passes his power to bring pressure upon Vichy and Madrid Governments increases rapidly.

6. I hope, Mr President, you will bear in mind the language I have held to Stalin supported by Harriman with your full approval. If 'Torch' collapses or is cut down as is now proposed, I should feel my position painfully affected. For all these reasons, I most earnestly beg that the memorandum may be reconsidered, and that the American Allied Commander-in-Chief may be permitted to go forward with the plans he has made, upon which we are all now working night and day. The Staffs are communicating similar views to their American colleagues.

---

eral Officer Commanding-in-Chief, East Africa, 1945–6. Governor of Gibraltar, 1947–52. General, 1949. Died in Gibraltar.

Winston S. Churchill to King George VI
(Churchill papers, 20/54)

27 August 1942

Sir,

Your Majesty's Ministers have asked me, on their behalf, to offer to your Majesties, to her Royal Highness the Duchess of Kent, and to all the Royal Family their deepest sympathy on the death, on active service, of his Royal Highness the Duke of Kent,[1] and to express their sense of the grievous loss which the Nation and Empire have suffered thereby.

With my humble duty,
I remain,
Your Majesty's faithful and devoted servant and subject
Winston S. Churchill

Winston S. Churchill to the Duke of Windsor
(Churchill papers, 20/88)

27 August 1942

I beg Your Royal Highness to accept my most profound sympathy in the tragic death of your gallant and much-loved brother. I can never forget the day which we all three spent together. My heart goes out to you in this blow which you have suffered. The King is in the deepest sorrow, and his grief is shared by the whole nation.[2]

---

[1] Prince George Edward Alexander Edmund, 1902–42. Fourth son of King George V. Served in the Royal Navy, 1921–7; on the staff of the Commander-in-Chief, Atlantic Fleet, 1927. Attached to the Foreign Office, 1929. Married Princess Marina of Greece, 1934. Created Duke of Kent, 1934. Privy Councillor, 1937. Group-Captain, Royal Air Force, 1937. Rear-Admiral, Major-General and Air Vice-Marshal, 1939. Governor-General Designate of Australia, 1938; prevented from taking up the post by the outbreak of war. Naval Intelligence Division, Admiralty, 1939–40. Air Commodore, Royal Air Force, 1940. Killed in an air crash in Scotland while flying to Iceland to make a tour of inspection, 25 August 1942. His son Prince Michael of Kent, born on 4 July 1942, was nine weeks old at the time of his father's death.

[2] The Duke of Windsor telegraphed from the Bahamas to Churchill: 'Deeply touched by your message of sympathy. My sorrow is great and my sense of loss profound and your message therefore is a source of much comfort to me at this sad time. Edward' (*Churchill papers, 20/79*).

Winston S. Churchill to William Mackenzie King and John Curtin
(Churchill papers, 20/79)

27 August 1942

Most Secret and Personal

Now that I am back in London, I hasten to give you some account of my discussions in Moscow.

1. Harriman and I arrived in Moscow at 5 p.m. on the 12th August and had a four-hour conference that evening with Stalin, Molotov and Voroshilov. At this meeting I explained at length:

(*a*) The reasons why we would not make an attack in force on France in 1942;

(*b*) The facts as to United States arrivals in the United Kingdom, and our own proposed expeditionary force; and

(*c*) The ruthless bombing of Germany.

Stalin did not agree with our reasons as to (*a*), and argued the other way, but finally he said that we had the right to decide. He attached the greatest importance to (*c*), which he knew to be having a tremendous effect in Germany. Courtesy and dignity prevailed, but everyone was glum.

2. I then told Stalin that we and the United States had a plan for an attack in North Africa in October. Stalin became intensely interested, and, after raising possible political objections as to the effect in France and as regards de Gaulle, summarised the reasons for this operation as follows: It would hit Rommel in the back, overawe Spain, produce fighting between Germans and Frenchmen in France and expose Italy to the whole brunt of the war. I added the shortening of the sea route through the Mediterranean. After further discussion, the meeting ended cordially. Harriman was a great help in this extremely serious and at one time critical discussion.

3. On the morning of the 13th August I had a general talk with Molotov, during which I pointed out how injurious it would be to the common cause if, owing to recriminations about the matter mentioned in paragraph 1 (*a*), we were forced to argue publicly against such enterprises. He listened affably, but contributed nothing.

4. At 11 p.m. on the 13th August we had a further meeting with Stalin and Molotov. Stalin handed me a memorandum generally expressing strong dissatisfaction at the decision of ourselves and the United States Government as to paragraph 1 (*a*) above. The memorandum stated, *inter alia*, that:

(i) The organisation of a second front in Europe in 1942 was pre-decided during Molotov's visit to London in June and expressed in the joint communiqué then published;

(ii) The refusal to do this inflicts a moral blow to the whole of Soviet public opinion.

5. I said that I would reply in writing. We argued for about two hours, during which Stalin said a great many disagreeable things. Finally, he said we could carry the matter no further, and then invited us to dinner in the evening of the 14th August. I accepted and, after an appeal to him, the talk became less tense and we agreed as to the exchange of information about military inventions. A meeting between his military authorities and our Generals for detailed discussions of the proposed operations we also arranged, and Stalin gave me reasons for his confidence in Russia's ability to hold the Caucasus mountain chain.

6. I sent a written reply to the Russian memorandum:

(i)   Setting out the advantages of the operation mentioned in paragraph 2 as compared with that referred to in paragraph 1 (*a*), and indicating that we and the United States Government had decided on the former and that preparations for it were proceeding with the utmost speed;

(ii)   Denying that any promise had been given as to undertaking the latter, and referring to a passage in a memorandum which I gave Molotov on the 10th June stating 'We can, therefore, give no promise';

(iii) Drawing attention to the advantages which have accrued and should continue to accrue from misleading the enemy as to our intentions;

(iv) Reaffirming our resolve to aid Russia by every practicable means.

7. The dinner on the 14th August passed off in a very friendly atmosphere, but without discussion of serious matters. On the 15th August, when I went to Stalin to wind up, we had an agreeable conversation which led to his asking me to his apartment in the Kremlin where I had dinner with him and Molotov and a talk lasting six hours, particularly concerning the help we can give as to supply routes for Russian armies. The greatest goodwill prevailed and for the first time we got on to easy and friendly terms. I got home at 3.30 a.m. and we left by plane at 5 a.m. with full military ceremonies.

8. On the whole, I am definitely encouraged by my visit to Moscow. There was never any suggestion about the Russians not fighting on, and I think Stalin has good confidence that he will win. I am sure that the disappointing news I brought could not have been imparted except by me personally without leading to really serious drifting apart. It was my duty to go. Now they know the worst, and having made their protest are

entirely friendly. This, in spite of the fact that this is their most anxious and agonising time. Moreover, I am sure that Stalin is entirely convinced of the great advantages of the proposal which I have put before him.

9. I, of course, rely on you to treat with the strictest secrecy what is said above as to possible future military operations

Oliver Harvey: diary
('The War Diaries of Oliver Harvey', page 153)

28 August 1942

[...]

I hear the PM was much shocked in Cairo by the slovenly dress of the Generals all in shorts cut like ballet dancers' skirts and open-neck shirts and no sleeves, in which they went out to dinner! He gave orders at once for this to be stopped.

Winston S. Churchill to General Hastings Ismay,
for the Chiefs of Staff Committee
(Churchill papers, 20/67)

28 August 1942
Most Secret

I am much concerned with the account of the Turkish position given me by the Turkish Ambassador, whom I saw this morning at the request of the Cabinet.

2. We should now prepare a scheme, on the assumption of definite success in the Western Desert by the middle of October, of sending more war material to Turkey. It ought to be possible to spare 200 tanks of the Valentine or other older type. These would be replaced in Egypt by the improved tanks now approaching in a regular stream. Similarly, 300 2.4 two-pounder A/T guns should be made available and 100 Bofors. If these were earmarked and prepared ready to move forward into Turkey the moment a favourable decision has been reached, they would be in Turkish hands by the end of October. This might make all the difference to the Turkish will-power to resist in a situation where the Russians may have lost the naval command of the Black Sea, and where Turkey may be subjected to very severe Axis pressure.

3. What is the objection to giving the Turks some RDF installations? The Germans surely know the secret, or have other equally satisfactory variants of their own.

4. We must proceed on the basis, which personally I adopt, that we trust Turkey. The whole Nile position would be greatly embarrassed if Turkey were forced to succumb.

5. Let me have a plan worked out on these lines for discussion.

Winston S. Churchill to John Curtin
(Churchill papers, 20/79)

29 August 1942
Most Secret and Personal

His Majesty's Government in the United Kingdom have heard with the deepest regret of the heavy blow sustained by Royal Australian Navy by the loss in action of the gallant ship HMAS *Canberra*. They realise fully how gravely this further loss has depleted the strength of the Royal Australian Navy.

2. Your Government will be aware that the Royal Navy is also seriously short of cruisers. Despite this, it is the unanimous desire of the War Cabinet that I should immediately offer to you, on behalf of His Majesty's Government, an 8-inch cruiser to replace HMAS *Canberra*. This offer is made freely, outright and without any conditions as regards operational control. The cruiser we offer is HMS *Shropshire*, which is expected to complete a refit, in which she will be brought thoroughly up to date, in about six months' time. In view of the time that it would take to get together an Australian crew and send them to this country, I hope that this arrangement will be convenient to you if you accept. Details can be settled later between the Australian Navy Board and the Admiralty.

3. I shall be much obliged if you will lay this offer before your Government and inform me of their views.

Winston S. Churchill to Pamela Gott [1]
(Churchill papers, 20/54)

29 August 1942

Dear Mrs Gott,

I met your late husband only the day before he was killed. I took occasion to have him drive back with me from General Auchinleck's Head-

[1] Pamela Frances Mary Gott, widow of General Gott. Her father, Brigadier-General Walpole Kays, CMG, had died only eight months earlier.

quarters in order that I might form an impression of him, and also ask him if he felt tired after all his long, hard, brilliant fighting and feats of arms which were the pride of the Desert Army. He inspired me at once with a feeling of confidence, and although he said he would be all the better for a few months' leave, I accepted his statement that he was feeling capable of going on, in view of the imminence of renewed battle as it then seemed. I therefore advised the Cabinet that he should be appointed to command the Eighth Army, feeling sure this was what the situation required, and the Army would welcome. The Cabinet had just endorsed my recommendation when they received my further telegram that he had been killed in action. I thought you would like to know this and that it was fitting I should place it on record.

I cannot attempt to measure the magnitude of your loss, but of this I am sure: that the nation's loss and that of the Desert Army is of the most grievous character. He has left few or none his like behind him, and his memory and prowess will be long recalled among his comrades and the men he led. The cause for which he gave his best and finally his life casts perhaps some consolation upon those who loved him. I beg you will accept my most heartfelt sympathy and that you will be strengthened to carry on to the end of the road.

Believe me,
Yours sincerely,
Winston S. Churchill

President Franklin D. Roosevelt to Winston S. Churchill
(Churchill papers, 20/90)

30 August 1942
Personal and Most Secret

THE NORTH AFRICAN LANDINGS

I have considered carefully your telegram in reference to the 'Torch' operation. It is my earnest desire to start the attack at the earliest possible moment. Time is of the essence, and we are speeding up preparations vigorously.

I feel very strongly that the initial attacks must be made by an exclusively American ground force, supported by your naval, transport, and air units. The operation should be undertaken on the assumption that the French will offer less resistance to us than they will to the British. I would even go so far as to say I am reasonably sure a simultaneous landing by British and Americans would result in full resistance by all French in Africa, whereas an initial American landing without British ground forces offers a real chance that there would be no French resistance, or only a token resistance. I need a week, if possible, after we land to consolidate the position for both of us by securing the non-resistance of the French. I sincerely hope I can get this.

Then your force can come in to the eastward. I realise full well that your landing must be made before the enemy can get there. It is our belief that German air and parachute troops cannot get to Algiers or Tunis in any large force for at least two weeks after the initial attack. Meanwhile your troops would be ashore, we hope, without much opposition, and would be moving eastward. As to the place of the landings, it seems to me that we must have a sure and permanent base on the north-west coast of Africa, because a single line of communications through the Straits is far too hazardous in the light of our limited joint resources.

I propose therefore that (*a*) American troops land simultaneously near Casablanca and near Oran; (*b*) that they seek to establish road and rail communication with each other back of the mountains. The distance is little more than 300 miles. This gives to the enterprise a supply base in Morocco, which is outside the Straits and can be used to reinforce and supply the operations in Algiers and Tunis. The real problem seems to be that there is not enough cover and combat loadings for more than two landings. I realise it would be far better to have three, with you handling the one to the eastward a week after we get it. To this end I think we should re-examine our resources and strip everything to the bone to make the third landing possible. We can give up the Russian convoy temporarily at that time and risk or hold up other merchant shipping.

It is essential of course that all ships now assigned to Eisenhower for his two landings remain intact. Hence the eastward landing must be made on ships not now available to 'Torch'. I will explore this at our end. Can we get an answer on this within forty-eight hours or less?

I want to emphasise however that under any circumstances one of our landings must be on the Atlantic.

The directive to the Commander-in-Chief of the operation should prescribe that the attack should be launched at the earliest practicable date. The date should be consistent with the preparation necessary for an operation with a fair chance of success, and accordingly it should be determined by the Commander-in-Chief; but in no event later than October 30. I still would hope for October 14.

Winston S. Churchill to President Franklin D. Roosevelt
(Churchill papers, 20/79)

30 August 1942
Personal and Most Secret
No. 140

RUSSIA

The project of placing on the southern flank of Russian armies a British and presently American Air Force must be viewed as a long-term policy in our co-operation with Russia and for the defence of the Persian oilfields. The main reasons appear to be:

(*a*) to strengthen the Russian air-power generally;

(*b*) to form the advance shield of all our interests in Persia and Abadan;

(*c*) for moral effect of comradeship with the Russians, which will be out of all proportion to the forces employed; and

(*d*) because this is no dispersion of forces, but a greater concentration on the supreme Allied Air Force target, namely, wearing down the German Air Force by daily fighting contact.

2. Following on the various references to this subject which occur in our correspondence, and to the favour with which you have viewed it in principle, I have committed His Majesty's Government in my talks with Stalin to the general policy and have stated that you also took a great interest in the matter. I now submit, Mr President, a formal draft, on which you may feel disposed to give me your decision:

(i) The proposal is to establish in Trans-Caucasia an Anglo-American Air Force to assist the Russian land and air forces in holding the line of the Caucasus mountains and the Black Sea coast. The necessary air forces would be withdrawn from Egypt as soon as the situation in the Western Desert is such that they can be spared from that front, and could be concentrated in the Baku–Batum area in about two months from that time.

(ii) This proposal has already been offered in general terms to Premier Stalin, who accepted it gratefully and indicated that the details of the plan should receive further study. In discussion between the CIGS, Air Marshal Tedder, and Marshal Voroshilov it was agreed that combined planning and preparation should start at once, and the suggestion put that Allied air representatives should go to Moscow for this purpose.

3. Subject to American agreement, the force envisaged would comprise the following units: eight short-range fighter squadrons, one long-

range fighter squadron, three light bomber squadrons, two medium bomber squadrons, one United States heavy bombardment group, and possibly, later, one general reconnaissance squadron.

4. Owing to the extreme difficulties which the lack of good ground communications will impose on the maintenance of this force, ample air transport will be essential for its maintenance. One United States transport group of approximately fifty aircraft is considered the minimum necessary for this purpose.

5. Thus the American contribution suggested is one heavy bombardment group now in Egypt and one transport group, which is not at present available in the Middle East. The former will require an adequate flow of aircraft and trained crews to meet attrition. In addition it is of the utmost importance that every effort should be made to ensure that at least the aircraft and air crews, both first-line and replacements, together with minimum maintenance parties of the United States Pursuit and Medium Bomber groups scheduled for the Middle East, should be operationally fit in Egypt by the dates agreed. Even if Rommel is driven out of Cyrenaica the air defence of Egypt and our long line of communications in the Western Desert will be a heavy commitment. It is also vitally important that the RAF allocations of American fighters for Egypt be fully and promptly supplied, since we must expect a high rate of attrition in the Caucasus area, not only in air fighting, but on account of the poor communications and lack of adequate repair facilities in that area.

6. The force will have to rely for the protection of its bases and line of communications mainly on the Russian forces, but we should be prepared to send light anti-aircraft units for the defence of aerodromes. We might also have to send some engineer units for work on aerodromes.

7. It is important that the ground echelon of the force should be kept as small as possible consistent with the effective operation of the aircraft, since it can only be concentrated and maintained at the expense of Russian supplies through the Persian Gulf route. The interference with these supplies should not be serious. The concentration of the force will involve a movement on the rail and sea communications between Iraq and the Caucasus of the order of 12,000 personnel, 2,000 vehicles, 4,000 tons of stores. Its subsequent maintenance, on the assumption that petrol and lubricants can be supplied by the Russians, should not exceed 200 tons a day, of which a substantial proportion should be lifted by air.

8. The force will operate under the strategic control of the Russian High Command, but will remain a homogenous Allied force under a British air officer, with the right of appeal to his own Government.

9. The foregoing should constitute the basis of instructions to a mission consisting of British and American Air Force officers, who should be dispatched forthwith to Russia to undertake the necessary planning, reconnaissance and practical preparations in combination with the Russians. It is urgently important that this be put in hand without delay.

Oliver Harvey: diary
('The War Diaries of Oliver Harvey', page 154)

30 August 1942

[...]

AE didn't arrive down till late from Chequers where PM and he had discussed 'Torch' with CIGS and Eisenhower. Rather inconclusively as Roosevelt hasn't yet replied to PM's message asking that date of Oct. 14 be fixed and that decision be taken to do Algiers and Oran, even if Casablanca is dropped.

We discussed it with Dill who told me 'he hated it'. He would prefer to concentrate in Egypt and Persia against German threats to the pipeline. The Americans, he said, both Marshall and Eisenhower, still prefer 'Sledgehammer'[1] on the ground that operation, though difficult, is nearer home and our resources and reserves, which wouldn't be diminished by distant overseas commitment, and it would inevitably make Germany fight in the air. But nobody seems to think it likely that we could stay there and the last thing we can stand is another Dunkirk. But 'Torch', as D says, is a very great gamble but with enormous stakes if successful – whole of North Africa in our hands.

PM had wanted to go and see Roosevelt but AE tried to dissuade him by offering to go himself.

If Torch fails, we are clearly in a frightful mess. PM has now promised Stalin that it shall be done – he is personally engaged. But it is very necessary that the plan should be studied from all angles and by the War Cabinet, which hasn't yet been done. Much will depend on the position in the Western Desert where Rommel (or his successor) is expected to attack very shortly. If we could defeat R, then the way would be open for 'Torch'.

---

[1] 'Sledgehammer': the proposed amphibious landing at Brest and Cherbourg in 1942.

War Cabinet: conclusions
(Cabinet papers, 65/27)

31 August 1942   10 Downing Street
6.30 p.m.

INDIA

The Prime Minister expressed gratification at the firmness with which the Government of India had dealt with the situation in India. The limited response to the revolutionary campaign of the Congress Party had provided a practical demonstration that Congress did not represent the masses of the Indian people.

Winston S. Churchill to Lord Cranborne[1]
(Churchill papers, 20/63)

31 August 1942

DEFENCE OF THE BAHAMAS

Am I not right in thinking that the only attack possible is by a party landed from a U-boat? If so, Government House seems to be the obvious quarry. A U-boat would not have the facilities for finding out where the Duke of Windsor was if he were not there or were moving about. The right rule is, one may always take a chance but not offer 'a sitter'. I am therefore in favour of putting an electrified fence round Government House and the other places mentioned, but not interfering with the Duke's liberty of movement otherwise than by informing him of the dangers. It is essential that the seat of government should be protected against a U-boat raiding force, and for this purpose additional platoons should be sent.

2. Why are not the 200 well-educated young male English idlers rounded up and made to do their bit?

Winston S. Churchill to President Franklin D. Roosevelt[2]
(Churchill papers, 20/79)

31 August 1942
Personal and Secret
No. 141

Rommel has begun the attack for which we have been preparing. An important battle may now be fought.

---

[1] Secretary of State for the Colonies.
[2] Churchill sent an identical telegram to Stalin.

Lord Linlithgow[1] to Winston S. Churchill
(Churchill papers, 20/79)

31 August 1942
Immediate
Personal

I am engaged here in meeting by far most serious rebellion since that of 1857 gravity and extent of which we have so far concealed from world for reason (of) military security. Mob violence remains rampant over large tracts of countryside and I am by no means confident that we may not see in September formidable attempt to renew this widespread sabotage our war effort. Lives of (?Europeans) in outlying places (?are) today in jeopardy. If we bungle this business we shall be India's (omission) as a base future allied operations and as thoroughfare for United States help to China. Throughout this most anxious crisis I have managed to hold together Indian members of my Executive Council, though several of them are in mortal terror of possible consequences to themselves of their having supported me in arresting Gandhi and Working Committee of Congress. There are circumstances in which I am now threatened by visitations from Wendell Wilkie[2] and Sherwood Eddy.[3] The latter threatens to come India in hope of helping by way of mediation (see telegram 4367 August 29 addressed to Foreign Office from Ambassador Washington).

Winston S. Churchill to Baron de Cartier de Marchienne[4]
(Churchill papers, 20/54)

31 August 1942

My dear Ambassador,

I thank you for your letter of July 7 in which you informed me of your Government's desire that His Majesty's Government should reconsider their decision on the question of despatching vitamins and milk products through the blockade to Belgium.

---

[1] Viceroy of India.

[2] Wendell Willkie, Roosevelt's personal emissary to Britain, China, and Soviet Union in 1940–1.

[3] George Sherwood Eddy, 1871–1963. Born in Leavenworth, Kansas. Educated at Yale University and Princeton Theological Seminary. In charge of student work for the YMCA in India, where he did missionary work, 1896–1911. YMCA Secretary for Asia, 1911. YMCA Secretary for the British Army during First World War. Author of *The Awakening of India* (1911); *The Students of Asia* (1915); *With Our Soldiers in France* (1917). Friends with Gandhi and Nehru. Died in Jacksonville, Illinois.

[4] Belgian Ambassador in London.

May I express my regret at the delay that there has been in answering your letter due to the very careful thought that has once more been given to this question and also to my absence from this country.

My colleagues and I have studied most carefully the considerations set forth in your letter of July 7, but to my great regret I can only repeat that the conclusions to which we have now come do still not enable us to modify our blockade policy at this stage. Although the present quantities envisaged by your Government are not great, it is not primarily with the direct benefit to the enemy of these supplies that we are concerned. Apart from the case of Greece, where exceptional conditions prevailed, the United Nations, standing firmly together, have succeeded in frustrating the manoeuvres of the enemy designed to throw upon them the burden of feeding the Allied occupied territories. You will, I know, realise that the success or failure of this manoeuvre is of vast importance in terms of the enemy's resources and ours, and there can be little doubt that the enemy would be quick to seize on the chance offered by a concession of the nature advocated by your Government. It would not only be open to him to represent that the United Nations have now accepted a general responsibility to contribute towards the supply of occupied Europe, but the enemy might equally well withhold the supplies which he at present furnishes to Belgium and other occupied territories – irrespective of whether these are the same kind as those which your Government proposes should be admitted through the blockade – in the confident expectation that he can force us to extend the concession.

Were the enemy to resort to either of these courses, you will, I feel sure, agree that His Majesty's Government, the Belgian Government and the other Allied Governments associated with them would be placed in an extremely difficult position; and it is in order to avoid giving the enemy the slightest loophole of this nature that my colleagues and I, however great our regret, feel obliged to adhere for the present to our original view.

Yours sincerely,
Winston S. Churchill

September
1942

Winston S. Churchill to President Franklin D. Roosevelt
(Churchill papers, 20/79)

1 September 1942
Personal and Most Secret
No. 142

We have carefully considered your No. 180. The Chiefs of Staff have also talked things over with Eisenhower.

2. We could not contest your wish if you so desire it to take upon the United States the whole burden, political and military, of the landings. Like you I assign immense importance to the political aspect. I do not know what information you have of the mood and temper of Vichy and North Africa, but, of course, if you can get ashore at the necessary points without fighting or only token resistance, that is the best of all. We cannot tell what are the chances of this.

3. I hope, however, that you have considered the following points.

(*a*) Will not British participation be disclosed by the assembly of British small craft and aircraft at Gibraltar for some time beforehand?

(*b*) Would it not be disclosed at the time of landing whatever flag we wear?

(*c*) Would not initial fighting necessarily be between French and British aircraft and French batteries and British ships?

(*d*) If the approach and landing take place in the dark, as is indispensable to surprise, how will the Americans be distinguished from British? In the night all cats are grey.

(*e*) What happens if, as I am assured is 4–1 probable, surf prevents disembarkation on Atlantic beaches?

4. Moreover if, contrary to your hopes, the landings are stubbornly opposed and even held up, we shall not be able to give you the follow-up help for some considerable time because all our assault vessels would have been used for your troops and our reinforcements would be embarked in vessels which can only enter by captured harbours. Thus, if the political bloodless victory, for which I agree with you there is a good chance, should go amiss, a military disaster of very great consequence will supervene. We could have stormed Dakar in September 1940 if we had not been cluttered up with preliminary conciliatory processes. It is that hard experience that makes our military experts rely so much upon the simplicity of force. Will you have enough American trained and equipped forces to do this all by yourselves, or at any rate to impress the enemy by the appearance of ample strength?

5. This sudden abandonment of the plan on which we have hitherto been working will certainly cause grievous delay. General Eisenhower says that 30th October will be the very earliest date. I myself think that it may well mean the middle of November. Orders were given to suspend loadings yesterday in order that, if necessary, all should be recast. I fear the substitution of November for October will open up a whole new set of dangers far greater than those which must anyhow be faced.

6. Finally, in spite of the difficulties it seems to us vital that Algiers should be occupied simultaneously with Casablanca and Oran. Here is the most friendly and hopeful spot where the political reaction would be most decisive throughout North Africa. To give up Algiers for the sake of the doubtfully practicable landing at Casablanca seems to us a very serious decision. If it led to the Germans forestalling us not only in Tunis but in Algeria, the results on balance would be lamentable throughout the Mediterranean.

7. Mr President, to sum up, 'Torch', like 'Gymnast' before it, has always been viewed as primarily a United States enterprise. We have accepted an American command and your leadership and we will do our utmost to make a success of any plan on which you decide. We must, however, say quite plainly that we are sure that the best course is to persevere along the general lines so clearly set out in the agreed directive handed to General Eisenhower on the 14th August, with or without the modifications suggested in the Chiefs of Staff's telegram No. COS (W) 265 of 29th August. I am sure that if we both strip ourselves to the bone as you say, we could find sufficient naval cover and combat loadings for simultaneous attempts at Casablanca, Oran and Algiers.

Winston S. Churchill to John Curtin
(Churchill papers, 20/79)

1 September 1942
Most Secret and Personal

I fully share your view of importance of providing sufficient air forces for the defence of Australia, and, as I assured you in my message of 6th August, our representatives in Washington are doing everything possible to ensure that the interests of Australia are adequately safeguarded. The ideal arrangements would be to provide sufficient aircraft to enable the RAAF to build up strength adequate for the defence of Australia without any dependence on United States assistance. Unfortunately the resources of the United Nations are inadequate for this to be possible and it will clearly be necessary to continue the present arrangements whereby the defence of Australia is conducted by RAAF and United States Air Forces in collaboration.

We understand that the plans of the United States Chiefs of Staff provide for a combined strength of over 1,100 aircraft in Australia by 1st April, 1943. This corresponds closely to the 71 squadrons referred to in your telegram. We consider that this should be adequate for the defence of Australia, especially when account is taken of another 1,000 aircraft which are to be provided in New Zealand and the South Pacific Islands. The proportion which will be RAAF is for the United States Chiefs of Staff to decide, but, as you know, our representatives have been maintaining maximum pressure to ensure that the RAAF get a fair share, and the proposal to turn over equipment from 10 United States squadrons to the RAAF is presumably the result of our joint efforts. In the circumstances I am reluctant to intervene with the President in this matter, but I can assure you that our representatives in Washington will continue to maintain pressure to see that RAAF secure largest possible share of resources in South-West Pacific area.

The three Spitfire squadrons were, as you say, a special measure of assistance from the United Kingdom to Australia and so they have always been regarded here. They will enable the RAAF to be built up more quickly than would otherwise have been possible, and will provide you with resources which are independent of American control. In view, however, of the general shortage of air forces throughout the world, it is understandable that the American Chiefs of Staff should take account of these squadrons in planning for the provision of air forces in your theatre. I do not think that it is a matter on which we can question their decision.

You mention the scale on which the Americans plan to provide aircraft to replace wastage. I understand that 20 per cent per month is the provisioning rate which they use for their own air forces throughout the world. It is certainly too low for a period of intensive operations, but, taken as an average over a long period, it does not seem unreasonable. We are having to make do with this rate of replacement for our units in Middle East on American types, as well as for the United States in that theatre.

Finally, I can assure you of my entire sympathy and anxiety to help in any way I can to strengthen Australia's defences. I do not think that the United States Chiefs of Staff are neglecting their responsibilities, and I think that we should be justified in relying on the action they are taking to provide air forces in South-West Pacific as being adequate to ensure Australia's defence, though admittedly not enough for a strategic offensive.

Pamela Gott to Winston S. Churchill
(Chartwell Trust)

1 September 1942

Waverley Avenue Lodge
Fleet
Hampshire

Dear Prime Minister,

I am so <u>very</u> grateful to you for writing to me, & for all you say about my Strafer – His last letter to me was written on August 5th, just before he saw you, & he said he would write & tell me all about it afterwards. I fear he must have waited to do this from Cairo – I have wondered so much if he knew he was to command the 8th Army. He had <u>absolutely</u> no ambition for himself – his only thought was to do his best, to win the war, & then to leave the Army & follow some profession which was <u>constructive</u>, & useful. He so hated the war and all the <u>destruction</u> it brought with it. 'To have led a useful life' was all he wanted to be able to feel when his life was ending. Surely he has indeed achieved this – I am <u>glad</u> you found him fit, & able to carry on – I believe it was only to me he admitted how tired he was – but he often said that as long as he was wanted & needed out there it wouldn't be right to stress the personal side & try to come home – & of course I understand. But it's a long time, nearly 4 years, & he's never seen our youngest child, who will be 3 next month – We are not meant to understand the ways of God, & as you say, no man can give more than his best, & his life for England – 'Who dies if England lives, who lives if England dies' (Possibly misquoted! But you know what I mean.)[1]

Strafer & I had <u>great</u> Faith (one of our Baby's names) & this, & great pride in my beloved Strafer, will surely help me still.

Your letter will be amongst the most precious of my possessions, one day when they are old enough will help to explain to our daughters how great a man their Father was.

Yours sincerely,
Pamela M. Gott

Winston S. Churchill to Sir Stafford Cripps
(Churchill papers, 20/56)

2 September 1942
Secret

I have been considering your long memorandum of July 30. Your remarks in paras 1 and 2 about the present state of public morale are of course matters of opinion; but we can all agree upon the good effect which would be produced by definite and decisive victories. Personally, I do not think the morale of the country is bad. On the contrary it stands up well in a long period of unsatisfactory results and many disappointments, in spite of the activities of a mischievous but happily small band of MPs and Peers, assisted by the *Daily Mirror* and *Daily Herald*. It must be remembered that the public do not know and cannot be told the military policies and plans upon which our energies are directed. It is therefore necessary that persons in responsible positions and possessing full knowledge should not allow themselves to be swayed by the passing gusts of public or Parliamentary feeling. In wartime no Government that shows itself susceptible to such influence would be able to steer a true course.

2. I do not think that your proposals about the central direction of the war would be helpful. The guiding principle of war direction is, in

[1] Rudyard Kipling, 'For All We Have And Are' (1914), fourth stanza:
No easy hope or lies
Shall bring us to our goal,
But iron sacrifice
Of body, will, and soul.
There is but one task for all –
One life for each to give.
Who stands if England fall?
Who dies if England live?

my opinion, the formulation of war plans by those who have the power and responsibility of executing them. Such men, whose thoughts are in contact at every moment with realities, go through a process incomparably more instructive than any that could be attained by irresponsible and academic speculations. This in no way disparages the functions of Planning Departments which, as you know, are organized with us upon a very large scale and are in high activity. To set up an independent War Planning Directorate of three persons 'of the calibre of the present Chiefs of Staff' as advisers to me, as Minister of Defence, would be vicious in principle. It would create two rival bodies, one irresponsible, one responsible, yet nominally of equal status. It would confront the War Cabinet and the Minister of Defence with the constant need of disregarding the advice of one or the other of these bodies. It would lead to immediate and violent friction. For instance, an Admiral would be appointed to tell the First Sea Lord how to move the Fleet; and an Air Marshal 'of equal calibre' to criticize by implication the Chief of the Air Staff; and similarly in the Army sphere. I am sure if you reflect upon the matter you will see the dangers and antagonisms inherent in such a system. Personally, having had very long experience in these matters, I should only work with and through responsible advisers, that is to say War Chiefs who can give effect to decisions taken and are accountable for results. Any clever person can make plans for winning the war if he has not to carry them out. This is to be encouraged in the Planning Departments, provided their status is definitely and effectively subordinated to the professional heads of the Service Departments. A policy of disembodied Brains Trust browsing about among our secrets and adding to the immense volume of Committees and their reports, is not to me an attractive proposition. There has never I think been a period in this war or the last, with both of which I am fully acquainted, where the relations between the Prime Minister and the three Service Chiefs were so good and smooth, or where there was such complete identity of view upon all the measures to be taken. Why, then, should I withdraw my confidence from these professional advisers, whom I consider are the best the Services can produce at the present time, in order to bestow it in part at least upon officers who are not only less responsible but less capable?

3. Finally, it is in my opinion a delusion to suppose that there is a large supply of officers 'of equal calibre' to the present Chiefs of Staff. Those who might be considered approaching this class would either be men who have already retired from the Services and are of an advanced age, or men who would be naturally the most likely successors to the present

professional heads. The implications attaching to this latter category are self-evident. We saw the mischiefs of all this when the complicated apparatus of the Versailles Council was created in 1918 in order to enable the Prime Minister to overcome the disagreements of Sir William Robertson whom he had not the political authority to dismiss.

4. I enclose a note on co-operation between the Services prepared in the War Cabinet Office and approved by General Ismay.

5. The organization of the scientific and inventive staff is, I understand, covered by the three Scientific Advisers to the Ministry of Production and the Advisory Body, over which I understand you are to preside, on scientific matters apart from those dealt with in the three Service Departments.

6. I entirely agree with what you say about the proliferation of Committees. You may be interested to read what I wrote on the 14th March, 1941, on this subject,[1] and of the results which followed from it. I agree that something in the nature of a continuous overhaul is required, and I have asked Sir Richard Hopkins[2] and Sir Edward Bridges[3] to draft a Minute which ensures this.

7. The other points which you raise as to the general efficiency of our administrative methods and the need for changes in personnel, should, I think, be considered by Sir Richard Hopkins. I am sending him a copy of this part of your Memorandum and asking him to submit a Note on it.

Oliver Harvey: diary
('The War Diaries of Oliver Harvey', page 155)

2 September 1942

We hear PM's heart is bad again. Sir C. Wilson[4] has said he really mustn't fly Atlantic again.

---

[1] War Cabinet Paper, 14 March 1941, 'Committees: Note by the Prime Minister, Addressed to Ministers in Charge of Departments' (*Churchill papers, 23/9*), reproduced in Martin Gilbert, *The Churchill War Papers*, Volume III, *The Ever-Widening War, 1941*, Volume XVI of *The Churchill Documents* (New York and London, 2001), page 354.

[2] Permanent Secretary at the Treasury.

[3] Secretary to the Cabinet.

[4] Sir Charles Wilson, later Lord Moran, the Prime Minister's personal physician

Lord Halifax[1] to Winston S. Churchill
(Churchill papers, 20/79)

2 September 1942
Immediate
Most Secret and Personal

Harriman told me this afternoon that he had as yet no detailed message to send you on 'Torch' but he was very hopeful of different points of view being brought together.

Urgency of decision was fully appreciated here.

Winston S. Churchill to John Llewellin[2]
(Churchill papers, 20/67)

2 September 1942

All their forecasts have been several times written down, and all their performances fall short of their reduced forecasts. The falling off in the heavy bombers is particularly serious. There is no justification for blaming holidays, as it is known beforehand that holidays will be taken in certain months.

The non-expansion of MAP[3] output is really very grave. What action do you propose? Please report to me. We can, if necessary, have the matter in Cabinet.

Winston S. Churchill to Sir Edward Beneš[4]
(Churchill papers, 20/54)

2 September 1942

My dear Excellency,

I write to thank you for the kind letter of greeting which you sent me on the 26 August on my return from Russia and the Middle East.

---

[1] Ambassador in Washington.

[2] Minister of Production.

[3] Ministry of Aircraft Production.

[4] Edvard Beneš, 1884–1948. Born in Bohemia, the son of a farmer. Educated in Prague, Berlin, and London. A leading member of the Czechoslovak National Council, Paris, 1917–18. Czech Minister for Foreign Affairs, 1918–35; Prime Minister, 1921–2. President of the Czechoslovak Republic, 1935–8. In exile as President of the Czechoslovak National Committee in London, 1939–45. Re-elected as President of the Republic, Prague, 1945. Resigned, 1948. Author of many books and pamphlets on the Czech question.

You already know my attitude toward the Munich Agreement. Two years ago I said publicly that it had been destroyed by the Germans. It therefore gives me particular satisfaction that our two Governments have formally placed on record their agreement that Munich can now be considered as dead between them.

The exchange of letters of August 5 is a further proof to the whole world that the days of compromise with aggression and tyranny are now long past. My hope is that it may also prove a source of inspiration and encouragement to your compatriots at home who are suffering so terribly under the German yoke. I look with you to the day of their liberation.

Yours sincerely,
Winston S. Churchill

Winston S. Churchill to Brendan Bracken[1]
(Churchill papers, 20/67)

2 September 1942

What are the arrangements for controlling broadcasts by British Service officers in the overseas Empire, such as that referred to in the attached extract[2] about a broadcast by General Wavell? In the United Kingdom a speech by a Minister not in the War Cabinet on such a topic would not be broadcast without reference to me, and I cannot agree to any lesser control outside this country. Pray make yourself responsible for ensuring, in consultation with the Secretaries of State concerned, that no permission is given for such broadcasts, save in accordance with arrangements approved by you. Any proposals for broadcasts by officers of the highest rank should be referred to me personally.

President Franklin D. Roosevelt to Winston S. Churchill
(Churchill papers, 20/79)

3 September 1942
Most Secret
No. 182

Your message of September 1 has been received and given careful consideration.

---

[1] Minister of Information.
[2] From the *Star* of 2 September 1942.

2. Your willingness to co-operate by agreeing that all initial landings will be made by United States ground forces is appreciated. It is true that British participation in the form of naval and air support will be disclosed to the defenders early in the operation. However, I do not believe that this will have quite the same effect that British forces making the first beach landing would have.

3. Bad surf conditions on the Atlantic beaches is a calculated risk. The use of numerous small lightly defended ports may be necessary.

4. It will be necessary to use all available combat loaders in the first assault. The assaulting troops, regardless of whether they are British or American, must seize a port before follow-up forces can be landed. Regardless of what troops arrive subsequent to the initial landing, the situation will be the same.

5. In view of your urgent desire that Algiers should be occupied simultaneously with Casablanca and Oran, we offer the following solution:

   (1) Simultaneous landings at Casablanca, Oran, and Algiers, with assault and immediate follow-up troops generally as follows:

     (*a*) Casablanca (United States troops): 34,000 in the assault and 24,000 in the immediate follow-up, to land at a port.

     (*b*) Oran (United States troops): 25,000 in the assault and 20,000 in the immediate follow-up, to land at a port.

     (*c*) Algiers (United States and British troops): in the beach landing 10,000 United States troops, followed within the hour by British troops, to make the landing secure, the follow-up to be determined by the Commander-in-Chief. This follow-up to land at a port in non-combat-loaded ships.

   (2) *Troops.* For the above landings the United States can furnish:

     (*a*) from the United States, the Casablanca force, and

     (*b*) from the United Kingdom, the Oran force and 10,000 men for the Algiers force.

As immediate follow-up forces we have one armoured division in the United States and one armoured division in the United Kingdom (both less elements included in the assault echelons), with supporting and service troops, including ground echelons of air units. Later, additional infantry and armoured divisions can be furnished from the United States and the remaining United States troops in the United Kingdom can be made available.

   (3) *Shipping.* The following shipping can be made available by the United States, to sail from United States ports October 20:

    (*a*) Combat loaders with a lift of 34,000 men.

    (*b*) Transports, other than combat loaders, with a lift of 52,000 men, with sufficient cargo vessels to support this personnel. In addition to this shipping there will be available in the United Kingdom United States transports with personnel lift of 15,000 and nine cargo vessels which have been previously set aside by agreement to transport United States troops from the United Kingdom for this operation. In round numbers, the shipping shown as available in the United States is estimated to be sufficient to move the first, second, and third convoys of the Casablanca force.

  (4) *Naval*. The United States cannot provide forces for escort and support in this operation in excess of those now available in the Atlantic, plus all ships which can be expedited in readiness for service, as is now being done.

  6. The above shows the total ground, naval, and shipping effort which the United States can put into this operation. If the operation is to be executed along the lines indicated, namely, simultaneous landings at Casablanca, Oran and Algiers, all the remaining requirements must be furnished from British sources. As we see it, this would mean, in general, that it will be necessary for you to furnish:

    (*a*) all shipping (including combat loaders) required for the Oran and Algiers forces, except the United States shipping now in the United Kingdom earmarked for 'Torch';

    (*b*) the additional troops required for the Algiers assault and follow-up forces; and

    (*c*) the naval forces required for the entire operation, less the United States naval force indicated above.

  7. In order that I may continue with vigorous preparations for the execution of 'Torch' at the earliest practicable date, please confirm by cable that the United Kingdom will provide the troop-lift, troops, naval forces, and shipping noted herein as necessary.

  8. I reiterate the belief expressed in my telegram of August 30, that the Commander-in-Chief should be directed to execute the operation at the earliest practicable date, and that this date should be fixed by him. I am convinced of the absolute necessity for an early decision. I feel that the operation as outlined herein is as far as I can go towards meeting your views, and it seems to me to be a practical solution which retains the Algiers operation and is sufficiently strong to be a good risk throughout.

9. Our latest and best information from North Africa is as follows:

    (a) An American expedition led in all three phases by American officers will meet little resistance from the French Army in Africa. On the other hand, a British-commanded attack in any phase or with the de Gaullist co-operation would meet with determined resistance [...]

Because of this information I consider it vital that some responsibility be placed [on] high Americans for relations with French military and civil authorities in Africa.

As you and I decided long ago, <u>we</u> were to handle the French in North Africa, while you were to handle the situation in Spain.

Winston S. Churchill to President Franklin D. Roosevelt
(Churchill papers, 20/79)

3 September 1942
Personal and Secret
No. 143

Your No. 182.

We have spent the day looking into physical possibilities. Accepting your general outlines we think that a working plan can be made on the basis that the emphasis is shifted somewhat, namely reducing Casablanca by ten or twelve thousand (making up deficiency in the follow ups). These troops with their combat loaded ships would give sufficient strength inside, while making the entire assault American. This evens up the three landings and gives the essential appearance of strength at all vital points. Without such a transference there is no hope of Algiers on account of shortage of combat loaders and landing craft. We all think this would be a great blemish to the plan.

2. Tomorrow we suggest that either General Clark or General Eisenhower should come with Admiral Ramsay[1] who knows the whole transportation escort story and the naval aspect from our end, and Mountbatten on the landing details which are crucial, party reaching you Sunday morning. We do not here know what naval forces you are able to supply. Please let these be imparted to Admiral Cunningham to whom in view of the importance of the operation we propose to give the naval command under the Allied C-in-C.

---

[1] Flag Officer, Expeditionary Force.

3. Delay due to change already extends three weeks. Free French have got inkling and are leaky. Every day saved is precious. We have therefore already ordered work to go forward on these lines but of course the decision rests with you.

General Sir Alan Brooke: diary
('War Diaries, Field Marshal Lord Alanbrooke', page 317)

3 September 1942

Arrived at COS to find that PM had just received President's reply to his wire!

He ordered us to meet him at 10 Downing St at 11 a.m. This was quite useless as the President's wire required examining with experts to arrive at implications. He kept us waiting till 11.15 then talked round the subject till 11.45 when Attlee, Eden and Oliver Lyttelton turned up. We then talked more hot air and at last I obtained leave to withdraw the COS to consider the matter and to report at 5 p.m. We sent at once for Eisenhower and Clark and also for Ramsay. The new plan contemplated an assault force of some 34,000 at Casablanca, where the surf will probably render a landing impossible, and only 10,000 at Algiers, which is the key to the whole front. We concluded that the Casablanca landing must be cut by some 10 to 12 thousand to make Algiers possible. PM and ministers agreed, he then took me and Eisenhower to draft reply to President suggesting this change. He is sending Eisenhower, Ramsay and Mountbatten to Washington and asked me whether I thought I ought to go over. I said I felt that main difference rested on matter of shipping, assault craft and naval cover, that I did not feel I could assist much, especially so in view of the fact that Dill is also going back and can deal with the major points.

John Martin: diary
(Sir John Martin papers)

4 September 1942   Chequers

PM had slight tonsillitis.

Winston S. Churchill to Chiang Kai-shek
(Churchill papers, 20/79)

4 September 1942　　　　　　　　　　　　　　　　Chequers

I am deeply grateful for your Excellency's message on the occasion of the third anniversary of the outbreak of war between this country and Germany. I welcome your tribute all the more coming as it does from the leader of a courageous and steadfast people, who have already withstood the onslaught of the Japanese aggressor for more than five long years. Their resistance owes much, as the British people well know, to your Excellency's resolution and unswerving loyalty to the cause of Freedom, to which we have both consecrated all our energies. With such a cause to inspire us, victory is certain, and when that day dawns, as dawn it will, the British people will be proud to acclaim the Chinese as fellow-architects to victory.

Winston S. Churchill to Lord Linlithgow
(Churchill papers, 20/79)

4 September 1942
Personal and Secret

THE SITUATION IN INDIA

We can, of course, deprecate at Washington in such a manner as probably to prevent the visits to India of Mr Wendell Willkie and Mr Sherwood Eddy. On the other hand, it is for consideration whether you could not captivate them and convert them if that is necessary. I had a great success here with Wendell Willkie, with whom I took the greatest trouble. He is a good dining companion and very ready to see things through our eyes. He has been a good friend to this country and to the Alliance.

2. I do not know Sherwood Eddy, but he is reported as friendly. I always make a point of seeing these prominent Americans and making sure that they get a good show, and the results have always been most satisfactory. Pray let me know how you feel about this.

3. On no account, however, should any foreign visitors be given access to any of the internees.

Winston S. Churchill to William Mackenzie King
(Churchill papers, 20/79)

4 September 1942
Most Secret and Personal
Decipher Yourself

ATLANTIC CONVOYS

With reference to paragraph 2 of my Most Secret and Personal Telegram No. 1900 of 27th August, one of our chief anxieties is lack of escorting craft. We would be grateful if you could lend us every available ship from both Canadian coasts capable of escorting, save those required to maintain the strength of the HX and SC convoy escorts, which are already dangerously weak. If you approve, our naval advisers could arrange details, including such questions as the date of return of such Canadian escort ships as you can spare.

President Franklin D. Roosevelt to Winston S. Churchill
(Churchill papers, 20/79)

4 September 1942
No. 183

Replying to your No. 143. We are getting very close together. I am willing to reduce the Casablanca force by the number of combat loaders capable of carrying a force of one regimental combat team. Approximately 5,000 men. Since a similar reduction was made in original Oran assault force this releases a total of British and United States combat loaders for some 10,000 men for use at Algiers. The combat loaded force of American troops can be used as the nucleus on which to complete that force. I am sure that the additional troops can be found in the United Kingdom.

I do not see advantage of Eisenhower or Clark coming over at this time. I know that they have heavy and pressing responsibilities in organising slowly arriving American forces and I am sure we have a full understanding of their view point. Furthermore, I do want to see Eisenhower later on before final take-off and two trips appear out of the question. We would be glad to see Ramsay and Mountbatten if you wish to send them but I do not desire that their visit shall cause any delay. I am directing all preparations to proceed. We should settle this whole thing with finality at once.

I hope to cable you today a list of United States naval craft which can be made available for the operation.

Winston S. Churchill to Brendan Bracken
(Churchill papers, 20/67)

4 September 1942
Most Secret

This is a very serious matter[1] and wears the aspect not only of indiscretion but of treachery. Let me know today who is the writer. Mr Duff Cooper should also be asked to report upon him. Who are the censors who let this through? While making these most searching and urgent enquiries, it is important not to raise a hullabaloo, which would only emphasise the significance of the disclosure.

It also should be asked what he means by the expression 'some diplomatic quarters'. I regard the matter as most urgent and important, and indeed the gravest one which I have ever referred to you.[2]

Winston S. Churchill to Sir James Grigg
(Churchill papers, 20/67)

4 September 1942
Strictly Personal

I see nothing in these reports[3] which would justify removing this officer from the command of his division on its proceeding on active service.

General Hobart bears a very high reputation, not only in the Service, but in wide circles outside. He is a man of quite exceptional mental attainments with great strength of character, and although he does not work easily with others, it is a great pity we have not more of his like in the Service. I have been shocked at the persecution to which he has been subjected.

[1] Telegram from the United Kingdom High Commissioner in Canada reporting that the *Ottawa Journal* had published a BUP (British United Press) message from London to the effect that relations between the United States and Vichy might soon be broken off, and that this rumour was coupled by a growing conviction in Great Britain that the Axis must be cleared out of North Africa by the British with the aid of the United States.

[2] Brendan Bracken responded that Field Marshal Smuts had also made reference to a coming offensive, to which Churchill replied: 'Field Marshal Smuts' reference meant, and was understood to mean, no more than an offensive through Egypt from Libya; whereas Russell's statement clearly comprises the western end of the Mediterranean.

'The Censor should certainly be dismissed. Russell should also be made to give us the name of the diplomat, under penalty of withdrawing his Press facilities' (Most Secret, 7 September 1942, *Churchill papers, 20/67*). Ned Russell was a BUP correspondent and chief of the London Bureau of the *New York Herald Tribune*.

[3] Medical Board report on General Hobart and letter from the Assistant Director of Medical Services of his division to General Anderson. Notwithstanding his reinstatement, at Churchill's insistence, after his forced early retirement in 1940, Hobart's opponents were making one last attempt to discredit him, using the medical reports mentioned here, which made reference to his relatively advanced age (he was 56).

I am quite sure that if, when I had him transferred from a corporal in the Home Guard to the command of one of the new armoured divisions, I had instead insisted upon his controlling the whole of the tank developments, with a seat on the Army Council, many of the grievous errors from which we have suffered would not have been committed. The High Commands of the Army are not a club. It is my duty and that of His Majesty's Government to make sure that exceptionally able men, even though not popular with their military contemporaries, should not be prevented from giving their services to the Crown.

Winston S. Churchill to Lord Trenchard
(Churchill papers, 20/54)

4 September 1942
Private

My dear Trenchard,

Many thanks for your interesting paper.[1] As you may have heard, I am a champion of Bomber Command, and I do my utmost to strengthen it in every way and to prevent it from being wrongfully inroaded upon.

While admitting and admiring the force of your arguments, I think you spoil a good case by overstating it. You certainly push it to lengths where very few people here or in the United States would agree with you. However, as I am most anxious to combat the attacks made upon what is called 'the luxury bombing of Germany' and the campaign of disparagement which has been pressed upon bombing from so many quarters, I am circulating your paper to the War Cabinet as I did a recent document by Air Marshal Harris.

---

[1] In a memorandum of 29 August 1942, circulated to selected recipients 'by direction of the Prime Minister' (*Cabinet papers, 66/28/29*), Trenchard argued against any 'large land operations on the Continent' as that would 'mean that our last bomb had been dropped on German territory and the whole of our air strength and that of the United States also will be needed to support a plan which, on the most favourable assumptions will be very difficult and costly in life and which might result in utter disaster... If we are to win the war in a reasonable time we must avoid entanglement in land campaigns on the mainland of Europe and instead put everything into air power (British and American) against the enemy's vital spots. If we can put such force into attack from the air German morale and ability to continue the war will be broken. To do this we must concentrate. We must give the fullest air support to fields in which the Army is already engaged and we must supply the demands for aircraft from India.

'On the other hand we have very considerable resources in trained personnel and material locked up in this country in the Army Co-operation Squadrons against some future time when we can send an Expeditionary Force to land where – in Europe?' (*Churchill papers 23/10*).

With regard to your last paragraph but one, it is very difficult to divorce the Head of the Executive in any country from the chief responsibility for the conduct of the war. In the United States and Russia the Head of the Executive is also Commander-in-Chief, although neither Mr Roosevelt nor Premier Stalin has any military experience or training. In this country it would be even more difficult to separate the chief constitutional authority from all control over the war sphere, which is identical with the whole life and fortunes of the nation. To pick an airman, give him plenary powers, and tell him to win the war is certainly a policy, but I wonder whether you have thought it out in all its implications. He would certainly have great difficulty with the other two Services. He would also have difficulty with the Allies, who adopt quite different systems, and particularly with the United States who hold rigidly to a subordinate Air Force. There might also be trouble with the House of Commons, the Cabinet, and all those sort of things. Should the right man be found, however, many of these difficulties could be overcome by his becoming at the same time, Prime Minister. If I were convinced that this solution would bring about a speedy victory, I should be very glad to make way for him. Would it be too much to enquire whom you have in mind? You say there are many. I was not aware that our Services were so rich in talent as to have a number of officers who have already commanded in this war, who take your view about the Air, and who are capable of being the 'one brain responsible for the purely military (in its widest sense) strategical conception of the war in Europe'.

> With good wishes,
> Yours sincerely,
> Winston S. Churchill

General Sir Alan Brooke: diary
('War Diaries, Field Marshal Lord Alanbrooke', page 318)

4 September 1942

We received rumours in the morning that the President would probably agree to our proposal except that he would only reduce the Casablanca attack by 5,000 men instead of 10 to 12 thousand. By the evening it looked as if I should be caught and fail to get off for my Saturday off! President's wire was reported to be coming in late that evening. Finally I escaped and went home feeling very weary![1]

[1]'Not till September 5th was the transatlantic essay competition, as Eisenhower called it, resolved. On that day the awaited cable arrived from the President – who for all his advisers' misgivings had never lost sight of the real objective – agreeing to transfer enough landing-craft from the Casa-

Winston S. Churchill to Sir Miles Lampson[1]
(Churchill papers, 20/79)

5 September 1942
Immediate
Secret

I hope you are taking trouble with Wendell Willkie, who is a good friend of our country. He should be given every chance to see the Front and anything else of interest that he desires. It is most important he should be warmly welcomed. You might mention him to Alexander if the latter is not too busy. Please also give him the warmest messages from me.

Winston S. Churchill to John Llewellin
(Churchill papers, 20/67)

5 September 1942

I attach the greatest importance to this subject.[2] We have made 20,000 2.4-pounder anti-tank guns. We are making another 11,000 for issue to infantry. At present these guns are smirched in reputation. It is of the utmost consequence that confidence should be restored. It can only be restored through the success and issue of the new ammunition. Pray give this your most earnest attention and report to me what you think can be done.

President Franklin D. Roosevelt to Winston S. Churchill
(Churchill papers, 20/79)

5 September 1942
No. 184

King reports maximum number of American naval vessels that can be made available for 'Torch' operation. One modern battleship, two old battleships, one aircraft carrier, two small converted aircraft carriers, tentative planes carried total seventy-eight fighters, thirty dive-bombers, two eight-inch cruisers, three large six-inch cruisers, forty destroyers, six fast minesweepers, total fifty-seven vessels.

---

blanca contingent to enable 10,000 British and American troops to land at Algiers' (Arthur Bryant, in *Turn of the Tide*, p. 494).

[1] Ambassador to Egypt and High Commissioner for the Sudan.

[2] The reference is to a minute of 4 September 1942 from the Controller-General of Munitions Production, Ministry of Supply, about special 2-pounder shot.

Winston S. Churchill to President Franklin D. Roosevelt
(Churchill papers, 20/79)

5 September 1942
Personal and Most Secret
No. 144

We agree to the military lay-out as you propose it. We have plenty of troops highly trained for landing. If convenient, they can wear your uniform. They will be proud to do so. Shipping will be all right.

2. I have just had your No. 184, and it is evident that you too have skinned yourselves to the bone. Unless we suffer serious losses in PQ, we consider that naval forces now jointly to be provided justify us in going full speed ahead with staging the operations.

3. I am sending Admiral Ramsay, with the agreement of General Eisenhower, over at once to furnish Admiral Cunningham with the means of going into naval details with you. It is imperative now to drive straight ahead and save every hour. In this way alone shall we realise your strategical design and the only hope of doing anything that really counts this year.

4. We strongly endorse the request which we understand Eisenhower has already made to Marshall that the force you are releasing from Casablanca may be sent over here complete with its regimental combat team.

Kindest regards.

President Franklin D. Roosevelt to Winston S. Churchill
(Churchill papers, 20/79)

5 September 1942
No. 185

Hurrah!

Winston S. Churchill to President Franklin D. Roosevelt
(Churchill papers, 20/79)

6 September 1942
Personal and Most Secret
No. 145

OK, full blast.

Winston S. Churchill: note
(Churchill papers, 20/63)

6 September 1942

PROTECTION OF DUKE OF WINDSOR

Any place near the sea used habitually must be protected properly. Voyages in small launches across U-boat areas cannot be allowed.

Winston S. Churchill to Josef Stalin
(Churchill papers, 20/79)

6 September 1942
Personal and Secret

Convoy PQ18 with 40 ships has started. As we cannot send our heavy ships within range of enemy shore-based aircraft, we are providing a powerful destroyer striking force, which will be used against the enemy's surface ships should they attack us east of Bear Island. We are also including in the convoy escort, to assist in protecting it against air attack, an auxiliary aircraft-carrier just completed. Further, we are placing a strong line of submarine patrols between the convoy and the German bases. The risk of an attack by German surface ships still, however, remains serious. This danger can only be effectively warded off by providing in the Barents Sea air striking forces of such strength that the Germans will not risk their heavy ships any more than we will risk ours in that area. For reconnaissance, we are providing eight Catalina flying-boats and three PRU Spitfires to operate from North Russia. To increase the scale of air attack, we have sent 32 torpedo-carrying aircraft which have suffered loss on the way, though we hope that at least 24 will be available for operation. These, with the 19 bombers, the 10 torpedo-carrying aircraft, the 42 short-range and 43 long-range fighters which we understand you are providing, will almost certainly not be enough to act as a final deterrent. What is needed is more long-range bombers. We quite understand that the immense pressure put upon you on the main line of battle makes it difficult to supply any more Russian army long-range bombers. But we must stress the great importance of this convoy, in which we are using seventy-seven warships, requiring to take in 15,000 tons of fuel during the operation. If you can transfer more long-range bombers to the north temporarily, please do so. It is most needful for our common interests.

2. Rommel's attack in Egypt has been sharply rebuffed, and I have good hopes may reach a favourable decision there during the present month.

3. The operation 'Torch' though set back about three weeks beyond the earliest date I mentioned to you, is on full blast.

4. I am awaiting the President's answer to definite proposals I have made him for bringing a British–American air contingent into action during the winter on your southern flank. He agrees in principle and I am expecting to receive his plans in detail. I will then cable you again. Meanwhile, I hope that planning with regard to air-fields and communications may proceed as was agreed, subject to your approval, by your officers while I was in Moscow. For this purpose we are anxious to send staff officers from Egypt to Moscow, in the first instance, as soon as you are ready for us to do so.

5. We are watching with lively admiration the continued magnificent resistance of the Russian armies. The German losses are certainly heavy and winter is drawing nearer. I shall give, when I address the House of Commons on Tuesday, an account of my visit to Moscow, of which I retain most pleasing memories, in what I hope you will regard as agreeable terms.

6. Please give my good wishes to Molotov and thank him for his congratulations on my safe return. May God prosper all our undertakings.

Winston S. Churchill to Brigadier Leslie Hollis
(Churchill papers, 20/67)

6 September 1942
Most Secret

There is no need for anyone to get excited for fear 'Torch' should happen too early. Intense efforts must be made to strike on 31st October. To ensure this, it would be well to aim at 29th October. I propose to telegraph to the President in this sense. Surely if the Americans can be ready at their end, we can conform at ours?

We must beware lest we give orders which lead to a general slacking off. If you announce 31st October as the earliest date, it will certainly be ten days later.

Please speak to me about this.

Winston S. Churchill to General Sir Harold Alexander
(Churchill papers, 20/79)

6 September 1942
Private and Personal

Your business seems to have gone remarkably well, thanks to the masterly handling of the troops and artillery. You have no doubt followed the sinkings of Rommel's vital ships and know how small his margin is. It seems most important not to let him get his second wind.

2. 'Torch' is on at full blast but delayed till early November.

3. All good wishes to you and Montgomery, and please give my compliments to Tedder and Coningham for their splendid contribution.

Winston S. Churchill to Admiral of the Fleet Sir Dudley Pound and
Air Chief Marshal Sir Charles Portal
(Churchill papers, 20/67)

6 September 1942

See Boniface 1371 – T.10.[1] This[2] is evidently an occasion for supreme effort, even at the risk of great sacrifices by the Navy and Air Force. Pray inform me tonight what action you are taking.[3]

Winston S. Churchill to Sir John Anderson
(Churchill papers, 20/67)

6 September 1942

Thank you very much for the trouble you have taken.[4] The fact remains that the Metropolitan Water Board are giving better treatment to a conscientious objector than to a young man who volunteered for the Army. This is a disgrace to any body of Englishmen, and is on a par with the same miserable sentiments which degraded our country before the war and played a recognisable part in bringing these miseries upon the world.

Your remark about stealing a march on their colleagues to be just requires amplification as follows: 'stealing a march *towards the enemy* on their colleagues'.

[1] Enigma decrypts.

[2] Sailing of an enemy convoy from Italy to North Africa.

[3] The convoy was attacked; three of its four merchant ships, laden with aviation fuel, were sunk.

[4] Minute of 3 September 1942 from Anderson (Lord President of the Council) about the treatment meted out by the Metropolitan Water Board to an employee who joined the Forces without the Board's sanction as compared with their attitude to an employee who was a conscientious objector.

As soon as I have got through with my speech I will take the matter up myself in writing with the Board, and unless I get satisfaction I shall publish the correspondence.

Winston S. Churchill to Members of the War Cabinet
(Cabinet papers, 66/28)

7 September 1942
Secret
War Cabinet Paper No. 395 of 1942

THE INDIAN REPRESENTATIVE AT THE WAR CABINET

We may expect the arrival, during this week, of His Highness the Maharaja Jam Sahib of Nawanagar and the Honourable Sir Ramaswami Mudaliar, representatives of India at the War Cabinet. The invitation was a generous gesture to loyal Indians, and we should make the most of it. They must be treated in every possible way as Dominion representatives, and I know my colleagues will show them every courtesy and consideration.

But let me sound one note of warning. Though I shall naturally invite them to attend our Monday Meetings on general war affairs, it must not be assumed that I shall feel able to invite them to Meetings when Indian affairs are to be discussed. We have already had several such meetings, and may have more, at which the presence of Indian representatives would be highly embarrassing. I suggest we should bear this point in mind in any personal conversations we may have with the Jam Sahib and Sir Ramaswami, and avoid giving them the impression that they have a right to attend all War Cabinet Meetings, or necessarily to be present when Indian matters are under discussion.

It will, of course, follow that they will not receive all papers circulated to War Cabinet Ministers. No doubt my colleagues will bear this also in mind. A Note is annexed indicating the classes of papers which they will receive.

Winston S. Churchill to President Franklin D. Roosevelt
(Churchill papers, 20/79)

7 September 1942
Personal and Secret
No. 146

First four ships carrying 193 Shermans and 28 SP 105's arrived 2nd and were unloaded in record time.

The rest are close behind. 24th, 2nd and 9th Brigades should all be fully equipped with these tanks in the next ten days. I am sure the troops will do full justice to these fine weapons. Remembering that dark Tobruk day, I am most grateful to you. I have good hopes about all the Egyptian fighting and believe Rommel is hard pressed.

Josef Stalin to Winston S. Churchill
(Churchill papers, 20/80)

8 September 1942
Personal and Secret
Decipher Yourself

I received your message on September 7. I understand all-importance of safe arrival of convoy PQ18 in Soviet Union and necessity of taking measure for its defence. Difficult as it is for us to transfer at the present moment an additional number of long-range bombers for this task, we have decided to do so. Today orders have been given to send additional long-range bombers for the purpose mentioned by you.

I wish you success in the outcome of operations against Rommel in Egypt, and also full success in Operation 'Torch'.

House of Commons: Debate
(Hansard)

8 September 1942
12 noon

DEBATE ON THE WAR SITUATION

The Prime Minister (Mr Churchill): Nine weeks have passed since I spoke here on the Vote of Censure. I am most grateful to the House for the substantial majority which they then gave to me and to the Government. Every proof that is given to the world of the inflexible steadfastness of Parliament and of its sense of proportion strengthens the British war effort in a definite and recognisable manner. Most particularly are such manifestations of our national will-power a help to the head of the British Government in time of war. The Prime Minister of the day, as head of the Executive, has to be from time to time in contact and correspondence with the Heads of the Executives of the great Allied States. President Roosevelt and Premier Stalin are not only Heads of the Executive but are Commanders-in-Chief of the Armed Forces. We work our affairs in a different way. The Prime Minister is the servant of the House and is liable to dismissal at a moment's notice by a simple vote. It is only possible for him to do what is necessary, and what has got to be done on occasion by somebody or other, if he enjoys, as I do, the support of an absolutely loyal and united Cabinet, and if he is refreshed and fortified from time to time, and especially in bad times, as I have been, by massive and overwhelming Parliamentary majorities. Then your servant is able to transact the important business which has to be done with confidence and freedom, and is able to meet people at the heads of the Allied countries on more or less equal terms, and on occasion to say 'Yes' and 'No' without delay upon some difficult questions. Thus we arrive, by our ancient constitutional methods, at practical working arrangements which show that Parliamentary democracy can adapt itself to all situations and can go out in all weathers. That is why I am especially grateful to the House for their unswerving support and for the large majority with which they rejected a hostile vote on the last occasion we were together.

Since that day and since the House separated there have been several important operations of war. The first of these has been the carrying into Malta of a convoy of supplies sufficient to ensure the life and resistance of that heroic island fortress for a good many months to come. This operation was looked forward to with a certain amount of anxiety on account of the great dangers to which many of His Majesty's most valuable ships must be exposed. For this purpose a powerful battle squadron, supported by three aircraft carriers trained to work in combination, and by powerful cruiser squadrons and flotillas were set in motion through the Straits of Gibraltar. At the same time the Malta Air Force was raised to a very high level of strength by the flying through of Spitfires from other carriers, so that an effective protective umbrella was spread around the island for a considerable distance and the local command of the air was effectively assured. The convoy was thus able to force its way through the extraordinary dangers which beset its passage from Sardinia onwards. Three or four hundred German and Italian shore-based bombers, torpedo planes and long-range fighters were launched against our armada – an enormous concourse of ships – and in the narrows, which were mined, it was attacked by E-boats[1] and U-boats. Severe losses were suffered both by the convoy and the escorting fleet. One aircraft-carrier, the *Eagle*, two cruisers and one destroyer were sunk and others damaged. But this price, although heavy, was not excessive for the result obtained, for Malta is not

---

[1] E-boat: the German *Schnellboot* or 'fast boat', a fast-moving surface attack craft.

only as bright a gem as shines in the King's Crown, but its effective action against the enemy communications with Libya and Egypt is essential to the whole strategic position in the Middle East. In the same operation one eight-inch Italian cruiser and one six-inch Italian cruiser were torpedoed and badly damaged and two U-boats were sunk. A most remarkable feature of this fighting was undoubtedly the defeat by gunfire, and by aircraft of the carriers, of the enemy's shore-based aircraft. Fifty-six Axis aircraft were shot down for certain and 15 others were probably destroyed. Of these 39 were shot down by carrier-borne aircraft of the Fleet and 17 by the 'Ack-Ack' guns of the ships of the convoy and of the escort. In addition, at least 16 were destroyed by aircraft from Malta, and all this loss was sustained by these very powerful shore-based squadrons, operating from bases in comparatively close proximity, without their being able to inflict by air action any appreciable damage upon the ships of war or the supply ships of the convoy – a remarkable fact.

Although the loss of the *Eagle* at the outset of the operation affected the combination of the three carriers on which much store was set – which always seemed to me, personally, to be of the highest importance and a new feature – we must regard the whole episode as a further proof of the value of aircraft carriers working together in combination at sea and also of the increasing power of the gunnery of the fleet and of the merchant vessels, which were all armed to the teeth and fought with customary determination. All of this fleet and the whole operation was led with the utmost discipline and determination, reflecting the highest credit on all officers and men concerned, both of the Royal Navy and Mercantile Marine and upon the skilful admirals in charge – Admiral Syfret, Admiral Burrough[1] and Admiral Lyster.

The second important operation was the attack upon Dieppe. It is a mistake to speak or write of this as 'a Commando raid', although some Commando troops distinguished themselves remarkably in it. The military credit for this most gallant affair goes to the Canadian troops, who formed five-sixths of the assaulting force, and to the Royal Navy, which carried them all there and which carried most of them back. The raid must be considered as a reconnaissance in force. It was a hard, savage clash such as are likely to become increasingly numerous as the War

---

[1] Harold Martin Burrough, 1888–1977. Gunnery Officer, HMS *Southampton*, Battle of Jutland, 1916. Commanded 5th Destroyer Flotilla, 1935–7; HMS *Excellent*, 1937–8. Rear-Admiral, 1939. Assistant Chief of the Naval Staff, 1939–40. Commanded Cruiser Squadron, 1940–2. Commanded Naval Forces, Algiers, 1942 (DSO). Vice-Admiral, 1942. Knighted, 1942. Flag Officer Commanding Gibraltar and Mediterranean Approaches, 1943–5 (bar to DSO). Allied Naval Commander-in-Chief, Expeditionary Force, 1945. British Naval Commander-in-Chief, Germany, 1945–6.

deepens. We had to get all the information necessary before launching operations on a much larger scale. This raid, apart from its reconnaissance value, brought about an extremely satisfactory air battle in the West which Fighter Command wish they could repeat every week. It inflicted perhaps as much loss upon the enemy in killed and wounded as we suffered ourselves. I, personally, regarded the Dieppe assault, to which I gave my sanction, as an indispensable preliminary to full-scale operations. I do not intend to give any information about these operations, and I have only said as much as I have because the enemy can see by his daily reconnaissances of our ports many signs of movements that we are unable to conceal from his photography. He is also aware of the steady and rapid influx into this Island of United States divisions and other troops, but what he does not know is how, when, where and with what forces and in what fashion he will be smitten. And on this point it is desirable that he should be left to his own ruminations, unassisted by British or American advice or comment.

Since the successful action off Midway Island, our American Allies, with the very active support of Australian Forces, have been engaged with the Japanese in the South-west Pacific, and in the course of these operations they have taken the offensive and occupied the Islands of Guadalcanal, Tulagi and other islands in the Solomons. They have, moreover, according to the reports which have already been seen in the Press, frustrated Japanese activities in Milne Bay. The fighting ashore, in which United States marines were prominent, and the fighting at sea have both been exceptionally bitter. In the fighting at sea His Majesty's Australian ship *Canberra* has been sunk, as has already been announced. His Majesty's Government considered that the Commonwealth Government should not bear this grievous loss, following the sinking of other gallant Australian ships. We have therefore decided to offer freely and unconditionally the transfer of His Majesty's eight-inch gun cruiser *Shropshire* to the Commonwealth Government. The offer has been most warmly received.

Since we were last together the tendencies of war have continued to move in our favour. Of the Russian Front, I will only at this moment say that it is the 8th of September. In other quarters the growing predominance of the Allied air power is continuous. From June onwards to the first week in September, just closed, we have discharged nearly double the bomb load upon Germany as was discharged in the corresponding period of last year, and that with much greater precision. A far larger proportion fell in built-up areas or hit the actual target. The United States daylight bombing is a new and increasingly important factor, and there is no doubt that both in accuracy of aim and in mutual defensive power new possibilities of air warfare are being opened by our American comrades and their Flying Fortresses.

The losses at sea are still very heavy, but I am glad to say that the months of July, August, and September so far as it has run, are a definite improvement on those which preceded them. This is due largely to the continued development and completion of the convoy system off the American coast, and this improvement has been effected in spite of heavy losses in war operations, such as the Russian and Malta convoys.

During these same months, the line of new building of merchant ships of the United Nations has definitely crossed and maintained itself on the graph above the line of sinkings. Warfare – and this is even more important, because offence is more important than defence, however successful – warfare on U-boats has been more successful than at any former period in the war. In fact, very few days have passed without one or more being sunk or damaged by us or our Allies. One would, of course, expect the U-boats to suffer heavier losses as there are more of them about, and I cannot say that the sinkings of U-boats have nearly kept pace with the believed and planned new construction. On the other hand, our heavy and successful bombing of the German shipbuilding yards will have an increasing effect upon future output and assembly of U-boats, and the part which the air is taking in the U-boat warfare grows more important with every week that passes.

We must regard the struggle at sea as the foundation of all the efforts of the United Nations. If they lost that, all else would be denied to them, but there is no reason to suppose that we have not the means of victory in our hands, provided that the utmost in human power is done here and in the United States.

Lastly, we may note that the ruthless unlimited German U-boat warfare and the outrages to which this gave vent, have brought us a new Ally, and in the dawn of the fourth year of the war we welcome the accession of Brazil to the ranks of the United Nations. We are entitled to regard this as a most helpful and encouraging event.

Continued efforts are made by us and our Allies to unify and concert the command and action of the United Nations, and particularly of their leading members. These efforts are made in spite of all the obvious difficulties which geography can interpose. During the month of July, President Roosevelt sent a most important mission to this country. No announcement of this was made at the time. The mission comprised General Marshall, the Head of the United States Army, Admiral King, the Head of the Navy, and Mr Hopkins, the President's Personal Representative. These gentlemen met in numerous conferences, not only the

British Chiefs of Staff, but the Members of the War Cabinet, and of the Defence Committee which is a somewhat smaller grouping of it. During a period of 10 days or more the whole field of the war was explored and every problem of importance in it was scrutinised and weighed. Decisions of importance were taken affecting the whole future general conduct of our operations not only in Europe but throughout the world. These decisions were in accordance with the wishes of President Roosevelt, and they received his final approval. Thus, by the end of July complete agreement on war policy and war plans had been reached between Great Britain and the United States. This agreement covers the whole field of the war in every part of the world, and also deals with the necessary productive and administrative measures which are required to enforce the combined policy and strategy which has been agreed upon.

Armed with this body of agreement between Great Britain and the United States, and invigorated by the good will of the House manifested at what was a particularly dark, unhappy and anxious moment, I took advantage of the Recess to visit the Army in the Middle East and to visit Premier Stalin in Moscow. Both these journeys seemed necessary in the public interest, and I believe that the results achieved, although now secret, will as they become apparent justify any trouble or expense incurred.

Travelling always in a Liberator bomber, it was possible to reach Cairo in an uncommonly short time. Before I left I had some reason to believe that the condition of the Desert Army and the troops in Egypt was not entirely satisfactory. The Eighth Army, or the Army of the Western Desert, or the Desert Army as I like to call it, had lost over 80,000 men. It had been driven back about 400 miles since May, with immense losses in munitions, supplies and transport. General Rommel's surprisingly rapid advance was only rendered possible because he used our captured stores and vehicles. In the battles around Gazala, in the stress of the retreat and the fighting at El Alamein, where General Auchinleck succeeded in stabilising the front, the structure of the Army had become much deranged. The divisional formations had been largely broken up, and a number of battle groups or other improvised formations had sprung into being piecemeal in the course of the hard fighting. Nevertheless, as I can myself testify, there was a universal conviction in officers and men of every rank that they could beat the Germans man to man and face to face. But this was coupled with a sense of being baffled and of not understanding why so many misfortunes had fallen upon the Army. The spirit of the troops was admirable, but it was clear to me that drastic changes were required in the High Command and that the Army must have a new start under new leaders. I was fortified in these conclusions by the advice of the Chief of the Imperial General Staff, who accompanied me, and also by the massive judgment of Field-Marshal Smuts, who flew from Cape Town to Cairo to meet me and also, of course, to see the South African divisions which he has sent into the line.

I, therefore, after many heart-searchings, submitted proposals to the War Cabinet for changing and remodelling the High Command. In these proposals, General Alexander, fresh from his brilliant uphill campaign in Burma – a most testing ordeal for any man – succeeded General Auchinleck, and General Gott, who was greatly trusted by the troops, was to command the Eighth Army. The Cabinet was in the act of endorsing these telegraphed recommendations when General Gott was killed by the enemy. I felt this very much, because I met him only the day before; I spent a long time in his company, and he seemed a most splendid man. General Montgomery, who now commands the Eighth Army, is one of our most accomplished soldiers, and we had need of him for certain purposes here at home. However, the imminent threat of battle in the Western Desert left us no choice but to call upon him. I am satisfied that the combination of General Alexander, as Commander-in-Chief, and General Montgomery under him commanding the Eighth Army, with General McCreery, an officer deeply versed in the handling of tanks, as Chief of the General Staff, is a team well adapted to our needs and the finest at our disposal at the present time. There were, of course a number of other changes. It is always painful making such changes, but in wartime individual feelings cannot be spared, and whatever is thought to be the best arrangement must be made without regard to persons, and must be made quickly. I hope the House will not press me to argue these matters on merits in detail, as I certainly should not be able to comply with their wish without detriment to the public interest.

Of General Auchinleck I will only say that he is an officer of the greatest distinction and of a character of singular elevation. He wrested victory for us at the battle of Sidi Rezegh in November, and in the early days of July he stemmed the adverse tide at El Alamein. He has at present, at his own request, gone on leave, and it is my hope that his services may be available later on in the war.

In spite of the heavy losses which I mentioned, the Army of the Western Desert is now stronger actually and relatively than it has ever been. In fact, so large have the new reinforcements which have reached this Army been, that what is to a large extent a new Army has been created while the fighting has actually been in progress. The principal measures which rendered this possible were taken before the disaster of Tobruk, and, indeed, before the opening of the battle at Gazala in May. They were part of the general preparation which, looking ahead, we made for the hazards and stresses of the Desert campaign of 1942. As far back as March last I asked President Roosevelt to lend me shipping to transport an additional 40,000 or 50,000 men to the Middle East so as to have something to veer and haul upon, so as to have a force which could be turned to the various theatres in which danger might develop. The President consented and placed at our disposal a number of American ships, and in consequence at the critical moment we had rounding the Cape a very large and well-equipped force which could be directed immediately to Egypt. It is to that that the improvement in our affairs, the maintenance of our affairs, in that region must largely be attributed. Besides this a broadening stream of drafts to replace casualties, of equipment, tanks, anti-tank guns, 'Ack-Ack' guns and vehicles of all kinds has been flowing from this country and from the United States to the Middle East, and we now have in Egypt a very good, strong, well-equipped and resolute Army barring the further advance of the invader.

In the Debate on the Vote of Censure on Thursday, 2nd July, some of the Opposition speakers seemed to think that the fall of Cairo and Alexandria was only a matter of days. 'Wait till Monday, wait till Tuesday', it was said, 'and events will reinforce our criticisms.' Well, we have waited, and now after more than two months I feel able to assure the House that they may be confident in our ability to maintain the successful defence of Egypt, not for days or for weeks, but for several months ahead. [Interruption.] I say several months ahead, but I might say more. Suffice it to say that.

I am strengthened in this view by the results of the heavy fighting of last week. Owing to the restraint and understatement which have been practised in the Middle East communiqués in deference to the taste of the House, the scale and intensity of these operations have not been realised, or have only now begun to be realised. General Rommel has been much hampered by the sinkings of so many of his supply ships by our submarines, as well as by the British and United States air attacks renewed again from Malta and also from Egypt. Under the inconveniences resulting from their pressure as we may suppose, he came round our Southern flank last Monday week in a major offensive with the whole German Afrika Korps, including the 90th Light Division, the two Panzer divisions and a large part of the 20th Italian Motorised Corps. We have not been able to keep our left hand upon the Qattara depression, which dies away at this point to the Eastward, and there was plenty of room for Rommel to execute such a manoeuvre. The Desert Army under its new command had, however, been reorganised in depth and had been reinforced by every brigade, by every tank and by every gun that could be hurried forward from the Delta. I had the good fortune to visit the troops on exactly the ground where this battle took place, and I must say it seemed to me very obliging of General Rommel to have come on to us just where all the preparations had been made for his hearty reception.

This desert warfare has to be seen to be believed. Large armies, with their innumerable transport and tiny habitations, are dispersed and scattered as if from a pepper-pot over the vast indeterminate slopes and plains of the desert, broken here and there only by a sandy crease or tuck in the ground or outcrop of rock. The ground in most places, especially on all commanding eminences, is rock with only an inch or two of sand on the top, and no cover can be obtained for guns or troops except by blasting. Scattered though the troops are, there is an elaborate system of signalling, the enormous development of which is incredible. The more improvements there are in our means of communication the more people are required to serve the Signals Branch. But owing to this elaborate system of signalling, in which tens of thousands of people are engaged, this army, scattered over these vast areas, can be moved and brought into action with extraordinary rapidity, and enormous distances can be covered by either side in what seemed a few years ago to be an incredibly short space of time.

It did not seem to our commanders that General Rommel would dare to bypass the Desert Army, with its formidable armoured striking power, and push on to Cairo, and in this they were right; but in order that the Desert Army should have the fullest freedom of manoeuvre a new Army has been brought into being along the line of the Nile and the Delta, where conditions prevail totally different from those which exist in the desert. In fact, you could not have a greater contrast in every military condition than is presented at the point where cultivation begins and the desert ends. Rommel was not, however, disposed to run the risk of going round and by-passing the Army, and he strove instead to repeat the tactics he had used at Gazala. He was met not only by British armour but by British artillery used on a scale hitherto unprecedented. We had many hundreds of 25-pounders, as good a field gun as exists in the world, as well as many hundreds of 6-pounder high velocity anti-tank guns in action. We had a good superiority in armour, though we were not quite equal in the heaviest-gunned tanks, and we had once again undoubted mastery in the air. The attack of the Axis army, which had been reinforced up to 12 divisions and had also very powerful artillery, with some superiority in medium guns, and powerful armoured forces, was first brought to an abrupt standstill and then pressed slowly and steadily back with heavy losses of tanks and vehicles of all kinds. We are entitled to consider this last week's fighting as distinctly not unsatisfactory, especially when we compare it with what our position was 2½ months ago. As to the future, I can only say that the Desert Army will welcome every opportunity of fighting that is offered to it and that further developments may be awaited with good heart by all who are watching events in that theatre.

The striking feature in this theatre is, of course, the outstanding strength and resiliency of our Air Force. Three-quarters of the Air Force is British, but there are also some most gallant and efficient Australian and South African squadrons and powerful United States air groups working with the Royal Air Force. Co-operation between the Air and the Army had been brought to the very highest degree in the days of General Auchinleck, and it is now renewed between Air Chief Marshal Tedder and General Alexander and Air Vice-Marshal Conyngham and General Montgomery. The Army and Air commanders in the field live and camp together in the same moving headquarters, and the Air Force rather than being divided among the troops is used as a whole in characteristic fashion for their benefit and, as far as I could see, not only for their benefit but to their very great satisfaction. The Air Force has played a decisive part throughout this campaign. Without its superior power, no one can say whether we should have got thus far. But the story is only half told and it would be inartistic to attempt to anticipate the further chapters which remain to be written.

Three times when I asked the question, 'What do you think of the dive bombers?' because I asked all sorts of questions of all sorts of people I got the answer, 'Which dive bombers?' from officers of different ranks. There is no doubt at all that our ground strafing aircraft and fighter bombers are achieving results at least equal to those of the Stukas without being vulnerable as the Stukas are when caught unprotected by their fighter escort. The most intense exertions have been made by all the air squadrons not only during the action but in the preparatory stages. I should not have thought it possible that such a high percentage of sorties could be maintained without detriment to health and efficiency. Nothing could exceed however the efficiency and ardour of all the airmen whom I saw, and nothing could exceed the admiration and good will in which the Air Force is held by their comrades in the Army. I took pains while I was there to visit and inspect almost every large formation, not only those at the front but others which were preparing in the rear. I spent five days in this way and was most kindly received by the troops, to whom I explained the extraordinary importance and significance of their task and its bearing upon the issues of the whole war. Their life in the fierce light of the desert, with its cool strong breezes, is hard but healthy. I have never seen an Army which deserved victory more, and I await with confident hope the further unfolding of the scroll of fate.

Apart from the changes in the High Command, I reached the conclusion that the Middle East Command was too extensive in itself, and that General Auchinleck had been unduly burdened by having to consider the problems of Persia and Iraq, some 600 or 700 miles away, at the same time that he had Rommel on his hands within 50 miles of Alexandria. I therefore obtained permission from my colleagues for the detaching of Persia and Iraq from the Middle Eastern Command and the making of a new and separate Command round the Tenth Army based on Basra and Baghdad. This sphere is given to Sir Henry Maitland-Wilson, who, from his command of the Ninth Army in Syria and Palestine, has already had opportunities of being thoroughly acquainted with the situation. The Tenth Army is being rapidly strengthened and, with the substantial Air Force which it will require, may eventually give support to the Russian left flank, and will in any case defend the soil of Persia.

During my visit to Cairo the Chief of the Imperial General Staff and I had the advantage of long consultations with General Wavell about India, with Lord Gort about Malta, and with General Platt about East Africa. In Cairo I was received by King Farouk and in Teheran by the Shah of Persia. Both these young rulers, who are also brothers-in-law, affirmed their loyalty to the cause of the United Nations, and the Shah of Persia was good enough to enter upon a most able exposition of the solid reasons which make the interests of Persia identical with the victory of Britain and her Allies.

The main purpose of my journey was, however, to visit Premier Stalin in Moscow. This was accomplished in two long flights with a break at Teheran. We flew across the two mountain systems, each about 300 miles wide, which lie South of the Caspian Sea and between which spread the plain and plateau of Persia. Some of these peaks go up to 18,000 or 19,000 feet, but as we flew by day we had no need to go higher than 13,000 feet. We flew across long stretches of the Caspian Sea up the Ural River towards Kuibyshev (formerly Samara) and reached Moscow in the afternoon.

In this part of my mission I was accompanied by Mr Averell Harriman, President Roosevelt's personal representative. The House will see that it was a great advantage to me to have the support of this most able and forceful man who spoke with the august authority of the President of the United States. We spent four days in conferences with Premier Stalin and Mr Molotov, sitting sometimes for five and six hours at a time, and we went into everything with the utmost candour and thoroughness. At the same time, the Chief of the Imperial General Staff and General Wavell, who accompanied me, had farther conferences with Marshals Voroshilov and Shaposhnikov and dealt with the more technical aspects of our joint affairs. Naturally I should not give any account of the subjects we discussed or still less of the conclusions which we reached. I have reported all these to the War Cabinet, and Mr Harriman has reported them to President Roosevelt, but all must remain secret.

I may say, however, that the Russians do not think that we or the Americans have done enough so far to take the weight off them. This is not at all surprising, in view of the terrific onslaught which they are enduring and withstanding with such marvellous tenacity. No one in the last war would have deemed it possible that Russia could have stood up as she has been doing to the whole weight of the Teutonic armies. I say the whole weight, because, although there are 40 to 45 Germans divisions facing us in the West and holding down the subjugated countries, these numbers are more than made up against Russia by Finnish, Hungarian, Rumanian and Italian troops who have been dragged by Hitler into this frightful welter. It is a proof of the increased strength which Premier Stalin has given to Russia that this prodigious feat of the resistance of Russia alone to the equivalent of the whole of the Teutonic Army has been accomplished for so long and with so great a measure of success. It is difficult to make the Russians comprehend all the problems of the sea and of the ocean. We are sea animals and the United States are to a large extent ocean animals. The Russians are land animals. Happily, we are all three air animals. It is difficult to explain fully all the different characteristics of the war effort of various countries, but I am sure that we made their leaders feel confidence in our loyal and sincere resolve to come to their aid as quickly as possible and in the most effective manner without regard to the losses or sacrifices involved so long as the contribution was towards victory.

It was an experience of great interest to me to meet Premier Stalin. The main object of my visit was to establish the same relations of easy confidence and of perfect openness which I have built up with President Roosevelt. I think that, in spite of the accident of the Tower of Babel, which persists as a very serious barrier in numerous spheres, I have succeeded to a considerable extent. It is very fortunate for Russia in her agony to have this great rugged war chief at her head. He is a man of massive outstanding personality, suited to the sombre and stormy times in which his life has been cast; a man of inexhaustible courage and will-power and a man direct and even blunt in speech, which, having been brought up in the House of Commons, I do not mind at all, especially when I have something to say of my own. Above all, he is a man with that saving sense of humour which is of high importance to all men and all nations, but particularly to great men and great nations. Stalin also left upon me the impression of a deep, cool wisdom and a complete absence of illusions of any kind. I believe I made him feel that we were good and faithful comrades in this war – but that, after all, is a matter which deeds not words will prove. One thing stands out in my mind above all others from this visit to Moscow – the inexorable, inflexible resolve of Soviet Russia to fight Hitlerism to the end until it is finally beaten down. Premier Stalin said to me that the Russian people are naturally a peaceful people, but the atrocious cruelties inflicted upon them by the Germans have roused them to such a fury of indignation that their whole nature is transformed.

As I flew back to Cairo across the vast spaces, back across the Caspian Sea and the mountain ranges and deserts, I bore with me the conviction that in the British Empire, the United States and the Soviet Union, Hitler has forged an alliance of partnership which is strong enough to beat him to the ground, and steadfast enough to persevere not only until his wickedness has been punished, but until some at least of the ruin he has wrought has been repaired.

We have recently been reminded that the third anniversary of the war has come and gone and that we are now entered upon the fourth year. We are indeed entitled, nay, bound to be thankful for the inestimable and measureless improvements in our position which have marked the last two years. From being all alone, the sole champion left in arms against Nazi tyranny, we are now among the leaders of a majestic company of States and nations, including the greatest nations of the world, the United States and Russia, all moving forward together until absolute victory is won, and not only won but established upon unshakable foundations. In spite of all the disappointing episodes, disasters and sufferings through which we have passed, our strength has grown without halt or pause, and we can see each day that not only our own power but the weight of the United States becomes increasingly effective in the struggle.

Apart from the physical and mortal dangers of the war through which we have made our way so far without serious injury, there was a political danger which at one time seemed to me, at any rate, to be a formidable threat. After the collapse of France, when the German armies strode on irresistibly in triumph and conquest, there seemed to be a possibility that Hitler might establish himself as a kind of Charlemagne in Europe and would unite many countries under German sway while at the same time pointing to our island as the author of the blockade and the cause of all their woes. That danger, such as it was, and I certainly did not think it negligible, has rolled away. The German is now more hated in every country in Europe than any race has been since human records began. In a dozen countries Hitler's firing-parties are at work every morning, and a dark stream of cold execution blood flows between the Germans and almost all their fellow-men. The cruelties, the massacres of hostages, the brutal persecutions in which the Germans have indulged in every land into which their armies have broken have recently received an addition in the most bestial, the most squalid and the most senseless of all their offences, namely, the mass deportation of Jews from France, with the pitiful horrors attendant upon the calculated and final scattering of families. This tragedy fills one with astonishment as well as with indignation, and it illustrates as nothing else can the utter degradation of the Nazi nature and theme, and the degradation of all who lend themselves to its unnatural and perverted passions.

When the hour of liberation strikes in Europe, as strike it will, it will also be the hour of retribution. I wish most particularly to identify His Majesty's Government and the House of Commons with the solemn words which were used lately by the President of the United States, namely, that those who are guilty of the Nazi crimes will have to stand up before tribunals in every land where their atrocities have been committed, in order that an indelible warning may be given to future ages and that successive generations of men may say, 'So perish all who do the like again'.

Mr Arthur Greenwood (Wakefield): I think my first word ought to be a word of welcome, on behalf of the Members of this House, to the Prime Minister upon his safe return from his most recent, no doubt not his last, adventurous journey, an adventurous journey which in his inimitable way he has so picturesquely described, and thereby enabled himself no doubt to avoid entering on some rather more controversial issues. I will in the few remarks that I shall make follow the Prime Minister's references. I think we have all heard with pride of the success, notwithstanding heavy punishment, of the latest Malta convoy, for if that small indomitable island were to go, it would perhaps be Rommel's greatest victory.

As regards Dieppe, the Prime Minister told us very little, and perhaps that is not surprising. Though we accept the assurance that this was a reconnaissance in force, I have no doubt myself that it provided experience in combined operations which will be needed in the further stages of the war. It is, of course, obvious that the Prime Minister cannot tell the

House how, when and where any further efforts of this kind, or greater ones, are to take place, but I noticed a phrase of his which I interpret in a generous manner. He spoke of Dieppe being a preliminary to full-scale operations. I have never myself joined in the demand for what is called a second front until such a new front could be successfully and permanently established, and it may well be that Dieppe has taught us a great deal as to our future operations.

I am glad the Prime Minister referred to the offensive action now being taken in the South-Western Pacific. The United States, like this country, got off on the wrong leg at the beginning of the war. For that, one does not attach any blame to any person, but it is a comfort now to know that the worst of the disasters may well be over in the Pacific. I wish that the Prime Minister, while he was roaming over that part of the globe, had referred to the recent victories in China, which have not perhaps received the attention in this part of the world that their intrinsic importance in my view demands. The Prime Minister's reference to increasing air raids was one which gives us considerable comfort. It is good to know that United States airmen and United States aircraft are taking part in ever-increasing numbers in both day and night raids, and out of their combined operations I have no doubt will come not double the strength but even more than double the strength of the two single air forces.

The sea situation, the right hon. Gentleman tells us, is somewhat better, that is to say, as I understood him, we are now producing rather more than we are losing, that our campaign against the U-boat is developing and heavy damage is being inflicted upon the enemy; but I submit that that is not enough. The right hon. Gentleman emphasised the overwhelming importance of sea-power for the United Nations, but merely to get on top of current losses does not do much to replace that vast amount of tonnage which has gone to the bottom of the sea in the last three years. Therefore, we must not, and I think the Prime Minister would be the last to suggest that we should, fall into a sense of easy complacency about the shipping situation which, after all, whatever may be said about the production of munitions, is really the major bottle-neck of the war today as regards its conduct overseas, and, indeed as regards its conduct over here should that become necessary. With the Prime Minister I welcome Brazil, that great country with enormous resources and with a strategic advantage over that of all other parts of North and South America, as an active ally in the present great struggle.

I assume from what the Prime Minister said about the American Mission that closer bonds of co-operation were forged during that visit. His reference, however, was merely to the agreement between this country and the United States. One may hope that such co-operation as has been achieved has met with the approval and support of our other Allies, and that the results of that Mission will be woven into the major strategy of the war. With regard to the Middle East, the right hon. Gentleman has admitted that the situation had become somewhat unsatisfactory. When the changes took place, the public impression was one of mystification. I think the right hon. Gentleman has cleared the situation today. If, in his judgment, confirmed by the judgment of the War Cabinet, men are unfitted, for one reason or another which is not necessarily a criticism of them personally, for particular posts, or if they have become stale or tired, it is clear that they should be replaced. The right hon. Gentleman has expressed his perfect confidence in the new Army leaders. I remember an earlier occasion when he spoke with great fervour of the qualities of General Auchinleck – sincerely and no doubt rightly. One hopes that this very brave, very sincere and able man will not be relieved from war service for all time, and that his experience can be re-employed.

The right hon. Gentleman really is a master of the meaningless phrase, which he uses quite deliberately. He said that the results of recent months in Egypt were definitely not unsatisfactory. It would have pleased the Committee had he been able to say that, even within limits, they were definitely satisfactory.

The Prime Minister: I can say that too.

Mr Greenwood: It would have convinced the Committee a little more had the right hon. Gentleman said it in his speech. After the ebb and flow, and the reverses that we have had, the public feel and they will certainly feel it even more keenly after the Prime Minister's speech that a definite advance ought soon to be made, in view of the very large reinforcements which, the Prime Minister told us, are now in that theatre of war.

As to Russia, it is perhaps in the nature of the case that the Prime Minister was uncommunicative. He did give us a picturesque account of his flight to Moscow, and then the door of the Kremlin closed, and we did not hear very much more about it. I think we can infer that the result of the discussions between Britain, the United States and the USSR will be a new and better understanding. I am quite sure that the public heard of the Prime Minister's visit to Russia with pleasure and gratitude for two reasons. In the first place, the British people feel in their hearts that, however much we have done for the USSR in material of all kinds, and it is not negligible – somehow it is not enough. That is the general feeling. One reason for the public appreciation of the Prime Minister's visit was, that out of this came the hope in people's minds that it might lead to closer co-operation in the war sphere.

Dr Haden Guest[1] (Islington, North): Have we a united strategy?

Mr Greenwood: I am just going to say a word on that point. The public of this country want to know whether Russia is now completely 100 per cent in accord with the major strategy which, in the early days – although it may have been modified – was agreed upon between this country and the United States. The second reason why the public were more than interested in the Prime Minister's visit was that they know that Anglo-Russian relations have been clouded for many years by mutual suspicion, created very largely on this side, but which, having regard to their treatment in the Press, the Russians maintained up to very recent days. If we can do something, as the Prime Minister has told us he has endeavoured to do with some success, to give the impression that we are not going to let the Russians down but are going to play fair by them, and that we are standing in with them in this struggle, it will not only add powerfully to the successful prosecution of the war but will lay the foundation of a permanent friendship after the war. In the years of the interregnum after the war, this will be vital to the maintenance of peace in Europe.

There is one aspect of the problem on which I would like to say a word or two. The British Trades Union Congress, which is the most powerful and most responsible trade union movement in the world, with its more than 6,000,000 members, is meeting in conference this week. Anybody who has read the president's address, the annual report or the agenda of resolutions, will find there an increasing toughness, an even stronger determination to secure, as far as possible, the effective prosecution of the war. The report of the Council records a year of great activity during which the Council have taken in very many ways their share of the burden of thought, advice and administration in all our war industries. Some of the resolutions seem to show that, without in any way wishing to minimise what has been done – we tend to do that too often – there is the view that labour, with its skill and experience, is not being used as fully as it should be. There is a wealth of experience and technical knowledge in the workshops and mines in this country which ought to be more fully mobilised for war purposes. That finds its expression in some of the resolutions of the Trades Union Congress. It is, or it may well

[1] Leslie Haden-Guest, 1877–1960. Registered as Licentiate, Royal College of Physicians, London, 1900. Served in the Royal Army Medical Corps in the Boer War and both world wars. Military Cross, 1917. Labour MP for Southwark North, 1923–7; for Islington North, 1937–50. Lieutenant, 1940. Officer in the Venerable Order of the Hospital of St John of Jerusalem, 1943. Created Baron, 1950. Lord in Waiting to the King, 1951. Assistant Opposition Whip in the House of Lords, 1951.

be, the last ounce of that effort which will make the difference between victory and defeat in Egypt. If that ounce of effort can be obtained, as I believe it can, by harnessing the skill, enthusiasm and determination of the workers to the full, in my view it ought to be done.

The right hon. Gentleman at the end of his speech referred to the fourth year of war.

Dr Haden Guest: On a point of Order. It is not very unusual for the Prime Minister to leave the House when the Leader of the Opposition is replying to his first speech? May I be informed whether he is coming back?

The Deputy-Chairman (Colonel Clifton Brown[1]): That is not a point of Order. The Leader of the House is here.

Mr Greenwood: I think, Colonel Clifton Brown, it is a point of hunger, hunger which I share myself. That brings me to the conclusion of my own statement. The fourth year of war opens on a scene which seems to me to offer possibilities of accomplishment which we have not hitherto had in any previous year of the war. I think we are entitled to expect something more than sad reverses, something more than rebuffs, in this fourth year of war. When the factories of the world are pouring out munitions on a scale unprecedented in the world's history, when the number of men under arms grows day by day to gigantic proportions, we can only hope that the leadership of this and others of the great Allied countries will be such that this fourth year of war will register events which will stand to our credit, and will bring nearer the successful conclusion of the war.

Mr Cary[2] (Eccles): I am sure that all hon. and right hon. Members of the Committee will have heard with perhaps even greater interest than on any other occasion the account which the Prime Minister has given of his most recent political tour. As my right hon. Friend the Member for Wakefield (Mr Greenwood) has just said, when the British public heard about it they were heartened and regarded it with the greatest satisfaction. The hazards of the journey were great and no doubt demanded great energy and endurance from my right hon. Friend the Prime Minister. But that sort of expedition seems to refresh my right hon. Friend rather than wear him out. May that long continue.

---

[1] Douglas Clifton Brown, 1879–1958. Educated at Trinity College, Cambridge. Conservative MP for Hexham, 1918–51. Deputy Speaker of the House of Commons, 1938–43. Privy Councillor, 1941. Speaker of the House of Commons, 1943–51. Created Viscount Ruffside, 1951.

[2] Robert Archibald Cary, 1898–1979. Educated at Sandhurst. On active service, 1916–18. General Staff, Iraq, 1920. Conservative MP for Eccles, 1935–45; for Manchester Withington, 1951–74. Parliamentary Private Secretary to the Civil Lord of Admiralty, 1939; to the Secretary of State for India, 1942–4; to the Minister of Health, 1951–2; to the Lord Privy Seal and Leader of the House, 1951–64. Knighted, 1945. Created Baronet, 1955.

Following my right hon. Friend's visits to President Roosevelt, it had been the wish of many Members of this House that the Prime Minister should seek an early opportunity to meet the head of the Russian State. Members will recall the opinion which was expressed by the Deputy Prime Minister in the Debate on 19th May, when he said that you could not get leaders or leaders' representatives together quickly today. Air transportation has not been the limiting factor in taking the Prime Minister to Washington and Moscow, in taking General Smuts to Egypt or General Chiang Kai-shek to Delhi, but the shortage of air transport equipment has been a grave handicap in many other directions – for essential personnel, mails and urgent battle equipment. I think that before we can begin to win this war at full flood much more will have to be done in that direction. I ask the Government to give it their fullest attention. The Empire, with its limitless frontiers of waterways and seaways, has the ideal geography for great seaplanes, and I hope this vital work will ultimately be planned at the centre by a central authority to which all the Empire Governments will subscribe.

I was pleased to hear the Prime Minister say that apart from Malta perhaps the most significant thing which has happened during the last four weeks has been the attack at Dieppe. Firstly, because it was the first real test of enemy defences, and secondly, because it provided a complete reversal of the long held military theory that the occupation of the Channel ports of the European coastline was fatal to the existence of Great Britain. No doubt the French General Staff, in the recommendation which it made to the French Government in June 1940, and which was passed on to our own Prime Minister in such insulting phraseology, believed that the ultimate resistance of Great Britain was out of the question. But two years later what do we now see? That these Islands have become a gigantic forward base and aerodrome against the Continent, and in addition that they have become a titanic workshop for munitions of all sorts, with a greater output per man-unit than any other Allied nation including America. This has been achieved in spite of the most vicious submarine and air attacks against our merchant shipping. All honour is due to the Royal Navy, which must remain the supreme Service of the Armed Forces of the Crown.

I agree with the Prime Minister that if from now on we play our cards well [...] there can be no question of how this war must end, not only ending in victory but promising the outright military defeat from the West of Hitler's Third Reich. Victory for us in the West has now become a legitimate ambition. I would ask other Allied nations to bear in mind that second fronts are not of limited application in geography, and that to continue to fight the enemy wherever he may appear or may be sought out is perhaps the best method of co-operation between the Allied nations.

At the beginning of the Recess in my own particular locality a large deputation waited upon the Lord Mayor of Manchester and asked for immediate action for the opening-up of a second front. The deputation claimed to represent 150,000 workers in surrounding industries. I think the time has come for a little straightforward speaking about this vital matter, which must do so much to shorten the war. No one, least of all the Prime Minister, would wish to damp down a natural desire for action. Surely he above all men would be the first to take some sudden action in removing any number of Nazis from the world, but my right hon. Friend has to put business before pleasure. I also hate the suggestion that the continuance of Russia's superb resistance is dependent or conditional upon something being done elsewhere. We have heard from the Prime Minister today of the superb leadership given to Russia by Premier Stalin. I have not the slightest doubt that that leadership will not fail.

When we do begin our attack in the West – call it a second front, call it what you will – we want our second front to be a freehold, not a tenancy. It will require better soldiers, better guns and better generalship than Germany's. It will require a level of training which will give us the advantage when the fight opens, and a margin of staying-power when it ends. Above all, we want to force the enemy to fight at the time, in the place and under the conditions best suited to ourselves. The period of 'dare' in fighting this war is long since over. Cold calculation and exact planning to defeat the counter-planning of the German general staff are the only method. The deciding battle of this war will be the great engagement which must take place between the British–American Army and the German Army. It is the battle the world is waiting for, and anyone can prophesy that the gaps in the man-power of all three nations engaged will, for many years after this war has ceased, be felt by those nations, and practically beyond repair. Many Members during the Recess have been heartened by seeing in so many parts of our country thousands of gallant American soldiers. We welcome them, and, as the Prime Minister has said, they represent a substantial fortification of our own efforts. The newspapers have catalogued a number of small isolated unfriendly incidents. It would indeed be strange if this sort of thing did not occur. But let us as a nation be at pains to be most tolerant and understanding hosts to these new Armies. This is the way I look at it. A high percentage of these men may not see the United States again, and Great Britain is the last free country many of them may know. I should like them to leave it, loving it and looking upon it as their own, and knowing it as the last free stronghold of democracy.

Sir Earle Page[1] a few weeks ago prophesied that this war would last 10 years, that the Allies would lose the first four years and the Germans would lose the last six. I would be astonished if the German nation could suffer six years in reverse. Another Empire statesman, Mr Nash,[2] who *The Times* described as a friendly critic, and who is a great friend of this country, took us to task for not taking more trouble with or, at this juncture, more interest in the problems of post-war reconstruction. I think it would be a great mistake to divert too many of our energies to that sort of work or even to divert the minds of our people to considering what might follow this war. There is confidence of the victory in the West, but also a tendency to oversimplify the circumstances of victory day by stating what we failed to do to Germany in 1918. Twenty-three years ago the French and ourselves had suffered millions of casualties, inflation had poisoned our financial system, our delicate capitalist business machinery, which alone sustained the enormous population of these Islands, was in ruins. Tens of thousands of men overseas wanted to come home, and many of their civilian relatives demanded the return home of their surviving men. In those circumstances exhaustion and war sickness were not all on the German side. If we had embarked on the occupation of Germany with a gigantic army of our own, a civilian army, for the purpose of civilising a demobilised and demoralised German army, I think it would have been a total failure.

Against what we did then such an occupation seems even now to me to be a fantastic alternative. Both our countries have terrible years ahead. Both sides are fighting for their lives. In my opinion it will go to the last bitter round, and the victor may have no more than a slender margin of staying-power left at the end. I would ask the Government not to associate themselves in any way with false hopes for the aftermath of victory. Rather let them devote all their energy to keeping the nation's will fixed on the one objective of overthrowing the Nazi tyranny by making all three Fighting Services the champions of every engagement. If the Government do that, they will have served their country well. As far as my own constituency is concerned, the Prime Minister and his colleagues still enjoy the full confidence of the people.

[1] Special Australian Envoy to the British War Cabinet, 1941–2; Member of the Australian War Council, 1942–5.

[2] Minister of New Zealand in the United States, 1942–4; Member of New Zealand War Cabinet, 1939–45.

Dr Haden Guest (Islington, North): The Prime Minister, in giving his resumé of the war situation today, has given us a vivid insight into a large number of matters over a very wide field, but I feel, and I am sure I speak for many in this House, that he has not given us enough detailed information on certain matters which the House and which the country will wish to have. Dealing with the arrangements in the Middle East – the Desert Army's affairs, as the Prime Minister described them – he gave us a good deal of detail. He described the arrangements of the Army. He made what to me was the very shocking revelation that Rommel was able to make his swift advance because of the equipment, ammunition, and supplies left behind by us. He gave us a great deal of detail about that campaign, and gave us – justifiably, so far as I am able to judge – by his words encouragement about the resisting powers of the Army defending Egypt, a point of defence vital for the whole of the world war.

When the Prime Minister dealt with the even more important matter of – I took down his own words at the time – the continuous effort to unify command between ourselves and the United States – those were the only two countries he mentioned at first – he told us that there had been a very important mission in this country in July last, that it spent, I think, 10 days here, in continuous consultation, and that a very great measure of understanding and agreement was reached. That is, to my thinking, one of the most important parts of the Prime Minister's speech. Complete understanding and agreement between all the United Nations is the most important need at the present time. When my right hon. Friend was speaking from these benches just now, I ventured to interject a question as to whether the Prime Minister, when he was in Russia, had arranged equally close collaboration with Premier Stalin, leading to a united strategy. It is this united strategy between ourselves, the United States, the USSR, and China – and I regret that China seems to have been rather left out of the picture – as well as the other United Nations, to which we must address our efforts.

I have been an advocate on public platforms of what is known as the second front, because I believe that Germany can be beaten and brought to her knees, as she must be, only by an attack on land in Europe from this country as well as the attack from the Soviet Union. But it is really incorrect to speak of a second front, because in this world war there is really only one front. It has different sections. There is the front of the oceans, in which we hold the offensive in our hands in nearly all places and in which our effort, I think, has been somewhat under-estimated. Were it not for the tremendous power of the British Navy, now fortu-nately added to by the American Navy, on the seas, the war could not have continued to this moment, whatever forces there had been on land. That front on the sea is of the first importance. But that other front on land, which stretches from the Arctic down through Leningrad and Moscow and Stalingrad, through the Caucasus and through the countries of the Near East, to Egypt and Libya, is of equal importance; and every part of that land front is as much our front as it is the front of the Soviet people.

The Soviet people at this moment are hotly contesting Stalingrad, where I understand there is a concentration of German troops, land forces and air forces, stronger than that which was in France at the time of the fall of France. Whether that is so or not, the concentration of German troops against Stalingrad is undoubtedly greater than anything we have seen in this war. The Russian troops there are not fighting an isolated battle for Stalingrad; they are not fighting merely to uphold the liberties and rights of the Soviet people; they are fighting a key battle in the world war, and what they do affects us as much as it does them. Until that realisation can enter into the minds of all of us we have not realised the meaning of this global war, as President Roosevelt calls it.

Is it true that there are on the Russian front at present 75 per cent of Germany's effective military forces and air forces? Is it true that with one-quarter of his forces Hitler is keeping all the rest of the world with which he is in immediate opposition engaged, keeping Europe in subjection, keeping our forces here inactive, keeping the Americans inactive, and also carrying on the strenuous attacks which Rommel is delivering in Egypt? If that is true, what is going to happen if Hitler can succeed in his clear, obvious, and simple plan of driving back the Russians to the Volga, and fortifying the Volga as his East wall, which he could maintain, according to competent military critics, with a comparatively small army, enabling him to turn the rest of his armies on to some other front? I do not say that he is going to turn the rest of his armies on to this country; no doubt the fortress of Great Britain would be by-passed. Where he might turn them is to the Near East and Iraq, to make a junction there with Japan. I do not think we have been given enough information by the Prime Minister as to these possibilities, and as to what we are doing. I have strongly advocated the opening of an offensive by this country, with the assistance of the Americans, on the Continent of Europe. I have advocated that because only by smashing the Germans on land will you beat these prodigiously well-armoured and well-generalled men. You cannot do it by this long-distance bombing of the cities of Germany, which may have excellent results on their production, and, therefore, on supplies in six, nine or 12 months' time, but which does not affect the immediate issue of the fighting on the Russian front, which is the front that matters. Cannot the Prime Minister give us some more explanation about that?

Cannot he also tell us why this Government, under this Prime Minister, which has been in existence now for two years and three months, is not more ready to take action on land than it is at present? I do not underrate the immense effort which this country has made. I do not underrate the tremendous effort we have made upon the sea – an effort which, as I said just now, I think has been underrated – which is just as important as the land front in Russia; but, after two years and three months of a Government pledged to an all-out war effort, we ought to be more ready than we are to strike a blow.

I do not doubt ultimate victory. I know the spirit of our people, of the Dominions, of the Soviet Union, of the Allied Nations and of the United States of America under their great leader, President Roosevelt, but I do not want this war to be prolonged for two, four, six or more years, but to be brought to an end at an earlier period. If we allow Hitler at the present time to immobilise the Russian Forces by building an east wall on the Volga river, who then could say how long this war will continue, if Hitler is then free to dispose of his effectives on any other front he pleases? Do not let us exaggerate, or rather do not let us minimise the very great advantages which Hitler obtains at the present time from having the whole effective production strength of Europe at his disposal. We know that there is sabotage, that there is 'Go Slow' and an unwillingness to co-operate, but not everywhere, and we know his difficulty in getting things done. But let us be so foolish or impotent as to allow Hitler to make a junction with the Japanese, and then he will have not only the productive power of Europe at his disposal but the national resources of the tropical world as well as the production resources here. This is a very real threat. Every competent military observer will, I believe, consider it to be at least a threat, and some consider it a very grave threat, and, if there is this possibility in front of us, the survey which the Prime Minister has given to us, fine and in some ways refreshing as it is, is not sufficient.

We are entitled to come back to the question with which I began and to which I hope we shall be given some answer at the end of the Debate – what progress has been made towards unifying the strategy of this country, the United States, the Soviet Union, China, and of all the United Nations in order that we may use all our resources at the point where the enemy is weakest and oppose him where he is strong with defensive forces, that we may have our forces concentrated and not dispersed, that they may be one spearhead directed at the German heart and not a whole flock of little arrows thrown around here, there and everywhere? We want to hit with all the Forces of the United Nations behind our Forces, and that can only be done if we have a united strategy and unity of command which will insist upon that being done.

Motion made, and Question, 'That the Chairman do report Progress, and ask leave to sit again' [Major Sir James Edmondson[1]], put, and agreed to.

Committee report Progress; to sit again upon the next Sitting Day.

Winston S. Churchill: recollection
(*'The Hinge of Fate', page 487*)

8 September 1942   10 Downing Street
8.30 p.m.

On September 8 Eisenhower and Clark dined with me. It was our regular Tuesday meeting. I had come back from speaking to the House of Commons upon the results of my recent journey. The main purpose of our talk that evening was to discuss the final date of attack in North Africa. The planners were still aiming at November 4. I asked 'Ike'[2] for his view. 'November 8 – sixty days from today' was his answer. The new delay was apparently due to the need for equipping the American regimental combat teams. I offered, as before, to place our highly trained Commandos in American uniform in order to avoid further delay. 'Ike' however was anxious to keep to the all-American character of the operation.

Harold Nicolson to Vita Sackville-West
(*'Harold Nicolson, Diaries and Letters', pages 239–40*)

9 September 1942

Winston was splendid yesterday. He reduced the art of understatement to a virtuosity such as I have never seen equalled. People were meaning to speak about the changes in command in Egypt, about the Dieppe raid, about the Second Front. But he took the wind so completely out of their sails that they tore up their notes and remained seated. The

---

[1] Albert James Edmondson, 1887–1959. Conservative MP for Banbury, 1922–45. Vice Chamberlain of the Household, 1939–42. Treasurer of the Household, 1942–5. Created Baron Sandford, 1945.
[2] General Eisenhower.

debate therefore collapsed. This would have been all right if Cripps had not profited by the occasion to give the House a rather sharp talking-to and to accuse them of preferring their luncheon to their duties. This has enraged everybody, and will, I fear, do the House much damage in the country. It was unfair of Cripps and unwise, unless he is aspiring to some form of dictatorship.

Harold Nicolson: diary
('Harold Nicolson, Diaries and Letters', page 240)

9 September 1942

[...] Guy[1] and I agreed that Cripps' attitude was probably wholly disinterested and sincere. He really believes that Winston is incapable of dealing with the home-front and that his handling of the minor problems of production and strategy is fumbling and imprecise. We agreed also that Cripps would find the atmosphere of Downing Street (with its late hours, casual talk, cigar smoke and endless whisky) most unpalatable, while Winston never regards with affection a man of such inhuman austerity as Cripps, and cannot work easily with people unless his sentiment as well as his respect is aroused. We also agreed that Cripps, who in his way is a man of great innocence and narrow vision, might be quite seriously unaware that his resignation would shake Winston very severely, that around him would gather all the elements of opposition, and that in the end he would create an 'alternative Government' and take Winston's place. At the same time we felt that there was a hope that if Winston would show real consideration to Cripps and give him a vital part in the direction of the war, then something might be done to avert this disaster.

I suggested to Guy that we should visit Violet[2] and tell her the whole story. She is the only outside person I know who is on terms of intimate friendship with Winston and also has the confidence of Stafford and Lady Cripps. We told her the story. She said that she was in an awkward position as Lady Cripps had taken her into her confidence and told her much the same. She could not betray this confidence, much as she agreed with our point of view. We arranged therefore that Violet would see Cripps or his wife, and ask whether she might say a word to Winston – a word of warning. Failing this, I should see Brendan Bracken.

---

[1] Guy Francis De Moncy Burgess, 1911–63. British-born intelligence officer and double agent, who worked for the Soviet Union. One of the Cambridge Five spy ring that betrayed Western secrets to the Soviets before and during the Cold War.
[2] Violet Bonham Carter.

Winston S. Churchill to Field Marshal Jan Smuts
(Churchill papers, 20/80)

9 September 1942
Most Secret and Personal

I am a bit worried by reports of your speech in Pretoria which contains references to North Africa being vital and other remarks about clearing the Mediterranean which do not seem to be localized to the eastern end. Pray forgive me, my dear friend, for bringing this to your notice.

Field Marshal Jan Smuts to Winston S. Churchill
(Churchill papers, 20/80)

9 September 1942
Most Secret and Personal
Immediate

Very sorry to have cauzed worry by my speech. From fuller report cabled by High Commissioner to Secretary of State you will see that I referred to Middle East and incidentally used term North Africa which in South Africa is generally used for Middle East. In brief cabled report you mention reference to Middle East must have been omitted. Any attempt at correction now might only increase suspicion and matter had better be left alone.

Your great speech in Commons yesterday has had wonderful effect in South Africa. Ends.

For summary of speech see my telegram No. 53.

Winston S. Churchill to Pieter Gerbrandy[1]
(Churchill papers, 20/54)

9 September 1942

MESSAGE TO THE DUTCH PRIME MINISTER IN EXILE

My dear Excellency,

I warmly thank you for your message of the 3rd September marking the commencement of the fourth year of war. I take this opportunity to salute the heroism of the Dutch people who in their mother country, and throughout the world, continue in steadfast comradeship with the peoples of the United Nations to defy the brutal powers of aggression. I

[1] Prime Minister of the Netherlands Government-in-Exile in London.

am confident that, inspired by the example of their Queen, the Dutch people under your leadership will go forward with us until the final destruction of the power of darkness.

Yours v. sincerely
Winston S. Churchill

Winston S. Churchill to Brigadier Leslie Hollis,
for the Chiefs of Staff Committee
(Churchill papers, 20/67)

9 September 1942

BOXING OF VEHICLES IN TRANSIT BY SEA

The Office of the Minister of Defence is to receive notice beforehand of every proposed shipment of unboxed vehicles to leave this country, together with a brief written statement by the Department concerned showing the reasons why boxing is not practicable.

2. The Air Ministry should report why they have so far ignored the instructions given to box as many vehicles as possible. Up to the end of July they have boxed none. Considering the strain on our shipping and the restrictions on life in this island the country has a right to expect the co-operation of Government Departments in economising shipping space.

Harold Nicolson: diary
('Harold Nicolson, Diaries and Letters', page 242)

10 September 1942

Violet tells me that she saw Lady Cripps this morning. Stafford had written a letter to the PM saying that he saw he was not being accorded 'full confidence'. He contends that Winston really runs the war by himself, that the War Cabinet has only met once during the last week, that he never sees Winston alone and that he is sacrificing his whole future merely for a shadow. He will, however, take a week's holiday and will not come to his decision until that is over.

Winston S. Churchill: speech
(Churchill papers, 9/158)

10 September 1942　　　　　　　　　　　　　　　Horse Guards Parade
6 p.m.

INSPECTION OF CIVIL SERVICE BATTALION, HOME GUARD

I congratulate you on the striking turn-out of this remarkable battalion. Philosophers have argued about whether the pen is mightier than the sword. But here we have both.

I wish to compliment you on the public spirit which has enabled you, by continuous sacrifice of your leisure and by attention to drill and training to produce a military unit which can take part in any game which may happen to be tried. The security of our Island from invasion cannot be achieved without the part played by those 1,750,000 men who do their regular work and, at the same time, are available at the shortest notice to defend their hearths and home. I am sure that however the winds may blow we shall see in this Island that we are in no need to ask favours of the enemy.

Sir Alexander Cadogan: diary
('The Diaries of Sir Alexander Cadogan', page 477)

10 September 1942

[...] Winston enjoying himself enormously, reviewing Home Guard on Horse Guards' Parade, with Marines' Band.

Winston S. Churchill to Major Desmond Morton[1]
(Churchill papers, 20/67)

10 September 1942

I expect it was my old idea of four States in a Confederation, of which three were Arab and one Jewish. I did, of course, advise Sir Edward Spears against drifting into the usual anti-Zionist and anti-Semitic channel which it is customary for British officers to follow. [2]

---

[1] Personal assistant to Churchill and his adviser on governments-in-exile.

[2] The reference is to a minute of 7 September 1942 from Major Morton about a telegram from Sir Edward Spears (No. 297 from Syria of 29 August 1942) saying that the Prime Minister had told him in Cairo something of how the problem of the Levant States might be settled after the war.

If there is any doubt about it, he should be asked what words he was referring to.

Winston S. Churchill to Brendan Bracken
(Churchill papers, 20/67)

10 September 1942

THE 'BLIMP' FILM

Pray propose to me the measures necessary to stop this foolish production[1] before it gets any further. I am not prepared to allow propaganda detrimental to the morale of the Army, and I am sure the Cabinet will take all necessary action. Who are the people behind it?

Winston S. Churchill to Gwilym Lloyd George
(Churchill papers, 20/76)

10 September 1942

CONFERENCE OF MINERS ON THE COAL SITUATION

Before I commit myself to come on Saturday, 19th September, will you let me know exactly what you want me to do? How long am I to speak, is it to be broadcast, where am I to speak, can I leave immediately after speaking, and so forth? Will you also show me the sort of thing you want me to say?[2]

---

[1] In the War Cabinet on 21 September 1942, the Secretary of State for War, Sir James Grigg, said 'that a film about "Colonel Blimp" was being made. Facilities had been asked for from the War Office. These had been refused, on the ground that the film was likely to bring ridicule upon the Army. The producers had nevertheless proceeded with the making of the film which was now at an advanced stage.

'There was no existing Defence Regulation under which the film could be suppressed. He understood that the Minister of Information was averse from taking the very wide powers which would be necessary to stop this film.

'More recently, however, an approach had been made to the financier who was backing the film, who had agreed that, when the film had reached the "rough-cut stage", it should be seen by representatives of the War Office and the Ministry of Information, and that, if they took the view the film was undesirable, he would arrange for it to be withdrawn.

'General agreement was expressed with the view that it was impossible to allow a film to be produced which was liable to undermine the discipline of the Army; and satisfaction was expressed that this could be achieved by the friendly arrangement outlined by the Secretary of State for War.'

[2] In the event, Churchill did not go to the conference.

Winston S. Churchill to A. V. Alexander
and Admiral Sir Henry Moore[1]
(Churchill papers, 20/67)

10 September 1942
Secret

SUCCESSOR TO ADMIRAL LEATHAM AS
VICE-ADMIRAL, MEDITERRANEAN

If you are satisfied that Admiral Bonham-Carter[2] is the best choice, I accept your view.

2. I do not wish Lord Gort to be pressed to render an adverse report formally against Admiral Leatham, who has done very good work and is moved only for the purposes of change. If, however, any such report is necessary, I am prepared to place on record that, from a variety of circumstances known to me, I have come to the conclusion that a change in the command is desirable at the present time.[3]

Winston S. Churchill to Air Chief Marshal Sir Charles Portal
(Churchill papers, 20/67)

10 September 1942

Make me out a list of the German towns bombed since 1st August, with the weight of bombs dropped on each and the number of aircraft used. I thought of sending it to Premier Stalin.

Winston S. Churchill to Air Chief Marshal Sir Charles Portal
(Churchill papers, 20/67)

10 September 1942

Air Marshal Harris spoke to me the other night about the large number of bomber crews sent to the Middle East which were not returned to this country after having delivered the machines.

---

[1] Vice-Chief of the Naval Staff.

[2] Stuart Sumner Bonham-Carter, 1889–1972. On active service, 1914–18 (despatches, DSO); commanded HMS *Intrepid* at Zeebrugge. Assistant Director of Naval Equipment, 1932–4. Commodore, Royal Naval Barracks, Chatham, 1937–9. Naval Secretary to the First Lord of the Admiralty (Churchill), 1939. Rear-Admiral, 3rd Battle Squadron, 1940. CB, 1941. Vice-Admiral, Malta, 1943. Knighted, 1943. Rear-Admiral, 18th Cruiser Squadron, 1944.

[3] Bonham-Carter succeeded Leatham as Vice-Admiral, Malta, in 1943.

In view of the great importance of increasing the strength of Bomber Command at home, please look into this and draft something to Tedder.

Winston S. Churchill: speech
(Hansard)

11 September 1942   House of Commons

The House will already have learned that His Majesty's Government recently decided to resume operations in Madagascar, and to seize key points on the West Coast of the island from which enemy submarines might operate against our shipping in the Mozambique Channel. Majunga, Morondava and Nosi Be were assaulted in the early hours of yesterday morning and captured with little opposition and light casualties. The town of Majunga surrendered during the course of the day, and the operations against Morondava and Nosi Be were also completely successful. The operations, in which all three Services co-operated, were carried out precisely according to plan. British, Union of South Africa, East African troops and South African Air Forces took part in the operations.

Winston S. Churchill to Colonel John Bevan[1]
(Churchill papers, 20/67)

11 September 1942
Most Secret

OPERATION 'TORCH' – COVER AND DECEPTION PLANS

This scheme seems well considered.

2. The only point about which I am doubtful is the last part of the paragraph 4. I have a great fear that with all the talk there is here and in the United States, the enemy will find out that we are going to North Africa. I still hope he will not find out we are going <u>inside</u> the Mediterranean, and will think the American attack is only from the Atlantic shore. I am afraid that if you start 'Cover' inside the Mediterranean after the Malta convoy idea is blown at the same time that there is a lot of suspi-

---

[1] John Henry Bevan, 1894–1978. Educated at Eton and Christ Church, Oxford. Served in the First World War with the Herts Regiment. Captain, 1916. Military Cross, 1917. Major, 1918. Joined the Territorial Army Reserve. Recalled, 1939, and served in MI5. Controlling Officer, May 1942. Played a central role in the development of strategic deception for the remainder of the war. CB, 1945.

cion about North Africa generally, it will direct the enemy's attention to O and A;[1] whereas, even if we fail to keep the general secrecy, this might escape notice and we might achieve our purpose. Do not speak to anyone about this, but think it over and seek an opportunity to talk to me. The matter is not urgent.

3. Is this 'Cover' being concerted with our American friends, and what are tales they are telling Washington? If necessary I could send the whole 'Cover' story to the President.

4. Have you seen my request to the Chiefs of the Staff which they are putting to the American Staffs about substituting the names: Dunkirk, Calais and Boulogne for the three principal names, from west to east, in 'Torch'?

5. Are we going to attempt a positive operation on the Norwegian coast, or not? Exactly what is the nature of our cover there, other than preparations and air reconnaissances? Let me know exactly what is being done, and report to me each week on the progress of our measures.

Winston S. Churchill to Lord Cranborne
(Churchill papers, 20/67)

11 September 1942

I have a very clear opinion that the case of Malta is unique, and that, on account of its superb exertions and shattering damage, the Imperial Government should assume responsibility for building it up.

I do not know why you wanted to get the Chancellor of the Exchequer[2] inclined against the proposal by sending him a copy of your minute before you had discussed it with me. The matter must now be raised in Cabinet. Perhaps you will bring it up at an early date. I am sending a copy of this minute to the Chancellor of the Exchequer.

---

[1] Oran and Algiers.
[2] Sir Kingsley Wood.

Winston S. Churchill to Sir James Grigg and General Hastings Ismay
(Churchill papers, 20/67)

11 September 1942
Personal

I am much impressed by the work and bearing of Colonel E. I. C. Jacob, RE.[1] He showed marked ability and competence when he accompanied me during my recent visit to the Middle East and Moscow.

I consider that the position he holds and the duties which he discharges in my Defence Office should carry with them the rank of Brigadier, and I should be glad if arrangements could be made for Colonel Jacob to be promoted to that rank. I do not contemplate being able to release him from his present duties for other service.

Winston S. Churchill to Admiral Sir Henry Moore
(Churchill papers, 20/67)

11 September 1942
Most Secret

I wish you to look in great detail into the 8-days' boiler cleaning and repair period. How many destroyers are involved? How many men in each destroyer are boiler cleaning? What is the total number of men in all the destroyers involved who would be boiler cleaning? Is this special work for engineers, or can it be done by able seamen? Are there any other boiler cleaners available in the Navy? Supposing that, say, 50 men in each destroyer are boiler cleaning and 20 destroyers are involved, this would be 1,000 men. Surely the depots, damaged ships refitting, &c., could provide 1,000 men, and these men be brought by special trains to the harbours so that the moment the destroyers come in the weary crews can walk off to their leave and rest, and the boiler cleaning is done by the special men. This should be under a small skeleton staff from the destroyers, to make sure that all is correctly done. An arrangement like this should save three days extra for rest, leaving five days for boiler cleaning. Therefore, on two 8-day periods there should be 6 days saving.

2. It is admitted that three days can be saved on the slow convoy by going the nearer route. Let me have the speed of advance each day for these convoys by each of the routes, showing how many days you have got in the totals for accidents of weather. I appreciate the point about being able to take a short cut, and having that up your sleeve.

[1] Military Assistant Secretary to the War Cabinet, 1939–45.

3. I cannot believe that we are unable to scrape two days off the ten days allowed for loadings. This gives a total of eleven days, which should make it possible to run PQ19 and yet do 'Torch' on the 4th November, which is the earliest date that the United States contingent sailing on the 20th October can arrive. As for other reasons I should be content with the 8th November as the firm, final date, there are four days to veer and haul upon.

Winston S. Churchill to Josef Stalin
(Churchill papers, 20/80)

12 September 1942
Personal and Secret

I am much obliged for the 48 long-range bombers, 10 torpedo bombers and the 200 fighters, including 47 long-range fighters which I now learn you are sending to help bring in PQ18.

2. I thought you might like to know the weight of bombs dropped by the Royal Air Force on Germany since 1st July this year. The total amount from 1st July to 6th September was 11,500 tons. The tonnage dropped on the more important targets was Duisburg 2,500 tons, Dusseldorf 1,250 tons, Saarbrucken 1,150 tons, Bremen and Hamburg 1,000 tons each, Osnabruck 700 tons, Kassel, Wilhelmshaven, Mainz, Frankfurt, all about 500 tons; Nuremberg received 300 tons and there were many other lesser tonnages. Included in the bombs dropped were six 8,000-lb bombs and 1,400 4,000-lb bombs. We have found that by using these with instantaneous fuses the bombs do not break up but explode most effectively, so that parachutes are not required.

Winston S. Churchill to William Mackenzie King
(Churchill papers, 20/80)

12 September 1942
Most Secret and Personal

Thank you for Canada's magnificent response to our appeal for assistance with escorting craft in our special operation. The 17 corvettes promised by the Chief of Naval Staff, Ottawa, in his telegram to First Sea Lord will make all the difference in the strength of our escorts.

We fully realise the added difficulties with which you will be faced in Canadian waters whilst these ships are away, and we will do our best to send them back to you as quickly as possible.

Winston S. Churchill to President Franklin D. Roosevelt
(Churchill papers, 20/80)

12 September 1942
Personal and Secret
No. 147

317 Shermans and 94 SP 105's which you so kindly gave me on that dark Tobruk day in Washington have now all safely arrived in Egypt. 82 Shermans have already been issued to the troops. It is proposed to arm three brigades with 94 each and the rest Crusaders, this being thought the best combination. Averell will tell you of our visit to these brigades. I now hear they have received these weapons with the greatest enthusiasm, and I trust it will not be long before I give you good accounts of their use.[1] As these tanks were taken from the hands of the American Army, perhaps you would show this message to General Marshall.

Winston S. Churchill to Sir Archibald Sinclair
(Churchill papers, 20/67)

13 September 1942
Most Secret

Many thanks for your paper on the expansion of Bomber Command. I am glad to see the great efforts which you and the Air Staff are making to improve the position. Will you please let me have your programme of expansion by squadrons?

2. Will you also let me know:

(a) How many bombers we have sent to the Middle East since 1st May, 1942, and

(b) How many crews of these bombers have been returned?

Tedder has got into the habit of keeping all, or nearly all, of the crews used for ferry purposes. This cannot be allowed. I had thought of sending him a telegram myself, but I await your reply to this.

---

[1] On September 8, Brooke had written to Churchill: 'The three brigades to be armed with Shermans have each received some. Their enthusiasm for this new equipment is outstanding, and officers and men much appreciate your message.'

Winston S. Churchill to A. V. Alexander
(Churchill papers, 20/67)

13 September 1942
Most Secret

BUILDING OF FLEET DESTROYERS

Supposing you build nothing but Hunts[1] and leave out the Intermediates[2] and the Fleet types, how many more Hunts should we get at the expense of how many of the larger kind?

2. The Naval Staff have still got in their minds the picture of another Battle of Jutland. But this is certainly not going to happen. On the other hand, the numbers for escort will be a desperate need in 1943, when we have double the number of U-boats operating and convoys have to be provided for all routes.

Winston S. Churchill to General Sir Alan Brooke
(Churchill papers, 20/67)

13 September 1942
Secret

You will see on other papers that General Alexander says that the date of 'Lightfoot'[3] will be delayed by the late battle. On the other hand, the enemy has been seriously weakened by that battle. If 'Lightfoot' is to straggle over into October, we must be careful not to ask Malta to do too much meanwhile, and General Alexander should be made aware of the fact that Malta cannot be run to a standstill.

Winston S. Churchill to Air Marshal Sir Arthur Harris
(Churchill papers, 20/67)

13 September 1942

You must be careful not to spoil a good case by overstating it. I am doing all I can to expand Bomber Command, and I set a high value on

[1] Hunts: a class of Royal Navy escort destroyer. Built 1939–43. Named after British fox hunts, they served extensively in the Second World War, particularly on the British East Coast and Mediterranean convoys.

[2] Intermediates: a class of smaller destroyers that could be built more quickly and cheaply than full-sized fleet destroyers, but were larger than the small 'Hunt' class. Initially suggested by Admiral Roger Backhouse in 1937, they first came into being as the 'O' Class of 1939. Twenty-six Intermediate class destroyers were ordered in the 1942 programme.

[3] 'Lightfoot': codename for 8th Army operations in the Western Desert in the autumn of 1942.

your action against Germany. I do not, however, think that air bombing is going to bring the war to an end by itself, and still less that anything that could be done with our existing resources could produce decisive results in the next twelve months.

Winston S. Churchill to Patrick Donner[1]
(Churchill papers, 20/54)

13 September 1942

My dear Donner,

The question of deportation[2] was very carefully considered by the Government of India, and they decided against it. There can be no question of changes now.

I am very glad you are pleased with the line I took.[3] It is extraordinary how startled some people are by the mere statement of obvious massive truths.

Yours v. sincerely,
Winston S. Churchill

General George C. Marshall to Winston S. Churchill
(Churchill papers, 20/80)

14 September 1942	Headquarters
Secret	European Theater of Operations
Personal	United States Army

The President gave me your message in regard to Sherman's and SP 10's in Egypt. I am very much relieved to learn that this material has

---

[1] Patrick William Donner, 1904–88. Educated abroad and at Exeter College, Oxford. Studied Imperial development and administration, 1928–30. Conservative MP for West Islington, 1931–5; Basingstoke Division of Hampshire, 1935–55. Hon. Secretary, India Defence League, 1933–5. Parliamentary Private Secretary to Sir Samuel Hoare, Home Secretary, 1939. Member of Advisory Committee on Education in the Colonies. Parliamentary Private Secretary to Colonel Oliver Stanley, Secretary of State for the Colonies, 1944. Director, National Review Ltd, 1933–47. Member Executive Council Joint East and Central African Board, 1937–54. Joined RAF Volunteer Reserve, 1939. Served at HQ Fighter Command; Acting Squadron Leader, 1941. Chairman, Executive Committee of the Men of the Trees, 1952–62. Knighted, 1953. Member of Art Panel of the Arts Council, 1963–66. High Sheriff of Hampshire, 1967–8.

[2] On 10 September Donner had put a Private Notice Question in Parliament suggesting 'the deportation of Gandhi and the Congress leaders to the Seychelles (or some other island)' distinct from India to show that 'we really mean business'.

[3] In a speech to the Commons on September 10, Churchill had argued that the Indian Congress Party did not represent all or even most of India because it was run by elite manufacturing and financial interests. Opposed to it were the Muslims and Untouchables, as well as certain Sikhs, Christians, and even some Hindus. It was, he insisted, impossible to understand the problem in India 'without the recognition of these basic data'.

reached the hands of your fighting men. Your generous words of appreciation will be given confidentially to the commanders of units from whom this material was taken and who, I know, will feel greatly honoured and fully compensated by receipt of your message.

Marshall

Winston S. Churchill to Brigadier Leslie Hollis
(Churchill papers, 20/67)

14 September 1942
Secret

Your paragraph 2 of attached.[1] I do not know why the emphasis is placed on light tanks. Considering the low value attached by the Army in the Middle East to the Valentines,[2] especially the Matildas, it ought to be possible to prepare 100 of these for Turkey. After all, if the Germans go into Turkey it will be with heavy tanks and not with light. Light tanks, on the other hand, will work very well with the 10th Army or in the defence of India, where they will probably not have heavy tanks to contend with at the outset. This should be reconsidered.

Your paragraph 3. Let me have a table showing what tanks are earmarked for the Middle East up to the end of the year, both from Britain and the United States, and what demand is made upon these to fulfil our somewhat modified pledge to General Smuts. Also any other projects for increasing tank units that you may have in mind.

Winston S. Churchill to L. S. Amery
(Churchill papers, 20/67)

14 September 1942

Please let me have a note on Mr Gandhi's intrigues with Japan and the documents which the Government of India published, or any other they possessed before on this topic. The note should not exceed three pages of open typescript.

---

[1] About supply of arms and equipment to Turkey.
[2] Valentines: British infantry tanks.

Winston S. Churchill to Anthony Eden
(Churchill papers, 20/67)

14 September 1942
Secret

I deplore these lengthy hypothetical discussions based on the suggestions 'if we lose Egypt' and 'if Russia collapses in the Caucasus'.

Who started telegram No. 1384?[1] Was it sent at the request of the
Chiefs of Staff? It has evidently encouraged Sir H. Knatchbull-Hugessen[2]
to spread himself in his usual length, and to give us a number of glimpses
of the obvious.

Lady Leslie[3] to Winston S. Churchill
(Churchill papers, 1/368)

14 September 1942   Glaslough,County Monaghan

Dearest Winston,

How much you travel! You take my breath away! I can't even keep pace
with your new hats – (I like the one Gen. Smuts gave you). You are really
splendid – and I am all puffed up with pride at your great achievements
– Yes – puffed out like an old pouter pigeon – I must have my clothes
let out! – I do wish I could have heard you in the HofC and seen your
equimatic[4] smile when you drove a point home with – swift irony –

Here we lead a sheltered life – which seems all wrong when there is
so much suffering in the world – but we keep the Home going & give
shelter to waifs & strays & Lame Dogs who need cheering & feeding up
– I read books I never had time to read – tear up old letters – enjoy the
memories they awake & even do a little music – Enclosed cutting of yr
Mother & the donkeys Mrs Ronalds gave us will amuse you – I remember the tandem but not the Kettle! – David Gray[5] (US Minister) comes

---

[1] From Foreign Office to Angora (Ankara), on the possibility of German pressure or attack on
Turkey and the question of Turkish resistance.

[2] Hughe Montgomery Knatchbull-Hugessen, 1886–1971. Entered the Foreign Office, 1908. British
Minister to the Baltic States, 1930–4; in Teheran, 1934–6. Knighted, 1936. Ambassador to China,
1936–7; to Turkey, 1939–44; to Brussels, 1944–7. In 1949 he published his memoirs, *Diplomat in
Peace and War*. Known, after secret documents in his possession had been stolen by the German spy
'Cicero' in Turkey, as 'Snatch'.

[3] Churchill's aunt (née Leonie Jerome).

[4] Although Lady Leslie wrote the word 'equimatic' perhaps she meant to write 'enigmatic' – unless,
in the context, she wanted to create a double irony, for the word itself is not in the dictionary.

[5] David Gray, 1870–1978. United States Minister in Dublin, 1940–7. Member of Roosevelt
family.

sometimes to see us – I like him he speaks his mind freely to the Head of this State[1] – There is an element of unrest here one is never sure how strong or how well equipped it is – the US soldiers dislike it –

Jack Leslie[2] & I are well – we march down hill serenely hand in hand – holding on to life to see the Allies Victorious! – We both send you our fondest Love.

Your devoted old Aunt
Leonie

Winston S. Churchill to Randolph S. Churchill
(Churchill papers, 1/369)

14 September 1942

My dear Randolph,

It may be that the craze for running Independent candidates has passed its zenith. We shall continue to oppose all Independent candidates, and I am sure the Party authorities will do their best. I have complete confidence in them.[3]

Your loving Father,
Winston S. Churchill

Winston S. Churchill to President Franklin D. Roosevelt
(Churchill papers, 20/80)

15 September 1942
Personal and Most Secret
No. 148

Averell, who arrived and stayed with me last night, gave me the latest news of you. He says trans-Persian Railway is settled. Please let me have your final plan.

---

[1] Eamon de Valera, Prime Minister of the Republic of Ireland.

[2] John Leslie, 1857–1944. Known as 'Jack'. Lieutenant, Grenadier Guards, 1877. On active service in Egypt, 1882; South Africa, 1900. Married Churchill's Aunt Leonie (Lady Randolph Churchill's sister), 1884. Lieutenant-Colonel Commanding 5th Royal Irish Fusiliers, 1900–8; retired with the rank of Colonel. Succeeded his father as 2nd Baronet, 1916. A Justice of the Peace for County Monaghan.

[3] Churchill was responding to a letter from his son dated September 9 (*CHAR 1/369/23–24*), in which Randolph lamented the recent success of Independent candidates in by-elections and suggested that Conservative Central Office was falling short in the task of selecting and campaigning for the return of Government-endorsed candidates.

2. I am hoping to receive your wishes about the Anglo-American Air Force on the Russian southern flank. I am not without hopes of a favourable decision in Egypt in the next few weeks. Unless we can offer Stalin something definite for, say, December, we shall not get the full facilities we need for preparing airfields, &c., thereabouts. Moreover, if we are able to make a firm offer, albeit contingent on favourable events in Egypt, it would be possible at the same time to ask for some favours for the Poles. Stalin has given us sixty thousand Poles with thirty thousand dependants, out of which two and a half divisions are being made, but no provision has been made for recruitment of further Poles, officers and men, to keep these forces going. Of these there are great numbers in various sorry plights throughout Russia. I thought we might help two birds with one piece of sugar.

3. I have had long conferences and conversations with Eisenhower and Clark, bringing in all our people as required with the sole aim of keeping to (for date see my next) for 'Torch' as now settled between us. If you can make it from your end, we will make it from this.

4. I entirely agree with your political outlook on 'Torch'. It is sound unless we are forestalled. There is no sign in any of the secret matter which I see that the enemy is aware, and the mood of France is now at its very best. I count the days.

5. In the whole of 'Torch', military and political, I consider myself your lieutenant, asking only to put my viewpoint plainly before you. We shall have a wireless station of overriding power available by zero, so that if you dictate your appeals to France and other propaganda material to gramophone records beforehand, these can be blared out over everything during the performance. We British will come in only as and when you judge expedient. This is an American enterprise in which we are your helpmeets.

6. I agree with you that de Gaulle will be an irritant, and his movement must be kept out. We do not yet know what the local generals will do, or whether perhaps you are going to bring Giraud[1] to the scene. At your leisure please let me know your ideas.

7. I repeat, the outlook seems good to me and will be bettered by good news from Egypt.

8. Bad news from the PQ Convoy, twelve being sunk by torpedo bombers already, and there are at least two more days to run in the danger zone. When we know the results of PQ18 we must decide about PQ19.

---

[1] Former commander of the French 7th Army. Taken prisoner 1940. Escaped 1942. Went on to command United French Armed Forces, 1943–4.

All preparations for this are going forward, but it looks almost impossible to fit in another PQ before 'Torch', and if the losses are very heavy this time it would not be worth trying. Should the decision be adverse to PQ19 you will have to help me with Stalin, and here again the offer of air support on the Russian southern flank may be important.

Kindest regards to all.

Winston S. Churchill to Sir Kingsley Wood
(Churchill papers, 20/67)

15 September 1942

Is Sir Archibald Carter[1] qualified in any way for the Customs? He was at the India Office, and then came to the Admiralty. I understand he has to be found employment for five years in order to qualify for a pension. He is certainly an able and agreeable man. But is this quite the way in which an appointment like the Customs should be filled?

Winston S. Churchill to General Hastings Ismay,
for the Chiefs of Staff Committee
(Churchill papers, 20/67)

16 September 1942

OPERATION 'JUPITER'

To keep contact with Russia and to keep the Russian armies equipped and in the field by a continued stream of supplies must be considered one of the three or four most important vital objects before us. For this the greatest sacrifices and exertions must be made by the Allies. The total defeat of Russia or the reduction of that country to a minor military factor would let the whole mass of the German armies loose upon us. The President has stated that he regards the maintenance of the PQ convoys as an operation of equal magnitude with 'Torch', although he is ready to skip one or perhaps two for the sake of 'Torch'.

[1] Richard Henry Archibald Carter, 1887–1958. A direct descendant of Samuel Pepys (Secretary of the Admiralty from 1673). Educated at Eton and Trinity College, Cambridge. Private Secretary to the Secretary of State for India, 1924–7. Secretary-General of the Indian Round Table Conference, 1930–1. Knighted, 1935. Assistant Under-Secretary of State for India, 1936. Permanent Secretary, Admiralty, 1936–40. Went to India in 1941 as Chairman of the Eastern Group Supply Council (Delhi). Chairman of the Board of Customs and Excise, London, 1942–7. Permanent Under-Secretary of State for India, 1947. Joint Permanent Under-Secretary of State for Commonwealth Relations, 1948. Chairman of the Monopolies and Restrictive Practices Commission, 1949–53.

2. The alternative before us is therefore:

(a) to go on with the PQ convoys (perhaps missing one or two) in addition to 'Torch' and all it implies, all through 1943. Indeed, the scale of the convoys must be increased. The Russians have been solemnly promised larger quotas, and they will become more dependent on imported arms as their own territory is reduced by enemy invasion; or

(b) to clear the Germans out of the north of Norway by some form of the operation 'Jupiter'.

When we consider the losses attendant on the sending of these convoys, that they have to take place at least three times in every two months, and the grievous consequences of our announcing, on the other hand, that we can send no more, it may well be that 'Jupiter', with all its cost and risk, will be found not only necessary but cheapest in the long run.

3. I have now read the McNaughton report,[1] which certainly does not err on the side of underrating the difficulties before us. Making allowances for this, the McNaughton report can be taken as a basis for further discussions.

4. When the winter comes the Russians must take the offensive against the German lines. Here in the North is as good a place as any, and, having regard to their vital need of Allied munitions, I have no doubt, after my conversations with Premier Stalin, that they not only will resist attacks upon the Murmansk and Archangel railways, but also would be willing to set on foot a heavy offensive towards Petsamo. At any rate, before dogmatising about it we must find out what they would be prepared to do. I am assuming however that they would not only bring enough forces to the North to attack the enemy, as proposed by General McNaughton, but also would if necessary undertake part of the landings themselves.

5. The fitting of Operation 'Jupiter' into our war plans can only be considered in relation to 'Torch'. We cannot yet judge what 'Torch' will involve. If the French come over to us the whole of the 'Torch' area may be formed up against Germany in a week, or even a night. If this were so, we should have harbours with proper defences, airfields, eight or nine French fleet divisions, a certain amount of air, and perhaps the French fleet in Toulon. In this case the British troops could be railed rapidly through to attack Tripoli from the west. There is no question of the Germans being able in the time mentioned – a fortnight, or even

---

[1] General McNaughton, the officer commanding Canadian troops in Britain, had been asked in July 1942 to undertake the preparation of a plan for 'Jupiter', to be carried out largely by Canadian troops.

a month – to mount and launch a heavy attack. They have not got, above all, the air force to spare. We must expect that very heavy operations in Egypt and Libya will have been already in progress. Therefore, I think, if things go well for us on the North African shore, it may be that a large number of assault ships and tank-landing craft will be free to go north for 'Jupiter'. To these would be added all the additions to our tank-landing force and assault ships, over and above those assigned to 'Torch', which were coming into Britain under 'Bolero' for the purposes of 'Round-up'. It is no use saying the Americans have cancelled all this, because we have not yet given them the reasons against such improvident action. I am sure I can claim from the United States for the purposes of 'Jupiter' all the craft which were being prepared under 'Bolero' for an April 'Round-up', or at any rate enough of them. I admit the escorts are the pinch.

6. On the other hand, if the French fight the Americans in 'Torch' and ask the Germans to come and help them, and the Germans come, or the Spaniards turn against us and we have to fight neck or nothing in the 'Torch' area, naturally in that case 'Jupiter' does not have to be argued about.

7. I have no doubt we could have a couple of Arctic-trained American divisions, and with the Canadian Corps, and also several Russian divisions, apart from the Russian offensive, we could get together quite enough forces to conquer the 'Jupiter' area. But if we don't make preparations, not mere paper plans, now (which, anyhow, may come in for 1943–4), order the equipment, train the troops, etc., we are not even going to have the option.

8. It follows that if 'Jupiter' as well as 'Torch' should get going there could be no 'Round-up' till 1944. This is already the United States view. But 'Torch' by itself is no substitute for 'Round-up'.

Winston S. Churchill to Anthony Eden and Brigadier Leslie Hollis,
for the Chiefs of Staff Committee
(Churchill papers, 20/67)

16 September 1942
Most Secret

We shall have to watch very carefully Spanish reactions to preparations for 'Torch' which will become evident at Gibraltar. I should like to have a short report on what we shall be putting into Gibraltar in preparation for 'Torch', with a time-table. How much of these preparations would exceed the normal for a big Malta convoy?

2. The arrival of large numbers of aircraft will be the crux of the problem, and the use of the neutral ground will be involved.

3. What will happen if, about a fortnight before zero 'Torch', the Germans put pressure on Spain for an explanation of these preparations and demand either that the neutral ground is cleared or that they are allowed to install their own aircraft in the Valencia airfields? What are the likely Spanish reactions to this pressure, and what should be our attitude? We might be faced with a show-down with Franco over this at an awkward moment. I think we should have our plans prepared.

Winston S. Churchill to President Franklin D. Roosevelt
(Churchill papers, 20/80)

16 September 1942
Most Secret
No. 150

The results of the first operations by your Flying Fortresses have been most encouraging. General Spaatz[1] has wisely been feeling his way, and they have not yet struck very deep. But we may hope that when they are available in sufficient numbers they will be able, with the help of their escorting fighters, to carry the air war into Germany by day on heavy scale. This would be a development of the highest importance.

2. In spite of the fact that we cannot make up more than 32 squadrons of bombers, instead of 42 last year, we know our night bomber offensive is having a devastating effect. Nuremberg, Mainz, Karlsruhe and Dusseldorf are the latest additions to the growing list of German cities to feel its weight, and the blows at Hamburg and Bremen cannot fail to have an effect on rate of U-boat building. I have told Air-Marshal Evill to send you a copy of a paper on our bomber offensive, recently prepared at my request by Air-Marshal Harris, who has almost unique qualifications to express an opinion on the subject. Out of zeal he has no doubt overstated a good case. None the less, the paper is an impressive contribution to thought on the subject.

3. If we can add continuity and precision to the attack by your bombers striking deep into the heart of Germany by day the effect would be

---

[1] Officer Commanding US 8th Air Force and Commanding General of the United States Army Air Forces in the European theatre.

redoubled. To do this effectively, and without prohibitive loss, they must have numbers to saturate and disperse the defences. And time is precious. A few hundred Fortresses this Autumn and Winter, while substantial German air forces are still held in Russia, may well be worth many more in a year's time, when the enemy may be able greatly to reinforce his Western air defences. Together we might even deal a blow at the enemy's air power from which he could never fully recover.

4. I hope you may consider it wise to build up General Spaatz's strength. We are following with admiration your fight in the Solomons. We must make 'Torch' a success. But I am sure we should be missing great opportunities if we did not concentrate every available Fortress and long-range escort fighter as quickly as possible for the attack on our primary enemy.

5. I cannot help feeling some concern at the extent to which the programme for the build-up of American air forces in this country is falling behind expectations, particularly in view of the withdrawal from the United Kingdom of over 800 British and American aircraft for 'Torch'. We had hoped to see twelve heavy groups and seven pursuit groups in the United Kingdom by the 1st of November. Obviously, the claims of 'Torch' will substantially reduce those figures, but I hope they will not be permitted to obscure the importance of keeping up and intensifying the direct pressure on Germany, for which the Fortress and the long-range fighter are indispensable. Moreover, the deliveries of American aircraft to the RAF in the Middle East show some startling deficiencies on the figures in the new air agreement which you and I initialled in June. This is especially serious in view of our possible minor commitments in the Caucasus this Winter. I know General Arnold is doing his best, and that the shortcomings are due to the failure of United States production to come up to schedule. After Dunkirk we gave our aircraft industry special priorities which resulted in a great acceleration in the curve of deliveries. I understand you are considering giving similar priorities for the time being to aircraft production; may I suggest that special emphasis should be laid on that of heavy bombers and pursuit aircraft to provide for a rapidly increasing intensity of air attack on Germany. I am told that the heavy bomber programme of the Army Air Force has been reduced from a figure of 117 groups by the end of 1943 to one of 65 groups, whereas that for dive bombers has been doubled. I wonder whether these priorities will be reconsidered in the light of the new turn in our strategy?

Winston S. Churchill to Randolph S. Churchill
(Churchill papers, 1/369)

16 September 1942

My dear Randolph,

I see that you are making speeches and writing articles about the future of the Conservative Party. Without going into the merits of the questions raised, I think it fair to let you know that it might become my duty, as Leader of the Party, to disavow your actions and to make it clear that I do not approve them. This would also apply to a by-election should you, as I am told, think of courting one at Preston.

It would of course be painful to me to be drawn into public opposition to you, but in the circumstances I should have no choice.

Your loving Father,
Winston S. Churchill

Winston S. Churchill to General Sir Harold Alexander
(Churchill papers, 20/80)

17 September 1942   10 Downing Street
Personal and Secret
To be deciphered by his personal Staff Officer only
No circulation

A great deal of consideration has been given to your paper, on which I sent you an interim reply. I now send you a minute which I am issuing to the Departments about Committees and a letter which Sir Richard Hopkins[1] is writing to the Permanent Heads of Departments. You will have seen from my previous printed minute that the evil of Committees has been already drastically struck at by me. But I quite agree that another stroke will be beneficial.

2. In sending you the note referred to in paragraph 4 of my minute of September 2 on your views about military reorganization I should perhaps have pointed out that this was not written for your eye, but I presumed you would rather see it as it was written.

3. I am sure you will agree that I have given very full and careful attention, in spite of the pressure of events, to the memorandum you were good enough to send me.

---

[1] Permanent Secretary at the Treasury.

Oliver Harvey: diary
(*'The War Diaries of Oliver Harvey', page 157*)

17 September 1942

A drive is being made, I'm glad to say, to intensify our bombing over Germany this winter. PM has appealed to Roosevelt to increase the American effort (which has not come up to promises given).

Madagascar operations proceeding well, at last almost a walk-over.[1] PM very tiresome over it, anxious to make terms with Anet,[2] the Vichy Governor, and keep de Gaulle out. But Anet is unreliable and 'wet'. We could never trust any terms he signed; he would remain Vichy's man. Also we are practically committed to handing it over sooner or later to de G.

PM as always blinded by his passions to his interests, now hates de Gaulle. But he is increasingly difficult to deal with in such matters, fussing over little points, reopening questions, up one day down the next.

Winston S. Churchill to Sir John Anderson and others[3]
(*Churchill papers, 20/67*)

17 September 1942
Action this Day

The following are only preliminary notes:

MAN-POWER

We have sent 6 divisions abroad since January, and we may easily have to send 5 or 6 more. We cannot confide the defence of Britain in 1943 unduly to American troops. The 9 beach divisions must be raised to the same level as the other mobile divisions in England. However, for this purpose the War Office must make a real contribution by a more efficient use of their man-power, both here and in the Middle East. At home, transport and rearward services can be pooled to a larger extent. In the Middle East, drafts must be saved by combing out the rearward personnel to fill the gaps in infantry. Unless there is goodwill in this and a genuine effort, it is very difficult to help the Army.

[1] In August, having failed to reach agreement with the Vichy Governor, the British Government had decided to occupy the whole island.

[2] Vichy Governor-General of Madagascar.

[3] Also sent to the Minister of Labour (Ernest Bevin), the Minister of Production (Oliver Lyttelton), the Secretary of State for Air (Sir Archibald Sinclair), the Secretary of State for War (Sir James Grigg), and Lord Cherwell.

2. A searching examination must be made of the wastage scales demanded. One does not see the prospect of any large numbers of our British divisions being continuously engaged with the enemy in the next six months.

3. We were told last year that a British division worked out at over 40,000 men. Let a table be prepared showing the number of divisions sent abroad since 1st January 1942, the number of men sent with each, and the number, if any, left behind. If this latter category is numerous, they could surely be used to improve the beach divisions. I repeat the Army must help itself if it is to be helped at all.

4. Let a table be prepared of the sorties per month or per quarter since His Majesty's present Government was formed, in relation to the total strength of the Air Force at home. My impression is that the ground proportion has grown unceasingly, both in relation to sorties and initial equipment.

5. Owing to our various disappointments as a result of shortfalls in the supply of aircraft, the Air Ministry's programme, Metropolitan Air Force only, is greatly reduced. Has a proportionate reduction been made in their demands for ground staff? It is quite certain, anyhow, that the demand of the Air Force as now presented must undergo a 50 per cent cut. The Air Ministry should find a way for doing this which least affects their sortie output. I must make it clear that those who do not try to make both ends meet and to save at every point are not helping the war effort of the country, observing that the man-power available can only meet one-half of the paper demand.

6. The reference in LMAB (42) 41 to 331 Aerodrome Defence battalions is a misnomer. 13,000 men, in addition to the 66,000 RAF ground personnel already serving, i.e., a total of 79,000 or, say, 80,000 were allocated to aerodrome defence. This number must be subjected to searching inquiry and compression. Lord Swinton[1] has recently asked not to be cumbered with white personnel for aerodrome defence on the West Coast, when he can, with native labour, make what he calls efficient arrangements. It does not follow that every airfield can be equally protected or that if we double the number of airfields we shall require double the number of ground air defence staff, or that the only defence must be the station personnel. Mobile columns of good troops can be kept in the neighbourhood and serve clusters of airfields.

7. MAP demands several hundred thousand more men, but their output continues to fall much below programmes drawn up quite recently.

[1] Cabinet Minister Resident in West Africa.

Let a table be prepared showing the proportion of men in MAP to the weekly tables of output in horse-power structure-weight which are furnished me. I repeat, it is an act of bad citizenship to ask for more than is necessary or to take a selfish and local view.

8. The Ministers of Production and Supply must revise their demands for man-power in respect of filling factories, observing we are firing practically nothing, and there seems no prospect in the next six months of continuous heavy firing.

9. In all the above at this stage only British Island man-power is to be considered.

Winston S. Churchill to Sir Archibald Sinclair
(Churchill papers, 20/67)

17 September 1942   Chequers
Action this Day
Personal and Secret
To be deciphered by his personal Staff Officer only

I am anxiously awaiting some account of your intentions. My understanding with you was the fourth week in September. Since then you have stated that the recent battle which greatly weakened the enemy has caused delay in regrouping, etc. I do not wish to know either your plan or the exact date, but I must know which week it falls in, otherwise I cannot form the necessary judgments affecting the general war.

Winston S. Churchill to Brendan Bracken
(Churchill papers, 20/67)

17 September 1942   Chequers
THE 'BLIMP' FILM

We should act not on the grounds of 'expressing harmful or misguided opinions', but on the perfectly precise point of 'undermining the discipline of the Army'. You and the Secretary of State should bring the matter before the Cabinet on Monday, when I have no doubt any special authority you may require will be given you. The Ministry of Information is the seat of the Censorship, and consequently you are the channel for any Cabinet decision on the subject.

Winston S. Churchill to Air Marshal Sir Arthur Harris
(Churchill papers, 20/67)

18 September 1942
Most Secret

Thank you for sending me General Arnold's paper.[1] I agree about strengthening the air attack on Germany and also that the Pacific should be regarded as a secondary theatre. Apart from this, I think the paper a very weak and sloppy survey of the war, and I am surprised that with his information he cannot produce something better. Both Germany and Japan, completely separated from one another, lie in the centre of large circles and can throw their strength outwards against any part of the circumferences. The Allies have not yet been able to gain the initiative, and are forced to make the best arrangements possible to meet a variety of dangers. However, these evils apply less to air power than to ground forces because, so long as our air forces are engaged with the enemy air force and are reducing the total sum of its strength in daily contact, it does not matter whether the bases from which they operate are dispersed or not. The wearing down of the enemy's air forces can be achieved from several different directions, just as batteries are dispersed the better to concentrate their fire.

General Arnold's arguments, if applied to our own case, would have abandoned the Middle East as a major theatre of war, and we should have had the Germans spread over great parts of Asia and Africa today. Nothing that could be done by Anglo-American aircraft bombing Germany would be the slightest compensation for injuries so fearful.

It is a great pity that General Arnold does not try first to send us two or three hundred of his big American bombers to expand our Bomber Command, after they have been adapted to night fighting. Failing this, he should send us as many American squadrons as he can to operate from this country, and teach them to fly by night. So far, his day bombing operations have been on a very petty scale.

I see he does not approve of the important operation which is pending,[2] which certainly shows him lacking in strategic and political sense, as it is the only practical step we can take at the present time, and one which, if successful, will produce profound reactions.

---

[1] Paper by the Commanding General of United States Air Forces, Henry Arnold, on plans for operation against the enemy, 3 September 1942.

[2] Operation 'Torch', the North Africa landings.

Sarah Churchill to Winston S. Churchill
(Churchill papers, 1/369)

18 September 1942   RAF Station
                                                                    Medmenham

Darling Papa,

Thank you so very much for your message to me.

While I realise how interesting and exciting it would be at Bomber Command, I know nothing about night photography.

I have been six months at my present job – interpreting day-light photographs, and feel I am just beginning to know something about it. I enjoy the work and it is in a section where the widest field of aerial photographing is covered.

As experience is one of the chief assets for any branch in this work I feel I would not be of much use to them at Bomber Command for at least two months – whereas they have allowed me to understand at Medmenham, that I am beginning to be useful to them, in a section from which they are losing quite a few who have to go overseas.

Could you explain this to Air Marshal Harris and thank him for his interest and kindness. You know how happy it makes me feel that you are interested in what I do – I'm afraid you have a poor picture from my incoherent accounts! But I love the work and feel I have a real job.

I hope your poor sore throat is better – please take care of yourself.

I love you very much.

                                                                    Sarah

Winston S. Churchill to Lord Halifax
(Churchill papers, 20/80)

19 September 1942
Personal and Most Secret

I hope you will not let yourself become unduly disturbed by superficial and uninstructed trends of American opinion about India. Our policy has been adopted with great deliberation and will not be changed in response to mere clamour.

2. We should certainly not tolerate any interference by foreign countries. I have made this quite clear to the President and to Chiang Kai-shek, the latter of whom sent some very foolish messages. If necessary, I shall come on the broadcast myself.

3. For the first time for fourteen sad years I received cordial House of Commons, and particularly Conservative, support for what I said about India last week. There was, of course, fretfulness from the usual softie and febrile elements, which had its reflection in the Left-Wing Press, but I doubt whether twenty will go into the Lobby against us when the expected debate comes on in a few weeks. How could anyone expect Indian Civil Servants and Police to do their duty against Gandhi and the Congress if all the time they knew we were seeking to negotiate with them, would install them in office and would leave our friends to their vengeance? The Viceroy and the Indian Government are doing extremely well and will be steadfastly supported.

4. I do not think I am out of touch with the total mind of the United States. It will soon have something else to occupy it than interfering with our business in India.

Winston S. Churchill to Brendan Bracken and Brigadier Leslie Hollis
(Churchill papers, 20/67)

19 September 1942
Most Secret

This involved story[1] does not clear up the matter at all. I presume you are keeping the Chiefs of Staff supplied with the material to answer JSM 389. (I wish to see the reply before it is dispatched.)

2. No speculation upon future operations is to be allowed to pass the Censors. In any case of doubt the message is to be held up until it has received the personal sanction of the Minister himself. I should be glad if the Minister would again see the newspaper proprietors and impress upon them the dangers of speculative articles upon future operations. It should be a point of honour to exclude them. You need not be too much afraid of seeming to confirm the rumours that have been circulated. The offence is equally heinous whether the rumours are true or false.

3. The British United Press seems to be very mischievous. I have lately noticed several offences committed in its telegrams. It is very easy for the Germans to introduce traitors and agents in our midst. The British United Press personnel and control should be subjected to considerable scrutiny.

---

[1] Minute of 18 September 1942 from the Director-General of the Ministry of Information, Cyril Radcliffe, commenting on JSM 389 about a British United Press message on the subject of future operations in North Africa.

4. Had such a message as that quoted in JSM 389 been sent, I am of opinion that the sender should be arrested under the Official Secrets Act or 18B or other emergency power and kept in complete seclusion for a considerable time. Let me know what powers are possessed.

5. The whole matter should be brought before the War Cabinet on Monday.

Sir Alexander Cadogan: diary
('The Diaries of Sir Alexander Cadogan', page 478)

19 September 1942

A. rang me up. He's been having trouble with PM, who wants to make peace with Vichy French in Madagascar. Why, I don't know – except that he says 'Annet's quite a good chap: Clemmie met him in a train somewhere once.' That doesn't seem good enough.

John Martin: diary
(Sir John Martin papers)

20 September 1942   Chequers

My turn has come round again already as Peck, though returned after his appendicitis, is not yet up to the succession of 3 a.m. bedtimes (or thereabout). Fortunately there is always a pause in the middle of the afternoon and I have my black eye-bandage with me so as to make the most of any such opportunity.

[...]

We had two American Ferry Command pilots here on Friday, who had flown the PM to Moscow in their Liberator. I was admitted a Short Snorter. The qualification is that you must have flown the Atlantic and the rule is that you must always carry about with you a dollar bill signed by the Short Snorters who admitted you and any others who may be added. If you meet another Short Snorter and challenge him to produce his bill and he can't, he has to pay a dollar to each Short Snorter present. The PM is a Short Snorter and has been caught in this way. All of which must sound, as it is, a little mad.

Winston S. Churchill to General Sir Harold Alexander
(Churchill papers, 20/80)

20 September 1942
Personal and Most Secret

I am greatly distressed to receive such bad news, for which I was not prepared, having regard to your strength compared with the enemy.

2. Were your attempts on Tobruk and Gialo related to this new retarded date or to an earlier one?

3. Is there not danger that the enemy will use the interval for fortifying himself in depth by blasting additional gun positions? What reinforcements does he expect and when, particularly the 22nd German Division?

4. The Chiefs of Staff must consider your new proposals in relation to the defence of Malta, for which it is not possible to run another convoy.

5. The present target date of 'Torch' is (see my next[1]), but it may well be (see ditto[2]). It is vital to influence French action in 'Torch' by a victory in Egypt. The date you mention does not give sufficient time for impression to soak in. Besides this, there is a further complication. We have to assemble so many vessels and aircraft in Gibraltar from the middle of October onwards that the disguise of this being another Malta convoy will no longer cover them. Demands may be made by Germany upon Spain to interfere with the neutral zone or the shipping in the Bay before the date of 'Torch' is reached. Spanish resistance to German pressure will be greatly strengthened by a British success in Egypt. The same applies to France in respect of these possible pre-'Torch' pressures.

6. The above will show you how our difficulties and anxieties are increased by the time taken to perfect your preparations.

Winston S. Churchill to Brigadier Leslie Hollis
(Churchill papers, 20/67)

20 September 1942

ASSISTANCE TO TURKEY

What reserves are to be provided for the formations at C on page 1?

2. By the end of this month Middle East were to have approximately 1,360 runners out of a total of about 2,500 tanks of all descriptions. In

---

[1] November 4.
[2] November 8.

addition, they are to receive in allocations from the United States and United Kingdom up to the end of 1942 approximately 2,500 brand-new tanks, including 2,000 Shermans. How is this great mass of 5,000 tanks to be distributed among the tank formations of the 8th Army? The allocations to Persia–Iraq are negligible. What formations of the 8th Army exist to take these tanks? I cannot accept that, out of such great resources, the detachment of Valentines and Matildas which I require for Turkey cannot be found. I had no idea such heavy reinforcements were coming from America. I cannot approve of heavy reserves being accumulated while front-line necessities are unmet.

At the end of October, unless we are defeated in the Western Desert, there must go to Turkey from Egypt 200 Valentines and Matildas or 2-pounder Crusaders, in addition to the light tanks from the United States. Have a plan for this worked out for me. If necessary, I will bring it before the War Cabinet. At the same time and on the above assumption, draft for me the substance of a telegram which I can send to Turkey. All this has got to be settled in the next few days.

Winston S. Churchill to Sir Archibald Sinclair
(Churchill papers, 20/67)

20 September 1942
Secret

EXPANSION OF BOMBER COMMAND AND RETURN
OF BOMBER CREWS FROM THE MIDDLE EAST

[...]

3. The fact that out of 316 bombers only 6 crews have returned to this country is really quite scandalous. You are getting a mass of sediment in the Middle East and are hampering your own development at home. Let me have a table showing the strength in squadrons, men and machines of the RAF in the Middle East on 1 September 1941, and on 1 September 1942.

War Cabinet: Confidential Annex
(Cabinet papers, 65/31)

21 September 1942   10 Downing Street
10 p.m.

The Prime Minister said that there were a number of important matters affecting future operations for discussion by the War Cabinet. He welcomed the presence of Sir Andrew Cunningham,[1] who could report at first hand on the position in Washington.

The Prime Minister said that the Americans stated that the date now fixed for this Operation was the 8th November. If we decided to send a further PQ convoy (PQ19) before Operation 'Torch', this would mean Operation 'Torch' would have to be delayed until either the 24th or 28th November, according to whether or not we intended to bring back the ships of PQ18 from North Russia.

The Prime Minister said that, in his view, to delay Operation 'Torch' until the 24th or 28th November would be to court disaster. He referred in particular to the rumours which were now in circulation regarding an impending operation. A good deal of this was, of course, inevitable when the size of the operation was taken into account. Furthermore, the weather would be worse as the winter went on. Three weeks had already been lost through the Americans having changed the plan of the operation – a change which we had had to accept. It was also significant that since a week ago, there had been a great change in the atmosphere at Washington, where the authorities were now full out on Operation 'Torch' and determined to make it a success.

Sir Andrew Cunningham confirmed this change of atmosphere, which was noticeable not only in the highest quarters, but also on lower levels.

The Prime Minister said that the first point on which a decision was called for from the War Cabinet was whether they were in agreement that Operation 'Torch' must be pushed forward at the earliest possible moment, irrespective of the effect on other operations.

The next question for a decision was what should be done about convoys to Russia. Up to the present, orders had been given that the loading of ships for PQ19 should proceed. The fact that this convoy was being loaded might be regarded by the enemy as preparation for an attack on Norway, and therefore also served the purpose of confusing the enemy as to our intentions.

The Prime Minister said that hitherto he had been principally influenced on this matter by the consideration that, if the Americans had said that Operation 'Torch' would have to be further postponed, there might have been time to fit in another convoy to North Russia before that operation had taken place. He had been anxious, therefore, to retain the option to run this convoy, so as not to fall between two stools.

---

[1] Head of the British Admiralty Delegation in Washington.

Finally, he had been unwilling to have to make it known to the Russians that the running of convoys to North Russia would be suspended, until this had become absolutely necessary.

The Prime Minister said that ten days ago the United States authorities had given orders that 180 Airacobra aircraft, loaded in ships forming part of the PQ19 convoy, should be unloaded, as they were required for Operation 'Torch'. In this matter we had been mainly carrying out instructions issued by the Americans. Nevertheless, the Russians had taken the matter very much amiss. M Maisky had been to see him that afternoon and had complained about this action. He (the Prime Minister) had told M Maisky that something much worse was in store for him than the action in regard to the Airacobras. It had been evident from M Maisky's attitude that the Russians would be greatly upset at the suspension of the convoys. He therefore asked the First Sea Lord to investigate whether any possible means could be found to continue sailings to North Russia, although on a greatly reduced scale.

The First Sea Lord said that he would certainly continue to investigate this matter. It must be realised, however, that any ships going to North Russia had to be prepared to meet three forms of attack: surface ships, U-boats, and aircraft.

The Prime Minister said that, in view of the very grim picture which the suspension of the convoys would present to Russia, it was clearly necessary to give further consideration to Operation 'Jupiter'. At his meeting with Premier Stalin in Moscow he had said that we would consider carrying out an operation with two British Divisions. Stalin had said that he would put in three Russian Divisions and had taken a hopeful view of the operation.

A Minute (D No 154/2) on Operation 'Jupiter', addressed by the Prime Minister on the 16th September to the Chiefs of Staff Committee, was then read to the War Cabinet. This Minute dealt with the prospects of Operation 'Jupiter', and commented on certain observations in General McNaughton's report on this operation.

The Prime Minister said that the Chiefs of Staff had examined this question very fully. On the whole, they took a rather unfavourable view of the possibility of being able to provide the necessary forces and particularly the shipping for 'Jupiter' in addition to 'Torch'.

The Prime Minister said that he had had a long conference that morning with the Chiefs of Staff, at which General Eisenhower and various United States Officers, and also Admirals Cunningham and Ramsay had been present. As a result of this meeting, drafts of three telegrams had been prepared:

(a) From the Prime Minister to President Roosevelt, dealing with the general position, including Operation 'Jupiter', the prospects of 'Round-Up', and of future PQ convoys.
(b) From the Prime Minister to Premier Stalin, in regard to Operation 'Jupiter'.
(c) From the Prime Minister to Premier Stalin, saying that PQ convoys must be suspended until January.

[...]

Sir Alexander Cadogan: diary
(*'The Diaries of Sir Alexander Cadogan'*, page 478)

21 September 1942

PM not v well, I think.

Sir Stafford Cripps to Winston S. Churchill
(*Churchill papers, 20/56*)

21 September 1942   Gwydyr House
Whitehall

My Dear Prime Minister,

When I joined the Cabinet seven months ago I hoped that I might be able to help the country by co-operating with you in the direction of the war effort, and there seemed to be a good prospect of this in the early days, especially before my visit to India.

Since my return last April there has been a change in our relationship and I do not now feel that you place reliance upon my help. I feel increasingly out of touch with your mind on a wide range of subjects of which, as Leader of the House of Commons, I should have an intimate knowledge.

Naturally I feel uneasy about the situation and, if you can spare me the time before long, I should much appreciate a talk with you upon this whole matter.

I am anxious, in the light of the developments over the last seven months, and in view of the heavy responsibilities which weigh upon us all, to know how you view the future.

I am sending you a note in reply to yours on the Minute which I sent you on July 30. I much appreciate the care which you have devoted to answering the various points which I raised. Perhaps we could have a word about some of these when we meet?

Yours Very Sincerely
Sir Stafford Cripps

Winston S. Churchill to Sir Stafford Cripps
(Churchill papers, 20/54)

22 September 1942

My dear Cripps,

I am surprised and somewhat pained to receive your letter. I was certainly not aware of any change in our relationship since you first took office seven months ago. I thought we were on the most cordial terms when I set out on my journey at the beginning of August. In the seven weeks that have passed since then I have been away for nearly a month, and you later for more than a week. Apart from Cabinets (of which we have had three, aggregating six hours and a half, in the last twenty-four hours) I always do my best to see my principal colleagues. I have always found our conversations agreeable and stimulating. I hope you will not fail to come and see me whenever you wish.

With regard to the further memorandum which you have been good enough to send me on the whole system and method by which, for good or for ill, I endeavour to discharge my task of presiding over the Government and the conduct of the war, no one knows better than you the controversial significance of all that you write. I also have convictions on these matters, which are the result of long experience and heavy responsibility. Another would no doubt do differently.

I do not intend to argue here, as it would be endless, but I am sure you would not underrate the wisdom, knowledge, and precision of mind of the First Sea Lord if you had worked with him as closely as I have under the hard stresses of his war. Indeed, I cannot help saying that I feel you are less than generous to the Admiralty achievement by which we have lived.

You ask me how I view the future. I view it with hope, and, I trust, with undiminished firmness of spirit. Great operations impend which are in full accordance with your own conceptions and on which we are all agreed. We must have the fibre and fortitude to endure the delays and await the outcome. As I myself find waiting more trying than action, I can fully understand the uneasiness you say you feel.

Yours very sincerely
Winston S. Churchill

Winston S. Churchill to President Franklin D. Roosevelt
(Churchill papers, 20/80)

22 September 1942
Personal and Most Secret
No. 151

Had long conference this morning with Eisenhower and your officers. Cunningham and Ramsay present and our Chiefs of Staff.

2. General Eisenhower announced that the final date for 'Torch' would be (see my following telegram[1]). Everything is being worked to this.

3. We now know that PQ18 carried 27 ships safely to Archangel and 13 are sunk. For PQ19, 40 ships are already loaded but it is impossible to send this convoy without throwing back the date of 'Torch' by three weeks. We all regard any delay in 'Torch' as inadmissible.

4. The time has therefore come to tell Stalin, first, that there will be no PQ19 and secondly, that we cannot run any more PQs till the end of the year, i.e., January. This is a formidable moment in Anglo-American-Soviet relations and you and I must be united in any statement made about convoys.

5. We are solemnly pledged to the supply of Russia and the most grave consequences might follow from failure to make good. For 1943 there may be two choices. First, to run from January onwards Arctic convoys under the present conditions of danger, waste and effort, observing that we used 77 warships for PQ18 and think ourselves fortunate to have lost no more than one-third of the merchant ships.

6. Secondly, the Operation called 'Jupiter'. It is more than doubtful whether the developments of 'Torch' will leave shipping and escort resources sufficient for 'Jupiter' unless you can help at any rate with the latter. We must, however, also know what importance Stalin would attach to the operation and what contribution he would make to it. See the account of my last conversation with him where I mentioned two divisions and he offered three. Our estimate here is that larger numbers

[1] November 8.

would be required, and I repeat the shipping problem is unsolved and is anyhow dependent on 'Torch' developments.

7. It seems to me that simply to tell him now no more PQs till 1943 is a great danger, and I therefore wish to open staff conversations on 'Jupiter' under all necessary reserves. See the telegram I propose to send to him after consulting Mackenzie King, which, as you will see, leaves both British and Soviet Governments free to decide when the result of the Joint Staffs study is completed. Of course, if you were able to take an interest in this it would be most helpful. As in a few days it will be necessary to unload and discharge PQ19 I felt this new project necessary to break the blow.

8. I gained the impression at the Conference that 'Roundup' was not only delayed or impinged upon by 'Torch' but was to be regarded as definitely off for 1943. This will be another tremendous blow for Stalin. Already Maisky is asking questions about the Spring offensive. I understood that the words of our agreement stood, namely, that all preparations should go forward in a balanced way as fast as possible. Under all circumstances it is indispensable to hold the Germans pinned on the Channel coast of France. However, Mountbatten says landing craft are not going forward as arranged, and, of course, the movement of American troops across the Atlantic will evidently be greatly reduced.

9. We ought now to make a new programme. So far, three United States divisions have arrived here, all of which will shortly leave for 'Torch'. We have sent six divisions from the United Kingdom and are holding four more ready for 'Torch'. If we are to be able to take advantage of a breakdown in enemy morale, or an undue weakening of their forces in Europe next Spring, or alternatively, if things go badly for us and we have to face the possibility of invasion, it will be necessary for you in the next six months to send at least eight United States divisions to the United Kingdom in addition to your air force programme. United States General Smith says that at least twenty ship-loads could be saved by use of the proportion of British equipment which we hope to be able to supply. Also these divisions can work up here almost as well as at home.

10. I can quite see how in the altered circumstances you would be inclined to shift the emphasis from building landing craft to escort vessels, but I hope this will not go too far and that you will give me a steady flow both of troops and landing craft up to the limit of shipping possibilities. Could you please send as soon as possible revised programmes of what we may expect in the next twelve months between now and next September under the 'Bolero'–'Roundup' scheme. Only then can we

make plans for our own safety and the accommodation of your men, apart altogether from enterprises such as 'Jupiter'. By a further rigorous handling of the British man-power problem we are hoping to bring the nine Beach divisions up to full field standard. It seems vital to all our plans not only that we should be free from the invasion menace but that the enemy should feel our pressure and we be able to take advantage of any serious deterioration in German morale. In this connexion every argument used for 'Sledgehammer' and/or 'Roundup' counts even more in 1943 and 1944 than it did in 1942 and 1943.

11. If 'Torch' proves hard and costly and if we have to fight French and Germans and perhaps Spaniards, there could, of course, be no question of 'Jupiter'. We British would require to reinforce 'Torch' from Great Britain. Thus it is all the more necessary that we receive the fullest flow of American divisions and air forces to the United Kingdom.

12. But there is a more favourable assumption to which personally I incline, namely, that by the end of November the United States with French assistance will be masters of French North Africa and that the British expedition will be striking from 'Torch' at Tripoli. General Alexander will attack in sufficient time to influence 'Torch' favourably should he be successful. His operation is called (see my telegram No. 153[1]). If all goes well on both operations we might control the whole North African shore by the end of the year, thus saving some of the masses of shipping now rounding the Cape. This is our first great prize.

13. It would then be open to us to decide on the next move. If the Russian need were sufficiently grave and their demands imperative we might decide to do 'Jupiter' instead of attacking the under-belly of the Axis by Sardinia, Sicily and even possibly Italy. We ought to have the option open which entails not only paper Staff studies but all such preparations as do not hamper our immediate agreed action.

14. To sum up, my persisting anxiety is Russia, and I do not see how we can reconcile it with our consciences or with our interests to have no more PQs till 1943, no offer to make joint plans for 'Jupiter', and no signs of a spring, summer or even autumn offensive in Europe. I should be most grateful for your counsel on all this. We wish urgently to send the telegram (of which copy follows separately) to Stalin, and hope that you will back it up as strongly and as soon as you can.

---

[1] Operation 'Lightfoot'.

Winston S. Churchill to Josef Stalin
(Churchill papers, 20/80)

22 September 1942

We have made the following estimate of German operational aircraft production which the Air Ministry believe is trustworthy. It may be of interest to you and I should be very glad to learn at your convenience how it squares with your own estimates of enemy output.

[. . .]

Winston S. Churchill to Anthony Eden
(Churchill papers, 20/67)

22 September 1942

I think it is a great mistake to let de Gaulle into Madagascar, which he will only use as another field for anti-British activities. Anyhow, we cannot take any decision until after we have reached a settlement with him about his recent misbehaviour.

It is quite possible that as the result of 'Torch' we may be in relation with a French anti-German organisation very much wider in its basis than that presided over by de Gaulle. It would be wise to keep options in our hands as long as possible.

Meanwhile, I agree with you that the term 'Governor-General' should not be used, but rather 'Officer in charge of Administration'.

Winston S. Churchill to Lord Woolton[1]
(Churchill papers, 20/67)

22 September 1942

PROPOSED PROHIBITION ON THE SALE
AND MANUFACTURE OF ICE CREAM

Without definite information as to the saving in transport and man-power, I cannot judge whether the destruction of this amenity was worth while.

I suppose the large numbers of American troops in this country will have their own arrangements made for them. They are great addicts of ice cream, which is said to be a rival to alcoholic drinks.

The step should not have been taken without the Cabinet having an opportunity to express an opinion.

[1] Minister of Food.

Winston S. Churchill to General Sir Harold Alexander
(Churchill papers, 20/80)

23 September 1942
Most Secret
Personal

Your No. CS1550. We are in your hands and, of course, a victorious battle makes amends for much delay. Whatever happens we shall back you up and see you through.

2. There is a point about the fortifications which the enemy will make in the interval which I should like to put to you. Instead of a crust through which a way can be cleared in a night, may you not find 25 miles of fortifications with blasted rock, gunpits and machine-gun posts? The tank was originally invented to clear a way for the infantry in the teeth of machine-gun fire. Now it is the infantry who will have to clear a way for the tanks, and it seems to me their task will be a very hard one now that fire power is so greatly increased. No doubt you are thinking about all this and how so to broaden your front of attack as to make your superior numbers felt.

3. The Germans seem very nervous about Crete and the islands. See Boniface[1] of today. Anything that can make them more nervous would act as good cover for 'Torch' as well as 'Lightfoot'. Let me know if you have any ideas.

General Sir Alan Brooke: diary
('War Diaries, Field Marshal Lord Alanbrooke', pages 323–4)

23 September 1942

[...] After lunch PM sent for me to discuss a reply wire he wanted to send to Alexander. I tried to stop him and told him that he was only letting Alex see that he was losing confidence in him which was a most disconcerting thing before a battle. He then started all his worst arguments about generals only thinking of themselves and their reputations, and never attacking unless matters were a certainty, and never prepared to take risks, etc, etc. He said this delay would result in Rommel fortifying a belt 20 miles deep by 40 miles broad that we should never break through owing to a series of Maginot defences etc etc! I had a very unpleasant ¾ hour! However, I succeeded in getting a very definite tempering of

---

[1] Enigma decrypts.

the message. After dinner at 10 pm I was sent for again, this time about tanks for Turkey. We had a hammer and tongs argument which ended in friendly terms.

Winston S. Churchill to Sir James Grigg, Sir Archibald Sinclair,
Lord Leathers, and General Ismay, for Chiefs of Staff
(Churchill papers, 20/67)

23 September 1942

BOXING OF LORRIES

The August figures show a welcome improvement and I am glad to see that the bulk of the so-called 'non-technical' War Office vehicles are being boxed. I trust that every effort will now be made to ship in boxes the largest possible proportion of 'technical' vehicles, cars and RAF vehicles, and to improve existing methods of boxing.

Winston S. Churchill to William Mackenzie King
(Churchill papers, 20/80)

24 September 1942
Personal and Secret

I am sorry about McNaughton. I thought that at this critical juncture in Anglo-American relations with the Soviets his personality and knowledge of the subject might have got a good plan worked out with the Russians, and on a far better basis than that on which his own study had been made. Moreover, as Commander-in-Chief of the Canadian Army he would no doubt have got access to Stalin himself, which will probably not be the case with any British general.

2. There would, of course, have been no question of any commitments being entered into by any Government, nor would the full freedom of Canadian action have been compromised in the slightest degree.

3. It is quite true that the arrival of the Canadian Commander-in-Chief in Moscow would have led the enemy to think that some joint operation for a second front in northerly latitudes was being planned. As you know, we are trying to spread that very idea as cover for 'Torch' and the Americans also are training an Arctic division with some ostentation. Thus exactly the right impression would have been given to mislead the enemy at this critical time.

4. Moreover, it so happens that this use of the 'Jupiter' operation as cover for 'Torch' would not compromise or hamper its eventual execution in reality after some months had passed. When the enemy saw 'Torch' become operative they would conclude that the McNaughton mission was part of the blind and would therefore cease to worry about the northern theatre, and meanwhile, if we had decided in favour of 'Jupiter' our preparations could continue.

5. No question had arisen or could arise between us for some time of Canadian troops being employed, or of General McNaughton being selected, and, in fact, we are preparing British divisions in Scotland for Arctic service as part of the cover.

6. Apart from all the above, which seems to me to fit together rather neatly, I am under dire necessity of convincing Premier Stalin of our resolve to help him to the utmost of our strength. We have now to suspend the PQ convoys for the sake of 'Torch'. This will be another heavy blow to Stalin. Russian resistance will only be maintained on a great scale if during 1943 we are able to keep a broad stream of supplies flowing in by the Arctic route from Britain and the United States. The whole burden of fighting these convoys through falls upon the Royal Navy (77 warships were used last time); and unless 'Jupiter' or something like it cleans up the Norwegian tip, the waste, loss and effort in munitions and naval power during 1943 will be paralysing to our action elsewhere. The first thing, however, was to get a good plan and find out what the Russians themselves could do. Stalin seemed very keen about it when we talked in Moscow, and I am of opinion that he might make a great effort, thus simplifying the whole business.

7. I would have put all these reasons to you when making my request if I had thought that the serious issues mentioned in your message would be raised simply by his visit. Of course, if after hearing them you still feel that McNaughton should not go, I will send someone else. I need not emphasise the extreme secrecy of all the foregoing.[1]

Kindest regards.

---

[1] On September 26, Churchill wrote to Mackenzie King: 'Your telegram No. 1917. If I had known that McNaughton was not keen on this Mission to try to make a plan, I would not have troubled you with my reasons for it. I only learned, however, of his attitude after my last message. Pray think no more about it.'

General Sir Alan Brooke: diary
('War Diaries, Field Marshal Lord Alanbrooke', page 324)

24 September 1942

[...]

I asked him if he had yet seen McNaughton's letter. He said he had not, and I told him the contents of it. He then became very worked up about the whole show and in the end was very pathetic. He said this machine of war with Russia at one end and America at the other was too cumbersome to run any war with. It was so much easier to do nothing! He could so easily sit and wait for work to come to him. Nothing was harder than doing things, and everybody did nothing but produce difficulties. He is a wonderful mixture and one never knows what mood he will be in next.[1]

[...]

Winston S. Churchill to Chiang Kai-shek
(Churchill papers, 20/54)

25 September 1942

My dear Generalissimo,

I take this further opportunity of sending greetings by the hand of the Delegation from the Parliament of the United Kingdom.

It is my hope that this mission of goodwill from the oldest and most important of our democratic institutions, whose servant I am, will be received in China in a very special sense as a gesture of friendship and solidarity from the people of this country to those of the great Republic that is ably served by Your Excellency.

Both in your land and ours the leaders are, I know, sustained in their heavy burden by the knowledge that they have behind them a people conscious that it is their own chosen way of life for which they are fighting, and not a system imposed upon them by tyranny.

The unbreakable tenacity with which the Chinese, British and other progressive nations are holding to this precious heritage of representative government is the assurance of our final victory over the forces of evil. In the confidence born of this belief I commend our Parliamentary

---

[1] 'Frequently in this oration he worked himself into such a state from the woeful picture he had painted that tears streamed down his face' (Alan Brooke, *Notes on My Life*, draft autobiography, 1954–6, Volume VII, page 536).

Delegation to your care, and I send my best wishes that Your Excellency may be long preserved in health and happiness.

Yours most cordially and sincerely,
Winston S. Churchill

Winston S. Churchill to Lord Gort
(Churchill papers, 20/80)

26 September 1942
Most Secret
Personal
Bigot[1]

I have read Rowntree's report. We are thinking about you every day, and everything in human power shall be done. We hope to run some ships through in the flurry of 'Torch'. All good wishes to you and Munster.[2]

Winston S. Churchill to General Hastings Ismay,
for the Chiefs of Staff Committee
(Churchill papers, 20/67)

26 September 1942
Most Secret

PIERS FOR USE ON FLAT BEACHES

It seems to me that we ought to have three or four miles of this pier tackle. It could of course be used in many places in short sections. Pray do not lightly turn this aside. We must, however, know what we should have to give up.

---

[1] 'Bigot': code word used at the start of any telegram relating to future operations. A 'Bigot' officer was one who knew the actual destination of a particular operation, in this case 'Torch' (North Africa).

[2] Geoffrey William Richard Hugh FitzClarence, 1906–75. Educated at Charterhouse. Succeeded his uncle as 5th Earl of Munster, 1928. Sat as a Conservative Peer in the House of Lords. Member of London County Council for North Paddington, 1931–7. A Lord-in-Waiting, 1932–8. Paymaster-General, 1938–9. Parliamentary Under-Secretary of State for War, February–September 1939. ADC and Military Assistant to Lord Gort, 1939. General Staff Officer to Malta, 1942. Parliamentary Under-Secretary of State for India and for Burma, 1943–4; Home Office, 1944–5; Colonial Office, 1951–4. Minister without Portfolio, 1954–7. Privy Councillor, 1954; KBE, 1957.

Winston S. Churchill to Sir John Anderson
(Churchill papers, 20/67)

26 September 1942

In trying to effect economy of fuel or labour on the Home Front, I hope you will bear in mind that these may react upon the efficiency of the workers. For instance, fewer bus services mean longer journeys, and tired workers arrive at their offices or plants. A business man could, of course, clean his own room and arrive an hour late at an important job, and so forth. I do not wish to dogmatise, but hope this point is being borne in mind.

Winston S. Churchill to Sir Stafford Cripps
(Churchill papers, 20/67)

26 September 1942

It would be a good thing to hear what the Commander-in-Chief, Bomber Command, thinks about it.[1] This we must have before the Cabinet decision is reopened. Personally, I think it very foolish to give this information to the enemy, and without a statement of the numbers taking part in the raid it is most misleading and needlessly distressing. I should have no difficulty in explaining the matter to the house.

Winston S. Churchill to Geoffrey Lloyd[2]
(Churchill papers, 20/67)

26 September 1942

It is of great importance to find means to dissipate fog at aerodromes so that aircraft can land safely. Let full experiments to this end be put in

---

[1] The reference is to a minute of 25 September 1942 from the Lord Privy Seal about the publication of aircraft losses.

[2] Geoffrey William Geoffrey-Lloyd, 1902–84. Educated at Harrow School and Trinity College, Cambridge. President of Cambridge Union, 1924. Unsuccessful Parliamentary candidate for Southwark (1924) and Birmingham Ladywood (1929). Private Secretary to Sir Samuel Hoare (Secretary of State for Air), 1926–9; to Stanley Baldwin (Prime Minister, then Leader of the Opposition), 1929–31. Conservative MP for Birmingham Ladywood, 1931–45; for Birmingham King's Norton, 1950–5; for Sutton Coldfield, 1966–74. Parliamentary Private Secretary to Stanley Baldwin (Lord President of the Council, then Prime Minister), 1931–5; Parliamentary Under-Secretary, Home Office, 1935–9. Chairman, Oil Control Board, 1935–45. Secretary for Mines, 1939–40. Secretary for Petroleum, 1940–2. Minister in Charge of Petroleum Warfare, 1940–5. Parliamentary Secretary (Petroleum), Ministry of Fuel and Power, 1942–5. Privy Councillor, 1943. Minister of Information, 1945. A Governor of the BBC, 1946–9. Minister of Fuel and Power, 1951–5. Minister of Education, 1957–9. President, Birmingham Conservative and Unionist Association, 1946–76. Created Baron, 1974. Chairman, Leeds Castle Foundation, 1974–84.

hand by the Petroleum Warfare Department with all expedition. They should be given every support.

President Franklin D. Roosevelt to Winston S. Churchill
(Churchill papers, 20/80)

27 September 1942   Washington DC
Most Secret
No. 187

I agree with you that the realities of the situation require us to give up PQ19. While I think that is a tough blow for the Russians, I nevertheless think that the purposes for which the escorts are to be used both as to time and place make that decision inevitable. PQ19 however would not have sailed under any circumstances for another ten days, and I feel very strongly that we should not notify the Russians until that time arrives and we know with finality that the convoy will not go. I can see nothing to be gained by notifying Stalin sooner than is necessary, and indeed much to be lost. Furthermore, I believe that within ten days we could come to a final conclusion regarding the Air Force in Trans-Caucasia, regarding which Stalin should be notified at the same time.

For security reasons I think it would be unwise to unload any of the ships at Iceland. While it is true that we are short of shipping, we probably do not need those particular ships for 'Torch' and I think we had better make the sacrifice of letting the ships remain idle in Iceland rather than risk giving the enemy the information that we are not running the next convoy. I believe that 'Torch' should not be delayed a single day. We are going to put everything into that enterprise, and I have great hopes for it.

I will be back in Washington Thursday, and will cable you then regarding the Air Force in the Caucasus and other matters. I am having a great trip. The training of our forces is far advanced and their morale excellent. Production is good, but must be better.

Winston S. Churchill to Vyacheslav Molotov
(Churchill papers, 20/80)

27 September 1942
Personal and Private

The Foreign Secretary tells me that he has sent you a message about the British Naval Hospital at Vaenga being ordered to close and go home. I should be glad if you would look into the matter personally yourself. Terrible cases of mutilation through frost-bite are now arriving back here, and I have to consider constantly the morale of the merchant seamen, who have hitherto gone so willingly to man the merchant ships to Russia. The British hospital unit was sent simply to help, and implied no reflection on Russian arrangements under the pressure of air bombardment, &c. It is hard on men in hospital not to have nurses who speak their own language. At any rate I hope you will give me some solid reason which I can give should the matter be raised in Parliament, as it very likely will be.

Winston S. Churchill to A. V. Alexander and
Admiral of the Fleet Sir Dudley Pound
(Churchill papers, 20/67)

27 September 1942

The report of 650 survivors being brought in from the *Laconia* and another ship shows that a very serious tragedy has taken place. Is it known what proportion of the rescued are Italian prisoners of war and what proportion are British personnel? There were nearly 3,000 people to be accounted for, so over 2,000 must have lost their lives.[1]

Winston S. Churchill to President Franklin D. Roosevelt
(Churchill papers, 20/80)

28 September 1942
Personal and Secret
No. 155

Your No. 187. Earliest date PQ19 could have sailed is October 2, i.e. five days from date of your message of September 27. However if you think well we can keep it, as if it really was sailing, till 7th or even later. Bulk of the ships are in Scottish ports. Agree it is most important to make a firm offer about Caucasus air support.

2. Am encouraged by the way our troops were received in Tananarive.

Kindest regards.

---

[1] The British troopship *Laconia*, carrying 463 officers and crew, 80 civilians, 286 British soldiers, 1,793 Italian prisoners of war, and 103 Polish soldiers, was attacked and sunk by a U-boat off the West African coast on 12 September. Over 1,600 of those on board perished, 1,420 of them Italian prisoners.

When the U-boat commander realized that the ships' occupants were mainly prisoners of war and civilians, he ordered operations to rescue survivors. The German vessels taking part in those operations subsequently came under US air attack, causing orders to be issued in Germany that U-boats were no longer to offer assistance to passengers of vessels attacked.

Winston S. Churchill to General Hastings Ismay,
for the Chiefs of Staff Committee
(Churchill papers, 20/67)

28 September 1942
Most Secret

Let me see what studies have been made so far for the exploitation of
'Torch' should it prove entirely successful. Sardinia, Sicily and Italy itself
have no doubt been considered. If things go well, we should not waste a
day but carry the war northwards with audacity. I am hoping that air plans
have already been made to bring Southern Italy under close bombing
attack as soon as we are established in Tunis. What arrangements have
been made with Lord Gort about the Malta force? Assuming that Tunis
comes over quietly and swiftly, what forces do we send forward to clear
up Tripoli?

Winston S. Churchill: recollection
('The Hinge of Fate', pages 472–3)

28 September 1942
1.30 p.m.

At one of our meetings, on September 28, I certainly rendered a
service to Bedell Smith[1] and his chief. It was not very late at night, but I
noticed that 'the Beetle', as he was also called, looked frightfully tired and
ill. I suggested that he should go to bed, but he insisted on remaining.
There was a moment when I thought he was going to faint and fall off
his chair. I therefore closed the discussion. On the way upstairs I asked
Eisenhower to come alone with me into the Cabinet room. I closed the
door and said, 'If you want Bedell in this battle you should send him to
hospital this very night, no matter what he says. Otherwise you will lose
him altogether.' Eisenhower acted with his customary decision. Next
day Bedell Smith was in hospital. He had to have two blood transfusions
in the next two days, and was kept a fortnight from all work and mostly
in bed. Thus he was able to play his important part in the design which
dominated our minds.

---

[1] Chief of Staff to Eisenhower.

War Cabinet: Confidential Annex
(Cabinet papers, 65/31)

28 September 1942   10 Downing Street
5.30 p.m.

[...]

The Prime Minister said that he had sent a Minute to the Chiefs of Staff on this question. He agreed that the present time was a bad moment at which to broach the diminution of supplies to Russia by the Persian gulf route. He thought that the situation in a fortnight's time would make it very much easier to reach a decision as to the proper line of action to be taken. Furthermore, any approach made to the Russian Government in a fortnight's time could, he hoped, be linked up with the proposal, which was already under discussion with President Roosevelt, to send a force of 20 British and American squadrons to the North Persian–Caucasus front.

Winston S. Churchill to General Hastings Ismay,
for the Chiefs of Staff Committee
(Churchill papers, 20/67)

28 September 1942
Most Secret

General Wilson's proposals for taking up advanced positions in Persia are sound in principle and seem to be well worked out. The price to be paid in cutting down Russian supplies is heavy, and the moment when PQ 19 is cancelled is by no means the best for notifying the Russians. The question is therefore one of timing, and the answer depends upon the view taken of the German advance into the Caucasus. In the six weeks that have passed since the CIGS and I were in Moscow, the Caucasus situation has improved markedly. More than forty of the sixty days which Premier Stalin told me he would have to hold out for, have passed. The Russian resistance has been most vigorous. Their artillery still commands the borders of Novorossisk. The intruders over the high passes made no headway. Snow is falling on the Caucasian mountains. The Grozny oilfield has not yet been taken. The fortifications which the CIGS saw just beginning on the Caspian shore must now be much further advanced. Personally I have always felt that the Russians would hold the line of the Caucasus mountains until the spring, and that Baku would not be taken this year. I must admit that this view is temperamental rather than scientific. Nevertheless, we must all feel that things have turned out better than many people expected.

2. In the light of the above, it would certainly seem that we could afford to wait for another fortnight before embarking on the forward move of the 10th Army. By the middle of October it should be possible to see more clearly over the whole scene, and I suggest we wait until then before addressing the Russians and the Americans on the subject of trans-Persian tonnages.

3. The President has now promised to give an answer, presumably favourable, about 'Velvet',[1] by the 7th October. A draft time-table should be prepared on the assumption that the answer is favourable. I am not clear whether the 20 squadrons of 'Velvet' involve all the aircraft, including the Army components, at the disposal of the 10th Army. They will certainly be in advance of it and a shield to it, and if things go badly they will fall back on it. It would be convenient to have all the air units set out on a table even before the President's message is received.

4. It is not yet necessary or possible to make up our minds what to do with the 10th Army if the German attack on Russia in 1942 should present itself as a definite failure. But this question will assume a greater precision when we see how 'Lightfoot' and 'Torch' go.

5. I hope General Wavell has been wise in proclaiming his intention to attack in Burma. The requests which he now makes for air support, &c., seem modest, and I should be glad to know they could be met.

6. When the Chiefs of the Staff have considered these matters, we ought to have a War Cabinet and Defence Committee meeting upon them.

Winston S. Churchill to Sir James Grigg and General Sir Alan Brooke
(Churchill papers, 20/67)

28 September 1942
Secret

I am not prepared to approve reserves of tanks of 90 per cent being assigned to some armoured divisions, while others have no tanks at all. When an army is expanding its armoured forces, as we are doing, every effort should be made to give priority to the initial equipment of all units, and it is only after these needs have been satisfied that the reserves can

---

[1] 'Velvet': the movement of Anglo-American forces to the Caucasus to support the Russians.

be built up. Of course, where the forces are in contact with the enemy, a large proportion of spare tanks must be provided.

2. In the Middle East all the Shermans should be put in the front line, the reserves being found by Grants. In any particular theatre where a large number of one mark of tank is used by several units, it would be well to make a general pool rather than to assign a fixed reserve to each unit. This applies particularly at home, where we have very large numbers of Churchills, of Crusaders and of Valentines. Here in this small island, where the units lie close to their large workshops, a very much lower standard is possible than in the Middle East or India. We cannot afford to have tanks standing idle on the one hand and formations left unequipped on the other.

3. I should be glad to have a statement of all the armoured units at home and abroad, formed and in formation, with their initial equipment and the actual numbers of tanks they have got, either with the units or in reserve.

*Winston S. Churchill to A. V. Alexander and
Admiral of the Fleet Sir Dudley Pound
(Churchill papers, 20/67)*

28 September 1942
Most Secret

Pray consider in what way the ships of PQ19 can best be used to make the enemy believe we intend to run another convoy. It will be a great advantage to us and, indeed, a help to 'Torch' if the Germans are induced to keep their submarines, aircraft and surface vessels in the north this winter, doing nothing because no convoys are running. Everything should therefore be done to favour the idea of an October convoy.

*Winston S. Churchill to Air Chief Marshal Sir Charles Portal
(Churchill papers, 20/67)*

28 September 1942
Secret

Everything in the Boniface shows the increasing dependence of the enemy on Tobruk as against Benghazi. It seems to me astonishing that the whole of the air forces which we and the Americans have in Egypt are not able to bring the work of this port, which lies so near them, to an end.

29 September 1942   House of Commons

The success of the initial landings[1] and the fact that they were accomplished with only the lightest casualties to both sides were due in great measure to the efficiency of the Royal Navy and the speed with which they ferried the troops on to the beaches at the right time.

After British troops had secured the port of Majunga, motorised units of the King's African Rifles disembarked for their advance on their capital 300 miles to the south. Their first objective was the 1,600 feet long suspension bridge over the Betsiboka River, 140 miles from Majunga. They reached this point at 9.30 am on the second day, and found that the Vichy French had cut the suspension cables. Although the centre span had collapsed into the water, the infantry crossed and secured a bridgehead against slight opposition. Very shortly afterwards, the advance on the capital was resumed.

On the 16th September M Annet, the Vichy French Governor of the island, broadcast an appeal for an armistice. One of our planes was sent to Tananarive to bring his plenipotentiaries to Majunga, where Lieut. General Sir William Platt received them on the 17th. The French were unable to accept our terms, however, and the delegates left the next morning. Earlier on that same morning our seaborne forces appeared off the east coast port of Tamatave and called upon the town to surrender. The commandant refused and fired on our envoys, but after a brief bombardment by His Majesty's ships, the white flag was hoisted over the town at 8 a.m. Our troops landed without incident and pursued the retiring French forces to Brickaville, the principal town on the railway from Tamatave to the capital, which they captured on the 19th.

At this time, our column from Majunga had reached a point some 40 miles north of Tananarive and here they met their first serious opposition. This was overcome in two sharp engagements on the 21st and 22nd, and our forces entered the capital at mid-day on the 23rd. They were received with strong demonstrations of good will and even enthusiasm. Operations against the remaining Vichy French forces south of the capital are

---

[1] On Madagascar.

proceeding. Resistance in the northern part of the island between Diego Suarez and Majunga has collapsed, and all is now quiet in this area.

I should mention that I received news this morning that Tulear, an important port in the southern portion of the island, surrendered to an ultimatum without any bombardment being necessary.

Harold Nicolson: diary
('Harold Nicolson, Diaries and Letters', page 242)

29 September 1942

Aneurin Bevan stands me a drink. He bewails the Government and says that we shall lose the war if Churchill stays. This is all very difficult to answer. I agree that very serious strategic and supply mistakes have been made, but this is inevitable. I still see Winston as the God of War.

Winston S. Churchill to Lady Leslie[1]
(Churchill papers, 1/368)

30 September 1942

Dearest Leonie,

I was so glad to see your vigorous and youthful handwriting again. It is a great pleasure to me to know that you follow my toils. It seems to me that the tide of destiny is moving steadily in our favour, though our voyage will be long and rough.

My love to Jack, and believe me,

Your always loving,
W.

Winston S. Churchill to Josef Stalin
(Churchill papers, 20/80)

30 September 1942
Most Secret and Personal

I have got the following information from the same source[2] that I used to warn you of the impending attack on Russia a year and a half

---

[1] This is Churchill's reply to his aunt's letter of 14 September: see page 1202 above.

[2] Enigma, although Churchill did not reveal this to the Soviets, telling them instead that the source was an agent secretly planted in Germany.

ago. I believe this source to be absolutely trustworthy. Pray let this be for your own eye.

1. Begins. Germans have already appointed an Admiral to take charge of naval operations in the Caspian. They have selected Makhach-Kala as their main naval base. About twenty craft including Italian submarines, Italian torpedo boats and mine-sweepers are to be transported by rail from Mariupol to the Caspian as soon as they have got a line open. On account of the icing-up of the Sea of Azov the submarines will be loaded before the completion of the railway line. Ends.

2. No doubt you are already prepared for this kind of attack. It seems to me to make all the more important the plan I mentioned to you of our reinforcing with American aid your Air Force in the Caspian and the Caucasus theatre by twenty British and American squadrons. I have never stopped working at this since we were together and I hope in a week or so to have the final approval of the President and to be able to make you a definite joint offer.

3. With regard to the 154 Aerocobras which have been unloaded from PQ19 I personally authorised this at the urgent request of General Marshall, the American Commander-in-Chief. They were American machines assigned to us and by us assigned to you. The American demand was urgent and explicit and was concerned with 'Torch'. General Marshall undertook to replace them via Alaskan route forthwith. I will telegraph you further within the next ten days.

October
1942

Winston S. Churchill: comment to Anthony Eden and Clement Attlee
('The War Diaries of Oliver Harvey', page 165)

1 October 1942   10 Downing Street

If 'Torch' fails, then I'm done for and must go and hand over to one of you.

Winston S. Churchill to Anthony Eden
(Churchill papers, 20/67)

2 October 1942

Your PM/42/200.[1]

1. Let me have a short description of what it can actually do, and also a good plan for using it during 'Torch'. My idea was, the President should let us have some records which could be let off at appropriate moments as General Eisenhower thought fit. In addition, I would, once the show was well started, have a go in French or English, as the case might be, to France.

2. Pray let me have the draft of the telegram I could send to the President asking for the extra valves.

---

[1] About 'Aspidistra', a high-power (500 kW) medium-wave broadcasting transmitter near Crowborough in the Ashdown Forest, Sussex. Used in black propaganda against Germany during the Second World War, including a classic 'man-in-the-middle' eavesdropping attack. Named after a popular foliage houseplant, Aspidistra used an antenna consisting of three guyed masts, each 110 metres tall. The transmitter building was in an underground shelter excavated by a Canadian Army construction unit. It went into service on 8 November 1942 and was used for several British propaganda operations during the Second World War, aiming (directly or indirectly) to undermine the credibility of the Nazi leadership by creating fear, uncertainty, and doubt in the minds of Germans listening to the broadcasts.

Vyacheslav Molotov to Winston S. Churchill
(Churchill papers, 20/80)

2 October 1942
Personal

In my letter to Mr Eden I asked him to acquaint you, Mr Prime Minister, with the contents of my reply on the question of the British medical personnel in Archangel and Voinga (Murmansk). I think that if you glance at the Memorandum of the Soviet Foreign Office of the 27th August and my letter of the 12th September addressed to the British Ambassador, Sir Archibald Clark Kerr, you will have the full information on the matter and will be in a position to draw the necessary conclusions as to the real state of affairs, particularly in regard to certain irregularities in the actions of the respective British naval authorities.[1] I think also that the solution of this question as set out in my message to Mr Eden corresponds to the wishes you have expressed.[2]

Sir Stafford Cripps to Winston S. Churchill
(Churchill papers, 20/56)

3 October 1942   Gwydyr House
Personal and Confidential   Whitehall

My dear Prime Minister,

In accordance with my promise when I saw you yesterday, I am writing to you about my position in the War Cabinet, which we have been discussing during the last few days.

You have not convinced me that the changes which I have suggested in the central direction of the war are unnecessary. I firmly believe that alterations of that nature are essential if we are to make the most of our war potential.

Such a conviction would have led me to ask you to place my resignation in the hands of HM the King, were it not for the special circumstances to which you and my other colleagues have drawn my attention.

I fully realise however, as you have impressed upon me, that this precise moment is one of great anxiety for the country and for the Government. In such circumstances it is clear that nothing avoidable should be done during these particular critical days by the suggestion of disunity or of differences as to the central direction of the war, which

---

[1] Churchill commented on Molotov's message: 'This grimace is a good example of how official jargon can be used to destroy any kind of human contact, or even thought itself' (*The Hinge of Fate*, page 516).

[2] See Churchill's note to Molotov of 27 September 1942, reproduced above (page 1234).

might disturb the morale of our fighting men or increase our international difficulties.

These temporary considerations seem to me to override even the necessity for the changes that I have suggested, and I have therefore decided that it is my duty, in the interests of the successful prosecution of the coming operations, to delay taking any further action as regards my position in the War Cabinet until the operations are at least well launched.

When the time arrives I will revert to this matter.

It is, I am sure, unnecessary for me to add that in the meantime I shall do my utmost to assist you in every possible way and that I shall give you my most energetic support wherever and whenever I can.

PS. I have shown this letter to Anthony Eden and Clem Attlee, and have told the other members of the War Cabinet of the general line of my action.

Winston S. Churchill to Sir Stafford Cripps
(Churchill papers, 20/56)

3 October 1942

My dear Stafford Cripps,

I am sure that you are right to withhold your resignation until the great operations upon which we have all agreed have been, as you say, at least well launched. The discussions attending your departure from the Government could not fail at the present time to be harmful to the public interest and to the safety of British and American troops. It would be very difficult for me to take part in them without saying something from which the enemy might draw conclusions. On the other hand, you are fully entitled to bring our differences to an issue at a later stage. Meanwhile I thank you for your assurance that you will give me all possible help in the interval, and I shall certainly reciprocate your aid and courtesy to the full.

Josef Stalin to Winston S. Churchill
(Churchill papers, 20/80)

3 October 1942   Kremlin
Personal and Secret   Moscow

I have to inform you that the situation in the Stalingrad area deteriorated since the beginning of September. The Germans were able to concentrate in this area great reserves of aviation and in this way managed to secure superiority in the air in the ratio 2:1. We had not enough fighters for the protection of our forces from the air. Even the bravest troops are helpless if they lack the air protection. We more particularly require Spitfires and Air-Cobras. I told about all that in great detail to Mr Wendell Wilkie.

2. The ships with arms arrived at Archangel and are being unloaded. This is a great help. In view however of the scarcity of tonnage we would be prepared temporary to forgo some forms of assistance and in this way to reduce the amount of tonnage necessary if there would be secured the increased number of the fighter aircraft. We would be prepared temporary to forgo our claims on tanks and artillery equipment if Great Britain and the USA could supply us with 800 fighters a month (approximately Great Britain 300 and the USA 500). Such a help would be more effective and would improve position at the front.

3. The information of your Intelligence to the effect that Germany manufactures not more than 1300 combat machines a month is not confirmed by our sources. According to our information the German aircraft works together with the works in the occupied countries engaged in making of aircraft parts are producing not less than 2500 combat machines a month.

Stalin

Winston S. Churchill to C. R. W. Nevinson[1]
(Churchill papers, 20/56)

3 October 1942[1]

Dear Mr Nevinson,

I am greatly obliged to you for your letter of September 26 and by the exceedingly kind thought which has prompted the gift of your fine paint-

---

[1] Christopher Richard Wynne Nevinson, 1889–1946. An English painter, often referred to by his initials as C. R. W. Nevinson. Son of the famous war correspondent and journalist Henry Nevinson. Educated at Uppingham School, St John's Wood School of Art, University College London and the Slade School of Art. Joined the Friends' Ambulance Brigade with his father, October 1914; served as a volunteer Red Cross ambulance driver transporting wounded soldiers from Dunkirk to a hospital in Malo-les-Bains. In early 1915 left France on sick leave and returned to London; later that year joined the Royal Army Medical Corps and worked at the General Hospital in Wandsworth. Discharged from Army due to ill-health, January 1916. Drew on his war experiences for a series of powerful paintings using Futurist techniques. First exhibition of war paintings, Leicester Galleries, 1916. Appointed an official war artist and returned to the front, 6 July to 5 August 1917, witnessing the preparations for the Passchendaele campaign. Of three paintings Nevinson produced under the group title *The Battlefields of Britain*, two were exhibited at the Royal Academy in 1942; the artist presented one to the nation in late 1942 and it hung in the Council Room of the Air Ministry for many years (as part of the Government Art Collection). Much of his work can be seen today in the Imperial War Museum and National Gallery in London as well as at the Metropolitan Museum in New York, the National Gallery of Wales, the Fitzwilliam Museum, Cambridge, and galleries in Manchester, Liverpool, Prague, and Zagreb.

ing 'Battlefields of Britain'. I accept your gift with much pleasure but I think that such a picture should not be retained as my private property but should rather become a public possession of the British Nation. I feel that it could not hang in any more appropriate place than in the Air Council Room at the Air Ministry, and the Secretary of State informs me that he would be delighted to arrange this. Both he and the Chief of the Air Staff have received the proposal with very great pleasure.

I am so sorry to hear that you are laid aside from your work with illness and send my best wishes for your recovery.

With my most grateful thanks.

Yours sincerely,
Winston S. Churchill

Winston S. Churchill to President Franklin D. Roosevelt
(Churchill papers, 20/88)

4 October 1942
Most Secret and Personal
No. 156

I have been furnished with a copy of the Progress Report which the Combined Production and Resources Board have submitted to you in response to your letter of 19th August. I have followed with interest the work of the Board since its inception in June, and I fully appreciate the importance to the success of their task of integrating the production programmes of the two countries, of a statement of requirements directly related to strategic needs. I also realise the formidable difficulties which stand in the way of the preparation of such a statement for a date so far ahead as 1st April, 1944. The progress towards the ideal at which the Board is aiming may well be slow.

2. In the meanwhile, it seems to me that there are certain features of our combined programmes which, if they are allowed to stand unmodified, must lead to a misdirection in 1943 of resources of materials and industrial capacity which we can ill afford. I think I can best illustrate my meaning by taking as examples the combined production programmes of tanks and of ball ammunition.

3. Our combined tank programme for 1943 allows for the production in the United States of some 31,000 light tanks and 45,000 medium and heavy tanks. In the United Kingdom the production will be 11,000 of all types. The total amounts to some 87,000 tanks, which I am advised would be sufficient to equip some 200 armoured divisions of 225 tanks each

with 100 per cent. reserves. This appears to me to be a provision on a scale out of all proportion to anything that might be brought to bear on the enemy in 1943. It was, of course, necessary for us to fix high targets in the early days, so as to get production moving on a great scale. Have we not now reached the time when we could, with advantage, scrutinise our targets more closely? In our efforts to reach to too great a height we may well exhaust an undue quantity of our resources.

4. A further effect of setting the targets of the main items of equipment too high is that everything else is then calculated in proportion. For example, the United States production in 1943 of ball ammunition will be about 20,000 million rounds of all calibres. That of the United Kingdom will be about 2,000 million rounds. Observing that the entire expenditure of ball ammunition by our army in the Middle East, from the beginning of the war to the present date, is little more than 200 million rounds, and remembering that the total expenditure of the American Expeditionary Force in the last war was around 1,000 million rounds, it would appear that we are making provision on a scale which is altogether too lavish.

5. I bring these matters to your attention because of my anxiety that, if inflated demands are given full rein, we shall create for ourselves unnecessary difficulties in the provision of raw materials and industrial capacity, and shall be unnecessarily curtailing our power to expand the production of such vital requirements as escort vessels, ships, and aircraft, of which it is almost impossible to have too many.

6. I am ready to co-operate in any way you may think desirable in scrutinising our programmes, so as to rectify those anomalies which may exist, and so as to ensure that our combined resources will be used to the best advantage.[1]

---

[1] On 13 October 1942, Roosevelt replied to Churchill, explaining that 'realising the acute shortages of materials, we have reduced our objectives for the medium and heavy tanks for 1943 to a total of 38,527 of which 4,500 are to be furnished to Russia and 23,108 are carried as to the requirements of the United Kingdom as fixed by the Joint Tank Committee which met here during the past summer. If the requirements for the United Kingdom are now in excess of operational needs, it will permit a reduction in our tank program. Our own requirements have been reduced to approximately 11,000 medium tanks for 1943, including maintenance and reserve.

'Our light tank program requires the production of approximately 16,501 tanks during 1943, of which 6,250 are required for the United Kingdom and for Russia.' In his final paragraph, Roosevelt wrote: 'I believe the Combined Production and Resources Board rather than questioning specific requirements items should analyse the total US and UK requirements which have been presented to them and then advise the Combined Chiefs of Staff if it is found that the realities of production make it necessary to revise them' ('Secret', *Churchill papers, 20/81*).

Winston S. Churchill to General Hastings Ismay,
for the Chiefs of Staff Committee
(Churchill papers, 20/67)

4 October 1942

I presume plans are in hand for accompanying 'Torch' with large-scale air diversions to tie the German Air Force to the French coast?

2. Would it not be well to have a certain number of American ships, not necessarily very powerful ones, showing the American flag in the British squadrons which might have to deal with the sortie of the Vichy Fleet from Toulon?

3. What is the truth of the newspaper rumours about French submarines being sent to Dakar?

General Archibald Wavell to Winston S. Churchill
(Churchill papers, 20/80)

5 October 1942   India
Personal
Secret
Immediate

I know that you are busy with most important affairs elsewhere but you may like to hear how things are going in India. I am sending official telegram to COS shortly.

2. You know I am trying to act offensively as soon as I can but, at the moment, prospects are not too bright. We are having very malarial autumn after heavy monsoon and sick rate is high. Internal situation still requires considerable number troops and communications to north-east India which are poor at best of times have not recovered from monsoon damage and Congress sabotage. This all means that preparations are retarded.

3. Akyab operation (my 23785/C 27/9 to COS). Palliser whom I sent to see Somerville has just returned and told me state of Eastern Fleet. Obvious that I can get little naval support before 1943 and shortage of small craft will make escort of my expedition rather precarious. My air is not coming up to expectation and percentage of serviceability of bombers especially is low for various reasons. Meanwhile Japanese are making aerodromes and air shelters in Burma on scale sufficient for several hundred aircraft and have definitely increased their air strength possibly up to about 200. Do not think they can spare large air force for Burma unless they make this their main effort. I shall keep on all preparations

for Akyab and carry it out whenever possible. Soon I hope but I must reckon up naval and air possibilities before I embark.

4. Stilwell is coming [to] Delhi next week and I will discuss plans fully with him. I am anxious to get close co-operation with Americans but Stilwell's position at Chungking and lack of combined command cause difficulties.

5. Am visiting Assam October 8 to 13 to see progress and shall fly Fort Hertz if weather favourable.

6. This may not sound very progressive but we are doing our best with our resources and conditions. Grateful for 29th Brigade and ships and landing craft which will all be very valuable.

President Franklin D. Roosevelt to Winston S. Churchill
(*'The Hinge of Fate', pages 516–17*)

5 October 1942[1]

I have gone over carefully your proposed message to Stalin of September 22.

I feel very strongly that we should make a firm commitment to put an Air Force in the Caucasus, and that that operation should not be contingent on any other.

The Russian front is today our greatest reliance, and we simply must find a direct manner in which to help them other than our diminishing supplies. We shall on our part undertake to replace in the Middle East all of our own planes which are transferred, and assist you in every way possible with your own air problems in the Middle East.[2]

So far as PQ19 is concerned, I feel most strongly that we should not tell Stalin that the convoy will not sail. After talk with Admiral King I would like to urge that a different technique be employed, in which evasion and dispersion are the guiding factors. Thus let PQ19 sail in successive groups, comprising the fastest ships now loaded and loading for Russia. These groups would comprise two or three ships each, supported by two or three escorts, and sail at twenty-four to forty-eight hour intervals. They might have to go without the full naval covering support that would pro-

[1] Date received: it had been sent three days earlier.

[2] On 7 October 1942 Field Marshal Sir John Dill, Head of the British Joint Staff Mission in Washington, wrote to Churchill: 'Hopkins mentioned incidentally that President has today given instructions that the production of combat aircraft in 1943 shall be set at one hundred thousand. This programme to take precedence where necessary over all other classes of production' (*Churchill papers, 20/81*).

tect the convoy from the *Tirpitz* or heavy cruisers, but that must simply be a risk that we have to take. We know that so far as air attack is concerned the weather would in all probability not be against us every day and the longer nights will be of help.

I believe we would stand a good chance of getting as high a proportion of the ships through as we did with PQ18. Under any circumstances I think it is better that we take this risk than endanger our whole relations with Russia at this time. I know that you and Pound will give this proposal of mine every consideration. I should tell you that our Ambassador [Admiral Standley[1]] has asked to come home to deliver in person a very important message, and I have some fears as to what that message might be.

I propose that you should send the following to Stalin:

'You will recall our conversation about putting a British–American Air Force in the Caucasus. I have examined this matter with the President, and we have determined to move to accomplish this without delay. I will let you know the extent of the Air Force that we can make available, and our plans for building the force up during succeeding months.'

Please let me know when you send [your] message to Stalin, and I will immediately send him a similar message, but I am certain both our messages should be so phrased as to leave a good taste in his mouth.

Winston S. Churchill to President Franklin D. Roosevelt
(Churchill papers, 20/80)

6 October 1942   10 Downing Street
Personal and Secret
No. 157

I have just received the telegram immediately following from Stalin.[2] It seems to me that in addition to 'Velvet' we ought to make a desperate effort to meet him as far as possible, and include the promise in our impending telegram about PQ19. This is becoming urgent now as much unloading has to be done and assembly of PQ ships complicates somewhat 'Torch'. Should be most grateful to hear from you at earliest.

---

[1] William Harrison Standley, 1872–1963. United States Admiral. Chief of Naval Operations, 1933–7. United States Ambassador to the Soviet Union, 1941–3.

[2] Stalin's message to Churchill of October 3, reproduced above (page 1245).

Elliott,[1] who is in great form, was with me last night together with Eisenhower and the American Eagle[2].[3]

Winston S. Churchill: note
(Cabinet papers, 65/28)

6 October 1942

Arrangements already made to sail about 10 ships from Iceland (C) during dark period 28th October to 8th November. These would sail singly at about 200 mile intervals with occasional larger gaps and rely on evasion and dispersion.

2. We had already considered sailing small groups with weak escort but in our view there is no half way between independent sailings and fighting through with full escorting forces.

3. Our reasons are:

(a) Possibilities of evasion are slight as German air reconnaissance for North Russian convoys is very intensive and anything in the nature of a group of ships would be continually shadowed.

(b) A group is more likely to draw attack by enemy surface vessels which are still waiting in their northern anchorages.

(c) Anything short of full covering support invites disaster both to the group and Naval forces.

(d) To send a total of 40 ships in groups of 2 or 3 ships with 2 or 3 escorts would employ as many escorts as were required for PQ18. 'Torch' is absorbing every available craft.

4. The voyage in anything but a full escorted convoy is so hazardous that it should only be undertaken by volunteers who clearly understand the risk. The chance of crews of stricken ships surviving when they take to their boats is remote.

---

[1] Elliott Roosevelt, 1910–90. Second child of President Franklin Delano Roosevelt and Eleanor Roosevelt. Served in the United States Air Corps during the Second World War, rising to the rank of Brigadier General. Wrote several books.

[2] General Mark (Wayne) Clark, Chief of Staff for United States ground forces in England (for European operations).

[3] On 7 October 1942, President Roosevelt telegraphed to Churchill: 'I forgot to tell you in my wire last night that we are prepared to send a Heavy Bomber Group to "Velvet" in addition to an Air Transport Group. I am anxious that we have on that Front a real Anglo-American Air Force. Under this plan you would provide the Fighters and the Medium or Light Bombers' ('Secret', *Churchill papers, 20/81*).

Winston S. Churchill to President Franklin D. Roosevelt
(Cabinet papers, 65/28)

7 October 1942
Personal and Secret
No. 159

There is no possibility of letting PQ19 sail in successive groups with reduced escorts as you suggest. Neither can the fact that the convoy is not sailing be concealed from the Russians any longer. Maisky is already aware of the position, though not officially informed, and I expect he has let Stalin know the general prospect. We are preparing ten ships to sail individually during the October dark. They are all British ships for which the crews will have to volunteer, the dangers being terrible, and their sole hope if sunk far from help being Arctic clothing and such heating arrangements as can be placed in the lifeboats. Absolutely nothing else is possible unless you are able to help by providing some American ships for independent sailing after November 9, should experience have proved that the chances are sufficiently good.

2. I believe that the blunt truth is best with Stalin, but there has been advantage in the delay of a fortnight in telling him, which you proposed. I feel strongly that he should be told now.

3. With regard to 'Velvet', nothing can move before the battle in Egypt. There is the danger that the Germans will pull their Air Force off Russia and turn it on to Egypt. There is also the probability that they will be forced anyway to turn a large proportion on to 'Torch'.

But, although we cannot be definite about an early date, it seems to me that we could be more definite as to the composition of the force. We have for weeks had the exact composition of the twenty squadrons planned out, subject to your concurrence and help. I should like to state the actual detail of the force and the time required for it to move and come into action.

4. I am puzzled to know what message Admiral Standley is bringing home to you, but I cannot believe it threatens a separate peace. So far the Russian campaign has been very adverse to Hitler, and though they are angry with us both they are by no means in despair.

5. If therefore we offer 'Velvet' as now defined, plus increased aircraft deliveries and the individual ships on the PQ route, I trust this will be sufficient to bridge the gap before 'Torch' opens.

President Franklin D. Roosevelt to Winston S. Churchill
(*Churchill papers, 20/81*)

7 October 1942
Most Secret
Personal
No. 190

Winant tells me that the *Chicago Tribune* has applied to Bracken for license to publish a daily paper in England primarily for the use of our troops. I earnestly hope that this application will not be approved.

The fact is that it should be turned down on the ground that the *Chicago Tribune* prints lies and deliberate misrepresentations in lieu of news.

Application can be rejected if you agree on the ground that the United States Government proposes to print a daily paper through an agency approved by you or a daily paper published by our Army or the troops themselves. Such as 'the Stars and Stripes' in Paris in 1918. I do not believe therefore that the application should be turned down on the lack of paper.

You will readily see that I do not trust the *Chicago Tribune* further than you can throw a bull by the tail but I do think we need a paper of our own for the soldiers in England.

Winston S. Churchill to President Franklin D. Roosevelt
(*Churchill papers, 20/88*)

7 October 1942
Personal and Secret
No. 161

Your 190. Bracken tells me that when he heard of the *Chicago Tribune*'s proposal he told some of the American correspondents that the Ministry of Information would not allow McCormick[1] to publish any paper in

---

[1] Robert Rutherford McCormick, 1880–1955. Editor and publisher. A Chicago newspaper baron and owner of the *Chicago Tribune*. Chairman of Board, *New York Daily News*. Educated at Ludgrove School, New Barnet; Groton School, Massachusetts; Yale College; Northwestern Law School. Alderman, Chicago, 1904; Member of the City Council, 1904–6. Admitted to Illinois Bar, 1908. Member of Chicago Bar Association. Member of law firm McCormick, Kirkland, Patterson and Fleming, 1908–20. President, *Chicago Tribune*, 1911; *Washington Times-Herald*, 1949–54. War correspondent with British, French, and Russians, 1915. Major, 1st Illinois Cavalry, Mexican border, 1916. Attached to General Pershing's staff, American Expeditionary Force, France. Adjutant, 57th Artillery Brigade. Lieutenant-Colonel, 122nd Field Artillery, US National Guard. Colonel, 61st Field Artillery, 1918. Colonel, General Staff, 1919. Commandant, Fort Sheridan, Illinois. DSM. Recommended for rank of General Officer by General Pershing, 1919.

England, on the ground that the *Chicago Tribune* had done everything in its power to injure the cause of the United Nations. No official application for facilities has yet been made. When it is, McCormick will be told that no opportunity will be given to him to reproduce in England the lies and misrepresentations which are the staple of the *Chicago Tribune*'s editorial policy.

Bracken told Eisenhower yesterday that every possible facility will be given to the American Army if it will produce a daily paper for the American troops.

Winston S. Churchill to General Archibald Wavell
(Churchill papers, 20/88)

7 October 1942
Personal

Thank you so much for your 24583/C. I am very glad you are pressing forward with your plans in spite of the absence of a firm guarantee of adequate reinforcements. We shall be able to see much more clearly in a few weeks, and larger decisions can then be taken.

2. I cannot help feeling much more comfortable about the Caucasus than when we were all in Moscow now nearly two months ago. Indeed, it looks as if Hitler's campaign against Russia in 1942 will be a great disappointment to him.

3. Everything here is rolling forward on the lines of which I told you. I am telling Ismay to send you an epitome of the recent telegrams I have exchanged with Stalin and the President. This will be for you and the Viceroy alone.

4. The personal matter which you mentioned to me is arranged and will be announced in the New Year List.[1]

Kindest regards.

---

[1] Wavell had hoped that his promotion to Field Marshal could be made before the New Year's Honours List, telegraphing to Churchill on 15 October 1942: '... I had hoped and still hope that you could announce it forthwith. After all I feel it was in 1941 that I earned it not in 1942, and that it will look rather like an old age pension in the New Year List. Life is uncertain and my military career is beginning to draw to an end. I confess I should like to enjoy prestige as long as possible. Also it might help in dealing with Americans and Chinese in forthcoming negotiations on Burma. Gingerbread is always gingerbread but may I have it with the gilt on please' (*Churchill papers, 20/81*). No gilt was forthcoming: the award was made in January 1943.

Winston S. Churchill to General Hastings Ismay,
for the Chiefs of Staff Committee
(Churchill papers, 20/67)

7 October 1942
Most Secret

Naturally I am very much in favour of the development of an amphibious striking force in this theatre.[1] I greatly regretted the manner in which the three Commandos we sent out with assault ships were frittered away, and also our fine Marine party put to no good use. I have always believed that operations of this character, whether against the island or in the rear of the enemy's position, ought to play an important part in the campaign. It seems all the more necessary that they should do so now that larger prospects are open.

2. The only thing that worries me is, what about Wavell's Akyab, &c. It would be a fine piece of work if we could manage to concentrate the MNBDO[2] without paralysing Wavell. Perhaps you will let me have a report.

Winston S. Churchill to Sir James Grigg and Sir Archibald Sinclair
(Churchill papers, 20/67)

7 October 1942
Secret

Whenever our Army is established on land, and is conducting operations against the enemy, the system of organisation and employment of the Royal Air Force should conform to that which has proved so successful in the Western Desert. The characteristics of this system are that the whole Air Force will be under the command of one Air Officer Commanding-in-Chief, whose relationship to the Army Commander-in-Chief will be that laid down in paragraphs 4 and 5 of my Directive of the 7th October, 1941. This fact must be the starting point in our inves-

---

[1] The Middle Eastern theatre.

[2] MNBDO: Mobile Naval Base Defence Organization. An unit about 8,000 strong, commanded by a Major-General of Royal Marines, and consisting of specialists, including engineers and mechanics; transport and crane drivers; armourers and gunners; surveyors and draughtsmen; bricklayers, masons, carpenters, plumbers, painters, decorators, and camouflage modellers; miners, blacksmiths, tinsmiths, and divers. The main function of the organization was to provide the Fleet with a base in any part of the world, whether on the coast of a mainland or on an island, within a week, and to defend it when prepared. The unit was carried in specially equipped merchant vessels.

tigation of the part to be played by the Royal Air Force in Continental operations based on the United Kingdom. I should like to see, set out in simple terms, the application of the Western Desert system to France. Let this statement be prepared and agreed by the time I return from the north.

2. Working backwards from the result which we must achieve in France, we can then determine how the awkward second phase, involving the spring across the Channel, can best be managed. Finally, we can see what arrangements should be made for the preparatory training period, so that there will be no break in the continuity throughout the three phases.

3. In the meanwhile, so that there may be no delay, and without prejudice to any final decision, the twelve Army Support Squadrons should begin forming in Army Co-operation Command as agreed upon between CIGS and CAS.

Winston S. Churchill to L. S. Amery
(Churchill papers, 20/67)

7 October 1942

The expression 'India shall have her complete freedom' is not a sensible one and does not conform to the Cripps paper, which indicates that the Constitution shall in the first place be within the British Commonwealth of Nations. It is not true, as stated in paragraph 3, that there is only one condition; there is a second, namely, that British responsibilities and obligations shall be honourably discharged. This covers the Princes and the Untouchables. It astonishes me that you should leave out these vital questions. I cannot accept responsibility for the document in its present form.[1]

---

[1] Letter of 5 October 1942 from the India Office enclosing copy of a note for the guidance of editors on the Indian constitutional issue.

Winston S. Churchill to Sir Edwin Lutyens[1]
(Churchill papers, 20/54)

7 October 1942

My dear Lutyens,

I am deeply honoured by the splendid work of art which you have presented to me in the name of the Royal Academy.[2]

Sir William Reid Dick[3] has produced a bust which certainly excites my warmest admiration, and which will long be treasured in my family.

Yours very Sincerely
Winston S. Churchill

Winston S. Churchill to Lord Halifax
(Churchill papers, 20/54)

7 October 1942

My dear Edward,

Thank you for your letter of September 25 about the suggestion that I might let the Library of Congress have the manuscript of the speech I delivered in the Senate Chamber last January.

I am flattered by MacLeish's[4] suggestion and loath to decline so courteous an invitation; but, in view of the similar requests received from time

---

[1] Edwin Landseer Lutyens, 1869–1944. Architect and artist. Educated privately. Member of Committee to advise Government of India as to site of Delhi, 1912. Architect for Government House, Imperial Delhi. Other works include Whitehall Cenotaph; British School of Art, Rome; British Pavilion, Paris; British Art Exhibition Building, Rome; Picture Gallery and South African War Memorial, Johannesburg; Head Offices of the Anglo-Persian Oil Company Ltd; New British Embassy, Washington. One of the principal architects for the Imperial War Graves Commission. Knighted, 1918. Member of the Royal Fine Art Commission, 1924. President of the Royal Academy, 1938. Hon. Member of the Royal Scottish Academy.

[2] A bronze head of Churchill by the sculptor William Reid Dick.

[3] William Reid Dick, 1879–1961. Educated at Glasgow School of Art. Exhibited at Royal Academy from 1905. Member of Royal Fine Art Commission, 1928. President, Royal Society of British Sculptors, 1933–8. Trustee, Tate Gallery, 1934–41. Knighted, 1935. Sculptor to King George VI, 1938–52. Queen's Sculptor in Ordinary for Scotland from 1952. Member of the Mint Advisory Committee. Trustee, Royal Academy. Albert Medal of Royal Society of Arts (presented by Princess Elizabeth), 1948.

[4] Archibald MacLeish, 1892–1982. Educated at the Hotchkiss School, Lakeville, Connecticut, and at Yale and Harvard Universities. Enlisted as Private, United States Army, 1917. Spent 12 months with American Expeditionary Force in France. Discharged with rank of Captain, 1919. An instructor in Government at Harvard, 1919–21. Practised law in Boston, 1923–30. Editor of *Fortune*, 1929–38. Librarian of Congress, 1939–44. Director, Office of Facts and Figures, 1941–2. Assistant Director, Office of War Information, 1942–3; Assistant Secretary of State, 1944–5. Chairman, American Delegation to London Conference of the United Nations to establish a Cultural and Educational Organisation, 1945. American Member, Executive Board UNESCO, 1946. Boylston Professor, Harvard University, 1949–62. President, American Academy of Arts and Letters, 1953–6. Simpson Lecturer, Amherst College, 1963–6. Presidential Medal of Free-

to time from other important Libraries and for other reasons, have felt it necessary for the present to maintain the rule that the original texts of my speeches (or photostat copies) cannot at this stage be given away.

I am so sorry to disappoint MacLeish but I am sure he will understand.

Why pull the sawdust out of the doll.[1]

Yours very Sincerely
Winston S. Churchill

Winston S. Churchill to Josef Stalin:
draft telegram from himself and President Franklin D. Roosevelt
(Churchill papers, 65/32)

8 October 1942

We shall attack in Egypt towards the end of this month and 'Torch' will begin early in November. The effect of these operations must be either:

(a) To oblige the Germans to send air and land forces to counter our move; or

(b) To compel them to accept the new position created by our success, which would then create a diversion by the threat of attack against Sicily and the south of Europe.

2. Our attack in Egypt will be in good force. 'Torch' will be a heavy operation in which, in addition to the United States Navy, 240 British warships and more than half a million men will be engaged. This is all rolling forward irrevocably.

3. The President and I are anxious to put an Anglo-American air force on your Southern flank and operate it under the strategic control of the Soviet High Command. This Force would consist of the following:

British: 9 Fighter Squadrons, 5 Bomber Squadrons.

United States: 1 Heavy Bombardment Group, 1 Transport Group.

Orders have been issued by us to assemble this force and take their station so that they would be available for combat early in the New Year. Most of this force will come from Egypt as soon they can be disengaged from the battle there, which we believe will be successful on our part.

dom, 1977. National Medal for Literature, 1978. Gold Medal for Poetry, American Academy and Institution, 1979.

[1] Churchill added this sentence in his own handwriting before signing the letter.

4. In the letter which M Maisky delivered to me on the 5th October you asked for a great increase in fighter aircraft supplied to Russia by this country and the United States. We will send you as soon as possible, by the Persian Gulf route, 150 Spitfires, with the equivalent of 50 more in the form of spares, to be sent as they become available, as a special reinforcement which we cannot repeat. This special reinforcement is over and above the protocol supplies by the Northern route so far as it can be used. President Roosevelt will cable separately about the United States contribution.

5. I was greatly relieved that so large a proportion of the last convoy reached Archangel safely. This success was achieved only because no less than 77 warships were employed on the operation. Naval protection will be impossible until our impending operations are completed. As the necessary escorts are withdrawn from 'Torch' they can again be made available in northern waters.

6. Nevertheless, we intend in the meanwhile to do our best to send you supplies by the Northern route by means of ships sailed independently instead of in escorted convoys. Arrangements have been made to sail ships from Iceland during the moonless period 28th October – 8th November. Ten of ours are preparing, in addition to what the Americans will do. The ships will sail singly, at about 200-mile intervals, with occasional larger gaps, and rely on evasion and dispersion.

7. We hope to resume the flow of supplies in strongly-escorted convoys from January 1943.

8. It would, of course, greatly help both you and us if the Germans could be denied the use of airfields in Northern Norway. If your Staffs could make a good plan the President and I would at once examine the possibility of co-operating up to the limit of our ability.

Winston S. Churchill to Sir Edward Bridges
(Churchill papers, 20/67)

8 October 1942

For your private information. I rate the capacity of a man to give a useful opinion on any question connected with war in accordance with the following three conditions:

First, courage and ability. Second, real experience of the fire. Third, peace-time Staff studies and routine promotion.

Winston S. Churchill to Anthony Eden
(Churchill papers, 20/67)

8 October 1942

In my opinion this is not the way this matter should have been handled. In the picture I make to myself of the Turk, comradeship, generosity, the impression of power and resources are what will count. I had never meant to mix this gift up with any bargain about chrome, about which they are obviously in great difficulties. When the Ambassador speaks about taking advantage to 'rub it in', he utterly misconceives the gesture. I took great trouble to get these tanks, &c. I am after the Turk; I am not after your chrome. I particularly asked that the two ideas should be kept quite separate.

I am very sorry about this. Do please see if you can get the issues on a right footing. We offer this hard-bought gift to Inönü. All that happens is, he is 'rather discomposed'. I should like to send the following telegram to Inönü:

The gift of arms from Britain to Turkey reported to you by the Ambassador on October 1 is meant by me as a token of comradeship and comprehension, and it is independent of every other consideration or matter in negotiation between our Governments.

Winston S. Churchill to Sir Archibald Sinclair and Ernest Bevin
(Churchill papers, 20/67)

8 October 1942

ROYAL AIR FORCE REGIMENT

I cannot agree that men under 25 should be employed on these highly localised duties. No more should be recruited at present. With regard to those now there, I am not certain under what tenure they are serving. Have we the power to transfer them to Army units? Please advise me. The transference should be made gradually, so as to avoid any shock to the formations. A period of four months would not be excessive for this.

2. The replacement of the under 25s would, of course, come from the older categories called up, and these should be supplied sufficiently to maintain the approved strength of the Royal Air Force Regiment. I shall be content if the total strength is allowed to run down from 79,000 to, say, 70,000.

3. Is it not very absurd that the officers of this ground service should be called pilot officers, flight-lieutenants, &c., when they have never flown and are never going to fly. No one ought to be called a pilot officer who has not flown or does not fly. Most people would be ashamed to call themselves pilots of the Royal Air Force when, in fact, they are never going to get off the ground. I wonder the pilots themselves do not feel rather scornful about this multiplication of borrowed plumes.[1]

Anthony Eden: diary
('The Eden Memoirs, The Reckoning', page 343)

8 October 1942

[...]

Max expressed concern at Winston's health and described him as 'bowed' and not the man he was. Brendan also said that W was very 'low' yesterday when Max saw him. I told him that his powers of recuperation were very great and I was not worried.[2]

Winston S. Churchill to Josef Stalin
(Churchill papers, 20/81)

9 October 1942
Personal and Secret

Further to paragraph 1 of my No. 251, my later information[3] shows that the German plans for sending shipping to the Caspian by rail have been suspended.

[1] The use of the nomenclature of 'Pilot Officer', 'Flying Officer' etc. for non-flying ranks was not unique to the RAF Regiment. The same practice applied to those serving in other ground-based divisions of the RAF, such as technical support, mechanical transport, RAF police, and administration.

[2] 'Beaverbrook came to see AE last night to tell him about the PM's suggestion that he should go to Moscow. PM was hunting about for someone to send and mentioned Lyttelton and then AE himself and when Beaverbrook said he didn't think the first would do or AE could be spared from here, PM suggested that B should go himself and told him to talk it over with AE. B made it quite clear to PM he didn't wish to go.

'B then went on to talk to AE about the future here. He said the PM was a "bent" man and couldn't be expected to last long. He had not been the same since his last journey. The future belonged to AE "but be careful of the Tory Party. Don't be too hard on them. Say what you like about the brave new world, but don't talk too much about controls after the war."

'AE was much intrigued and amused by this conversation and he asked me what I thought was the B's motive, which baffled him. I said I thought he had been looking round to see who would be the successor to Winston and found that AE was the best runner. He hated Cripps. He wishes therefore to pose as AE's patron and backer, and then no doubt when AE became PM, he would hope to run him' (*The War Diaries of Oliver Harvey*, pages 167–8).

[3] From Enigma.

Winston S. Churchill to General Sir Harold Alexander
(Churchill papers, 20/81)

10 October 1942
Private

ACTION AT MUNASSIB

Your CS/1570. Thank you very much. I was anxious to know what lay behind the crust. The raid of the Sussex also seemed to be very good. If you think it worth while, give my compliments to the company concerned.

2. You will no doubt have seen the recent highly satisfactory MK[1] about enemy shortages and sickness. Everything is rolling forward here.

3. Hope you will see something of Duncan Sandys during his visit. Every good wish.

President Franklin D. Roosevelt to Winston S. Churchill
(Churchill papers, 20/81)

10 October 1942
Most Secret
Personal
No. 194

Replying to your 163 I am making a radio disc immediately and incidentally while your French grammar is better than mine my accent is most alluring.

Roosevelt

Clementine Churchill to Winston S. Churchill
(Baroness Spencer-Churchill papers)

10 October 1942   10 Downing Street

My Darling,

I'm having a bad disappointment: I have a cold & sore throat & now my temperature has begun to rise indicating a slight influenza – so I can't come up for the Edinborough function. I was to have travelled up last night with Eva Rosebery[2] & had to send her a note at the last moment to

---

[1] MK: the prefix given to the special messages from the Bletchley decoding centre.

[2] Eva Isabel Marion Bruce, 1892–1987. Daughter of Henry Bruce, 2nd Baron Aberdare, and his wife Constance. Married, first, Algernon Strutt, 3rd Baron Belper, 1911 (divorced, 1922); second,

the train. Then – I hoped to travel up tonight arriving at Dalmeny Sunday morning. But I cannot. Wow! I did so much want to see you receive the Freedom of Edinburgh – my native capital! except that like Lady Baldwin[1] I'm really a London born cockney! Don't forget if you contact Eva Rosebery that she is Lady Digby's sister & therefore Pamela's Aunt.

Pamela is taking the Baby[2] down to Chequers on Monday & staying the night & settling him & his Nanny there for 3 weeks or so.

I'm sending this up & I'm told you will get it tomorrow Sunday afternoon – I hope I will be getting better by then.

Tender Love my Darling & I hope you are better throat & all.

Your loving
CLEMMIE
drooping [drawing of cat] Cat

Winston S. Churchill to Clement Attlee
(Churchill papers, 20/67)

11 October 1942

DIEPPE AND CHANNEL ISLAND CHAININGS[3]

I earnestly hope my colleagues will not be led by this specious pretext up the paths of appeasement. For us to invite, at German dictation, a neutral State to examine the conduct of our troops in the field would be to accept humiliation which I am certain would arouse the deepest anger in Britain and also in Russia. Any such process is only a step to mediate peace. I must warn my colleagues against these dangers in the face of a faithless and merciless enemy.

Albert Primrose, 6th Earl of Rosebery, 1924. Justice of the Peace for Buckinghamshire. Created Dame, 1955.

[1] Lucy Ridsdale, 1859–1945. Daughter of Edward Lucas Jenks Ridsdale and Esther Lucy Thacker of Rottingdean. Married, 1892, Stanley Baldwin (Prime Minister, 1923–4, 1924–9, 1935–7). A keen dancer and sportswoman; member of the White Heather Club, the first women's cricket club. Created Dame, 1937. Styled as Countess of Bewdley, 1937. Founder of the Anaesthetics Appeal Fund of the National Birthday Trust Fund and associated with the Lucy Baldwin machine for self-administration of nitrous-oxide/oxygen analgesia in obstetrics. Involved in Young Women's Christian Association and other charitable bodies for women.

[2] The younger Winston Churchill, Randolph and Pamela's son, born 1940.

[3] During the Dieppe raid of August 19, Allied troops tied the hands of some captured German soldiers. In response, Germany chained 1,376 prisoners of war. Britain and Canada subsequently chained up an equal number of German prisoners. The Canadian High Commissioner suggested the neutral Swiss investigate in order to resolve the issue. On December 12, Britain and Canada released the Axis prisoners from their chains. The Nazis refused to follow suit.

2. I think we should wait and see what happens. The Germans have made a great mistake in threatening to chain three times as many. It will expose them to considerable administrative difficulties, and should they push matters as far and numbers become very large they will lose much-needed labour in the fields and mines. There would be no objection to the protecting power ascertaining from both sides the numbers actually chained, the methods of chaining, whether this is temporary or permanent, &c.

3. We must not on any account put ourselves in the position where the Germans can blackmail us, by threatening to maltreat our prisoners, into having neutral enquiries into all methods of waging war. But that is what would happen if we were to accept the pusillanimous line suggested by the Canadian Government. We have far more at stake numerically than all the Dominions together. I hope, therefore, that the Cabinet will on no account weaken.

Winston S. Churchill to Clement Attlee
(Churchill papers, 20/67)

11 October 1942

FURTHER NOTE

Two entirely different questions are raised. First, the treatment of prisoners of war; and secondly the conduct of troops fighting in the field.

The laws of war expressly forbid the linking of the treatment of prisoners of war with the incidents of fighting in the field.

We could never admit the right of the enemy to claim that a neutral should sit in judgment on the conduct of our troops in the field. To do so would enable this procedure to be put into operation by Germany whenever they were dissatisfied with the way in which the fighting was carried on.

What would the Germans say if we asked that a neutral power should sit in judgment on the manner in which they have treated the Russian prisoners, whom they have shot by scores of thousands in cold blood; or Yugoslav prisoners upon whom the most frightful atrocities have been inflicted?

Winston S. Churchill: speech
(BBC Written Archives Centre)

12 October 1942   Usher Hall
Edinburgh

FREEDOM OF THE CITY OF EDINBURGH

I have never before been made a Freeman of any city, and though, during the War, I have been complimented by a number of invitations which I greatly value, your Freedom is the only one I have felt for myself so far able to receive in the hard press of events. It seemed to me that Edinburgh, the ancient capital of Scotland, enshrined in the affections of the Scottish race all over the world, rich in memories and tradition, immortal in its collective personality, stands by itself; and therefore I am here today to be refreshed by your very great kindness and inspiration, and to receive the all too flattering tribute from my old friend, Willie Y. Darling, your Lord Provost.[1]

The old quarrels, the age-old feuds which rent our island, have been ended centuries ago by the Union of the Crowns, and by the happy fulfilment of the prophecy that wherever the Stone of Scone shall rest the Scottish race shall reign.

The whole British Empire, and most of all, the United Kingdom of Great Britain and Northern Ireland, owes an inestimable debt to our King and Queen. In these years of trial and storm they have shared to the full the perils, the labours, the sorrows and the hopes of the British nation. I have seen the King, gay, buoyant and confident, when the stones and rubble of Buckingham Palace lay newly scattered in heaps upon its lawns. We even today are mourning the King's brother, who was killed on active service on a Highland hillside. You here in Scotland and in Edinburgh must especially rejoice in the charm and grace of a Scottish Queen whom Scotland has given to us all for this time of crisis.

I could not, as First Minister, come to Edinburgh, a city which has always been proud of its Royal connection, without expressing your sentiments of

---

[1] William Young Darling, 1885–1962. Educated at James Gillespie's School, Daniel Stewart's College and Heriot-Watt College, Edinburgh University. Trained for business in Edinburgh and London; held variety of appointments in Ceylon and Australia up to 1913. Enlisted in the ranks of the Black Watch, 1914; commissioned in the Royal Scots. Served 1915–17 in France, Salonika, Gallipoli (evacuation), Egypt (Military Cross and bar, despatches). ADC, 1918–19, in France, Belgium, and Germany. Served in Ireland, 1920–2. Resumed business career, 1922. Member, Edinburgh Town Council, 1933; City Treasurer, 1937–40. National Government Candidate, West Lothian, 1937. Chief Air Raid Warden, 1938–9. District Commissioner, South Eastern Scotland, 1939–41. Lord Provost of Edinburgh, 1941–4. Chairman, Scottish Council on Industry, 1942–6. Director, Royal Bank of Scotland, 1942–57. Conservative MP for South Edinburgh, 1945–57.

loyalty and devotion to our beloved Sovereign and his Consort, and paying them the tribute which their virtues and their actions alike deserve.

I come to you straight from a visit to the Fleet. I have spent the last few days going over a great many of our ships, some great, some small, some fresh from action in the Mediterranean, others from fighting their way through with the Russian convoys. I could not imagine a greater contrast between this Fleet in a harbour somewhere in Scotland and the Desert Army which I was visiting for two or three days some seven weeks ago. The scene, the light, the colour, the elements, the uniforms, the weapons, all were utterly different, but there was one feature which was not different – the spirit was the same. The Desert Army was confident that it would stand an unbreakable barrier between Rommel and the Nile Valley, and the Fleet is sure that once again it will stand between Continental tyrant and the dominion of the world.

I have myself some ties with Scotland which are to me of great significance – ties precious and lasting. First of all, I decided to be born on St. Andrew's Day – and it was to Scotland I went to find my wife, who is deeply grieved not to be here today through temporary indisposition. I commanded a Scottish battalion of the famous 21st Regiment for five months in the line in France in the last war. I sat for 15 years as the representative of 'Bonnie Dundee', and I might be sitting for it still if the matter had rested entirely with me. But although I have found what I trust is a permanent happy home in the glades of Epping Forest, I still preserve affectionate memories of the banks of the Tay. Well, here you will admit are some ties to unite me to Scotland, and now today you have given me a new one which I shall value as long as I live.

We call ourselves in our grand alliance the United Nations. Here, indeed, in Scotland is an example of national unity. Our present Secretary of State, our good and faithful friend, Tom Johnston, has inaugurated a notable experiment in forming an unofficial All-Party Council of State of which every living ex-Secretary of State for Scotland[1] is a member. Such brotherhood and comradeship have yielded excellent results.

---

[1] The office of Secretary of State for Scotland lay vacant from 1746 until 1885, when a new office of Secretary for Scotland was created. This was upgraded in 1926 to the original title of Secretary of State for Scotland. Since 1885 there had been 23 incumbents, of whom six were still living on 12 October 1942. These were Robert Munro, later 1st Baron Alness (Liberal), 1916–22; Archibald Sinclair, Viscount Thurso (Leader of the Liberal Party), 1931–2; Walter Elliot (Scottish Unionist), 1936–8; David John Colville, later 1st Baron Clydesmuir (Scottish Tory), 1938–40; Ernest Brown (Leader of the Liberal Nationals), 1940–1; and Thomas Johnston (Labour), 8 February 1941 to 23 May 1945.

From every quarter come reports that the people of Scotland are in good heart. They are also, I am glad to learn, in good health. Here, in the fourth year of the world war, more people in Scotland are getting three square meals than ever before was known. In Glasgow, the school medical authorities report that in the last year, 1941, the latest for which we have received the figures, the average net increase in the weight of school entrants above the figures for the five years 1935–1939 was 1 lb. And boys of 13 years of age were nearly 3 lbs. heavier than those in the same period before the war.

The whole country is pulling together as it has never done before in its history. Cruel blows like the loss of the original 51st Division in France have been borne with fortitude and silent dignity. A new 51st Division has been born, and will sustain the reputation and avenge the fortunes of its forerunner. The air bombing was endured with courage and resource. In all the Services, air and land and sea, in the merchant ships, in all the many forms of service which this great struggle has called forth, Scotsmen have gained distinction. You may indeed repeat with assurance the poet's lines:

> Gin dangers dare we'll thole our share,
> Gie's but the weapons, we've the will
> Beyont the main to prove again
> Auld Scotland counts for something still.[1]

Let us then for a moment cross the main and take a wider view. Our enemies have been more talkative lately. Ribbentrop, Göring, Hitler have all been making speeches which are of interest because they reveal with considerable frankness their state of mind.

There is one note which rings though all these speeches; it can be clearly heard above their customary boastings and threats – the dull, low, whining note of fear. They are all speeches of men conscious of guilt and conscious also of the law. How different from the tone of 1940 when France was struck down, when Western Europe was subjugated, when Mussolini hastened to stab us in the back, when Britain stood all alone, the sole champion in arms for the freedom and inheritance of mankind! How different are these plaintive speeches and expostulations from what we used to hear in those days!

Evidently something has happened in these two years to make these evildoers feel that aggression, war, bloodshed, the trampling down of the weak, may not be after all the whole story. There may be another

---

[1] These are the last four lines of 'A Sough o' War' ['A Sigh of War'] by Charles Murray

side to the account. It is a long account, and it is becoming pretty clear that the day is coming when it will have to be settled. The most striking and curious part of Hitler's speech was his complaint that no one pays sufficient attention to his victories.

'Look at all the victories I have won,' he exclaims in effect. 'Look at all the countries I have invaded and struck down. Look at the thousands of kilometres that I have advanced into the lands of other people. Look at the booty I have gathered, and all the men I have killed and captured. Contrast these exploits with the performances of the Allies. Why are they not down-hearted and dismayed? How do they dare to keep up their spirits in the face of my great success and their many misfortunes?'

I have not quoted his actual words. I have given their meaning and their sense. That is his complaint. This is the question which puzzles him and angers him. It strikes a chill into his marrow, because in his heart he knows that with all his tremendous victories and vast conquests his fortunes have declined, his prospects have darkened to an immeasurable degree in the last two years, while at the same time Britain, the United States, Russia, and China have moved forward through tribulation and sorrow, steadily forward, steadily onward, from strength to strength. He sees with chagrin and amazement that our defeats are but stepping-stones to victory, and that his victories are only the stepping-stones to ruin.

It was apparent to me that this bad man saw quite clearly the shadow of slowly and remorselessly approaching doom, and he railed at fortune for mocking him with the glitter of fleeing success. But, after all, the explanation is not difficult.

When peaceful nations like the British and the Americans, very careless in peacetime about their defences, care-free, unsuspecting nations, peoples who have never known defeat – improvident nations I will say, feckless nations, nations who despise the military art and thought war so wicked that it could never happen again – when nations like these are set upon by highly-organised, heavily-armed conspirators, planning and calculating in secret for years on end, exalting war as the highest form of human effort, glorifying slaughter and aggression, prepared and trained to the last point science and discipline can carry them, is it not natural that the peaceful, unprepared, improvident peoples should suffer terribly and that the wicked, scheming aggressors should have their reign of savage exaltation?

Ah! But that is not the end of the story. It is only the first chapter. If the great, peaceful Democracies could survive the few years of the aggressors' attack, another chapter had to be written. It is to that chapter we shall come in due time.

It will ever be the glory of this Island and its Empire that we stood alone for one whole year of mortal peril, and gained the time for the good cause to arm, to organise and slowly bring the conjoined, united, irresistible forces of outraged civilisation to bear upon the criminals. That is our greatest glory.

Fear is the motive which inspires Hitler's latest outrages. From the North Cape in Norway to the Spanish frontier near Bayonne, a distance apart from its inner indentations of nearly 2,000 miles, the German invading armies are holding down by brute force and terrorism the nations of Western Europe. Norway, Denmark, Holland, Belgium, France – all are in Hitler's grip, all are seething with the spirit of revolt and revolution. Except in Denmark, whose turn will come,[1] the Nazi firing parties are busy. Every day innocent hostages and prominent citizens are arrested haphazard and taken out and shot in cold blood, and every day hatred of the German race and name burns fiercer in the hearts of these ancient, famous States and peoples.

The British Commando raids at different points along this enormous length of coast, although so far only the forerunner of what is to come, inspire the author of so many crimes and miseries with lively anxiety. His soldiers dwell among populations who would kill them with their hands if they got the chance, and will kill them one at a time when they do get the chance. In addition, there comes out of the sea from time to time a hand of steel which plucks the German sentries from their posts with growing efficiency, amid the joy of the whole countryside.

In his fear and spite, Hitler turns upon the prisoners of war who are in his camps and in his power, just as he takes innocent hostages from his prisons in Norway, Belgium, Holland, France, to shoot them in the hope of breaking the spirit of their countrymen. So in flattest breach of the few conventions which still hold across the lines of world war, he vents his cruel fear and anger upon the prisoners of war and casts them in chains. I have always expected that this war would become worse in severity as the guilty Nazis feel the ring of doom remorselessly closing in upon them. Here in the West we have seen many savage, bestial acts, but nothing that has happened in the West so far can compare with the

---

[1] Organized sabotage, directed by Allied agents from Britain, against the Nazi occupation of Denmark, had begun in August 1942, and Danish resistance increased dramatically in late 1942 and into 1943. When the Danish Government rejected German demands including the trial of saboteurs in Nazi courts, it was dissolved by the Nazis on 29 August 1943 and replaced by military dictatorship.

wholesale massacre, not only of soldiers, but of civilians and women and children, which has characterised Hitler's invasion of Russia. In Russia and in his reigns of terror in Poland and Yugoslavia, tens of thousands have been murdered in cold blood by the German Army and by the special police battalions and brigades which accompany it everywhere and take a leading part in the frightful butchery perpetrated behind the front. For every one execution Hitler has ordered in the West he has carried out two hundred – it may be many more – in Eastern and Central Europe. On the first day after he entered Kiev he shot upwards of 54,000 persons.

I say to show weakness of any kind to such a man is only to encourage him to further atrocities. And you may be assured that no weakness will be shown.

There is another reason, apart from his perverted instincts, why Hitler has begun large-scale maltreatment of British prisoners of war: he wishes to throw a new topic into the arena of world discussion, and so divert men's eyes from the evident failure so far – I always say so far – of his second vast campaign against Russia.

The heroic defence of Stalingrad – the fact that the splendid Russian armies are everywhere intact, unbeaten, and unbroken, nay, counterattacking with amazing energy along the whole front from Leningrad to the Caucasus Mountains, the fearful losses suffered by the German troops, the near approach of another Russian winter – all these grim facts, which cannot be concealed, cast their freezing shadow upon the German people already wincing under the increasing impact of British bombing. The German people turn with a stony gaze upon the leader who has brought all this upon them, and dumbly, for they dare not speak aloud, they put the terrible question – 'Why did you go there? Why did you invade Russia?'

Already Field-Marshal Göring has made haste to point out that this decision was Hitler's alone, that Hitler alone conducts the war, and that the Generals of the German Army are only assistants who carry out his orders. Already Himmler, the police butcher, has been decorated, honoured and promoted in token not only of the importance of his work in shooting and hanging thousands of Russian prisoners of war and in torturing Polish, Czechoslovaks, Yugoslavs, and Greeks, but of the increasing need for his devilish arts to be employed in the homeland of Germany itself. Evidently in such a plight it would be natural for Hitler to raise a stir in some other quarter, and what could be more attractive to such a being than to mishandle captives who are powerless in his hands? There are other matters which should cause Hitler and his guilty but somewhat ridiculous confederate, Mussolini, to ask themselves uncomfortable questions.

The U-boat warfare still remains the greatest problem of the United Nations, but there is no reason whatever why it should not be solved by the prodigious measures of offence, of defence, and of replacement on which Britain, Canada and, above all, the United States, are now engaged. The months of August and September have been, I will not say the best, but the least bad months since January. These months have seen the new building of merchant ships which substantially outweigh the losses.

They have seen the greatest tonnage of British bombs dropped upon Germany. They have covered the most numerous safe arrivals of United States troops in the British Isles. They have marked a definite growth of Allied air superiority over Germany, Italy and Japan.

In these same months, far away in the Pacific, the Australians, with our American Allies, have made a good advance in New Guinea. It is not my habit to encourage light or vain expectations, but these are solid and remarkable facts.

Surveying both sides of the account – the good and the bad, with equal composure and coolness – we must see that we have reached a stern and sombre moment in the war, one which calls in a high degree for firmness of spirit and constancy of soul.

The excitement and the emotion of those great days when we stood alone and unaided against what seemed overwhelming odds and, single-handed, saved the future of the world are not present now. We are surrounded by a concourse of Governments and nations, all of us bound together in solemn unbreakable alliance, bound together by ties not only of honour but of self-preservation. We are able to plan our slow but sure march onward. Deadly dangers still beset us. Weariness, complacency, or discord, squabbles over petty natures, would mar our prospects.

We must all drive ourselves to the utmost limit of our strength. We must preserve and refine our sense of proportion. We must strive to combine the virtues of wisdom and of daring. We must move forward together, united and inexorable.

Thus, with God's blessing, the hopes which are now justified, which we are now entitled to feel, will not fail or wither. The light is broadening on the track, and the light is brighter too. Among the qualities for which Scotland is renowned, steadfastness holds perhaps the highest place.

Be steadfast, then, that is the message which I bring to you, that is my invocation to the Scottish people, here in this ancient capital city, one of whose burgesses I now have the honour to be. Let me use the words of your famous minstrel – he is here today[1] – words which have given comfort and renewed strength to many a burdened heart:

Keep right on to the end of the road,

Keep right on to the end.

Winston S. Churchill: speech
('Winston S. Churchill, His Complete Speeches', volume 6, page 6684)

12 October 1942   Edinburgh

CIVIL DEFENCE WORKERS INSPECTION

This fine sample – for it is no more than a sample – of your Air Raid Precautions, and those engaged in them, give one confidence that should the enemy renew his attacks upon our cities – as he may do in the future – Edinburgh will be prepared to meet whatever his malice may bring. I saw a statement made the other day that the attack which may be expected this winter would make all previous attacks look like a picnic. I don't agree with that. The power of the enemy is less than it was – very much less than it was, comparatively to our power and methods of dealing with enemy night raids. At the same time it seems to me possible that, having failed in other quarters, he may attempt to make some small return for the good services which we are rendering him in the continuous bombing of German towns, which will go forward on an increasing scale from now until the end of the war. But you must be ready here – and you are ready – to meet any emergency that may come, with the customary efficiency and management for which the Scottish administration and people are distinguished. I thank you.

Winston S. Churchill to General Sir Harold Alexander
(Churchill papers, 20/81)

12 October 1942

Most Secret and Private

I have given directions for more exactly textual MK's to be sent from now on. I trust you are getting all these yourself and taking all precautions.[2]

---

[1] Harry MacLennan Lauder, 1870–1950. As a boy, worked in a flax mill and then, for ten years, in a coal mine. Made his career as a comedian and songwriter. First appeared on the stage in Scotland, 1882; in London, 1900. Organized concerts for charitable purposes, 1914–18; also gave concerts on the Western Front. Knighted, 1919. His songs included 'I love a lassie' and 'Stop yer tickling, Jock'. His only son, Captain John Lauder, was killed in action on the Western Front in December 1916.

[2] Desmond Morton noted at the bottom of Churchill's telegram: 'Defence Registry. This telegram is not to be distributed. Will you please return this copy to me.'

Winston S. Churchill to Brigadier Ian Jacob[1]
(Churchill papers, 20/67)

12 October 1942

CHURCHILL TANKS

I want reports of definite authenticity. Ask for reports through the CIGS from the divisions who are using them. What are the complaints about their firing defects?

Your skinny summary adds nothing to my general knowledge.

Winston S. Churchill to Anthony Eden
(Churchill papers, 20/67)

12 October 1942

But have you seen the recent telegrams from General Platt showing the immense friction that will be caused by the abrupt or premature infusion of de Gaullists? We must gain time so as to allow 'Torch' to operate. This is in the interests of 'Torch' no less than of your policy in Madagascar.

Winston S. Churchill to Sir James Grigg
(Churchill papers, 20/56)

12 October 1942
Personal

Why should courts-martial be held in public on all occasions? Is this the law? Surely we have power to withhold publicity, on military grounds. In this case the military ground is that the publication of these cases will no doubt enhance our reputation here for the proper control of our own officers, but that the facts, detached from our treatment of them, will be used as dangerous propaganda, and also may react unfavourably upon the treatment of our numerous prisoners of war in German hands.

I have never heard of courts-martial being held in public as an ordinary rule, nor of reporters being admitted or wanting to be admitted to them.

---

[1] Military Assistant Secretary to the War Cabinet.

Sir Alexander Cadogan: diary
('The Diaries of Sir Alexander Cadogan', page 483)

12 October 1942

Cabinet 10.30 (p.m.) to discuss 'shackling' of prisoners. PM just back from Edinburgh in a silly fighting mood. On A's[1] instructions I timidly put up suggestion for appeal to Protecting Power. To my surprise, it went, and we drafted statement for PM in House tomorrow.

[...]

Winston S. Churchill: speech
(Hansard)

13 October 1942   House of Commons

His Majesty's Government have never countenanced any general order for the tying-up of prisoners on the field of battle. Such a process, however, may be necessary from time to time under stress of circumstances, and may indeed be in the best interest of the safety of the prisoners themselves. The Geneva Convention upon the treatment of prisoners of war does not attempt to regulate what happens in the actual fighting. It is confined solely to the treatment of prisoners who have been securely captured and are in the responsible charge of the hostile Government. Both His Majesty's Government and the German Government are bound by this Convention. The German Government, by throwing into chains 1,376 British prisoners of war for whose proper treatment they are responsible, have violated Article 2 of the aforesaid Convention. They are thus attempting to use prisoners of war as if they were hostages upon whom reprisals can be taken for occurrences on the field of battle with which the said prisoners can have had nothing to do. This action of the German Government affronts the sanctity of the Geneva Convention, which His Majesty's Government have always been anxious to observe punctiliously.

His Majesty's Government have therefore approached the protecting Power and invited that Power to lay before the German Government our solemn protest against this breach of the Geneva Convention and to urge them to desist from it, in which case the counter measures of a similar character which His Majesty's Government felt themselves forced to take in order to protect their prisoners of war in enemy hands will immediately be withdrawn.

[1] Anthony Eden's.

Until we learn from the protecting Power the result of his protest, I have no further statement to make upon the subject, and I should strongly deprecate any discussion which might be prejudicial to the action of the protecting Power and consequently to the interests of the prisoners of war of both belligerent countries.

Harold Nicolson: diary
('Harold Nicolson, Diaries and Letters', page 250)

13 October 1942

Winston makes a statement about the chaining of the prisoners. He has evidently realised that the House and country feel that he has made a mistake in ordering reprisals, and he announces that he has applied to the Swiss Government asking them to use their good offices. He deprecates any further discussion, and when Cunningham-Reid[1] gets up to ask a supplementary,[2] he is howled down. Winston has been with the Fleet and has wisely taken Cripps with him. The latter has returned bubbling with pleasure and renewed confidence. I do not think we shall hear any more about resignation for the moment.

Dine with Tilea. The other man there is the head of the Polish FO, Jan Wizelaki.[3] They are both much impressed by the altered tone of Hitler's speeches. It is evident to their minds that the Germans now realise they cannot win and are concentrating on the thought that they cannot lose. If our campaign in Africa comes off, then we shall win the war by next winter. If not, then it may go on till 1943. I call this most optimistic. Wizelaki calculates (having spent months on working out the figures with the military staff) that the Russian casualties (i.e. irreplaceable) must be between 6,500,000 and 7,500,000 and the German, on any computation, more than they lost in the whole of the last war.

---

[1] Alec Stratford Cunningham-Reid, 1895–1977. On active service with the Royal Engineers and Royal Flying Corps, 1914–18 (despatches, DFC). Conservative MP for Warrington, 1922–3, 1924–9; for St Marylebone, 1932–45 (sitting as an Independent, 1942–5).

[2] Cunningham-Reid's question was: 'In view of today's reported reactions from Australia can the Prime Minister say whether it is probable that any Australian prisoners in German hands have been chained?'

[3] Jan Wszelaki, 1894–1965. Polish diplomat and scholar. Served in the Polish Ministry of Foreign Affairs from 1918. Before the Second World War he held diplomatic posts in Moscow and London, and was also an economic adviser to the Polish Government. Deputy Secretary-General of the Polish Government-in-Exile in London, 1939–44. Representative in the United States of the Polish Government-in-Exile, 1944–50. A member and Executive Director of the Polish Institute of Arts and Sciences of America, 1962–5.

Winston S. Churchill: broadcast appeal
(*'Winston S. Churchill, His Complete Speeches'*, volume 6, page 6685)

13 October 1942

BOOKS FOR THE ARMED FORCES

For the men and women of the forces at home and abroad I make an appeal to which every family in the Kingdom can respond. I do not ask for money. I ask only for books, magazines, and periodicals.

If you had seen, as I have seen on my many visits to the forces, and particularly in the Middle East, the need for something to read during the long hours off duty and the pleasure and relief when that need is met, you would gladly look, and look again, through your bookshelves and give what you can. If you hesitate to part with a book which has become an old friend, you can be sure that it will be a new friend to men on active service.

The procedure is quite simple. Almost any post office will take your books and magazines if handed in unwrapped, unstamped, and unaddressed. They will then be distributed to all the services where most required. Malta, the Middle East, Iceland, and a dozen other places abroad will welcome your gifts, and there are lonely stations at home to be supplied.

Will you contribute from your shelves, and remember when you buy a book or a magazine that there are many waiting to read it after you?

Sir Alexander Cadogan: diary
(*'The Diaries of Sir Alexander Cadogan'*, page 483)

13 October 1942

[...]

Bobbety[1] tried to impress Cabinet with <u>his</u> (Colonial) difficulties. Said black official at CO had always lunched at a certain restaurant which now, because it was patronised by US Officers, kept him out. PM said 'That's all right: if he takes a banjo with him they'll think he's one of the band'! I with difficulty slipped my piece in. No one took any notice, but the eventual solution was quite sensible.

---

[1] Viscount Cranborne, Secretary of State for the Colonies.

War Cabinet: conclusions
(Cabinet papers, 65/28)

13 October 1942   Prime Minister's Room
                                                   House of Commons

(1) There was general agreement that the attitude of the United States Army to this question was a factor of great importance, which must be given due weight in determining the British attitude to coloured American troops.

(2) In particular, it was generally agreed that it was desirable that the people of this country should avoid becoming too friendly with coloured American troops.

(3) On the other hand, the recommendation made at the conclusion of the Secretary of State for War's Memorandum that the personnel of the Army, including ATS, should be educated to adopt towards the United States coloured troops the attitude of the United States Army authorities as at present worded went too far. (The Secretary of State for War[1] agreed that some amendment of his paper was called for in this respect.) While it was right that our troops and our people should be educated to know what the American attitude was, it was equally important that the Americans should recognise that we had a different problem as regards our coloured people and that *modus vivendi* between the two points of view should be found.

(4) Turning to the practical issues involved, it was agreed that we need not, and should not, object to the Americans making full use of administrative arrangements for the segregation of their coloured troops. But they must not expect our authorities, civil or military, to assist them in enforcing a policy of segregation.

(5) It was clear that, so far as concerned admission to canteens, public houses, theatres, cinemas, and so forth, there would, and must, be no restriction of the facilities hitherto extended to coloured persons as a result of the arrival of United States troops in this country.

(6) A certain number of instances had arisen in which well-intentioned persons had extended invitations to American white and coloured troops at the same time. These occurrences could be avoided if those who wished to extend hospitality to American troops were encouraged to ask for guidance or to consult the authorities before making arrangements.

---

[1] Sir James Grigg.

(7) The Secretary of State for the Colonies[1] expressed some uneasiness at the point made under (2) above, namely, that the people of this country should avoid becoming too friendly with coloured American troops. He thought that this involved some departure from the attitude hitherto adopted towards coloured British subjects who came to this country, and that there was a risk of creating an atmosphere which would give offence to the coloured people now in this country and lead to their becoming a focus of discontent when they returned to their homes in the Colonies.

(8) The suggestion was made that it would be desirable to refer in future to 'American negroes' rather than to 'United States coloured troops'.

Winston S. Churchill: engagement cards[2]
(Thompson Papers)

14 October 1942

7 p.m. Col. Bevan,[3] Col. Dudley Clarke,[4] Major Fleming.[5]

Lord Alanbrooke: recollection
('War Diaries, Field Marshal Lord Alanbrooke', page 329)

[14 October 1942]

[...] I had now received a detailed plan of Monty's attack and also probable date. He asked me to take every possible care that no details of this plan leaked out. As I had no confidence in Winston's ability to keep anything secret I decided not to tell him about this plan. I knew,

---

[1] Viscount Cranborne.

[2] For a meeting to plan deception of the enemy on a massive scale – for example, creating fake Army divisions to convince the Nazis that British North Africa was much stronger than in fact it was.

[3] Colonel John Henry Bevan, senior intelligence officer with key role in strategic deception.

[4] Dudley Wrangel Clarke, 1899–1974. Educated at Charterhouse and Royal Military Academy, Woolwich. Served in the First World War with Royal Flying Corps and Royal Artillery. Iraq Rebellion, 1920 (Medal and clasp). Palestine Rebellion, 1936 (Brevet Major, Medal and clasp). General Staff, 1936–47. Served with Middle East Forces, 1939–40; in Norway, 1940; in Mediterranean Theatre, 1940–5 (despatches, OBE, CBE, CB, Africa Star, Italy medal, US Legion of Merit). Set up deception organization known as 'A' Force. Head of Public Opinion Research Department at Conservative Central Office, 1948–52. Wrote *Seven Assignments* (1948); *The Eleventh at War* (1952); *Golden Arrow* (1955).

[5] Peter Fleming, 1907–71. Writer and intelligence officer. Elder brother of the writer Ian Fleming. Educated at Eton and Christ Church, Oxford. Joined staff of *The Spectator*, 1931. Special correspondent for *The Times*, 1932–5, travelling to Brazil and China; wrote several books on his travels. Joined staff of *The Times*, 1936. Joined Grenadier Guards, 1939. Worked in intelligence throughout the war. Appointed Head of Deception by Wavell, 1942. After the war, returned to journalistic and historial writing.

however, that I should have difficulties as Winston was continually fretting to advance the date and asking me why we were not being informed of the proposed date of attack. I had to judge between the relative importance of maintaining complete secrecy and on the other hand of stopping Winston from wiring to Alex and Monty upsetting their plans with his impatience.

War Cabinet: conclusions
(Cabinet papers, 65/28)

14 October 1942   10 Downing Street
5.30 p.m.

When the Germans had first announced their decision to tie the hands of 1,370 British prisoners, it had been necessary to reach an immediate decision as to what action we should take. The question had been brought up unexpectedly at the War Cabinet, and he offered an apology to Mr Bruce[1] that he had not been present when the matter had been considered on that occasion.

The decision to order the manacling of an equivalent number of German prisoners had given rise to a sharp division of opinion. The present position was a delicate one. We had asked the Protecting Power to lay a protest before the German Government against their breach of the Geneva Convention by attempting to use prisoners of war as hostages against whom reprisals could be taken. It was most undesirable that the matter should be the subject of public discussion at this juncture. The House of Commons on the previous day had assented to this view. If the matter could be kept quiet for a few days longer, a new situation might well arise, in which some new step might be possible. He believed that the German threat that, if we tied up 1,370 German prisoners, they would tie up three times as many had been, from the enemy's point of view, a mistake. It was surely significant that, although three days had now elapsed, there had been no announcement that this threat had been carried out. Such a step presented very serious administrative difficulties, and he expected that the German Government were now being faced with remonstrances from those who would have to carry it out.

The Prime Minister therefore hoped that the matter could be left as it stood for a day or so, no further decision being taken in the meantime. If the German Government were to say that, if we would take the

---
[1] Stanley Bruce, Representative of Australia in the British War Cabinet.

initiative and would cancel the orders given for tying the hands of 1,370 prisoners, they would do likewise, he would be ready to take the course. If, on the other, the German Government announced that they were proceeding with their intention of tying up three times as many prisoners as we had tied up, the whole matter would have to be fully considered, in consultation with the representatives of the Dominions, before any further decision was reached.

Harold Nicolson: diary
('Harold Nicolson, Diaries and Letters', page 251)

14 October 1942

[...] In the evening I get Jack Macnamara[1] to meet John Sparrow.[2] Jack feels that there is a great wastage of man-power in the Air Force and that it should be combed out. He had lunched today with Winston at Downing Street *en famille*. He had been horrified by Winston's indiscretion in front of the servants. He spoke of everything. In the end Winston agreed with Jack's view about the Air Force. Jack feels that Winston does not usually like soldiers. He was rather shocked by (a) his indiscretion; (b) his egoistic and dictatorial manner; and (c) the immense amount of port and brandy he consumed.[3]

[1] John Robert Jermain Macnamara, 1905–44. Known as 'Jack'. Educated at Haileybury; member of the Officer Training Corps. Joined the Territorial Army as a 2nd Lieutenant in the 3rd London Regiment, 1924. Conservative MP for Chelmsford, 1935. Joint Secretary, with the Liberal MP Wilfrid Roberts, of the Basque Children Committee. Colonel of the Royal Ulster Rifles (the London Irish Rifles), Italy, 1944. Killed in action during the fighting in northern Italy, December 1944. Laid to rest in Forli War Cemetery.

[2] John Hanbury Angus Sparrow, 1906–92. Educated at Winchester and New College, Oxford. Entered the Army as a Private on the outbreak of war in 1939. Commissioned in the Coldstream Guards, 1940. Moved to the War Office, 1941. Assistant Adjutant-General with special responsibility for morale. Lieutenant-Colonel. OBE, 1946. Warden of All Souls College, Oxford, 1952–77.

[3] On 15 October 1942 Colonel Macnamara wrote to Churchill: 'First of all thank you very much for so kindly asking me to lunch on Wednesday. I much appreciated it.

'I have, as you asked, put down on paper the outline of the subjects which we discussed. I have purposely avoided detail as I know that you will have so much to read. I could give details if desired.

'I feel that there is a very serious wastage of man-power in the RAF, and I feel that the RAF could transfer on loan to the Army 100,000 first class men.

'I did not mention myself, but you kindly did, and I therefore take this opportunity of reminding you that you said you would do your best to arrange for me to take an active part in this war very soon' ('Confidential', *Churchill papers, 20/97*). Churchill immediately arranged for Macnamara to be transferred to a course at the Senior Staff College. On 16 October 1942 Macnamara wrote to Churchill's Parliamentary Private Secretary, Harvie-Watt: 'Winston said he would do this for me. He said it was high time I was given a change as I had served so loyally during all the long, dull years.' Macnamara continued to hope for an active command. On 24 October 1942, Churchill wrote to General Ismay: 'I shd like to meet his desire for fighting' (*Churchill papers, 20/97*). Eventually Macnamara was appointed

Harry Hopkins to Winston S. Churchill
(Churchill papers, 20/81)

14 October 1942
Secret
Personal

I have been giving careful consideration to going to England at this time and it seems to me that there is no awfully good reason why I should make the trip now. The most serious problems with which we have to deal immediately are in the field of production and I am sure those can be ironed out between Lyttelton[1] and Nelson.[2] Nelson can not get away for a while and we are expecting Lyttelton soon and I am sure he should come along whenever it is convenient, the sooner the better.

I hope you will not get disturbed about the article in *Life* magazine. It in no sense represents American public opinion. It does represent the private views of Henry Luce, the Publisher.[3]

I have had good talks with Halifax, Dill, Macready, and Sinclair lately. The President is in good health and spirits.

There may be reasons in your mind for my coming to England at once with which I am not fully acquainted but there is so much to do here that I do not wish to come unless it is important to you and the President.

My son Robert[4] is in the Army in England.

Mrs Roosevelt is looking forward to seeing you and Clemmie. She is anxious to have a trip that is free from official business as possible. I have told her that Clemmie knows more than anybody else about the kind of things that she will want to see.

Assistant Commandant, Middle East Combined Training Centre, and then Chief of Staff to Headquarters, Land Forces Adriatic. He was killed on a visit to his old unit, the 1 London Irish Rifles.

[1] British Minister of Production.

[2] Donald Marr Nelson, Director of Priorities, United States Office of Production Management, and Executive Director of Supplies, Priorities and Allocations Board.

[3] On 12 October 1942, *Life* published an article entitled 'An Open Letter from the Editors of *Life* to the People of England'. It was critical of Britain's colonial policies and accused it of failing to see the bigger picture, warning: 'If your strategists are planning a war to hold the British Empire together they will sooner or later find themselves strategizing alone . . . this is a war by free men to establish freedom more firmly, and over a wider area, on this earth.'

[4] Robert Hopkins, 1921–2007. One of Harry Hopkins' three sons. Educated at the University of North Carolina. Worked as a researcher for the 'March of Time' newsreel service until volunteering for the Army at the outset of the Second World War. Served in the Signal Corps as a photographer and cameraman in North Africa. Filmed the Casablanca Conference between President Roosevelt and Prime Minister Winston Churchill, 1943. Recorded Allied campaigns in Sicily and other parts of Italy, 1943–4, and the meetings of Roosevelt, Churchill, and Stalin in Teheran and Yalta, 1945. Sent to England in 1944 to film preparations for the Normandy invasion. After the war, worked in Hollywood as a screenwriter at 20th Century Fox Film Corporation; as a radio producer for the Marshall Plan in Paris; and as a writer of *Fodor's Guide to France*. In the 1950s he joined the CIA, where he worked until his retirement in 1980. After retirement he set up the Harry Hopkins Public Service Institute in Washington.

Your femme General Knox[1] has been here. All your British Officers seem to be marrying American gals but this time the gals haven't any money repeat any money.

Give my love to Clemmie.

Harry

Winston S. Churchill to Admiral John Tovey[2]
(Churchill papers, 20/81)

14 October 1942
Personal and Most Secret

I greatly enjoyed my visit to the Fleet, and all of us are most grateful to you for your hospitality.

Admiral John Tovey to Winston S. Churchill
(Churchill papers, 20/81)

15 October 1942
Personal

Thank you for your kind message. It is good to know that your brief stay with us provided a refreshing break for you, but it is for us to thank you both for the privilege of entertaining you and for the honour conferred on the Fleet by the visit of yourself and the Lord Privy Seal. Your presence with us has been an encouragement and inspiration to all.

Winston S. Churchill to Admiral of the Fleet Sir Dudley Pound
(Churchill papers, 20/67)

15 October 1942
Action this Day

See Admiral Harwood's[3] telegram about the French Fleet in Alexandria. We want to get them on our side as 'Lightfoot'[4] and 'Torch'[5] develop. Superior force is a powerful persuader. Pray consider urgently sending *Warspite* or *Valiant* from Kilindini to arrive at Alexandria a few

[1] Jean Marcia Marshall, 1908–93. Daughter of G. G. Leith Marshall. Wife of Squadron-Leader G. R. M. Knox. Temporary Chief Controller, and War Substantive Controller, Auxiliary Territorial Service, 1941–3. Held the rank of Major-General. CBE, 1943. Visited the White House at the time Hopkins wrote to Churchill. In 1945 she married the 3rd Baron Swaythling (Stuart Albert Samuel Montagu).

[2] Commander-in-Chief, Home Fleet.

[3] Vice-Admiral and Commander-in-Chief, Mediterranean Station.

[4] 'Lightfoot': the 8th Army's imminent operations in the Western Desert.

[5] 'Torch': the Allied landings in French North Africa, also planned for autumn 1942.

days before 'Torch' or in whatever is in the best timing. Harwood could send a few destroyers from his scanty stock to pick her up in the Red Sea, if possible in the Gulf of Aden. She is a fast ship and could look after herself up to there. I hate to see ships standing idle at a crisis. According to my ideas the whole lot should go, including the carrier. The appearance of this fleet at Alexandria would start up all these ideas about Crete and Italy which are helpful to 'Torch'. How many destroyers has Harwood got and how far south could they get in time?

Winston S. Churchill to Sir James Grigg
(Churchill papers, 20/67)

15 October 1942

It has been reported to me by an officer now serving with the Royal Air Force Regiment in Ireland that American officers are never invited to British officers' messes, either Army or RAF, and that Americans are, generally speaking, left to fend for themselves. This is a grave reflection on our comradeship and common courtesy.

Pray let me have a report.

Winston S. Churchill to General Wladyslaw Sikorski[1]
(Churchill papers, 20/54)

15 October 1942

My dear General,

Thank you so much for your letter of the 13th October and for being so kind as to send me the beautifully worked Polish shield as a present from the First Rifle Brigade in memory of your visit and mine to the Polish Army in Scotland.[2]

I particularly enjoyed the visit which we paid together to your troops and am so glad to possess this fine piece of workmanship to remind me of it. Will you please convey to the Officers and men of the First Rifle Brigade my warm thanks for sending it to me.

Yours very sincerely,
Winston S. Churchill

---

[1] Prime Minister of the Polish Government-in-Exile and Commander-in-Chief of the Polish Army.

[2] A gilt shield, set with an oval icon of the Madonna and Child. The presentation inscription on the reverse reads: 'In memory of the visit of the Polish Army in Scotland, from the 1st Rifle Brigade. October 23rd 1940.'

Winston S. Churchill to Harry Hopkins
(Churchill papers, 20/81)

16 October 1942
Personal and Secret

We are, of course, frightfully anxious about the future American Air Programme and what our assignments in it are to be. We thought that a qualitative review was much more necessary than stepping up the total target figures. Winant and Averell are both deeply informed on these matters and have, no doubt, been in communication with the President. At their suggestion I got into touch with Rickenbacker[1] and found that he and I were in pretty close agreement, first on the great importance of the United States being prepared if necessary for the immediate development of bombers suitable for use at night; and, secondly, on the urgency of developing production of the Mustang Fighter with Merlin 61 and later the Griffin engine. This, in Portal's view, would be far ahead of anything in the fighter line you have in hand. Whether the Fortresses and Liberators will be able to bomb far into Germany by day is one of the great tactical questions of the war and one that is at present unanswered. If the answer should unhappily be negative, and if it proves impossible to suppress the revealing flames from the exhausts, then I am afraid that much of your vast future production of these types may be unsuitable for the decisive European theatre for which the highest possible performance in fighters is also necessary.

2. I must also say to you, for your eye alone and only to be used by you in your high discretion, that the very accurate results so far achieved in the daylight bombing of France by your Fortresses under most numerous fighter escort, mainly British, does not give our experts the same confidence as yours in the power of the day bomber to operate far into Germany. We do not think the claims of fighters shot down by Fortresses are correct, though made with complete sincerity, and the dangers of daylight bombing will increase terribly once outside fighter protection and as the range lengthens. It is of next year and 1944 I am thinking rather than this. There is the utmost goodwill and comradeship between all ranks of both our Services, and, of course, the views we have formed may be wrong. All the same, I am deeply concerned, and as these mat-

---

[1] Edward Vernon Rickenbacker, 1890–1973. Known as 'Eddie'. Joined US Army, 1917. Top US fighter ace of the First World War. During the Second World War, worked for the United States Government to encourage support for the war among both civilians and the military. Visited Britain in 1942 on an official mission authorized by Henry L. Stimson, United States Secretary of War.

ters are so deadly and there is such danger of giving offence, I wanted greatly to go into it all with you while time remains and before large mass production is finally fixed.

3. I am also oppressed with the heavy U-boat sinkings and the biting need for more long-range aircraft to harry the U-boats in their passage out and home from the Biscay ports and northabout between Iceland and the Faroes, and to strike at the packs collecting round the slow convoys in mid-Atlantic. It would be of the greatest possible help to us if you could give us at least another 50 Liberators fitted with your latest short-wave ASV[1] to help the direct offensive against U-boats, which is complementary to the important bombing of the building yards and Biscay bases, and enables us to sink an occasional crew as well as destroying and often damaging the vessels. I fear this also would be a ticklish matter to raise, but if these additional 50 Liberators were sent over at once they would not only be of great value in the U-boat campaign but would undoubtedly play an important part in ensuring the safety of the 'Torch' convoys.

4. As you have so much to do in Washington I could not press you to come during these critical days, unless you feel the need from what I have said. I will, therefore, send Lyttelton, who will be armed with precise figures, towards the beginning of November and with him either Portal or Freeman, in order to discuss both the munitions programme and the air policy. Let me know if this will be in time and before binding final commitments are made.

5. I was riled by the Brokaws disagreeable views,[2] but was comforted by the vigorous American rejoinders which were made to them. I am so glad to learn the President is in good health and spirits. We shall need all our buoyancy in the near future, about which my hopes are high.

6. I am hoping Mrs Roosevelt will stay with us at Chequers for her first weekend, and am concerting plans with Winant which I think she will like. Clemmie is looking forward so much to meeting her. I am getting into touch with Robert[3] at once.

Kindest regards to you both.

---

[1] ASV: Air to Surface Vessel, radar for maritime patrol aircraft.
[2] The reference is to Henry Luce, Founder and Editor of *Life*, and his wife Clare Booth Luce (née Brokaw), who wrote articles for the magazine.
[3] Hopkins' son, at this point serving with the Army in England.

Winston S. Churchill to General Sir William Platt
(Churchill papers, 20/81)

16 October 1942

I take this opportunity of offering you my most cordial congratulations upon the success of your Madagascar task. Exceptional zeal and enterprise were shown by you and the naval authorities in undertaking this campaign in spite of the very great reductions you had to suffer in the forces available. The efficiency and thoroughness with which the operations were prepared, and the speed and vigour with which they were carried though, are highly creditable to all ranks, in particular to your staff and above all to yourself.

2. Please let me have your advice as to when this message should be published.

Winston S. Churchill to General Hastings Ismay
(Churchill papers, 20/67)

16 October 1942

Please make sure that I have a daily report on the Russian weather conditions along the whole front at Murmansk, Archangel, Leningrad, Moscow, Stalingrad, and in the Caucasus. The best possible will do.

Winston S. Churchill to Anthony Eden
(Churchill papers, 20/67)

16 October 1942
Action this Day

TIMING (GENERAL LEGENTILHOMME AND GENERAL DE GAULLE: MADAGASCAR)[1]

Some of these telegrams I have seen to General Platt make me fear we are getting on a bit too quickly. Please let me have your reply to my

---

[1] See Oliver Harvey's diary entry of 18 May 1942, reproduced at page 688 above. In his minute 'Timing' (*Churchill papers, 20/67*), Churchill sets out a proposed timetable for the installation of General Legentilhomme as Governor of Madagascar: '1. Tell French leaders by "the middle of next week" (around 21 October) that the British find it agreeable to have Legentilhomme become governor of Madagascar. 2. "A little later" Legentilhomme could be installed without setting up a new administration. 3. About "the middle of November" de Gaulle can announce that he appointed Legentilhomme as governor.'

minute about 'Timing'. Madagascar must be the sop to soothe de Gaulle for not being in 'Torch', and must not be given prematurely.

2. The first thing is to feed Legentilhomme up to him gently and hang the preliminary discussion on Legentilhomme's personality. This would be much better than drawing up detailed agreements.

Pray let me hear from you.

Winston S. Churchill to Sir Archibald Sinclair
(Churchill papers, 20/67)

16 October 1942
Secret

RAISING BOMBER COMMAND TO 50 SQUADRONS

I agree that the development of the Airborne Division may be retarded for two months within the limits you suggest; but it will certainly have to be expanded and pressed forward in the spring, as it may have a great strategic and political rôle to play in the summer of 1943.

2. I hope it will not be necessary to withdraw any of the airmen now lent to industry except in very special cases of key men, without whom more bombers cannot be flown. Anyhow this should be the last source to tap.

3. Subject to the above, your proposals seem to me admirably conceived to secure the massive war objective in view. The papers must now be brought before the Chiefs of Staffs Committee, as both the other Services are affected.

Anthony Eden: recollection
('The Eden Memoirs, The Reckoning', page 344)

17 October 1942

We reached London and met, at No.10 Downing Street, Lieutenant-General Dwight D. Eisenhower, Allied Commander-in-Chief, Major-General Mark Clark, his deputy, and Brigadier-General Bedell Smith, his Chief of Staff. Our own Chiefs of Staff also attended and we agreed that contact should be made with Giraud[1] only, but that there would be no change in the chain of command for 'Torch'. Giraud's representatives in

---

[1] Henri-Honoré Giraud: former commander of the French 7th Army who would go on to command United French Armed Forces, 1943–4.

Algiers having suggested that a secret American mission should be sent to meet them, General Clark was asked to handle this.

Winston S. Churchill to Josef Stalin
(Churchill papers, 20/81)

18 October 1942
Most Secret and Personal

Please convey following from Prime Minister to Premier Stalin.
Begins.
My 268.
I should have added that the 150 Spitfires are all armed with 2 cannons and 4 machine guns.
Ends.

Winston S. Churchill to President Franklin D. Roosevelt
(Churchill papers, 20/81)

18 October 1942
Personal and Secret
No. 168

I am perturbed by the 100 Octane position. Demands increase and stocks diminish. Your authorities are considering proposals to increase plant capacity beyond present programme and to accelerate plant construction already under way. This is necessary to meet demands on a basis agreed by your Air Staff and ours. Can you hasten a favourable decision and so ease our anxieties about the United Kingdom, Egypt and India?

Winston S. Churchill to Lord Cranborne
(Churchill papers, 20/67)

18 October 1942

COMBINED PUBLICITY FOR THE THREE ARMED SERVICES

This would mean a very great derangement and disturbance out of all proportion to the results in view. Each Service Department would put up a desperate fight for its own publicity, especially in the Air Ministry. I do not think it is going badly as it is, although the Air Ministry are very conscientious in filling up their daily advertising space whether much has happened or not.

Upon the whole, therefore, my feeling is that it is better not to make a change. I have, however, marked your paper to the COS Committee. There is, of course, tremendous pressure at the present moment.

Winston S. Churchill to Anthony Eden
(Churchill papers, 20/67)

18 October 1942

'THE FOUR-POWER PLAN'; 'ORGANISATION OF THE WORLD
AFTER THE WAR'

Naturally, many people have views on these topics and I have no doubt I myself shall find something to say about them when the time comes.

Any conclusions drawn now are sure to have little relation to what will happen. It is even dangerous to discuss some aspects of the problem, for instance, the position of Russia. It may be that the problem will be simplified because the collapse of Hitler would still leave heavy campaigns to be undertaken against Japan. We should aid the United States to the utmost in this great American interest, and a successful joint war against Japan would form a very good background for collaboration about the settlement of Europe, the British Empire, India and other things like that. Meanwhile, I hope that these speculative studies will be entrusted mainly to those on whose hands time hangs heavy, and that we shall not overlook Mrs Glass's[1] Cookery Book recipe for jugged hare – 'First catch your hare'.

Oliver Harvey: diary
('The War Diaries of Oliver Harvey', page 170)

19 October 1942

PM, to whom AE handed a copy of his paper on Four Power post-war policy on Friday, has sent a foolish and denigrating minute, hoping that such matters be left to those who have nothing else to do. Unfortunately the three, the PM, Smuts and AE weren't able to have the discussion

---

[1] Hannah Glasse was the author of a popular treatise on cookery, *The Art of Cookery, Made Plain and Easy*, first published in 1747, in which the extravagance of French cooks was severely condemned. The proverb 'First catch your hare' is not found in her book, but (as the *Dictionary of National Biography* notes) 'her words "Take your hare when it is cased" [i.e. skinned] may have suggested it'.

about it I had hoped. 'Torch' affairs intervened and they talked of little else. AE is much annoyed at this further example of the PM's blockading of postwar questions and means to send a firm reply. We must get on with this.

Winston S. Churchill to Admiral of the Fleet Sir Dudley Pound
(Churchill papers, 20/67)

19 October 1942
Secret

'THE NEEDS OF THE NAVY'

Your DC (S) (42) 88, paragraph 23, last sentence. Surely it is misleading to group 'destroyers and larger types' in a paper which centres mainly on the anti-U-boat war? The destroyers must be considered with corvettes, sloops, armed trawlers, &c. Let me now have your total numbers of the above:

(*a*) built and building,
(*b*) in service   January 1, 1942
                   January 1, 1943
                   July 1, 1943
                   January 1, 1944

Anybody reading the sentence referred to in its context would think that we should be no stronger actually (I do not mean relatively) in anti-U-boat craft in January 1944 than today.

2. I was concerned about the future development of our anti-U-boat flotillas, but was reassured by an Admiralty statement showing the immense increase in A/S craft of all kinds expected from the United States, apart from our own construction during 1943. You have not reported to me any diversion of these by the United States Government.

3. By all means, if you wish, make a similar calculation for the strength of the Fleet at the dates mentioned in vessels larger than destroyers. Show also what losses you expect in each class on the basis of previous losses. I must say that we cannot be sure that we shall lose an equal number of battleships each year. We might lose more, or we might lose less. Losses in cruisers and aircraft carriers, as well as destroyers and anti-U-boat craft, may average out fairly evenly.

4. With regard to the aircraft carriers, there is no dispute that you should have as many as you can get, both by home conversion and from the United States. I understood that the Admiralty were satisfied that their

needs were being met in this respect as far as was humanly possible. I am not aware that your programme of aircraft carrier construction has been restricted. On the contrary, was it not the Cabinet who pressed you to add it the other day? I am ready at any time to consider methods of increasing the number above the 28 which you expect to have at the end of 1943.

5. *Paragraph* 25. Have you made any allowance for monthly losses in the estimate, and also for damage done to the enemy constructional yards and training establishments by our bomber offensive?

6. *Paragraph* 26. You say there will only be 600 escort vessels (which I presume are the same as A/S vessels) out of 1,050 required in British operational areas. What is the comparable figure today?

7. *Paragraph* 27, *last sentence.* It is new to me that the opening up of the Mediterranean will be a heavy blow to the Navy. I had always thought it was one of the greatest boons. Undoubtedly the North African coast will require to be strongly manned with Coastal aircraft so as to give fighter protection to convoys going through. But if our campaign in the Mediterranean theatre should prosper, these forces will move northwards and the enemy's power be eradicated with immense easement both to our air and sea resources.

8. *Paragraph* 29. An Admiralty paper which says: 'We secured the United Kingdom from invasion' runs the risk of being thought to overlook the part played in 1940, and indeed at the present time, by the RAF.

9. *Paragraph* 40. In my opinion, the Admiralty are themselves very largely to blame for the present unsatisfactory condition of the aircraft of the Fleet Air Arm. I should at any time have been ready to help secure deliveries, but by not having a clear view of what was wanted, by repeated alterations, and the attempt to pile up inordinate reserves, you have somewhat crippled yourselves. Our latest discussion on this subject was about inordinate reserves. If there are any other measures required to overtake the arrears in naval aircraft, please bring them forward, and I will myself take it up with MAP.

10. *Paragraph* 40. *Sub-Section* (*iii*). I should be glad to know what is involved in the new air stations and minor repair yards at home and abroad, and what are the estimates of the personnel and cost required for them. I am referring the air claims which you make to the Air Ministry for their comments.

11. Generally speaking, I do not think there was any need to deploy all the arguments about the importance of sea power and sea communications in order to advance a series of proposals which could quite well have been considered on their merits. Everyone knows that the U-boat menace

remains our greatest danger. I am certainly prepared to assist you in the specific needs which you state, but I doubt very much whether the overriding priorities which you ask for in paragraph 33 should be accorded.

Winston S. Churchill to Sir Stafford Cripps
(Churchill papers, 20/67)

19 October 1942

NAVY–AIR CO-OPERATION

It may be said of this paper 'it contains some things that are trite and some things that are true, but what is true is trite and what is not trite is not true' (Balfour).

2. I do not see what you mean by saying 'a decision ought to be arrived at'. The point at issue is not whether we should give everything to Tovey or everything to Harris. We have a great lay-out of forces, land, sea and air, in continual contact with the enemy. The emphasis has to be changed from time to time. This emphasis reduces itself in practice to comparatively small dimensions, and it is, in fact, only gradually that the bias can be altered. I endeavour to advise the Cabinet on such practical issues as emerge.

3. I do not see any need to circulate Tovey's paper. The First Lord can do so if he wishes, but he has already circulated a paper of his own covering the same ground. Tovey's paper damns itself by describing our bombing of Germany as 'a luxury' (paragraph 17). This was the Fleet Street line a few months ago.

Winston S. Churchill to General Sir Harold Alexander
(Churchill papers, 20/81)

20 October 1942
Immediate
Most Secret
'Bigot'[1]

Events are moving in our favour both in North Africa and Vichy France, and 'Torch' goes forward steadily and punctually. But all our hopes are centred upon the battle you and Montgomery are going to fight. It may well be the key to the future. Give my warmest regards to

---

[1] Code word used at the start of any telegram relating to future operations.

Montgomery and also Coningham.[1] Let me have the word ZIP[2] when you start.

[...]

Winston S. Churchill to A. V. Alexander and
Admiral of the Fleet Sir Dudley Pound
(Churchill papers, 20/67)

20 October 1942

FALL OF SINGAPORE

It is singular that Admiral Layton[3] makes no reference to the failure to provide defences for Singapore Fortress from land attack. In paragraph 29 he writes:

'... so the army retired to Singapore, which the Japanese reduced, for all that it was heavily fortified and nominally defended by nearly 100,000 troops, in a matter of 48 hours by the simple expedient of landing in the least likely places'.

This seems to be the only reference to the fortification of the Island or to the gorge of the Fortress. It is an extraordinary instance of mental blind spot which seems to have affected all concerned.

2. There is no advantage in circulating this report or entering upon correspondence with the Admiral at so busy a time. It should be put by till the end of the war.[4]

---

[1] Arthur Coningham, commanding air forces working with 8th Army in North Africa.

[2] 'ZIP': codeword used to indicate that the Second Battle of El Alamein had commenced (chosen by Churchill from 'the clothes I so often wore', specifically his favoured one-piece suit with a zipper down the front).

[3] Commander-in-Chief, China Station, 1940–2; Ceylon, 1942–5.

[4] Admiral Layton's war diary. Among the daily logs, Layton gives a detailed analysis of Allied naval strategy. He states his reasons for going into great detail about Singapore: 'I feel it is necessary to remark at some length on the operations in Malaya and the defence of Singapore for two reasons. The first is that I was the only one of the three Commanders who drew up the original Tactical Appreciation for the defence of Malaya who remained to see it put into execution. I therefore was in a unique position to see both theory and practice. The second is that, of the Commanders of Services in Malaya who were responsible for the operations in the opening weeks of the campaign, I alone remain in a position to report.'

Winston S. Churchill to Anthony Eden
(Churchill papers, 20/67)

21 October 1942

HONOURS

I trust that you will be able to meet my wishes and include a CMG for Hillgarth[1] in the next Honours List. I am surprised, indeed, that the honour asked for is so modest, considering the altogether exceptional quality of the services which this officer has rendered and his remarkable personality and standing. I should, in fact, have thought a KCMG would have been more appropriate.

If you do not wish his name to be on the Foreign Office list, I am quite willing to provide for him on my own list.[2]

Winston S. Churchill to President Franklin D. Roosevelt
(Churchill papers, 20/81)

21 October 1942
Most Secret and Personal
No. 169

I am convinced that the danger of offensive action by the French Fleet in the Mediterranean would be markedly reduced by the showing of the American flag by United States warships inside the Mediterranean, particularly in view of the recent developments which the American Eagle is now testing.

2. The attachment of four American destroyers to the British naval units inside the Mediterranean would be enough. They would be replaced in the American Atlantic flotilla by corresponding number of British destroyers, and should not be required for more than four or five days.

3. I am sure that the administrative and command difficulties of this arrangement could easily be overcome, even at this late hour, and I beg you to give the matter your personal attention. Cunningham[3] would like it.

[1] Alan Hugh Hillgarth, 1899–1978. Entered the Royal Navy as a cadet at the Osborne Naval College at the age of eight. Wounded at the Dardanelles, 1915. Vice-Consul, Palma, Majorca, 1932–7; Consul, 1937–9. Naval Attaché, Madrid, 1939–43. Chief of Intelligence Staff, Eastern Fleet, 1943–4. Chief of British Naval Intelligence, Eastern Theatre, 1944–6. For five years after the Second World War he was Churchill's principal informant on Intelligence matters (a full account of which is given in David Stafford, *Churchill and Secret Service*, London, 1997).

[2] Hillgarth was appointed CMG in the Foreign Office Honours List on 1 January 1943. Immediately after Hillgarth in the Foreign Office List for 1 January 1943 was another notable contributor to British Intelligence work, Alfred Dilwyn Knox Esq., recognized 'For services to the Foreign Office'. Knox was a Classicist who used his linguistic skills in breaking the Enigma codes.

[3] Naval Commander-in-Chief, Expeditionary Force, North Africa.

Winston S. Churchill to Admiral of the Fleet Sir Dudley Pound
(Churchill papers, 20/67)

21 October 1942
Secret

U-BOAT THREAT AGAINST 'TORCH'

I discussed the air protection of the convoys last night with General Eisenhower and Admiral Cunningham. General Eisenhower professed himself ready to make all American Liberators and Fortresses available for anti-U-boat work, even at the expense of the American daylight bombing effort, either against the Biscayan ports or operating from Land's End, which Admiral Cunningham said was perfectly possible. It was agreed that Cunningham should, after consultation at the Admiralty, make a definite proposal to General Eisenhower.

2. In addition to the above, is there not an offer from General Arnold to lend some long-range reconnaissance aircraft to us, to be based on Gibraltar? I presume these would be Catalinas.

3. The above should be cleared up before an inroad is made upon our Lancasters, which will be so injurious to the bombing attack on Germany.

4. If we have an unopposed landing at Dunkirk (T),[1] air bases can immediately be established there from which reconnaissance of the greatest value can be made effective.

Winston S. Churchill to Anthony Eden
(Churchill papers, 20/67)

21 October 1942
Most Secret

ANTHONY EDEN'S 'FOUR POWER PLAN'

You are, of course, perfectly entitled to print and circulate to the War Cabinet this document. In spite of the pressure of events, I will endeavour to write a reply. It sounds very simple to pick out these four Big Powers. We cannot, however, tell what sort of a Russia and what kind of Russian demands we shall have to face. A little later on it may be possible. As to China, I cannot regard the Chungking Government as representing a great world Power. Certainly there would be a faggot vote[2] on the side of the United States in any attempt to liquidate the British Overseas Empire.

---

[1] The deceptive codename for the 'Torch' landings in North Africa.

[2] 'Faggot vote': a vote taking advantage of a legal loophole to gain a desired outcome. For example, in the case of a property qualification, a large landowner might give land temporarily to tenants who would then vote according to his wishes, after which the land would be returned to the origi-

2. I must admit that my thoughts rest primarily in Europe – the revival of the glory of Europe, the parent continent of the modern nations and of civilisation. It would be a measureless disaster if Russian barbarism overlaid the culture and independence of the ancient States of Europe. Hard as it is to say now, I trust that the European family may act unitedly as one under a Council of Europe. I look forward to a United States of Europe in which the barriers between the nations will be greatly minimised and unrestricted travel will be possible. I hope to see the economy of Europe studied as a whole. I hope to see a Council consisting of perhaps ten units, including the former Great Powers, with several confederations – Scandinavian, Danubian, Balkan, &c. – which would possess an international police and be charged with keeping Prussia disarmed. Of course, we shall have to work with the Americans in many ways, and in the greatest ways, but Europe is our prime care and we certainly do not wish to be shut up with the Russians and the Chinese when Swedes, Norwegians, Danes, Dutch, Belgians, Frenchmen, Spaniards, Poles, Czechs and Turks will have their burning questions, their desire for our aid and their very great power of making their voices heard. It would be easy to dilate upon these themes. Unhappily the war has prior claims on your attention and on mine.

3. I am, by the way, increasingly inclined to think there has been a change in the Russian internal situation. It may be that Stalin has had to cede some of his powers to the military. I am sure we should be wise to wait longer before trying to formulate conclusions.

Winston S. Churchill to Sir John Anderson[1] and Lord Leathers[2]
(Churchill papers, 20/67)

21 October 1942

I am distressed to see the queues for buses lengthening again in a very pronounced manner. The reduction in bus services is bound to affect the war effort. It seems to easy to make a boast of saving this or that amount of petrol by inflicting hardship and forcing austerity, and yet how heavy is the price when people arrive at their work or homes tired out, and so reduce their output and efficiency. I know of nothing in the petrol situation which could justify this blow at our output.

nal owner. The implication seems to be that lesser powers such as China would vote in accordance with American wishes on matters such as the end of the British Raj in India in order to gain favour with the United States.

[1] Lord President of the Council.

[2] Minister of War Transport.

2. Economies in fuel are very desirable and certainly should be enforced by precept and example. Is it true, however, that there has been a great epidemic of colds this month in consequence? Of course, the loss of workers through needless illness is war waste of a most expensive kind. I gather that the coal situation is improving slightly. What arrangements are to be made for moderate central heating in November?

3. The climax of folly seems to be reached by the gentleman who writes in the papers proposing that the use of lifts should be restricted, pointing out that if you walk up eight flights of stairs you save the use of electricity for the lift which would keep an electric light burning for so many hours. But this takes no note of the condition of exhaustion of people made to climb several times a day up many flights of stairs, and the bad effect on their office work. If it comes to that, why not stop the trains and let people walk and carry their baggage with them, as they did in the good old days? We are a modern community at war, and not Hottentots or Esquimaux. I hope, therefore, it will not be imagined that simply cutting off facilities and imposing hardships produces increased war output, which is the sole aim. There is an optimum in these matters, and I do not think we are very far off it.

4. I should like to see what Lord Leathers proposes to say in his broadcast.[1]

Winston S. Churchill to Lord Cherwell
(Churchill papers, 20/67)

21 October 1942

I notice a new method of presenting returns which is creeping in. This takes the form of putting the grand total first and all details in inverted order beneath it. There may be some case in logic for such a system, but it is entirely contrary to all usage, and has an unnatural and baffling effect when presented to people who have been accustomed to add up and write the total at the bottom.

Let me know how far this inflection has permeated and which are the branches that use it. It may still be possible to arrest it. Is it a fad of the Central Statistical Branch? Fads of this kind should not be allowed to cause inconvenience in time of war.

---

[1] Proposed broadcast about winter transport.

Winston S. Churchill to Lord Portal [1]
(Churchill papers, 20/67)

22 October 1942
Secret

REBUILDING OF THE HOUSE OF COMMONS

Pray examine and make proposals upon a project for beginning the rebuilding of the House of Commons as soon as possible.

What demands would be made on labour and what time would be required:

(*a*) to make the Chamber habitable;

(*b*) to decorate it as it was before?

The existing site, foundations and size should all be preserved, but, as you will see by reference to Questions and Answers given in the House, the ventilation might be improved, and perhaps some further accommodation given to the distinguished visitors and the public.

It has occurred to me that a great deal could be done in restoring the foundations and outer structure and putting the roof on, even while the war is going forward, without any very heavy demands on labour. It is a great public need to have the Chamber restored, and if we wait till the end of the war it may be years before we can sit with reasonable comfort and efficiency. The whole character of Parliament is affected by the Chamber.

The matter should be kept secret at the present stage. Anyhow, it is very unlikely the enemy will hit the same place twice. A preliminary report is all that is required in the first instance.

General Sir Harold Alexander to Winston S. Churchill
(Churchill papers, 20/81)

23 October 1942
7.45 p.m.
Most Immediate
Most Secret
Personal

ZIP 2200 hours local time today.

---

[1] Minister of Works and Planning.

Winston S. Churchill to President Franklin D. Roosevelt
(Churchill papers, 20/81)

23 October 1942
Personal and Secret
No. 170

The battle in Egypt began tonight at 8 p.m. London time. The whole force of the army will be engaged. I will keep you informed. A victory there will be most fruitful to our main enterprise. All the Shermans and 105 SB's[1] which you gave me on that dark Tobruk morning will play their part.

Winston S. Churchill to Anthony Eden
(Churchill papers, 20/67)

23 October 1942
Most Secret

The Takoradi route is strained to its full by the need of supporting 'Lightfoot', and anything that may follow from it. I have, however, referred your paper to the Chief of the Air Staff for his views on all points in it affecting the air.

2. I am meditating another telegram to Stalin, asking exactly what he means by his reply: 'Thank you', and whether it is the reply to the long telegram I sent him in agreement with the President of the United States. I had expected that, at any rate in regard to the placing of the 20 squadrons in Southern Russia, we should have had some details as to the collaboration so urgently needed with the Russians in choosing the landing grounds and making the administrative arrangements. I am also asking the President whether he has had any reply to his telegram which was parallel to mine and, if so, what it is.

3. It will be better to wait until after 'Lightfoot' has started before addressing Stalin.

---

[1] This is an error for 'SPs': 'self-propelled' guns.

Winston S. Churchill to A. V. Alexander
(Churchill papers, 20/55)

24 October 1942

My dear First Lord,

I was sorry to see that you looked very tired the other night at the Cabinet in the Central War Room. I hope you will not hesitate to take a rest and at any rate not add to your burdens by extraneous engagements. After a bad dose of 'flu, or something like it, which you have had, it would be sensible to take a little well-earned holiday.

I am writing to the Minister of War Transport to say that I consider in a case like this your wishes should have been met, and that I hope in future consideration will be given to them.[1]

Yours very sincerely,
Winston S. Churchill

Winston S. Churchill: memorandum for the War Cabinet
(Churchill papers, 23/10)

24 October 1942
Most Secret

POLICY FOR THE CONDUCT OF THE WAR

Pearl Harbour and the entry of the United States into the war on one side, while Japan broke out upon us on the other, opened an entirely new phase of the war. I proceeded with professional advisers to Washington in order to concert future action with President Roosevelt. We were all agreed that the overthrow of Hitler was the prime objective, both in magnitude and in time, and that Japan must be held as far as possible until the defeat of Germany and Italy enabled our whole force to be turned upon her.

2. At this time the President showed himself already deeply interested in the plan for American intervention in French North Africa by landings at Casablanca or Tangier. This operation was called 'Gymnast'. General Auchinleck was then advancing towards Benghazi and Agedabia and we had the hope that his operation, called 'Crusader', would be followed by 'Acrobat', namely the advance of our Desert Army to Tripoli. 'Gymnast'

---

[1] Alexander had asked the Minister of Transport, Lord Leathers, if a sleeper car could be attached to a train he was taking to the Midlands. This would have meant removing a passenger car. Churchill sent a note to Leathers stating that while he understood wartime constraints he hoped Alexander's wishes would be granted if possible. Leathers replied that 'the really critical objection was the use of an extra engine' which was required by the added weight. Other routes with first-class sleeping cars were offered to Alexander but he declined them, preferring to keep to his original schedule.

was explored at Washington but before any definite decision could be taken General Auchinleck's forces were thrown back to the Gazala position. All prospects of 'Acrobat' were closed and 'Gymnast' faded a good deal. However, both the President and I continued to regard it as the main and most attractive form of the first American impact upon the Western theatre of war.

3. In April 1942, General Marshall came over to England with a plan for a mass invasion of the Continent by Anglo-American forces in April 1943. The Defence Committee were in complete agreement with this conception of a great campaign for the liberation of Europe. For this there were solid arguments. The British Isles are the best assembly point for a great mass of American troops and have already a considerable British Army. The Pas de Calais is the only place where the whole power of the British Metropolitan Air Force, which must in any case be located here with any American accessions, can be thrown immediately and directly into the conflict. On the other hand, the enemy know this, and have concentrated very strong air and ground forces in this area, and fortified it with the utmost care. The tides and beaches are unfavourable, the ports shallow and mined or destroyed. General Marshall's plan also contemplated a landing from England into Northern France in 1942 while Germany was busy in Russia. The shortage of landing craft in 1942 made this smaller operation extremely doubtful. Nevertheless, we agreed with General Marshall that we should proceed with plans for the seizing in 1942 of bridgeheads ('Sledgehammer') as a preliminary for 1943, and anyhow for a great assault on the Continent in 1943. The name of the main operation is 'Roundup', and the administrative preparation, which is vast in extent, is called 'Bolero'.

4. It soon became apparent that the 1942 operation would have little chance of success, unless the Germans were completely demoralised and virtually in collapse, observing that it would have to be either an assault on the Pas de Calais, where the enemy is strongest and conditions are most adverse, or, alternatively, an opposed landing at some point outside air cover. Personally I was sure that the newly raised United States formations, as well as our own somewhat more matured forces, could not establish themselves on the French coast, still less advance far inland, in the teeth of well-organised German opposition.

5. Accordingly I went to Washington in June 1942 and expressed these doubts to the President and General Marshall. I also enlarged on the possibilities of 'Gymnast' and pressed that it should be explored carefully and conscientiously. In deference to the American reluctance

to abandon 'Sledgehammer', it was agreed that further resolute efforts should be made to overcome the obvious dangers and difficulties of the enterprise, and that, if a sound and sensible plan could be contrived, we should not hesitate to give effect to it. It was also agreed that, as an alternative for 1942, the 'Gymnast' plan should be completed in all details as soon as possible. In the above, I was guided by the advice of our expert authorities, and sustained by the opinion of my colleagues in the War Cabinet.

6. On my return to England our further studies convinced us that 'Sledgehammer' held out no prospects of success. Accordingly, General Marshall and Admiral King came to London at our invitation towards the end of July for the second London Conference. We all unitedly dissuaded them from 'Sledgehammer' in 1942 (about which they were themselves beginning to feel uneasy), while urging that general preparation on a large scale for 'Roundup' should continue. As an alternative to 'Sledgehammer', we begged them to throw their whole weight into an enlarged 'Gymnast' as our 1942 operation. After long discussions, which are in my colleagues' memory, complete agreement was reached between all authorities, British and American, political and military. Since then preparations have gone forward without ceasing, both for 'Gymnast', which was rechristened 'Torch', and through 'Bolero', for the building up of 'Roundup', though at a much later date in 1943 than April.

7. The Russians meanwhile, completely ignorant of amphibious warfare and wilfully closing their eyes to the German strength on the French northern coast, continued to clamour for 'a second front in Europe'. On this we have protected ourselves by written declarations from all reproach of breach of faith. M Molotov knew when he returned to Russia in June exactly how we stood about invading Northern France.

8. In order to convince our Russian ally that we had in no way broken faith to him, and to persuade him of the virtues of 'Torch' (which now included action *inside* the Mediterranean), I went to Moscow in the middle of August where everything was plainly and even brutally explained. M Stalin, while expressing dissatisfaction at the aid we were giving to Russia, was in my opinion convinced of what he called 'the military correctness' of 'Torch'. So much for the past.

9. People say there ought to be a comprehensive plan of the war as a whole, and that all the United Nations ought to participate in it. There has always been on our part, since the United States entry, a perfectly clear view. I have never varied on the main points. We have at length got a large measure of agreement and co-operation from the United

States. Everything is now moving forward into action. Our plan is in the first place 'Torch', with its forerunner 'Lightfoot'. The success of these operations will dictate our main action in 1943. Not only shall we open a route under air protection through the Mediterranean, but we shall also be in a position to attack the under-belly of the Axis at whatever may be the softest point, i.e., Sicily, Southern Italy or perhaps Sardinia; or again, if circumstances warrant, or as they may do, compel, the French Riviera or perhaps even, with Turkish aid, the Balkans. However this may turn out, and it is silly to try to peer too far ahead, our war from now on till the summer of 1943 will be waged in the Mediterranean theatre.

10. It will still be necessary to maintain a strong Army in Great Britain and to insist upon adequate United States reinforcements being assembled here. 'Bolero' must continue at full blast, and we must persuade the Americans not to discard 'Roundup' albeit much retarded. Thus we shall have in Great Britain ample troops to defend the Island against a German invasion and to pin down large forces on the northern coast of France. We shall also be ready to take advantage of a German collapse. In any case we should have a mass of troops in Great Britain ready to move to the Mediterranean theatre, or even possibly to the Arctic ('Jupiter').

11. All these matters have been sedulously thrashed out by the Chiefs of Staff, the Defence Committee and the War Cabinet, and I have heard of no difference in principle amongst them.

12. There preys upon us as the greatest danger to the United Nations, and particularly to our Island, the U-boat attack. The Navy call for greater assistance from the Air. I am proposing to my colleagues that we try for the present to obtain this extra assistance mainly from the United States, and that we encroach as little as possible upon our Bomber effort against Germany, which is of peculiar importance during these winter months. I have, on the contrary, asked for an increase in the Bomber effort, rising to 50 squadrons by the end of the year. Thereafter our bombing power will increase through the maturing of production. It may be that early in 1943 we shall have to damp down the Bomber offensive against Germany in order to meet the stress and peril of the U-boat war. I hope and trust not, but by then it will be possible at any rate to peg our bomber offensive at a higher level than at present. The issue is not one of principle, but of emphasis. At present, in spite of U-boat losses, the Bomber offensive should have first place in our air effort.

13. To sum up, our policy remains unaltered. Germany is the prime objective and Japan must be held. Our tasks are these:

(1) To preserve the United Kingdom and our communications.

(2) 'Lightfoot' and 'Torch' and their exploitation.

(3) 'Bolero', for a retarded but still paramount 'Roundup.'

(4) The Bomber offensive against Germany, minus any inroads that may have to be made upon it next year in order to meet the U-boat menace.

(5) Supplies to Russia by the Arctic route, with the possibility of 'Jupiter' always borne in mind should the Russians offer a major contribution to it.

(6) The gathering of air and land forces south of Turkey and the Caspian, capable of either sustaining the Southern Russian flank and/or influencing Turkey, or, alternatively, if things go badly, defending Persia, Syria, Iraq and Palestine.

(7) Subject to prior claims, preparing for an attack on the Japanese communications via the Burma Road, by the recovery of Burma.

14. There are many minor but still important matters which should be mentioned in any complete review. But what is set down here is surely quite enough.

Winston S. Churchill to President Franklin D. Roosevelt
(Churchill papers, 20/81)

24 October 1942
Private and Secret
No. 171

I am delighted that Mrs Roosevelt has arrived safely, though she was delayed by weather for two days at Foynes.[1] My wife and I are looking forward so much to her coming at the weekend. Thank you indeed for the letter which she brought me from you.[2] I am convinced that better days are coming in. I am pressing Smuts to go to you. He has been a great help here and is, I believe, one of the finest men in the world.

---

[1] Foynes, in south-west Ireland, was the main aviation hub connecting Europe and America (frequently used by flying boats). Irish coffee was invented here by Joe Sheridan when whiskey was mixed in coffee to warm a group of rain-soaked American travellers.

[2] Reproduced here as the immediately following document.

President Franklin D. Roosevelt to Winston S. Churchill
(Churchill papers)

24 October 1942[1]

Dear Winston,

I confide my Missus to take care of you and Mrs Churchill. I know our better halves will hit it off beautifully.

All well here, though I am worried about the SW Pacific. Every day we are killing a number of Jap ships and planes, but there is no use blinking at the fact that we are greatly outnumbered.

My trip to the west coast was well worth while and the people are all right – not the newspaper owners. You have that headache too.

Take care of yourself.

As ever
Franklin D. Roosevelt

Winston S. Churchill to Harry Hopkins
(Churchill papers, 20/81)

24 October 1942

Robert inspected Dover with me today and is coming to spend the weekend. He is a charming boy.

Winston S. Churchill to President Franklin D. Roosevelt
(Churchill papers, 20/81)

24 October 1942
Personal and Secret
No. 172

You have seen my message to Stalin which I sent you for your concurrence and despatched on the 8th October (our series message No. 167). There is also the telegram you sent him quoted in your No. 193 to me.

On the same day that I sent my long telegram I sent a short one to him imparting a piece of secret news. On the 13th October I received the somewhat cryptic answer 'Thank you.' Otherwise I have had no response.

We asked our Ambassador to which telegram the 'Thank you' referred. Molotov's private secretary, though repeatedly pressed, has given an evasive answer. But Maisky has now indicated in response to an indirect

[1] Date of receipt; sent by Roosevelt on October 19.

enquiry that he regards Stalin's reply as referring to the longer message. Have you had any answer to your message quoted in your 193?

Meanwhile, fourteen days have passed and no progress has been made in the necessary arrangements with the Russians for choosing landing groups, &c., to enable our 20 squadrons to take station on the Russian southern flank in January. Nor have we received any comment from Moscow on the other parts of the message affecting the 150 plus equivalent spare parts for 50 Spitfires offered by us, all mounting cannon guns.

Lastly we are sending, both of us, our ships in the dark period of October by the Arctic Route hoping to get a good many through to Murmansk or Archangel. Yet this effort on our part entails a considerable Russian movement of aircraft and submarines to help these brave ships in.

As I say, I have received nothing but this cryptic 'Thank you.' Baffling as all this is we are persevering because of the splendid fighting of the Russian Armies. I wonder whether anything has occurred inside the Soviet animal to make it impossible for Stalin to give an effective reply. It may be that the Russian Army has acquired a new footing in the Soviet machine. All this chatter about Hess[1] may be another symptom. I am frankly perplexed and would be grateful for your thoughts at the earliest moment because time is passing.[2]

Winston S. Churchill to President Franklin D. Roosevelt
(Churchill papers, 20/81)

24 October 1942
Personal and Secret
No. 173

I have seen M Boheman,[3] the Swedish Secretary-General, several times during his visit here and consider him a remarkable man. He virtually combines in Sweden the permanent guidance of the Foreign Office with a kind of Secretaryship to the Cabinet. He is thoroughly well-disposed

[1] Rudolf Hess, 1894–1987. Hider's Political Secretary, 1920–31. Deputy Leader of the German Nazi Party, 1934–41. Flew from Germany to Britain, 10 May 1941, landing by parachute. Interned as a prisoner of war, 1941–5. In late October 1942, Moscow made five separate accusations within two days that back in May 1941 Britain had intended using Hess to negotiate peace with Hitler.

[2] Churchill informed the War Cabinet of this episode, and of his telegram to Roosevelt, at the War Cabinet meeting on 26 October 1942.

[3] Erik Carlsson Boheman, 1895–1979. Studied law in Stockholm, 1918. Attaché for Swedish diplomatic missions to Paris and London. Permanent position in State Department, 1921. Envoy to Istanbul, Sofia, Athens, Warsaw, Bucharest. Cabinet Secretary, 1938–45. Swedish Ambassador to London, 1947–8; to Washington, 1948–58. Liberal MP, 1959–70. President of the Upper Chamber of the Swedish Parliament, 1965–70.

to our cause, though very guarded on account of the danger in which Sweden lies. He is now going to the United States, and I trust you will find an opportunity of having a talk with him.

2. I feel it most important that Sweden should be in with us all before the end, though the moment for bringing her in must be wisely chosen.[1]

President Franklin D. Roosevelt to Winston S. Churchill
(Churchill papers, 20/81)

24 October 1942
Most Secret
No. 198

I have been canvassing this morning the possibilities of increasing our escort vessels and merchant ships for 1943 and I am convinced that by making some readjustments we can build at least 70 more escort vessels than we now plan in 1943 and something more than 2,000,000 additional dead weight tons of merchant ships which would enable us to transport before the end of 1943 more than 500,000 additional soldiers abroad with their equipment and maintain them. I have felt for a long time that our airplane program was dragging here and I took the bull by the horns the other day and told them they had to build 100,000 combat planes in 1943. Since that time I have held numerous conferences about it and have agreed this morning to reduce it to 82,000 combat planes but I am telling our production people that I want that many combat planes actually delivered in 1943 and it is not merely a goal to shoot at. The types of course must be decided by the military with appropriate conferences with you. I will talk to Lyttelton about this when he gets here. I have no additional news about Guadalcanal but you of course know that we are hard pressed there. I am sure you are keeping my wife's official business to the minimum. I would appreciate it if you would let me know occasionally how things are going for her. Harry and I are going off for a quiet week end. All good luck in the Libyan Desert.

---

[1] Churchill's hopes were not to be fulfilled. Sweden remained neutral for the duration of the war.

Winston S. Churchill to Brendan Bracken
(Churchill papers, 20/67)

24 October 1942

Pray stop any repetition of any *New Statesman* comments[1] outside the country till you have been personally consulted on the text of each message. You can recur to me at any hour of the night or day.

Winston S. Churchill to Sir Archibald Sinclair
(Churchill papers, 20/67)

24 October 1942
Secret

BOMBING OF GIEN[2]

I do not feel this is a very convincing answer. You make a lot of the War Cabinet decision not being repealed till 2nd February, 1942, but you had only to ask at any time to have it reconsidered. You have always asked me when you wanted anything in particular. I am sure that if I or the War Cabinet had known that there was a concentration of some 2,000 AFVs[3] parked at this place, they would have urged you to go for them.

2. Nor is the argument that 'Gien is a small target and extremely difficult to find' very valid, because when you did go, you found it all right. The Target Committee seem to have been at fault in this matter. I am not at all surprised that it has caused unfavourable comment. I wish you had consulted me.

---

[1] Churchill had seen a telegram from Sir Horace Seymour, the British Minister to China, protesting about an 'unhelpful' aticle in the *New Statesman* on British policy in India (*Premier papers, 4/26/8*). The article, which was republished in the October 6 issue of the *Daily Globe* in Ironwood, Michigan, argued that the British Government had dealt lackadaisically with India's plea to create a national government that could defend its own people, resulting in Indian hostility towards Great Britain and an increased likelihood that a Japanese attack against India could not be repulsed.

[2] Sinclair had been subjected to critical questioning in the House of Commons about an air attack on the occupied French town of Gien, and the apparent failure to launch the bombing mission in time to damage a large number of tanks before their transfer to the North African theatre.

[3] AFVs: armoured fighting vehicles.

Winston S. Churchill to Anthony Eden
(Churchill papers, 20/67)

24 October 1942
Secret

POSSIBILITY OF SPAIN TAKING HOSTILE ACTION
DURING 'TORCH'

I entirely agree. Will you please draw up a short note which I can
send to General Eisenhower showing the interpretation we put on his
expression: 'go sour'. I am sure he will agree it was a loose expression,
and ought not to remain the basis of our correspondence.

2. Please bear in mind that the President has several times said that
we are responsible for the Spanish side, and he for the French.

3. Considering how near we are now getting to zero, I think the position looks very good. As I told you on the telephone, the American Eagle
met those people and reports he had a very satisfactory interview. He is
now returning.

Winston S. Churchill to Lord Cherwell[1]
(Churchill papers, 20/67)

24 October 1942
Secret

I am anxious to survey the whole position afresh, with a view to issuing
a general directive covering the calendar year 1943. For this purpose you
should assemble the salient facts under the following heads:

(i) *Navy.* Here supreme priority should be given:
    (*a*) to all anti-U-boat craft,
    (*b*) to aircraft-carriers of all types, and
    (*c*) to 'Vanguard'.[2]

(ii) *Army.*
    (*a*) Since the beginning of the year we have sent 7 divisions
    abroad; and now for 'Torch' 4 are earmarked, total 11. It
    will be necessary to bring 6 of the 9 Beach Divisions up to
    full standard and to free them from draft finding. For this
    purpose 3 other Beach Divisions and one additional new

[1] Personal assistant to Churchill and head of his statistical section.

[2] HMS *Vanguard*: a British battleship, the largest and fastest of the Royal Navy's Dreadnoughts. It
was laid down in 1941 and finally launched in late 1944. Its construction was given a high priority
in order to counter the strength of German and Japanese fleets.

division will be used. (See the paper by Secretary of State for War.) This should give, including Canadians and Poles, 23 divisions by April next. It is most necessary that 8 United States divisions should have arrived by then. The target for home defence and to pin the enemy in the Pas de Calais may be considered as 30 divisions, as desired by Commander-in-Chief, Home Forces. This does not mean that 30 is accepted as an irreducible minimum defence, but only as desirable. I should be prepared to draw on this up to at least 5 divisions for overseas reinforcements if necessary.

(*b*) The rearward services of these forces must be clearly set forth, after the cuts which the Secretary of State is proposing to make in them, which I highly approve, in a form in which they can be scrutinised.

(*c*) Besides the 23 British divisions at home and in Northern Ireland, we must maintain in the Middle East, west of the Suez Canal, about 10 divisions; and east of it, including 3 Polish divisions, and in India, about 6; the whole in addition to Malta, Gibraltar, Cyprus, Aden, East Africa, Madagascar, &c., garrison forces.

(*d*) Of the divisions in the Middle East and India, it will be sufficient to assume that 12 will be in continuous action and the others in roulement. The divisions in the 'Torch' theatre, namely, 4 and possibly 6, must be considered in constant action. Of those at home, we should assume 6 in constant action and rely on accumulated stocks for the rest.

(*e*) Casualties should be calculated on the basis of one-third of our total forces being in constant action from January 1943 onwards. The above data are for consideration. On what basis are the War Office going now?

(iii) *Air.* The maximum expansion possible must be made, priorities being given:

(*a*) to the equipment of the aircraft carriers, with properly scrutinised reserves.

(*b*) to the long-range heavy bombers, the test being the potential bomb discharge upon Germany or Italy month by month.

(*c*) to additional assistance to the anti-U-boat warfare.

(*d*) to fighters, in which qualitative improvement is indispensable, and

(*e*) to Army Co-operation as now agreed.

(On the above, see my draft minute now under examination in the Defence Office.)

(iv) *Merchant shipbuilding.*

    (*a*)   We must try to achieve 1,250,000 tons in the year.

    (*b*)   Repairs have, however, priority over new merchant building. What is the position about repairs, turn-round, and generally in the Battle of the Atlantic sphere? What expectations have we got from the United States? Nothing definite has been settled about this, and we must insist upon our quota.

    (*c*)   A separate calculation should be made showing the relief which would be afforded if we were able to re-open the Mediterranean.

(v) *Tonnage and troop movements.* We must consider the maintenance of the above armies abroad, and also strive for an import of 27 million. (See my printed paper on this subject of about three months ago.)

(vi) I have in no way given up the idea of 'Roundup' in August or September, provided the German demoralisation is adequate. For this purpose the maximum importation of landing-craft must be obtained from the United States, and all preparations under 'Bolero' must go forward. It may be, however, that much of this effort will be drawn away, either to 'Torch' or possibly even some to 'Jupiter'.

There must be no closing-down of 'Bolero' and no abandoning of 'Roundup', though the date is retarded from April to August or September. Some saving in man-power should result from the retardation of the date of arrival of American contingents.

(vii) Provision must be made in our supply services for 1943 for the Russian quota, for large additional supplies to Turkey, and for the equipment of the Poles. The additional assistance of the United States must be invoked for Turkey, who, I hope, will be induced to enter the war on our side during 1943. How does this stand now?

(viii) *Food.* Estimates should be obtained of the amount of home-grown food to be expected in 1943, with figures showing the increases since pre-war as well as the proposed imports. We cannot contemplate a further reduction in the standard of living.

(ix) *Man-Power.* What is the lay-out of man-power on the present basis, to which it is proposed this directive will give certain qualifications?

(x) *Coal.* What target should we aim at in 1943? What are our prospects?

(xi) *Oil.* We must endeavour to add at least a million tons to our reserves in this year. What does this necessitate in tankers, the American pipe-line, &c.? It is most undesirable to enforce further restrictions.

Any other spheres which I may have overlooked. When you have assembled the salient facts over these fields, I will endeavour to redraft this statement in the form of a directive.

Winston S. Churchill to Randolph S. Churchill[1]
(Churchill papers, 20/65)

24 October 1942

All my thoughts and love go with you.[2]

Winston S. Churchill to Anthony Eden
(Churchill papers, 20/67)

25 October 1942
Most Secret

DISARMING THE PERSIAN ARMY

I cannot help feeling that this is a squalid business. We have overrun Persia by force and made her into an Ally. All we do for her is to wheedle and extract such few arms as her troops have. Why should we now make a fight for this small packet of rifles, and even threaten force? This policy of disarming his army will offend the Shah very much. We ought, on the contrary, to try to build up the Persian army and offer instructors, and make them into a more effective fighting force.

*Winston S. Churchill to Admiral of the Fleet Sir Dudley Pound
and Air Chief Marshal Sir Charles Portal*
(Churchill papers, 20/67)

26 October 1942
Secret

The movement of *Tirpitz* and *Scheer* to Trondheim calls for every effort to strike them while there. Pray let me know in writing, or, if you prefer it, orally, what you have in mind.[3]

---

[1] Randolph Churchill, who was serving as an Intelligence officer in the Commando Brigade, was among the British soldiers who took part in the North African landings. That morning he reported to his father: 'Well here we are safe and sound in the anchorage to the west of Algiers. Nearly everything has gone according to plan.'

[2] Randolph Churchill replied: 'Thank you. Good luck and love.'

[3] Despite more than one attempt (see note on page 144 and pages 385–6 above), the *Tirpitz* was not finally sunk until November 1944. The pocket battleship *Scheer* was sunk in April 1945 while in Kiel for repair.

Winston S. Churchill to Sir Archibald Sinclair[1]
and Air Chief Marshal Sir Charles Portal
(Churchill papers, 20/67)

26 October 1942
Most Secret

The Secretary of State's minute of the 23rd October. It is much better at the present time to persuade the Americans to use Flying Fortresses and Liberators to give additional protection to convoys for 'Torch' (assuming, of course, that they can make the distances), though this may be at the expense of their daylight raiding of France. I hope that, having got them on to the trade routes for this purpose, they will remain there and help to control the Bay of Biscay, both against U-boats and enemy blockade runners. The alternative would be to take more Lancaster squadrons from Bomber Command, which I have been trying my best to prevent for a long time past. It is in this sense that I have spoken to General Eisenhower and Admiral Cunningham.

2. I have not raised with any American authority the question of whether the 'daylight penetration' of Germany is a sound operation. The position remains as stated in my telegram to the President, which CAS saw and approved.

3. I am not at all convinced of the soundness of the Secretary of State's minute of the 23rd October, either on the merits of the 'daylight penetration' policy or on the tactics we should pursue towards the Americans. There is no need, however, to discuss that now.

Winston S. Churchill to Air Chief Marshal Sir Charles Portal
(Churchill papers, 20/67)

26 October 1942

It seems to me essential that we should see beforehand what is going to be said to the troops.[2] This rule might be waived in the case of the Archbishop of Canterbury and Sir Stafford Cripps. In all other cases it should be enforced, and most particularly in the case of Sir Richard Acland,[3] who, I should have thought, is utterly unfit to speak to soldiers.

---

[1] Churchill also sent a copy of this minute to Air Marshal Harris.

[2] The Archbishop of Canterbury had invited the Prime Minister to give a talk in connection with a series of lectures to be given at the RAF station at Yatesbury, Wiltshire.

[3] Richard Thomas Dyke Acland, 1906–90. Son of the liberal politician Sir Francis Acland. Stood unsuccessfully for Parliament as a Liberal, 1929 and 1931. Liberal MP for Barnstaple, 1935–40.

Winston S. Churchill to Vice-Admiral Lord Louis Mountbatten
and General Hastings Ismay,
for the Chiefs of Staff Committee
(Churchill papers, 20/67)

26 October 1942
Most Secret

SNOW PLOUGHS

It is of the utmost importance that these vehicles should be brought into existence at the earliest moment, and that their preparation should not be delayed by premature discussion as to where they will be used. Pray draft me a telegram on which I can base a personal message to the President.

Even if it is not possible to do 'Jupiter' in 1942–43, it may be just as desirable in 1943–44. If we do not make the weapons now, we shall never even have an option open to us on future plans.

Winston S. Churchill to Vice-Admiral Lord Louis Mountbatten
(Churchill papers, 20/67)

26 October 1942
Private

I thought Noel Coward's film 'In Which We Serve' was rather more mixed than when I saw it the first time. It is conceived in the spirit of a dream passing before a man in the early stages of drowning, but in some respects the chronology is disturbed. There should be a few captions to say whether it was Crete or the North Sea where they were fighting. The two operations are so mixed up now that most people would find it difficult to follow them separately. There was at first a caption saying 'Crete 1941', but this seems to have been dropped out of the later edition.

As you took an interest in the film, perhaps it would be well for you to have a talk with the author on the subject.

Succeeded his father as 15th Baronet, 1939. Labour MP, 1947–55. Senior Lecturer, St Luke's College of Education, 1959–74.

Winston S. Churchill to Major-General Swinton[1]
(Churchill papers, 20/54)

26 October 1942

My dear Swinton,

I am grateful to you for the gift of the new and enlarged edition of the 'Green Curve'.[2]

I always admired the prophetic touch in some of your earlier stories, and the country is probably indebted more than it knows to the stimulus given by them and your other writing. The book, embellished as it is by your newer tales, will, I feel sure, be an inspiration to yet another generation, and it will certainly find a welcome and an honourable place on my shelves.

Yours sincerely,
Winston S. Churchill

Winston S. Churchill to President Franklin D. Roosevelt
(Churchill papers, 20/88)

26 October 1942
No. 174

I hear that you would prefer to omit from the British message to the Spanish Government a reference to the participation of British forces in 'Torch'.

I am satisfied that it is important to inform both the Spanish and Portuguese Governments of British participation, if only to remove any suspicions about the object of our own concentrations at Gibraltar and to lend force to the assurances we are giving them. The considerations which apply to the handling of the French do not necessarily apply to that of the Spaniards and Portuguese, for which you agreed that we should be primarily responsible.

---

[1] Ernest (Dunlop) Swinton, 1868–1951. Educated at Rugby, Cheltenham, and Royal Military Academy, Woolwich. Entered the Army (Royal Engineers), 1888. Captain, 1899. Major, 1906. Lieutenant-Colonel, 1915. Served in South Africa, 1899–1902 (DSO, 1900). Instrumental in the development of the tank during the First World War: raised the Heavy Section Machine Gun Corps, 1916 (renamed the Royal Tank Corps, 1917). Assistant Secretary, Committee of Imperial Defence and War Cabinet, 1916. CB, 1917. Retired from the Army with rank of Major-General, 1919. Controller of Information Department of Civil Aviation, 1919–21. Knighted, 1923. Chichele Professor of Military History, Oxford University, 1925–39. Colonel Commandant, Royal Tanks Corps, 1934–8.

[2] *The Green Curve* was a collection of stories on the future of warfare written by Ernest Swinton and first published by Faber & Faber in 1909.

There will be no question of our publishing the full text of our declarations to Spain and Portugal on zero-day. All that we should make public would be the substance, omitting any passages, such as those about British participation which would not be in accord with the general line we are both taking in public in the first stage of the operation.

We should, of course, say to both Spaniards and Portuguese that what we tell them about our share in the operation is for their strictly confidential information.

I hope that with this explanation you will agree to the retention of the original text, to which we attach importance.

Similar considerations apply to any message to Dr Salazar.[1]

War Cabinet: conclusions
(Cabinet papers, 65/28)

27 October 1942   10 Downing Street

[...]

The Prime Minister said that he had undertaken to speak at a meeting, to be held in the Central Hall, Westminster, on Saturday, the 31st October, at 10.30 a.m., which was to be attended by representatives of miners and mine managers drawn from every pit in the country.

The Prime Minister said that it would be a very great advantage if Field-Marshal Smuts were willing to accompany him to that meeting and make a short speech. The proceedings at the meeting would not be reported in the Press and he intended to speak mainly about the progress of the war, though he would, of course, make it clear that increased coal output was necessary if our military plans were to go forward without interruption.

Field-Marshal Smuts said that he would be very pleased to attend the meeting.

The Prime Minister said that, if other members of the War Cabinet were free to attend, he would be glad of their support on this occasion.

---

[1] Antonio de Oliveira Salazar, 1889–1970. Portuguese Minister of Finance, 1928–32. Prime Minister, and dictator, of Portugal, 1932–68. Served as his own Foreign Minister, 1936–47, and his own War Minister, 1936–44. Incapacitated by a stroke, 1968.

Winston S. Churchill to President Franklin D. Roosevelt
(Churchill papers, 20/81)

27 October 1942   10 Downing Street
Personal and Secret
No. 175

Mrs Roosevelt has, I think, enjoyed her first three days in England. She spent Sunday with us at Chequers and went to see my wife's maternity hospital. She went with my wife today [to] a long round of Women's Army Services. She seems extremely well and in the best of spirits. By official engagements I suppose you mean ceremonial affairs. These can be cut to any extent. But Mrs Roosevelt has an immense programme of official engagements in the sense of scheduled appointments to see things. I have urged her to apply to me in any case where she wanted to have them cancelled or warded off. I also urged the importance of keeping a good many days spare so that she could do whatever she felt inclined. Elliott[1] came to luncheon Sunday. I will telegraph again in a day or two.

Winston S. Churchill to President Franklin D. Roosevelt
(Churchill papers, 20/81)

27 October 1942
Personal and Secret
No. 178

I like your Press release very much and deem it admirably conceived for its purpose. I have only two suggestions: for 'Egyptian campaign' read 'British campaign in Egypt', and at the end add 'and prove the first historic step to the liberation and restoration of France'.

Winston S. Churchill to Anthony Eden
(Churchill papers, 20/67)

27 October 1942
Most Secret

I am sure it would be a great mistake to run after the Russians in their present mood; and still less to run around with them chasing a chimera.

---

[1] The President's son.

By all means let the Lord Privy Seal[1] focus and refresh in our minds the Hess story. When it is ready, the Cabinet can consider whether the facts should be imparted to the Russian Government. I assure you the only thing that will do any good is fighting hard and winning victories. A great deal of fighting is now going on, and more is to come. Should success crown our efforts, you will find we shall be in a very different position. Meanwhile I should treat the Russians coolly, not getting excited about the lies they tell, but going steadily on with our task. You must remember the Bolsheviks have undermined so many powerful Governments by lying, machine-made propaganda, and they probably think they make some impression on us by these methods.

2. I am awaiting the President's answer to my query about whether he has heard from Stalin in reply to his and my telegrams. As soon as I hear, I will draft a telegram to Stalin myself. It will be quite short, asking if his 'Thank you' was in reply to my long telegram, and if so, what steps does he propose to take about the twenty squadrons on the southern flank, anything additional about the Spitfires which we are sending, and the ships which are to slip through, one by one, in the dark period. Now that *Tirpitz* has gone south to Trondheim, it may be possible after the first part of 'Torch' is over to reconsider the convoy question, but the problem will still be escort craft.

3. On another subject, did you see that Willkie said that the offensive in Egypt was due to pressure of public opinion? I am thinking of sending him a personal telegram on this. I am anxious not to lose him entirely. If the President liked it, I would invite him over here. It is not necessary, however, to hurry this. We must let events speak. Words do not count now as much as they do in time of peace. What matters is action.

President Franklin D. Roosevelt to Winston S. Churchill
(Churchill papers, 20/81)

27 October 1942
No. 200
Personal
Most Secret

Replying to your 174 of October 26th I am in agreement therewith regarding your messages to Franco and Salazar in both of which

---

[1] Sir Stafford Cripps.

I hope you will stress the fact that the expedition is under American command.

Winston S. Churchill to William Mackenzie King,
Peter Fraser, and John Curtin
(Churchill papers, 20/81)

28 October 1942
Most Secret and Personal

The great battle in Egypt has opened well, although one cannot yet forecast its result. The enemy are short of ammunition and fuel, and we have just destroyed a most important tanker on which they were counting. Our forces are substantially superior in the air, in armour, including best armour, in artillery fire and in numbers, and they have far easier lines of communication. Rommel is seriously ill and has only been brought back as an extreme measure. In Alexander and Montgomery we have Generals determined to fight the battle out to the very end. Should they succeed, it will be very difficult for the enemy army to make a good retreat on account of his shortage of transport and fuel. It is therefore much better for us to fight him to a finish on this ground than further west.

(to 2 only)

2. You will have seen with pride and pleasure all that your valiant New Zealanders are doing and the part they are playing in what may well be a memorable event.

(to 3 only)

2. You will have observed with pride and pleasure the distinguished part which the 9th Australian Division are playing in what may be an event of first magnitude.

(to all)

Ends

Winston S. Churchill to William Mackenzie King,
Peter Fraser, and John Curtin
(Churchill papers, 20/81)

28 October 1942

About the tying up of prisoners, we are, as you know, awaiting the reply of the German Government to our representations and protest conveyed to them by the Swiss Government. As soon as we receive it we will communicate with you again. In no case should we take any further measures without full discussion with you.

2. I have the strong impression that the original order for tying up prisoners came from Hitler and is a sign of his rage and fury, and that it encountered a good deal of passive opposition, not only from the German Foreign Office but from the German military authorities under whom the prison camps now fortunately are. Hitler or the German Government then sought to widen the issue by indulging in a campaign of atrocity allegations, and a week ago it looked as if this might be the prelude to a general denunciation by them of the Geneva Convention with the intention of using prisoners of war for all kinds of work or for some other reason. But this again seems to have encountered considerable resistance in German military and diplomatic circles. At any rate, nothing has happened yet. I have the feeling, which I must admit is based largely on instinct, that the German answer may take the form of demanding solemn assurances as to the strict maintenance of the Geneva Convention, which assurances we should of course immediately give.

3. I remain hopeful that with time and patience we shall succeed in relieving our officers and men from the affront to which they have been subjected.

Winston S. Churchill to Lord Gort
(Churchill papers, 20/81)

28 October 1942
Personal and Secret
Bigot

MALTA

All our main plans are working out steadily. The prospects of 'Torch' encountering only weak opposition have sensibly improved. The battle in Egypt has opened well.

2. The work you are doing in animating the magnificent resistance of the Island and its effective intervention on the enemy's line of communications commands general admiration.

3. Your name will be submitted to the King for promotion to the rank of Field Marshal in the New Year Honours List.

Every good wish.

Winston S. Churchill to General Sir Alan Brooke
(Churchill papers, 20/67)

28 October 1942

TELEGRAM TO BE SENT TO GENERAL ALEXANDER

The Foreign Secretary and I are agreed that this or something like it should be sent in view of the evident slowing down of the battle. The last Cositrep is particularly disquieting. I am calling a meeting at 12.30 tomorrow, and will be glad if you will let me have your views then. It is most necessary that the attack should be resumed before 'Torch'. A stand-still now will be proclaimed as a defeat. We consider the matter most grave.

General Sir Alan Brooke: diary
('War Diaries, Field Marshal Lord Alanbrooke', page 335)

29 October 1942

Before I got up this morning I was presented with a telegram which PM wanted to send Alexander! Not a pleasant one and brought about purely by the fact that Anthony Eden had come round late last night to have a drink with him and had shaken his confidence in Montgomery and Alexander, and had given him the impression that the Middle East offensive was petering out!!

During COS, just while we were having the final interview with Eisenhower, I was sent for by the PM and had to tell him fairly plainly what I thought of Anthony Eden's ability to judge a tactical situation at this distance!

Then at 12.30 we had a COS meeting under PM attended by Smuts, Attlee, Eden and Oliver Lyttelton. Here again the whole question of the Middle East situation was raised. Eden made a statement as to his worst fears. I refuted this statement and the PM then turned to Smuts who (thank God) said, 'You are aware, Prime Minister, that I had no opportunity of discussing this matter with the CIGS, but I am in entire agreement with all the opinions he has expressed!!' This settled the situation, and I was very grateful to him.

[. . .]

Lord Alanbrooke: recollection
(*'War Diaries, Field Marshal Lord Alanbrooke', pages 335–6*)

[29 October 1942]

When I went to see Winston, having been sent for from the COS meeting, I was met with a flow of abuse of Monty. What was my Monty doing now, allowing the battle to peter out (Monty was always my Monty when he was out of favour!). He had done nothing now for the last three days, and now he was withdrawing troops from the front. Why had he told us he would be through in seven days if all he intended to do was to fight a half hearted battle? Had we not got a single general who could even win one single battle? etc, etc. When he stopped to regain his breath I asked him what had suddenly influenced him to arrive at these conclusions. He said that Anthony Eden had been with him last night and that he was very worried with the course the battle was taking, and that neither Monty nor Alex was gripping the situation and showing a true offensive spirit. The strain of the battle had had its effect on me, the anxiety was growing more and more intense every day and my temper was on edge. I felt very angry with Eden and asked Winston why he consulted his Foreign Secretary when he wanted advice on strategic and tactical matters. He flared up and asked whether he was not entitled to consult whoever he wished! To which I replied he certainly could, provided he did not let those who knew little about military matters upset his equilibrium. He continued by stating that he was dissatisfied with the course of the battle and would hold a COS meeting under his Chairmanship at 12.30 to be attended by some of his colleagues.

At 12.30 we met and he turned to Eden and asked him to express his views. To which Anthony said that he considered that Monty was allowing the battle to peter out, that he had done nothing for the last three days and that now he was withdrawing formations to the rear. I was then asked by Winston what my views were. I replied that the Foreign Secretary's view of the battle must have been very superficial if he had come to the conclusions he had just expressed. He had said that during 3 days Monty had done nothing; he had therefore evidently failed to observe that during that period Monty had withstood a series of determined counterattacks delivered by Rommel, none of which had made any head way. During that period Rommel had therefore suffered very heavy casualties, all of which played an important part in securing ultimate success in this battle. And again, I said since the Foreign Secretary had been a Staff Captain in the last war he must be familiar with administrative matters.

(Winston was always drawing my attention to the fact that Eden had been a Staff Captain and therefore familiar with military matters!) Had he not observed that Monty's attack had advanced the front several thousand yards, did he not remember this entailed a forward move of artillery and the establishment of new stocks of ammunition before another attack could be staged? Finally the Foreign Secretary accused Monty of withdrawing formations. Had he forgotten that the fundamental principle of all strategy and tactics lay in immediately forming new reserves for the next blow? I then went on to say that I was satisfied with the course of the battle up to the present and that everything I saw convinced me that Monty was preparing for his next blow.

We have seen in the diary how fortunate I was to have Smuts' full support. The flow of words from the mouth of that wonderful statesman was as if oil had been poured on troubled waters! The temperamental film-stars returned to their tasks – peace reigned in the dove cot!

Personally however I was far from being at peace. I had my own doubts and my own anxieties as to the course of events, but these had to be kept entirely to myself. On returning to my office I paced up and down, suffering from a desperate feeling of loneliness. I had, during that morning's discussion, tried to maintain an exterior of complete confidence. It had worked, confidence had been restored. I had told them what I thought Monty must be doing, and I knew Monty well, but there was still just the possibility that I was wrong and that Monty was beat. The loneliness of those moments of anxiety, when there is no one one can turn to, have to be lived through to realize their intense bitterness.

Winston S. Churchill to General Sir Harold Alexander
(Churchill papers, 20/81)

29 October 1942
Immediate
Most Secret
Private
Bigot

The Defence Committee of the War Cabinet congratulate you on the resolute and successful manner in which you and General Montgomery have opened the decisive battle which is now proceeding. They feel that the general situation justifies all the risks and sacrifices involved in its relentless prosecution. We assure you that you will be supported, whatever the cost, in all the measures which you are taking to shake the life out of Rommel's army and make this a fight to a finish.

2. You have no doubt seen Boniface, particularly Nos. QT/4474, QT/4592, QT/4599, QT/4642, QT/4644 and 4682. The brilliant success of the Air in sinking the vitally-needed tankers, the conditions of intense strain and anxiety behind the enemy's front, give us solid grounds for confidence in your final success. We should be grateful for any general outline you may care to give of your immediate intentions, over and above what is contained in the Cositreps.

3. Meanwhile 'Torch' is moving forward so far with complete secrecy and good fortune, and the date will be punctually kept.

4. For yourself and Montgomery alone. Clarke[1] visited 'Torch' area and held long conference with friendly generals. We have every reason to hope, and indeed believe, that very little opposition will be encountered and that powerful aid will be forthcoming. Thus events may move more rapidly – perhaps far more rapidly – than we had planned. Decisive reactions may be looked for in France. Nothing sinister has yet cropped up from Spain. We have no evidence that the enemy have any idea of what is coming and certainly not of its imminence or scale. The fact of your battle continuing at full blast will play a vital part.

Every good wish to you both.

Winston S. Churchill to President Franklin D. Roosevelt
(Churchill papers, 20/81)

29 October 1942
Personal and Secret
No. 176

Your No. 203.[2] I am deeply grateful for your help. General Alexander has just telegraphed that it is impossible to withdraw this division during the battle. Later on, if Curtin insists, it will have to go, but I trust your telegram will be decisive.

---

[1] United States General Mark (Wayne) Clark (misspelling in original).

[2] Roosevelt's telegram to the Prime Minister of Australia strongly urging Curtin not to withdraw the 9th Australian Division from the Middle Eastern theatre and offering an extra US division for the defence of Australia.

Winston S. Churchill to the Most Reverend William Temple [1]
(Churchill papers, 20/54)

29 October 1942

My dear Archbishop,

I cannot refrain from sending, through you, to the audience which is assembling under your Chairmanship at the Albert Hall today to protest against Nazi atrocities inflicted on the Jews, the assurance of my warm sympathy with the objects of the meeting. The systematic cruelties to which the Jewish people – men, women, and children – have been exposed under the Nazi regime are amongst the most terrible events of history, and place an indelible stain upon all who perpetrate and instigate them. Free men and women denounce these vile crimes, and when this world struggle ends with the enthronement of human rights, racial persecution will be ended.

Yours sincerely,
Winston S. Churchill

Winston S. Churchill to Lord Gort
(Churchill papers, 20/81)

30 October 1942
Most Secret
Private
Bigot

'Torch' is moving forward so far with complete secrecy and good fortune, and the date will be punctually kept.

2. For yourself alone, an American General of high rank visited 'Torch' area and held a long conference with friendly generals. We have every reason to hope, and indeed believe, that very little opposition will be encountered and that powerful aid will be forthcoming. Thus events may move more rapidly – perhaps far more rapidly – than we had planned. Decisive reactions may be looked for in France. Nothing sinister has yet cropped up from Spain. We have no evidence that the enemy had any idea of what is coming and certainly not of its imminence or scale. Bear all this in mind when thinking about 'Breastplate'.[2]

---

[1] Archbishop of Canterbury.

[2] 'Breastplate': plan for amphibious Allied assault on Tunisia from Malta. Rendered unnecessary by Allied success in closing in on the Axis beachhead in Tunisia.

Winston S. Churchill to Dr Chaim Weizmann[1]
(Churchill papers, 20/81)

30 October 1942

My thoughts are with you on this anniversary.[2] Better days will surely come for your suffering people and for the great cause for which you have fought so bravely. All good wishes.

Winston S. Churchill to Air Chief Marshal Sir Arthur Tedder
(Churchill papers, 20/81)

30 October 1942

Many congratulations on the magnificent way in which you are cutting to the enemy in the air, on the ground and on the sea. Pray give my compliments to Coningham and also to all the officers and men who welcomed me so cordially in the desert. I was sure then that great days lay ahead. Those days have come, and you are all playing a glorious part in them.

Winston S. Churchill to President Franklin D. Roosevelt
(Churchill papers, 20/81)

30 October 1942
Most Secret and Personal
No. 177

Although I understand from Mountbatten that the Plough Scheme[3] as originally conceived is not a practicable proposition this winter, I am convinced that it is of the utmost importance that the development and production of the vehicle should not be delayed.

---

[1] Chaim Weizmann, 1874–1952. Born in Russia. Educated in Germany. Reader in Bio-chemistry, University of Manchester, 1906. Naturalized as a British subject, 1910. Director, Admiralty Laboratories, 1916–19. President of the World Zionist Organization, and of the Jewish Agency for Palestine, 1921–31, 1935–46. Chairman, Board of Governors, Hebrew University of Jerusalem, 1932–50. Adviser to the Ministry of Supply, London, 1939–45. First President of the State of Israel from 1949 until his death. His eldest son, Flight Lieutenant Michael Weizmann, RAF, was killed in action in 1942.

[2] The reference is to the imminent 25th anniversary of the Balfour Declaration of 2 November 1917, in which the British Foreign Secretary, Arthur Balfour, had asserted that 'His Majesty's Government view with favour the establishment in Palestine of a national home for the Jewish people.'

[3] See page 1315 above [Churchill to Mountbatten of 26 October].

I am sure that even if its employment is impossible in the near future, it is essential that every opportunity should be taken to improve upon the present design so that we shall be fully prepared to grasp our opportunity when it occurs as it certainly will.

General Sir Harold Alexander to Winston S. Churchill
and General Sir Alan Brooke
(Churchill papers, 20/81)

30 October 1942
Immediate
Most Secret
Private

Montgomery and I fully agreed utmost pressure of our offensive must be maintained. Enemy minefields and anti-tank guns have caused a lot of trouble and delay. We are now, however, about to put in a large scale attack with infantry and tanks to break a way through for the Tenth Corps. If this is successful it will have far reaching results.

Winston S. Churchill to General Hastings Ismay,
for the Chiefs of Staff Committee
(Churchill papers, 20/67)

30 October 1942
Most Secret

PROVISION OF SHIPPING FOR OPERATION 'BACKBONE'[1]

This is a very serious matter. As long as the plans are hypothetical and are only brought into being as the result of some great new crisis happening once the large operation is launched, there would be no objection to our obtaining the assignment of these ships from the United States. On the other hand, if it is now intended to unload the ships with Russian munitions lying at Kirkwall at once, this will bring about a renewed crisis in our relations with Russia, and I am sure that the President should be made aware of the seriousness of this. Moreover, the Foreign Secretary

---

[1] 'Backbone': plan to strike Spanish troops if they massed in Spanish Morocco in order to join the Axis in the fight during or after 'Torch'. This contingency plan included a diversion of PQ ships to supply the operation. By February 1943 it became clear that Spain was not a serious threat and preparations for 'Backbone' were stopped.

and the Cabinet would have to be consulted and agree. The unloading of these ships will be taken by the Russians as an abandonment of the attempt to supply them with munitions northabout.

I hope this matter may be reviewed again by the Chiefs of Staff and General Eisenhower. I fully agree that we cannot do any more.

Winston S. Churchill: note[1]
(Churchill papers, 20/67)

30 October 1942

The position of foreign and neutral Ambassadors in this country enables them to report to their Governments anything they may hear about our plans and military affairs. They necessarily and naturally have easy access to high official as well as social circles. This applies not only to the Great Powers but to the Embassies of the smaller countries and, of course, to the representative of Southern Ireland. The greatest discretion must be observed by all Ministers and military and civil officers in any conversations with them. It must be remembered that some of them have no interest in our fortunes, and gain credit with their Governments by any tit-bits they can pick up. The utmost reserve is therefore enjoined. Any conversation which should arise of the slightest significance should be reported to the Foreign Secretary, who is the proper channel through which the Diplomatic Corps should be informed.

Winston S. Churchill to Lord Cranborne
(Churchill papers, 20/67)

30 October 1942

CHAINING OF PRISONERS OF WAR

I am very reluctant to give Hitler a triumph and admit ourselves wrong. I would rather Canada acted independently, though I doubt if she will do so. I have had no answer from Mackenzie King to my telegram.

The idea of giving up all hope of getting our men released is very painful to me. It is a terrible thing to have one's will-power broken by the enemy. It reacts on every form and every phase of the struggle. Of

[1] Sent to Sir Edward Bridges and General Ismay with the instruction: 'Pray circulate the following in high official circles.'

course if you desire to reopen the discussion in Cabinet, arrangements can be made, but I hope you will not think this necessary.

Winston S. Churchill to Anthony Eden
(Churchill papers, 20/67)

30 October 1942
Most Secret

I agree with Major Morton in thinking that the President's remarks[1] are out of date and overdone. I could send him a tactful telegram suggesting a toning-down. If you think well, let me know. As it stands, it will infuriate the Fighting French beyond words.

Winston S. Churchill to Anthony Eden and Sir Alexander Cadogan
(Churchill papers, 20/67)

30 October 1942
Most Secret

I am all for the President representing 'Torch' as a 'second front'. It was the American communiqué that got us into trouble during Molotov's visit, and that they should get out of it is all to the good. Moreover, it ('Torch') is our major contribution at the present time, and I personally am certainly going to speak of it as a full discharge of our obligations as Allies to Russia. I entirely agree with the view taken by the Foreign Secretary. Any propaganda policy in contradiction to this must be dimmed.

2. On the strategic point, I propose to make it clear when the time comes, probably about the middle of next month, that we are mounting a great attack in England and to favour the idea that 'Sledgehammer' and 'Roundup' are still alive and even kicking. In fact, as you know, I have always regarded the holding front we maintain here and the overseas flanking move by the south as part of one integral operation.

---

[1] President Roosevelt's message to Marshal Pétain, and his message to General Franco and Dr Salazar, in connection with 'Torch'.

Sarah Churchill to Winston S. Churchill
(Churchill papers, 1/369)

30 October 1942   RAF Station
Medmenham
Marlow
Buckinghamshire

My darling Papa,

You know that it is impossible to thank you enough for the financial arrangement you have made for me. It is so sweet of you to think of it, amidst so many other worries. It will be the most tremendous help. Thank you darling so very much. Wow!

It was lovely seeing you last Sunday. You seemed in good spirits and health.

I saw Randolph for a few minutes before he left. He looked so much better and calmer. He loves you very much as indeed we all do.

Your very loving 'Lieut'
Sarah

Air Chief Marshal Arthur Tedder to Winston S. Churchill
(Churchill papers, 20/82)

31 October 1942
Personal and Secret

On behalf of all of us I wish to thank you most sincerely for your inspiring message of encouragement. We are all at full throttle and determined to make a job of it.

General Sir Harold Alexander to Winston S. Churchill
(Churchill papers, 20/82)

31 October 1942
Personal

Thank you for your encouraging message. Enemy is fighting desperately, but we are hitting him hard and continuously, and boring into him without mercy. Have high hopes he will crack soon.

Winston S. Churchill: speech
(*'Winston S. Churchill, His Complete Speeches'*, volume 6, pages 6687–92)

31 October 1942   Central Hall
11 a.m.Westminster

COAL-OWNERS AND MINERS CONFERENCE[1]

War is made with steel, and steel is made with coal. This is the first
and only industry I have addressed as an industry during the time of my
responsibility. I am doing so because coal is the foundation and, to a very
large extent, the measure of our whole war effort. I thought it would be
a good thing if we met in private. The Press are our good friends, they
play their part in the battle, a valuable part and an indispensable part,
but the difficulty about making reported speeches is – look at all the ears
that listen; look at the different audiences that have to be considered!
So, if you will allow me to say so, I thought it would be a compliment to
the coal industry if I, in my position, and the other Ministers who are
here, came and had a talk in private with you about our great affairs. Of
course, I cannot see the whole of the coal industry, but I have come here
to give you first-hand guidance, and I am going to ask you to go back to
your pits as the ambassadors of His Majesty's Government, to tell them
the impressions you have formed and assist to the utmost in promoting
the common cause.

I am very glad indeed to see the success Gwilym[2] is making of his
extremely hard job. He bears a name which is a household word, and he
is adding the distinction which a second generation can impart to such a
name: the distinction of great services rendered by the father, sustained
and carried forward by the son. I am told that in the few months since
he has been Minister of Fuel, Power and Light, out of 1,600 Pit Production Committees he has actually visited and addressed 714. No one can
say that he is sparing himself, and no one can say that his exertions have
gone without response. The output has improved in recent weeks, and
I well know what an effort that must require because of the adverse circumstances which war-time conditions impose upon production, but still
it is not enough. As he told you just now, the great munition plants are
coming into production. Factories, plants and mills begun two years ago
are now completed. The population has been assembled, the workers
are there, and the great wheels are turning, turning out the apparatus
of war, and they are consuming in many cases 40 per cent more fuel,

---

[1] Some 3,000 miners were present to hear Churchill speak.
[2] Major Gwilym Lloyd George.

largely in the form of gas, than was the case last year. This comes to us at a time of special necessity. We are making the utmost economies compatible with the health and welfare of the people in the consumption of fuel, but such economies as we can make cannot achieve the results necessary to bridge the gap between the growing consuming power of the great war plants and the existing supply. Besides, I do not want to cut the cottage homes too sharply. The people must have warmth for their spirits and for the war efficiency, and one can easily go too far in that direction.

The White Paper has placed the coal industry upon the basis of national service for the duration of the war, and for a further period until Parliament has reviewed the scheme in the light of the experience gained. I therefore come here today to call upon everyone in that industry, managements and miners alike, hand in hand to sweep away all remaining obstacles to maximum production. That is the object with which this meeting is called, but here let me say this. I am very sorry that we have had to debar so many miners from going to the war in the Armed Forces. I respect their feelings, but we cannot afford it; we cannot allow it. Besides the need for their services in the pits, there is danger in the pits too, and where there is danger there is honour. 'Act well thy part, there all the honour lies', and that is the motto I want to give out to all those who in an infinite variety of ways are playing an equally worthy part in the consummation of our high purpose.

But I have not come to address you mainly about coal. I have come to talk mainly about war, and that is why I brought the Field-Marshal[1] with me. It was a surprise, but also a prize. He and I are old comrades. I cannot say there has never been a kick in our gallop. I was examined by him when I was a prisoner of war, and I escaped; but we made an honourable and generous peace on both sides, and for the last forty years we have been comrades working together. I was very glad to entice him over here. He has great duties to discharge in South Africa. He holds that gateway to our brothers in Australia and New Zealand and the Middle East. He holds that gateway faithfully and surely, for – to quote his own phrase, although not everybody knows it is his own phrase – for the British Commonwealth of Nations, and, as you all feel he may justly say, for purposes which are wider and larger and longer even than the British Commonwealth of Nations.

You, Major Lloyd George, have spoken about the past, about the crisis of 1940, and we ought from time to time to look back to that astonishing

[1] Smuts.

experience in our lives. Unprepared, almost unarmed, left alone, this country never flinched. With one voice it defied the tyrant. That was indeed our finest hour, and it was from that hour that our deliverance came. We had in this small Island lost in the northern mists, rendered a service to the whole world which will be acknowledged even when a thousand years have passed.

This brings me to a point which I will venture to mention. I do not think the British have any need to apologise for being alive. When I see critics in other countries, and not only in other countries, and a stream of criticism which would suggest that we are an unworthy nation; that we were an exploiting nation; that our contribution to world progress has been wanting, nothing is less true. Well was it for Europe, well was it for the world, that the light shone out which the British people had carefully nourished, that a light shone out from this Island to guide them all forward upon their paths. Therefore, I am not going to apologise, and I have to pick up my words carefully here, for the fact that we are alive, still alive and kicking. But, Mr Chairman,[1] I frankly admit that we owe much to the mistakes of our enemies. We have made mistakes, we have made miscalculations; but we are being saved from the consequences of our shortcomings by the incomparably greater mistakes and blunders which these all-wise glittering dictators have perpetrated. Look at the mistake that Hitler made in not trying invasion in 1940. Mind you, he tried, tentatively, but the Royal Air Force crushed him. He did attempt to destroy our air fields, our air organisation and our aircraft factories; he tried; but I have often asked myself what would have happened if he had in fact put three-quarters of a million on board all the barges and boats and let them stream across and taken the chance of losing three-quarters of them. There would have been a terrible shambles in this country, because we had hardly a weapon; we had not at that time fifty tanks, whereas we now have 10,000 or 12,000. We had not at that time fifty tanks; we had a couple of hundred field guns, some of them brought out of the museums; we had lost all our equipment at Dunkirk and in France; and indeed we were spared an agonising trial. Of course, we should have gone on fighting, but modern weapons, the weapons made, forged and shaped by modern science and industry, give a terrible advantage against people almost entirely without them, however brave they may be, however ready to give their lives, however proud to give their lives they may be. Well, at any rate, without entering into an attempt to pass upon final judgment on whether he would have succeeded or not,

[1] Gwilym Lloyd George.

I am quite content that he did not try, or that he did not try more than he did. But what about the next mistake? I am bound to say I thought it very likely in the early Summer that he would attack Turkey and try to by-pass Russia, but it soon became clear, some weeks before, that he intended to invade Russia in order to steal the larger part of the Russian cornlands and factories and to make it into a great slave area ruled by the *Herrenvolk*; but he reckoned without his host. He invaded Russia to find a nation of people ready to fight and die with a valour and steadfastness which none can excel. That was a great mistake. Another mistake was his forgetting about the Russian Winter. You know, it gets cold there, very cold indeed. The snow falls down and lies on the ground, and an icy wind blows in across the Steppes. He overlooked that point, and I expect he has overlooked it again, now that his second campaign against Russia is ending in frustration. Another mistake of our foes was made by Japan when they attacked the United States at Pearl Harbour instead of attacking us alone who were already busy with Italy and Germany in Europe. It was most fortunate that, led away by their dark conspiracies and schemes, dizzy and dazzled from poring over plans, they sprang out upon a peaceful nation with whom they were at that time in peaceful parley, and were led away and tottered over the edge and, for the sake of sinking half a dozen ships of war and beating up a naval port, brought out against them the implacable energies and the measureless power of the 130 million educated people who live in the United States. We have much to be thankful for.

I sometimes have a feeling, in fact I have it very strongly, a feeling of interference. I want to stress that. I have a feeling sometimes that some guiding hand has interfered. I have the feeling that we have a guardian because we serve a great cause, and that we shall have that guardian so long as we serve that cause faithfully. And what a cause it is! One has only to look at the overwhelming evidence which pours in day by day of the bestial cruelties of the Nazis and the fearful misery of Europe in all the lands into which they have penetrated; the people ground down, exploited, spied upon, terrorised, shot by platoons of soldiers, day after day the executions, and every kind of petty vexation added to those dark and bloody acts of terrorism. Think what they would do to us if they got here. Think what they would do to us, we who have barred their way to the loot of the whole world, we whom they hate the most because they dread and envy us the most. Think what they would do to us.

I said just now that we have had to forbid miners to go into the Armed Forces, and how much I feel we owe you an apology for that, but I must now say that, with my responsibilities, I cannot let miners who have been trained as soldiers leave the Army in large numbers. The miners are amongst the best fighting men we have. The Army needs them, and you would wreck every platoon and every section if you pulled out those men who have made their friends and made their comradeships and know the work and have been trained for over two years in many cases. I have to think of the strength and efficiency of the Army. First, we have to ward off invasion. That for the moment is not a danger, but danger may come back. First we have to ward off invasion all through the Summer and Winter of 1940 and through the Spring and Summer of 1941, and then after the attack began on Russia, we were easier in that respect, but we had to be ready for it; and now we are again thinking about invasion, but invasion the other way round, invasion not to conquer and pillage, invasion to liberate and rescue. That is what is in our minds. All Europe is seething under the Nazi yoke. The Army must be ready. It must be ready when the opportunity comes, as come it will, so some must stay in the pits and others must stay in the Army. Both are needed, both are equally needed, and for both there is equal credit.

Now let me speak about the dangers which lie ahead. The first of all our dangers is the U-boat peril. That is a very great danger. Our food, our means of making war, our life, all depend upon the passage of ships across the sea. The whole power of the United States to manifest itself in this war depends upon the power to move ships across the sea. Their mighty power is restricted, it is restricted by those very oceans which have protected them. The oceans which were their shield have now become a bar, a prison house, through which they are struggling to bring armies, fleets, and air forces to bear upon the great common problems we have to face. Now we see our way through. I saw that with all solemnity and sobriety. We see our way through. Although it is true that there will be many more U-boats working next year than there are now, and there may be 300 to 400 at work now, yet we have a vast construction of escort vessels, submarine-hunting vessels, afoot, as well as replacements of merchant ships; and in the United States, which has resources in steel far greater than ours and which is not so closely and deeply involved at present, a programme on astronomical lines has been developed and is being carried forward in the construction both of escort vessels and of merchant ships. But what a terrible waste it is to think of all these great ships that are sunk, full of priceless cargoes, and how necessary it is to make that extra intensification of effort which will enable us to get ahead and to establish more complete mastery and so save these ships from being sunk, as well as adding new ones to the Fleet, by which alone the victory of the good cause can be achieved.

There is a second danger. You must never underrate the power of the German machine. It is the most terrible machine that has been created. After the last war they kept the brains of the German Army together. They kept their Great Staff together. Although their weapons were taken away, this tremendous association of people who think about nothing but war, studying war, ruthless scientific war, was held together, thousands of them, and they were able to train and build up an army which, as you saw, in a few weeks shattered to pieces the once famous Army of France, and which has marched in country after country and laid it low, and laid low every form of opposition, and only now in the vast spaces of Russia is confronted with this immense and valiant race which has stood against them; only now has the resistance of superior numbers made them pay the terrible toll of probably over 4,000,000 lives or men disabled; only now; but do not let us delude ourselves. Hitler lies in the centre, and across all the great railway lines of Europe he can move very rapidly forces from one side to the other. He may close down one front and open up on another. He has now, across in France and the Low Countries, a German Army as large as we have in this country, apart of course from the Home Guard. That is our great standby against parachute invasion. When I see the number of Divisions there are in France and realise that he can bring back in a few months, at any time in the Spring, 60 or 70 more Divisions, while perhaps lying quiescent or adopting a defensive attitude or perhaps giving some ground on the Russian front, I cannot feel that the danger of invasion can be put out of our minds. After all, if these men can strike us and strike us at the heart, the world is theirs. We are the target. We are the prize. We have sent and are sending many troops away. We are fighting very hard in Egypt now. The battle has only just begun. It is going to be a fight through to a finish. We have sent half a million men from this country to Egypt, to India, to the great regions which lie south of the Caspian Sea, during this present year alone. We must be ready. We must be ready here at the centre, not only to take advantage of any weakness on their part, but to be prepared to ward off any counter-stroke which they may cast upon us. Do not let people suggest to you that the major dangers of this war are past. We got through one supreme crisis where we might have been snuffed out, and now I do not think such a crisis can recur only because we are armed, because we are ready, because we are organised, because we have the weapons, because we have great numbers of trained men. But do not let us suppose that the dangers are past, even though the mortal danger was warded off two years ago.

There is a third danger, and it presents itself in a less precisely defined form. The last hope of the guilty Huns is a stalemate. Their idea has been made very plain in a series of speeches all delivered in the last month by Hitler, Göring, Goebbels and others, all defining and describing one conception, the idea of making a vast fortress of the greater part of Europe, with the Russian cornfields worked by slaves from the subjugated nations and by the prisoners of war, of whom they have several million, of organising a great European arsenal out of all the factories of the conquered countries, of starving and disciplining everyone in the great fortress area in order to feed the master race, and so hold out for years hoping that we shall get tired and fall out amongst ourselves and make a compromise peace, which means, and can only mean, that they will begin again. That is the third danger, and in some ways I think you will admit it is the most insidious of all.

How, then, are we to make sure of shortening the War? It is said we ought to concert our war plans. Well, everyone would agree to that. There is an obstacle, however, which should not escape attention – geography. You remember that thing we used to learn at school – all those maps; geography. We do the best we can to get over geography. The Field-Marshal and I fly to and fro wherever we have to go, for no other purpose than to bring into the closest possible concert the plans of the principal different nations on whom our alliance depends, and one of these fine days – mark my words – you will see whether we have been idle and whether we are quite incapable of design and action.

My Lords and Gentlemen, we have great Allies. We are no longer alone. Thirty nations march with us. Russia has come in, the United States have come in, there is another great ally on the way – supremacy in the air. We have got that supremacy in Egypt now. Presently we shall have it everywhere. Already we are blasting their war industries, already they are receiving what they gave, with interest – with compound interest. Soon they will get a bonus. Help us in all this. I know you will. All depends upon inflexible willpower based on the conviction shared by a whole people that the cause is good and righteous. Let it be the glory of our country to lead this world out of the dark valley into the broader and more genial sunshine. In the crisis of 1940, it is no more than the sober truth to say, we saved the freedom of mankind. We gave Russia time to arm, and the United States to organise; but now it is a long cold strain we have to bear, harder perhaps for the British to bear than the shocks which they know so well how to take. We must not cast away our great deliverance; we must carry our final work to its final conclusion. We shall not fail, and then some day, when children ask 'What did you do to win this inheritance for us, and to make our name so respected among men?' one will say: 'I was a fighter pilot'; another will say: 'I was in the Submarine Service'; another: 'I marched with the Eighth Army'; a fourth will say; 'None of you could have lived without the convoys and the Merchant Seamen'; and you in your turn will say, with equal pride and with equal right: 'We cut the coal.'

. . . D.In the name of His Majesty's Government, representing all Parties, and personally, from the bottom of my heart, I thank you most profoundly.

Winston S. Churchill to Sir Stafford Cripps
(Churchill papers, 20/67)

31 October 1942
Most Secret

DISPOSITION AND EMPLOYMENT OF EASTERN FLEET[1]

We were not strong enough to fight the Japanese Fleet when it entered the Bay of Bengal accompanied by five aircraft-carriers, in the early days of April, and it was necessary to withdraw to the African Coast. Directions were given to form a strong, balanced Eastern Fleet by the end of July, comprising three armoured aircraft-carriers, the battleships *Warspite, Valiant, Rodney, Nelson,* and four 'R' Class battleships together with the cruisers and flotillas. This fleet would certainly have advanced to Ceylon and Trincomalee and been ready to dispute the command of the Bay of Bengal. However, events, as you might have observed, took a different course. The Japanese did not press their attack upon India. Their naval war effort was, and is, concentrated mainly in the Pacific (the Coral Sea, Midway Island and the Solomons). At the same time the operation 'Torch' required the withdrawal of two out of the three carriers, and now the sinkings off the Cape have also required the temporary withdrawal of all the destroyers with this fleet. It exercises a general deterrent against surface raiders, because the enemy do not know where it may be or how large it is. It has rendered the Madagascar operation possible. It is not, however, in a condition to take offensive action, although individual

[1] Sir Stafford Cripps had written to Churchill criticizing the disposition and employment of the Eastern Fleet as lacking in 'common sense'.

'R' Class battleships sometimes accompany convoys. The losses in the Mozambique Channel and in the Indian Ocean have not been particularly severe, but, since they have been inflicted almost entirely by Japanese U-boats, the remedy would not be the use of the fleet but the provision of destroyer escorts. I am surprised that you do not realise how fully our destroyers are employed as all this has been apparent from the papers at your disposal. In fact, in spite of occasional losses, the whole vast flow of convoys has moved safely to and from the Middle East.

2. I had looked forward to re-forming the Eastern Fleet after the operation 'Torch' by returning to it the two carriers, *Malaya*, and some flotillas. It now seems, however, that our carriers will have to go to a different destination. Nevertheless, I hope it may be possible at the beginning of the New Year to advance to the Ceylon bases (which have already been visited several times by Admiral Somerville) and afford naval support to the offensive operations which we hope to see launched against the Japanese in Burma. I had asked the Admiralty whether the battleships should not enter the Eastern Mediterranean by the Suez Canal as part of the impending operations, but they convinced me that this evident localisation and presentment of the fleet outside the Indian Ocean would relieve the Japanese from the deterrent effect which it undoubtedly still exercises, even in its present incomplete condition.

3. I hope you will be careful not to allow this explanation, which I hope is not lacking 'common sense', and in which the Admiralty concur, to fall into any hands except your own.

Winston S. Churchill to President Franklin D. Roosevelt
(Churchill papers, 20/54)

31 October 1942
Most Secret

My dear Mr President,

Oliver Lyttelton will talk to your officers about production in its various aspects as they affect the layout we now have to make on what are our last remaining reserves of manpower; but I hope you will let me discuss with you some of the major points governing our joint action in the war.

First of all, I put the U-boat menace. This, I am sure, is our worst danger. It is horrible to me that we should be budgeting jointly for a balance of shipping on the basis of 700,000 tons a month loss. True it is not yet as bad as that. But the spectacle of all these splendid ships being built, sent to sea crammed with priceless food and munitions, and being sunk – three or four every day – torments me day and night. Not only does this attack cripple our war energies and threaten our life, but it arbitrarily limits the might of the United States coming into the struggle. The Oceans which were your shields threaten to become your cage.

Next year there will be many more U-boats, and they will range far more widely. No Ocean passage will be safe. All focal points will be beset and will require long range air protection. I expect all convoys will have to have anti-U-boat escorts, and often auxiliary aircraft carriers, throughout the greater part of their journeys, and fast convoys will have to be arranged for the ships at present routed independently. How are we to find the craft for this?

Nothing is more clearly proved than the efficacy of the convoy system. The marvellous recovery of your Atlantic shore is one proof. The immunity hitherto enjoyed by the vast and numerous troop convoys with ample escorts, is another. We are doing all we can to strike at the U-boat bases and U-boat plants, and you are proposing to base stronger bomber forces here to multiply our effort. All the same, it is <u>escorts</u> that we need, even more than merchant ships. We want both, but I am all with those who say, 'A ship not sunk in 1943 is worth two built for 1944'.

Therefore I submit to you for your good judgment the maximum allocation of steel for merchant shipbuilding, and then out of that, the maximum construction of escort vessels which engine capacity will allow. From the important measures which you have lately taken, I am sure your mind is moving in exactly the same direction.

We must ask for a fair share of the merchant shipping and of the escort vessels. All our labour and capacity is engaged in the war effort. We have had to sacrifice 100,000 tons of merchant shipbuilding in order to get more corvettes, and we cannot hope to produce more than 1,100,000 British gross tons of new merchant ships in the calendar year 1943. We have lost enormously in ships used in the common interest, and we trust to you to give us a fair and just assignment of your new vast construction to sail under our own flag.

We have agreed together that the escort vessels should be in the common pool, to be drawn upon in accordance with strategic requirements. In January, 1942, you accepted a requisition bringing the total of escort vessels to be built on our behalf to 300, 150 to be delivered in 1943 and 150 in 1944. Since then we have sent some assistance to the successful conflict you have waged against the U-boats on the east coast. The balance of strategic needs is such that we do not expect even the majority of these craft, but we ask most earnestly for a distribution of long range escort vessels from the common pool in the ratio of 1 to Britain to 1.37 to the United States, which is the ratio of our shortages mutually agreed. We are counting on this.

We have been so well treated by you in tanker tonnage, that it is with diffidence that I mention the figure of one million tons additional, which is what we need in 1943.

Mr President, I cannot cut the food consumption here below its present level. We need to import 27,000,000 tons for our food and war effort in 1943. More than three-quarters of our immense marine is engaged in war transport of one kind or another. We are asking for 2,500,000 dead weight non-tanker tonnage to be assigned to us from the beginning of 1943 from your new construction. Our stocks are running down with dangerous rapidity. Any further inroads upon them, except for some great emergency, would be highly improvident. These Islands are the assembly base for the war against Hitler; many of your troops will be here; and we must have a margin in case of a renewed 'blitz' on the Mersey and the Clyde, or exceptional concentration of U-boats on the Atlantic routes. Rather than cut any further on the food of the people, I should be forced to reduce our general contribution to the overseas war effort.

(ii) I send you herewith my direction for 1943 about the British Army. During 1942 we have sent abroad six Divisions apart from the five either on the sea or earmarked for 'Torch'. We may easily have to send two, or even four, more at short notice, and we shall be ready to do so. To help fill this gap, I am bringing up (as you will see from the paper) the nine 'Beach' Divisions, six to full standard, and freeing the other three with one additional for the draft-finding process for overseas, so exhausting to military efficiency. But the paper will speak for itself in detail, and I am sure you will feel it is a considerable contribution to the struggle.

I have not yet heard from you in reply to that part of my long telegram about Russia which dealt with the need to place more American divisions in this country, and to go forward with 'Bolero' for a retarded 'Round-up'. I had hoped to have, even on the new layout, seven or eight United States Divisions in these Islands by April, and we are still making preparations on a very large scale for the reception of a great American Army. I recognise that shipping is the limiting factor. Practically only the two Queens[1] are running now. I trust however you will allow your officers to discuss with ours the whole process of moving continuously Divisions at the fastest rate into these Islands, and thus make us both able to push our forces outwards where needed, as well as making the forward striking base safe, and holding the enemy pinned on the French shore.

(iii) Lastly, I come to the Air. Oliver Lyttelton is also thoroughly informed about this, and I have already communicated with Harry on the subject. An ever increasing weight of bomb discharge upon Germany and Italy must be our unrelenting aim. In our view, night bombing has already yielded results which justify it being backed by the United States, at any rate as a follow-up to your day bombing. But also the anti-U-boat war will require many long range flying boats and aircraft. So far as fighters are concerned, our opinion is that the latest British Spitfires and the improved American Mustang will hold the leadership in 1943.

Lyttelton is fully authorised to discuss all the above matters with you, and he is in full possession of our views. He will be with you during tremendous days, about which I shall be telegraphing to you pretty constantly. I pray that this great American enterprise, in which I am your Lieutenant and in which we have the honour to play an important part, may be crowned by the success it deserves. So far, all promises well.

I hope also to report to you about the Battle in Egypt, which is now entering upon a more important phase.

Believe me, always your most sincere friend,
Winston S. Churchill

---

[1] RMS *Queen Elizabeth* and RMS *Queen Mary*.

November
1942

Winston S. Churchill to President Franklin D. Roosevelt
(Churchill papers, 20/88)

1 November 1942
Most Secret

My wife and I have had the pleasure of seeing a good deal of Mrs Roosevelt in the last week, and my wife escorted her to Canterbury and Dover in my train on Friday. Dover is, of course, within range of the enemy artillery, but all passed off happily. It was lucky Friday was chosen instead of the next day, for Canterbury was then quite heavily bombed in a daylight raid as you will have seen.[1] Mrs Roosevelt has been winning gold opinions here from all for her kindness and her unfailing interest in everything we are doing. I think she has been impressed herself, and we are most grateful for her visit and for all the encouragement it is giving to our women workers. I did my best to advise a reduction of her programme and also interspersing it with blank days, but I have not met with success, and Mrs Roosevelt proceeds indefatigably. My wife is writing to you by the earliest plane and will give you more details. I only wish you were here yourself. I hope that may come to pass one day.

2. Meanwhile General Smuts seems much more inclined to accept your invitation to go to the United States. He has, of course, great responsibilities in South Africa, where his personality has held the fort. I hope, however, he may be persuaded to go. There are things he could say to the American people about the British Empire or Commonwealth of Nations which we could not say ourselves with equal acceptance. Naturally people are much hurt over here by the Luce–Willkie line.[2]

---

[1] In a surprise raid on Saturday, 31 October 1942, 62 German aircraft bombed Canterbury in the largest daylight raid on England since 1940. The streets were busy with shoppers: over 30 people were killed and more than 100 injured.

[2] Henry Luce, who had made his opposition to British imperial policy plain in, for example, the *Life* article of 12 October 1942 (see note on page 1282 above), had been a close adviser to the

3. Oliver Lyttelton leaves today. He brings you a personal letter from me to which I attach very great importance. I am sure you will read it with your invariable friendship and kindness to me.

4. The battle in Egypt is now rising to its climax, and our hopes are higher than I dare say.

Winston S. Churchill: War Cabinet paper
(Churchill papers, 23/10)

1 November 1942
Most Secret

ARMY STRENGTHS

We have now in Great Britain and Northern Ireland (including Canadian and Allied troops) 8 armoured divisions, 14 standard motorised infantry divisions, 1 Royal Marine division and 1 airborne division, total 24 fully mobile divisions, well equipped with guns and transport, with an average strength of about 15,300 men, with 9 corps organisations and corps troops (53,000). We have 3 brigade groups with artillery and engineers, which are equivalent to another fully mobile division. Of the 14 standard infantry divisions 5 have been reorganised in the past year to include a tank, instead of an infantry brigade, thus increasing their striking power. There are also 9 lower establishment divisions, averaging about 10,000 organised for semi-mobile defence with reduced scales of artillery and engineers and little transport. In addition, there are 3 armoured, 5 tank and 10 infantry brigades not included in divisions and 17 un-brigaded battalions; furthermore, 95 home defence and young soldiers' battalions are employed on vulnerable points and airfield defence.

2. During 1942 we have sent abroad 1 armoured and 5 infantry divisions which are not included above; also 252,000 men in non-divisional units and drafts. Under orders for overseas are 2 armoured, 2 infantry and 1 Royal Marine divisions: total 11 divisions. Of these 5 divisions must be taken from those given in paragraph 1 and will require their quota of corps, army, anti-aircraft and base units. These additional forces for overseas service could only be found at the expense of troops in the United Kingdom; and it is necessary to take steps to build up the forces remaining.

Republican candidate Wendell Willkie in the 1940 American presidential election. Although a supporter of US financial and material assistance to Britain and France in their struggle against Nazi Germany, Willkie had spoken out strongly against British colonial practices in his campaign speeches, many of them written by Luce.

3. It is proposed to transform the forces remaining in the United Kingdom, after despatch of 5 divisions mentioned above, into 7 armoured divisions (increase of 1 Canadian armoured division), 18 standard motorised infantry divisions and 1 airborne division, total 26 fully mobile divisions. The 3 brigade groups will remain as at present. Of 18 standard divisions 7 will include tank brigades and 6 will be transformed from lower establishment divisions brought up in strength. There will be a reserve organisation consisting of 4 divisions and 1 officer training brigade, whose main task will be to complete the training of reinforcements for the considerable forces overseas instead of our having, as at present, to find these men from the mobile divisions to the continuous detriment of their efficiency.

Independent tank and armoured brigades will be reduced to 2 and infantry brigades not in divisions to 5. Battalions for vulnerable points and airfield defence will be reduced to 24 and the task of guarding aerodromes handed over mainly to the RAF Regiment.

The foregoing will constitute the Home Field Army which can be reckoned as the equivalent of 33 divisions.

4. The object of these changes is to increase the war-power of the Army by concentrating scattered defensive elements into proper formations which can be turned later on into forces for overseas operations. There will be an increase in divisions with an armoured element and additional field, anti-tank and flak artillery will be provided.

5. No reduction in the force mentioned in paragraph 3 is compatible with our war needs; indeed, it is necessary that rearward services should be provided in 1943 for as many of the divisions as possible with a view to passing to the offensive on the Continent of Europe or elsewhere. To maintain the Army, to provide for the replacement of casualties as they occur and to build up the necessary units for offensive action, there will be required an intake to the Army averaging 45,000 men per month from November till April 1943, when a further review will be made.

6. ADGB[1] has been reduced to 280,000 men by using women and Home Guards to the maximum extent possible under present circumstances. 76,000 at least of the 280,000 will be formed into mobile flak units to accompany any Field Army divisions used for offensive operations, and further examination is being made to reduce overheads and make additional savings in the number of fit men employed on anti-aircraft defences in the United Kingdom. The anti-aircraft force is formed into 7 groups which are the equivalent of 12 divisions.

[1] ADGB: Air Defence of Great Britain.

7. The Army of the Nile has lost the services of the Australian corps with 2 Australian divisions, and the remaining Australian division will be returned to Australia in 1943. Also the 70th British Division was sent to India to assist in meeting the Japanese threat to Burma and Ceylon. These reductions have been offset by the arrival in the Middle East of the 8th British Armoured Division, and 44th and 51st British Infantry Divisions. A separate Command has been established for Persia and Iraq to which the 5th British Division from India and the 56th now at sea have been assigned.

8. It is proposed to reorganise the forces in the Middle East to include 3 British armoured and 2 South African armoured divisions, 2 British, 1 New Zealand, 2 Indian and the equivalent of 2 Allied divisions of Fighting French and Greek troops; total 12 divisions.

9. The Army in Persia and Iraq will comprise 1 Indian armoured division and 1 British armoured brigade, 2 British, 3 Indian divisions and the Polish Army of the East of 2 divisions and 2 tank brigades; total, 9 divisions. Grand total field divisions in North Africa, Palestine and Syria, Persia and Iraq: 26 divisions.

10. For the defence of India there will be assembled and ready by next Spring 1 Indian armoured division and 2 tank brigades, 2 British divisions and 1 brigade group, 10 complete Indian divisions and the equivalent of 2 further divisions in brigade groups, &c. This excludes troops for defence of the North-West Frontier and for Internal Security, which amount to the equivalent of 4 divisions and 92 battalions; the whole totalling 20 divisions. There are, in addition, 2 Chinese divisions which are in process of being formed and equipped.

11. There remain our garrisons abroad, to wit:

Gibraltar and Malta – the equivalent of 2 divisions.
East Africa, including Madagascar – that of 3 ½
West Africa and minor garrisons – that of 3 ½
Total division-equivalent of garrisons, 9.

12. We have suffered grievous losses in Malaya, Burma, and the Middle East, including the loss of 4 complete divisions at Singapore and 1 South African division in Tobruk. In spite of this, the total strength of British, Dominion, and Allied forces has been maintained at the equivalent of approximately 100 divisions. In maintaining our fighting strength, India has provided the greatest contribution and has expanded by several divisions, but we have had to find British cadres for these divisions.

13. If we estimate our Army in divisions or their equivalent, the general lay-out for 1943 is as follows:

United Kingdom	33
Under orders for overseas operations	5
Anti-aircraft divisions	12
Army of the Nile	12
Army of Persia and Iraq	9
Army of India	20
Garrisons in Africa and elsewhere	9
Grand total	100

It must be realised that, in setting out the numerical distribution of forces in equivalent divisions, anti-aircraft and static troops have been included where the total numbers of such troops approximately equal a division. These divisions are not provided with artillery, engineers and signals and cannot be counted on as field divisions. The number of field divisions are specifically mentioned in paragraphs 2, 3, 8, 9 and 10.

14. It is our duty to develop, equip and maintain all these units during 1943.

Winston S. Churchill to Major Desmond Morton
(Churchill papers, 20/67)

1 November 1942

Is there no arrangement by which all Intelligence of the Departments is brought together? How is it that I am not supplied with this series of telegrams?[1] Find out also about the one on pink paper which General Smuts had about the effect of the air attack on Northern Italy. It may be that these are a special Air Force line, different from the series of which you sometimes send me flimsies. If so, you are to see that line on my behalf and weed out ones of special interest or importance, so as not to burden me too much. In case you require authority, draft a minute accordingly for my signature.

You may also redraft your minute flagged 'B',[2] to bring it up to date, and then return to me.

---

[1] Telegrams from Naval, Military, and Air Attachés abroad sent directly to their Directors of Intelligence.

[2] Minute of 20 January 1941 about the organisation of Intelligence.

Winston S. Churchill to Lord Louis Mountbatten
and Brigadier Ian Jacob
(Churchill papers, 20/67)

1 November 1942
Secret

We must be careful not to make heavy weather over the manning of landing craft. No doubt there must be a nucleus of skilled personnel to handle them and keep the engines in order. They do not have to be kept up, however, like a fleet or flotilla, as they are only needed for a special operation and, if all goes well, only for the preliminary stages of that. If it were decided that the time had come for such an operation, both the Fleet and the Army would have to provide men specially for the month or three weeks concerned. We could not possibly afford to tie up a large mass of men indefinitely waiting for the chance of a big cross-Channel operation. First, let us get the craft and, meanwhile, make a scheme to put them into skeleton preparation capable of being brought up to fuller strength as the moment comes nearer. In trying to be perfect you will spoil the whole thing.

Winston S. Churchill to John Stourton[1]
(Churchill papers, 20/54)

1 November 1942
Private

Dear Mr Stourton,

I have referred your letter of October 30 to the Secretary of State for War for his consideration.

We have not the same control over the Canadian Army as over our own troops. This is a fact which must be accepted.

With regard to equalizing the spending power of the British and American troops, everyone can see this would be a good thing. We are not however in a position to give directions to the United States. This power was lost, as you will remember, some 150 years ago, and I think it is highly unlikely it will be resumed. When I made inquiries as to whether an agreement could be reached, I was informed that the pay of American

---

[1] John Joseph Stourton, 1899–1992. Educated at Downside. Lieutenant, 10th Royal Hussars, 1918. Served in the North Russian Relief Force at Archangel, 1919. Conservative MP for South Salford, 1931–45. Served with the Army in the Second World War; Major, Royal Norfolk Regiment. Secretary, Conservative Foreign Affairs Committee, 1944–5.

forces is based on legislation by Congress, and that any attempt to raise the matter would be ill-received and quite ineffectual.

Equality of sacrifice is certainly the ideal at which the United Nations should aim. Whether we shall achieve that ideal is quite another matter. Opinions might differ about the facts, and I expect the Russians would have something to say. I do the best I can to get these problems solved in a satisfactory manner, but anyone who thinks we are in a position to give orders over the whole area of the United Nations is adrift from reality.

Yours very faithfully,
Winston S. Churchill

Winston S. Churchill to Brendan Bracken
(Churchill papers, 20/67)

1 November 1942

Who was the censor who passed the Willkie article for *Collier's Magazine*? You say the Egyptian censor. What do you mean by that? Was he a British officer, or is there an American censorship for American articles? Let me know the authority and the name.

I asked for this information last week. Please treat it as urgent, as I wish to communicate with Mr Willkie on the matter, in which I think he has reasonable grounds for complaint.

Winston S. Churchill to Field Marshal Jan Smuts
(Churchill papers, 20/54)

1 November 1942

My dear Smuts,

Thank you so much for sending me the manuscript of your speech.[1] I am having it bound and am going to have it preserved with the other historic treasures at Chequers.

Yours v. sincerely
Winston S. Churchill

---

[1] Smuts' address to House of Commons on 21 October 1942, in which he spoke of the end of Britain's defensive stage of the war, and of the beginning of its offensive stage. He labelled the fight against Hitler the darkest page in modern history, and called for a 'new fight to death for man's rights and liberties'.

Oliver Harvey: diary
(*'The War Diaries of Oliver Harvey'*, page 175)

2 November 1942

POSSIBLE VISIT BY CHURCHILL TO WASHINGTON DC

[...] the PM is particularly keen to go again now, and the PM's doctor has urged strongly against any more flying. AE would go over after 'Torch' and discuss both military operations and postwar, the former subject being obvious and unassailable, the latter to be kept secret if necessary.

[...]

Sir Alexander Cadogan: diary
(*'The Diaries of Sir Alexander Cadogan'*, page 488)

3 November 1942

'C' had news, which he 'phoned me this morning, which certainly seems to show Rommel is in a fix. I am *inclined* to think that R cries 'wolf' to get more help sent him. [...]

Cabinet this morning about 'Atlantic Co-operation'. PM of course excited about Egyptian news, and his excitement took the not unexpected form of 'Damn Europe: we'll be strong enough to go our own way'.[...]

Winston S. Churchill to President Franklin D. Roosevelt
(*Churchill papers, 20/82*)

3 November 1942
Personal and Secret
No. 182

The Battle of Egypt goes well. We have good hopes of breaking the enemy's lines in the northern sector, with consequences which may well be far-reaching.

2. Will you allow me to say that your proposed message to Petain seems to me too kind. His stock must be very low now. He has used his reputation to do our cause injuries no lesser man could have done. I beg you to think of the effect on the de Gaullists, to whom we have serious obligations and who have now to go through the great trial of being kept outside. I am advised that unfavourable reactions would be produced

in various other quarters. Of course it is absolutely right to send him a friendly message, but will you consider toning it down a bit.

3. Giraud has wirelessed us saying he has decided to come over at once and asking for an airplane to fetch him to Gibraltar. Eisenhower[1] has replied advising that he uses the British submarine under a United States captain which is already off the coast.

Winston S. Churchill to President Franklin D. Roosevelt
(Churchill papers, 20/82)

3 November 1942
Personal and Secret
For yourself alone
No. 183

The reports from Egypt now justify confidence in a decisive victory. In the event of a satisfactory break through in the north it will be very difficult for Rommel to disengage his Army, particularly the eight unmotorized divisions to the southwards.

2. I am so glad to see that your news from the Solomons and New Guinea is also so much better.

Winston S. Churchill to Duncan Sandys
(Churchill papers, 20/82)

3 November 1942
Personal and Secret

Should be glad to know how you are getting on and whether you have seen anything of the battle. I hope so. The news we have of it is very good. PJ[2] has agreed to fortnightly meetings of the Army Council at which all important decisions of the Executive Committee will be reviewed. I see no reason why you should not continue your tour as you plan though you will no doubt arrange with the Secretary of State yourself. Diana has just been with me, and all is well at home.

---

[1] On 6 November 1942 General Eisenhower telegraphed to Churchill: 'I should like once again to express to you personally my grateful thanks for your constant support and encouragement during the last few months. We are of good heart and have every confidence that good fortune will continue to be ours' ('Personal', *Churchill papers, 20/82*).

[2] Sir [Percy] James Grigg, Secretary of State for War.

Winston S. Churchill to Sir James Grigg
(Churchill papers, 20/54)

3 November 1942

My dear Grigg,

I am very much obliged to you for meeting my wishes on the constitutional points raised in my letter to you of October 27,[1] and I hope that now matters will run smoothly and to your liking.

Thank you also for your personal letter about the reorganization of the Army and my directive thereupon. I hope indeed we shall be able to find the ways and means.

Yours sincerely,
Winston S. Churchill

Winston S. Churchill and Clementine Churchill to Lord Halifax
(Churchill papers, 20/57)

3 November 1942

I beg you accept our deepest sympathy with you in the loss of your gallant son[2] in this great battle, which will not be fought in vain.

Winston and Clementine Churchill

Lord and Lady Halifax to Winston S. Churchill
and Clementine Churchill
(Churchill papers, 20/57)

3 November 1942
Personal

We are deeply grateful to you both. With you we pray for victory in Africa which may bring lightening of your great burdens

Edward and Dorothy

---

[1] In this letter Churchill lamented the decreasing frequency of meetings of the Army Council during Grigg's tenure as Secretary of State for War, and the consequent diminished role of Parliamentary Ministers (as opposed to civil servants and military officers) in Army administration. He urged Grigg to remedy the situation, pointing out the need to 'ensure that the Parliamentary Ministers are enabled to perform their due part in the work of the [War] Office'.

[2] Francis Hugh Peter Courtenay Wood, 1916–42. 2nd son of Viscount Halifax. Educated at Eton. Major in the Queen's Own Yorkshire Dragoons. Killed in action in Egypt, 26 October 1942.

Winston S. Churchill to General Sir Harold Alexander
(Churchill papers, 20/82)

4 November 1942
Immediate
Bigot

I send you my heartfelt congratulations on the splendid feat of arms achieved by the Eighth Army under the command of your brilliant lieutenant, Montgomery, in the Battle of Egypt. Although the fruits may take some days or even weeks to gather it is evident that an event of the first magnitude has occurred which will play its part in the whole future course of the World War.

2. If the reasonable hopes of your telegram are maintained, and wholesale captures of the enemy and a general retreat are apparent, I propose to ring the bells all over Britain for the first time this war. Try to give me the moment to do this in the next few days. At least 20,000 prisoners would be necessary. You will realise that such a demonstration would be timely in the immediate advent of 'Torch', both in encouraging our friends in the 'Torch' area and in taking the enemy's eye off what is coming to him next quite soon.

3. 'Kingpin'[1] is proposing to embark tonight in one of our submarines to go to Gibraltar and meet 'Ikey'. He will definitely head the movement in the 'Torch' area under the Supreme United States Command.[2]

All 'Torch' movements are proceeding with precision and hitherto amazing secrecy. We shall all have to take a new view of the general position before very long.

Winston S. Churchill: recollection
('The Hinge of Fate', page 114)

4 November 1942

U-BOAT WARFARE

So menacing were the conditions in the outer waters beyond the range of air cover that on November 4 I personally convened a new Anti-U-boat

---

[1] General Giraud.

[2] On 8 November 1942, thanking Churchill for a message of greeting (see page 1368 below), General Giraud replied: 'Thank you for your kind telegram. I too remember our frank talks at Metz. Like you, through difficulties and trials, I have never had any doubt of the final victory. I am certain today that, thanks to the efforts of all, Alsace and Lorraine will remain French' (*Churchill papers, 20/82*).

Committee to deal specially with this aspect. The power of this body to take far-reaching decisions played no small part in the conflict. In a great effort to lengthen the range of our Radar-carrying Liberator aircraft, we decided to withdraw them from action for the time needed to make the necessary improvements. As part of this policy the President at my request sent all suitable American aircraft, fitted with the latest type of Radar, to work from the United Kingdom. Thus we were presently able to resume operations in the Bay of Biscay in greater strength and with far better equipment. This decision, and other measures taken in November 1942, were to reap their reward in 1943.

Winston S. Churchill to General Sir Harold Alexander
(Churchill papers, 20/82)

4 November 1942
Most Secret and Personal

ROMMEL'S REPORT OF A SHORTAGE
OF FUEL OIL AND MUNITIONS

Presume you have read all the 'Boniface' including especially No. QT5086[1] sent you night of 2nd.
Kindly acknowledge Clear the Line.[2]

Winston S. Churchill to President Franklin D. Roosevelt
(Churchill papers, 20/82)

4 November 1942
Personal and Secret
No. 184

I have just received the following from General Alexander. We are not proclaiming anything at present. Begins: After twelve days of heavy and violent fighting 8th Army has inflicted a severe defeat on the enemy's German and Italian forces under Rommel's command in Egypt. The

---

[1] An emergency message from Rommel announcing that his army was 'no longer in a position to prevent a further attempt by strong enemy tank formations to break through' and that, in view of the obstacles to withdrawal, 'in spite of the heroic resistance and the excellent spirit of the troops the possibility of the gradual annihilation of the army must be faced' (Hinsley et al., *British Intelligence in the Second World War*, Volume II, page 448).

[2] General Alexander replied: 'Have read all the Boniface' ('Most Secret, Personal', *Churchill papers, 20/82*).

enemy's front has broken and British armoured formations in strength have passed through and are operating in the enemy's rear areas. Such portions of the enemy's forces as can get away are in full retreat and are being harassed by our armoured and mobile forces and by our Air Forces. Other enemy divisions are still in position endeavouring to stave off defeat and these are likely to be surrounded and cut off.

The RAF has throughout given superb support to the land battle and are bombing the enemy's retreating columns incessantly.

Fighting continues. Ends.

I feel sure you will regard this as a good prelude to 'Torch'.

Winston S. Churchill to William Mackenzie King
(Churchill papers, 20/82)

4 November 1942
Most Secret and Personal

I really do hope you will not press me too hard about these 400 prisoners, whom you can tie up as loosely as you please. Very great events are impending, and we may feel much easier in a little while. The Hitler movement to accuse us of atrocities and to repudiate the Geneva Convention is dying down. Our firm attitude has made its impression on the German Foreign Office and German High Command. It would be a thousand pities to give in to this bully and make a feature of it at this juncture. Such an advertised surrender might well lead to a prolongation of these indignities on your men and ours. I shall certainly ask Parliament next week to wait longer for the results of the Swiss mediation, and I have very little doubt that the House of Commons will accord us this help in our responsibilities and difficulties. Better days are coming. All good wishes.

Winston S. Churchill to the Most Reverend William Temple[1]
(Churchill papers, 20/54)

4 November 1942
Private and Secret

My dear Archbishop,

We are still waiting for a reply from the German Government to the communication we addressed to them on the 13th of October.

---

[1] Archbishop of Canterbury.

Meanwhile no further reprisals have been taken by the German Government so far as I am aware and we, having made our protest, have no intention of proceeding further upon that course. Moreover the campaign of alleged atrocities by Great Britain to which the German propaganda has lent itself and which has seemed to be the prelude to a repudiation by them of the Geneva Convention has died down. The Cabinet have decided to wait longer for the German reply before taking any action and this is the view which I shall express to the House of Commons. I have no doubt that the publication at the date you propose of the Resolution which you have been good enough to send me will be detrimental to the chances of obtaining a reciprocal removal of the restraints inflicted upon a small number of prisoners by each side which was begun by the Germans. For this however the responsibility will not rest with His Majesty's Government.

Let me thank you for your courtesy in communicating your intentions.

Yours sincerely,
Winston S. Churchill

General Sir Alan Brooke: diary
(*'War Diaries, Field Marshal Lord Alanbrooke'*, *page 338*)

4 November 1942

[...] Sent for by PM at 10.20 a.m. to show me an intercept of Hitler saying to Rommel that he was to hold on and that his men should select between 'death and victory'. PM delighted. At 3.30 p.m. he sent for me again to discuss the prospect of ringing church bells. I implored him to wait a little longer till we were quite certain that we should have no cause for regretting ringing them. More good reports from Alex during afternoon. At 11 p.m. sent for again by PM who was busy dictating messages to Roosevelt, Stalin, Dominions, Commanders, etc. He was in great state of excitement. Anthony Eden came in later, also Brendan Bracken who was mainly interested in results of American election which has gone badly for Roosevelt. But PM refused to be depressed by this!

[...]

Winston S. Churchill to Josef Stalin
(Cabinet papers, 65/28)

5 November 1942
Most Immediate
Personal and Secret

I promised to tell you when our Army in Egypt had gained a decisive victory over Rommel. General Alexander now reports that the enemy's front is broken and that he is retreating westwards in considerable disorder. Apart from the troops in the main battle, there are six Italian and two German divisions in the desert to the south of our advance along the coast. These have very little mechanical transport or supplies, and it is possible that a very heavy toll will be taken in the next few days. Besides this, Rommel's only line of retreat is along the coastal road, which is now crammed with troops and transport and under the continuous attack of our greatly superior Air Force.

2. Most Secret – for yourself alone. 'Torch' is imminent on a very great scale. I believe the political difficulties about which you expressed concern have been satisfactorily solved. The military movement is proceeding with precision.

3. I am most anxious to proceed with the placing of the 20 British and American squadrons on your southern flank as early as possible. President Roosevelt is in full accord and there is no danger now of a disaster in Egypt. Before anything can be done however it is necessary that detailed arrangements should be made about landing grounds, etc., between your Officers and ours.

Kindly let me know as soon as possible how you would like this consultation to be arranged. The squadrons it is proposed to send were stated in my telegram of 8th October (Foreign Office No. 268) in accordance with which we have been making such preparations as were possible pending arrangements with you.

4. Let me further express to you, Premier Stalin, and to M Molotov our congratulations on the ever-glorious defence of Stalingrad and on the decisive defeat of Hitler's second campaign against Russia. I should be glad to know from you how you stand in the Caucasus.

5. All good wishes for your anniversary.[1]

---

[1] The 25th anniversary of the foundation of the Soviet Union in November 1917.

Winston S. Churchill to President Franklin D. Roosevelt
(Churchill papers, 20/82)

5 November 1942
Personal and Secret
No. 185

It will be necessary for me to explain 'Torch' to de Gaulle some-time during D minus 1 when it is certain the weather is all right. You will remember that I have exchanged letters with him of a solemn kind in 1940 recognising him as the Leader of Free Frenchmen. I am confident his military honour can be trusted. I will however take all precautions.

2. I shall explain to him that the reason I have not mentioned 'Torch' to him is that it is a United States enterprise and a United States secret, and that the reason he and his friends are not in on it is not any want of goodwill on our joint part towards him and his Movement, but because of the local complications in the 'Torch' area and the need to have as little fighting as possible. I am arranging to let him announce General Legentilhomme as Governor-General of Madagascar sometime Friday. This we have been keeping for his consolation prize. It will be a proof that we do not think of throwing over the Free French. As for his relations with Giraud I should think myself they will join forces politically though under what conditions I cannot foresee. I hope you will approve of the course I propose.

Winston S. Churchill to General Bernard Montgomery
(Churchill papers, 20/82)

5 November 1942
Most Secret
Immediate

I send you my warmest congratulations on your wonderful work, both in reviving the spirits of the Eighth Army and in your masterly conduct of the battle.

Winston S. Churchill to Admiral Henry Harwood[1]
(Churchill papers, 20/82)

5 November 1942
Immediate. Hush.
Personal

Our victory in Egypt and the impending reactions to 'Torch' may give an opportunity for bringing Admiral Godfroy to see his duty to France in its true light.[2] You must watch this moment with the greatest vigilance. We shall also be watching it from here. Your personal influence as one sailor to another may go far. Keep close to him these days and let me know his mood, also that of his officers and men.

2. It seems to me certain that the Germans will overrun Unoccupied France on the morrow of 'Torch' and that Vichy will collapse, possibly even there will be resistance to the Germans.

Winston S. Churchill to Anthony Eden
(Churchill papers, 20/67)

5 November 1942

Although the World War is proceeding with diverse episodes of interest cropping up from time to time, the entire politics of the Foreign Office with Turkey are expressed in the one word 'chrome'. I thought you told me you were going to wind this up, but your pertinacious secretariat and your verbose Ambassador[3] continue to wear out the cipher staff and aggravate the paper shortage, to say nothing of wearing out my eyesight, by endless disputation.

King George VI to Winston S. Churchill
(Churchill papers, 20/67)

5 November 1942   Buckingham Palace

My dear Winston,

I must send you my warmest congratulations on the great Victory of the 8th Army in Egypt. I was overjoyed when I received the news and so was everybody else. In our many talks together over a long period I knew that the elimination of the Afrika Corps, the threat to Egypt, was your <u>one</u> aim, the most important of all the many other operations with which you

---

[1] Vice-Admiral and Commander-in-Chief, Mediterranean Station.

[2] Godfroy, who commanded the demilitarized French fleet in Alexandria, joined the Free French in 1943.

[3] Sir Hughe Knatchbull-Hugessen.

have had to deal. When I look back and think of all the many arduous hours of work you have put in, and the many miles you have travelled, to bring this battle to such a successful conclusion you have every right to rejoice; while the rest of our people will one day be very thankful to you for what you have done. I cannot say more. At last the Army has come into its own, as it is their victory primarily, ably helped by the forces of the air, and of those that work under the surface of the sea.

I am so pleased that everybody is taking this victory in a quiet and thankful way, though their rejoicing is very deep and sincere.

I remain,
Yours very sincerely,
GEORGE RI

Winston S. Churchill to General Charles de Gaulle
(Churchill papers, 20/54)

5 November 1942
Secret

My dear General,

Thank you very much for your letter of congratulation.

The fruits of the victory have yet to be gathered, but they may well be abundant. Your military eye will no doubt observe the extremely compromised position of all the Axis divisions south of the break-through, and also the ordeal which awaits the whole of Rommel's army as they flee westwards on the coastal road. It will, I am sure, give you the same pleasure as it does me to see the Boche getting a taste of the medicine with which they have dosed others so mercilessly.

Both your Fighting French Brigades are well forward in the hunt on the southern flank.

Yours sincerely
Winston S. Churchill

Winston S. Churchill to Randolph S. Churchill
(Churchill papers, 20/65)

5 November 1942
Personal and Secret

Tell Colonel Glendinning[1] that the victory in Egypt is very great and will be greater. Thinking much of you. Love from all.

[1] Colonel William Glendinning, Officer Commanding Commando No. 1 of Special Services Brigade, 1940–2; Second-in-Command of Special Services Brigade, 1942.

Sir Alexander Cadogan: diary
(*'The Diaries of Sir Alexander Cadogan'*, page 489)

5 November 1942

[...]

PM v. over-excited. Night before last he sent for 'C' at 11 p.m. About 11.15 he said 'You look v. tired; you'd better go to bed'. 'C' admitted he was, and would. At 2.15 a.m. PM rang him up to ask a quite unnecessary question – and then apologised!

General Sir Harold Alexander to Winston S. Churchill
(*Churchill papers, 20/82*)

6 November 1942
Most Immediate
Personal

Ring out the bells! Prisoners estimated now 20,000, tanks 350, guns 400, MT[1] several thousand. Our advanced mobile forces are south of Mersa Matruh. 8th Army is advancing.

Winston S. Churchill to Richard Casey
(*Churchill papers, 20/82*)

6 November 1942
Immediate
Bigot
Personal and Most Secret

We are not telling de Gaulle anything until 'Torch' is lit. Nothing therefore must be said to Catroux[2] in advance. The reason which we shall give for this is that it is an American secret, and an American expedition, and the President insisted on secrecy.

---

[1] MT: Motor transport (vehicles).

[2] Georges Catroux, 1877–1969. A professional soldier, he spent most his career in Syria, where in 1930 a young staff officer, Captain de Gaulle, was much impressed by his ability to arouse local sympathy and respect. As Governor-General of Indo-China in 1940, he was the only French pro-consul and the only *général d'armée* to join de Gaulle, for which he was condemned to death by Vichy. In 1941 he was appointed by de Gaulle to command the Free French forces against the Vichy forces in the Syrian campaign. Free French representative in Algeria, 1943. Ambassador to Moscow, 1945–8. Honorary British knighthood, 1946. Governor-General of Algeria, 1956.

Winston S. Churchill to President Franklin D. Roosevelt
(Churchill papers, 20/82)

6 November 1942
Most Secret and Personal
No. 186

As at present arranged no reference will be made to the participation of British Divisions in 'Torch', as distinct from the supporting action by the Royal Navy and the Royal Air Force, before your press release. It would greatly help me if you could let me know at what time you intend to issue this. I would then follow up your press release with a statement of my own.

2. Since in your press release you are referring to the participation of British Divisions, I much hope that you will reconsider your decision not to allow the use of the leaflet submitted by Eisenhower making known the arrival of British troops in Algeria. I feel that this leaflet should not be held up more than 24 or at the most 48 hours after British troops have landed.

3. I am still sorry about de Gaulle. Of course we control all his telegrams outwards. But we are ready to accept your view. All goes well.

Oliver Harvey: diary
('The War Diaries of Oliver Harvey', page 177)

6 November 1942

[…]

Giraud is believed to be arriving at Gibraltar tonight. De Gaulle is only to be told of 'Torch' on Sunday. We wanted to tell him the evening before but Roosevelt won't hear of it.

The armada is now well into the Mediterranean, the largest expedition that has ever set sail, 500,000 men. It has eluded the pack of German submarines lying off Gibraltar but it now comes within range of bombers from Sardinia and Sicily. The Germans are concentrating all they can there but our ships have large forces of fighters in carriers.

Winston S. Churchill to General Sir Harold Alexander
(Churchill papers, 20/82)

6 November 1942
Most Secret
Important
Bigot
Personal

I shall be making an important statement to Parliament on the battle of Egypt on November 11th. Try to send me the latest information to reach me night of 10th, including best possible estimate of casualties given and taken and anything else which you think helpful. I should welcome a good account.

2. My regards to Montgomery. He has been magnificent. I wish I could have been with you both in these great days.

3. All well so far with 'Torch', and weather promising.

Lady Leslie to Winston S. Churchill
(Churchill papers, 1/368)

6 November 1942   Glaslough
                                         County Monaghan

Beloved Winston,

We are all rejoicing over the news from Libya – the tide is turning – and I like to think of how pleased you must be!

Your visit to the Desert is having good Results. Harold Alexander is not only very able – but also lucky.

This is no letter dearest. Only a wave of Love and Congratulations.

                                                 Leonie[1]

Harold Nicolson: diary
('Harold Nicolson, Diaries and Letters', pages 257–8)

6 November 1942

At 1.15 I stroll across to Downing Street where I am to lunch. As I have time at my disposal, I shall record what happened in full detail.

---

[1] Churchill replied by telegram, written out in his own hand: 'Thank you so much dear Leonie' (*Churchill papers, 1/368*).

I turned into Downing Street where there is a barrier with barbed wire and police. I waved my blue pass and was not interrupted.... I enter No.10. Attlee is there and waves. Eden is hurrying along the passage... I go downstairs to the basement where the Churchills are living, since the upper floors have been knocked about. They made it very pretty with chintz and flowers and good furniture and excellent French pictures not only the moderns, but Ingres and David.

I find Lady Kitty Lambton[1] and Lady Furness[2] and Clemmie Churchill. We are given sherry. Eddy Marsh[3] comes in, and then the Private Secretary, Martin a neat alert young man: I should say Winchester, New College and Treasury.[4] He tells us not to wait for Winston, as he is late. We go into luncheon: sea-kale, jugged hare and cherry tart. Not well done. In a few minutes Winston comes in. He is dressed in his romper suit of Air Force blue and he carries a letter in his hand. He kisses Kitty Lambton. 'Good to have you here, Kitty. You must tell me about France.' He is introduced to Lady Furness. 'Good morning, Eddy.' 'Good morning, Harold.' He half bows and smiles, accenting the first syllable of 'morning'. He gives the letter to Clemmie. It is a long letter from the King written in his own handwriting, and saying how much he and the Queen have been thinking of Winston these glorious days. Winston is evidently pleased. 'Every word', he mutters, 'in his own hand.'

Kitty Lambton and Lady Furness have just escaped from the South of France. Lady Kitty has clearly known Winston from childhood and treats him with gay familiarity which is only slightly overdone. Lady Furness has

[1] Katherine de Vere Beauclerk, 1877–1958. Daughter of William Ameleus Aubrey de Vere Beauclerk, 10th Duke of St Albans. Married Henry Charles Somers Augustus Somerset, 1896. Divorced, 1920. Married Major-General Sir William Lambton, 1921.

[2] Thelma Morgan, 1904–70. Born in Lucerne, Switzerland. Thelma and her twin sister, Gloria, both prominent and glamorous figures in high society in London in the 1920s and early 1930s, were daughters of Harry Hays Morgan, an American diplomat who served as United States Consul in Buenos Aires and in Brussels. Briefly a film producer and actress, having founded Thelma Morgan Pictures at the age of 17, in 1923, and starred that year in a film produced by her own company, *Aphrodite*. She also had small parts in the films *Enemies of Women* (1923), *So This Is Marriage?* (1924), and *Any Woman* (1925). Married, first, James Converse (divorced); second, the shipping magnate the 1st Viscount Furness, 1926.

[3] Edward Howard Marsh, 1872–1953. Educated at Westminster and Trinity College, Cambridge. Entered the Colonial Office as a 2nd Class Clerk, 1896. Assistant Private Secretary to Neville Chamberlain, 1900; to Oliver Lyttelton, 1903. 1st Class Clerk, 1905. Private Secretary to Winston Churchill, 1905 (accompanying him on his visit to East Africa and Uganda, 1907–8), 1917–22. CMG, 1908. Assistant Private Secretary to Herbert Asquith, 1915–16; to the Duke of Devonshire, 1922–4; to J. H. Thomas, 1924, 1929–36; to Malcolm MacDonald, 1936–7. CB, 1918. KCVO, 1937. Trustee of the Tate Gallery, 1937–44. Chairman of the Contemporary Art Society, 1937–52. Vice-President of the Royal Society of Literature, 1943.

[4] Actually Edinburgh Academy, Corpus Christi College, Oxford, and the Dominions and Colonial Offices.

been brought by Lady Kitty and is nervous. I sit between her and Mrs Winston. Winston talks to Lady Kitty and I talk hard to Lady Furness, as she is frightened of the gigantic figure on her right, and Winston is bad at putting people at their ease. Nor does Clemmie Churchill help much. Winston stops talking to Lady Kitty and gazes round the table with his curious eyes. They are glaucous and look dead. When he gazes at people like that, there is no light either of interest or intelligence in his eyes. There is a faint expression of surprise, as if he were asking, 'What the hell is this man doing here?' There is a faint expression of angered indignation, as if he were saying, 'What damned cheek coming to luncheon here!' There is a mask of boredom and another mask or film of obstinacy, as if he were saying, 'These people bore me and I shall refuse to be polite.' And with it all, there are films of stubbornness, perhaps even a film of deep inner thought. It is very disconcerting. Then suddenly he will cease thinking of something else, and the film will part and the sun comes out. His eyes then pucker with amusement or flash with anger. At moments they have a tragic look. Yet these passing moods and phases do not flash across each other: they move slowly and opaquely like newts in a rather dim glass tank.

Lady Kitty chaffs him. She says that *Malbrouk s'en va-t-en guerre* refers, not to his well-known ancestor, but to some Saracen of the name of Ma'barak who attacked the Crusaders. She tells him that he owed nothing to the Churchill blood but it is the Jeromes who have brought in genius, as to Shane Leslie[1] and Clare Sheridan. 'I am proud,' he says, 'very proud of my American blood, but do not impute Shane to me.'

He turns to me and thanks me for my article on his oratory. I say I hope that I was right in saying that he was not a born orator. 'You are perfectly right,' he mumbles. 'Not born in the very least just hard, hard work.' He then talks to us about the battle. He begins with the first two battles of Alamein. 'I refuse', he says, 'to call it El Alamein. Like those asses who talk about Le Havre. *Havre* the place is to any decent man. Now this third battle must not be called Alamein. It must be called "The Battle

---

[1] John Randolph Leslie, 1885–1971. Known as 'Shane'. 3rd Baronet; Maternal first cousin of Winston Churchill. Educated at Ludgrove School, Eton, and King's College, Cambridge. Converted to Roman Catholicism, 1908. Parliamentary candidate, Irish Nationalist Party, 1910. Volunteer, British Ambulance Corps, 1913–15. Aide to British Ambassador to United States, 1916–17. Editor, *Dublin Review*, 1916–26. Privy Chamberlain of the Sword and Cape to Pope Pius XI, 1922. Founding Member of Irish Academy of Letters, 1932. Rosenbach Fellow in Bibliography, University of Pennsylvania, 1933–4. Professor, University of Notre Dame, 1934–5. Honorary Doctor of Laws, Notre Dame, 1935. Captain, Home Guard, 1939–46. Succeeded his father as 3rd Baronet, 1944. Author of over 40 volumes, including poetry, novels, memoirs, short stories, biographies, and other non-fiction. Close friend and mentor to F. Scott Fitzgerald.

of Egypt". Harold, see to that at once. Tell your people henceforward to call it the Battle of Egypt.' He tells us at length how he decided to remove Auchinleck and how he broke the news to him. 'It was a terrible thing to have to do. He took it like a gentleman. But it was a terrible thing. It is difficult to remove a bad General at the height of a campaign: it is atrocious to remove a good General. We must use Auchinleck again. We cannot afford to lose such a man from the fighting line.' He admits that he wanted Gott for the 8th Army. 'I saw that Army. It was a broken, baffled Army, a miserable Army. I felt for them with all my heart. I made my decision. I telegraphed to the Cabinet. I then took off all my clothes and rolled in the surf. Never have I had such bathing. And when I got back to Cairo, I heard at the Embassy that night that Gott was dead. I sent for Montgomery. I gather that there was some confusion and difficulty between him and Auchinleck. But by then the die was cast, and I, after all, was having my row with Jo [Stalin].'

He speaks of the battle. He thinks that the enemy is done. He thinks Rommel was right to abandon the Italians. 'That was the correct military decision, but it makes excellent propaganda for us.' He warms to the subject. 'The enemy', he says, 'were stuck to the Alamein position like limpets to a rock. We cut them out' – at that he makes a gesture of someone cutting a limpet off a rock with a knife – 'we detached them utterly. And what happens to a limpet when it loses its rock? It dies a miserable death. Thirst comes to it, aching, inescapable thirst. I should not like our armies to be suffering what the Afrika Korps will suffer in these days.' He does not think that Rommel can make much of a stand before Halfaya, or even there. 'The next days will show. There is more jam to come. Much more jam. And in places where some of you least expect.'

Brendan Bracken then comes in and Winston tells him to arrange for all the bells in England to be tolled on Sunday. Some hesitation is expressed by all of us. 'Not at all,' says Winston, 'not at all. We are not celebrating final victory. The war will still be long. When we have beaten Germany, it will take us two more years to beat Japan. Nor is that a bad thing. It will keep America and ourselves together while we are making peace in Europe. If I am still alive, I shall fling all we have into the Pacific.'

Lady Kitty interrupts him to complain about the BBC. With a grin he waves her on to me. 'Here, Kitty, is the BBC in person. Fling your darts.' But all she says is that we are wrong to talk of an increase in juvenile delinquency and venereal disease. It gives a bad impression abroad. Winston contradicts her. 'Not in the least. We speak for ourselves. We are not dependent on what others say.' I ask her whether it is not a fact that after the French collapse, the BBC was the only hope of France. 'Of course,' she says. 'Your people have done well,' says Winston. 'Very well indeed.'

At that moment Mary Churchill comes in in ATS uniform. She flings her arms round Winston's neck and hugs him. 'Daddy', she says, 'think of it. I have 48 hours leave and shall come to Chequers.' He beams at her.

We then go. He comes up with us to the ground floor and opens the door of the Cabinet Room. He stands there with the Corinthian columns showing inside. 'There is more news to come soon,' he says. 'More jam. Remember that.' And he goes in smiling grimly.

Mary Churchill: diary
(Mary Soames, 'Clementine Churchill', page 356)

6 November 1942

[...] the party broke up, Mummie being violent (quite rightly I thought) with Papa who wanted to have all the bells rung on Sunday.

Winston S. Churchill to Josef Stalin
(Churchill papers, 20/82)

7 November 1942
Immediate
Most Secret
Personal and Secret

You have no doubt realised that when Hitler despairs of taking Baku he will try to wreck it by air attack. Pray accept this from me.[1]

Winston S. Churchill to General Henri-Honoré Giraud
(Churchill papers, 20/82)

7 November 1942

As a fellow escapee I am delighted that we are at work together again. I remember all our talks at Metz.[2] For 35 years I have had faith in France, and I rejoice that our two nations and the United States are now going to strike the first great blow together for the recovery of Alsace-Lorraine.

---

[1] Information based on Enigma decrypts.
[2] In 1936.

Winston S. Churchill to General Sir Harold Alexander
(Churchill papers, 20/82)

7 November 1942
Personal
Most Secret
Bigot

Your No. 68827. The results so far are splendid and I am publishing your figures today in order to influence Spanish policy at this decisive moment.

2. On reflection I have decided not to ring the bells till after 'Torch' is ashore in case of some accident which would cause distress. Next week I expect to do so.

Averell Harriman to Winston S. Churchill
(Churchill papers, 20/82)

7 November 1942
Personal

I have watched with increasing elation the reports of the mounting successes of your troops in the desert. Now that victory is in your grasp I want to send my personal congratulations to you for the wisdom and determination of your leadership in this great struggle over the past two years beginning in the summer of 1940 when you sent forward the first reinforcements to Wavell continuing month by month ever since against all obstacles of limited resources and transport and of dangers at home and culminating finally in the part you played in the selection of the Command and in the inspiration you gave the troops on your visit to Cairo. To your indomitable leadership goes the lion's share of the glory of the victory.

With my personal and affectionate regards.

Averell[1]

---

[1] Churchill replied by telegram on 8 November 1942: 'Thank you so much, my friend' ('Personal', *Churchill papers, 20/82*).

General George C. Marshall to Winston S. Churchill
(Churchill papers, 20/82)

7 November 1942
Personal

Having been privileged to witness your courage and resolution on the day of the fall of Tobruk I am unable to express to the full my delight over the news from the Middle East and my admiration for the British Army.

Winston S. Churchill to General Dwight D. Eisenhower
(Churchill papers, 20/82)

7 November 1942
Most Secret
Personal

I feel the Rock of Gibraltar will be safe in your hands.

Sir Walter Monckton: article
('Sunday Times', 7 November 1942)[1]

7 November 1942

[...]
Whichever way one looks at this victory it has been based upon a stupendous effort by all concerned at home and in the Middle East. And it could not have been done unless there had been someone who believed wholeheartedly in this offensive campaign: who had the vision and imagination to see it and who could impart to the others his own enthusiastic faith in the possibilities which lay ahead. It is in this connection that the Prime Minister's visit to the Middle East ought to be remembered. I believe that in its conception, as in the drive and direction which impelled it, this victory ought to be known as Churchill's Victory.

---

[1] Churchill was shown a copy of Walter Monckton's article, entitled 'Makers of Victory', with the final paragraph – printed here – boxed in red.

Winston S. Churchill to General George C. Marshall
(Churchill papers, 20/82)

8 November 1942
Personal

I am most grateful to you for your message. I was indeed touched at the time of Tobruk by the kindness and delicacy you all showed.

2. We may now be very hopeful of the Egyptian and Libyan war. The enemy's armour is virtually obliterated and will be difficult to replace rapidly. Your Shermans played a great part and are at the top of the hunt.

3. Let me congratulate you on all the news so far received of the great events taking place in French North Africa. We shall find the problems of success not less puzzling though more agreeable than those we have hitherto surmounted together. You have got a grand trio in Ike, the American Eagle and the Bulldog. It would be a great comfort to see you here again. The whole scene will have to be reviewed.

General Bernard Montgomery to Winston S. Churchill
(Churchill papers, 20/82)

8 November 1942
Most Secret
Immediate

Thank you for your message and congratulations. 8th Army is driving ahead westwards and destroying the enemy wherever met. Our objective is the removal of the Germans and Italians from North Africa, and we will not rest till we have achieved it.

Josef Stalin to Winston S. Churchill
(Cabinet papers, 65/28)

8 November 1942   Kremlin
Personal and Secret   Moscow

Your message received on the 5th November.

2. My congratulations on the successful development of the military operations in Egypt. Let me express my confidence that now you will be able to completely annihilate the Rommel's gang and his Italian allies.

3. We all here hope for the success of the 'Torch'.

4. Many thanks for your communication that you and President Roosevelt have decided to send in the near future to our Southern front the 20 British and American squadrons. A speedy arrival of these 20 squadrons would be a very valuable help. The necessary consultation between the British, American and Soviet representatives on the preliminary arrangements could be best organised at first in Moscow and later in case of need direct in the Caucasus. I am already informed that the USA will send for this purpose the General E. E. Andler.[1] I will wait for your communication on who will be appointed to represent Great Britain.

5. The situation on our Caucasian front deteriorated somewhat as compared with October. The Germans succeeded in capturing the town Nalchik. They are approaching Vladikavkas[2] where severe fighting is going on at present. Our difficulty here is our weakness in the fighter aircraft.

6. Let me express my gratitude for your congratulations in connection with the anniversary of the USSR.

Winston S. Churchill to General Hastings Ismay,
for the Chiefs of Staff Committee
(Churchill papers, 20/67)

9 November 1942

This report[3] follows, in the main, lines on which there will be general agreement. It is, in my opinion, unduly negative. There is a prevailing inhibition against facing the Germans anywhere except on the other side of salt water. The criticism 'Safety First' would certainly be made against it.

2. To make no more use of the success of 'Torch' and 'Lightfoot' in 1943 than the occupation of Sicily and Sardinia would be most regrettable. I should be very sorry to see this report being accepted as the limit of our action. It must be remembered we have already committed ourselves with the Americans to 'Roundup' in 1943. This was an operation

[1] Elmer Edward Adler, 1892–1970. Born in Buffalo, New York. Graduated from West Point, 1913. Joined the United States Army Air Force, 1918. Served in the Philippines, 1925–8. Major, 1940. In 1941 promoted Brigadier-General (temporary) and appointed Chief of the Air Section and chief representative of the commanding general of the USAAF in Africa, the Middle East, and India. In June 1942, travelled to the Middle East as commanding general of the Air Service Command with the 9th Air Force. Travelled to Russia in late 1942 with the object of creating a US air presence in the Caucasus.

[2] Soviet forces halted the German forces' drive towards the oilfields of Grozny and Baku near Vladikavkaz towards the end of 1942.

[3] COS (42) 345 (O), 'American–British Strategy. Report by Chiefs of Staff'.

on the greatest scale which, nevertheless, the Chiefs of Staff considered feasible. The interposition of 'Torch' is no excuse for lying down during 1943, content with descents on Sicily and Sardinia and a few more operations like Dieppe (which can hardly be taken as a pattern).

3. The effort for the campaign of 1943 should clearly be a strong pinning down of the enemy in Northern France and the Low Countries by continuous preparations to invade, and a decisive attack on Italy, or, better still, Southern France, together with operations not involving serious shipping expense, and other forms of pressure to bring in Turkey, and operate over land with the Russians into the Balkans.

4. This report also seems written in an atmosphere which assumes that we can go on spending twelve or thirteen millions a day and losing fifty or sixty thousand tons of shipping a month indefinitely. Great danger of a stalemate, which is Germany's last hope, would arise if this kind of mood prevails. I could not agree that it should go to the United States and be laid before the Combined Staffs there until it has been fully discussed by the War Cabinet. Moreover, it requires to be reviewed in the light of the success gained in 'Torch' now plainly in sight after one day's campaign. If French North Africa is going to be made an excuse for locking up great forces on the defensive and calling it 'a commitment', it would be better not to go there at all. In a month French North Africa should be comfortably and securely in Allied hands, and a considerable French force developed there. We must then go forward to the attack on islands, with the object of preparing the way for a very large-scale offensive on the underbelly of the Axis in 1943.

5. Is it really to be supposed that the Russians will be content with our lying down like this during the whole of 1943, while Hitler had a third crack at them? However alarming the prospect may seem, we must make an attempt to get on to the mainland and fight in the line against the enemy in 1943.

Harold Nicolson: letter to his wife
('Harold Nicolson, Diaries and Letters', pages 261–2)

9 November 1942   4 King's Bench Walk
London EC4

But what a brilliant bit of timing and strategy it all is! I envy Winston at the Guildhall. I envy him in the House. But how he has deserved it all!

War Cabinet: conclusions
(Cabinet papers, 65/28)

9 November 1942   10 Downing Street
6 p.m.

[...]

The Prime Minister said that he and the Foreign Secretary had seen General de Gaulle the previous day in regard to the operations in North Africa. General de Gaulle had been most co-operative, and the broadcast which he had made the previous evening had been very helpful. On this account it was the more desirable that an early announcement should be made of a decision to hand over to the French National committee the civil administration of Madagascar.

[...]

John Martin: letter to Rosalind Julia Ross
(Sir John Martin papers)

10 November 1942

[...] For the Lord Mayor's luncheon the PM and Mrs Churchill drove into the City in an open car, while Harvie Watt and I followed in a closed one behind. On the suggestion of the Remembrancer loud-speaker vans had announced his coming and we made a triumphal progress along the Strand and Fleet Street, up Ludgate Hill and past St Paul's. There were huge and enthusiastic crowds, with scarcely enough police to control them, and at the last stage we had some difficulty getting through. The luncheon went very well – an unusually sumptuous repast for these days. [...]

Winston S. Churchill: speech
(BBC Written Archives Centre)

10 November 1942   Mansion House
                                                     London

I notice, my Lord Mayor, by your speech that you had reached the conclusion that the news from the various fronts has been somewhat better lately. In our wars the episodes are largely adverse, but the final results have hitherto been satisfactory. Away we dash over the currents that may swirl around us, but the tide bears us forward on its broad, resistless flood.

In the last war the way was uphill almost to the end. We met with continual disappointments, and with disasters far more bloody than anything we have experienced so far in this one. But in the end all the oppositions fell together, and all our foes submitted themselves to our will.

We have not so far in this war taken as many German prisoners as they have taken British, but these German prisoners will no doubt come in in droves at the end just as they did last time. I have never promised anything but blood, tears, toil, and sweat. Now, however, we have a new experience. We have victory, a remarkable and definite victory. The bright gleam has caught the helmets of our soldiers, and warmed and cheered all our hearts.

The late M Venizelos[1] observed that in all her wars England – he should have said Britain, of course – always wins one battle – the last. It would seem to have begun rather earlier this time. General Alexander, with his brilliant comrade and lieutenant, General Montgomery, has gained a glorious and decisive victory in what I think should be called the Battle of Egypt. Rommel's army has been defeated. It has been routed. It has been very largely destroyed as a fighting force.

This battle was not fought for the sake of gaining positions or so many square miles of desert territory. General Alexander and General Montgomery fought it with one single idea. They meant to destroy the armed force of the enemy, and to destroy it at the place where the disaster would be most far-reaching and irrecoverable.

All the various elements in our line of battle played their parts – Indian troops, Fighting French, the Greeks, the representatives of Czechoslovakia and the others who took part. The Americans rendered powerful and invaluable service in the air. But as it happened, as the course of the battle turned, it has been fought throughout almost entirely by men of British blood from home and from the Dominions on the one hand, and by Germans on the other. The Italians were left to perish in the waterless desert or surrender as they are doing.

The fight between the British and the Germans was intense and fierce in the extreme. It was a deadly grapple. The Germans have been outmatched and outfought with the very kind of weapons with which they had beaten down so many small peoples, and also large unprepared peoples. They have been beaten by the very technical apparatus on which they counted to gain them the domination of the world. Especially is

---

[1] Eleutherios Venizelos, 1864–1936. Prime Minister of Greece, 1910–15. Forced to resign by King Constantine, May 1915. Prime Minister for the second time, August–October 1915. Subsequently Prime Minister, 1917–20, 1928–32, 1933.

this true of the air and of the tanks and of the artillery, which has come back into its own on the battlefield. The Germans have received back again that measure of fire and steel which they have so often meted out to others.

Now this is not the end. It is not even the beginning of the end. But it is, perhaps, the end of the beginning. Henceforth Hitler's Nazis will meet equally well armed, and perhaps better armed troops. Henceforth they will have to face in many theatres of war that superiority in the air which they have so often used without mercy against others, of which they boasted all round the world, and which they intended to use as an instrument for convincing all other peoples that all resistance to them was hopeless. When I read of the coastal road crammed with fleeing German vehicles under the blasting attacks of the Royal Air Force, I could not but remember those roads of France and Flanders, crowded, not with fighting men, but with helpless refugees – women and children – fleeing with their pitiful barrows and household goods, upon whom such merciless havoc was wreaked. I have, I trust, a humane disposition, but I must say I could not help feeling that what was happening, however grievous, was only justice grimly reclaiming her rights.

It will be my duty in the near future to give to Parliament a full and particular account of these operations. All I will say of them at present is that the victory which has already been gained gives good prospect of becoming decisive and final so far as the defence of Egypt is concerned.

But this Battle of Egypt, in itself so important, was designed and timed as a prelude and counterpart of the momentous enterprise undertaken by the United States at the western end of the Mediterranean – an enterprise under United States command in which our Army, Air Force, and, above all, our Navy, are bearing an honourable and important share. Very full accounts have been published of all that is happening in Morocco, Algeria, and Tunis. The President of the United States, who is Commander-in-Chief of the armed forces of America, is the author of this mighty undertaking, and in all of it I have been his active and ardent lieutenant.

You have no doubt read the declaration of President Roosevelt, solemnly endorsed by His Majesty's Government, of the strict respect which will be paid to the rights and interests of Spain and Portugal, both by America and Great Britain. Towards those countries our only policy is that they shall be independent and free, prosperous and at peace. Britain and the United States will do all that they can to enrich the economic life of the Iberian Peninsula. The Spaniards especially, after all their troubles, require and deserve peace and recuperation.

At this time our thoughts turn towards France, groaning in bondage under the German heel. Many ask themselves the question: Is France finished? Is that long and famous history, adorned by so many manifestations of genius and valour, bearing with it so much that is precious to culture and civilisation, and above all to the liberties of mankind – is all that now to sink for ever into the ocean of the past, or will France rise again and resume her rightful place in the structure of what may one day be again the family of Europe? I declare to you here, on this considerable occasion, even now when misguided or suborned Frenchmen are firing upon their rescuers, I declare to you my faith that France will rise again. While there are men like General de Gaulle and all those who follow him – and they are legion throughout France – and men like General Giraud, that gallant warrior whom no prison can hold, while there are men like those to stand forward in the name and in the cause of France, my confidence in the future of France is sure.

For ourselves we have no wish but to see France free and strong, with her Empire gathered round her and with Alsace-Lorraine restored. We covet no French possession; we have no acquisitive appetites or ambitions in North Africa or any other part of the world. We have not entered this war for profit or expansion, but only for honour and to do our duty in defending the right.

Let me, however, make this clear, in case there should be any mistake about it in any quarter. We mean to hold our own. I have not become the King's First Minister in order to preside over the liquidation of the British Empire. For that task, if ever it were prescribed, someone else would have to be found, and, under democracy, I suppose the nation would have to be consulted. I am proud to be a member of that vast commonwealth and society of nations and communities gathered in and around the ancient British monarchy, without which the good cause might well have perished from the face of the earth. Here we are, and here we stand, a veritable rock of salvation in this drifting world.

There was a time, not long ago, when for a whole year we stood all alone. Those days, thank God, have gone. We now move forward in a great and gallant company. For our record we have nothing to fear, we have no need to make excuses or apologies. Our record pleads for us, and will gain gratitude in the breasts of free men and women in every part of the world.

As I have said, in this war we desire no territorial gains and no commercial favours; we wish to alter no sovereignty or frontier for our own benefit or profit. We have come into North Africa shoulder to shoulder with our American friends and Allies for one purpose, and one purpose only – namely, to gain a vantage ground from which to open a new front against Hitler and Hitlerism, to cleanse the shores of Africa from the stain of Nazi and Fascist tyranny, to open the Mediterranean to Allied sea power and air power, and thus effect the liberation of the peoples of Europe from the pit of misery into which they have been cast by their own improvidence and by the brutal violence of the enemy.

These two African undertakings, in the east and in the west, were part of a single strategic and political conception which we have laboured long to bring to fruition, and about which we are now justified in entertaining good and reasonable confidence. Thus, taken together, they were two aspects of a grand design, vast in its scope, honourable in its motive, noble in its aim. The British and American affairs continue to prosper in the Mediterranean, and the whole event will be a new bond between the English-speaking peoples and a new hope for the whole world.

I recall to you some lines of Byron, which seem to me to fit the event, the hour, and the theme:

> Millions of tongues record thee, and anew
> Their children's lips shall echo them, and say
> 'Here, where the sword united nations drew,
> Our countrymen were warring on that day!'
> And this is much, and all which will not pass away.[1]

Josef Stalin to Winston S. Churchill
(Churchill papers, 20/82)

10 November 1942   Kremlin
Personal   Moscow

We are delighted at your successes in Libya and at the successful beginning of the 'Torch'. I wish you full victory.

Many thanks for your warning concerning Baku. We are taking the necessary measures to combat the danger.

---

[1] George Gordon, Lord Byron, *Childe Harold's Pilgrimage*, Canto the Third, stanza XXXV.

Winston S. Churchill to President Franklin D. Roosevelt
(Cabinet papers, 20/82)

11 November 1942
Personal and Secret
No. 188

It is surely of the highest importance to unify in every possible way all Frenchmen who regard Germany as the foe. The invasion of Unoccupied France by Hitler should give the opportunity for this. You will I am sure realize that His Majesty's Government are under quite definite and solemn obligations to de Gaulle and his Movement. We must see they have a fair deal. It seems to me that you and I ought to avoid at all costs the creation of rival French émigré governments each favoured by one of us. We must try to fuze all anti-German French forces together, and make a united Government. This may take some time and nothing must prejudice the military operations, but we ought to make it clear to all parties what we want and what we are going to work for.

Winston S. Churchill: speech
(Hansard)

11 November 1942   House of Commons

The Prime Minister: The custom has always been to compliment the Mover and Seconder of the Address upon the speeches which they have delivered and very often those compliments have been well founded. I am sure that the House, without distinction of party, will feel that that is the case today. My hon. Friend the Member for South Bristol (Mr Walkden[1]) speaks as the representative of one of the great trade unions of the country, those institutions which lie so near the heart and core of our social life and progress and have proved that stability and progress can be combined. He speaks in that capacity, and my hon. and gallant Friend the Member for Stafford (Major Thorneycroft[2]), who has not been very long in this House, has already begun to find his feet here, and the speech which he has made today gives every assurance that he will play a valuable and increasing part in our Debates. I should like to express to both hon. Members my acknowledgements of the extremely

---

[1] Alexander George Walkden, 1873–1951. Fourth General Secretary of the Railway Clerks' Association, 1906–36. Labour MP for Bristol South, 1929–31, 1935–45. Created Baron, 1945.

[2] Peter Thorneycroft, 1909–94. Conservative MP for Stafford, 1938–45; for Monmouth, 1945–66. Parliamentary Secretary, 1945. President of Board of Trade, 1951–7. Chancellor of the Exchequer, 1957–8. Minister of Aviation, 1960–2. Minister of Defence, 1962–4. Secretary of State for Defence, 1964. Created Baron, 1967.

kind and complimentary remarks which they have made about me. Really their whole outlook has been one of extreme benevolence to the Government, to its head, to our fortunes in war and also to the admirable constituencies which they represent. I thank them both for the part which they have played.

There are a number of announcements which should be made about the Business of the House, about the course of the Debate on the Address, about the measures which the Government will take to appropriate and monopolise the time of the House as is usual on these occasions, and also about the somewhat greater latitude which we shall have to give to what may be called legislation not wholly free from controversy but carrying with it a broad measure of general approval. These statements I shall, with the permission of the House, ask my right hon. Friend the Leader of the House to make at the close of my remarks. They belong entirely to the sphere of House of Commons business, and I am today to deal with other matters more remote from this Chamber, though not more remote from our minds.

We meet in a time of great stress when events are moving very fast and when final views cannot easily or lightly be taken. I have however to tell the House about the great Battle of Egypt, which is a British victory of the first order, and also about the other half of the combination, namely, the United States and British intervention in North Africa. There are three points which must be duly examined in matters of this magnitude and violence. First, the time required for preparation. Secondly, the need of combination and concert. And thirdly, the importance of surprise. I will address myself to these points in the course of my statement. Here let me say that the pressure at present is extreme and I must ask for the indulgence of the House if in any part of my statement I should lack full historical precision. I have not had the time to give the mature consideration to the exact balance between the different elements and forces involved that would be possible in ordinary times. I do the best I can.

Taking the question of the time, it is not generally realised how much time these great operations take to mount. For instance, the British divisions which have reinforced the 8th Army for this battle left England in May or early June. Most of the 6-pounders we are now and have been using in so many hundreds were despatched before the fall of Tobruk. This also applies to the more heavily armoured and more heavily gunned British tanks. As for the American tanks – the admirable Shermans – they came to us in the following way. On that dark day when the news of the fall of Tobruk came in, I was with President Roosevelt in his room at the White House. The House knows how bitter a blow this was. But nothing could have exceeded the delicacy and kindness of our American friends and Allies. They had no thought but to help. Their very best tanks – the Shermans – were just coming out of the factories. The first batch had been newly placed in the hands of their divisions who had been waiting for them and looking forward to receiving them. The President took a large number of these tanks back from the troops to whom they had just been given. They were placed on board ship in the early days of July and they sailed direct to Suez under American escort for a considerable part of the voyage.

The President also sent us a large number of self-propelled 105 mm guns, which are most useful weapons for contending with the 88 mm high velocity guns, of which the Germans have made so much use. One ship in this convoy – this precious convoy – was sunk by a U-boat, but immediately, without being asked, the United States replaced it with another ship carrying an equal number of these weapons. All these tanks and high velocity guns played a recognisable part, indeed an important part, in General Alexander's battle.

When I was in Egypt in the early days of August I visited myself every unit which was to be armed with these tanks and guns, some of them the most seasoned regiments we have, including the Yeomanry Division. But, alas, they had no weapons adequate for the fight, and even those they had had been taken away from them in the stress of General Auchin-leck's battle. I was able to tell those troops that the very finest weapons that existed would soon be in their possession; that these came direct from the President and that, meanwhile, they must prepare themselves by every form of exercise and training for their use when they were delivered. That was at the beginning of August. But none of these units was ready to fight in the repulse of Rommel's attack in the second battle of El Alamein, although all of them were ready for action by 23rd October when we began what I call the Battle of Egypt. Thus, you will see that the decision taken by the President on 20th June took four months to be operative, although the utmost energy and speed were used at each stage. Records were broken at every point in the unloading and fitting-up of the weapons and in their issue to the troops, but it was indispensable that the men should also have reasonable training in handling them. One may say, in fact, that between taking the decision for reinforcing the Middle East for a great operation and the reinforcements coming into action a period of five months or even more has been required.

Thus, before the Vote of Censure in the early days of July, all measures in our power had already been taken first to repel the enemy's further assault and, secondly, to take decisive offensive action against him. See then how silly it is for people to imagine that Governments can act on impulse or in immediate response to pressure in these large-scale offensives. There must be planning, design and forethought, and after that a long period of silence, which looks – I can quite understand it – to the ordinary spectator as if it were simply apathy or inertia, but which is in fact steady indispensable preparation for the blow. Moreover, you have first to get sufficient ascendancy even to prepare to strike such a blow.

I am certainly not one of those who need to be prodded. In fact, if anything, I am a prod. My difficulties rather lie in finding the patience and self-restraint to wait through many anxious weeks for the results to be achieved. And because a Government cannot at every moment give an explanation of what it is doing and what is going on, it would be, and it will be, a great mistake to assume that nothing is being done. In my view, everything in human power was done, making allowance for the fallibility of human judgment. We recreated and revivified our war-battered Army, we placed a new Army at its side, and rearmed it on a gigantic scale. By these means we repaired the disaster which fell upon us and converted the defence of Egypt into a successful attack.

Of course, if we had not had the disaster, the measures taken in the hopes of better fortune would have carried us by now far on the road to Tripoli, but what was prepared to lead on to success came in as a means of retrieving failure. The failure has delayed our operations. Our position, in time, has been set back. Still there are consolations. The losses to the enemy in all this Egyptian fighting have been very heavy. He could not have found a worse place to lose a battle. The cost to him of maintaining this African campaign has been exorbitant. One in every three of his ships, with their sorely needed cargoes, has gone to the bottom of the sea, through our submarines and our Air Force, and the resources of German and Italian shipping are most severely strained. Now in this battle the enemy's losses have been mortal so far as this theatre is concerned, and he has had to employ a great part of his air force, including one-third of his transport and long-range reconnaissance planes, merely to keep his army supplied with food, ammunition and fuel. His air effort against Russia was definitely affected during all these last three months. His U-boat activities in the Mediterranean have been considerably reduced. Great as has been the cost and the burden to us of the African campaign, many as have been its disappointments and mistakes, it has from first to last been an immense drain upon German and Italian resources and the most effective means we have yet had of drawing a portion of the enemy's strength and wrath away from Russia upon ourselves.

Another important point to remember is the need of combining and concerting the operations of the various Allies and making them fit together into a general design, and to do this in spite of all the hard accidents of war and the incalculable interruptions of the enemy. One great obstacle to the constant unity of the Allies is geography. We stand around the circumference of the circle. The main enemy lies in the centre. A vast void separates us from the other war, in which we are equally interested, proceeding in the Pacific theatre. Hitler can summon quite easily a conference in Berlin or anywhere he chooses in Central Europe and can bring together, apart from Japan, all those concerned in the war effort of the Axis Powers, without these representative authorities being subject to any serious inconvenience, or being even temporarily detached from the tasks each of them has in hand. For us, through geography, joint consultation is far more difficult. President Roosevelt has not found it possible to leave the United States nor Premier Stalin to leave Russia. Therefore, I have had to make journeys in each direction, carrying with me to and fro most important military authorities and other experts and to labour so far as possible to bring all our plans into concert and harmony. We have brought them for the time being into some harmony.

So far as Russia is concerned, her course and position were fixed. The Soviets had to repel the terrific onslaught of Germany. They have been completely absorbed in their own defence and, in defending themselves, they have rendered an incomparable service to the common cause. They have rendered this service by killing or permanently putting out of action far more millions than Germany lost during the whole of the last war. I recognise the force of all that Premier Stalin said in his last speech about the enormous weight that has been thrown on Russia. My heart has bled for Russia. I have felt what almost every one in this House must have felt, that intense desire that we should be suffering with her and that we should take some of the weight off her. Everything that he said about the burden thrown on them, the disproportionate burden, is perfectly true. It is evident however that Russia is at least three times as strong a living organism as she was in the last war. The idea that Russia could withstand the whole of the German Army in the last war was never for a moment entertained. Then she had only a small fraction of the German power but now she has the whole weight of it, and as for any that is employed on this side or in the conquered countries, that is more than made up for by the horde of divisions provided by Finland, Rumania, Hungary and others of the Nazi-ridden or Fascist-ridden States. The Russians have borne the burden and the heat of the day, and I think it absolutely natural on their part, and fully within their rights, for them to make the very strong and stark assertions which they have made. Our need was to help them but to help them in a manner effective and suitable. It might have been a relief to our feelings – at least in the early stages – if we had delivered a premature attack across the Channel, if we had had, for instance, a dozen Dieppes on one day and a couple of Dunkirks a week or two later. But a disaster of that character would have been of no help to Russia. It would have been the greatest disservice to Russia. But the attack which will be made in due course across the Channel or the North Sea requires an immense degree of preparation, vast numbers of special landing craft and a great Army trained division by division in amphibious warfare. All this is proceeding, but it takes time. Of course, should the enemy become demoralised at any moment, the same careful preparations would not be needed. Risks could be run on a large scale. But this is certainly not the case at the present time. There is a German Army in France as large, apart from the Home Guard, as ours in Great Britain. It is not so well equipped as the British or American troops, but it contains many veteran German soldiers, many experienced officers who have taken part in the overthrow and massacre of a dozen countries. It has ample weapons of the latest type; it has the aid of the immense fortifications erected along the Channel and North Sea coasts. There are also the extraordinary and peculiar difficulties attendant on all landings across the sea in the teeth of opposition – the chances of weather in this somewhat variable Northern climate, the difficulty of reconciling tides and moons, of catching at one moment high visibility from the air and smooth water for the landing craft. There are many other factors. I could speak for an hour upon them, but I do not intend to labour the matter, certainly not in Public Session, because a great many of these difficulties it will be our duty to overcome. But all of them constitute a problem which make the processes of moving an Army across the Channel from one side to the other – it cuts both ways – a problem which, happily for us, has never yet been solved in war.

It would have been most improvident for us to attempt such an enterprise before all our preparations were ready. They have very greatly advanced. Enormous installations have been and are being brought into existence at all our suitable ports, but no one would have been justified, nor indeed would it have been physically possible, in making an effective invasion of the Continent during the summer or autumn of 1942.

Here let me say a word about pressure. No amount of pressure by public opinion or from any other quarter would make me, as the person chiefly responsible, consent to an operation which our military advisers had convinced me would lead to a great disaster. I should think it extremely dishonourable and indeed an act of treason to the nation to allow any un-instructed pressure however well meant, or sentimental feelings however honourable, to drive me into such reckless or wanton courses. Again and again, with the full assent of my colleagues in the War Cabinet, I have instructed the Chiefs of the Staff that in endeavouring to solve their problems they should disregard public clamour, and they know that His Majesty's Government, resting securely upon this steady House of Commons, is quite strong enough to stand like a bulkhead between the military authorities and the well-meant impulses which stir so many breasts. It is not for me to claim the whole responsibility for what has not been done, but I should be quite ready and well content to bear it.

Why then, it will be said, did you allow false hopes to be raised in Russian breasts? Why then did you agree with the United States and Russia to a communiqué which spoke of a second front in Europe in 1942? I must say quite frankly that I hold it perfectly justifiable to deceive the enemy even if at the same time your own people are for a while misled. There is one thing however which you must never do, and that is to mislead your Ally. You must never make a promise which you do not fulfil. I hope we shall show that we have lived up to that standard. All British promises to Russia have been made in writing or given across the table in recorded conversations with the Soviet representative. In June I gave the Russian Government a written document making it perfectly clear that, while we were preparing to make a landing in 1942, we could not promise to do so. Meanwhile, whether or not we were going to attack the Continent in August, September or October, it was of the utmost consequence to Russia that the enemy should believe that we were so prepared and so resolved. Only in this way could we draw and keep the largest possible number of Germans pinned in the Pas de Calais, along the coast of France and in the Low Countries. We have drawn and have kept at least 33 German divisions in the West, and one-third of the German bomber air force is there, and this bomber force is not being used to bomb us to any extent. Why? It was being saved up for these very landings should they occur on the beaches, and they have remained, playing no effective military part for a considerable time. We ourselves are also engaging, including the Middle East and Malta fighting, more than half of the whole fighter strength of Germany.

In addition, there are 10 German divisions in Norway. The main part of the German fleet has been for some months tied to the Northern fjords. There are about 350 of their best aircraft gathered up in the Far North to impede our convoys to Russia. Here is another front we have found it very costly to maintain. Let me tell you about that. Of the 19 convoys we have sent to Russia, every one has been an important fleet operation, because the enemy's main fleet was close at hand. The latest one required the use of 77 ships of war, apart altogether from the supply ships. The Foreign Secretary if he is well enough – my right hon. Friend has a temporary indisposition today – or if not, the Undersecretary of State for Foreign Affairs, will recount in some detail later on in the Debate the immense output of munitions which we have sent to Russia during a period when we ourselves were being vehemently reproached, and naturally reproached, for the comparative ill-equipment of our own troops. Indeed I think that the effort and achievement of this country, industrial, naval, and military, during the year 1942 should be a source of pride and thanksgiving, not only to all in these Islands, but to our Allies both in the East and in the West.

Now, I come to the great enterprise which has just been unfolded. On my first visit to Washington after the United States was attacked by Japan, Germany and Italy, President Roosevelt favoured the idea that French North Africa was specially suitable for American intervention in the Western theatre. This view was fully shared by us. However, it was clearly the duty both of Britain and of the United States to exhaust every possibility of carrying more direct aid to Russia by means of a liberating descent upon France. Both plans were therefore studied by the Staffs with the utmost attention, and preparations were made for both possibilities, either alternatively or simultaneously. Personally, I have always considered the Western front as one. We hold a very powerful enemy army pinned on the French shores, and every week our preparations to strike it will increase and develop. At the same time we make this wide encircling movement in the Mediterranean, having for its primary object the recovery of the command of that vital sea, but also having for its object the exposure of the under-belly of the Axis, especially Italy, to heavy attack. That seemed from the beginning of this year to be the correct strategy. The establishment of a Mediterranean as well as an Atlantic or Channel front would obviously give us wide freedom of manœuvre. Our sea power and the gradual development of our amphibious power enabled both operations to be contemplated on a very large scale. The 18th and 19th century battles were fought on fronts of six or seven miles, but the same principles apply on fronts which nowadays extend for 2,000 miles or more.

As the year advanced it became clear that the provision of landing craft would not be on a sufficiently large scale to enable a heavy intervention to take place across the Channel in the favourable weather months of 1942.

General Marshall, the Head of the American Army, with which is included the American Air Force, paid two visits to this country, the first in April, the second in July; and on the second occasion he was accompanied by Admiral King, the Commander-in-Chief of the American Navy. It was decided on this second occasion to hold the enemy on the French shore and to strike at his Southern flank in the Mediterranean through North Africa. In this decision the British and American Staffs were wholly united, and their views were shared and adopted by the President and the British War Cabinet. Orders were issued accordingly with extreme urgency at the end of July. Here I should like to say that in the planning of this joint operation the American and British staff officers, of whom many scores have been employed night and day, have worked together like a band of brothers. The comprehension which exists, the give and take, the desire to be first in giving quick service, are very marked, and will be an invaluable ingredient in our future tasks and our future achievements. Orders for the North African expedition were accordingly issued at the end of July.

As a very important part of this North African operation, it was necessary to bring the British 8th Army into a condition to regain the initiative and to resume the offensive in Egypt. At that time there was very great anxiety about our ability even to hold the front at El Alamein. However, General Auchinleck, that fine officer, succeeded in stemming the enemy's advance. The powerful reinforcements, which I have mentioned, of men and material had arrived or were on the water close at hand, and the troops were being equipped with all the latest material which was pouring in, and were rapidly fitting themselves for a renewal of the conflict on a great scale.

As I was far from satisfied with the conditions reported to prevail in the 8th Army and was concerned about its confidence in the higher command, I thought it my duty to visit this Army, taking with me the Chief of the Imperial General Staff, Sir Alan Brooke, in whose judgment I have the greatest confidence, in order that together we could see the situation on the spot and take any decisions which might be found necessary.

There was an even greater need for such a journey. Although, as I have said, we have told the Soviet Government that we could make no promise to attack across the Channel in 1942, but only that we would do our utmost to overcome the difficulties of such an operation, and as we had now settled not to make the attempt in the Autumn of 1942, but, on the other hand, to make an enveloping attack on North Africa, it was necessary to explain the whole position to Premier Stalin. I thought it better – and my colleagues pressed this view upon me – that I should deal with this matter personally, face to face, rather than leave it to the ordinary diplomatic channels. It was a very serious conversation which I had to undertake. I therefore sought and obtained the approval of the War Cabinet to make the journey which I described to the House when I came back about six weeks ago. I am sure that the course adopted prevented a great deal of friction and ill feeling between us and our Russian Allies, and I was very glad to read Mr Stalin's statement when he said: 'There followed another important step, the visit to Moscow of the British Prime Minister, Mr Churchill, in the course of which a complete understanding was reached concerning the relations between the two countries.' I assure the House I have a solid belief in the wisdom and good faith of this outstanding man, and although the news that I brought was not welcome and was not considered by them adequate, nevertheless the fact remains that we parted good friends, and, in the words which Mr Stalin uses, a complete understanding exists between us. The Russians bore their disappointment like men. They faced the enemy, and now they have reached the winter successfully, although we were unable to give them that help which they so earnestly demanded and which we, had it been physically practicable, would so gladly have accorded.

I have already told the House about the changes which, with the approval of the Cabinet and with the advice of the Chief of the Imperial General Staff, I made in the Middle East Command and in the Command of the 8th Army. In order that General Alexander should concentrate his whole attention upon the main object, he was relieved of all responsibility for Persia and Iraq. When you have a wild beast in your back garden like Rommel, you do not want to be worrying about things that are going on a thousand miles away. A new Command came into being there, which is now becoming a powerful force under General Maitland-Wilson. I can now read to the House the actual directive which I gave to General Alexander on 10th August, before leaving Cairo for Russia. It has at least the merit of brevity: '1. Your prime and main duty will be to take or destroy at the earliest opportunity the German–Italian Army commanded by Field Marshal Rommel, together with all its supplies and establishments in Egypt and Libya.' '2. You will discharge, or cause to be discharged such other duties as pertain to your Command without prejudice to the task described in paragraph 1, which must be considered paramount in His Majesty's interests.' The General may very soon be sending along for further instructions. In spite of the strain to which General Alexander had been subjected in the hard, adverse campaign in Burma, from which he had emerged with so much credit although he had nothing but retreat and misfortune, he accepted the new duties with ardour. Under him, commanding the 8th Army, was placed that remarkable soldier, General Montgomery. These two officers set up their headquarters in the desert, and Air Vice-Marshal Coningham, who commands the air forces in the battle there, was in the same little circle of lorries, wagons and tents in which they live. In a very short time an electrifying effect was produced upon the troops, who were also reinforced by every available man and weapon. Meanwhile, in the rearward areas, the intensive training of the formations to be armed with the new American and British weapons proceeded ceaselessly. All these changes had to be made in the face of an imminent attack by Rommel's army, the preparations for which were plainly apparent. In order that the Desert Army should have the fullest freedom of manœuvre and not have to fall back if its Southward flank were turned – because the line did not extend completely to the Qattara Depression; there was an open flank – every preparation was made to defend Cairo by the assembly of a considerable force, by the mobilising of every man from the rearward Services, exactly as we should do in England in the case of invasion, by the preparation of defence works along the line of the Nile, and by the use of inundations. All this was set in train. The new Command having been installed, my work there was done, and I returned to give my report to the House.

During the night of 30th–31st August, when the moon was already on the wane, Rommel's threatened attack was delivered. Quite rightly from his point of view, he did not by-pass the army to strike at Cairo, although the road seemed open. We thought he might, but he did not. He did not care to leave behind him the Desert Army now that it was reinforced by the 44th Division, which is commanded with distinction by our Deputy Serjeant at Arms (Major-General Hughes[1]) and which was largely reorganised and regrouped. Pivoting on the Italians in the coastal area, he therefore attacked on the Southern flank with all his armour and most of his Germans. Then followed the second Battle of Alamein, the first being General Auchinleck's which stemmed the tide in July. Rommel found himself immediately confronted with stern resistance and with artillery, used on the largest scale and abundantly supplied with ammuni-

[1] Ivor Thomas Percival Hughes, 1897–1962. Commanding Officer, 4th Battalion Queen's Royal Regiment, 1937–9; 1st Battalion 6th Queen's Royal Regiment, 1939–40. Acting Commanding Officer, 31st Brigade, 1939. Commanding Officer, 219th Independent Brigade, 1940–1. Commanding Officer, 131st Brigade, 1941–2. General Officer Commanding 44th Division, North Africa, 1942–3; XXV Corps and Cyprus, 1943. Head of Military Liaison in Greece, Yugoslavia and, Albania, 1944–5.

tion. He did not press the issue to extremes, and after about three days he withdrew. Our losses were about 2,000. His were considerably heavier, especially a disproportionate loss in tanks.

The narrowness of the passage between the sea and the Qattara Depression, which had proved so serviceable to us when we were resisting Rommel's attacks in both the defensive Battles of Alamein, became of course a most serious adverse factor to our advance when we ourselves were ready in our turn to assume the offensive. Our attack had to fit in harmoniously with the great operation in French North Africa to which it was a prelude. We had to wait till our troops were trained in the use of the new weapons which were arriving. We had to have a full moon on account of the method of attack. All these conditions were satisfiable around 23rd October. Meanwhile, however, we knew that the enemy was turning the position in front of us into a veritable fortress, blasting gun-pits and trenches in the solid rock, laying enormous and elaborate minefields and strengthening himself in every manner both by air and sea transport, in spite of the heavy toll exacted by our Air Force and our submarines. An attack by us round the enemy's Southern flank led into difficult country, with no threat to his communications. On the other hand, to blast a hole by a frontal attack in the North by the sea was a most forbidding task. However, when I spent a night on 19th August with Generals Alexander and Montgomery in their desert headquarters, General Montgomery, with General Alexander's full assent, expounded in exact detail the first stages of the plan which has since in fact been carried out. It was an anxious matter. In the last war we devised the tank to clear a way for the infantry, who were otherwise held up by the intensity of machine-gun fire. On this occasion it was the infantry who would have to clear the way for the tanks, to break through the crust and liberate the superior armour. This they could only do in the moonlight, and for this they must be supported with a concentration of artillery more powerful than any used in the present war. On a six-mile front of attack we had a 25-pounder gun, or better, every 23 yards. It is true that in the later barrages of 1918, at the Hindenburg Line, and other long prepared positions, a concentration of one gun to every 15 yards was attained. But the field guns of those days were 18-pounders. Our 25-pounders are heavier, and we also believe they are the best field guns in the world. It was necessary to effect penetration of about 6,000 yards at the first stroke in order to get through the hostile minefields, trenches and batteries. In the last war it was nearly always possible to make this initial penetration. In those days the artillery having blasted the gap, the next step was to gallop the cavalry through what was called the 'G in Gap'. But this was never done as the horsemen were soon brought to a standstill by the machine-gun posts in the rear. Horses were shot and the whole possibility of exploiting the breach passed away. Times have changed however. We have a steel machine cavalry now which, once a path is cleared through the mines and anti-tank guns, can certainly go forward against machine-gun posts to encounter whatever mobile forces of the enemy may lie beyond. That is the difference in this matter between the two wars. I feel sure the House will be glad that I should put these points to them because in all that has been written – and so much has been written – about this battle these points which touch the sequence and articulation of events have not been made very clearly.

For the purpose of turning to full account the breach we made an entirely new Corps, the 10th, was formed consisting of two British Armoured Divisions and the New Zealand Division – that 'ball of fire' as it was described to me by those who had seen it work. This very powerful force of between 40,000 and 50,000 men, including all the best tanks, the Grants and the Shermans, was withdrawn from the battle front immediately after Rommel's repulse in the second battle of Alamein and devoted itself entirely to intensive training, exercises and preparation. It was this thunderbolt hurled through the gap which finished Rommel and his arrogant army.

The success of all these plans could not have been achieved without substantial superiority in the air. The Royal Air Force which had a substantial proportion of American-manned squadrons with it had first to attain ascendancy over the opposing air force. Having attained this ascendancy it was used behind the lines to reduce the all-important supplies of fuel and ammunition without which the Germans could not effectively resist. It was also used in the battle itself to break up any threatening counter-attacks before they could develop thus giving the troops time to consolidate the positions won. By reaching out far to the rear of the retreating army air power completely disorganised the enemy's withdrawal and once again by the destruction of his mechanised transport prevented the bringing of fuel and ammunition to the front. When we retreated all those hundreds of miles from Tobruk at such speed what saved us was superior air power. What has consummated Rommel's ruin is that he has had to make this ruinous and speedy retreat with a superior air force hammering him and hampering him at every stage. In Air Marshal Tedder and Air Vice-Marshal Coningham we have two air leaders of the very highest quality, not technicians, but warriors who have worked in perfect harmony with the generals, and the manner in which in this Egyptian campaign the arrangements between the air and the military have been perfected has given a model which should be followed in all combined operations in the future.

It is true we had gathered superior forces, but all this would have been futile but for the masterly military conception of the commanders, the attention to detail which characterised their preparations and the absolute ruthlessness with which their forces were engaged, not only at the point of rupture but in gripping the enemy along the entire battle front. This battle is in fact a very fine example of the military art as developed under modern conditions. The skill of the commanders was rivalled by the conduct of their troops. Everyone testifies to the electrifying effect which the new Command had upon the Army. This noble Desert Army, which has never doubted its power to beat the enemy and whose pride had suffered cruelly from retreats and disasters which they could not understand, regained in a week its ardour and self-confidence. Historians may explain Tobruk. The 8th Army has done better: it has avenged it. Very full accounts have been given of the course of the battle during the 12 days' vehement fighting by the intrepid reporters and photographers who have been given a free run over the field at the risk of their lives. I am only concerned at the moment with its sequence and articulation.

From the moment that the seaward flank of the enemy was broken and the great mass of our armour flowed forward and successfully engaged the Panzer divisions the fate of the Axis troops to the southward, amounting to six Italian divisions, largely motorised, was sealed. As our advance reached El Daba and later Fuka, their lines of supply and of retreat were equally severed. They were left in a waterless desert to perish or surrender. At Fuka a grim action was fought on a smaller scale, but with unexampled ardour on both sides between the British armour and the remnants of the German Panzer Army. In this action particularly, the British and Germans had it all to themselves. The Germans were almost entirely destroyed, only remnants escaping to Mersa Matruh where again no halting-place was found.

It is impossible to give a final estimate of the enemy's casualties. General Alexander's present estimate, which reached me late last night, is that 59,000 Germans and Italians have been killed, wounded and taken prisoner. Of these 34,000 are Germans, and 25,000 Italians. Of course there are many more Italians who may be wandering about in the desert and every effort is being made to bring them in. The enemy also lost irretrievably about 500 tanks and not fewer than 1,000 guns of all types from 47 mm upwards. Our losses though severe and painful have not been unexpectedly high having regard to the task our troops were called upon to face. They amount to 13,600 officers and men. They were spread over the whole Army. Fifty-eight per cent. of them are British troops from the United Kingdom, with a much larger proportion of officers owing to all the armoured formations being British. Australian, New Zealand and South African troops were in the forefront of the break-through. Of the three British infantry Divisions, the 51st Division, which bore the brunt, has gained further honour for Scotland and the Highlands. The 50th and 44th Divisions also acquitted themselves with distinction. The 4th Indian Division and the Fighting French and Greek Brigades all played their part with the utmost alacrity. The pursuit has now rolled far to the West, and I cannot pretend to forecast where it will stop or what will be left of the enemy at the end of it. The speed of advance of our pursuing troops exceeds anything yet seen in the several ebbs and flows of the Libyan battlefields. Egypt is already clear of the enemy; we are advancing into Cyrenaica, and we may rely upon our generals and upon the Air Force to accomplish amazing feats now that the main force of the enemy has been broken and they have before them the opportunity of regaining in a few weeks, perhaps in much less than that, ground which otherwise might have taken long campaigns to reconquer.

Taken by itself, the Battle of Egypt must be regarded as an historic British victory. In order to celebrate it directions are being given to ring the bells throughout the land next Sunday morning, and I should think that many will listen to their peals with thankful hearts.

Mr George Griffiths[1] (Hemsworth): At what time?

The Prime Minister: That will be notified through the agency of the BBC, for everyone's convenience; and also to explain that the bells are not being rung on account of invasion.

While I do not want to detain the House too long, I must say one word about the third of these elements I mentioned, a word about surprise and strategy. By a marvellous system of camouflage complete tactical surprise was achieved in the desert. The enemy suspected, indeed knew, that an attack was impending, but where and when and how it was coming were hidden from him. The 10th Corps which he had seen from the air exercising 50 miles in the rear moved silently away in the night, but leaving an exact simulacrum of its tanks where it had been, and proceeded to

[1] George Griffiths, 1880–1945. Labour MP for Hemsworth, 1934–45.

its points of attack. The enemy suspected that the attack was impending but did not know how, when or where, and above all he had no idea of the scope upon which he was to be assaulted.

But what was done by the Desert Army in the field was accomplished upon a far vaster scale here at home and in the United States in the gigantic Anglo-American descent upon North Africa. Here again Hitler knew that something was brewing, but what, he could not guess. He naively complained of 'military idiots' and drunkards – he is quite uncivil from time to time – the working of whose tortuous minds he and his staffs were unable to discern. In fact however while he was thus wondering, the largest amphibious operation ever conceived was about to sail for a strategic area of cardinal importance, which it reached without the slightest warning and where the ships succeeded in making their landfall.

There is a great advantage, I think, in our not publishing the shipping losses. The Germans tell their own tales, which make no difference to the mentality and steadfastness of our people, but the Germans become the victims of their own lies. They have exaggerated continuously. The losses are heavy enough in all conscience, but they have continuously exaggerated them, and consequently I do not think they believed that we had the shipping for any operation on such a scale as is now being employed. None the less, the greatest credit is due to the many hundreds of people in Britain and in the United States – hundreds, there may be more – who necessarily had to be informed because of the part they played in the preparations or who could have inferred from the duties given to them what was in the wind. A tribute is also due to the Press for the extreme discretion which they practised, and which they were asked to practise, in avoiding all speculation upon dangerous topics. These are important matters and will be helpful in the future. Democracies have to show that they are not incapable of keeping their war secrets. Here is a fine example.

I have completed my account of these operations. I thought it right to go into the details of them because I know the deep interest which the House takes in these matters, and also the very large number of Members who have practical experience of war. What is happening now? We of course foresaw the reactions which the entry of American and British Forces into North Africa would produce on various countries affected. First of all there was Italy, which will now come to a much fuller and better realisation of the trials of war and of the unwisdom of entering a war when you think your antagonist is prostrate. It will bring home to the people of Italy as a whole a very much clearer realisation of the trials and horrors of war than they have had the opportunity of experiencing up to now. Today the news reaches us that Hitler has decided to overrun all France, thus breaking the Armistice which the Vichy Government had kept with such pitiful and perverted fidelity, at a horrible cost, even sacrificing their ships and sailors to fire upon American rescuing troops as they arrived. Even while they were doing that for the sake of this Armistice they have been stricken down by their German taskmasters.

This surely is the moment for all Frenchmen worthy of the name to stand together and to be truly united in spirit. Their trials will be many, and the difficulties into which individuals will be thrown in the circumstances which may overtake them are unimaginable. Nevertheless, here is the moment for all Frenchmen to sink personal feuds and rivalries and to think, as General de Gaulle is thinking, only of the liberation of their native land. I must however confess freely to the House that I have not sufficient information at the moment about what is happening in France to add anything to the accounts which are being made public hour by hour. Only at the moment when I entered the House news reached me that in North Africa Casablanca had capitulated to the United States. Another message was that Bougie has been occupied, further to the east of Algiers, by an amphibious expedition. Oran is already in the possession of the Allies. Algiers has been for three days in their possession. All the vital landing ports in North Africa are in Allied hands.

The House may be sure that many things are going to happen in the next few days, and I should be merely presuming if I attempted to give my own opinion upon the situation which will develop in North Africa, in France or in Italy, except that we shall shortly have far greater facilities for bombing Italy than ever existed before. That is not a matter of speculation.

I have now given to the House the best account I can, amid the press of events, of these remarkable transactions, which I venture to hope have already been highly beneficial to our interests and to our cause. We are entitled to rejoice only upon the condition that we do not relax. I always liked those lines by the American poet, Walt Whitman. I have several times repeated them. They apply today most aptly. He said: '...
Now understand me well – it is provided in the essence of things that from any fruition of success, no matter what, shall come forth something to make a greater struggle necessary.' The problems of victory are more agreeable than those of defeat, but they are no less difficult. In all our efforts to recapture the initiative we shall be confronted with many perplexing choices and many unavoidable hazards, and I cannot doubt that we shall meet with our full share of mistakes, vexations and disap-

pointments. We shall need to use the stimulus of victory to increase our exertions, to perfect our systems, and to refine our processes. In that spirit, sustained by the unswerving support of the House of Commons, we shall bend again to our task.

Henry Channon: diary
('Chips', page 341)

11 November 1942

[...] Winston followed and for 76 minutes we had a dramatic treat, as he described the African landings, the victory in Egypt, etc. But whilst vivid and boisterous, he said nothing, or little, that one had not heard on the wireless. Indeed, events just now seem to happen with such dramatic celerity and frequency, that we are breathless. The Germans have occupied Tunisia, the Italians have taken the Riviera. Darlan is rumoured to be treating with us. We listened enthralled. At last I crept away, and slept solidly in the library for 20 minutes, and when I returned, Winston was winding up. It was a creditable, indeed amazing, performance, for an overworked man of 68. He was cheered when he sat down, and the House emptied, or almost. [...]

Winston S. Churchill to William Mackenzie King
(Churchill papers, 20/82)

12 November 1942

I have heard of the success of the Canadian Third Victory Loan and of the great response which the Canadian people have made. I send to them through you many warmest congratulations. Hitler has good reason to know the might of Canada's armed forces, of her ships and planes and weapons of war. Her sailors, soldiers and airmen have answered every call in all parts of the world. Her workers in shipyards and munition factories have delivered and are delivering their full measure. From her coasts, prairies, forests and mines come many of the resources on which the United Nations depend in their battle for freedom. Canada's unbending will to share to the full the burden and sacrifices of the war is manifest. She has accepted the challenge which threatens all freedom-loving peoples alike and her people have given proof of their readiness to make every contribution to victory which victory demands.

Winston S. Churchill to General Hastings Ismay,
for the Chiefs of Staff Committee
(Churchill papers, 20/67)

12 November 1942

AIRCRAFT 'TUGS' FOR GLIDERS

I am disquieted by these notes which Lord Cherwell, at my request, has put before me. You may remember that the Lord Privy Seal recently raised the question of the excessive construction of gliders. As you know, I think they will play their part when demoralisation sets in; but I am worried by the difficulty of storing these wooden machines and the very heavy drain upon the bomber offensive. It is all a question of balance and emphasis.

2. I am sure it requires review. I do not want the Chiefs of the Staff in this operational crisis to be unduly burdened with this. It would be better that the Vice-Chiefs should give it a special examination, which, of course, should not take more than two sittings. Their report would give us something to work upon. We might look very foolish if we had a lot of these things standing out in the rain and spoiling when no opportunity for their offensive use occurred. My feeling is at present that the 'Horsa' programme should be curtailed.

Winston S. Churchill to the Chiefs of Staff Committee
(Churchill papers, 20/67)

12 November 1942
Action this Day

We cannot divest ourselves of responsibility for the convoy from the East to Malta. If it is to sail on the 15th, what arrangements are made to protect it against surface attack by the Italian fleet? Is it to approach Malta in darkness or in daylight? What protection would it have against bombers from Crete, and generally until it gets under the Malta air umbrella? This is no time to throw away four fast heavily-laden ships. Will the airfield at Derna be working by the time the convoy gets there? If it is not, we ought to wait a few more days till it is. The prospects in Cyrenaica are now so good that there is no need for forlorn, desperate adventures. Admiral Harwood should submit his scheme, showing exactly his daylight and darkness passage, and how he plans to get through.

2. It is, of course, of the utmost importance that Lord Gort should intervene by air in Tunis. But I do not think we ought simply to leave the

responsibility of using up his petrol to him. What view do the Chiefs of Staff take about the amount he should keep in hand?

3. It would seem that everything should be calculated from the date when the Derna airfield is effectively occupied.

George Harvie-Watt: report
(Premier papers, 4/64/6)

13 November 1942

[...]

The House has been in a buoyant mood this week. Your speech on Wednesday and events in North Africa have cheered Members up tremendously. Your Speech was generally acclaimed an outstanding success. Many of your former critics in conversation with me have said that they are delighted that you have had this successful break. Clement Davies, Hore Belisha and Shinwell are among those who have said that events have justified your policy and that their criticism was merely to get a more vigorous prosecution of the war. I doubt very much however if they are likely to remain stalwart supporters for long.

The subsequent Debate on the Address was somewhat unreal – Members had really nothing to say. Most speakers paid high tribute to you.

Winston S. Churchill to President Franklin D. Roosevelt
(Churchill papers, 20/82)

13 November 1942
Personal and Secret
No. 189

Thank you very much for all you say. Our enterprises have prospered beyond our hopes and we must not neglect the good gifts of fortune. All our three Generals are splendid, and relations with ours are perfect.

2. Everything you say in your paragraph beginning (quote) it is hoped (unquote) down to the words (quote) Germany's flank (unquote) is in absolute harmony with our views.[1] I shall spend all this weekend with our Chiefs of the Staff reviewing the whole scene, which may be more clear then than now. On Sunday morning we will confer with General Smith, and I hope early next week to send you our views.

---

[1] 'It is hoped that you with your Chiefs of Staff in London and I with the Combined Staff here may make a survey of the possibilities including forward movement directed against Sardinia, Sicily, Italy, Greece, and other Balkan areas, and including the possibility of obtaining Turkish support for an attack through the Black Sea against Germany's flank.'

3. Meanwhile let me say that nothing pleases me more than to read what you say about trying to bring Turkey in. Our minds have indeed moved together on this, as in so much else. It seems to me there are four stages:

   (a) The clearance of the North African coast and the opening of the Mediterranean for military traffic.

   (b) A guarantee to Turkey by Great Britain, Russia and the United States of her territorial integrity and status quo.

   (c) The rapid stocking-up of Turkey with British and American arms, particularly tanks, flak and anti-tank guns.

   (d) The movement of Air forces to the Russian Southern flank, which must in any case be pressed forward at once, and the gathering during the winter of a considerable army in Syria.

I hope next week to make you specific proposals and suggestions.

4. Rommel's Panzer Army is reduced to a few thousand men with barely a score of tanks and guns. It looks as if he would have to clear out of Cyrenaica altogether and try to make a stand at Agheila and in the Gulf of Sirte.

5. The reaction in Spain has been excellent and in France all to the good. We hope soon to turn the bombing heat on to Italy.

6. I am still deeply anxious about the U-boat depredations, and I beg you to give favourable consideration to the letter I sent you by Oliver Lyttelton.[1]

All good wishes.

Winston S. Churchill to General Dwight D. Eisenhower
(Churchill papers, 20/82)

13 November 1942
Personal and Secret

Accept my warmest congratulations on the brilliant success of your operations, and my best thanks for all the kind thing you say in your No. 297. I am sure you are right in feeling that the utmost risks should be run to profit by this happy turn of fortune, and that intense efforts should be made to secure the mastery in the tip of Tunis, and the capture of Tripoli [. . .]

2. The President, whose views I share to the full, has asked me to confer with the British Chiefs of Staff about the future while he does the same

[1] This is the letter referred to in paragraph 3 of Churchill's cable to Roosevelt of 1 November 1942, reproduced at page 1345 above.

at Washington. Accordingly I am holding a conference on Saturday, and have invited General Smith to join us on Sunday morning.

3. It looks as if Rommel and his panzer army, now reduced to a few thousand men with about 20 tanks and guns, will be cleared out of Cyrenaica altogether, and will try to stand at Agheila. Alexander and Montgomery are hunting him hard.

4. Give my congratulations to General Clark on his splendidly-earned promotion to Lieutenant-General, of which I read in the newspapers.

5. I send you a copy of my telegram to the President about De Gaulle, to which he has replied in very favourable terms agreeing to a De Gaullist emissary being sent to try to fix things amicably with Giraud.[1]

6. Every good wish. If I can help in any way, count on me.

Winston S. Churchill to General Hastings Ismay
(Churchill papers, 20/67)

13 November 1942

I saw the Jefferis gun last week.[2] It appears to be a powerful weapon, which would enable infantry to face tank attack.

How many have been ordered?

When will they be delivered?

How is it proposed to distribute them?

I should hope that the Middle East and India would receive their quota at a very early date.

Pray let me have a report.

---

[1] '[M]y telegram to the President' of 11 November 1942; see page 1379 above. Roosevelt replied on November 12: 'I wholly agree that we must prevent rivalry between the French émigré factions and I have no objection to a de Gaulle Emissary visiting Kingpin in Algiers.'

[2] Known as the PIAT (Projector, Infantry, Anti-Tank): a British anti-tank weapon developed during the Second World War. It consisted of a steel tube, trigger mechanism, and firing spring, and was based on the spigot mortar system. Instead of using a propellant to fire a round directly, the spring was cocked and tightened. When the trigger was pulled, it released the spring, which pushed the spigot forward into the rear of the bomb. This detonated the propellant in the bomb itself, which was then thrown forward off the spigot. It possessed an effective range of approximately 100 yards (90 metres). This system gave the PIAT had several advantages, including a lack of muzzle smoke to reveal the position of the user, the option to fire it from inside buildings, and an inexpensive barrel. However, there were countervailing disadvantages, including difficulty in cocking the weapon, the bruising the user received when firing it, and problems with its penetrative power. The PIAT entered service in 1943, and was first used during the Allied invasion of Sicily that year. It remained in use with British and Commonwealth forces until the early 1950s, when it was replaced by the American bazooka.

Winston S. Churchill to Lord Selborne[1]
(Churchill papers, 20/67)

13 November 1942

It seems most important to intensify the operations in the newly-occupied regions of France in order to make the relations between the torpid French and the German invaders as unpleasant as possible.

Pray let me know what you are doing or propose to do.

Winston S. Churchill to Josef Stalin
(Churchill papers, 20/82)

13 November 1942
Most Immediate
Personal and Secret

Many thanks for your messages of the 8th and 10th November which have both reached me.

2. I have appointed Air Marshal Drummond[2] to represent Great Britain in the Staff discussions between the Soviet, American and British representatives on the preliminary arrangements for the employment of the 20 British and American squadrons on your Southern front. Air Marshal Drummond has been ordered to leave Cairo for Moscow with a small party of Staff Officers forthwith.

3. Important success has rewarded our operations both in Egypt and French North Africa. We have already penetrated deeply into Cyrenaica. Tobruk has just been recaptured. The so-called Panzer Army is now reduced to a very small, hard-pressed band with hardly a score of tanks, and we are in hot pursuit. It seems to me almost certain that Benghazi will soon be recovered and the enemy will try to escape into Tripolitania holding a line at Agheila. He is already evacuating stores from Benghazi, and is endeavouring to open new improvised and restricted bases in the Gulf of Sirte.

4. The 'Torch' is flaming well, and General Eisenhower and our own Commanders have every hope of obtaining complete control of French North Africa and building up a superior Air power at the tip of Tunisia.

---

[1] Minister of Economic Warfare.

[2] Peter Roy Maxwell Drummond, 1894–1945. Born in Perth, Western Australia. Educated at Scotch College, Perth. Served with Australian Imperial Forces, Egypt, and Gallipoli, 1914–15; Royal Flying Corps and RAF, Palestine, 1916–18; Sudan, 1919–20 (Military Cross, despatches twice, DSO and bar 1918, Medal with clasp). OBE, 1921. Graduated from RAF Staff College, 1923; from Imperial Defence College, 1930; Deputy Air Officer Commanding-in-Chief, Royal Air Force, Middle East, 1941–3. CB, 1941. KCB, 1943. Air Member for Training on the Air Council from 1943.

This is all in the intention of further aggressive operations. All the great troop convoys have moved or are moving so far safely across the ocean and from Great Britain. We hope to create a strong anti-German French Army in North Africa under General Giraud.

5. The political reactions in Spain and Portugal have been most satisfactory, and the danger of Gibraltar harbour and air-field being rendered unusable has ceased for the present to be a grave anxiety. The German invasion of Vichy France, which was foreseen by us and also by you in our conversation is all to the good. The poisonous and paralyzing influence of Vichy on the French nation will decline, and the whole people will soon learn to hate the Germans as much as they are hated in the occupied zone. The future of the Toulon fleet is obscure. The Germans have not felt themselves strong enough to demand its surrender, and are reported to intend to respect the entrenched camp of Toulon. Admiral Darlan, who is in our power, has asked the fleet to sail for West African ports. Whether this order will be obeyed is still doubtful.

6. A great reversal of the situation along the whole African shore has taken place and may be counted on. If we can open passage for military traffic through the Mediterranean, our shipping problem will be greatly eased and we shall come into far closer contact with Turkey than has hitherto been possible. I am in communication with President Roosevelt who is delighted at the success of American enterprise. The whole position must be reviewed in a few days, with the intention of further vehement action. I will let you know as soon as possible what our ideas for the future are. You know I am sure how anxious we are to take off you some of the undue weight which you have steadfastly borne in these last hard months. Meanwhile I am proceeding on the assumption that you are still confident the Caucasus range will not be penetrated in the winter months.

Josef Stalin to Winston S. Churchill
(Churchill papers, 20/83)

14 November 1942　　　　　　　　　　　　　　　　Kremlin
Personal and Secret　　　　　　　　　　　　　　　Moscow

Many thanks for your message of the 13th November.

We all here delighted at your successes in Libya and at the successes of the British–American forces in the French North Africa. Let me congratulate you from the bottom of my heart on your victory and wish you further successes

In the last few days we succeeded in stopping the Germans near Vladikavkas and in stabilising the situation there. Vladikavkas is in our hands and, it seems to me, will remain in our hands. We are taking all possible measures to keep our positions in the Northern Caucasus.

We hope to start our winter campaign in the near future. The exact moment of the beginning depends on weather which is beyond our power. I will regularly inform you on the course of the operations.

Stalin

Winston S. Churchill to Admiral of the Fleet Sir Dudley Pound
(Churchill papers, 20/67)

14 November 1942
Secret

I am most anxious to run a Russian convoy late in December. For this purpose the United States must be asked to make available for our needs at least 20 or 25 destroyers, which they can easily save from the excessive escorts which they are using for the big troop convoys for 'Torch'. Such a request might well be coupled with our meeting their wishes in regard to the two aircraft carriers. If we had another 25 destroyers in our hands, we should be much easier.

Winston S. Churchill to Sir Stafford Cripps
(Churchill papers, 20/67)

14 November 1942
Secret

ANTI U-BOAT WARFARE COMMITTEE

I think it would be a mistake to set up the kind of body you suggest.[1] The Admiralty would, I am sure, resent anything like continuous tutelage or supervision. Moreover, the men you would be seeing would be those engaged in handling the matter; at least, those are the only ones worth dealing with.

You will find that the discussions which take place at my weekly meetings, focussed as they will be by Sir Edward Bridges and Lord Cherwell, will have the effect of clearing up inter-departmental difficulties and

---

[1] Referring to a minute from the Lord Privy Seal suggesting that a smaller body sit continuously, reporting weekly or fortnightly to the larger body.

heating up the activities of the branches of the Admiralty and Air Ministry concerned.

I hope the Field-Marshal[1] and you had an interesting visit yesterday to the Admiralty. You must not underrate this enormous, intricate, high-speed organisation, which has borne us thus far so well. It is capable of stimulus and improvement, and that is what we are trying to effect. At any rate, let us see how the Committee gets on.

Winston S. Churchill to Air Chief Marshal Sir Charles Portal
(Churchill papers, 20/54)

14 November 1942
Private and Personal

My dear Portal,

Of course my first wish is to help you in your all-important work, but I must say the more I ponder on the proposed changes, the less I like them.

It seems to me a very great pity to move Tedder from the Middle East, where he has now learned thoroughly the desert conditions, and knows all the personalities and the whole problem. It will take a new man at least six months to acquire this knowledge.

The same applies to moving Sholto Douglas from the Fighter Command, of which he is complete master, having had two years' experience.

The routine of Service movements and promotions must give way in time of war to having the great functions in practised and experienced hands. We change far too often. Surely you could find some other officer besides Tedder who could act as your Vice-Chief and help you in your very heavy work. Would Air Marshal Evill[2] be any good? I met him the last time I was in Washington. But anyhow, I am sure there must be others.

Yours very sincerely,
Winston S. Churchill

[1] Smuts.
[2] Air Marshal Evill, Head of the Royal Air Force delegation in Washington, was indeed appointed Vice-Chief of the Air Staff in 1943.

Anthony Eden: diary
(*'The Eden Memoirs, The Reckoning'*, page 348)

14 November 1942

LUNCHEON ALONE WITH CHURCHILL AT CHEQUERS

[...] He began to talk of reconstruction. Paper and pens were produced and we sat until 4 p.m. W. anxious to put the changes through next week. In particular he doesn't want to go on in uncertainty as to Cripps' attitude.

Oliver Harvey: diary
(*'The War Diaries of Oliver Harvey'*, pages 185–6)

15 November 1942

[...] Eisenhower confesses that he is at the mercy of Darlan and therefore he is obliged to reach agreement with him. He says he is quite certain what he has done is right, Cunningham agrees with him and no one not on the spot can understand. What a document! What a confession! Appeasement and nothing else. What is this agreement worth? And what harm won't it do us everywhere else? Compromising with Frenchmen who have betrayed us and killed our men, for military necessity. It is Munich reasoning over again.

We are all very worried here, from Alec Cadogan downwards. PM has sent a message to Roosevelt saying our doubts and fears have not been removed by this report, asking him to consult us about long-term arrangements and urging danger that we are being double-crossed.

Winston S. Churchill to President Franklin D. Roosevelt
(*Churchill papers, 20/83*)

15 November 1942
Urgent
Personal and Most Secret
No. 190

General Eisenhower's No. 527 on political arrangements in French North Africa.[1]

---

[1] Eisenhower's message emphasized the delicacy of the political situation in North Africa, pointing out that the French leaders – including Giraud – all agreed that only Darlan had 'an obvious right to assume the Marshal's mantle in North Africa'. He cautioned strongly against repudiating Darlan, emphasizing that to do so would gravely endanger French cooperation in the region and

1. We cannot say that our doubts or anxieties are removed by what is proposed or that the solution will be permanent or healthy. Nevertheless, in view of the dominating importance of speed and of the fact that the Allied Commander-in-Chief's opinion is so strongly and ably expressed and that it is endorsed by our officers, including Admiral Cunningham, who were with him on the spot we feel we have no choice but to accept General Eisenhower's arrangements for maintaining local and interim equilibrium and for securing the vital positions in Tunis.

2. We feel sure you will consult us on the long-term steps pursuing always the aim of uniting all Frenchmen who will fight Hitler.

3. Great care must be taken that we are not double-crossed. There were some disquieting evidences in our Magics[1] two days ago. On the other hand we have these men in our power and should be vigilant lest they escape from us.

4. We do not see any need to publish the press release contained in General Eisenhower's No. 544 or anything like it at present, pending further developments in Tunis and Dakar, and hope our views may be met.

5. To save time we are repeating this telegram to you to General Eisenhower for his immediate information.

Winston S. Churchill to General Sir Harold Alexander
(Churchill papers, 20/83)

15 November 1942
Most Immediate
Personal and Most Secret

We hope to be masters of Tunisia pretty soon but the communications with Tripolitania are said to be so poor that about three months would be required to bring a division and a half or two divisions to bear on Tripoli town from the west. A demonstration with a smaller force would no doubt be arranged a good deal earlier. To take Tripoli from the west might mean burdening our shipping with greater weight of transport and rearward services than would be necessary if we were only concerned with Tunisia. We must save all we can for other enterprises. On the other hand we know the enemy has resolved not to stand decisively

the chances of victory in Tunisia, as well as losing the Toulon fleet. See *The Papers of Dwight David Eisenhower: The War Years*, Volume II, Baltimore, 1970, pages 706–10.

[1] Magic: the term used by American forces for the cryptanalysis of Japanese ciphers. The effort was led by William Friedman, who was able to replicate the 'PURPLE' machine, the Japanese encryption device, and intercept Japanese diplomatic messages.

against you at Agheila but rather at Misurata. In these circumstances how do you feel about taking Tripoli yourself? And how long do you think you would require? Should be glad to have your best estimate as soon as possible.

Oliver Harvey: diary
(*'The War Diaries of Oliver Harvey'*, *page 187*)

16 November 1942

[...] AE disturbed at the differences between himself and the PM over foreign affairs, 'just like with Neville Chamberlain again'. He was annoyed because Kingsley Wood has had a paper written up in the Treasury against his Four Power Plan. KW plays up to the PM who doesn't discourage him.

AE spoke of going to India himself! I said that was nonsense. No one going to India now could ever be PM. He could resign again if he must but he must remain in England. His future was to be PM of England and only someone who had been in this country in the vital years would be PM. He exaggerated his differences with the PM. He should talk to him heart to heart. The PM loved him as a son and spoke of him as his successor. He alone of his colleagues was listened to by the PM in military matters. He should have it out with him and demand more support for himself in foreign affairs as against the KWs who were the PM's enemies anyway.

Winston S. Churchill to President Franklin D. Roosevelt
(*Churchill papers, 20/83*)

17 November 1942
Personal and Secret
No. 192

I am so glad to read about this splendid American naval victory in the Solomons.[1] Pray accept my warmest congratulations and thanks.

---

[1] The Battle of Guadalcanal, fought near the island of Guadalcanal from 12 to 15 November 1942, between Japanese and Allied (primarily US) naval forces. The Japanese attempted to land infantry on the island and to bombard the Allied-held airfield called Henderson Field, but the naval group was intercepted by Allied forces. Over a period of several days, with much of the action taking place at night, the Japanese were kept from Henderson Field and lost most of their transports in the engagement. The Allied naval forces suffered 9 sunk and 9 damaged ships, while the Japanese fleet suffered 26 sunk and 12 damaged vessels. This marked a decisive strategic victory for Allied forces, and the last major Japanese assault and reinforcement action of the war on Guadalcanal and the surrounding waters.

Winston S. Churchill to President Franklin D. Roosevelt
(Churchill papers, 20/83)

17 November 1942
Personal and Secret
No. 193

I ought to let you know that very deep currents of feeling are stirred by the arrangement with Darlan. The more I reflect upon it the more convinced I become that it can only be a temporary expedient justifiable solely by the stress of battle. We must not overlook the serious political injury which may be done to our cause, not only in France but throughout Europe, by the feeling that we are ready to make terms with the local Quislings. Darlan has an odious record. It is he who has inculcated in the French Navy its malignant disposition by promoting his creatures to command. It is but yesterday that French sailors were sent to their death against your line of battle off Casablanca and now, for the sake of power and office, Darlan plays the turncoat. A permanent arrangement with Darlan or the formation of a Darlan Government in French North Africa would not be understood by the great masses of ordinary people whose simple loyalties are our strength.

2. My own feeling is that we should get on with the fighting and let that overtake the parleys, and we are all very glad to hear that General Eisenhower expects to be able to order the leading elements of our First Army to attack the Germans in Tunis and Bizerta in the course of the next few days.

Winston S. Churchill to the Chiefs of Staff
(Churchill papers, 20/83)

17 November 1942

PLANS AND OPERATIONS IN THE MEDITERRANEAN,
MIDDLE EAST AND NEAR EAST

In settling what to do in a vast war situation like this, it may sometimes be found better to take a particular major operation to which one is committed and follow that through vigorously to the end, making other things subordinate to it, rather than to assemble all the data from the whole world scene in a baffling array. After the needs of the major operation have been satisfied so far as possible, other aspects of the war will fall into their proper places. Moreover, it is by the continued stressing of the major operation that our will may be imposed upon the enemy and the initiative regained.

2. The paramount task before us is, first, to conquer the African shores of the Mediterranean and set up there the naval and air installations which are necessary to open an effective passage through it for military traffic; and secondly, using the bases on the African shore, to strike at the under-belly of the Axis in effective strength and in the shortest time.

3. There are therefore two phases – consolidation and exploitation. Dealing with consolidation first, we may hope that General Alexander will become master of the whole of Cyrenaica during the present month, and that he will be pressing the enemy in the Agheila position or even at Sirte. We may also assume that in the same period or not long after the American and British forces will become masters of the whole of French North Africa including Tunis, provided they press forward with their present energy and violence.

4. It will be necessary to set up Air stations at suitable intervals along all the African shore in our power, but particularly and urgently in the Tunis tip. The largest installations for American bombers ought to be set up here so that long-range bombers sent by the United States to North Africa, together with American bombers already based on the Middle East can operate against Italian targets. The United States form of daylight attack would have its best chance in the better weather of the Mediterranean.

5. The bombing weight of the British night attack should be brought to bear on Italy whenever the weather is more favourable than for bombing Germany. Every endeavour should be made to make Italy feel the weight of the war. All the industrial centres should be attacked in an intense fashion, every effort being made to render them uninhabitable and to terrorize and paralyze the population. I have asked for a scheme of desirable targets in Italy.

6. It will no doubt be necessary also to act against the Catania and Cagliari airfields so as to keep down the attack on Tunis in the period of consolidation.

7. As soon as we are sure of ourselves, and consolidated, in French North Africa, including especially Tunis, two successive operations present themselves. The first is the advance to Tripoli. It is possible that General Alexander may be able to take this important prize from the East, and I have asked him how he feels about it, and how long he thinks it would require; but we must also be prepared for a rapid advance from the West. Would General Anderson's[1] two British Divisions be sufficient, assuming

---

[1] Kenneth Anderson, commander of the 1st Army in Operation 'Torch'.

that Tunis itself can be held by American and French Allied troops? I
should like the best possible estimate of the time that this will take.

8. The second immediate objective is obviously either Sardinia or Sicily.
The possession of either of these Islands and of the airfields in the South
would create an Air triangle, in which we should fight for and secure
Air mastery. Moreover from either of them continuous intensified short-
range attacks on Naples, Rome, and the Italian fleet bases would raise
the war against Italy to an intense degree. Let an immediate report be
prepared in order that a decision can be taken. Whichever it may be, the
fight for Air control in the Central Mediterranean should be undertaken
as a great Air battle with extreme priority, the fullest advantage being
taken of the Axis shortage of aircraft.

9. The swift success in French North Africa has completely changed
the character of the problem which we had been bound to face in that
region. We need no longer contemplate a protracted campaign against
French in Algeria, nor immediate trouble with the Spaniards in Morocco.
On the contrary, all is well in Algeria, and a French army will be coming
into existence, fed by Allied munitions at our discretion. An examination
should be made as to how the follow-up 'Torch' convoys can be drastically reduced and revised. Will the four British Divisions now in North
Africa or under orders to go there be required for 'Torch'? It should be
possible sensibly to reduce the 'tail' of these divisions, thus saving escorts
for other purposes, including, in the following order:

(a) Sardinia or Sicily
(b) Restoration of the British Trans-Atlantic convoys up to standard
      strength.
(c) Resumption of the PQ convoys in the latter part of December.

To facilitate these vital needs, and to provide the large Naval, particularly anti-submarine, forces which will be required, together with the
necessary air forces, to secure a safe passage through the Mediterranean,
United States naval help will be urgently needed. Cannot the American
Naval authorities reduce the strength of their follow-up trans-Atlantic
convoys and can the American 'tail' be reduced in the same way as I
hope the British 'tail' will be combed?

10. What are General Eisenhower's wishes about the force to attack
Sardinia or Sicily? There are two British Divisions of the First Army, as
well as the two others which are standing by. Is there any need to put
the first two into North Africa? Can they not be combat loaded here?
Are the losses among our combat loaders crippling? How serious are
they? There are great advantages and saving of time in going straight

from the United Kingdom to the landing in Sardinia or Sicily. We must expect a steady reinforcement of both islands by the enemy, and speed will make our task definitely lighter. Note that the preparations to attack Sardinia may take as long as those to attack Sicily, and that Sicily is by far the greater prize.

Decisions on all the above are needed within the next week.

11. The relief and re-supplying of Malta should follow naturally from the operations now in progress or in prospect in the Central Mediterranean, and the immediate needs of the island are being dealt with on an effective scale. It would be well, when circumstances and shipping permit, to exchange the Units who have long been in the fortress for some of those who have been in the Desert, and vice versa.

12. I have received a telegram from the President containing the following paragraph:

'It is hoped that you with your Chiefs of Staff in London and I with the Combined Staff here may make a survey of the possibilities including forward movement directed against Sardinia, Sicily, Italy, Greece and other Balkan areas and including the possibility of obtaining Turkish support for an attack through the Black Sea against Germany's flank.'

I endorse the above conception by the President. The first part of the President's wishes are being studied by the Combined Staffs in Washington, and are the subject of the foregoing paragraphs for our discussions.

13. The second part relating to Turkey is also of vital importance, though it is a slower process. A supreme and prolonged effort must be made to bring Turkey into the war in the Spring. We must expect that our naval forces and shipping, landing craft, etc. will be fully engaged in the Central Mediterranean, and that only minor amphibious facilities will be available in the Levant. Access can however be had to Turkey by the railways through Syria as well as by coastal shipping, and by a gradual build-up of Air protection not only Adalia but the Dardanelles itself might become open to supplies for Turkey. Troops can move by rail and road from Syria.

I wish to record my opinion that Turkey may be won if the proper measures are taken. Turkey is an Ally. She will wish to have a seat among the victors at the Peace Conference. She has a great desire to be well-armed. Her Army is in good order except for the specialized modern weapons, in which the Bulgarians have been given so great an advantage by the Germans. The Turkish Army has been mobilised for nearly three years, and is warlike. Hitherto Turkey has been restrained by fear from fulfilling her obligations, and we have taken an indulgent view of her policy on account of our own inability to help. The situation has now changed. By the destruction of Rommel's Army, large forces may presently become available in Egypt and Cyrenaica. By a strengthened Russian resistance and a possible counterstroke in the Caucasus, which we should urge upon the Russians with all emphasis, great easement will be secured in Persia and the Tenth Army may be drawn upon. There is also the Ninth Army in Syria. From all these sources it should be possible, on the assumption of the Russians maintaining themselves in the Caucasus north of the mountain line and holding the Caspian, to build up a powerful British land and air force to assist the Turks. A target date for the concentration should be April or May. Let me have proposals.

14. The following is the order of procedure, political and military:

(a) Turkey should be offered a Russian–American–British guarantee of territorial integrity and status quo. The Russians have already agreed with us upon this. The addition of the United States would probably be a decisive reassurance. This should be followed by the despatch to Turkey of a strong Anglo-American Military Mission.

(b) All through the winter from now on, Turkey must be equipped from Egypt and from the United States with tanks, A/T and AA guns, and active construction of airfields must be undertaken. We have been working upon airfield construction in Turkey for two years. What progress has been made so far? Now that Rommel has been beaten, there is evidently a surplus of material in Egypt. We had over 2,500 tanks at the disposal of the Middle East Army. Much enemy material has been captured, both German and Italian. This is also true of A/T and AA guns. Experts must be provided to assist the Turks in learning to use and maintain this material. A ceaseless flow of weapons and equipment must go into Turkey. We have already promised a consignment, but the moment Turkey agrees secretly with the plan above, greater quantities must be sent. What is the capacity of the railways from Syria to the Bosphorus and the Dardanelles? It would seem a great mistake to attack Rhodes and other islands in enemy hands in the Eastern Mediterranean until we have got Turkey on our side. Any attacks can then be supported by heavy shore-based Air power. We have to creep round this coast by land and sea, building up our Air as we go.

(c) In conjunction with the above, we should urge the Russians to develop their strength on their southern flank, to try to clear the Caucasus, to regain Novorossisk and, above all, to resume at the earliest date their intentions explained to me by Premier Stalin, of striking south-west from the region north of Stalingrad towards Rostov on the Don. An ultimate result of these operations, if successful, would be the opening of the Dardanelles under heavy Air protection, to the passage of supplies to Russian Black Sea ports, and to any naval assistance the Russians might require in the Black Sea.

(d) Lastly, all being well we should assemble in Syria the British and Imperial forces mentioned in preceding paragraphs.

Winston S. Churchill to President Franklin D. Roosevelt
(Churchill papers, 20/83)

17 November 1942
Personal and Secret
No. 194

Your 210 and 211.

As promised in Paragraph 2 of my 189, I am sending you in my immediately following telegram the text of a note which I have given to the British Chiefs of Staff.[1]

2. The Chiefs of Staff are in general agreement with this note and are busily engaged in studying the implications of the various possibilities which it contemplates. I will send you the results as soon as possible.

3. Meanwhile you might find it convenient to let the Combined Chiefs of Staff see my note before their discussions. This would facilitate and hasten the agreement which we must reach between ourselves before we send a joint Mission to Moscow.

4. Thank you so much for your statement about Darlan. This puts it all right for us.

Winston S. Churchill to General Hastings Ismay,
for the Chiefs of Staff Committee and John Llewellin[2]
(Churchill papers, 20/67)

17 November 1942

CHIEFS OF STAFF REPORT ON AIRBORNE FORCES

This is all a question of balance and emphasis. I have, as you know, always been anxious to have a well-found airborne division, but there is no prospect in the near future of our being able to provide the necessary

[1] Reproduced here as the immediately preceding item.
[2] Minister of Aircraft Production.

aircraft for a force of the size contemplated by the War Office. Moreover, I am worried by the excessive construction of gliders and the difficulty of storing these wooden machines. We might look very foolish if we had a lot of these things standing out in the rain spoiling when no opportunity for their offensive use occurred. We should find out at once how many C47s we may expect to get from the United States, as we cannot accept a heavy drain upon our bomber offensive. In any event, I am sure that the Horsa programme will have to be drastically curtailed.

2. Our immediate target should be the creation of a force of the dimensions recommended by CAS in paragraph 10 of his note, i.e., two parachute brigades, plus a small gliderborne force to lift the heavier supporting weapons and vehicles which cannot be dropped by parachute. Let the details be worked out forthwith between the War Office and Air Ministry and a report made. A stand-still order for gliders should be issued at once.

3. The whole position should be re-examined in about six months' time say, the 1st June.

Winston S. Churchill to Air Chief Marshal Sir Charles Portal and to General Hastings Ismay, for the Chiefs of Staff Committee
(Churchill papers, 20/67)

17 November 1942

I should find it very difficult to advise the Cabinet to make any delay in giving this support to the Russians. 'Velvet'[1] has always been studied by Tedder as a separate operation after the main battle was won. He has now 1,200 aircraft ready or at 14 days. The enemy have 300. There can be no grounds for not sparing about 250. If it were only a question of delaying the departure of the American heavy bombers, they could be put late in the schedule and do a little more bombing for General Alexander before they leave. I do not think the arrangement ought to be upset.

---

[1] 'Velvet': the movement of Anglo-American forces to the Caucasus to support the Russians.

Winston S. Churchill to Lord Portal[1]
(Churchill papers, 20/67)

17 November 1942
Secret

The King has an idea that, if President Roosevelt came over here, he might be accommodated at Admiralty House. I am sure the First Lord would be agreeable. The ground floor could be arranged as one large suite for the President, and there is a shelter handy, apart from the Admiralty Citadel.

Pray look into this and report.

War Cabinet: conclusions
(Cabinet papers, 65/28)

18 November 1942   Prime Minister's Room
12 noon   House of Commons

BRITISH COLONIAL POLICY

The War Cabinet had some discussion in connection with the criticisms of British Colonial Policy now current in the United States.

The Prime Minister thought that it might be a good plan that a full statement should be drawn up for publication on the development of the British Colonial Empire, vindicating our past and present policy, and indicating the probable trends of future policy.

The Secretary of State for the Colonies[2] said that an opportunity might soon occur, as he understood that a motion on this subject was to be put on the Paper in the House of Lords.[3] He would like to make a full statement in answer to this motion.

The War Cabinet expressed itself in favour of his proposal.

---

[1] Minister of Works and Planning.

[2] Viscount Cranborne.

[3] On 3 December 1942, the House of Lords considered a motion put down three weeks previously by the Earl of Listowel, concerning whether His Majesty's Government 'can make a statement on colonial policy in accord with the provisions of the Atlantic Charter'. However, it was noted that by that date Viscount Cranborne was no longer the Secretary of State for the Colonies (having been replaced by Colonel Oliver Stanley on November 22), and that therefore discussion of the matter in the House of Lords would be 'less useful . . . because the Colonial Office is no longer represented here by either of its Ministerial chiefs'.

Winston S. Churchill: speech
('Winston S. Churchill, His Complete Speeches', volume 6, page 6709)

18 November 1942   Harrow School
3.30 p.m.   Harrow

I have come down here twice before during the war to refresh myself by singing these songs with you, songs that I know so well and love so much. The first time I came, two years ago, it was rough weather for most of you. Some of you are here today who had been out on the tiles putting out the incendiaries, but all were very proud of having had the honour of being under the fire of the enemy at such an early age – a very great privilege and a piece of good fortune. Many of those who were here then have now gone into the services, and some may already be fighting. If the war goes on, as go on it may, it may be that some of you who are here will also take your place in one of the various services with which we confront the enemy, and in which we defend our cause.

You have visitors here now in the shape of a sister-school – Malvern. I must say I think this is a very fine affair – to meet the needs of war, to join forces, to share alike, like two regiments that serve side by side in some famous brigade, and never forget it for a hundred years after. I was very sorry that I myself had to be responsible for giving some instructions in regard to one of our establishments which made it necessary to take over Malvern at comparatively short notice. But everyone at Harrow will, I know, make it his business to let his friends and guests carry away with them a memory which will make its mark definitely on the relationship of the two Schools – and, no doubt, to give them a beating in any of the games which you play.

Two years have passed since we stood alone. No one can doubt that we are in a better position now than we were when I came here those two years ago, when we sang many of these songs. Certainly I think the songs are very important. I enjoy them very much. I know many of them by heart. I was telling the Head Master[1] just now that I could pass an examination in some of them. They are a great treasure and possession of Harrow School, and keep the flame burning in a marvellous manner.

---

[1] Ralph Westwood Moore, 1906–53. Educated at Wolverhampton Grammar School and Christ Church, Oxford (Scholar). First Class Honours Classical Moderations, 1926. First Class Literae Humaniores, 1928. Assistant Master, Rossall School, 1928–31. Sixth Form Master, Shrewsbury School, 1931–8. Head Master, Bristol Grammar School, 1938–42. Headmaster, Harrow School, 1942–53. Member, BBC General Advisory Council, 1952. Member of the Hispanic Council. Member of the Councils of St Mary's and of Charing Cross Hospital Medical Schools.

Many carry them with them all their lives. You have the songs of Bowen[1] and Howson[2] (whom I remember well as House Masters here) with the music of John Farmer[3] and Eaton Faning.[4] They are wonderful; marvellous; more than could be put into bricks and mortar, or treasured in any trophies of silver or gold. They grow with the years. I treasure them and sing them with joy. When I was asked two years ago to come here, I said I would only come on one condition: 'You make the boys sing to me.' And if you ask me next year I will come. I hope we shall have something better to sing about; but it is not so bad. The progress we have made is very great. We were all alone, but we went on. We could not say how it was, by what means or method we should come out of our troubles. All we knew was that we should fight to the end. Now we are a great company of allied nations. We are moving forward to success and victory. As the Head Master was saying, General Alexander is a Harrow boy, and I remember him speaking to me only a short while ago with great keenness about his Harrow days.

These are very grateful thoughts, and I am entitled to bring them to your notice. We are moving forward. Far be it from me to say how long the road will be, or how great the effort will be. I cannot tell, but certainly from everything that has happened in the past we should draw encouragement and the means of keener exertion. The path leads forward; we are making our way through the dark valley. We are coming out of the wood gradually, although there are many dangers. There may be many appearances of light which turn out to be deceptive, yet nevertheless I do feel I can assure you that we are moving forward, stronger every month, and with more knowledge and confidence and power, and that the day will shortly come, through our qualities, through the qualities of the British race as much as through any other cause, when we shall reach a broader and brighter light, which when once it has shone will never be quenched.

[1] Edward Ernest Bowen, 1836–1901. Educated at King's College London and Trinity College, Cambridge (Scholar and Fellow). Master at Harrow School from 1859. On the staff of the *Saturday Review*, 1861. Stood (unsuccessfully) against A. J. Balfour as Liberal parliamentary candidate for Hertford, 1880.

[2] Edmund Whytehead Howson, 1855–1905. Fellow of King's College, Cambridge, author, and Assistant Master at Harrow School.

[3] John Farmer, 1835–1901. Composed oratorios and cantatas, as well as chamber and church music. While head of music at Harrow School he composed the school song 'Forty Years On' with Bowen.

[4] Eaton Faning, 1850–1927. English composer and teacher. Attended the Royal Academy of Music where one of his teachers was Arthur Sullivan. Later taught at the Royal Academy of Music, the Guildhall School of Music, and the Royal College of Music. Served as Director of Music at Harrow School, 1885–1901.

Winston S. Churchill to General Sir Harold Alexander
(Churchill papers, 20/83)

18 November 1942
Immediate
Most Secret and Personal

The magnificent and relentless pursuit you and Montgomery have organised far exceeds all hopes and forecasts. Therefore do not imagine that in asking these questions I am implying the slightest criticism. Could you however tell me what chance there is of cutting off those of the enemy forces who cannot do a Dunkirk from Benghazi by the movements you have now launched via Mekili and Msus? You will have noticed in the 'Boniface'[1] the expression 'Land bridge' near Agedabya. Also that the enemy have dreaded this southward move, and that owing to sinkings of oil ships and other failures in supply the Afrika Corps is 'nearly incapable of movement'. Secondly, please give me a short account of the Agheila position, especially the terrain of its landward flank. Is it a difficult position to turn? I have the feeling from all I read that the enemy is very hard pressed.

All my congratulations and good wishes.

Winston S. Churchill to President Franklin D. Roosevelt
(Churchill papers, 20/83)

18 November 1942
Personal and Most Secret
No. 196

I know your earnestness about sending another convoy to North Russia as soon as possible. We can have 31 ships ready to sail from Iceland on 22nd December.[2]

2. As *Tirpitz, Hipper* and two small enemy cruisers are stationed in Norway, it is essential to have with the convoy, in addition to their close escort, a striking force of 16 destroyers to deal with the German surface forces.

---

[1] 'Boniface': German military reports intercepted between 10 and 18 November 1942 spoke of tankers being sunk, a 'catastrophic' fuel situation, the army being virtually immobilized, and sightings of British forces south of Benghazi (Hinsley et al., *British Intelligence in the Second World War*, Volume II, pages 454–5).

[2] The next convoy to Russia in fact sailed from Liverpool on 15 December 1942. This was the first in the second series, known as the JW/RA convoys (JW outbound, RA inbound). These convoys, which ran until the end of the war, were accompanied by larger destroyers than the PQ convoys, the last of which (PQ18) had sailed in September 1942.

3. We can provide the close escort for the convoy but, owing to 'Torch' commitments and the casualties to destroyers in that operation, we can only provide 17 out of the 29 destroyers required for a screen for the Battlefleet and cruisers and the destroyer striking force mentioned above.

4. I am reluctant to risk sending this convoy unless we give it adequate protection. It is hoped therefore that you would be prepared to send 12 long endurance destroyers to assist in passing the convoy in.

5. It would be desirable for your destroyers to arrive at Scapa by 7th December in order to give time for them to get accustomed to working with our Fleet.

Winston S. Churchill to General Hastings Ismay,
for the Chiefs of Staff Committee
(Churchill papers, 20/67)

18 November 1942
Action this Day
Most Secret

Although I have asked that the tail of 'Torch' should be combed in the light of the changed character of the campaign we must expect in North Africa, I had not contemplated that the number of British and American divisions earmarked for the Western and Central Mediterranean should be reduced. Some of the latter divisions may be combat-loaded and sent to new points of attack, if these points are open in time, but I am assuming that in principle the whole operation of 'Torch' as planned, with all its follow-up, less combing is going forward. Make sure nothing is done contrary to this without letting me know beforehand.

2. Under the agreements made about 'Roundup' and 'Bolero' with General Marshall we were to have by the 1st April, 1943, 27 American and 21 British divisions ready for the Continent, together with all the necessary landing craft, &c. This task was solemnly undertaken and an immense amount of work has been done. General Marshall in July argued in favour of even beginning the attack on the Continent in August or September by means of operation 'Sledgehammer'. This we argued against, and it was abandoned for very good reasons by agreement. We then went on to 'Torch', which is now in progress. But 'Torch' is only 13 divisions, whereas we had been prepared to move 48 divisions against the enemy in 1943. We have therefore reduced our striking intent against the enemy from the days of 'Roundup' by 35 divisions. Allowance should no

doubt be made for the larger distances from here to 'Torch' compared with those across the Channel. However, the fact remains that we and the Americans have enormously reduced our estimate of the effort it is possible for us to make in 1943. We have given Stalin to understand that the great attack on the Continent will come in 1943, and we are now working on a basis of 35 divisions short of what was purposed in the period April–July, or, in other words, little more than a quarter.

3. It is no use blinking at this or imagining that the discrepancy will not be perceived. I have no doubt myself that we and General Marshall over-estimated our capacity as measured by shipping and also by the rate at which United States forces as well as special landing craft, &c., could be ready. But there is a frightful gap between what the Chiefs of the Staff contemplated as reasonable in the summer of 1942 for the campaign of 1943 and what they now say we can do in that campaign. I am not making any criticisms, because I am in this myself to the full. But I feel we have got to get much closer to grips with this whole business. I fear I shall have to go to the United States in the near future. No doubt we were planning too much for 1943 in the summer, but we are certainly planning too little now. I must repeat that 'Torch' is no substitute for 'Roundup'. It must also be remembered that we had proposed to continue the campaign in the Middle East while 'Roundup' was going forward, and now we have an easement there through the virtual destruction of Rommel. We have, in fact, pulled in our horns to an almost extraordinary extent, and I cannot imagine what the Russians will say or do when they realise it. My own position is that I am still aiming at a 'Roundup' retarded till August. I cannot give this up without a massive presentation of facts and figures which prove physical impossibility. These figures will, however, if they prove the case, stultify our ambitions and judgement of this summer, and that of the Americans.

4. We must now grapple with the bomber offensive for 1943 and 1944. At the moment the impression is that it has petered out. The weather is given as a reason. Certainly, there have been very few and only small raids in the last two months, when we had been led to believe that the longer nights would facilitate even greater operations than in the summer. It would be very much better to aim at a smaller target total for 1944 and make sure of hitting it than to give way to the pleasures of megalomania. Before I can commit myself to a target of 4,000 to 6,000 British and American heavy bombers operative against Germany either from this country or in the Mediterranean, I must know exactly what this means quarter by quarter in the shipment of air groundsmen, stores and petrol.

The Air Ministry should produce the best estimate and forecast they can in the next day or two and we can check up upon it later.

Winston S. Churchill to Anthony Eden
(Churchill papers, 20/67)

18 November 1942

As long as Darlan is the French political and civil head our representative should call on him.

2. Generally speaking, now that the situation has been made satisfactory by the President's statement, we should get what advantage we can out of the connection. Of course, if Darlan renders effective service against the Germans, that would have to be set to his credit.

Winston S. Churchill to Sir James Grigg and General Sir Alan Brooke
(Churchill papers, 20/67)

18 November 1942
Action this Day

I see General Anderson[1] has given another interview today, reported in the evening papers. In the first interview he was to 'kick Rommel in the pants'. In the second one he is to 'kick him out of Africa'. It is unlikely that he will be within 800 miles of Rommel.

2. I should be much obliged if you would instruct this officer not to give Press interviews without obtaining permission in each case beforehand.

President Franklin D. Roosevelt to Winston S. Churchill
(Churchill papers, 20/83)

18 November 1942
Urgent
Personal and Secret
No. 213

I too have encountered the deep currents of feeling about Darlan. I felt I should act fast so I have just given out a statement at my press conference which I hope you will like and I trust it will be accepted at face value. It follows in my 214.

---

[1] Lieutenant-General Władysław Anders, CB; a General in the Polish Army who fought alongside the Allies in the Second World War.

Winston S. Churchill to President Franklin D. Roosevelt
(Churchill papers, 20/83)

19 November 1942
Personal and Secret
No. 200

Your public statement about Darlan has settled the matter in the best possible way. I am anxious however as you and Eisenhower that we should profit to the full in the actions which are impending by French co-operation. Also I fully recognize that if Darlan and Company render real services during the operations, these would naturally count in their favour. I feel pretty sure we are looking at it from exactly the same point of view.

Every good wish.

President Franklin D. Roosevelt to Winston S. Churchill
(Churchill papers, 20/83)

19 November 1942   Washington DC
Personal and Most Secret
No. 218

Replying to your message No. 196 of November 18 I am in complete agreement that every effort should be made to send another convoy to Russia at the earliest possible date.

It is noted that you can make available escort vessels for the close escort and some for the covering and striking forces but you feel that 12 additional destroyers are necessary for adequate protection. You are familiar with the necessity of our radical reductions of escort forces even to retaining in the Atlantic destroyers urgently required in the Pacific in order to provide escort vessels for 'Torch'. The movement of essential follow up convoys from America to Africa is contingent upon availability of escort vessels and the 'Torch' operation must be adequately supported.

Destroyer losses and damage to destroyers in recent naval operations in the Pacific have been so serious as to necessitate an immediate return of the destroyers borrowed from the Pacific for 'Torch'. This will leave in the Atlantic only minimum requirements for follow up convoys to Africa and makes it impossible for us to provide the destroyers for the Russian convoy suggested in your message number 196. I wish I could send you a more favourable answer.

President Roosevelt

Winston S. Churchill to Sir Stafford Cripps
(Churchill papers, 20/54)

19 November 1942
Private and Personal

My dear Stafford,

Surveying the war at this present moment, it seems to me that the production of aircraft and the development of radio technique lie at the very heart of our affairs. If you were willing to take the Ministry of Aircraft Production you could, in my opinion, render a very great service to the country and its cause. Without undervaluing the work of the present Minister, which has resulted in a large expansion, I am sure that there is no one who could bring to bear upon this group of problems the personal force and powers comparable to those with which you are gifted.

Although it might at first sight seem that by leaving your present post for a great administrative Department you would be stepping down in the political hierarchy, I know you would not be influenced by that. Moreover, in my opinion the work you would do would be more important even than the Leadership of the House of Commons which, under wartime conditions, is not a full occupation.

You would of course succeed Colonel Llewellin as Chairman of the Radio Board, and I should wish you to continue to assist me as Vice-Chairman of the Anti-U-boat Warfare Committee.

This new work would I think bring us more closely together even than heretofore, on account of my duties as Minister of Defence. At any rate I hope you will give very careful consideration to this proposal, which is conceived solely to meet a most serious war need.

Yours very sincerely
Winston S. Churchill

Winston S. Churchill to President Franklin D. Roosevelt[1]
(Churchill papers, 20/83)

20 November 1942
Secret
No. 202

One of the most potent weapons for hunting the U-Boat and protecting our convoys is the long range aircraft fitted with ASV[2] equipment.

---

[1] This telegram was sent via Harry Hopkins.
[2] ASV: Air to Surface Vessel radar for maritime patrol aircraft.

2. The German U-Boats have recently been fitted with a device enabling them to listen to our 1½ metre ASV equipment and thus dive to safety before our aircraft can appear on the scene. As the result our day patrols in the Bay[1] have become largely ineffective in bad weather and our night patrols, with searchlight aircraft, have been rendered almost entirely useless. Sightings of U-Boats have accordingly declined very sharply from 120 in September to 57 in October. No improvement can be expected until aircraft fitted with a type of ASV to which they cannot at present listen called 'centimetre ASV' become available.

3. One of the main objects of patrolling the Bay is to attack U-Boats in transit to and from the American Atlantic seaboard. This region is doubly urgent now so many American 'Torch' convoys pass in the vicinity.

4. We can deal with the inner zone of the Bay of Biscay by modifying and diverting to our Wellingtons a form of centimetre ASV which has been developed as a target location device for our heavy bombers.

5. A more difficult situation arises in the outer zone of the Bay where aircraft of longer range fitted with centimetre ASV are essential.

6. The very heavy sinkings in Mid-Atlantic have forced us to convert our own Liberators for work in this area. This leaves us with no aircraft with adequate range for the outer zone of the Bay, unless to make a further diversion from the small force of long range bombers responsible for the air offensive against Germany. Even if this diversion were made a considerable time would necessarily elapse before the essential equipment could be modified and installed.

7. I am most reluctant to reduce the weight of bombs we are able to drop on Germany as I believe it is of great importance that this offensive should be maintained and developed to the utmost of our ability throughout the winter months. I would, therefore, ask you Mr President to consider the immediate allocation of some 30 Liberators with centimetre ASV equipment from the supplies which I understand are now available in the United States. These aircraft would be put to work immediately, in an area where they would make a direct contribution to the American war effort.

[1] The Bay of Biscay.

Winston S. Churchill to President Franklin D. Roosevelt[1]
(Churchill papers, 20/83)

20 November 1942
Personal and Secret
No. 203

This is a Most Secret telegram. After arrival this morning I had a long talk with Eisenhower and Cunningham, which I summarise for your information. As regards coming operation next Sunday or Monday it is doubtful whether Anderson is strong enough to take Hizerta but Tunis appears more hopeful. In any case every effort will be made to press enemy into as small an area or bridgehead as possible so that air and other attack may finish him later.

Further south attempt will be made to clean up small pockets of enemy at Sfax and elsewhere, but no large forces will be employed in Tripoli direction at present. Sea losses so far have been made good. Loss of personnel and ships have been compensated by equal number of French ships acquired, and for every merchant vessel lost a U-boat has been sunk. As regards Darlan statements published have had unsettling effect on local French leaders and it would be dangerous to go further on these lines.

Nogues has threatened to resign and as he controls Morocco population results of such a step might be far reaching. From point of view of securing French cooperation and stabilising situation nothing could be worse than impression that we were merely using leaders to discard them as soon as they have served our purpose. There can be no doubt that Darlan and his friends have burnt their boats and are doing their best to fight the Axis and consolidate French behind us in this fight. French are cooperating in non-combatant tasks and even fighting on small scale, but their fighting value is at present low for want of proper arms. Darlan was not Eisenhower's choice but that of other French leaders some of whom were his enemies and our strong supporters and who all agreed that his leadership in cooperation was essential for our operations. It would be great mistake to create impression that he is to be discarded at early date. Military situation may call for his retention for fairly long period and meanwhile impression to contrary should not be publicly created.

---

[1] This is the text of a telegram from Smuts, forwarded to Roosevelt by Churchill with the following prefatory note: 'Following from Smuts who spent this morning 20th at Gibraltar Headquarters. I am in full agreement with him.'

I explained to Eisenhower that I do not think there was any intention to repeat or go beyond statements already made which were only intended to correct impression that political accord with Vichy elements had been come to. Future political arrangements should be left to governments concerned and agreement of French amongst themselves. I think it would be wise to pass on to President Roosevelt my strong impression that further anti-Darlan statements might be harmful to our cause, and indeed are not called for.

Josef Stalin to Winston S. Churchill
(Churchill papers, 20/83)

20 November 1942
Personal and Secret

We began offensive operations in the Stalingrad area – in the North Western and in the Southern sections of the front. The first stage of these offensive operations has as its task to capture the Railway line Stalingrad–Lihaya and to dislocate communications of the Stalingrad group of the German forces. In the North Western section the German front is broken on the stretch of 22 kilometres and in the Southern section on the stretch of 12 kilometres. The operations are developing not badly.

Stalin

Winston S. Churchill to Sir Edward Bridges
(Churchill papers, 20/67)

21 November 1942
Most Secret

You know what has been arranged about Sir Stafford Cripps.[1] I propose that as a consequence, Lord Cranborne should take the Privy Seal and lead the House of Lords and give up the Colonial Office to a new Minister. Mr Herbert Morrison would join the War Cabinet in place of Sir Stafford Cripps.

2. The War Cabinet is the responsible repository of power. I do not want to add to its numbers, in view of the strong arguments and public desire that it should be kept small. On the other hand, I consider that Sir Stafford Cripps, Lord Cranborne as Leader of the House of Lords, and Sir Archibald Sinclair as Leader of the Liberal Party, should 'sit in' on all

[1] That is, that he should be appointed Minister of Aircraft Production.

occasions except at meetings called 'War Cabinet Only'. This would, I think, be most agreeable and convenient, and would not raise any question of the balance of Parties. The three Ministers concerned would have all the papers circulated to the War Cabinet, except any in regard to which special exception is made. Pray let me have your views on this, and how it should be implemented. In my opinion no formal announcement is necessary. We should merely let the new practice grow by custom.

3. This increase in the numbers at War Cabinet meetings will revive the need for a greater use being made of the Defence Committee, both Operational and Supply.

Winston S. Churchill to Sir James Grigg
(Churchill papers, 20/67)

21 November 1942

I was shocked to hear yesterday, when visiting the 53rd Division, that an Army Council instruction had been issued three days ago ordering the immediate removal of all regimental shoulder-badges. Both the General commanding the division[1] and the Commander-in-Chief, Home Forces,[2] expressed to me their surprise and regret. There is no doubt that it will be extremely unpopular and tend to destroy that regimental *esprit de corps* upon which all armies worthy of the name are founded. I was also told that the Army Council instruction was accompanied by a notification that no discussion of it was to be allowed. Who is responsible for this? I fear it is the Adjutant-General.[3] If so, it would confirm much that I have heard of his outlook upon the Army.

---

[1] Robert Knox Ross, 1893–1951. Educated at Cheltenham College and Royal Military College, Sandhurst. Entered the Army, 1913. Lieutenant, 1914. Captain, 1915. Served in the First World War, 1914–18 (despatches thrice; DSO; Military Cross): with British Expeditionary Force, 1916–18; with Egyptian Expeditionary Force, 1918–19. Adjutant, 2nd Battalion The Queen's Royal Regiment, 1919–22. Served in Waziristan, 1920–1 (Medal and two bars). Attached to Egyptian Army and Sudan Defence Force, 1923–2. Major, 1931. Lieutenant-Colonel, 1937. Commanded 2nd Battalion The Queen's Royal Regiment (West Surrey), 1937–9. Served in the Second World War, 1939–45; in Palestine, 1939–40 (despatches, Medal). Colonel, 1940. Commander 160 (SW) Infantry Brigade, 1940–2. Acting Major-General, 1942. Commander 53rd (Welsh) Division, 1942–5. Major-General, 1944. British Liberation Army, 1944–5. CB, 1945. Awarded Legion of Honour, Croix de Guerre. Commander, Aldershot and Hants District, 1945–6. Retired, 1946.

[2] Bernard Paget.

[3] Ronald Forbes Adam, 1885–1982. Educated at Eton and Royal Military Academy, Woolwich. Commissioned in 1903 into the Royal Artillery. Posted to India (Royal Horse Artillery), then France, Belgium, and Italy during the First World World War. Major, 1916. DSO, despatches thrice. OBE, 1919. After First World War held number of successively more senior staff postings at the War Office. Succeeded as 2nd Baronet, 1926. Instructor at the Army Staff College, 1932–5. Commander, Royal Artillery, 1st Division, 1936. Commander of the Staff College, Camberley

I hope you will give directions to cancel the instruction before great harm is done.

Winston S. Churchill to Lord Woolton
(Churchill papers, 20/67)

21 November 1942

I hope it is not true that we are enforcing a whole set of vexatious regulations of this kind.[1] It is absolutely contrary to logic and good sense that a person may not give away or exchange his rations with someone who at the moment he feels has a greater need. It strikes at neighbourliness and friendship. I should be so sorry to see the great work you have done spoilt by allowing these officials, whose interests are so deeply involved in magnifying their functions and their numbers, to lead you to strike a false note.

The matter must be brought before the Cabinet next week, unless you can reassure me.

Winston S. Churchill: recollection
('The Hinge of Fate', pages 502–3)

[22 November 1942]

SIR STAFFORD CRIPPS

Although he was no longer willing to accept the full responsibilities entailed by membership of the War Cabinet itself, I was anxious to find some other field of service within the Government in which his talents and energies could continue to be used. In November, when the battle in Africa was fairly launched, I prevailed upon him to take Ministerial charge of the Ministry of Aircraft Production, an office which he held with increasing skill and effectiveness until the end of the war. I am glad to be able to acknowledge my sense of obligation to him for the loyal and efficient service which he rendered as a Production Minister during those three difficult years. Elsewhere in this book I have said that an

---

(Major-General), 1937. Deputy to Chief of the Imperial General Staff Lord Gort, 1938. General Officer Commanding-in-Chief Northern Command, 1940. Adjutant-General, the second military member of the Army Council and a key role with responsibility for all personnel, administration and organizational matters, 1941. Retired, 1946. GCB, 1946.

[1] The reference is to a cutting from *The Times* of 21 November 1942 about the ban on exchanges of rationed food. The article was headed 'Exchanging Food Rations. Readers' Criticisms of the Ban'.

exalted brooding over the work of others is only too often the lot of a Minister without departmental duties. For a man of his keen intellect, as yet untempered by administrative experience, his exalted ideals, and his skill in theoretical exposition, this form of activity held a strong though dangerous appeal. His great intellectual energy needed to be harnessed to a more practical task; and the success which he achieved as Minister of Aircraft Production, no less than the sense of frustration which he suffered as Lord Privy Seal, only deepens my regret that he should have declined my original proposal that he should join the Government in the first instance as Minister of Supply.

Winston S. Churchill to President Franklin D. Roosevelt
(Churchill papers, 20/83)

22 November 1942
Personal and Secret
No. 205

General de Gaulle wished on November 21 to broadcast, through the BBC, the following statement (see my next telegram) denouncing the maintenance of the Vichy regime in North Africa. I felt that, in view of impending operations, I should not allow anything that might compromise arrangement made by Eisenhower with Darlan or prejudice the military situation. I accordingly vetoed the broadcast, which will not now be made. De Gaulle was told that as the operations were under the United States Command I felt bound to take your opinion before agreeing to anything which might be detrimental to them. If your view was that broadcasts of this kind were undesirable at the moment, being your ardent and active lieutenant I should bow to your decision without demur.

Winston S. Churchill to William Mackenzie King
(Churchill papers, 20/83)

23 November 1942
Most Secret and Personal

I am seriously concerned at recent heavy losses from convoys in the centre of the transatlantic route. Experience has shown the great protection given by air escorts, which can keep U-boats down by day and so make the gathering of packs extremely difficult.

2. Until auxiliary aircraft-carriers can be made available we must rely on long-range shore-based aircraft. All available auxiliary carriers are now being used for combined operations, and in any case there will not be sufficient for all convoys for many months. We intend to increase petrol tankage of some Liberator aircraft to give an operational range of 2,300 sea-miles, but to reach all convoys these very long-range aircraft would have to operate from airfields on your side of the Atlantic as well as from Iceland (C) and Northern Ireland.

3. We are therefore most anxious to make use of Goose Airfield, in Labrador, for these long-range aircraft on anti-submarine operations, and request that the necessary refuelling and servicing facilities should be made available as early as possible. We would require similar facilities at Gander, and ask that the same steps be taken there. We might later wish to send a Coastal Command squadron to operate from these bases. In the meantime any extension of the range at which Canadian aircraft can go to the assistance of threatened convoys would be of great value in reducing losses.

Winston S. Churchill to Josef Stalin
(Churchill papers, 20/83)

24 November 1942
Personal and Most Secret

It gave me the very greatest pleasure to receive your warm and heart-felt congratulations. I regard our trustful personal relations as most important to the discharge of our duties to the great masses whose lives are at stake.

2. Although the President is unable with great regret to lend me twelve American destroyers for which I asked, I have now succeeded in making arrangements to sail a convoy of over thirty ships from Iceland on December 22. The Admiralty will concert the operation with your officers as before. The Germans have moved the bulk of their aircraft from the north of Norway to the south of Europe as a result of 'Torch'. On the other hand the German surface forces in Norway are still on guard. The Admiralty are pleased so far with the progress of the QP convoy which has been helped by bad weather and is now under the protection of our cruisers which have been sent out to meet it.

3. I have communicated to President Roosevelt some preliminary ideas about Turkey, and have found that he independently had formed

very similar views. It seems to me that we ought all of us to make a new intense effort to have Turkey enter the war on our side in the Spring. For this purpose I should like the United States to join in an Anglo-Soviet guarantee of the territorial integrity and status of Turkey. This would bring our three countries all into line, and the Americans count for a lot with the Turks. Secondly, we are already sending Turkey a considerable consignment of munitions including 200 tanks from the Middle East. During the winter by land route, or coasting up the Levant, I shall keep on sending supplies of munitions to Turkey together if permitted with experts in plain clothes for training and maintenance purposes. Thirdly, I hope by the early Spring to assemble a considerable army in Syria drawn from our Eighth, Ninth and Tenth Armies, so as to go to the help of Turkey if either she were threatened or were willing to join us. It is evident that your operations in the Caucasus or north of it may also exercise a great influence. If we could get Turkey into the war we could not only proceed with operations designed to open the shipping route to your left flank on the Black Sea but we could also bomb heavily from Turkish bases the Roumanian oilfields which are of such vital importance to the Axis in view of your successful defence of the main oil supplies of the Caucasus. The advantage of a movement into Turkey is that it proceeds mainly by land and can be additional to offensive action in the Central Mediterranean which will absorb our seapower and much of our Air power.

4. I have agreed to President Roosevelt's suggestion that we each send in the near future, if agreeable to you, two high British Officers and two Americans to Moscow to plan this part of the war in 1943. Pray let me know if you agree.

5. I hope you realize, Premier Stalin, that shipping is our limiting factor. In order to do 'Torch' we have had to cut our trans-Atlantic escorts so fine that the first half of November has been our worst month so far. We and the Americans have budgeted to lose at the rate of 700,000 tons a month and still improve our margin. Over the year the average loss has not been quite so bad as that, but this first fortnight in November is worse. You who have so much land may find it hard to realise that we can only live and fight in proportion to our sea communications.

6. Do not be disturbed about the rogue Darlan. We have thrown a large Anglo-American army into French North Africa and are getting a very firm grip. Owing to the non-resistance of the French army and now to its increasing support, we are perhaps fifteen days ahead of schedule. It is of the utmost consequence to get the Tunisian tip and the naval base of

Bizerta at the earliest moment. The leading elements of our First Army will probably begin their attack immediately. Once established there with overpowering Air, we can bring the war home to Mussolini and his Fascist gang with an intensity not yet possible.

7. At the same time, by building up a strong Anglo-American army and Air Force in Great Britain and making continuous preparations along our south-eastern and southern coasts, we keep the Germans pinned in the Pas de Calais, etc. and are ready to take advantage of any favourable opportunity. And all the time our bombers will be blasting Germany with ever-increasing violence. Thus the halter will tighten upon the guilty doomed.

8. The glorious news of your offensive is streaming in. We are watching it with breathless attention. Every good wish.[1]

Winston S. Churchill to President Franklin D. Roosevelt
(Churchill papers, 20/54)

24 November 1942
Personal and Secret
No. 211

We have had a letter from General Hartle[2] stating that under directive from the United States War Department (quote) any construction in excess of the requirements for a force of 427,000 must be accomplished entirely by your own labour and with your own materials and that Lend-Lease materials cannot be furnished in these instances (unquote). This has caused us very great concern, not so much from the standpoint of

---

[1] Paragraph 8 is written in Churchill's own hand. It is most likely that he was referring to the Soviet counter-offensive within the Battle of Stalingrad. This counter-offensive, launched on 19–20 November 1942, involved both a northern and a southern offensive. By November 23 the two elements had linked up west of the German forces and the encirclement of the German 4th and 6th Armies was complete. The Russian encirclement proved effective in the defence of Stalingrad, which would be a turning point in the war.

[2] Russell Peter Hartle, 1889–1961. Commanding Officer, 65th Infantry Regiment, US Army, 1939–40; Puerto Rico Mobile Force, 1940–1. In January 1942, brought the US 34th Division to Northern Ireland: the first large concentration of US troops to arrive in the United Kingdom. Commanding General, V Corps, May 1942. Deputy Commander of US troops in the European Theatre of Operations, under General Eisenhower, November 1942. Reassigned to Camp Fannin, Texas, to train replacement troops, 1943–5. Retired, 1946.

Lend-Lease but on grounds of grand strategy. We have been preparing under 'Bolero' for 1,100,000 men, and this is the first intimation we have had that this target is to be abandoned. We had no knowledge that you had decided to abandon forever 'Round-Up', and all our preparations were proceeding on a broad front under 'Bolero'.

2. It seems to me that it would be a most grievous decision to abandon 'Round-Up'. 'Torch' is no substitute for 'Round-Up' and only engages 13 divisions as against the 48 contemplated for 'Round-Up'. All my talks with Stalin, in Averell's presence, were on the basis of a postponed 'Round-Up'. But never was it suggested that we should attempt no second front in Europe in 1943 or even 1944.

3. Surely, Mr President, this matter requires most profound consideration. I was deeply impressed with all General Marshall's arguments that only by 'Round-Up' could the main forces be thrown into France and the Low Countries, and only in this area could the main strength of the British Metropolitan and United States Overseas Air forces be brought into action. One of the arguments we used against 'Sledgehammer' was that it would eat up in 1942 the seed-corn needed for the much larger 'Round-Up' in 1943. No doubt we have all been sanguine of our shipping resources, but that is a matter which time can correct. Only by the building up of a 'Round-Up' force here as rapidly and regularly as other urgent demands on shipping allow can we have the means of coming to grips with the main strength of the enemy and liberating the European nations. It may well be that, try as we will, our strength will not reach the necessary levels in 1943. But if so it becomes all the more important to make sure we do not miss 1944.

4. Even in 1943 a chance may come. Should Stalin's offensive reach Rostov-on-the-Don, which is his aim, a first-class disaster may overtake the German southern armies. Our Mediterranean operations following on 'Torch' may drive Italy out of the war. Widespread demoralization may set in among the Germans, and we must be ready to profit by any opportunity which offers.

5. I do beg of you, Mr President, to let me know what has happened. At present we are completely puzzled by this information and the manner in which it has reached us. It seems to me absolutely necessary either that General Marshall and Admiral King with Harry should come over here or that I should come with my people to you.

Winston S. Churchill to John Curtin
(Churchill papers, 20/83)

24 November 1942
Personal and Secret

To Mr Curtin,

Your Johcu No. 45 and President Roosevelt's telegram of 1st November. We recognise, of course, that the withdrawal of the 9th Australian Division from the Mediterranean theatre rests with the Commonwealth Government. However, the United States forces are now heavily engaged both in helping to defend Australia and in mastering French North Africa as a prelude to further action in Europe. They are therefore entitled to have the opportunity of considering the position as a whole and of making any representations to you which they may think desirable.

2. It seems probable that the Eastern Mediterranean will be the scene of large-scale action in the early Spring and the position of Turkey is of peculiar interest. If the 9th Australian Division is withdrawn to Australia, it will, of course, have to be replaced in the Middle East either by British or American forces. In the present acute and aggravated shipping stringency it will be necessary to save tonnage as much as possible. For instance, it might be most economical to move one of the American divisions in Australia or destined for the Pacific direct to Suez, where they could pick up the 9th Australian Division on the return journey. There might be no other way of maintaining the necessary strength in the Middle East. On the other hand, it might be possible to carry the Australians away from the Middle East as an isolated shipping operation. This, again, would have to be at the expense of our general power to move troops about the world and would have to be considered in relation to the dominating military exigencies. The matter is one on which the Combined Chiefs of Staff at Washington, who alone have the central point of view, should in the first instance advise.

3. So far as we are concerned, we shall, of course, not oppose your wishes, although we greatly regret the departure from the Middle Eastern theatre of a Division which has rendered distinguished service. The object should be to bring the greatest number of the United Nations divisions into contact with the enemy, and certainly it would appear more helpful to the common cause if fresh troops were moved from the United States into the Pacific and into action against Japan than that troops already engaged with the enemy in another part of the world should be withdrawn.

4. As I know the great importance which you have always attached to American opinion and how much you value the substantial aid they have given to the defence of Australia, I feel bound to put these points before you.

Winston S. Churchill to Peter Fraser
(Churchill papers, 20/83)

24 November 1942
Personal and Secret

I should very much regret to see the New Zealand Division quit the scene of its glories, but I quite understand your feelings and how embarrassing to you would be the withdrawal of the 9th Australian Division. I am having the whole situation reviewed by the Chiefs of Staff in London. In the meanwhile, I send you a copy of the telegram I have today despatched to Mr Curtin. I am sure it would be a mistake for Australia and New Zealand to ignore the opinion of the United States military authorities, having regard to the great contribution they are now making to the defence of the Southern Pacific and the still greater efforts we must expect from them.

Winston S. Churchill to President Franklin D. Roosevelt[1]
(Churchill papers, 20/88)

24 November 1942
Personal and Secret
No. 210

The time has come, I feel, when I must raise with you the question of the return of the 2nd New Zealand Division from the Middle East. In doing so, I assure you that the exigencies of the war situation, both in this part of the world and in the North African theatre, are fully in my mind. We in New Zealand have for some considerable time been of the opinion that, in view of the growing difficulties of the man-power position and of our increased and increasing commitments in the Pacific area, this request should be made by my colleagues, and I also felt that to do so in the adverse circumstances which existed hitherto in the Middle

---

[1] This is the text of a telegram from Peter Fraser, Prime Minister of New Zealand, forwarded to Roosevelt by Churchill with the prefatory note: 'Following is text of Pefra No. 8'. 'Pefra' = Peter Fraser.

East and in Russia would be inappropriate. It was always my intention, however, at the proper time, and when the situation in Egypt became easier, to place the whole position before you. As late as August of this year, when approval was given for the despatch of reinforcements for the Middle East, it was felt that the urgent needs of that theatre outweighed those of the area in which New Zealand itself was situated. Now, however, with the launching of the most promising Anglo-American offensive, the immediate security of the Middle East, which we have always regarded as being of such vital importance, appears for all practical purposes to have been achieved, and, with the accession of large new forces from the United States and Britain, the presence of one New Zealand Division in this theatre becomes a matter of diminishing importance. Here, in the Pacific, on the other hand, we are faced not only with the possibility of Japanese launching further offensive action, both to retrieve the situation arising from her recent set-back, and to take advantage of the preoccupations of the United Nations in Europe and in Africa, but also with what we regard as the necessity on the part of the United Nations to launch a counter-offensive at the earliest possible date. In either case it is felt that the place of the 2nd Division is here in the South Pacific.

Now that the New Zealand Army and Air Forces have, at our own request, been placed under the Commander of the South Pacific area, we anticipate that increasingly heavy demands will inevitably be made upon the resources of this Dominion, both in man-power and materials. Already, as you are aware, we have, in response to requests from the Commander, South Pacific Area, readily and promptly agreed to send a New Zealand Division for service in the Islands, part of which has already proceeded to its several destinations. In addition to our Army commitments it has been decided that the New Zealand Air Force also should be trained and equipped to undertake an offensive role in the Pacific, and for some time now, I should add, a large proportion of our limited force of modern aircraft have been operating in Guadalcanal and Esperitu Santo and other Pacific Islands. New Zealand is now endeavouring to complete preparations for an Air Force of 16 Squadrons for service in the Pacific, with an ultimate aim of achieving a 30-Squadron Air Force.

You will appreciate that, with our extremely limited man-power resources, which have now reached straining point, it is not possible for us to maintain two divisions overseas, and an adequate home defence force together with our air commitments; which include, of course, the Empire Air Training Scheme, and our comparatively small but increasingly useful naval units. We have, in fact, reached the limit of our man-power resources in New Zealand. Up to the present we have taken over 163,000 men and 5,000 women from industry. We now find ourselves unable to reach the establishment which our Chiefs of Staff laid down as the minimum force required for the defence of the Dominion. There is also the question of production of food and other supplies, both for the United Kingdom and the South Pacific area. The United States Forces are becoming increasingly dependent upon the resources of the Dominion for those essential supplies and services which we must endeavour to provide under the mutual aid agreement. Already, in order to maintain production, it has become necessary to strip the army of a large number of its personnel and return such men to industry, and we now are forced, in considering the needs of essential industry and our commitments in respect of the armed forces, to come to the decision to reduce establishment below the level which our Military Advisers regard as sufficient.

I think I should tell you also of the attitude of the New Zealand people, both Maori and European generally, towards the return of the Division from overseas. The main body left New Zealand three years ago next January, and the greater proportion of the men now fighting in the Middle East have been absent from New Zealand for well over two years. There is general feeling in the country, particularly in view of the extremely heavy casualties which our Division has suffered – some 18,500 so far out of a total of 43,500 sent to the Middle East – that our men have a strong claim to return, and, further, that our own tried and well-trained troops should be used for the defence of New Zealand in the Pacific area.

And, finally, I must draw your attention to the effect on New Zealand public opinion of the possible withdrawal of the Ninth Australian Division from the Middle East, concerning which Mr Curtin has now sent me (corrupt group), you will appreciate that it would be absolutely impossible for the New Zealand Government to resist the strong feeling to which I have referred should it become known that all three Australian Divisions have returned. I feel bound, therefore, to place the whole matter fully and frankly before you and to ask that, as soon as circumstances permit, effect should be given to this request.

That there will be difficulties and embarrassments I fully realise, and particularly in regard to shipping, but I hope that it will be possible for some adequate and early provision to be made. The urgent question at the moment is, of course, the despatch of the reinforcements which we had undertaken to send to the Middle East and for which transport is already bound for New Zealand. It will be necessary, therefore, to give further consideration to this matter upon receipt of your reply to this telegram.

I would like, in conclusion, to make it plain that it is not our intention to regard the 2nd NZEF as a force to be stationed permanently in New Zealand itself. We are firmly convinced that a long and difficult conflict with the Japanese lies ahead, irrespective of the success of any operations against Italy and Germany, and that the United Nations must, at the earliest possible date, make a forward move against Japan. We would wish to participate in any such offensive in the Pacific to the fullest extent of our capacity.

Dominion has, I hope, given unmistakable evidence of its fixed determination to fight this war through to the end, and the losses we have suffered in successive campaigns are proof of the spirit of the New Zealand people and of their willingness to make every sacrifice to this end.

I know you will appreciate the reasons which induce me to raise this matter and that you will give to it your full and sympathetic consideration.[1]

Winston S. Churchill to President Franklin D. Roosevelt
(Churchill papers, 20/88)

24 November 1942

Your No. 220 of 20th November. I cannot do better than send you the two telegrams I have despatched to Mr Curtin and Mr Fraser respectively. We cannot, of course, in any way oppose in principle the withdrawal of either or both of these divisions, but you who have a great army in the Pacific theatre and have assumed a considerable measure of responsibility for the defence of Australasia have every right to express an opinion, more especially as American armies are also engaged in North Africa and it is arguable their position might be affected. Moreover, there is a great case against the uneconomical use of our limited shipping. It therefore seems to me that the view taken by General Marshall is sound and the Combined Chiefs of Staff should lay their view before the Dominion Governments concerned. We are very grateful to the United States for the help you are giving to the defence of Australia and New Zealand while our own troops are so fully engaged with the enemy in other quarters.

---

[1] On 24 November 1942, Churchill telegraphed to General Alexander: 'I am still steadily resisting both here and through the President the withdrawal of either or both of these Divisions. Anyhow I hope to save the New Zealanders' (*Churchill papers, 20/88*).

Winston S. Churchill: note for the War Cabinet
(Churchill papers, 23/10)

25 November 1942
Most Secret
War Cabinet Paper No. 546 of 1942

POSITION OF ITALY

I am in general agreement with the conclusions of the Foreign Secretary's paper WP (42) 545. It is, however, in my opinion, premature to assume that no internal convulsion in Italy could produce a Government which would make a separate peace. If we increase the severity of our pressure upon Italy, the desire and indeed the imperative need of getting out of the war will come home to all the Italians, including the rank and file of the Fascist party. Should Italy feel unable to endure the continued attacks which will be made upon her from the air, and presently, I trust, by amphibious operations, the Italian people will have to choose between, on the one hand, setting up a Government under someone like Grandi to sue for a separate peace, or, on the other, submitting to a German occupation, which would merely aggravate the severity of the war.

2. I do not share the view that it is in our interests that the Germans should occupy and take over Italy. We may not be able to prevent it. It is still my hope that the Italians themselves will prevent it, and we should certainly do what we can to further this move. If there was a revolution in Italy and an Armistice Government came into power, it is at least arguable that the German interests would be as well served by standing on the Brenner as by undertaking the detailed defence of Italy against the wishes of its people, and possibly of a provisional Government.

3. When a nation is thoroughly beaten in war it does all sorts of things which no one would imagine beforehand. The sudden, sullen, universal, simultaneous way in which Bulgaria – Government, Army and people alike – cut out in 1918 remains in my memory. Without caring to make any arrangements for their future or for their safety, the troops simply marched out of the lines and dispersed to their homes, and King Ferdinand[1] fled. A Government headed by a peasant leader remained to await the judgment of the victors.

Similarly the French, at Bordeaux and after, committed acts which, both in their folly and abjectness, were difficult to believe.

---

[1] King Ferdinand I of Bulgaria, 1861–1948. Born Prince Ferdinand Maximilian Karl Leopold Maria of Saxe-Coburg and Gotha. Prince Regent (the Knjaz) and later Tsar of Bulgaria (reigned 1887–1918). Also an author, botanist, and entomologist.

4. Therefore I would not rule out the possibilities of a sudden peace demand being made by Italy, and I agree with the United States policy of trying to separate the Italian people from their Government. The fall of Mussolini, even though precaution may have been taken against it beforehand, might well have a decisive effect upon Italian opinion. The Fascist chapter would be closed. One tale would be finished and another would begin. I consider it would be well to drop leaflets over all Italian towns that are bombed, on the theme 'One man alone is the cause of your sufferings – Mussolini'.

5. It is to be observed that we are under no obligations to offer any terms to the vanquished, should they sue for them. That decision must be taken when and if we are offered their surrender, and in the meanwhile we certainly ought not to make promises, as some of the American propaganda leaflets have seemed to do.

Winston S. Churchill to General Sir Harold Alexander
(Churchill papers, 20/83)

25 November 1942
Most Secret

Presume you have read Boniface QT/6839 WD/1252 paraphrased to you on 24/11. I can if you wish send you the whole text in sections, also QT/6845 WD/1253. These seem to be of profound importance and I should like to know whether they make any difference to your target date for attack.[1]

Winston S. Churchill to General Hastings Ismay,
for the Chiefs of Staff Committee
(Churchill papers, 20/67)

25 November 1942
Action this Day

This[2] appears to be manifest nonsense. It is entirely contrary to nearly all the Boniface stuff. There was, however, one telegram about the Italian

---

[1] In QT/6839 WD/1252, Rommel, defending Tripolitania on the Agheila line, wrote to Hitler that his Panzer Army's fuel would be exhausted in a few days.

[2] Telegram R.3504 of November 24 from Adjutant-General, War Department, Washington, to US forces in London, about an imminent attack by the Axis in Tunisia.

railways being so congested with troop movements that air force personnel was to be flown direct from an airfield in North Italy. It would be worth while therefore to have a few salient facts checked as to shipping, landing facilities, harbour space, &c., in order to show the limits of possibilities in the next week or fortnight.

Winston S. Churchill to General Sir Alan Brooke
(Churchill papers, 20/67)

25 November 1942

I asked C to draw your attention particularly to Bonifaces of today, which bear on all this. Let us discuss it tomorrow.

Winston S. Churchill to Herbert Morrison[1]
(Churchill papers, 20/67)

25 November 1942

I understand that fire watchers have been instructed to wait 7 minutes (or until the bomb explodes) before approaching a fire, unless a 4½ inch brick wall is conveniently sited, from behind which it can be attacked. Will it not usually in this time either have burnt out harmlessly or have started a fire too big to be put out with a stirrup pump?

Any addition to the necessary strains of war weighs heavily on people's shoulders, and if it is universal the effect on war output may be alarming. If, as I understand, firewatching at present adds about 12 hours of duty a week to the longish hours already worked by most men, I should like you to consider whether some relaxation could not be made, at any rate in the less vulnerable areas and in quiet times like the present.

Winston S. Churchill to General Sir Alan Brooke

(Churchill papers, 20/67)

25 November 1942
Action this Day

Are we not dispersing this army rather rapidly?[2] If 9th Australian and 2nd New Zealand Divisions leave and now two South Africans, and then

---

[1] Minister of Home Security.

[2] The reference is to Telegram CS/1709 of 23 November 1942, from Commander-in-Chief, Middle East, about the return to South Africa from the Middle East of the 1st South African Division for leave and re-formation on the basis of two armoured divisions.

there is to be cannibalisation, what is going to be left? It seems to me that we have got to think of the whole picture in relation to the next six months. Please report. I am disquieted.

Winston S. Churchill to Field Marshal Sir John Dill
(Churchill papers, 20/83)

26 November 1942
Most Secret
Important
Personal

Reference JSM 496. I visualise Special Service Force playing vital role in possible ultimate re-conquest of Norway, and wish you therefore to press most strongly for their retention in this role.

2. Development of various types of plough should be pressed on, such as light reconnaissance plough, armoured reconnaissance plough and load-carrying plough. These ploughs might be of the greatest value for equipping British and American Arctic Divisions who are at present understood to be relying largely on wheeled vehicles.

3. Target date for planning should be October 1943.[1]

President Franklin D. Roosevelt to Winston S. Churchill
(Churchill papers, 20/83)

26 November 1942
Personal and Secret
No. 222

In reply to your 211. We of course have no intention of abandoning 'Round-Up'. No one can possibly know now whether or not we may have the opportunity to strike across the Channel in 1943 and if the opportunity comes we must obviously grasp it. However the determination as to the size of the force which we should have in 'Bolero' in 1943 is a matter which should require our joint strategic considerations. It is

---

[1] After Churchill had telegraphed Roosevelt with specific reference to the 'Plough project', the President replied: 'Reference your No. 177 concerning the Plough project, the vehicle will be produced on schedule and the special service force will have the vehicles for use this winter. Development of improved design now in progress and test will be made this winter for possible production for future use. The training of the special group of United States and Canadian soldiers is proceeding vigorously' ('Personal and Most Secret', 2 December 1942, *Churchill papers, 20/84*).

my present thought that we should build up as rapidly as present active operations permit a growing striking force in the United Kingdom to be used quickly in event of German collapse or a very large force later if Germany remains intact and assumes a defensive position.

The conclusions of the Combined Chiefs of Staff at the meeting last summer in London indicated that the mounting of 'Torch' necessarily postponed the assembling of the required forces in the United Kingdom. In view of our requirements for the initiation and maintenance of 'Torch' our studies indicated that we could not send forces and material to the United Kingdom at this time in excess of that stated by General Hartle. Until we have provided adequately against the possible reactions from Spanish Morocco, and are clear as to the situation in Tunisia, North Africa must naturally take precedence. We are far more heavily engaged in the Southwest Pacific than I anticipated a few months ago. Nevertheless, we shall continue with 'Bolero' as rapidly as our shipping and other resources permit. I believe that as soon as we have knocked the Germans out of Tunisia, and have secured the danger against any real threat from Spain, that we should proceed with a military strategical conference between Great Britain, Russia and the United States. I am hoping that our military position in Africa will be such that a conference might be held in a month or six weeks. Our own combined Chiefs of Staff will, I believe, have a recommendation for us within a few days as to what the next steps should be, but I feel very strongly that we have got to sit down at the table with the Russians. My notion would be a conference in Cairo or Moscow: that each of us would be represented by a small group meeting very secretly: that the conclusions of the conference would of course be approved by the three of us. I would probably send Marshall to head up our group but I presume that all services should be represented. I think it would be wise to keep the numbers down to three from each of us.

I have given Oliver[1] some private messages to you which I do not wish to put on the cables and he will be returning I believe next Monday. I hope that all of his problems will have been substantially resolved.

Will you let me know as soon as you can what you think of my proposal.

[1] Lyttelton.

Winston S. Churchill to President Franklin D. Roosevelt
(Churchill papers, 20/83)

26 November 1942
Secret
No. 213

My No. 211. In conference with Major-General Smith,[1] who has just returned from Gibraltar and was out of England when we received General Hartle's letter, we have learnt that there is no change in the general plan of 'Bolero' and 'Roundup', and that the letter quoted related only to the rate at which accommodation should be provided for the build-up. I am very glad this misunderstanding has been cleared away and that we are as ever in closest agreement.

Winston S. Churchill to President Franklin D. Roosevelt
(Churchill papers, 20/84)

26 November 1942
Personal and Secret
No. 214

Thank you so much about my 211. As I cabled you last night, we are in full agreement.

2. I entirely agree in principle that there should be a conference with the Russians, but I doubt very much whether a conference on general war policy, apart from some special point, between officers would be of much value. Certainly if a Russian delegation went to Cairo, which I deem unlikely, they would be so tied up that they would have to refer every point of substance back to Stalin at Moscow. If the conference were held in Moscow there would be less delay, but I trust that before British and United States Missions went to Moscow they would have a joint and agreed view, to serve at least as a basis for discussion. I hope also that if General Marshall were sent by you he would not by-pass this country.

3. I think I can tell you in advance what the Soviet view will be. They will say to us both (quote) How many German divisions will you be engaging in the summer of 1943? How many have you engaged in 1942? (unquote). They will certainly demand a strong second front in 1943 by the heavy invasion of the Continent either from the west or from the south or from both. This sort of argument, of which I had plenty in Moscow, requires to be met either by principals or by naval and shipping authorities who

---

[1] General Walter Bedell Smith.

would certainly have to be present. It would be very difficult to spare all our Chiefs for so long at this time.

4. Stalin talked to me in Moscow in the sense of being willing to come to meet you and me somewhere this winter, and he mentioned Iceland. I pointed out that England was no farther and more convenient. He neither accepted nor rejected the idea. At the same time, apart from the climate, there is a lot to be said for a new triple Atlantic Conference in Iceland. Our ships might lie together in Halfjord and we would place a suitable ship at Stalin's disposal wearing the Soviet flag pro tem. He talked with some zest of his desire to fly and of his confidence in the Russian machines. Only at a meeting between principals will real results be achieved. What about proposing it for January? By that time Africa should be cleared and the great battle in South Russia decided.

5. I may add that if ever I can persuade you to come to Iceland I shall never be satisfied unless you look in on this small place before returning.

Lady Leslie to Winston S. Churchill
(Churchill papers, 1/368)

26 November 1942 Glaslough
County Monaghan

A Happy Birthday to you My darling Winston – and may Providence continue watching over you – You will be overwhelmed by thousands of good wishes and the gratitude of multitudes will be showered on you – and you richly deserve – I hope it makes up in a way for the dark Hours you have had to pass through.

God bless you.

Yr. devoted
Leonie

George Harvie-Watt: report
(Premier papers, 4/64/6)

27 November 1942

[...]

The Government changes have been well received by the House. Some surprise was expressed at the inclusion of Morrison in the War Cabinet, in view of his heavy departmental commitments and also at the apparent relegation of Llewellin to America. The main criticisms which have been made are:

1. The War Cabinet now consists, with the exception of Sir John Anderson, of Ministers with departmental responsibilities and,

2. The extreme right wing Tories have pointed out that all the principal industrial departments of the Government, with the exception of Supply and Production, are now in the hands of the Socialists; the Board of Trade, the Ministry of Aircraft Production, the Ministry of Labour, and the Supply department of the Admiralty under the First Lord.

War Cabinet: conclusions
(Cabinet papers, 65/28)

27 November 1942   10 Downing Street
11.30 a.m.

The Prime Minister said that it was important not to make any public statement underrating the conception or the achievements of the League of Nations until we were in a position to make positive suggestions for something to put in its place.

Josef Stalin to Winston S. Churchill
(Churchill papers, 20/84)

27 November 1942   Kremlin
Personal and Secret   Moscow

Many thanks for your message which I received on the 25th November. I fully share your view on the importance of developing our personal relations.

2. I am grateful to you for the measures you are taking to send a new big convoy to Archangel. I realise that in view of the considerable naval operations in the Mediterranean Sea this constitutes great difficulty for you.

3. I am in full agreement with you and President Roosevelt on the question of Turkey. It would be desirable to do everything possible to have Turkey enter the war on our side in the spring. This would be of great importance in order to accelerate the defeat of Hitler and his accomplices.

4. It seems to me that the Americans used Darlan not badly in order to facilitate the occupation of the Northern and Western Africa. The military diplomacy must be able to use for military purposes not only Darlans but 'even the devil himself and his grandma' Maisky's footnote: this is a strong Russian proverb.

5. I paid close attention to your communication that you and Americans do not relax preparations along your south-eastern and southern coasts in order to keep the Germans pinned in the Pas de Calais etc. and that you are ready to take advantage of any favourable opportunity. I hope this does not mean that you change your mind with regard to your promise given in Moscow to establish a second front in Western Europe in the spring of 1943.

6. I am in full agreement with President Roosevelt's suggestion and your wish to arrange in Moscow conversations of the representatives of the three General Staffs to prepare the respective military plans for 1943. We are ready to meet the British and American representative whenever you wish.

7. In the Stalingrad operations we were so far successful partly because of snowfall and fog which hindered the activities of the German aviation.

8. We have intention to start in the next few days active operations on the central front in order to pin here the enemy forces and to prevent the transfer of any portion of them to the south.

Winston S. Churchill to Lord Leathers
(Churchill papers, 20/67)

28 November 1942

Pray convey to all those in your Department who have contributed to the success of 'Torch' my warm congratulations and thanks for the part they played in the preparation and movement of this great armada. It owed much to their skill, industry and reticence and they share in the honour of a great achievement.

Winston S. Churchill to Anthony Eden and Brendan Bracken
(Churchill papers, 20/67)

28 November 1942

It would be much better for General de Gaulle not to broadcast before he goes to the United States.[1] He will only complicate his affairs there. Of course, if he were inclined to make a really helpful broadcast, that would be different. This present one is out of date. Moreover, we do not need his help in getting round the Darlan issue, and we should not be likely to get it if we did.

[1] Referring to a letter from the Foreign Office of 27 November 1942 about a proposed broadcast by General de Gaulle on North Africa.

My talks with him and Catroux went extremely well, but do not lead me to modify the above.

Winston S. Churchill: War Cabinet paper
(Churchill papers, 23/10)

28 November 1942
Most Secret
War Cabinet Paper No. 556 of 1942

MAN-POWER

The available resources of man-power for the period the lst July, 1942, to the end of 1943 fall short of the stated demands of the Services and of the munitions industries by at least 1,089,000.[1] The existing programme on which these demands are based must therefore be revised. This revision will take into account the following:

2. The greatest danger which now confronts us is the U-boat peril. We must expect attack by increasingly large numbers and spread over wider areas. The highest priority must therefore be accorded to vessels and weapons for use against the U-boat. No construction of merchant shipbuilding below 1,100,000 tons or slowing down of repair work can be accepted.

The Admiralty must save labour at the cost of some retardation in other parts of the programme, particularly in the construction of men-of-war of the larger categories (battleships and cruisers). If necessary, some of the larger vessels must be put into reserve. The R battleships should be considered in this connection.

3. It is unlikely that the enemy will again be able to bring to bear against this country as heavy a weight of air attack as two years ago, still less to keep it up so long. Further reductions should therefore be made in Civil Defence and in ADGB and still greater use should be made of the Home Guard for duties with the latter. The reserves of anti-aircraft ammunition in this country do not need to increase with the number of AA guns. We shall not require to fire more rounds than we fired in the blitz of two years ago. A considerable number of anti-aircraft equipments will be needed for the defence of the North African coast and for supply to Turkey. This must also be at the expense of ADGB.

---

[1] The estimate of 939,000 given in paragraph 7 of WP (42) 539 took into account the arbitrary cut of 150,000 mentioned in paragraph 3 of that paper.

4. It can be assumed as a working rule that invasion or large-scale airborne attack are unlikely. This assumption must be constantly reviewed. Meanwhile it will enable reductions to be made in the upkeep of our static defences. For example, the RAF Regiment and coast defences can be reduced. Again, the Home Guard should not be raised above the ceiling of 1¾ million, and of this number, say, ½ million should be temporarily relegated to a reserve from which they can be recalled as and when required.

5. The assumption already made by the War Office that, with the exception of the forces in or destined for the North African and Mediterranean areas, the British Armies will not be engaged on a large scale with heavy casualties and expenditure of ammunition before the end of June 1943 can be accepted. The wastage occurring in the first nine months of 1943 will be met from men called up before the end of 1942. The Army will also benefit largely from the economies resulting from the assumptions in (3) and (4) above. These factors, together with a drastic pruning of the staffs, also of ancillary units and establishments, and a definite reduction in the establishments of Corps, Army, and line of communication units, should enable the Army during 1943 to form and maintain the organisation set out in my WP (42) 504.

6. The results of (3), (4) and (5) will enable a substantial reduction to be made in the War Office demands on the Ministry of Supply, more particularly in miscellaneous stores and equipment. It is incumbent on the Army authorities to see that these demands are reduced as soon as possible. So great is the stringency of man-power that only by this means can a reduction be avoided in the effective fighting strength of the Army.

7. The demands of the Royal Air Force and of the Ministry of Aircraft Production should be governed by the fact that it is more important at present to increase the output of aircraft than the number of officers and other ranks in the RAF. A cut in the demands of the RAF for air ground staff cannot be avoided. By concentrating on essentials, the most effective use must be made of that which is available.

8. Chemical warfare supplies are now approaching their very high target figure; and while special items should be taken care of, and the power to open out production if necessary should be retained, a very general curtailment should be possible.

9. In the light of the above, I put before my colleagues and the Chiefs of Staff for their earnest consideration the following proposed reductions in their demands:

(In thousands.)

	Original Demands			Cut Proposed	
Admiralty	Men	287		Men	60
			} 323			} 75
	Women	36		Women	15
		186 (shipbuilding)			
Army	Men	649		Men	300
			} 809			} 380
	Women	160		Women	80
Supply		148			215
RAF	Men	365		Men	185
			} 472			} 225
	Women	107		Women	40
MAP		603			75
Civil Defence		13			*100
Miscellaneous		135			19
		——			——
		2,689			1,089

* This is in addition to existing arrangements for the withdrawal of 20,000 men and 4,000 women from Civil Defence. Taking account of the new demand for 13,000 women for these Services, the *net* reduction now proposed is 113,000.[1]

10. Even the estimate of man-power supply at 1,600,000 may well prove beyond our powers. The health and efficiency of the people must not be damaged by new stresses. The work of the central departments of government must not be deranged for the sake of getting a few hundred highly trained individuals on to the barrack square. We have no choice but to spread the inevitable reduction of new demands in the least harmful manner. Thus, although the task before my colleagues presents great difficulties and will involve many inconveniences and indeed hardships, I ask them, both to accept the reductions, and to apply them with the best housekeeping ingenuity, so as to keep all we can of the increased offensive power of the Services.

11. Every effort must also be made by the Minister of Production, aided by the Minister of Labour and National Service and the Supply Ministers, to make the necessary adjustments and simplifications in existing programmes in such a way that the quality of our equipment is made the highest aim, that the production of obsolescent and redundant stores is cut out, and that the call-up of fit men works the minimum of evil. If by careful planning further economy of labour can be made in the muni-

---

[1] This seems to be a miscalculation or typing error: the figures in the table and accompanying footnote imply a net reduction of 111,000.

tion industries, the armed forces will receive the benefit in the shape of increased intakes for the second half of 1943.

Any reductions in supply will relieve the Import Programme and shipping stringency. These should be noted by the Ministry of War Transport.

12. The assumptions and figures in this Note relate to the period up to 31st December, 1943, and Departments should frame their long-term plans on this basis. The position will, however, be reviewed before the end of June 1943, in the light of strategic developments.

Winston S. Churchill to Vernon Bartlett[1]
(Churchill papers, 20/55)

28 November 1942
Private

My dear Bartlett,

I have read your article in today's *News Chronicle* and I want to tell you how sensible and helpful I find it. You have made a valuable contribution to a difficult matter.[2]

Yours sincerely,
Winston S. Churchill

Winston S. Churchill: speech
(BBC Written Archives Centre)

29 November 1942 Chequers
(recorded live)

Two Sundays ago all the bells rang to celebrate the victory of our desert Army at Alamein. Here was a martial episode in British history which deserved a special recognition. But the bells also carried with their clashing joyous peals our thanksgiving that, in spite of all our errors and shortcomings, we have been brought nearer to the frontiers of deliverance. We have not reached those frontiers yet, but we are becoming ever more

[1] Charles Vernon Oldfield Bartlett, 1894–1983. On active service, 1914–16. Joined the *Daily Mail*, 1916; Reuters Agency, 1917; *The Times*, 1919. London director of the League of Nations, 1922–32. A regular broadcaster on foreign affairs from 1928. On the staff of the *News Chronicle*, 1934–54. Independent Progressive MP for Bridgwater, 1938–50. Author of some 28 books. CBE, 1956.

[2] Bartlett's article, entitled 'Darlan is Proving a Useful Weapon', argued in favour of the decision to use Darlan's leadership and influence to strengthen the Allies' position in North Africa. For the full article, see Churchill Archives, *CHAR 20/55/93-6*.

entitled to be sure that the awful perils which might well have blotted out our life and all that we love and cherish will be surmounted, and that we shall be preserved for further service in the vanguard of mankind.

We have to look back along the path we have trodden these last three years of toil and strife, to value properly all that we have escaped and all that we have achieved. No mood of boastfulness, of vain glory, of over-confidence must cloud our minds; but I think we have a right which history will endorse to feel that we had the honour to play a part in saving the freedom and the future of the world. That wonderful association of States and races spread all over the globe called the British Empire or British Commonwealth if you will; I do not quarrel about it; and above all, our small Island, stood in the gap alone in the deadly hour. Here we stood, firm though all was drifting; throughout the British Empire no one faltered. All around was very dark. Here we kept the light burning which now spreads broadly over the vast array of the United Nations: that is why it was right to ring out the bells, and to lift our heads for a moment in gratitude and in relief, before we turn again to the grim and probably long ordeals which lie before us and to the exacting tasks upon which we are engaged.

Since we rang the bells for Alamein, the good cause has prospered. The Eighth Army has advanced nearly four hundred miles, driving before them in rout and ruin the powerful forces, or the remnants of the powerful forces, which Rommel boasted and Hitler and Mussolini believed would conquer Egypt. Another serious battle may be impending at the entrance to Tripolitania. I make it a rule not to prophesy about battles before they are fought. Everyone must try to realise the immense distances over which the North African war ranges, and the enormous labours and self-denial of the troops who press forward relentlessly, twenty, thirty, forty and sometimes fifty miles in a single day. I will say no more than that we may have the greatest confidence in Generals Alexander and Montgomery, and in our soldiers and airmen who have at last begun to come into their own.

At the other side of Africa, a thousand miles or more to the westward, the tremendous joint undertaking of the United States and Britain which was fraught with so many hazards has also been crowned with astonishing success. To transport these large armies of several hundred thousand men, with all their intricate elaborate modern apparatus, secretly across the seas and oceans, and to strike to the hour, and almost to the minute, simultaneously at a dozen points, in spite of all the U-boats and all the chances of weather, was a feat of organisation which will long be studied with respect. It was rendered possible only by one sovereign fact – namely the perfect comradeship and understanding prevailing between the British and American staffs and troops. This majestic enterprise is under the direction and responsibility of the President of the United States, and our First British Army is serving under the orders of the American Commander-in-Chief, General Eisenhower, in whose military skill and burning energy we put our faith, and whose orders to attack we shall punctually and unflinchingly obey. Behind all lies the power of the Royal Navy, to which is joined a powerful American Fleet; the whole under the command of Admiral Cunningham, and all subordinated to the Allied Commander-in-Chief.

It was not only that the U-boats were evaded and brushed aside by the powerfully-escorted British and American convoys; they were definitely beaten in the ten-days' conflict that followed the landings, both inside and outside the Mediterranean. Here was no more secrecy. We had many scores of ships continuously exposed; large numbers of U-boats were concentrated from all quarters; our destroyers and corvettes and our aircraft took up the challenge and wore them down and beat them off. For every transport or supply ship we have lost, a U-boat has been sunk or severely damaged; for every ton of Anglo-American shipping lost so far in this expedition, we have gained perhaps two tons in the shipping acquired or recovered in the French harbours of North and West Africa. Thus, in this respect, as Napoleon recommended, war has been made to support war.

General Alexander timed his battle at Alamein to suit exactly this great stroke from the West, in order that his victory should encourage friendly countries to preserve their strict neutrality, and also to rally the French Forces in North-West Africa to a full sense of their duty and of their opportunity. Now, at this moment, the First British Army is striking hard at the last remaining footholds of the Germans and Italians in Tunisia. American, British and French troops are pressing forward side by side, vying with each other in a general rivalry and brotherhood. In this there lies the hope and the portent of the future.

I have been speaking about Africa, about the 2,000 miles of coastline fronting the underside of subjugated Europe. From all this we intend, and I will go so far as to say we expect, to expel the enemy before long. But Africa is no halting-place: it is not a seat but a springboard. We shall use Africa only to come to closer grips. Anyone can see the importance to us of re-opening the Mediterranean to military traffic and saving the long voyage round the Cape. Perhaps by this short cut and the economy of shipping resulting from it, we may strike as heavy a blow at the U-boats as has happened in the whole war; but there is another advantage to be gained by the mastery of the North African shore: we open the air battle upon a new front. In order to shorten the struggle, it is our duty to engage the enemy in the air continuously on the largest scale and at the highest intensity. To bring relief to the tortured world, there must be the maximum possible air fighting. Already, the German Air Force is a wasting asset; their new construction is not keeping pace with their losses; their front line is weakening both in numbers and, on the whole, in quality. The British, American and Russian Air Forces, already together far larger, are growing steadily and rapidly; the British and United States expansion in 1943 will be, to put it mildly, well worth watching: all we need is more frequent opportunities of contact. The new air front, from which the Americans and also the Royal Air Force are deploying along the Mediterranean shore, ought to give us these extra opportunities abundantly in 1943. Thirdly, our operations in French North Africa should enable us to bring the weight of the war home to the Italian Fascist state, in a manner not hitherto dreamed of by its guilty leaders, or still less by the unfortunate Italian people Mussolini has led, exploited and disgraced. Already the centres of war industry in Northern Italy are being subjected to harder treatment than any of our cities experienced in the winter of 1940. But if the enemy should in due course be blasted from the Tunisian tip, which is our aim, the whole of the South of Italy – all the naval bases, all the munition establishments and other military objectives wherever situated – will be brought under prolonged, scientific, and shattering air attack.

It is for the Italian people, forty millions of them, to say whether they want this terrible thing to happen to their country or not. One man, and one man alone, has brought them to this pass. There was no need for them to go to war; no one was going to attack them. We tried our best to induce them to remain neutral, to enjoy peace and prosperity and exceptional profits in a world of storm. But Mussolini could not resist the temptation of stabbing prostrate France, and what he thought was helpless Britain, in the back. Mad dreams of imperial glory, the lust of conquest and of booty, the arrogance of long-unbridled tyranny, led him to his fatal, shameful act. In vain I warned him: he would not hearken. On deaf ears and a stony heart fell the wise, far-seeing appeals of the American President. The hyena in his nature broke all bounds of decency and even commonsense. Today his Empire is gone. We have over a hundred Italian generals and nearly three hundred thousand of his soldiers in our hands as prisoners of war. Agony grips the fair land of

Italy. This is only the beginning, and what have the Italians to show for it? A brief promenade by German permission along the Riviera; a flying visit to Corsica; a bloody struggle with the heroic patriots of Yugoslavia; a deed of undying shame in Greece; the ruins of Genoa, Turin, Milan; and this is only a foretaste. One man and the regime he has created have brought these measureless calamities upon the hard-working, gifted, and once happy Italian people, with whom, until the days of Mussolini, the English-speaking world had so many sympathies and never a quarrel. How long must this endure?

We may certainly be glad about what has lately happened in Africa, and we may look forward with sober confidence to the moment when we can say: one continent relieved. But these successes in Africa, swift and decisive as they have been, must not divert our attention from the prodigious blows which Russia is striking on the Eastern Front. All the world wonders at the giant strength which Russia has been able to conserve and to apply. The invincible defence of Stalingrad is matched by the commanding military leadership of Stalin. When I was leaving the Kremlin in the middle of August, I said to Premier Stalin: 'When we have decisively defeated Rommel in Egypt, I will send you a telegram.' And he replied: 'When we make our counteroffensive here' (and he drew the arrow on the map), 'I will send you one.' Both messages have duly arrived, and both have been thankfully received.

As I speak, the immense battle, which has already yielded results of the first magnitude, is moving forward to its climax; and this, it must be remembered, is only one part of the Russian front, stretching from the White Sea to the Black Sea, along which, at many points, the Russian armies are attacking. The jaws of another Russian winter are closing on Hitler's armies – a hundred and eighty German divisions, many of them reduced to little more than brigades by the slaughters and privations they have suffered, together with a host of miserable Italians, Rumanians, and Hungarians, dragged from their homes by a maniac's fantasy: all these as they reel back from the fire and steel of the avenging Soviet Armies must prepare themselves with weakened forces and with added pangs for a second dose of what they got last year. They have, of course, the consolation of knowing that they have been commanded and led, not by the German General Staff, but by Corporal Hitler himself.

I must conduct you back to the West to France, where another vivid scene of this strange melancholy drama has been unfolded. It was foreseen when we were planning the descent upon North Africa that this would bring about immediate reactions in France. I never had the slightest doubt myself that Hitler would break the Armistice, overrun all France, and try to capture the French fleet at Toulon; such developments were to be welcomed by the United Nations, because they entailed the extinction for all practical purposes of the sorry farce and fraud of the Vichy Government. This was a necessary prelude to that reunion of France without which French resurrection is impossible. We have taken a long step towards that unity. The artificial division between occupied and unoccupied territory has been swept away. In France all Frenchmen are equally under the German yoke, and will learn to hate it with equal intensity. Abroad all Frenchmen will fire at the common foe. We may be sure that after what has happened, the ideals and the spirit of what we have called Fighting France will exercise a dominating influence upon the whole French nation. I agree with General de Gaulle that the last scales of deception have now fallen from the eyes of the French people; indeed, it was time.

'A clever conqueror,' wrote Hitler in *Mein Kampf*,

will always, if possible, impose his demands on the conquered by instalments. For a people that makes a voluntary surrender saps its own character, and with such a people you can calculate that none of those oppressions in detail will supply quite enough reason for it to resort once more to arms.

How carefully, how punctiliously he lives up to his own devilish doctrines! The perfidy by which the French fleet was ensnared is the latest and most complete example. That fleet, brought by folly and by worse than folly to its melancholy end, redeemed its honour by an act of self-immolation, and from the flame and smoke of the explosions at Toulon, France will rise again.

The ceaseless flow of good news from every theatre of war, which has filled the whole month of November, confronts the British people with a new test. They have proved that they can stand defeat; they have proved that they can bear with fortitude and confidence long periods of unsatisfactory and unexplained inaction. I see no reason at all why we should not show ourselves equally resolute and active in the fact of victory. I promise nothing. I predict nothing. I cannot even guarantee that more successes are not on the way. I commend to all the immortal lines of Kipling:

If you can dream – and not make dreams your master;
If you can think – and not make thoughts your aim;
If you can meet with Triumph and Disaster
And treat those two impostors just the same

– there is my text for this Sunday's sermon, though I have no licence to preach one. Do not let us be led away by any fair-seeming appearances of fortune; let us rather put our trust in those deep, slow-moving tides that have borne us thus far already, and will surely bear us forward, if we know how to use them, until we reach the harbour where we would be.

I know of nothing that has happened yet which justifies the hope that the war will not be long, or that bitter and bloody years do not lie ahead. Certainly the most painful experiences would lie before us if we allowed ourselves to relax our exertions, to weaken the discipline, unity and order of our array, if we fell to quarrelling about what we should do with our victory before that victory had been won. We must not build on hopes or fears, but only on the continued faithful discharge of our duty, wherein alone will be found safety and peace of mind. Remember that Hitler with his armies and his secret police holds nearly all Europe in his grip. Remember that he has millions of slaves to toil for him, a vast mass of munitions, many mighty arsenals, many fertile fields. Remember that Göring has brazenly declared that whoever starves in Europe, it will not be the Germans. Remember that these villains know their lives are at stake. Remember how small a portion of the German Army we British have yet been able to engage and to destroy. Remember that the U-boat warfare is not diminishing but growing, and that it may well be worse before it is better. Then, facing the facts, the ugly facts as well as the encouraging facts, undaunted, then we shall learn to use victory as a spur to further efforts, and make good fortune the means of gaining more.

This much only will I say about the future, and I say it with an acute consciousness of the fallibility of my own judgment. It may well be that the war in Europe will come to an end before the war in Asia. The Atlantic may be calm, while in the Pacific the hurricane rises to its full pitch. If events should take such a course, we should at once bring all our forces to the other side of the world, to the aid of the United States, to the aid of China, and above all to the aid of our kith and kin in Australia and New Zealand, in their valiant struggle against the aggressions of Japan. While we were thus engaged in the Far East, we should be sitting with the United States and with our ally Russia and those of the United Nations concerned, shaping the international instruments and national settlements which must be devised if the free life of Europe is ever to rise again, and if the fearful quarrels which have rent European civilisation are to be prevented from once more disturbing the progress of the world. It seems to me that should the war end thus, in two successive stages, there will be a far higher sense of comradeship around the council table than existed among the victors at Versailles. Then the danger had passed away. The common bond between the Allies had snapped. There was no sense of corporate responsibility such as exists when victorious nations who are masters of one vast scene are, most of them, still waging war side by side in another. I should hope, therefore, that we shall be able to make better solutions – more far-reaching, more lasting solutions – of the problems of Europe at the end of this war than was possible a quarter of a century ago. It is not much use pursuing these speculations farther at this time. For no one can possibly know what the state of Europe or of the world will be, when the Nazi and Fascist tyrannies have been finally broken. The dawn of 1943 will soon loom red before us, and we must brace ourselves to cope with the trials and problems of what must be a stern and terrible year. We do so with the assurance of ever-growing strength, and we do so as a nation with a strong will, a bold heart and a good conscience.

Sir Alexander Cadogan: diary
('The Diaries of Sir Alexander Cadogan', page 498)

29 November 1942

Winston broadcasting at 9. Quite good – sober jubilation – no rash promises.

[...]

Lord and Lady Halifax to Winston S. Churchill
(Churchill papers, 20/84)

29 November 1942   Washington DC
Personal

All our best wishes. We have just listened to your excellent broadcast and hope you will have still better story to tell in your next birthday talk. Best of luck.

Edward, Dorothy.

Harry Hopkins to Winston S. Churchill
(Churchill papers, 20/84)

29 November 1942   Washington DC

Dear Winston,

Your friend his wife and mine have listened to your speech. Mussolini did not like it. We did.

Harry

Winston S. Churchill to General Hastings Ismay,
for the Chiefs of Staff Committee
(Churchill papers, 20/67)

29 November 1942
Action this Day
Most Secret

Paragraph 9. Are we really going to give supreme priority to the arrival in this country of masses of American air groundsmen, while the United States Air Force have not shown themselves possessed of any machines capable of bombing Germany either by night or by day? Much doubt is also thrown upon those curious looking Lightnings. It is the greatest pity to choke up all our best airfields. Surely it would be much better to bring over half a dozen extra American divisions, including armour, and to encourage the American air effort to develop mainly in North Africa.

2. Paragraph 11. I really do not think this paragraph will do. See Stalin's telegram to me which I circulated yesterday. The paragraph is a practical abandonment of any resolute effort to form a second front in 1943. I certainly think we should make all plans to attack the French coast either in the Channel or in the Bay of Biscay, and that July 1943 should be fixed as the target date. Judging from the conditions on the Russian front, it does not look as if Hitler will be able to bring back any large force from the east to the west. He has now to watch the southern coast of France as well. The battles on the Russian front have already greatly modified and may fundamentally change the situation.

3. Apart from these points I am in agreement with the paper.

Sir Stafford Cripps to Winston S. Churchill
(Churchill papers, 20/56)

29 November 1942

My Dear Prime Minister,

I send you my very best wishes for your birthday and for your continued vigour and good health.

It has been a privilege for me to work under you through the last 9 months and however much we may differ in outlook on certain matters it has been a great joy to me to witness your tireless work for victory.

As you now enter upon a new year of effort you must be vastly and rightly stimulated by the result of all your hard and incessant work through the dark days of defeat and disappointment.

May God guard and guide you in the days to come.

Yours very sincerely
Stafford Cripps

War Cabinet: conclusions
(Cabinet papers, 65/28)

30 November 1942

The Prime Minister read to the War Cabinet a very cordial telegram which he had received from M Stalin, dated 28th November, in reply to a telegram from himself dated 24th November.

In this telegram M Stalin expressed gratitude for the decision to send a new big convoy to Archangel; agreement with the policy towards Turkey; and understanding of the use made by the Americans of Darlan in order to facilitate the occupation of Northern and Western Africa.

M Stalin had referred to the paragraph in the Prime Minister's telegram in which he had stated that by building up a strong American Army and Air Force in Great Britain and making continuous preparations along our South-Eastern and Southern coasts we kept the Germans pinned in the Pas de Calais. M Stalin hoped that this did not mean that the Prime Minister had changed his mind with regard to his promise, given in Moscow, to establish a Second Front in Europe in the Spring of 1943.

The Prime Minister said that the changed situation made it all the more incumbent upon us to start a Second Front in Europe in 1943. Our present activities in the Mediterranean, important though they were, could only be regarded as an inadequate contribution compared with the efforts which Russia was making.

President Franklin D. Roosevelt to Winston S. Churchill
(Churchill papers, 23/10)

30 November 1942   The White House
Personal and Most Secret   Washington DC

My dear Winston,

I presume that we shall never satisfy ourselves as to the relative need of merchant ships *versus* escort vessels. In this case I believe we should try to have our cake and eat it too.

At any rate, we are moving aggressively here to increase both of these programs and have given them the highest priority for material and machine tools.

So far as merchant shipping is concerned, we have, after re-examination of our steel plate problem and other facilities, determined to increase it to 18,800,000 deadweight tons in 1943. I intend to raise this to 20 million tons if, after re-examination by our people, it should prove possible.

Of one thing I think you can be sure: that we will build in this country a minimum of 18,800,000 tons of merchant shipping of all kinds. Your offices here will keep you informed of the types of ships that are being built, and, naturally, I would welcome your judgement in regard to this, because it is very important that we have a proper balance between tankers, cargo vessels and transports.

I agree that this is the time for me to reply to you concerning the very urgent requirements of the British shipping program in 1943.

I have had the 27 million ton figure of imports to the British Isles examined rather hurriedly here by our own people and they are satisfied that this figure is substantially correct.

Our joint war effort requires that this pipe-line of material and food to Britain be maintained; that the moving of this tonnage at reasonably even levels is a matter of primary importance. I recognize it as such.

I am well aware of the concern with which your Government faces the serious net losses in tonnage to your merchant fleet. It is a net loss which persists, and I think we must face the fact that it may well continue through all of next year. I therefore want to give you the assurance that from our expanding fleet you may depend on the tonnage necessary to meet your import program.

Accordingly, I am instructing our Shipping Administration to allocate through the machinery of the Combined Shipping Adjustment Board enough dry-cargo tonnage out of the surplus shipbuilding to meet your imports, the supply and maintenance of your armed forces and other services essential to maintaining the war effort of the British Common-wealth, to the extent that they cannot be transported by the fleet under British control.

I have been given to understand by our combined shipping people that an average of nearly 300,000 tons each month of carrying capac-ity will have to be used to supplement the tonnage already engaged on behalf of the British war effort. Because of the commitments already made, the allocation of ships during the next three months must of necessity be less than the average for the whole period.

We may hope for a substantial reduction in this if we can make our way through the Mediterranean. Furthermore, I think that you and I should insist that every possible economy is exercised by our shipping and military authorities.

You will, I am sure, agree that emergencies may develop which may require me to divert for our own military purposes tonnage which it is now contemplated will be utilized for imports to Great Britain. There will, no doubt, be other cases in which we shall wish jointly to confer relative to vital military uses of merchant tonnage.

I want you to know that any important diversions of tonnage will be made only with my personal approval because I am fully cognizant of the fact that your Government may feel that decisions might be made to divert tonnage in contravention of the policy which I am laying down in this letter. (See enclosure.)[1]

The allocation of tonnage month by month must be worked out by the Combined Shipping Adjustment Board. And hence I confine myself to the above statement of policy. I wish to give you the definite assurance, subject to the qualifications I have indicated, that your requirements will be met.

We have increased our escort program recently by 70 for 1943, so that we should turn out 336 escort vessels during the next calendar year. I am asking Admiral King to confer with your representatives here and make arrangements about the distribution of these ships.

The problem of getting our troops to England is a serious one. I rec-ognize that there must be a minimum joint force there, well equipped and prepared to meet any eventuality.

While 'Roundup' seems more and more difficult, I do not think it should be taken off the boards by any means. We never can tell when

---

[1] Memorandum from the President to Admiral Land of the US Navy (*Churchill papers, 23/10*), assert-ing the supplementing of the British merchant fleet as 'one of the top military necessities of the war' and requesting to be consulted prior to any diversion of shipbuilding allocated for this purpose.

the opportunity may come for us to strike across the Channel, and if that opportunity comes we must be ready to take it. Obviously, however, the success of our joint enterprise in North Africa requires us to review the movement of our troops during the next few months. We need to come to an early decision as to what our next steps are going to be, and upon that decision must rest the determination of the number of American divisions that should be in England. We have this whole matter very much in mind here, and our Chiefs of Staff have it under constant consideration.

As you know, we have recently agreed upon a program of 82,000 combat planes. There have been misgivings in some quarters about the size of this program. I have none. We simply must get a complete domination of the air next year, even though other important things give way.

One thing is sure: that the aircraft must be brought to bear on the enemy at the earliest possible moment, and, if there are competent British and Russian crews to fight these planes and you can get at the enemy quicker and just as effectively as we can, then I have no hesitancy in saying that you and the Russians should have the planes you need.

We must give consideration to the shipping difficulties that are met when we send our United States air forces great distances. We have heavy commitments in the Southwest Pacific. We are rapidly assuming similar commitments in North Africa, and the bombing of Germany and Italy, whether from England or Russia, must be an unrelenting and constant business.

There have been many conferences taking place here between our respective representatives regarding the distribution of aircraft. I am in accord with the agreement that has been reached. Oliver will tell you of this. A detailed memorandum of the agreement will follow in a few days. Oliver has impressed upon me the necessity of making an early decision regarding the distribution of our combined aircraft production. I think the decisions that we have come to regarding aircraft are of the highest importance.

I am told that there is a substantial meeting of minds between your representatives and ours relative to the medium tank. I must confess that I think we are both underrating the need for these medium tanks. It is quite possible that the Russians may again press for large increases in medium tanks and I have a feeling that we are cutting our pattern pretty thin. I am asking General Marshall to explore this once more. I should think it would be no great strain on our production to get a few more thousand medium tanks in 1943.

I understand that some of your ground force requirements have not yet been discussed with my officers. These are being considered. Every effort will be made to include your essential requirements in our Army Supply Programme and I have asked to have a report of these further discussions submitted to me as early as possible.

I also recognise that your own production for Navy, Army and Air, and for the minimum needs of the civilian population, requires an assured flow of materials, machine tools, components and complementary items from America. These supplies, unless unforeseen circumstances intervene, will be maintained.

In conclusion, I want you to feel that this letter, together with the agreements that Oliver is taking home with him, gives you the assurances that you need in planning your own production, and that you may regard them as a firm base upon which to make the allocations of your remaining reserves of manpower.

As ever yours,
Franklin D. Roosevelt

PS – I forgot to say: Russia asks [for] 500 transport planes as a prime necessity. Let us remember that we *may* have to revise that item.

FDR

Field Marshal Jan Smuts to Winston S. Churchill
(Churchill papers, 20/84)

30 November 1942   Pretoria
Immediate   South Africa

Salute and Best Wishes to the youthful veteran of 68 coupled with warm congratulations on your brilliant war survey last night. I have returned from my English visit confident that you, in company with the other grand leaders of the United Nations, will yet, under Heaven's blessing, lead us to one of the greatest victories in world history.

General George C. Marshall to Winston S. Churchill
(Churchill papers, 20/56)

30 November 1942   Washington DC
Secret

Your masterly review of the present war situation certainly proves you to be 'two hundred per cent fit'. My deep and heartfelt congratulations on your birthday.

King George VI to Winston S. Churchill
(Churchill papers, 1/368)

30 November 1942   Buckingham Palace
Telegram

The Queen and I send you our heartfelt good wishes for your birthday.

George RI

December
1942

War Cabinet: conclusions
(Cabinet papers, 65/28)

1 December 1942   10 Downing Street
6 p.m.

[...]

The Prime Minister said that although clearly no assurance could be given that the enemy would not retaliate upon us for the heavy air attacks which we had made on Germany and Italy, nevertheless it was necessary to make some reductions in our defensive services in order to increase our offensive strength.

Winston S. Churchill to General Sir Alan Brooke
(Churchill papers, 20/67)

1 December 1942
Most Secret

The role of the Tenth Army is dependent upon the Russian defence of the Caucasus. Since we formed it in August, a vast favourable change has taken place, and it may be that before the end of the year all danger to Persia and Iraq will have rolled far to the westward.

2. Our policy towards Turkey may require that a large portion of the Tenth Army should be available to help the Turks. In view of the victories gained by the Allies both to the north and south of Turkey, the idea of Turkey opening a path voluntarily to the Germans need no longer be entertained.

3. Will you let me have a report showing how you could move four to six divisions of the Tenth Army westward into Syria and Turkey? Could they be maintained in Syria, or how many of them? How fast could they

move into Turkey by rail if desired? Let a scheme be worked out having as its target date six divisions in Western Turkey by the 1st May. It is not necessary to go into this in undue detail.

Winston S. Churchill to General Sir Alan Brooke
(Churchill papers, 20/67)

1 December 1942
Most Secret

Should we be successful in expelling the enemy from the Tunisian tip and in building up a really powerful American air force on the French North African shore, it ought not to be necessary to keep more than six United States or British divisions in French North Africa, aided by four or five French divisions, which by then will have proved their loyalty. Still less is it necessary to transport to the 'Torch' area all the vast apparatus, Corps, Army and L of C[1] personnel, which would have been appropriate to a prolonged campaign fought over great distances against French, Germans and Italians already strongly established. The situation in North Africa is already entirely different from what was expected and with air power and sea power and French assistance no large number of divisions should be locked up there, nor should these divisions have the full battle mobility previously required.

2. I am therefore not accepting General Eisenhower's estimate of ten divisions. I am also feeling uncertain about 'Brimstone'.[2] The price may be too heavy and the delay too long. We cannot afford to waste the summer and our shipping in campaigning in 'Brimstone'. It may be that we should close down the Mediterranean activities by the end of June with a view to 'Roundup' in August. The issues will have to be settled on the highest levels after we have reached agreement among ourselves. We cannot possibly be content with locking up large forces in French North Africa and some subsequent 'Brimstone' operations. See paragraph marked 'A':[3] we do not need to build up vehicles and stores to the full

---

[1] L of C: lines of communication.

[2] 'Brimstone': the capture of Sardinia.

[3] Churchill is responding to Brooke's minute of 25 November 1942, itself a response to Churchill's minute 546/2 of November 23. A and B refer to the latter: in paragraph 1 (here called A), Churchill states that the divisions placed in North Africa were designed to fight 'heavy opposition', but with all resistance now having ceased 'except in the Tunis tip', those troops need no longer be stationed in North Africa. In paragraph B he states that Brimstone would divert forces and shipping originally provided for Torch rather than add new resources on top of Torch. He emphasized that he never meant the Anglo-American army to stay in North Africa: 'It is a springboard and not a sofa' (*Churchill papers, 20/67*).

8. If you are in favour of this exchange Pound will settle details with King.[1]

Winston S. Churchill to Field Marshal Jan Smuts
(Churchill papers, 20/84)

2 December 1942
Secret and Personal

We were rather surprised by your decision to bring the whole 1st South Africa Division back to South Africa for leave and reorganisation. We had thought that only a portion were to go. Shipping them back will be a further strain on our resources. Australian 9th Division has been recalled and probably New Zealand Division will follow. We shall have to cannibalise at least one of the British divisions owing to reduction in WS convoys. The 8th Army will be woefully reduced.

Naturally I shall help to the full in anything you decide.

Winston S. Churchill to John Curtin
(Churchill papers, 20/84)

2 December 1942
Most Secret and Personal

THE RETURN OF THE 9TH AUSTRALIAN DIVISION

I and my professional advisers are very sorry that you continue to press for the move of the 9th Australian Division, which we do not consider is in accordance with the general strategic interests of the United Nations.

2. Nevertheless, in accordance with your wishes, I shall recommend to the President that the 9th Australian Division returns to Australia as soon as shipping can be provided. This will probably be early in the New Year. I may say that it will involve a loss to us in personnel shipping lift of 10,000 men in the WS convoys and 20,000 in the trans-Atlantic build-up for the invasion of the Continent.

3. Reference your paragraph 8. We very much regret that we cannot arrange for the equipment of your division to be returned to Australia.

[1] On 5 December 1942, Roosevelt telegraphed to Churchill: 'The early arrival of *Illustrious* in Pearl Harbour is looked forward to with anticipation' ('Personal and Most Secret', *Churchill papers, 20/84*). Churchill later recalled: 'Admiral King was however unwilling to spare the *Ranger*, and in consequence we could only send the *Victorious*. She left the Home Fleet for Pearl Harbour in December' (*Closing the Ring*, page 20).

We could not face the cost to our offensive operations of the cargo and MT shipping necessary for this movement.

4. You will like to know that in response to an urgent request by the Americans for naval help in the Pacific, we are proposing to offer them the two modern armoured aircraft carriers *Victorious* and *Indomitable*, under the command of a British admiral, for service under American orders in the Pacific. These are among the most vital units we possess. We have only four of this class. We are asking for *Ranger* from the Atlantic in exchange. I hope this movement will provide an additional and important reinsurance for the safety of Australia.

Winston S. Churchill to Peter Fraser
(Churchill papers, 20/84)

2 December 1942
Most Secret and Personal

[...]

2. The fact that we are losing the Australian Division makes the retention of the New Zealand Division in the Middle East even more necessary for us, though I quite understand your difficulties.

3. The return of the New Zealand Division would involve a further loss in shipping lift of 10,000 men in WS convoys and 40,000 in the trans-Atlantic build-up for the invasion of the Continent. The reason for the loss of lift for the move of the New Zealand Division being greater than that for the move of the Australian Division is because the big personnel ships happen to be arriving at Suez at a convenient time for the move of the latter. They would have to return from Australia to move the New Zealand Division. I could not, therefore, commit myself to any definite date for the shipping.

President Franklin D. Roosevelt to Winston S. Churchill
(Churchill papers, 20/84)

3 December 1942
Personal and Secret
No. 224

I have been giving a good deal of thought to our proposed joint conference with the Russians and I agree with you that the only satisfactory scale in North Africa. And 'B': I do not think 'Brimstone' is worth a lift of 90,000 men four months hence.

Winston S. Churchill to President Franklin D. Roosevelt
(Churchill papers, 23/10)

2 December 1942
Personal and Most Secret
No. 216

I give below the text of telegrams exchanged between me and Premier Stalin.[1]

2. Please note particularly the last sentence of paragraph 5 of Stalin's message. The chances of 'Roundup' may be greatly improved by the present battles on the Russian front.

3. It seems to me that the whole question ought to be re-examined in the light of Russian victories. It would be unwise in my view for us to send separate delegations to Moscow without having decided what we are going to do about 'Roundup', which is almost the sole thing they will want to know.

4. I hope, therefore, that you will allow General Marshall and Admiral King to come over here, if possible with Harry, at the earliest moment.

5. I still cherish the hope of an Iceland meeting after the ground has been fully explored.

Winston S. Churchill to President Franklin D. Roosevelt
(Churchill papers, 20/84)

2 December 1942
Personal and Secret
No. 217

Ever since we received a request for carrier reinforcement for your Pacific Fleet we have been earnestly seeking to meet your wishes. We did not feel able to come to a decision about these very few vital units until we knew how our carriers had fared in the restricted and dangerous waters in which they had to operate for 'Torch'.

---

[1] See Churchill's telegram to Stalin of 24 November 1942, and Stalin's reply of November 27 (pages 1430–2 above).

2. The hazards of 'Torch' are not yet ended, as our build-up of shore-based aircraft will not enable the withdrawal for some time of the two carriers now employed on 'Torch'.

Knowing, however, how urgently you require a reinforcement of carriers in the Pacific, we are prepared to take a risk now and come to a decision as to what assistance we can give you.

3. As you are aware, our carrier strength consists of the following:

(a) Four long endurance Armoured Fleet Carriers:

Victorious – Efficient and just withdrawn from 'Torch'.

Illustrious – Efficient and the only carrier now with the Eastern Fleet.

Indomitable – Undergoing after action repairs, and will not be worked up before February.

Formidable – Now employed on 'Torch' but has turbine trouble and must go into dockyard hands for 6 or 7 weeks as soon as possible.

(b) One short endurance Fleet Carrier, *Furious*, which is now employed on 'Torch'.

(c) An aircraft repair ship, *Unicorn*, which can operate about 25 aircraft, but will not be ready for service until early February.

4. In the hope that your operations in the South Pacific will prevent the Japanese from making serious raids into the Indian Ocean we are prepared to take the serious risk of withdrawing *Illustrious* from the Eastern Fleet, and give Admiral Somerville the *Unicorn* and an auxiliary carrier. We are also prepared to withdraw *Victorious* from the Home Fleet and to send you both *Victorious* and *Illustrious* if you can allow *Ranger* to join the Home Fleet.

5. In view of the vital importance of the Atlantic communication, the necessity of supporting the North Russian convoys, the possible appearance of *Graf Zeppelin* at the end of the year, and the present condition of *Indomitable* and *Formidable*, we could not release both *Victorious* and *Illustrious* without the addition of *Ranger* to the Home Fleet.

6. I am much in favour of sending you two carriers rather than one if this can be managed, as this will not only give you increased strength but would allow the two ships to work as a tactical unit, which would appear to be necessary as neither ship carries sufficient aircraft to operate singly.

I would propose to send Admiral Lyster,[1] who is known to a good many of your officers, in command.

7. It is considered necessary for both ships to proceed to Pearl Harbour, where they should arrive about the end of December, to adjust their complement of aircraft.

[1] Vice-Admiral Lumley Lyster, Flag Officer, Aircraft Carriers, Home Fleet.

way of coming to the vital strategic conclusions the military situation requires is for you and me to meet personally with Stalin. My thought would be that each of us could be accompanied by a very small staff made up of our top Army, Air and Naval Chiefs of Staff. I should bring Harry and Averell but no State Department representative although I believe we should arrive at tentative procedures to be adopted in event of a German collapse. I should like to see the conference held about January 15th or soon thereafter. Tunis and Bizerta should have been cleared up and Rommel's army liquidated before the conference. As to the place, Iceland or Alaska are impossible for me at this time of year and I believe equally so for Stalin. I should prefer a secure place south of Algiers or in or near Khartoum. I don't like mosquitoes. I think the conference should be very secret and that the press should be excluded. I would question the advisability of Marshall and the others going to England prior to the conference because I do not want to give Stalin the impression that we are settling everything between ourselves before we meet him.

I think that you and I understand each other so well that prior conferences between us are unnecessary and when the time comes we can work things out from day to day. Our military people will also be in close co-operation at all times from now on.

I think that this conference may well result in knocking out Germany sooner than we anticipated. As you know Stalin has already agreed to a purely military conference to be held in Moscow and I have today sent him a message urging him to meet you and me. I believe he will accept.

I prefer a comfortable oasis to the raft at Tilsit.

Winston S. Churchill to President Franklin D. Roosevelt
(Churchill papers, 20/84)

3 December 1942
Personal and Secret
No. 220

OPERATION 'VELVET': ANGLO-AMERICAN FORCE
TO THE CAUCASUS

We have had the following exchange of telegrams with Air Marshal Drummond[1] in Moscow. Extract from OZ 2077 of 1st December to Drummond (Begins) The operational and administrative advantages to

[1] Deputy Air Officer Commanding-in-Chief, Royal Air Force, Middle East, 1941–3. British representative in the staff discussions with Soviet and American representatives on arrangements for the deployment of British and American squadrons on the southern Russian front.

the RAF in the Middle East of Russian alternative proposal of number of aircraft equivalent to 'Velvet' force and your suggested compromise are fully realised, but these alternatives would not achieve the overriding political benefits which were the object of the original plan. It was hoped that by sending 'Velvet' force to Caucasus an example would be given of Allied forces working hand in hand with the Russians for the same military objectives and under unity of strategic control on a bigger scale than anything yet attempted. Not only would there have been practical co-operation on a considerable scale but there might also have developed a genuine spirit of comradeship in arms which would have opened up considerable possibilities in the political and military fields. This spirit was very evident in the Russian Navy as a result of our small fighter force going to North Russia in 1941. Para.2 The replacement of the whole or the greater part of 'Velvet' force by the equivalent in aircraft would not have this effect and would destroy the whole raison d'etre of the plan. There would be the further risk that if we only gave aircraft on this occasion we might let ourselves in for sending 'Velvet' force as well at a later stage in the war if the situation in Caucasus should deteriorate. Provision of aircraft is also bound to leave Middle East short at least in certain types and so cause the dismounting of squadrons. (Ends)

Following is Drummond's reply dated 2nd December (Begins) Your OZ 2077 1st December gives me political background which I needed. It is already clear beyond question that the Russians will not resume discussions and will not allow us to proceed to the Caucasus to arrange any further details for the establishment and operation of the force until they are convinced that we shall not agree to their alternative proposal of providing aircraft in lieu of the force. I must, therefore, preface my renewed approach with a reasoned refusal to entertain their alternative proposal. Even so I do not think they will accept this unless I can assure them that it is the agreed decision of the joint British and American Govts. (?) I, therefore, suggest that I be authorised to convey to the Russians as from the Anglo/American Governments a reply in the sense of Paras. 2, 3, 4 and 5 following. Para.2 The British and American Governments cannot agree to disarm twenty two fully operational squadrons in order to provide aircraft for the Red Air Force additional to those already promised and being supplied. Para. 3 At the present date, the military situation in the Caucasus appears to be not unfavourable and there is, therefore, less urgent need for the Anglo-American Force to be provided. These units would however, prove a most valuable asset in any offensive operations which the Russian High Command may undertake on the Caucasus front in the Spring 1943. In the meanwhile these squadrons can be usefully employed in the operations now proceeding in N. Africa. Para.4 The Anglo-American proposal, therefore, is that the complete Anglo-American Force as originally accepted by Premier Stalin should be despatched to the Russian Southern front at a time which will permit it to be fully operational by early April 1943. For this purpose detailed arrangements for the reception of the force must now be undertaken by the Allied Staffs and all administrative arrangements including predumping must proceed in the Caucasus and in N. Persia. The basis of these arrangements has already been most amicably agreed between representatives of the Red Army Air Force and my Mission. The principles agreed to in Moscow should now be applied in the Caucasus and a nucleus Anglo American Headquarters should be set up at Caucasus GHQ forthwith. It is desired to perfect these administrative preparations now so that the force can move in at short notice. Para.5 If this later date for the arrival of the force in the Caucasus is agreed a longer period is available for assembling supplies for it. In consequence the proportional interruption of the flow of aid over the Trans-Persian Railway to Russia will be smaller. We compute that there would be a twelve per cent interruption in January, a ten per cent interruption in February, a nine per cent interruption in March and thereafter less than eight per cent monthly. Moreover, if in the meanwhile the Russians will develop or allow us to develop the road Rowandaz – Lake Urmia we may be able to maintain the force without any interference with the flow of Russian aid (?). Para.6 I would re-emphasize that General Falalaev has clearly indicated that the Russian High Command will not engage in further discussion of the original project unless and until a firm Anglo/American Government refusal to consider the Russian alternative proposal is received. (Ends)

It seems to me that the situation is changing so rapidly that we should do well to let a week or so pass before ourselves taking steps to break the deadlock. We have made an offer which could only be fulfilled by heavy sacrifices on our part. We made that offer largely to take the edge off various Russian disappointments about the Second Front in 1942, about the PQ convoys, etc. and to show that we really wished to help. The offer stands. Since it was made immense improvements have occurred in the Russian position which have already altered and may completely change the strategic situation on the Russian Southern Front. At the same time by the Anglo-American successes along the whole North African Front we have shown the Russians that we are active comrades in the war and they are impressed by this. I do not wish to force upon them what it costs us so much to give. I consider therefore that Air Marshal Drummond and your representative, General Adler,[1] might mark time a little on the ground defined in Air Marshal Drummond's telegram without bringing matters to a sharp point. Meanwhile the strategic situation will be clarifying itself and we can make the arrangements for the Conference proposed in your No. 224, about which I am sending you a separate telegram. It seems to me that 'Velvet' might well be brought into the general scheme and should be decided at this Conference. In the meanwhile all preparations for 'Velvet' should go forward so far as they rest with Britain and the United States.

Winston S. Churchill to Josef Stalin
(Churchill papers, 20/84)

3 December 1942
Most Secret and Personal

The President tells me he has proposed a meeting for us three in January somewhere in North Africa. This is far better than the Iceland project we talked over in Moscow. You could get to any point desired in three days, I in two and the President in about the same time as you. I earnestly hope you will agree. We must decide at the earliest moment the best way of attacking Germany in Europe with all possible force in 1943. This can only be settled between the heads of Governments and States with their high expert authorities at their side. It is only by such a meeting that the full burden of the war can be shared according to capacity and opportunity.

Winston S. Churchill to President Franklin D. Roosevelt
(Churchill papers, 20/84)

3 December 1942
Personal and Secret
No. 219

Your 224. I am delighted at your proposal which is the only way of making a good plan for 1943. At present we have no plan for 1943 which is on the

---

[1] Commanding general of US Air Service Command. US representative in the staff discussions with Soviet and British representatives on arrangements for the deployment of British and American squadrons on the southern Russian front.

scale or up to the level of events. It is grand of you to come and I will meet you anywhere. I am telegraphing Stalin to reinforce your invitation.

2. Meanwhile I deprecate sending our military representatives to Moscow. It will only lead to a deadlock and queer the pitch. We still think that Marshall, King and Arnold should come here in advance so that at least we have some definite plans as a basis for discussion when we all meet in January 'somewhere in Africa'. Otherwise Stalin will greet us with the question 'Have you then no plan for the second front in Europe you promised me for 1943.'

3. Khartoum is at your disposal and would be most satisfactory as regards weather, security and communications. I will report on accommodation tomorrow. We should be honoured to be the hosts. I am not informed, though quite ready to learn, about the oases south of Algiers. Marrakesh I can personally vouch for as regards accommodation, climate and, barring any extraordinary lapse, weather.

4. A supreme war conference, as this would be, ought to have the necessary staffs. For ourselves I should like to bring Eden from the War Cabinet with me and three Chiefs or Vice-Chiefs of the Staff, supported by a powerful secretariat, cypher staff, map room, etc. say about twenty-five.

5. As to timing, the sooner the better. Every day counts. We may reasonably expect that Tunis will be settled by the end of December and Tripolitania by the end of January. We ought not to be dependent on the actual working out of these operations. All prospect of attack in Europe in 1943 depends on early decision.

6. However everything hangs on whether 'Barkis is willin''.[1]

Winston S. Churchill: note by the Minister of Defence
(Churchill papers, 23/10)

3 December 1942   10 Downing Street
Most Secret
Chiefs of Staff Paper No. 429 (Operations) of 1942

In April last General Marshall unfolded to us the plan subsequently called 'Roundup', of which 'Bolero' is the administrative counterpart. A massive argument was that 'Roundup' is the only way in which large American and British forces can be brought into direct contact with

---

[1] 'Barkis is willin'': a quotation from Charles Dickens' novel *David Copperfield*, drawing a parallel between the drawn-out courtship of two of the characters and the uncertainty of Stalin's response to the Anglo-American proposal.

the enemy, and the British Metropolitan and United States Overseas Air Forces exercise their maximum power. American military opinion was solidly ranged behind this enterprise, and since then preparations under 'Bolero' have gone forward steadily, subject only to 'Torch'. As an addition to 'Roundup', 'Sledgehammer' was proposed in July. It was agreed by the combined staffs that 'Torch' should be executed instead of 'Sledgehammer'. Meanwhile 'Bolero' was to continue with preparations for a retarded or opportunist 'Roundup'.

2. However, the opinion was held by the American Staffs that the abandonment of 'Sledgehammer' and the adoption of 'Torch' in fact rendered 'Roundup' impossible in 1943, even though retarded. One reason for this was the probability of Russia being so seriously weakened that Hitler could bring back very large armies from the east, thus making the forces available for 'Roundup' in 1943 altogether insufficient. They also founded their opinion on the fact that the assembly of forces for 'Roundup' would be so delayed by the diversion of shipping to 'Torch', that we should not be strong enough during the 1943 season to effect an entry into the Continent, even against comparatively weak forces. The American Military Staff thus foresaw their troops being held idle in the United Kingdom, a situation which the President and General Marshall were anxious to avoid.

3. Besides the above, the shipping stringency has become pronounced. The progress of constructing landing-craft and training crews has been slowed down, if not largely arrested. 'Torch' is in full progress with its serious demands on shipping, and we have in prospect the variants of 'Brimstone' which, though secondary, are substantial operations.

4. On the other hand, the Russians have been led to believe that we were going to open 'a Second Front in 1943'. 'Roundup' was explained to them by me in the presence of the United States representative, Mr Harriman. These conversations at Moscow were duly reported to the President. I feel that Premier Stalin would have grave reasons to complain if our land offensive against Germany and Italy in 1943 were reduced to the scale of about 13 divisions instead of nearly 50, which have been mentioned to him. Moreover, apart from any Russian obligations, I feel that our offensive war plans for 1943 are on altogether too small a scale compared with the resources and power of Britain and the United States.

5. Recent most important events have altered, and are altering, the data on which thought on both sides of the Atlantic has hitherto proceeded. The Russians have not been defeated or weakened in the

campaign of 1942. On the contrary, it is Hitler who has been defeated and the German Army which has been very grievously reduced. See the statement of General von Thoma that the 180 German divisions on the Russian front are in many cases little more than brigades. The demoralization among the Hungarian, Rumanian and Italian troops on the eastern front is marked. The Finns are no longer fighting except for a few mountain troops.

6. The great battles now in progress at Stalingrad and in the central sector of the Russian front have not yet been decided. It may well be that the Russian offensives will produce far-reaching effects upon the German power. If the Sixth German Army, which is now encircled before Stalingrad, is destroyed, the Russian southern offensive may reach its objective at Rostov-on-the-Don. In this case, the position of the three remaining German armies in the Northern Caucasus, already closely engaged by the Russians, may be seriously and perhaps even mortally compromised, again with measureless results. The Russian offensive in the central sector and the counter-attacks they are making at many points along the front may lead to a withdrawal of the German line to winter positions. The winter will impose formidable privations and ordeals upon the weakened German armies, in spite of the better railway system they now have. Before the end of 1942 it may be possible for us to draw with certainty at least the conclusion:

That no important transfers of German troops can be made in 1943 from the Eastern to the Western theatre.

This would be a new fact of the first magnitude.

7. The operation 'Torch' has prospered beyond all reasonable expectation, and by the end of the year we may be masters of the whole of French North-West Africa including Tunisia. At the same time, the Eighth Army may have destroyed the remnants of Rommel's forces and be themselves advancing towards Tripoli. In this case future operations in the Mediterranean may not require more than 5 United States divisions already landed or at sea, the 2 British divisions already landed, the 2 more under orders from 'Backbone'[1] or 'Brimstone', the 51st and 44th British Infantry Divisions, the 4th and 10th Indian Divisions, the 1st, 7th and 10th Armoured Divisions and the Australian and New Zealand divisions, whose withdrawal must be resisted as far as possible. To these should be added 5 French divisions in French North-West Africa, making a total for the Mediterranean of 23 divisions.

[1] 'Backbone': planned operation against Spanish Morocco.

8. The improved position in the Caucasus should permit the 6 British or British Indian divisions of the Tenth Army, plus the 2 Polish divisions (total 8 divisions), to throw their weight to the westward and participate in the Turkey plan. It might, however, be necessary to reinforce India with one or two of these divisions if a diversionary invasion were threatened by Japan. Subject to this, the total number of divisions in the Mediterranean and Levant would be 31. This force should be sufficient for all operations in the Mediterranean theatres to be undertaken in 1943.

9. The events which have taken place in France[1] have compelled the Germans, in order to defend the southern coasts of France, to withdraw 11 divisions from the 40 which stood opposite Britain in France and the Low Countries. Their task of maintaining internal security in France has been rendered more onerous. They will probably be compelled to find another 4 or even 6 divisions to protect and hold down Italy against the menace of 'Torch', 'Brimstone', &c., and to garrison Sicily and perhaps Sardinia. The Yugoslav resistance continues, and no relief can be expected by the Axis in any part of the Balkan Peninsula. On the contrary, they have the need to reinforce Greece, Rumania and Bulgaria on account of the general situation as well as of the possible entry of Turkey against them, for which we are to work. None of these facts were present when 'Roundup' and 'Sledgehammer' were considered at the London conferences of July.

10. I am therefore of opinion that the whole position must be completely resurveyed, with the object of finding means of engaging United States and British armies directly upon the Continent. For this purpose the assumptions set forth in the preceding paragraphs should be accepted as data. Besides these, it should be assumed that the North African shore is adequately equipped with Air forces, and that the Mediterranean is open for military traffic by the end of March, thus securing a substantial relief in shipping; that any 'Brimstone' operations are concluded by the beginning of June; and that all landing-craft, &c., needed for 'Roundup' should be back in Great Britain by the end of June; that July should be devoted to preparation and rehearsal; and that August or, if the weather is adverse, September should be taken as the striking target.

11. For this purpose there should be assembled in this country by the beginning of July 15 British and 20 United States Divisions – total, 35, of which 12 should be Armoured. There should be held ready in the United States 15 additional Divisions (of which 5 Armoured). These

---

[1] In November and early December Nazi Germany invaded and took over previously unoccupied southern France. Prior to this, Vichy forces had maintained internal security in this region.

would proceed direct to France after the invasion has secured the necessary deep-water landing ports. There should also be provided sufficient United States reinforcements for the British Air Force to ensure the maintenance of a two-to-one superiority in the West. At the same time the development of the United States air power from Tunis should enable a very heavy extra drain to be made upon the enemy's air force in Italy, Sicily, &c.

12. To sum up, the target schedule should be:

End of 1942:
Occupation of Tunisia and completion of 'Torch'.
Entry of the British Eighth Army into Tripolitania.
Resumption of PQ Convoys.

End of January:
Capture of Tripoli and total clearance of North African shore from Axis Forces.

End of March:
Completion of air build-up along African shore and opening of Mediterranean for military traffic.

End of May:
Completion of any 'Brimstone' or similar operation.
Culminations of policy of bringing Turkey into the war and movement of the Tenth Army to the Turkish theatre.

End of June:
Completion of concentration in Great Britain of all landing-craft, whether from Mediterranean or United States.
Concentration of the Anglo-American Expeditionary Army in Great Britain.
Suspension of PQ Convoys.

End of July:
Completion of all preparations for 'Roundup' and assembly in United States of the 15 supporting Divisions.

August and September:
Action.

Winston S. Churchill to Sir John Anderson
(Churchill papers, 20/67)

3 December 1942
Action this Day

In my personal minute M. 543/2 of 23rd November, I said that I was in favour of the Archbishop of Canterbury's request that the bells should be rung on Christmas Day and that I did not think that the invasion danger warranted the maintenance of this ban. I trust that Commander-in-Chief, Home Forces,[1] is not raising objection on military grounds. If so, please let me know immediately. I shall be seeing him before the weekend and would be very ready to put the position to him.

Winston S. Churchill to Sir Archibald Sinclair and
Air Chief Marshal Sir Charles Portal
(Churchill papers, 20/67)

3 December 1942

BOMBING POLICY

Is 3,000 tons a month the maximum you can discharge in the next few months? I thought you were aiming at bigger figures than that.

2. The heat should be turned on Italy in the manner proposed by you at present, but Germany should not be entirely neglected. I am looking forward to a big raid on Berlin this month if conditions are favourable.

3. Our policy can be reviewed and changed from time to time as may be desired.

4. The Secretary of State[2] might, if he felt inclined, supply the War Cabinet with a short statement, as the matter was mentioned to them.

Admiral François Darlan to Winston S. Churchill
('Their Finest Hour', pages 203–5)

4 December 1942   Algiers

Dear Mr Prime Minister,

On June 12, 1940, at Briare, at the headquarters of General Weygand, you took me aside and said to me: 'Darlan, I hope you will never surrender the Fleet.' I answered you: 'There is no question of doing so; it

---

[1] Sir Bernard Paget.
[2] Secretary of State for Air, Sir Archibald Sinclair.

would be contrary to our naval traditions and honour'. The First Lord of the Admiralty, Alexander, and the First Sea Lord, Pound, received the same reply on June 17, 1940, at Bordeaux, as did Lord Lloyd. If I did not consent to authorise the French Fleet to proceed to British ports, it was because I knew that such a decision would bring about the total occupation of Metropolitan France as well as North Africa.

I admit having been overcome by a great bitterness and a great resentment against England as the result of the painful events which touched me as a sailor; furthermore it seemed to me that you did not believe my word. One day Lord Halifax sent me word by M Dupuy that in England my word was not doubted, but that it was believed that I should not be able to keep it. The voluntary destruction of the Fleet at Toulon has just proved that I was right, because even though I no longer commanded, the Fleet executed the orders which I had given and maintained, contrary to the wishes of the Laval Government. On the orders of my chief, the Marshal,[1] I was obliged, from January 1941 to April 1942, to adopt a policy which would prevent France and its Empire from being occupied and crushed by the Axis Powers. This policy was by the force of events opposed to yours. What else could I do? At that time you were not able to help us, and any gesture towards you would have led to the most disastrous consequences for my country. If we had not assumed the obligation to defend the Empire by our own forces (I always refused German aid, even in Syria) the Axis would have come to Africa and our own Army would have been discarded; the First British Army undoubtedly would not be before Tunis today with French troops at its side to combat the Germans and Italians.

When the Allied Forces landed in Africa on November 8 I at first executed the orders I had received. Then as soon as this became impossible I ordered the cessation of the fighting in order to avoid unnecessary bloodshed and a fight which was contrary to the intimate sentiments of those engaged. Disavowed by Vichy and not wishing to resume the fight, I placed myself at the disposition of the American military authorities, only in that way being able to remain faithful to my oath. On November 11 I learned of the violation of the Armistice Convention by the Germans, the occupation of France, and the solemn protest of the Marshal. I then considered that I could resume my liberty of action, and that, remaining faithful to the person of the Marshal, I could follow that road which was most favourable to the welfare of the French Empire, that of the fight against the Axis. Supported by the high authorities of French Africa and

[1] Pétain.

by public opinion, and acting as the eventual substitute of the Chief of State, I formed the High Commissariat in Africa and ordered the French forces to fight at the side of the Allies. Since then French West Africa has recognised my authority. I should never have been able to accomplish this result if I had not acted under the aegis of the Marshal and if I were simply represented as a dissident. I have the conviction that all Frenchmen who now fight against Germany each in his own manner will finally achieve a general reconciliation, but I believe that for the moment they must continue their separate action. There is a certain resentment, notably in French West Africa, which is too active for me to obtain more, as you know. I follow my role without attacking anyone; I ask for reciprocity. For the moment the only thing that counts is to defeat the Axis; the French people when liberated will later choose their political *régime* and their leaders.

I thank you, Mr Prime Minister, for having associated yourself with President Roosevelt in declaring that, like the United States, Great Britain wishes the integral re-establishment of French sovereignty as it existed in 1939. When my country has recovered its integrity and its liberty my only ambition will be to retire with the sentiment of having served it well.

Please accept, Mr Prime Minister, the assurances of my highest consideration.

Francois Darlan, Admiral of the Fleet

Winston S. Churchill to Hugh Dalton[1]
(Churchill papers, 20/67)

4 December 1942

I am told that the whole of the Army have been made to strip off their regimental badges, at great detriment to *esprit de corps*. As many of the soldiers paid for these badges themselves, there has been a lot of distress caused. The War Office state the Board of Trade have informed them that the amount of material and labour used to make these badges (most of which are already in existence) is more than we can afford in the present stringency.

Will you let me know exactly what the burden is? It must be taken into account that a great deal can be done by regimental and local arrangements. It would seem to me this was a very small proportion of the Army

---

[1] President of the Board of Trade.

clothing. Let me know exactly what the Board of Trade said to the War
Office which led them to this step.

Winston S. Churchill: speech
(*'Winston S. Churchill, His Complete Speeches'*, volume 6, pages 6716–17)

5 December 1942   Town Hall Steps,
                                                                   Bradford

It is a pleasure for me to come to Bradford. I have a memory and a
connection with the city which goes back a long time, because fifty years
ago my father, Lord Randolph Churchill, had the great ambition of representing the Central Division of this city, and he would undoubtedly
have been your Member had he not died very suddenly. I have always
felt a connection with your great city on that account.

The last time I came here I came in a time – 28 years ago – of bitter
internal struggle.[1] We were all divided and were fiercely ranged against
one another. Parties were facing each other with clenched teeth, and they
even seemed to be drifting into violence and broils inside the State. It was
a very hard, stern time, but one which our institutions – our broad-based
free, democratic institutions – enabled us to pass through and overcome
and to settle our problems.

Now, I come and there is no division. All are united like one great family; all are standing together, helping each other, taking their share and
doing their work, some at the front, some under the sea or on the sea in
all weathers, some in the air, some in the coal mines, great numbers in
the shops, some in the homes all doing their bit, and every one of you
entitled to ask himself every morning or every evening: 'Am I rowing my
weight in the boat?' and if you can answer that searching question 'Yes,
I am,' then, believe me, all are bearing their part, each and every one
is bearing his or her part, in one of the greatest struggles that have ever
glorified, torn, and dignified the human race.

Now, we have just passed through the month of November, usually
a month of fogs and gloom, but, on the whole, a month I have liked
a good deal better than some other months we have seen during the
course of this present unpleasantness; a month in which our affairs have
prospered, in which our soldiers and sailors and airmen have been victorious, in which our gallant Russian Ally has struck redoubtable blows

[1] The reference is to Churchill's previous visit to Bradford in March 1914, when he made a
speech relating to Ulster.

against the common enemy, and in which our American Allies and our kith and kin far off in the Pacific Ocean, in Australia and New Zealand, have also seen their efforts crowned with a considerable measure of success. A great month, this last month of November.

But I must tell you, and I know you will not mind my saying it, because I do not think it is wise to deal in smooth words or airy promises, that you must be on your guard not to let the good fortune that has come to us be anything else but a means of striking harder. The struggle is approaching its most tense period. The hard core of Nazi resistance and villainy is not yet broken in upon. We have to gather up all our strength.

If by any chance unexpected good tidings come to us, that would be a matter which we could rejoice at, but which we must not count upon. We count upon our strong right arms, upon our honest, hard-working hearts; we count upon our courage, which has not been found wanting either in domestic or foreign stresses during the whole course of this war. These are the simple virtues which our island race has cultured and nurtured during many generations, and these are the virtues which will bear us through all struggles and in which we must put our faith.

We have broken into North Africa, with our American Allies, and now we have, in a short time, advanced from the Atlantic Ocean almost to the centre of the Mediterranean, a distance of nearly 900 miles; but there are still twenty miles to go, and very hard fighting will take place before that small distance is overcome and the violence and military power of the enemy there has been beaten down and driven into the sea. I do not doubt of the result, but I cannot leave you to suppose that it will be easily achieved. Away on the other side of North Africa, our armies are advancing, taking thousands of prisoners and driving the enemy before them; but here again hard fighting is to be expected. But during this month, when so much fighting has been carried on by the British and Americans, there has been a feeling of gladness that we, too, are engaging the enemy closely and not leaving the entire burden to be borne by the Russians, who have carried this immense struggle through the whole of this year and a large part of last year. They are defending their own country; we are defending our own country; but we are all of us defending something which is, I won't say dearer, but greater than a country, namely, a cause. That cause is the cause of freedom and of justice; that cause is the cause of the weak against the strong; it is the cause of law against violence, of mercy and tolerance against brutality and iron-bond tyranny. That is the cause that we are fighting for. That is the cause which is moving slowly, painfully but surely, inevitably and inexorably forward to victory; and when the victory is gained you will find that you are I will not say in a new world, but a better world; you are in a world which can be made more fair, more happy, if only all the peoples will join together to do their part, and if all classes and all parties stand together to reap the fruits of victory as they are standing together to bear, and to face, and to cast back the terrors and menaces of war.

Our enemies are very powerful; they dispose of many millions of soldiers; they have millions of prisoners whom they, in many cases, use like slaves; they have rich lands which they have conquered; they have large, gifted populations in their grip; they have a theme of their own which is the Nazi theme of tyranny, the domination of a race by the shameful idolatry of a single man, a base man, lifted almost to the stature of a god by his demented and degraded worshippers; they have this ideal of the suppression of the individual citizen, man and woman, to be a mere chattel in a State machine.

All this is, in our view, at stake, but our enemies are powerful. They consider that they will have the strength to wear us out even if they cannot beat us down. Their hope is now to prolong the struggle so that perhaps differences will arise between friends and allies, so that perhaps democracies whom they despise and whom they underrate will weary of the war.

So I say to you all here in Bradford what I said when I was here nearly thirty years ago: Let us go forward together and put the great principles we support to the proof.

Winston S. Churchill to Peter Fraser
(Churchill papers, 20/84)

6 December 1942
Most Secret and Personal

All my colleagues and I are very deeply grateful to you and to the Government and people of New Zealand for the most generous manner in which you have responded to our appeal to allow the glorious New Zealand division to represent the Dominion on the African battlefield. Naturally you are free to reconsider your decision at any time, and especially if your own situation deteriorates. I am sure the President of the United States will share our feelings here of admiration for New Zealand and all that she stands for.

2. It looks as if Rommel will not stand at Agheila, and by the time this reaches you he may well be taking another big bound backwards. We shall follow hot-foot on his heels. A second British convoy has arrived at Malta from Alexandria, and the haunting anxiety that the fortress would be starved out, which we have endured for so many months, and for the sake of which we have made such heavy sacrifices both in warships and supply vessels, has been swept away. In Tunisia our vanguards have been sharply checked, and it will be necessary to go over to the defensive for a week or more while Air and armour come up from the main body. It was quite right to go on pell-mell while the going was good, and thereby we have gained an immense amount of territory including seaports from which we can strike with surface craft at the enemy convoys. Everything will be done to drive the Axis out of Tunisia at the earliest moment. The war in that theatre is very costly for them on account of the immense toll we shall levy on their reinforcements.

3. The United States have preferred to have one British armoured carrier and keep their own *Ranger* instead of sending us *Ranger*[1] and taking two armoured carriers from us. We should have preferred the latter plan because it would have given us more say in the tasks to be set us. Still, there will be two more carriers in the Pacific as a result of the moves.

Kindest regards and all good wishes.

Winston S. Churchill to President Franklin D. Roosevelt
(Churchill papers, 20/84)

6 December 1942

I feel it is right that I should address you, Mr President, on this day, since our country no less than the United States was the object of the infamous outrage of a year ago. The injuries that we have all suffered at the hands of Japan during the past year are grievous indeed. The peoples of the British Commonwealth of Nations are deeply conscious of their duty. We look forward one and all to the day when our full strength can be joined to that of our United States, Dutch and Chinese Allies for the utter and final destruction of Japan's aggressive power.

[1] United States aircraft carrier and Flagship of the US Atlantic Fleet.

President Franklin D. Roosevelt to Winston S. Churchill
(Churchill papers, 20/84)

6 December 1942
Emergency
Personal and Most Secret
No. 227

Replying to your 220, I agree with you that our two representatives in Moscow mark time in relation to 'Velvet'. On the other hand, I would not wish to give them any authority to call that enterprise off because it seems to me to have great political and possibly military advantages.

Winston S. Churchill to President Franklin D. Roosevelt
(Churchill papers, 20/84)

6 December 1942
Personal and Secret
No. 223

I entirely agree.

Josef Stalin to Winston S. Churchill
(Churchill papers, 20/84)

6 December 1942
Personal and Secret

Your message of the 4th December[1] received.

I welcome the idea of a meeting between the Heads of the Governments of the three countries being arranged in order to fix a common line of military strategy.

To my great regret however I will not be in a position to leave the Soviet Union. Time presses us and it would be impossible for me to be absent even for a day as it is just now that important military operations of our winter campaign are developing. These operations will not be relaxed in January, probably to the contrary.

I am waiting your reply to the paragraph of my preceding letter dealing with the establishment of the second front in Western Europe in the spring of 1943.

[1] Dated December 3 above.

The operations in the Stalingrad area as well as on the Central front are developing. In the Stalingrad area we are keeping a large group of the German troops surrounded and we hope to annihilate them completely.

Stalin

Winston S. Churchill to General Sir Harold Alexander
(Churchill papers, 20/88)

6 December 1942

Presume you will have read 'Boniface' numbers QT 7789 and QT 7903, which certainly reveal a condition of weakness and counter-order among the enemy of a very remarkable character.[1]

Winston S. Churchill to General Hastings Ismay,
for the Chiefs of Staff Committee
(Churchill papers, 20/67)

6 December 1942

This[2] is, of course, sound so far as concerns the landing ships and craft required for the actual spearhead of assault. If it is attempted to apply these high-grade conditions to all movements from one shore to the other, the only result will be to render operations of this character utterly impossible. The maxim 'Nothing avails but perfection' may be spelt shorter, 'Paralysis'.

---

[1] Enigma decrypts at this time revealed the many and grave supply problems afflicting Axis forces in late November and December. 'By 5 December five shiploads of stores for the Panzer Army were waiting in Italy, but only two medium-sized ships were available...On 5 December the Enigma disclosed the complete strength and supply return for the Panzer Army and the GAF for 1 December. The Panzer Army, now reduced to 54 tanks and to a little Italian armour (42 medium tanks), had no reserves of fuel and was desperately short of ammunition. The GAF had fuel and one day's operations and could not undertake adequate reconnaissance' (Hinsley et al., *British Intelligence in the Second World War*, Volume II, pages 456–8).

[2] Telegram COS (W) 380, regarding the lessons to be learned from the Dieppe raid of August 1942 in connection with landing ships and craft.

Winston S. Churchill to Admiral of the Fleet Sir Dudley Pound
(Churchill papers, 20/67)

6 December 1942
Action this Day

Apparently from the attached telegram Harwood is going to use *Orion*[1] and seven destroyers to convoy back empty merchant ships from Malta to Alexandria, after which the escort will return to Malta. But this is the week of all others when the Malta surface force (Force K) must strike upon the communications of the Axis forces in Tunis. A week or ten days later will be too late. Infinite harm will be done and the whole battle compromised.

2. This also is the time for Admiral Cunningham to use his cruisers and destroyers, even at heavy risk, against enemy convoys. These vessels could never play so useful a part as in stopping the reinforcements of the enemy during the battle. The first duty of the Navy for the next ten days is to stop the reinforcements to Tunisia. This duty should be discharged even at a heavy cost.

Winston S. Churchill to Lord Portal
(Churchill papers, 20/67)

6 December 1942

This seems all right, but is movement possible *on the level* through the basement from Admiralty House to the citadel part of the Admiralty? Could a connection be made? Our guest could then be wheeled swiftly to a safe place.[2] It is essential that there should be complete security.

Winston S. Churchill to General Dwight D. Eisenhower
(Churchill papers, 20/84)

7 December 1942
Most Urgent
Personal and Secret

It is very good of you to telegraph to me so fully. I am filled with admiration by the brilliant advance you have made and <u>not</u> at all disappointed

---

[1] HMS *Orion*: a Leander-class light cruiser for the Royal Navy laid down in 1931 and commissioned in 1934. Served in the Mediterranean for most of the war. Decommissioned, 1947. Scrapped, 1949.

[2] Plans were being made for a possible visit by President Roosevelt.

by the check our vanguards have received in their audacious attempt to seize the maximum territory possible before enemy resistance is solidified. You were absolutely right to run all risks and the opposite policy would have denied us invaluable gains.

2. From this somewhat detached summit it seems that protracted fighting in the Tunisian tip must be very costly for the Axis <u>not</u> only at the front but even more on their harassed communications. You may count on our doing everything in human power to support your operations and vindicate your strategy.

3. I am sorry you should have been bothered in the midst of an exciting battle by all this Darlan business. I shall cover your necessary action to the best of my ability feeling sure you will avoid formal long term commitments. I gather from today's telegrams that arrangements are being reached about Dakar. Anyhow please think of me as a fairly solid fortification covering your rear and go for the swine in front with a blithe heart.

All good wishes to you and the Eagle.[1]

I do <u>not</u> know what has happened to the Bulldog.[2]

4. Alexander will be on the job again pretty soon.

5. In the middle of your Tunis Battle, I also agree entirely with you about <u>not</u> bombing the remnants of the Toulon Fleet.

Winston S. Churchill to General Sir Harold Alexander
(Churchill papers, 20/84)

7 December 1942
Most Immediate
Most Secret and Personal

Your CS/1718.[3]

I am sure you are watching them like a cat does a mouse. It is a great help to me in my work when you keep in touch.

---

[1] General Clark.
[2] General Bedell Smith.
[3] Telegram T1670/2 from General Alexander to the Prime Minister of December 6, outlining plans for further advance of 8th Army towards Tripoli.

Winston S. Churchill to Field Marshal Jan Smuts
(Churchill papers, 20/84)

7 December 1942
Immediate
Most Secret

I am profoundly touched by the kindness of your statement which will be of real help to me.[1]

2. Our vanguards in Tunisia have been sharply checked but it was quite right to push while the going was good and we have gained an immense amount of valuable territory. The Tunisian tip is a very good place to fight the Hun as they get so well bled on their communications. Alexander will soon be on the job again too.

Winston S. Churchill to the War Cabinet
(Churchill papers, 23/10)

7 December 1942
Secret
War Cabinet Paper No. 567 of 1942

SERVICE REQUIREMENTS

The man-power and raw materials shortage makes it absolutely imperative to ensure that the requirements of the Service Departments are not in excess of needs. The following instances – and there may be others – raise doubt as to whether this has been fully realised:

(i) We had in stock in this country on the 1st October 100,000 tons of obsolescent 500-lb GP bombs and 22,000 tons of 250-lb GP bombs. Expenditure between the 1st July and the 1st October averaged roughly 600 tons a month of the former and 70 tons a month of the latter. Assuming that we continue to drop this obsolescent type of bomb at the same rate, we had, therefore on that date about 14 years' supply of the 500-lb type and 30 years' supply of the 250-lb type in stock. Abroad we had about 20,000 tons of the 500-lb bombs and 18,500 tons of the 250-lb bombs. Expenditure appears to be about 400 tons a month of each, so that abroad we had something like 4 years' supply.

[1] The reference is most likely to Smuts' birthday wishes and statement of confidence in Churchill (see page 1464 above).

Although 33,000 tons of our home stocks of the 500-lb bomb and 12,500 tons of the 250-lb bomb are listed as 'tactical reserves against invasion', the total quantities do not seem to justify production at the rate which has until recently been going on, namely about 6,000 tons a month, requiring about 4,000 tons of steel. It appears that the Secretary of State for Air has recently stated that he wanted no more of these bombs, but apparently production has not yet been stopped.

It is, of course, true that the Air Ministry hoped for a bigger expansion of the RAF than has actually been possible, but should they not have stopped the output of this obsolescent type of bomb much earlier?

(ii) We have a total world-wide stock of 75 million rounds of gun ammunition; expenditure on the Western Front in 1918 was 65 million rounds. Planned production in the United Kingdom next year is 70 million rounds. 100,000 tons of steel are allocated monthly to shells and at least 400,000 people will be engaged on their manufacture.

(iii) Of the ammunition stocks 6.85 million rounds are 3.7 AA ammunition. The highest expenditure in any one month of the blitz on England was 140,000 rounds, at which rate our present stocks are equal to 50 months' supply. Our planned production in 1943 is 310,000 rounds per month.

(iv) The War Office plan to issue 9½ million suits of battle dress in 1943. We have produced more than 22 million to date, and are making about 450,000 per month.

(v) Greatcoats are normally reckoned in the Army to last 4½ years. We have made 8½ million to date, and are producing at the rate of 90,000 per month. The War Office plan to issue 3 million greatcoats in 1943.

Desirable as it may be to have a smart, well-turned-out Army, it must be remembered that all the 40 million civilians get only about the same amount of wool and cotton as the Services and are to be allowed only about the same amount of labour for converting the stuff into clothing.

2. The general stringency is now such that the Services can no longer have all they would like, but must be content with what we can afford. I propose that the Minister of Production[1] should investigate in broad general terms with the various Departments what would be the effect on the efficiency of the Services concerned if the rate of production of all items in the Ministry of Supply save a few obvious items such as tanks, 17-pdrs, AT ammunition, were cut down by one-third, and how much man-power and materials and ship tonnage would thereby be saved in the Ministry of

[1] Oliver Lyttelton.

Supply. A similar investigation should be made as regards the output of items other than ships produced by the Admiralty and other than aircraft produced by MAP. In this investigation it might be assumed that all GP bombs should be stopped completely. These investigations would cover both operational and non-operational requirements (e.g. clothing).

Naturally, small bottleneck items should not be dealt with in these surveys. The investigation should proceed on broad general lines with a desire to discover the amount of man-power and materials and ship tonnage which could be set free for the Services by reducing their equipment.

Winston S. Churchill to General Hastings Ismay,
for the Chiefs of Staff Committee
(Churchill papers, 20/67)

7 December 1942
Most Secret

HABBAKUK[1]

I attach the greatest importance to the prompt examination of these ideas, and every facility should be given to CCO[2] for developing them. He will report to me weekly on the setting-up of the organisation and the preliminary work.

2. I do not, of course, know anything about the physical properties of a lozenge of ice 5,000 feet by 2,000 feet by 100 feet, or how it resists particular stresses, or what would happen to an iceberg of this size in rough Atlantic weather, or how soon it would melt in different waters at different periods of the year. The advantages of a floating island or islands, even if only used as refuelling depots for aircraft, are so dazzling that they do not at the moment need to be discussed. There would be no difficulty in finding a place to put such a 'stepping-stone' in any of the plans of war now under consideration.

3. The scheme is only possible if we make nature do nearly all the work for us and use as our materials sea water and low temperature. The scheme will be destroyed if it involves the movement of very large numbers of men and a heavy tonnage of steel or concrete to the remote recesses of the Arctic night.

[1] 'Habbakuk': the proposal to use artificial icebergs as staging posts for aircraft in the Atlantic.
[2] Chief of Combined Operations, Admiral Lord Louis Mountbatten.

4. Something like the following procedure suggests itself to me. Go to an icefield in the far north which is six or seven feet thick but capable of being approached by ice-breakers; cut out the pattern of the ice-ship on the surface; bring the right number of pumping appliances to the different sides of the ice-deck; spray salt water on continually so as to increase the thickness and smooth the surface. As this process goes on the berg will sink lower in the water. There is no reason why at the intermediate stages a trellis-work of steel cables should not be laid to increase the rate of sinking and give stability. The increasing weight and depth of the berg will help to detach the structure from the surrounding ice-deck. It would seem that at least 100 feet in depth should be secured. The necessary passages of oil fuel storage and motive power can be left at the proper stages. At the same time, somewhere on land the outfit of huts, workshops and so forth will be made. When the berg begins to move southward, so that it is clear of the ice floes, vessels can come alongside and put all the equipment, including ample flak, on board.

Anthony Eden: diary
('The Eden Memoirs, The Reckoning', page 356)

7 December 1942

Oliver[1] lunched with me. Maisky turned up at No. 10 with message from Joe.[2] This was disappointing as to meeting.[3] Winston asked me to stay when he had gone and began to argue that Thursday's debate[4] must be postponed. I contested this, and argument got us nowhere. I told him House would resent postponement and country's suspicions of Darlan business be increased. He said that my leadership of the House was 'febrile', and that not one person in a hundred was worried about Darlan anyway.

[...]

---

[1] Lyttelton.
[2] Stalin, saying that he could not leave the front.
[3] Of Churchill, Roosevelt, and Stalin.
[4] The Secret Session debate, scheduled for December 10, on the developments in North Africa.

Clementine Churchill to Winston S. Churchill
(Churchill papers, 20/98)

8 December 1942

Winston,

You will remember that Margot was very anxious that we should go and see a play called 'Flare Path'[1] (It is very good) produced by her son Puffin.[2] She now writes to say that if we do not go soon the play will be taken off.

The play is at six, so one would have dinner afterwards. I can see no day this week except Friday – on which afternoon we should be going to Chequers. What about next week? Would you like to go on Monday evening, the 14th, or Wednesday the 16th?

Clemmie

Winston S. Churchill to Clementine Churchill
(Churchill papers, 20/98)

8 December 1942

I cannot escape any of these days – except this Friday – and that is putting off going down to Chequers.

Clementine Churchill to Margot, Countess of Oxford and Asquith
(Churchill papers, 20/98)

9 December 1942

Dearest Margot,

I am so very disappointed as I should have loved to take Winston to 'Flare Path', but he simply cannot make it. I suggested three evenings next week, but he cannot escape on any of these days from his over-mastering work. I am so sorry.

I have seen it myself and thought it was a beautiful play. It is a real loss to Winston as he loves the theatre.

Yours affectionately,
CSC

---

[1] *Flare Path*: a play written by Terence Rattigan (1911–77) in 1941. The story is about a love triangle between a pilot, his wife, and a film star. It takes place in a hotel near Bomber Command.

[2] Hon. Anthony Asquith, 1902–68. Known as 'Puffin'. Son of 1st Earl and Countess of Oxford and Asquith. Educated at Winchester and Balliol College, Oxford. Film director. A Governor of British Film Institute. President, Association of Cinematograph, Television, and Allied Technicians. Fellow, British Film Academy. Commander of the Order of Al Merito della Repubblica (Italy).

Winston S. Churchill to President Franklin D. Roosevelt
(Churchill papers, 20/84)

9 December 1942
Personal and Secret
No. 226

I should like to read your No. 214 to the House in Secret Session on Thursday as there is a good deal of uneasiness about Darlan which the reading of the above message would clear away. There is nothing in it which could be harmful even if published but you may be sure Parliament will observe the strictest secrecy.

President Franklin D. Roosevelt to Winston S. Churchill
(Churchill papers, 20/84)

9 December 1942
Personal and Most Secret
No. 232

Very glad to have you read my no. 214 in Secret Session Thursday.

You might add from me if you wish that General Eisenhower has definite instructions from me to enter into no agreement or bilateral contract with Admiral Darlan, but that all decisions by Eisenhower shall be unilateral on our part, and shall take the form of announcements from the military Commander-in-Chief of our armed forces.

Furthermore I hope you will call attention to the fact that Dakar instead of being a menace is today open to use by British and American ships and planes in the prosecution of the war.

Winston S. Churchill to President Franklin D. Roosevelt
(Cabinet papers, 65/28)

9 December 1942
Personal and Secret
No. 227

SOL[1]

I have been disturbed by reports received during the last few days from North Africa about conditions in French Morocco and Algeria.

---

[1] SOL: Service d'ordre legionnaire (Legionary Order of Service). A French Fascist militia, created by Joseph Darnand (1897–1945), that collaborated with Nazi Germany and fought the French Resistance. After 'Torch' stripped Vichy France of control of North Africa, SOL was granted autonomy from Vichy, whereupon it took the name Milice française (French Militia).

These reports, which come from independent and reliable sources, all paint the same picture of the results which follow from our inability in existing circumstances to exercise a proper control over the local French authorities in internal matters. You are, I am sure, fully aware of this state of affairs, but I think it my duty to let you know the position as it appears in the light of our own reports.

2. These reports show that the SOL and kindred Fascist organisations continue their activities and victimise our former French sympathisers, some of whom have not yet been released from prison. The first reaction of these organisations to the Allied landing was, rightly, one of fear, but it seems that they have now taken courage to regroup themselves and continue their activities. Well-known German sympathisers who had been ousted have been reinstated. Not only have our enemies been thus encouraged, but our friends have been correspondingly confused and cast down. There have been cases of French soldiers being punished for desertion because they tried to support the Allied forces during their landing.

3. There is an almost complete absence of control on the Franco-Spanish frontier. The result of this is that undesirables of all sorts, including Axis agents, cross the frontier in both directions, carrying information to the enemy and preparing trouble for us throughout North Africa. Unless proper control is instituted soon, our military operations may be endangered and we may witness sabotage in North Africa on a large scale and other incidents of a serious nature which may culminate in risings in various parts of North Africa. There is no Allied control of postal and telegraph censorship, and therefore nothing to stop enemy agents from writing and telegraphing information to Europe. One informant, for example, states that certain Germanophile Spanish consuls in the French Zone send full reports about the military situation by telephone and telegraph to the Spanish High Commissioner at Tetuan.

4. Veiled anti-Allied propaganda continues in the press and on the radio and positive enemy propaganda increases daily.

5. In short, elements hostile to the United Nations are being consolidated within the administration and conditions are being created which will make North Africa a favourable resort for Axis trouble-makers. If we were to suffer serious setbacks in Tunisia, the Axis may be relied upon to exploit the situation to the full, and there is no knowing what difficulties we may not then encounter even at the hand of those Frenchmen who now appear to be co-operating with us.

6. It occurs to me that there is one step that we might usefully take, and that is to see that such good friends of ours as Generals Bethouard[1] and Mast[2] are appointed to high military commands in Morocco. Mast is at present serving as Giraud's liaison officer at Allied Headquarters, while Bethouard has been sent to Gibraltar to perform non-existent liaison duties. It is a pity that men like these, who took such grave risks on our behalf, should not be in active employment. Bethouard, who commanded a division at Casablanca, would be particularly useful in Morocco, where a man of his stamp seems to be badly needed.

7. All of this reinforces the need for immediate political and administrative help for Eisenhower. As you know, we are very ready to give any assistance in our power.

Winston S. Churchill: speech
('Secret Session Speeches')

10 December 1942   House of Commons

ADMIRAL DARLAN AND THE NORTH AFRICAN LANDINGS

I have first of all an announcement to make about the unshackling of prisoners. Last week the Germans officially informed the International Red Cross that they intended to unshackle all prisoners for the Christmas week. We had previously suggested to the protecting power that they should ask both countries to unshackle and we had told them that we would immediately comply with such a request. The protecting power has now made the request and instructions have been given by us to unshackle the German prisoners in our hands on December 12. I do not know what the response of the Germans to the protecting power will be, but in view of their statement about unshackling for Christmas there certainly seems a good chance that they will relieve our officers

---

[1] Antoine Béthouart, 1889–1982. General Officer Commanding 1st Light Chasseurs Division in Norway, and French Expeditionary Force, 1940. Commanding Officer Subdivision Morocco, 1940–2. Head of French Military Mission to the United States, 1942–3. Chief of National Defence Staff and Chief of Staff, 1st Army, 1944. General Officer Commanding French troops in Austria, 1945–6. Retired, 1950.

[2] Charles Emmanuel Mast, 1889–1977. French Military Attaché to Tokyo, 1932–7. Commanding Officer, 137th Infantry Regiment, 1938. General Officer Commanding 3rd North African Infantry Division, 1940. Imprisoned after Battle of France, 1940–1. Released and made General Officer Commanding March Division Algeria, 1941; Casablanca, 1942. Head of French Military Mission to Syria and Egypt, 1943. Resident-General of Tunisia, 1943–7. Director of Institut des Hautes Études de Défense Nationale (Institute of Higher National Defense Studies), 1947–50. Retired, 1950.

and men from the indignities they so wrongfully inflicted upon them. At any rate, that is what we are going to do.

I should like to make it clear that we have never had any object but to get our men unchained and it remains to be seen whether we shall achieve that object or not. There has never been in our minds any thought of reprisals in the sense of inflicting cruelty for cruelty's sake. On the other hand, it does not do to give way to a bully like Hitler. I am aware that many good people have criticized the action we took, but it may be that that action and the timing of its cessation will produce the result we aimed at, namely, the relief of our men. If so, it will be a matter for general satisfaction. In order that the Swiss action may have the best chance of success, the House will realize the importance of discretion in public discussion during the next few days.

I now come to certain aspects of the considerable enterprise which we and the United States have launched in French Northwest Africa, to which for convenience some months ago I gave the code name of 'Torch'.

On August 26, on my return from Moscow I telegraphed as follows to President Roosevelt:

As I see this operation, it is primarily political in its foundations. The first victory we have to win is to avoid a battle. The second, if we cannot avoid it, to win it. In order to give us the best chances of the first victory we must (a) present the maximum appearance of overwhelming strength at the moment of the first attack, and (b) attack at as many places as possible. This is an absolutely different kind of operation from the Dieppe business. There we were up against German efficiency and the steel-bound, fortified coasts of France. In 'Torch' we have to face, at the worst, weak, divided opposition and an enormous choice of striking points at which to land. Risks and difficulties will be doubled by delay and will far outstrip increase of our forces. Careful planning in every detail, safety first in every calculation, far-seeing provisions for a long-term campaign, to meet every conceivable adverse contingency, however admirable in theory, will ruin the enterprise in fact.

In order to lighten the burden of responsibility on the military commanders, I am of opinion that you and I should lay down the political data and take the risk upon ourselves. In my view, it would be reasonable to assume (a) that Spain will not go to war with Britain and the United States on account of 'Torch'; (b) that it will be at least two months before the Germans can force their way through Spain or procure some accommodation from her; (c) that the French resistance in North Africa will be largely token resistance, capable of being overcome by the suddenness and scale of the attack, and that thereafter the North African French may actively help us under their own Commanders; (d) that Vichy will not declare war on the United States and Great Britain; (e) that Hitler will put extreme pressure on Vichy, but that in October he will not have the forces available to overrun unoccupied France while at the same time we keep him pinned in the Pas de Calais, etc.

The last of these forecasts was falsified because the French never made any resistance to the overrunning of the Unoccupied Zone, but all the others have so far been borne out by events. I quote them to show how much politics, apart from strategy, were involved in our joint plan, and how we hoped to reduce bloodshed and risk of failure to a minimum by utilizing the help of Frenchmen who were then in the service of the Vichy government. Into this scheme of things there swam quite unexpectedly, as I shall presently relate, the very important figure of Admiral Darlan.

I do not at all wonder that this Darlan business has caused a good deal of concern in this country, and I am glad to give an explanation of it. The question, however, which we must ask ourselves is not whether we like or do not like what is going on, but what are we going to do about it. In war it is not always possible to have everything go exactly as one likes. In working with allies it sometimes happens that they develop opinions of their own. Since 1776 we have not been in the position of being able to decide the policy of the United States. This is an American expedition in which they will ultimately have perhaps two or three times as large ground forces as we have, and three times the air force. On sea the proportion is overwhelmingly in our favour, and we have, of course, given a vast amount of organization and assistance in every way. Nevertheless, the United States regards this as an American expedition under the ultimate command of the President of the United States, and they regard Northwest Africa as a war sphere which is in their keeping, just as we regard the eastern Mediterranean as a theatre for which we are responsible. We have accepted this position from the outset and are serving under their command. That does not mean we have not got a great power of representation, and I am, of course, in the closest touch with the President. It does mean, however, that neither militarily nor politically are we directly controlling the course of events. It is because it would be highly detrimental to have a debate upon American policy or Anglo-American relations in public that His Majesty's government have invited the House to come into Secret Session. In Secret Session alone can the matter be discussed without the risk of giving offence to our great Ally and also of complicating the relationships of Frenchmen, who, whatever their past, are now firing upon the Germans.

I hold no brief for Admiral Darlan. Like myself he is the object of the animosities of Herr Hitler and of Monsieur Laval. Otherwise I have nothing in common with him. But it is necessary for the House to realize that the government and to a large extent the people of the United States do not feel the same way about Darlan as we do. He has not betrayed them. He has not broken any treaty with them. He has not vilified them. He has not maltreated any of their citizens. They do not think much of him, but they do not hate him and despise him as we do over here. Many of them think more of the lives of their own soldiers than they do about the past records of French political figures. Moreover, the Americans have cultivated up to the last moment relations with Vichy, which were of a fairly intimate character and which in my opinion have conduced to our general advantage. At any rate, the position of the Americans at Vichy gave us a window on that courtyard which otherwise would not have existed.

Admiral Leahy[1] has been Ambassador to Vichy until quite recently. He lived on terms of close intimacy with Marshal Pétain. He has at all times used his influence to prevent Vichy France becoming the ally of Germany or declaring war upon us when we have had to fire on Vichy troops at Oran or Dakar, in Syria or in Madagascar. On all these occasions I have believed, and have recorded my opinion beforehand, that France would not declare war; but a factor in forming that opinion was the immense American influence upon all Frenchmen, which influence, of course, increased enormously after the United States entered the war. Admiral Leahy is a close friend of President Roosevelt and was recently appointed his personal Chief of the Staff. The attitude of the United States executive and State Department towards Vichy and all its works must be viewed against this background.

Since we broke with Vichy in 1940, this country has had no contacts with French North Africa, or only very slender and hazardous secret contacts. The Americans, on the other hand, have roamed about Morocco, Algiers, and Tunisia without the slightest impediment, with plenty of money and with a policy of trade favours to bestow. They have worked all this time, both before and after they came into the war, to predispose

[1] United States Naval Chief of Staff.

French North Africa to them, to have the closest observation of the country, to have a strong footing there, and to make all kinds of contacts with all kinds of people, especially important military and civil functionaries. When we began to plan this expedition with them they redoubled their efforts not only to acquire information and to create good will, but also to make a regular conspiracy among the high French officers there to come over with their troops to the Allies, should an American landing take place.

Great Britain is supposed in American circles to be very unpopular with the French. I do not think it is true, and certainly our troops have had the very best reception in Northwest Africa once we got ashore. Nevertheless, as we had been firing on the French on so many different occasions and in so many places, it was not worth while to contest the point. The whole enterprise therefore was organized on the basis not only of American command but of having Americans everywhere in evidence at the crucial moment of landing. If you keep in your mind the supreme object, namely, the destruction of Hitler and Hitlerism, there is no room for small points of national self-assertiveness. As long as the job is done, it does not matter much who gets the credit. We have no need to be anxious about the place which our country will occupy in the history of this war, nor, when the facts are known, about the part which we have played in the great enterprise called 'Torch'.

I now turn to examine a peculiar form of French mentality, or rather of the mentality of a large proportion of Frenchmen in the terrible defeat and ruin which has overtaken their country. I am not at all defending or still less eulogizing this French mentality. But it would be very foolish not to try to understand what is passing in other people's minds and what are the secret springs of action to which they respond. The Almighty in His infinite wisdom did not see fit to create Frenchmen in the image of Englishmen. In a state like France, which has experienced so many convulsions – Monarchy, Convention, Directory, Consulate, Empire, Monarchy, Empire, and finally Republic – there has grown up a principle founded on the *droit administratif* which undoubtedly governs the action of many French officers and officials in times of revolution and change. It is a highly legalistic habit of mind and it arises from a subconscious sense of national self-preservation against the dangers of sheer anarchy. For instance, any officer who obeys the command of his lawful superior or of one whom he believes to be his lawful superior is absolutely immune from subsequent punishment. Much, therefore, turns in the minds of French officers upon whether there is a direct, unbroken chain of lawful command, and this is held to be more important by many Frenchmen than moral, national, or international considerations. From this point of view many Frenchmen who admire General de Gaulle and envy him in his role nevertheless regard him as a man who has rebelled against the authority of the French state, which in their prostration they conceive to be vested in the person of the antique defeatist who to them is the illustrious and venerable Marshal Pétain, the hero of Verdun and the sole hope of France.

Now, all this may seem very absurd to our minds. But there is one aspect about it which is important to us. It is in accordance with orders and authority transmitted or declared to be transmitted by Marshal Pétain that the French troops in Northwest Africa have pointed and fired their rifles against the Germans and Italians instead of continuing to point and fire their rifles against the British and Americans. I am sorry to have to mention a point like that, but it makes a lot of difference to a soldier whether a man fires his gun at him or at his enemy; and even the soldier's wife or father might have a feeling about it, too.

It was the opinion of those officers who were ready to come over to our side that any admixture of de Gaullist troops at the outset would destroy all hope of a peaceful landing. Although we were prepared to bear down all opposition and in fact did overcome a very considerable degree of opposition, it is my duty to confess that neither we nor the Americans were looking for additional trouble, there being quite enough going about at the present time. The Americans, who, as I have said, were in command from the beginning, for their part refused to allow the slightest intervention of de Gaullists into this theatre.

There was, however, one French figure upon whom our hopes were set: General Giraud, a very senior French officer who was taken prisoner before the French surrender in 1940 while fighting gallantly in a tank and who a few months ago made his second remarkable and dramatic escape from German captivity. Giraud is an undoubted hero of the French Army. General Juin,[1] who commanded the important Algiers garrison and Army Corps, was ready to act as his lieutenant. From our point of view there was nothing wrong with General Giraud. We, therefore, at General

---

[1] Alphonse-Pierre Juin, 1888–1967. French Chief of Staff, North African Theatre, 1939. Imprisoned after Battle of France, 1940–1. Released, and made General Officer Commanding-in-Chief, Morocco, 1941. Commander-in-Chief, North Africa, 1942–3. General Officer Commanding French Expeditionary Corps in Italy, 1943–4. Chief of National Defence Staff, 1944–7. Resident-General of Morocco, 1947–51. Member of the Supreme War Council, 1948–54. President of Chief of Staffs' Committee, 1951–3. Marshal of France, 1952. Commander-in-Chief, Allied Forces Central Europe, 1953–6. Member of the Supreme National Defence Council, 1958–60.

Eisenhower's request, sent a British submarine under the American flag to cruise off the French Riviera coast and on the night of November 6, two days before the dawn of zero, we picked up the General, took him out to sea, transferred him to a seaplane, and brought him to Gibraltar, where he arrived on the afternoon of the seventh. We all thought General Giraud was the man for the job and that his arrival would be electrical. In this opinion General Giraud emphatically agreed and he made the most sweeping demands for plenary authority to be given to him as Supreme Commander-in-Chief of all the forces in or ever to be brought into Northwest Africa. Some hours passed in persuading him to reduce these claims to the bounds of reason.

Under the influence of General Juin, Algiers surrendered on the evening of the eighth. By the afternoon of the ninth, General Clark had established Allied Advanced Headquarters there. Here was found Admiral Darlan, who had been in our hands, though treated with all consideration since the day before. He had come back after his official tour to visit his son, who is said to be dying.

The landing at Casablanca was proceeding very slowly in the face of obstinate opposition. Large numbers of ships crammed with troops were lolling about outside the range of the forts and the U-boats were arriving on the scene in ever-increasing numbers. On four days out of five off Casablanca the surf is too great for landing on the beaches. The Americans had hitherto been astonishingly favoured by fortune in the weather, but it might have broken at any moment, and, if so, the greater part of the armada off Casablanca would have to crowd into the bay at Gibraltar or go on cruising about in the open sea among the U-boats. Although Oran capitulated on the tenth, the landing facilities there would have been wholly insufficient to deal except very slowly with double the force which we had already assigned for it. Indecisive and protracted operations in this area would have put a peculiar stress on Spain, whose interests were affected and whose fears and appetites alike might easily have been excited. It was therefore of the utmost importance to bring the fighting at Casablanca to a close as soon as possible. Of course, looking back on all these events after they have turned out right, it is not easy to recall how hazardous they looked to us, to the American Chiefs of the Staff, or to General Eisenhower beforehand and while they were going on. The United States might have lost ten thousand to twenty thousand men drowned by U-boats apart from the fighting on the beaches and the fire of the harbour batteries. Moreover, the need for speed in the whole campaign was intensely felt by us all.

Morocco and Algeria were only stepping stones to the real prize, which is Tunisia, which held and holds the key to the central Mediterranean. To get eastward with the utmost rapidity was only possible if the French would not only cease fighting, but would abstain from sabotaging railways and roads and actively assist in unloading the ships. Delay in getting eastward would give the Germans the time to fly and ferry over a powerful army, and every day lost might mean a week's heavy fighting with thousands of extra casualties. This was the situation on the tenth with which General Clark at Algiers and his superior General Eisenhower at Gibraltar had to deal.

All the high French authorities in Tunis, Algeria, and Morocco had been invited to Algiers, and most of them had complied. Darlan, Giraud, Juin, Noguès,[1] Châtel,[2] and various others were gathered. Admiral Esteva,[3] in whom we had great hopes, was held in Bizerta by the enemy. These Frenchmen wrangled together in the most bitter manner. But under the vehement pressure of United States' General Clark for a decision one way or the other, Giraud and all the other French authorities present agreed to accept Darlan as their leader and custodian of the mystical authority of the Marshal and the honour of France. Darlan, although virtually a prisoner, at first refused to do anything, but eventually, late in the afternoon, he agreed to accept General Clark's terms and to send orders by air to stop all French resistance to the Allied forces. All fighting at Casablanca thereafter ceased, though whether as the result of Darlan's order is not known, and the heavy American disembarkations began. The provisional emergency agreement made in these circumstances by General Clark and Admiral Darlan was approved, for what it was worth, by General Eisenhower. This was the beginning of the relationship with Darlan.

Next day, the eleventh, another great event occurred. Hitler overran unoccupied France in the teeth of the protests of the venerable and illustrious Marshal. This constituted a breach of the armistice. The French officers considered themselves released from its conditions. All bets were

---

[1] Auguste Noguès, 1876–1971. Commander-in-Chief of the French Forces in North Africa and Resident-General, Morocco. On 19 June 1940 de Gaulle had telegraphed to him his willingness to serve under him if he would reject the armistice. On 25 June Noguès telegraphed to the Government at Bordeaux that he was ready to continue the war. Two days later he telegraphed again, giving his support to the armistice and to Pétain, who retained him in his North African command.

[2] Yves-Charles Châtel, 1865–1944. A civilian; Governor-General of Algeria, 1941–3.

[3] Jean-Pierre Esteva, 1880–1951. French Admiral. Commander of French Naval Forces South at Toulon, 1939. After the fall of France, became Resident General of Tunisia, 1940–3. Retired, 1943. After liberation of France, arrested for failure to resist German build-up in Tunisia. Sentenced to life imprisonment. Released in 1950 owing to failing health.

off. There was a new deal. It could be said that the venerable and illustrious Marshal was no longer a free agent. His authority was therefore even more clearly held to reside in Admiral Darlan. Darlan was the only authority plainly derived from Marshal Pétain. General Giraud could not claim that authority. He had left France without the permission of Marshal Pétain and even, as was suggested, breaking his written promise to him. The remarkable thing is that General Giraud was himself impressed by the arguments of the other Frenchmen. He was quite soon convinced that he had no power whatever to influence the decision and, more than that, he seems to have felt himself at a disadvantage compared with these other Frenchmen who could prove they had obeyed the orders emanating legally from the head of the state.

On the thirteenth General Eisenhower, with Admiral Cunningham, arrived at Algiers from Gibraltar for the first time and began more formal conversations with General Clark, Admiral Darlan, General Giraud, and other French high officers. His object now was not merely to obtain a cessation of resistance but to bring the whole French military and administrative machine actively over to our side.

On the fourteenth, he telegraphed to the Combined Chiefs of Staff in Washington under whom he is serving that he had reached an agreement with the Frenchmen; that they would accept only Darlan's leadership and that Darlan would co-operate with the Allied army. The main point was that General Eisenhower recognized Admiral Darlan as the supreme French authority in Northwest Africa. This was not a treaty. It was an arrangement made by the American Commander-in-Chief in the field with the local authorities to facilitate the safe landing of his troops and the eastward movement of his army. Not only all the American generals but Admiral Cunningham, who knows the Mediterranean from end to end and who had been in the 'Torch' enterprise for several months, and also the representatives of the Foreign Office and the State Department who were present, strongly urged acceptance of the subsequent written agreement by their governments. All the French forces and officials came over to our side, thus relieving the Americans of the anxieties and difficulties which a forcible taking over of the administration of these vast regions would have imposed upon them and us, and of the still more imminent risk of sabotage of our communications to the eastward. Giraud was appointed by Darlan Commander-in-Chief and hastened to rally the French troops to their new allegiance. The French garrison in Tunis, who had made no resistance to the German landings, which had already begun there, marched out of the city to the westward and took up positions facing east against the Germans. Fraternization ensued between the British, American, and French soldiers. The populace, whose sympathies were never in doubt, but who in some places seemed sunk in coma and in bewilderment, became enthusiastic, and the whole enterprise proceeded with speed and vigor. So much for what happened on the spot.

In these emergency transactions His Majesty's government had not been consulted in any way; nor did we know the details of all the violent events which were happening. The decision which the President had to take was whether to disavow or endorse what his General had done. He backed him up. The question before us was whether we should repudiate General Eisenhower at the risk of a very serious break with the United States. I have no doubt whatever that we should have been very careless of the lives of our men and of the interests of the common cause if we had done anything of the kind. However, on November 17 I telegraphed to the President in the following sense:

> I ought to let you know that very deep currents of feeling are stirred by the arrangement with Darlan. The more I reflect upon it the more convinced I become that it can only be a temporary expedient justifiable solely by the stress of battle. We must not overlook the serious political injury which may be done to our cause, not only in France but throughout Europe, by the feeling that we are ready to make terms with the local Quislings. A permanent arrangement with Darlan or the formation of a Darlan government in French North Africa would not be understood by the great masses of ordinary people whose simple loyalties are our strength.
>
> My own feeling is that we should get on with the fighting and let that overtake the parleys, and we are all very glad to hear that General Eisenhower expects to be able to order the leading elements of our First Army to attack the Germans in Tunis and Bizerta in the course of the next few days.

On this the President a few hours later made the statement to his press conference which was published and gave so much general satisfaction. To me he telegraphed at midnight on the seventeenth the text of the statement he had just given out at his press conference:

> I have accepted General Eisenhower's political arrangements for the time being in Northern and Western Africa. I thoroughly understand and approve the feeling in the United States and Great

Britain, and among all the other United Nations, that in view of the history of the past two years no permanent arrangement should be made with Admiral Darlan. People in the United Nations likewise would never understand the recognition of a reconstituting of the Vichy government in France or in any French territory. We are opposed to Frenchmen who support Hitler and the Axis.

No one in our Army has any authority to discuss the future government of France and the French Empire. The future French government will be established not by any individual in metropolitan France or overseas but by the French people themselves after they have been set free by the victory of the United Nations. The present temporary arrangement in North and West Africa is only a temporary expedient, justified solely by the stress of battle.

The present temporary arrangement has accomplished two military objectives. The first was to save American and British lives on the one hand and French lives on the other hand. The second was the vital factor of time. The temporary arrangement has made it possible to avoid a 'mopping up' period in Algiers and Morocco which might have taken a month or two to consummate. Such a period would have delayed the concentration for the attack from the west on Tunis, and we hope on Tripoli.

Every day of delay in the current operation would have enabled the Germans and Italians to build up a strong resistance, to dig in and make a huge operation on our part essential before we could win. Here again, many more lives will be saved under the present speedy offensive than if we had had to delay it for a month or more. It will also be noted that French troops under the command of General Giraud have already been in action against the enemy in Tunisia, fighting by the side of American and British soldiers for the liberation of their country. Admiral Darlan's proclamation assisted in making a 'mopping up' period unnecessary. Temporary arrangements made with Admiral Darlan apply, without exception, to the current local situation only. I have requested the liberation of all persons in Northern Africa who had been imprisoned because they opposed the efforts of the Nazis to dominate the world, and I have asked for the abrogation of all laws and decrees inspired by Nazi governments or Nazi ideologists. Reports indicate that the French of North Africa are subordinating all political questions to the formation of a common front against the common enemy.

It seemed to me that these statements by the President safeguard what I may call the long-term policy, and we should do very well to rest upon them. I must, however, say that personally I consider that in the circumstances prevailing General Eisenhower was right, and even if he was not quite right I should have been very reluctant to hamper or impede his action when so many lives and such vitally important issues hung in the balance. I do not want to shelter myself in any way behind the Americans or anyone else.

Now, how far are we committed to Admiral Darlan? There is no doubt that if you ask for a man's help and he gives it in a manner that is most valuable to you, on the faith of an agreement entered into amid dangers which are thereby relieved, you have contracted a certain obligation towards him. I do not want the House to have any illusions about this. Both governments had undoubtedly the right to reject General Eisenhower's agreement with Admiral Darlan, but in view of what had happened it is perfectly clear that a certain obligation had been contracted towards him. More than that, we had benefited greatly from the assistance we had received. I do not consider that any long-term or final agreement has been entered into. I do not consider that the agreement is a document to be interpreted by legalistic processes. It is a question of fair dealing, and of this General Eisenhower is in the first instance the judge. He states that he does not consider that he is in any way bound permanently to Admiral Darlan. He claims that he has the sole right of interpretation. Darlan and the other French leaders are certainly in his power, and I for my part hope that he will interpret his obligations in a reasonable and honourable manner, even to a man like Darlan.

Since then events have moved at a gallop. The American and British armies, several hundreds of thousands strong, with all their complicated and ponderous tackle, have now landed and are in control of the whole of French Northwest Africa, an area over nine hundred miles long from west to east, with the exception only of the twenty or thirty miles of the Tunisian tip on which the Germans and Italians are endeavouring to build up an array and where the Germans are desperately and vigorously resisting. The whole French Army and administration are working wholeheartedly on the side of the Allies. It is much too late for their leaders to turn back now. We need their aid, but they are in our power. The French troops have fought well on two occasions. On the first, six hundred of them repelled a German attack without yielding an inch of ground, although they suffered twenty-five per cent casualties. On the second, supported by United States artillery and some parachutists, they destroyed a German battle group at Faid and took the position together with one hundred prisoners, mostly German. They are guarding a long line from about forty miles south of the Mediterranean down to the Tripolitanian frontier, holding back the German and Italian patrols and pressing forward as far as their strength allows towards Sfax and Gabès. As our troops come up we shall reinforce them strongly. Meanwhile Admiral Darlan succeeded in bringing the whole of French West Africa, including the key strategic base of Dakar, to our side against the enemy. I asked the President whether I might refer to certain secret telegrams and I have just received the following from him:

> You might add from me if you wish that General Eisenhower has definite instructions from me to enter into no agreement or bilateral contract with Admiral Darlan, but that all decisions by Eisenhower shall be unilateral on our part, and shall take the form of announcements from the military Commander-in-Chief of our Armed Forces. Furthermore, I hope you will call attention to the fact that Dakar, instead of being a menace, is today open to use by British and American ships and planes in the prosecution of the war.

The advantages of Dakar coming over are enormous, and saved us a costly and perhaps bloody expedition. We are to have all the facilities of the port. The United States deal for us in the matter; they have adopted the claims the Admiralty made and we are to share with them all these facilities. The powerful modern battleship *Richelieu* can go to the United States to be completed. Other French vessels are being formed into a squadron which obeys the orders of Admiral Darlan. Darlan is actively endeavouring through his emissaries to persuade Admiral Godfrey, who commands the French squadron interned in Alexandria Harbour, and is paid by us, to come out on our side. So far he has not succeeded, but we are hopeful. Questions of honour appear to be specially complicated in this case.

All this is done in the sacred name of the Marshal, and when the Marshal bleats over the telephone orders to the contrary and deprives Darlan of his nationality, the Admiral rests comfortably upon the fact or fiction, it does not much matter which, that the Marshal is acting under the duress of the invading Hun, and that he, Darlan, is still carrying out his true wishes. In fact, if Admiral Darlan had to shoot Marshal Pétain he would no doubt do it in Marshal Pétain's name.

While all this has been going on, Admiral Darlan was naturally some-what affected by the President's outspoken declaration and other state-ments which reached his ears. It may be of interest to hear a letter which he wrote to General Clark. We are not called upon to approve or sympa-thize with his position, but it is just as well to understand it:

Monsieur le General,

Information from various sources tends to substantiate the view that 'I am only a lemon which the Americans will drop after they have squeezed it dry'.

In the line of conduct which I have adopted out of pure French patriotic feeling, in spite of the serious disadvantages which it entails for me, at the moment when it was extremely easy for me to let events take their course without my intervention, my own personal position does not come into consideration.

I acted only because the American government has solemnly undertaken to restore the integrity of French sovereignty as it existed in 1939, and because the armistice between the Axis and France was broken by the total occupation of metropolitan France, against which the Marshal has solemnly protested.

I did not act through pride, ambition, nor calculation, but because the position which I occupied in my country made it my duty to act.

When the integrity of France's sovereignty is an accomplished fact and I hope that it will be in the least possible time it is my firm intention to return to private life and to end my days, in the course of which I have ardently served my country, in retirement.

During the last summer I have established close and friendly relations with General Eisenhower. I do not think I can give a better general pic-ture of the situation than the latest message which he has sent to me. It was dispatched on December 5:

In the political field it is easily evident that our war communications system has not served us well in trying to keep you fully informed. This has been aggravated by the fact that difficulties in censorship here have permitted rumours to go out that have no foundation in truth. Among these stories is one that the American military authorities are dealing with Darlan about matters that have noth-ing to do with the local military situation, and are supporting his claims to a permanent authority rather than as merely the tempo-rary head of the local government. Nothing could be further from the fact. Admiral Cunningham, Mr Mack,[1] Brigadier Whiteley,[2] and other British officers are kept closely and intimately informed of all moves made, both in our local dealings with Darlan and in the weary process we have been going through in straightening out the Dakar tangle. At every meeting with Darlan, I tell him that so far as this headquarters is concerned, he is at the head of a local *de facto* organization by means of which we are enabled to secure the co-operation, both military and civil, that we need for the prosecution of this campaign. He knows I am not empowered to go further than this.

I assure you again that we are not entering a cabal designed to place Darlan at the head of anything except the local organization. Here he is entirely necessary, for he and he alone is the source of every bit of practical help we have received. If you will contemplate the situation existing along our lines of communication, which extend five hundred miles from here through mountainous country to Tunisia, you will understand that the local French could, without fear of detection, so damage us that we would have to retreat hurriedly back to ports from which we could supply ourselves by sea. Giraud quickly gave up trying to help us and it was only through Darlan's help that we are now fighting the Boche in Tunisia instead of somewhere in the vicinity of Bone or even west of that. It appears to us that both Boisson[3] and Darlan are committed irrevocably to an Allied victory...

The military prospects depend upon several factors, of which the most important is our ability to build up fighter cover for our ground troops. This, in turn, depends upon getting supplies, establishing forward fields, and maintaining a rapid flow of fighter craft until the battle is won. It depends also upon weather, until we can get steel mats on all our mud fields. The next thing we must do is

---

[1] William H. B. Mack, Foreign Office French Department. Civil Liaison officer in Algiers.

[2] Sir John Francis Martin Whiteley, 1896–1970. Deputy Director of Organization, Middle East Command, 1940–2. Brigadier-General, Staff 8th Army, North Africa, 1942. Deputy Chief of Staff, Middle East, 1942–3. Deputy Chief of Staff, Allied Forces Headquarters, 1943–4. Chief Army Instructor at Imperial Defence College, 1945. Commandant of Canadian Army Staff College, Canada, 1947–9. Deputy Chief of the Imperial General Staff, War Office, 1949–53. Head of Joint British Services Mission to Washington, 1953–6. Retired, 1956.

[3] Pierre François Boisson, 1894–1948. Governor-General of French West Africa, 1938–9, 1940–3; of French Equatorial Africa, 1939–40. High Commissioner at Dakar. Initially loyal to Vichy regime; opposed Allies during the Battle of Dakar, September 1940. On 7 December 1942, transferred loyalty to Admiral Darlan and the Allies. Described by de Gaulle in his memoirs as the man 'whom Roosevelt expected one day to open to him the gates of Africa' (*The Call to Honour*, page 210).

to get forward every available scrap of ground reinforcement and replacements for troops now on the line, who need a short rest. In addition, we must get our communication lines to work so well that all ground and air troops will be assured of adequate reserves when more intensive fighting starts again. The third great factor is our ability to prevent rapid reinforcement by the enemy. Our bombing fields are now so far removed from targets that the scale of our air bombing is not what we should like, but we are doing our best. Finally, during all this we must provide adequate protection for our land and sea lines of communication, especially our ports. All these jobs strain our resources and keep everyone going at top speed, but we shall yet get them done. But all this shows you how dependent we are upon French passive and active co-operation and, so far, we have no evidence of reluctance on Darlan's part to help us.

It is very necessary that the two governments and, if I may say so, the President and I, keep very closely together, as we are doing. After all, what is it we want? We want the maximum possible united French effort against the common enemy. This, I believe, can be achieved, but it can only be achieved gradually and it will best be achieved by the action of Frenchmen. If Admiral Darlan proceeds to render important services, he will undoubtedly deserve consideration in spite of his record, but that consideration gives him no permanent claims even upon the future of the French possessions which have rallied to him, still less upon the future of France.

The Germans by their oppression will soon procure for us the unity of metropolitan France. That unity can now only take an anti-German form. In such a movement the spirit of the Fighting French must be continually in the ascendant. Their reward will come home on the tide. We must try to bring about as speedily as possible a working arrangement and ultimately a consolidation between all Frenchmen outside the German power. The character and constitution of Admiral Darlan's government must be continuously modified by the introduction of fresh and, from our point of view, clean elements. We have the right and I believe we have the power to effect these necessary transformations so long as Great Britain and the United States act harmoniously together. But meanwhile, above all, let us get on with the war.

I must say I think he is a poor creature with a jaundiced outlook and disorganized loyalties who in all this tremendous African episode, west and east alike, can find no point to excite his interest except the arrangements made between General Eisenhower and Admiral Darlan.

The struggle for the Tunisian tip is now rising to its climax and the main battle impends. Another trial of strength is very near on the frontiers of Cyrenaica. Both these battles will be fought almost entirely by soldiers from this island. The 1st and 8th British Armies will be engaged to the full. I cannot take my thoughts away from them and their fortunes, and I expect that will be the feeling of the House of Commons.

The House will, I believe, feel that it is being well and faithfully served by His Majesty's government. I ask them to support us in refusing to do anything at this juncture which might add to the burdens and losses of our troops. I ask them to give their confidence to the government and to believe in their singleness and inflexibility of purpose. I ask them to treat with proper reprobation that small, busy and venomous band who harbour and endeavour to propagate unworthy and unfounded suspicions, and so to come forward unitedly with us in all the difficulties through which we are steadfastly and successfully making our way.

Winston S. Churchill: speech – words omitted from the published version
(Churchill papers, 9/156)

10 December 1942   House of Commons

ADMIRAL DARLAN AND THE NORTH AFRICAN LANDINGS

I must now say a word about General de Gaulle. On behalf of His Majesty's Government I exchanged letters with him in 1940 recognising him as the Leader of all Free Frenchmen wherever they might be, who would rally to him, in support of the Allied cause. We have most scrupulously kept our engagements with him and have done everything in our power to help him. We finance his Movement. We have helped his operations. But we have never recognised him as representing France. We have never agreed that he and those associated with him, because they were right and brave at the moment of French surrender, have a monopoly on the future of France. I have lived myself for the last 35 years or more in a mental relationship and to a large extent in sympathy with an abstraction called France. I still do not think it is an illusion. I cannot feel that de Gaulle is France, still less that Darlan and Vichy are France. France is something greater, more complex, more formidable than any of these sectional manifestations.

I have tried to work as far as possible with General de Gaulle, making allowances for his many difficulties, for his temperament and for the limitations of his outlook. In order to sustain his Movement at the moment of the American occupation of French North Africa and to console him and his friends for their exclusion from the enterprise we agreed to his nominee, General le Gentilhomme, being proclaimed as High Commissioner for Madagascar, although this adds somewhat to our difficulties in pacifying that large island, which oddly as it seems to us would much prefer Darlan. We are at the present time endeavouring to rally Jibuti to the Free French Movement. Therefore I consider that we have been in every respect faithful in the discharge of our obligations to de Gaulle, and we shall so continue to the end.

However now we are in Secret Session the House must not be led to believe that General de Gaulle is an unfaltering friend of Britain. On the contrary, I think he is one of those good Frenchmen who have a traditional antagonism engrained in French hearts by centuries of war against the English. On his way back from Syria in the summer of 1941 through the French Central and West African Colonies he left a trail of anglophobia behind him. On August 25, 1941, he gave an interview to the Correspondent of the *Chicago Daily News* at Brazzaville in which he suggested that England coveted the African Colonies of France, and said:

England is afraid of the French Fleet. What in effect England is carrying out is a war-time deal with Hitler in which Vichy serves as a go-between.

He explained that Vichy served Germany by keeping the French people in subjection and England by keeping the fleet out of German hands. All this and much more was very ungrateful talk, but we have allowed no complaint of ours to appear in public.

Again this year in July General de Gaulle wished to visit Syria. He promised me before I agreed to facilitate his journey, which I was very well able to stop, that he would behave in a helpful and friendly manner, but no sooner did he get to Cairo than he adopted a most hectoring attitude and in Syria his whole object seemed to be to foment ill-will between the British military and the Free French civil administrations and state the French claims to rule Syria at the highest, although it had been agreed that after the war, and as much as possible even during the war, the Syrians are to enjoy their independence.

I continue to maintain friendly personal relations with General de Gaulle and I help him as much as I possibly can. I feel bound to do this because he stood up against the Men of Bordeaux and their base surrender at a time when all resisting will-power had quitted France. All the same, I could not recommend you to base all your hopes and confidence upon him, and still less to assume at this stage that it is our duty to place, so far as we have the power, the destiny of France in his hands. Like the President in the telegram I have read, we seek to base ourselves on the will of the entire French nation rather than any sectional manifestations even the most worthy.

Winston S. Churchill to President Franklin D. Roosevelt
(Churchill papers, 20/84)

10 December 1942
Personal and Secret
No. 228

I have never seen the House so unanimous as it was today in Secret Session. I explained the whole story to them and they understood it as well as you and I do ourselves. Your message was much appreciated. I am going to send you a message tomorrow about Joe. I suspect he thought he would have put across [two missing words] him by us both (quote) No second front in 1943 (unquote) and that he thought he might just as well get that by post as verbally. We have got to go into the whole of this matter again. I am most grieved not to meet you and still hope we may fix it. But anyhow in the interval surely you will let Marshall, Arnold and King come over here with Harry to survey the new scene with your faithful friends. Every day counts.

Harold Nicolson: diary
('Harold Nicolson, Diaries and Letters', page 266)

10 December 1942

Secret Session on North Africa and Darlan. It is opened by Winston who speaks for an hour, and I have never heard him more forceful, informative or convincing. He refers to Pétain (whose name he pronounces as 'Peatayne') as that 'antique defeatist'. He convinces us (a) that we were never consulted about the Darlan move; (b) that when it happened, he himself realised at once what trouble would be caused, and warned Roosevelt accordingly; (c) that it is purely temporary. [...]

Winston S. Churchill: recollection
('The Hinge of Fate', page 576)

10 December 1942

I do not remember any speech out of hundreds which I made where I felt opinion change so palpably and decisively. This was no case for applause, but only for results. The Commons were convinced, and the fact that all further Parliamentary opposition stopped after the Secret Session quenched the hostile Press and reassured the country. There was also the growing exhilaration of victory after so many hard months of disappointment or defeat.

David Lloyd George to Winston S. Churchill
(Sir John Martin papers)

10 December 1942   10 Downing Street

A REMARK AT LUNCHEON

I've had my show. This is your show and I don't want to interfere with it.

Winston S. Churchill to John Curtin
(Churchill papers, 20/88)

10 December 1942
Most Secret and Personal

Thank you very much for the very full explanation of your difficulties which you have been kind enough to send me. The fact that the New Zealand Division is to remain in the Middle East makes it easier for us to meet your wishes. Shipping will be arranged at the end of January to repatriate all you wish in personnel and for the minimum equipment which you require. I am having your list examined by the Staffs and the details will be communicated to you as soon as possible. The 9th Australian Division will carry with them from the African Desert a splendid reputation and the honour of having played a leading part in a memorable victory for the Empire and the common cause.

2. The United States have preferred to have one British armoured carrier and keep their own *Ranger* instead of sending us *Ranger* and taking two armoured carriers from us. We should have preferred the latter plan,

because it would have given us more say in the tasks to be set us. Still, there will be two more carriers in the Pacific as a result of the moves.

All good wishes.

Winston S. Churchill to General Sir Harold Alexander
(Churchill papers, 20/84)

11 December 1942
Immediate
Private and Most Secret

It might be well for you to give a friendly hint from me to General Montgomery about the disadvantages of his making confident statements that he will beat and out-wit Rommel before the impending battle has been fought. I hear a certain amount of unfavourable comment from those who have the highest admiration for Montgomery's military qualities. Will he not seem foolish if as is possible there is no battle at Agheila and Rommel slips away.[1]

Winston S. Churchill to Field Marshal Sir John Dill
(Churchill papers, 20/84)

11 December 1942
Immediate
Personal and Most Secret

[...]

2. The great thing is to build up a powerful long-range bombing force in the Tunisian tip when we get it (bracket) repeat (bracket) when we get it. Britain and USA must not resign themselves to playing the minor hand in 'Brimstone'[2] and 'Husky'[3] unless we are absolutely sure we cannot assume the major role in the Channel and thereabouts.

[...]

---

[1] On 16 December 1942, Alexander telegraphed to Churchill: 'I have myself given your message to Montgomery and trust that all will be well in future. The reporters statement was inaccurate and should have referred to the battle of El Alamein and not to Agheila. Montgomery tells me that he made no such boast about the latter' ('Private and Most Secret', *Churchill papers, 20/85*).

[2] 'Brimstone': capture of Sardinia.

[3] 'Husky': capture of Sicily.

Winston S. Churchill to Sir James Grigg
(Churchill papers, 20/67)

11 December 1942

REMOVAL OF REGIMENTAL BADGES

I have several times made it plain that I do not approve of measures which tend to weaken the pride of officers and soldiers in their regiments. I spoke to the Adjutant-General[1] about this some time ago in connection with drafting. Of course, in the stress of world war it may be necessary to post men to units different from those which they joined or from those which represent the part of the country from which they come. This process should be kept at a minimum. The fact, however, that there must be a good deal of it makes it all the more indispensable to invest all combatant units with a clear sense of individual characteristics and distinction. The above applies particularly to the units serving in the Home Forces and Northern Ireland, who are not in contact with the enemy, and have to endure a long and trying period of waiting.

2. Badges and distinguishing marks, whether divisional or regimental, have an important military value and are well worth the modest expense that they entail. The proof of the desire and need for badges is found in the fact that a considerable number of regiments and corps have provided them at their own expense in spite of War Office discouragement. The recent order which instructed all units to divest themselves of these badges, many of which the men had paid for themselves, has caused a great deal of needless heart-burning and is, in my opinion as Minister of Defence, definitely detrimental to morale. When I visited the Welsh Division they were in process of being stripped of their badges, and the Divisional Commander,[2] as well as many of the regimental officers, in reply to my questions and with my full authorisation, expressed their regret at this deprivation and informed me that it caused distress among the troops. The Commander-in-Chief, Sir Bernard Paget, who was with me, expressed similar views and should certainly have been consulted before any such sweeping step was taken.

3. The argument about expense and the time it would take to make the issue is based on wrong and needlessly extravagant assumptions. The report, which has been furnished me at my request by the Minister of Supply,[3] shows that the War Office based their objections on the

[1] Ronald Adam.
[2] Robert Ross.
[3] Sir Andrew Duncan.

facts, first, that the whole army must have the flashes; secondly, that a preference was expressed that all these flashes should be embroidered; and, thirdly, that 20,400,000 flashes would be required. Even on this extravagant basis, adopted as it might well seem to make difficulties, only 85,000 yards of cotton cloth would be required for a long time to come, as compared with a normal consumption of about 8 million yards of cloth a week. If the badges are printed instead of being embroidered, the labour needed will be the equivalent of 65 men and 102 women working for one week, and the Ministry of Supply estimate that it would take six months and not four years, as estimated by you, to complete the above demand. Samples of the printed flashes, for which I called, are attached to this minute.

4. I also attach a statement I have received from the President of the Board of Trade, which shows that the matter was not raised by the Board of Trade as a necessary step in public economy.

5. Accordingly, I have reached the conclusion that the wearing of the badges, &c., should be resumed from the 1st January, 1943. Those units which already possess badges should be authorised to mount them at that date, whether they are embroidered or not. An issue of printed badges should be made with the utmost speed to the other units. The issue will, in the first instance, be limited to the personnel of the combatant units in the United Kingdom, beginning first with the divisions of the Home Forces and Northern Ireland. As the total number of men in the Home Forces and Northern Ireland is stated by the War Office to be about 710,000, I do not see why so extravagant a figure as 20,400,000 badges should be required. At four per man, this would amount to 3 million only. However, 10 million should be ordered to provide for unforeseen contingencies and wearing out. Rather than not have the badges or flashes at all, it would be well to have them mounted on one shoulder only, thus halving the expense and labour. This, however, is so modest that the question need not be raised in 1943.

6. I have also considered the argument which you advance, that the discipline of the Army will be affected if directions recently given by the War Office are countermanded. I do not consider there is any valid force in this. The War Office frequently make mistakes which entail alterations of policy. In this particular case the War Office has departed from the whole policy laid down by Mr Eden when Secretary of State for War. Moreover, by fixing the date as the 1st January, an interval of several weeks is provided between the latest Army Council instruction and the announcement of the new policy.

7. Should you desire to bring the matter before the Cabinet, I will arrange to have a special meeting next Tuesday morning, at which I should ask my colleagues to sustain my decision as Minister of Defence. I may add that I have already ascertained that it would be agreeable to His Majesty The King as Head of the Army if the troops could be permitted to resume their badges.

Winston S. Churchill to President Franklin D. Roosevelt
(Churchill papers, 20/85)

12 December 1942
Most Secret and Personal
No. 230

The only question which the Russians will ask or the only one that matters will be 'Are you going to make a Second Front in 1943 and when and with what forces?'. I cannot answer this except jointly with you because the forces we British can dispose of are obviously insufficient. Therefore, we cannot reply to Stalin's question until our staffs have explored the possibilities together and hence my strong wish that your friends should come here. If this is not agreeable I am willing to come to you. We are all here sure that a talk whether at Moscow or Khartoum among the three staffs apart from the Heads of Governments would not be useful.

Winston S. Churchill to Josef Stalin
(Churchill papers, 20/85)

12 December 1942
Personal and Most Secret

In your message to me of November 27 in the last sentence of paragraph 5, and also in your message of December 6, you ask specifically about a second front in 1943. I am not able to reply to this question except jointly with the President of the United States. It was for this reason that I so earnestly desired a meeting between the three of us. We both understand the paramount military reasons which prevent you from leaving Russia while conducting your great operations. I am in constant communication with the President in order to see what can be done.

Winston S. Churchill to Anthony Eden
(Churchill papers, 20/67)

13 December 1942

PROPOSAL OF ARCHDUKE ROBERT OF AUSTRIA[1]
FOR AN AUSTRIAN 'ALLIED' FORCE

Of course, it would be a very good thing to have an Austrian unit if it could be managed without too much trouble. I am extremely interested in Austria, and hope that Vienna may become the capital of a great Confederation of the Danube. It is perfectly true that Europe left Austria to her fate in a pusillanimous manner in 1938. The separation of the Austrians and Southern Germans and the Prussians is essential to the harmonious reconstitution of Europe.

2. How many Austrians are there in England that would be affected?

3. I should like to have something better to say than this to my correspondent.[2]

Winston S. Churchill to General Sir Alan Brooke and General Ismay,
for the Chiefs of Staff Committee
(Churchill papers, 20/67)

13 December 1942

UNITED KINGDOM AND UNITED STATES CONVOYS
TO NORTH AFRICA

Out of over 34,000 men in KMS[3] 5 and KMS 6 assigned to the Eastern Task Force, which is the only one engaged or likely to be engaged, there are less than 9,000 fighting troops, including both a new unit and reinforcements. This is the crisis period of the Tunisian battle. I doubt very much whether we and the Americans have yet brought more than 15,000 actual fighting men into contact with the enemy out of, perhaps, a quarter of a million landing or about to land.

---

[1] Robert of Austria-Este, 1915–96. Son of Emperor Karl I of Austria and Princess Zita. Prince Imperial of Austria, Prince Royal of Hungary and Bohemia. Created Archduke of Austria-Este by his father, 1917.

[2] The reference is to a draft reply from the Foreign Office to a letter of 19 November 1942 from Archduke Robert to the Prime Minister.

[3] KMS: the code for convoys heading from the United Kingdom to the Mediterranean that travelled at a slow pace. Thus KMS means Kingdom to Mediterranean Slow. There were also KMF convoys that travelled fast. Return trips were known as MKS and MKF.

2. KMS 5 has passed out of our control. Is it not possible and would it not be well to find two or three more ships and get a Brigade Group of the 46th Division out with the Christmas convoy? Ought we not to include another two or three thousand reinforcements as well? When there are two or three hundred thousand men in or approaching the theatre it seems an awful pity to stake the fortunes of battle on the very small spearhead at present available for the Eastern Task Force. Observe: I am not proposing to cut the enormous non-combatant tail which fills up KMS 5 and KMS 6, but only to make sure there are some teeth to bite the enemy with. It is the teeth that we always run short of, and however good the supply, the Signals, the Pioneers, the RE and the hospitals are, there must always somewhere up in front be a certain number of people who actually are engaged in trying to kill the enemy with the weapons which they hold.

President Franklin D. Roosevelt to Winston S. Churchill
('The Hinge of Fate', page 600)

14 December 1942
Private

In spite of Stalin's inability to meet with us, I think we should plan a meeting at once with our respective military staffs. I should like to meet in Africa about January 15. There is, I believe, a satisfactory and safe place just north of Casablanca. It might be wise for some of our military men to precede us by a few days to clear the ground. I should think if we could have four or five days together we could clear up all of our business. Will you let me know what you think of this?

Winston S. Churchill to Lord Halifax
(Churchill papers, 20/85)

14 December 1942
Personal and Secret

NETHERLANDS GOVERNMENT PROTEST
AGAINST DARLAN ARRANGEMENTS

I have never seen the House so unanimous, and I am not conscious of any political difficulties. Of course there are certain sections of the Press and public who want to have the advantages of Darlan without Darlan. I would make a public statement were it not that I do not wish to give unnecessary importance to this one feature in our great African campaign.

Winston S. Churchill to William Mackenzie King
(Churchill papers, 20/88)

14 December 1942

AIRCRAFT FOR CONVOY PROTECTION IN MID-ATLANTIC

Thank you for your telegram No. 259 and for the assurance of your help. We recognise the value of the patrols done by your squadrons, and we realise the handicaps imposed by high winds and the moderate range of their aircraft. Experience with HX 217[1] during the last two days has demonstrated once again the immense value of air protection at very long range. The help you can give us by allowing us to use 'Goose' and 'Gander'[2] for servicing and refuelling our Liberators will be invaluable, and I would ask you to let our staffs arrange this together as soon as possible. If you agree, they could also discuss the subsequent movement of a Coastal Command squadron to 'Goose'.

2. I regret that at present we can do nothing to meet your request for very long-range aircraft. The number of Liberators we have is at present too small to allow us to base any of them permanently in the Western Atlantic. We realise, however, the desirability of doing so, and hope that the supply of suitable aircraft will eventually make this possible.

Sir Alexander Cadogan: diary
('The Diaries of Sir Alexander Cadogan', page 499)

14 December 1942
5.30 pm Cabinet

[...] Tunisia not going well, so PM on his usual (and to me well-founded) complaint that, out of about 110,000 men there, there are only about 10,000 fighting men.
[...]

---

[1] HX convoys originally headed from Halifax, Nova Scotia, to the UK. After the United States entered the war, they left from New York. HX 217 was a convoy that left New York on 27 November 1942 and arrived in Liverpool on December 14. The Commodore's report stated: 'This has been a most interesting convoy and is the best example I have yet seen of good co-operation between Escort, Convoy and Aircraft and the proper use of those instruments, devices and weapons supplied to Escort, Convoy and Aircraft for the undoing of the enemy. I feel sure much may be learnt from the study of these particular attacks and counter attacks and convoy procedure' (*Admiralty papers, 199/717*).

[2] 'Goose' and 'Gander': two Canadian forces bases located in, respectively, Happy Valley, Goose Bay, Newfoundland, and Gander, Labrador. They were major connecting points for flights to and from Great Britain.

President Franklin D. Roosevelt to Winston S. Churchill
(Churchill papers, 20/85)

15 December 1942
Personal and Most Secret
No. 234

I am sending you a letter by courier in regard to our future plans. You should get it in three or four days, weather permitting.

Winston S. Churchill to Members of the War Cabinet
(Churchill papers, 23/10)

15 December 1942
Most Secret
War Cabinet Paper No. 583 of 1942

UNITED KINGDOM – INVASION IN 1943

I am in full accord with the conclusions of the Chiefs of the Staff, and I recommend that they should be endorsed by my colleagues in the War Cabinet.

2. It is, of course, understood that our immunity from invasion even in 1943 depends upon the maintenance of a good army strong enough to make it useless for the enemy to come except in numbers large enough to furnish effective targets, on sea and in the invasion ports, for our Navy and Air Force.

3. Whereas in the summer of 1940 we could only bomb the invasion ports by night, our fighter cover has now become strong enough to protect British and American bombers operative by day. Thus those invasion ports from Dunkirk to Dieppe inclusive which were the greatest danger to us and were nearest to Kent and Sussex, and thus to London, are now almost certainly denied to the enemy, who is thus forced to cross broader waters with additional weather risks and offering further opportunities to the Navy. Should any offensive operations undertaken by us in 1943 bring about a further relative weakening of the enemy's Air Force, the foregoing considerations would be enhanced.

4. While I am entirely in favour of a definite diminution in the scale of defence for airfields and vulnerable points against airborne descents, the possibility of vicious raids cannot be excluded. It would be well if the Chiefs of the Staff would draw up a statement of the actual measures and reductions it is proposed to enforce, as a consequence of their conclusions, at the above points and also along the coasts.

5. The conversion of the army to the offensive phase is urgent and should be pressed forward with the utmost vigour and contrivance. It is certainly not sufficient that only 9 divisions should be available for offensive action by the 1st July, and that 15 cannot be obtained before the 1st October. A special study should be made to bring the October figure forward to July.

6. While it is necessary that these conclusions should become known to a wide circle of officers, stringent instructions should be issued that they are to be kept absolutely secret. No officer is to use in public any language compatible with the idea that all danger of invasion is gone, and the Minister of Information[1] should endeavour to dissuade the Press from making any statements of this character, which can only have a discouraging effect upon the large numbers of troops and Civil Defence personnel involved in Home Defence, on whose untiring vigilance and efficiency our safety from month to month depends.

Winston S. Churchill to William Phillips[2]
(Churchill papers, 20/54)

15 December 1942

My dear Mr Phillips.

There are serious things beneath the surface of this old book.[3] When I went out as a Subaltern to India in 1896, I was advised to read it by one of the wisest Civil Servants in India, who had been a friend of my family.[4] I thought it might interest you to read it on the journey out, as

[1] Brendan Bracken.

[2] William Phillips, 1878–1968. Educated at Harvard. US diplomat. Secretary in London to Joseph Hodges Choate, US Ambassador to the United Kingdom. Worked for the Ambassador to China in Beijing. Returned to work in London, 1909. Assistant Secretary of State, 1917–20. Minister Plenipotentiary to Netherlands and Luxemburg, 1920. Under-Secretary of State, 1922–4. Ambassador to Belgium, 1924–7. Minister to Canada, 1927–9. Ambassador to Italy, 1936–41. Chief of United States Office of Strategic Services in London, 1942. Appointed as a personal representative of President Franklin D. Roosevelt, serving in India, 1942. Special Advisor on European political matters to General Eisenhower, with the rank of Ambassador, 1943. Retired in 1944. Briefly returned to diplomatic life in 1945 as a special assistant to Secretary of State Edward R. Stettinius. Served on the Anglo-American Committee on Palestine, 1946.

[3] *Twenty-One Days in India: Being the Tour of Sir Ali Baba, KCB*, by George Abereigh-Mackay. A tongue-in-cheek series of sketches of nineteenth-century colonial life in India, originally published in *Vanity Fair* and so popular that it ran to six editions.

[4] Probably William Beresford, 1847–1900. Served in the 9th Queen's Royal Lancers during the Zulu and Afghan Wars. Victoria Cross. Military Secretary to Viceroys of India Lords Dufferin and Lansdowne. Major, 1884. Colonel, 1891. Knight Commander of the Order of the Indian Empire. Married Lillian, widow of George Spencer-Churchill, 8th Duke of Marlborough. Churchill stayed with his regiment near Beresford for six months immediately before departing for India as a

it is a book famous in a small circle and supposed to give very briefly a sweeping glance at a vast, marvellous scene. Pray do not however suspect me of anything but literary taste. The author deals with a world that has passed away, and this is the only copy I could get.

All good wishes for your journey.

Yours very sincerely,

Winston S. Churchill

Winston S. Churchill to General Dwight D. Eisenhower
(Churchill papers, 20/85)

16 December 1942
Most Secret
Priority

I read with great interest your appreciation in Review No. 25 and felt heartfelt satisfaction at your resolve to come to grips. Boniface shows the hard straits of the enemy, the toll taken of his supplies by submarines and surface ships, and especially the effect which our bombing is having upon his congested ports. It seems to me, speaking of course as a layman, that it is wise to keep the enemy bleeding and burning up his strength, even if we sustain equal losses. Thus a larger animal crushes the life out of a weaker and never gives him the chance to gather strength for a spring.

2. I have much admired the way you have pressed forward so vehemently to the East, and am sure this was right whatever the immediate results might be. We can reinforce much faster than the enemy, and consequently it pays us to engage and wear him down, like Grant and the Confederates in 1864. As I thought perhaps you might be getting a little short in actual fighting units, I asked the Chiefs of Staff to add a Brigade Group of the 46th Division to KM 6. I am very glad to have found it possible to make these arrangements without detriment to the very numerous servicing and supply units and details which are already on the way or allotted.

3. Like General Marshall, I am concerned that you should be so much occupied with political matters when the only thing that matters is the battle. I hope arrangements may be made by our two Governments to devolve some of this burden on to other shoulders while leaving you the necessary ultimate control on military grounds. I am sure you will feel

young officer, and visited Beresford frequently; he said in *My Early Life* that Beresford's opinions were deeply practical and that he was never tired of listening to his wisdom.

that you have not been harassed by me, and that you know I stand here between you and trouble.

All good wishes.

Winston S. Churchill to President Franklin D. Roosevelt
(Churchill papers, 20/85)

16 December 1942
Most Secret and Personal
No. 232

Your No. 234.

I am anxiously awaiting the arrival of your courier. Our affairs are so inter-dependent that I cannot make any plans or even think ahead until I know your wishes.

2. Thank you so much for your long letter about Lyttelton's affairs to which I am preparing a full answer.

We are most grateful to you for all your help.

General Dwight D. Eisenhower to Winston S. Churchill
(Churchill papers, 20/85)

16 December 1942   Algiers
Private and Most Secret

[...]

2. With warm regard and deep respect, thanks for your message of 16th. I assure you that none of us has ever for a moment thought that you were in any way harassing us or our efforts. To the contrary, we have confidently felt that you have always understood our problems and were devoting your full energies to our support. I am particularly pleased that you are able to arrange for speeding up the arrival of a brigade of the 46th Division, as I anticipate hard fighting and a need for more combat strength. Weather precluded bombing operations today, but yesterday we apparently hurt the enemy considerably. I hope we can get at his ports again tomorrow.

3. I know that you are anxious to see our ground force moving ahead once more and assure you again that we are equally anxious. Our pitifully inadequate L of C is <u>not</u> an alibi, but just a hard fact that we have to meet and overcome. This minute, while we are working it to capacity,

we are confronted by Giraud with a demand that we pass forward one of his Moroccan Divisions which, unfortunately, has no AT or Flak, making it of little use in open country. Although it is apparently composed of fine fighting men, its movement and its later maintenance simply add to our burdens. If I had two battalions each of Flak and AT to give him this minute, I would pay any price within my power. As it is, we have to try to secure his consent to postponing the movement, because blunt refusal might cause repercussions in the region his light forces are covering for us. This merely illustrates some of the difficulties we encounter on the Political – Military front. These people are poor and have suffered much humiliation and are therefore excessively proud, and the matter cannot be handled on a straight military basis. I learn also that Giraud is counting on bringing into North Africa some 40,000 and 50,000 troops from Dakar and this, under current conditions, would be a calamity. I am sure, though, that Boisson will not agree to such a movement for a long time to come.

4. There has been no considerable change reported in the battlefront since the withdrawal in which combat team B lost so heavily by bogging of vehicles. Its remaining strength was reported to CCS and now I am scraping the bottom of the barrel to build it back to respectable strength. This job is held up by delays in unloading at Oran, and by lack of trains. But we keep plugging.

Winston S. Churchill to the War Cabinet
(Churchill papers, 23/10)

16 December 1942   10 Downing Street
Most Secret
War Cabinet Paper No. 580 of 1942

AIR POLICY

The bombing offensive over Germany and Italy must be regarded as our prime effort in the Air. It is of the utmost importance that this should not fall away during these winter months, when the strain of the Russian and Anglo-American offensives will be heavy on the German and Italian peoples. To maintain a steady crescendo is an offensive measure of the highest consequence. Arrangements have been set on foot for raising Bomber Command to 50 Squadrons by the end of the year, and all the necessary action has been taken to ensure that this target is in fact reached.

2. The United States are persevering with the idea of the daylight bombing of Germany by means of Flying Fortresses and Liberators in formation without escort. This policy and our official attitude towards the United States Air Force and Government about it require examination in two states. First, what is the truth; secondly, what to say or do about it. The Air Ministry must be careful not to mix these processes. They must not allow purely technical and military judgements to be clouded or distorted by the fear that if the Americans were offended by our telling them what we feel to be the truth, Admiral King would get the power to send everything off to the Pacific. Any mixing of the technical and political functions prevents the Cabinet from getting the best service in either.

3. The brute fact remains that the American bombers so far have rarely gone beyond the limits of strong British fighter escort. Their bombing of the U-boat bases in the Biscay ports has been ineffectual or at the most has yielded very small results. Even when hits have been secured from a high level, the bombs have not penetrated the heavily armoured shelters. A certain amount of inconvenience may have been caused in these ports, but there has been no appreciable diminution in the number of U-boats using them. They have not so far dropped a single bomb on Germany. The effect of the American bombing effort in Europe and Africa, judged by the number of sorties, the number of bombs and the results observed, compared with the very large quantities of men and material involved, has been very small indeed. And this after a year of United States war.

4. On the other hand, it should not be overlooked that the American bombing force in Great Britain has been continually depleted in the interests of 'Torch'; that they make large claims of killing enemy fighters, which, even if reduced to one-third, are still appreciable; that they have sometimes been attacked without fighter escort and have given a good account of themselves without disproportionate loss; and finally, that the accuracy of their high-level bombing is remarkable, especially if they are not interfered with at the moment of discharge.

5. Listening to all I can hear from every source, I have, during the two months of writing this paper, become increasingly doubtful of the daylight bombing of Germany by the American method. The danger of their having all their ammunition teased out of them by minor attacks by enemy fighters increases with every mile of penetration. To minimise this they now propose to have one in three (presently it may be one in two) Fortresses carrying no bombs but only ammunition. This, of course,

reduces the effective bomb-load proportionately while not reducing the number of aircraft exposed to danger. Against this must be counted any enemy fighters shot down.

6. If the American plan proves a failure, the consequences will be grievous. In the first place, it will be a heavy shock to public opinion in America. In the second place, American industry is already largely committed, and becoming increasingly committed on a vast scale, to the production of heavy bombers which are not fitted for night bombing. Thirdly, we shall have brought over and maintained in this country large numbers of personnel on our best airfields, thus adding to the length of our own attacking journeys without being able to count upon any corresponding return in their assistance in our Air offensive on Germany. Many of our airfields in United States occupation are being used for little more than training.

7. We should, of course, continue to give the Americans every encouragement and help in the experiment which they ardently and obstinately wish to make, but we ought to try to persuade them to give as much aid as possible (a) to sea work, and (b) to night bombing, and to revise their production, including instruments, and training for the sake of these objects. I have already in my telegram to Mr Hopkins and in my conversation with Captain Rickenbacker at the desire of Mr Winant put these views forward as tactfully as possible.

8. There is, of course, the alternative to which I have called attention in my note to the Chiefs of the Staff on plans and operations in the Mediterranean, Middle East and Near East (WP(42)543), that 'The United States form of daylight attack would have its best chance in the better weather of the Mediterranean.'

9. All these matters require earnest attention, especially in connection with the consideration being given by the Chiefs of the Staff to the paper 'An Estimate of the effects of an Anglo-American Bomber Offensive against Germany' (COS(42)379(O)), since it would clearly be disastrous to undertake the gigantic commitment involved in building up an Anglo-American Bomber force of 5,000 to 6,000 heavy bombers without being absolutely sure that the American bombers were capable of sustained attack, without disproportionate loss, on Germany.

10. The United States have affirmed their decision to produce 82,000 combat planes in 1943, and the Minister of Production[1] has returned with firm agreements regarding the distribution of these aircraft. It will be seen from paragraph 12 of Appendix B of his Report (WP(42)568) that

[1] Oliver Lyttelton.

'Every effort is being made to make United States heavy bombers suitable for night bombing. A comparatively simple modification has been evolved which gives reasonable hope of success. Modification sets are now being tried out both in this country and in America.' This work should be given highest priority and progress reports made at short intervals.

11. In fighter aircraft, qualitative superiority is vital and fashions must improve even at some expense in numbers. Technical mastery must be achieved even at a great cost. A different set of considerations governs the development of bomber aircraft. The varying difficulty of the tasks set them enables older types to play a part for longer, though at a greater price in casualties. It must never be forgotten that the success of the bomber effort is measured by the weight of bombs discharged. With the fighters it is *technical Leadership*, and for the bombers, *bulk Deliveries*. Whereas in fighter aircraft we have enough in hand to look some distance ahead, we are terribly behindhand in Bombing expansion. The maintenance of the bomb deliveries on Germany and their steady increase are imperative. No alteration should be made in our bomber production which is inconsistent with a steadily rising bomb delivery potential. We cannot, for instance, slack off for the next six months in order to make a great splash in the autumn of 1943, or sacrifice 1943 for the sake of 1944 or 1945. The process of bombing has to be continuous and cumulative, and all programmes must conform to it. The Wellingtons must not be prematurely discarded until it can be shown that concentration upon the Lancasters, which is evidently in itself most desirable, causes no falling-off in bomb deliveries on Germany. We must scrutinise carefully the effect on our estimated bomb deliveries on Germany, especially in 1943, of the various proposals for alterations in our heavy bomber programme (see WP(42)526. 'Policy for the replacement of the Wellington and the Warwick', and WM(42)147th Conclusions, Minute 1, paragraph *(b)*, 'Switch off Stirling and other capacity to the manufacture of Lancaster').

12. The development of the Fleet Air Arm since the war began has not been satisfactory. For nearly two years it has been evident that every aircraft carrier requires, first and foremost, a section of the highest grade fighter aircraft which can be flown on and off a ship (see my memorandum DO(42)49). This remains the paramount object, and the highest priority should continue to be given to the supply of the best fighter types to the carriers. In this I am now prepared to include all carriers, whether armoured, intermediate or auxiliary. This does not, however, mean that inordinate reserves should be built up all over the world. However desirable it might be for the Navy to have an outfit of aircraft in every port, we

cannot at the present time afford to have a lot of aircraft standing idle. The War Cabinet on the 22nd September (WM(42) 128th Conclusions, Minute 2) approved the proposals made by the Minister of Production regarding the scale of reserves for Fleet Air Arm aircraft.

We have to try to find the best compromise between scales that are wasteful of aircraft and carriers idle through lack of them. I propose to keep this matter under periodic review. Presently we shall be better off.

13. The development of the Merchant Aircraft Carriers is also most important as an anti-U-boat weapon.

14. In all carriers of the regular and intermediate types, more emphasis should be placed at present upon the proportion of fighters compared with torpedo-carrying planes. (The Admiralty would require a higher ratio of torpedo-carrying planes if the carriers moved East to undertake operations against the Japanese naval units.) We are not inferior in gunpower to the enemy and his surface ships are not our danger. It is the attack from the air and by the U-boats that requires tireless attention. The use of the fighter aircraft in larger proportions by our carriers is not a defensive symptom, since its object is to enable the Fleet to take bolder offensive action.

Winston S. Churchill to Sir James Grigg
(Churchill papers, 20/67)

16 December 1942
Action this Day

Pray send round samples of the printed and embroidered slip-on regimental flashes to which you refer in the first paragraph of your minute of the 14th December.

2. Let me have the text of the original instruction issued by your predecessor, together with the War Office files upon which he took this decision.

3. What is General Paget's explanation of the non-enforcement of this instruction until the order sent out by him in July 1942?

4. What were the circumstances which led to the issue of the Army Council Instruction of last month? Pray let me see the War Office files on this subject. Was General Paget consulted before this instruction was issued?

5. It was, of course, from General Paget, when I inspected the 53rd Division, that I learnt of the distress to the troops by the enforcement

of the order, and he certainly expressed himself in a manner which led me to believe that he greatly regretted it.

6. It seems to me that, if the Commander-in-Chief has condoned over a great many months the numerous breaches of this order which you mention it was hard on the units concerned to enforce so sudden a change of policy.

7. You do not reply in your minute of 14.12.42 to any of the points dealt with in paragraphs 1, 2, 3, 4 and 5 of my minute of 11.12.42, although these dealt with the bulk of your minute of 9.12.42. Perhaps you would be good enough to do this.

8. I should be glad if you would also explain to me why the Guards are to be specially favoured in this matter. Has a special permission been granted to them, and, if so, on what grounds? I should have thought that line regiments and especially national regiments like the Welsh or the Scots were even more anxious for the support to *esprit de corps* and the expression of individuality which the enjoyment of distinctive badges confers.

9. I can quite see that the difficulty is one into which you have got yourself by making the enforcement of this wrong principle a matter of prestige, and I should be willing to allow a longer interval to elapse before the general mounting of badges is authorised.

Winston S. Churchill to President Franklin D. Roosevelt
(Churchill papers, 20/85)

17 December 1942
Personal and Most Secret
No. 233

I am most grateful for the assistance you have given us by establishing a pool of oil in New York from which our tankers can draw. Without this assistance our oil position would soon have become grave in the extreme.

Unfortunately, despite this new arrangement, our consumption will continue to exceed imports, and it is clear that very early steps are necessary not only to check this drain but also to build up stocks, which are at a dangerously low level.

2. If the present situation is allowed to persist, our stocks will be reduced in the coming months to such a degree that it may be necessary to restrict the movements of our warships and oil burning ships, which would affect the North Russian and 'Torch' convoys.

3. I am advised that this serious state of affairs has arisen as a result of the lengthened turn-round of tankers occasioned by the extension of the convoy system to the Gulf of Mexico and Caribbean, accentuated by the unexpectedly large demands of oil supplies to the 'Torch' area which under present arrangements can only be made from the United Kingdom resources.

4. Drastic measures are obviously necessary to remedy this situation and proposals which have been worked out by the Admiralty and Ministry of War Transport are contained in my immediately following telegram.[1]

5. One of the proposed measures is that as you have assumed responsibility for the civil administration of North Africa, you should also assume responsibility for the supply of petroleum products both civil and military to this area. I very much hope you will be able to agree to this though we cannot offer you any assistance in providing escorts for the tankers so employed.

6. In view of the urgency of preventing our position from deteriorating further, I should be grateful if the proposals contained in paragraph 5 above and in my immediately following telegram could be given very early consideration.

Winston S. Churchill to William Mackenzie King
(Churchill papers, 20/88)

17 December 1942
Most Secret and Personal

I am sending you copies of my telegrams Nos. 233 and 234 (see my immediately following telegram) to the President of the United States regarding the serious position of the United Kingdom oil stocks.

2. You will have noted that the Admiralty propose that the eight British manned escort groups should operate the trans-Atlantic convoys, accepting the shorter lay-over entailed, and that the four groups of escort vessels

---

[1] On 17 December 1942, in his Telegram No. 234, Churchill telegraphed to Roosevelt: 'With reference to my immediately preceding telegram, the following are the measures proposed for arresting the decline of the UK oil stocks.

'2 (a) To institute direct tanker convoys every 20 days between the Dutch West Indies and the United Kingdom, by which we should hope to improve our imports by 100,000 tons a month.

'(b) To find the escorts for these convoys by a further opening of the cycle of the trans-Atlantic convoys from 8 to 10 days, which will enable 4 groups of escort vessels to be released.

'3 By the opening of the trans-Atlantic cycle to 10 days, it will be possible to operate these convoys with 8 groups of escorts by accepting a shorter period of lay over between voyages and it is proposed that the 8 British manned groups should be employed on this duty' (*Churchill papers, 20/85*).

released as a result of opening out the trans-Atlantic cycle should comprise the three Canadian and one American groups. The Admiralty further propose that these latter should be temporarily employed, together with some of the seventeen Canadian corvettes you have already lent us in escorting the 'Torch' build-up convoys between the United Kingdom and Gibraltar in order to enable the necessary long-endurance escorts to be made available for the tanker convoys.

3. A careful analysis of attacks on our trans-Atlantic convoys has clearly shown that in those cases where heavy losses have occurred, lack of training of the escorts, both individually and as a team, has been largely responsible for these disasters.

4. I appreciate the grand contribution of the Royal Canadian Navy to the Battle of the Atlantic, but the expansion of the Royal Canadian Navy has created a training problem which must take some time to solve.

5. An advantage of the Admiralty proposal is, therefore, that until your training facilities are built up it will afford the Canadian and American groups an opportunity of using the unique training facilities available on this side of the Atlantic which their employment on the shorter voyage between the United Kingdom and Gibraltar and the longer lay-over in the United Kingdom will enable them to do.

6. I trust, therefore, that you will see your way to agree to these proposals, since there is no question that we must put a stop to the heavy toll which the U-boats are taking from our Atlantic convoys, and this can only be achieved by training our escorts to the highest possible pitch of efficiency.

Winston S. Churchill to Sir Kingsley Wood,[1] Anthony Eden,[2]
Sir William Jowitt,[3] and Hugh Dalton[4]
(Churchill papers, 20/67)[5]

17 December 1942

I hope that in studying the various proposals for social reform, land development, &c., you are giving full consideration to our post-war financial position. The implications of these schemes must be related to the cost of the armed forces which it will be necessary to maintain, and to the prospects of restoring our export trade. Nothing would be more danger-

[1] Chancellor of the Exchequer.
[2] Foreign Secretary.
[3] Paymaster-General.
[4] President of the Board of Trade.
[5] A copy of this note was sent to Sir John Anderson, Lord President of the Council.

ous than for people to feel cheated because they had been led to expect attractive schemes which turn out to be economically impossible.

What progress has been made in the talks with the Americans? The vital question of the rapid restoration of our export trade must depend on the result of these conversations, and no doubt you are examining all possible markets. This work will be of value whatever international trading arrangements are agreed upon. Pray consider these matters at your convenience.

Winston S. Churchill to the Most Reverend William Temple
(Churchill papers, 20/54)

17 December 1942

My dear Archbishop,

I have now been able to consider, in consultation with the authorities concerned, the proposals in your letter of November 16 about the ringing of Church bells.

I regret that it is not considered possible to accept the proposal that the ban should be completely removed and that, beginning with Christmas Day, the bells should ring as usual to summon people to worship. There are two main objections to such a course. The first is that no satisfactory alternative to bells as a warning signal has been found; the second that such a step would, it is thought, be interpreted as a token that the Government had discounted the danger of invasion or air-borne attack, and that this would have a most serious effect on the morale and keenness of the Home Guard and other organizations, whose purpose is to be ready to deal with such eventualities. Very great importance is attached to this psychological factor.

But no objection is seen to the bells being rung on special occasions, such as Christmas Day, provided that notice is given to the public beforehand, though not too long beforehand. If, as I hope, this is agreeable to you, I suggest that you should get into touch with the Home Secretary about the necessary announcement regarding the change and about details such as the arrangements for giving notice to the public this Christmas and on any future special occasion on which it is proposed to ring the bells.

I am very much obliged to you for raising this important matter.

Yours v. sincerely,
Winston S. Churchill

War Cabinet: Confidential Annex
(Cabinet papers, 65/32)

18 December 1942
5.30 p.m.

[...]

The Prime Minister said that we were under an obligation to send material to the Russians, and he would like to inform M Stalin that we were making arrangements to send convoys in January (in two parts), in February, and in March. Every endeavour must be made to fulfil our obligations and to send high priority supplies to the Russians. We were not, however, under any obligation to supply Russia with 6-pdr. tanks up to the full number of tanks provided in the Protocol. If the United States were sending goods across the North Pacific, we must reconcile ourselves to smaller convoys going to North Russia. He asked the Secretary of State for Foreign Affairs to consider the matter with the Allied Supplies Executive and to submit a Report, for consideration by the War Cabinet, setting out what we could send to Russia during January, February and March, in fulfilment of our obligations, and the implications of the course proposed.

The Prime Minister said that it was significant that the Japanese were not interfering with the transit to Russia of goods on the route West Coast of the United States to Vladivostok in ships which had only recently been transferred from the American to the Russian flag. He would be glad if the Foreign Secretary would consider what light this threw on Japan's attitude.

Winston S. Churchill to A. V. Alexander and
Admiral of the Fleet Sir Dudley Pound
(Churchill papers, 20/67)

18 December 1942

Many thousands of British soldiers have been three and four years in the Middle East and in India who would no doubt very much like to come home and be given leave before resuming their duties. I do not know why special favour should be shown to the Navy. Many of the soldiers have, in fact, probably been more often in action. How much petrol will be used in bringing the *Valiant* home and sending her back merely for the purpose of giving leave? Have we a right to make this movement?

2. It certainly would be a very sensible thing to bring the old Rs.[1] back and lay them up in some safe harbour, using the crews to man new vessels. They are only coffin ships and a cause of grievous anxiety the moment any modern enemy vessel appears. If these ships are brought home one by one, the crews who have been shipwrecked or have been out a particularly long time could be given passages in them.

3. I am certainly very glad that *Anson* or *Howe* should play a part in the Mediterranean.

Winston S. Churchill to A. V. Alexander and
Admiral of the Fleet Sir Dudley Pound
(Churchill papers, 20/67)

19 December 1942

I am still grieved to see our submarines described as 'P.212' &c., in the daily returns. I thought you told me that you would give them names. It is in accordance with the tradition of the Service and with the feelings of the officers and men who risk their lives in these vessels. Not even to give them a name is derogatory to their devotion and sacrifice.

Anthony Eden: diary
('The Eden Memoirs, The Reckoning', pages 358–9)

19 December 1942

Winston rang up once or twice to conjecture the contents of the note this weather-bound courier is to bring.[2] He expects a rendezvous, since only the answer 'yes' or 'no' is required, according to Hopkins. The delay is maddening for no plans for the future can be made meanwhile. 'I don't know whether I should stand on my head or sit on my tail,' Winston complained this morning.

In the evening he rang up to give me good news of German difficulties on Tripoli front.

[...]

---

[1] Rs: the Revenge Class (also listed as Royal Sovereign Class) battleships, built during the First World War.
[2] From Roosevelt.

Winston S. Churchill to Harry Hopkins
(Churchill papers, 20/85)

20 December 1942
Personal and Secret

No courier in sight today. Could you state identity number of Aircraft or port of arrival?

Harry Hopkins to Winston S. Churchill
(Churchill papers, 20/85)

20 December 1942
Personal

Courier further delayed and we will cable message if he does not arrive on twenty first.

Winston S. Churchill to Clare Sheridan
(Churchill papers, 1/368)

20 December 1942

My dear Clare,

I was delighted to be of any help, and I think you have produced a very fine piece of work.[1] I should certainly like to have a replica of the head in bronze, but I am not going to allow you to be put to any expense in the matter. I do not know whether £100 would be of any use in this direction. If so, I will send you a cheque at once.

I so greatly value the charming miniature you gave me of my Mother. It is always by my bedside. I have such vivid memories of her.

Keep in touch.

Yours affectionately,
W.

All good wishes for Christmas and the New Year.

---

[1] Clare Sheridan's busts of Churchill are today at Blenheim Palace, Harrow School, and Chartwell.

Winston S. Churchill to President Franklin D. Roosevelt
(Churchill papers, 20/85)

21 December 1942
Personal and Most Secret
No. 238

Yes certainly. The sooner the better. I am greatly relieved. It is the only thing to do. All arrangements here will be made on basis that it is a staff meeting only. Suggested code name 'Symbol'.[1]

Winston S. Churchill to General Hastings Ismay,
for the Chiefs of Staff Committee
(Churchill papers, 20/67)

21 December 1942
Secret

DIEPPE

Although for many reasons everyone was concerned to make this business look as good as possible, the time has now come when I must be informed more precisely about the military plans.

2. Who made them? Who approved them? What was General Montgomery's part in it? And General McNaughton's[2] part? What is the opinion about the Canadian generals selected by General McNaughton? Did the General Staff check the plans? At what point was VCIGS[3] informed (in CIGS's absence)?

3. At first sight it would appear to a layman very much out of accord with the accepted principles of war to attack the strongly fortified town front without first securing the cliffs on either side, and to use our tanks in frontal assault off the beaches by the Casino, &c., instead of landing them a few miles up the coast and entering the town from the back.

4. You should first collect through the Defence Office the ascertainable facts about this, and I will then consider whether there should be a more formal inquiry and what form it should take.

---

[1] 'Symbol': the Casablanca Conference, at which Roosevelt and Churchill were to meet in January 1943.

[2] General Officer Commanding the Canadian Corps, 1940–2. General Officer Commanding-in-Chief, First Canadian Army, 1942–4.

[3] Vice-Chief of the Imperial General Staff, Sir Archibald Edward Nye.

Winston S. Churchill to General Sir Harold Alexander
(Churchill papers, 20/85)

22 December 1942
Important
Most Secret
Personal

I am disappointed that you do not keep me more fully informed about your prospects and intentions. It would be a help to me in my work if you kept more in touch.

President Franklin D. Roosevelt to Winston S. Churchill
('The Hinge of Fate', pages 598–600)

[Delivered 23 December 1942[1]]   The White House
Private   Washington DC

Dear Winston,

I have not had an answer to my second invitation to our Uncle Joe, but, on the assumption that he will again decline, I think that in spite of it you and I should get together, as there are things which can be definitely determined only by you and me in conference with our Staff people. I am sure that both of us want to avoid the delays which attended the determination on 'Torch' last July.

1. On the grounds of vile climate and icing on the wings, Iceland must be definitely out for both of us.

2. England must be out for me for political reasons.

3. There will be a commotion in this country if it is discovered that I have flown across any old seas. Therefore Bermuda would be just as much out for me as Africa. However, on condition that I can get away in absolute secrecy and have my trip kept secret until I get back, I have just about made up my mind to go along with the African idea – on the theory that public opinion here will gasp, but be satisfied when they hear about it after it is over.

4. One mitigating circumstance would be the knowledge that I had seen our military leaders in North and West Africa, and that is why I think it would be best if we could meet somewhere in that neighbourhood instead of Khartoum. Incidentally, I could actually see some of our troops.

[1] This letter had been sent from Washington on 14 December 1942 and delivered personally to Churchill nine days later.

5. Incidentally also it would do me personally an enormous amount of good to get out of the political atmosphere of Washington for a couple of weeks.

6. My thought is, therefore, that if the time suits your plans we could meet back of Algiers or back of Casablanca about January 15th. That would mean that I would leave about January 11th, and pray for good weather. My route would be either from here to Trinidad and thence to Dakar and thence north, or from here to Natal (Brazil), and across to Liberia or Freetown, and north from there.

7. In view of Stalin's absence, I think you and I need no Foreign Affairs people with us, for our work will be essentially military. Perhaps your three top men and my three top men could meet at the same place four or five days in advance of our arrival and have plans in fairly good tentative shape by the time we get there. I asked General [Bedell] Smith, who left here four or five days ago, to check up confidentially on some possible tourist oasis as far from any city or large population as possible. One of the dictionaries says 'an oasis is never wholly dry'. Good old dictionary!

8. Here is an alternative plan in case Uncle Joe says he will meet us about March 1st:

I would suggest that your Staff people and mine should meet with the Russian Staff people somewhere in Africa, or even as far as Baghdad, and come to certain recommendations which would at least get the preliminaries of new moves started. The three of us could, when we meet, close up the loose ends, and also take up some of the post-war matters.

With my warm regards,
As ever yours,
Franklin D. Roosevelt

Winston S. Churchill to President Franklin D. Roosevelt
(Churchill papers, 20/85)

23 December 1942
Personal and Secret
No. 240

Your courier has arrived. I like it all. I will discreetly contact General Smith.

Winston S. Churchill to General Hastings Ismay,
for the Chiefs of Staff Committee
(Churchill papers, 20/67)

24 December 1942
Most Secret

From time to time references to German designs on the Balearic Islands[1] appear in the newspapers. We know from the Thoma conversations how the German Staff view their second line of defences in the Mediterranean, namely, the islands: Rhodes, Crete, Sicily, Sardinia; and it certainly would not be out of harmony with this conception if they tried to add the Balearics to the line.

I should like a short study to be made of this danger and anything we could do to stop it.

Winston S. Churchill to Clement Attlee and Anthony Eden
(Churchill papers, 20/67)

24 December 1942
Action this Day

I still do not think this is good enough.[2] It all seems impeccable on paper, but in the result we are frustrated. Many a war has been lost by taking 'No' for an answer. I do not regard the neutrality of the Iberian Peninsula as hanging in the balance, nor that we have to '*try*' to maintain Portuguese neutrality. It is better than ever before. A considerably stronger effort can be made than mere representations. Having regard to the general position of the war the Portuguese are more likely to defer to our pressure in respect of Lorenzo Marques, which Smuts could certainly overrun, than to the vague German threat of heavy invasion of Spain, which is not at all likely to be made good during these winter months. Now is the time.

2. We should try to arrive at our objective by means less formal than those General Smuts suggests. First, we should put very hard pressure on the Portuguese both at Lisbon and in South Africa. Secondly, SOE[3] should, if possible, by the connivance or at least with the acquiescence

---

[1] A group of islands off the eastern coast of the Spanish mainland, the chief of them being Mallorca, Menorca, Ibiza, and Formentera.

[2] Minute of 18 December 1942 from the Dominions Secretary, Clement Attlee, about the possibility of making representations to the Portuguese Government concerning Axis submarine activity in the Mozambique Channel.

[3] SOE: the Special Operations Executive.

of the Portuguese East Africa Government, build up at once a strong organisation in all the ports and along the coast in question. We should insist on the fullest liberty of inspection of all German activities. The German consuls should be marked down and ringed around with spies and agents. A system of plain clothes coastal patrols should, if possible, be instituted. The question of German consulates sending messages in cypher should be examined. The Portuguese are on our side, want us to win and will help us as much as they dare; but as we are very gentle while the enemy is aggressive, they drift along the line of least resistance. This process ought to come to an end. The time has come when we can afford to make Lorenzo Marques fear us more than they do the Germans.

3. I should be very glad to see the Foreign Secretary, the Dominions Secretary, the First Lord and MEW[1] at 12.30 pm today. I hope this may be convenient.

Winston S. Churchill to President Franklin D. Roosevelt
(Churchill papers, 20/85)

25 December 1942
Personal
No. 241

Last year I passed a happy Christmas in your home and now I send my heartfelt wishes to you and all around you on this brighter day than we have yet seen. My wife joins with me in this message to you and Mrs Roosevelt.

Winston and Clementine Churchill

President Franklin D. Roosevelt to Winston S. Churchill
(Churchill papers, 20/59)

25 December 1942
Personal
No. 244

The Roosevelts send the Churchills warm personal Christmas greetings.

The old team-work is grand.

Roosevelt

---

[1] MEW: Minister for Economic Warfare, the Earl of Selborne.

Winston S. Churchill to General George C. Marshall
(Churchill papers, 20/85)

26 December 1942
Secret
Personal (eyes only)

My sincere thanks to you and the War Department for the magnificent globe which General Hartle presented to me yesterday on your behalf. It will be a fine addition to No. 10 Downing Street where it will occupy a very special place. We have marched resolutely together through this past difficult year, and it will be of deep interest to me to follow on the Globe the great operations all over the world which will bring us final victory. Pray accept my best wishes for 1943 and my kind regards.

Winston S. Churchill to Sir James Grigg
and General Sir Alan Brooke
(Churchill papers, 20/67)

26 December 1942
Secret

11TH ARMOURED DIVISION

The Tunisian tip in which this division will operate with other troops is about 35 miles deep by 55 miles broad. It, therefore, bears no resemblance to the vast distances of the Western Desert. On the other hand, it may have to face permanent fortifications at Bizerta and strong field positions around Tunis. It may be needed to support an infantry breakthrough. For all these purposes heavy weapons and thick armour are required. No question is raised of standard establishments but of creating a particular instrument for a special task.

2. I am glad you are able to add 36 6-pounder tanks by increasing the troops from three to four. I wish you to consider urgently whether we cannot add a fourth regiment of 6-pounder tanks as a self-contained unit of the divisional reserve. Best of all would be if this unit could be A22s, because in punching through the defences of Bizerta or Tunis and in street fighting this tank alone has the necessary armour. Lord Leathers[1] informs me that the addition to the convoy would not be more than two or at the most three ships. We thus increase the punch enormously. However, perhaps the

---

[1] Minister of War Transport.

landing facilities at Algiers and still more at Bone could not handle 40-ton tanks. Nevertheless, this would be the tool for the job. The additional regiment, apart from its special workshops and spare parts, would not require any additional overheads in the divisional organisation.

3. In AT and flak units this division must be regarded as exceptional. In view of the importance of its mission, other units in the Home Army may be drawn upon temporarily. The Divisional Commander[1] has shown me, at my request, the letter which he has already written to the War Office. I certainly think that all his AT weapons should at least be 6-pounder, and I hope it may be possible to add a dozen 17-pounders in view of the fact that the delay will certainly bring more German Tigers to the scene.

4. Considering the vitally important part that this division may be called upon to play in February or at the latest March, it is necessary to give it an altogether special outfit. This should certainly include the support company of mortars. Pray let me have a scheme for effecting the above, or as much of it as is practicable. There must be no retardation in the sailing date of this division in consequence of any of the above changes without my being duly informed.

5. Besides all this, I should be willing to ask the President to send two or three hundred Shermans out to Algeria so that our 6th Armoured Division could work into these regiment by regiment as the withdrawals from the front line rendered possible. We cannot go on with these Gazala defeat outfits without exposing ourselves to very grave Parliamentary censure.

Winston S. Churchill to Sir John Anderson
(Churchill papers, 20/67)

26 December 1942

SICKNESS

According to the figures supplied by the Health Insurance Approved Societies to the Government Actuary, the average number of people away from work owing to minor illness has increased in the last year by more than a quarter. If this applies to the whole working population it is equivalent to having 80,000 less people working than would normally be the case. It may well be that such absenteeism is due, in part at any rate, to causes other than deterioration of health, but such a notable increase

---

[1] Montagu Brocas Burrows, 1894–1967.

may be an indication of the danger of imposing more and more hard-ships on the civil population.

Winston S. Churchill to President Franklin D. Roosevelt
(Churchill papers, 20/85)

27 December 1942
Personal and Secret
No. 242

SITUATION IN FRENCH NORTH AFRICA
AFTER ASSASSINATION OF ADMIRAL DARLAN[1]

Your 245. As I told Harry I had already asked United States Head-quarters, London, to delay plane which was carrying de Gaulle for forty-eight hours as it is essential to see how 'Torch' situation develops. De Gaulle sent on 25th through American Embassy message repeated in my immediately following to Giraud. It seems to me that we ought to try above anything to bring them all together and have some French nucleus solid and united to work with. I am seeing de Gaulle today and will cable you further.

2. I am sure that North African settlement cannot be held up for 'Symbol'.

We have received news that Kingpin[2] has been unanimously elected High Commissioner and C-in-C by the French group of notabilities. I have already informed Eisenhower that so far as we are concerned we entirely agree with this solution.

3. War Cabinet attach much importance to Macmillan's appointment[3] and arrival. We feel quite unrepresented there yet our fortunes are deeply involved and we are trying to make a solid contribution to your enterprise. Murphy's appointment[4] has already been announced and I

[1] Darlan was assassinated on 24 December 1942 when a member of the Resistance, Ferdinand Bonnier La Chapelle (1922–42), entered his headquarters and shot him. Churchill later wrote: 'Darlan's murder, however criminal, relieved the Allies of their embarrassment at working with him, and at the same time left them with all the advantages he had been able to bestow during the vital hours of the Allied landings' (*The Hinge of Fate*, page 578).

[2] General Giraud.

[3] On December 22 Harold Macmillan was appointed British Minister Resident at Allied Head-quarters, North-West Africa, with a brief as political adviser to the Supreme Allied Commander in North Africa, General Eisenhower.

[4] Robert Daniel Murphy, 1894–1978. Educated at Marquette Academy and University and George Washington University. Assistant Chief, Treasury Department, 1919–20. Vice-consul, Zürich, 1921; Munich, 1921–5. Consul, Seville, 1925. Department of State, 1926–30. Consul, Paris, 1930–6. First Secretary, Paris, 1936–9. Counsellor, Paris, 1940. Chargé d'Affaires, Vichy,

hope you will agree to my publishing Macmillan's appointment. He will be, I am sure, a help. He is animated by the friendliest feelings towards the United States, and his mother hails from Kentucky.

General Sir Harold Alexander to Winston S. Churchill
(Churchill papers, 20/85)

27 December 1942
Most Immediate
Personal and Most Secret

Eighth Army are now regrouping and dumping for next attack against Buerat position. Intention is to press down Tripoli road in conjunction with a wide turning movement with armour and mobile forces to reach Tripoli in one bound. Target date about January 20th. Hope to seize Tripoli by February 1st. As you know, enemy may withdraw, but 30 Corps is operating in such a way as not to frighten enemy in order to try and keep him in Buerat area. A forward move in strength cannot be made before January 14th.

Winston S. Churchill to General Sir Harold Alexander
(Churchill papers, 20/88)

27 December 1942
Personal and Most Secret

Many thanks for your CS/1779.[1] 'Boniface' shows the enemy in great anxiety and disarray at Buerat, and under lively fear of being cut off there by an enveloping movement from the south which he expected might become effective as early as 26th December. Reading 'Boniface', after discounting enemy's natural tendency to exaggerate his difficulties in order to procure better supplies, I cannot help hoping that you may find it possible to strike earlier than the date mentioned in paragraph

July 1940. Detailed November 1940 by President Roosevelt to investigate conditions in French North Africa. February 1941, concluded economic accord with General Maxime Weygand, providing limited United States economic assistance for French North Africa. Effected preparations for Allied landings in North Africa, November 1942. In December 1942, conducted negotiations for entry of French West Africa into war; appointed President's Personal Representative with rank of Minister to French North Africa.

[1] General Alexander's telegram of 24 December 1942 to the Prime Minister and Chief of the Imperial General Staff, giving details of planned operations in the approach to Tripoli.

6.[1] Thus the great honour of taking Tripoli would probably fall to the 8th Army.

2. All good wishes for Christmas and the New Year.

Please keep me informed.

Winston S. Churchill to General Hastings Ismay,
for the Chiefs of Staff Committee
(Churchill papers, 20/67)

27 December 1942
Action this Day
Most Secret

It seems to me that you are over-weighting 'Brimstone' to such an extent as to kill it. It may be this is right. Certainly if the sum of all American fears is to be multiplied by the sum of all British fears, faithfully contributed by each Service, the project is not worth the cost and trouble. The delay in taking the Tunisian tip in any case throws out all previous calculations.

'Husky' alone gives a worth-while prize, even if we have to wait till May. Moreover, the PQ convoys could then run regularly at least till the end of March.

War Cabinet: conclusions
(Cabinet papers, 65/28)

28 December 1942   10 Downing Street
5.30 p.m.

[...]

The Prime Minister said that on the previous day he had discussed with General de Gaulle the situation in North Africa resulting from the assassination of Admiral Darlan. De Gaulle thought it of first importance to create a strong, united, national French authority. He was quite ready to work with General Giraud, but regarded him as qualified for a military rather than a political rôle. He was also willing to work with Noguès, but less ready to co-operate with Boisson· though in the last resort he could

[1] Paragraph 6 read: 'Impossible yet to give a firm date for the attack on Buerat position, but if the enemy stands, I do not think it can be before the end of January.'

probably be persuaded to do so. He had suggested an early meeting with General Giraud. The latter, while agreeing in principle, had replied that the moment was not opportune.

President Roosevelt had suggested that de Gaulle should postpone his proposed visit to the United States until the situation in North Africa had clarified.

The President had also suggested that, for the same reason, the appointment of a British Political Representative to General Eisenhower's headquarters in North Africa should be postponed. The Prime Minister had telegraphed to the President urging that this appointment should not be further delayed.

It was the general view of the War Cabinet that the political situation in North Africa should not be allowed to drift.

The Prime Minister read out the terms of a telegram which he proposed to send to President Roosevelt, giving him an account of his conversations with de Gaulle, and adding that he strongly favoured an early meeting between de Gaulle and Giraud.

The War Cabinet:

Took note of this statement and approved the terms of the telegram which the Prime Minister proposed to send to President Roosevelt.

[...]

War Cabinet: Confidential Record
(Cabinet papers, 65/28)

28 December 1942   10 Downing Street
5.30 p.m.

A general discussion ensued as to the position in Tunisia.

The Prime Minister said that General Eisenhower, who had originally intended to launch an attack in the near future, had now abandoned this plan and thought that, owing to weather conditions, an attack could not be made for some time, possibly for two months. In the meantime the enemy was continuing to reinforce his forces in Tunisia, which might also be reinforced by the bulk of Rommel's forces from Tripolitania.

The Prime Minister also said that there were indications in General Eisenhower's telegram that matters were not running too smoothly between ourselves and the Americans in North Africa. Furthermore, units were being split up, and the situation seemed not unlike that in the 8th Army at the time when he had visited Egypt in the summer.

The Prime Minister said that he proposed to take an opportunity in the course of the next few days of discussing the situation with some of his colleagues, and thereafter he might find it necessary to address a communication on the subject to President Roosevelt.

Winston S. Churchill to General Sir Harold Alexander
(Churchill papers, 20/85)

28 December 1942
Immediate
Personal and Most Secret

Thank you very much for giving me your programme which will be kept strictly secret. It will be very fine if you can pull this off. I think myself that Rommel is off to the rescue of Tunisia and pastures new.

2. I am far from happy about the First Army and the Americans. Eisenhower is reconciling himself to a two months delay, due allegedly to rainy weather, before making a main offensive against Tunis and Bizerta. Meanwhile he proposes to operate with US and French troops against Axis communications SE of Tebessa. The delay will give the enemy time to strengthen himself, albeit by a costly process. 46th British Infantry and 11th British Armoured Divisions come in on our side.

3. On your programme you might be able to join the party too. I presume that all the advantages of your getting Tripoli and opening it as a new base have been studied in detail by the Joint C-in-Cs Cairo. I should be glad to hear from you about this at your leisure.

The above is for you and Montgomery alone.

Winston S. Churchill to President Franklin D. Roosevelt
(Churchill papers, 20/85)

28 December 1942
Personal and Secret
No. 244

I had some long talks yesterday with Generals de Gaulle and D'Astier,[1] the latter just returned from Algiers. De Gaulle holds it of first importance

[1] François d'Astier de Vigerie, 1886–1956. Educated at Lycée Janson de Sailly and Military Academy of Saint Cyr. Entered French Army, 1908; Air Force, 1916. Captain, 1917. Took part in military operations in Morocco commanding aviation centres of Fes, 1927–9 (despatches; promoted Lieutenant-Colonel). Major-General, 1939. Promoted to Lieutenant-General and took

to create a strong, united, National French authority. He is anxious to meet Giraud, in whom he sees the Commander who will lead the French troops to the liberation of France after North Africa has been cleared. He considers that Giraud is more suited for military than for political functions. He is quite ready to work with Noguès but apparently less so with Boisson, though I cannot think he would be obstinate about it.

I must say I strongly favour a meeting between de Gaulle and Giraud as soon as possible, before rivalries crystallize.

Winston S. Churchill to Sir James Grigg
(Churchill papers, 20/67)

28 December 1942
Action this Day

REGIMENTAL BADGES

In your minute of 23rd December, paragraph 2, you say that the Army Council Instruction of 27th December, 1941, was intended to codify existing instructions in a single document and not to lay down any new rules, and that it was never formally submitted to the then Secretary of State.[1] This no doubt explains why the Commander-in-Chief, Home Forces,[1] took no steps to enforce it. The question therefore does not turn on this Army Council Instruction of December 1941, but deals with the practice which has grown up and continued in the Army without any official check of allowing regiments to mount distinguishing badges. Mr Eden tells me that he was strongly in favour of regimental badges and gave instructions accordingly. Therefore it seems to me, on your own showing, that units had no grounds for supposing that they were 'disobeying orders'. In this view they were no doubt confirmed by the action of the Commander-in-Chief, Home Forces, who allowed the healthy practice to continue unchecked. I have no doubt he did this because he thought the stripping off of the badges a purposeless and wrong proceeding. In consequence many units, out of their *esprit de corps*, in some cases at their

command of the Air Force, 1939. Appointed head of the Air Operations Area North, 1939. On 4 July 1940 refused to obey order to attack English ships stationed in Gibraltar; relived of command. Assistant to General de Gaulle, Commander-in-Chief of Free French Forces, and a member of the High Military Committee in London, December 1942. Took part in mission to Algiers, 19–22 December 1942. Commander of French military forces in Britain, July 1943. Senior Commander of French troops in Britain, October 1943. Military Delegate to the London Action Committee in France and delegate to Inter-Allied High Command for matters of military administration in France on the northern theatre operations, December 1943. Mission to Spain, June 1944; joined General de Gaulle after liberation of Paris, 1944.

[1] Sir Bernard Paget.

own expense, were wearing these badges without the slightest injury to discipline and with general advantage to the Army. In October 1942 the imperative orders to strip them off were issued as an Army Council Instruction and, although the Commander-in-Chief, Home Forces, did not approve of it, the required stripping was done, with consequent distress to the troops. In view of the fact that successive Commanders-in-Chief had countenanced the practice for so long a period, you have no right to question the discipline of the troops or to use such a word about them as 'disobedience'.

2. The strongly-worded Army Council Instruction of October 1942 ought not to have been settled by the military members alone. This was exactly one of those cases which affect morale and nationalist and territorial feelings, in which the Parliamentary Ministers should have been consulted. Moreover, I must express the opinion that artillery officers are not particularly qualified to judge the feelings of Regiments of the Line, as the conditions in the Royal Regiment of Artillery are wholly different. For this reason the post of Adjutant-General should be filled whenever possible by an Infantry officer possessing regimental experience.

3. I may add that there are no grounds of reason or of justice for favouring the Guards and Household Cavalry as against the Line. If such indulgences are good for the Guards they are also good for the Line. Indeed, Line Regiments with county or nationalist associations would seem to have an even greater claim and need for them than the Grenadier and Coldstream Guards, who are recruited from all over the country.

4. The badges have now been all stripped off, and I agree that an interval should elapse before they are restored. But I wish them to be restored at an early date. The standard flashes mentioned in your paragraph 1, of which samples have been sent me, are certainly as unattractive as possible, and I do not wonder they have not been generally adopted. An effort should be made to produce a more attractive pattern for all standard badges, and surely, except for Rifle Regiments, red is preferable to black. Units which have at their own expense provided themselves with embroidered badges, thus showing their spirit and pride in their regiment, should certainly be permitted to resume them, and new applications from other units to supply themselves with approved badges by regimental arrangement should be favourably considered. I hope you will therefore present me with a scheme showing how and when effect can be given to the very strong opinion which I hold about the importance of regimental associations to an Army serving under the conditions of Home Forces.

5. If you desire to appeal against my decision to the War Cabinet, I will have a special meeting called for Thursday next at 5.30. I trust, however, that you will not think it necessary to inflict this upon us at so busy a time. Meanwhile, I shall be glad if you will collect for me as many samples as possible of the embroidered badges mounted by units during the period of condonation and let me have a detailed statement of the dates when these badges were first mounted by the units concerned.

Winston S. Churchill to Josef Stalin
(Churchill papers, 20/85)

29 December 1942
Personal, Private and Most Secret

We are deeply encouraged by the growing magnitude of your victories in the south.[1] They bear out all that you told me at Moscow. The results may be very far-reaching indeed.

2. The Axis are making good their bridgehead on the Tunisian tip, which we nearly managed to seize at the first rush. It now looks as if the fighting there will continue through January and February. I hope that General Alexander's army will be masters of Tripoli early in February. Rommel will very likely withdraw towards the Tunisian tip with his forces, which amount to about 70,000 German troops and as many Italians, two-thirds of all of them administrative. The warfare on the African coast is very costly to the enemy on account of heavy losses in transit and at the ports. We shall do our utmost to finish it as quickly as possible.

3. The December PQ convoy has prospered so far beyond all expectation. I have now arranged to send a full convoy of thirty or more ships through in January, though whether they will go in one portion or in two is not yet settled by the Admiralty.

4. For yourself alone, I am going to visit President Roosevelt soon in order to settle our plans for 1943. My supreme object is for the British and Americans to engage the enemy with the largest numbers in the shortest time. The shipping stringency is most severe. I will inform you what passes.

---

[1] Having encircled the German 6th Army during the Battle of Stalingrad, Soviet anti-aircraft fire and aircraft were gravely hampering German attempts to resupply their forces by air. On December 24 a Soviet raiding force captured Tatsinskaya, a major Luftwaffe air base, ending its capability to supply the 6th Army.

*Winston S. Churchill to members of the War Cabinet
and the Chiefs of Staff Committee*
(Churchill papers, 23/10)

29 December 1942
Most Secret
Chiefs of Staff Paper No. 485 (Operations) of 1942

BRITISH STRATEGY IN 1943

A prime object of British and United States strategy in 1943 should be to bring the maximum force into contact with the enemy, both on the ground and in the air. Only in this way can we achieve the wearing-down of the enemy's air force and play our part equally with the armies of our Russian ally. Our action in the various theatres now under discussion should have continuous regard to this prime object.

2. By the great operation of 'Torch' we have placed ourselves in a position to threaten or attack the enemy both from the West and from the South. We ought to take the fullest advantage of this. Once we have cleared the North African shore, several important alternative enterprises are open in the Central Mediterranean, and the success of the Russian armies presents us with favourable possibilities in the Near East. Unless, however, during the summer and autumn we also engage the enemy from the West, we shall not be able to bring the most important part of our forces into play. The British Metropolitan and American Overseas Air Forces in the United Kingdom will be limited to bombing only. Our resources in small shipping will not be utilized. The weight of the British Home Army and of the American forces to be gathered in Britain will not count. Thus we shall have failed to engage the enemy with our full strength, and may even fail to keep him pinned down in the West while we attack in the South.

3. The questions therefore arise whether combined and concurrent operations can be organized from the West and the South and, if the answer is affirmative, which theatre should be considered the major or the minor, and how the emphasis and priorities should be cast. The plan should be framed as a whole with the object of utilizing all our forces and with the best timing. It should be possible to make a good programme.

4. In the southern or Mediterranean theatre it should be observed that the case for 'Husky' in preference to 'Brimstone' is strengthened (a) by the increased scale and time now said to be required for 'Brimstone', and (b) by the delay in taking the Tunisian tip. If we have to wait so long as April, May or June there will be time to make the larger-scale prepara-

tions which 'Husky' entails. Such an arrangement would also enable the PQ convoys, which must be considered as a major war operation, to be provided at least up till the end of March.

Winston S. Churchill to Sir Edward Campbell[1]
(Churchill papers, 20/54)

29 December 1942

My dear Campbell,

I was so very grieved to hear of the death of your son.[2] I know how great a gap this will leave in your family and how little any words of mine can help to comfort you. But you must take consolation in the knowledge that he has rendered distinguished service wherever he has been and that he could have given his life for no better or greater cause.

With heartfelt sympathy.

Yours sincerely,
Winston S. Churchill

Winston S. Churchill to King George VI
(Churchill papers, 20/54)

29 December 1942

Sir,

Since our conversation at luncheon today, I have examined, in consultation with the Chancellor of the Exchequer, the details of the case brought against Mr Noel Coward.[3] The Chancellor and Sir Richard Hopkins[4] contend that it was one of substance and that the conferment

---

[1] Edward Campbell, 1879–1945. Conservative MP for Camberwell North West, 1924–9; for Bromley, 1930–45.

[2] Gillian Lorne Campbell, 1920–42. Son of Sir Edward and Lady Campbell of Bromley. Joined the RAF Volunteer Reserve as an airman under training and was called up on 1 September 1939. On completion of training he was commissioned Flight Lieutenant and joined 236 Squadron on August 1940. With 272 Squadron flying Beaufighters, 1941 (DFC). Posted to Boscombe Down for flight testing, 1942. Killed 23 December when flying Spitfire Mk. 9 BS139.

[3] Noël Pierce Coward, 1899–1973. Educated at Chapel Road School and privately. First appeared on stage, 1910. Rose to international fame as actor and playwright in the 1920s. On outbreak of war in 1939, served for a time in Bureau of Propaganda and then in the Secret Service, including intelligence gathering in the United States. In 1941, prosecuted for contravening currency regulations. Produced the iconic wartime films *In Which We Serve* (1942), *This Happy Breed* (1943), and *Brief Encounter* (1945). He eventually received a knighthood in 1969.

[4] Permanent Secretary to the Treasury.

of a Knighthood upon Mr Coward so soon afterwards would give rise to unfavourable comment.

With considerable personal reluctance I have therefore come to the conclusion that I could not advise Your Majesty to proceed with this proposal on the present occasion.

With my humble duty, I remain

Your Majesty's faithful subject and servant,
Winston S. Churchill

King George VI to Winston S. Churchill [1]
(Churchill papers, 20/59)

30 December 1942   Buckingham Palace

My dear Winston,

Thank you for your letter. I quite understand that it is not possible to carry out our intentions now. I have read your speech (which I now return) with the greatest interest. I am sure the House now has a very clear idea of the political make up of France.

I am sorry you have all the worry over Tunisia & I do wish we had more of our own fighting troops there.

Thank you for sending me the Presidents (courier) letter to read.

All my best wishes to you for 1943 & may it be a happier one for all of us.

I am

Yours very sincerely
George RI

Winston S. Churchill to President Franklin D. Roosevelt
(Churchill papers, 20/88)

30 December 1942
Personal and Most Secret
No. 247

My dear Mr President,

The letter which Oliver Lyttelton brought and the associated agreements about Air and Ground force equipment are very welcome. I am deeply grateful. These Washington discussions and the conclusions

---

[1] This note was handwritten by the King.

reached show that our departments and yours are developing a closer understanding of each other's problems and getting nearer to a common view of the war. This is essential to success.

2. The Agreements arranged by Lyttelton, together with the assurances of your letter, give me a basis on which to allocate our reserves of man-power in full confidence that our British effort will be effectively balanced and rightly applied. We have now taken our decisions, I will not burden you with details. In broad terms we calculate that between midsummer 1942 and December 1943 we may he able to draft into the Services and draw into munition production some 1,600,000 extra men and women. Considering the degree of mobilisation already achieved in the past three years this is a large figure, and to reach it will mean a further straitening of living conditions and will call upon all the nation's latent resources. But it is less by 1,100,000 than is asked for by the Services and those responsible for our munition production whose combined requirements total 2,700,000. We have therefore had to ration our reserves of man-power and confine the programmes to essentials without allowing any margins for insurance or contingencies.

3. The following is what we have decided. First, we must give the Navy all they need for the anti-U-boat war up to the limit of our shipbuilding capacity and the resources which you can assign to us. The Admiralty will get the men for manning the ships but they must reduce their industrial requirements by labour economies in the shipyards and workshops, even though this means slowing down somewhat the building of big ships. Escort vessels will have the highest priority in the Navy's programme, and I am obliged to you for the allocations made to us from the pool.

4. Secondly, we shall strain every nerve to prevent labour shortage from checking the expansion of our aircraft industry. Our policy, subject to the limitations of training, technical problems, the availability of management and the supply of material and machines, will be to move labour into the factories as fast as it can be absorbed. The RAF, which has been taking in recruits on a large scale, will be able to use effectively all the aircraft which we can make or which you will send us under the new agreement, or more. But, like other services, it will have to be economical in its use of man-power and even reduce some of its defensive services, such as the balloon barrage and air field guards.

5. There are two things concerning the aircraft programme about which I am greatly concerned: one is the Fleet Air Arm and the other is transport aircraft. I have the impression that neither of our countries is devoting enough of its aircraft production to either of these two objects.

We must be certain that we have enough Fleet Air Arm type aircraft to match the carrier programmes in the two countries, and, as things are, it looks as if we might fall behind. Again, the experiences of both the Egyptian and North African campaigns emphasise the great value of transport aircraft, and I am personally much impressed with the Russian argument with which they back their demands for further transport aircraft. It may be that their power to start a successful offensive in 1943 will depend upon increasing our ability to supply them with transport aircraft to supplement their rather rudimentary communications. As you know, we ourselves are woefully short of transport aircraft, but we are providing them with 100 Albemarles for conversion for this purpose. I believe there are proposals in the United States for building wooden aircraft, and I feel that, if you could personally stimulate this production, it might prove a decision of the highest strategic importance.

6. Third, we have had to limit the Army's man-power intake considerably, and we are having to curtail our plans for producing Army equipment. The Army will take its cut where it hurts least; we can now run more risk in thinning out the home defences, and generally in combing the Army's tail, in order to sharpen its teeth. Here and there, as in the Middle East, we shall have to make two divisions into one by compression. But at home the main decision is to convert the Home Army to an offensive basis with a possible increase in its striking power. We shall be able to reduce the numbers in the factories making ground equipment, partly because the personnel is becoming more efficient and output per head is rising, partly because the initial equipment of the Army is in many items nearly complete and we are reaching the point where we can maintain it on a reduced output. We have been fortified in taking the decision to reduce the labour at the disposal of the Ministry of Supply by the agreements which Oliver Lyttelton brought back covering tanks and other Army supplies. In the circumstances, we shall rely heavily upon your medium tanks; I agree with your view that some increase in your programme would be wise.

7. Lastly shipping. Here again we are fortified by your assurance that our 27-million-ton import programme will be met, as well as our other essential needs. This is an undertaking of the highest importance to these islands. You may rest assured that we shall do our utmost to limit the demands of the British import programme upon the common pool of shipping. We are now running down our stocks, and we shall make what economies we can. But these devices only give us a little relief for a little while. You have warned me that the early months of 1943 will be

difficult. This I fully understand. But I must tell you frankly that the prospect in the next few months is going to be more acute than we expected
when the figures were prepared which Lyttelton took to Washington.
American shipbuilding has turned your own *net* losses of the spring into a
surplus. British and Allied *net* losses are, however, very serious indeed. In
November, for example, admittedly a bad month, losses from all causes
of American-controlled and United Nations' tonnage other than our
own were 260,000 dw tons, against which, excluding the Todd ships[1] for
us, you built 850,000 tons dw, giving a net gain of 590,000 tons. Losses
of British-controlled tonnage, on the other hand, were 850,000 tons dw
(100,000 due to 'Torch'), against which new construction of British and
Canadian yards, plus the Todd contracts, gave us 250,000 tons, leaving
us a net loss of 600,000 tons. With this position before us you will understand how vital it is that the reinforcement of our depleted shipping
resources should not be deferred. The situation which we now foresee
will only give us imports over the five months November to March at the
rate of 17 million tons a year. This is indeed a grim prospect, and one
which means for us dangerous and difficult decisions between military
operations, food and raw materials.

8. The suggested average supplement figure of 300,000 tons of dry-cargo
carrying capacity each month will only be enough if certain conditions are
fulfilled. First and foremost, we must be able to load a sufficient proportion of our total import on the North Atlantic seaboard or at other near
or convenient sources of supply. Our joint machinery will examine this
and other technical aspects, but in thanking you for the directions which
you have given, I must sound the alarm of mortal urgency. I am relieved by
knowing that you will keep this whole business constantly under your own
eye and that no further important diversion of tonnage to military purposes
will be made without your personal direction after I have had my say.

9. I was also reassured by your resolve to raise the shipbuilding programme to 20,000,000 dead-weight tons, if it should prove feasible; and,
as we live and fight upon our shipping, I hope you will be able to give
me some good news about the result of this enquiry. Indeed, any news
of progress on this would be helpful.

---

[1] Todd Shipyards Corporation, one of the major US shipbuilding companies, had major contracts
during the Second World War with the British Purchasing Commission. Cargo ships constructed in
the United States to supplement British construction were thus known as 'Todd ships'. Churchill
here includes Todd ships in the figures for British losses since, although built in the United States,
they fell under British control. (Records relating to Todd ships can be found in *Ministry of Transport
papers, 9/3368.*)

10. In conclusion, Mr President, let me emphasize the fact that our whole man-power lay-out is based upon striking the strongest blows we can in 1943. We will run the utmost risk for this; but unless our shipping resources are, in fact repaired as you so kindly propose, I shall be forced immediately to reduce the British war effort in oversea theatres even though this involves prolongation of the war and leaves you a greater portion of the burden we are eager to share.

Believe me,

Always your most sincere friend,
Winston S. Churchill

Winston S. Churchill to President Franklin D. Roosevelt
(Churchill papers, 20/85)

30 December 1942
Through Admiral Kirk[1] Personally
Most Secret and Personal
No. 248

I sent Brigadier Jacob to North Africa on Christmas Day to consult with Generals Eisenhower and Smith about arrangements for 'Symbol'. Jacob has now telegraphed that they have found admirable accommodation and that General Smith who is in full agreement is telegraphing the results of their reconnaissance to you.

2. I do not think we can do better than accept these proposals, and as time is short, I am going ahead on the assumption that you approve.

3. My intention is that HMS *Bulolo*, which is a specially fitted Headquarter Ship, should leave the UK on about 4th January with the more junior Staff Officers of my delegation, cypher staff, clerical staff, etc. *Bulolo* will be berthed in the harbour and serve as Signal Ship.

4. In your 242[2] you suggested that some of our Military men should precede us by a few days to clear the ground. I entirely agree, and will arrange for British Chiefs of Staff to arrive by air at rendezvous on whatever day it may be possible for American Chiefs of Staff to reach there. Can you give me a date?

---

[1] Alan Goodrich Kirk, Chief of Staff to Admiral Stark, Commander, United States Naval Forces in Europe.

[2] President Roosevelt's letter to Churchill delivered on December 23 (see pages 1543–4 above).

5. It would also be helpful if you could let me know as soon as possible your own programme and I will make my own arrangements accordingly.

6. Many thanks about Macmillan. I agree to what you say about Eisenhower's final authority.[1]

Winston S. Churchill to the War Cabinet
(Churchill papers, 23/10)

30 December 1942   10 Downing Street
Secret
War Cabinet Paper No. 613 of 1942

HOME FOOD PRODUCTION

I have asked the Minister of Agriculture and Fisheries,[2] the Secretary of State for Scotland[3] and the Home Secretary[4] to epitomise the results of their labours on the land. The achievement in increasing our home-grown food and thus saving over 10 million tons of imports must be regarded as a very direct and vital contribution to our survival and ultimate victory. I feel sure my colleagues would wish a formal expression of the approval of the War Cabinet to be conveyed to the Ministers concerned, and that they should in turn make this known throughout their Departments and among their voluntary assistants.

President Franklin D. Roosevelt to Winston S. Churchill
(Churchill papers, 20/85)

31 December 1942
Personal and Secret
No. 248

Arrangements for 'Symbol' satisfactory. Our Chiefs of Staff will arrive twelfth and I will follow two days later so that we could all meet together

---

[1] On December 29 Roosevelt sent a telegram accepting Macmillan's designation as Minister Resident at Allied Headquarters, with the rider that Eisenhower 'will continue to have full veto power over all Civil Officials in the area of operations' (*Churchill papers, 20/85*).

[2] Robert Spear Hudson, 1886–1957. Educated at Eton and Magdalen College, Oxford. Attaché, Diplomatic Service, 1911; First Secretary, 1920–3. Conservative MP for Whitehaven, 1924–9; for Southport, 1931–52. Parliamentary Secretary, Ministry of Labour, 1931–5. Minister of Pensions, 1935–6. Secretary, Department of Overseas Trade, 1937–40. Privy Councillor, 1938. Minister of Shipping, April–May 1940. Minister of Agriculture and Fisheries, 1940–5. Created Viscount, 1952.

[3] Thomas Johnston.

[4] Herbert Morrison.

on fifteenth. I believe our Staffs can cover the ground in a two day preliminary conference.

The prospect pleases me.

Winston S. Churchill to President Franklin D. Roosevelt
(Churchill papers, 20/85)

31 December 1942
Personal and Most Secret
No. 249

I send you some of my thoughts on our present difficulties with the
French.

We ought not to accept the suggestion that our armies in North West
Africa are on the same footing as they were in France in 1918. We were
not invited but fought our way on shore with the loss of 2,000 men.
Therefore the Allied Commander-in-Chief, representing you as head
of our joint enterprise in these regions, must be supreme in all matters
military and civil, of course without prejudice to the territorial sovereignty
of France reviving when the war is over.

2. Giraud is in my opinion quite unsuited to the discharge of civil
responsibilities. He is a brave, capable, flamboyant soldier and it is his
duty to animate and lead the French armies in this theatre under Eisenhower's orders.

3. A civil regime should be set up in whatever form is found locally
convenient, in which Murphy and Macmillan should have, as you suggested, a veto as well as powers of guidance and initiation veiled under
appropriate forms.

4. I trust Eisenhower will soon be freed from the distraction of local
French politics, the rate of exchange, problems of French sovereignty,
etc. I am most anxious about the military situation. If Nehring[1] can get
enough transport (dash) a big if (dash) he might bring off the same
kind of attack along the sea flank that Alexander and Montgomery did
at Alamein, with the disastrous results to all our forces to the southward
that befell the Italians. The danger to our First Army, or rather Corps,
for it is no more, seems to me far more serious than anything which
threatens us on the southern flank. Only a Supreme Commander like

[1] Walther Kurt Nehring, 1892–1983. Commander, 5th Panzer Regiment, 1935–9. Chief of Staff,
XIX Corps, Poland–France, 1939–40. General Officer Commanding 18th Panzer Division, 1940–2;
Africa Corps and LXXXX Corps, 1942; XXIV Panzer Corps, 1943–5. Deputy General Officer Com-
manding 4th Panzer Army and General Officer Commanding XXXVII Panzer Corps, 1944.

Eisenhower, concentrating his whole thought upon the fighting, can cope with these military perils.

5. For you alone. Alexander and Montgomery hope to have Tripoli early in February. Rommel will most likely make his way with his remnants, some of which are formidable, to Tunisia. We hope to be hard at his tail in superior force, and I am encouraging General Alexander to press forward to the utmost.

6. We are putting hard pressure on de Gaulle to shut his Brazzaville mouth,[1] and I am suggesting that Swinton[2] has a talk with Boisson.

Winston S. Churchill to General Sir Harold Alexander
and General Bernard Montgomery
(Churchill papers, 20/105)

31 December 1942
Most Secret
Immediate
Private

I send you herewith extracts from various telegrams which have passed between us and General Eisenhower or the Combined Chiefs of the Staff about Tunisia, in order that you may have this whole situation in your mind. It seems to me that Eisenhower's northern flank might well be attacked with greater results than his southern flank. In fact it has an Alamein look about it. The one comfort is that the enemy is not yet very mobile. It would indeed be a glory to the Desert Army if they struck the decisive blow in Tunisia after a pursuit unparalleled in war. Even if Tunis does not take a nasty turn March might well be in time.

2. Most particularly secret. An Anglo-American Staff Conference of the highest importance will be held near Casablanca during the third week of January. I expect to arrive 14th and hope that you will find it possible to meet me there then. I propose later to visit your Army. It is only a night's flight either way.

3. Give my warmest regards to Montgomery and tell him how splendid we all think his work has been.

The supreme prize lies ahead.

---

[1] French broadcasts were being made from the major Free French radio station at Brazzaville and from Accra attacking the authority of Governor Boisson. The British owned the broadcast equipment at Accra and allowed the French to use it. Churchill attempted to put pressure on de Gaulle to halt the Brazzaville broadcasts, using British ownership of Accra radio as leverage.

[2] Lord Swinton, Cabinet Minister Resident in West Africa.

Winston S. Churchill to General Dwight D. Eisenhower
(Churchill papers, 20/88)

31 December 1942

My immediately following, drafted by the Foreign Office, will show you that we have in no way let you down.[1] I have also today personally telegraphed to Boisson, in spite of his bad record, as follows:

The way to clear up all misunderstandings and arrive at a good plan for the common cause is for you to meet Lord Swinton personally wherever it can best be arranged and as soon as possible.

2. I do hope you will not be distracted from the fighting by interminable French intrigues.

I am deeply concerned about the unfavourable turn in Tunisia, and our Staffs take an even more serious view. The danger is on the seaward flank. It seems to me vital to create an effective reserve as far east as possible.

3. For yourself alone. Alexander hopes to capture Tripoli early in February. Rommel will probably make his way into Tunisia, but we shall try to follow hard at his tail with stronger forces from the Desert Army.

4. Meanwhile, you should soon have the leading brigade of the 46th British Infantry Division. We are also sending the brigade of Churchill tanks in the convoy leaving about the 20th instant. The rest of the 46th Division should be with you during January, and we are pushing the 11th Armoured Division, which has been much more heavily armed out to you as fast as is humanly possible. Nothing matters now but the battle in the Tunisian Tip.

5. All good wishes for the New Year.

I am looking forward to 'Symbol'.

Winston S. Churchill to Anthony Eden
(Churchill papers, 20/67)

31 December 1942

I am doubtful whether your reply will do the job.[2] I think we ought (i) to try to bring Swinton and Boisson together to settle up on the spot;

---

[1] On December 30, Eisenhower had relayed to General Ismay (in Telegram T.1775/2) Boisson's concerns that Britain was not fully implementing agreed arrangements for the cessation of propaganda activity and exchange of prisoners in French West Africa.

[2] Minute of 31 December 1942 from the Foreign Secretary with draft telegram to Lord Swinton about the alleged continuance of broadcasts in French from the British station at Accra attacking Governor Boisson's authority.

and (ii) to compel de Gaulle to make Brazzaville lay off, under penalty
of forfeiting British recognition.

Winston S. Churchill to Lord Swinton
(Churchill papers, 20/85)

31 December 1942
Most Immediate
Most Secret and Personal

Until further instructed the Accra radio should stop all controversial
references to French politics, and in addition should make it clear that
Accra radio is quite separate from Brazzaville.

We are taking up Brazzaville strongly with de Gaulle here. You should
pass the following to Boisson from me.

Winston S. Churchill to Governor-General Pierre Boisson
(Churchill papers, 20/85)

31 December 1942
Most Immediate

The way to clear up all misunderstandings and arrive at a good plan
for the common cause is for you to meet Lord Swinton personally wherever it can best be arranged, and as soon as possible.

Appendices

Appendix A: Members of the Cabinet, 1942

WAR CABINET

Prime Minister and Minister of Defence
  Winston S. Churchill
Deputy Prime Minister and Secretary of State for Dominion Affairs
  Clement Attlee (from 19 February 1942)
Lord President of the Council
  Sir John Anderson
Lord Privy Seal
  Clement Attlee
  Sir Stafford Cripps (from 19 February 1942)
Leader of the House of Commons
  Winston S. Churchill
  Sir Stafford Cripps (from 19 February 1942)
  Anthony Eden (from 22 November 1942)
Secretary of State for Foreign Affairs
  Anthony Eden
Chancellor of the Exchequer
  Sir Kingsley Wood (until 19 February 1942)
Secretary of State for the Home Department and Minister
  of Home Security
  Herbert Morrison (from 22 November 1942)
Minister of Labour and National Service
  Ernest Bevin
Minister of Supply
  Lord Beaverbrook (until 4 February 1942)
Minister of War Production
  Lord Beaverbrook (from 4 February 1942)

Minister of Production
  Oliver Lyttelton (from 19 February 1942)
Minister without Portfolio
  Mr Arthur Greenwood (until 19 February 1942)
Minister of State in the Middle East
  Oliver Lyttelton (until 19 February 1942)
  Richard Casey (from 18 March 1942)

OTHER MINISTERS, 1942

First Lord of the Admiralty
  A. V. Alexander
Minister of Agriculture and Fisheries
  Robert Hudson
Secretary of State for Air
  Sir Archibald Sinclair
Minister of Aircraft Production
  Colonel J. T. C. Moore-Brabazon
  Colonel J. J. Llewellin (from 22 February 1942)
  Sir Stafford Cripps (from 22 November 1942)
Secretary of State for Burma and India
  L. S. Amery
Chancellor of the Duchy of Lancaster
  Alfred Duff Cooper
Chancellor of the Exchequer
  Sir Kingsley Wood (from 19 February 1942)
Secretary of State for the Colonies
  Lord Moyne
  Viscount Cranborne (from 22 February 1942)
  Colonel Oliver Stanley (from 22 November 1942)
Secretary of State for Dominion Affairs
  Viscount Cranborne (until 19 February 1942)
Minister of Economic Warfare
  Hugh Dalton
  Viscount Wolmer (from 22 February 1942; later Earl of Selborne)
President of the Board of Education
  R. A. Butler
Minister of Food
  Lord Woolton

Minister of Fuel and Power (created 3 June 1942)
  Major Gwilym Lloyd George
Minister of Health
  Ernest Brown
Secretary of State for the Home Department and Minister
  of Home Security
  Herbert Morrison (until 22 November 1942)
Leader of the House of Lords
  Lord Moyne
  Viscount Cranborne (from 22 February 1942)
Minister of Information
  Brendan Bracken
Lord Chancellor
  Viscount Simon
Lord Privy Seal
  Viscount Cranborne (from 22 November 1942)
Minister without Portfolio
  Sir William Jowitt (from 30 December 1942)
Paymaster-General
  Lord Hankey
  Sir William Jowitt (from 4 March 1942)
  Lord Cherwell (from 20 December 1942)
Minister of Pensions
  Sir Walter Womersley
Postmaster-General
  Mr W. S. Morrison
Secretary of State for Scotland
  Thomas Johnston
Minister of Supply
  Sir Andrew Duncan (from 4 February 1942)
President of the Board of Trade
  Sir Andrew Duncan
  Colonel J. J. Llewellin (from 4 February 1942)
  Hugh Dalton (from 22 February 1942)
Secretary of State for War
  Captain H. D. R. Margesson
  Sir James Grigg (from 22 February 1942)
Minister of War Transport
  Lord Leathers

Minister of Works and Planning
  Lord Reith
  Lord Portal (from 22 February 1942)

Law officers:
Attorney-General
  Sir Donald Somervell
Lord Advocate
  J. S. C. Reid
Solicitor-General
  Sir William Jowitt
  Sir David Maxwell Fyfe (from 4 March 1942)
Solicitor-General for Scotland
  Sir David King Murray

Ministers overseas:
Minister Resident for Supply in Washington
  Colonel J. J. Llewellin (from 22 November 1942)
Minister Resident at Allied Force Headquarters,
  Mediterranean Command
  Harold Macmillan (from 30 December 1942)
Minister Resident in West Africa
  Viscount Swinton (from 8 June 1942)
Deputy Minister of State Resident in the Middle East
  Lord Moyne (from 28 August 1942)

Appendix B

CODE NAMES

Acrobat: advance from Cyrenaica into Tripolitania, launched on 11 January 1942.

Anakim: plan to recapture Burma, beginning with a seaborne invasion in early 1943, and re-open the overland supply line to China.

Anklet: allied naval and commando raid on the Lofoten Islands, 26 December 1941, to intercept the flow of Swedish iron ore to Germany along the Norwegian coast.

Aspidistra: a high-power (500 kW) medium-wave broadcasting transmitter near Crowborough in the Ashdown Forest, Sussex.

Backbone: plan to strike Spanish troops if they massed in Spanish Morocco in order to join the Axis in the fight during or after 'Torch'.

Bigot: code word used at the start of any telegram relating to future operations. A 'Bigot' officer was one who knew the actual destination of a particular operation.

Bolero: administrative preparations for the opening of a 'second front' in north-west Europe, involving the movement of United States ground forces and equipment across the Atlantic to Britain.

Boniface: signals intelligence gained from decrypts of coded German information.

Bonus: plan to seize Vichy-held Madagascar (later called Operation 'Ironclad').

Breastplate: plan for amphibious Allied assault on Tunisia from Malta.

Brimstone: capture of Sardinia.

Colonel White: Clementine Churchill.

Crusader: operation in the Western Desert, launched 24 January 1942.

Dynamo: evacuation of the Dunkirk beachhead in June 1940.

Force H[ypo]: a British naval formation created in 1940 to replace French naval power in the western Mediterranean that had been removed by the French armistice with Nazi Germany.

Gymnast: British plan for an amphibious landing in French North Africa in the spring of 1942 to bring United States ground forces into action against Germany and Italy and end the Vichy Government's control of Morocco and Tunisia. Later developed into 'Torch', the landings that took place from 8 to 16 November 1942.

Habbakuk: proposal to use artificial icebergs as staging posts for aircraft in the Atlantic.

Harpoon: British supply convoy of six merchant ships, sailing from Gibraltar to Malta (5–15 June 1942).

Husky: capture of Sicily.

Imperator: plan (conceived in response to the repeated Soviet calls for a second front) to land an army division and armoured units on the Channel coast of France, carry out a two- or three-day raid and then re-embark.

Ironclad (formerly Bonus): invasion of Madagascar to replace the Vichy administration there with Free French rule.

Jackpot: British landing on Norway's largest island, Spitzbergen, bordering the Arctic Ocean, the Greenland Sea, and the Norwegian

Sea. Spitzbergen was not then occupied by the Germans (who had conquered Norway in May–June 1940), and German installations on the island had been destroyed in August 1941 by a ten-day combined British, Canadian, and Norwegian commando raid.

Jubilee (formerly Rutter): British and Canadian landing at Dieppe, planned in April 1942, for implementation at the end of June, and eventually carried out on 19 August 1942.

Jupiter: planned operations in northern Norway, including an attempt to secure Petsamo in combination with Soviet forces.

Lightfoot: 8th Army operations in the Western Desert in the autumn of 1942.

Magic: term used by American forces for the cryptanalysis of Japanese ciphers.

Magnet: Anglo-American operations to move United States ground forces into Northern Ireland as part of the build-up for subsequent operations on the European mainland.

Market Garden: airborne landings in Arnhem, September 1944.

Mohican: original name of 'Torch', the landings in North Africa carried out from 8 to 16 November 1942.

Overlord: Normandy landings of June 1944.

Pedestal: August 1942 supply convoy to Malta.

Performance: breakout on 1–4 April 1942 from the Swedish port of Gothenburg, where they were interned, to the United Kingdom, of ten Norwegian merchant ships, supported on the second day of the breakout by six British destroyers and RAF Fighter and Coastal Command.

Roundup: plan for the liberation of France in 1943.

Rubble: operation in which Norwegian merchant ships based in the Swedish port of Gothenburg ran the German naval blockade, escorted by the Royal Navy, in 1941.

Rutter: original name of 'Jubilee', British and Canadian landing at Dieppe.

Semi-Gymnast: North African landings with French co-operation (which never took place).

Sledgehammer: proposed amphibious landing at Brest and Cherbourg in 1942.

Super-Gymnast: despatch, authorised on 13 January 1942, of 21,000 United States troops with aircraft and other equipment from the East Coast of the United States to Australia.

Super Roundup: final development of Operation 'Roundup', involving a substantial Allied landing in northern France as soon as possible after Operation 'Torch' (scheduled for the summer of 1943). Eventually postponed in January 1943 in favour of Operation 'Husky' against Sicily.

Symbol: the Casablanca Conference, at which Roosevelt and Churchill were to meet in January 1943.

Torch: Allied landings in French North Africa, 8–16 November 1942.

Tube Alloys: British work on what would become the atomic bomb, which from late 1941 had involved British and Canadian scientists working in collaboration with counterparts in the United States.

Velvet: movement of Anglo-American forces to the Caucasus to support the Russians.

Vigorous: supply convoy of 11 supply ships, sailing from Alexandria to Malta (11–16 June 1942).

ZIP: code word used to indicate that the Second Battle of El Alamein had commenced

Appendix C

ABBREVIATIONS

A: Antananarivo, capital of Madagascar
AA: anti-aircraft
ABDA: American, British, Dutch, Australian
ABDACOM: American–British–Dutch–Australian Command
Ack-ack: anti-aircraft (defence, weapons)
ADC: aide-de-camp
ADGB: Air Defence of Great Britain
AFC: Air Force Cross
AFV: armoured fighting vehicle
A/Midget: anti-midget-submarine
ANZAC: Australian and New Zealand Army Corps
ARP: Air Raid Precautions
AS, A/S: anti-submarine
ASU: Air Storage Units (aircraft in storage); Air Support Units
ASV: Air to Surface Vessel (radar)
AT, A/T: anti-tank
ATFERO: Atlantic Ferry Organization

ATS: Auxiliary Territorial Service
BAOR: British Army of Occupation on the Rhine
BBC: British Broadcasting Corporation
BDE: British Destroyer Escort
BOAC: British Overseas Airways Corporation
B of T: Board of Trade
BUP: British United Press (press agency)
C: Head of the Secret Intelligence Service
CAS: Chief of the Air Staff
CB: Companion of the Order of the Bath
CBE: Commander of the Order of the British Empire
CBS: Columbia Broadcasting System
CCO: Chief of Combined Operations
CGGS: Chief of the (proposed) Great General Staff
CH: Companion of Honour
CIA: Central Intelligence Agency
CIGS: Chief of the Imperial General Staff
C in C: Commander-in-Chief
CMG: Companion of the Order of St Michael and St George
DBE: Dame Commander of the Order of the British Empire
DCI: Director of Central Intelligence
DE: Destroyer Escort
DFC: Distinguished Flying Cross
D-notice: Defence Notice; a formal request to the media not to publish
   material deemed to be sensitive in defence terms
DS: Diego Suarez
DSC: Distinguished Service Cross
DSM: Distinguished Service Medal
DSO: Distinguished Service Order
E-boat: German *Schnellboot* or 'fast boat', a fast-moving surface attack
   craft
EPT: Export Programme Targets
GAF: German Air Force
GBE: Knight Grand Cross of the Order of the British Empire
GC: George Cross
GCB: Knight Grand Cross of the Order of the Bath
GHQ: General Headquarters
GMCG: Knight Grand Cross of the Order of St Michael and St
   George
GP: general purpose

H2S: an airborne, ground-scanning radar system for the RAF

Halpro Force: Halverson Provisional Detachment: specially trained United States bomber unit, commanded by Colonel Harry A. Halverson

HE: high explosive

HMS: His Majesty's Ship

HQ: headquarters

HRH: His Royal Highness

HX convoys: convoys headed from Halifax Nova Scotia to the UK

IBRD: International Bank for Reconstruction and Development

IMF: International Monetary Fund

IRA: Irish Republican Army

JW/RA convoys: second series of supply convoys to Russia, from December 1942 (JW outbound, RA inbound)

KBE: Knight Commander of the Order of the British Empire

KC: King's Counsel

KCB: Knight Commander of the Order of the Bath

KCMG: Knight Commander of the Order of St Michael and St George

KCVO: Knight Commander of the Royal Victorian Order

KMF: Kingdom to Mediterranean Fast, code for fast convoys heading from the United Kingdom to the Mediterranean. Return trips were known as MKF.

KMS: Kingdom to Mediterranean Slow, code for convoys heading from the United Kingdom to the Mediterranean at a slow pace. Return trips were known as MKS. There were also KMF convoys that travelled fast. Return trips were known as MKS and MKF

LAA: light anti-aircraft (guns)

LDV: Local Defence Volunteers

LLD: Doctor of Laws

L of C: line(s) of communication

LVF: Légion des Voluntaires Français, French unit of German army

MA: Master of Arts

MAP: Ministry of Aircraft Production

MBE: Member of the Order of the British Empire

MC: medium capacity/medium case (bomb)

MD1: Ministry of Defence 1, an experimental establishment located at Whitchurch, Buckinghamshire

MEW: Minister/Ministry of Economic Warfare

MI5: Military Intelligence 5, a branch of the Secret Intelligence Service

MK: prefix given to the special messages from the Bletchley decoding centre
MNBDO: Mobile Naval Base Defence Organization
MP: Member of Parliament
MT: motor transport
M/V: merchant vessel
MVO: Member of the Royal Victorian Order
NATO: North Atlantic Treaty Organisation
OBE: Officer of the Order of the British Empire
ORP: Okret Rzeczypospolitej Polskiej (Ship of the Polish Republic)
OSS: [US] Office of Strategic Services
OTU: Operational Training Unit.
PC: Privy Councillor
PEP: Political and Economic Planning
PIAT: Projector, Infantry, Anti-Tank, a British anti-tank weapon
PM: Prime Minister
Port T: Trincomalee
PPF: Parti Populaire Français, ultra-nationalist French party
PQ convoys: supply convoys to Russia via the northern Arctic route
    (up to September 1942)
PRU: Photographic Reconnaissance Unit (RAF)
Q: Quartermaster (supply)
QC: Queen's Counsel
RAC: Royal Armoured Corps
RAF: Royal Air Force
RAOC: Royal Army Ordnance Corps
RASC: Royal Army Service Corps
R Class: Revenge Class (battleships)
RDF: Radio Direction Finding (radar)
RE: Royal Engineers
RMS: Royal Mail Ship
RN: Royal Navy
RNVR: Royal Naval Volunteer Reserve
rr: railroad
SA: South Africa
SAA: small arms ammunition
SAS: Special Air Service
Sitrep: situation report
SOE: Special Operations Executive
SOL: Service d'ordre legionnaire, French Fascist militia

SP: self-propelled (gun)

SS (British): Secret Service

SS (German): *Schutzstaffel* (special police)

T: tank; Tamatave, port on the Indian Ocean coast of Madagascar

U-boat: German *Unterseeboot*, submarine

UNESCO: United Nations Educational, Scientific and Cultural Organisation

UNRRA: United Nations Relief and Rehabilitation Administration

USAAF: United States Army Air Forces

USS: United States Ship

UWWP: Under Water Working Party

VC: Victoria Cross

WAAF: Women's Auxiliary Air Force

WO: War Office

WS convoys: 'Winston's Specials': convoys to the East from August 1940 to August 1943

WSC: Churchill's initials, with which he habitually signed his many thousands of minutes

WVS: Women's Voluntary Service

YMCA: Young Men's Christian Association

YWCA: Young Women's Christian Association

Maps

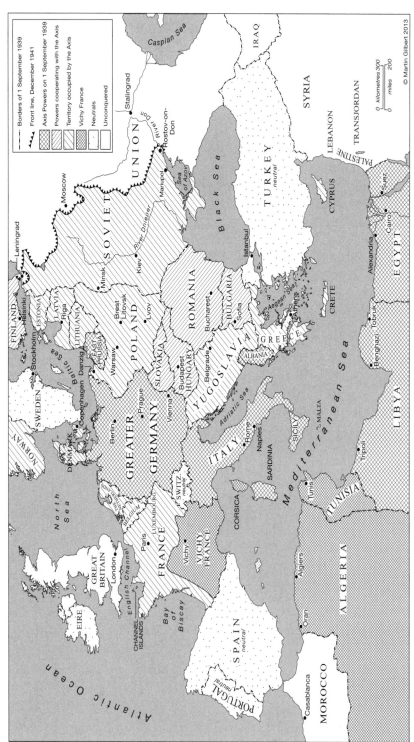

1. German Europe

Borders of 1 September 1939
Front line, December 1941
Axis Powers on 1 September 1939
Powers cooperating with the Axis
Territory occupied by the Axis
Vichy France
Neutrals
Unconquered

© Martin Gilbert 2013

0 kilometres 300
0 miles 200

Atlantic Ocean

North Sea

GREAT BRITAIN
London
EIRE
English Channel
CHANNEL ISLANDS
Bay of Biscay

NORWAY
SWEDEN
Stockholm
Baltic Sea
DENMARK
Copenhagen
Berlin
GREATER GERMANY
Prague
Vienna

FINLAND
Helsinki
Leningrad
ESTONIA
LATVIA
Riga
LITHUANIA
EAST PRUSSIA
Danzig
Warsaw
POLAND
Brest Litovsk
Minsk

SOVIET UNION
Moscow
River Don
Stalingrad
Rostov-on-Don
Caspian Sea

Kiev
River Dnieper
Lvov
Mariupol
Sea of Azov

BELGIUM
LUXEMBOURG
Paris
FRANCE
Vichy
VICHY FRANCE
SWITZ. neutral

SLOVAKIA
Budapest
HUNGARY
ROMANIA
Bucharest
Belgrade
YUGOSLAVIA
Sofia
BULGARIA

Black Sea
Istanbul
TURKEY neutral

ITALY
Rome
Naples
SARDINIA
CORSICA
Adriatic Sea
ALBANIA
GREECE
Aegean Sea
Piraeus
CRETE

SYRIA
LEBANON
PALESTINE
TRANSJORDAN
CYPRUS
Suez
Cairo
Alexandria
EGYPT

IRAQ

SPAIN neutral
PORTUGAL neutral

SICILY
MALTA
Mediterranean Sea
Tunis
TUNISIA
Tripoli
LIBYA
Benghazi
Tobruk

MOROCCO
Casablanca
ALGERIA
Algiers
Oran

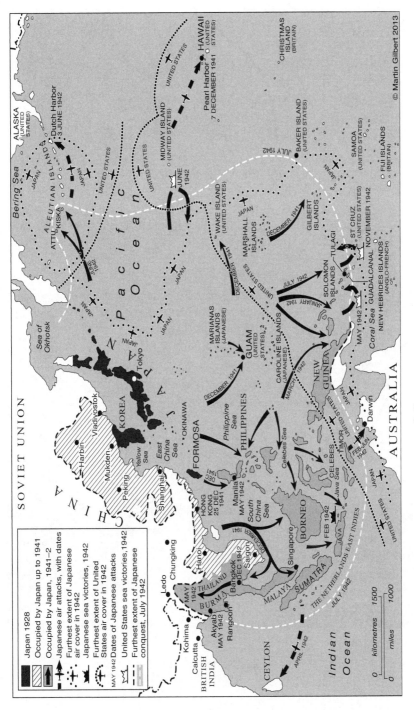

2. Japanese conquests

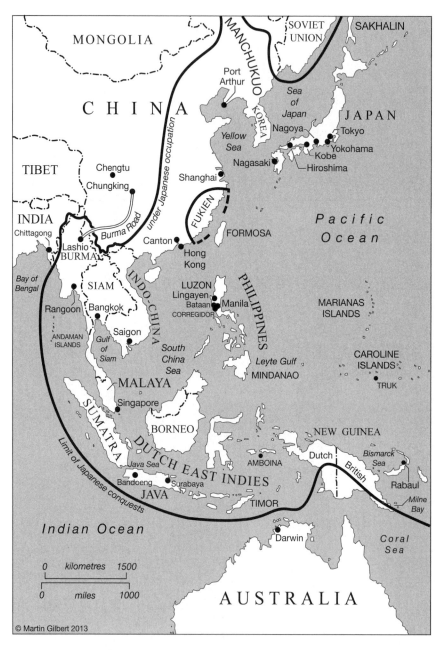

3. The Far East

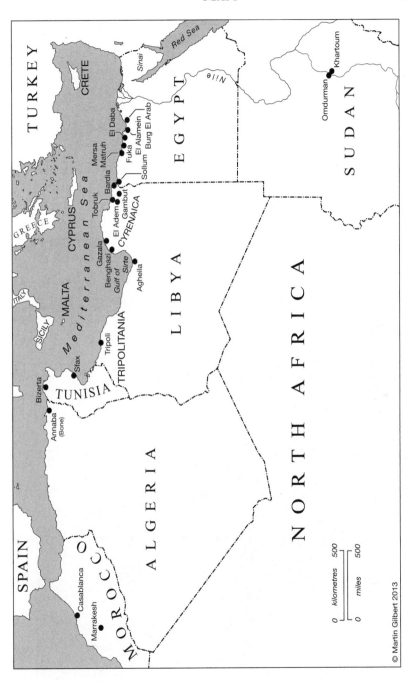

4. North Africa

© Martin Gilbert 2013

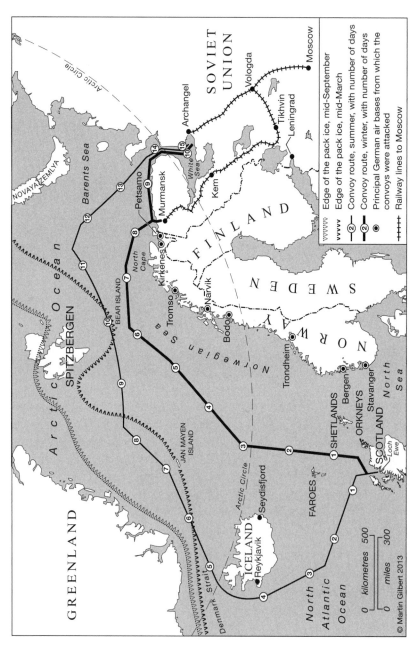

5. Scandinavia

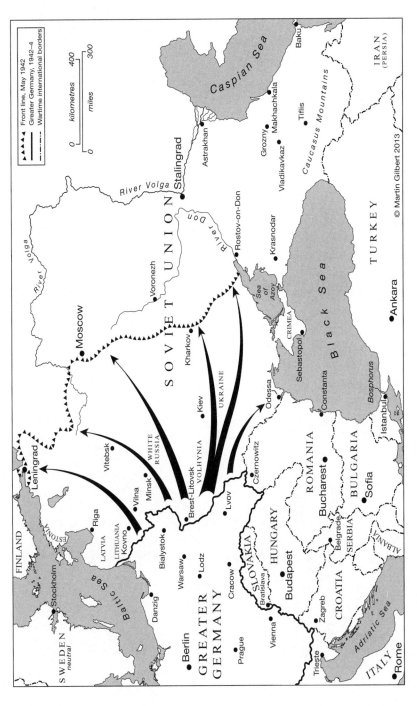

6. The Balkans and the Caucasus

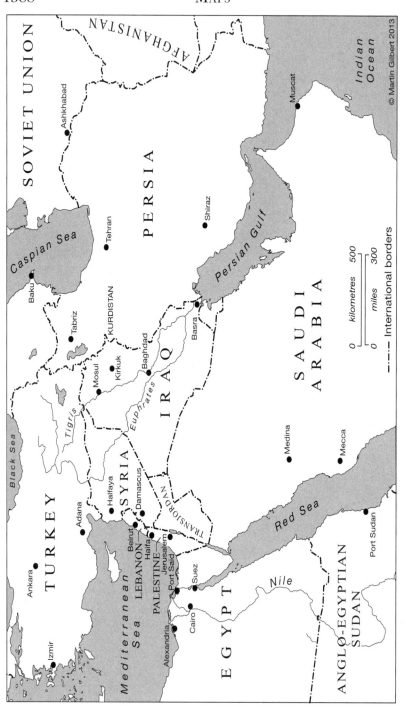

7. The Middle East

Velikiye Luki

Polotsk

Vitebsk

Orsha   Smolensk

Minsk

Mogilev

B E L A R U S

Bobruisk

Bryansk

Gomel

Kalinin

Rzhev

Vyazma

Moscow

Vladimir

Kaluga

Ryazan

Orel

Yelets

S O V I E T   U N I O N

UKRAINE

Voronezh

Dnieper

Kiev

Belgorod

Kharkov

Poltava

Don River

Lugansk

Zaporozhye

Taganrog

Don River

Rostov-on-Don

Azov

Yelsk

Gulf of
Perekop

Sea of Azov

CRIMEA

Kerch

Feodosiya

Black
Sea

Sebastopol

0   kilometres 150

0   miles   100

© Martin Gilbert 2013

Legend:

▲▲▲▲▲ The German front line on 7 December 1941

⬅ Soviet counter-attacks, January–May 1942

ՄՄՄՄՄ German defensive lines breached,
January–May 1942

➤ German counter-attacks, May–June 1942

△△△△△ The front line by the end of June 1942

Soviet partisans active behind German
lines, January–June 1942

Evacuation of Soviet forces from
Sebastopol, 30 June – 3 July 1942

8. The Eastern Front

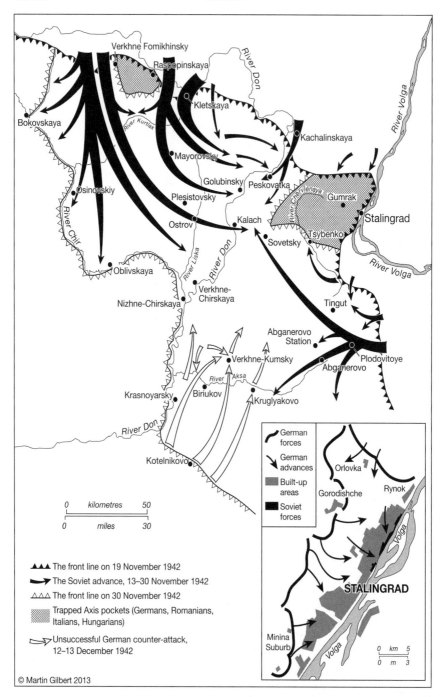

© Martin Gilbert 2013

9. The battle for Stalingrad

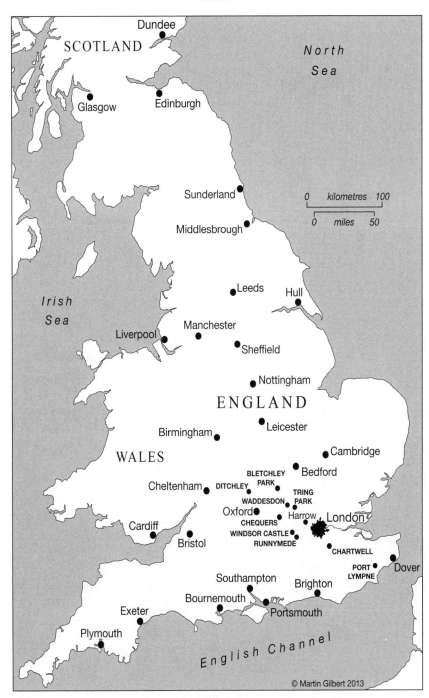

10. Great Britain

Legend:
- International borders 2013
- German Concentration Camps

Baltic Sea

North Sea

POLAND

Hamburg
Neuengamme

Belower Forest

Ravensbrück

Bergen-Belsen

Sachsenhausen

River Oder

Gardelegen

Berlin

Brandenburg · Wannsee

THE NETHERLANDS

River Rhine

BELGIUM

River Elbe

Bernberg

Mittelbau-Dora

Zeithain

Buchenwald

G E R M A N Y

Sonnenstein

Hadamar

LUXEMBOURG

CZECH REPUBLIC

Flossenbürg

Heidelberg

Nuremberg

FRANCE

Stuttgart

River Danube

Grafeneck

Dachau

Munich

0 kilometres 200
0 miles 100

AUSTRIA

SWITZERLAND

© Martin Gilbert 2013

11. Germany

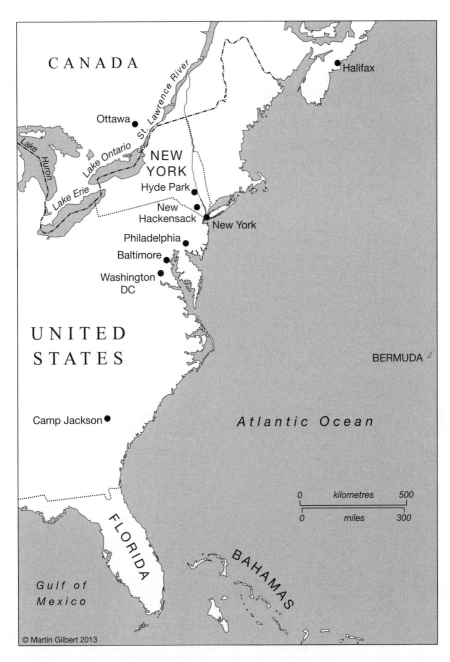

12. The eastern seaboard of the United States

Index